Weiss Ratings' Guide to Property and Casualty Insurers

Weiss Ratings' Guide to Property and Casualty Insurers

A Quarterly Compilation of Insurance Company Ratings and Analyses

Summer 2018

GREY HOUSE PUBLISHING

Weiss Ratings
4400 Northcorp Parkway
Palm Beach Gardens, FL 33410
561-627-3300

WeissRatings
Independent. Unbiased. Accurate. Trusted.

Published by Grey House Publishing, Inc., located at 4919 Route 22, Amenia, NY 12501; telephone 518-789-8700. Grey House Publishing neither guarantees the accuracy of the data contained herein nor assumes any responsibility for errors, omissions or discrepancies. Grey House Publishing accepts no payment for listing; inclusion in the publication of any organization, agency, institution, publication, service or individual does not imply endorsement of the publisher.

Grey House
Publishing
4919 Route 22
PO Box 56
Amenia, NY 12501-0056

Edition No. 97, Summer 2018

ISBN: 978-1-68217-810-2
ISSN: 2158-5989

Contents

Terms and Conditions

This document is prepared strictly for the confidential use of our customer(s). It has been provided to you at your specific request. It is not directed to, or intended for distribution to or use by, any person or entity who is a citizen or resident of or located in any locality, state, country or other jurisdiction where such distribution, publication, availability or use would be contrary to law or regulation or which would subject Weiss Ratings or its affiliates to any registration or licensing requirement within such jurisdiction.

No part of the analysts' compensation was, is, or will be, directly or indirectly, related to the specific recommendations or views expressed in this research report.

This document is not intended for the direct or indirect solicitation of business. Weiss Ratings and its affiliates disclaims any and all liability to any person or entity for any loss or damage caused, in whole or in part, by any error (negligent or otherwise) or other circumstances involved in, resulting from or relating to the procurement, compilation, analysis, interpretation, editing, transcribing, publishing and/or dissemination or transmittal of any information contained herein.

Weiss Ratings has not taken any steps to ensure that the securities or investment vehicle referred to in this report are suitable for any particular investor. The investment or services contained or referred to in this report may not be suitable for you and it is recommended that you consult an independent investment advisor if you are in doubt about such investments or investment services. Nothing in this report constitutes investment, legal, accounting or tax advice or a representation that any investment or strategy is suitable or appropriate to your individual circumstances or otherwise constitutes a personal recommendation to you.

The ratings and other opinions contained in this document must be construed solely as statements of opinion from Weiss Ratings, and not statements of fact. Each rating or opinion must be weighed solely as a factor in your choice of an institution and should not be construed as a recommendation to buy, sell or otherwise act with respect to the particular product or company involved.

Past performance should not be taken as an indication or guarantee of future performance, and no representation or warranty, expressed or implied, is made regarding future performance. Information, opinions and estimates contained in this report reflect a judgment at its original date of publication and are subject to change without notice. Weiss Ratings offers a notification service for rating changes on companies you specify. For more information visit WeissRatings.com or call 1-877-934-7778. The price, value and income from any of the securities or financial instruments mentioned in this report can fall as well as rise.

This document and the information contained herein is copyrighted by Weiss Ratings, LLC. Any copying, displaying, selling, distributing or otherwise reproducing or delivering this information or any part of this document to any other person entity is prohibited without the express written consent of Weiss Ratings, LLC, with the exception of a reviewer or editor who may quote brief passages in connection with a review or a news story, is prohibited.

Message To Insurers

All survey data received on or before May 21, 2018 has been considered or incorporated into this edition of the Directory. If there are particular circumstances which you believe could affect your rating, please use the online survey (http://weissratings.com/survey/) or e-mail Weiss Ratings, LLC (insurancesurvey@weissinc.com) with documentation to support your request. If warranted, we will make every effort to incorporate the changes in our next edition.

Welcome to Weiss Ratings'
Guide to Property and Casualty Insurers

Most people automatically assume their insurance company will survive, year after year. However, prudent consumers and professionals realize that in this world of shifting risks, the solvency of insurance companies can't be taken for granted.

If you are looking for accurate, unbiased ratings and data to help you choose property and casualty insurance for yourself, your family, your company or your clients, Weiss Ratings' *Guide to Property and Casualty Insurers* gives you precisely what you need.

In fact, it's the only source that currently provides ratings and analyses on over 2,000 property and casualty insurers.

Weiss Ratings' Mission Statement

Weiss Ratings' mission is to empower consumers, professionals, and institutions with high quality advisory information for selecting or monitoring a financial services company or financial investment.

In doing so, Weiss Ratings will adhere to the highest ethical standards by maintaining our independent, unbiased outlook and approach to advising our customers.

Why rely on Weiss Ratings?

Weiss Ratings provides fair, objective ratings to help professionals and consumers alike make educated purchasing decisions.

At Weiss Ratings, integrity is number one. Weiss Ratings never takes a penny from insurance companies for issuing a rating. We publish Weiss Safety Ratings without regard for insurers' preferences. However, other rating agencies like A.M. Best, Fitch, Moody's and Standard & Poor's are paid by insurance companies for their ratings and may even suppress unfavorable ratings at an insurer's request.

Our ratings are reviewed and updated more frequently than the other agencies' ratings. You can be sure that the information you receive is accurate and current, providing you with advance warning of financial vulnerability early enough to do something about it.

Other rating agencies focus primarily on a company's current claims paying ability and consider only mild economic adversity. Weiss Ratings also considers these issues, but our analysis also covers a company's ability to deal with severe economic adversity and a sharp increase in claims.

Our use of more rigorous standards stems from the viewpoint that an insurance company's obligations to its policyholders should not depend on favorable business conditions. An insurer must be able to honor its policy commitments in bad times as well as good.

Our rating scale, from A to F, is easy to understand. Only a few outstanding companies receive an A (Excellent) rating, although there are many to choose from within the B (Good) category. An even larger group falls into the broad average range which receives C (Fair) ratings. Companies that demonstrate marked vulnerabilities receive either D (Weak) or E (Very Weak) ratings.

How to Use This Guide

The purpose of the *Guide to Property and Casualty Insurers* is to provide policyholders and prospective policy purchasers with a reliable source of insurance company ratings and analyses on a timely basis. We realize that the financial strength of an insurer is an important factor to consider when making the decision to purchase a policy or change companies. The ratings and analyses in this Guide can make that evaluation easier when you are considering:

- Homeowners insurance

- Business insurance

- Auto insurance

- Workers' compensation insurance

- Product liability insurance

- Medical malpractice and other professional liability insurance

This Guide does not include companies that strictly provide life and health insurance or annuities. For information on those companies, please refer to our *Guide to Life and Annuity Insurers*. Also, only a few of the property and casualty companies in this Guide provide any form of health insurance. For a complete listing of health insurance providers, please refer to our *Guide to Health Insurers*.

The rating for a particular company indicates our opinion regarding that company's ability to meet its commitments to the policyholder – not only under current economic conditions, but also during a declining economy or in the event of a sharp increase in claims. Such an increase in claims and related expenses may be triggered by any number of occurrences including a strong earthquake or hurricane, rising medical or legal costs, or large court awards. The safest companies, however, should be prepared to deal with harsh and unforeseen circumstances.

To use this Guide most effectively, we recommend you follow the steps outlined below:

Step 1   To ensure you evaluate the correct company, verify the company's exact name and state of domicile as it was given to you or appears on your policy. Many companies have similar names but are not related to one another, so you want to make sure the company you look up is really the one you are interested in evaluating.

Step 2   Turn to Section I, the Index of Companies, and locate the company you are evaluating. This section contains all companies analyzed by Weiss Ratings including those that did not receive a Safety Rating. It is sorted alphabetically by the name of the company and shows the state of domicile following the name for additional verification. Once you have located your specific company, the first column after the state of domicile shows its Weiss Safety Rating. Turn to *About Weiss Safety Ratings* for information about what this rating means. If the rating has changed since the last issue of this Guide, a downgrade will be indicated with a down triangle ▼ to the left of the company name; an upgrade will be indicated with an up triangle ▲.

Step 3   Following Weiss Safety Rating are some of the various indexes that our analysts used in rating the company. Refer to the Critical Ranges in our Indexes table for an interpretation of which index values are considered strong, good, fair or weak. You can also turn to the introduction of Section I to see what each of these factors measures. In most cases, lower-rated companies will have a low index value in one or more of the factors shown. Bear in mind, however, that a Safety Rating is the result of a complex propriatary quantitative and qualitative analysis which cannot be reproduced using only the data provided here.

Step 4   Our analysts evaluate a great number of ratios and performance measures when assigning a rating. The right hand page of Section I shows you some of the key financial ratios we consider. Again, refer to the introduction of Section I for a description of each ratio.

Step 5   Some insurers have a bullet ● preceding the company name on the right hand page of Section I. This means that more detailed information about the company is available in Section II. If the company you are evaluating is identified with a bullet, turn to Section II, the Analysis of Largest Companies, and locate it there (otherwise skip to step 8). Section II contains the largest insurers rated by Weiss Ratings, regardless of rating. It too is sorted alphabetically by the name of the company.

Step 6   Once you have identified your company in Section II, you will find its Safety Rating and a description of the rating immediately to the right of the company name. Then, below the company name is a description of the various rating factors that were considered in assigning the company's rating. These factors and the information below them are designed to give you a better feel for the company and its strengths and weaknesses. See the Section II introduction to get a better understanding of what each of these factors means.

Step 7   To the right, you will find a five-year summary of the company's Safety Rating, capitalization and income. Look for positive or negative trends in these data. Below the five-year summary, we have included a graphic illustration of the most critical factor or factors impacting the company's rating. Again, the Section II introduction provides an overview of the content of each graph or table.

Step 8   If the company you are evaluating is not highly rated and you want to find an insurer with a higher rating, turn to the page in Section V that has your state's name at the top. This section contains those Recommended Companies (rating of A+, A, A- or B+) that are licensed to underwrite insurance in your state, sorted by rating. Then turn to the page in Section IV that shows the type of insurance you are interested in at the top. Insurers appearing on both lists will be those Recomended Companies which are licensed to sell that particular type of insurance in your state. From here you can select a company and then refer back to Sections I and II to analyze it.

Step 9   If you decide that you would like to contact one of Weiss Recommended Companies about obtaining a policy or for additional information, refer to Section III. Following each company's name is its address and phone number to assist you in making contact.

Step 10 In order to use Weiss Safety Ratings most effectively, we strongly recommend you consult the Important Warnings and Cautions listed. These are more than just "standard disclaimers"; they are very important factors you should be aware of before using this Guide. If you have any questions regarding the precise meaning of specific terms used in the Guide, refer to the Glossary.

Step 11 The Appendix contains information about State Guaranty Associations and the types of coverage they provide to policyholders when an insurance company fails. Keep in mind that while guaranty funds have now been established in all states, many do not cover all types of insurance. Furthermore, all of these funds have limits on their amount of coverage. Use the table to determine whether the level of coverage is applicable to your policy and the limits are adequate for your needs. You should pay particular attention to the notes regarding coverage limitations.

Step 12 If you want more information on your state's guaranty fund, call the State Commissioner's Office directly.

Step 13 Keep in mind that good coverage from a state guaranty association is no substitute for dealing with a financially strong company. Weiss Ratings only recommends those companies which we feel are most able to stand on their own, even in a recession or downturn in the economy .

Step 14 Make sure you stay up to date with the latest information available since the publication of this Guide. For information on how to set up a rating change notification service, acquire follow-up reports, or receive a more in-depth analysis of an individual company, call 1-877-934-7778 or visit www.weissratings.com.

Data Sources: Annual and quarterly statutory statements filed with state insurance commissioners and data provided by the insurance companies being rated. The National Association of Insurance Commissioners has provided some of the raw data. Any analyses or conclusions are not provided or endorsed by the NAIC.

Date of data analyzed December 31, 2017 unless otherwise noted.

About Weiss Safety Ratings

The Weiss Ratings of insurers are based upon the annual and quarterly financial statements filed with state insurance commissioners. This data may be supplemented by information that we request from the insurance companies themselves. However, if a company chooses not to provide supplemental data, we reserve the right to rate the company based exclusively on publicly available data.

The Weiss Ratings are based on a complex analysis of hundreds of factors that are synthesized into a series of indexes: capitalization, investment safety (life, health and annuity companies only), reserve adequacy (property and casualty companies only), profitability, liquidity, and stability. These indexes are then used to arrive at a letter grade rating. A weak score on any one index can result in a low rating, as financial problems can be caused by any one of a number of factors, such as inadequate capital, unpredictable claims experience, poor liquidity, speculative investments, inadequate reserving, or consistent operating losses.

Our **Capital Index** gauges capital adequacy in terms of each insurer's ability to handle a variety of business and economic scenarios as they may impact investment performance, claims experience, persistency, and market position. The index combines two Risk-Adjusted Capital ratios as well as a leverage test that examines pricing risk.

Our **Investment Safety Index** measures the exposure of the company's investment portfolio to loss of principal and/or income due to default and market risks. Each investment area is rated by a factor that takes into consideration both quality and liquidity. (This factor is measured as a separate index only for life, health, and annuity insurers.)

Our **Reserve Adequacy Index** measures the adequacy of the company's reserves and its ability to accurately anticipate the level of claims it will receive. (This factor is measured as a separate index only for property and casualty insurers.)

Our **Profitability Index** measures the soundness of the company's operations and the contribution of profits to the company's financial strength. The profitability index is a composite of five sub-factors: 1) gain or loss on operations; 2) consistency of operating results; 3) impact of operating results on surplus; 4) adequacy of investment income as compared to the needs of policy reserves (life, health and annuity companies only); and 5) expenses in relation to industry norms for the types of policies that the company offers.

Our **Liquidity Index** evaluates a company's ability to raise the necessary cash to settle claims and honor cash withdrawal obligations. We model various cash flow scenarios, applying liquidity tests to determine how the company might fare in the event of an unexpected spike in claims and/or a run on policy surrenders.

Our **Stability Index** integrates a number of sub-factors that affect consistency (or lack thereof) in maintaining financial strength over time. These sub-factors will vary depending on the type of insurance company being evaluated but may include such things as 1) risk diversification in terms of company size, group size, number of policies in force, types of policies written, and use of reinsurance; 2) deterioration of operations as reported in critical asset, liability, income and expense items, such as surrender rates and premium volume; 3) years in operation; 4) former problem areas where, despite recent improvement, the company has yet to establish a record of stable performance over a suitable period of time; 5) a substantial shift in the company's operations; 6) potential instabilities such as reinsurance quality, asset/liability matching, and sources of capital; and 7) relationships with holding companies and affiliates.

In order to help guarantee our objectivity, we reserve the right to publish ratings expressing our opinion of a company's financial stability based exclusively on publicly available data and our own proprietary standards for safety.

Each of these indexes is measured according to the following range of values.

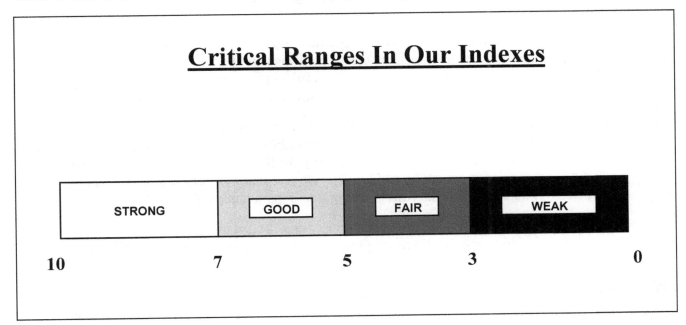

What Our Ratings Mean

A   **Excellent.** The company offers excellent financial security. It has maintained a conservative stance in its investment strategies, business operations and underwriting commitments. While the financial position of any company is subject to change, we believe that this company has the resources necessary to deal with severe economic conditions.

B   **Good.** The company offers good financial security and has the resources to deal with a variety of adverse economic conditions. It comfortably exceeds the minimum levels for all of our rating criteria, and is likely to remain healthy for the near future. However, in the event of a severe recession or major financial crisis, we feel that this assessment should be reviewed to make sure that the firm is still maintaining adequate financial strength.

C   **Fair.** The company offers fair financial security and is currently stable. But during an economic downturn or other financial pressures, we feel it may encounter difficulties in maintaining its financial stability.

D   **Weak.** The company currently demonstrates what, in our opinion, we consider to be significant weaknesses which could negatively impact policyholders. In an unfavorable economic environment, these weaknesses could be magnified.

E   **Very Weak.** The company currently demonstrates what we consider to be significant weaknesses and has also failed some of the basic tests that we use to identify fiscal stability. Therefore, even in a favorable economic environment, it is our opinion that policyholders could incur significant risks.

F   **Failed.** The company is deemed failed if it is either 1) under supervision of an insurance regulatory authority; 2) in the process of rehabilitation; 3) in the process of liquidation; or 4) voluntarily dissolved after disciplinary or other regulatory action by an insurance regulatory authority.

+   The **plus sign** is an indication that the company is in the upper third of the letter grade.

-   The **minus sign** is an indication that the company is in the lower third of the letter grade.

U   **Unrated.** The company is unrated for one or more of the following reasons: (1) total assets are less than $1 million; (2) premium income for the current year was less than $100,000; (3) the company functions almost exclusively as a holding company rather than as an underwriter; (4) in our opinion, we do not have enough information to reliably issue a rating.

How Our Ratings Differ From Those of Other Services

Weiss Safety Ratings are conservative and consumer-oriented. We use tougher standards than other rating agencies because our system is specifically designed to inform risk-averse consumers about the safety of property and casualty insurers.

Our rating scale (A to F) is easy to understand by the general public. Users can intuitively understand that an A+ rating is at the top of the scale rather than in the middle like some of the other rating agencies.

Other rating agencies give top ratings more generously so that most companies receive excellent ratings.

More importantly, other rating agencies focus primarily on a company's *current* claims paying ability or consider only relatively mild economic adversity. We also consider these scenarios but extend our analyses to cover a company's ability to deal with severe economic adversity and potential liquidity problems. This stems from the viewpoint that an insurance company's obligations to its policyholders should not be contingent upon a healthy economy. The company must be capable of honoring its policy commitments in bad times as well.

Looking at the insurance industry as a whole, we note that several major rating firms have poor historical track records in identifying troubled companies. The 1980s saw a persistent decline in capital ratios, increased holdings of risky investments in the life and health industry as well as recurring long-term claims liabilities in the property and casualty industry. The insurance industry experienced similar issues before and during the Great Recession of 2007-2009. Despite these clear signs that insolvency risk was rising, other rating firms failed to downgrade at-risk insurance companies. Instead, they often rated companies by shades of excellence, understating the gravity of potential problems.

Other ratings agencies have not issued clear warnings that the ordinary consumer can understand. Few, if any, companies receive "weak" or "poor" ratings. Surely, weak companies do exist. However, the other rating agencies apparently do not view themselves as consumer advocates with the responsibility of warning the public about the risks involved in doing business with such companies.

Additionally, these firms will at times agree *not* to issue a rating if a company denies them permission to do so. In short, too often insurance rating agencies work hand-in-glove with the companies they rate.

At Weiss Ratings, although we seek to maintain good relationships with the firms, we owe our primary obligation to the consumer, not the industry. We reserve the right to rate companies based on publicly available data and make the necessary conservative assumptions when companies choose not to provide additional data we might request.

Comparison of Insurance Company Rating Agency Scales				
Weiss Ratings [a]	**Best** [a]	**S&P**	**Moody's**	**Fitch**
A+, A, A-	A++, A+	AAA	Aaa	AAA
B+, B, B-	A, A-	AA+, AA AA-	Aa1, Aa2, Aa3	AA+, AA, AA-
C+, C, C-	B++, B+,	A+, A, A-, BBB+, BBB, BBB-	A1, A2, A3, Baa1, Baa2, Baa3	A+, A, A-, BBB+, BBB, BBB-
D+, D, D-	B, B- C++, C+, C, C-	BB+, BB, BB-, B+, B, B-	Ba1, Ba2, Ba3, B1, B2, B3	BB+, BB, BB-, B+, B, B-
E+, E, E- F	D E, F	CCC R	Caa, Ca, C	CCC+, CCC, CCC- DD

[a] Weiss Ratings and Best use additional symbols to designate that they recognize an insurer's existence but do not provide a rating. These symbols are not included in this table.

Rate of Insurance Company Failures

Weiss Ratings provides quarterly Safety Ratings for thousands of insurance companies each year. Weiss Ratings strives for fairness and objectivity in its ratings and analyses, ensuring that each company receives the rating that most accurately depicts its current financial status, and more importantly, its ability to deal with severe economic adversity and a sharp increase in claims. Weiss Ratings has every confidence that its Safety Ratings provide an accurate representation of a company's stability.

In order for these ratings to be of any true value, it is important that they prove accurate over time. One way to determine the accuracy of a rating is to examine those insurance companies that have failed, and their respective Weiss Safety Ratings. A high percentage of failed companies with "A" ratings would indicate that Weiss Ratings is not being conservative enough with its "secure" ratings, while conversely, a low percentage of failures with "vulnerable" ratings would show that Weiss Ratings is overly conservative.

Over the past 29 years (1989–2017) Weiss Ratings has rated 637 insurance companies, for all industries, that subsequently failed. The chart below shows the number of failed companies in each rating category, the average number of companies rated in each category per year, and the percentage of annual failures for each letter grade.

	Safety Rating	Number of Failed Companies	Average Number of Companies Rated per year	Percentage of Failed Companies per year (by ratings category)*
Secure	A	1	153	0.02%
	B	6	1,111	0.02%
	C	70	1,610	0.15%
Vulnerable	D	278	744	1.29%
	E	282	217	4.48%

A=Excellent, B=Good, C=Fair, D=Weak, E=Very Weak

On average, only 0.09% of the companies Weiss Ratings rates as "secure" fail each year. On the other hand, an average of 2.01% of the companies Weiss Ratings rates as "vulnerable" fail annually. That means that a company rated by Weiss Ratings as "Vulnerable" is 21.7 times more likely to fail than a company rated as "Secure".

When considering a Weiss Safety Rating, one can be sure that they are getting the most fair, objective, and accurate safety rating available anywhere.

*Percentage of Failed Companies per year = (Number of Failed Companies) / [(Average Number of Companies Rated per year) x (years in study)]

Data as of December 2017 for Life and Annuity Insurers and Property & Casualty Insurers
Data as of December 2016 for Health Insurers

What Does Average Mean?

At Weiss Ratings, we consider the words average and fair to mean just that – average and fair. So when we assign our ratings to insurers, the largest percentage of companies receives an average C rating. That way, you can be sure that a company receiving Weiss B or A rating is truly above average. Likewise, you can feel confident that companies with D or E ratings are truly below average.

Percentage for Property and Casualty Insurers in Each Rating Category

Current Weiss Ratings Distribution

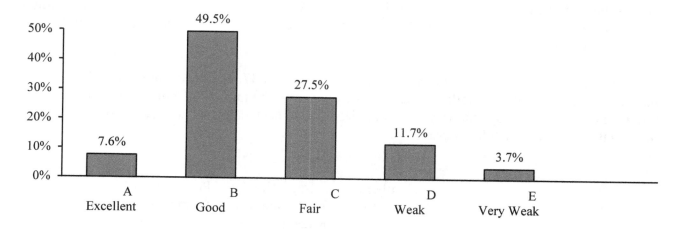

Important Warnings and Cautions

1. A rating alone cannot tell the whole story. Please read the explanatory information contained in this publication. It is provided in order to give you an understanding of our rating philosophy, as well as paint a more complete picture of how we arrive at our opinion of a company's strengths and weaknesses.

2. Weiss Safety Ratings represent our opinion of a company's insolvency risk. As such, a high rating means we feel that the company has less chance of running into financial difficulties. A high rating is not a guarantee of solvency nor is a low rating a prediction of insolvency. Weiss Safety Ratings are not deemed to be a recommendation concerning the purchase or sale of the securities of any insurance company that is publicly owned.

3. Company performance is only one factor in determining a rating. Conditions in the marketplace and overall economic conditions are additional factors that may affect the company's financial strength. Therefore, a rating upgrade or downgrade does not necessarily reflect changes in the company's profits, capital or other financial measures, but may be due to external factors. Likewise, changes in Weiss indexes may reflect changes in our risk assessment of business or economic conditions as well as changes in company performance.

4. All firms that have the same Safety Rating should be considered to be essentially equal in strength. This is true regardless of any differences in the underlying numbers which might appear to indicate greater strengths. Weiss Safety Rating already takes into account a number of lesser factors which, due to space limitations, cannot be included in this publication.

5. A good rating requires consistency. If a company is excellent on four indicators and fair on one, the company may receive a fair rating. This requirement is necessary due to the fact that fiscal problems can arise from any *one* of several causes including speculative investments, inadequate capital resources or operating losses.

6. We are an independent rating agency and do not depend on the cooperation of the companies we rate. Our data are derived, from annual and quarterly financial statements that we obtain from federal regulators and filings with state insurance commissioners. The latter may be supplemented by information insurance companies voluntarily provide upon request. Although we seek to maintain an open line of communication with the companies, we do not grant them the right to stop or influence publication of the ratings. This policy stems from the fact that this publication is designed for the protection of the consumer.

7. Affiliated companies do not automatically receive the same rating. We recognize that a troubled company may expect financial support from its parent or affiliates. Weiss Safety Ratings reflect our opinion of the measure of support that may become available to a subsidiary, if the subsidiary were to experience serious financial difficulties. In the case of a strong parent and a weaker subsidiary, the affiliate relationship will generally result in a higher rating for the subsidiary than it would have on a stand-alone basis. Seldom, however, would the rating be brought up to the level of the parent. This treatment is appropriate because we do not assume the parent would have either the resources or the will to "bail out" a troubled subsidiary during a severe economic crisis. Even when there is a binding legal obligation for a parent corporation to honor the policy obligations of its subsidiaries, the possibility exists that the subsidiary could be sold and lose its parental support. Therefore, it is quite common for one affiliate to have a higher rating than another. This is another reason why it is especially important that you have the precise name of the company you are evaluating.

Section I

Index of Companies

An analysis of all rated and unrated

U.S. Property and Casualty Insurers.

Companies are listed in alphabetical order.

Section I Contents

This section contains the key rating factors and performance measures for all rated and unrated insurers analyzed by Weiss Ratings. An explanation of each of the footnotes and stability factors appears at the end of this section.

Left Pages

1. Insurance Company Name
The legally registered name, which can sometimes differ from the name that the company uses for advertising. If you cannot find the company you are interested in, or if you have any doubts regarding the precise name, verify the information with the company before looking the name up in this Guide. Also, determine the domicile state for confirmation. (See column 2.)

2. Domicile State
The state which has primary regulatory responsibility for the company. It may differ from the location of the company's corporate headquarters. You do not have to be living in the domicile state to purchase insurance from this firm, provided it is licensed to do business in your state.

3. Safety Rating
Our rating is measured on a scale from A to F and considers a wide range of factors. Please see *What Our Ratings Mean* for specific descriptions of each letter grade. Also, refer to how our ratings differ from those of other rating agencies. Most important, when using this rating, please be sure to consider the warnings regarding the ratings' limitations and the underlying assumptions. Notes in this column refer to the date of the data included in the rating evaluation and are explained.

4. Total Assets
All assets admitted by state insurance regulators in millions of dollars through the most recent quarter available. This includes investments and current business assets such as receivables from agents and reinsurers.

The overall size is an important factor which affects the ability of a company to manage risk. Generally speaking, risks can be more effectively diversified by large companies. Because the insurance business is based on probability, the number of policies must be large enough so that actuarial statistics are valid. The larger the number of policyholders, the more reliable the actuarial projections will be. A large company with a correspondingly large policy base can spread its risk and minimize the effects of claims experience that exceeds actuarial expectations.

5. Capital and Surplus
The company's statutory net worth in millions of dollars through the most recent quarter available. Consumers may wish to limit the size of any policy so that the policyholder's maximum potential claims do not exceed approximately 1% of the company's capital and surplus. For example, when buying a policy from a company with capital and surplus of $10,000,000, the 1% limit would be $100,000. (When performing this

calculation, do not forget that figures in this column are expressed in millions of dollars.)

6. Net Premium

The amount of insurance premiums received from policyholders less any premiums that have been transferred to other companies through reinsurance agreements. This figure is updated through the most recent annual report available.

Generally speaking, companies with large net premium volume generally have more predictable claims experience.

Critical Ranges In Our Indexes and Ratios

Indicators	Strong	Good	Fair	Weak
Risk-Adjusted Capital Ratio #1	—	1.0 or more	0.75 - 0.99	0.74 or less
Risk-Adjusted Capital Ratio #2	1.0 or more	0.75 - 0.99	0.5 - 0.74	0.49 or less
Capitalization Index	6.9 – 10	4.9 - 6.8	2.9 - 4.8	Less than 2.9
Reserve Adequacy Index	6.9 – 10	4.9 - 6.8	2.9 - 4.8	Less than 2.9
Profitability Index	6.9 – 10	4.9 - 6.8	2.9 - 4.8	Less than 2.9
Liquidity Index	6.9 – 10	4.9 - 6.8	2.9 - 4.8	Less than 2.9
Stability Index	6.9 – 10	4.9 - 6.8	2.9 - 4.8	Less than 2.9

7. Net Income

The company's profit for the period. Profit is defined as revenues minus expenses. In the case of an insurance company, revenues include premiums and investment income, and expenses include claims payments and underwriting expenses.

8. Capitalization Index

An index that measures the adequacy of the company's capital resources to deal with a variety of business and economic scenarios. It combines Risk-Adjusted Capital Ratios #1 and #2 as well as a leverage test that examines pricing risk. (See the table above for the ranges which we believe are critical.)

9. Reserve Adequacy Index

An index that uses annual and quarterly data to measure the adequacy of the company's reserves. Reserves are funds the company sets aside to cover unsettled claims it estimates each year. Included are claims that the company has already received but have not yet been settled and claims that they expect to receive, but which have not yet been reported.

If a company consistently estimates its claims accurately, that is good. Or if it errs on the side of being conservative and overestimates its claims from time to time, that is even better. Either case will cause this index to move higher.

On the other hand, some companies may have trouble accurately predicting the claims they will have to pay. Others may intentionally underestimate their claims to inflate their profits for stockholders or to make their capital appear higher than it really is. In either case, inadequate reserve levels will result in a low Reserve Adequacy Index.

If a company has chronically deficient reserves, it calls into question the company's ability to manage its policy risk effectively.

10. Profitability Index

An index that uses annual and quarterly data to measure the soundness of the company's operations and the contribution of profits to the company's fiscal strength. The Profitability Index is a composite of five factors: (1) gain or loss on underwriting; (2) gain or loss on overall operations; (3) consistency of operating results; (4) impact of operating results on surplus; and (5) expenses in relation to industry averages for the types of policies that the company offers.

11. Liquidity Index

An index which uses annual and quarterly data to measure the company's ability to raise the necessary cash to settle claims. Sometimes a company may appear to have the necessary resources to pay claims on paper, but in reality, it may be unable to raise the necessary cash. This can occur, for example, when a company is owed a great deal of money from its agents or reinsurers, or when it cannot sell its investments at the prices at which they are valued in the company's financial statements.

We look at various cash flow scenarios. Then we apply liquidity tests which tell us how the company might fare in each of those circumstances.

12. Stability Index

An index which uses annual and quarterly data to integrate a number of factors such as: (1) risk diversification in terms of company size, number of policies in force, use of reinsurance, and single largest risk exposure; (2) deterioration of operations as reported in critical asset, liability, income, or expense items such as premium volume and/or surplus (See the table prior page for the levels which we believe are critical.)

13. Stability Factors

Indicates those specific areas that have negatively impacted the company's Stability Index.

Right Pages

1. Risk-Adjusted Capital Ratio #1

This ratio examines the adequacy of the company's capital base and whether the company has sufficient capital resources to cover potential losses which might occur in an average recession or other moderate loss scenario. Specifically, the figure, calculated from annual and quarterly data, answers the question: For every dollar of capital that we feel would be needed, how many dollars in capital resources does the company actually have?

You may find that some companies have unusually high levels of capital. This often reflects special circumstances related to the small size or unusual operations of the company.

See the table prior page for the levels which we believe are critical. See the Appendix for more details on how this ratio is calculated.

2. Risk-Adjusted Capital Ratio #2

This is similar to the Risk-Adjusted Capital Ratio #1. But in this case, the question relates to whether the company has enough capital cushion to withstand a *severe* recession or other severe loss scenario.

See the table prior page for the levels which we believe are critical. See the Appendix for more details on how this ratio is calculated.

3. Premium to Surplus

The ratio of net premiums written compared to the company's capital and surplus level. This ratio, calculated from the company's annual report, answers the question: For every dollar of capital and surplus, how many dollars of premium does the company take in? Results of over 300% are considered perilous and could indicate that the insurer does not have adequate capital to support the volume of business that it is underwriting. A large figure could also help explain why a company has poor results on its risk-adjusted capital tests.

4. Reserves to Surplus

The ratio of reserves for expected claims compared to the company's capital and surplus level. If a company does not set aside enough reserves, it may have to withdraw capital to pay claims. This ratio, calculated from the annual report, is a rough measure of how much capital cushion the company has against claims reserves. The industry average is around 180%.

High ratios signify that reserve deficiencies would have a strong impact on capital and could help explain why a company has poor risk-adjusted capital results.

5. One-Year Reserve Development

The percentage increase or decrease in the company's annual reserve estimate compared to the previous year. If last year's estimate is below that of this year, this will result in a positive ratio meaning that the company underestimated its future claims and set aside insufficient reserves. Making this error consistently is viewed negatively because it means the company is inflating its income and capital.

| 6. | **Two-Year Reserve Development** | This ratio is similar to the One-Year Reserve Development ratio. However, instead of comparing the latest estimates with those from the prior year, it compares them to the estimates from two years ago. |

Again, a positive ratio means the company underestimated its reserve needs while a negative ratio indicates that reserve needs were overestimated.

| 7. | **Loss Ratio** | The ratio of claims paid to premiums collected, calculated from the annual report, measures the company's underwriting profits. Needless to say, if an insurer pays out a very high percentage of what it collects, there may not be enough left over for other expenses, let alone enough to build the company's capital and financial strength over time. |

| 8. | **Expense Ratio** | The ratio of overhead expenses to premiums collected, calculated from the annual report, and answers the question: How many cents is the company paying out in executive salaries, agents' commissions, and other administrative expenses for every dollar in premiums that it collects from policyholders? A low Expense Ratio is good for both the company and its policyholders because it means that the company is efficient and can utilize more of each premium dollar to pay claims. A high Expense Ratio is a bad sign because it signals that too much of the company's premiums are being used for things which do not directly benefit its policyholders. |

| 9. | **Combined Ratio** | The sum of the Loss Ratio and the Expense Ratio. The Combined Ratio shows how much the company is paying out in administrative expenses and claims for every dollar of premium collected. |

Values over 100% indicate that the company is losing money on its underwriting. This is very common in the industry, but it's still a sign of possible weakness.

Underwriting losses can often be offset by income the company realizes on its investments. This is especially true for companies that issue policies on which they do not have to pay claims for several years (long-tail policies). With these policies, the premiums can be invested in order to earn income for the company until the claims are paid.

| 10. | **Cash from Underwriting** | The ratio of cash received from premiums (net of reinsurance) to cash outlays for claims and underwriting expenses, compiled from the annual report. A figure under 100% indicates that the company is paying out more in claims and expenses than it is receiving in premiums, whereas a figure over 100% indicates a positive cash flow. A negative figure generally indicates that the company has sold more business to a reinsurance company than it has taken in during the current year. |

When a company has a positive net cash flow from its underwriting, it can generate additional funds for investing. On the other hand, if net cash flow is negative, the company may have to rely on its investment income to make up the shortfall. And if that isn't enough, it may even have to sell assets to meet its obligations.

11. Net Premium Growth

The annual percentage change in net premiums compared to the previous year. A company can increase its premium volume by: (1) issuing more new policies; (2) raising its rates; or (3) selling less of its insurance to other insurance companies. Slow and steady growth is healthy but rapid growth is often an indicator of trouble ahead. It may mean that the company is underpricing as a means of gaining market share. Indeed, a high percentage of insurance company failures are related to rapid growth. Regulators consider a fluctuation of more than 33% as a cautionary flag.

A rapid decline in premium volume is also a negative sign. It indicates that the company is losing its customer base. However, if the decline is the result of premium redistribution among a group of affiliates, the significance of the decline is minimal.

12. Investments In Affiliates

The percentage of the company's investment portfolio from the annual report dedicated to investments in affiliates. These investments can be bonds, preferred and common stocks, as well as other vehicles which many insurance companies use to invest in – and establish a corporate link with – affiliated companies. Large investments of this type can pose problems as these investments often produce no income and can be difficult to sell.

Footnotes:

(1)   Data items shown are from the company's 2016 annual statutory statement except for Risk-Adjusted Capital Indexes 1 and 2, Profitability Index, Investment Safety Index, Liquidity Index and Stability Index which have been updated using the company's September 2016 quarterly statutory statement. Other more recent data may have been factored into the rating when available.

(2)   Data items shown are from the company's 2016 annual statutory statement except for Risk-Adjusted Capital Indexes 1 and 2, Profitability Index, Investment Safety Index, Liquidity Index and Stability Index which have been updated using the company's June 2017 quarterly statutory statement. Other more recent data may have been factored into the rating when available.

(3)   Data items shown are from the company's 2016 annual statutory statement except for Risk-Adjusted Capital Indexes 1 and 2, Profitability Index, Investment Safety Index, Liquidity Index and Stability Index which have been updated using the company's March 2017 quarterly statutory statement. Other more recent data may have been factored into the rating when available.

(4)   Data items shown are from the company's 2016 annual statutory statement. Other more recent data may have been factored into the rating when available.

(5)   These companies have data items that are older than September 30, 2016. They will be unrated (U) if they are not failed companies (F).

Stability Factors

(A)   Stability Index was negatively impacted by the financial problems or weaknesses of a parent or **affiliate** company.

(C)   Stability Index was negatively impacted by past results on our Risk-Adjusted **Capital** tests. In general, the Stability Index of any company can be affected by past results even if current results show improvement. While such improvement is a plus, the improved results must be maintained for a period of time to assure that the improvement is not a temporary fluctuation. During a five-year period, the impact of poor past results on the Stability Index gradually diminishes.

(D)   Stability Index was negatively impacted by limited **diversification** of general business, policy, and/or investment risk. This factor especially affects smaller companies that do not issue as many policies as larger firms. It can also affect firms that specialize in only one line of business.

(E)   Stability Index was negatively impacted due to a lack of operating **experience**. The company has been in operation for less than five years. Consequently, it has not been able to establish the kind of stable track record that we believe is needed to demonstrate financial permanence and strength.

(F)   Stability Index was negatively impacted by negative cash **flow**. In other words, the company paid out more in claims and expenses than it received in premiums and investment income.

(G)   Stability Index was negatively impacted by fast asset or premium **growth**. Fast growth can pose a serious problem for insurers. It is generally achieved by offering policies with premiums that are too low, benefits that are too costly, or agents commissions that are too high. Due to the highly competitive nature of the insurance marketplace, rapid growth has been a factor in many insurance insolvencies.

(L)   Stability Index was negatively impacted by results on our **liquidity** tests. While the company may have sufficient cash flow to meet its current obligations, it could encounter difficulties under adverse scenarios, such as a dramatic increase in claims.

(O)   Stability Index was negatively impacted by significant changes in the company's business **operations**. These changes can include shifts in the kinds of insurance offered by the company, a temporary or permanent freeze on the sale of new policies, or recent release from conservatorship. In these circumstances, past performance cannot be a reliable indicator of future financial strength.

(R)   Stability Index was negatively impacted by concerns about the financial strength of its **reinsurers**.

(T)   Stability Index was negatively impacted by significant **trends** in critical asset, liability, income or expense items. Examples include fluctuations in premium volume, changes in the types of investments the company makes, and changes in the types of policies the company writes.

(Z)   This company is unrated due to data, as received by Weiss Ratings, that are either incomplete in substantial ways or contains items that, in the opinion of Weiss Ratings analysts, may not be reliable.

INSURANCE COMPANY NAME	DOM. STATE	RATING	TOTAL ASSETS ($MIL)	CAPITAL & SURPLUS ($MIL)	ANNUAL NET PREMIUM ($MIL)	NET INCOME ($MIL)	CAPITAL-IZATION INDEX (PTS)	RESERVE ADQ INDEX (PTS)	PROFIT-ABILITY INDEX (PTS)	LIQUIDITY INDEX (PTS)	STAB. INDEX (PTS)	STABILITY FACTORS
1ST ATLANTIC SURETY CO	NC	D+	4.1	2.4	0.8	0.7	9.5	5.0	5.6	9.6	1.7	DT
1ST AUTO & CASUALTY INS CO	WI	C	25.5	11.0	22.4	-0.2	7.3	6.7	2.5	2.6	3.8	DFLR
1ST CHOICE ADVANTAGE INS CO	PA	C	21.6	7.5	14.0	-0.2	7.1	4.2	2.7	4.4	3.6	DLR
21ST CENTURY ADVANTAGE INS CO	MN	B	29.6	29.7	0.0	0.3	10.0	4.6	6.0	10.0	4.2	DT
21ST CENTURY ASR CO	DE	B	70.5	70.4	0.0	0.6	10.0	4.6	5.8	10.0	4.6	DT
21ST CENTURY AUTO INS CO OF NJ	NJ	U	--	--	--	--	N/A	--	--	--	--	Z
21ST CENTURY CASUALTY CO	CA	B	12.5	12.5	0.0	0.1	10.0	4.6	6.0	10.0	4.7	D
21ST CENTURY CENTENNIAL INS CO	PA	B	601.1	601.1	0.0	5.1	8.3	4.6	6.4	10.0	5.3	T
21ST CENTURY INDEMNITY INS CO	PA	B	69.3	69.3	0.0	1.7	10.0	4.6	6.7	10.0	4.3	DT
21ST CENTURY INS CO	CA	B	997.9	996.1	0.0	24.0	10.0	4.6	6.9	10.0	6.0	
21ST CENTURY INS CO OF THE SW	TX	U	--	--	--	--	N/A	--	--	--	--	Z
21ST CENTURY NATIONAL INS CO INC	NY	B	25.4	25.4	0.0	1.1	10.0	4.6	6.7	10.0	5.2	DT
21ST CENTURY NORTH AMERICA INS	NY	B	594.6	572.1	0.0	7.5	10.0	4.9	6.0	7.0	5.8	T
21ST CENTURY PACIFIC INS	CO	B	44.4	44.4	0.0	0.3	10.0	4.6	5.8	10.0	4.3	DFT
21ST CENTURY PINNACLE INS CO	NJ	B	42.9	42.8	0.0	0.4	10.0	4.6	5.6	10.0	4.4	DT
21ST CENTURY PREFERRED INS CO	PA	B	42.4	42.4	0.0	0.7	10.0	4.6	6.1	10.0	5.4	DT
21ST CENTURY PREMIER INS CO	PA	B-	289.3	289.3	0.0	4.6	10.0	4.6	6.3	10.0	4.9	T
21ST CENTURY SECURITY INS CO	PA	B	200.8	200.6	0.0	2.0	10.0	4.6	5.9	10.0	4.6	DT
21ST CENTURY SUPERIOR INS CO	CA	U	--	--	--	--	N/A	--	--	--	--	Z
▲360 INS CO	WY	B	33.6	24.0	8.7	0.5	10.0	6.1	5.7	7.5	4.1	DGOT
7710 INS CO	SC	D+	14.8	6.3	8.9	-0.5	2.2	3.6	2.1	7.0	2.2	CDFG
▲A CENTRAL INS CO	NY	C	118.3	41.4	52.6	1.6	9.0	6.1	6.8	6.4	3.5	T
▼A-ONE COMM INS RRG GROUP INC	TN	E	22.0	5.2	11.7	-1.3	0.1	2.1	2.8	7.7	0.2	CDGT
ACA FINANCIAL GUARANTY CORP	MD	U	--	--	--	--	N/A	--	--	--	--	Z
ACADEMIC HLTH PROFESSIONALS INS	NY	E-	330.7	-73.1	51.4	6.6	0.0	3.8	0.9	7.2	0.0	CRT
▲ACADEMIC MEDICAL PROFESSIONALS RRG	VT	D	4.8	2.4	1.0	0.1	3.6	8.4	5.3	9.6	1.5	DGT
ACADIA INS CO	NH	C	164.3	53.6	0.0	0.8	10.0	N/A	6.4	9.0	4.3	
▼ACCC INS CO	TX	E+	279.0	52.1	258.0	-12.2	1.9	0.5	1.9	0.0	0.8	CFL
▲ACCEPTANCE CASUALTY INS CO	NE	D+	162.5	67.2	61.2	0.3	7.0	4.2	4.4	7.3	2.5	GRT
ACCEPTANCE INDEMNITY INS CO	NE	C-	330.6	181.6	89.0	7.3	6.7	4.9	4.6	6.4	2.7	FR
ACCEPTANCE INS CO	NE	F	11.4	3.0	0.0	-4.8	2.2	0.3	0.1	10.0	0.0	CDFR
ACCESS HOME INS CO	LA	C	37.8	12.8	13.1	1.1	6.3	6.5	8.5	7.1	3.3	D
▼ACCESS INS CO	TX	F (1)	214.1	30.6	46.1	-2.9	4.8	2.4	2.9	6.6	3.5	CFRT
ACCIDENT FUND INS CO OF AMERICA	MI	B-	3,664.5	994.7	1,319.1	126.3	6.5	4.8	8.9	6.9	4.6	GR
ACCIDENT INS CO	NM	E	87.3	26.4	13.1	-1.2	0.4	0.1	2.1	8.2	0.1	CFRT
▲ACCREDITED SURETY & CAS CO INC	FL	B-	148.7	54.5	8.6	3.4	9.4	6.1	8.3	9.4	5.2	DG
ACE AMERICAN INS CO	PA	B-	13,606.0	2,531.8	2,002.6	401.0	7.1	6.0	3.9	6.8	4.9	R
ACE FIRE UNDERWRITERS INS CO	PA	C	119.9	78.1	10.8	1.4	10.0	6.0	6.9	8.1	3.9	RT
ACE INS CO OF THE MIDWEST	IN	C	68.8	37.9	0.0	1.3	10.0	4.6	2.6	6.7	3.9	FT
ACE P&C INS CO	PA	B-	8,693.1	1,970.3	1,894.4	157.9	8.1	6.0	5.2	6.6	4.9	R
ACIG INS CO	IL	D+	503.4	143.0	78.0	4.9	7.2	7.0	6.4	6.6	2.2	R
ACSTAR INS CO	IL	C+	52.6	23.6	0.8	1.6	9.4	8.7	3.6	10.0	4.7	DR
▲ACUITY A MUTUAL INS CO	WI	A-	3,960.1	1,819.8	1,374.3	145.8	9.4	8.9	8.8	6.7	7.0	
ADDISON INS CO	IA	C+	125.3	48.1	40.8	1.5	9.5	8.1	6.9	6.8	4.8	T
▲ADIRONDACK INS EXCHANGE	NY	C+	326.3	100.6	127.5	4.8	7.8	4.9	4.9	5.5	4.5	FR
ADM INS CO	AZ	C	103.1	23.1	0.0	-0.7	9.4	N/A	3.6	0.0	3.7	DFLT
ADMIRAL INDEMNITY CO	DE	C	59.5	42.8	0.0	0.9	10.0	N/A	7.1	10.0	4.2	R
ADMIRAL INS CO	DE	C	749.4	666.0	0.0	10.4	8.2	N/A	7.3	7.0	4.1	AR
ADRIATIC INS CO	ND	C	95.4	75.2	26.4	5.7	10.0	8.0	8.7	7.1	4.0	R
ADVANCED PROVIDERS INS RRG INC	AZ	D	1.5	1.4	0.1	0.1	10.0	4.8	3.8	9.8	1.3	DT
▲ADVANTAGE WORKERS COMP INS CO	IN	B	508.1	215.5	68.2	5.6	7.1	5.8	4.6	7.0	4.1	T
▲AEGIS HEALTHCARE RRG INC	DC	D+	5.0	2.9	1.0	-0.1	7.8	9.6	3.3	6.8	1.9	DR

See Page 27 for explanation of footnotes and Page 28 for explanation of stability factors.
Arrows denote recent upgrades ▲ or downgrades ▼   (see Section VII for explanations)

30

www.weissratings.com

RISK ADJ. RATIO #1	CAPITAL RATIO #2	PREMIUM TO SURPLUS (%)	RESV. TO SURPLUS (%)	RESV. DEVELOP. 1 YEAR (%)	RESV. DEVELOP. 2 YEAR (%)	LOSS RATIO (%)	EXP. RATIO (%)	COMB RATIO (%)	CASH FROM UNDER-WRITING (%)	NET PREMIUM GROWTH (%)	INVEST. IN AFFIL (%)	INSURANCE COMPANY NAME
3.6	3.3	34.9	7.6	0.3	-6.1	8.2	50.4	58.6	125.5	-37.3	0.0	1ST ATLANTIC SURETY CO
1.5	1.2	204.9	61.6	-3.0	-4.1	73.8	33.0	106.8	85.6	-0.6	0.0	1ST AUTO & CASUALTY INS CO
1.5	1.0	188.2	71.8	1.0	11.7	81.4	25.0	106.4	98.8	8.1	0.0	1ST CHOICE ADVANTAGE INS CO
268.7	134.3	N/A	N/A	N/A	N/A	N/A	N/A	N/A	38.7	0.0	0.0	21ST CENTURY ADVANTAGE INS CO
269.5	134.7	N/A	N/A	N/A	N/A	N/A	N/A	N/A	N/A	0.0	0.0	21ST CENTURY ASR CO
N/A	N/A	--	--	--	--	--	--	--	--	--	--	21ST CENTURY AUTO INS CO OF NJ
316.5	158.3	N/A	N/A	N/A	N/A	N/A	N/A	N/A	N/A	0.0	0.0	21ST CENTURY CASUALTY CO
1.8	1.8	N/A	N/A	N/A	N/A	N/A	N/A	N/A	2.3	0.0	59.7 ●	21ST CENTURY CENTENNIAL INS CO
280.4	140.2	N/A	N/A	N/A	N/A	N/A	N/A	N/A	N/A	0.0	0.0	21ST CENTURY INDEMNITY INS CO
119.1	54.7	N/A	N/A	N/A	N/A	N/A	N/A	N/A	N/A	0.0	0.0 ●	21ST CENTURY INS CO
N/A	N/A	--	--	--	--	--	--	--	--	--	--	21ST CENTURY INS CO OF THE SW
101.1	50.5	N/A	N/A	N/A	N/A	N/A	N/A	N/A	N/A	0.0	0.0	21ST CENTURY NATIONAL INS CO INC
5.9	5.6	N/A	2.7	0.3	1.1	N/A	N/A	N/A	-0.2	0.0	17.7 ●	21ST CENTURY NORTH AMERICA INS
264.3	132.2	N/A	N/A	N/A	N/A	N/A	N/A	N/A	N/A	0.0	0.0	21ST CENTURY PACIFIC INS
257.9	128.9	N/A	N/A	N/A	N/A	N/A	N/A	N/A	N/A	0.0	0.0	21ST CENTURY PINNACLE INS CO
178.2	89.1	N/A	N/A	N/A	N/A	N/A	N/A	N/A	N/A	0.0	0.0	21ST CENTURY PREFERRED INS CO
4.5	4.5	N/A	N/A	N/A	N/A	N/A	N/A	N/A	6.9	0.0	24.1 ●	21ST CENTURY PREMIER INS CO
8.5	8.3	N/A	N/A	N/A	N/A	N/A	N/A	N/A	N/A	0.0	12.7	21ST CENTURY SECURITY INS CO
N/A	N/A	--	--	--	--	--	--	--	--	--	--	21ST CENTURY SUPERIOR INS CO
5.2	3.5	36.5	18.8	-1.1	1.1	82.6	14.5	97.1	155.5	31.4	0.0	360 INS CO
0.6	0.3	140.6	62.1	-3.3	-1.1	55.6	43.0	98.6	80.5	60.2	0.0	7710 INS CO
3.1	2.4	127.1	81.7	-0.6	0.6	67.2	31.9	99.1	108.1	5.4	0.0	A CENTRAL INS CO
0.1	0.1	227.7	196.3	53.3	40.2	95.5	18.4	113.9	198.5	99.8	0.0	A-ONE COMM INS RRG GROUP INC
N/A	N/A	--	--	--	--	--	--	--	--	--	--	ACA FINANCIAL GUARANTY CORP
-0.1	-0.1	-70.2	-532.1	15.7	24.9	98.4	8.0	106.4	121.0	-20.4	-0.1	ACADEMIC HLTH PROFESSIONALS INS
0.8	0.5	42.4	55.7	-3.9	-7.3	54.7	36.7	91.4	187.2	32.4	0.0	ACADEMIC MEDICAL PROFESSIONALS
5.8	5.3	N/A	N/A	N/A	N/A	N/A	N/A	N/A	80.9	0.0	0.0	ACADIA INS CO
0.3	0.3	495.6	278.1	79.8	105.5	90.8	13.8	104.6	88.2	-12.1	0.0	ACCC INS CO
1.6	1.0	91.0	69.5	0.2	11.9	73.3	30.7	104.0	268.5	26.5	0.0	ACCEPTANCE CASUALTY INS CO
1.3	1.0	49.0	37.4	0.1	7.0	73.2	30.7	103.9	94.8	26.0	21.9	ACCEPTANCE INDEMNITY INS CO
0.6	0.2	N/A	254.4	76.7	83.5	N/A	N/A	N/A	-0.4	0.0	0.0	ACCEPTANCE INS CO
2.1	1.2	102.7	10.2	-3.2	-1.3	34.2	58.7	92.9	114.0	-9.2	0.0	ACCESS HOME INS CO
0.9	0.7	138.4	88.9	40.3	22.6	102.0	15.9	117.9	87.7	-16.4	0.0	ACCESS INS CO
1.1	0.9	132.6	161.6	-4.6	-3.7	59.8	26.6	86.4	202.0	42.6	15.2 ●	ACCIDENT FUND INS CO OF AMERICA
0.2	0.1	49.8	170.3	-42.6	119.0	69.4	59.6	129.0	10.1	-6.9	0.0	ACCIDENT INS CO
6.2	3.9	15.8	23.7	-0.3	-0.5	1.9	32.6	34.5	-15.1	-6.4	0.0	ACCREDITED SURETY & CAS CO INC
1.4	1.0	79.1	142.7	-1.1	2.3	83.9	22.7	106.6	112.4	8.3	14.6 ●	ACE AMERICAN INS CO
13.3	10.8	13.9	25.0	-0.2	0.4	83.9	17.6	101.5	91.6	8.3	0.0	ACE FIRE UNDERWRITERS INS CO
8.0	7.2	N/A	6.9	N/A	N/A	N/A	N/A	N/A	-28.3	100.0	0.0	ACE INS CO OF THE MIDWEST
2.5	1.7	96.1	173.5	-1.2	2.8	83.9	20.0	103.9	102.1	8.3	2.8 ●	ACE P&C INS CO
2.1	1.3	54.6	168.1	-22.7	-52.2	75.6	40.6	116.2	100.6	12.1	0.0	ACIG INS CO
4.1	2.7	3.4	50.1	-2.1	-5.6	-20.4	136.7	116.3	52.7	-28.7	0.0	ACSTAR INS CO
4.5	2.7	75.5	71.9	-6.3	-7.9	62.0	31.1	93.1	114.6	4.4	0.0 ●	ACUITY A MUTUAL INS CO
4.3	3.0	84.8	96.7	-2.5	-2.3	72.8	30.4	103.2	108.7	5.6	0.0	ADDISON INS CO
2.2	1.6	126.8	56.4	1.8	-6.0	66.7	34.4	101.1	94.9	18.1	9.0	ADIRONDACK INS EXCHANGE
2.8	2.5	N/A	N/A	N/A	N/A	N/A	N/A	N/A	96.4	0.0	0.0	ADM INS CO
13.5	12.1	N/A	N/A	N/A	N/A	N/A	N/A	N/A	72.7	0.0	0.0	ADMIRAL INDEMNITY CO
1.6	1.7	N/A	N/A	N/A	N/A	N/A	N/A	N/A	N/A	0.0	49.8 ●	ADMIRAL INS CO
11.2	7.0	35.0	8.3	-5.5	-5.5	43.4	29.3	72.7	145.3	6.6	0.0	ADRIATIC INS CO
8.3	7.3	10.4	1.5	0.3	-3.5	2.8	78.9	81.7	139.1	-4.6	0.0	ADVANCED PROVIDERS INS RRG INC
1.5	1.0	31.7	124.4	-3.8	-16.2	66.2	35.2	101.4	115.0	-3.3	0.0	ADVANTAGE WORKERS COMP INS CO
1.9	1.5	34.4	59.9	-18.3	-22.7	57.0	44.0	101.0	95.8	11.2	0.0	AEGIS HEALTHCARE RRG INC

999 + Denotes number greater than 999.9%
999 - Denotes number less than -999.99%
● Bullets denote a more detailed analysis is available in Section II.

INSURANCE COMPANY NAME	DOM. STATE	RATING	TOTAL ASSETS ($MIL)	CAPITAL & SURPLUS ($MIL)	ANNUAL NET PREMIUM ($MIL)	NET INCOME ($MIL)	CAPITAL-IZATION INDEX (PTS)	RESERVE ADQ INDEX (PTS)	PROFIT-ABILITY INDEX (PTS)	LIQUIDITY INDEX (PTS)	STAB. INDEX (PTS)	STABILITY FACTORS
▼AEGIS SECURITY INS CO	PA	D+	148.7	53.7	104.3	-2.8	2.0	7.9	3.3	0.7	2.7	CLR
AETNA INS CO OF CT	CT	U	--	--	--	--	N/A	--	--	--	--	Z
AF&L INS CO	PA	U (1)	--	--	--	--	N/A	--	--	--	--	Z
▲AFFILIATED FM INS CO	RI	C+	3,163.0	1,779.9	457.9	-17.0	8.9	6.2	7.7	6.8	4.5	R
AFFILIATES INS CO	IN	U	--	--	--	--	N/A	--	--	--	--	Z
AFFILIATES INS RECIPROCAL A RRG	VT	B-	7.3	5.8	0.4	0.5	9.1	6.0	5.2	10.0	3.5	D
AFFINITY MUTUAL INS CO	OH	C-	13.9	8.2	4.4	0.0	8.0	6.9	3.7	6.8	2.7	DFR
AFFIRMATIVE CASUALTY INS CO	LA	F (5)	35.4	28.0	0.0	0.0	10.0	4.6	3.9	7.0	0.0	FGRT
AFFIRMATIVE DIRECT INS CO	NY	F	5.1	5.0	0.0	0.0	10.0	N/A	3.4	7.0	0.0	DT
▲AGCS MARINE INS CO	IL	C-	312.1	196.5	0.0	10.0	10.0	4.0	6.8	7.0	3.3	R
▲AGENCY INS CO OF MD INC	MD	B-	177.4	43.9	141.0	3.5	5.4	5.8	8.8	4.8	5.3	CL
AGENT ALLIANCE INS CO	AL	C	67.2	51.0	0.0	1.3	10.0	N/A	8.0	6.7	4.0	T
▲AGENTS MUTUAL INS CO	AR	D+	4.5	2.7	1.7	0.4	5.0	7.0	8.9	6.5	1.9	DR
AGIC INC	FL	U	--	--	--	--	N/A	--	--	--	--	Z
▲AGRI GENERAL INS CO	IA	C	99.7	87.8	0.0	3.8	10.0	3.6	2.7	10.0	3.5	RT
AGRI INS EXCHANGE RRG	IN	C	19.3	16.1	0.9	1.1	7.4	8.7	8.6	9.4	3.6	D
AGRICULTURAL WORKERS MUT AUTO INS	TX	B-	90.5	37.6	39.5	0.8	7.1	5.9	4.5	6.2	4.5	FR
AGSECURITY INS CO	OK	C+	57.4	32.1	19.4	0.3	9.7	8.6	4.7	6.8	4.6	
AIG INS CO - PR	PR	B- (1)	150.1	86.7	14.8	-11.5	10.0	7.7	2.8	8.7	4.4	T
AIG PROPERTY CASUALTY CO	PA	C	444.0	416.8	-481.9	203.8	10.0	3.1	1.9	0.0	4.2	AFLT
AIG SPECIALTY INS CO	IL	C+	115.6	83.0	0.0	-2.8	10.0	3.7	6.0	6.9	4.7	A
AIMCO MUTUAL INS CO	NC	U	--	--	--	--	N/A	--	--	--	--	Z
▲AIOI NISSAY DOWA INS CO LTD	GU	C-	35.6	13.8	11.3	1.3	7.4	9.3	8.9	9.1	3.2	D
▲AIOI NISSAY DOWA INS CO OF AMERICA	NY	B-	137.7	64.1	25.2	2.6	10.0	8.9	7.0	7.1	5.3	T
AIX SPECIALTY INS CO	DE	B-	56.9	46.1	0.0	1.2	10.0	N/A	4.0	7.6	5.3	
▲ALABAMA MUNICIPAL INS CORP	AL	B-	120.1	55.0	34.6	6.0	8.5	9.3	8.8	7.2	4.9	R
ALAMANCE FARMERS MUTUAL INS CO	NC	B-	8.9	6.1	3.4	0.4	7.3	6.6	5.4	6.6	3.5	D
ALAMANCE INS CO	IL	C-	466.3	370.5	29.8	9.1	7.7	7.7	5.8	7.0	2.6	R
▲ALASKA NATIONAL INS CO	AK	B+	1,004.7	480.3	226.8	59.4	9.4	9.4	8.9	7.5	6.5	T
ALASKA TIMBER INS EXCHANGE	AK	C	15.6	7.9	3.6	0.1	8.3	9.4	3.6	7.4	2.7	DR
ALEA NORTH AMERICA INS CO	NY	U	--	--	--	--	N/A	--	--	--	--	Z
ALFA ALLIANCE INS CORP	VA	B	37.2	20.9	13.3	0.2	9.6	7.7	6.5	6.7	5.8	D
▲ALFA GENERAL INS CORP	AL	B+	101.6	51.6	53.2	2.3	9.0	7.9	4.9	5.8	6.4	DL
ALFA INS CORP	AL	B	95.8	43.6	39.9	0.5	9.6	7.7	3.4	6.6	6.0	
▲ALFA MUTUAL FIRE INS CO	AL	B+	770.4	437.7	399.0	2.0	8.4	7.7	6.3	5.1	6.5	L
▲ALFA MUTUAL GENERAL INS CO	AL	A-	115.4	61.9	53.2	2.3	9.0	7.7	6.5	6.3	6.9	
ALFA MUTUAL INS CO	AL	B	1,344.9	499.5	691.5	-9.5	7.2	7.8	3.6	2.8	6.0	L
ALINSCO INS CO	TX	C	69.8	15.2	14.1	2.9	7.0	N/A	9.7	8.8	2.5	DT
▲ALL AMERICA INS CO	OH	A-	291.6	156.6	106.5	5.8	10.0	9.0	8.4	6.8	6.9	
▲ALLEGANY CO-OP INS CO	NY	B-	55.4	36.5	14.1	2.1	9.1	4.1	8.0	6.7	5.3	DF
ALLEGHENY CASUALTY CO	NJ	C	36.1	22.6	29.4	0.6	4.3	7.3	5.7	6.8	4.3	CDF
▲ALLEGHENY SURETY CO	PA	D+	4.4	2.5	1.3	0.3	7.2	3.6	3.6	6.7	2.0	DRT
ALLEGHENYPOINT INSURANCE CO	PA	B-	34.1	17.5	0.0	0.1	10.0	N/A	7.8	10.0	4.8	DFT
▲ALLEGIANT INS CO INC A RRG	HI	D-	30.8	13.3	7.4	2.5	1.6	0.8	9.0	8.3	0.9	D
ALLIANCE INDEMNITY CO	KS	C+	10.5	7.0	4.0	0.1	10.0	7.7	7.6	6.9	3.9	DR
ALLIANCE INS CO	KS	C	25.7	11.7	15.9	0.3	8.1	8.6	8.0	6.5	3.8	DR
▲ALLIANCE OF NONPROFITS FOR INS RRG	VT	C+	106.8	38.2	32.0	2.7	7.3	6.2	8.4	7.0	4.5	R
ALLIANCE UNITED INS CO	CA	C	652.9	198.6	640.2	49.7	5.1	3.7	4.1	0.7	3.7	L
ALLIANZ GLOBAL RISKS US INS CO	IL	C	7,625.6	1,850.6	2,048.5	226.9	4.2	9.8	4.5	5.7	4.3	CRT
ALLIANZ UNDERWRITERS INS CO	IL	C-	95.2	73.5	0.0	1.8	10.0	N/A	7.5	8.3	3.1	RT
ALLIED EASTERN INDEMNITY CO	PA	B-	95.6	15.5	20.8	1.7	5.7	4.9	6.4	6.0	5.3	D
ALLIED GUARANTY INS CO RRG	NV	D	12.7	2.7	5.0	0.6	5.3	3.6	9.8	2.2	0.6	DFLT

See Page 27 for explanation of footnotes and Page 28 for explanation of stability factors.

32

www.weissratings.com

Arrows denote recent upgrades ▲ or downgrades ▼ (see Section VII for explanations)

RISK ADJ. RATIO #1	CAPITAL RATIO #2	PREMIUM TO SURPLUS (%)	RESV. TO SURPLUS (%)	RESV. DEVELOP. 1 YEAR (%)	RESV. DEVELOP. 2 YEAR (%)	LOSS RATIO (%)	EXP. RATIO (%)	COMB RATIO (%)	CASH FROM UNDER-WRITING (%)	NET PREMIUM GROWTH (%)	INVEST. IN AFFIL (%)	INSURANCE COMPANY NAME
0.5	0.3	194.1	47.9	-4.9	-1.1	47.6	50.2	97.8	114.2	37.7	16.4	AEGIS SECURITY INS CO
N/A	N/A	--	--	--	--	--	--	--	--	--	--	AETNA INS CO OF CT
N/A	N/A	--	--	--	--	--	--	--	--	--	--	AF&L INS CO
3.6	2.2	25.7	35.6	-2.1	-1.5	103.3	27.0	130.3	94.9	8.1	0.0 •	AFFILIATED FM INS CO
N/A	N/A	--	--	--	--	--	--	--	--	--	--	AFFILIATES INS CO
3.9	2.4	6.4	12.1	-1.7	-1.7	59.1	36.3	95.4	162.6	0.0	0.0	AFFILIATES INS RECIPROCAL A RRG
2.7	1.7	53.6	18.7	-5.6	-12.2	46.6	58.7	105.3	86.8	2.4	0.0	AFFINITY MUTUAL INS CO
4.8	4.2	N/A	-0.1	N/A	N/A	N/A	N/A	N/A	193.2	0.0	29.1	AFFIRMATIVE CASUALTY INS CO
134.7	60.7	N/A	N/A	N/A	N/A	N/A	N/A	N/A	N/A	0.0	0.0	AFFIRMATIVE DIRECT INS CO
22.7	20.4	N/A	N/A	N/A	N/A	N/A	N/A	N/A	-36.0	0.0	0.6	AGCS MARINE INS CO
1.0	0.8	321.2	134.9	-2.8	-6.0	72.3	22.6	94.9	119.5	25.1	0.0	AGENCY INS CO OF MD INC
16.4	14.8	N/A	N/A	N/A	N/A	N/A	N/A	N/A	260.4	0.0	0.0	AGENT ALLIANCE INS CO
1.3	0.9	60.7	5.7	-2.5	1.7	48.5	20.9	69.4	132.2	2.2	0.0	AGENTS MUTUAL INS CO
N/A	N/A	--	--	--	--	--	--	--	--	--	--	AGIC INC
32.1	14.3	N/A	5.2	N/A	N/A	N/A	N/A	N/A	26.4	0.0	0.0	AGRI GENERAL INS CO
2.0	1.2	5.9	15.6	-3.6	-5.8	-11.2	33.8	22.6	477.7	-1.6	0.0	AGRI INS EXCHANGE RRG
1.6	1.2	105.0	23.7	2.8	1.5	67.4	24.2	91.6	107.3	1.9	15.1	AGRICULTURAL WORKERS MUT AUTO
4.5	2.8	60.6	24.1	-0.8	-0.1	65.2	31.6	96.8	97.5	33.5	0.0	AGSECURITY INS CO
9.6	5.8	16.2	12.6	-1.9	-3.7	8.5	48.7	57.2	145.6	-7.2	1.4	AIG INS CO - PR
79.6	49.3	-115.6	N/A	N/A	N/A	N/A	37.7	N/A	-11.4	-159.8	0.0 •	AIG PROPERTY CASUALTY CO
21.8	19.6	N/A	N/A	N/A	N/A	N/A	N/A	N/A	N/A	0.0	0.0	AIG SPECIALTY INS CO
N/A	N/A	--	--	--	--	--	--	--	--	--	--	AIMCO MUTUAL INS CO
2.0	1.2	82.1	18.8	-2.8	-2.2	39.0	35.4	74.4	135.1	23.4	0.0	AIOI NISSAY DOWA INS CO LTD
6.2	4.2	39.3	82.9	-6.1	-9.8	62.9	29.2	92.1	116.3	1.1	0.0	AIOI NISSAY DOWA INS CO OF AMERICA
18.3	16.4	N/A	N/A	N/A	N/A	N/A	N/A	N/A	N/A	0.0	0.0	AIX SPECIALTY INS CO
2.6	2.2	62.9	84.9	-7.7	-4.1	63.2	24.8	88.0	146.4	5.4	0.0	ALABAMA MUNICIPAL INS CORP
1.9	1.2	56.4	8.1	-3.6	-4.5	35.7	61.0	96.7	108.0	8.2	0.0	ALAMANCE FARMERS MUTUAL INS CO
1.4	1.4	8.0	19.7	-1.2	-2.3	46.0	53.8	99.8	77.0	6.8	59.8 •	ALAMANCE INS CO
4.2	2.9	47.2	79.6	-8.4	-14.4	48.2	27.3	75.5	130.7	2.4	0.0 •	ALASKA NATIONAL INS CO
2.4	1.8	45.9	91.1	-5.7	-6.2	63.3	25.9	89.2	123.1	-6.3	0.0	ALASKA TIMBER INS EXCHANGE
N/A	N/A	--	--	--	--	--	--	--	--	--	--	ALEA NORTH AMERICA INS CO
4.3	2.9	63.5	23.9	-1.2	-2.9	74.0	32.6	106.6	97.6	8.2	0.0	ALFA ALLIANCE INS CORP
3.5	2.4	103.2	36.4	-1.8	-3.5	75.6	29.4	105.0	103.1	8.2	0.0 •	ALFA GENERAL INS CORP
3.8	2.7	91.5	32.5	-1.3	-2.8	75.8	27.3	103.1	147.9	8.2	0.0	ALFA INS CORP
2.4	2.0	91.1	31.9	-2.0	-2.8	75.1	29.6	104.7	98.1	8.2	21.3 •	ALFA MUTUAL FIRE INS CO
4.3	2.9	85.9	30.1	-1.9	-2.6	75.1	29.7	104.8	99.0	8.2	0.6 •	ALFA MUTUAL GENERAL INS CO
1.3	1.1	138.4	51.6	-2.9	-3.5	75.4	29.5	104.9	105.2	8.2	34.9 •	ALFA MUTUAL INS CO
1.3	1.0	92.7	24.6	N/A	N/A	86.2	-23.4	62.8	882.1	0.0	0.0	ALINSCO INS CO
6.4	4.4	68.0	43.9	-2.2	-7.5	65.0	33.1	98.1	101.7	7.8	0.1 •	ALL AMERICA INS CO
3.9	2.4	38.7	18.0	2.9	13.7	55.1	37.4	92.5	82.1	4.7	0.0	ALLEGANY CO-OP INS CO
0.7	0.6	129.8	N/A	N/A	-0.1	N/A	97.9	97.9	99.2	-7.8	0.0	ALLEGHENY CASUALTY CO
1.5	1.2	50.8	40.9	-1.6	-1.5	0.9	84.0	84.9	96.7	-12.6	0.0	ALLEGHENY SURETY CO
5.5	5.0	N/A	N/A	N/A	N/A	N/A	N/A	N/A	622.9	0.0	0.0	ALLEGHENYPOINT INSURANCE CO
0.5	0.4	55.6	84.4	10.0	29.0	43.0	13.3	56.3	212.3	16.8	0.0	ALLEGIANT INS CO INC A RRG
5.7	4.2	56.8	18.2	-1.9	-1.9	68.7	30.4	99.1	100.0	4.2	0.0	ALLIANCE INDEMNITY CO
2.4	1.8	135.5	43.5	-4.6	-4.8	68.7	30.4	99.1	100.0	4.2	0.0	ALLIANCE INS CO
1.6	1.3	83.9	131.0	N/A	-0.8	65.5	30.3	95.8	125.6	6.9	0.0	ALLIANCE OF NONPROFITS FOR INS
1.0	0.8	322.3	156.5	N/A	3.9	81.4	21.6	103.0	98.2	23.3	0.0	ALLIANCE UNITED INS CO
0.8	0.6	110.7	194.7	-2.9	-40.9	77.2	37.6	114.8	106.5	-3.6	26.6 •	ALLIANZ GLOBAL RISKS US INS CO
19.9	17.9	N/A	N/A	N/A	N/A	N/A	N/A	N/A	-208.1	0.0	0.0	ALLIANZ UNDERWRITERS INS CO
1.0	0.8	134.1	137.4	-7.5	-5.3	62.2	25.9	88.1	159.5	-0.8	0.0	ALLIED EASTERN INDEMNITY CO
1.0	0.7	185.1	5.9	5.6	N/A	65.4	3.6	69.0	181.1	0.0	0.0	ALLIED GUARANTY INS CO RRG

999 + Denotes number greater than 999.9%
999 - Denotes number less than -999.99%
• Bullets denote a more detailed analysis is available in Section II.

INSURANCE COMPANY NAME	DOM. STATE	RATING	TOTAL ASSETS ($MIL)	CAPITAL & SURPLUS ($MIL)	ANNUAL NET PREMIUM ($MIL)	NET INCOME ($MIL)	CAPITAL-IZATION INDEX (PTS)	RESERVE ADQ INDEX (PTS)	PROFIT-ABILITY INDEX (PTS)	LIQUIDITY INDEX (PTS)	STAB. INDEX (PTS)	STABILITY FACTORS
ALLIED INS CO OF AMERICA	OH	C+	78.3	14.4	0.0	0.1	8.1	N/A	7.1	7.0	3.2	DFGT
ALLIED P&C INS CO	IA	B	400.3	60.4	0.0	2.2	10.0	N/A	6.5	6.7	5.4	F
ALLIED PREMIER INS A RRG	CT	E (1)	3.0	1.1	-0.3	0.5	3.3	3.6	0.4	8.0	0.0	DEFG
ALLIED PROFESSIONALS INS CO RRG	AZ	C-	48.2	21.5	9.0	1.4	6.7	2.3	6.1	8.1	3.2	DR
▲ALLIED SERVICES RRG	SC	E+	6.2	4.1	1.0	0.3	7.0	9.5	5.6	7.1	0.5	D
ALLIED TRUST INS CO	TX	C-	28.0	12.0	15.6	-3.7	3.5	3.6	2.6	6.9	2.3	CDGT
ALLIED WORLD ASR CO (US) INC	DE	B-	337.7	140.7	43.7	-2.3	10.0	5.9	4.2	8.8	4.6	AR
ALLIED WORLD INS CO	NH	C	1,788.1	1,011.6	196.5	-12.9	7.7	6.0	3.4	7.4	3.4	AR
ALLIED WORLD NATL ASR CO	NH	C	320.9	153.7	43.7	-3.2	10.0	5.9	3.9	7.7	4.0	AR
▲ALLIED WORLD SPECIALTY INS CO	DE	B+	829.1	419.2	109.2	-9.7	8.3	5.9	4.3	8.2	6.5	
ALLIED WORLD SURPLUS LINES INS	AR	C	263.3	96.5	43.7	-2.4	9.2	5.9	3.9	8.5	4.2	R
ALLMERICA FINANCIAL ALLIANCE INS CO	NH	C+	19.5	19.5	0.0	0.4	10.0	N/A	5.6	7.0	4.4	DR
ALLMERICA FINANCIAL BENEFIT INS CO	MI	C+	45.3	45.3	0.0	0.8	10.0	N/A	7.4	7.0	4.5	R
ALLSTATE COUNTY MUTUAL INS CO	TX	B	14.7	14.7	0.0	0.1	10.0	N/A	6.2	10.0	5.0	D
▲ALLSTATE F&C INS CO	IL	B-	245.1	239.5	0.0	3.6	10.0	N/A	7.2	10.0	4.9	
ALLSTATE INDEMNITY CO	IL	B	115.2	102.8	0.0	1.6	10.0	N/A	3.3	7.0	5.4	FT
▲ALLSTATE INS CO	IL	B+	48,302.5	17,454.4	29,252.0	2,874.4	7.8	6.1	8.2	5.4	6.5	L
▲ALLSTATE NJ INS CO	IL	A-	2,485.7	831.1	1,128.8	166.8	8.3	8.2	6.6	6.5	7.1	
▲ALLSTATE NJ P&C INS CO	IL	B-	76.1	75.1	0.0	1.0	10.0	N/A	7.3	7.0	4.9	
ALLSTATE NORTH AMERICAN INS CO	IL	U	--	--	--	--	N/A	--	--	--	--	Z
ALLSTATE NORTHBROOK INDEMNITY CO	IL	B-	59.0	58.7	0.0	0.8	10.0	N/A	7.3	7.0	4.1	T
ALLSTATE P&C INS CO	IL	B	236.7	215.8	0.0	3.0	10.0	N/A	5.4	10.0	6.1	FT
ALLSTATE TEXAS LLOYDS	TX	B	17.3	17.2	0.0	0.1	10.0	N/A	6.3	10.0	5.3	D
ALLSTATE VEHICLE & PROPERTY INS CO	IL	B	63.1	55.2	0.0	0.8	10.0	N/A	8.0	10.0	4.9	FT
ALPHA P&C INS CO	WI	B	30.1	13.4	0.0	0.3	10.0	N/A	5.6	7.0	4.9	DR
▲ALPS PROPERTY & CASUALTY INS CO	MT	B-	131.2	40.7	32.5	3.4	8.1	7.9	6.9	7.5	5.3	T
▲ALTERRA AMERICA INS CO	DE	B	392.6	223.0	29.0	32.6	7.7	7.0	6.0	6.9	5.2	FT
AMALGAMATED CASUALTY INS CO	DC	B-	59.7	42.6	13.4	-2.7	9.7	7.7	3.8	7.0	4.4	DFT
AMBAC ASR CORP SEGREGATED ACCT	WI	U	--	--	--	--	N/A	--	--	--	--	Z
AMBAC ASSURANCE CORP	WI	E	5,455.7	699.6	36.6	123.7	2.8	3.0	3.3	9.0	-0.5	CFRT
▲AMCO INS CO	IA	B-	959.3	209.8	0.0	2.4	10.0	N/A	3.9	7.0	5.0	F
AMERICA FIRST INS CO	NH	C+	15.0	14.9	0.0	0.3	10.0	N/A	6.8	7.0	4.6	DRT
AMERICA FIRST LLOYD'S INS CO	TX	C+	6.9	6.4	0.0	0.0	10.0	N/A	6.3	7.0	3.1	DRT
▼AMERICAN ACCESS CASUALTY CO	IL	D	420.6	62.4	372.8	0.8	1.6	1.9	3.8	0.7	2.2	CLT
AMERICAN AGRI BUSINESS INS CO	TX	C+	715.2	31.5	0.0	3.7	7.9	N/A	8.9	7.0	4.5	R
▲AMERICAN AGRICULTURAL INS CO	IN	B+	1,338.9	584.8	363.5	-8.6	8.0	7.0	5.7	6.9	6.5	
AMERICAN ALLIANCE CASUALTY CO	IL	D	38.3	10.3	24.2	0.0	1.4	0.9	4.2	7.1	1.4	CDGT
AMERICAN ALTERNATIVE INS CORP	DE	C	590.3	201.7	0.0	32.1	10.0	N/A	8.9	8.3	3.7	R
AMERICAN ASSOC OF ORTHODONTIST RRG	AZ	C	48.2	17.2	6.5	1.7	7.1	10.0	8.4	8.2	3.6	DR
AMERICAN AUTOMOBILE INS CO	MO	C	126.0	78.0	0.0	0.8	10.0	N/A	2.6	7.0	3.4	FR
AMERICAN BANKERS INS CO OF FL	FL	B	2,353.4	561.8	996.8	141.5	8.1	8.0	8.4	6.2	5.8	A
AMERICAN BUILDERS INS CO	DE	C	146.3	42.0	24.6	2.8	9.5	9.0	8.9	6.9	3.5	R
AMERICAN BUILDERS INS CO RRG INC	AL	D	1.2	0.6	0.9	0.0	0.9	3.9	2.4	7.1	1.2	CDGT
AMERICAN BUS & MERCANTILE INS MUT	DE	C	68.8	32.8	2.2	-1.3	1.8	3.2	3.5	6.9	3.9	CDR
AMERICAN CAPITAL ASSR CORP	FL	B	122.6	64.2	34.6	2.0	10.0	9.4	3.3	6.8	5.5	F
AMERICAN CAR DEALERS RRG INC	HI	U (1)	--	--	--	--	N/A	--	--	--	--	Z
AMERICAN CASUALTY CO OF READING	PA	C	142.2	142.2	0.0	2.3	8.7	N/A	5.2	7.7	3.8	AR
▲AMERICAN COASTAL INS CO	FL	B	327.2	160.2	130.8	17.7	9.2	5.9	3.7	7.0	5.5	
AMERICAN COMMERCE INS CO	OH	B-	340.7	101.4	194.3	-2.0	8.2	4.1	2.8	2.4	4.8	L
AMERICAN COMPENSATION INS CO	MN	D	73.9	54.3	0.0	0.5	10.0	N/A	6.1	7.0	2.1	R
▲AMERICAN CONTRACTORS INDEMNITY CO	CA	B+	338.3	128.6	18.1	13.7	10.0	9.6	8.4	8.7	6.5	T
AMERICAN CONTRACTORS INS CO RISK	TX	D-	36.4	10.3	0.0	0.5	8.8	N/A	8.6	9.3	1.2	DGR

See Page 27 for explanation of footnotes and
Page 28 for explanation of stability factors.
Arrows denote recent upgrades ▲ or downgrades ▼   (see Section VII for explanations)

34

www.weissratings.com

RISK ADJ. RATIO #1	CAPITAL RATIO #2	PREMIUM TO SURPLUS (%)	RESV. TO SURPLUS (%)	RESV. 1 YEAR (%)	DEVELOP. 2 YEAR (%)	LOSS RATIO (%)	EXP. RATIO (%)	COMB RATIO (%)	CASH FROM UNDER-WRITING (%)	NET PREMIUM GROWTH (%)	INVEST. IN AFFIL (%)	INSURANCE COMPANY NAME
1.9	1.7	N/A	N/A	N/A	N/A	N/A	N/A	N/A	100.2	0.0	0.0	ALLIED INS CO OF AMERICA
5.4	4.8	N/A	N/A	N/A	N/A	N/A	N/A	N/A	-12.2	0.0	3.7	ALLIED P&C INS CO
1.9	1.7	-38.8	322.2	-198.9	N/A	103.8	-918.7	-814.9	-6.9	-106.0	0.0	ALLIED PREMIER INS A RRG
1.3	0.9	42.2	93.3	-7.7	4.9	51.3	45.6	96.9	132.7	-30.7	0.0	ALLIED PROFESSIONALS INS CO RRG
1.6	1.2	25.3	38.1	-4.2	-25.3	56.4	25.2	81.6	150.8	0.8	0.0	ALLIED SERVICES RRG
0.8	0.4	129.6	25.5	-1.5	N/A	62.1	46.1	108.2	165.3	685.7	0.0	ALLIED TRUST INS CO
5.0	3.5	31.0	69.1	1.8	3.9	85.6	29.4	115.0	94.4	-1.4	0.0	ALLIED WORLD ASR CO (US) INC
1.5	1.4	19.4	43.3	1.1	2.2	85.6	29.3	114.9	94.4	-1.4	50.2 ●	ALLIED WORLD INS CO
5.5	3.9	28.4	63.3	1.6	4.0	85.6	29.4	115.0	94.2	-1.4	0.0	ALLIED WORLD NATL ASR CO
2.2	1.8	26.0	58.0	1.5	3.3	85.6	29.4	115.0	94.2	-1.4	28.0 ●	ALLIED WORLD SPECIALTY INS CO
3.4	2.4	45.3	100.8	2.6	5.6	85.6	29.4	115.0	94.4	-1.4	0.0	ALLIED WORLD SURPLUS LINES INS
90.3	41.6	N/A	N/A	N/A	N/A	N/A	N/A	N/A	N/A	0.0	0.0	ALLMERICA FINANCIAL ALLIANCE INS CO
90.2	42.2	N/A	N/A	N/A	N/A	N/A	N/A	N/A	N/A	0.0	0.0	ALLMERICA FINANCIAL BENEFIT INS CO
99.2	49.6	N/A	N/A	N/A	N/A	N/A	N/A	N/A	N/A	0.0	0.0	ALLSTATE COUNTY MUTUAL INS CO
114.1	50.1	N/A	N/A	N/A	N/A	N/A	N/A	N/A	159.7	0.0	0.0 ●	ALLSTATE F&C INS CO
38.1	34.2	N/A	N/A	N/A	N/A	N/A	N/A	N/A	772.0	0.0	0.0	ALLSTATE INDEMNITY CO
2.0	1.5	167.6	98.0	-2.3	-0.7	69.4	25.4	94.8	109.4	2.7	12.8 ●	ALLSTATE INS CO
2.3	1.9	135.8	146.0	-4.0	-6.9	60.0	23.6	83.6	116.4	-3.1	4.9 ●	ALLSTATE NJ INS CO
175.6	89.7	N/A	N/A	N/A	N/A	N/A	N/A	N/A	157.3	0.0	0.0	ALLSTATE NJ P&C INS CO
N/A	N/A	--	--	--	--	--	--	--	--	--	--	ALLSTATE NORTH AMERICAN INS CO
175.9	87.9	N/A	N/A	N/A	N/A	N/A	N/A	N/A	N/A	0.0	0.0	ALLSTATE NORTHBROOK INDEMNITY CO
59.9	48.1	N/A	N/A	N/A	N/A	N/A	N/A	N/A	-194.7	0.0	0.0	ALLSTATE P&C INS CO
108.3	54.1	N/A	N/A	N/A	N/A	N/A	N/A	N/A	N/A	0.0	0.0	ALLSTATE TEXAS LLOYDS
26.8	24.1	N/A	N/A	N/A	N/A	N/A	N/A	N/A	999 +	0.0	0.0	ALLSTATE VEHICLE & PROPERTY INS CO
4.2	3.8	N/A	N/A	N/A	N/A	N/A	N/A	N/A	-115.8	0.0	0.0	ALPHA P&C INS CO
2.6	1.8	79.9	139.0	-2.8	-0.9	64.8	32.8	97.6	120.2	6.2	1.0	ALPS PROPERTY & CASUALTY INS CO
4.4	2.6	13.0	62.5	-17.4	-31.7	-7.5	28.4	20.9	48.1	-60.7	0.0 ●	ALTERRA AMERICA INS CO
3.7	2.8	31.5	19.0	1.3	-1.1	96.0	32.8	128.8	89.5	17.0	0.0	AMALGAMATED CASUALTY INS CO
N/A	N/A	--	--	--	--	--	--	--	--	--	--	AMBAC ASR CORP SEGREGATED ACCT
0.7	0.3	5.2	407.0	22.0	-76.0	360.5	-387.8	-27.3	15.8	-19.1	11.2 ●	AMBAC ASSURANCE CORP
6.7	6.1	N/A	N/A	N/A	N/A	N/A	N/A	N/A	-54.8	0.0	13.8	AMCO INS CO
131.2	65.5	N/A	N/A	N/A	N/A	N/A	N/A	N/A	N/A	0.0	0.0	AMERICA FIRST INS CO
31.7	28.5	N/A	N/A	N/A	N/A	N/A	N/A	N/A	N/A	0.0	0.0	AMERICA FIRST LLOYD'S INS CO
0.3	0.3	597.1	318.9	44.6	22.1	77.8	21.2	99.0	111.0	25.9	0.0	AMERICAN ACCESS CASUALTY CO
2.2	1.5	N/A	N/A	N/A	N/A	N/A	N/A	N/A	N/A	0.0	0.0	AMERICAN AGRI BUSINESS INS CO
2.4	1.7	62.2	99.4	-1.9	-12.5	87.7	21.0	108.7	99.0	6.7	0.1 ●	AMERICAN AGRICULTURAL INS CO
0.3	0.3	233.7	115.4	39.1	63.6	71.2	26.8	98.0	116.5	42.3	0.0	AMERICAN ALLIANCE CASUALTY CO
17.3	15.3	N/A	N/A	N/A	N/A	N/A	N/A	N/A	-32.9	0.0	0.0	AMERICAN ALTERNATIVE INS CORP
1.6	1.2	37.9	134.8	-55.9	-84.1	23.0	41.2	64.2	128.0	-5.1	0.0	AMERICAN ASSOC OF ORTHODONTIST
11.9	10.7	N/A	N/A	N/A	N/A	N/A	N/A	N/A	344.6	0.0	0.0	AMERICAN AUTOMOBILE INS CO
3.1	2.2	177.4	30.6	-1.8	-4.5	48.7	32.4	81.1	119.7	8.9	0.8 ●	AMERICAN BANKERS INS CO OF FL
4.1	2.9	58.5	82.0	-3.5	-7.1	61.9	21.1	83.0	176.9	10.4	0.0	AMERICAN BUILDERS INS CO
0.3	0.2	154.1	23.0	-8.3	-39.2	31.1	27.9	59.0	225.0	0.0	0.0	AMERICAN BUILDERS INS CO RRG INC
0.5	0.3	6.8	101.7	8.5	8.1	169.7	50.1	219.8	87.2	-38.7	39.6	AMERICAN BUS & MERCANTILE INS MUT
5.8	5.5	53.9	11.7	-9.8	-8.1	56.9	42.1	99.0	77.0	-9.8	0.0	AMERICAN CAPITAL ASSR CORP
N/A	N/A	--	--	--	--	--	--	--	--	--	--	AMERICAN CAR DEALERS RRG INC
2.1	2.1	N/A	N/A	N/A	N/A	N/A	N/A	N/A	N/A	0.0	51.1	AMERICAN CASUALTY CO OF READING
3.0	2.4	81.6	23.6	-1.2	4.3	36.7	46.3	83.0	108.1	-1.1	0.0	AMERICAN COASTAL INS CO
2.1	1.8	191.6	97.9	5.9	5.4	79.9	23.9	103.8	107.8	0.4	0.0	AMERICAN COMMERCE INS CO
4.1	4.0	N/A	N/A	N/A	N/A	N/A	N/A	N/A	81.9	0.0	28.4	AMERICAN COMPENSATION INS CO
12.1	8.9	14.1	12.1	-8.3	-22.7	-2.0	55.5	53.5	79.2	-6.3	0.0 ●	AMERICAN CONTRACTORS INDEMNITY
2.4	2.2	N/A	N/A	N/A	N/A	N/A	N/A	N/A	313.6	0.0	0.0	AMERICAN CONTRACTORS INS CO RISK

999 + Denotes number greater than 999.9%
999 - Denotes number less than -999.99%
● Bullets denote a more detailed analysis is available in Section II.

INSURANCE COMPANY NAME	DOM. STATE	RATING	TOTAL ASSETS ($MIL)	CAPITAL & SURPLUS ($MIL)	ANNUAL NET PREMIUM ($MIL)	NET INCOME ($MIL)	CAPITAL-IZATION INDEX (PTS)	RESERVE ADQ INDEX (PTS)	PROFIT-ABILITY INDEX (PTS)	LIQUIDITY INDEX (PTS)	STAB. INDEX (PTS)	STABILITY FACTORS
▼AMERICAN COUNTRY INS CO	IL	D-	109.7	18.3	57.2	-9.1	0.7	0.7	1.9	0.5	1.0	CDFL
AMERICAN ECONOMY INS CO	IN	B-	72.3	68.8	0.0	1.2	10.0	N/A	6.5	7.0	5.3	AFT
AMERICAN EMPIRE INS CO	OH	C	21.5	21.0	-3.6	1.9	10.0	3.5	4.4	2.9	3.5	DFLR
▼AMERICAN EMPIRE SURPLUS LINES INS CO	DE	C-	467.9	153.7	89.0	9.6	6.0	1.9	5.0	6.5	2.9	R
AMERICAN EQUITY INS CO	AZ	U	--	--	--	--	N/A	--	--	--	--	Z
AMERICAN EQUITY SPECIALTY INS CO	CT	B	78.4	27.3	22.8	1.9	8.1	8.0	4.3	7.3	5.8	D
AMERICAN EUROPEAN INS CO	NH	B-	138.1	57.8	26.3	-1.9	7.9	5.9	2.7	7.2	4.6	FR
▲AMERICAN EXCESS INS EXCHANGE RRG	VT	C	308.3	177.8	20.3	19.7	9.2	6.8	3.6	7.2	3.5	R
AMERICAN FAMILY HOME INS CO	FL	C+	423.2	178.4	173.3	-2.5	8.4	8.0	5.1	6.4	4.4	T
AMERICAN FAMILY INS CO	WI	B	64.8	24.2	0.0	0.6	10.0	N/A	7.7	6.1	4.8	DGT
▲AMERICAN FAMILY MUTL INS CO SI	WI	A-	17,157.4	6,631.4	8,605.2	103.3	7.7	8.1	6.1	5.7	7.1	
AMERICAN FARMERS & RANCHERS	OK	C	159.4	72.4	126.2	5.8	8.2	9.5	8.8	5.1	3.5	R
AMERICAN FEDERATED INS CO	MS	C+	40.7	13.1	19.5	3.2	5.2	7.7	4.2	6.8	4.3	D
AMERICAN FEED INDUSTRY INS CO RRG	IA	U (5)	--	--	--	--	N/A	--	--	--	--	Z
AMERICAN FIRE & CASUALTY CO	NH	C-	46.2	40.7	0.0	0.6	10.0	N/A	6.3	7.0	3.1	AR
AMERICAN FOREST CASUALTY CO RRG	VT	D+	9.2	4.6	2.1	0.1	7.5	9.4	5.9	6.4	2.3	DFR
▲AMERICAN FREEDOM INS CO	IL	B	51.6	21.4	10.8	2.5	8.2	7.0	8.8	6.6	4.1	DFT
AMERICAN GUARANTEE & LIABILITY INS	NY	C+	259.2	184.5	0.0	4.3	10.0	N/A	6.3	7.0	4.7	R
AMERICAN HALLMARK INS CO OF TX	TX	B	423.5	131.8	124.3	0.8	7.6	4.5	5.3	6.7	6.1	F
AMERICAN HEARTLAND INS CO	IL	D	18.3	3.0	11.9	-0.1	2.2	7.1	2.9	6.5	1.8	C
AMERICAN HOME ASR CO	NY	C	25,639.7	6,237.8	5,030.6	-393.2	7.7	3.0	3.3	6.3	4.2	AF
AMERICAN INDEPENDENT INS CO	PA	D+(1)	108.0	6.3	15.8	-2.3	5.6	1.8	1.0	0.0	2.4	CDFG
AMERICAN INS CO	OH	C-	112.7	66.7	0.0	-0.9	10.0	N/A	1.9	7.0	3.1	RT
AMERICAN INTEGRITY INS CO OF FL	FL	C+	246.3	74.0	126.4	2.6	7.7	2.9	8.8	3.5	4.8	L
▲AMERICAN INTER FIDELITY EXCHANGE	IN	B-	105.6	29.2	49.9	3.1	5.2	4.5	8.8	6.7	4.8	CGR
AMERICAN INTERSTATE INS CO	NE	B-	1,234.5	382.1	274.6	65.5	7.8	9.4	6.7	7.0	4.6	R
▲AMERICAN INTERSTATE INS CO OF TX	TX	B+	68.1	27.3	16.7	3.0	7.5	9.4	8.0	7.0	6.5	D
AMERICAN LIBERTY INS CO	UT	E	19.3	3.5	7.4	0.7	0.3	0.2	2.8	6.6	0.3	CDGR
AMERICAN MEDICAL ASR CO	IL	U	--	--	--	--	N/A	--	--	--	--	Z
AMERICAN MERCURY INS CO	OK	B	368.7	175.4	169.9	26.6	8.9	5.7	6.3	6.2	6.0	
AMERICAN MERCURY LLOYDS INS CO	TX	B	6.3	5.5	0.0	0.0	10.0	N/A	6.5	7.0	4.9	D
AMERICAN MILLENNIUM INS CO	NJ	D	34.4	8.7	10.1	0.6	1.1	1.7	8.3	6.7	1.5	CDRT
AMERICAN MINING INS CO	IA	B-	40.8	26.4	0.0	0.5	10.0	N/A	6.8	9.9	4.9	
AMERICAN MODERN HOME INS CO	OH	C+	1,030.7	378.8	305.0	-8.3	7.9	7.7	3.4	6.4	4.2	R
AMERICAN MODERN INS CO OF FLORIDA	FL	B-	35.4	10.9	12.8	-0.7	7.1	8.3	4.7	6.0	4.4	DF
AMERICAN MODERN LLOYDS INS CO	TX	C	11.6	4.2	0.0	0.1	8.4	N/A	4.7	9.1	3.3	DFT
AMERICAN MODERN PROPERTY &	OH	B	34.1	16.9	3.2	0.1	10.0	7.4	7.2	6.9	4.0	DGT
AMERICAN MODERN SELECT INS CO	OH	C	222.3	59.5	32.1	2.8	10.0	7.7	8.3	7.0	3.9	T
AMERICAN MODERN SURPLUS LINES INS	OH	B	62.7	28.4	32.1	-1.0	7.3	8.1	3.9	6.7	5.4	DT
AMERICAN MUTUAL SHARE INS CORP	OH	C-	257.8	235.0	0.2	1.1	10.0	9.3	6.8	10.0	2.0	F
AMERICAN NATIONAL GENERAL INS CO	MO	B	109.5	65.5	43.3	-1.3	10.0	8.1	4.7	6.6	6.1	
AMERICAN NATIONAL LLOYDS INS CO	TX	B	86.7	66.6	23.2	-1.3	10.0	6.0	4.7	6.9	6.1	F
▲AMERICAN NATIONAL PROPERTY & CAS CO	MO	B+	1,418.0	656.5	623.1	13.4	8.1	8.3	6.7	6.0	6.5	
AMERICAN NATL COUNTY MUT INS CO	TX	B	25.6	10.9	0.0	0.3	8.1	N/A	6.7	7.2	4.7	D
AMERICAN PACIFIC INS CO	HI	U	--	--	--	--	N/A	--	--	--	--	Z
▲AMERICAN PET INS CO	NY	C	75.9	37.2	205.5	7.5	3.5	5.9	9.0	0.0	3.5	CGLT
AMERICAN PHYSICIANS ASR CORP	MI	U	--	--	--	--	N/A	--	--	--	--	Z
▲AMERICAN PLATINUM PROP & CAS INS CO	FL	B-	22.4	16.6	3.7	-0.6	10.0	6.1	4.2	8.1	5.1	D
AMERICAN PROPERTY INS	NJ	D+	24.7	8.6	12.3	1.3	2.0	7.0	5.3	6.6	2.2	CDGR
AMERICAN RELIABLE INS CO	AZ	B	219.2	84.4	59.4	-2.5	8.2	5.6	4.2	6.5	5.0	FT
AMERICAN RESOURCES INS CO INC	OK	D	23.1	3.8	10.7	-2.6	1.1	4.6	0.7	5.4	1.6	CDFR
▲AMERICAN RISK INS CO	TX	C-	31.1	12.0	17.0	0.3	5.2	3.2	7.5	7.1	3.2	DF

See Page 27 for explanation of footnotes and   36   www.weissratings.com
Page 28 for explanation of stability factors.
Arrows denote recent upgrades ▲ or downgrades ▼   (see Section VII for explanations)

RISK ADJ. RATIO #1	CAPITAL RATIO #2	PREMIUM TO SURPLUS (%)	RESV. TO SURPLUS (%)	RESV. DEVELOP. 1 YEAR (%)	RESV. DEVELOP. 2 YEAR (%)	LOSS RATIO (%)	EXP. RATIO (%)	COMB. RATIO (%)	CASH FROM UNDER-WRITING (%)	NET PREMIUM GROWTH (%)	INVEST. IN AFFIL (%)	INSURANCE COMPANY NAME
0.2	0.2	313.6	213.9	75.9	91.5	95.1	25.1	120.2	99.7	32.6	0.0	AMERICAN COUNTRY INS CO
5.9	5.8	N/A	N/A	N/A	N/A	N/A	N/A	N/A	N/A	0.0	17.6	AMERICAN ECONOMY INS CO
86.1	56.8	-17.3	N/A	N/A	N/A	N/A	N/A	N/A	-11.2	-139.3	0.0	AMERICAN EMPIRE INS CO
1.3	0.8	57.9	169.0	12.2	39.8	89.6	11.8	101.4	112.2	7.1	4.9	AMERICAN EMPIRE SURPLUS LINES INS
N/A	N/A	--	--	--	--	--	--	--	--	--	--	AMERICAN EQUITY INS CO
2.5	1.7	83.5	136.9	-1.8	-2.9	69.5	29.1	98.6	108.3	4.9	0.0	AMERICAN EQUITY SPECIALTY INS CO
2.0	1.6	45.5	80.3	3.8	5.1	80.4	38.2	118.6	83.5	-1.2	17.1	AMERICAN EUROPEAN INS CO
3.9	2.7	11.4	67.7	-6.9	-6.9	50.8	27.4	78.2	72.6	-6.7	0.0	AMERICAN EXCESS INS EXCHANGE RRG
3.6	2.5	97.2	22.9	-2.4	-3.5	60.4	45.9	106.3	120.8	-7.3	9.0	AMERICAN FAMILY HOME INS CO
4.2	3.8	N/A	N/A	N/A	N/A	N/A	N/A	N/A	-77.6	0.0	0.0	AMERICAN FAMILY INS CO
1.9	1.4	129.8	65.1	0.9	-2.3	77.2	28.6	105.8	95.9	18.0	15.6 •	AMERICAN FAMILY MUTL INS CO SI
2.7	2.0	174.4	34.7	0.1	-5.3	67.3	26.8	94.1	106.2	5.9	7.8	AMERICAN FARMERS & RANCHERS
0.8	0.7	148.4	3.2	-0.6	-1.5	5.2	77.3	82.5	121.6	6.2	0.0	AMERICAN FEDERATED INS CO
N/A	N/A	--	--	--	--	--	--	--	--	--	--	AMERICAN FEED INDUSTRY INS CO RRG
25.1	22.6	N/A	N/A	N/A	N/A	N/A	N/A	N/A	N/A	0.0	0.0	AMERICAN FIRE & CASUALTY CO
1.9	1.5	45.7	65.0	-5.8	-16.8	75.3	35.1	110.4	88.2	11.4	0.0	AMERICAN FOREST CASUALTY CO RRG
4.2	3.0	50.6	58.3	-1.9	-3.3	67.5	36.7	104.2	75.5	-69.8	0.0	AMERICAN FREEDOM INS CO
23.4	21.1	N/A	N/A	N/A	N/A	N/A	N/A	N/A	85.4	0.0	0.0	AMERICAN GUARANTEE & LIABILITY INS
1.6	1.3	94.3	95.7	9.2	9.2	79.1	25.1	104.2	87.1	1.0	26.3	AMERICAN HALLMARK INS CO OF TX
0.4	0.4	399.9	376.9	-18.7	-46.8	55.7	39.1	94.8	113.0	46.7	0.0	AMERICAN HEARTLAND INS CO
2.3	1.4	80.6	194.2	3.4	11.9	96.3	31.9	128.2	26.0	-19.7	0.6 •	AMERICAN HOME ASR CO
0.4	0.3	136.5	109.0	19.7	29.1	106.4	23.8	130.2	194.7	-8.2	21.6	AMERICAN INDEPENDENT INS CO
10.5	9.5	N/A	N/A	N/A	N/A	N/A	N/A	N/A	-1.5	0.0	0.0	AMERICAN INS CO
2.0	1.6	170.8	69.7	18.9	27.0	71.8	26.1	97.9	108.3	11.3	0.0	AMERICAN INTEGRITY INS CO OF FL
1.4	0.9	171.0	142.2	7.0	14.0	72.9	22.6	95.5	140.0	37.3	0.0	AMERICAN INTER FIDELITY EXCHANGE
1.9	1.5	71.9	144.8	-6.8	-18.5	60.5	23.3	83.8	132.7	-5.9	11.3 •	AMERICAN INTERSTATE INS CO
1.9	1.5	61.1	115.0	-5.9	-16.9	60.6	23.6	84.2	129.5	-5.8	0.0 •	AMERICAN INTERSTATE INS CO OF TX
0.2	0.1	210.8	226.0	27.7	145.0	63.6	19.0	82.6	111.8	13.2	0.0	AMERICAN LIBERTY INS CO
N/A	N/A	--	--	--	--	--	--	--	--	--	--	AMERICAN MEDICAL ASR CO
3.5	2.8	96.8	40.7	3.0	2.9	72.4	26.0	98.4	101.6	-4.1	12.7	AMERICAN MERCURY INS CO
17.2	15.4	N/A	N/A	N/A	N/A	N/A	N/A	N/A	188.9	0.0	0.0	AMERICAN MERCURY LLOYDS INS CO
0.3	0.2	115.8	134.2	22.2	34.5	87.3	9.1	96.4	119.9	-1.1	0.0	AMERICAN MILLENNIUM INS CO
9.0	8.1	N/A	N/A	N/A	N/A	N/A	N/A	N/A	131.0	0.0	0.0	AMERICAN MINING INS CO
1.9	1.6	80.5	19.0	-1.9	-2.6	60.4	46.5	106.9	61.6	-7.3	40.6 •	AMERICAN MODERN HOME INS CO
2.4	1.5	118.3	27.9	-3.1	-5.0	60.4	47.2	107.6	92.7	-7.3	0.0	AMERICAN MODERN INS CO OF FLORIDA
2.1	1.9	N/A	N/A	N/A	N/A	N/A	N/A	N/A	-22.8	0.0	0.0	AMERICAN MODERN LLOYDS INS CO
5.3	4.7	18.9	4.5	-0.5	-0.7	60.4	42.5	102.9	866.7	-7.3	0.0	AMERICAN MODERN PROPERTY &
6.2	4.8	54.0	12.7	-1.4	-2.2	60.4	37.6	98.0	284.1	-7.3	0.0	AMERICAN MODERN SELECT INS CO
2.6	1.6	113.0	26.7	-2.7	-3.9	60.4	46.7	107.1	81.6	-7.3	0.0	AMERICAN MODERN SURPLUS LINES
10.7	9.7	0.1	7.1	-3.9	-10.4	204.5	911.0	999 +	2.0	-9.3	8.9 •	AMERICAN MUTUAL SHARE INS CORP
5.0	3.7	66.1	31.4	2.3	-3.4	86.9	24.3	111.2	98.4	23.9	0.0	AMERICAN NATIONAL GENERAL INS CO
9.1	6.6	34.8	9.2	0.4	-0.6	92.5	27.8	120.3	83.3	9.5	0.0	AMERICAN NATIONAL LLOYDS INS CO
2.1	1.7	94.9	44.9	-3.9	-4.8	74.1	27.8	101.9	102.6	14.8	19.3 •	AMERICAN NATIONAL PROPERTY & CAS
2.9	1.7	N/A	N/A	N/A	N/A	N/A	999 +	999 +	173.6	0.0	0.0	AMERICAN NATL COUNTY MUT INS CO
N/A	N/A	--	--	--	--	--	--	--	--	--	--	AMERICAN PACIFIC INS CO
0.9	0.5	552.5	30.2	-0.8	2.7	73.0	20.1	93.1	108.8	33.2	0.0	AMERICAN PET INS CO
N/A	N/A	--	--	--	--	--	--	--	--	--	--	AMERICAN PHYSICIANS ASR CORP
7.5	3.9	22.1	8.7	-0.8	-0.5	81.7	47.3	129.0	89.0	-2.2	0.0	AMERICAN PLATINUM PROP & CAS INS
0.5	0.3	143.7	59.8	2.6	2.2	48.9	33.0	81.9	162.8	14.8	0.0	AMERICAN PROPERTY INS
2.8	1.7	70.4	83.4	0.7	-3.2	81.8	37.1	118.9	66.7	-11.7	2.0	AMERICAN RELIABLE INS CO
0.4	0.2	280.7	298.0	35.0	28.8	83.0	49.7	132.7	81.3	-9.2	0.0	AMERICAN RESOURCES INS CO INC
1.1	0.8	141.7	31.6	-8.3	-10.3	58.7	39.1	97.8	94.3	5.0	0.0	AMERICAN RISK INS CO

999 + Denotes number greater than 999.9%
999 - Denotes number less than -999.99%
• Bullets denote a more detailed analysis is available in Section II.

INSURANCE COMPANY NAME	DOM. STATE	RATING	TOTAL ASSETS ($MIL)	CAPITAL & SURPLUS ($MIL)	ANNUAL NET PREMIUM ($MIL)	NET INCOME ($MIL)	CAPITAL-IZATION INDEX (PTS)	RESERVE ADQ INDEX (PTS)	PROFIT-ABILITY INDEX (PTS)	LIQUIDITY INDEX (PTS)	STAB. INDEX (PTS)	STABILITY FACTORS
AMERICAN RISK MGMT RRG INC	TN	D	4.0	1.5	2.0	0.0	5.6	3.6	3.5	7.9	1.4	DGT
▲AMERICAN ROAD INS CO	MI	B-	711.9	270.4	160.0	9.5	10.0	6.1	7.5	7.0	4.5	R
AMERICAN SAFETY INS CO	GA	C	16.7	16.2	0.0	0.4	10.0	N/A	3.9	7.0	3.7	DR
AMERICAN SAFETY RRG INC	VT	D+(1)	7.7	5.6	0.3	0.0	5.3	9.6	1.8	6.9	2.1	DFGR
AMERICAN SECURITY INS CO	DE	B-	1,376.3	506.3	849.2	91.8	7.7	6.4	3.4	3.2	5.1	AFL
AMERICAN SELECT INS CO	OH	C	271.5	123.7	92.9	-0.3	9.1	8.3	6.8	6.7	4.1	T
AMERICAN SENTINEL INS CO	PA	C-	43.3	17.8	25.2	2.7	3.2	8.0	8.2	6.0	3.1	CD
AMERICAN SERVICE INS CO	IL	D	207.7	42.2	95.4	-15.2	3.0	0.9	3.1	3.9	1.8	GLRT
AMERICAN SOUTHERN HOME INS CO	FL	C	135.3	47.3	25.7	0.0	9.3	7.6	7.8	7.3	3.8	T
AMERICAN SOUTHERN INS CO	KS	C+	115.4	43.3	53.4	6.3	8.0	8.2	8.6	6.1	4.5	R
AMERICAN SPECIAL RISK INS CO	DE	U	--	--	--	--	N/A	--	--	--	--	Z
AMERICAN STANDARD INS CO OF OH	WI	B	13.0	8.7	0.0	0.5	10.0	N/A	8.0	6.7	4.7	DT
AMERICAN STANDARD INS CO OF WI	WI	B+	400.9	347.6	0.0	4.5	10.0	N/A	6.9	7.0	6.4	FT
AMERICAN STATES INS CO	IN	B-	143.5	133.0	0.0	1.5	10.0	N/A	6.9	7.0	5.3	A
AMERICAN STATES INS CO OF TX	TX	B	14.2	12.4	0.0	0.3	10.0	N/A	7.3	7.0	4.7	DR
AMERICAN STATES LLOYDS INS CO	TX	B	3.7	3.7	0.0	0.1	10.0	N/A	6.7	7.0	4.1	DRT
AMERICAN STATES PREFERRED INS CO	IN	B-	23.5	22.3	0.0	0.3	10.0	N/A	6.3	7.0	5.2	AD
AMERICAN STEAMSHIP O M PROT & IND AS	NY	D+	249.4	74.8	66.2	20.5	7.0	5.0	5.0	5.3	2.6	FR
AMERICAN STRATEGIC INS CO	FL	C	1,223.1	508.1	779.5	-22.7	8.3	9.3	5.1	6.4	3.8	T
AMERICAN SUMMIT INS CO	TX	C+	40.9	22.8	26.3	0.7	8.4	7.6	3.3	6.5	4.5	DR
AMERICAN SURETY CO	IN	C	14.2	10.5	11.4	0.9	6.1	9.2	5.1	6.7	3.1	D
AMERICAN TRADITIONS INS CO	FL	C+	69.0	19.9	33.3	0.4	5.2	5.0	4.8	7.0	4.7	DFGR
AMERICAN TRANSIT INS CO	NY	E+	287.5	76.8	333.6	13.5	0.7	0.1	3.2	6.4	0.4	CGRT
▼AMERICAN TRUCKING & TRANSP INS RRG	MT	E-	41.1	2.4	16.1	-5.7	0.0	4.9	0.3	2.8	0.1	CDGL
AMERICAN UNDERWRITERS INS CO	AR	D+	5.9	5.0	0.0	0.0	10.0	N/A	3.4	10.0	2.5	DRT
AMERICAN WEST INS CO	ND	C	18.1	12.4	13.9	0.4	4.4	6.4	8.2	2.4	4.3	CDL
AMERICAN WESTERN HOME INS CO	OK	C	162.7	71.1	57.8	-1.0	9.0	7.8	5.2	6.7	3.9	T
AMERICAN ZURICH INS CO	IL	C+	332.8	234.9	0.0	3.6	10.0	N/A	7.4	7.5	4.7	R
AMERICAS INS CO	DC	C	16.6	7.4	3.1	-0.2	8.2	5.6	2.5	7.1	2.8	DFRT
AMERIPRISE INS CO	WI	B	50.1	48.3	0.0	1.0	10.0	N/A	6.6	10.0	5.4	
AMERISURE INS CO	MI	B-	875.0	241.8	244.6	2.1	8.2	5.2	6.1	6.6	4.7	FR
AMERISURE MUTUAL INS CO	MI	B-	2,369.8	982.5	546.3	35.8	8.3	5.8	6.9	6.8	4.7	T
AMERISURE PARTNERS INS CO	MI	C+	88.2	24.0	24.5	-0.2	7.4	5.4	4.4	6.5	4.5	DF
AMERITRUST INS CORP	MI	D+	13.8	12.6	0.0	0.4	10.0	1.9	1.9	6.1	2.6	DRT
AMEX ASSURANCE CO	IL	B	218.2	175.8	176.5	53.4	10.0	6.9	3.9	7.4	5.9	
▲AMFED CASUALTY INS CO	MS	C	5.9	5.1	0.0	0.0	10.0	N/A	7.5	7.0	3.5	DFRT
▲AMFED NATIONAL INS CO	MS	D	65.7	34.5	10.0	2.3	3.7	1.9	8.1	7.1	1.4	DF
▲AMFIRST SPECIALTY INS CO	MS	D+	2.7	2.4	-0.9	0.0	10.0	N/A	6.5	7.0	2.3	DFT
AMGUARD INS CO	PA	C	878.8	168.7	202.5	20.1	5.5	9.3	8.8	7.1	3.4	GRT
AMICA MUTUAL INS CO	RI	B+	5,384.6	2,669.5	2,273.9	82.7	8.2	8.3	5.5	5.3	6.8	L
▲AMICA P&C INS CO	RI	B	84.1	79.7	0.0	0.7	10.0	4.9	6.4	10.0	5.5	FT
AMSHIELD INS CO	MO	U	--	--	--	--	N/A	--	--	--	--	Z
AMTRUST INS CO OF KANSAS INC	KS	B-	106.2	63.9	35.4	29.3	9.7	7.1	9.9	2.4	3.9	GLRT
ANCHOR GENERAL INS CO	CA	C	98.2	20.9	40.7	-1.3	6.7	4.2	2.6	1.0	3.5	DFLR
ANCHOR P&C INS CO	FL	D	79.8	25.2	31.5	-29.8	0.9	1.5	1.8	3.8	1.6	CFLT
ANCHOR SPECIALTY INS CO	TX	C	18.6	10.1	4.0	-4.0	5.2	4.5	2.4	4.7	3.5	DFLR
ANPAC LOUISIANA INS CO	LA	B	134.7	70.5	60.6	2.7	9.3	6.4	4.3	6.3	6.2	
▲ANSUR AMERICA INS CO	MI	B+	121.2	46.7	50.7	4.3	10.0	9.3	8.8	6.6	6.5	D
ANTHRACITE MUTUAL FIRE INS CO	PA	C-	4.3	4.3	0.4	0.2	10.0	6.0	7.9	9.2	3.3	D
ANTILLES INS CO	PR	C (1)	69.9	39.3	26.0	-4.3	5.0	7.7	2.5	5.5	3.7	RT
APOLLO CASUALTY CO	IL	E (1)	15.3	4.9	8.8	-1.3	0.7	1.3	0.5	0.0	0.1	CDFG
APOLLO MUTUAL FIRE INS CO	PA	C-	4.2	4.1	0.1	0.1	10.0	5.0	6.9	10.0	2.2	D

See Page 27 for explanation of footnotes and Page 28 for explanation of stability factors.

38

www.weissratings.com

Arrows denote recent upgrades ▲ or downgrades ▼   (see Section VII for explanations)

RISK ADJ. RATIO #1	CAPITAL RATIO #2	PREMIUM TO SURPLUS (%)	RESV. TO SURPLUS (%)	RESV. DEVELOP. 1 YEAR (%)	RESV. DEVELOP. 2 YEAR (%)	LOSS RATIO (%)	EXP. RATIO (%)	COMB RATIO (%)	CASH FROM UNDER-WRITING (%)	NET PREMIUM GROWTH (%)	INVEST. IN AFFIL (%)	INSURANCE COMPANY NAME
1.2	0.9	133.6	104.4	2.2	N/A	63.7	52.3	116.0	147.0	-26.1	0.0	AMERICAN RISK MGMT RRG INC
22.3	11.9	59.2	1.7	N/A	0.6	95.4	0.7	96.1	98.5	1.6	0.0 •	AMERICAN ROAD INS CO
31.2	11.3	N/A	N/A	N/A	N/A	N/A	N/A	N/A	N/A	0.0	0.0	AMERICAN SAFETY INS CO
1.1	0.9	5.2	36.5	4.7	-16.3	168.4	194.7	363.1	36.4	-37.2	0.0	AMERICAN SAFETY RRG INC
2.0	1.5	167.7	42.2	-2.3	-3.8	62.5	45.6	108.1	75.4	-10.2	12.9 •	AMERICAN SECURITY INS CO
3.6	2.4	75.0	71.1	0.2	-2.2	73.5	34.5	108.0	99.6	2.6	0.0	AMERICAN SELECT INS CO
0.7	0.5	141.3	48.1	-5.4	-1.3	47.5	49.2	96.7	112.9	-0.2	0.0	AMERICAN SENTINEL INS CO
0.6	0.5	226.0	154.1	62.8	83.7	95.1	25.1	120.2	116.7	32.6	0.0	AMERICAN SERVICE INS CO
3.5	2.8	54.3	12.8	-1.4	-2.1	60.4	44.9	105.3	742.2	-7.3	13.0	AMERICAN SOUTHERN HOME INS CO
2.4	1.9	123.1	94.1	-6.4	-5.8	64.3	30.5	94.8	109.0	3.7	15.5	AMERICAN SOUTHERN INS CO
N/A	N/A	--	--	--	--	--	--	--	--	--	--	AMERICAN SPECIAL RISK INS CO
6.6	5.9	N/A	N/A	N/A	N/A	N/A	N/A	N/A	999 +	0.0	0.0	AMERICAN STANDARD INS CO OF OH
50.4	45.3	N/A	N/A	N/A	N/A	N/A	N/A	N/A	81.8	0.0	0.0 •	AMERICAN STANDARD INS CO OF WI
53.6	48.2	N/A	N/A	N/A	N/A	N/A	N/A	N/A	N/A	0.0	0.0	AMERICAN STATES INS CO
19.0	17.1	N/A	N/A	N/A	N/A	N/A	N/A	N/A	N/A	0.0	0.0	AMERICAN STATES INS CO OF TX
263.1	131.5	N/A	N/A	N/A	N/A	N/A	N/A	N/A	N/A	0.0	0.0	AMERICAN STATES LLOYDS INS CO
44.9	40.4	N/A	N/A	N/A	N/A	N/A	N/A	N/A	N/A	0.0	0.0	AMERICAN STATES PREFERRED INS CO
1.5	1.1	88.4	177.8	-13.3	0.6	43.6	50.4	94.0	86.4	-22.1	2.3	AMERICAN STEAMSHIP O M PROT & IND
2.2	1.8	153.4	32.0	-5.8	-11.8	71.0	31.6	102.6	108.4	26.1	1.2 •	AMERICAN STRATEGIC INS CO
2.3	1.9	115.5	14.3	-2.6	-1.0	62.1	35.3	97.4	98.7	-1.1	0.0	AMERICAN SUMMIT INS CO
0.9	0.8	108.7	10.2	-4.6	-9.7	6.7	87.7	94.4	99.0	5.4	0.0	AMERICAN SURETY CO
0.9	0.7	167.2	50.0	-2.9	0.8	66.0	30.1	96.1	94.5	17.3	0.0	AMERICAN TRADITIONS INS CO
0.2	0.2	434.4	176.4	169.1	359.0	68.6	26.9	95.5	116.6	16.2	0.0	AMERICAN TRANSIT INS CO
0.0	0.0	674.4	999 +	70.6	1.7	125.1	20.5	145.6	107.4	25.3	0.0	AMERICAN TRUCKING & TRANSP INS
11.8	10.6	N/A	N/A	N/A	N/A	N/A	N/A	N/A	30.3	0.0	0.0	AMERICAN UNDERWRITERS INS CO
0.8	0.6	111.8	11.8	-4.5	-5.1	68.7	24.6	93.3	109.7	43.4	0.0	AMERICAN WEST INS CO
4.8	2.9	81.2	19.2	-2.0	-3.0	60.4	46.4	106.8	95.8	-7.3	0.0	AMERICAN WESTERN HOME INS CO
7.1	6.8	N/A	N/A	N/A	N/A	N/A	N/A	N/A	276.8	0.0	15.0 •	AMERICAN ZURICH INS CO
3.2	2.8	41.9	22.1	-2.3	6.4	50.4	70.7	121.1	81.8	-55.3	6.1	AMERICAS INS CO
69.9	32.2	N/A	N/A	N/A	N/A	N/A	N/A	N/A	N/A	0.0	0.0	AMERIPRISE INS CO
2.5	1.7	101.2	172.1	7.5	7.5	74.3	29.9	104.2	92.8	0.3	0.0 •	AMERISURE INS CO
2.4	1.9	55.6	94.6	4.4	4.6	74.3	30.0	104.3	106.4	0.3	13.0 •	AMERISURE MUTUAL INS CO
1.7	1.2	102.0	173.5	7.5	7.4	74.3	29.8	104.1	83.2	0.3	0.0	AMERISURE PARTNERS INS CO
11.3	6.4	N/A	N/A	N/A	N/A	N/A	N/A	N/A	-422.5	0.0	0.0	AMERITRUST INS CORP
9.1	5.3	100.4	18.7	0.3	0.2	46.0	12.2	58.2	177.3	-0.5	0.0	AMEX ASSURANCE CO
15.7	14.1	N/A	N/A	N/A	N/A	N/A	N/A	N/A	136.1	0.0	0.0	AMFED CASUALTY INS CO
0.8	0.5	28.9	64.2	-8.3	-19.8	38.7	45.6	84.3	67.7	-5.6	9.1	AMFED NATIONAL INS CO
12.7	7.4	-36.9	N/A	N/A	N/A	N/A	-3.7	N/A	158.9	-159.7	0.0	AMFIRST SPECIALTY INS CO
0.9	0.8	120.1	131.9	-6.8	-8.6	58.1	24.7	82.8	166.2	26.0	0.0	AMGUARD INS CO
2.6	1.7	85.2	46.2	-5.1	-5.3	79.9	23.3	103.2	102.9	9.0	8.4 •	AMICA MUTUAL INS CO
59.4	38.1	N/A	N/A	N/A	N/A	N/A	N/A	N/A	-874.3	0.0	0.0	AMICA P&C INS CO
N/A	N/A	--	--	--	--	--	--	--	--	--	--	AMSHIELD INS CO
6.1	5.5	55.4	N/A	-163.4	-107.5	74.0	-54.3	19.7	241.0	-43.6	0.0	AMTRUST INS CO OF KANSAS INC
1.1	0.9	194.7	114.0	6.5	12.1	75.0	31.2	106.2	97.4	-18.6	25.0	ANCHOR GENERAL INS CO
0.3	0.2	124.9	76.9	47.3	32.1	165.0	43.4	208.4	57.0	26.4	0.0	ANCHOR P&C INS CO
1.1	0.7	39.9	25.2	-7.9	-2.7	161.1	38.3	199.4	60.9	-6.1	0.0	ANCHOR SPECIALTY INS CO
4.1	2.8	86.0	48.7	-0.3	1.5	75.9	23.4	99.3	108.5	12.5	0.0	ANPAC LOUISIANA INS CO
5.1	3.8	108.5	75.3	-10.4	-11.0	59.0	32.3	91.3	106.2	5.7	0.0 •	ANSUR AMERICA INS CO
10.8	6.3	9.6	0.6	N/A	0.3	32.7	40.2	72.9	120.6	7.2	0.0	ANTHRACITE MUTUAL FIRE INS CO
2.4	1.5	60.9	6.9	-0.7	-1.3	51.2	71.2	122.4	94.9	-15.5	0.0	ANTILLES INS CO
0.8	0.6	450.9	330.1	33.2	48.7	110.1	28.9	139.0	107.7	66.6	0.0	APOLLO CASUALTY CO
7.6	5.0	3.4	0.1	-0.1	-0.1	24.4	86.3	110.7	90.4	1.7	0.0	APOLLO MUTUAL FIRE INS CO

999 + Denotes number greater than 999.9%
999 - Denotes number less than -999.99%

• Bullets denote a more detailed analysis is available in Section II.

INSURANCE COMPANY NAME	DOM. STATE	RATING	TOTAL ASSETS ($MIL)	CAPITAL & SURPLUS ($MIL)	ANNUAL NET PREMIUM ($MIL)	NET INCOME ($MIL)	CAPITAL-IZATION INDEX (PTS)	RESERVE ADQ INDEX (PTS)	PROFIT-ABILITY INDEX (PTS)	LIQUIDITY INDEX (PTS)	STAB. INDEX (PTS)	STABILITY FACTORS
APPALACHIAN INS CO	RI	C	326.0	204.4	70.8	-13.1	9.5	3.9	4.2	6.7	3.9	FR
▲APPLIED MEDICO LEGAL SOLUTIONS RRG	AZ	C+	152.8	45.6	45.1	1.7	7.3	5.0	6.4	7.3	4.5	FR
▲APPLIED UNDERWRITERS CAPTIVE RISK	IA	C	847.1	74.3	0.0	4.4	7.4	7.0	6.7	7.0	3.5	T
▲ARAG INS CO	IA	B	82.9	61.3	85.1	13.2	9.5	8.2	9.4	6.2	5.5	
ARBELLA INDEMNITY INS CO	MA	C	53.1	17.2	23.3	2.0	7.7	8.2	5.5	6.5	3.4	DR
ARBELLA MUTUAL INS CO	MA	C+	1,462.6	621.1	590.6	49.2	8.5	8.0	5.7	6.5	4.3	R
ARBELLA PROTECTION INS CO	MA	C+	325.7	104.6	124.3	10.4	9.1	8.2	6.0	6.1	4.3	R
ARCH EXCESS & SURPLUS INS CO	MO	U	--	--	--	--	N/A	--	--	--	--	Z
ARCH INDEMNITY INS CO	MO	B-	102.3	31.0	0.0	4.2	10.0	N/A	5.7	9.2	3.7	RT
ARCH INS CO	MO	C	3,921.9	929.8	-549.1	71.1	7.9	9.6	8.6	6.4	3.4	RT
ARCH MORTGAGE GUARANTY CO	WI	B	50.9	49.2	0.1	0.0	10.0	3.6	3.9	9.9	4.7	DGT
▲ARCH MORTGAGE INS CO	WI	B	2,134.6	471.9	416.2	12.1	7.7	5.8	3.8	9.1	4.5	GRT
ARCH REINS CO	DE	C-	1,987.8	1,287.6	193.9	17.7	7.8	8.1	7.5	7.0	2.7	R
▲ARCH SPECIALTY INS CO	MO	B+	483.4	300.7	0.0	5.7	10.0	6.0	6.2	7.5	6.5	FT
ARCH STRUCTURED MRTG INS CO	NC	U	--	--	--	--	N/A	--	--	--	--	Z
ARCHITECTS & ENGINEERS INS CO	DE	C	22.5	10.8	1.6	0.6	9.9	6.1	8.2	9.1	3.0	DFR
▲ARCOA RRG INC	NV	D-	19.4	8.2	12.2	1.4	1.2	5.0	9.3	6.9	1.1	CD
ARDELLIS INSURANCE LTD		E	8.5	8.3	0.4	-0.1	10.0	N/A	3.7	9.1	0.0	DT
▲ARECA INS EXCHANGE	AK	B-	28.4	20.3	4.2	0.5	10.0	6.4	4.5	7.5	4.4	DR
ARGONAUT GREAT CENTRAL INS CO	IL	D+	40.8	27.3	0.0	0.5	10.0	N/A	6.9	7.0	2.4	R
ARGONAUT INS CO	IL	C	1,820.4	872.8	302.0	2.7	7.2	3.5	6.5	6.9	3.3	R
ARGONAUT LTD RISK INS CO	IL	U	--	--	--	--	N/A	--	--	--	--	Z
ARGONAUT-MIDWEST INS CO	IL	D	22.9	17.8	0.0	0.3	10.0	N/A	7.1	10.0	2.3	DR
ARGONAUT-SOUTHWEST INS CO	IL	U	--	--	--	--	N/A	--	--	--	--	Z
ARGUS FIRE & CASUALTY INS CO	FL	F	3.6	3.3	0.0	-2.0	10.0	4.6	2.7	10.0	0.0	DFT
ARI CASUALTY CO	NJ	U	--	--	--	--	N/A	--	--	--	--	Z
ARI INS CO	PA	D	72.8	17.1	-2.6	-2.5	4.5	3.6	2.0	0.0	2.1	DFLR
ARISE BOILER INSPECT & INS CO RRG	KY	B-	4.2	3.2	1.0	0.4	10.0	8.5	8.2	9.0	3.5	D
▲ARIZONA AUTOMOBILE INS CO	AZ	C+	41.3	9.2	11.3	0.0	8.1	8.1	5.7	5.9	3.1	DFGR
ARIZONA HOME INS CO	AZ	D	28.8	19.0	9.4	0.9	7.1	8.1	8.3	6.7	2.2	DR
ARKANSAS MUTUAL INS CO	AR	D	2.7	1.7	-0.1	-0.5	10.0	5.1	0.5	7.0	1.9	DFT
▲ARMED FORCES INS EXCHANGE	KS	B	139.4	67.5	67.9	2.0	8.6	8.3	3.3	6.3	5.5	
ARROW MUTUAL LIABILITY INS CO	MA	B-	45.9	30.4	6.8	-0.2	8.7	8.4	3.9	6.9	5.1	DF
ARROWOOD INDEMNITY CO	DE	D	1,211.0	183.2	-0.2	-58.1	0.3	3.5	1.4	9.2	1.8	CFRT
ARROWOOD SURPLUS LINES INS CO	DE	U	--	--	--	--	N/A	--	--	--	--	Z
ARTISAN & TRUCKERS CASUALTY CO	WI	C	346.2	65.6	51.8	5.2	10.0	6.2	8.9	6.8	3.6	R
▲ASCENDANT COMMERCIAL INS INC	FL	D	64.0	11.3	25.1	1.0	1.9	1.4	7.9	6.7	1.5	CD
ASCENT INSURANCE CO	IL	U	--	--	--	--	N/A	--	--	--	--	Z
ASHLAND MUTUAL FIRE INS CO OF PA	PA	U	--	--	--	--	N/A	--	--	--	--	Z
ASHMERE INS CO	FL	D+	18.0	6.7	10.8	-2.2	2.1	3.6	1.4	7.0	2.6	CDFG
▼ASI ASR CORP	FL	B-	128.4	45.1	72.4	-2.9	8.6	9.4	3.3	6.3	5.1	FG
ASI HOME INS CORP	FL	B-	17.6	15.9	1.6	0.6	10.0	3.6	4.0	9.1	5.2	D
ASI LLOYDS	TX	D+	222.7	91.4	127.9	-3.7	8.5	8.6	3.8	6.6	2.7	FR
▼ASI PREFERRED INS CORP	FL	C+	106.7	33.6	51.5	-9.1	7.4	9.3	3.0	6.3	4.5	F
ASI SELECT AUTO INS CORP	CA	C	18.3	18.0	0.1	-4.8	10.0	N/A	2.6	10.0	2.7	DFT
▲ASI SELECT INS CORP	DE	C	28.7	20.2	5.3	-0.9	10.0	5.4	3.7	7.0	3.5	DGT
ASOC DE SUSCRIPCION CONJUNTA DEL	PR	C- (1)	122.3	36.0	62.4	2.6	10.0	7.7	1.9	6.7	3.1	FT
▼ASPEN AMERICAN INS CO	TX	C+	903.9	506.3	86.5	-5.5	7.6	3.0	3.6	8.3	4.5	R
▼ASPEN SPECIALTY INS CO	ND	D	401.7	139.2	41.6	-9.5	1.5	3.8	3.7	6.9	2.2	CR
ASPEN SPECIALTY RRG INC	DC	U (1)	--	--	--	--	N/A	--	--	--	--	Z
ASPIRE GENERAL INS CO	CA	C-	22.7	8.4	10.7	-0.3	3.6	4.7	1.8	6.8	2.3	DGT
ASSET PROTECTION PROGRAM RRG INC	SC	U	--	--	--	--	N/A	--	--	--	--	Z

See Page 27 for explanation of footnotes and Page 28 for explanation of stability factors.
Arrows denote recent upgrades ▲ or downgrades ▼   (see Section VII for explanations)

40   www.weissratings.com

RISK ADJ. RATIO #1	CAPITAL RATIO #2	PREMIUM TO SURPLUS (%)	RESV. TO SURPLUS (%)	RESV. DEVELOP. 1 YEAR (%)	RESV. DEVELOP. 2 YEAR (%)	LOSS RATIO (%)	EXP. RATIO (%)	COMB RATIO (%)	CASH FROM UNDER-WRITING (%)	NET PREMIUM GROWTH (%)	INVEST. IN AFFIL (%)	INSURANCE COMPANY NAME
4.3	2.6	34.6	34.3	N/A	-3.3	108.4	28.9	137.3	84.0	7.0	0.0	APPALACHIAN INS CO
1.7	1.1	99.0	153.2	-0.3	5.6	74.3	30.6	104.9	79.8	49.1	0.0	APPLIED MEDICO LEGAL SOLUTIONS
2.3	1.2	N/A	88.7	-32.4	-57.4	N/A	N/A	N/A	-28.7	0.0	0.0	APPLIED UNDERWRITERS CAPTIVE RISK
4.1	2.6	138.7	29.4	-1.0	-0.6	46.4	33.3	79.7	129.1	11.1	0.0	ARAG INS CO
2.3	1.5	135.2	79.3	-5.1	-8.6	60.0	34.4	94.4	97.7	-4.6	0.0	ARBELLA INDEMNITY INS CO
2.6	2.0	95.1	55.8	-3.8	-6.3	60.0	33.6	93.6	107.9	-4.6	13.8 ●	ARBELLA MUTUAL INS CO
3.9	2.5	118.9	69.7	-4.5	-7.4	60.0	34.1	94.1	104.3	-4.6	0.0	ARBELLA PROTECTION INS CO
N/A	N/A	--	--	--	--	--	--	--	--	--	--	ARCH EXCESS & SURPLUS INS CO
4.0	3.6	N/A	6.3	N/A	N/A	N/A	N/A	N/A	-19.0	0.0	0.0	ARCH INDEMNITY INS CO
2.5	2.3	-59.1	43.2	-102.5	-83.4	132.5	-34.7	97.8	103.5	-169.2	13.7 ●	ARCH INS CO
47.5	41.6	0.3	0.1	-0.1	N/A	4.4	548.0	552.4	25.5	-52.7	0.0	ARCH MORTGAGE GUARANTY CO
3.0	2.2	88.2	45.9	-11.5	-16.6	17.6	45.6	63.2	999 +	370.8	0.0 ●	ARCH MORTGAGE INS CO
1.5	1.5	15.1	32.3	-1.3	-3.3	60.3	37.6	97.9	95.0	-10.1	52.9 ●	ARCH REINS CO
5.7	4.6	N/A	14.9	0.2	0.1	999 +	999 +	999 +	-48.0	-106.1	0.0 ●	ARCH SPECIALTY INS CO
N/A	N/A	--	--	--	--	--	--	--	--	--	--	ARCH STRUCTURED MRTG INS CO
4.2	3.0	14.6	34.7	3.4	2.3	70.0	8.4	78.4	33.9	2.6	0.0	ARCHITECTS & ENGINEERS INS CO
0.4	0.3	148.2	130.1	-1.3	-12.8	43.5	43.7	87.2	148.7	16.9	0.0	ARCOA RRG INC
13.5	9.3	4.8	2.8	N/A	N/A	159.1	7.6	166.7	90.3	0.0	0.0	ARDELLIS INSURANCE LTD
6.5	3.7	20.7	29.8	0.9	-2.7	58.5	40.3	98.8	239.1	-2.6	0.0	ARECA INS EXCHANGE
9.7	8.7	N/A	N/A	N/A	N/A	N/A	N/A	N/A	-28.3	0.0	2.6	ARGONAUT GREAT CENTRAL INS CO
1.3	1.1	34.6	56.0	2.6	7.1	71.0	37.1	108.1	113.2	35.0	33.7 ●	ARGONAUT INS CO
N/A	N/A	--	--	--	--	--	--	--	--	--	--	ARGONAUT LTD RISK INS CO
11.5	10.3	N/A	N/A	N/A	N/A	N/A	N/A	N/A	-0.1	0.0	0.0	ARGONAUT-MIDWEST INS CO
N/A	N/A	--	--	--	--	--	--	--	--	--	--	ARGONAUT-SOUTHWEST INS CO
26.0	23.4	N/A	4.1	-0.2	-0.1	N/A	N/A	N/A	N/A	0.0	0.0	ARGUS FIRE & CASUALTY INS CO
N/A	N/A	--	--	--	--	--	--	--	--	--	--	ARI CASUALTY CO
1.8	1.4	-15.0	N/A	-929.4	999 +	176.3	-39.3	137.0	9.6	-109.5	15.4	ARI INS CO
4.9	4.1	31.2	5.5	-4.6	-5.2	2.6	55.6	58.2	184.7	13.1	0.0	ARISE BOILER INSPECT & INS CO RRG
1.9	1.7	123.5	90.5	-2.7	-3.8	67.5	33.1	100.6	95.4	21.8	0.0	ARIZONA AUTOMOBILE INS CO
1.8	1.1	49.8	14.6	-4.2	-4.1	67.8	22.1	89.9	110.8	-1.1	0.0	ARIZONA HOME INS CO
4.8	4.3	-7.3	N/A	N/A	N/A	N/A	-567.5	-567.5	-386.6	93.7	0.0	ARKANSAS MUTUAL INS CO
2.9	2.0	100.6	25.0	-5.2	-2.1	64.6	39.7	104.3	98.2	-1.3	4.2	ARMED FORCES INS EXCHANGE
3.2	2.1	22.3	37.3	-1.1	-8.5	96.3	17.6	113.9	88.6	7.2	0.0	ARROW MUTUAL LIABILITY INS CO
0.2	0.1	-0.1	493.7	11.0	19.4	999 +	999 +	999 +	-0.9	-501.3	7.6	ARROWOOD INDEMNITY CO
N/A	N/A	--	--	--	--	--	--	--	--	--	--	ARROWOOD SURPLUS LINES INS CO
6.2	4.7	79.0	46.2	0.6	-3.0	70.4	17.5	87.9	121.5	7.7	0.0	ARTISAN & TRUCKERS CASUALTY CO
0.5	0.3	222.2	226.5	25.8	22.1	71.4	19.3	90.7	132.5	35.2	0.0	ASCENDANT COMMERCIAL INS INC
N/A	N/A	--	--	--	--	--	--	--	--	--	--	ASCENT INSURANCE CO
N/A	N/A	--	--	--	--	--	--	--	--	--	--	ASHLAND MUTUAL FIRE INS CO OF PA
0.5	0.3	160.9	37.4	N/A	N/A	73.2	31.9	105.1	97.9	N/A	0.0	ASHMERE INS CO
2.6	2.0	160.5	45.2	-3.5	-11.1	76.6	36.8	113.4	79.3	-4.1	0.0	ASI ASR CORP
18.8	14.7	10.4	1.6	-1.6	-0.3	23.0	41.8	64.8	104.9	-19.4	0.0	ASI HOME INS CORP
2.4	2.0	139.9	30.2	-5.8	-3.8	75.8	30.5	106.3	103.6	6.0	0.0	ASI LLOYDS
1.9	1.5	153.3	31.9	-3.4	-4.5	54.5	68.7	123.2	70.6	-3.1	0.0	ASI PREFERRED INS CORP
3.5	3.5	0.7	N/A	N/A	N/A	48.6	999 +	999 +	0.4	0.0	0.0	ASI SELECT AUTO INS CORP
7.9	5.1	26.4	5.9	-0.7	-0.2	116.1	14.0	130.1	94.8	187.5	0.0	ASI SELECT INS CORP
4.5	3.2	61.1	9.1	-4.9	-0.6	74.7	25.1	99.8	77.9	-38.4	0.0	ASOC DE SUSCRIPCION CONJUNTA DEL
1.8	1.4	17.1	38.0	12.1	34.1	95.6	14.6	110.2	197.6	-3.6	29.0 ●	ASPEN AMERICAN INS CO
0.3	0.3	29.9	123.3	43.6	23.8	125.4	4.4	129.8	212.6	-33.8	0.0	ASPEN SPECIALTY INS CO
N/A	N/A	--	--	--	--	--	--	--	--	--	--	ASPEN SPECIALTY RRG INC
0.8	0.5	128.1	51.5	-3.5	-5.0	81.8	18.7	100.5	152.1	71.3	0.0	ASPIRE GENERAL INS CO
N/A	N/A	--	--	--	--	--	--	--	--	--	--	ASSET PROTECTION PROGRAM RRG INC

999 + Denotes number greater than 999.9%
999 - Denotes number less than -999.99%
● Bullets denote a more detailed analysis is available in Section II.

INSURANCE COMPANY NAME	DOM. STATE	RATING	TOTAL ASSETS ($MIL)	CAPITAL & SURPLUS ($MIL)	ANNUAL NET PREMIUM ($MIL)	NET INCOME ($MIL)	CAPITAL-IZATION INDEX (PTS)	RESERVE ADQ INDEX (PTS)	PROFIT-ABILITY INDEX (PTS)	LIQUIDITY INDEX (PTS)	STAB. INDEX (PTS)	STABILITY FACTORS
ASSN CASUALTY INS CO	TX	C	46.8	18.3	20.8	-0.3	8.2	6.0	3.9	6.2	3.9	D
ASSN OF CERTIFIED MTG ORIG RRG	NV	D	2.5	1.2	0.2	0.1	8.3	3.6	5.4	10.0	1.1	DFT
ASSOCIATED EMPLOYERS INS CO	MA	C	6.8	6.0	0.0	0.1	10.0	N/A	8.0	7.0	3.5	DR
ASSOCIATED INDEMNITY CORP	CA	C	106.4	90.0	0.0	0.7	10.0	N/A	6.7	7.0	4.2	RT
▼ASSOCIATED INDUSTRIES INS CO INC	FL	C-	245.0	48.4	30.3	24.7	8.5	7.1	2.0	1.8	3.2	FLRT
ASSOCIATED INDUSTRIES OF MA MUT INS	MA	B-	625.2	237.0	142.2	21.3	8.3	9.4	8.8	6.7	4.5	R
ASSOCIATED LOGGERS EXCHANGE	ID	C	37.6	14.3	11.8	-0.1	5.5	6.6	7.6	6.6	3.5	DR
ASSOCIATED MUTUAL INS CO	NY	C	28.5	9.5	8.6	0.3	4.9	3.5	3.3	6.9	2.9	CDR
ASSURANCEAMERICA INS CO	NE	D+	79.8	18.7	43.6	5.1	4.4	6.6	6.5	6.6	2.4	DGR
ASSURED GUARANTY CORP	MD	C-	3,126.7	2,073.2	21.6	219.1	10.0	1.5	6.9	9.4	2.9	AFRT
ASSURED GUARANTY MUNICIPAL CORP	NY	D+	5,479.6	2,253.9	261.8	152.4	7.8	4.7	6.1	9.5	2.4	ACRT
▲ASURE WORLDWIDE INS CO	MI	B	44.0	18.8	19.0	1.7	9.4	9.3	8.8	6.7	5.4	D
ATAIN INS CO	TX	C	88.2	52.2	12.9	1.5	9.2	6.0	6.8	7.1	4.0	DR
ATAIN SPECIALTY INS CO	MI	C	387.9	190.8	73.1	-1.0	7.5	6.0	6.9	6.9	3.8	R
ATLANTA INTERNATIONAL INS CO	NY	C	96.2	27.0	14.3	9.0	8.2	6.1	7.1	7.3	4.3	GRT
▲ATLANTIC BONDING CO	MD	D	9.5	8.7	0.5	0.2	7.5	6.0	3.9	7.0	1.5	DF
ATLANTIC CASUALTY INS CO	NC	B-	286.4	108.8	84.4	5.4	7.8	9.3	8.6	7.0	4.5	R
▲ATLANTIC CHARTER INS CO	MA	B	178.4	56.6	65.3	17.9	6.5	9.9	9.4	6.8	5.5	T
ATLANTIC SPECIALTY INS CO	NY	C+	2,259.6	618.1	555.8	-118.9	7.0	3.3	2.6	6.8	4.6	FR
ATLANTIC STATES INS CO	PA	B-	793.2	223.2	451.6	-0.3	8.4	5.8	6.8	6.1	4.7	R
▲ATRADIUS TRADE CREDIT INS CO	MD	C+	117.5	64.5	20.1	3.3	10.0	5.0	3.5	7.0	4.5	R
ATRIUM INS CORP	NY	U	--	--	--	--	N/A	--	--	--	--	Z
ATTORNEYS INS MUTUAL	DC	C-	11.5	6.3	2.4	-0.2	8.5	9.4	2.2	8.6	2.5	DR
ATTORNEYS INS MUTUAL RRG	HI	C-	20.3	8.8	2.7	0.0	5.0	8.2	5.5	9.0	2.8	DFR
▲ATTORNEYS LIAB ASR SOCIETY INC RRG	VT	D+	2,045.4	759.5	199.2	75.3	3.9	3.2	6.4	7.0	2.4	R
ATTPRO RRG RECIPROCAL RRG	DC	D	3.0	1.0	0.1	-0.1	7.3	4.9	1.9	7.8	1.2	DFGT
▲AUSTIN MUTUAL INS CO	MN	D+	59.2	49.5	0.0	4.7	10.0	3.5	8.7	8.2	2.5	R
AUTO CLUB CASUALTY CO	TX	U	--	--	--	--	N/A	--	--	--	--	Z
AUTO CLUB COUNTY MUTUAL INS CO	TX	D+	108.7	8.3	0.0	0.1	5.6	N/A	6.3	9.0	2.7	D
AUTO CLUB FAMILY INS CO	MO	C	114.7	49.8	38.1	-0.1	8.6	6.0	6.9	6.4	3.8	T
AUTO CLUB GROUP INS CO	MI	C+	365.6	130.1	151.1	5.3	9.5	4.8	5.7	6.4	4.8	
AUTO CLUB INDEMNITY CO	TX	B+	25.7	5.5	0.0	0.1	7.6	N/A	6.4	7.9	5.0	D
AUTO CLUB INS ASSN	MI	B	4,292.9	1,924.0	1,597.5	158.4	7.9	4.9	6.9	6.2	4.9	R
▲AUTO CLUB INS CO OF FL	FL	B+	377.9	165.9	197.6	-5.9	9.3	9.1	6.3	6.3	6.5	F
AUTO CLUB PROPERTY & CASUALTY INS	MI	C	91.2	33.4	43.2	1.3	8.4	4.7	5.5	6.4	3.9	T
▲AUTO CLUB SOUTH INS CO	FL	B	134.7	58.5	63.2	2.0	9.1	6.1	6.8	6.1	5.5	
▲AUTO-OWNERS INS CO	MI	A	15,390.4	10,633.7	3,576.5	445.0	8.6	6.2	8.1	6.8	7.5	
AUTO-OWNERS SPECIALTY INS CO	DE	U	--	--	--	--	N/A	--	--	--	--	Z
AUTOMOBILE CLUB INTERINSURANCE	MO	C	422.3	198.3	152.6	-0.8	7.9	6.0	3.5	5.8	4.2	
AUTOMOBILE INS CO OF HARTFORD CT	CT	B	1,028.4	305.9	312.8	22.8	8.3	8.3	4.4	6.8	6.0	
AVEMCO INS CO	MD	B-	87.6	56.2	23.9	3.0	10.0	9.3	6.7	6.8	5.3	T
▲AVENTUS INSURANCE CO	TX	C+	33.5	20.8	4.9	2.2	10.0	6.9	8.6	7.1	4.2	DFR
▲AVIATION ALLIANCE INS RRG INC	MT	D	2.9	1.1	1.9	0.1	0.0	0.4	1.9	0.0	1.0	CGLT
AVIVA INS CO OF CANADA (US BR)	NY	U	--	--	--	--	N/A	--	--	--	--	Z
AWBURY INS CO	DE	U	--	--	--	--	N/A	--	--	--	--	Z
AXA ART INS CORP	NY	C	12.7	10.8	-1.4	-1.0	10.0	8.0	2.0	7.0	3.3	DFRT
AXA INS CO	NY	C-	237.5	135.4	54.5	10.0	9.3	6.4	8.1	8.8	3.3	R
AXIS INS CO	IL	B	1,465.3	544.7	336.8	-29.8	7.7	6.9	3.1	6.7	5.2	AF
AXIS REINS CO	NY	C+	3,227.4	966.8	612.5	-9.8	7.8	9.3	4.6	6.8	4.2	AFR
AXIS SPECIALTY INS CO	CT	U	--	--	--	--	N/A	--	--	--	--	Z
AXIS SURPLUS INS CO	IL	C+	459.2	173.4	48.2	-2.9	10.0	8.0	3.2	6.8	4.2	R
BADGER MUTUAL INS CO	WI	C+	180.7	69.9	87.5	2.7	8.3	3.3	5.6	6.2	4.6	R

See Page 27 for explanation of footnotes and Page 28 for explanation of stability factors.
Arrows denote recent upgrades ▲ or downgrades ▼   (see Section VII for explanations)

42

www.weissratings.com

RISK ADJ. RATIO #1	CAPITAL RATIO #2	PREMIUM TO SURPLUS (%)	RESV. TO SURPLUS (%)	RESV. DEVELOP. 1 YEAR (%)	RESV. DEVELOP. 2 YEAR (%)	LOSS RATIO (%)	EXP. RATIO (%)	COMB RATIO (%)	CASH FROM UNDER-WRITING (%)	NET PREMIUM GROWTH (%)	INVEST. IN AFFIL (%)	INSURANCE COMPANY NAME
2.4	1.7	113.5	92.8	3.5	2.0	82.2	28.8	111.0	106.1	6.1	0.0	ASSN CASUALTY INS CO
2.0	1.8	15.5	5.6	-0.7	N/A	24.1	25.9	50.0	-180.2	-7.4	0.0	ASSN OF CERTIFIED MTG ORIG RRG
16.7	15.0	N/A	N/A	N/A	N/A	N/A	N/A	N/A	32.3	0.0	0.0	ASSOCIATED EMPLOYERS INS CO
28.8	25.9	N/A	N/A	N/A	N/A	N/A	N/A	N/A	-39.1	0.0	0.0	ASSOCIATED INDEMNITY CORP
4.1	3.0	62.7	N/A	-211.8	-200.8	76.5	-35.7	40.8	49.6	-65.4	3.1	ASSOCIATED INDUSTRIES INS CO INC
2.6	1.9	60.0	118.4	-7.1	-15.0	67.1	22.0	89.1	115.2	3.6	2.6 ●	ASSOCIATED INDUSTRIES OF MA MUT
1.3	0.8	82.2	151.3	8.8	7.0	84.3	22.1	106.4	109.5	-1.1	1.7	ASSOCIATED LOGGERS EXCHANGE
0.9	0.6	90.4	123.3	8.6	17.2	63.2	39.5	102.7	108.1	3.5	0.0	ASSOCIATED MUTUAL INS CO
0.7	0.6	233.6	93.8	-4.9	-0.2	67.9	11.4	79.3	115.1	72.3	7.3	ASSURANCEAMERICA INS CO
12.2	7.8	1.0	6.5	-1.3	-13.9	113.0	203.3	316.3	14.3	-62.8	3.4 ●	ASSURED GUARANTY CORP
2.2	1.5	11.6	28.1	8.0	11.6	164.1	-70.7	93.4	121.5	82.5	16.8 ●	ASSURED GUARANTY MUNICIPAL CORP
3.8	2.8	101.3	70.3	-9.8	-10.2	59.0	32.3	91.3	112.1	5.7	0.0	ASURE WORLDWIDE INS CO
3.4	2.5	24.7	47.7	N/A	2.1	87.1	29.6	116.7	105.6	-7.1	0.0	ATAIN INS CO
1.7	1.3	38.3	73.8	N/A	3.4	87.0	27.5	114.5	99.4	-7.1	14.7	ATAIN SPECIALTY INS CO
2.1	1.7	53.2	12.5	N/A	-65.7	78.3	10.9	89.2	165.8	182.1	0.0	ATLANTA INTERNATIONAL INS CO
2.2	1.3	6.0	2.0	0.9	-0.7	15.4	110.3	125.7	149.5	-16.3	0.0	ATLANTIC BONDING CO
1.9	1.5	77.6	118.0	-7.4	-15.5	54.8	37.9	92.7	121.8	13.8	0.0	ATLANTIC CASUALTY INS CO
1.5	1.1	115.4	171.5	-28.1	-50.2	41.2	25.6	66.8	127.4	6.6	0.0	ATLANTIC CHARTER INS CO
1.3	1.0	89.9	134.8	14.2	19.4	85.3	44.0	129.3	83.0	0.5	12.5 ●	ATLANTIC SPECIALTY INS CO
2.7	1.9	202.3	113.3	1.0	0.9	69.3	32.2	101.5	106.8	5.9	0.0 ●	ATLANTIC STATES INS CO
7.7	5.7	31.2	14.7	-9.2	2.1	34.1	43.9	78.0	83.0	10.4	0.0	ATRADIUS TRADE CREDIT INS CO
N/A	N/A	--	--	--	--	--	--	--	--	--	--	ATRIUM INS CORP
2.8	2.0	38.5	41.4	-9.0	-11.2	44.8	62.0	106.8	120.2	2.6	0.0	ATTORNEYS INS MUTUAL
1.2	0.8	30.4	55.9	-2.1	-2.1	71.8	48.8	120.6	66.1	-14.3	0.0	ATTORNEYS INS MUTUAL RRG
0.7	0.6	26.2	124.5	-19.5	-25.3	43.3	17.4	60.7	107.0	-3.4	32.7 ●	ATTORNEYS LIAB ASR SOCIETY INC
1.3	1.2	8.7	12.7	-0.1	-0.2	82.6	33.7	116.3	21.7	24.3	0.0	ATTPRO RRG RECIPROCAL RRG
16.3	7.9	N/A	N/A	N/A	N/A	N/A	N/A	N/A	-38.5	0.0	0.0	AUSTIN MUTUAL INS CO
N/A	N/A	--	--	--	--	--	--	--	--	--	--	AUTO CLUB CASUALTY CO
0.9	0.8	N/A	N/A	N/A	N/A	N/A	N/A	N/A	-67.7	0.0	0.0	AUTO CLUB COUNTY MUTUAL INS CO
3.1	2.0	76.6	29.5	0.3	1.6	79.6	20.7	100.3	110.3	11.1	0.0	AUTO CLUB FAMILY INS CO
3.2	2.7	116.2	93.8	-0.1	0.5	72.2	28.1	100.3	107.0	7.1	0.0	AUTO CLUB GROUP INS CO
1.5	1.3	N/A	N/A	N/A	N/A	N/A	N/A	N/A	-155.2	0.0	0.0 ●	AUTO CLUB INDEMNITY CO
2.1	1.6	83.0	67.9	N/A	0.4	72.2	28.2	100.4	102.2	7.1	16.4 ●	AUTO CLUB INS ASSN
3.3	2.6	119.1	56.4	-2.6	-7.8	86.7	21.1	107.8	97.1	6.2	0.0 ●	AUTO CLUB INS CO OF FL
2.4	2.0	129.3	94.7	-1.0	0.3	72.1	28.1	100.2	102.9	7.1	0.0	AUTO CLUB PROPERTY & CASUALTY INS
2.6	2.3	108.1	55.5	-1.0	-0.9	78.9	20.6	99.5	110.3	9.0	0.0	AUTO CLUB SOUTH INS CO
2.3	2.0	33.6	21.7	-1.0	-1.8	59.0	31.0	90.0	115.1	11.1	28.4 ●	AUTO-OWNERS INS CO
N/A	N/A	--	--	--	--	--	--	--	--	--	--	AUTO-OWNERS SPECIALTY INS CO
2.1	1.5	76.9	29.6	0.2	1.3	79.6	20.7	100.3	107.5	11.1	16.5	AUTOMOBILE CLUB INTERINSURANCE
2.7	1.8	102.3	167.6	-2.2	-3.5	69.5	29.3	98.8	107.7	4.9	0.0 ●	AUTOMOBILE INS CO OF HARTFORD CT
3.1	2.9	42.6	22.4	-2.3	-16.3	51.0	40.1	91.1	118.9	-9.0	21.2	AVEMCO INS CO
7.7	7.0	23.7	10.7	-7.4	-10.2	46.0	20.9	66.9	75.0	-49.0	0.0	AVENTUS INSURANCE CO
0.0	0.0	170.1	148.9	146.4	191.5	71.0	18.0	89.0	122.5	64.4	0.0	AVIATION ALLIANCE INS RRG INC
N/A	N/A	--	--	--	--	--	--	--	--	--	--	AVIVA INS CO OF CANADA (US BR)
N/A	N/A	--	--	--	--	--	--	--	--	--	--	AWBURY INS CO
16.0	14.4	-13.1	N/A	-6.7	-5.2	54.0	-43.4	10.6	-156.7	-250.5	0.0	AXA ART INS CORP
3.4	2.5	40.2	24.0	-2.7	-4.8	36.6	65.0	101.6	90.6	4.7	0.0	AXA INS CO
2.0	1.5	61.8	103.8	-1.5	-7.8	77.0	38.2	115.2	65.7	7.4	21.3 ●	AXIS INS CO
2.6	1.5	63.3	160.6	-2.6	-9.0	79.1	33.7	112.8	82.3	15.2	0.0 ●	AXIS REINS CO
N/A	N/A	--	--	--	--	--	--	--	--	--	--	AXIS SPECIALTY INS CO
6.0	3.8	27.8	46.9	-1.1	-3.4	80.1	37.2	117.3	96.0	12.1	0.0	AXIS SURPLUS INS CO
3.0	1.8	125.2	74.7	2.5	11.1	71.4	29.6	101.0	97.4	0.0	0.0	BADGER MUTUAL INS CO

999 + Denotes number greater than 999.9%
999 - Denotes number less than -999.99%
● Bullets denote a more detailed analysis is available in Section II.

INSURANCE COMPANY NAME	DOM. STATE	RATING	TOTAL ASSETS ($MIL)	CAPITAL & SURPLUS ($MIL)	ANNUAL NET PREMIUM ($MIL)	NET INCOME ($MIL)	CAPITAL-IZATION INDEX (PTS)	RESERVE ADQ INDEX (PTS)	PROFIT-ABILITY INDEX (PTS)	LIQUIDITY INDEX (PTS)	STAB. INDEX (PTS)	STABILITY FACTORS
▲BALBOA INS CO	CA	C	77.9	78.0	-0.1	0.2	10.0	5.9	3.2	7.0	3.5	DFRT
▲BALDWIN MUTUAL INS CO	AL	C	12.2	9.7	3.5	0.7	10.0	9.3	8.4	7.2	2.9	D
BALTIMORE EQUITABLE SOCIETY	MD	U	--	--	--	--	N/A	--	--	--	--	Z
BANKERS INDEPENDENT INS CO	PA	C (1)	20.8	3.8	11.6	-1.6	2.3	1.3	0.8	0.0	3.5	CDFG
BANKERS INS CO	FL	C	149.4	77.9	37.1	-2.7	7.3	3.8	4.9	6.9	4.1	FR
▲BANKERS SPECIALTY INS CO	LA	B	55.6	45.3	9.7	0.3	6.2	7.7	4.0	5.9	5.5	CD
BANKERS STANDARD INS CO	PA	C	762.9	167.8	162.4	4.5	7.9	6.0	8.4	6.5	4.0	FR
BAR PLAN MUTUAL INS CO	MO	C	41.9	15.6	9.5	-1.5	5.7	5.9	2.4	7.0	3.8	DFR
BAR PLAN SURETY & FIDELITY CO	MO	C	5.5	4.5	0.5	0.3	10.0	8.1	7.9	9.9	3.3	DOR
▲BAR VERMONT RRG INC	VT	C-	31.9	21.5	2.0	3.5	7.8	8.3	6.7	9.3	2.9	DR
BARNSTABLE COUNTY INS CO	MA	C	25.0	22.7	1.9	1.0	10.0	7.3	8.0	8.9	4.4	DR
BARNSTABLE COUNTY MUTUAL INS CO	MA	B	112.7	90.8	18.3	3.6	9.2	7.5	8.0	7.3	5.0	T
BATTLE CREEK MUTUAL INS CO	NE	C	8.2	5.9	0.0	0.2	10.0	3.5	6.9	6.9	3.6	DFRT
BAY INS RRG INC	SC	U	--	--	--	--	N/A	--	--	--	--	Z
BAY STATE INS CO	MA	B-	573.2	367.9	84.4	10.8	7.9	7.5	7.9	7.0	4.8	T
BCS INS CO	OH	B	276.6	147.0	98.6	13.9	10.0	6.9	3.9	6.6	5.4	R
BEACONHARBOR MUTUAL RRG	ME	U	--	--	--	--	N/A	--	--	--	--	Z
BEAR RIVER MUTUAL INS CO	UT	B	279.0	121.2	160.1	2.3	8.2	8.0	3.3	4.9	6.2	L
BEARING MIDWEST CASUALTY CO	KS	C	7.6	5.8	0.0	0.1	10.0	N/A	6.5	7.0	2.9	DT
▲BEAZLEY INS CO	CT	B	317.1	120.1	65.4	-0.9	9.1	8.1	3.6	7.0	5.5	
BEDFORD PHYSICIANS RRG INC	VT	C-	43.1	9.1	11.0	-0.2	3.7	5.9	3.9	10.0	2.8	DFR
BEDIVERE INS CO	PA	D+	240.1	108.0	0.1	-2.9	2.0	5.1	1.9	9.1	2.5	CFRT
▲BELL UNITED INS CO	NV	B-	34.8	21.8	4.7	-1.0	7.9	9.4	4.6	9.1	4.7	D
▲BENCHMARK INS CO	KS	B	347.3	98.8	57.4	11.3	8.0	6.9	8.9	7.8	4.1	RT
BENEFIT SECURITY INS CO	IL	B-	9.3	4.8	1.6	0.6	7.5	7.0	8.0	7.3	3.5	D
BERKLEY ASR CO	IA	C-	72.5	54.8	0.0	1.0	10.0	N/A	6.4	7.0	2.9	RT
BERKLEY INS CO	DE	B	18,358.6	5,479.6	5,594.5	698.9	7.2	7.9	7.0	6.7	5.2	A
BERKLEY NATIONAL INS CO	IA	C	145.9	51.1	0.0	0.8	10.0	N/A	5.9	7.0	4.3	
BERKLEY REGIONAL INS CO	DE	C+	762.9	728.0	0.0	13.2	8.1	N/A	7.7	10.0	4.4	AR
BERKLEY REGIONAL SPCLTY INS CO	DE	C	63.1	57.3	0.0	1.4	10.0	N/A	7.6	7.0	4.2	
BERKSHIRE HATHAWAY DIRECT INS CO	NE	C	151.8	135.8	0.6	2.1	10.0	4.1	3.4	10.0	3.7	DGT
BERKSHIRE HATHAWAY ASR CORP	NY	A+	2,223.5	1,799.8	9.0	421.3	9.4	4.6	8.7	10.0	7.2	T
BERKSHIRE HATHAWAY HOMESTATE INS	NE	C+	2,938.5	1,660.7	494.0	272.7	7.7	8.1	8.3	8.3	4.4	R
BERKSHIRE HATHAWAY SPECIALTY INS CO	NE	C+	4,950.5	3,749.6	356.0	46.3	9.4	4.6	4.0	9.6	4.6	GRT
BITCO GENERAL INS CORP	IL	B	943.6	293.6	356.3	15.7	7.8	8.5	6.7	6.6	6.2	AG
BITCO NATIONAL INS CO	IL	B	427.6	155.8	5.0	24.2	8.1	6.1	6.8	6.9	4.5	AFT
BLACK DIAMOND INS CO	NV	U (5)	--	--	--	--	N/A	--	--	--	--	Z
BLACKBOARD INSURANCE CO	DE	C	57.0	43.2	3.5	-7.8	10.0	4.8	2.5	8.9	3.3	DFGR
BLACKBOARD SPECIALTY INS CO	DE	B-	149.1	91.1	12.8	-16.2	8.2	4.6	2.6	6.9	3.8	FGT
▲BLOOMFIELD MUTUAL INS CO	MN	C	12.6	9.7	3.4	0.6	10.0	7.7	8.3	6.7	2.9	D
▲BLOOMINGTON COMP INS CO	MN	B-	16.6	14.0	0.0	0.1	10.0	N/A	6.1	7.0	4.9	DFR
BLUE HILL SPECIALTY INS CO	IL	U	--	--	--	--	N/A	--	--	--	--	Z
BLUE RIDGE INDEMNITY CO	WI	C	6.9	6.8	0.0	0.0	10.0	3.9	4.2	7.0	2.7	DRT
▲BOND SAFEGUARD INS CO	SD	C	90.8	39.4	44.4	6.5	7.3	4.6	7.0	7.5	3.5	R
BONDED BUILDERS INS CO RRG	NV	D+	3.6	2.0	0.9	0.2	7.8	6.9	8.6	8.3	2.3	DT
BONDEX INS CO	NJ	B-	8.8	3.5	3.8	-0.2	6.0	9.1	4.3	8.6	3.5	DGT
▲BOSTON INDEMNITY CO INC	SD	C-	7.8	4.5	1.6	-1.1	7.6	6.8	2.2	7.3	2.2	DFT
▲BREMEN FARMERS MUTUAL INS CO	KS	C+	44.6	22.6	25.9	2.0	8.0	8.9	8.8	5.9	4.5	DR
BRETHREN MUTUAL INS CO	MD	B	274.8	134.1	119.7	5.9	9.6	4.7	6.8	6.7	6.3	
BRIAR CREEK MUTUAL INS CO	PA	C	14.9	12.0	2.3	0.4	10.0	6.2	8.0	7.0	3.1	DR
▲BRICKSTREET MUTUAL INS CO	WV	B	2,270.7	798.7	354.5	30.5	8.1	9.5	8.4	6.9	5.5	T
BRIDGEFIELD CASUALTY INS CO	FL	C	56.9	46.7	0.0	0.7	10.0	N/A	4.9	7.0	4.3	R

See Page 27 for explanation of footnotes and Page 28 for explanation of stability factors.

44

www.weissratings.com

Arrows denote recent upgrades ▲ or downgrades ▼   (see Section VII for explanations)

RISK ADJ. RATIO #1	CAPITAL RATIO #2	PREMIUM TO SURPLUS (%)	RESV. TO SURPLUS (%)	RESV. DEVELOP. 1 YEAR (%)	RESV. DEVELOP. 2 YEAR (%)	LOSS RATIO (%)	EXP. RATIO (%)	COMB RATIO (%)	CASH FROM UNDER-WRITING (%)	NET PREMIUM GROWTH (%)	INVEST. IN AFFIL (%)	INSURANCE COMPANY NAME
3.4	3.4	-0.1	3.6	1.1	1.7	999 +	961.7	-123.2	465.5	14.2	31.8	BALBOA INS CO
6.0	4.9	36.2	3.0	-1.3	-1.5	22.2	54.6	76.8	126.1	-12.3	0.0	BALDWIN MUTUAL INS CO
N/A	N/A	--	--	--	--	--	--	--	--	--	--	BALTIMORE EQUITABLE SOCIETY
0.4	0.3	261.7	194.6	33.1	50.1	109.3	26.7	136.0	102.3	45.8	0.0	BANKERS INDEPENDENT INS CO
1.6	1.4	47.7	55.1	8.1	17.6	56.4	63.2	119.6	97.5	4.0	33.2	BANKERS INS CO
1.0	0.9	21.5	7.1	0.1	-0.3	57.9	43.8	101.7	101.9	3.7	70.3	BANKERS SPECIALTY INS CO
2.4	1.6	96.8	174.6	-1.5	3.2	83.9	17.6	101.5	69.6	8.3	0.0	BANKERS STANDARD INS CO
1.3	0.9	60.5	118.2	3.0	-10.5	85.6	39.4	125.0	82.1	-5.1	14.2	BAR PLAN MUTUAL INS CO
10.3	9.2	10.4	9.3	-4.0	-6.9	15.1	19.8	34.9	385.0	9.0	0.0	BAR PLAN SURETY & FIDELITY CO
2.5	1.5	9.2	18.4	-2.2	-4.0	26.0	81.5	107.5	92.5	-2.0	0.0	BAR VERMONT RRG INC
7.7	4.6	8.4	1.1	-0.3	-0.4	24.9	51.8	76.7	122.3	7.3	0.0	BARNSTABLE COUNTY INS CO
3.1	2.6	20.1	4.0	-1.4	-1.9	35.7	50.8	86.5	115.1	4.1	21.4	BARNSTABLE COUNTY MUTUAL INS CO
7.1	6.4	N/A	N/A	N/A	N/A	N/A	N/A	N/A	391.1	0.0	0.0	BATTLE CREEK MUTUAL INS CO
N/A	N/A	--	--	--	--	--	--	--	--	--	--	BAY INS RRG INC
2.6	1.6	22.9	16.3	-0.7	-0.5	64.3	41.0	105.3	118.4	4.4	0.0 ●	BAY STATE INS CO
10.4	5.8	67.1	20.1	-7.1	-7.4	57.9	29.1	87.0	106.6	-3.1	0.3	BCS INS CO
N/A	N/A	--	--	--	--	--	--	--	--	--	--	BEACONHARBOR MUTUAL RRG
2.5	1.7	132.0	54.4	2.4	-4.2	84.5	24.4	108.9	98.1	15.9	0.0	BEAR RIVER MUTUAL INS CO
8.7	7.8	N/A	N/A	N/A	N/A	N/A	N/A	N/A	N/A	0.0	0.0	BEARING MIDWEST CASUALTY CO
3.3	2.3	54.5	77.1	-3.1	-5.3	58.9	46.9	105.8	102.5	-12.0	0.0	BEAZLEY INS CO
0.7	0.6	120.5	370.6	-5.2	14.7	95.6	6.9	102.5	-6.6	2.7	0.0	BEDFORD PHYSICIANS RRG INC
0.6	0.3	0.1	103.6	1.8	-7.9	999 +	999 +	999 +	1.2	-31.0	18.1	BEDIVERE INS CO
1.9	1.5	21.5	59.4	3.6	-0.4	123.5	20.9	144.4	94.7	11.7	0.0	BELL UNITED INS CO
2.3	1.6	58.1	64.2	-2.3	-5.8	60.1	16.1	76.2	203.2	25.6	0.0	BENCHMARK INS CO
2.0	1.5	33.6	45.6	-18.9	-30.5	-6.9	71.5	64.6	144.1	-0.7	0.0	BENEFIT SECURITY INS CO
16.8	15.1	N/A	N/A	N/A	N/A	N/A	N/A	N/A	N/A	0.0	0.0	BERKLEY ASR CO
1.3	1.1	102.1	173.2	-0.7	-2.9	60.4	33.3	93.7	112.7	-2.0	20.7 ●	BERKLEY INS CO
5.8	5.2	N/A	N/A	N/A	N/A	N/A	N/A	N/A	68.1	0.0	0.0	BERKLEY NATIONAL INS CO
1.5	1.7	N/A	N/A	N/A	N/A	N/A	N/A	N/A	-6.0	0.0	48.0 ●	BERKLEY REGIONAL INS CO
33.9	30.5	N/A	N/A	N/A	N/A	N/A	N/A	N/A	N/A	0.0	0.0	BERKLEY REGIONAL SPCLTY INS CO
5.9	3.5	0.5	0.3	N/A	N/A	109.3	-49.4	59.9	79.6	104.1	0.0	BERKSHIRE HATHATWAY DIRECT INS
4.4	2.6	0.5	1.7	N/A	N/A	20.0	12.8	32.8	267.1	205.7	0.0 ●	BERKSHIRE HATHAWAY ASR CORP
2.9	1.6	29.7	47.0	-4.9	-6.1	61.1	21.1	82.2	144.2	11.9	0.0 ●	BERKSHIRE HATHAWAY HOMESTATE
4.6	2.7	9.5	11.3	0.3	N/A	84.6	25.8	110.4	158.7	33.1	0.0 ●	BERKSHIRE HATHAWAY SPECIALTY INS
2.4	1.5	121.4	175.3	-4.1	-6.1	74.1	26.3	100.4	134.2	53.9	0.0 ●	BITCO GENERAL INS CORP
3.5	1.9	3.2	159.9	6.0	7.6	76.2	17.5	93.7	6.0	-96.7	0.0	BITCO NATIONAL INS CO
N/A	N/A	--	--	--	--	--	--	--	--	--	--	BLACK DIAMOND INS CO
4.1	3.3	8.1	8.1	-0.9	-0.5	113.6	240.7	354.3	28.6	32.8	0.0	BLACKBOARD INSURANCE CO
2.0	1.8	14.1	26.8	-1.1	0.3	113.9	140.0	253.9	44.6	-30.4	31.8	BLACKBOARD SPECIALTY INS CO
9.4	5.6	35.4	5.5	-0.4	-1.5	56.2	33.2	89.4	107.3	-12.5	0.0	BLOOMFIELD MUTUAL INS CO
15.6	14.0	N/A	N/A	N/A	N/A	N/A	N/A	N/A	175.5	0.0	0.0	BLOOMINGTON COMP INS CO
N/A	N/A	--	--	--	--	--	--	--	--	--	--	BLUE HILL SPECIALTY INS CO
124.4	56.3	N/A	N/A	N/A	N/A	N/A	N/A	N/A	N/A	100.0	0.0	BLUE RIDGE INDEMNITY CO
1.6	1.3	112.7	50.5	-11.4	-16.3	21.1	58.4	79.5	164.6	-2.2	0.0	BOND SAFEGUARD INS CO
3.1	2.5	47.7	11.7	-4.8	-5.2	4.9	56.3	61.2	166.3	15.8	0.0	BONDED BUILDERS INS CO RRG
1.0	0.8	109.2	20.1	-11.8	-10.3	5.0	80.0	85.0	106.8	191.4	0.0	BONDEX INS CO
1.9	1.6	34.6	24.8	-3.2	-2.8	70.0	101.4	171.4	55.1	-21.9	0.0	BOSTON INDEMNITY CO INC
2.2	1.9	114.3	15.1	-3.5	-8.9	66.3	27.4	93.7	106.5	0.0	0.0	BREMEN FARMERS MUTUAL INS CO
4.4	2.7	89.3	43.5	0.9	1.2	64.8	34.0	98.8	108.2	4.9	0.0	BRETHREN MUTUAL INS CO
5.7	3.4	19.1	5.5	-1.2	-1.4	43.1	40.5	83.6	123.5	0.0	0.0	BRIAR CREEK MUTUAL INS CO
2.8	1.8	44.4	136.2	-17.0	-27.2	61.0	43.4	104.4	123.1	4.9	2.6 ●	BRICKSTREET MUTUAL INS CO
18.9	17.0	N/A	N/A	N/A	N/A	N/A	N/A	N/A	469.9	0.0	0.0	BRIDGEFIELD CASUALTY INS CO

999 + Denotes number greater than 999.9%
999 - Denotes number less than -999.99%
● Bullets denote a more detailed analysis is available in Section II.

INSURANCE COMPANY NAME	DOM. STATE	RATING	TOTAL ASSETS ($MIL)	CAPITAL & SURPLUS ($MIL)	ANNUAL NET PREMIUM ($MIL)	NET INCOME ($MIL)	CAPITAL-IZATION INDEX (PTS)	RESERVE ADQ INDEX (PTS)	PROFIT-ABILITY INDEX (PTS)	LIQUIDITY INDEX (PTS)	STAB. INDEX (PTS)	STABILITY FACTORS
BRIDGEFIELD EMPLOYERS INS CO	FL	B-	122.4	116.1	0.0	1.7	9.5	N/A	5.6	7.0	4.9	R
BRIERFIELD INS CO	MS	C-	13.5	9.1	0.0	0.2	10.0	N/A	6.4	9.1	3.2	DR
BRISTOL WEST CASUALTY INS CO	OH	D+	18.9	8.9	0.0	0.0	10.0	5.0	5.7	7.9	2.5	DR
BRISTOL WEST INS CO	OH	D+	145.8	46.2	0.0	0.4	10.0	4.6	4.4	7.3	2.6	R
▲BRISTOL WEST PREFERRED INS CO	MI	C+	22.6	11.8	0.0	0.1	10.0	6.2	6.1	6.9	4.5	DFR
BRITISH AMERICAN INS CO	TX	C+ (1)	56.3	31.5	3.8	-0.6	5.4	4.5	5.1	8.6	3.4	DRT
BROADLINE RRG INC	VT	C	100.1	27.8	18.8	-0.9	7.1	7.0	2.5	5.6	4.1	D
BROADWAY INS & SURETY CO	NJ	D (4)	2.7	1.7	0.8	0.2	9.2	3.6	8.6	9.6	1.3	DT
BROOKWOOD INS CO	IA	U	--	--	--	--	N/A	--	--	--	--	Z
BROOME CO OPERATIVE INS CO	NY	C	22.8	14.9	6.8	0.6	9.4	7.9	8.1	6.8	3.5	D
BROTHERHOOD MUTUAL INS CO	IN	B+	644.9	266.2	361.8	8.7	8.0	4.3	8.3	5.1	6.5	L
BTTS INS RRG GROUP INC	SC	U	--	--	--	--	N/A	--	--	--	--	Z
▼BUCKEYE STATE MUTUAL INS CO	OH	C	55.0	19.0	37.8	-0.2	7.1	8.6	2.3	2.4	3.6	DFLR
BUCKS COUNTY CONTRIBUTIONSHIP	PA	U	--	--	--	--	N/A	--	--	--	--	Z
▲BUILD AMERICA MUTUAL ASR CO	NY	C-	515.0	427.3	8.6	-25.4	10.0	N/A	2.5	10.0	3.0	FGT
BUILDERS INS (A MUTUAL CAPTIVE CO)	GA	C	634.4	280.7	168.6	16.8	8.1	9.3	8.6	6.9	3.5	R
▲BUILDERS MUTUAL INS CO	NC	A	859.6	358.2	307.2	41.8	8.0	6.7	8.8	6.7	7.5	
▲BUILDERS PREMIER INS CO	NC	B-	12.2	12.0	0.0	0.2	10.0	N/A	6.9	10.0	4.6	D
BUILDING INDUSTRY INS ASSN INC	VA	E (1)	23.3	5.1	13.8	1.1	0.1	0.3	2.9	0.4	0.3	CDGL
BUNKER HILL INS CAS CO	MA	C	12.2	6.4	4.8	1.0	7.4	6.9	5.3	7.0	3.6	DF
BUNKER HILL INS CO	MA	C	55.7	34.6	-3.1	2.5	7.5	6.6	6.9	7.5	4.2	FRT
BUNKER HILL PREFERRED INS CO	MA	D+	11.6	5.9	8.5	0.7	7.4	3.6	8.9	7.1	1.1	DT
BUNKER HILL PROPERTY INS CO	MA	D+	11.6	5.9	8.5	0.7	7.4	3.6	8.9	7.1	1.1	DT
BUNKER HILL SECURITY INS CO	MA	D+	11.7	5.9	8.5	0.7	7.4	3.6	8.9	7.1	1.1	DT
BURLINGTON INS CO	IL	C-	345.0	178.7	42.2	2.1	9.8	8.7	5.7	7.3	2.6	FR
▲BUSINESSFIRST INS CO	FL	B	45.0	17.4	13.1	0.9	7.5	6.9	8.4	6.4	5.3	D
CA CASUALTY COMP INS CO	CA	U	--	--	--	--	N/A	--	--	--	--	Z
CALIFORNIA AUTOMOBILE INS CO	CA	B	802.1	188.2	675.3	-26.4	5.3	3.4	3.2	0.9	5.4	CL
▼CALIFORNIA CAPITAL INS CO	CA	C-	538.4	219.8	219.9	-65.2	7.3	3.8	1.8	5.8	3.1	FR
▼CALIFORNIA CAS GEN INS CO OF OREGON	OR	C-	111.0	19.1	43.0	-5.2	5.7	6.1	1.5	3.1	3.2	DFLR
CALIFORNIA CASUALTY & FIRE INS CO	CA	C	68.0	16.1	35.8	-4.2	5.9	6.1	1.6	5.1	3.4	DFR
CALIFORNIA CASUALTY INDEMNITY EXCH	CA	C+	575.9	241.6	250.8	-22.8	7.7	6.1	2.2	5.0	4.4	FR
▼CALIFORNIA CASUALTY INS CO	OR	C	92.1	55.1	28.7	-3.2	7.9	6.0	2.4	6.6	3.7	R
CALIFORNIA GENERAL UNDERWRITERS INS	CA	B	21.8	21.3	0.2	0.6	10.0	5.7	6.8	10.0	5.4	DT
▲CALIFORNIA HEALTHCARE INS CO INC RRG	HI	B	127.2	58.3	15.3	2.7	10.0	9.6	8.1	7.7	5.5	T
CALIFORNIA INS CO	CA	B	1,021.4	622.6	307.5	97.2	9.8	6.2	8.9	7.9	5.4	R
▲CALIFORNIA MEDICAL GROUP INS CO RRG	AZ	E+	16.1	4.9	5.3	0.3	6.3	10.0	5.2	7.8	0.5	DR
▲CALIFORNIA MUTUAL INS CO	CA	C	15.7	11.8	4.3	0.3	9.3	6.5	6.8	6.9	3.1	DR
▲CALLICOON CO-OPERATIVE INS CO	NY	B-	32.5	26.7	5.1	1.3	10.0	7.5	8.3	7.0	5.0	D
CAMBRIA COUNTY MUTUAL INS CO	PA	U	--	--	--	--	N/A	--	--	--	--	Z
CAMBRIDGE MUTUAL FIRE INS CO	MA	B-	1,012.4	579.5	197.0	56.7	8.0	7.6	7.0	7.1	4.8	T
CAMERON MUTUAL INS CO	MO	C+	83.5	34.5	58.9	-3.4	7.5	6.6	3.1	4.9	4.1	FLR
CAMERON NATIONAL INS CO	MO	C-	11.0	10.7	0.0	0.2	10.0	N/A	8.1	10.0	3.3	DR
▲CAMICO MUTUAL INS CO	CA	C+	91.9	41.0	33.1	3.0	8.1	4.0	6.6	6.7	4.5	R
▲CAMPMED CAS & INDEM CO INC OF MD	NH	B-	20.1	20.1	0.0	0.4	10.0	N/A	5.6	10.0	4.9	DR
CANAL INDEMNITY CO	SC	B	49.5	47.3	0.0	1.6	10.0	N/A	6.9	10.0	5.1	DT
CANAL INS CO	SC	B	827.7	453.6	219.4	22.8	8.5	4.9	5.6	7.0	5.8	F
CANOPIUS US INS INC	DE	B	211.4	122.2	35.3	8.3	8.5	6.9	3.7	7.2	6.0	
CAPACITY INS CO	FL	D	22.2	10.2	8.9	0.2	2.0	3.2	8.4	6.0	2.1	CD
▲CAPITOL CASUALTY CO	NE	B-	32.3	29.8	0.7	1.2	8.3	7.3	6.9	9.3	5.0	D
CAPITOL COUNTY MUTUAL FIRE INS CO	TX	C	9.6	6.2	0.0	-0.6	7.4	4.8	1.4	7.7	3.4	DFRT
CAPITOL INDEMNITY CORP	WI	C	592.8	265.3	189.8	11.2	7.3	4.8	5.7	6.7	4.1	R

See Page 27 for explanation of footnotes and
Page 28 for explanation of stability factors.

46

www.weissratings.com

Arrows denote recent upgrades ▲ or downgrades ▼   (see Section VII for explanations)

RISK ADJ. RATIO #1	CAPITAL RATIO #2	PREMIUM TO SURPLUS (%)	RESV. TO SURPLUS (%)	RESV. DEVELOP. 1 YEAR (%)	RESV. DEVELOP. 2 YEAR (%)	LOSS RATIO (%)	EXP. RATIO (%)	COMB RATIO (%)	CASH FROM UNDER-WRITING (%)	NET PREMIUM GROWTH (%)	INVEST. IN AFFIL (%)	INSURANCE COMPANY NAME
2.7	2.6	N/A	N/A	N/A	N/A	N/A	N/A	N/A	999 +	0.0	38.4	BRIDGEFIELD EMPLOYERS INS CO
6.7	6.0	N/A	N/A	N/A	N/A	N/A	N/A	N/A	149.3	0.0	0.0	BRIERFIELD INS CO
3.6	3.3	N/A	N/A	N/A	-0.1	N/A	N/A	N/A	999 +	0.0	0.0	BRISTOL WEST CASUALTY INS CO
5.1	4.6	N/A	3.0	-0.1	N/A	N/A	N/A	N/A	999 +	0.0	0.0	BRISTOL WEST INS CO
4.6	4.2	N/A	0.9	-0.6	-1.6	N/A	N/A	N/A	-40.6	0.0	0.0	BRISTOL WEST PREFERRED INS CO
0.9	0.7	11.4	65.0	1.0	-1.4	65.9	28.1	94.0	95.1	-14.8	0.0	BRITISH AMERICAN INS CO
1.5	1.0	67.6	223.5	1.6	1.6	108.0	7.1	115.1	166.2	1.1	0.0	BROADLINE RRG INC
3.9	3.4	45.4	7.6	N/A	N/A	-1.5	48.9	47.4	189.2	-0.7	0.0	BROADWAY INS & SURETY CO
N/A	N/A	--	--	--	--	--	--	--	--	--	--	BROOKWOOD INS CO
4.0	2.6	45.9	20.8	-2.6	-4.5	59.1	34.0	93.1	111.2	2.9	0.0	BROOME CO OPERATIVE INS CO
2.2	1.6	135.9	48.9	6.1	9.0	66.4	31.6	98.0	103.0	6.1	0.0 ●	BROTHERHOOD MUTUAL INS CO
N/A	N/A	--	--	--	--	--	--	--	--	--	--	BTTS INS RRG GROUP INC
1.4	1.0	199.1	52.0	9.7	-1.0	77.1	32.5	109.6	88.9	-7.8	15.7	BUCKEYE STATE MUTUAL INS CO
N/A	N/A	--	--	--	--	--	--	--	--	--	--	BUCKS COUNTY CONTRIBUTIONSHIP
12.4	11.7	2.0	N/A	N/A	N/A	N/A	400.5	400.5	28.0	-24.1	0.0 ●	BUILD AMERICA MUTUAL ASR CO
2.4	1.8	60.1	97.6	-4.2	-9.1	62.2	30.6	92.8	132.5	8.9	12.4 ●	BUILDERS INS (A MUTUAL CAPTIVE CO)
2.5	1.7	85.8	104.6	-4.8	0.7	54.8	30.7	85.5	129.2	8.0	1.6 ●	BUILDERS MUTUAL INS CO
109.5	54.7	N/A	N/A	N/A	N/A	N/A	N/A	N/A	N/A	0.0	0.0	BUILDERS PREMIER INS CO
0.1	0.1	270.6	155.0	65.0	101.1	58.8	39.4	98.2	107.8	26.8	0.0	BUILDING INDUSTRY INS ASSN INC
1.8	1.2	75.4	27.4	-16.8	-4.8	39.6	35.5	75.1	106.5	-17.3	0.0	BUNKER HILL INS CAS CO
1.4	1.3	-9.0	5.1	-3.1	-1.2	39.6	-50.2	-10.6	-33.0	-116.8	55.7	BUNKER HILL INS CO
1.5	1.2	143.8	29.7	-18.3	N/A	39.6	20.3	59.9	416.7	0.0	0.0	BUNKER HILL PREFERRED INS CO
1.5	1.2	143.8	29.7	-18.3	N/A	39.6	20.3	59.9	408.7	0.0	0.0	BUNKER HILL PROPERTY INS CO
1.5	1.2	143.8	29.7	-18.3	N/A	39.6	20.3	59.9	411.2	0.0	0.0	BUNKER HILL SECURITY INS CO
3.7	3.0	23.6	57.9	-3.8	-6.2	45.7	57.9	103.6	76.4	7.0	0.0	BURLINGTON INS CO
1.7	1.3	75.2	91.4	-6.0	-8.3	64.7	28.9	93.6	112.7	6.7	0.0	BUSINESSFIRST INS CO
N/A	N/A	--	--	--	--	--	--	--	--	--	--	CA CASUALTY COMP INS CO
1.1	0.7	358.7	146.4	10.6	19.7	85.5	23.3	108.8	104.0	12.5	3.1	CALIFORNIA AUTOMOBILE INS CO
1.6	1.2	100.0	94.2	13.2	17.4	100.6	35.7	136.3	85.2	-1.7	20.7	CALIFORNIA CAPITAL INS CO
1.2	0.8	224.7	101.4	1.5	1.0	88.4	25.9	114.3	93.1	3.6	0.0	CALIFORNIA CAS GEN INS CO OF
1.2	0.8	222.8	100.6	1.5	1.0	88.4	25.9	114.3	92.6	3.6	0.0	CALIFORNIA CASUALTY & FIRE INS CO
1.7	1.4	103.8	46.9	0.8	0.5	88.4	25.9	114.3	89.3	3.6	30.2 ●	CALIFORNIA CASUALTY INDEMNITY
1.6	1.5	52.0	23.5	0.4	0.2	88.4	25.9	114.3	99.0	3.6	48.4	CALIFORNIA CASUALTY INS CO
16.3	9.7	1.0	2.3	1.3	2.2	177.1	42.0	219.1	139.8	-47.6	0.0	CALIFORNIA GENERAL UNDERWRITERS
4.4	3.0	26.2	85.8	-10.7	-23.1	80.1	15.4	95.5	101.0	9.1	0.4	CALIFORNIA HEALTHCARE INS CO INC
4.1	3.3	49.4	50.6	-0.7	2.5	50.0	22.0	72.0	208.1	20.6	0.0 ●	CALIFORNIA INS CO
1.1	0.9	109.1	188.1	-61.5	-59.2	42.9	12.7	55.6	252.2	2.7	0.0	CALIFORNIA MEDICAL GROUP INS CO
3.9	2.5	36.3	7.3	-2.1	-3.8	50.8	47.9	98.7	100.9	8.1	2.2	CALIFORNIA MUTUAL INS CO
12.8	8.8	19.0	8.4	-0.4	-1.1	42.9	37.4	80.3	134.7	0.4	0.0	CALLICOON CO-OPERATIVE INS CO
N/A	N/A	--	--	--	--	--	--	--	--	--	--	CAMBRIA COUNTY MUTUAL INS CO
2.6	1.6	34.0	24.1	-0.9	-0.7	64.3	41.0	105.3	118.8	4.4	0.0 ●	CAMBRIDGE MUTUAL FIRE INS CO
1.8	1.3	170.5	62.8	-5.1	-5.4	74.3	32.9	107.2	91.7	2.4	15.8	CAMERON MUTUAL INS CO
50.2	27.8	N/A	N/A	N/A	N/A	N/A	N/A	N/A	-634.8	0.0	0.0	CAMERON NATIONAL INS CO
2.6	1.7	80.7	79.8	-0.7	5.9	57.2	35.9	93.1	109.5	7.4	1.2	CAMICO MUTUAL INS CO
78.7	35.5	N/A	N/A	N/A	N/A	N/A	N/A	N/A	N/A	0.0	0.0	CAMPMED CAS & INDEM CO INC OF MD
5.7	3.2	N/A	N/A	N/A	N/A	N/A	N/A	N/A	-9.6	0.0	0.0	CANAL INDEMNITY CO
3.0	2.0	48.4	50.4	1.3	6.0	75.6	31.2	106.8	90.8	4.5	6.4 ●	CANAL INS CO
3.5	2.2	28.9	53.4	-11.8	-22.6	31.3	45.6	76.9	117.3	20.1	0.0	CANOPIUS US INS INC
0.5	0.4	87.1	50.2	10.1	18.7	56.5	44.9	101.4	123.1	-0.1	0.0	CAPACITY INS CO
3.2	1.9	2.2	0.6	-0.6	-0.7	15.8	78.7	94.5	107.3	27.5	0.0	CAPITOL CASUALTY CO
1.3	1.2	N/A	N/A	1.2	2.0	N/A	N/A	N/A	-18.7	0.0	59.4	CAPITOL COUNTY MUTUAL FIRE INS CO
1.5	1.1	71.6	72.0	-0.7	-2.6	55.6	43.4	99.0	115.7	8.4	19.7 ●	CAPITOL INDEMNITY CORP

999 + Denotes number greater than 999.9%
999 - Denotes number less than -999.99%
● Bullets denote a more detailed analysis is available in Section II.

INSURANCE COMPANY NAME	DOM. STATE	RATING	TOTAL ASSETS ($MIL)	CAPITAL & SURPLUS ($MIL)	ANNUAL NET PREMIUM ($MIL)	NET INCOME ($MIL)	CAPITAL-IZATION INDEX (PTS)	RESERVE ADQ INDEX (PTS)	PROFIT-ABILITY INDEX (PTS)	LIQUIDITY INDEX (PTS)	STAB. INDEX (PTS)	STABILITY FACTORS
CAPITOL INS CO	PA	E-	12.2	-2.3	8.8	-4.2	0.0	0.2	0.3	7.0	0.8	CDFR
CAPITOL PREFERRED INS CO	FL	C	56.4	26.5	14.8	-0.8	7.3	6.6	6.3	6.4	4.2	FR
CAPITOL SPECIALTY INS CORP	WI	C+	150.2	58.9	40.7	1.8	9.0	4.7	5.1	6.8	4.6	R
CAPSON PHYSICIANS INS CO	TX	D	28.7	5.0	12.7	-2.9	1.2	2.7	1.3	5.2	1.5	CDF
CAR RRG INC	TN	D	1.7	1.3	0.8	0.0	7.2	3.6	3.0	5.2	1.0	DGT
CARE RRG INC	DC	D+	21.2	4.8	6.8	-0.1	4.6	7.0	3.9	5.9	2.3	DFR
▲CARE WEST INS CO	CA	C	129.9	37.9	27.2	5.9	6.5	5.0	8.7	6.8	3.5	R
CARECONCEPTS INS INC A RRG	MT	F (5)	3.8	0.4	1.3	0.0	0.7	3.9	0.9	4.1	0.0	CDFG
▲CAREGIVERS UNITED LIAB INS CO RRG	SC	C	43.6	27.7	5.2	3.0	8.8	9.3	7.3	8.4	3.5	DR
CARIBBEAN AMERICAN PROPERTY INS CO	PR	C	59.4	20.5	34.0	3.4	2.5	7.0	4.4	1.3	4.3	CDGL
▲CARING COMMUNITIES RECIP RRG	DC	B	91.2	54.7	10.3	3.5	8.5	8.1	8.8	8.9	5.5	T
CAROLINA CASUALTY INS CO	IA	C	176.4	103.4	0.0	2.7	10.0	N/A	6.4	7.0	4.3	FR
CAROLINA FARMERS MUTUAL INS CO	NC	C-	9.8	7.6	3.2	1.3	8.1	7.4	6.0	7.7	2.5	DR
▲CAROLINA MUTUAL INS INC	NC	B	94.7	49.4	32.4	5.7	8.6	9.7	8.8	7.1	5.4	T
▲CASCO INDEMNITY CO	ME	B-	32.0	14.3	17.7	1.1	8.8	9.3	8.7	6.5	4.9	DR
CASSATT RISK RETENTION GROUP INC	VT	D+	12.5	3.7	0.1	0.0	7.8	4.8	3.7	10.0	2.2	DR
CASTLE KEY INDEMNITY CO	IL	B	16.8	10.8	0.0	0.2	10.0	N/A	7.4	8.9	4.9	DF
▲CASTLE KEY INS CO	IL	B+	362.5	216.2	122.6	6.7	10.0	6.4	8.6	6.7	6.4	F
CASTLEPOINT FLORIDA INS	FL	F (5)	10.0	7.3	-1.0	0.0	7.3	3.5	2.3	0.0	0.0	DFGL
CASTLEPOINT INS CO	NY	F (5)	178.4	17.4	-33.8	0.0	2.0	0.9	0.1	3.0	0.0	CDFL
▲CASUALTY CORP OF AMERICA	OK	D	13.9	4.6	13.8	1.4	2.2	1.6	4.2	2.6	1.5	CDGL
CASUALTY UNDERWRITERS INS CO	UT	D+	5.1	4.5	1.1	0.1	7.8	3.6	5.9	7.0	2.0	DGRT
▲CATASTROPHE REINS CO	TX	C	2,013.8	1,886.9	147.0	114.8	10.0	5.5	8.9	9.1	3.5	T
CATAWBA INS CO	SC	U	--	--	--	--	N/A	--	--	--	--	Z
▲CATERPILLAR INS CO	MO	B+	790.6	347.9	212.3	32.3	9.4	6.3	8.9	7.0	6.5	
CATLIN INDEMNITY CO	DE	C	108.9	67.1	5.4	-0.4	7.4	5.9	3.6	7.0	3.6	T
▲CATLIN INS CO	TX	C+	181.6	55.9	37.8	-7.6	6.9	3.2	2.9	7.0	4.4	FRT
CATLIN SPECIALTY INS CO	DE	C+	588.2	244.0	64.8	-7.8	8.4	4.0	3.8	7.5	4.3	FRT
CATTLEMANS INS CO A RRG	MT	U (5)	--	--	--	--	N/A	--	--	--	--	Z
▲CBIA COMP SERVICES INC	CT	C	24.9	11.0	4.6	1.9	6.5	9.9	6.6	6.7	2.9	DFR
CELINA MUTUAL INS CO	OH	C	76.8	33.4	43.1	-0.3	8.1	8.5	7.6	5.6	4.1	R
▲CEM INS CO	IL	C-	45.9	12.0	23.8	1.3	7.1	2.6	8.3	5.1	3.1	DGR
▲CENSTAT CASUALTY CO	NE	B-	25.3	18.2	2.1	0.7	10.0	7.6	7.7	8.4	5.3	D
CENTAURI NATIONAL INSURANCE CO	LA	D+	10.7	6.4	0.2	0.3	10.0	N/A	5.9	8.3	1.1	DT
CENTAURI SPECIALTY INS CO	FL	C	143.4	35.4	62.2	-1.5	5.0	5.3	3.6	5.2	4.2	CFOR
▲CENTENNIAL CASUALTY CO	AL	B	125.2	82.9	10.7	3.5	8.4	4.6	8.5	7.3	5.5	D
▲CENTER MUTUAL INS CO	ND	B-	57.7	29.1	28.0	1.6	9.1	8.4	5.7	6.3	5.1	T
CENTER VALLEY MUTUAL FIRE INS CO	PA	D+	2.6	2.5	0.1	0.1	10.0	N/A	5.6	10.0	2.0	D
CENTRAL CO-OPERATIVE INS CO	NY	C	20.2	12.5	7.9	1.6	9.3	6.4	8.6	6.9	3.1	DR
▲CENTRAL MUTUAL INS CO	OH	B+	1,618.4	822.0	559.1	34.9	8.8	9.1	8.5	6.6	6.5	
▲CENTRAL PA PHYSICIANS RRG INC	SC	C+	54.4	22.6	11.5	0.5	7.4	4.4	5.3	6.9	4.5	DF
CENTRAL STATES INDEMNITY CO OF	NE	C+	542.1	466.0	64.0	63.6	9.3	7.3	6.8	8.4	4.5	R
CENTRE COUNTY MUTUAL FIRE INS CO	PA	D+	7.0	4.1	3.0	0.3	6.4	6.7	7.1	6.0	2.1	D
CENTRE INS CO	DE	U	--	--	--	--	N/A	--	--	--	--	Z
CENTURION CASUALTY CO	IA	B-	39.8	39.5	9.9	5.6	10.0	7.2	1.9	8.9	5.0	D
▲CENTURION MEDICAL LIAB PROTECT RRG	AZ	C	21.0	12.6	6.0	0.1	10.0	7.0	8.7	8.8	3.3	DR
▲CENTURY CASUALTY CO	GA	D	1.2	1.1	-0.2	-1.3	10.0	3.4	0.5	0.3	1.5	FLRT
CENTURY INDEMNITY CO	PA	U	--	--	--	--	N/A	--	--	--	--	Z
▲CENTURY INS CO GUAM LTD	GU	D+	29.2	17.8	8.1	3.0	8.0	4.2	8.3	7.0	2.5	D
CENTURY MUTUAL INS CO	NC	C-	10.3	8.4	2.5	0.4	7.1	6.1	5.6	6.7	2.7	D
CENTURY SURETY CO	OH	C	101.1	97.6	0.0	14.6	8.0	2.5	2.4	7.0	3.5	DRT
CENTURY-NATIONAL INS CO	CA	C-	135.8	41.3	-48.1	14.7	9.8	6.7	1.9	0.0	3.1	LT

See Page 27 for explanation of footnotes and Page 28 for explanation of stability factors.
Arrows denote recent upgrades ▲ or downgrades ▼   (see Section VII for explanations)
48
www.weissratings.com

RISK ADJ. RATIO #1	CAPITAL RATIO #2	PREMIUM TO SURPLUS (%)	RESV. TO SURPLUS (%)	RESV. DEVELOP. 1 YEAR (%)	RESV. DEVELOP. 2 YEAR (%)	LOSS RATIO (%)	EXP. RATIO (%)	COMB RATIO (%)	CASH FROM UNDER-WRITING (%)	NET PREMIUM GROWTH (%)	INVEST. IN AFFIL (%)	INSURANCE COMPANY NAME
-0.1	-0.1	-386.1	-402.9	213.6	264.1	133.2	14.8	148.0	66.7	14.0	0.0	CAPITOL INS CO
1.7	1.2	55.7	27.2	0.1	-6.8	124.9	-13.0	111.9	57.0	11.8	3.3	CAPITOL PREFERRED INS CO
3.9	2.3	69.0	67.3	-0.4	-1.2	55.9	43.1	99.0	124.6	8.4	0.0	CAPITOL SPECIALTY INS CORP
0.4	0.2	252.9	328.2	59.4	35.3	82.5	41.6	124.1	84.4	1.2	0.0	CAPSON PHYSICIANS INS CO
1.5	1.1	59.8	30.5	-3.8	N/A	69.1	24.8	93.9	126.4	111.9	0.0	CAR RRG INC
1.0	0.7	141.9	248.0	-32.1	-28.0	75.1	30.7	105.8	68.9	-2.8	0.0	CARE RRG INC
1.9	1.2	71.7	190.7	-14.9	-33.9	58.0	22.9	80.9	121.7	-4.4	0.0	CARE WEST INS CO
0.1	0.1	202.6	370.2	28.7	-7.5	73.4	65.4	138.8	82.2	-9.5	0.0	CARECONCEPTS INS INC A RRG
3.4	2.1	18.7	48.0	-3.8	-12.4	70.4	14.9	85.3	227.8	1.7	0.0	CAREGIVERS UNITED LIAB INS CO RRG
0.6	0.4	165.2	24.3	-2.5	0.5	54.0	32.2	86.2	108.7	12.1	0.0	CARIBBEAN AMERICAN PROPERTY INS
2.3	2.0	18.8	31.3	0.8	-1.3	55.4	23.0	78.4	561.0	9.8	24.9	CARING COMMUNITIES RECIP RRG
13.2	11.9	N/A	N/A	N/A	N/A	N/A	N/A	N/A	999 +	0.0	0.0	CAROLINA CASUALTY INS CO
3.3	2.0	41.4	1.8	-2.0	-0.7	29.8	29.8	59.6	136.1	-2.7	0.0	CAROLINA FARMERS MUTUAL INS CO
3.0	2.5	65.6	58.8	-10.9	-27.0	47.6	29.3	76.9	125.9	-1.1	0.0	CAROLINA MUTUAL INS INC
3.2	2.3	123.3	57.4	-8.0	-8.2	60.4	33.9	94.3	105.7	5.7	0.0	CASCO INDEMNITY CO
1.6	1.5	2.7	1.7	N/A	N/A	100.0	-38.0	62.0	-215.7	0.0	0.0	CASSATT RISK RETENTION GROUP INC
6.2	5.6	N/A	N/A	N/A	N/A	N/A	N/A	N/A	-4.6	0.0	0.0	CASTLE KEY INDEMNITY CO
4.5	3.7	56.7	22.6	-1.1	-4.6	71.3	27.6	98.9	91.5	-0.1	6.4 ●	CASTLE KEY INS CO
7.8	7.0	-14.3	N/A	-7.0	9.7	13.1	-156.6	-143.5	46.3	-119.4	0.0	CASTLEPOINT FLORIDA INS
1.2	0.8	-418.8	N/A	253.5	71.5	108.5	-15.2	93.3	-35.1	-122.8	9.4	CASTLEPOINT INS CO
0.7	0.5	298.4	85.9	-2.0	-11.8	71.1	17.0	88.1	104.8	19.3	0.0	CASUALTY CORP OF AMERICA
2.1	1.5	23.4	10.0	1.6	N/A	85.9	17.6	103.5	159.7	366.6	16.3	CASUALTY UNDERWRITERS INS CO
15.2	9.1	7.8	1.9	N/A	-1.7	39.3	0.3	39.6	644.8	-0.8	0.0 ●	CATASTROPHE REINS CO
N/A	N/A	--	--	--	--	--	--	--	--	--	--	CATAWBA INS CO
3.5	2.6	61.0	6.0	-0.2	0.4	78.2	11.9	90.1	135.2	17.5	0.0 ●	CATERPILLAR INS CO
1.3	1.3	8.1	16.4	0.3	1.3	81.9	29.6	111.5	51.1	29.0	54.5	CATLIN INDEMNITY CO
1.8	1.0	67.7	137.7	2.6	11.2	81.9	36.1	118.0	218.3	29.0	0.0	CATLIN INS CO
3.0	2.2	26.6	54.0	1.1	4.7	81.9	33.5	115.4	23.1	29.0	15.3 ●	CATLIN SPECIALTY INS CO
N/A	N/A	--	--	--	--	--	--	--	--	--	--	CATTLEMANS INS CO A RRG
1.9	1.2	41.9	113.4	-12.9	-32.5	45.9	29.4	75.3	87.9	-8.0	0.0	CBIA COMP SERVICES INC
2.7	1.7	129.2	40.6	-3.7	-8.0	73.8	30.9	104.7	99.4	9.0	0.0	CELINA MUTUAL INS CO
1.2	1.0	198.3	53.0	20.4	9.8	70.5	20.6	91.1	130.1	66.5	0.0	CEM INS CO
8.6	7.2	11.6	10.7	-2.4	-2.8	55.3	27.3	82.6	122.5	-19.1	0.0	CENSTAT CASUALTY CO
4.7	4.2	2.4	0.8	N/A	N/A	42.6	-254.5	-211.9	-290.6	0.0	0.0	CENTAURI NATIONAL INSURANCE CO
1.0	0.6	175.6	56.8	-3.7	-0.1	79.3	36.8	116.1	94.6	-21.5	5.3	CENTAURI SPECIALTY INS CO
3.3	1.9	12.9	6.3	-0.6	N/A	63.5	19.1	82.6	144.3	4.2	0.0	CENTENNIAL CASUALTY CO
3.5	2.4	96.1	26.9	-0.4	-4.5	70.2	27.0	97.2	103.0	5.9	0.0	CENTER MUTUAL INS CO
25.0	22.7	5.0	N/A	N/A	N/A	16.9	79.8	96.7	101.9	-18.6	0.0	CENTER VALLEY MUTUAL FIRE INS CO
3.9	2.7	63.5	12.5	-1.7	0.4	38.2	35.5	73.7	136.3	15.3	0.0	CENTRAL CO-OPERATIVE INS CO
2.9	2.2	68.0	43.9	-2.4	-8.2	65.0	33.0	98.0	104.5	7.8	11.3 ●	CENTRAL MUTUAL INS CO
1.9	1.4	50.7	92.0	7.5	11.3	76.8	34.3	111.1	71.1	-1.5	0.0	CENTRAL PA PHYSICIANS RRG INC
3.9	2.5	13.7	1.6	N/A	-0.1	66.1	53.0	119.1	86.4	7.4	3.2 ●	CENTRAL STATES INDEMNITY CO OF
1.5	0.9	71.8	16.5	3.2	-1.2	57.2	34.0	91.2	115.0	5.0	0.0	CENTRE COUNTY MUTUAL FIRE INS CO
N/A	N/A	--	--	--	--	--	--	--	--	--	--	CENTRE INS CO
12.9	11.5	25.1	0.7	-0.6	-0.1	4.1	17.7	21.8	443.9	-3.3	0.0	CENTURION CASUALTY CO
5.8	4.3	47.6	30.5	9.9	5.4	60.5	34.3	94.8	149.3	-9.3	0.0	CENTURION MEDICAL LIAB PROTECT
38.6	34.7	-18.5	N/A	36.6	30.7	999 +	-207.7	999 +	0.6	-787.4	0.0	CENTURY CASUALTY CO
N/A	N/A	--	--	--	--	--	--	--	--	--	--	CENTURY INDEMNITY CO
3.4	2.0	45.2	16.3	5.4	1.5	36.1	37.0	73.1	126.8	6.2	0.0	CENTURY INS CO GUAM LTD
1.4	1.0	29.9	4.0	-1.7	-0.9	52.1	45.1	97.2	101.3	12.6	0.0	CENTURY MUTUAL INS CO
1.6	1.6	N/A	N/A	N/A	N/A	N/A	N/A	N/A	38.5	0.0	59.6	CENTURY SURETY CO
5.0	4.5	-116.6	N/A	-1.0	-5.5	59.4	-38.4	21.0	91.8	-122.9	0.0	CENTURY-NATIONAL INS CO

999 + Denotes number greater than 999.9%
999 - Denotes number less than -999.99%
● Bullets denote a more detailed analysis is available in Section II.

INSURANCE COMPANY NAME	DOM. STATE	RATING	TOTAL ASSETS ($MIL)	CAPITAL & SURPLUS ($MIL)	ANNUAL NET PREMIUM ($MIL)	NET INCOME ($MIL)	CAPITAL-IZATION INDEX (PTS)	RESERVE ADQ INDEX (PTS)	PROFIT-ABILITY INDEX (PTS)	LIQUIDITY INDEX (PTS)	STAB. INDEX (PTS)	STABILITY FACTORS
▲CGB INS CO	IN	D+	550.2	159.8	0.0	8.6	10.0	3.6	8.2	7.0	2.5	GT
CHARITABLE SERVICE PROVIDERS RRG	AZ	U (5)	--	--	--	--	N/A	--	--	--	--	Z
CHARTER INDEMNITY CO	TX	B	11.1	7.1	0.0	0.3	10.0	N/A	3.7	10.0	4.1	DRT
CHARTER OAK FIRE INS CO	CT	B	925.9	227.4	290.0	18.3	7.7	8.5	3.8	6.5	5.9	
CHAUTAUQUA PATRONS INS CO	NY	C	22.0	11.9	8.0	0.1	8.1	6.1	6.1	6.6	3.2	DFR
CHEROKEE GUARANTEE CO INC A RRG	AZ	E	22.9	3.8	9.6	-0.1	0.1	1.9	5.4	7.2	0.1	CDGT
▲CHEROKEE INS CO	MI	B	541.6	197.8	186.4	25.5	7.8	4.4	6.7	6.0	5.5	
▲CHERRY VALLEY COOPERATIVE INS CO	NY	D+	2.0	1.5	0.5	0.0	7.8	6.1	4.3	9.0	1.9	DRT
CHESAPEAKE EMPLOYERS INS CO	MD	B	2,317.8	695.3	220.1	140.6	7.4	9.5	7.1	7.0	6.3	T
CHICAGO INS CO	IL	C	77.2	66.5	0.0	-0.2	10.0	N/A	7.6	7.0	4.2	DRT
CHUBB CUSTOM INS CO	NJ	B-	389.2	223.3	25.4	10.3	10.0	7.9	8.5	7.2	4.9	T
CHUBB INDEMNITY INS CO	NY	B	397.6	171.8	25.4	10.4	10.0	8.0	8.8	6.9	6.0	T
CHUBB INS CO OF NJ	NJ	B	97.2	35.6	0.0	0.5	10.0	N/A	6.9	7.0	5.4	DF
CHUBB INS CO OF PR	PR	B (2)	146.4	49.3	63.8	0.6	7.3	9.5	7.2	7.0	4.3	T
CHUBB LLOYDS INS CO OF TX	TX	B	52.8	5.4	0.0	0.0	5.0	N/A	6.4	7.0	4.9	CDFG
CHUBB NATIONAL INS CO	IN	B	406.1	171.5	25.4	10.4	10.0	8.0	8.8	6.9	6.0	T
CHUNG KUO INS CO LTD GUAM BRANCH	GU	C+(2)	41.6	26.1	16.5	2.7	7.8	9.1	8.4	9.0	3.2	DGT
CHURCH INS CO	NY	U	--	--	--	--	N/A	--	--	--	--	Z
▲CHURCH MUTUAL INS CO	WI	B+	1,739.8	703.7	730.4	28.5	8.3	8.1	6.3	6.5	6.5	
CIM INS CORP	MI	C	17.7	17.5	0.0	0.1	10.0	N/A	6.1	7.0	3.3	DRT
CIMARRON INSURANCE CO	AZ	U	--	--	--	--	N/A	--	--	--	--	Z
CINCINNATI CASUALTY CO	OH	B	433.6	392.3	0.0	21.0	10.0	N/A	8.0	10.0	5.8	
CINCINNATI EQUITABLE INS CO	OH	U	--	--	--	--	N/A	--	--	--	--	Z
CINCINNATI INDEMNITY CO	OH	A-	133.0	100.0	0.0	4.0	10.0	N/A	7.9	7.2	6.9	F
CINCINNATI INS CO	OH	A	12,914.9	5,093.6	4,624.9	401.2	7.9	8.2	8.6	6.2	7.6	
▲CINCINNATI SPECIALTY UNDERWRITER	DE	A	820.6	436.0	219.1	58.5	8.3	9.4	8.8	7.0	7.5	
CIRCLE STAR INS CO A RRG	VT	D	3.1	1.9	0.5	0.7	10.0	9.3	9.8	9.9	1.6	DT
CITATION INS CO (MA)	MA	C+	256.5	71.1	160.6	-1.2	7.8	4.2	2.6	3.8	4.6	L
▲CITIES & VILLAGES MUTUAL INS CO	WI	B-	52.1	28.6	13.9	-0.7	5.2	6.2	4.1	6.9	5.0	CD
CITIZENS INS CO OF AM	MI	B	1,559.4	699.5	773.2	93.7	9.9	8.0	7.3	6.1	5.2	
CITIZENS INS CO OF IL	IL	C+	5.4	5.4	0.0	0.1	10.0	N/A	7.8	7.0	3.6	DR
CITIZENS INS CO OF OHIO	OH	C	14.7	14.7	0.0	0.4	10.0	N/A	4.7	7.0	4.2	D
CITIZENS INS CO OF THE MIDWEST	IN	C	61.0	59.4	0.0	1.0	10.0	N/A	7.4	7.0	4.3	
CITIZENS PROPERTY INS CORP	FL	A+(1)	11,362.5	6,456.7	552.6	-944.2	10.0	5.8	3.6	9.3	7.5	FT
CITIZENS UNITED RECIP EXCH	NJ	D	59.6	14.1	26.5	-8.5	1.8	1.2	1.2	2.8	2.2	CDFL
CITY NATIONAL INS CO	TX	C	19.1	12.0	10.8	-0.1	10.0	5.0	3.7	8.7	3.0	GRT
CIVIC PROPERTY & CASUALTY CO INC	CA	C+	268.9	116.1	141.8	1.4	9.7	5.9	5.2	6.4	4.7	FR
▼CIVIL SERVICE EMPLOYEES INS CO	CA	C	217.2	94.4	121.0	-18.4	8.2	6.0	2.2	6.0	4.1	FR
CLAIM PROFESSIONALS LIAB INS CO RRG	VT	D+	4.7	2.9	0.7	0.0	8.6	7.0	8.3	9.0	2.0	DR
▲CLAVERACK CO-OPERATIVE INS CO	NY	D+	3.1	1.6	0.0	0.0	9.4	9.4	2.9	7.9	1.9	DFT
▲CLEAR BLUE INS CO	IL	C+	56.0	45.7	0.0	0.6	10.0	4.6	4.0	10.0	3.5	GT
CLEAR BLUE SPECIALTY INS CO	NC	C+	106.5	104.2	0.0	0.3	8.5	2.8	6.1	10.0	3.7	GRT
CLEAR SPRING P&C CO	TX	D-	79.1	52.7	21.0	-4.6	10.0	5.1	2.2	7.8	1.0	GRT
CLEARPATH MUTUAL INSURANCE CO	KY	U	--	--	--	--	N/A	--	--	--	--	Z
CLEARWATER SELECT INS CO	CT	D	1,279.8	519.2	215.4	25.8	6.2	3.5	8.7	9.1	1.7	R
CLERMONT INS CO	IA	C	27.4	23.3	0.0	0.5	10.0	N/A	7.2	10.0	4.2	DR
CLINIC MUTUAL INS CO RRG	HI	U (5)	--	--	--	--	N/A	--	--	--	--	Z
▲CLOISTER MUTL CAS INS CO	PA	C+	9.9	9.8	0.1	0.1	10.0	7.2	4.3	10.0	4.4	D
CM REGENT INS CO	PA	B-	190.9	81.4	0.0	13.4	9.3	9.7	8.1	7.5	3.9	RT
CM SELECT INSURANCE CO	WI	U	--	--	--	--	N/A	--	--	--	--	Z
CM VANTAGE SPECIALTY INS CO	WI	B	61.7	53.2	0.0	0.6	10.0	N/A	4.9	8.5	4.3	FT
CMIC RRG	DC	C+(1)	5.4	2.8	0.3	0.0	8.1	4.9	4.1	9.2	3.3	DGT

See Page 27 for explanation of footnotes and
Page 28 for explanation of stability factors.

50

www.weissratings.com

Arrows denote recent upgrades ▲ or downgrades ▼   (see Section VII for explanations)

RISK ADJ. RATIO #1	CAPITAL RATIO #2	PREMIUM TO SURPLUS (%)	RESV. TO SURPLUS (%)	RESV. DEVELOP. 1 YEAR (%)	RESV. DEVELOP. 2 YEAR (%)	LOSS RATIO (%)	EXP. RATIO (%)	COMB RATIO (%)	CASH FROM UNDER-WRITING (%)	NET PREMIUM GROWTH (%)	INVEST. IN AFFIL (%)	INSURANCE COMPANY NAME
7.9	3.9	N/A	N/A	N/A	N/A	N/A	N/A	N/A	N/A	0.0	0.0	CGB INS CO
N/A	N/A	--	--	--	--	--	--	--	--	--	--	CHARITABLE SERVICE PROVIDERS RRG
5.5	5.0	N/A	N/A	N/A	N/A	N/A	N/A	N/A	6.9	0.0	0.0	CHARTER INDEMNITY CO
2.2	1.4	127.5	209.0	-2.6	-4.1	69.5	29.5	99.0	96.8	4.9	0.0 •	CHARTER OAK FIRE INS CO
2.6	1.7	67.5	31.9	-0.5	1.7	67.4	39.7	107.1	90.7	-4.7	0.0	CHAUTAUQUA PATRONS INS CO
0.1	0.1	256.2	476.3	116.2	121.4	107.4	-2.6	104.8	174.1	174.8	0.0	CHEROKEE GUARANTEE CO INC A RRG
3.0	1.7	94.2	136.3	-1.6	3.5	93.7	9.1	102.8	109.1	-2.1	0.0	CHEROKEE INS CO
2.3	1.5	30.7	26.9	3.0	-0.4	77.1	24.1	101.2	322.9	4.5	0.0	CHERRY VALLEY COOPERATIVE INS CO
2.7	1.6	31.7	178.4	-18.6	-29.4	51.8	27.9	79.7	90.2	-7.3	0.0 •	CHESAPEAKE EMPLOYERS INS CO
26.5	23.8	N/A	N/A	N/A	N/A	N/A	N/A	N/A	20.5	0.0	0.0	CHICAGO INS CO
13.4	8.3	11.4	32.3	-1.4	-3.3	62.6	25.4	88.0	120.8	-19.9	0.0 •	CHUBB CUSTOM INS CO
11.2	7.0	14.8	42.0	-1.8	-4.4	62.6	25.4	88.0	175.6	-19.9	0.0	CHUBB INDEMNITY INS CO
4.9	4.4	N/A	N/A	N/A	N/A	N/A	N/A	N/A	N/A	0.0	0.0	CHUBB INS CO OF NJ
1.4	1.1	125.7	122.5	-5.5	-13.9	30.9	68.6	99.5	114.3	0.0	0.0	CHUBB INS CO OF PR
0.8	0.7	N/A	N/A	N/A	N/A	N/A	N/A	N/A	N/A	0.0	0.0	CHUBB LLOYDS INS CO OF TX
11.2	6.9	14.8	42.0	-1.8	-4.3	62.6	25.4	88.0	116.0	-19.9	0.0	CHUBB NATIONAL INS CO
3.6	2.4	70.7	13.0	-10.6	-11.5	29.4	40.6	70.0	113.3	3.8	0.0	CHUNG KUO INS CO LTD GUAM BRANCH
N/A	N/A	--	--	--	--	--	--	--	--	--	--	CHURCH INS CO
2.5	1.8	103.8	72.9	0.6	-3.2	66.6	31.3	97.9	111.3	13.1	8.8 •	CHURCH MUTUAL INS CO
268.8	241.9	N/A	N/A	N/A	N/A	N/A	N/A	N/A	-5.0	0.0	0.0	CIM INS CORP
N/A	N/A	--	--	--	--	--	--	--	--	--	--	CIMARRON INSURANCE CO
10.0	5.8	N/A	N/A	N/A	N/A	N/A	N/A	N/A	-81.7	0.0	0.0 •	CINCINNATI CASUALTY CO
N/A	N/A	--	--	--	--	--	--	--	--	--	--	CINCINNATI EQUITABLE INS CO
11.5	6.6	N/A	N/A	N/A	N/A	N/A	N/A	N/A	-48.2	0.0	0.0 •	CINCINNATI INDEMNITY CO
2.2	1.6	90.8	93.8	-2.1	-4.3	67.5	30.3	97.8	109.8	5.3	10.0 •	CINCINNATI INS CO
3.3	2.5	50.2	59.9	-7.7	-18.7	41.4	30.5	71.9	173.4	15.4	0.0 •	CINCINNATI SPECIALTY UNDERWRITER
4.0	3.6	24.7	32.6	-4.8	-11.7	40.2	-148.9	-108.7	-82.2	5.7	0.0	CIRCLE STAR INS CO A RRG
1.8	1.5	225.9	115.5	7.3	6.1	79.9	25.5	105.4	99.1	0.4	0.0	CITATION INS CO (MA)
1.1	0.7	48.7	66.8	9.4	6.8	76.1	28.5	104.6	120.2	0.0	4.7	CITIES & VILLAGES MUTUAL INS CO
4.3	2.9	110.5	59.7	-1.9	-3.6	61.6	26.6	88.2	113.9	8.3	0.0 •	CITIZENS INS CO OF AM
253.2	126.6	N/A	N/A	N/A	N/A	N/A	N/A	N/A	N/A	0.0	0.0	CITIZENS INS CO OF IL
67.6	30.2	N/A	N/A	N/A	N/A	N/A	N/A	N/A	N/A	0.0	0.0	CITIZENS INS CO OF OHIO
75.6	33.4	N/A	N/A	N/A	N/A	N/A	N/A	N/A	N/A	0.0	0.0	CITIZENS INS CO OF THE MIDWEST
16.7	8.2	7.5	9.7	1.0	1.4	82.0	43.3	125.3	71.8	-4.4	0.0	CITIZENS PROPERTY INS CORP
0.4	0.3	188.1	214.3	44.8	51.0	103.3	33.8	137.1	65.0	-29.9	0.0	CITIZENS UNITED RECIP EXCH
6.3	5.7	89.8	5.8	0.3	-0.1	49.4	28.8	78.2	131.3	740.3	0.0	CITY NATIONAL INS CO
4.0	2.9	122.2	72.2	-0.3	1.3	69.5	32.9	102.4	93.9	-3.9	0.0	CIVIC PROPERTY & CASUALTY CO INC
2.2	1.8	128.2	59.4	1.9	2.6	83.5	32.7	116.2	95.4	19.6	18.1	CIVIL SERVICE EMPLOYEES INS CO
4.2	2.7	22.8	25.7	-0.7	-6.5	55.3	51.7	107.0	132.0	5.4	0.0	CLAIM PROFESSIONALS LIAB INS CO
2.8	2.5	N/A	5.9	-10.4	-36.5	N/A	N/A	N/A	33.6	100.0	0.0	CLAVERACK CO-OPERATIVE INS CO
18.6	16.7	N/A	N/A	N/A	N/A	N/A	N/A	N/A	0.8	0.0	0.0	CLEAR BLUE INS CO
2.1	2.0	N/A	13.1	13.2	24.8	N/A	N/A	N/A	3.9	0.0	44.0	CLEAR BLUE SPECIALTY INS CO
5.0	4.5	39.9	12.7	N/A	N/A	67.1	44.2	111.3	134.2	0.0	0.0	CLEAR SPRING P&C CO
N/A	N/A	--	--	--	--	--	--	--	--	--	--	CLEARPATH MUTUAL INSURANCE CO
1.5	1.1	41.5	123.1	-6.7	-12.7	60.3	25.8	86.1	131.4	9.5	14.7 •	CLEARWATER SELECT INS CO
18.0	16.2	N/A	N/A	N/A	N/A	N/A	N/A	N/A	51.7	0.0	0.0	CLERMONT INS CO
N/A	N/A	--	--	--	--	--	--	--	--	--	--	CLINIC MUTUAL INS CO RRG
15.7	7.0	1.5	0.3	-0.3	-0.3	8.5	165.1	173.6	56.6	6.1	0.0	CLOISTER MUTL CAS INS CO
5.6	3.3	N/A	94.6	-10.6	-32.6	28.2	169.9	198.1	105.8	-100.1	0.0	CM REGENT INS CO
N/A	N/A	--	--	--	--	--	--	--	--	--	--	CM SELECT INSURANCE CO
24.5	22.1	N/A	N/A	N/A	N/A	N/A	N/A	N/A	17.2	0.0	0.0	CM VANTAGE SPECIALTY INS CO
3.2	2.8	10.3	20.0	3.0	-0.1	-253.1	-234.9	-488.0	43.2	199.9	0.0	CMIC RRG

999 + Denotes number greater than 999.9%
999 - Denotes number less than -999.99%
• Bullets denote a more detailed analysis is available in Section II.

INSURANCE COMPANY NAME	DOM. STATE	RATING	TOTAL ASSETS ($MIL)	CAPITAL & SURPLUS ($MIL)	ANNUAL NET PREMIUM ($MIL)	NET INCOME ($MIL)	CAPITAL-IZATION INDEX (PTS)	RESERVE ADQ INDEX (PTS)	PROFIT-ABILITY INDEX (PTS)	LIQUIDITY INDEX (PTS)	STAB. INDEX (PTS)	STABILITY FACTORS
COAST NATIONAL INS CO	CA	D+	589.8	434.8	0.0	8.8	10.0	4.6	6.6	10.0	2.7	R
COASTAL AMERICAN INS CO	MS	C-	9.7	4.0	5.8	-0.5	5.0	8.2	4.1	6.2	2.3	D
▲COASTAL SELECT INS CO	CA	C-	105.9	35.2	47.0	0.5	1.3	7.6	3.6	0.3	2.9	CLR
CODAN INS CO LTD	NY	U	--	--	--	--	N/A	--	--	--	--	Z
▲COFACE NORTH AMERICA INS CO	MA	C+	135.9	47.1	49.7	6.8	7.8	7.0	3.2	7.3	4.5	FR
COLISEUM REINS CO	DE	U	--	--	--	--	N/A	--	--	--	--	Z
COLLEGE LIAB INS CO LTD RRG	HI	D	14.2	5.2	4.2	0.1	1.7	6.0	1.7	6.0	1.7	CD
COLLEGE RRG INC	VT	C	28.4	10.2	6.0	0.2	7.1	5.9	6.8	7.2	3.0	D
COLONIAL AMERICAN CAS & SURETY CO	MD	C+	25.1	23.4	0.0	0.5	10.0	N/A	7.0	7.0	4.6	DR
COLONIAL COUNTY MUTUAL INS CO	TX	B	130.0	13.9	0.0	0.0	7.6	N/A	3.9	7.0	4.9	D
▲COLONIAL LLOYDS	TX	C	9.7	6.8	0.7	0.4	10.0	4.8	5.9	9.1	3.5	D
COLONIAL MORTGAGE INS CO	TX	U	--	--	--	--	N/A	--	--	--	--	Z
COLONIAL SURETY CO	PA	B-	62.0	40.5	10.7	4.3	10.0	9.3	8.8	8.1	5.3	D
COLONY INS CO	VA	C	1,698.6	424.5	285.6	18.4	7.4	9.2	8.6	6.9	3.3	R
COLONY SPECIALTY INS CO	OH	D+	67.9	23.7	0.0	0.8	9.4	N/A	7.2	7.7	2.4	DR
COLORADO CASUALTY INS CO	NH	C+	24.9	24.8	0.0	0.3	10.0	N/A	6.4	7.0	4.1	DRT
▲COLORADO FARM BUREAU MUTUAL INS CO	CO	C+	81.3	35.4	26.1	0.2	8.7	9.4	3.9	6.7	4.5	
COLUMBIA CASUALTY CO	IL	C	245.2	245.0	0.0	6.5	10.0	N/A	6.1	9.5	3.9	AR
COLUMBIA FEDERAL INS CO	DC	D+	3.4	2.5	0.8	0.1	7.1	6.9	6.8	6.4	1.8	DFT
COLUMBIA INS CO	NE	U	--	--	--	--	N/A	--	--	--	--	Z
▲COLUMBIA LLOYDS INS CO	TX	B-	50.4	27.8	22.1	3.2	6.0	6.9	8.9	6.5	5.2	F
COLUMBIA MUTUAL INS CO	MO	B-	381.2	172.9	152.4	-7.5	8.0	6.2	4.0	6.2	4.7	R
COLUMBIA NATIONAL INS CO	NE	C+	90.7	36.9	39.2	-0.1	9.0	6.1	4.9	6.5	4.7	
▲COLUMBIA NATIONAL RRG INC	VT	E+	2.0	1.3	0.3	0.1	10.0	N/A	8.3	10.0	0.5	DT
COMCARE PRO INS RECIPROCAL RRG	VT	D+	5.7	2.6	2.7	-0.7	2.7	3.2	1.9	2.0	2.1	CDLT
COMMERCE & INDUSTRY INS CO	NY	C	419.6	414.8	0.0	2.4	10.0	4.0	1.9	6.8	4.2	AT
▲COMMERCE INS CO	MA	B-	2,246.1	626.3	1,290.8	18.4	8.0	4.2	3.8	3.2	4.8	L
COMMERCE WEST INS CO	CA	C	182.3	54.2	107.1	2.8	8.2	4.1	4.1	5.0	4.3	
COMMERCIAL ALLIANCE INS CO	TX	C	104.9	46.2	44.2	1.0	6.7	3.4	6.6	6.7	3.8	R
COMMERCIAL CASUALTY INS CO	IN	U	--	--	--	--	N/A	--	--	--	--	Z
COMMERCIAL HIRECAR INS CO RRG	TN	D	6.9	2.0	4.1	0.2	4.2	3.6	4.8	6.7	1.3	DGT
COMMERCIAL MUT INS CO	GA	F (5)	0.0	0.0	7.9	0.0	0.0	2.3	0.1	0.0	0.0	CDFL
COMMONWEALTH CASUALTY CO	AZ	E	31.4	8.7	35.2	-6.2	0.0	3.9	2.0	0.0	0.3	CDGL
COMMONWEALTH INS CO OF AMERICA	DE	U	--	--	--	--	N/A	--	--	--	--	Z
COMMUNITIES OF FAITH RRG INC	SC	C	14.1	13.0	1.1	1.1	9.4	8.1	7.0	9.3	3.3	DR
COMMUNITY BLOOD CENTERS EXCHANGE	IN	C	19.3	15.6	2.4	1.3	9.0	9.3	7.1	7.6	3.7	DR
▲COMMUNITY CARE RRG INC	DC	D+	9.3	2.7	1.6	0.0	7.3	3.8	7.3	7.9	1.9	DT
COMMUNITY HEALTH ALLIANCE RECIP RRG	VT	U	--	--	--	--	N/A	--	--	--	--	Z
▲COMMUNITY HOSPITAL ALTERNATIVE RRG	VT	B	251.1	140.3	37.8	23.8	9.5	9.6	8.9	7.2	5.5	T
COMMUNITY INS CO (PA)	PA	D	5.8	3.3	2.3	-0.3	7.3	5.0	1.9	7.0	1.2	DFGR
COMMUNITY INS CORP	WI	C+	7.6	6.1	0.0	0.1	10.0	N/A	6.5	7.0	3.8	DR
COMMUNITY MUTUAL INS CO	NY	D+	2.0	1.2	0.0	0.1	10.0	5.1	6.2	9.6	1.4	DFRT
COMPASS INS CO	NY	U	--	--	--	--	N/A	--	--	--	--	Z
COMPASS SPCLTY INS RRG INC	TN	D	5.4	1.8	4.1	0.1	2.8	3.6	4.3	9.0	1.1	DGT
▼COMPTRUST AGC MUT CAPTIVE INS CO	GA	C-	32.5	10.5	18.7	0.5	2.8	9.4	3.1	6.3	3.1	CDT
COMPUTER INS CO	RI	U	--	--	--	--	N/A	--	--	--	--	Z
▲COMPWEST INS CO	CA	B	251.1	137.7	15.6	5.2	10.0	5.9	8.3	6.8	5.5	T
CONCORD GENERAL MUTUAL INS CO	NH	B-	518.0	301.8	170.4	15.0	8.2	8.4	7.6	6.7	4.6	T
▲CONEMAUGH VALLEY MUTUAL INS CO	PA	C+	14.5	7.0	3.3	0.5	9.0	6.4	8.0	6.7	3.8	DFR
▲CONIFER INS CO	MI	D	121.3	35.8	62.5	-7.0	1.5	3.1	2.9	3.5	1.4	CGL
CONNECTICUT MEDICAL INS CO	CT	B	504.1	307.3	28.3	-6.3	6.6	6.9	4.3	7.1	5.9	F
CONSOLIDATED INS CO	IN	C	14.6	13.4	0.0	0.1	10.0	N/A	6.2	10.0	4.3	DR

See Page 27 for explanation of footnotes and Page 28 for explanation of stability factors.
Arrows denote recent upgrades ▲ or downgrades ▼ (see Section VII for explanations)

52

www.weissratings.com

RISK ADJ. CAPITAL RATIO #1	CAPITAL RATIO #2	PREMIUM TO SURPLUS (%)	RESV. TO SURPLUS (%)	RESV. DEVELOP. 1 YEAR (%)	RESV. DEVELOP. 2 YEAR (%)	LOSS RATIO (%)	EXP. RATIO (%)	COMB RATIO (%)	CASH FROM UNDER-WRITING (%)	NET PREMIUM GROWTH (%)	INVEST. IN AFFIL (%)	INSURANCE COMPANY NAME
8.1	7.5	N/A	N/A	N/A	N/A	N/A	N/A	N/A	-8.7	0.0	11.8 ●	COAST NATIONAL INS CO
1.0	0.5	144.1	14.6	-6.8	-7.5	54.6	51.6	106.2	102.7	30.0	0.0	COASTAL AMERICAN INS CO
0.4	0.3	133.7	31.4	2.7	-0.9	65.2	28.8	94.0	120.6	17.9	0.0	COASTAL SELECT INS CO
N/A	N/A	--	--	--	--	--	--	--	--	--	--	CODAN INS CO LTD
2.1	1.5	105.5	88.8	-24.7	-12.4	45.5	41.0	86.5	89.1	-6.3	0.0	COFACE NORTH AMERICA INS CO
N/A	N/A	--	--	--	--	--	--	--	--	--	--	COLISEUM REINS CO
0.4	0.3	80.4	131.7	1.7	5.4	97.6	17.8	115.4	92.8	22.7	0.0	COLLEGE LIAB INS CO LTD RRG
1.3	1.1	58.7	114.7	-4.6	1.3	82.2	22.7	104.9	109.7	2.2	0.0	COLLEGE RRG INC
36.3	32.7	N/A	N/A	N/A	N/A	N/A	N/A	N/A	35.0	0.0	0.0	COLONIAL AMERICAN CAS & SURETY CO
1.5	1.3	N/A	N/A	N/A	N/A	N/A	N/A	N/A	48.6	0.0	0.0	COLONIAL COUNTY MUTUAL INS CO
7.2	6.5	10.8	3.6	-1.4	-5.7	60.3	2.7	63.0	218.6	48.2	0.0	COLONIAL LLOYDS
N/A	N/A	--	--	--	--	--	--	--	--	--	--	COLONIAL MORTGAGE INS CO
6.0	4.2	26.3	25.1	-5.0	-13.8	6.0	40.4	46.4	150.3	8.4	0.0	COLONIAL SURETY CO
1.8	1.2	67.3	109.5	-4.8	-6.3	56.8	41.4	98.2	130.9	9.1	5.0 ●	COLONY INS CO
3.8	2.6	N/A	N/A	N/A	N/A	N/A	N/A	N/A	-310.3	0.0	0.0	COLONY SPECIALTY INS CO
193.9	96.9	N/A	N/A	N/A	N/A	N/A	N/A	N/A	N/A	0.0	0.0	COLORADO CASUALTY INS CO
2.9	2.2	73.8	25.3	-5.7	-17.8	82.6	22.0	104.6	101.4	0.6	1.7	COLORADO FARM BUREAU MUTUAL INS
63.9	28.0	N/A	N/A	N/A	N/A	N/A	N/A	N/A	N/A	0.0	0.0 ●	COLUMBIA CASUALTY CO
1.7	1.0	33.3	35.5	-0.6	4.0	91.5	19.2	110.7	76.6	1.0	0.0	COLUMBIA FEDERAL INS CO
N/A	N/A	--	--	--	--	--	--	--	--	--	--	COLUMBIA INS CO
1.4	1.1	79.6	11.1	-2.7	-19.5	56.1	23.8	79.9	103.9	0.1	36.5	COLUMBIA LLOYDS INS CO
1.9	1.6	88.1	72.1	2.7	1.6	82.2	29.7	111.9	107.3	6.1	24.6	COLUMBIA MUTUAL INS CO
3.1	2.3	106.3	86.9	3.3	1.9	82.2	28.8	111.0	95.6	6.1	0.0	COLUMBIA NATIONAL INS CO
4.0	3.6	25.4	N/A	N/A	N/A	N/A	33.4	33.4	320.9	25.0	0.0	COLUMBIA NATIONAL RRG INC
0.6	0.4	106.0	66.3	29.4	29.4	123.8	15.1	138.9	100.7	26.8	0.0	COMCARE PRO INS RECIPROCAL RRG
22.6	23.2	N/A	N/A	N/A	N/A	N/A	N/A	N/A	N/A	100.0	5.2 ●	COMMERCE & INDUSTRY INS CO
2.0	1.6	206.1	105.3	6.8	5.7	79.9	22.9	102.8	97.5	0.4	3.4 ●	COMMERCE INS CO
2.1	1.8	197.4	100.9	6.7	5.9	79.9	18.1	98.0	103.1	0.4	0.0	COMMERCE WEST INS CO
1.7	1.0	95.7	73.0	0.2	11.9	73.3	30.7	104.0	125.1	26.5	0.0	COMMERCIAL ALLIANCE INS CO
N/A	N/A	--	--	--	--	--	--	--	--	--	--	COMMERCIAL CASUALTY INS CO
0.9	0.5	200.4	55.3	-0.7	N/A	49.5	18.7	68.2	282.4	164.1	0.0	COMMERCIAL HIRECAR INS CO RRG
0.0	0.0	544.6	674.2	9.5	40.7	76.4	80.1	156.5	91.3	-17.7	0.0	COMMERCIAL MUT INS CO
0.0	0.0	405.3	153.4	23.7	5.2	91.1	26.9	118.0	101.6	40.6	0.0	COMMONWEALTH CASUALTY CO
N/A	N/A	--	--	--	--	--	--	--	--	--	--	COMMONWEALTH INS CO OF AMERICA
4.3	2.6	8.8	8.2	-3.7	-6.4	-2.0	46.1	44.1	127.9	4.2	0.0	COMMUNITIES OF FAITH RRG INC
3.0	2.3	15.6	11.8	-1.3	-4.3	17.9	43.9	61.8	141.3	28.2	0.0	COMMUNITY BLOOD CENTERS
1.5	1.2	57.9	165.2	-30.9	-6.7	79.9	21.9	101.8	753.3	-38.1	0.0	COMMUNITY CARE RRG INC
N/A	N/A	--	--	--	--	--	--	--	--	--	--	COMMUNITY HEALTH ALLIANCE RECIP
4.1	2.9	26.9	76.2	-8.3	-11.0	40.7	16.7	57.4	149.0	-2.7	0.0	COMMUNITY HOSPITAL ALTERNATIVE
2.0	1.3	69.0	16.3	3.1	-0.6	52.5	75.6	128.1	89.1	43.1	0.0	COMMUNITY INS CO (PA)
10.5	9.4	N/A	N/A	N/A	N/A	N/A	N/A	N/A	5.7	0.0	0.0	COMMUNITY INS CORP
3.6	3.2	N/A	N/A	N/A	N/A	N/A	N/A	N/A	999 +	0.0	9.6	COMMUNITY MUTUAL INS CO
N/A	N/A	--	--	--	--	--	--	--	--	--	--	COMPASS INS CO
0.7	0.4	229.0	66.5	12.7	N/A	57.6	21.3	78.9	276.7	355.3	0.0	COMPASS SPCLTY INS RRG INC
0.6	0.4	178.9	154.5	-11.9	-18.4	55.3	46.8	102.1	119.6	16.2	0.0	COMPTRUST AGC MUT CAPTIVE INS CO
N/A	N/A	--	--	--	--	--	--	--	--	--	--	COMPUTER INS CO
15.1	13.1	11.3	11.8	-0.3	-0.2	59.8	26.7	86.5	95.7	-67.8	0.0	COMPWEST INS CO
2.8	1.8	56.5	20.4	-2.7	-6.1	62.5	34.1	96.6	101.5	4.8	6.3 ●	CONCORD GENERAL MUTUAL INS CO
3.5	2.4	47.4	15.9	3.7	2.8	47.3	45.6	92.9	83.5	-6.9	0.0	CONEMAUGH VALLEY MUTUAL INS CO
0.4	0.3	174.3	134.7	25.6	33.7	70.8	42.3	113.1	131.4	8.9	0.0	CONIFER INS CO
1.1	0.9	9.2	47.8	2.4	1.5	126.9	43.5	170.4	55.9	-17.1	0.0 ●	CONNECTICUT MEDICAL INS CO
26.2	23.6	N/A	N/A	N/A	N/A	N/A	N/A	N/A	N/A	0.0	0.0	CONSOLIDATED INS CO

999 + Denotes number greater than 999.9%
999 - Denotes number less than -999.99%
● Bullets denote a more detailed analysis is available in Section II.

INSURANCE COMPANY NAME	DOM. STATE	RATING	TOTAL ASSETS ($MIL)	CAPITAL & SURPLUS ($MIL)	ANNUAL NET PREMIUM ($MIL)	NET INCOME ($MIL)	CAPITAL-IZATION INDEX (PTS)	RESERVE ADQ INDEX (PTS)	PROFIT-ABILITY INDEX (PTS)	LIQUIDITY INDEX (PTS)	STAB. INDEX (PTS)	STABILITY FACTORS
▲CONSTITUTION INS CO	NY	C+	25.4	22.7	0.8	1.6	10.0	4.9	8.6	6.9	3.5	DT
CONSUMER SPECIALTIES INS CO RRG	VT	D+	4.1	2.2	0.5	-0.4	7.4	8.5	1.6	9.3	2.0	DFRT
CONSUMERS COUNTY MUTUAL INS CO	TX	D	261.6	2.3	0.0	0.0	0.7	N/A	6.2	2.9	1.8	CFLT
▼CONSUMERS INS USA INC	TN	C+	65.7	26.2	21.7	-2.6	8.0	5.2	2.8	6.5	4.4	R
▲CONTINENTAL CASUALTY CO	IL	B-	43,528.3	10,726.2	6,015.6	953.2	7.8	6.6	5.4	6.9	4.8	AR
CONTINENTAL DIVIDE INS CO	CO	C+	18.4	13.3	0.0	0.4	10.0	N/A	8.9	7.0	4.7	D
CONTINENTAL HERITAGE INS CO	FL	C	29.6	25.1	7.4	-0.8	9.4	7.2	4.5	7.0	2.8	DGRT
CONTINENTAL INDEMNITY CO	IA	C	227.6	115.2	65.9	18.5	9.1	6.3	8.9	8.1	3.8	R
CONTINENTAL INS CO	PA	C	1,775.7	1,558.1	0.0	58.5	10.0	3.7	6.5	7.0	4.3	AR
CONTINENTAL INS CO OF NJ	NJ	C	19.1	19.0	0.0	0.3	10.0	N/A	6.7	10.0	3.8	ADR
CONTINENTAL MUTUAL INS CO	PA	D	1.9	1.4	1.7	0.0	7.0	6.3	8.4	6.5	1.9	DRT
CONTINENTAL RISK UNDERWRITERS RRG	NV	U (5)	--	--	--	--	N/A	--	--	--	--	Z
CONTINENTAL WESTERN INS CO	IA	C	214.8	93.9	0.0	2.1	10.0	N/A	6.9	9.1	4.3	
▲CONTINUING CARE RRG INC	VT	E+	4.2	1.4	3.9	-0.2	1.4	0.7	1.3	2.3	0.5	CDLR
CONTRACTORS BONDING & INS CO	IL	B	211.8	114.9	69.1	10.4	10.0	9.3	6.2	6.9	5.9	
CONTRACTORS INS CO OF NORTH AMER	HI	C-	37.1	20.1	2.2	-5.7	6.1	5.9	2.0	10.0	3.3	DFT
▲CONTROLLED RISK INS CO OF VT RRG	VT	B	60.9	40.7	21.6	1.8	9.1	6.5	8.0	6.9	5.4	DR
▲CONVENTUS INTER-INS	NJ	B	93.2	41.5	13.7	1.3	10.0	9.4	6.7	7.5	5.4	DR
COOPERATIVA D SEGUROS MULTIPLES D	PR	B- (1)	518.2	151.1	198.4	12.0	8.1	6.2	4.1	7.0	4.0	RT
COPIC A RRG	DC	U	--	--	--	--	N/A	--	--	--	--	Z
▼COPIC INS CO	CO	B+	603.2	297.7	100.3	7.3	9.9	9.3	4.3	7.5	6.8	
COPPERPOINT AMERICAN INS CO	AZ	C+	6.5	5.4	0.0	0.0	10.0	N/A	3.9	7.0	3.6	DF
COPPERPOINT CASUALTY INS CO	AZ	C+	7.1	4.5	0.0	-0.1	10.0	N/A	3.6	10.0	3.5	D
COPPERPOINT GENERAL INS CO	AZ	B-	15.3	9.4	0.0	-0.2	10.0	N/A	3.2	10.0	4.4	D
▲COPPERPOINT INDEMNITY INS CO	AZ	C+	11.0	7.4	0.0	-0.2	10.0	N/A	3.6	7.0	4.1	D
COPPERPOINT MUTUAL INS CO	AZ	A+	3,694.0	1,466.9	244.9	74.4	8.3	6.7	6.7	7.1	8.5	
COPPERPOINT NATIONAL INS CO	AZ	C	7.3	4.5	0.0	-0.1	10.0	N/A	2.9	9.3	3.5	D
COPPERPOINT PREMIER INS CO	AZ	U	--	--	--	--	N/A	--	--	--	--	Z
COPPERPOINT WESTERN INS CO	AZ	B-	8.6	5.0	0.0	-0.2	10.0	N/A	3.3	10.0	3.6	D
COREPOINTE INS CO	DE	C-	37.9	13.4	1.6	2.6	10.0	9.9	1.9	6.2	2.7	DFRT
CORNERSTONE MUTUAL INS CO	GA	F (5)	0.0	0.0	7.9	0.0	0.3	3.2	0.8	0.1	0.3	CDFL
▼CORNERSTONE NATIONAL INS CO	MO	D+	25.2	7.6	19.9	-1.1	5.2	6.9	1.5	0.9	2.7	DFLR
COUNTRY MUTUAL INS CO	IL	A-	4,850.2	2,567.6	2,314.8	113.3	10.0	5.3	6.8	6.1	7.3	
COUNTRY-WIDE INS CO	NY	D-	229.5	34.7	96.2	0.9	1.1	0.4	2.0	4.1	0.9	CFLR
COUNTRYWAY INS CO	NY	C	28.2	23.8	0.0	0.6	10.0	N/A	6.2	7.0	3.8	D
COUNTY HALL INS CO INC A RRG	NC	D	18.9	5.9	12.9	0.1	3.1	3.6	4.3	8.8	1.0	DGT
COURTESY INS CO	FL	B	906.6	401.7	229.6	14.2	10.0	6.0	8.3	6.9	5.1	
COVENANT INS CO	CT	C	89.3	28.8	38.9	3.3	7.8	8.3	5.8	6.3	3.7	T
▲COVERYS RRG INC	DC	C	28.8	12.1	1.5	-1.5	7.4	4.9	2.9	9.2	2.5	DGT
COVERYS SPECIALTY INS CO	NJ	B	64.6	51.1	0.0	1.1	10.0	N/A	4.9	7.0	4.3	T
▲COVINGTON SPECIALTY INS CO	NH	B+	97.9	47.3	14.2	1.3	10.0	5.9	5.3	6.9	6.5	DF
CPA MUTL INS CO OF AM (A RRG)	VT	C-	16.2	5.9	3.7	0.4	5.4	6.4	2.2	6.6	2.4	DFR
CRESTBROOK INS CO	OH	B	176.1	86.8	0.0	5.2	10.0	N/A	4.6	6.9	4.5	AFGT
CRONUS INSURANCE CO	TX	C+	28.8	22.3	8.9	2.0	10.0	N/A	8.9	7.1	4.6	DGT
▼CROSSFIT RRG INC	MT	E+	7.6	1.6	2.4	-0.4	0.5	1.9	1.8	1.3	0.8	CDLT
▲CROWN CAPTIVE INS CO	GA	D+	2.3	1.2	0.9	0.2	7.1	7.0	8.6	9.1	1.5	DGT
CROWN CAPTIVE INS CO INC	DC	D	5.0	1.7	3.1	-0.3	4.6	5.8	2.2	5.2	1.8	DFT
CRUDEN BAY RRG INC	VT	D	17.3	5.0	2.0	-2.0	7.0	10.0	2.3	7.5	1.9	D
CRUM & FORSTER INDEMNITY CO	DE	D+	53.9	17.5	18.7	1.6	7.1	6.1	6.9	8.4	2.7	DR
CRUM & FORSTER INS CO	NJ	D+	53.2	18.1	18.7	0.6	7.2	6.1	5.9	9.0	2.7	D
CRUM & FORSTER SPECIALTY INS CO	DE	D+	68.8	50.3	0.0	-0.2	10.0	N/A	6.4	10.0	2.7	FR
▼CRUSADER INS CO	CA	C+	110.8	50.4	31.6	-6.2	9.3	6.3	2.5	6.9	4.4	FR

See Page 27 for explanation of footnotes and Page 28 for explanation of stability factors.

Arrows denote recent upgrades ▲ or downgrades ▼   (see Section VII for explanations)

54

www.weissratings.com

RISK ADJ. RATIO #1	CAPITAL RATIO #2	PREMIUM TO SURPLUS (%)	RESV. TO SURPLUS (%)	RESV. DEVELOP. 1 YEAR (%)	RESV. DEVELOP. 2 YEAR (%)	LOSS RATIO (%)	EXP. RATIO (%)	COMB RATIO (%)	CASH FROM UNDER-WRITING (%)	NET PREMIUM GROWTH (%)	INVEST. IN AFFIL (%)	INSURANCE COMPANY NAME
7.9	6.0	3.7	8.3	-4.3	-9.9	2.3	208.6	210.9	198.9	-83.5	0.0	CONSTITUTION INS CO
1.7	1.2	22.8	67.7	-5.1	-7.6	94.0	88.7	182.7	66.4	-0.3	0.0	CONSUMER SPECIALTIES INS CO RRG
0.2	0.2	0.1	N/A	N/A	N/A	N/A	999 +	999 +	89.7	0.0	0.0	CONSUMERS COUNTY MUTUAL INS CO
2.4	1.6	82.7	70.7	3.8	1.6	83.5	42.0	125.5	93.3	1.1	0.0	CONSUMERS INS USA INC
1.9	1.5	56.1	162.8	-4.0	-5.6	79.7	32.2	111.9	88.0	0.3	11.1 ●	CONTINENTAL CASUALTY CO
8.6	7.8	N/A	14.9	N/A	N/A	N/A	N/A	N/A	17.8	0.0	0.0	CONTINENTAL DIVIDE INS CO
3.3	2.6	29.2	3.2	-3.0	-0.2	7.2	69.2	76.4	133.5	118.2	0.0	CONTINENTAL HERITAGE INS CO
3.6	2.9	57.2	58.6	-0.7	3.3	50.2	21.9	72.1	200.6	20.6	0.0	CONTINENTAL INDEMNITY CO
6.5	5.1	N/A	51.4	1.4	9.6	N/A	N/A	N/A	-68.7	0.0	10.3 ●	CONTINENTAL INS CO
55.9	24.3	N/A	N/A	N/A	N/A	N/A	N/A	N/A	N/A	0.0	0.0	CONTINENTAL INS CO OF NJ
1.1	1.0	115.7	4.4	-2.3	-1.8	24.5	76.8	101.3	99.3	2.4	0.0	CONTINENTAL MUTUAL INS CO
N/A	N/A	--	--	--	--	--	--	--	--	--	--	CONTINENTAL RISK UNDERWRITERS
10.2	9.1	N/A	N/A	N/A	N/A	N/A	N/A	N/A	96.5	0.0	0.0	CONTINENTAL WESTERN INS CO
0.3	0.3	289.9	158.8	42.4	87.3	56.3	36.2	92.5	111.6	-17.8	0.0	CONTINUING CARE RRG INC
4.9	3.8	60.1	47.6	-3.2	-8.7	39.0	47.1	86.1	123.4	2.0	0.0	CONTRACTORS BONDING & INS CO
1.5	0.8	11.1	64.0	9.9	18.9	324.4	47.0	371.4	51.4	-29.6	0.0	CONTRACTORS INS CO OF NORTH
2.7	2.4	53.1	38.4	-2.4	-0.8	33.2	62.1	95.3	96.9	4.2	0.0	CONTROLLED RISK INS CO OF VT RRG
4.5	3.7	33.1	71.6	-8.6	-14.5	62.8	35.7	98.5	116.9	-9.7	0.0	CONVENTUS INTER-INS
2.6	1.7	133.7	24.0	-2.1	-5.0	62.8	36.6	99.4	99.9	12.5	5.9	COOPERATIVA D SEGUROS MULTIPLES
N/A	N/A	--	--	--	--	--	--	--	--	--	--	COPIC A RRG
4.3	2.9	33.7	71.5	-3.2	-8.9	72.2	18.7	90.9	118.9	-0.1	0.0 ●	COPIC INS CO
11.4	10.3	N/A	N/A	N/A	N/A	N/A	N/A	N/A	-33.4	0.0	0.0	COPPERPOINT AMERICAN INS CO
5.1	4.6	N/A	N/A	N/A	N/A	N/A	N/A	N/A	20.4	0.0	0.0	COPPERPOINT CASUALTY INS CO
5.5	5.0	N/A	N/A	N/A	N/A	N/A	N/A	N/A	62.3	0.0	0.0	COPPERPOINT GENERAL INS CO
6.3	5.7	N/A	N/A	N/A	N/A	N/A	N/A	N/A	-129.9	0.0	0.0	COPPERPOINT INDEMNITY INS CO
2.8	1.9	16.7	138.2	-1.2	-1.5	72.7	36.4	109.1	82.0	-1.1	6.2 ●	COPPERPOINT MUTUAL INS CO
4.7	4.2	N/A	N/A	N/A	N/A	N/A	N/A	N/A	123.0	0.0	0.0	COPPERPOINT NATIONAL INS CO
N/A	N/A	--	--	--	--	--	--	--	--	--	--	COPPERPOINT PREMIER INS CO
4.2	3.8	N/A	N/A	N/A	N/A	N/A	N/A	N/A	155.8	0.0	0.0	COPPERPOINT WESTERN INS CO
3.6	3.3	12.3	1.8	-413.9	-387.0	78.0	89.4	167.4	25.1	-84.0	12.2	COREPOINTE INS CO
0.1	0.1	172.5	213.5	6.7	29.5	76.4	86.4	162.8	67.9	-17.7	0.0	CORNERSTONE MUTUAL INS CO
0.8	0.7	263.2	143.3	10.5	-6.8	92.0	25.2	117.2	67.8	-30.6	0.0	CORNERSTONE NATIONAL INS CO
4.6	3.2	90.2	43.6	-0.8	-0.5	73.4	28.2	101.6	97.5	14.4	3.8 ●	COUNTRY MUTUAL INS CO
0.3	0.2	277.1	353.7	26.4	56.3	93.8	8.2	102.0	77.3	6.1	1.3	COUNTRY-WIDE INS CO
17.5	15.7	N/A	N/A	N/A	N/A	N/A	N/A	N/A	57.0	0.0	0.0	COUNTRYWAY INS CO
0.7	0.4	219.5	79.0	-0.5	N/A	59.9	24.6	84.5	346.1	261.1	0.0	COUNTY HALL INS CO INC A RRG
7.7	4.5	57.2	6.0	0.4	0.5	85.0	5.7	90.7	165.1	78.3	0.0 ●	COURTESY INS CO
2.5	1.6	135.1	79.2	-5.2	-8.7	60.0	34.4	94.4	107.1	-4.6	0.0	COVENANT INS CO
1.7	1.2	12.5	45.1	-1.2	0.4	233.8	15.2	249.0	-36.7	67.1	0.0	COVERYS RRG INC
18.2	16.4	N/A	N/A	N/A	N/A	N/A	N/A	N/A	146.5	0.0	0.0	COVERYS SPECIALTY INS CO
5.2	3.6	30.1	43.4	2.3	2.1	73.7	28.4	102.1	86.8	-3.4	0.0 ●	COVINGTON SPECIALTY INS CO
1.0	0.8	63.7	109.4	6.1	-0.5	83.9	24.3	108.2	92.3	-6.9	0.0	CPA MUTL INS CO OF AM (A RRG)
10.1	9.1	N/A	N/A	N/A	N/A	N/A	N/A	N/A	34.6	0.0	0.0	CRESTBROOK INS CO
4.1	3.6	40.0	N/A	N/A	N/A	N/A	-10.5	-10.5	999 +	0.0	0.0	CRONUS INSURANCE CO
0.2	0.1	149.5	144.3	7.3	14.7	60.0	54.8	114.8	161.5	-5.4	0.0	CROSSFIT RRG INC
1.5	1.0	74.3	74.5	-3.7	-14.3	59.2	16.5	75.7	214.2	40.9	0.0	CROWN CAPTIVE INS CO
0.8	0.7	190.8	186.6	-11.0	-32.5	73.7	39.8	113.5	93.5	-14.8	0.0	CROWN CAPTIVE INS CO INC
1.2	1.0	39.6	218.7	-53.2	-86.9	231.6	11.1	242.7	109.3	0.0	0.0	CRUDEN BAY RRG INC
1.8	1.0	106.5	147.6	-1.1	-2.9	64.7	35.3	100.0	104.4	3.5	0.0	CRUM & FORSTER INDEMNITY CO
1.9	1.1	102.9	142.6	-1.0	-2.6	64.7	35.1	99.8	102.8	3.5	0.0	CRUM & FORSTER INS CO
15.0	13.5	N/A	N/A	N/A	N/A	N/A	N/A	N/A	-27.2	0.0	0.0	CRUM & FORSTER SPECIALTY INS CO
2.8	2.5	62.7	80.6	11.7	8.8	94.1	31.7	125.8	82.3	-3.1	0.0	CRUSADER INS CO

999 + Denotes number greater than 999.9%
999 - Denotes number less than -999.99%
● Bullets denote a more detailed analysis is available in Section II.

INSURANCE COMPANY NAME	DOM. STATE	RATING	TOTAL ASSETS ($MIL)	CAPITAL & SURPLUS ($MIL)	ANNUAL NET PREMIUM ($MIL)	NET INCOME ($MIL)	CAPITAL- IZATION INDEX (PTS)	RESERVE ADQ INDEX (PTS)	PROFIT- ABILITY INDEX (PTS)	LIQUIDITY INDEX (PTS)	STAB. INDEX (PTS)	STABILITY FACTORS
CRYSTAL RIDGE SPCLTY INS CO	IL	U	--	--	--	--	N/A	--	--	--	--	Z
CRYSTAL RUN RECIPROCAL RRG	VT	U	--	--	--	--	N/A	--	--	--	--	Z
CSAA AFFINITY INS CO	AZ	C	224.3	149.3	56.5	-3.4	10.0	6.1	3.8	6.8	3.5	R
CSAA FIRE & CASUALTY INS CO	IN	C	116.6	46.1	18.8	-0.9	10.0	6.1	4.6	6.0	3.9	F
▲CSAA GENERAL INS CO	IN	C+	361.8	142.1	112.9	-5.9	10.0	6.2	3.3	6.4	4.4	
CSAA INS EXCHANGE	CA	B-	7,168.5	3,224.6	3,541.5	-184.2	8.6	6.3	2.6	5.1	4.8	R
CSAA MID-ATLANTIC INS CO	AZ	C-	38.1	23.6	11.3	-0.6	10.0	6.1	3.9	6.8	3.2	DR
CSAA MID-ATLANTIC INS CO OF NJ	NJ	C-	52.6	22.4	22.6	-2.5	8.5	6.3	2.5	6.2	3.2	D
▼CSE SAFEGUARD INS CO	CA	C	102.9	33.8	60.4	-9.0	8.3	5.9	2.1	6.4	3.6	R
CUMBERLAND INS CO	NJ	B-	104.7	55.7	21.4	0.8	10.0	8.0	6.9	7.0	4.8	DR
CUMBERLAND MUTUAL FIRE INS CO	NJ	B-	287.2	170.5	97.9	11.7	8.5	6.1	8.1	6.8	4.8	R
CUMIS INS SOCIETY INC	IA	A-	2,002.8	911.0	906.7	45.0	10.0	9.2	8.7	6.2	7.2	
CUMIS MORTGAGE REINS CO	WI	C+	37.3	31.8	4.9	-0.4	10.0	3.6	3.8	7.4	3.1	DGT
CUMIS SPECIALTY INS CO INC	IA	B	57.0	55.5	0.0	1.9	10.0	3.9	5.4	10.0	4.1	DT
CUSA RRG INC	VT	E	3.6	2.0	1.5	0.0	8.0	N/A	3.8	7.0	0.0	DT
CYPRESS INS CO	CA	C+	1,764.8	519.2	450.1	105.0	6.3	9.4	8.7	8.1	4.4	T
CYPRESS P&C INS CO	FL	C	89.3	26.1	36.9	-2.5	7.2	7.0	1.9	6.4	3.4	F
CYPRESS TEXAS INS CO	TX	D	63.2	12.1	22.7	-0.7	2.8	9.2	2.0	7.1	2.0	DF
DAILY UNDERWRITERS OF AMERICA	PA	C+	47.1	34.7	13.6	2.2	9.0	3.4	8.8	7.6	4.8	D
DAIRYLAND COUNTY MUTUAL INS CO OF TX	TX	B	21.0	12.5	0.0	0.0	10.0	N/A	5.2	2.6	4.9	DGL
▲DAIRYLAND INS CO	WI	A-	1,400.7	477.0	368.9	29.4	9.4	7.9	5.6	6.8	7.2	
DAKOTA FIRE INS CO	ND	C	242.3	71.7	104.9	6.2	8.0	8.7	8.5	6.3	4.4	T
DAKOTA TRUCK UNDERWRITERS	SD	C+	125.4	48.3	38.5	4.7	8.1	6.7	8.9	6.6	4.4	R
▲DAN RRG INC	SC	D+	2.5	1.0	-0.2	0.0	7.6	3.6	3.5	9.1	1.4	DFT
DANBURY INS CO	MA	C	13.2	8.0	4.3	0.5	9.5	7.9	6.5	6.9	3.7	DR
DANIELSON NATIONAL INS CO	CA	U	--	--	--	--	N/A	--	--	--	--	Z
▼DB INS CO LTD (US BRANCH)	HI	E+	283.4	78.8	99.8	0.4	2.6	0.5	2.8	6.5	0.8	R
▲DB INS CO LTD US GUAM BRANCH	GU	B	78.8	46.2	14.8	3.4	10.0	8.3	8.7	7.4	5.5	T
DE SMET FARM MUTUAL INS CO OF SD	SD	C+	27.9	17.4	12.7	0.8	7.9	5.8	6.9	6.4	4.1	DR
DE SMET INS CO OF SD	SD	C	16.0	6.7	10.5	-0.5	7.3	8.4	2.9	6.0	3.7	DR
DEALERS ASR CO	OH	B-	117.1	67.3	16.1	4.4	10.0	3.6	8.8	8.5	4.7	R
DEALERS CHOICE MUTUAL INS INC	NC	C-	23.7	9.7	5.1	1.8	5.1	7.0	4.8	6.4	2.7	DF
DELAWARE GRANGE MUTUAL FIRE INS CO	DE	D	1.6	1.4	0.2	0.1	8.4	5.2	8.0	9.1	1.2	DRT
DELPHI CASUALTY CO	IL	D (1)	2.3	2.1	-0.6	0.0	9.3	1.2	3.4	2.7	2.2	DFGL
DELTA FIRE & CAS INS CO	GA	C-	7.8	5.8	2.0	-0.3	7.8	8.4	3.9	6.5	2.9	DFR
DELTA LLOYDS INS CO OF HOUSTON	TX	U	--	--	--	--	N/A	--	--	--	--	Z
DENTISTS BENEFITS INS CO	OR	C	19.0	13.2	3.9	0.5	9.1	6.8	7.6	7.8	3.6	D
DENTISTS INS CO	CA	B	351.6	198.0	66.7	6.9	8.1	8.2	6.8	6.9	6.0	T
DEPOSITORS INS CO	IA	B-	291.1	38.9	0.0	2.2	10.0	N/A	7.0	10.0	5.1	F
DEVELOPERS SURETY & INDEMNITY CO	CA	D	620.7	102.1	209.4	-18.8	0.2	9.9	3.9	7.0	2.1	CGRT
DIAMOND INS CO	IL	D	47.3	9.6	17.4	0.8	1.9	4.2	5.2	3.5	1.9	CDFL
▼DIAMOND STATE INS CO	IN	C	97.4	38.5	28.5	-2.4	7.6	6.5	2.9	6.7	4.2	FRT
DIRECT AUTO INS CO	IL	D	63.7	12.1	36.2	0.6	2.4	10.0	8.7	7.9	2.3	CD
DIRECT GENERAL INS CO	IN	C-	188.9	44.8	-146.2	21.5	8.6	4.5	1.9	0.0	3.1	FLRT
DIRECT GENERAL INS CO OF LA	LA	C-	5.5	3.7	-4.1	0.3	9.0	4.2	1.7	0.6	3.2	DFLR
DIRECT GENERAL INS CO OF MS	MS	C-	23.0	4.9	-14.0	1.3	7.2	5.9	1.9	0.0	3.2	DFLR
DIRECT INS CO	TN	C-	64.7	23.7	-33.7	2.9	8.2	6.0	4.2	2.3	3.2	DFLR
DIRECT NATIONAL INS CO	AR	C+	17.1	5.6	-5.4	0.7	7.6	6.0	2.3	5.6	3.6	DFRT
DISCOVER P&C INS CO	CT	C+	135.4	61.8	32.0	3.4	10.0	7.7	5.0	7.0	4.7	T
DISCOVER SPECIALTY INS CO	CT	C+	108.2	36.6	32.0	2.6	8.6	8.1	4.0	7.0	4.7	
▲DISCOVERY INS CO	NC	C	30.2	13.6	23.5	1.9	7.6	9.4	6.0	2.4	3.2	DL
▲DIST-CO INS CO INC A RRG	HI	E+	3.4	3.1	0.3	0.3	10.0	5.2	6.4	9.3	0.5	DT

RISK ADJ. RATIO #1	CAPITAL RATIO #2	PREMIUM TO SURPLUS (%)	RESV. TO SURPLUS (%)	RESV. DEVELOP. 1 YEAR (%)	RESV. DEVELOP. 2 YEAR (%)	LOSS RATIO (%)	EXP. RATIO (%)	COMB RATIO (%)	CASH FROM UNDER-WRITING (%)	NET PREMIUM GROWTH (%)	INVEST. IN AFFIL (%)	INSURANCE COMPANY NAME
N/A	N/A	--	--	--	--	--	--	--	--	--	--	CRYSTAL RIDGE SPCLTY INS CO
N/A	N/A	--	--	--	--	--	--	--	--	--	--	CRYSTAL RUN RECIPROCAL RRG
3.3	3.1	37.8	20.0	-1.1	-1.1	85.6	26.5	112.1	100.0	7.6	23.5	CSAA AFFINITY INS CO
6.0	5.4	40.8	21.6	-1.2	-1.2	85.6	23.0	108.6	58.3	7.6	0.0	CSAA FIRE & CASUALTY INS CO
5.4	3.8	79.5	42.1	-2.2	-2.1	85.6	22.6	108.2	104.8	7.6	0.0	CSAA GENERAL INS CO
3.1	2.0	109.8	58.1	-3.1	-3.0	85.6	26.9	112.5	96.3	7.6	3.3 •	CSAA INS EXCHANGE
5.9	4.2	47.9	25.3	-1.4	-1.4	85.6	26.1	111.7	94.9	7.6	0.0	CSAA MID-ATLANTIC INS CO
2.8	2.0	100.9	53.4	-2.7	-2.6	85.6	26.3	111.9	92.9	7.6	0.0	CSAA MID-ATLANTIC INS CO OF NJ
2.7	1.8	179.0	82.9	2.6	4.6	83.5	32.7	116.2	114.9	19.6	0.0	CSE SAFEGUARD INS CO
6.4	3.9	38.5	64.8	-1.7	-1.7	74.8	32.9	107.7	94.4	-3.8	0.0	CUMBERLAND INS CO
2.5	2.1	57.4	28.4	-0.5	1.3	53.4	36.2	89.6	104.5	2.3	20.8	CUMBERLAND MUTUAL FIRE INS CO
4.7	3.5	99.5	46.5	-4.2	-8.5	68.5	27.4	95.9	111.4	10.5	5.1 •	CUMIS INS SOCIETY INC
7.5	6.7	15.6	1.1	-0.8	-0.4	5.0	81.2	86.2	259.0	82.0	0.0	CUMIS MORTGAGE REINS CO
98.3	52.3	N/A	N/A	N/A	N/A	N/A	N/A	N/A	999 +	0.0	0.0	CUMIS SPECIALTY INS CO INC
2.7	1.6	74.4	7.9	N/A	N/A	66.0	2.9	68.9	N/A	0.0	0.0	CUSA RRG INC
1.5	1.1	86.7	186.7	-18.6	-27.3	64.0	19.5	83.5	187.0	5.0	8.2 •	CYPRESS INS CO
1.5	1.1	141.6	63.9	1.3	4.7	58.3	57.4	115.7	79.1	4.1	0.0	CYPRESS P&C INS CO
0.7	0.4	187.4	75.3	3.5	-19.3	72.9	33.6	106.5	78.7	-10.9	0.0	CYPRESS TEXAS INS CO
3.6	2.6	39.3	14.5	1.9	8.2	51.1	31.8	82.9	127.9	8.2	0.0	DAILY UNDERWRITERS OF AMERICA
5.8	5.2	N/A	N/A	N/A	N/A	N/A	N/A	N/A	105.4	0.0	0.0	DAIRYLAND COUNTY MUTUAL INS CO OF
4.0	2.5	77.3	120.5	-1.4	-2.9	74.8	28.6	103.4	101.5	4.7	0.0 •	DAIRYLAND INS CO
2.6	1.7	146.3	146.1	-4.1	-7.9	64.2	32.2	96.4	104.3	4.4	0.0	DAKOTA FIRE INS CO
2.2	1.8	79.5	106.3	-4.7	-7.7	67.3	20.9	88.2	128.6	5.0	7.4	DAKOTA TRUCK UNDERWRITERS
1.5	1.4	-22.7	4.5	0.7	N/A	-15.2	109.8	94.6	82.2	-792.5	0.0	DAN RRG INC
4.5	3.0	54.4	19.8	-1.9	-3.2	49.2	41.1	90.3	113.4	1.3	0.0	DANBURY INS CO
N/A	N/A	--	--	--	--	--	--	--	--	--	--	DANIELSON NATIONAL INS CO
0.7	0.4	126.6	173.2	-1.9	55.7	73.0	30.2	103.2	98.6	10.6	0.0	DB INS CO LTD (US BRANCH)
8.3	5.0	32.0	7.3	-1.7	-1.8	20.8	45.1	65.9	128.0	1.0	0.0	DB INS CO LTD US GUAM BRANCH
2.0	1.7	73.3	16.6	-4.6	3.2	67.7	25.2	92.9	98.9	-1.4	24.9	DE SMET FARM MUTUAL INS CO OF SD
1.6	1.2	156.2	97.3	-1.0	-6.8	94.0	15.7	109.7	99.7	3.2	0.0	DE SMET INS CO OF SD
9.9	6.6	24.0	0.5	-0.1	N/A	13.2	32.3	45.5	244.5	42.2	0.0	DEALERS ASR CO
1.4	0.9	52.6	138.3	-25.1	-46.4	61.9	28.8	90.7	66.2	-23.7	0.0	DEALERS CHOICE MUTUAL INS INC
3.1	1.9	14.6	1.9	-0.8	-0.6	41.6	50.7	92.3	142.2	2.1	0.0	DELAWARE GRANGE MUTUAL FIRE INS
18.5	16.7	-26.6	N/A	N/A	N/A	76.1	8.1	84.2	32.1	-120.9	0.0	DELPHI CASUALTY CO
1.8	1.5	34.2	4.8	-3.6	-4.5	28.7	94.6	123.3	79.2	2.3	23.9	DELTA FIRE & CAS INS CO
N/A	N/A	--	--	--	--	--	--	--	--	--	--	DELTA LLOYDS INS CO OF HOUSTON
3.8	2.5	29.4	23.6	0.6	3.0	58.8	36.7	95.5	127.4	-15.9	0.0	DENTISTS BENEFITS INS CO
2.4	1.7	33.7	46.6	0.4	-0.7	82.8	23.6	106.4	104.6	5.0	12.1	DENTISTS INS CO
3.7	3.3	N/A	N/A	N/A	N/A	N/A	N/A	N/A	-587.8	0.0	2.9	DEPOSITORS INS CO
0.2	0.1	205.1	328.8	93.8	-198.0	60.9	21.9	82.8	-10.3	N/A	5.2	DEVELOPERS SURETY & INDEMNITY CO
0.6	0.4	180.2	274.3	-2.8	31.0	64.5	31.9	96.4	87.1	-11.9	0.0	DIAMOND INS CO
2.3	1.4	74.0	87.7	0.5	-2.3	81.8	39.6	121.4	81.4	-11.7	0.0	DIAMOND STATE INS CO
0.6	0.5	300.5	310.1	-56.2	-80.9	57.6	37.0	94.6	142.3	26.8	0.0	DIRECT AUTO INS CO
4.6	4.2	-326.4	N/A	N/A	3.8	N/A	0.1	N/A	17.6	-145.2	0.0	DIRECT GENERAL INS CO
5.1	4.6	-108.9	N/A	N/A	4.5	N/A	N/A	N/A	-17.8	-141.7	0.0	DIRECT GENERAL INS CO OF LA
1.4	1.3	-286.3	N/A	N/A	3.4	N/A	-0.1	N/A	35.1	-149.7	0.0	DIRECT GENERAL INS CO OF MS
4.0	3.6	-142.4	N/A	N/A	1.9	N/A	N/A	N/A	34.3	-150.1	0.0	DIRECT INS CO
2.1	1.9	-95.8	N/A	N/A	7.2	N/A	N/A	N/A	40.1	-146.6	0.0	DIRECT NATIONAL INS CO
5.4	3.5	51.8	84.8	-1.1	-1.8	69.5	28.5	98.0	106.8	4.9	0.0	DISCOVER P&C INS CO
3.0	2.0	87.3	143.0	-1.8	-3.0	69.5	29.1	98.6	109.2	4.9	0.0	DISCOVER SPECIALTY INS CO
3.3	1.8	173.0	28.6	-4.9	-10.3	74.9	17.8	92.7	99.2	14.7	0.0	DISCOVERY INS CO
9.7	5.7	8.9	2.9	-1.1	-0.9	1.2	38.0	39.2	643.0	-37.2	0.0	DIST-CO INS CO INC A RRG

999 + Denotes number greater than 999.9%
999 - Denotes number less than -999.99%
• Bullets denote a more detailed analysis is available in Section II.

INSURANCE COMPANY NAME	DOM. STATE	RATING	TOTAL ASSETS ($MIL)	CAPITAL & SURPLUS ($MIL)	ANNUAL NET PREMIUM ($MIL)	NET INCOME ($MIL)	CAPITAL- IZATION INDEX (PTS)	RESERVE ADQ INDEX (PTS)	PROFIT- ABILITY INDEX (PTS)	LIQUIDITY INDEX (PTS)	STAB. INDEX (PTS)	STABILITY FACTORS
▲DISTRICTS MUTL INS & RISK MGMT	WI	C	25.6	15.1	5.7	1.8	8.8	9.5	6.3	7.6	3.4	D
DOCTORS & SURGEONS NATL RRG IC	VT	F (5)	9.1	1.1	5.4	0.0	1.0	4.3	0.6	7.3	0.0	CFGT
DOCTORS CO AN INTERINS	CA	B-	4,409.2	2,138.8	595.9	149.0	7.9	8.7	4.8	7.1	4.7	R
▲DOCTORS CO RRG A RECIPROCAL	DC	C	27.8	15.0	7.2	1.0	8.4	3.6	3.5	9.5	2.5	DGT
DOCTORS DIRECT INS INC	IL	C	13.5	5.9	1.7	-0.9	3.7	5.8	2.3	6.9	2.6	CDFR
DOCTORS PROF LIAB RRG INC	NC	D	5.3	1.9	2.4	-0.1	5.3	3.6	3.4	9.1	1.1	DGT
DORCHESTER INS CO LTD	VI	C	32.9	17.1	3.5	0.4	9.8	9.4	7.9	7.0	4.0	DFGR
DORCHESTER MUTUAL INS CO	MA	C	99.7	46.6	32.1	2.1	8.3	6.3	6.9	6.8	4.3	R
DORINCO REINS CO	MI	C-	1,547.9	579.7	157.3	112.1	7.5	9.3	8.6	6.8	2.6	F
▲DRIVE NEW JERSEY INS CO	NJ	B	186.4	35.9	33.6	4.0	9.9	6.6	8.5	6.7	5.2	T
DRYDEN MUTUAL INS CO	NY	B	217.7	144.7	63.1	12.3	10.0	6.0	8.8	7.0	6.0	
DTRIC INS CO LTD	HI	C	129.5	44.9	46.1	0.1	7.2	9.4	3.6	6.7	4.0	FR
DTRIC INS UNDERWRITERS LTD	HI	C	13.5	5.1	0.0	0.2	8.7	N/A	7.8	6.9	3.5	DR
DUBOIS MEDICAL RRG	DC	C	13.2	9.5	1.1	-0.2	9.7	8.9	5.8	8.1	2.9	D
EAGLE BUILDERS INS CO RRG INC	NC	D	2.5	1.5	0.8	0.0	10.0	N/A	3.2	9.1	0.6	DT
▼EAGLE WEST INS CO	CA	C-	117.9	35.2	57.7	-17.3	6.1	3.2	1.5	3.9	2.9	FL
EAGLESTONE REINS CO	PA	C	6,138.8	1,982.1	-0.1	123.7	1.1	1.6	3.7	7.0	4.2	CT
▲EASTERN ADVANTAGE ASR CO	PA	B	61.2	14.9	17.9	1.2	5.3	4.7	8.8	6.3	5.1	CD
EASTERN ALLIANCE INS CO	PA	D	341.5	109.3	99.8	9.3	8.1	4.8	8.9	6.3	1.9	R
EASTERN ATLANTIC INS CO	PA	C-	69.4	33.5	18.4	1.3	7.9	6.0	3.8	6.8	3.2	D
▲EASTERN DENTISTS INS CO RRG	VT	B	58.2	25.4	11.1	0.7	7.9	9.4	8.5	7.1	4.9	D
EASTERN MUTUAL INS CO	NY	C	26.6	17.3	6.1	0.9	10.0	9.0	8.6	6.9	4.0	D
EASTGUARD INS CO	PA	D+	180.6	52.1	57.9	6.5	1.9	8.7	8.9	7.0	2.5	CGR
▼ECHELON P&C INS CO	IL	E	14.6	2.4	7.0	-1.8	0.1	1.4	0.8	2.6	0.2	CDLR
ECOLE INS CO	AZ	D	15.1	7.7	3.9	0.2	1.5	6.8	4.6	7.3	2.0	CDT
ECONOMY FIRE & CAS CO	IL	B-	511.9	390.6	0.0	18.0	10.0	N/A	6.8	7.0	5.1	
ECONOMY PREFERRED INS CO	IL	B	61.2	14.0	0.0	0.3	8.4	N/A	7.6	7.0	4.9	DG
ECONOMY PREMIER ASR CO	IL	B	80.9	47.0	0.0	1.6	10.0	N/A	6.1	7.0	5.7	T
EDISON INS CO	FL	D+	65.9	21.1	32.5	-2.2	0.9	3.1	3.4	1.3	2.4	CDGL
ELECTRIC INS CO	MA	C+	1,424.1	491.5	279.1	32.6	8.8	9.3	3.8	6.8	3.4	R
ELEPHANT INS CO	VA	C	215.9	56.9	72.8	-16.1	7.0	6.0	2.3	3.2	4.3	FLT
ELITE TRANSPORTATION RRG INC	VT	E-	9.3	-2.4	5.1	-4.4	0.0	0.4	0.4	7.0	0.0	CDFT
ELIZABETHTOWN INS CO	DE	U (5)	--	--	--	--	N/A	--	--	--	--	Z
ELLINGTON MUTUAL INS CO	WI	D+	6.4	3.8	2.7	-0.5	7.2	6.9	3.2	6.2	2.2	DFR
EMC PROPERTY & CASUALTY CO	IA	C	88.5	82.9	0.0	2.2	10.0	4.7	6.4	7.0	4.2	T
EMC REINS CO	IA	B-	492.3	215.7	132.3	1.2	8.0	9.3	8.1	6.6	4.8	T
EMCASCO INS CO	IA	B-	510.9	156.5	217.8	13.1	8.1	8.7	8.6	6.4	4.8	T
EMERGENCY CAP MGMT LLC A RRG	VT	D	9.1	3.4	3.0	0.6	2.1	3.1	3.9	6.8	2.0	CDG
EMERGENCY MEDICINE PROFESSIONAL	NV	C	18.7	8.3	5.5	-0.3	7.1	9.4	5.4	6.7	4.2	DFR
EMERGENCY PHYSICIANS INS RRG	VT	C	22.9	8.1	4.6	-1.6	3.4	5.0	1.9	6.9	2.9	CDFR
EMPIRE BONDING & INS CO	NY	B-	4.0	2.5	1.0	0.3	10.0	7.6	8.7	9.3	3.5	D
EMPIRE FIRE & MARINE INS CO	NE	C+	50.9	39.4	0.0	0.7	10.0	N/A	3.9	7.0	4.6	FRT
EMPIRE INDEMNITY INS CO	OK	C+	61.7	52.4	0.0	0.8	10.0	N/A	6.7	7.0	4.6	R
EMPIRE INS CO	NY	U	--	--	--	--	N/A	--	--	--	--	Z
EMPLOYERS ASSURANCE CO	FL	C	484.8	189.6	86.8	14.0	8.8	7.6	4.6	6.8	3.3	R
EMPLOYERS COMPENSATION INS CO	CA	A-	1,091.0	345.3	253.3	48.4	7.6	7.8	7.3	7.0	6.9	
EMPLOYERS FIRE INS CO	PA	U	--	--	--	--	N/A	--	--	--	--	Z
▲EMPLOYERS INS CO OF NV	NV	C	577.5	198.7	130.3	25.8	7.1	7.8	2.8	7.0	3.5	RT
EMPLOYERS INS OF WAUSAU	WI	B-	6,056.4	1,521.5	2,284.0	-48.1	8.0	5.7	5.0	6.2	5.1	A
EMPLOYERS MUTUAL CAS CO	IA	B-	3,404.4	1,436.6	1,172.9	59.3	8.0	7.9	8.1	6.3	4.8	R
EMPLOYERS NATIONAL INS CO (MN)	OK	U	--	--	--	--	N/A	--	--	--	--	Z
EMPLOYERS PREFERRED INS CO	FL	C	966.4	158.8	253.3	28.5	4.5	7.8	3.3	6.2	3.3	CRT

See Page 27 for explanation of footnotes and   58   www.weissratings.com
Page 28 for explanation of stability factors.
Arrows denote recent upgrades ▲ or downgrades ▼   (see Section VII for explanations)

RISK ADJ. CAPITAL RATIO #1	RATIO #2	PREMIUM TO SURPLUS (%)	RESV. TO SURPLUS (%)	RESV. 1 YEAR (%)	DEVELOP. 2 YEAR (%)	LOSS RATIO (%)	EXP. RATIO (%)	COMB RATIO (%)	CASH FROM UNDER-WRITING (%)	NET PREMIUM GROWTH (%)	INVEST. IN AFFIL (%)	INSURANCE COMPANY NAME
3.9	2.4	38.0	45.7	-18.9	-22.3	37.7	49.6	87.3	110.4	5.9	0.0	DISTRICTS MUTL INS & RISK MGMT
0.2	0.2	302.1	366.1	-138.9	-29.6	67.7	32.1	99.8	80.1	44.6	0.0	DOCTORS & SURGEONS NATL RRG IC
2.1	1.6	27.9	72.8	-3.2	-6.0	77.0	24.8	101.8	109.7	-1.1	14.7 ●	DOCTORS CO AN INTERINS
4.1	2.6	47.7	27.5	2.5	2.2	164.0	-39.9	124.1	-79.6	568.5	0.0	DOCTORS CO RRG A RECIPROCAL
0.7	0.5	29.1	98.7	20.0	18.2	131.6	67.4	199.0	52.3	-24.1	0.0	DOCTORS DIRECT INS INC
1.2	0.7	122.4	55.0	-0.9	N/A	66.3	25.7	92.0	403.1	188.2	0.0	DOCTORS PROF LIAB RRG INC
4.2	2.8	20.2	28.3	0.1	-8.5	58.0	56.0	114.0	82.4	-11.9	0.0	DORCHESTER INS CO LTD
2.7	1.9	69.0	45.7	-2.1	-6.2	57.2	39.4	96.6	124.5	7.0	7.4	DORCHESTER MUTUAL INS CO
2.9	1.9	27.1	137.5	-13.7	-17.5	72.8	20.6	93.4	102.3	-8.9	0.0 ●	DORINCO REINS CO
3.8	3.2	93.6	68.2	-4.0	-6.1	65.9	18.8	84.7	138.9	9.4	0.0	DRIVE NEW JERSEY INS CO
7.6	5.0	43.6	19.4	1.9	1.1	40.2	39.7	79.9	120.0	3.3	0.0	DRYDEN MUTUAL INS CO
2.6	1.7	102.7	96.4	-4.3	-25.2	66.3	35.1	101.4	95.0	-4.3	5.1	DTRIC INS CO LTD
2.3	2.1	N/A	N/A	N/A	N/A	N/A	N/A	N/A	192.2	0.0	0.0	DTRIC INS UNDERWRITERS LTD
4.2	2.8	11.9	30.0	-1.2	-1.9	127.7	23.4	151.1	88.9	17.0	0.0	DUBOIS MEDICAL RRG
3.4	3.1	50.0	1.1	N/A	N/A	40.0	-4.0	36.0	257.1	0.0	0.0	EAGLE BUILDERS INS CO RRG INC
1.4	0.8	163.6	154.1	20.0	27.8	100.6	35.7	136.3	85.2	-1.7	0.0	EAGLE WEST INS CO
0.3	0.2	N/A	279.8	-1.7	18.4	382.2	999 +	999 +	N/A	-103.2	0.0 ●	EAGLESTONE REINS CO
1.2	1.0	119.9	100.7	-3.9	0.5	65.1	24.2	89.3	139.7	5.0	0.0	EASTERN ADVANTAGE ASR CO
2.2	1.7	91.4	79.2	-2.3	0.6	66.0	24.9	90.9	102.1	2.1	0.0	EASTERN ALLIANCE INS CO
2.3	1.6	54.9	66.5	-10.9	2.8	65.1	37.7	102.8	93.9	1.7	0.0	EASTERN ATLANTIC INS CO
1.8	1.5	43.6	91.3	-5.5	-15.2	49.2	45.2	94.4	117.0	3.3	0.0	EASTERN DENTISTS INS CO RRG
4.5	2.9	35.1	22.9	-4.3	-8.2	53.7	37.0	90.7	114.9	2.6	0.3	EASTERN MUTUAL INS CO
0.4	0.3	111.0	120.7	-6.3	-8.0	57.8	24.0	81.8	133.7	26.0	0.0	EASTGUARD INS CO
0.1	0.1	289.8	284.9	23.5	48.0	95.1	36.4	131.5	98.4	-5.2	1.2	ECHELON P&C INS CO
0.3	0.3	50.3	56.7	-7.3	-10.1	81.5	12.8	94.3	191.2	-9.3	0.0	ECOLE INS CO
6.5	5.9	N/A	N/A	N/A	N/A	N/A	N/A	N/A	N/A	0.0	15.7 ●	ECONOMY FIRE & CAS CO
2.1	1.9	N/A	N/A	N/A	N/A	N/A	N/A	N/A	N/A	0.0	0.0	ECONOMY PREFERRED INS CO
9.3	8.4	N/A	N/A	N/A	N/A	N/A	N/A	N/A	N/A	0.0	0.0	ECONOMY PREMIER ASR CO
0.3	0.2	154.3	67.0	5.3	3.4	85.2	24.5	109.7	140.2	17.1	0.0	EDISON INS CO
3.8	2.2	56.8	158.4	-5.0	-13.2	82.3	24.0	106.3	89.8	-15.3	2.3 ●	ELECTRIC INS CO
1.5	1.1	127.9	51.3	2.6	0.1	87.6	35.2	122.8	79.5	7.5	0.0	ELEPHANT INS CO
-0.1	-0.1	-210.3	-430.4	332.1	132.1	147.0	11.7	158.7	69.6	-16.8	0.0	ELITE TRANSPORTATION RRG INC
N/A	N/A	--	--	--	--	--	--	--	--	--	--	ELIZABETHTOWN INS CO
1.8	1.1	72.6	8.2	-2.4	-4.1	76.8	41.8	118.6	84.4	10.4	0.0	ELLINGTON MUTUAL INS CO
50.9	44.8	N/A	N/A	N/A	N/A	N/A	N/A	N/A	N/A	100.0	0.0	EMC PROPERTY & CASUALTY CO
2.4	1.7	61.3	102.3	-1.8	-9.8	88.3	22.9	111.2	102.8	0.9	0.0	EMC REINS CO
2.8	1.9	139.2	138.9	-3.9	-7.6	64.2	32.2	96.4	104.3	4.4	0.0	EMCASCO INS CO
0.6	0.3	88.1	146.8	-0.3	-3.0	60.8	10.4	71.2	442.3	116.8	0.0	EMERGENCY CAP MGMT LLC A RRG
1.5	1.0	65.6	69.2	23.5	-17.3	75.6	35.2	110.8	79.8	-8.3	0.0	EMERGENCY MEDICINE PROFESSIONAL
0.6	0.5	56.8	146.1	14.8	21.6	96.2	41.5	137.7	40.1	15.0	0.0	EMERGENCY PHYSICIANS INS RRG
4.2	3.8	38.7	7.3	N/A	-2.3	7.4	46.2	53.6	195.7	12.0	0.0	EMPIRE BONDING & INS CO
15.2	13.6	N/A	N/A	N/A	N/A	N/A	N/A	N/A	160.7	0.0	0.0	EMPIRE FIRE & MARINE INS CO
22.7	20.4	N/A	N/A	N/A	N/A	N/A	N/A	N/A	-25.5	0.0	0.0	EMPIRE INDEMNITY INS CO
N/A	N/A	--	--	--	--	--	--	--	--	--	--	EMPIRE INS CO
3.1	2.2	45.8	109.4	-0.8	-1.2	59.8	30.3	90.1	100.4	4.2	0.0	EMPLOYERS ASSURANCE CO
2.0	1.4	73.3	175.2	-1.2	-2.3	59.8	30.4	90.2	109.7	4.2	0.0 ●	EMPLOYERS COMPENSATION INS CO
N/A	N/A	--	--	--	--	--	--	--	--	--	--	EMPLOYERS FIRE INS CO
2.0	1.3	65.6	156.7	-1.5	-0.9	59.8	29.4	89.2	108.2	4.2	0.0	EMPLOYERS INS CO OF NV
2.3	1.6	150.1	206.7	4.4	5.0	79.5	29.0	108.5	100.0	7.7	2.8 ●	EMPLOYERS INS OF WAUSAU
2.1	1.6	81.6	83.0	-1.8	-4.1	69.7	31.2	100.9	102.3	4.4	18.5 ●	EMPLOYERS MUTUAL CAS CO
N/A	N/A	--	--	--	--	--	--	--	--	--	--	EMPLOYERS NATIONAL INS CO (MN)
0.9	0.6	159.5	381.2	-3.2	-2.7	59.8	30.2	90.0	124.3	4.2	0.0	EMPLOYERS PREFERRED INS CO

999 + Denotes number greater than 999.9%
999 - Denotes number less than -999.99%
● Bullets denote a more detailed analysis is available in Section II.

INSURANCE COMPANY NAME	DOM. STATE	RATING	TOTAL ASSETS ($MIL)	CAPITAL & SURPLUS ($MIL)	ANNUAL NET PREMIUM ($MIL)	NET INCOME ($MIL)	CAPITAL- IZATION INDEX (PTS)	RESERVE ADQ INDEX (PTS)	PROFIT- ABILITY INDEX (PTS)	LIQUIDITY INDEX (PTS)	STAB. INDEX (PTS)	STABILITY FACTORS
ENCOMPASS FLORIDIAN INDEMNITY CO	IL	U	--	--	--	--	N/A	--	--	--	--	Z
ENCOMPASS FLORIDIAN INS CO	IL	U	--	--	--	--	N/A	--	--	--	--	Z
ENCOMPASS HOME & AUTO INS CO	IL	B-	19.1	18.1	0.0	0.3	10.0	N/A	7.1	7.0	4.9	D
ENCOMPASS INDEMNITY CO	IL	B	27.9	25.8	0.0	0.4	10.0	N/A	5.7	10.0	5.7	DT
ENCOMPASS INDEPENDENT INS CO	IL	B-	6.2	6.1	0.0	0.2	10.0	N/A	3.5	7.0	3.8	D
ENCOMPASS INS CO	IL	C+	9.4	9.1	0.0	0.2	10.0	N/A	3.9	7.0	4.3	D
▲ENCOMPASS INS CO OF AM	IL	B-	20.2	19.8	0.0	0.5	10.0	N/A	5.2	7.0	4.9	D
ENCOMPASS INS CO OF MA	MA	C+	6.1	5.9	0.0	0.1	10.0	N/A	3.9	7.0	3.6	DT
ENCOMPASS INS CO OF NJ	IL	C+	24.6	24.4	0.0	0.4	10.0	N/A	3.4	7.0	4.5	DT
ENCOMPASS PROP & CAS INS CO OF NJ	IL	C+	11.1	11.0	0.0	0.2	10.0	N/A	3.4	7.0	4.6	D
ENCOMPASS PROPERTY & CASUALTY CO	IL	B-	10.2	9.8	0.0	0.2	10.0	N/A	4.8	10.0	4.4	D
ENDEAVOUR INS CO	MA	C+	6.3	6.3	0.0	0.1	10.0	N/A	7.5	7.0	3.8	DR
▲ENDURANCE AMERICAN INS CO	DE	B	1,794.7	426.9	321.9	-11.9	7.4	5.7	4.2	6.7	5.5	G
▲ENDURANCE AMERICAN SPECIALTY INS CO	DE	B-	453.7	100.0	164.0	-6.0	5.5	4.7	4.0	6.7	5.2	F
ENDURANCE ASR CORP	DE	A-	2,059.0	891.5	377.8	-11.3	8.0	8.6	4.8	7.4	7.2	
▲ENDURANCE RISK SOLUTIONS ASR CO	DE	B-	255.9	68.3	121.5	-4.7	5.4	4.5	4.0	5.9	5.1	C
ENUMCLAW P&C INS CO	OR	C+	8.2	8.1	0.0	0.1	10.0	N/A	6.4	7.0	4.1	D
EQUITABLE LIABILITY INS CO	DC	D	2.5	1.1	0.9	-0.1	7.1	9.5	2.5	8.4	1.3	DFT
EQUITY INS CO	TX	C	86.1	30.4	62.1	-0.5	7.2	6.0	3.5	5.5	3.2	R
▲ERIE & NIAGARA INS ASSN	NY	B+	234.3	160.5	70.8	13.0	10.0	6.0	8.8	6.9	6.5	
ERIE INS CO	PA	B-	1,039.0	374.3	331.5	22.1	10.0	7.8	8.4	6.5	4.9	T
ERIE INS CO OF NEW YORK	NY	B	112.9	33.4	33.1	1.5	9.5	7.9	8.0	6.5	5.1	T
ERIE INS EXCHANGE	PA	B	16,974.6	8,802.8	6,264.4	628.9	9.5	7.7	8.6	6.4	5.1	
ERIE INS P&C CO	PA	B-	110.4	12.6	0.0	0.2	7.4	N/A	7.1	7.0	4.7	D
ESSENT GUARANTY INC	PA	A-	1,756.6	761.0	423.3	261.8	10.0	5.3	9.6	7.6	6.7	GT
ESSENT GUARANTY OF PA INC	PA	B	93.1	45.5	12.0	10.3	10.0	5.3	8.2	8.0	5.9	D
ESSENTIA INS CO	MO	C	81.8	31.1	-13.2	5.6	10.0	3.6	4.3	6.8	4.0	AFRT
ESURANCE INS CO	WI	C	191.5	165.2	0.0	1.4	10.0	N/A	4.9	10.0	3.9	R
ESURANCE INS CO OF NJ	WI	C	14.0	12.0	0.0	0.1	10.0	N/A	6.0	7.0	3.9	DR
ESURANCE P&C INS CO	WI	C	115.2	42.8	0.0	0.5	10.0	N/A	7.6	6.7	3.9	FR
ETHIO-AMERICAN INS CO	GA	D+	10.7	3.1	5.8	-0.4	5.6	4.2	2.2	6.9	2.2	DF
EULER HERMES NORTH AMERICA INS CO	MD	B	445.6	157.6	102.9	16.6	10.0	9.1	8.7	7.8	6.0	T
EVER-GREENE MUTUAL INS CO	PA	C	6.4	6.3	0.4	0.4	10.0	7.3	8.7	9.3	3.5	D
EVEREST DENALI INSURANCE CO	DE	U	--	--	--	--	N/A	--	--	--	--	Z
EVEREST INDEMNITY INS CO	DE	C	212.5	65.9	0.0	7.7	10.0	3.5	8.7	6.6	3.9	FR
▼EVEREST NATIONAL INS CO	DE	C	808.5	156.0	0.0	24.8	10.0	2.6	5.4	7.0	4.0	FRT
EVEREST PREMIER INSURANCE CO	DE	B-	25.7	25.3	0.0	0.3	10.0	N/A	4.9	10.0	5.0	DT
EVEREST REINS CO	DE	B-	9,486.1	3,391.9	1,741.2	-391.4	8.0	6.3	5.3	6.6	4.7	FRT
EVEREST SECURITY INS CO	GA	C	36.3	23.6	0.0	2.2	10.0	3.6	8.7	7.0	3.7	DFR
EVERETT CASH MUTUAL INS CO	PA	B-	131.7	62.9	63.2	2.5	8.1	6.0	6.2	6.0	4.6	R
EVERGREEN NATIONAL INDEMNITY CO	OH	C	48.1	34.5	11.7	3.8	8.8	8.9	7.9	7.1	4.2	R
EVERGREEN USA RRG INC	VT	U (4)	--	--	--	--	N/A	--	--	--	--	Z
EVERSPAN FINANCIAL GUARANTEE CORP	WI	U	--	--	--	--	N/A	--	--	--	--	Z
EXACT PROPERTY & CASUALTY CO INC	CA	C+	267.7	116.1	141.8	1.7	9.7	5.9	5.2	6.5	4.7	FR
EXCALIBUR NATIONAL INS CO	LA	C-	14.5	7.2	8.9	-1.0	5.0	3.6	1.9	8.2	2.3	DGT
EXCALIBUR REINS CORP	PA	U (5)	--	--	--	--	N/A	--	--	--	--	Z
EXCELA RECIPROCAL RRG	VT	E	12.7	2.0	3.7	-1.0	0.2	0.2	1.9	7.0	0.3	CDGT
EXCELSIOR INS CO	NH	C	36.7	35.9	0.0	0.4	10.0	N/A	6.3	7.0	4.3	R
EXCESS SHARE INS CORP	OH	C	53.3	21.8	1.8	0.5	10.0	9.1	5.8	10.0	4.3	D
EXECUTIVE INS CO	NY	U	--	--	--	--	N/A	--	--	--	--	Z
▲EXECUTIVE RISK INDEMNITY INC	DE	B	3,231.3	1,489.6	406.2	131.3	9.4	8.7	8.6	6.9	5.5	F
EXECUTIVE RISK SPECIALTY INS CO	CT	B-	288.7	184.7	25.4	10.0	10.0	8.0	8.7	8.0	4.9	F

See Page 27 for explanation of footnotes and Page 28 for explanation of stability factors.

Arrows denote recent upgrades ▲ or downgrades ▼   (see Section VII for explanations)

60

www.weissratings.com

RISK ADJ. RATIO #1	CAPITAL RATIO #2	PREMIUM TO SURPLUS (%)	RESV. TO SURPLUS (%)	RESV. DEVELOP. 1 YEAR (%)	RESV. DEVELOP. 2 YEAR (%)	LOSS RATIO (%)	EXP. RATIO (%)	COMB RATIO (%)	CASH FROM UNDER-WRITING (%)	NET PREMIUM GROWTH (%)	INVEST. IN AFFIL (%)	INSURANCE COMPANY NAME
N/A	N/A	--	--	--	--	--	--	--	--	--	--	ENCOMPASS FLORIDIAN INDEMNITY CO
N/A	N/A	--	--	--	--	--	--	--	--	--	--	ENCOMPASS FLORIDIAN INS CO
40.9	36.8	N/A	N/A	N/A	N/A	N/A	N/A	N/A	999 +	0.0	0.0	ENCOMPASS HOME & AUTO INS CO
35.2	31.7	N/A	N/A	N/A	N/A	N/A	N/A	N/A	-234.4	0.0	0.0	ENCOMPASS INDEMNITY CO
114.5	103.1	N/A	N/A	N/A	N/A	N/A	N/A	N/A	N/A	0.0	0.0	ENCOMPASS INDEPENDENT INS CO
97.1	75.6	N/A	N/A	N/A	N/A	N/A	N/A	N/A	N/A	0.0	0.0	ENCOMPASS INS CO
98.9	48.9	N/A	N/A	N/A	N/A	N/A	N/A	N/A	999 +	0.0	0.0	ENCOMPASS INS CO OF AM
97.9	88.1	N/A	N/A	N/A	N/A	N/A	N/A	N/A	N/A	0.0	0.0	ENCOMPASS INS CO OF MA
114.7	57.2	N/A	N/A	N/A	N/A	N/A	N/A	N/A	326.3	0.0	0.0	ENCOMPASS INS CO OF NJ
103.1	51.0	N/A	N/A	N/A	N/A	N/A	N/A	N/A	510.0	0.0	0.0	ENCOMPASS PROP & CAS INS CO OF NJ
57.2	51.5	N/A	N/A	N/A	N/A	N/A	N/A	N/A	-131.0	0.0	0.0	ENCOMPASS PROPERTY & CASUALTY
88.3	43.2	N/A	N/A	N/A	N/A	N/A	N/A	N/A	N/A	0.0	0.0	ENDEAVOUR INS CO
2.7	1.7	75.4	75.0	4.7	6.7	94.1	12.0	106.1	106.2	26.8	12.0 ●	ENDURANCE AMERICAN INS CO
1.6	0.9	164.0	163.1	6.5	9.2	94.1	12.0	106.1	72.2	26.8	0.0	ENDURANCE AMERICAN SPECIALTY INS
1.8	1.6	42.4	67.8	-1.9	-5.9	72.9	32.2	105.1	132.8	26.4	30.5 ●	ENDURANCE ASR CORP
1.5	0.8	177.9	176.9	7.0	10.0	94.1	12.0	106.1	110.5	26.8	0.0	ENDURANCE RISK SOLUTIONS ASR CO
93.5	57.4	N/A	N/A	N/A	N/A	N/A	N/A	N/A	N/A	0.0	0.0	ENUMCLAW P&C INS CO
1.4	1.0	83.6	129.6	8.6	-15.5	74.0	36.7	110.7	68.9	-19.5	0.0	EQUITABLE LIABILITY INS CO
1.1	1.1	204.0	93.1	5.3	3.4	88.7	14.0	102.7	94.5	16.4	0.0	EQUITY INS CO
7.3	4.8	44.1	13.2	0.4	0.7	43.4	38.3	81.7	131.0	6.5	0.1 ●	ERIE & NIAGARA INS ASSN
5.3	3.7	88.5	57.8	-1.0	-2.5	68.6	27.9	96.5	105.6	6.0	5.0 ●	ERIE INS CO
4.1	2.8	99.2	64.8	-1.2	-2.8	68.6	27.9	96.5	103.5	6.0	0.0	ERIE INS CO OF NEW YORK
4.1	2.7	71.2	46.4	-0.9	-2.2	68.6	27.9	96.5	106.6	6.0	4.5 ●	ERIE INS EXCHANGE
1.4	1.2	N/A	N/A	N/A	N/A	N/A	N/A	N/A	N/A	0.0	0.0	ERIE INS P&C CO
13.1	7.5	55.6	4.8	-1.5	-1.2	5.2	25.1	30.3	409.3	24.3	0.0 ●	ESSENT GUARANTY INC
7.0	6.3	26.4	3.0	-1.1	-1.4	2.4	29.8	32.2	288.1	-18.9	0.0	ESSENT GUARANTY OF PA INC
4.5	4.1	-42.6	N/A	N/A	-0.4	N/A	51.3	N/A	-364.4	-149.2	0.0	ESSENTIA INS CO
3.2	3.1	N/A	N/A	N/A	N/A	N/A	N/A	N/A	101.8	0.0	38.6	ESURANCE INS CO
16.2	14.5	N/A	N/A	N/A	N/A	N/A	N/A	N/A	N/A	0.0	0.0	ESURANCE INS CO OF NJ
5.5	4.9	N/A	N/A	N/A	N/A	N/A	N/A	N/A	-24.1	0.0	0.0	ESURANCE P&C INS CO
1.1	0.8	186.8	170.4	2.0	-4.0	79.8	29.3	109.1	96.9	-11.9	0.0	ETHIO-AMERICAN INS CO
6.6	4.1	65.3	32.1	-6.5	-3.8	52.1	24.2	76.3	124.6	25.6	0.0	EULER HERMES NORTH AMERICA INS
80.1	40.9	6.3	0.4	-0.3	-0.5	20.3	23.4	43.7	218.5	0.0	0.0	EVER-GREENE MUTUAL INS CO
N/A	N/A	--	--	--	--	--	--	--	--	--	--	EVEREST DENALI INSURANCE CO
6.9	6.2	N/A	N/A	N/A	N/A	N/A	N/A	N/A	64.2	0.0	0.0	EVEREST INDEMNITY INS CO
9.9	8.9	N/A	N/A	N/A	N/A	N/A	N/A	N/A	130.3	0.0	0.0	EVEREST NATIONAL INS CO
98.3	45.2	N/A	N/A	N/A	N/A	N/A	N/A	N/A	268.4	0.0	0.0	EVEREST PREMIER INSURANCE CO
2.4	1.6	51.3	107.9	-3.9	-6.9	105.2	43.5	148.7	47.2	-15.1	4.5 ●	EVEREST REINS CO
8.5	7.7	N/A	N/A	N/A	N/A	N/A	N/A	N/A	347.2	0.0	0.0	EVEREST SECURITY INS CO
2.4	1.7	100.4	52.8	4.0	4.2	72.9	27.5	100.4	107.6	3.1	6.8	EVERETT CASH MUTUAL INS CO
3.1	2.2	33.9	13.3	-7.8	-8.7	7.7	68.3	76.0	131.7	-3.2	0.0	EVERGREEN NATIONAL INDEMNITY CO
N/A	N/A	--	--	--	--	--	--	--	--	--	--	EVERGREEN USA RRG INC
N/A	N/A	--	--	--	--	--	--	--	--	--	--	EVERSPAN FINANCIAL GUARANTEE
4.0	2.9	122.2	72.2	-0.3	1.3	69.5	32.9	102.4	94.3	-3.9	0.0	EXACT PROPERTY & CASUALTY CO INC
1.0	0.5	124.5	9.9	-0.1	N/A	51.8	43.0	94.8	119.2	284.6	0.0	EXCALIBUR NATIONAL INS CO
N/A	N/A	--	--	--	--	--	--	--	--	--	--	EXCALIBUR REINS CORP
0.1	0.1	186.3	532.6	82.8	91.7	121.9	9.0	130.9	232.1	14.5	0.0	EXCELA RECIPROCAL RRG
95.6	77.2	N/A	N/A	N/A	N/A	N/A	N/A	N/A	N/A	0.0	0.0	EXCELSIOR INS CO
4.8	4.3	8.4	10.5	-6.2	-9.3	3.3	90.9	94.2	107.6	7.9	0.0	EXCESS SHARE INS CORP
N/A	N/A	--	--	--	--	--	--	--	--	--	--	EXECUTIVE INS CO
3.3	2.7	27.3	77.4	-3.7	-8.3	62.6	25.4	88.0	73.0	-19.9	13.8 ●	EXECUTIVE RISK INDEMNITY INC
8.6	5.4	13.7	39.0	-1.6	-4.0	62.6	25.4	88.0	71.0	-19.9	0.0	EXECUTIVE RISK SPECIALTY INS CO

999 + Denotes number greater than 999.9%
999 - Denotes number less than -999.99%
● Bullets denote a more detailed analysis is available in Section II.

INSURANCE COMPANY NAME	DOM. STATE	RATING	TOTAL ASSETS ($MIL)	CAPITAL & SURPLUS ($MIL)	ANNUAL NET PREMIUM ($MIL)	NET INCOME ($MIL)	CAPITAL-IZATION INDEX (PTS)	RESERVE ADQ INDEX (PTS)	PROFIT-ABILITY INDEX (PTS)	LIQUIDITY INDEX (PTS)	STAB. INDEX (PTS)	STABILITY FACTORS
EXPLORER INS CO	CA	C	401.3	143.5	145.1	18.3	7.2	6.4	8.9	6.6	3.7	R
FACILITY INS CORP	TX	U	--	--	--	--	N/A	--	--	--	--	Z
FACTORY MUTUAL INS CO	RI	B-	19,155.5	12,501.8	2,894.6	-333.4	8.3	6.2	5.1	6.8	4.7	R
FAIR AMERICAN INS & REINS CO	NY	B-	211.3	193.9	4.0	3.8	10.0	5.1	3.6	9.7	5.3	
FAIR AMERICAN SELECT INS CO	DE	B	112.8	102.8	2.5	-0.5	10.0	4.6	6.8	7.6	4.7	GT
FAIRMONT FARMERS MUTUAL INS CO	MN	C+	35.4	20.3	16.2	0.5	10.0	7.7	8.7	6.8	4.3	D
FAIRWAY PHYSICIANS INS CO RRG	DC	E- (2)	9.5	0.0	3.8	-0.1	2.1	1.1	0.2	2.3	0.0	CDFG
FALCON INS CO	IL	D+	37.1	11.3	15.3	0.2	2.7	2.9	3.2	6.5	2.3	CDFT
▲FALLS LAKE FIRE & CASUALTY CO	CA	C+	88.0	15.3	4.9	0.6	7.7	3.7	4.3	8.5	3.1	DGT
FALLS LAKE GENERAL INS CO	OH	C	12.2	5.3	2.5	0.2	7.2	8.6	4.2	7.2	2.9	DT
▲FALLS LAKE NATIONAL INS CO	OH	B	321.9	58.1	5.8	0.7	7.3	8.5	7.2	7.0	5.3	T
FAMILY SECURITY INS CO	HI	C+	83.7	22.0	70.9	-1.4	4.0	5.8	3.6	6.5	3.2	CDGT
▲FARM BU TOWN & COUNTRY INS CO OF MO	MO	B+	421.4	191.3	216.1	5.8	9.0	7.6	8.5	5.4	6.5	L
FARM BUREAU CNTY MUTUAL INS CO OF	TX	C	18.8	6.0	0.0	0.1	8.5	N/A	6.0	7.0	3.6	D
▲FARM BUREAU GENERAL INS CO OF MI	MI	B+	719.9	321.1	350.9	14.3	9.9	6.2	6.9	5.7	6.5	L
FARM BUREAU INS OF NC INC	NC	B	10.0	9.7	0.0	0.2	10.0	N/A	7.1	7.0	4.3	D
FARM BUREAU MUTUAL INS CO OF AR	AR	B	408.6	253.3	197.6	13.5	10.0	7.9	8.9	6.1	6.1	
FARM BUREAU MUTUAL INS CO OF ID	ID	B	467.0	241.0	197.7	-13.6	8.7	6.0	3.6	6.0	4.7	F
▲FARM BUREAU MUTUAL INS CO OF MI	MI	B+	782.4	406.5	352.7	29.1	10.0	8.4	8.7	6.0	6.5	
▲FARM BUREAU P&C INS CO	IA	A-	2,532.4	1,303.7	1,238.8	117.1	10.0	8.2	8.9	6.0	7.2	
▲FARM CREDIT SYS ASSOC CAPTIVE INS CO	CO	B	113.3	84.4	17.3	5.4	10.0	9.3	7.3	7.2	5.5	D
FARM FAMILY CASUALTY INS CO	NY	B+	1,241.7	481.4	444.4	57.6	9.7	9.3	8.4	6.6	6.8	
FARMERS & MECH MU I ASN OF CECIL CTY	MD	D	1.1	0.4	0.7	0.1	7.2	7.7	2.3	7.0	0.9	DFRT
FARMERS & MECH MUTUAL INS CO	PA	B	6.4	5.5	0.3	0.2	8.0	5.2	8.3	7.6	4.5	AD
FARMERS & MECHANICS FIRE & CAS INS	WV	C	12.8	5.3	6.5	0.2	7.2	5.8	4.9	6.0	3.6	DR
▲FARMERS & MECHANICS MUTUAL IC OF WV	WV	B	70.1	51.2	22.0	2.1	10.0	6.1	8.1	6.8	5.4	R
▲FARMERS & MERCHANTS MUTUAL FIRE I C	MI	B-	32.2	27.1	3.8	1.0	9.8	4.6	8.0	7.0	4.9	DFR
FARMERS ALLIANCE MUTUAL INS CO	KS	B-	319.2	175.7	139.2	5.3	10.0	8.0	7.9	6.5	4.7	R
FARMERS AUTOMOBILE INS ASN	IL	B+	1,226.6	480.7	491.0	13.9	8.0	7.8	4.1	6.2	6.0	
FARMERS FIRE INS CO	PA	C	31.2	15.6	15.1	1.2	7.7	5.6	5.8	7.0	3.6	DR
FARMERS INS CO	KS	C+	291.8	105.8	106.4	1.0	10.0	5.8	5.2	6.8	4.7	R
FARMERS INS CO OF AZ	AZ	C+	44.0	4.2	0.0	0.0	4.4	N/A	3.9	2.5	3.3	CDLR
▲FARMERS INS CO OF FLEMINGTON	NJ	B-	70.6	30.3	21.9	1.4	7.2	8.5	8.7	7.2	5.1	T
FARMERS INS CO OF IDAHO	ID	C+	188.6	70.4	106.4	0.9	9.0	5.9	4.9	6.5	4.6	FR
FARMERS INS CO OF OREGON	OR	B	1,634.6	529.6	992.9	15.5	8.2	5.6	5.3	5.9	5.4	FR
FARMERS INS CO OF WA	WA	B-	528.5	205.8	283.7	5.6	9.2	5.9	5.6	6.0	4.9	FR
FARMERS INS EXCHANGE	CA	C	16,164.8	4,203.1	7,340.6	-65.4	5.3	5.4	3.7	2.6	4.3	FLR
FARMERS INS HAWAII INC	HI	B	100.6	95.0	0.0	0.7	10.0	4.6	3.4	10.0	5.6	FT
FARMERS INS OF COLUMBUS INC	OH	C+	260.2	101.0	141.8	1.8	9.2	5.9	5.2	6.5	4.7	FR
FARMERS MUTUAL F I C OF MCCANDLESS	PA	C-	11.9	6.9	5.6	0.2	7.2	6.0	8.3	6.0	2.5	DFR
FARMERS MUTUAL F I C OF OKARCHE OK	OK	C	19.2	13.5	8.1	-0.4	8.7	6.1	5.9	6.3	3.5	DF
▲FARMERS MUTUAL F I C OF SALEM CTY	NJ	B	158.7	81.0	41.4	3.7	9.6	9.0	8.3	7.0	5.5	T
▲FARMERS MUTUAL FIRE INS CO OF	PA	C+	35.4	25.1	9.5	2.2	8.6	8.4	8.8	7.1	4.4	DR
FARMERS MUTUAL HAIL INS CO OF IA	IA	B-	752.1	450.9	452.8	32.6	7.6	7.9	5.7	2.8	4.6	LR
FARMERS MUTUAL INS CO	WV	C	17.3	12.0	5.8	1.0	10.0	5.2	8.7	7.4	3.1	DR
▲FARMERS MUTUAL INS CO OF ELLINWOOD	KS	D	5.2	3.2	2.7	0.4	8.0	4.4	5.4	6.4	1.5	DR
FARMERS MUTUAL INS CO OF MI	MI	D-	2.0	1.2	1.3	0.1	7.0	5.7	3.2	7.2	1.0	DRT
▲FARMERS MUTUAL INS CO OF NE	NE	B+	680.3	353.4	343.5	22.0	10.0	6.3	6.1	6.1	6.5	
FARMERS MUTUAL OF TENNESSEE	TN	C	22.6	13.4	11.5	-0.6	8.2	6.4	3.8	6.7	3.5	DFR
FARMERS NEW CENTURY INS CO	IL	C+	185.5	70.8	106.4	0.8	9.0	5.9	4.9	6.5	4.7	FR
FARMERS REINS CO	CA	C+	202.0	77.5	78.7	-3.3	10.0	4.9	1.9	6.3	4.4	T
FARMERS SPECIALTY INS CO	MI	B-	51.5	17.4	0.0	0.4	10.0	N/A	7.1	10.0	3.8	DFT

See Page 27 for explanation of footnotes and
Page 28 for explanation of stability factors.

62

www.weissratings.com

Arrows denote recent upgrades ▲ or downgrades ▼   (see Section VII for explanations)

RISK ADJ. RATIO #1	CAPITAL RATIO #2	PREMIUM TO SURPLUS (%)	RESV. TO SURPLUS (%)	RESV. DEVELOP. 1 YEAR (%)	RESV. DEVELOP. 2 YEAR (%)	LOSS RATIO (%)	EXP. RATIO (%)	COMB RATIO (%)	CASH FROM UNDER-WRITING (%)	NET PREMIUM GROWTH (%)	INVEST. IN AFFIL (%)	INSURANCE COMPANY NAME
1.8	1.3	101.1	161.0	-4.9	-4.1	65.8	23.2	89.0	153.3	-0.6	0.0	EXPLORER INS CO
N/A	N/A	--	--	--	--	--	--	--	--	--	--	FACILITY INS CORP
2.3	1.8	23.2	28.3	-0.3	-1.9	109.1	30.6	139.7	103.1	3.6	20.4 •	FACTORY MUTUAL INS CO
55.7	37.5	2.1	3.3	-0.2	-0.4	50.7	49.6	100.3	118.5	3.6	0.0	FAIR AMERICAN INS & REINS CO
28.6	22.7	2.4	4.0	0.5	-0.2	143.5	53.6	197.1	147.3	8.8	0.0	FAIR AMERICAN SELECT INS CO
5.8	3.3	80.0	16.3	-2.4	-1.1	67.5	32.0	99.5	111.6	2.1	0.0	FAIRMONT FARMERS MUTUAL INS CO
-0.1	-0.1	119.7	267.0	32.0	73.6	89.7	56.6	146.3	78.6	-63.8	0.0	FAIRWAY PHYSICIANS INS CO RRG
0.6	0.4	134.8	80.2	31.3	27.3	100.2	1.5	101.7	75.3	-2.4	0.0	FALCON INS CO
1.9	1.5	32.3	70.5	-0.5	-2.9	67.0	25.6	92.6	507.2	-43.7	0.0	FALLS LAKE FIRE & CASUALTY CO
1.6	1.1	46.5	101.4	-0.9	-5.1	67.0	26.4	93.4	98.0	-39.0	0.0	FALLS LAKE GENERAL INS CO
1.2	1.2	9.9	21.6	-0.2	-0.9	67.0	26.3	93.3	-24.5	-1.1	68.9	FALLS LAKE NATIONAL INS CO
0.7	0.6	321.7	34.9	2.7	0.6	60.8	19.8	80.6	214.7	271.9	0.0	FAMILY SECURITY INS CO
3.4	2.3	113.0	39.2	-2.0	-1.9	82.2	19.5	101.7	100.3	7.2	4.7 •	FARM BU TOWN & COUNTRY INS CO OF
2.1	1.9	N/A	N/A	N/A	N/A	N/A	N/A	N/A	N/A	0.0	0.0	FARM BUREAU CNTY MUTUAL INS CO OF
4.4	3.0	109.3	56.6	2.7	1.8	74.3	26.0	100.3	105.1	4.3	0.0 •	FARM BUREAU GENERAL INS CO OF MI
96.1	50.7	N/A	N/A	N/A	N/A	N/A	N/A	N/A	N/A	0.0	0.0	FARM BUREAU INS OF NC INC
6.3	4.6	78.0	9.3	-2.1	-1.7	74.7	20.5	95.2	101.7	0.1	0.5 •	FARM BUREAU MUTUAL INS CO OF AR
2.5	2.1	82.0	36.0	1.6	-0.4	88.9	26.8	115.7	89.7	5.3	21.1 •	FARM BUREAU MUTUAL INS CO OF ID
4.9	3.3	86.8	48.1	-0.5	-3.1	65.6	30.2	95.8	102.0	-1.3	0.0 •	FARM BUREAU MUTUAL INS CO OF MI
4.6	3.5	95.0	35.1	-3.4	-5.8	66.3	26.6	92.9	102.5	2.0	5.8 •	FARM BUREAU P&C INS CO
9.0	5.9	20.5	33.5	-0.8	-9.9	78.2	9.3	87.5	148.6	6.5	0.0	FARM CREDIT SYS ASSOC CAPTIVE INS
4.7	3.0	92.3	104.6	-8.6	-14.2	60.0	30.9	90.9	113.8	3.6	0.0 •	FARM FAMILY CASUALTY INS CO
1.5	1.1	153.8	10.1	-2.2	-5.0	40.5	36.6	77.1	93.0	62.1	0.0	FARMERS & MECH MU I ASN OF CECIL
2.8	1.6	4.7	2.9	-0.6	-1.0	62.9	29.4	92.3	96.1	3.6	0.0	FARMERS & MECH MUTUAL INS CO
1.4	1.2	122.6	46.9	-2.0	-8.9	68.0	28.2	96.2	100.8	3.1	0.0	FARMERS & MECHANICS FIRE & CAS INS
4.2	3.0	43.0	7.6	-0.4	-0.1	54.5	36.7	91.2	106.8	6.2	8.4	FARMERS & MECHANICS MUTUAL IC OF
4.8	2.9	14.1	2.0	-0.1	N/A	56.4	48.7	105.1	85.3	-1.4	0.0	FARMERS & MERCHANTS MUTUAL FIRE I
4.8	3.7	79.2	25.4	-2.7	-2.7	68.7	30.4	99.1	99.0	4.2	6.7	FARMERS ALLIANCE MUTUAL INS CO
1.9	1.6	102.1	84.8	-4.2	-1.4	74.2	28.5	102.7	98.3	0.0	23.1 •	FARMERS AUTOMOBILE INS ASN
2.5	1.7	96.8	26.6	-4.7	3.8	57.1	37.9	95.0	103.9	0.4	0.0	FARMERS FIRE INS CO
4.8	3.4	100.6	62.7	0.1	2.3	69.8	33.1	102.9	98.4	-3.9	0.0	FARMERS INS CO
0.7	0.6	N/A	N/A	N/A	N/A	N/A	N/A	N/A	-29.4	0.0	0.0	FARMERS INS CO OF AZ
1.9	1.1	72.4	77.4	-9.9	-2.3	58.3	38.2	96.5	111.2	-3.9	0.0	FARMERS INS CO OF FLEMINGTON
3.3	2.3	151.0	89.2	-0.4	1.6	69.4	32.9	102.3	94.7	-3.9	0.0	FARMERS INS CO OF IDAHO
2.6	1.8	187.5	115.2	N/A	3.7	69.7	32.9	102.6	94.2	-3.9	0.0 •	FARMERS INS CO OF OREGON
3.6	2.5	137.9	81.5	-0.4	1.5	69.5	33.0	102.5	94.6	-3.9	0.0	FARMERS INS CO OF WA
0.8	0.7	174.6	112.2	0.5	5.4	70.0	33.8	103.8	92.4	-3.9	47.9 •	FARMERS INS EXCHANGE
8.8	8.6	N/A	N/A	N/A	N/A	N/A	N/A	N/A	N/A	0.0	11.6	FARMERS INS HAWAII INC
3.5	2.5	140.5	83.0	-0.4	1.5	69.4	32.9	102.3	94.2	-3.9	0.0	FARMERS INS OF COLUMBUS INC
1.9	1.2	80.7	13.9	4.3	2.4	69.6	35.8	105.4	94.5	0.3	0.0	FARMERS MUTUAL F I C OF
3.4	2.1	59.6	4.4	-1.1	0.8	70.7	43.2	113.9	83.3	-3.9	0.0	FARMERS MUTUAL F I C OF OKARCHE
4.3	2.7	51.1	54.7	-3.8	-7.1	59.2	33.6	92.8	109.2	2.7	0.0	FARMERS MUTUAL F I C OF SALEM CTY
3.3	2.0	38.0	9.0	-2.0	-4.5	45.3	31.7	77.0	126.2	2.6	0.0	FARMERS MUTUAL FIRE INS CO OF
2.0	1.4	100.4	37.4	-5.5	-5.6	72.8	19.6	92.4	115.3	35.5	34.3 •	FARMERS MUTUAL HAIL INS CO OF IA
5.0	3.1	48.1	1.9	-1.4	-0.7	26.3	53.3	79.6	127.6	3.5	0.0	FARMERS MUTUAL INS CO
3.5	2.2	85.6	3.5	1.2	0.6	45.2	38.3	83.5	115.0	-0.8	5.7	FARMERS MUTUAL INS CO OF
1.8	1.2	103.3	1.0	1.6	0.5	24.8	56.7	81.5	139.0	32.9	0.0	FARMERS MUTUAL INS CO OF MI
4.3	3.0	97.2	25.7	-1.3	0.4	69.2	26.0	95.2	103.8	4.9	0.0 •	FARMERS MUTUAL INS CO OF NE
3.2	2.1	85.7	12.7	-4.9	-4.5	67.8	39.5	107.3	88.5	1.3	0.4	FARMERS MUTUAL OF TENNESSEE
3.3	2.3	150.2	88.7	-0.4	1.6	69.4	32.9	102.3	94.8	-3.9	0.0	FARMERS NEW CENTURY INS CO
5.0	3.4	101.5	49.2	1.4	1.0	N/A	26.8	N/A	138.9	0.0	0.0	FARMERS REINS CO
3.4	3.1	N/A	N/A	N/A	N/A	N/A	N/A	N/A	112.9	0.0	0.0	FARMERS SPECIALTY INS CO

999 + Denotes number greater than 999.9%
999 - Denotes number less than -999.99%
• Bullets denote a more detailed analysis is available in Section II.

INSURANCE COMPANY NAME	DOM. STATE	RATING	TOTAL ASSETS ($MIL)	CAPITAL & SURPLUS ($MIL)	ANNUAL NET PREMIUM ($MIL)	NET INCOME ($MIL)	CAPITAL-IZATION INDEX (PTS)	RESERVE ADQ INDEX (PTS)	PROFIT-ABILITY INDEX (PTS)	LIQUIDITY INDEX (PTS)	STAB. INDEX (PTS)	STABILITY FACTORS
▲FARMERS UNION MUTUAL INS CO	MT	B-	66.4	37.8	23.9	2.3	10.0	6.9	8.3	7.0	5.3	T
▲FARMERS UNION MUTUAL INS CO	ND	B	121.3	69.8	66.3	5.6	10.0	7.9	8.6	6.8	5.5	T
FARMERS UNION MUTUAL INS CO	AR	D	4.8	2.1	2.3	0.1	5.6	5.6	2.9	7.0	1.5	DFT
FARMINGTON CASUALTY CO	CT	B	1,031.4	274.5	337.9	25.6	7.8	8.5	4.2	6.7	6.0	
▲FARMINGTON MUTUAL INS CO	WI	E+	8.2	6.9	1.1	0.0	9.1	4.6	6.9	6.9	0.5	DFR
FARMLAND MUTUAL INS CO	IA	B	559.9	163.6	188.7	-4.2	9.4	5.9	3.2	6.0	5.9	AF
FB INS CO	KY	U	--	--	--	--	N/A	--	--	--	--	Z
▼FBALLIANCE INS CO	IL	B-	43.9	43.1	0.5	-4.3	10.0	3.6	2.2	10.0	3.5	DFT
▲FBALLIANCE INS INC	VA	D+	4.8	4.5	0.0	0.0	10.0	N/A	4.9	10.0	2.5	DT
FCCI ADVANTAGE INS CO	FL	U	--	--	--	--	N/A	--	--	--	--	Z
FCCI COMMERCIAL INS CO	FL	U	--	--	--	--	N/A	--	--	--	--	Z
FCCI INS CO	FL	C+	2,067.1	594.5	799.5	24.5	7.8	6.3	4.7	6.5	4.2	R
▼FD INS CO	FL	C	12.9	11.1	0.0	0.5	10.0	10.0	2.4	7.0	2.9	DT
▲FDM PREFERRED INS CO	NY	C	10.0	3.9	1.9	0.9	5.1	9.3	8.8	9.0	3.2	CD
▼FEDERAL INS CO	IN	C+	21,770.0	7,296.7	3,532.5	4,948.1	7.3	8.5	2.2	6.6	4.5	FT
FEDERATED MUTUAL INS CO	MN	B	5,847.9	3,362.5	1,538.1	156.4	9.5	8.8	8.4	6.8	5.4	T
FEDERATED NATIONAL INS CO	FL	C	575.8	162.2	350.6	-13.9	4.5	5.8	3.6	4.2	4.3	CFLR
▲FEDERATED RURAL ELECTRIC INS EXCH	KS	B+	553.2	203.1	122.1	33.0	8.9	9.4	8.9	6.8	6.5	
FEDERATED SERVICE INS CO	MN	B-	450.4	244.5	128.2	16.2	10.0	9.3	8.8	6.7	5.2	F
▲FFVA MUTUAL INS CO	FL	B	336.2	164.3	112.0	12.7	8.5	8.8	8.9	6.6	5.5	T
FFVA SELECT INSURANCE CO	FL	U	--	--	--	--	N/A	--	--	--	--	Z
FHM INS CO	FL	C	72.3	34.6	27.3	-3.4	7.6	6.4	2.4	6.6	4.1	FR
FIDELITY & DEPOSIT CO OF MARYLAND	MD	C+	214.0	171.2	0.0	2.7	10.0	N/A	6.4	7.0	4.6	R
FIDELITY & GUARANTY INS	WI	C+	151.3	89.0	22.8	3.6	10.0	7.4	4.8	8.3	4.7	
FIDELITY & GUARANTY INS CO	IA	C+	20.1	17.7	0.0	0.4	10.0	N/A	3.8	7.0	3.4	DT
FIDELITY MOHAWK INS CO	NJ	U	--	--	--	--	N/A	--	--	--	--	Z
FIDUCIARY INS CO OF AMERICA	NY	F (3)	38.5	-160.6	0.0	-2.1	0.0	0.2	0.2	0.0	0.0	CLRT
FINANCIAL AMERICAN PROP & CAS INS CO	TX	C-	10.2	8.0	0.2	-0.8	9.0	6.1	2.0	8.4	2.8	DFRT
▲FINANCIAL CASUALTY & SURETY INC	TX	C+	24.3	16.5	12.6	-0.3	7.4	9.3	5.2	7.5	3.9	DF
FINANCIAL GUARANTY INS CO	NY	E	2,340.2	66.4	6.7	8.8	0.0	2.1	2.9	2.6	0.0	CFLR
FINANCIAL INDEMNITY CO	IL	B-	102.8	20.4	0.0	0.8	8.9	N/A	3.4	7.0	5.1	D
▲FINANCIAL PACIFIC INS CO	CA	B+	261.4	97.6	81.5	3.6	9.7	8.0	7.2	6.5	6.4	
▲FINGER LAKES FIRE & CASUALTY CO	NY	B-	43.9	30.2	10.1	1.5	9.2	6.0	8.1	6.9	5.0	D
FINIAL REINS CO	CT	D+	1,265.4	780.4	0.2	289.5	9.9	4.6	3.8	10.0	2.5	RT
FIRE DISTRICTS INS CO	NY	C	15.2	6.1	2.9	1.5	5.3	9.3	8.8	8.0	3.5	CD
▲FIRE DISTRICTS OF NY MUT INS CO INC	NY	B-	94.5	39.8	14.5	9.2	7.4	6.5	8.6	7.6	5.2	D
FIRE INS EXCHANGE	CA	C+	2,863.8	787.2	1,063.9	-9.8	5.2	5.6	3.9	2.9	4.8	LR
FIREMANS FUND INDEMNITY CORP	NJ	C+	15.8	14.9	0.0	-0.2	10.0	N/A	4.0	7.0	4.4	DT
▲FIREMANS FUND INS CO	CA	C+	2,110.0	1,387.4	0.0	99.2	10.0	5.1	3.6	7.0	4.4	FRT
FIREMANS FUND INS CO OF HI INC	HI	C+	12.4	9.1	0.0	-0.1	10.0	N/A	3.9	7.0	4.3	DRT
FIREMENS INS CO OF WASHINGTON DC	DE	C	91.9	33.2	0.0	0.7	10.0	N/A	6.3	10.0	4.2	
▲FIRST ACCEPTANCE INS CO	TX	C-	243.5	66.1	186.2	2.3	5.8	3.8	1.6	1.1	3.0	LR
▲FIRST ACCEPTANCE INS CO OF GEORGIA	GA	C-	89.6	20.5	73.4	0.3	3.3	3.2	2.4	0.6	2.9	CDFL
▼FIRST ACCEPTANCE INS CO OF TN INC	TN	D	27.5	6.7	22.6	0.2	3.2	3.7	1.6	0.0	2.0	CDFL
FIRST AMERICAN PROP & CAS INS CO	CA	C	97.1	41.4	55.4	-1.5	7.0	4.4	3.0	3.2	3.6	FLR
FIRST AMERICAN SPECIALTY INS CO	CA	C	126.7	51.1	71.1	-9.1	6.7	5.0	3.9	2.7	3.6	FLR
FIRST BENEFITS INS MUTUAL INC	NC	D	45.9	10.1	17.8	1.1	2.4	9.9	8.6	6.7	2.3	CD
FIRST CHICAGO INS CO	IL	D	81.5	18.3	54.3	3.0	4.8	6.7	8.7	5.2	2.3	DR
▲FIRST CHOICE CASUALTY INS CO	NV	C	14.1	5.1	5.4	0.3	5.4	5.0	3.5	7.1	2.9	CD
FIRST COLONIAL INS CO	FL	B	300.3	133.6	28.3	-16.9	10.0	6.0	2.1	6.7	5.3	F
FIRST COMMUNITY INS CO	FL	C	99.4	38.0	49.8	-2.1	8.5	5.9	5.3	6.7	4.1	R
FIRST DAKOTA INDEMNITY CO	SD	C	52.1	15.6	17.3	1.4	6.3	6.9	8.9	6.6	4.3	DR

See Page 27 for explanation of footnotes and Page 28 for explanation of stability factors.

64

www.weissratings.com

Arrows denote recent upgrades ▲ or downgrades ▼   (see Section VII for explanations)

RISK ADJ. CAPITAL RATIO #1	CAPITAL RATIO #2	PREMIUM TO SURPLUS (%)	RESV. TO SURPLUS (%)	RESV. DEVELOP. 1 YEAR (%)	RESV. DEVELOP. 2 YEAR (%)	LOSS RATIO (%)	EXP. RATIO (%)	COMB RATIO (%)	CASH FROM UNDER- WRITING (%)	NET PREMIUM GROWTH (%)	INVEST. IN AFFIL (%)	INSURANCE COMPANY NAME
4.3	3.1	63.2	30.7	2.8	0.2	56.4	33.5	89.9	130.4	3.6	-1.5	FARMERS UNION MUTUAL INS CO
4.6	3.7	95.0	13.3	-1.9	-3.1	58.0	32.2	90.2	118.4	6.2	0.0	FARMERS UNION MUTUAL INS CO
1.1	0.8	110.5	4.5	-2.2	2.5	52.4	44.3	96.7	88.8	24.0	0.0	FARMERS UNION MUTUAL INS CO
2.3	1.5	123.1	201.8	-2.5	-4.2	69.5	29.2	98.7	108.6	4.9	0.1 •	FARMINGTON CASUALTY CO
4.0	2.4	15.9	1.2	-0.7	N/A	94.5	44.0	138.5	58.3	2.0	0.0	FARMINGTON MUTUAL INS CO
3.6	2.6	115.3	93.3	0.2	1.9	81.1	30.4	111.5	92.0	-3.2	0.0	FARMLAND MUTUAL INS CO
N/A	N/A	--	--	--	--	--	--	--	--	--	--	FB INS CO
8.6	7.7	1.2	0.2	-0.1	N/A	49.9	966.5	999 +	5.4	373.7	10.5	FBALLIANCE INS CO
34.0	30.6	N/A	N/A	N/A	N/A	N/A	N/A	N/A	-98.6	0.0	0.0	FBALLIANCE INS INC
N/A	N/A	--	--	--	--	--	--	--	--	--	--	FCCI ADVANTAGE INS CO
N/A	N/A	--	--	--	--	--	--	--	--	--	--	FCCI COMMERCIAL INS CO
2.1	1.5	134.5	154.0	-4.6	5.6	68.6	31.2	99.8	112.9	6.6	6.9 •	FCCI INS CO
22.3	20.1	N/A	5.0	N/A	-197.1	N/A	N/A	N/A	111.0	100.0	0.0	FD INS CO
1.8	0.6	49.1	132.8	-12.7	-12.8	42.2	22.1	64.3	121.5	-7.7	0.0	FDM PREFERRED INS CO
1.4	1.1	48.4	143.3	-4.0	-7.9	59.7	27.8	87.5	77.3	-25.0	27.3 •	FEDERAL INS CO
3.2	2.6	45.7	46.1	-2.4	-5.3	70.9	25.0	95.9	113.0	5.3	16.9 •	FEDERATED MUTUAL INS CO
1.0	0.7	216.1	84.3	4.6	5.1	75.6	34.7	110.3	95.4	7.5	2.6	FEDERATED NATIONAL INS CO
3.4	2.3	60.1	135.8	-12.3	-19.7	74.0	15.3	89.3	125.7	-1.1	0.0 •	FEDERATED RURAL ELECTRIC INS EXCH
8.2	5.4	52.4	52.8	-2.7	-6.0	70.9	23.6	94.5	75.8	-21.0	0.0 •	FEDERATED SERVICE INS CO
2.7	2.1	68.2	76.5	-3.7	-10.4	62.8	25.7	88.5	112.8	-1.3	1.8	FFVA MUTUAL INS CO
N/A	N/A	--	--	--	--	--	--	--	--	--	--	FFVA SELECT INSURANCE CO
1.9	1.3	78.8	91.2	7.6	-2.4	79.2	33.4	112.6	80.5	-1.2	0.0	FHM INS CO
7.7	7.4	N/A	N/A	N/A	N/A	N/A	N/A	N/A	0.4	0.0	13.7	FIDELITY & DEPOSIT CO OF MARYLAND
10.7	7.1	25.7	42.0	-0.6	-1.0	69.5	30.0	99.5	120.5	4.9	0.0	FIDELITY & GUARANTY INS
22.0	19.8	N/A	N/A	N/A	N/A	N/A	N/A	N/A	91.0	0.0	0.0	FIDELITY & GUARANTY INS CO
N/A	N/A	--	--	--	--	--	--	--	--	--	--	FIDELITY MOHAWK INS CO
-16.2	-14.6	N/A	N/A	N/A	N/A	N/A	N/A	N/A	N/A	0.0	0.0	FIDUCIARY INS CO OF AMERICA
2.4	2.3	1.9	1.7	-0.6	-0.8	20.4	993.3	999 +	49.9	-85.6	0.0	FINANCIAL AMERICAN PROP & CAS INS
1.8	1.5	76.6	17.1	-13.2	-15.6	33.1	69.6	102.7	94.9	-14.8	0.0	FINANCIAL CASUALTY & SURETY INC
0.1	0.0	10.1	999 +	999 +	999 +	801.8	350.6	999 +	2.8	-25.7	1.4	FINANCIAL GUARANTY INS CO
2.4	2.2	N/A	N/A	N/A	N/A	N/A	N/A	N/A	18.3	0.0	0.0	FINANCIAL INDEMNITY CO
4.3	3.0	83.5	95.2	-2.4	-2.0	72.8	30.5	103.3	91.5	5.6	0.0 •	FINANCIAL PACIFIC INS CO
3.8	2.4	33.5	14.8	-0.6	2.1	50.5	35.5	86.0	105.1	3.5	0.0	FINGER LAKES FIRE & CASUALTY CO
5.9	2.9	N/A	55.1	-4.8	-0.2	999 +	169.4	999 +	-52.3	-99.7	0.0 •	FINIAL REINS CO
1.9	0.7	47.5	128.4	-12.4	-11.7	42.2	19.6	61.8	157.7	-7.7	0.0	FIRE DISTRICTS INS CO
2.2	1.6	36.6	124.1	-7.1	-5.8	47.1	20.4	67.5	155.4	-7.7	10.9	FIRE DISTRICTS OF NY MUT INS CO INC
0.8	0.7	135.1	86.5	0.4	4.1	70.0	32.8	102.8	121.7	-3.9	61.1 •	FIRE INS EXCHANGE
38.5	34.6	N/A	N/A	N/A	N/A	N/A	N/A	N/A	27.8	0.0	0.0	FIREMANS FUND INDEMNITY CORP
3.9	3.6	N/A	N/A	N/A	N/A	N/A	N/A	N/A	320.7	100.0	33.9 •	FIREMANS FUND INS CO
8.6	7.7	N/A	N/A	N/A	N/A	N/A	N/A	N/A	5.8	0.0	0.0	FIREMANS FUND INS CO OF HI INC
4.6	4.1	N/A	N/A	N/A	N/A	N/A	N/A	N/A	283.4	0.0	0.0	FIREMENS INS CO OF WASHINGTON DC
0.9	0.8	281.8	158.1	-4.0	20.3	79.4	21.0	100.4	97.3	-5.6	13.8	FIRST ACCEPTANCE INS CO
0.6	0.5	357.7	200.7	-5.4	31.9	79.4	21.0	100.4	86.6	-5.6	0.0	FIRST ACCEPTANCE INS CO OF
0.5	0.5	338.4	189.8	-4.4	24.6	79.4	21.0	100.4	84.0	-5.6	0.0	FIRST ACCEPTANCE INS CO OF TN INC
1.6	1.0	134.0	42.9	4.5	10.0	77.7	35.0	112.7	84.6	-6.3	0.0	FIRST AMERICAN PROP & CAS INS CO
1.6	0.9	139.3	51.1	3.1	-0.6	90.9	34.6	125.5	88.1	3.4	0.0	FIRST AMERICAN SPECIALTY INS CO
0.7	0.5	175.7	259.8	-17.7	-45.8	70.3	28.4	98.7	100.4	-3.0	0.0	FIRST BENEFITS INS MUTUAL INC
0.9	0.6	296.6	217.0	-6.1	-5.4	59.2	31.8	91.0	116.1	15.7	6.5	FIRST CHICAGO INS CO
1.2	0.5	106.1	128.3	-5.1	-16.5	62.2	37.5	99.7	180.3	-18.6	0.0	FIRST CHOICE CASUALTY INS CO
4.7	4.0	21.2	11.5	2.1	2.7	140.3	53.5	193.8	24.4	-26.2	0.0	FIRST COLONIAL INS CO
2.6	1.9	131.1	50.8	0.8	5.6	67.7	38.7	106.4	101.7	23.4	0.0	FIRST COMMUNITY INS CO
1.1	0.9	111.0	149.7	-6.6	-11.4	67.3	21.0	88.3	131.0	5.0	0.0	FIRST DAKOTA INDEMNITY CO

999 + Denotes number greater than 999.9%
999 - Denotes number less than -999.99%
• Bullets denote a more detailed analysis is available in Section II.

INSURANCE COMPANY NAME	DOM. STATE	RATING	TOTAL ASSETS ($MIL)	CAPITAL & SURPLUS ($MIL)	ANNUAL NET PREMIUM ($MIL)	NET INCOME ($MIL)	CAPITAL-IZATION INDEX (PTS)	RESERVE ADQ INDEX (PTS)	PROFIT-ABILITY INDEX (PTS)	LIQUIDITY INDEX (PTS)	STAB. INDEX (PTS)	STABILITY FACTORS
FIRST F&C INS OF HI INC	HI	C	9.3	9.3	0.0	-0.8	10.0	N/A	2.9	7.0	3.8	DR
FIRST FINANCIAL INS CO	IL	C-	538.9	429.6	22.3	12.8	7.3	7.7	6.2	7.2	2.6	R
FIRST FLORIDIAN AUTO & HOME INS CO	FL	B	259.6	188.3	51.3	3.1	10.0	6.1	4.4	7.1	5.8	
FIRST FOUNDERS ASR CO	NJ	D+	5.6	4.6	0.4	0.2	10.0	6.1	8.3	9.1	2.3	D
▲FIRST GUARD INS CO	AZ	B	31.9	28.7	24.2	3.1	10.0	7.4	8.9	7.5	5.0	T
FIRST INDEMNITY INS OF HI INC	HI	C	7.6	7.6	0.0	0.1	10.0	N/A	4.0	7.0	3.9	DR
▲FIRST INDEMNITY OF AMERICA INS CO	NJ	C-	11.9	7.1	7.6	1.1	5.7	4.3	7.7	5.9	2.4	DR
FIRST INS CO OF HI LTD	HI	C	661.6	281.5	204.9	15.9	10.0	6.9	6.1	6.7	4.2	R
FIRST JERSEY CASUALTY INS CO INC	NJ	U	--	--	--	--	N/A	--	--	--	--	Z
FIRST LIBERTY INS CORP	IL	C+	22.3	22.3	0.0	0.1	10.0	N/A	5.7	10.0	4.4	AD
▲FIRST MEDICAL INS CO RRG	VT	B-	114.1	56.7	11.2	6.5	8.6	8.7	4.3	9.0	5.1	D
▲FIRST MERCURY INS CO	DE	C+	97.6	52.7	0.0	1.1	10.0	N/A	4.2	7.0	4.5	ART
FIRST MUTUAL INS CO	NC	D+	6.7	5.3	1.4	0.3	10.0	7.3	8.2	9.3	2.3	DR
FIRST NATIONAL INS CO OF AMERICA	NH	B	57.7	57.5	0.0	1.0	10.0	N/A	6.7	7.0	5.5	A
▲FIRST NET INS CO	GU	C	18.5	12.4	6.2	1.3	8.5	4.3	5.7	6.8	3.4	DF
▼FIRST NONPROFIT INS CO	DE	C-	41.1	15.7	9.0	3.6	8.9	5.1	1.9	1.7	3.1	DFLR
FIRST PROFESSIONALS INS CO INC	FL	U	--	--	--	--	N/A	--	--	--	--	Z
FIRST PROTECTIVE INS CO	FL	U	--	--	--	--	N/A	--	--	--	--	Z
FIRST SECURITY INS OF HI INC	HI	C	5.6	5.6	0.0	-0.2	10.0	N/A	3.5	7.0	3.6	DR
FIRST SPECIALTY INS CORP	MO	C	171.9	73.3	0.0	3.8	10.0	3.8	5.9	6.7	4.2	FRT
FIRST STATE INS CO	CT	U	--	--	--	--	N/A	--	--	--	--	Z
▲FIRST SURETY CORP	WV	C	37.7	13.8	2.1	1.2	8.7	5.3	4.5	9.6	2.3	DGRT
FIRST WASHINGTON INS CO	DC	U	--	--	--	--	N/A	--	--	--	--	Z
FIRSTCOMP INS CO	NE	B	261.3	110.7	43.7	16.1	7.8	9.4	3.8	6.9	6.0	
FIRSTLINE NATIONAL INS CO	MD	C+	102.8	57.7	42.4	2.6	8.9	6.1	8.2	6.8	4.7	T
FITCHBURG MUTUAL INS CO	MA	C+	140.2	65.7	45.9	3.1	9.0	6.3	6.9	6.9	4.3	R
FLAGSHIP CITY INS CO	PA	C+	50.1	12.7	0.0	0.2	8.7	N/A	7.1	7.0	4.5	DF
FLORIDA FAMILY INS CO	FL	B	106.8	55.6	54.0	-0.2	8.6	6.3	5.2	5.6	6.1	F
FLORIDA FARM BU CASUALTY INS CO	FL	B-	558.0	277.4	263.5	-5.0	10.0	7.8	4.1	6.3	4.8	F
FLORIDA FARM BUREAU GENERAL INS CO	FL	B	12.0	10.7	0.0	0.3	10.0	N/A	6.9	7.0	4.5	D
▲FLORIDA LAWYERS MUTUAL INS CO	FL	B-	90.6	51.9	12.3	4.9	9.4	9.4	8.7	8.9	4.9	DR
▲FLORIDA PENINSULA INS CO	FL	B	304.7	108.9	100.9	-4.1	7.8	5.5	4.9	6.9	5.5	F
FLORIDA SELECT INS CO	FL	F (5)	0.0	0.0	-0.3	0.0	0.0	5.0	1.9	7.0	0.0	CDFT
▼FLORIDA SPECIALTY INS CO	FL	D	45.5	15.0	17.8	-5.7	4.0	6.0	1.1	2.6	2.3	DFLR
FLORISTS INS CO	IL	C	5.7	5.3	0.0	0.2	10.0	N/A	3.5	6.8	3.6	DRT
▲FLORISTS MUTUAL INS CO	IL	C	130.6	27.1	21.1	0.9	7.7	4.8	3.0	6.8	3.5	
FMH AG RISK INS CO	IA	B	123.2	114.4	0.0	2.8	10.0	4.7	3.6	7.0	6.1	FT
FMI INS CO	NJ	B-	53.5	46.3	0.0	0.6	7.6	N/A	6.9	7.0	5.0	F
FOREMOST COUNTY MUTUAL INS CO	TX	C+	81.8	5.5	0.0	0.5	4.0	N/A	8.9	9.2	3.5	CD
FOREMOST INS CO	MI	B	2,316.6	1,165.6	0.0	44.4	10.0	7.2	7.7	9.9	5.5	T
FOREMOST LLOYDS OF TEXAS	TX	C+	58.6	5.0	0.0	0.3	4.2	N/A	8.4	7.9	3.5	CD
FOREMOST P&C INS CO	MI	C+	56.2	18.3	0.0	0.2	10.0	N/A	6.2	10.0	4.6	D
FOREMOST SIGNATURE INS CO	MI	C+	61.9	20.2	0.0	0.2	10.0	N/A	5.9	7.8	4.6	DF
FORESTRY MUTUAL INS CO	NC	B-	61.0	24.1	21.0	0.7	7.3	9.6	8.5	6.6	4.7	DR
FORT WAYNE MEDICAL ASR CO RRG	AZ	D+	4.1	2.6	0.9	0.2	8.0	5.6	6.2	7.2	2.0	D
FORTRESS INS CO	IL	B-	142.2	64.7	22.6	2.0	5.0	5.3	4.8	7.4	4.7	CD
FORTUITY INS CO	MI	B	44.7	19.4	19.0	1.7	9.5	9.3	8.8	6.7	5.5	D
FOUNDERS INS CO (IL)	IL	C	166.7	72.7	48.6	2.3	9.8	4.6	3.6	6.7	4.2	R
FOUNDERS INS CO (NJ)	NJ	C	6.6	6.6	0.0	0.1	10.0	N/A	4.2	10.0	3.8	D
FOUNDERS INS CO OF MI	MI	U	--	--	--	--	N/A	--	--	--	--	Z
FRANDISCO P&C INS CO	GA	B-	117.8	91.6	29.3	10.3	10.0	6.2	8.6	6.9	4.5	T
FRANK WINSTON CRUM INS CO	FL	C-	101.0	21.3	19.8	2.7	5.1	3.3	7.6	7.1	3.3	DR

See Page 27 for explanation of footnotes and Page 28 for explanation of stability factors.
Arrows denote recent upgrades ▲ or downgrades ▼ (see Section VII for explanations)

66

www.weissratings.com

RISK ADJ. RATIO #1	CAPITAL RATIO #2	PREMIUM TO SURPLUS (%)	RESV. TO SURPLUS (%)	RESV. DEVELOP. 1 YEAR (%)	RESV. DEVELOP. 2 YEAR (%)	LOSS RATIO (%)	EXP. RATIO (%)	COMB RATIO (%)	CASH FROM UNDER-WRITING (%)	NET PREMIUM GROWTH (%)	INVEST. IN AFFIL (%)	INSURANCE COMPANY NAME
125.9	62.9	N/A	N/A	N/A	N/A	N/A	N/A	N/A	N/A	0.0	0.0	FIRST F&C INS OF HI INC
1.2	1.2	5.2	12.8	-0.9	-1.5	45.8	54.8	100.6	79.7	6.8	78.2 ●	FIRST FINANCIAL INS CO
11.9	9.1	27.2	22.2	-0.5	2.6	87.3	22.8	110.1	84.6	-7.8	0.0	FIRST FLORIDIAN AUTO & HOME INS CO
9.1	6.1	8.5	7.1	-1.4	-2.3	17.9	65.9	83.8	121.0	2.5	0.0	FIRST FOUNDERS ASR CO
11.8	6.1	84.4	5.2	-0.9	-1.9	61.7	19.7	81.4	129.0	8.2	0.0	FIRST GUARD INS CO
125.4	62.7	N/A	N/A	N/A	N/A	N/A	N/A	N/A	N/A	0.0	0.0	FIRST INDEMNITY INS OF HI INC
1.1	0.8	106.1	30.5	-8.3	-9.9	30.3	64.2	94.5	116.1	5.6	0.0	FIRST INDEMNITY OF AMERICA INS CO
5.1	3.4	72.8	83.2	-2.9	0.2	66.6	32.4	99.0	99.2	-0.2	3.8 ●	FIRST INS CO OF HI LTD
N/A	N/A	--	--	--	--	--	--	--	--	--	--	FIRST JERSEY CASUALTY INS CO INC
80.4	40.2	N/A	N/A	N/A	N/A	N/A	N/A	N/A	N/A	0.0	0.0	FIRST LIBERTY INS CORP
2.5	2.0	19.8	72.8	-1.4	-1.3	96.3	4.8	101.1	69.9	6.7	0.0	FIRST MEDICAL INS CO RRG
8.5	7.6	N/A	N/A	N/A	N/A	N/A	N/A	N/A	-23.4	0.0	0.0	FIRST MERCURY INS CO
9.6	7.2	26.2	1.8	0.2	-0.9	43.9	28.0	71.9	156.7	-4.9	0.0	FIRST MUTUAL INS CO
149.9	75.1	N/A	N/A	N/A	N/A	N/A	N/A	N/A	N/A	0.0	0.0	FIRST NATIONAL INS CO OF AMERICA
3.9	2.7	50.1	11.7	2.0	1.2	42.5	43.4	85.9	79.9	-3.4	0.0	FIRST NET INS CO
3.1	2.2	57.4	N/A	-425.4	-510.3	60.2	73.9	134.1	43.4	-66.5	12.5	FIRST NONPROFIT INS CO
N/A	N/A	--	--	--	--	--	--	--	--	--	--	FIRST PROFESSIONALS INS CO INC
N/A	N/A	--	--	--	--	--	--	--	--	--	--	FIRST PROTECTIVE INS CO
186.7	93.3	N/A	N/A	N/A	N/A	N/A	N/A	N/A	N/A	0.0	0.0	FIRST SECURITY INS OF HI INC
6.2	3.2	N/A	33.5	4.4	7.7	999 +	999 +	999 +	-66.2	-276.6	0.0	FIRST SPECIALTY INS CORP
N/A	N/A	--	--	--	--	--	--	--	--	--	--	FIRST STATE INS CO
3.3	2.2	15.0	20.5	2.0	8.9	39.9	29.0	68.9	213.3	2.8	0.0	FIRST SURETY CORP
N/A	N/A	--	--	--	--	--	--	--	--	--	--	FIRST WASHINGTON INS CO
2.3	1.5	39.5	96.1	-10.1	-15.5	36.4	28.6	65.0	120.0	-1.8	0.0	FIRSTCOMP INS CO
3.6	2.4	73.5	66.9	-1.2	0.6	61.0	35.5	96.5	117.8	8.6	0.0	FIRSTLINE NATIONAL INS CO
3.1	2.3	69.9	46.3	-1.9	-6.3	57.2	39.1	96.3	118.5	4.6	6.1	FITCHBURG MUTUAL INS CO
2.3	2.1	N/A	N/A	N/A	N/A	N/A	N/A	N/A	N/A	0.0	0.0	FLAGSHIP CITY INS CO
2.3	2.0	97.1	17.1	-1.7	-3.8	59.3	45.5	104.8	88.7	-3.8	17.7	FLORIDA FAMILY INS CO
4.5	3.6	95.0	45.4	-0.8	-2.2	88.5	19.5	108.0	91.3	5.0	2.9 ●	FLORIDA FARM BU CASUALTY INS CO
19.5	17.5	N/A	N/A	N/A	N/A	N/A	N/A	N/A	N/A	0.0	0.0	FLORIDA FARM BUREAU GENERAL INS
4.3	2.7	23.6	45.7	-12.7	-17.8	35.9	25.0	60.9	149.1	5.3	1.5	FLORIDA LAWYERS MUTUAL INS CO
1.9	1.5	92.6	82.8	4.3	1.4	81.0	34.6	115.6	81.8	-8.2	7.7	FLORIDA PENINSULA INS CO
-1.9	-1.7	2.3	-16.5	8.4	0.3	537.6	-780.2	-242.6	28.4	0.0	0.0	FLORIDA SELECT INS CO
0.8	0.6	118.3	25.4	5.2	1.8	71.8	72.6	144.4	58.3	-40.1	0.0	FLORIDA SPECIALTY INS CO
31.2	28.1	N/A	N/A	N/A	N/A	N/A	N/A	N/A	165.4	0.0	0.0	FLORISTS INS CO
2.6	1.7	77.8	121.1	-1.6	-3.4	74.8	28.6	103.4	159.9	4.7	4.9	FLORISTS MUTUAL INS CO
51.8	46.6	N/A	N/A	N/A	N/A	N/A	N/A	N/A	728.6	0.0	0.0	FMH AG RISK INS CO
2.2	1.3	N/A	N/A	N/A	N/A	N/A	N/A	N/A	N/A	0.0	0.0	FMI INS CO
0.7	0.6	N/A	N/A	N/A	N/A	N/A	N/A	N/A	-9.6	0.0	0.0	FOREMOST COUNTY MUTUAL INS CO
12.8	8.6	N/A	0.2	N/A	-0.1	N/A	N/A	N/A	-18.1	0.0	4.2 ●	FOREMOST INS CO
0.7	0.6	N/A	N/A	N/A	N/A	N/A	N/A	N/A	15.5	0.0	0.0	FOREMOST LLOYDS OF TEXAS
3.3	3.0	N/A	N/A	N/A	N/A	N/A	N/A	N/A	-12.3	0.0	0.0	FOREMOST P&C INS CO
3.4	3.1	N/A	N/A	N/A	N/A	N/A	N/A	N/A	2.5	0.0	0.0	FOREMOST SIGNATURE INS CO
1.6	1.2	87.0	87.3	-5.0	-8.2	67.4	35.2	102.6	109.6	-10.8	6.3	FORESTRY MUTUAL INS CO
2.2	1.6	33.5	32.0	5.2	10.4	41.3	48.8	90.1	97.3	-2.5	0.0	FORT WAYNE MEDICAL ASR CO RRG
1.0	0.7	34.9	90.6	-0.7	-2.0	73.2	29.9	103.1	114.7	-2.5	0.0	FORTRESS INS CO
3.9	2.9	98.0	68.0	-9.4	-9.8	59.0	32.3	91.3	112.1	5.7	0.0	FORTUITY INS CO
4.4	3.1	66.8	89.0	-0.7	-1.6	64.4	33.1	97.5	108.5	9.5	4.4	FOUNDERS INS CO (IL)
85.1	41.3	N/A	N/A	N/A	N/A	N/A	N/A	N/A	87.4	0.0	0.0	FOUNDERS INS CO (NJ)
N/A	N/A	--	--	--	--	--	--	--	--	--	--	FOUNDERS INS CO OF MI
10.1	8.3	32.0	2.3	-1.2	-1.5	13.6	54.8	68.4	147.0	-8.6	0.0	FRANDISCO P&C INS CO
1.2	0.7	92.8	110.9	2.2	11.5	57.0	31.7	88.7	104.7	-3.4	0.0	FRANK WINSTON CRUM INS CO

999 + Denotes number greater than 999.9%
999 - Denotes number less than -999.99%
● Bullets denote a more detailed analysis is available in Section II.

INSURANCE COMPANY NAME	DOM. STATE	RATING	TOTAL ASSETS ($MIL)	CAPITAL & SURPLUS ($MIL)	ANNUAL NET PREMIUM ($MIL)	NET INCOME ($MIL)	CAPITAL-IZATION INDEX (PTS)	RESERVE ADQ INDEX (PTS)	PROFIT-ABILITY INDEX (PTS)	LIQUIDITY INDEX (PTS)	STAB. INDEX (PTS)	STABILITY FACTORS
▲FRANKENMUTH MUTUAL INS CO	MI	B+	1,351.0	606.7	494.6	44.9	9.3	9.2	8.7	6.7	6.5	
FRANKLIN CASUALTY INS CO RRG	VT	D+	34.3	4.5	3.5	0.3	5.3	9.5	8.7	8.3	2.2	DR
FRANKLIN INS CO	PA	C	31.4	13.3	10.2	0.5	8.5	7.9	6.9	7.1	3.7	DR
FRANKLIN MUTUAL INS CO	NJ	B	1,080.4	793.8	119.8	37.9	8.2	7.9	8.1	7.9	5.6	T
FREDERICK MUTUAL INS CO	MD	C-	42.5	19.2	17.7	0.3	7.3	4.1	1.9	6.5	3.1	DF
FREEDOM ADVANTAGE INS CO	PA	D+	9.6	4.3	2.5	0.2	6.7	7.0	5.8	6.5	2.2	DFR
FREEDOM SPECIALTY INS CO	OH	B	57.9	22.1	0.0	0.7	10.0	N/A	8.2	8.1	5.7	DF
FREMONT INS CO	MI	D	158.6	48.3	64.8	2.3	9.0	4.7	6.0	6.1	1.7	R
FRIENDS COVE MUTUAL INS CO	PA	C-	6.0	3.5	2.9	0.2	7.5	5.8	5.1	6.5	2.1	DFR
FRONTLINE INS UNLIMITED CO	IL	U	--	--	--	--	N/A	--	--	--	--	Z
▲FULMONT MUTUAL INS CO	NY	D	2.9	0.9	1.2	-0.2	5.2	2.6	1.4	6.7	1.0	DFRT
▲GABLES RRG INC	VT	E+	9.1	4.7	3.4	1.1	7.4	5.0	3.3	7.0	0.5	D
GALEN INS CO	MO	F (3)	9.3	-2.3	1.2	-0.1	0.0	4.8	0.0	7.0	0.0	CDFG
GARRISON P&C INS CO	TX	B	2,277.8	851.4	1,616.1	19.2	8.1	7.8	4.8	2.4	6.3	L
▼GATEWAY INS CO	MO	D-	84.4	12.2	38.2	-5.9	0.9	0.8	1.8	3.3	1.2	CDGL
GEICO ADVANTAGE INS CO	NE	B	2,911.8	1,633.4	1,228.7	-235.1	8.7	6.1	3.1	7.0	4.9	FGT
▲GEICO CASUALTY CO	MD	C+	3,526.8	1,108.2	2,171.2	-95.9	7.4	9.4	2.9	2.5	4.5	L
GEICO CHOICE INS CO	NE	B+	1,134.6	483.1	665.7	-55.2	8.0	6.2	3.2	2.8	5.0	GLT
GEICO COUNTY MUTUAL INS CO	TX	C	156.4	5.0	0.0	0.0	2.8	N/A	3.9	0.0	2.8	CDGL
GEICO GENERAL INS CO	MD	B+	167.6	166.8	0.0	1.0	10.0	N/A	8.0	7.0	5.3	
GEICO INDEMNITY CO	MD	B	10,162.5	6,256.3	2,808.3	1,480.9	8.0	9.3	8.7	6.5	5.3	T
▲GEICO MARINE INS CO	MD	B-	149.5	54.3	57.6	9.7	7.7	8.1	4.9	2.3	3.9	FGLR
GEICO SECURE INS CO	NE	A-	625.3	335.0	294.1	-6.9	8.2	5.6	4.2	5.6	5.7	GT
▲GEISINGER INS CORP RRG	VT	D+	23.7	11.8	1.3	0.1	10.0	4.5	5.8	9.0	2.5	DR
▲GEM STATE INS CO	ID	C	12.3	9.1	4.1	-0.1	9.1	6.1	6.9	6.8	2.9	DF
GEMINI INS CO	DE	C	108.6	57.0	0.0	1.3	10.0	N/A	6.5	7.0	4.3	R
▲GENERAL AUTOMOBILE INS CO	WI	B-	98.7	37.4	-43.2	4.6	8.7	3.6	3.9	5.1	4.9	T
GENERAL CASUALTY CO OF WI	WI	C+	797.4	251.0	366.1	-10.5	7.2	6.8	2.8	4.0	4.5	FLR
GENERAL CASUALTY INS CO	WI	C	9.5	7.6	0.0	0.0	10.0	4.0	2.3	7.0	2.8	DRT
GENERAL INS CO OF AM	NH	B-	118.9	107.7	0.0	0.8	10.0	N/A	6.1	7.0	5.3	AF
GENERAL REINS CORP	DE	C+	16,507.9	11,392.5	885.6	300.5	7.3	7.7	5.8	8.7	4.6	GR
GENERAL SECURITY IND CO OF AZ	AZ	C-	365.7	49.5	8.7	-2.1	7.1	6.4	3.3	6.8	3.0	FRT
GENERAL SECURITY NATIONAL INS CO	NY	C-	416.1	121.7	77.8	-17.8	7.2	8.2	4.4	6.9	3.3	R
GENERAL STAR INDEMNITY CO	DE	C	931.6	677.1	85.2	92.8	9.9	8.5	7.2	9.8	4.0	R
GENERAL STAR NATIONAL INS CO	DE	B-	237.8	185.1	11.3	34.6	10.0	8.6	6.7	10.0	4.9	DR
GENERALI - US BRANCH	NY	C	63.3	34.1	0.5	-4.7	4.4	3.3	3.3	7.0	3.9	CRT
GENESEE PATRONS COOP INS	NY	D+	10.7	6.0	4.9	0.3	7.9	6.3	8.0	6.7	2.4	DR
GENESIS INS CO	DE	C	184.7	127.0	9.5	-1.2	10.0	8.7	5.3	10.0	4.3	DFR
GENEVA INS CO	IN	D+(1)	4.1	1.6	3.4	0.1	4.1	3.4	2.1	2.2	1.4	DFGL
GENWORTH FINANCIAL ASR CORP	NC	U	--	--	--	--	N/A	--	--	--	--	Z
GENWORTH MORTGAGE INS CORP	NC	C	3,346.0	1,366.5	683.2	449.3	8.0	6.1	7.9	7.0	4.0	R
GENWORTH MORTGAGE REINS CORP	NC	B	15.3	11.3	0.8	0.5	10.0	4.8	3.8	8.3	4.6	AD
▲GENWORTH MTG INS CORP OF NC	NC	B	394.9	191.4	73.7	61.7	8.7	6.9	7.3	6.9	5.4	T
GEORGIA CASUALTY & SURETY CO	GA	C	41.3	19.1	16.2	0.2	9.0	6.1	5.3	6.6	3.8	D
GEORGIA DEALERS INS CO	GA	U	--	--	--	--	N/A	--	--	--	--	Z
GEORGIA FARM BUREAU CASUALTY INS CO	GA	B	3.6	3.5	0.0	0.0	10.0	N/A	4.1	10.0	4.6	DT
▲GEORGIA FARM BUREAU MUTUAL INS CO	GA	C+	670.3	238.5	373.9	16.0	7.7	4.3	3.6	5.8	4.5	F
GEORGIA MUNICIPAL CAPTIVE INS CO	GA	D+	11.1	3.9	2.8	0.5	6.1	7.0	7.3	7.0	2.1	D
GEORGIA TRANSPORTATION CAPTIVE INS	GA	D	2.9	1.5	0.8	0.0	7.4	9.3	8.3	8.4	1.3	DT
GEOVERA INS CO	CA	D+	92.6	24.1	36.9	0.7	0.8	7.6	3.6	0.0	2.9	CDLR
GEOVERA SPECIALTY INS CO	DE	C	90.2	19.2	17.2	0.3	1.6	7.4	3.7	0.0	3.9	CDLR
GERMAN AMERICAN FARM MUTUAL	TX	B-	4.7	3.3	1.0	0.1	10.0	6.2	4.5	9.2	3.5	D

See Page 27 for explanation of footnotes and
Page 28 for explanation of stability factors.

Arrows denote recent upgrades ▲ or downgrades ▼   (see Section VII for explanations)

68

www.weissratings.com

RISK ADJ. RATIO #1	CAPITAL RATIO #2	PREMIUM TO SURPLUS (%)	RESV. TO SURPLUS (%)	RESV. DEVELOP. 1 YEAR (%)	RESV. DEVELOP. 2 YEAR (%)	LOSS RATIO (%)	EXP. RATIO (%)	COMB RATIO (%)	CASH FROM UNDER-WRITING (%)	NET PREMIUM GROWTH (%)	INVEST. IN AFFIL (%)	INSURANCE COMPANY NAME
3.1	2.5	81.5	56.5	-7.9	-8.2	59.0	32.3	91.3	114.6	5.7	14.0 •	FRANKENMUTH MUTUAL INS CO
1.0	0.9	77.9	153.4	-0.1	-18.7	50.9	37.8	88.7	101.3	15.8	0.0	FRANKLIN CASUALTY INS CO RRG
3.2	2.2	76.5	87.1	-2.2	-2.1	72.8	30.5	103.3	111.3	5.6	0.0	FRANKLIN INS CO
2.9	1.9	15.1	13.6	-2.0	-3.4	49.8	32.7	82.5	115.0	0.5	6.4 •	FRANKLIN MUTUAL INS CO
2.0	1.1	92.4	53.4	-2.6	7.1	62.7	46.8	109.5	80.4	-5.3	0.0	FREDERICK MUTUAL INS CO
2.0	1.3	57.4	98.5	-0.5	-9.5	67.5	39.1	106.6	73.7	-27.8	0.0	FREEDOM ADVANTAGE INS CO
4.2	3.8	N/A	N/A	N/A	N/A	N/A	N/A	N/A	-20.5	0.0	0.0	FREEDOM SPECIALTY INS CO
2.9	2.4	134.1	98.2	-1.0	0.4	72.1	28.1	100.2	97.2	7.1	0.0	FREMONT INS CO
2.2	1.4	81.3	7.1	-0.4	-0.3	45.8	46.0	91.8	92.2	-0.6	0.0	FRIENDS COVE MUTUAL INS CO
N/A	N/A	--	--	--	--	--	--	--	--	--	--	FRONTLINE INS UNLIMITED CO
1.1	0.6	132.1	144.9	4.6	37.2	99.6	28.5	128.1	51.9	-20.9	10.7	FULMONT MUTUAL INS CO
1.6	1.3	73.6	80.7	-1.9	7.2	44.8	9.7	54.5	205.8	3.9	0.0	GABLES RRG INC
-0.0	-0.0	-59.6	-502.5	164.5	25.1	152.1	194.5	346.6	40.4	-79.3	0.0	GALEN INS CO
2.3	1.7	189.8	89.9	-2.1	-2.3	88.2	12.8	101.0	105.7	17.4	0.0 •	GARRISON P&C INS CO
0.2	0.2	312.7	213.3	72.2	91.0	95.1	25.1	120.2	122.9	32.6	0.0	GATEWAY INS CO
4.0	2.8	75.2	33.0	-2.1	-3.4	106.5	23.2	129.7	87.8	55.9	0.0 •	GEICO ADVANTAGE INS CO
1.7	1.3	195.9	96.2	-1.0	-4.9	90.5	15.9	106.4	104.7	18.4	0.0 •	GEICO CASUALTY CO
2.2	1.6	137.8	53.3	-1.3	-3.2	94.0	17.5	111.5	98.8	41.9	0.0 •	GEICO CHOICE INS CO
0.5	0.4	N/A	N/A	N/A	N/A	N/A	N/A	N/A	250.3	0.0	0.0	GEICO COUNTY MUTUAL INS CO
150.2	75.1	N/A	N/A	N/A	N/A	N/A	N/A	N/A	N/A	0.0	0.0 •	GEICO GENERAL INS CO
2.4	1.7	44.9	25.6	-0.6	-1.4	82.9	12.6	95.5	112.1	10.4	13.2 •	GEICO INDEMNITY CO
1.9	1.4	106.1	25.2	-2.7	-2.4	89.9	22.9	112.8	76.3	38.2	0.0 •	GEICO MARINE INS CO
2.6	1.8	87.8	32.1	-0.8	-1.3	83.7	18.9	102.6	106.1	37.4	0.0 •	GEICO SECURE INS CO
4.4	3.9	10.7	4.2	N/A	N/A	40.1	50.4	90.5	121.6	2.9	0.0	GEISINGER INS CORP RRG
3.7	2.3	44.6	7.3	-0.7	0.5	86.5	30.8	117.3	88.3	6.0	0.0	GEM STATE INS CO
8.3	7.5	N/A	N/A	N/A	N/A	N/A	N/A	N/A	N/A	0.0	0.0	GEMINI INS CO
4.9	4.4	-115.7	N/A	15.8	18.7	N/A	N/A	N/A	102.6	-144.5	0.0	GENERAL AUTOMOBILE INS CO
1.6	1.1	145.9	121.9	-4.6	-14.7	75.6	31.2	106.8	85.7	-0.9	24.7 •	GENERAL CASUALTY CO OF WI
10.4	9.3	N/A	N/A	N/A	N/A	N/A	N/A	N/A	N/A	100.0	0.0	GENERAL CASUALTY INS CO
7.4	7.2	N/A	N/A	N/A	N/A	N/A	N/A	N/A	N/A	0.0	13.1	GENERAL INS CO OF AM
1.3	1.2	7.8	34.1	-1.3	-2.2	92.8	30.0	122.8	90.3	61.0	50.5 •	GENERAL REINS CORP
1.6	1.0	17.5	94.1	0.5	1.5	117.7	100.7	218.4	9.3	-52.1	0.0	GENERAL SECURITY IND CO OF AZ
1.9	1.1	64.0	136.5	-1.0	-3.3	80.9	45.9	126.8	122.4	-5.7	0.0	GENERAL SECURITY NATIONAL INS CO
4.7	2.9	12.6	21.2	-4.1	-7.7	60.4	35.6	96.0	117.3	25.8	0.0 •	GENERAL STAR INDEMNITY CO
8.2	5.3	6.1	20.9	-2.1	-6.1	56.5	41.7	98.2	121.4	10.4	0.0	GENERAL STAR NATIONAL INS CO
0.8	0.6	1.6	41.5	16.5	18.0	999 +	70.8	999 +	115.1	-22.5	0.3	GENERALI - US BRANCH
2.4	1.5	82.6	12.0	-1.4	0.2	60.6	30.2	90.8	113.5	13.0	0.0	GENESEE PATRONS COOP INS
6.6	4.6	7.5	37.6	0.1	-6.2	109.4	27.5	136.9	61.1	10.1	0.0	GENESIS INS CO
0.7	0.7	223.4	87.3	24.2	14.4	68.3	36.5	104.8	88.4	-22.3	0.0	GENEVA INS CO
N/A	N/A	--	--	--	--	--	--	--	--	--	--	GENWORTH FINANCIAL ASR CORP
2.8	2.4	50.0	29.2	-4.9	-5.9	15.5	24.7	40.2	159.2	1.1	14.7 •	GENWORTH MORTGAGE INS CORP
8.8	7.9	7.0	3.0	2.3	3.6	46.8	8.3	55.1	123.5	-24.0	0.0	GENWORTH MORTGAGE REINS CORP
3.3	2.8	38.5	30.3	-5.0	-4.7	16.5	0.4	16.9	180.8	7.4	14.6	GENWORTH MTG INS CORP OF NC
3.2	2.3	84.4	69.0	2.7	1.5	82.2	30.0	112.2	98.9	6.1	0.0	GEORGIA CASUALTY & SURETY CO
N/A	N/A	--	--	--	--	--	--	--	--	--	--	GEORGIA DEALERS INS CO
173.5	81.2	N/A	N/A	N/A	N/A	N/A	N/A	N/A	N/A	0.0	0.0	GEORGIA FARM BUREAU CASUALTY INS
2.4	1.8	156.8	70.9	-0.5	3.8	78.5	23.2	101.7	92.1	-16.9	1.6 •	GEORGIA FARM BUREAU MUTUAL INS
1.9	0.7	71.6	167.3	-9.1	-30.5	75.7	14.3	90.0	146.2	1.7	0.0	GEORGIA MUNICIPAL CAPTIVE INS CO
2.1	1.2	50.8	74.5	0.5	-1.6	75.1	25.0	100.1	105.3	-1.3	0.0	GEORGIA TRANSPORTATION CAPTIVE
0.3	0.2	153.4	36.0	3.1	-1.0	65.2	28.8	94.0	118.2	17.9	0.0	GEOVERA INS CO
0.4	0.3	89.7	21.1	1.8	-0.6	65.2	28.8	94.0	145.5	17.9	0.0	GEOVERA SPECIALTY INS CO
6.1	5.3	29.0	9.1	-0.8	0.7	72.2	18.8	91.0	102.6	13.2	0.0	GERMAN AMERICAN FARM MUTUAL

999 + Denotes number greater than 999.9%
999 - Denotes number less than -999.99%
• Bullets denote a more detailed analysis is available in Section II.

INSURANCE COMPANY NAME	DOM. STATE	RATING	TOTAL ASSETS ($MIL)	CAPITAL & SURPLUS ($MIL)	ANNUAL NET PREMIUM ($MIL)	NET INCOME ($MIL)	CAPITAL-IZATION INDEX (PTS)	RESERVE ADQ INDEX (PTS)	PROFIT-ABILITY INDEX (PTS)	LIQUIDITY INDEX (PTS)	STAB. INDEX (PTS)	STABILITY FACTORS
▲GERMAN MUTUAL INS CO	OH	D+	45.0	18.7	22.1	1.7	7.6	6.1	5.2	6.7	2.5	DR
▲GERMANIA FARM MUTUAL INS ASN	TX	C+	395.7	192.6	200.6	10.6	7.2	5.9	5.3	4.3	4.5	LR
GERMANIA FIRE & CASUALTY CO	TX	C	32.8	9.2	26.6	-2.6	5.8	5.6	1.6	1.2	3.9	DFLR
GERMANIA INS CO	TX	C+	82.6	51.5	25.6	4.1	10.0	6.0	8.9	6.7	4.9	R
▼GERMANIA SELECT INS CO	TX	C	211.2	61.1	170.2	-9.1	7.7	5.8	2.1	1.5	4.1	FLR
GERMANTOWN INS CO	PA	C+	98.2	50.1	32.3	3.5	10.0	6.3	8.0	6.7	4.7	T
▲GERMANTOWN MUTUAL INS CO	WI	B	113.0	61.7	47.9	4.6	10.0	8.9	8.6	6.2	5.5	
GLENCAR INSURANCE CO	WI	U	--	--	--	--	N/A	--	--	--	--	Z
GLOBAL HAWK INS CO RRG	VT	E-	59.6	7.1	19.8	-6.4	0.0	0.3	0.9	7.4	0.1	CDFR
GLOBAL HAWK PPTY CAS INS CO	DE	U	--	--	--	--	N/A	--	--	--	--	Z
GLOBAL INS CO	GA	U (5)	--	--	--	--	N/A	--	--	--	--	Z
▼GLOBAL LIBERTY INS CO OF NY	NY	D-	71.4	15.1	40.3	-5.1	2.1	0.8	2.0	5.2	1.2	DFRT
GLOBAL REINS CORP OF AM	NY	D+	236.9	100.8	0.1	15.0	7.3	8.9	2.2	8.5	2.7	DFGR
GNY CUSTOM INS CO	AZ	B+	60.5	54.0	3.2	1.2	10.0	5.0	6.9	9.2	6.5	D
▲GOAUTO INS CO	LA	D+	52.6	16.0	28.7	6.0	2.8	6.3	2.9	6.1	2.5	CDRT
▲GOLDEN BEAR INS CO	CA	B	154.9	53.8	35.5	2.0	7.4	9.8	8.6	7.3	5.5	T
GOLDEN EAGLE INS CORP	NH	C	59.2	57.0	0.0	-0.3	10.0	N/A	4.8	7.0	4.0	DRT
▼GOLDEN INS CO A RRG	NC	E+	15.2	2.2	4.2	-0.6	0.3	1.3	1.5	7.5	0.5	CDFT
GOLDSTREET INS CO	NY	U	--	--	--	--	N/A	--	--	--	--	Z
▲GOOD SHEPHERD RECIPROCAL RRG	SC	D+	10.9	8.3	2.6	1.9	4.9	4.8	9.1	9.2	2.5	DG
GOODVILLE MUTUAL CAS CO	PA	B	274.0	160.5	125.4	7.7	10.0	6.1	8.8	6.8	6.0	
GOTHAM INS CO	NY	C	299.3	79.0	90.6	3.8	7.1	3.8	4.3	7.1	4.1	G
GOVERNMENT EMPLOYEES INS CO	MD	B	33,381.7	20,424.2	7,722.5	4,378.3	8.5	9.2	8.7	6.7	5.3	T
GOVERNMENT ENTITIES MUTUAL INC	DC	U (5)	--	--	--	--	N/A	--	--	--	--	Z
GOVERNMENTAL INTERINS	IL	B	64.6	49.2	5.5	1.6	10.0	8.3	5.7	7.3	5.6	DF
▲GOVT TECHNOLOGY INS CO RRG INC	NV	E+	1.2	0.8	0.8	0.0	7.0	N/A	6.3	5.8	0.5	DFT
GRACO RRG INC	SC	U	--	--	--	--	N/A	--	--	--	--	Z
▲GRAIN DEALERS MUTUAL INS CO	IN	C	12.4	10.8	0.0	1.4	10.0	N/A	7.1	8.8	3.4	DR
GRANADA INS CO	FL	E+	42.3	13.5	11.8	1.3	1.6	0.6	5.4	7.9	0.6	DFGR
GRANGE INDEMNITY INS CO	OH	C	58.5	58.3	-18.7	4.2	10.0	4.6	8.7	6.7	4.2	FT
GRANGE INS ASSN	WA	B-	295.2	136.8	165.4	-12.4	8.6	5.8	3.2	5.9	4.7	R
GRANGE INS CO OF MI	OH	C	44.5	44.4	-11.7	2.5	10.0	4.6	8.5	6.8	4.2	FT
GRANGE MUTUAL CAS CO	OH	B	2,552.6	1,214.5	1,186.5	104.2	8.5	6.1	8.7	6.4	5.0	
GRANGE MUTUAL FIRE INS CO	PA	D+	5.1	4.1	1.2	0.4	9.3	7.4	8.4	7.1	2.1	DR
▲GRANGE P&C INS CO	OH	B	44.2	44.2	-9.3	2.3	10.0	4.6	8.8	6.9	5.5	FT
GRANITE MUTUAL INS CO	VT	C+	4.6	4.6	0.0	0.1	10.0	N/A	6.3	7.0	3.5	DR
▲GRANITE RE INC	OK	B	60.9	41.6	26.2	9.2	7.4	10.0	8.7	6.9	5.4	DGR
GRANITE STATE INS CO	IL	B-	35.8	33.8	0.0	2.1	10.0	N/A	6.8	7.0	5.1	
GRANWEST P&C	WA	C	23.8	20.9	0.0	0.4	10.0	6.6	6.5	9.5	3.5	DFRT
GRAPHIC ARTS MUTUAL INS CO	NY	C+	157.6	60.5	48.6	2.5	10.0	6.5	6.9	6.8	4.4	T
▲GRAY CASUALTY & SURETY CO	LA	C+	18.2	14.8	2.6	0.2	10.0	3.6	4.2	9.1	4.5	DR
GRAY INDEMNITY CO	TX	U	--	--	--	--	N/A	--	--	--	--	Z
▲GRAY INS CO	LA	B-	299.8	119.0	67.4	0.0	7.4	3.6	6.7	6.9	4.7	R
GRAY INS CO OF LOUISIANA	LA	U	--	--	--	--	N/A	--	--	--	--	Z
GREAT AMERICAN ALLIANCE INS CO	OH	C	27.9	27.9	0.0	0.6	10.0	N/A	3.9	7.0	4.3	AR
GREAT AMERICAN ASR CO	OH	C+	18.5	18.5	0.0	0.2	10.0	N/A	4.4	7.0	4.4	ADR
GREAT AMERICAN CASUALTY INS CO	OH	U	--	--	--	--	N/A	--	--	--	--	Z
GREAT AMERICAN CONTEMPORARY INS CO	OH	U	--	--	--	--	N/A	--	--	--	--	Z
GREAT AMERICAN E & S INS CO	DE	C	48.4	47.8	0.0	0.8	10.0	N/A	6.0	7.0	4.0	AR
GREAT AMERICAN FIDELITY INS CO	DE	C	48.5	48.0	0.0	0.9	10.0	N/A	6.0	7.0	4.0	ADR
GREAT AMERICAN INS CO	OH	B	7,076.5	1,668.4	2,728.8	446.6	7.5	6.5	7.1	6.7	5.3	A
GREAT AMERICAN INS CO OF NEW YORK	NY	C	49.7	49.2	0.0	0.8	10.0	N/A	6.2	7.0	4.3	AR

See Page 27 for explanation of footnotes and Page 28 for explanation of stability factors.

70

www.weissratings.com

Arrows denote recent upgrades ▲ or downgrades ▼   (see Section VII for explanations)

RISK ADJ. CAPITAL RATIO #1	CAPITAL RATIO #2	PREMIUM TO SURPLUS (%)	RESV. TO SURPLUS (%)	RESV. DEVELOP. 1 YEAR (%)	RESV. DEVELOP. 2 YEAR (%)	LOSS RATIO (%)	EXP. RATIO (%)	COMB. RATIO (%)	CASH FROM UNDER-WRITING (%)	NET PREMIUM GROWTH (%)	INVEST. IN AFFIL (%)	INSURANCE COMPANY NAME
2.4	1.6	118.1	40.1	-1.7	-3.1	68.5	27.4	95.9	110.5	7.2	0.0	GERMAN MUTUAL INS CO
1.3	1.2	104.2	9.8	-1.5	0.4	69.4	26.1	95.5	103.3	5.4	47.9	GERMANIA FARM MUTUAL INS ASN
1.0	0.8	288.4	94.4	5.0	4.9	88.6	25.0	113.6	91.2	33.8	0.0	GERMANIA FIRE & CASUALTY CO
4.4	3.7	49.8	28.2	-0.8	1.2	55.6	27.8	83.4	125.9	5.3	0.0	GERMANIA INS CO
1.7	1.4	278.4	90.2	1.7	6.0	81.1	27.9	109.0	94.2	11.2	1.4	GERMANIA SELECT INS CO
4.7	3.5	64.4	38.1	-1.7	-2.3	64.1	28.3	92.4	104.9	4.9	0.0	GERMANTOWN INS CO
6.5	4.5	77.6	33.5	-11.8	-12.2	61.1	30.7	91.8	105.0	2.4	0.0	GERMANTOWN MUTUAL INS CO
N/A	N/A	--	--	--	--	--	--	--	--	--	--	GLENCAR INSURANCE CO
0.0	0.0	278.4	492.1	277.0	271.7	116.7	24.8	141.5	92.7	-14.6	0.0	GLOBAL HAWK INS CO RRG
N/A	N/A	--	--	--	--	--	--	--	--	--	--	GLOBAL HAWK PPTY CAS INS CO
N/A	N/A	--	--	--	--	--	--	--	--	--	--	GLOBAL INS CO
0.5	0.3	266.4	185.7	46.7	75.6	91.9	26.7	118.6	96.5	11.6	0.0	GLOBAL LIBERTY INS CO OF NY
4.0	2.0	0.1	126.4	-12.0	-10.8	999 +	999 +	999 +	0.7	439.8	0.0	GLOBAL REINS CORP OF AM
22.5	18.2	5.9	8.0	N/A	0.3	64.0	30.4	94.4	119.4	10.6	0.0 ●	GNY CUSTOM INS CO
0.7	0.6	179.6	82.2	-0.3	-2.5	107.7	-32.6	75.1	118.4	30.2	0.0	GOAUTO INS CO
1.8	1.2	65.9	131.0	-20.5	-52.7	67.8	29.9	97.7	162.2	24.9	0.0	GOLDEN BEAR INS CO
73.7	66.3	N/A	N/A	N/A	N/A	N/A	N/A	N/A	N/A	0.0	0.0	GOLDEN EAGLE INS CORP
0.1	0.1	194.4	266.3	43.8	33.7	111.5	22.4	133.9	92.4	-10.3	0.0	GOLDEN INS CO A RRG
N/A	N/A	--	--	--	--	--	--	--	--	--	--	GOLDSTREET INS CO
1.2	1.0	31.2	31.4	-10.1	-2.4	20.6	9.9	30.5	477.2	48.6	0.0	GOOD SHEPHERD RECIPROCAL RRG
5.3	3.5	78.1	26.5	-1.1	-2.0	68.5	27.4	95.9	110.5	7.2	0.0	GOODVILLE MUTUAL CAS CO
1.5	1.0	114.8	193.2	5.0	10.0	64.4	31.6	96.0	216.1	22.9	0.0	GOTHAM INS CO
3.3	2.0	37.8	27.3	-0.1	-0.8	87.3	7.8	95.1	110.6	10.5	0.6 ●	GOVERNMENT EMPLOYEES INS CO
N/A	N/A	--	--	--	--	--	--	--	--	--	--	GOVERNMENT ENTITIES MUTUAL INC
8.1	6.0	11.3	20.5	-4.7	-5.7	49.1	58.6	107.7	65.2	-3.8	0.0	GOVERNMENTAL INTERINS
1.4	1.0	106.2	N/A	N/A	N/A	46.6	57.5	104.1	86.3	166.0	0.0	GOVT TECHNOLOGY INS CO RRG INC
N/A	N/A	--	--	--	--	--	--	--	--	--	--	GRACO RRG INC
18.0	16.2	N/A	N/A	N/A	N/A	N/A	N/A	N/A	-18.8	0.0	0.0	GRAIN DEALERS MUTUAL INS CO
0.9	0.6	87.6	121.3	19.4	39.4	90.7	-1.6	89.1	61.2	16.3	0.0	GRANADA INS CO
95.1	44.6	-32.0	N/A	N/A	N/A	N/A	N/A	N/A	-30.7	-139.9	0.0	GRANGE INDEMNITY INS CO
2.7	2.0	120.9	53.1	5.0	2.4	84.3	27.2	111.5	95.1	7.3	8.3	GRANGE INS ASSN
110.5	55.0	-26.3	N/A	N/A	N/A	N/A	N/A	N/A	-29.9	-139.9	0.0	GRANGE INS CO OF MI
2.6	1.9	97.7	55.2	-1.8	-2.8	64.6	28.3	92.9	116.5	20.7	13.0 ●	GRANGE MUTUAL CAS CO
4.3	2.6	29.1	1.7	-0.7	-1.3	24.6	49.8	74.4	125.3	12.8	0.0	GRANGE MUTUAL FIRE INS CO
86.2	40.1	-21.2	N/A	N/A	N/A	N/A	N/A	N/A	-40.0	-139.9	0.0	GRANGE P&C INS CO
106.3	55.1	N/A	N/A	N/A	N/A	N/A	N/A	N/A	N/A	0.0	0.0	GRANITE MUTUAL INS CO
2.6	2.1	62.9	26.7	-49.7	-69.3	-3.3	57.6	54.3	136.4	1.3	0.0	GRANITE RE INC
48.1	39.0	N/A	N/A	N/A	N/A	N/A	N/A	N/A	N/A	0.0	0.0	GRANITE STATE INS CO
21.3	19.2	N/A	N/A	N/A	-4.1	N/A	N/A	N/A	N/A	0.0	0.0	GRANWEST P&C
4.5	3.1	80.3	106.9	-0.9	-1.9	64.4	33.1	97.5	108.4	9.5	2.5	GRAPHIC ARTS MUTUAL INS CO
6.5	4.5	17.8	15.4	N/A	0.2	35.8	53.1	88.9	97.2	18.2	0.0	GRAY CASUALTY & SURETY CO
N/A	N/A	--	--	--	--	--	--	--	--	--	--	GRAY INDEMNITY CO
1.8	1.2	56.6	134.9	N/A	N/A	68.7	42.0	110.7	92.0	16.0	10.6	GRAY INS CO
N/A	N/A	--	--	--	--	--	--	--	--	--	--	GRAY INS CO OF LOUISIANA
130.9	65.4	N/A	N/A	N/A	N/A	N/A	N/A	N/A	N/A	0.0	0.0	GREAT AMERICAN ALLIANCE INS CO
171.3	83.2	N/A	N/A	N/A	N/A	N/A	N/A	N/A	N/A	0.0	0.0	GREAT AMERICAN ASR CO
N/A	N/A	--	--	--	--	--	--	--	--	--	--	GREAT AMERICAN CASUALTY INS CO
N/A	N/A	--	--	--	--	--	--	--	--	--	--	GREAT AMERICAN CONTEMPORARY INS
100.0	51.8	N/A	N/A	N/A	N/A	N/A	N/A	N/A	N/A	0.0	0.0	GREAT AMERICAN E & S INS CO
97.7	50.6	N/A	N/A	N/A	N/A	N/A	N/A	N/A	N/A	0.0	0.0	GREAT AMERICAN FIDELITY INS CO
1.8	1.3	163.6	193.9	1.3	0.3	62.1	31.0	93.1	129.5	10.4	8.1 ●	GREAT AMERICAN INS CO
87.1	45.8	N/A	N/A	N/A	N/A	N/A	N/A	N/A	N/A	0.0	0.0	GREAT AMERICAN INS CO OF NEW

999 + Denotes number greater than 999.9%
999 - Denotes number less than -999.99%
● Bullets denote a more detailed analysis is available in Section II.

INSURANCE COMPANY NAME	DOM. STATE	RATING	TOTAL ASSETS ($MIL)	CAPITAL & SURPLUS ($MIL)	ANNUAL NET PREMIUM ($MIL)	NET INCOME ($MIL)	CAPITAL-IZATION INDEX (PTS)	RESERVE ADQ INDEX (PTS)	PROFIT-ABILITY INDEX (PTS)	LIQUIDITY INDEX (PTS)	STAB. INDEX (PTS)	STABILITY FACTORS
GREAT AMERICAN LLOYDS INS CO	TX	U	--	--	--	--	N/A	--	--	--	--	Z
GREAT AMERICAN PROTECTION INS CO	OH	U	--	--	--	--	N/A	--	--	--	--	Z
GREAT AMERICAN SECURITY INS CO	OH	C	15.5	15.5	0.0	0.2	10.0	N/A	3.7	7.0	3.2	ADRT
GREAT AMERICAN SPIRIT INS CO	OH	C	17.1	17.1	0.0	0.2	10.0	N/A	3.7	7.0	3.3	ADRT
GREAT DIVIDE INS CO	ND	C	254.1	69.2	0.0	1.5	10.0	N/A	6.3	7.0	4.3	FR
GREAT FALLS INS CO	ME	D+	13.4	5.8	3.0	2.3	5.2	6.4	5.4	7.3	2.2	D
GREAT LAKES MUTUAL INS CO	MI	C-	12.6	8.9	3.7	1.0	10.0	8.6	8.8	7.6	2.7	D
GREAT MIDWEST INS CO	TX	B	215.3	107.0	73.0	-1.0	8.0	3.5	3.6	7.2	5.6	F
▲GREAT NORTHERN INS CO	IN	B	1,698.4	557.4	203.0	65.2	9.1	9.2	8.7	6.9	5.5	T
GREAT NORTHWEST INS CO	MN	C-	19.4	7.7	0.0	0.5	9.5	4.2	6.2	10.0	3.3	DR
GREAT PLAINS CASUALTY INC	IA	C+	23.5	21.0	4.8	2.2	10.0	8.5	8.9	7.8	4.0	D
GREAT WEST CASUALTY CO	NE	B	2,133.2	626.0	900.4	62.7	8.4	9.1	8.2	6.4	6.2	A
GREATER NEW YORK MUTUAL INS CO	NY	B-	1,057.8	503.2	266.4	21.7	8.4	5.9	8.1	6.9	4.7	R
▲GREEN HILLS INS CO A RRG	VT	E+	12.3	4.9	4.0	2.2	7.0	10.0	3.4	6.6	0.5	D
GREEN MOUNTAIN INS CO	VT	B	13.4	12.8	0.0	0.3	9.8	N/A	7.5	7.0	4.6	D
GREEN TREE PERPETUAL ASR CO	PA	U	--	--	--	--	N/A	--	--	--	--	Z
▲GREENVILLE CASUALTY INS CO INC	SC	C	9.5	5.9	4.8	0.2	7.9	4.3	2.9	5.6	2.9	DFT
GREENWICH INS CO	DE	C	1,250.4	359.9	253.3	-11.0	7.5	6.3	3.9	6.7	3.8	AR
GREYHAWK INSURANCE CO	CO	U	--	--	--	--	N/A	--	--	--	--	Z
GREYHAWK SPECIALTY INS CO	RI	U	--	--	--	--	N/A	--	--	--	--	Z
GRINNELL COMPASS INC	IA	U	--	--	--	--	N/A	--	--	--	--	Z
GRINNELL MUTUAL REINS CO	IA	B-	1,179.7	613.7	595.8	39.2	9.6	8.0	8.8	6.1	4.7	R
GRINNELL SELECT INS CO	IA	C	37.8	20.0	0.0	0.4	10.0	N/A	3.0	10.0	3.9	DFT
▲GROWERS AUTOMOBILE INS ASN	IN	C-	8.1	6.9	0.1	0.1	7.5	5.0	4.7	10.0	2.1	DT
GUARANTEE CO OF NORTH AMERICA USA	MI	B	230.5	190.0	54.5	15.6	10.0	6.3	8.4	9.2	6.0	
GUARANTEE INS CO	FL	F (3)	400.4	50.5	103.4	3.1	0.8	0.2	2.6	0.5	0.0	CFLR
▼GUARDIAN INS CO	VI	C-	37.2	11.5	16.0	-1.1	7.3	5.8	2.0	7.9	3.3	D
GUIDEONE AMERICA INS CO	IA	C+	12.1	11.0	0.0	0.2	10.0	N/A	6.6	7.0	4.5	DR
GUIDEONE ELITE INS CO	IA	C+	30.0	25.5	0.0	0.4	10.0	N/A	7.3	7.0	4.6	R
▼GUIDEONE MUTUAL INS CO	IA	C	1,049.1	363.1	260.5	-85.5	7.1	6.6	1.8	6.0	3.8	FR
▲GUIDEONE NATIONAL INS CO	IA	B-	52.8	48.6	0.0	0.9	10.0	N/A	7.9	10.0	4.9	
▼GUIDEONE P&C INS CO	IA	C+	378.4	204.2	81.4	-22.4	8.0	6.3	2.4	6.5	4.8	FR
▼GUIDEONE SPECIALTY MUTUAL INS CO	IA	C	226.6	79.3	65.1	-16.6	7.2	6.7	2.0	6.0	3.9	FR
GUILDERLAND REINS CO	NY	U	--	--	--	--	N/A	--	--	--	--	Z
GUILFORD INS CO	IL	C-	371.3	272.5	29.8	4.3	7.9	7.9	5.6	7.0	2.6	FR
GULF BUILDERS RRG INC	SC	F (5)	0.0	0.0	-0.1	0.0	3.0	4.6	0.8	10.0	0.0	FGT
GULF GUARANTY INS CO	MS	C	4.5	3.9	0.4	0.1	10.0	6.2	3.8	9.1	2.9	DF
GULF STATES INS CO (LA)	LA	D+	6.4	5.1	1.1	0.0	10.0	N/A	3.9	9.5	2.4	DT
GULF UNDERWRITERS INS CO	CT	U	--	--	--	--	N/A	--	--	--	--	Z
▼GULFSTREAM P&C INS CO	FL	C+	110.1	31.5	59.6	0.6	7.5	8.7	2.9	7.3	4.7	
▲GUTHRIE RRG	SC	C+	57.9	19.9	7.8	5.1	7.4	9.4	6.5	7.8	4.0	D
▲HALIFAX MUTUAL INS CO	NC	D+	9.7	4.9	4.2	0.3	7.6	8.6	6.4	7.2	2.2	DR
HALLMARK COUNTY MUTUAL INS CO	TX	C	5.8	5.5	0.0	0.0	10.0	N/A	5.3	7.4	3.6	DFR
HALLMARK INS CO	AZ	D+	308.4	96.0	117.0	0.7	7.9	4.4	6.0	6.8	2.2	R
HALLMARK NATIONAL INS CO	AZ	C	87.0	24.1	36.6	0.1	7.7	4.3	4.0	7.1	4.0	DR
▲HALLMARK SPECIALTY INS CO	OK	B	250.9	57.4	87.7	0.0	7.8	4.1	4.1	6.6	5.5	
HAMDEN ASR RRG INC	VT	U	--	--	--	--	N/A	--	--	--	--	Z
HANOVER AMERICAN INS CO	NH	C	29.3	29.3	0.0	0.6	10.0	N/A	5.6	7.0	4.3	R
HANOVER FIRE & CASUALTY INS CO	PA	D+	5.8	3.3	4.2	0.1	5.3	6.4	7.9	6.7	2.1	DR
▼HANOVER INS CO	NH	B-	7,748.1	2,071.7	3,337.1	270.1	7.1	3.1	5.6	5.9	5.1	A
HANOVER LLOYDS INS CO	TX	C+	6.2	6.2	0.0	0.1	10.0	N/A	7.1	7.0	3.8	DR
HANOVER NATIONAL INS CO	NH	U	--	--	--	--	N/A	--	--	--	--	Z

See Page 27 for explanation of footnotes and   72   www.weissratings.com
Page 28 for explanation of stability factors.
Arrows denote recent upgrades ▲ or downgrades ▼   (see Section VII for explanations)

RISK ADJ. RATIO #1	CAPITAL RATIO #2	PREMIUM TO SURPLUS (%)	RESV. TO SURPLUS (%)	RESV. DEVELOP. 1 YEAR (%)	2 YEAR (%)	LOSS RATIO (%)	EXP. RATIO (%)	COMB RATIO (%)	CASH FROM UNDER-WRITING (%)	NET PREMIUM GROWTH (%)	INVEST. IN AFFIL (%)	INSURANCE COMPANY NAME
N/A	N/A	--	--	--	--	--	--	--	--	--	--	GREAT AMERICAN LLOYDS INS CO
N/A	N/A	--	--	--	--	--	--	--	--	--	--	GREAT AMERICAN PROTECTION INS CO
223.0	111.5	N/A	N/A	N/A	N/A	N/A	N/A	N/A	N/A	0.0	0.0	GREAT AMERICAN SECURITY INS CO
218.0	109.0	N/A	N/A	N/A	N/A	N/A	N/A	N/A	N/A	0.0	0.0	GREAT AMERICAN SPIRIT INS CO
7.0	6.3	N/A	N/A	N/A	N/A	N/A	N/A	N/A	999 +	0.0	0.0	GREAT DIVIDE INS CO
1.8	0.9	51.6	54.5	-1.8	-5.7	82.6	-62.3	20.3	160.0	-1.0	0.0	GREAT FALLS INS CO
6.8	4.1	41.4	12.7	-2.2	-6.0	32.1	35.1	67.2	149.3	-4.3	0.0	GREAT LAKES MUTUAL INS CO
2.6	1.6	68.3	62.0	2.8	16.3	75.8	29.5	105.3	89.3	-15.3	0.5	GREAT MIDWEST INS CO
4.7	2.9	36.4	103.4	-4.6	-11.2	62.6	25.4	88.0	105.6	-19.9	0.0 ●	GREAT NORTHERN INS CO
2.9	2.6	N/A	3.8	-0.4	-2.4	N/A	N/A	N/A	47.5	0.0	0.0	GREAT NORTHWEST INS CO
5.8	3.4	22.7	5.7	-3.5	-4.3	30.6	11.8	42.4	164.9	-8.7	0.0	GREAT PLAINS CASUALTY INC
3.2	1.9	143.8	138.2	-1.9	-2.5	75.3	21.8	97.1	113.6	8.3	0.0 ●	GREAT WEST CASUALTY CO
2.2	1.9	52.9	72.0	-0.1	2.9	64.0	29.3	93.3	119.4	10.6	15.7 ●	GREATER NEW YORK MUTUAL INS CO
1.6	1.0	82.9	80.8	-32.4	-56.3	-7.3	23.8	16.5	257.9	2.4	0.0	GREEN HILLS INS CO A RRG
4.9	2.8	N/A	N/A	N/A	N/A	N/A	N/A	N/A	N/A	0.0	0.0	GREEN MOUNTAIN INS CO
N/A	N/A	--	--	--	--	--	--	--	--	--	--	GREEN TREE PERPETUAL ASR CO
2.0	1.8	80.3	23.3	10.5	8.5	58.8	37.7	96.5	87.3	-8.8	56.4	GREENVILLE CASUALTY INS CO INC
1.5	1.3	70.4	115.2	-2.6	-2.6	76.8	25.4	102.2	136.5	26.6	26.3 ●	GREENWICH INS CO
N/A	N/A	--	--	--	--	--	--	--	--	--	--	GREYHAWK INSURANCE CO
N/A	N/A	--	--	--	--	--	--	--	--	--	--	GREYHAWK SPECIALTY INS CO
N/A	N/A	--	--	--	--	--	--	--	--	--	--	GRINNELL COMPASS INC
4.5	3.2	97.1	47.7	-1.0	-3.3	73.2	26.2	99.4	107.7	7.1	2.4 ●	GRINNELL MUTUAL REINS CO
6.1	5.4	N/A	N/A	N/A	N/A	N/A	N/A	N/A	999 +	0.0	0.0	GRINNELL SELECT INS CO
2.3	1.4	1.5	0.1	-0.2	-1.3	79.6	110.5	190.1	58.1	-6.1	0.0	GROWERS AUTOMOBILE INS ASN
8.2	6.2	28.7	4.6	-1.7	-1.4	16.3	58.8	75.1	138.9	18.2	0.0	GUARANTEE CO OF NORTH AMERICA
0.2	0.1	203.6	129.9	71.9	122.0	82.0	31.6	113.6	65.4	59.5	8.2	GUARANTEE INS CO
1.5	1.2	139.1	34.5	3.1	4.3	65.7	43.7	109.4	184.7	-14.0	7.5	GUARDIAN INS CO
23.5	21.1	N/A	N/A	N/A	N/A	N/A	N/A	N/A	54.1	0.0	0.0	GUIDEONE AMERICA INS CO
18.3	16.5	N/A	N/A	N/A	N/A	N/A	N/A	N/A	153.3	0.0	0.0	GUIDEONE ELITE INS CO
1.4	1.0	71.7	132.3	8.8	3.9	108.9	33.1	142.0	74.7	-26.4	22.4 ●	GUIDEONE MUTUAL INS CO
36.7	31.1	N/A	N/A	N/A	N/A	N/A	N/A	N/A	-85.3	0.0	0.0	GUIDEONE NATIONAL INS CO
2.0	1.6	39.8	73.5	5.2	2.3	108.9	33.4	142.3	73.2	-26.4	26.9	GUIDEONE P&C INS CO
1.7	1.1	82.1	151.4	9.9	4.6	108.9	33.4	142.3	74.1	-26.4	8.2	GUIDEONE SPECIALTY MUTUAL INS CO
N/A	N/A	--	--	--	--	--	--	--	--	--	--	GUILDERLAND REINS CO
1.6	1.6	10.9	26.9	-1.6	-3.1	46.5	53.9	100.4	77.7	6.8	49.8 ●	GUILFORD INS CO
0.5	0.5	-52.9	20.2	-3.2	-0.7	27.2	-79.2	-52.0	1.0	-167.1	0.0	GULF BUILDERS RRG INC
9.1	6.4	9.7	0.9	-0.7	-0.9	29.7	82.9	112.6	41.9	-9.4	0.0	GULF GUARANTY INS CO
5.4	3.9	21.7	2.8	N/A	N/A	44.7	26.7	71.4	179.1	0.0	0.0	GULF STATES INS CO (LA)
N/A	N/A	--	--	--	--	--	--	--	--	--	--	GULF UNDERWRITERS INS CO
1.5	1.3	189.5	43.2	-7.6	-1.9	63.6	37.8	101.4	104.0	-2.9	0.0	GULFSTREAM P&C INS CO
1.7	1.3	39.0	170.3	-19.8	-14.1	59.9	5.1	65.0	323.8	2.1	0.0	GUTHRIE RRG
2.2	1.5	84.2	8.9	-2.7	-4.7	58.3	28.3	86.6	113.6	8.6	0.0	HALIFAX MUTUAL INS CO
36.3	32.7	N/A	N/A	N/A	N/A	N/A	N/A	N/A	N/A	0.0	0.0	HALLMARK COUNTY MUTUAL INS CO
2.2	1.5	121.8	123.7	11.6	11.7	79.1	26.6	105.7	102.7	1.0	9.7	HALLMARK INS CO
2.3	1.4	151.6	153.9	14.6	14.9	79.1	27.2	106.3	106.3	1.0	0.0	HALLMARK NATIONAL INS CO
2.4	1.5	152.8	155.1	15.3	15.4	79.1	27.3	106.4	99.0	1.0	0.0	HALLMARK SPECIALTY INS CO
N/A	N/A	--	--	--	--	--	--	--	--	--	--	HAMDEN ASR RRG INC
80.0	37.2	N/A	N/A	N/A	N/A	N/A	N/A	N/A	N/A	0.0	0.0	HANOVER AMERICAN INS CO
0.9	0.7	124.8	14.3	-1.2	-0.2	17.1	81.3	98.4	102.5	-7.2	0.0	HANOVER FIRE & CASUALTY INS CO
1.3	1.0	161.1	159.3	4.7	17.4	66.4	33.7	100.1	109.1	5.2	19.1 ●	HANOVER INS CO
71.6	31.7	N/A	N/A	N/A	N/A	N/A	N/A	N/A	N/A	0.0	0.0	HANOVER LLOYDS INS CO
N/A	N/A	--	--	--	--	--	--	--	--	--	--	HANOVER NATIONAL INS CO

999 + Denotes number greater than 999.9%
999 - Denotes number less than -999.99%
● Bullets denote a more detailed analysis is available in Section II.

INSURANCE COMPANY NAME	DOM. STATE	RATING	TOTAL ASSETS ($MIL)	CAPITAL & SURPLUS ($MIL)	ANNUAL NET PREMIUM ($MIL)	NET INCOME ($MIL)	CAPITAL-IZATION INDEX (PTS)	RESERVE ADQ INDEX (PTS)	PROFIT-ABILITY INDEX (PTS)	LIQUIDITY INDEX (PTS)	STAB. INDEX (PTS)	STABILITY FACTORS
HANOVER NJ INS CO	NH	U	--	--	--	--	N/A	--	--	--	--	Z
HARBOR INS CO	OK	D+	11.2	3.6	5.1	0.5	7.6	7.0	5.6	7.6	2.1	D
HARCO NATIONAL INS CO	IL	B-	606.1	204.1	156.3	1.2	6.8	4.6	6.7	6.3	4.3	GRT
HARFORD MUTUAL INS CO	MD	B-	467.1	232.0	134.5	7.8	8.4	6.1	8.1	7.0	4.7	R
HARLEYSVILLE INS CO	OH	C	167.8	27.9	0.0	2.3	9.5	N/A	6.6	6.3	3.8	A
HARLEYSVILLE INS CO OF NEW YORK	OH	C	59.4	24.4	0.0	0.6	10.0	N/A	6.1	7.0	3.8	DR
▼HARLEYSVILLE INS CO OF NJ	NJ	C-	61.6	22.0	0.0	3.8	10.0	N/A	1.9	7.0	3.2	ADT
▼HARLEYSVILLE LAKE STATES INS CO	MI	C-	36.2	19.3	0.0	4.3	10.0	N/A	2.0	7.0	3.3	ADT
HARLEYSVILLE PREFERRED INS CO	OH	C	118.3	51.2	0.0	1.1	10.0	N/A	5.1	7.0	3.8	A
HARLEYSVILLE WORCESTER INS CO	OH	C	181.7	59.4	0.0	3.9	10.0	N/A	3.9	7.0	3.8	A
HARTFORD ACCIDENT & INDEMNITY CO	CT	B	11,906.6	2,833.4	3,499.7	468.1	7.4	5.8	3.6	6.6	5.5	A
HARTFORD CASUALTY INS CO	IN	B	2,352.3	886.5	588.8	76.7	9.9	5.9	5.2	6.8	5.9	A
▼HARTFORD FIRE INS CO	CT	C+	22,855.3	9,916.0	4,442.9	1,257.1	7.8	5.9	3.0	6.9	4.8	AR
HARTFORD INS CO OF IL	IL	B	3,965.3	1,253.5	1,081.3	129.7	9.0	5.8	4.8	6.7	5.7	A
HARTFORD INS CO OF THE MIDWEST	IN	B	636.9	507.8	53.5	17.3	10.0	5.0	7.9	7.5	5.8	A
HARTFORD INS CO OF THE SOUTHEAST	CT	B	192.2	63.4	53.5	7.0	8.7	5.8	8.3	6.7	5.8	A
HARTFORD LLOYDS INS CO	TX	B	76.4	73.8	1.1	2.7	10.0	4.6	7.8	9.4	5.8	A
▼HARTFORD SM BOIL INSPECTION & INS	CT	B-	1,213.5	503.6	676.3	35.9	8.1	8.5	3.3	6.7	5.1	
▲HARTFORD SM BOIL INSPECTION IC OF CT	CT	B	15.3	13.0	-7.7	3.1	10.0	7.8	1.9	6.5	4.0	FT
HARTFORD UNDERWRITERS INS CO	CT	B	1,675.9	581.6	428.2	56.2	9.4	5.9	4.4	6.8	5.9	A
HARTLAND MUTUAL INS CO	ND	C	13.0	8.5	5.2	1.1	9.9	7.4	6.5	7.9	2.7	D
▲HASTINGS MUTUAL INS CO	MI	B+	932.1	446.2	406.6	21.2	10.0	6.5	8.2	6.6	6.5	
▲HAULERS INS CO	TN	B	77.8	42.9	38.2	4.3	9.8	7.0	6.5	6.3	5.5	F
▲HAWAII EMPLOYERS MUTUAL INS CO	HI	B	396.9	237.7	68.2	4.8	10.0	6.0	6.8	7.0	5.5	
▲HAWAIIAN INS & GUARANTY CO LTD	HI	B	28.4	14.4	11.7	0.4	8.4	6.6	8.0	7.0	5.0	D
HAWKEYE-SECURITY INS CO	WI	C	14.8	13.2	0.0	0.1	10.0	N/A	5.8	7.0	3.1	DRT
HAY CREEK MUTUAL INS CO	MN	D+	5.9	3.3	2.8	0.2	9.4	6.5	8.6	6.8	2.1	D
HCC SPECIALTY INS CO	OK	B-	22.0	16.9	0.0	0.3	10.0	N/A	6.2	10.0	4.9	DFR
HDI GLOBAL INS CO	IL	C	414.8	166.4	5.5	10.5	9.1	6.1	8.9	8.7	3.6	FGRT
HDI SPECIALTY INSURANCE CO	IL	B	48.5	47.4	0.0	0.4	10.0	N/A	4.7	10.0	4.2	DT
HEALTH CARE CASUALTY RRG INC	DC	U	--	--	--	--	N/A	--	--	--	--	Z
▲HEALTH CARE INDEMNITY INC	CO	C	326.4	116.0	23.2	10.5	7.2	9.6	3.4	6.9	3.5	FR
▲HEALTH CARE INDUSTRY LIAB RECIP INS	DC	C	50.5	17.2	3.9	0.4	8.9	6.4	7.3	7.3	3.5	DR
HEALTH CARE INS RECPL	MN	C-	27.2	8.4	7.1	0.4	5.6	9.8	3.8	6.8	2.9	DR
▲HEALTH CARE MUT CAPTIVE INS CO	GA	D+	11.9	6.3	4.9	1.0	7.1	9.6	8.5	6.9	2.4	DR
HEALTH PROVIDERS INS RECIPROCAL RRG	HI	B-	79.7	58.1	5.4	0.8	10.0	8.9	6.1	7.0	4.8	DFR
HEALTHCARE PROFESSIONAL INS CO INC	NY	D+	214.4	70.7	1.8	5.0	5.4	9.7	8.5	6.4	2.6	DFRT
▼HEALTHCARE PROVIDERS INS EXCH	PA	F (2)	32.6	6.0	-23.1	0.8	0.1	0.9	0.4	9.5	0.1	CFGR
▲HEALTHCARE UNDERWRITERS GRP MUT	OH	B	86.2	47.4	16.4	0.3	10.0	9.0	4.0	6.9	5.5	DF
▲HEALTHCARE UNDERWRITING CO RRG	VT	D+	154.9	34.0	47.2	11.3	3.1	2.6	3.8	7.6	2.5	
▲HEARTLAND MUTUAL INS CO	MN	D+	7.6	4.8	4.6	0.4	10.0	7.8	8.6	6.1	2.3	DF
▼HEREFORD INS CO	NY	D-	199.9	35.8	85.0	6.1	5.0	0.7	5.8	7.0	1.1	R
HERITAGE CASUALTY INS CO	KS	U	--	--	--	--	N/A	--	--	--	--	Z
▲HERITAGE INDEMNITY CO	CA	B-	68.6	17.7	-39.0	13.5	9.7	7.1	1.9	6.8	4.9	DFRT
▲HERITAGE P&C INS CO	FL	B-	618.4	186.0	317.3	7.6	5.3	4.5	4.3	5.8	5.1	CF
HERMITAGE INS CO	NY	F (5)	167.6	10.7	-32.3	0.0	5.2	0.9	0.1	2.3	0.0	DFLR
HIGH POINT P&C INS CO	NJ	B	360.6	336.6	0.0	9.1	7.5	N/A	6.2	7.0	5.5	T
▲HIGH POINT PREFERRED INS CO	NJ	B+	310.0	186.6	112.6	31.6	8.9	8.8	8.1	7.0	6.2	T
HIGH POINT SAFETY & INS CO	NJ	B-	67.5	55.3	0.0	1.2	10.0	N/A	8.2	7.0	5.0	
HIGHLANDS INS CO	TX	F (5)	0.0	0.0	40.8	0.0	0.0	0.7	0.0	1.9	0.0	CDFL
HIGHMARK CASUALTY INS CO	PA	C	268.1	185.3	185.7	6.1	9.5	6.9	7.7	4.7	4.2	LR
HINGHAM MUTUAL FIRE INS CO	MA	C+	68.8	44.0	21.0	2.0	8.9	7.8	5.3	6.8	4.7	R

See Page 27 for explanation of footnotes and Page 28 for explanation of stability factors.

Arrows denote recent upgrades ▲ or downgrades ▼   (see Section VII for explanations)

74   www.weissratings.com

RISK ADJ. RATIO #1	CAPITAL RATIO #2	PREMIUM TO SURPLUS (%)	RESV. TO SURPLUS (%)	RESV. DEVELOP. 1 YEAR (%)	RESV. DEVELOP. 2 YEAR (%)	LOSS RATIO (%)	EXP. RATIO (%)	COMB RATIO (%)	CASH FROM UNDER-WRITING (%)	NET PREMIUM GROWTH (%)	INVEST. IN AFFIL (%)	INSURANCE COMPANY NAME
N/A	N/A	--	--	--	--	--	--	--	--	--	--	HANOVER NJ INS CO
1.7	1.5	142.5	55.0	-10.1	-20.0	65.8	26.8	92.6	107.7	4.9	0.0	HARBOR INS CO
1.4	1.0	76.6	58.5	0.1	9.3	73.3	30.7	104.0	103.0	26.6	14.1	HARCO NATIONAL INS CO
2.4	1.9	58.0	49.9	-0.9	0.4	61.0	33.9	94.9	126.0	8.9	14.7 •	HARFORD MUTUAL INS CO
2.9	2.6	N/A	N/A	N/A	N/A	N/A	N/A	N/A	999 +	0.0	0.0	HARLEYSVILLE INS CO
4.7	4.2	N/A	N/A	N/A	N/A	N/A	N/A	N/A	72.1	0.0	0.0	HARLEYSVILLE INS CO OF NEW YORK
3.9	3.5	N/A	N/A	N/A	N/A	N/A	N/A	N/A	1.4	0.0	0.0	HARLEYSVILLE INS CO OF NJ
6.1	5.4	N/A	N/A	N/A	N/A	N/A	N/A	N/A	999 +	0.0	0.0	HARLEYSVILLE LAKE STATES INS CO
6.8	6.1	N/A	N/A	N/A	N/A	N/A	N/A	N/A	52.6	0.0	0.0	HARLEYSVILLE PREFERRED INS CO
6.4	5.8	N/A	N/A	N/A	N/A	N/A	N/A	N/A	336.2	0.0	0.0	HARLEYSVILLE WORCESTER INS CO
1.7	1.2	123.5	225.9	-1.0	2.5	68.7	29.8	98.5	110.1	1.6	8.9 •	HARTFORD ACCIDENT & INDEMNITY CO
4.5	2.9	66.4	121.5	-0.6	1.5	68.7	28.6	97.3	110.1	1.6	0.0 •	HARTFORD CASUALTY INS CO
1.8	1.6	44.8	84.8	2.0	2.9	75.1	25.9	101.0	105.8	1.6	27.8 •	HARTFORD FIRE INS CO
3.5	2.3	86.3	157.8	-0.8	2.0	68.7	29.8	98.5	110.1	1.6	0.0 •	HARTFORD INS CO OF IL
27.3	18.0	10.5	19.3	-0.1	0.3	68.7	15.5	84.2	110.1	1.6	0.0 •	HARTFORD INS CO OF THE MIDWEST
3.4	2.2	84.4	154.4	-0.8	2.3	68.7	28.0	96.7	110.1	1.6	0.0	HARTFORD INS CO OF THE SOUTHEAST
83.0	45.2	1.5	2.7	N/A	N/A	68.7	-5.3	63.4	110.1	1.6	0.0	HARTFORD LLOYDS INS CO
1.9	1.7	134.3	30.7	-3.1	-5.4	33.1	45.4	78.5	109.2	49.7	16.7 •	HARTFORD SM BOIL INSPECTION & INS
17.4	15.6	-58.9	N/A	N/A	-2.4	40.0	43.4	83.4	-131.2	-143.3	0.0	HARTFORD SM BOIL INSPECTION IC OF
3.9	2.6	73.6	134.7	-0.6	1.7	68.7	27.7	96.4	110.1	1.6	0.0 •	HARTFORD UNDERWRITERS INS CO
4.8	3.2	61.6	8.1	1.0	-0.3	42.2	37.1	79.3	118.8	-5.7	0.8	HARTLAND MUTUAL INS CO
5.3	3.5	91.1	59.6	-3.4	-4.5	66.0	30.8	96.8	108.1	1.2	0.0 •	HASTINGS MUTUAL INS CO
3.7	2.9	89.0	48.3	-5.7	-13.1	66.9	25.8	92.7	89.9	1.0	0.0	HAULERS INS CO
5.3	3.6	28.7	50.6	-1.3	0.7	71.6	32.5	104.1	109.2	-5.1	0.0 •	HAWAII EMPLOYERS MUTUAL INS CO
2.6	1.9	81.1	32.4	-4.2	-8.8	53.9	44.4	98.3	108.7	9.8	0.0	HAWAIIAN INS & GUARANTY CO LTD
22.3	20.0	N/A	N/A	N/A	N/A	N/A	N/A	N/A	N/A	0.0	0.0	HAWKEYE-SECURITY INS CO
3.8	3.4	84.0	9.8	-5.2	-7.1	56.2	36.4	92.6	111.5	5.6	0.0	HAY CREEK MUTUAL INS CO
11.0	9.9	N/A	N/A	N/A	N/A	N/A	N/A	N/A	-32.5	0.0	0.0	HCC SPECIALTY INS CO
2.7	2.4	3.3	20.8	0.8	2.2	191.2	-204.9	-13.7	23.1	2.6	16.1	HDI GLOBAL INS CO
65.6	29.2	N/A	N/A	N/A	N/A	50.0	464.7	514.7	-418.2	0.0	0.0	HDI SPECIALTY INSURANCE CO
N/A	N/A	--	--	--	--	--	--	--	--	--	--	HEALTH CARE CASUALTY RRG INC
1.5	1.2	20.0	184.9	-14.4	-13.8	77.4	20.5	97.9	35.7	7.7	0.0	HEALTH CARE INDEMNITY INC
3.0	2.4	22.5	50.7	-1.7	-1.5	76.9	13.8	90.7	111.8	6.5	0.0	HEALTH CARE INDUSTRY LIAB RECIP
1.2	0.8	84.5	200.6	-1.9	-46.6	77.8	26.2	104.0	122.1	-0.2	0.0	HEALTH CARE INS RECPL
1.8	1.4	78.0	70.2	-7.7	-45.4	53.6	27.7	81.3	125.0	0.2	0.0	HEALTH CARE MUT CAPTIVE INS CO
6.9	5.1	9.3	29.7	-1.4	-1.9	94.6	41.5	136.1	70.7	-32.4	0.0	HEALTH PROVIDERS INS RECIPROCAL
1.2	0.9	2.5	192.7	-15.7	-23.3	52.8	360.2	413.0	60.8	-91.5	0.0	HEALTHCARE PROFESSIONAL INS CO
0.2	0.1	-440.6	620.7	-56.1	4.5	40.8	6.3	47.1	-126.2	-192.1	0.0	HEALTHCARE PROVIDERS INS EXCH
4.0	3.4	34.6	59.8	-1.9	-3.4	65.7	50.6	116.3	84.5	2.5	0.0	HEALTHCARE UNDERWRITERS GRP
0.9	0.8	138.7	296.6	-20.5	38.2	73.2	5.1	78.3	161.5	4.0	0.0	HEALTHCARE UNDERWRITING CO RRG
5.3	4.8	94.1	0.8	-2.4	-3.1	59.1	31.1	90.2	91.6	9.2	0.0	HEARTLAND MUTUAL INS CO
1.0	0.7	237.6	315.9	29.7	59.9	81.4	13.0	94.4	141.2	17.7	0.0	HEREFORD INS CO
N/A	N/A	--	--	--	--	--	--	--	--	--	--	HERITAGE CASUALTY INS CO
3.1	2.8	-221.2	N/A	-611.3	-755.6	90.5	16.5	107.0	-402.4	-12.8	0.0	HERITAGE INDEMNITY CO
1.5	0.8	170.6	74.9	6.5	13.2	70.0	45.2	115.2	61.1	-0.5	0.0	HERITAGE P&C INS CO
1.2	1.1	-431.0	N/A	-101.2	69.8	108.5	-15.2	93.3	-35.1	-119.2	0.0	HERMITAGE INS CO
1.3	1.3	N/A	N/A	N/A	N/A	N/A	N/A	N/A	N/A	0.0	77.8 •	HIGH POINT P&C INS CO
3.5	2.6	60.3	27.0	-2.8	-6.9	39.0	25.2	64.2	151.3	-3.8	4.6 •	HIGH POINT PREFERRED INS CO
5.5	3.2	N/A	N/A	N/A	N/A	N/A	N/A	N/A	N/A	0.0	0.0	HIGH POINT SAFETY & INS CO
-0.0	-0.0	196.4	999 +	74.9	99.7	109.3	70.8	180.1	41.8	-86.8	0.0	HIGHLANDS INS CO
7.0	3.9	100.2	34.1	0.1	-9.2	78.9	19.3	98.2	103.0	-14.8	0.0	HIGHMARK CASUALTY INS CO
3.3	2.5	47.6	17.3	-1.6	-2.8	49.2	41.3	90.5	114.5	1.3	15.0	HINGHAM MUTUAL FIRE INS CO

999 + Denotes number greater than 999.9%
999 - Denotes number less than -999.99%
• Bullets denote a more detailed analysis is available in Section II.

INSURANCE COMPANY NAME	DOM. STATE	RATING	TOTAL ASSETS ($MIL)	CAPITAL & SURPLUS ($MIL)	ANNUAL NET PREMIUM ($MIL)	NET INCOME ($MIL)	CAPITAL- IZATION INDEX (PTS)	RESERVE ADQ INDEX (PTS)	PROFIT- ABILITY INDEX (PTS)	LIQUIDITY INDEX (PTS)	STAB. INDEX (PTS)	STABILITY FACTORS
HIROAD ASSURANCE CO	IL	U	--	--	--	--	N/A	--	--	--	--	Z
HISCOX INS CO	IL	C+	330.0	95.8	85.5	6.8	4.2	5.8	6.1	7.1	4.5	CGRT
▲HLTHCR PROVIDERS INS CO	SC	C+	81.5	50.8	9.9	5.0	9.3	9.4	8.7	7.9	4.5	DR
HOCHHEIM PRAIRIE CASUALTY INS CO	TX	C	81.9	32.7	50.9	-2.0	7.7	9.4	4.6	4.5	3.5	LR
▲HOCHHEIM PRAIRIE FARM MUT INS ASN	TX	D+	122.7	53.7	86.1	-4.2	7.0	5.0	2.0	1.0	2.5	FLR
HOME CONSTRUCTION INS CO	NV	U (5)	--	--	--	--	N/A	--	--	--	--	Z
HOME STATE COUNTY MUTUAL INS CO	TX	C-	81.2	8.4	4.8	0.4	4.8	6.7	8.7	7.0	3.2	DRT
HOME VALUE INS CO	OH	F (5)	0.0	0.0	0.0	0.0	8.4	N/A	0.9	10.0	0.0	DFGT
▲HOME-OWNERS INS CO	MI	A	2,323.7	1,158.1	905.8	55.1	10.0	6.1	8.8	6.8	7.5	
HOMELAND INS CO OF DE	DE	B	52.8	52.7	0.0	0.7	10.0	N/A	6.4	7.0	5.6	D
HOMELAND INS CO OF NY	NY	C	118.2	115.6	0.0	0.7	8.8	N/A	6.0	7.0	4.3	R
HOMEOWNERS CHOICE ASR CO INC	AL	U (5)	--	--	--	--	N/A	--	--	--	--	Z
HOMEOWNERS CHOICE PROP & CAS INS	FL	C	411.3	152.8	188.4	-10.5	7.9	4.0	3.9	7.0	3.8	
▼HOMEOWNERS OF AMERICA INS CO	TX	D	56.4	19.9	4.4	-1.0	7.4	6.3	6.3	0.0	2.0	DFGL
HOMESHIELD FIRE & CASUALTY INS CO	OK	U	--	--	--	--	N/A	--	--	--	--	Z
HOMESITE INDEMNITY CO	WI	C	51.9	40.4	0.0	0.2	10.0	3.6	6.5	8.2	3.5	R
HOMESITE INS CO	WI	C	155.8	88.0	0.0	1.0	10.0	3.6	6.8	7.0	3.6	FRT
HOMESITE INS CO OF CA	CA	C	64.3	37.2	0.0	0.1	10.0	3.6	6.4	6.8	3.5	FRT
HOMESITE INS CO OF FL	IL	C	16.8	11.1	0.0	0.1	10.0	3.6	6.0	8.0	3.5	DR
HOMESITE INS CO OF GA	GA	C	27.4	22.1	0.0	0.4	10.0	N/A	8.1	9.8	3.5	DRT
HOMESITE INS CO OF IL	IL	C	11.9	9.5	0.0	0.1	10.0	3.6	6.5	10.0	3.5	DR
HOMESITE INS CO OF NY	NY	C	37.8	18.7	12.2	0.4	8.5	3.6	8.8	7.5	3.3	DGRT
HOMESITE INS CO OF THE MIDWEST	WI	C	449.7	102.9	0.0	0.1	10.0	5.1	6.6	6.3	3.8	FR
▲HOMESITE LLOYDS OF TEXAS	TX	C+	31.2	16.1	0.0	0.2	10.0	3.6	7.8	7.0	3.2	DFRT
HOMESTEAD INS CO	PA	D	4.9	3.5	0.8	0.2	7.7	5.8	3.2	7.8	1.3	DGRT
HOMESTEAD MUTUAL INS CO	WI	C	10.2	7.8	2.3	0.2	8.0	6.1	5.3	6.8	2.7	DT
HOOSIER INS CO	IN	C	7.8	7.3	0.0	0.1	10.0	3.9	2.1	7.0	2.7	DRT
HORACE MANN INS CO	IL	B	526.7	190.6	270.5	8.7	8.2	8.2	6.1	5.2	5.7	AL
HORACE MANN LLOYDS	TX	B-	4.5	3.0	0.0	0.1	10.0	N/A	7.2	7.0	3.8	D
HORACE MANN P&C INS CO	IL	B	304.7	125.9	174.2	8.1	8.0	8.2	6.3	4.3	5.5	AL
HORIZON MIDWEST CASUALTY CO	KS	D	2.7	2.6	0.0	0.0	10.0	N/A	6.4	7.0	2.0	DT
HOSPITALITY INS CO	CT	C+	10.5	7.8	0.0	0.1	10.0	N/A	3.4	7.0	4.2	DFT
HOSPITALITY MUT CAPT INS CO	GA	F (5)	0.0	0.0	2.5	0.0	0.0	5.8	2.5	0.0	0.0	CDFG
HOSPITALITY MUTUAL INS CO	MA	C	68.9	27.2	17.6	0.6	4.3	4.1	3.1	6.8	4.0	CD
▲HOSPITALITY RRG INC	VT	D	6.9	2.9	3.6	0.0	5.0	3.6	3.7	9.0	1.5	DGT
HOSPITALS INS CO	NY	C-	1,671.8	584.0	178.9	62.5	6.8	9.8	8.6	6.9	3.2	R
▲HOUSING & REDEVELOPMENT INS EXCH	PA	C+	44.1	16.5	24.2	0.6	5.1	5.3	5.7	6.2	3.7	CDR
▲HOUSING AUTHORITY PROP A MUTUAL CO	VT	B+	181.9	118.5	52.3	-0.4	10.0	8.2	5.3	6.9	6.5	
▲HOUSING AUTHORITY RISK RET GROUP	VT	B	313.6	186.9	34.8	5.1	9.3	9.0	3.6	7.2	5.5	
▲HOUSING ENTERPRISE INS CO	VT	B-	78.3	33.6	25.4	1.3	5.3	7.0	5.0	6.5	5.1	C
HOUSING SPECIALTY INS CO	VT	C+	18.1	16.3	1.4	-0.1	10.0	3.6	3.9	8.8	3.3	DT
HOUSTON CASUALTY CO	TX	B-	3,382.8	1,865.1	863.0	120.8	7.8	7.6	5.0	6.6	4.9	R
HOUSTON GENERAL INS EXCH	TX	U (1)	--	--	--	--	N/A	--	--	--	--	Z
HOUSTON SPECIALTY INS CO	TX	B	455.8	261.3	91.3	19.6	6.4	5.5	5.9	6.7	6.1	C
HOW INS CO A RRG	VA	U (5)	--	--	--	--	N/A	--	--	--	--	Z
HPIC RRG	SC	D	1.8	1.6	0.0	-0.1	10.0	3.6	2.3	9.3	1.4	DFGT
HSB SPECIALTY INS CO	CT	B	56.2	50.7	0.0	0.4	10.0	N/A	5.6	10.0	4.3	DFT
HUDSON EXCESS INS CO	DE	B	76.7	59.1	0.0	3.2	10.0	N/A	8.4	10.0	4.2	T
HUDSON INS CO	DE	C-	1,204.1	428.4	198.4	30.7	8.3	7.7	4.8	8.2	3.3	R
HUDSON SPECIALTY INS CO	NY	D+	367.8	195.4	52.7	-1.9	9.6	8.3	6.2	9.6	2.6	R
HUTTERIAN BRETHREN MUTUAL INS CORP	IL	D	3.3	3.1	0.3	0.2	10.0	5.7	5.1	10.0	2.0	DT
HYUNDAI MARINE & FIRE INS CO LTD	CA	B	103.5	52.8	29.2	1.0	9.8	6.4	6.2	7.8	5.7	

See Page 27 for explanation of footnotes and Page 28 for explanation of stability factors.

76

www.weissratings.com

Arrows denote recent upgrades ▲ or downgrades ▼   (see Section VII for explanations)

RISK ADJ. RATIO #1	CAPITAL RATIO #2	PREMIUM TO SURPLUS (%)	RESV. TO SURPLUS (%)	RESV. DEVELOP. 1 YEAR (%)	RESV. DEVELOP. 2 YEAR (%)	LOSS RATIO (%)	EXP. RATIO (%)	COMB RATIO (%)	CASH FROM UNDER-WRITING (%)	NET PREMIUM GROWTH (%)	INVEST. IN AFFIL (%)	INSURANCE COMPANY NAME
N/A	N/A	--	--	--	--	--	--	--	--	--	--	HIROAD ASSURANCE CO
0.8	0.6	89.3	93.0	9.3	7.0	70.6	21.2	91.8	148.5	21.7	7.0	HISCOX INS CO
4.3	2.6	19.5	45.9	-7.2	-12.7	33.6	37.0	70.6	123.4	-3.2	0.0	HLTHCR PROVIDERS INS CO
2.0	1.4	156.0	69.5	4.5	-2.1	88.8	21.4	110.2	96.3	18.1	0.8	HOCHHEIM PRAIRIE CASUALTY INS CO
1.1	1.0	160.4	12.2	-2.4	-6.1	89.7	24.9	114.6	85.2	10.5	35.8	HOCHHEIM PRAIRIE FARM MUT INS ASN
N/A	N/A	--	--	--	--	--	--	--	--	--	--	HOME CONSTRUCTION INS CO
1.0	0.9	57.4	42.8	8.2	2.6	98.2	-10.6	87.6	87.7	-0.9	0.0	HOME STATE COUNTY MUTUAL INS CO
0.4	0.4	0.3	N/A	N/A	N/A	999 +	999 +	999 +	0.2	0.0	0.0	HOME VALUE INS CO
5.8	4.4	78.2	53.4	1.1	-0.2	71.1	25.4	96.5	108.4	8.9	0.0 ●	HOME-OWNERS INS CO
70.4	31.9	N/A	N/A	N/A	N/A	N/A	N/A	N/A	N/A	0.0	0.0	HOMELAND INS CO OF DE
2.2	2.2	N/A	N/A	N/A	N/A	N/A	N/A	N/A	N/A	0.0	47.3	HOMELAND INS CO OF NY
N/A	N/A	--	--	--	--	--	--	--	--	--	--	HOMEOWNERS CHOICE ASR CO INC
2.3	1.8	123.3	54.6	7.3	12.4	69.8	47.1	116.9	101.4	-13.2	0.0	HOMEOWNERS CHOICE PROP & CAS INS
1.7	1.2	22.3	13.7	-1.1	-5.1	197.8	-52.8	145.0	97.5	25.8	0.0	HOMEOWNERS OF AMERICA INS CO
N/A	N/A	--	--	--	--	--	--	--	--	--	--	HOMESHIELD FIRE & CASUALTY INS CO
15.9	14.3	N/A	N/A	N/A	N/A	N/A	N/A	N/A	160.1	0.0	0.0	HOMESITE INDEMNITY CO
11.9	10.7	N/A	N/A	N/A	N/A	N/A	N/A	N/A	-401.2	0.0	0.0	HOMESITE INS CO
8.8	7.9	N/A	N/A	N/A	N/A	N/A	N/A	N/A	-5.0	0.0	0.0	HOMESITE INS CO OF CA
6.8	6.2	N/A	N/A	N/A	N/A	N/A	N/A	N/A	654.7	0.0	0.0	HOMESITE INS CO OF FL
14.3	12.8	N/A	N/A	N/A	N/A	N/A	N/A	N/A	9.7	0.0	0.0	HOMESITE INS CO OF GA
11.9	10.7	N/A	N/A	N/A	N/A	N/A	N/A	N/A	5.0	0.0	0.0	HOMESITE INS CO OF IL
2.8	2.0	65.5	14.7	0.5	N/A	61.4	26.4	87.8	153.6	5.6	0.0	HOMESITE INS CO OF NY
10.9	9.8	N/A	N/A	N/A	N/A	N/A	N/A	N/A	39.2	0.0	0.0	HOMESITE INS CO OF THE MIDWEST
5.5	4.9	N/A	N/A	N/A	N/A	N/A	N/A	N/A	-167.3	0.0	0.0	HOMESITE LLOYDS OF TEXAS
2.8	1.4	22.5	41.0	0.9	0.8	44.1	41.2	85.3	301.1	0.0	0.0	HOMESTEAD INS CO
2.7	1.7	28.9	3.4	-0.6	0.1	59.1	41.2	100.3	100.6	5.1	0.0	HOMESTEAD MUTUAL INS CO
27.5	24.8	N/A	N/A	N/A	N/A	N/A	N/A	N/A	N/A	100.0	0.0	HOOSIER INS CO
3.0	2.0	141.9	56.3	0.2	-1.6	76.9	26.2	103.1	98.7	4.5	0.0	HORACE MANN INS CO
4.8	4.3	N/A	N/A	N/A	N/A	N/A	N/A	N/A	15.1	0.0	0.0	HORACE MANN LLOYDS
2.8	1.9	138.3	54.9	0.2	-1.5	76.9	26.2	103.1	98.6	4.5	0.0	HORACE MANN P&C INS CO
46.8	42.1	N/A	N/A	N/A	N/A	N/A	N/A	N/A	N/A	0.0	0.0	HORIZON MIDWEST CASUALTY CO
8.5	5.0	N/A	N/A	N/A	N/A	N/A	N/A	N/A	-641.7	0.0	0.0	HOSPITALITY INS CO
0.1	0.1	408.3	213.6	77.4	0.4	85.4	54.4	139.8	89.5	84.7	0.0	HOSPITALITY MUT CAPT INS CO
0.9	0.6	64.9	115.9	6.1	20.6	73.3	37.8	111.1	108.4	4.6	12.4	HOSPITALITY MUTUAL INS CO
1.0	0.6	125.7	40.1	1.4	N/A	60.5	21.8	82.3	156.9	351.2	0.0	HOSPITALITY RRG INC
1.3	1.1	30.6	164.2	-13.3	-26.8	63.8	3.7	67.5	163.2	-6.8	0.0 ●	HOSPITALS INS CO
1.0	0.6	146.8	119.7	20.3	14.2	72.9	28.3	101.2	98.6	6.5	0.0	HOUSING & REDEVELOPMENT INS EXCH
3.4	3.0	44.1	29.9	-3.3	-2.8	70.2	35.3	105.5	112.6	20.1	14.8 ●	HOUSING AUTHORITY PROP A MUTUAL
3.2	2.5	18.6	48.7	-9.8	-5.3	49.2	42.5	91.7	96.5	11.5	12.7	HOUSING AUTHORITY RISK RET GROUP
1.4	0.8	75.4	85.8	-17.9	-14.4	67.5	34.9	102.4	99.3	-7.9	0.0	HOUSING ENTERPRISE INS CO
9.8	6.4	8.4	5.4	-1.7	-0.6	55.3	84.1	139.4	80.4	18.1	0.0	HOUSING SPECIALTY INS CO
1.8	1.5	46.3	44.3	-3.6	-2.8	64.6	22.2	86.8	118.6	0.3	36.8 ●	HOUSTON CASUALTY CO
N/A	N/A	--	--	--	--	--	--	--	--	--	--	HOUSTON GENERAL INS EXCH
1.0	1.0	35.0	24.4	-1.7	3.5	50.6	30.4	81.0	104.6	-18.3	50.7 ●	HOUSTON SPECIALTY INS CO
N/A	N/A	--	--	--	--	--	--	--	--	--	--	HOW INS CO A RRG
4.8	4.7	0.8	2.5	-7.4	3.5	999 +	999 +	616.4	-38.8	-74.3	0.0	HPIC RRG
31.1	28.0	N/A	N/A	N/A	N/A	N/A	N/A	N/A	723.1	0.0	0.0	HSB SPECIALTY INS CO
18.1	16.3	N/A	2.7	N/A	N/A	N/A	N/A	N/A	-70.2	0.0	0.0	HUDSON EXCESS INS CO
2.1	1.8	46.3	44.6	-2.9	-3.4	67.8	18.1	85.9	120.9	25.1	31.5 ●	HUDSON INS CO
3.1	2.7	27.0	44.9	-2.1	-6.4	65.2	51.3	116.5	93.4	-0.7	19.8	HUDSON SPECIALTY INS CO
10.3	6.6	9.9	3.7	-0.7	-1.1	40.3	10.4	50.7	235.9	10.8	0.0	HUTTERIAN BRETHREN MUTUAL INS
4.9	2.8	55.4	47.4	-0.2	3.9	61.4	32.8	94.2	135.8	14.9	0.0	HYUNDAI MARINE & FIRE INS CO LTD

999 + Denotes number greater than 999.9%
999 - Denotes number less than -999.99%
● Bullets denote a more detailed analysis is available in Section II.

INSURANCE COMPANY NAME	DOM. STATE	RATING	TOTAL ASSETS ($MIL)	CAPITAL & SURPLUS ($MIL)	ANNUAL NET PREMIUM ($MIL)	NET INCOME ($MIL)	CAPITAL- IZATION INDEX (PTS)	RESERVE ADQ INDEX (PTS)	PROFIT- ABILITY INDEX (PTS)	LIQUIDITY INDEX (PTS)	STAB. INDEX (PTS)	STABILITY FACTORS
▲ICI MUTUAL INS CO A RRG	VT	B+	367.6	273.1	28.6	8.9	10.0	8.7	8.3	7.7	6.5	F
ICW NATIONAL INSURANCE CO	CA	U	--	--	--	--	N/A	--	--	--	--	Z
ID COUNTIES RISK MGMT PROGRAM UNDW	ID	C	73.2	25.2	25.1	-9.5	5.9	4.7	2.2	6.2	3.5	FR
▲IDS PROPERTY CASUALTY INS CO	WI	B	1,789.9	780.6	957.4	-9.7	8.7	3.8	3.7	5.2	5.4	FLR
IFA INS CO	NJ	F (4)	3.0	-4.3	0.6	-7.0	0.0	0.3	0.0	7.0	0.0	CDFR
▲IL STATE BAR ASSOC MUTUAL INS CO	IL	B-	80.2	38.5	16.2	2.8	9.3	9.4	8.5	8.3	5.3	D
▲ILLINOIS CASUALTY CO	IL	B-	124.1	50.8	46.0	1.3	7.9	9.4	6.1	6.6	5.1	T
ILLINOIS EMCASCO INS CO	IA	B-	378.7	116.2	161.3	9.8	8.1	8.6	8.6	6.4	4.8	T
ILLINOIS FARMERS INS CO	IL	C+	246.7	84.0	106.4	-0.4	7.2	5.8	3.2	6.6	4.7	FR
▲ILLINOIS INS CO	IA	B	60.4	36.1	22.0	4.4	8.1	6.3	8.9	8.9	5.5	D
ILLINOIS NATIONAL INS CO	IL	B-	55.4	41.3	0.0	2.7	10.0	N/A	5.9	7.0	5.1	
ILLINOIS UNION INS CO	IL	C	447.0	130.6	0.0	1.8	10.0	N/A	3.6	6.9	4.0	FR
IMPERIAL F&C INS CO	LA	C-	109.9	25.3	0.0	0.0	9.7	4.6	2.6	6.0	3.0	GRT
IMPERIUM INS CO	TX	C-	373.7	166.5	94.6	-2.2	6.0	1.7	3.3	6.6	2.9	FR
IMT INS CO	IA	B	396.0	175.5	232.6	-6.3	9.1	5.0	5.3	6.0	6.0	
INDEMNITY CO OF CA	CA	C	10.8	5.7	1.1	2.1	8.8	9.4	1.9	8.0	3.5	DRT
INDEMNITY INS CO OF NORTH AMERICA	PA	C	485.5	130.0	108.2	2.1	8.3	6.0	8.3	6.7	4.0	R
INDEMNITY NATIONAL INS CO	MS	C	68.1	50.1	10.3	-1.3	9.3	9.4	6.4	8.3	2.7	DGRT
INDEPENDENCE AMERICAN INS CO	DE	B-	112.9	72.1	110.8	8.7	8.2	5.6	8.8	6.0	4.8	R
▲INDEPENDENCE CASUALTY INS CO	MA	C	4.7	4.7	0.0	0.1	10.0	N/A	7.4	7.0	3.5	DR
▲INDEPENDENT MUTUAL FIRE INS CO	IL	B-	52.2	46.3	4.1	0.8	7.7	4.6	6.6	7.3	5.3	DF
INDEPENDENT SPECIALTY INS CO	DE	C	69.5	48.4	32.4	-0.6	10.0	3.6	4.3	7.1	3.9	AGRT
INDIAN HARBOR INS CO	DE	C-	242.1	47.5	42.2	-2.2	8.2	6.4	4.0	8.5	3.0	AR
▲INDIANA FARMERS MUTUAL INS CO	IN	B+	433.3	210.3	211.3	19.6	8.4	7.0	8.7	5.7	6.5	L
INDIANA INS CO	IN	C	69.7	66.8	0.0	0.2	10.0	N/A	6.5	7.0	4.3	R
INDIANA LUMBERMENS MUTUAL INS CO	IN	C	57.0	16.6	16.4	0.9	7.4	6.3	4.2	6.9	3.9	DFRT
INFINITY ASSURANCE INS CO	OH	B-	7.0	5.5	1.4	0.1	10.0	5.2	5.1	6.8	3.6	AD
INFINITY AUTO INS CO	OH	C	11.6	7.6	1.4	0.1	10.0	5.1	5.4	6.8	4.1	ADF
INFINITY CASUALTY INS CO	OH	B-	7.6	6.0	1.4	0.1	10.0	5.2	5.3	6.8	3.8	AD
INFINITY COUNTY MUTUAL INS CO	TX	C	74.3	5.1	0.0	0.0	3.8	N/A	5.5	9.6	2.9	CDGT
INFINITY INDEMNITY INS CO	IN	C	6.3	4.5	1.4	0.1	10.0	5.2	3.8	6.8	3.5	AD
INFINITY INS CO	IN	B	2,043.1	660.1	1,374.4	67.9	7.9	6.7	5.4	4.1	5.3	AL
INFINITY PREFERRED INS CO	OH	C	4.6	3.2	1.4	0.1	10.0	6.2	3.7	6.7	3.2	AD
INFINITY SAFEGUARD INS CO	OH	C+	5.0	3.5	1.4	0.1	10.0	6.1	3.8	6.7	3.2	ADT
INFINITY SECURITY INS CO	IN	C	5.7	4.3	1.4	0.1	10.0	5.2	3.9	6.8	3.3	AD
INFINITY SELECT INS CO	IN	B-	6.9	5.1	1.4	0.1	10.0	5.2	4.9	6.8	3.6	AD
INFINITY STANDARD INS CO	IN	C	7.2	5.5	1.4	0.1	10.0	5.2	5.4	6.8	3.6	AD
▲INLAND INS CO	NE	C+	300.7	252.9	0.7	8.5	8.5	3.6	6.9	10.0	4.5	R
INLAND MUTUAL INS CO	WV	C-	7.0	6.4	0.4	0.1	10.0	7.9	6.9	8.7	2.5	DR
INNOVATIVE PHYSICIAN SOLUTIONS RRG	VT	E	5.2	1.2	1.3	-0.2	0.0	1.7	1.6	6.4	0.1	CDFT
INS CO OF GREATER NY	NY	C+	128.0	64.2	31.7	2.6	10.0	5.9	7.9	6.9	4.7	T
INS CO OF ILLINOIS	IL	B	23.3	21.1	0.0	0.2	10.0	N/A	6.1	7.0	4.1	ADT
INS CO OF NORTH AMERICA	PA	C	999.4	251.2	270.6	6.0	7.7	6.0	8.1	6.6	4.1	R
INS CO OF THE AMERICAS	FL	U (2)	--	--	--	--	N/A	--	--	--	--	Z
INS CO OF THE SOUTH	GA	D+	51.5	14.6	35.8	0.8	2.4	6.3	8.6	2.9	2.4	CDL
INS CO OF THE WEST	CA	C	2,570.2	1,034.2	807.7	91.1	7.4	6.4	8.9	6.6	3.7	R
INS PLACEMENT FACILITY OF PA	PA	E-	6.9	-3.1	7.0	0.4	0.0	4.5	0.1	7.3	0.0	CDFT
INSPIRIEN INS CO	AL	C-	34.1	15.5	4.9	-2.1	7.4	9.4	2.1	7.3	3.3	DFR
INSUREMAX INS CO	IN	U	--	--	--	--	N/A	--	--	--	--	Z
▲INSURORS INDEMNITY CO	TX	C	39.7	21.1	15.7	1.2	7.9	9.3	8.5	7.3	3.5	D
INSURORS INDEMNITY LLOYDS	TX	C	5.0	2.7	0.0	0.0	10.0	N/A	4.3	8.8	3.0	DR
INTEGON CASUALTY INS CO	NC	C	26.3	6.4	0.0	0.1	8.0	N/A	3.6	7.0	3.7	DRT

See Page 27 for explanation of footnotes and
Page 28 for explanation of stability factors.

78

www.weissratings.com

Arrows denote recent upgrades ▲ or downgrades ▼   (see Section VII for explanations)

RISK ADJ. RATIO #1	CAPITAL RATIO #2	PREMIUM TO SURPLUS (%)	RESV. TO SURPLUS (%)	RESV. DEVELOP. 1 YEAR (%)	RESV. DEVELOP. 2 YEAR (%)	LOSS RATIO (%)	EXP. RATIO (%)	COMB RATIO (%)	CASH FROM UNDER-WRITING (%)	NET PREMIUM GROWTH (%)	INVEST. IN AFFIL (%)	INSURANCE COMPANY NAME
10.7	6.5	10.5	21.2	-4.6	-5.8	38.3	40.2	78.5	82.1	-6.6	-0.4 •	ICI MUTUAL INS CO A RRG
N/A	N/A	--	--	--	--	--	--	--	--	--	--	ICW NATIONAL INSURANCE CO
1.1	0.8	99.4	116.7	-1.1	9.5	114.8	26.4	141.2	78.2	3.0	0.0	ID COUNTIES RISK MGMT PROGRAM
2.9	2.3	122.6	78.3	2.3	-0.8	92.2	17.5	109.7	89.5	-10.1	3.1 •	IDS PROPERTY CASUALTY INS CO
-0.6	-0.4	-15.0	-169.1	125.5	241.6	536.0	426.0	962.0	9.5	-95.6	0.0	IFA INS CO
4.1	2.7	42.2	75.0	-17.2	-21.7	52.3	30.4	82.7	119.9	3.9	0.0	IL STATE BAR ASSOC MUTUAL INS CO
3.2	2.5	90.6	80.8	-12.5	-17.3	65.6	35.7	101.3	100.5	6.4	0.0	ILLINOIS CASUALTY CO
2.7	1.8	138.8	138.6	-3.9	-7.5	64.2	32.2	96.4	104.3	4.4	0.0	ILLINOIS EMCASCO INS CO
1.2	1.1	126.6	78.7	0.1	2.7	69.8	33.0	102.8	97.3	-3.9	37.4	ILLINOIS FARMERS INS CO
2.4	2.0	60.8	62.3	-0.7	3.3	50.2	21.9	72.1	213.9	20.6	0.0	ILLINOIS INS CO
14.4	12.9	N/A	N/A	N/A	N/A	N/A	N/A	N/A	N/A	0.0	0.0	ILLINOIS NATIONAL INS CO
11.9	8.3	N/A	25.3	N/A	N/A	N/A	N/A	N/A	-2.8	0.0	0.0	ILLINOIS UNION INS CO
3.1	2.7	N/A	N/A	N/A	N/A	N/A	N/A	N/A	999 +	0.0	0.0	IMPERIAL F&C INS CO
1.1	0.8	56.8	93.3	11.1	27.4	96.3	23.7	120.0	80.9	5.3	36.3	IMPERIUM INS CO
3.7	2.4	132.5	50.6	6.2	8.0	78.9	30.4	109.3	99.7	6.5	0.5	IMT INS CO
2.3	2.1	19.7	N/A	-45.7	-49.2	2.7	123.7	126.4	138.8	-70.9	0.0	INDEMNITY CO OF CA
2.8	1.8	83.3	150.3	-1.2	2.7	83.9	17.6	101.5	98.0	8.3	0.0	INDEMNITY INS CO OF NORTH AMERICA
5.1	3.4	20.6	6.1	-12.7	-16.9	-28.4	49.9	21.5	296.8	670.5	0.0	INDEMNITY NATIONAL INS CO
2.5	1.7	153.8	45.2	-0.5	4.1	47.0	45.7	92.7	109.1	21.5	0.0	INDEPENDENCE AMERICAN INS CO
112.3	55.6	N/A	N/A	N/A	N/A	N/A	N/A	N/A	N/A	0.0	0.0	INDEPENDENCE CASUALTY INS CO
2.4	1.4	8.9	0.6	-0.1	-0.2	30.2	100.2	130.4	76.4	13.1	0.0	INDEPENDENT MUTUAL FIRE INS CO
9.8	5.7	66.9	4.3	0.2	-0.1	49.4	28.8	78.2	141.5	0.0	0.0	INDEPENDENT SPECIALTY INS CO
2.8	1.7	88.8	145.4	-3.4	-3.4	76.8	26.9	103.7	136.5	26.6	0.0	INDIAN HARBOR INS CO
3.6	2.1	100.5	43.4	-8.9	-14.5	63.5	30.1	93.6	102.1	6.4	0.0 •	INDIANA FARMERS MUTUAL INS CO
5.4	5.2	N/A	N/A	N/A	N/A	N/A	N/A	N/A	N/A	0.0	19.3	INDIANA INS CO
2.1	1.3	98.8	100.6	1.9	4.9	64.4	32.8	97.2	97.9	11.0	12.9	INDIANA LUMBERMENS MUTUAL INS CO
9.5	8.5	25.2	12.4	-0.3	-0.3	77.1	17.8	94.9	99.3	-0.4	0.0	INFINITY ASSURANCE INS CO
5.9	5.3	18.4	9.0	-0.2	-0.2	77.1	17.8	94.9	66.4	-0.4	0.0	INFINITY AUTO INS CO
9.7	8.7	23.0	11.3	-0.3	-0.3	77.1	17.8	94.9	94.5	-0.4	0.0	INFINITY CASUALTY INS CO
0.6	0.6	N/A	N/A	N/A	N/A	N/A	N/A	N/A	N/A	0.0	0.0	INFINITY COUNTY MUTUAL INS CO
6.7	6.0	30.7	15.1	-0.4	-0.3	77.1	17.8	94.9	97.1	-0.4	0.0	INFINITY INDEMNITY INS CO
1.8	1.6	208.2	102.5	-2.4	-2.4	77.1	17.7	94.8	100.7	-0.4	3.1 •	INFINITY INS CO
5.6	5.0	43.5	21.4	-0.5	-0.5	77.1	17.8	94.9	100.3	-0.4	0.0	INFINITY PREFERRED INS CO
5.8	5.2	40.2	19.8	-0.4	-0.4	77.1	17.8	94.9	97.2	-0.4	0.0	INFINITY SAFEGUARD INS CO
7.5	6.7	32.6	16.0	-0.4	-0.3	77.1	17.8	94.9	100.3	-0.4	0.0	INFINITY SECURITY INS CO
7.6	6.9	27.0	13.3	-0.3	-0.3	77.1	17.8	94.9	113.9	-0.4	0.0	INFINITY SELECT INS CO
8.7	7.8	25.1	12.4	-0.3	-0.3	77.1	17.8	94.9	111.0	-0.4	6.9	INFINITY STANDARD INS CO
3.6	2.1	0.3	0.9	N/A	N/A	1.5	97.3	98.8	92.8	64.6	0.0 •	INLAND INS CO
5.2	3.0	6.2	3.3	-1.0	-2.5	40.7	57.9	98.6	104.6	2.3	0.0	INLAND MUTUAL INS CO
0.1	0.0	109.0	268.0	7.1	29.0	71.3	42.7	114.0	91.7	1.3	0.0	INNOVATIVE PHYSICIAN SOLUTIONS
3.8	3.2	49.4	67.2	-0.1	2.6	64.0	30.4	94.4	119.4	10.6	0.0	INS CO OF GREATER NY
27.0	24.3	N/A	N/A	N/A	N/A	N/A	N/A	N/A	N/A	0.0	0.0	INS CO OF ILLINOIS
2.2	1.4	107.7	194.4	-1.6	3.4	83.9	18.9	102.8	116.6	8.3	0.0 •	INS CO OF NORTH AMERICA
N/A	N/A	--	--	--	--	--	--	--	--	--	--	INS CO OF THE AMERICAS
0.5	0.4	246.0	32.6	2.0	1.6	48.3	40.1	88.4	124.3	17.8	0.0	INS CO OF THE SOUTH
1.8	1.4	78.1	124.4	-3.8	-3.1	65.8	23.2	89.0	143.4	-0.6	10.2 •	INS CO OF THE WEST
3.3	3.0	35.3	62.1	3.3	8.7	35.3	62.1	97.4	89.8	-5.0	0.0	INS PLACEMENT FACILITY OF PA
-0.5	-0.4	-226.3	-21.1	3.3	8.7	35.3	62.1	97.4	89.8	-5.0	0.0	INS PLACEMENT FACILITY OF PA
1.5	1.2	31.7	100.7	1.9	-5.9	91.7	74.5	166.2	70.6	-18.3	0.0	INSPIRIEN INS CO
N/A	N/A	--	--	--	--	--	--	--	--	--	--	INSUREMAX INS CO
2.2	1.6	74.3	38.7	-8.4	-9.9	38.5	52.4	90.9	129.5	2.5	7.4	INSURORS INDEMNITY CO
3.3	3.0	N/A	N/A	N/A	N/A	N/A	N/A	N/A	-77.2	0.0	0.0	INSURORS INDEMNITY LLOYDS
1.8	1.6	N/A	N/A	N/A	N/A	N/A	N/A	N/A	93.0	0.0	0.0	INTEGON CASUALTY INS CO

999 + Denotes number greater than 999.9%
999 - Denotes number less than -999.99%
• Bullets denote a more detailed analysis is available in Section II.

INSURANCE COMPANY NAME	DOM. STATE	RATING	TOTAL ASSETS ($MIL)	CAPITAL & SURPLUS ($MIL)	ANNUAL NET PREMIUM ($MIL)	NET INCOME ($MIL)	CAPITAL-IZATION INDEX (PTS)	RESERVE ADQ INDEX (PTS)	PROFIT-ABILITY INDEX (PTS)	LIQUIDITY INDEX (PTS)	STAB. INDEX (PTS)	STABILITY FACTORS
INTEGON GENERAL INS CORP	NC	C	95.0	6.7	0.0	0.4	4.7	N/A	3.7	2.5	2.7	CDGL
INTEGON INDEMNITY CORP	NC	C	185.5	20.3	0.0	-1.0	7.7	N/A	2.6	6.5	3.6	DGRT
▲INTEGON NATIONAL INS CO	NC	B-	3,766.0	970.4	1,384.4	145.4	7.1	4.4	4.0	5.5	4.7	GRT
INTEGON PREFERRED INS CO	NC	C	99.8	6.5	0.0	0.3	4.4	N/A	3.6	0.0	3.7	CDFG
INTEGRA INS INC	MN	D	1.8	1.8	2.8	0.1	3.6	N/A	3.7	2.4	1.6	DLT
INTEGRAND ASR CO	PR	C (1)	126.9	56.7	44.3	1.7	8.1	5.8	2.7	6.5	3.5	RT
▲INTEGRITY MUTUAL INS CO	WI	B	109.3	53.7	50.4	3.4	8.6	6.1	8.6	6.8	5.5	
▲INTEGRITY P&C INS CO	WI	C-	14.0	14.0	-3.3	0.7	10.0	4.6	8.8	6.0	3.1	DFT
INTEGRITY SELECT INSURANCE CO	WI	D	5.1	5.1	0.0	0.1	10.0	N/A	4.9	7.0	0.9	DT
▲INTERBORO INS CO	NY	C	79.7	42.8	26.1	1.7	8.7	8.2	8.3	6.8	3.5	RT
INTERINS EXCHANGE	CA	B+	10,404.3	6,637.9	3,623.1	71.8	9.6	6.0	6.9	6.5	5.8	
▲INTERNATIONAL FIDELITY INS CO	NJ	B	219.8	94.2	102.3	8.5	7.5	9.3	5.4	6.7	5.5	
INTERSTATE FIRE & CAS CO	IL	C-	150.0	70.1	0.0	-0.4	10.0	N/A	2.5	7.8	3.2	RT
INTREPID INS CO	IA	U	--	--	--	--	N/A	--	--	--	--	Z
IOWA AMERICAN INS CO	IA	B	24.3	7.6	7.2	-1.0	8.1	6.2	2.3	6.5	4.7	D
▼IOWA MUTUAL INS CO	IA	B-	93.9	28.1	21.7	-3.0	7.3	6.2	2.4	6.2	5.1	F
IQS INS RRG INC	VT	D	1.6	1.1	0.4	0.0	9.5	5.8	3.6	8.0	1.1	DT
IRONSHORE INDEMNITY INC	MN	B-	185.8	99.2	24.1	-11.3	8.7	4.4	2.1	1.3	4.9	LRT
IRONSHORE RRG (DC) INC	DC	D	2.0	1.4	0.0	-0.5	7.2	3.9	2.5	9.0	1.4	DFT
IRONSHORE SPECIALTY INS CO	AZ	C-	491.6	297.2	50.8	-29.5	9.2	4.6	2.6	6.9	2.8	FRT
ISLAND HOME INS CO	GU	D (1)	23.9	12.1	31.5	3.4	7.9	3.3	4.5	2.3	1.5	DGLT
ISLAND INS CO LTD	HI	B-	330.4	115.5	100.9	9.9	9.0	9.4	3.8	6.9	4.8	R
ISLAND PREMIER INS CO LTD	HI	C	10.5	5.9	0.0	0.2	10.0	N/A	7.7	10.0	3.6	DF
ISMIE INDEMNITY CO	IL	C	53.8	52.4	0.5	0.2	10.0	N/A	6.8	10.0	3.9	DT
ISMIE MUTUAL INS CO	IL	B-	1,403.5	695.5	133.4	12.4	10.0	9.4	7.1	7.9	4.6	FR
IU HEALTH RRG INC	SC	D+	5.6	2.8	0.0	0.0	9.5	N/A	1.9	7.0	2.0	DR
▲JAMES RIVER CASUALTY CO	VA	B-	44.7	17.3	7.4	0.8	7.4	8.6	7.3	6.9	5.3	D
JAMES RIVER INS CO	OH	C	630.4	161.1	128.3	31.2	7.2	8.4	7.5	7.7	4.0	GR
JEFFERSON INS CO	NY	C	104.6	65.8	121.2	6.5	7.5	7.4	8.7	6.1	3.5	R
JEWELERS MUTUAL INS CO	WI	B	442.4	282.5	196.3	23.5	10.0	7.6	8.7	6.8	6.3	T
JM SPECIALTY INSURANCE CO	WI	U	--	--	--	--	N/A	--	--	--	--	Z
JM WOODWORTH RRG INC	NV	U	--	--	--	--	N/A	--	--	--	--	Z
▲JUNIATA MUTUAL INS CO	PA	C-	9.8	5.9	5.1	0.0	8.3	5.9	4.9	6.9	2.4	DFR
KAMMCO CASUALTY CO	KS	D	6.3	4.8	0.0	-0.2	10.0	N/A	3.5	9.3	2.3	DT
KANSAS MEDICAL MUTUAL INS CO	KS	B	155.0	97.5	20.4	1.1	10.0	8.0	2.9	6.9	5.5	D
KANSAS MUTUAL INS CO	KS	C-	15.3	9.7	7.0	0.5	10.0	8.1	8.3	7.0	2.8	D
KEMPER FINANCIAL INDEMNITY CO	IL	U	--	--	--	--	N/A	--	--	--	--	Z
KEMPER INDEPENDENCE INS CO	IL	B	97.5	8.8	0.0	0.5	6.5	N/A	5.3	7.0	4.3	DR
KENSINGTON INS CO	NY	D	13.9	3.8	6.0	-1.3	2.3	2.6	2.4	7.0	2.2	CDF
▲KENTUCKIANA MEDICAL RRG & INS CO INC	KY	D	53.9	39.1	4.5	2.8	8.2	7.0	7.5	8.7	1.5	DRT
KENTUCKY EMPLOYERS MUTUAL INS	KY	B	994.0	206.7	154.7	10.7	7.0	4.9	5.6	6.9	6.2	
KENTUCKY FARM BUREAU MUTUAL INS CO	KY	B	2,505.4	1,374.7	999.1	71.0	10.0	7.8	6.9	6.2	4.8	
KENTUCKY HOSPITAL INS CO RRG	KY	C-	17.7	8.3	2.7	0.5	7.2	9.6	5.1	8.5	2.6	DFR
KENTUCKY NATIONAL INS CO	KY	C-	34.9	11.4	31.1	1.1	3.0	5.5	6.1	0.9	3.0	CDLR
KESWICK GUARANTY INC	VI	B-	5.8	5.8	0.3	0.3	9.3	4.6	8.5	7.4	3.5	D
▼KEY INS CO	KS	D-	37.6	7.5	57.9	-0.2	0.3	1.3	3.5	0.0	1.1	CDLT
KEY RISK INS CO	IA	C	45.0	31.6	0.0	0.8	10.0	N/A	7.3	10.0	4.2	R
▲KEYSTONE MUTUAL INS CO	MO	E+	3.3	0.5	2.1	-0.1	0.4	0.2	2.8	7.6	0.5	CDGT
KEYSTONE NATIONAL INS CO	PA	B-	19.9	10.0	2.5	0.4	10.0	7.6	7.9	7.6	4.3	DR
KINGSTONE INSURANCE CO	NY	C	197.0	101.3	92.9	7.9	8.1	4.2	8.8	7.0	4.3	GR
KINSALE INS CO	AR	B	578.1	213.8	189.5	23.8	7.0	9.3	8.9	7.4	4.6	T
KNIGHT SPECIALTY INS CO	DE	B	82.3	51.4	0.0	1.1	8.6	N/A	6.8	7.0	4.1	DT

See Page 27 for explanation of footnotes and Page 28 for explanation of stability factors.

Arrows denote recent upgrades ▲ or downgrades ▼   (see Section VII for explanations)

www.weissratings.com

RISK ADJ. RATIO #1	CAPITAL RATIO #2	PREMIUM TO SURPLUS (%)	RESV. TO SURPLUS (%)	RESV. DEVELOP. 1 YEAR (%)	RESV. DEVELOP. 2 YEAR (%)	LOSS RATIO (%)	EXP. RATIO (%)	COMB RATIO (%)	CASH FROM UNDER- WRITING (%)	NET PREMIUM GROWTH (%)	INVEST. IN AFFIL (%)	INSURANCE COMPANY NAME
0.7	0.7	N/A	N/A	N/A	N/A	N/A	N/A	N/A	166.4	0.0	0.0	INTEGON GENERAL INS CORP
1.5	1.4	N/A	N/A	N/A	N/A	N/A	N/A	N/A	-935.6	0.0	44.1	INTEGON INDEMNITY CORP
1.8	1.3	142.7	76.8	-1.5	3.3	76.2	21.7	97.9	91.1	-9.0	4.9 •	INTEGON NATIONAL INS CO
0.7	0.6	N/A	N/A	N/A	N/A	N/A	N/A	N/A	18.5	0.0	0.0	INTEGON PREFERRED INS CO
0.6	0.5	152.6	N/A	N/A	N/A	N/A	98.3	98.3	104.3	3.5	0.0	INTEGRA INS INC
2.1	1.5	71.6	32.8	-0.8	3.7	63.9	35.4	99.3	101.7	13.9	0.2	INTEGRAND ASR CO
2.5	2.1	93.7	52.0	-1.7	-2.7	64.6	27.8	92.4	119.5	30.4	19.7	INTEGRITY MUTUAL INS CO
63.7	29.9	-23.4	N/A	N/A	N/A	N/A	N/A	N/A	-43.0	-139.9	0.0	INTEGRITY P&C INS CO
161.4	80.6	N/A	N/A	N/A	N/A	N/A	N/A	N/A	N/A	0.0	0.0	INTEGRITY SELECT INSURANCE CO
3.6	3.0	60.9	27.3	-1.8	-2.2	74.1	35.8	109.9	95.7	-22.4	0.0	INTERBORO INS CO
4.5	2.7	54.6	21.0	0.2	1.1	79.6	20.7	100.3	104.9	11.1	1.0 •	INTERINS EXCHANGE
1.6	1.4	108.5	9.4	-10.1	-14.3	11.9	76.2	88.1	118.8	3.8	12.2	INTERNATIONAL FIDELITY INS CO
8.6	7.7	N/A	N/A	N/A	N/A	N/A	N/A	N/A	-127.3	0.0	0.0	INTERSTATE FIRE & CAS CO
N/A	N/A	--	--	--	--	--	--	--	--	--	--	INTREPID INS CO
2.3	1.7	95.5	81.6	4.2	1.7	83.5	41.9	125.4	97.6	1.1	0.0	IOWA AMERICAN INS CO
1.7	1.2	77.1	65.9	3.4	1.4	83.5	42.0	125.5	89.0	1.1	15.2	IOWA MUTUAL INS CO
3.5	2.6	39.9	33.0	8.0	-11.6	51.8	44.8	96.6	192.0	0.1	0.0	IQS INS RRG INC
2.8	2.7	24.3	N/A	N/A	N/A	84.8	161.4	246.2	999 +	-46.2	0.0	IRONSHORE INDEMNITY INC
1.8	1.4	1.0	33.6	22.8	20.8	385.1	999 +	999 +	21.1	-88.1	0.0	IRONSHORE RRG (DC) INC
4.7	4.4	17.1	N/A	N/A	N/A	93.8	225.7	319.5	-58.5	-53.7	0.0 •	IRONSHORE SPECIALTY INS CO
2.3	1.2	232.4	37.2	N/A	N/A	71.9	17.6	89.5	106.7	12.9	0.0	ISLAND HOME INS CO
3.5	2.3	87.3	119.2	-6.2	-12.5	63.8	31.0	94.8	116.2	-0.1	4.9	ISLAND INS CO LTD
4.1	3.7	N/A	N/A	N/A	N/A	N/A	N/A	N/A	N/A	0.0	0.0	ISLAND PREMIER INS CO LTD
52.0	34.2	0.9	N/A	N/A	N/A	N/A	143.2	N/A	98.9	0.0	0.0	ISMIE INDEMNITY CO
4.4	3.7	19.2	81.3	-5.6	-11.0	71.7	41.0	112.7	71.9	-10.8	4.4 •	ISMIE MUTUAL INS CO
2.9	2.6	N/A	N/A	N/A	N/A	N/A	N/A	N/A	N/A	0.0	0.0	IU HEALTH RRG INC
1.7	1.2	42.8	93.3	-0.7	-4.0	67.0	24.3	91.3	104.1	-35.3	0.0	JAMES RIVER CASUALTY CO
1.6	1.1	79.7	116.4	10.0	-1.0	95.7	-23.8	71.9	372.8	101.2	5.7	JAMES RIVER INS CO
1.7	1.4	184.3	13.0	-0.9	-1.2	34.3	55.9	90.2	117.4	26.0	0.0	JEFFERSON INS CO
4.6	3.1	69.5	9.9	-0.8	-1.8	42.8	41.5	84.3	123.4	8.7	4.2 •	JEWELERS MUTUAL INS CO
N/A	N/A	--	--	--	--	--	--	--	--	--	--	JM SPECIALTY INSURANCE CO
N/A	N/A	--	--	--	--	--	--	--	--	--	--	JM WOODWORTH RRG INC
2.7	1.8	86.0	5.6	4.9	4.3	57.7	42.8	100.5	96.9	1.3	0.0	JUNIATA MUTUAL INS CO
8.2	7.4	N/A	N/A	N/A	N/A	N/A	N/A	N/A	77.3	0.0	0.0	KAMMCO CASUALTY CO
7.5	5.0	21.0	32.4	-3.0	-3.6	83.5	31.9	115.4	94.5	4.2	-2.5	KANSAS MEDICAL MUTUAL INS CO
3.9	3.3	71.8	9.9	-2.9	-3.8	62.5	25.8	88.3	110.1	0.6	0.0	KANSAS MUTUAL INS CO
N/A	N/A	--	--	--	--	--	--	--	--	--	--	KEMPER FINANCIAL INDEMNITY CO
1.0	0.9	N/A	N/A	N/A	N/A	N/A	N/A	N/A	19.1	0.0	0.0	KEMPER INDEPENDENCE INS CO
0.7	0.4	157.2	163.1	9.5	12.4	77.3	47.2	124.5	70.3	-7.6	0.0	KENSINGTON INS CO
2.3	1.7	11.5	36.8	-5.2	-12.4	51.1	28.2	79.3	119.3	5.1	0.0	KENTUCKIANA MEDICAL RRG & INS CO
1.4	1.0	74.8	291.1	17.0	13.7	85.3	25.9	111.2	103.2	5.9	0.0	KENTUCKY EMPLOYERS MUTUAL INS
6.1	4.1	72.7	30.3	-1.1	-2.4	78.5	20.3	98.8	101.6	6.5	0.7 •	KENTUCKY FARM BUREAU MUTUAL INS
1.5	1.1	32.8	108.0	-22.1	-36.0	68.5	28.2	96.7	62.5	29.5	0.0	KENTUCKY HOSPITAL INS CO RRG
0.7	0.5	273.0	86.8	1.4	-3.0	68.8	28.9	97.7	104.9	14.5	12.7	KENTUCKY NATIONAL INS CO
4.5	2.6	5.2	1.5	1.4	1.7	22.5	45.1	67.6	140.5	-26.2	0.0	KESWICK GUARANTY INC
0.1	0.1	768.7	314.4	66.2	63.5	82.9	19.1	102.0	102.4	9.9	0.0	KEY INS CO
11.2	10.1	N/A	N/A	N/A	N/A	N/A	N/A	N/A	219.6	0.0	0.0	KEY RISK INS CO
0.3	0.2	439.1	226.4	62.2	224.4	47.4	49.9	97.3	126.7	19.7	0.0	KEYSTONE MUTUAL INS CO
4.2	3.5	25.0	8.0	-0.4	-3.2	51.2	35.5	86.7	185.2	12.8	0.0	KEYSTONE NATIONAL INS CO
3.5	2.4	91.7	31.6	-1.1	1.1	44.2	36.9	81.1	140.6	40.9	1.0	KINGSTONE INSURANCE CO
1.9	1.0	88.6	125.1	-8.1	-13.3	58.9	23.7	82.6	177.8	13.3	0.0	KINSALE INS CO
3.5	2.0	N/A	N/A	N/A	N/A	N/A	N/A	N/A	-118.6	0.0	0.0	KNIGHT SPECIALTY INS CO

999 + Denotes number greater than 999.9%
999 - Denotes number less than -999.99%
• Bullets denote a more detailed analysis is available in Section II.

INSURANCE COMPANY NAME	DOM. STATE	RATING	TOTAL ASSETS ($MIL)	CAPITAL & SURPLUS ($MIL)	ANNUAL NET PREMIUM ($MIL)	NET INCOME ($MIL)	CAPITAL-IZATION INDEX (PTS)	RESERVE ADQ INDEX (PTS)	PROFIT-ABILITY INDEX (PTS)	LIQUIDITY INDEX (PTS)	STAB. INDEX (PTS)	STABILITY FACTORS
KNIGHTBROOK INS CO	DE	D	159.3	71.1	17.1	7.2	4.9	0.5	2.9	6.6	2.2	DFGR
KOOKMIN BEST INS CO LTD US BR	NY	E+	273.9	115.1	33.7	-10.3	1.9	0.4	1.9	6.7	0.5	FRT
▲LACKAWANNA AMERICAN INS CO	PA	B+	89.8	43.8	23.0	2.6	9.1	6.5	8.6	6.8	6.3	
LACKAWANNA CASUALTY CO	PA	B-	240.2	93.1	80.8	6.5	7.1	6.7	8.1	6.0	4.5	R
LACKAWANNA NATIONAL INS CO	PA	B-	38.9	16.2	11.5	1.2	7.6	6.6	8.9	6.8	4.9	DRT
LAFAYETTE INS CO	LA	B-	221.2	91.4	71.3	2.6	9.6	8.0	6.9	6.7	5.2	T
LAKE STREET RRG INC	VT	D	2.4	1.7	0.7	0.3	8.9	7.1	5.4	9.8	1.3	DGT
▲LAKEVIEW INS CO	FL	B-	33.8	17.2	18.0	0.1	8.4	6.3	5.6	6.1	5.2	DF
LAMMICO	LA	B	432.9	238.8	47.1	7.6	10.0	8.7	8.1	8.6	6.1	T
▲LAMMICO RRG INC	DC	C	6.0	5.6	0.0	0.1	10.0	5.3	3.8	10.0	3.5	D
LAMORAK INS CO	PA	U	--	--	--	--	N/A	--	--	--	--	Z
▲LANCER INDEMNITY CO	NY	B-	30.2	11.6	4.8	0.5	6.0	4.1	5.5	6.9	4.6	DRT
▼LANCER INS CO	IL	B-	689.1	209.4	253.5	15.5	8.1	3.3	6.1	6.7	5.2	
LANCET IND RRG INC	NV	E- (1)	18.2	3.6	17.2	0.2	0.3	1.2	1.8	1.3	0.1	CFGL
▲LANDCAR CASUALTY CO	UT	B-	44.5	16.9	11.1	-0.7	7.0	6.0	4.9	6.8	4.6	D
LANDMARK AMERICAN INS CO	NH	C	355.2	184.6	39.2	6.9	10.0	7.8	3.4	7.0	3.5	AR
LAUNDRY OWNERS MUTUAL LIAB INS ASN	PA	C-	16.9	9.2	4.2	0.9	8.1	9.6	8.6	6.9	2.8	DR
LAWYERS MUTUAL INS CO	CA	B	342.2	239.9	34.7	14.1	10.0	9.3	8.7	7.6	6.1	T
LAWYERS MUTUAL INS CO OF KENTUCKY	KY	C	23.2	11.1	5.0	0.6	8.4	9.7	8.2	7.0	3.1	DFR
▲LAWYERS MUTUAL LIAB INS CO OF NC	NC	B	109.5	81.3	15.8	4.9	10.0	9.3	8.8	7.4	5.5	D
LCTA CASUALTY INS CO	LA	B-	71.0	33.2	22.3	0.3	7.6	3.6	4.4	6.7	3.9	DFT
LCTA SPECIALTY INSURANCE CO	LA	D+	7.2	5.4	0.0	0.1	10.0	N/A	5.2	10.0	1.0	DT
▼LE MARS INS CO	IA	C	66.1	23.4	39.5	-1.7	7.5	5.8	2.5	6.1	4.1	DR
▲LEAGUE OF WI MUNICIPALITIES MUT INS	WI	B	70.7	38.8	24.5	4.7	8.5	9.6	8.9	7.0	5.2	T
LEATHERSTOCKING COOP INS CO	NY	C+	43.4	23.3	18.8	3.4	7.6	9.1	8.9	6.8	4.3	DR
▲LEBANON VALLEY INS CO	PA	C+	26.5	12.7	8.7	1.1	7.6	9.4	6.1	6.8	4.5	DR
LEGAL MUTUAL LIAB INS SOCIETY OF MD	MD	U (5)	--	--	--	--	N/A	--	--	--	--	Z
LEMIC INS CO	LA	F (5)	0.0	0.0	15.4	0.0	0.0	1.6	0.1	7.0	0.0	CDFR
LEMONADE INS CO	NY	D+	25.2	17.0	8.3	-15.7	2.2	3.6	0.9	8.4	1.3	CDFG
LEON HIX INS CO	SC	D	3.6	3.4	0.2	0.0	10.0	N/A	5.5	10.0	2.1	DT
LEXINGTON INS CO	DE	C	21,180.1	5,441.9	4,215.0	-243.1	7.5	3.0	2.7	5.3	4.2	FR
▲LEXINGTON NATIONAL INS CORP	FL	D	61.9	19.3	12.9	0.4	7.4	6.0	7.4	7.1	1.5	DR
▲LEXON INS CO	TX	C	244.5	68.0	70.5	2.4	7.3	3.9	7.9	8.2	3.5	R
LIBERTY AMERICAN INS CO	FL	U (5)	--	--	--	--	N/A	--	--	--	--	Z
LIBERTY AMERICAN SELECT INS CO	FL	U (5)	--	--	--	--	N/A	--	--	--	--	Z
LIBERTY COUNTY MUTUAL INS CO	TX	C-	7.5	5.1	0.0	-0.1	10.0	N/A	3.4	7.0	2.6	DFT
LIBERTY FIRST RRG INS CO	UT	F (5)	0.0	0.0	2.5	0.0	0.2	0.5	1.9	8.5	0.0	CDGR
LIBERTY INS CORP	IL	C	260.1	245.1	0.0	3.1	10.0	N/A	7.0	10.0	4.3	A
LIBERTY INS UNDERWRITERS INC	IL	C	264.1	127.4	0.0	1.1	10.0	N/A	6.1	10.0	4.3	AFRT
LIBERTY LLOYDS OF TX INS CO	TX	B	6.6	6.5	0.0	0.1	10.0	N/A	6.4	7.0	4.3	D
LIBERTY MUTUAL FIRE INS CO	WI	B-	6,038.9	1,412.8	2,284.0	-31.0	7.7	5.7	5.0	6.0	5.0	A
LIBERTY MUTUAL INS CO	MA	B	46,020.8	14,531.3	14,275.1	-908.4	5.9	5.9	2.9	5.6	5.3	AC
LIBERTY MUTUAL MID ATLANTIC INS CO	MA	C	22.8	20.3	0.0	0.5	10.0	N/A	7.6	10.0	4.3	D
LIBERTY MUTUAL PERSONAL INS CO	MA	B	12.8	12.8	0.0	0.1	10.0	N/A	7.3	7.0	4.0	DG
LIBERTY NORTHWEST INS CORP	OR	C	59.9	55.5	0.0	-0.4	10.0	N/A	4.2	7.0	4.3	R
LIBERTY PERSONAL INS CO	NH	C	17.0	16.4	0.0	0.1	10.0	N/A	6.8	7.0	4.3	D
LIBERTY SURPLUS INS CORP	NH	C	139.7	91.6	0.0	-3.3	10.0	N/A	3.7	6.9	4.3	AFT
▼LIGHTHOUSE CASUALTY CO	IL	E+	35.6	8.1	30.7	-2.8	0.8	0.4	2.8	4.6	0.7	CDFG
LIGHTHOUSE PROPERTY INS CORP	LA	B-	100.9	24.2	50.9	-2.7	6.6	6.1	5.1	7.2	4.7	D
LIGHTNING ROD MUTUAL INS CO	OH	B-	300.3	176.8	116.8	5.7	10.0	7.8	8.2	6.9	4.7	T
▲LION INS CO (FL)	FL	B+	264.3	96.9	27.1	6.6	8.6	8.7	8.7	8.3	5.1	T
LITITZ MUTUAL INS CO	PA	B-	304.7	210.5	76.3	7.3	7.7	7.6	6.8	6.3	4.7	AR

See Page 27 for explanation of footnotes and
Page 28 for explanation of stability factors.

82

www.weissratings.com

Arrows denote recent upgrades ▲ or downgrades ▼   (see Section VII for explanations)

RISK ADJ. RATIO #1	CAPITAL RATIO #2	PREMIUM TO SURPLUS (%)	RESV. TO SURPLUS (%)	RESV. DEVELOP. 1 YEAR (%)	2 YEAR (%)	LOSS RATIO (%)	EXP. RATIO (%)	COMB RATIO (%)	CASH FROM UNDER- WRITING (%)	NET PREMIUM GROWTH (%)	INVEST. IN AFFIL (%)	INSURANCE COMPANY NAME
1.2	0.9	24.0	50.2	6.7	60.0	71.1	45.5	116.6	33.9	121.6	2.8	KNIGHTBROOK INS CO
0.6	0.4	29.3	116.3	2.9	3.3	97.8	54.9	152.7	40.8	33.0	0.0	KOOKMIN BEST INS CO LTD US BR
3.1	2.5	52.6	64.9	N/A	0.2	78.0	17.6	95.6	114.6	-0.2	0.0 ●	LACKAWANNA AMERICAN INS CO
1.2	1.0	86.8	110.0	-0.2	0.5	78.0	17.8	95.8	116.4	-0.2	29.5	LACKAWANNA CASUALTY CO
1.8	1.5	71.2	85.4	N/A	0.2	78.0	17.6	95.6	115.1	-0.2	0.0	LACKAWANNA NATIONAL INS CO
4.3	2.9	78.0	88.9	-2.3	-2.1	72.8	30.4	103.2	108.4	5.6	0.0	LAFAYETTE INS CO
3.2	2.2	39.5	38.7	0.1	-46.9	41.6	20.9	62.5	324.6	95.3	0.0	LAKE STREET RRG INC
2.2	1.9	104.9	18.5	-1.9	-4.1	59.3	45.5	104.8	88.7	-3.8	0.0	LAKEVIEW INS CO
5.7	4.3	19.7	65.0	-2.4	-6.1	73.9	27.5	101.4	99.6	-5.5	0.1 ●	LAMMICO
28.8	25.9	0.3	1.5	-0.1	-0.2	202.4	-559.7	-357.3	-288.3	8.1	0.0	LAMMICO RRG INC
N/A	N/A	--	--	--	--	--	--	--	--	--	--	LAMORAK INS CO
1.4	0.8	41.1	87.2	-2.5	-5.8	54.3	44.2	98.5	142.7	-49.2	0.0	LANCER INDEMNITY CO
2.6	1.8	121.0	167.0	1.1	11.2	68.3	29.5	97.8	107.0	-2.8	0.0	LANCER INS CO
0.1	0.1	381.3	259.5	258.7	286.1	120.0	19.3	139.3	95.4	104.6	10.7	LANCET IND RRG INC
1.4	1.0	65.3	16.1	1.4	0.8	111.6	7.1	118.7	103.3	4.5	0.0	LANDCAR CASUALTY CO
10.2	6.3	21.3	39.0	-1.1	-3.8	82.6	28.0	110.6	140.9	2.4	0.0	LANDMARK AMERICAN INS CO
2.8	2.2	46.1	64.0	-3.5	-22.2	50.8	38.9	89.7	120.9	-8.4	0.0	LAUNDRY OWNERS MUTUAL LIAB INS
9.5	5.8	14.5	29.0	-5.2	-11.1	51.6	16.0	67.6	124.9	-1.5	0.1 ●	LAWYERS MUTUAL INS CO
3.3	2.2	45.0	76.1	-11.9	-20.5	74.4	22.0	96.4	70.2	9.6	0.0	LAWYERS MUTUAL INS CO OF
6.6	4.3	19.4	18.5	-1.1	-6.2	49.9	29.4	79.3	104.6	8.3	3.0	LAWYERS MUTUAL LIAB INS CO OF NC
2.1	1.7	67.1	69.2	1.9	N/A	55.0	46.6	101.6	90.9	-1.1	9.0	LCTA CASUALTY INS CO
8.2	7.4	N/A	N/A	N/A	N/A	N/A	N/A	N/A	101.6	0.0	0.0	LCTA SPECIALTY INSURANCE CO
2.0	1.3	168.6	79.5	-2.2	-0.5	76.2	30.4	106.6	104.6	21.3	0.0	LE MARS INS CO
3.1	2.3	63.0	71.2	-9.6	-21.4	60.1	15.7	75.8	123.4	1.6	4.0	LEAGUE OF WI MUNICIPALITIES MUT INS
2.1	1.4	80.9	34.1	-8.1	-9.6	46.3	29.0	75.3	147.4	13.7	0.0	LEATHERSTOCKING COOP INS CO
1.7	1.3	68.3	49.7	-7.0	-21.9	43.0	45.2	88.2	104.8	2.7	0.0	LEBANON VALLEY INS CO
N/A	N/A	--	--	--	--	--	--	--	--	--	--	LEGAL MUTUAL LIAB INS SOCIETY OF
-0.0	-0.0	-739.3	999 +	53.8	50.0	121.0	52.5	173.5	71.1	-29.6	0.0	LEMIC INS CO
0.5	0.4	48.9	0.3	-0.1	N/A	74.4	197.4	271.8	14.3	N/A	0.0	LEMONADE INS CO
32.2	29.0	5.7	1.7	N/A	N/A	72.2	15.3	87.5	422.1	0.0	0.0	LEON HIX INS CO
2.0	1.3	77.5	186.8	-9.7	10.3	90.8	38.5	129.3	50.4	-12.9	0.8 ●	LEXINGTON INS CO
1.4	1.2	66.9	1.3	-4.4	2.3	0.7	99.0	99.7	96.2	-3.1	19.3	LEXINGTON NATIONAL INS CORP
1.5	1.2	103.5	46.6	-9.0	-6.2	22.9	73.3	96.2	133.5	-5.3	0.0	LEXON INS CO
N/A	N/A	--	--	--	--	--	--	--	--	--	--	LIBERTY AMERICAN INS CO
N/A	N/A	--	--	--	--	--	--	--	--	--	--	LIBERTY AMERICAN SELECT INS CO
6.1	5.5	N/A	N/A	N/A	N/A	N/A	N/A	N/A	N/A	0.0	0.0	LIBERTY COUNTY MUTUAL INS CO
-0.3	-0.2	149.9	267.7	21.4	98.2	41.3	11.6	52.9	222.4	-50.3	0.0	LIBERTY FIRST RRG INS CO
82.2	71.4	N/A	N/A	N/A	N/A	N/A	N/A	N/A	N/A	0.0	0.0 ●	LIBERTY INS CORP
13.6	12.2	N/A	N/A	N/A	N/A	N/A	N/A	N/A	999 +	0.0	0.0	LIBERTY INS UNDERWRITERS INC
269.9	134.9	N/A	N/A	N/A	N/A	N/A	N/A	N/A	N/A	0.0	0.0	LIBERTY LLOYDS OF TX INS CO
2.0	1.4	161.7	222.6	4.8	5.4	81.2	29.0	110.2	99.9	7.7	4.7 ●	LIBERTY MUTUAL FIRE INS CO
0.9	0.8	98.2	135.3	2.7	3.0	79.5	30.4	109.9	99.1	7.7	43.6 ●	LIBERTY MUTUAL INS CO
23.9	21.5	N/A	N/A	N/A	N/A	N/A	N/A	N/A	N/A	0.0	0.0	LIBERTY MUTUAL MID ATLANTIC INS CO
196.7	98.3	N/A	N/A	N/A	N/A	N/A	N/A	N/A	N/A	0.0	0.0	LIBERTY MUTUAL PERSONAL INS CO
3.8	3.7	N/A	N/A	N/A	N/A	N/A	N/A	N/A	N/A	0.0	27.0	LIBERTY NORTHWEST INS CORP
64.4	57.9	N/A	N/A	N/A	N/A	N/A	N/A	N/A	-52.2	0.0	0.0	LIBERTY PERSONAL INS CO
14.0	12.6	N/A	N/A	N/A	N/A	N/A	N/A	N/A	79.9	0.0	0.0	LIBERTY SURPLUS INS CORP
0.2	0.2	378.8	176.6	75.7	108.1	69.5	37.0	106.5	92.4	64.4	0.0	LIGHTHOUSE CASUALTY CO
1.3	1.0	210.0	41.4	2.8	0.3	61.3	42.9	104.2	112.8	27.7	0.0	LIGHTHOUSE PROPERTY INS CORP
5.2	3.3	66.1	30.2	-1.8	-2.7	69.8	30.6	100.4	103.2	3.8	0.1	LIGHTNING ROD MUTUAL INS CO
3.4	2.0	28.0	54.5	-3.3	-7.6	34.4	41.1	75.5	142.3	-4.2	0.0 ●	LION INS CO (FL)
2.6	1.6	36.3	10.8	0.2	-1.8	68.3	35.4	103.7	101.6	-0.1	0.0	LITITZ MUTUAL INS CO

999 + Denotes number greater than 999.9%
999 - Denotes number less than -999.99%
● Bullets denote a more detailed analysis is available in Section II.

INSURANCE COMPANY NAME	DOM. STATE	RATING	TOTAL ASSETS ($MIL)	CAPITAL & SURPLUS ($MIL)	ANNUAL NET PREMIUM ($MIL)	NET INCOME ($MIL)	CAPITAL-IZATION INDEX (PTS)	RESERVE ADQ INDEX (PTS)	PROFIT-ABILITY INDEX (PTS)	LIQUIDITY INDEX (PTS)	STAB. INDEX (PTS)	STABILITY FACTORS
LITTLE BLACK MUTUAL INS CO	WI	D+	5.6	2.7	2.6	-1.5	4.5	6.0	2.6	1.5	2.1	DFLR
LIVINGSTON MUTUAL INS CO	PA	C	3.5	1.7	0.4	0.0	8.8	6.5	3.9	7.1	2.3	DGT
LM GENERAL INS CO	IL	B-	11.2	10.9	0.0	0.2	10.0	4.8	6.7	10.0	4.5	DF
LM INS CORP	IL	C	124.0	116.5	0.0	-0.8	10.0	N/A	5.6	10.0	4.3	A
LM P&C INS CO	IN	U	--	--	--	--	N/A	--	--	--	--	Z
LOCUST MUTUAL FIRE INS CO	PA	D	1.3	1.3	0.0	0.0	7.6	4.7	3.6	7.0	1.2	DFT
▲LONE STAR ALLIANCE INC A RRG	DC	D+	9.9	2.8	0.7	-0.3	2.8	4.4	3.1	10.0	2.0	CDFT
LOUISIANA FARM BUREAU CAS INS CO	LA	B	12.2	11.5	0.0	0.3	10.0	N/A	7.5	7.0	4.5	D
LOUISIANA FARM BUREAU MUTUAL INS CO	LA	B	228.3	147.4	82.7	11.1	10.0	8.0	8.9	6.7	6.2	T
LOYA CASUALTY INS CO	CA	D	120.1	23.2	140.5	-6.0	2.8	4.2	1.1	0.9	2.0	CDL
▲LOYA INS CO	TX	D+	289.7	112.1	305.7	1.6	6.4	3.1	2.0	2.7	2.5	L
LR INS INC	DE	U	--	--	--	--	N/A	--	--	--	--	Z
▲LUBA CASUALTY INS CO	LA	B+	228.7	98.6	73.2	7.4	8.3	9.3	8.8	6.9	6.5	
▲LUBA INDEMNITY INS CO	LA	D+	5.3	5.0	0.0	0.0	10.0	N/A	4.9	9.5	2.5	DT
LUMBER MUTUAL INS CO	MA	F (5)	0.0	0.0	0.0	0.0	0.3	2.4	1.8	9.1	0.0	CFGR
LUMBERMENS UNDERWRITING ALLIANCE	MO	F (5)	354.2	-41.9	63.8	0.0	0.0	4.1	0.1	7.0	0.0	CDFR
LUTHERAN MUTUAL FIRE INS CO	IL	C	10.7	10.4	0.3	0.0	10.0	5.0	5.1	7.0	3.0	D
LVHN RRG	SC	U	--	--	--	--	N/A	--	--	--	--	Z
LYNDON SOUTHERN INS CO	DE	B	191.9	51.5	105.1	3.3	7.5	5.0	8.3	6.2	5.8	
MA EMPLOYERS INS CO	MA	C	4.4	3.7	0.0	0.0	10.0	N/A	6.3	10.0	3.3	DR
▲MACHINERY INS INC	FL	D	3.0	2.8	0.5	0.2	10.0	N/A	6.1	8.7	1.4	D
MADA INS EXCHANGE	MN	U	--	--	--	--	N/A	--	--	--	--	Z
MADISON MUTUAL INS CO	IL	B-	66.3	39.9	33.7	-2.2	8.5	5.5	3.2	6.1	4.9	FR
MADISON MUTUAL INS CO	NY	C+	15.1	10.5	4.6	1.0	10.0	7.6	7.8	6.9	3.0	DR
MAG MUTUAL INS CO	GA	B-	1,718.5	850.0	263.9	29.4	9.5	9.3	6.3	7.1	4.7	R
▼MAIDEN RE NORTH AMERICA INC	MO	C+	1,298.9	301.7	468.3	16.9	5.4	3.1	5.0	5.5	4.8	
▲MAIDSTONE INS CO	NY	D-	56.7	14.6	31.0	-1.6	2.9	7.0	0.7	5.6	1.0	DFR
▲MAIN STREET AMER PROTECTION INS CO	FL	C+	23.3	23.1	0.0	0.4	10.0	N/A	7.6	7.0	3.2	DGT
MAIN STREET AMERICA ASR CO	FL	C	44.0	43.6	0.0	0.6	10.0	N/A	5.5	9.3	3.8	
▲MAISON INS CO	LA	B-	92.0	38.7	50.1	-2.3	6.5	5.2	3.4	6.9	4.9	GT
MAKE TRANSPORTATION INS INC RRG	DE	D	7.1	2.5	3.2	0.4	5.3	7.0	8.9	7.7	1.8	DGRT
MANHATTAN RE-INS CO	DE	F (5)	0.0	0.0	0.0	0.0	5.6	9.8	0.8	9.2	2.0	FRT
▲MANUFACTURERS ALLIANCE INS CO	PA	C	219.4	75.8	60.7	3.7	7.5	2.7	5.9	6.4	3.5	AR
▲MANUFACTURING TECHNOLOGY MUT INS	MI	B	63.0	29.0	19.9	1.1	7.2	9.7	8.9	6.9	5.1	D
MAPFRE INS CO	NJ	C	80.5	21.2	47.6	-0.5	7.0	3.9	3.1	4.2	3.4	DLR
MAPFRE INS CO OF FLORIDA	FL	C	107.5	30.2	67.4	-1.3	7.4	4.3	2.5	4.6	3.4	L
MAPFRE INS CO OF NY	NY	C+	154.1	42.4	99.1	-0.6	7.7	4.2	2.5	4.0	4.7	L
MAPFRE PAN AMERICAN INS CO	PR	C (1)	38.3	13.2	7.7	2.2	5.6	7.3	7.0	6.3	2.4	CDGT
MAPFRE PRAICO INS CO	PR	C (1)	435.2	128.7	183.3	-33.2	7.0	8.3	3.8	5.6	2.9	FT
MAPLE VALLEY MUTUAL INS CO	WI	C	14.8	10.0	5.5	0.4	9.3	7.4	6.0	7.2	2.9	DR
MARATHON FINANCIAL INS INC RRG	DE	D+	3.3	1.9	0.3	-0.1	8.1	7.4	2.5	9.3	1.7	DFRT
MARKEL AMERICAN INS CO	VA	C	585.5	179.9	300.7	-3.1	7.1	9.4	6.0	6.8	3.7	AGRT
MARKEL GLOBAL REINS CO	DE	B+	2,180.9	904.3	613.6	-32.8	7.0	7.5	3.8	6.9	6.5	GT
▲MARYSVILLE MUTUAL INS CO	KS	B-	51.1	31.7	25.2	2.4	8.8	6.2	8.8	6.3	5.1	T
MASSACHUSETTS BAY INS CO	NH	C+	65.2	65.2	0.0	1.4	10.0	N/A	6.5	7.0	4.7	R
MASSACHUSETTS HOMELAND INS CO	MA	F (5)	8.9	8.3	0.0	0.0	10.0	N/A	4.5	7.0	0.0	DFGR
MAXUM CASUALTY INS CO	CT	C+	27.6	17.3	-29.6	1.5	10.0	6.0	3.9	7.0	4.8	DFRT
MAXUM INDEMNITY CO	CT	C	137.3	104.3	-155.6	7.0	10.0	7.0	3.0	7.0	4.0	RT
MAYA ASR CO	NY	E+	16.7	3.0	11.8	0.1	0.0	0.1	4.8	6.5	0.4	CDGT
MBIA INS CORP	NY	E+	262.4	236.5	40.7	107.1	1.3	1.3	1.3	0.2	0.4	CFLT
MCIC VERMONT INC RRG	VT	C	1,922.5	655.9	337.6	44.6	1.0	1.7	4.5	6.7	3.4	CR
MCMILLAN WARNER MUTUAL INS CO	WI	C	18.5	10.7	7.8	-0.4	8.1	7.7	5.0	6.6	3.0	DFR

See Page 27 for explanation of footnotes and
Page 28 for explanation of stability factors.

Arrows denote recent upgrades ▲ or downgrades ▼   (see Section VII for explanations)

84

www.weissratings.com

RISK ADJ. CAPITAL RATIO #1	CAPITAL RATIO #2	PREMIUM TO SURPLUS (%)	RESV. TO SURPLUS (%)	RESV. DEVELOP. 1 YEAR (%)	RESV. DEVELOP. 2 YEAR (%)	LOSS RATIO (%)	EXP. RATIO (%)	COMB RATIO (%)	CASH FROM UNDER-WRITING (%)	NET PREMIUM GROWTH (%)	INVEST. IN AFFIL (%)	INSURANCE COMPANY NAME
0.9	0.6	94.3	14.8	0.3	1.2	119.5	40.3	159.8	65.0	0.5	0.0	LITTLE BLACK MUTUAL INS CO
2.6	2.3	23.9	9.4	-0.9	-1.2	81.4	20.8	102.2	203.8	-17.8	0.0	LIVINGSTON MUTUAL INS CO
97.7	78.5	N/A	0.4	N/A	N/A	N/A	N/A	N/A	999 +	0.0	0.0	LM GENERAL INS CO
58.9	53.0	N/A	N/A	N/A	N/A	N/A	N/A	N/A	N/A	0.0	0.0	LM INS CORP
N/A	N/A	--	--	--	--	--	--	--	--	--	--	LM P&C INS CO
2.2	1.3	3.6	N/A	N/A	-0.7	52.4	115.1	167.5	51.7	10.1	0.0	LOCUST MUTUAL FIRE INS CO
0.6	0.4	23.9	70.2	8.1	8.6	229.7	-96.7	133.0	-299.4	-3.8	0.0	LONE STAR ALLIANCE INC A RRG
36.0	32.4	N/A	N/A	N/A	N/A	N/A	N/A	N/A	N/A	0.0	0.0	LOUISIANA FARM BUREAU CAS INS CO
6.0	5.1	56.1	9.9	-0.9	-1.6	65.7	20.6	86.3	112.0	-1.6	5.1	LOUISIANA FARM BUREAU MUTUAL INS
0.5	0.4	605.5	339.3	3.9	26.4	75.4	33.4	108.8	103.7	-7.1	0.0	LOYA CASUALTY INS CO
1.0	0.9	272.8	141.2	0.7	23.1	65.5	35.7	101.2	109.9	-12.1	18.8	LOYA INS CO
N/A	N/A	--	--	--	--	--	--	--	--	--	--	LR INS INC
2.6	2.0	74.2	89.7	-11.2	-16.1	53.6	34.8	88.4	109.5	-1.5	2.6 •	LUBA CASUALTY INS CO
39.0	35.1	N/A	N/A	N/A	N/A	N/A	N/A	N/A	757.7	0.0	0.0	LUBA INDEMNITY INS CO
0.1	0.1	0.7	407.0	33.1	32.6	999 +	999 +	999 +	0.4	146.2	54.4	LUMBER MUTUAL INS CO
-0.3	-0.2	-283.3	-645.8	3.0	15.1	97.4	177.7	275.1	71.0	-23.8	0.0	LUMBERMENS UNDERWRITING
13.3	8.6	2.9	0.4	0.2	-0.1	62.7	108.6	171.3	58.2	-1.8	0.0	LUTHERAN MUTUAL FIRE INS CO
N/A	N/A	--	--	--	--	--	--	--	--	--	--	LVHN RRG
2.3	1.4	204.3	27.1	1.6	1.3	48.3	40.2	88.5	115.5	17.8	0.0	LYNDON SOUTHERN INS CO
11.6	10.5	N/A	N/A	N/A	N/A	N/A	N/A	N/A	999 +	0.0	0.0	MA EMPLOYERS INS CO
9.8	7.1	16.7	0.9	N/A	N/A	-0.2	58.0	57.8	180.4	15.6	0.0	MACHINERY INS INC
N/A	N/A	--	--	--	--	--	--	--	--	--	--	MADA INS EXCHANGE
3.1	2.0	84.4	26.7	-1.6	-1.7	84.6	25.7	110.3	93.4	7.9	0.0	MADISON MUTUAL INS CO
5.1	3.3	43.4	8.9	-0.4	-1.6	37.3	37.9	75.2	133.2	14.0	0.0	MADISON MUTUAL INS CO
3.7	2.6	31.0	63.5	-2.1	-4.3	73.2	22.9	96.1	108.9	8.2	5.0 •	MAG MUTUAL INS CO
1.2	0.8	155.2	188.9	14.2	28.3	78.9	24.5	103.4	99.7	8.1	0.0 •	MAIDEN RE NORTH AMERICA INC
0.6	0.4	212.8	186.4	-12.8	-34.7	77.7	30.6	108.3	72.2	-20.1	0.0	MAIDSTONE INS CO
91.1	42.2	N/A	N/A	N/A	N/A	N/A	N/A	N/A	N/A	0.0	0.0	MAIN STREET AMER PROTECTION INS
43.0	21.0	N/A	N/A	N/A	N/A	N/A	N/A	N/A	127.1	0.0	0.0	MAIN STREET AMERICA ASR CO
2.0	1.1	129.5	11.7	-10.5	-3.3	46.1	42.6	88.7	111.7	62.7	0.0	MAISON INS CO
1.1	0.7	127.8	68.5	-9.7	-28.8	59.2	10.0	69.2	192.6	153.0	0.0	MAKE TRANSPORTATION INS INC RRG
2.4	0.9	-0.2	102.5	-76.7	-71.0	999 +	999 +	999 +	0.9	-120.0	0.0	MANHATTAN RE-INS CO
1.8	1.3	80.0	134.6	5.1	11.9	76.4	22.9	99.3	120.2	14.5	6.7	MANUFACTURERS ALLIANCE INS CO
2.0	1.5	68.6	84.7	-16.2	-29.5	48.4	19.2	67.6	155.0	-0.4	0.0	MANUFACTURING TECHNOLOGY MUT
1.2	1.0	224.3	114.6	7.0	6.3	79.9	23.3	103.2	101.4	0.4	0.0	MAPFRE INS CO
1.5	1.2	223.4	114.2	7.1	6.6	79.9	25.3	105.2	99.4	0.4	0.0	MAPFRE INS CO OF FLORIDA
1.7	1.4	233.8	119.5	7.1	6.3	79.9	24.8	104.7	101.5	0.4	0.0	MAPFRE INS CO OF NY
0.9	0.5	64.8	1.8	-0.5	-0.6	20.1	1.1	21.2	424.7	190.9	0.0	MAPFRE PAN AMERICAN INS CO
1.1	0.7	113.2	44.5	-4.6	-4.7	48.9	46.0	94.9	96.6	11.8	0.0	MAPFRE PRAICO INS CO
3.7	2.6	55.2	8.2	-2.2	-0.3	60.5	32.9	93.4	108.1	3.3	0.0	MAPLE VALLEY MUTUAL INS CO
3.4	2.4	15.9	N/A	-1.2	-1.1	-15.6	146.8	131.2	69.5	80.9	0.0	MARATHON FINANCIAL INS INC RRG
1.4	1.0	167.1	120.3	-16.1	-21.4	65.0	34.8	99.8	156.4	41.7	0.0	MARKEL AMERICAN INS CO
1.3	1.0	67.9	82.1	N/A	-1.5	76.6	34.6	111.2	143.8	140.9	13.3 •	MARKEL GLOBAL REINS CO
2.9	2.1	79.6	7.0	0.1	-0.8	62.2	26.1	88.3	112.7	9.3	0.0	MARYSVILLE MUTUAL INS CO
85.8	39.8	N/A	N/A	N/A	N/A	N/A	N/A	N/A	N/A	0.0	0.0	MASSACHUSETTS BAY INS CO
30.8	27.1	N/A	N/A	N/A	N/A	N/A	N/A	N/A	N/A	0.0	0.0	MASSACHUSETTS HOMELAND INS CO
8.0	7.2	-171.5	N/A	-121.3	-68.3	98.7	0.9	99.6	999 +	-304.2	0.0	MAXUM CASUALTY INS CO
24.3	21.9	-149.2	N/A	-104.9	-57.0	98.7	1.1	99.8	99.7	-304.3	20.2	MAXUM INDEMNITY CO
0.1	0.1	394.5	408.9	117.0	161.1	144.6	-37.6	107.0	174.2	92.6	0.0	MAYA ASR CO
0.5	0.1	17.2	-334.9	148.6	39.9	288.6	3.3	291.9	6.1	-21.8	2.3 •	MBIA INS CORP
0.3	0.2	51.5	175.7	2.9	-3.9	100.7	12.7	113.4	133.6	16.7	0.0 •	MCIC VERMONT INC RRG
2.4	1.8	73.1	12.1	-2.0	-3.1	78.4	35.4	113.8	84.8	11.8	0.0	MCMILLAN WARNER MUTUAL INS CO

999 + Denotes number greater than 999.9%
999 - Denotes number less than -999.99%
• Bullets denote a more detailed analysis is available in Section II.

INSURANCE COMPANY NAME	DOM. STATE	RATING	TOTAL ASSETS ($MIL)	CAPITAL & SURPLUS ($MIL)	ANNUAL NET PREMIUM ($MIL)	NET INCOME ($MIL)	CAPITAL-IZATION INDEX (PTS)	RESERVE ADQ INDEX (PTS)	PROFIT-ABILITY INDEX (PTS)	LIQUIDITY INDEX (PTS)	STAB. INDEX (PTS)	STABILITY FACTORS
▲MD RRG INC	MT	C	27.5	17.9	6.4	2.0	9.6	9.7	8.6	9.0	3.5	DGR
MDADVANTAGE INS CO OF NJ	NJ	C	336.8	150.9	29.5	7.5	8.5	9.3	8.3	7.7	3.5	T
MDOW INS CO	TX	B-	17.9	14.7	0.0	1.1	10.0	N/A	8.9	9.2	4.5	DF
MED MAL RRG INC	TN	D	4.0	1.6	0.1	0.1	8.1	6.0	4.1	10.0	1.3	DFT
MEDCHOICE RRG INC	VT	D	2.6	1.9	0.1	0.0	10.0	3.6	3.0	10.0	2.2	DT
MEDICAL ALLIANCE INS CO	IL	C-	9.2	5.3	2.7	0.3	9.6	N/A	5.4	9.0	2.4	DFR
MEDICAL INS EXCHANGE OF CALIFORNIA	CA	B	405.4	183.9	50.6	4.4	9.9	9.1	6.0	7.2	6.0	F
MEDICAL LIABILITY ALLIANCE	MO	B	83.3	59.5	11.3	3.2	10.0	8.7	8.3	7.3	5.8	D
MEDICAL LIABILITY MUTUAL INS CO	NY	D+	5,430.6	2,204.6	409.9	120.2	7.9	9.5	8.7	7.8	2.4	FR
MEDICAL MUTUAL INS CO OF MAINE	ME	B	312.8	178.3	34.5	6.4	10.0	9.3	8.3	8.7	6.0	T
MEDICAL MUTUAL INS CO OF NC	NC	B-	598.1	288.7	95.0	22.5	9.9	9.4	7.7	8.7	4.5	R
MEDICAL MUTUAL LIAB INS SOC OF MD	MD	B-	825.0	414.3	101.0	7.8	10.0	9.4	7.6	7.7	4.6	R
MEDICAL PROFESSIONAL MUTUAL INS CO	MA	B-	3,134.7	1,638.9	305.1	46.4	8.0	9.3	6.8	7.5	4.5	R
MEDICAL PROTECTIVE CO	IN	B	3,318.0	2,021.0	240.0	83.3	9.3	9.6	8.7	8.8	5.5	T
MEDICAL PROVIDERS MUTUAL INS CO RRG	DC	D+	7.9	3.0	1.1	0.0	7.8	9.5	2.9	8.9	2.1	DR
MEDICAL SECURITY INS CO	NC	C+	32.0	16.7	0.0	0.2	10.0	6.7	5.0	10.0	4.5	DFRT
MEDICUS INS CO	TX	B-	38.2	33.3	0.0	1.2	10.0	N/A	5.3	10.0	3.9	DFRT
▼MEDMAL DIRECT INS CO	FL	C+	43.3	16.8	12.1	-3.7	4.6	4.2	3.3	6.9	4.4	CD
MEDMARC CASUALTY INS CO	VT	C	295.6	203.5	33.8	3.0	8.5	8.9	7.9	7.0	4.1	R
▲MEDPRO RRG	DC	C	98.6	6.6	3.0	-0.2	4.8	9.3	3.6	9.1	2.7	CDT
MEDSTAR LIABILITY LTD INS CO INC RRG	DC	U (5)	--	--	--	--	N/A	--	--	--	--	Z
MEEMIC INS CO	MI	C	286.9	83.6	107.9	3.6	9.2	4.7	5.8	6.1	4.2	T
▲MEMBERS INS CO	NC	C	34.3	13.4	21.4	0.5	7.0	8.1	4.3	2.9	3.5	DL
MEMBERSELECT INS CO	MI	B-	546.9	159.5	194.3	6.6	9.3	4.8	5.6	6.3	4.9	
MEMIC CASUALTY CO	NH	B-	64.8	30.0	17.2	0.1	6.4	6.2	4.2	7.0	5.3	DG
MEMIC INDEMNITY CO	NH	C	528.6	147.5	195.9	1.8	6.1	6.4	6.5	6.6	3.2	R
MENDAKOTA INS CO	MN	B	11.1	9.4	0.0	0.1	10.0	N/A	6.0	7.0	4.4	DR
▲MENDOTA INS CO	MN	C-	118.6	26.2	113.7	-12.3	0.7	2.2	1.4	0.0	3.2	CFLR
MENNONITE MUTUAL INS CO	OH	C	29.0	15.7	15.3	0.7	8.4	6.3	8.7	6.3	3.6	D
▲MENTAL HEALTH RISK RETENTION GROUP	VT	C+	30.1	17.8	4.0	0.9	9.1	9.7	8.8	9.2	3.9	D
MERASTAR INS CO	IL	B-	39.6	12.5	0.0	0.6	9.5	N/A	7.4	7.0	4.5	DR
MERCED PROPERTY & CASUALTY CO	CA	C+	23.4	16.8	6.1	-0.2	10.0	8.0	3.7	6.9	4.8	DR
MERCER INS CO	PA	C+	269.0	107.1	91.7	2.8	7.9	8.0	5.9	6.7	4.4	R
MERCER INS CO OF NJ INC	NJ	C	92.2	34.9	30.6	1.3	8.6	8.1	6.9	6.8	3.8	R
MERCHANTS BONDING CO (MUTUAL)	IA	B	200.4	121.2	88.6	13.1	8.7	8.7	8.7	6.8	6.0	T
MERCHANTS MUTUAL INS CO	NY	B-	533.6	203.5	155.0	11.2	9.0	5.9	7.6	6.9	4.6	R
▲MERCHANTS NATIONAL BONDING INC	IA	B-	35.5	15.6	12.1	1.8	7.7	6.9	8.7	6.8	4.2	DRT
▲MERCHANTS NATIONAL INS CO	NH	B+	136.0	55.3	44.3	2.6	7.6	5.6	5.9	6.8	6.5	D
▲MERCHANTS PREFERRED INS CO	NY	B+	76.4	30.1	22.1	1.6	8.9	5.9	7.9	6.8	6.3	D
MERCHANTS PROPERTY INS CO OF IN	IN	U	--	--	--	--	N/A	--	--	--	--	Z
▲MERCURY CASUALTY CO	CA	B+	1,877.6	1,071.8	680.7	115.1	7.7	5.5	6.6	6.8	6.5	
MERCURY COUNTY MUTUAL INS CO	TX	B	11.7	4.8	0.0	0.0	8.9	N/A	3.5	7.0	4.9	D
▲MERCURY INDEMNITY CO OF AMERICA	FL	C	52.3	38.4	0.0	-1.4	10.0	N/A	3.9	7.0	3.5	
MERCURY INDEMNITY CO OF GEORGIA	GA	B	16.2	11.0	0.0	0.2	10.0	N/A	6.5	7.0	4.9	DT
MERCURY INS CO	CA	B+	1,708.0	609.8	1,624.5	60.8	7.5	4.4	3.9	2.5	6.6	L
▲MERCURY INS CO OF FL	FL	B-	43.0	42.7	0.0	0.9	10.0	N/A	6.7	10.0	3.9	DT
MERCURY INS CO OF GA	GA	B	22.2	19.0	0.0	0.7	10.0	N/A	7.7	7.0	5.4	DT
MERCURY INS CO OF IL	IL	B	36.3	34.5	0.0	0.5	8.3	N/A	6.9	8.5	6.0	DF
MERCURY NATIONAL INS CO	IL	U	--	--	--	--	N/A	--	--	--	--	Z
MERIDIAN SECURITY INS CO	IN	C	137.7	72.9	0.0	1.2	10.0	N/A	6.8	6.8	3.6	R
MERITPLAN INS CO	CA	U	--	--	--	--	N/A	--	--	--	--	Z
MERRIMACK MUTUAL FIRE INS CO	MA	B-	1,728.2	1,100.6	281.4	20.7	7.7	7.5	7.8	7.0	4.8	T

See Page 27 for explanation of footnotes and Page 28 for explanation of stability factors.

Arrows denote recent upgrades ▲ or downgrades ▼   (see Section VII for explanations)

86

www.weissratings.com

RISK ADJ. RATIO #1	CAPITAL RATIO #2	PREMIUM TO SURPLUS (%)	RESV. TO SURPLUS (%)	RESV. DEVELOP. 1 YEAR (%)	RESV. DEVELOP. 2 YEAR (%)	LOSS RATIO (%)	EXP. RATIO (%)	COMB RATIO (%)	CASH FROM UNDER-WRITING (%)	NET PREMIUM GROWTH (%)	INVEST. IN AFFIL (%)	INSURANCE COMPANY NAME
3.9	2.7	35.6	44.6	-17.8	-31.8	49.5	12.5	62.0	157.9	65.7	0.0	MD RRG INC
2.5	2.1	19.5	103.3	-5.0	-13.8	61.1	37.4	98.5	83.1	-14.5	0.0	MDADVANTAGE INS CO OF NJ
14.3	12.9	N/A	N/A	N/A	N/A	N/A	N/A	N/A	97.7	0.0	0.0	MDOW INS CO
2.0	1.8	5.1	33.8	-10.6	-20.1	-88.1	114.1	26.0	-40.5	-39.3	0.0	MED MAL RRG INC
6.0	5.4	3.0	1.9	0.1	N/A	252.1	-153.6	98.5	6.9	10.4	0.0	MEDCHOICE RRG INC
3.2	2.8	50.4	N/A	N/A	N/A	19.1	70.3	89.4	83.7	-0.3	0.0	MEDICAL ALLIANCE INS CO
4.1	3.0	27.5	71.9	-6.8	-11.3	78.3	19.2	97.5	94.6	1.1	2.0	MEDICAL INS EXCHANGE OF
7.8	5.1	19.0	30.7	-4.8	-4.9	46.9	18.1	65.0	180.5	3.5	0.0	MEDICAL LIABILITY ALLIANCE
2.1	1.8	18.6	131.4	-6.4	-21.5	85.3	32.0	117.3	76.2	4.1	0.2 ●	MEDICAL LIABILITY MUTUAL INS CO
6.6	4.6	19.4	51.6	-3.4	-6.1	70.3	26.7	97.0	114.8	-5.1	0.0	MEDICAL MUTUAL INS CO OF MAINE
4.1	2.9	32.9	64.1	-8.6	-16.9	60.4	13.9	74.3	155.3	-16.9	3.1 ●	MEDICAL MUTUAL INS CO OF NC
3.6	3.3	24.4	46.1	-8.6	-16.4	49.6	17.5	67.1	145.2	-3.1	14.6 ●	MEDICAL MUTUAL LIAB INS SOC OF MD
1.9	1.6	18.6	81.7	-3.6	-7.1	82.4	28.7	111.1	175.1	21.9	24.3 ●	MEDICAL PROFESSIONAL MUTUAL INS
3.9	2.5	11.9	40.8	-4.7	-8.6	58.0	14.0	72.0	143.0	-6.2	0.0 ●	MEDICAL PROTECTIVE CO
1.7	1.5	38.1	138.7	-20.8	-16.2	61.6	25.5	87.1	225.0	-6.5	0.0	MEDICAL PROVIDERS MUTUAL INS CO
5.6	5.0	N/A	0.1	0.2	0.1	N/A	N/A	N/A	999 +	100.0	0.0	MEDICAL SECURITY INS CO
20.8	16.3	N/A	14.0	N/A	N/A	N/A	N/A	N/A	-313.2	0.0	0.0	MEDICUS INS CO
0.9	0.7	71.6	110.5	21.4	19.1	99.0	40.8	139.8	101.6	-3.7	0.0	MEDMAL DIRECT INS CO
2.3	2.0	16.6	32.1	-3.5	-8.7	60.8	34.0	94.8	113.9	-0.2	27.9	MEDMARC CASUALTY INS CO
0.8	0.7	44.7	118.8	-2.3	-1.5	88.3	27.7	116.0	341.0	10.4	0.0	MEDPRO RRG
N/A	N/A	--	--	--	--	--	--	--	--	--	--	MEDSTAR LIABILITY LTD INS CO INC
3.1	2.5	129.0	94.5	-1.0	0.3	72.1	28.1	100.2	107.5	7.1	0.0	MEEMIC INS CO
1.5	1.0	159.8	46.4	-3.0	-2.5	75.9	23.3	99.2	99.1	9.2	0.0	MEMBERS INS CO
3.1	2.5	121.8	98.4	-0.1	0.5	72.2	28.1	100.3	102.9	7.1	0.0	MEMBERSELECT INS CO
1.9	0.9	57.3	80.7	-5.6	-4.3	76.6	25.1	101.7	161.2	24.7	0.0	MEMIC CASUALTY CO
1.1	0.8	132.8	178.7	-2.8	1.5	77.4	24.7	102.1	130.6	16.9	0.0	MEMIC INDEMNITY CO
14.3	12.9	N/A	N/A	N/A	N/A	N/A	N/A	N/A	8.1	0.0	0.0	MENDAKOTA INS CO
0.3	0.3	433.4	207.0	42.4	35.1	94.4	21.4	115.8	88.7	-1.1	36.7	MENDOTA INS CO
2.7	1.9	97.4	13.8	2.7	1.3	54.0	38.6	92.6	105.7	13.4	0.0	MENNONITE MUTUAL INS CO
3.6	2.4	22.3	52.5	-14.3	-31.2	21.1	29.5	50.6	191.5	-2.1	0.0	MENTAL HEALTH RISK RETENTION
2.9	2.6	N/A	N/A	N/A	N/A	N/A	N/A	N/A	0.8	0.0	0.0	MERASTAR INS CO
6.4	3.9	36.1	11.0	-4.6	-6.2	61.2	52.1	113.3	95.9	23.9	0.0	MERCED PROPERTY & CASUALTY CO
1.9	1.6	85.6	97.6	-2.4	-2.0	72.8	30.5	103.3	110.8	5.6	18.8	MERCER INS CO
3.5	2.5	87.7	99.9	-2.6	-2.4	72.8	30.2	103.0	122.5	5.6	0.0	MERCER INS CO OF NJ INC
2.6	2.1	73.1	15.5	-3.6	-7.9	8.3	69.3	77.6	129.9	10.6	5.2	MERCHANTS BONDING CO (MUTUAL)
2.8	2.3	76.2	103.1	-1.5	-1.3	58.5	35.6	94.1	110.1	5.8	12.6	MERCHANTS MUTUAL INS CO
1.7	1.4	77.6	16.5	-3.9	-8.5	8.3	69.3	77.6	120.4	10.6	0.0	MERCHANTS NATIONAL BONDING INC
1.8	1.6	80.0	97.0	-1.4	-1.1	58.5	35.6	94.1	109.8	5.8	25.9 ●	MERCHANTS NATIONAL INS CO
3.6	2.6	73.6	89.2	-1.3	-0.8	58.5	35.6	94.1	112.9	5.8	0.0 ●	MERCHANTS PREFERRED INS CO
N/A	N/A	--	--	--	--	--	--	--	--	--	--	MERCHANTS PROPERTY INS CO OF IN
1.7	1.5	63.5	42.9	1.7	6.0	79.3	25.2	104.5	95.1	-9.6	35.5 ●	MERCURY CASUALTY CO
2.5	2.2	N/A	N/A	N/A	N/A	N/A	N/A	N/A	45.5	0.0	0.0	MERCURY COUNTY MUTUAL INS CO
13.4	12.0	N/A	N/A	N/A	N/A	N/A	N/A	N/A	-63.2	0.0	0.0	MERCURY INDEMNITY CO OF AMERICA
7.0	6.3	N/A	N/A	N/A	N/A	N/A	N/A	N/A	2.3	0.0	0.0	MERCURY INDEMNITY CO OF GEORGIA
1.4	1.3	266.4	102.7	4.9	9.9	74.3	24.3	98.6	106.1	4.1	0.0 ●	MERCURY INS CO
79.7	52.9	N/A	N/A	N/A	N/A	N/A	N/A	N/A	-120.8	0.0	0.0	MERCURY INS CO OF FL
18.3	15.5	N/A	N/A	N/A	N/A	N/A	N/A	N/A	113.2	0.0	0.0	MERCURY INS CO OF GA
2.0	1.8	N/A	N/A	N/A	N/A	N/A	N/A	N/A	5.2	0.0	49.0	MERCURY INS CO OF IL
N/A	N/A	--	--	--	--	--	--	--	--	--	--	MERCURY NATIONAL INS CO
9.8	8.8	N/A	N/A	N/A	N/A	N/A	N/A	N/A	266.5	0.0	0.0	MERIDIAN SECURITY INS CO
N/A	N/A	--	--	--	--	--	--	--	--	--	--	MERITPLAN INS CO
1.8	1.4	25.6	18.1	-0.7	-0.5	64.3	41.0	105.3	121.8	4.4	24.3 ●	MERRIMACK MUTUAL FIRE INS CO

999 + Denotes number greater than 999.9%
999 - Denotes number less than -999.99%
● Bullets denote a more detailed analysis is available in Section II.

INSURANCE COMPANY NAME	DOM. STATE	RATING	TOTAL ASSETS ($MIL)	CAPITAL & SURPLUS ($MIL)	ANNUAL NET PREMIUM ($MIL)	NET INCOME ($MIL)	CAPITAL- IZATION INDEX (PTS)	RESERVE ADQ INDEX (PTS)	PROFIT- ABILITY INDEX (PTS)	LIQUIDITY INDEX (PTS)	STAB. INDEX (PTS)	STABILITY FACTORS
MESA UNDERWRITERS SPECIALTY INS CO	NJ	C	340.0	89.9	118.5	10.3	7.9	9.3	8.8	6.5	3.6	R
MET LLOYDS INS CO OF TX	TX	B	94.4	18.6	0.0	0.5	8.7	N/A	7.7	7.0	5.4	D
▼METROMILE INS CO	DE	D	41.4	12.9	33.5	-0.3	1.3	3.6	2.0	2.9	2.0	CDGL
METROPOLITAN CASUALTY INS CO	RI	B	234.9	68.4	0.0	1.7	10.0	N/A	7.7	7.0	5.6	
METROPOLITAN DIRECT PROP & CAS INS	RI	B	173.8	44.8	0.0	0.9	10.0	N/A	7.7	7.0	5.9	
METROPOLITAN GENERAL INS CO	RI	B	42.4	36.7	0.0	0.8	10.0	N/A	5.9	7.0	5.8	D
METROPOLITAN GROUP PROP & CAS INS	RI	B	687.0	386.2	0.0	12.8	10.0	3.6	5.9	7.0	5.4	
METROPOLITAN P&C INS CO	RI	B-	6,107.4	2,265.5	3,617.6	246.2	7.9	7.8	5.3	3.2	5.3	L
MFS MUTUAL INS CO	IA	C-	4.2	3.1	1.2	0.3	6.9	6.1	4.5	5.9	2.0	DR
MGA INS CO	TX	C	299.4	107.3	287.2	18.1	7.1	4.1	7.1	3.6	3.9	LR
▲MGIC ASSURANCE CORP	WI	C	17.8	14.4	2.4	0.3	10.0	6.1	5.9	9.6	3.0	DGT
MGIC CREDIT ASR CORP	WI	U	--	--	--	--	N/A	--	--	--	--	Z
MGIC INDEMNITY CORP	WI	D+	147.2	92.9	8.1	3.2	10.0	5.2	2.9	9.2	2.4	AD
▲MGIC REINS CORP OF WI	WI	D+	588.2	193.2	121.1	34.9	5.1	6.1	4.9	6.8	2.4	T
MIAMI MUTUAL INS CO	OH	B	61.2	27.5	35.9	-0.3	7.9	8.5	5.9	5.6	5.9	D
MIC GENERAL INS CORP	MI	C	57.2	27.3	0.0	0.3	10.0	N/A	6.8	9.1	3.3	FGRT
MIC P&C INS CORP	MI	C	99.7	55.2	0.0	0.3	10.0	N/A	6.1	10.0	3.8	FRT
MICHIGAN COMMERCIAL INS MUTUAL	MI	C-	75.2	16.1	35.0	-1.6	3.1	4.6	1.8	5.7	2.9	CDR
MICHIGAN INS CO	MI	C+	154.4	52.8	76.2	7.9	9.1	8.6	8.2	6.5	4.6	T
▲MICHIGAN MILLERS MUTUAL INS CO	MI	C+	187.6	60.0	63.9	6.5	8.1	3.2	2.9	6.6	4.5	R
▲MICHIGAN PROFESSIONAL INS EXCHANGE	MI	B-	104.5	48.9	16.6	3.6	7.9	9.4	4.1	7.0	4.9	DR
MICO INS CO	OH	U	--	--	--	--	N/A	--	--	--	--	Z
MID AMERICAN FIRE & CAS CO	NH	U	--	--	--	--	N/A	--	--	--	--	Z
MID-CENTURY INS CO	CA	B	3,941.6	1,077.6	2,269.6	48.2	7.6	5.9	6.4	4.4	5.6	FL
MID-CENTURY INS CO OF TX	TX	U	--	--	--	--	N/A	--	--	--	--	Z
MID-CONTINENT CAS CO	OH	C+	527.9	178.8	118.6	12.1	4.0	3.3	8.0	6.9	4.4	CR
▲MID-CONTINENT EXCESS & SURPLUS INS	DE	B-	18.6	18.1	0.0	0.3	10.0	N/A	6.9	7.0	5.1	D
MID-CONTINENT INS CO	OH	C	21.1	20.6	0.0	0.5	10.0	4.6	6.1	7.0	3.4	DRT
MID-HUDSON CO-OPERTIVE INS CO	NY	C	28.2	12.1	14.2	0.2	6.7	5.8	6.8	6.5	3.3	DR
MIDDLE STATES INS CO	OK	C-	6.1	5.5	1.8	0.0	9.8	5.9	3.9	7.5	2.4	DG
▲MIDDLESEX INS CO	WI	B+	764.3	244.3	210.8	11.2	8.8	8.0	5.4	6.8	6.5	
MIDROX INS CO	NY	D+	8.8	4.1	3.4	0.5	7.9	8.1	5.9	6.8	2.1	DR
MIDSOUTH MUTUAL INS CO	TN	C	27.4	11.8	9.4	0.3	4.2	9.3	5.1	7.0	2.5	CDT
▲MIDSTATE MUTUAL INS CO	NY	B-	42.5	28.1	11.3	0.9	10.0	7.5	8.0	6.9	5.0	D
MIDSTATES REINS CORP	IL	U	--	--	--	--	N/A	--	--	--	--	Z
MIDVALE INDEMNITY CO	WI	D-	14.5	13.3	0.0	0.1	10.0	4.6	6.7	6.6	1.0	DFRT
MIDWEST BUILDERS CASUALTY MUTUAL	KS	B	103.3	54.5	34.6	2.3	7.9	7.0	7.8	6.8	5.6	T
MIDWEST EMPLOYERS CAS CO	DE	C+	168.8	106.8	0.0	3.1	10.0	N/A	7.2	10.0	4.3	R
▲MIDWEST FAMILY MUTUAL INS CO	IA	B	242.6	68.9	136.6	6.2	7.9	6.9	8.9	6.3	5.5	
▲MIDWEST INS CO	IL	C+	96.4	38.2	23.0	3.0	7.3	4.9	8.4	6.9	4.5	R
MIDWEST INS GROUP INC RRG	VT	D	7.0	1.8	2.2	0.0	2.0	10.0	4.0	7.1	1.4	CDRT
MIDWESTERN EQUITY TITLE INS CO	IN	D+	4.3	3.5	0.1	0.1	7.8	3.6	7.6	10.0	2.1	DR
MIDWESTERN INDEMNITY CO	NH	C	28.1	27.8	0.0	0.2	10.0	N/A	6.0	7.0	4.3	DRT
MILBANK INS CO	IA	C+	635.9	154.0	273.4	4.5	7.1	5.0	5.2	6.1	4.3	AR
▲MILFORD CASUALTY INS CO	DE	B	44.8	25.3	15.0	6.9	9.3	7.1	8.5	0.9	5.4	DLRT
▲MILLERS CAPITAL INS CO	PA	B	145.9	71.8	54.2	3.9	9.3	9.3	6.0	6.7	5.5	
MILLERS CLASSIFIED INS CO	IL	F (5)	2.7	0.0	-0.4	0.0	2.4	7.0	0.1	5.1	0.0	CFRT
MILLERS FIRST INS CO	IL	F (5)	7.8	-4.0	0.0	0.0	0.0	4.8	0.1	7.0	0.0	CDRT
MILLVILLE INS CO OF NY	NY	C-	2.9	2.7	0.0	0.0	10.0	N/A	6.3	7.0	2.3	DT
MILLVILLE MUTUAL INS CO	PA	C+	92.6	60.5	32.2	5.1	10.0	6.3	8.8	6.9	4.3	T
MINNESOTA LAWYERS MUTUAL INS CO	MN	B	188.7	99.8	33.7	7.7	9.7	8.8	8.6	6.9	6.2	T
MISSISSIPPI FARM BUREAU CAS INS CO	MS	B-	438.2	289.6	168.0	27.1	10.0	7.7	8.9	6.7	4.8	T

See Page 27 for explanation of footnotes and
Page 28 for explanation of stability factors.
Arrows denote recent upgrades ▲ or downgrades ▼   (see Section VII for explanations)

88

www.weissratings.com

RISK ADJ. CAPITAL RATIO #1	CAPITAL RATIO #2	PREMIUM TO SURPLUS (%)	RESV. TO SURPLUS (%)	RESV. DEVELOP. 1 YEAR (%)	RESV. DEVELOP. 2 YEAR (%)	LOSS RATIO (%)	EXP. RATIO (%)	COMB RATIO (%)	CASH FROM UNDER- WRITING (%)	NET PREMIUM GROWTH (%)	INVEST. IN AFFIL (%)	INSURANCE COMPANY NAME
2.6	1.8	131.9	176.2	-1.7	-7.1	58.7	33.5	92.2	104.7	6.0	0.0	MESA UNDERWRITERS SPECIALTY INS
2.3	2.1	N/A	N/A	N/A	N/A	N/A	N/A	N/A	N/A	0.0	0.0	MET LLOYDS INS CO OF TX
0.4	0.2	259.8	108.0	3.0	N/A	107.2	-5.6	101.6	115.8	636.4	0.0	METROMILE INS CO
7.1	6.4	N/A	N/A	N/A	N/A	N/A	N/A	N/A	N/A	0.0	0.0	METROPOLITAN CASUALTY INS CO
4.8	4.3	N/A	N/A	N/A	N/A	N/A	N/A	N/A	N/A	0.0	0.0	METROPOLITAN DIRECT PROP & CAS
22.1	19.9	N/A	N/A	N/A	N/A	N/A	N/A	N/A	N/A	0.0	0.0	METROPOLITAN GENERAL INS CO
35.2	29.1	N/A	N/A	N/A	N/A	N/A	N/A	N/A	N/A	0.0	0.0 ●	METROPOLITAN GROUP PROP & CAS
1.9	1.5	159.7	69.1	-0.6	-0.1	71.5	26.5	98.0	101.7	1.7	21.3 ●	METROPOLITAN P&C INS CO
1.6	1.0	39.0	2.4	-2.1	-0.4	57.3	43.9	101.2	85.2	2.1	0.0	MFS MUTUAL INS CO
1.1	1.0	267.6	88.0	1.7	2.0	65.3	27.5	92.8	114.9	19.5	0.0	MGA INS CO
7.3	6.7	16.6	0.1	0.2	-1.2	2.8	7.5	10.3	262.2	33.7	0.0	MGIC ASSURANCE CORP
N/A	N/A	--	--	--	--	--	--	--	--	--	--	MGIC CREDIT ASR CORP
13.4	12.0	8.8	2.3	-1.1	-1.0	2.6	87.2	89.8	513.9	-18.3	0.0	MGIC INDEMNITY CORP
1.5	1.3	62.7	81.6	-25.2	-45.9	8.3	68.7	77.0	110.4	6.0	0.0	MGIC REINS CORP OF WI
2.5	1.6	130.6	41.1	-3.7	-8.1	73.8	30.9	104.7	99.0	9.0	0.0	MIAMI MUTUAL INS CO
5.9	5.3	N/A	N/A	N/A	N/A	N/A	N/A	N/A	-58.4	0.0	0.0	MIC GENERAL INS CORP
8.9	8.0	N/A	N/A	N/A	N/A	N/A	N/A	N/A	-329.3	0.0	0.0	MIC P&C INS CORP
0.6	0.5	217.3	271.4	2.6	-7.8	75.1	32.5	107.6	98.8	-4.6	0.0	MICHIGAN COMMERCIAL INS MUTUAL
3.8	2.6	144.3	95.9	-13.8	-12.0	54.1	32.7	86.8	129.4	1.8	0.0	MICHIGAN INS CO
2.9	1.9	106.6	110.3	-2.7	4.2	58.7	35.8	94.5	113.0	10.5	0.0	MICHIGAN MILLERS MUTUAL INS CO
2.1	1.6	33.9	90.4	-0.2	-13.3	92.5	9.4	101.9	136.8	13.2	0.0	MICHIGAN PROFESSIONAL INS
N/A	N/A	--	--	--	--	--	--	--	--	--	--	MICO INS CO
N/A	N/A	--	--	--	--	--	--	--	--	--	--	MID AMERICAN FIRE & CAS CO
2.0	1.4	210.6	131.2	-1.0	1.5	69.3	33.0	102.3	90.9	-3.9	8.5 ●	MID-CENTURY INS CO
N/A	N/A	--	--	--	--	--	--	--	--	--	--	MID-CENTURY INS CO OF TX
0.8	0.5	66.3	157.0	4.0	13.2	60.7	38.5	99.2	98.1	-2.2	11.1	MID-CONTINENT CAS CO
79.3	71.4	N/A	N/A	N/A	N/A	N/A	N/A	N/A	N/A	0.0	0.0	MID-CONTINENT EXCESS & SURPLUS
91.1	66.7	N/A	N/A	N/A	N/A	N/A	N/A	N/A	N/A	100.0	0.0	MID-CONTINENT INS CO
1.4	0.9	117.9	41.5	9.5	5.9	60.9	37.4	98.3	104.4	4.8	0.0	MID-HUDSON CO-OPERTIVE INS CO
4.2	2.8	31.7	10.8	1.1	2.2	75.2	25.4	100.6	109.4	50.8	0.0	MIDDLE STATES INS CO
3.3	2.2	86.3	134.4	-1.5	-3.2	74.8	28.6	103.4	102.8	4.7	4.1 ●	MIDDLESEX INS CO
2.7	1.8	82.3	22.3	-8.1	-3.4	45.0	34.4	79.4	109.4	-1.2	0.0	MIDROX INS CO
0.9	0.6	79.4	65.5	-2.6	-17.3	65.4	35.0	100.4	124.7	-0.2	0.0	MIDSOUTH MUTUAL INS CO
4.7	3.2	40.2	18.3	0.8	-1.0	61.6	36.5	98.1	98.5	0.1	0.0	MIDSTATE MUTUAL INS CO
N/A	N/A	--	--	--	--	--	--	--	--	--	--	MIDSTATES REINS CORP
26.2	23.6	N/A	N/A	N/A	N/A	N/A	N/A	N/A	999 +	0.0	0.0	MIDVALE INDEMNITY CO
2.2	1.8	63.4	67.4	-4.6	-7.9	58.7	26.1	84.8	122.9	26.4	9.3	MIDWEST BUILDERS CASUALTY MUTUAL
7.1	9.4	N/A	N/A	N/A	N/A	N/A	N/A	N/A	706.8	0.0	0.0	MIDWEST EMPLOYERS CAS CO
2.2	1.6	198.3	124.9	-10.2	-18.4	67.6	23.9	91.5	121.8	16.5	5.2	MIDWEST FAMILY MUTUAL INS CO
2.4	1.4	60.1	103.3	-14.4	-13.9	60.0	33.7	93.7	138.0	1.7	0.0	MIDWEST INS CO
0.4	0.3	120.2	195.7	-20.8	-65.4	69.3	35.4	104.7	124.0	13.2	0.0	MIDWEST INS GROUP INC RRG
2.5	1.5	2.5	N/A	N/A	N/A	9.8	82.2	92.0	113.3	0.3	0.0	MIDWESTERN EQUITY TITLE INS CO
3.6	3.5	N/A	N/A	N/A	N/A	N/A	N/A	N/A	N/A	0.0	29.9	MIDWESTERN INDEMNITY CO
1.7	1.1	177.5	176.9	-7.2	-3.0	72.2	35.1	107.3	104.4	-1.9	0.0	MILBANK INS CO
5.3	4.5	59.3	N/A	-160.1	-94.8	82.8	-2.0	80.8	133.0	-65.5	0.0	MILFORD CASUALTY INS CO
3.0	2.6	75.5	48.3	-1.8	-7.3	51.0	43.3	94.3	117.5	9.9	0.0	MILLERS CAPITAL INS CO
0.1	0.1	-78.8	746.7	-6.6	-14.0	357.3	-361.7	-4.4	-3.5	-106.7	0.0	MILLERS CLASSIFIED INS CO
-1.5	-1.3	N/A	N/A	N/A	N/A	N/A	N/A	N/A	N/A	-100.0	0.0	MILLERS FIRST INS CO
26.5	23.8	N/A	N/A	N/A	N/A	N/A	N/A	N/A	122.7	0.0	0.0	MILLVILLE INS CO OF NY
5.0	3.4	53.2	16.4	-1.6	-2.9	51.8	28.9	80.7	126.3	6.5	3.3	MILLVILLE MUTUAL INS CO
4.8	3.0	33.8	54.5	-6.0	-11.5	57.0	24.2	81.2	124.4	2.0	0.0	MINNESOTA LAWYERS MUTUAL INS CO
6.6	5.6	58.0	8.1	-1.2	-3.2	61.0	22.2	83.2	115.3	-1.9	0.0 ●	MISSISSIPPI FARM BUREAU CAS INS CO

999 + Denotes number greater than 999.9%
999 - Denotes number less than -999.99%
● Bullets denote a more detailed analysis is available in Section II.

INSURANCE COMPANY NAME	DOM. STATE	RATING	TOTAL ASSETS ($MIL)	CAPITAL & SURPLUS ($MIL)	ANNUAL NET PREMIUM ($MIL)	NET INCOME ($MIL)	CAPITAL-IZATION INDEX (PTS)	RESERVE ADQ INDEX (PTS)	PROFIT-ABILITY INDEX (PTS)	LIQUIDITY INDEX (PTS)	STAB. INDEX (PTS)	STABILITY FACTORS
MISSOURI DOCTORS MUTUAL INS CO	MO	E-	4.4	-0.1	3.5	-0.2	0.0	0.3	0.0	7.0	0.2	CDFT
▲MISSOURI HOSPITAL PLAN	MO	B-	207.4	160.3	20.1	2.9	8.6	6.7	4.2	7.0	5.3	F
MISSOURI PHYSICIANS ASSOCIATES	MO	U	--	--	--	--	N/A	--	--	--	--	Z
▲MISSOURI PROFESSIONALS MUTUAL INS	MO	D	13.0	0.1	6.1	0.3	0.0	0.2	1.0	7.0	0.6	CDFR
MISSOURI VALLEY MUTUAL INS CO	SD	D+	6.3	3.6	3.6	0.1	9.5	6.3	8.5	6.1	2.1	DR
▲MITSUI SUMITOMO INS CO OF AMER	NY	A-	975.8	371.9	201.3	30.2	9.4	9.3	8.6	7.0	7.0	
▲MITSUI SUMITOMO INS USA INC	NY	B-	139.3	64.5	25.2	2.4	10.0	8.9	6.5	8.6	5.1	T
MLM RRG INC	DC	U	--	--	--	--	N/A	--	--	--	--	Z
MMG INS CO	ME	B	276.6	99.3	171.7	2.2	8.8	4.3	6.6	6.0	5.9	
▲MMIC INS INC	MN	B+	682.7	362.6	96.8	43.1	7.9	9.3	8.7	7.0	6.5	T
MMIC RRG INC	DC	U	--	--	--	--	N/A	--	--	--	--	Z
▲MO EMPLOYERS MUTUAL INS CO	MO	B+	695.0	252.8	238.5	10.7	8.0	9.3	7.6	6.5	6.5	
MODERN USA INS CO	FL	B-	64.4	19.7	28.8	0.5	5.9	4.4	4.6	7.3	4.3	DFT
MONARCH NATIONAL INS CO	FL	C	39.2	25.8	8.5	-5.7	8.3	3.6	2.0	6.7	3.6	DFGT
MONROE GUARANTY INS CO	IN	C	52.5	54.0	0.0	1.0	10.0	N/A	6.2	10.0	3.5	R
MONTAUK RRG	VT	E	3.2	2.9	0.2	-0.1	10.0	N/A	3.1	7.0	0.0	DT
▼MONTEREY INS CO	CA	C-	78.7	21.9	39.7	-12.2	4.7	3.2	1.4	3.5	3.1	DFL
MONTGOMERY MUTUAL INS CO	MA	C	54.0	52.7	0.0	0.9	10.0	N/A	6.8	7.0	4.3	DR
MONTOUR MUTUAL INS CO	PA	U	--	--	--	--	N/A	--	--	--	--	Z
MORTGAGE GUARANTY INS CORP	WI	D+	4,756.2	1,620.4	866.3	271.7	7.3	4.8	5.3	6.8	2.4	AR
MOTOR CLUB INS CO	RI	B	53.5	51.6	1.1	0.8	9.3	3.6	6.9	9.3	4.1	DT
MOTORISTS COMMERCIAL MUTUAL INS CO	OH	A-	368.8	147.5	133.6	-22.4	8.4	6.3	3.2	6.2	6.9	F
▼MOTORISTS MUTUAL INS CO	OH	C+	1,370.8	460.7	494.7	-92.4	7.9	6.3	2.2	6.0	4.5	F
▲MOTORS INS CORP	MI	D+	2,030.5	867.8	394.1	76.2	10.0	6.4	6.7	7.5	2.5	R
MOUND PRAIRIE MUTUAL INS CO	MN	D+	7.7	4.9	3.2	0.6	8.9	5.9	4.8	7.1	2.2	D
MOUNT VERNON FIRE INS CO	PA	C	775.0	579.4	70.9	148.2	8.0	8.4	8.6	9.0	4.3	R
MOUNT VERNON SPECIALTY INS CO	NE	B-	62.3	61.2	0.4	-2.3	7.4	N/A	4.0	9.2	4.1	DFGT
MOUNTAIN LAKE RRG INC	VT	D	1.6	0.9	0.1	-0.2	8.0	8.8	1.7	7.7	1.0	DFT
MOUNTAIN LAUREL ASR CO	OH	C	183.4	69.3	202.9	9.7	7.4	8.6	8.9	1.8	3.6	LR
▲MOUNTAIN LAUREL RRG INC	VT	E+	22.4	10.1	4.8	2.9	4.8	9.7	4.4	7.7	0.5	D
MOUNTAIN STATES COMM INS CO	NM	U	--	--	--	--	N/A	--	--	--	--	Z
MOUNTAIN STATES HEALTHCARE RECIP	MT	D+	111.9	22.5	24.9	-4.4	3.4	2.8	1.2	6.6	2.5	CDF
MOUNTAIN STATES INDEMNITY CO	NM	C	16.3	11.0	-1.0	1.0	10.0	4.5	1.9	0.7	3.6	DFLR
MOUNTAIN VALLEY INDEMNITY CO	NY	D	64.1	20.3	14.2	-1.1	8.6	4.6	4.9	6.9	1.7	DRT
MOUNTAIN WEST FARM BU MUTUAL INS CO	WY	B	382.9	154.6	166.5	10.3	7.5	9.3	3.8	5.0	6.0	L
MOUNTAINPOINT INS CO	AZ	C-	12.2	12.1	0.0	0.1	10.0	N/A	4.0	10.0	3.0	DRT
MOWER COUNTY FARMERS MUT INS CO	MN	D+	5.5	3.8	2.4	0.3	10.0	7.7	8.6	6.7	2.1	DF
MSA INS CO	SC	B-	18.8	18.7	0.0	0.3	10.0	N/A	6.8	7.0	4.9	D
MT HAWLEY INS CO	IL	C	945.8	441.2	227.7	19.3	8.1	9.1	4.2	6.9	4.0	AR
▲MT MORRIS MUTUAL INS CO	WI	C+	40.7	20.0	21.7	1.6	7.4	4.6	8.4	5.9	4.0	DR
MT WASHINGTON ASR CORP	NH	C	7.0	3.6	0.0	0.0	10.0	N/A	7.1	6.1	3.2	DR
▲MULTINATIONAL INS CO	PR	C	71.4	14.7	19.5	0.2	5.0	3.3	3.9	8.6	3.5	CDG
MUNICH REINS AMERICA INC	DE	C+	18,585.6	4,019.2	4,167.9	-617.2	7.6	8.8	2.6	6.7	4.4	R
▲MUNICIPAL ASR CORP	NY	E+	823.6	270.4	0.7	32.3	10.0	N/A	1.9	10.0	0.5	T
▲MUNICIPAL MUTUAL INS CO	WV	B-	38.5	25.7	13.4	0.2	8.7	8.0	4.6	6.8	4.9	D
MUNICIPAL PROPERTY INS CO	WI	C-	14.2	8.8	6.8	0.2	6.7	3.6	4.0	6.5	2.3	DFT
MUTUAL BENEFIT INS CO	PA	B-	228.8	101.5	94.3	7.1	9.0	9.0	8.4	6.6	4.7	R
MUTUAL FIRE INS CO OF S BEND TOWNSHP	PA	D+	3.6	3.6	0.1	0.1	10.0	5.0	6.8	10.0	2.1	D
▲MUTUAL INS CO OF AZ	AZ	B+	1,105.9	665.4	95.8	23.4	10.0	9.3	8.0	7.7	6.5	T
▲MUTUAL OF ENUMCLAW INS CO	OR	B+	748.3	338.3	395.8	7.5	9.8	6.3	4.5	6.1	6.5	F
MUTUAL OF WAUSAU INS CORP	WI	C+	25.0	15.9	9.5	-0.3	8.2	7.6	5.1	6.6	4.3	D
▲MUTUAL RRG INC	HI	B-	111.4	53.0	23.6	3.6	10.0	9.6	8.6	7.8	4.9	R

See Page 27 for explanation of footnotes and
Page 28 for explanation of stability factors.

Arrows denote recent upgrades ▲ or downgrades ▼   (see Section VII for explanations)

90

www.weissratings.com

RISK ADJ. RATIO #1	CAPITAL RATIO #2	PREMIUM TO SURPLUS (%)	RESV. TO SURPLUS (%)	RESV. DEVELOP. 1 YEAR (%)	RESV. DEVELOP. 2 YEAR (%)	LOSS RATIO (%)	EXP. RATIO (%)	COMB RATIO (%)	CASH FROM UNDER-WRITING (%)	NET PREMIUM GROWTH (%)	INVEST. IN AFFIL (%)	INSURANCE COMPANY NAME
-0.0	0.0	999 +	999 +	999 +	931.5	51.1	53.9	105.0	74.4	-9.6	0.0	MISSOURI DOCTORS MUTUAL INS CO
2.4	2.0	12.6	22.1	0.2	-1.5	61.8	2.6	64.4	155.7	5.7	28.1	MISSOURI HOSPITAL PLAN
N/A	N/A	--	--	--	--	--	--	--	--	--	--	MISSOURI PHYSICIANS ASSOCIATES
0.0	0.0	999 +	999 +	999 +	397.8	72.6	30.3	102.9	73.9	-25.5	46.3	MISSOURI PROFESSIONALS MUTUAL INS
3.8	3.0	99.7	9.7	0.4	-1.5	63.6	36.3	99.9	99.5	5.6	0.0	MISSOURI VALLEY MUTUAL INS CO
4.0	2.5	54.1	114.2	-8.7	-14.2	62.9	29.2	92.1	116.2	1.1	0.0 ●	MITSUI SUMITOMO INS CO OF AMER
6.2	4.2	39.0	82.4	-5.9	-9.5	62.9	29.5	92.4	115.8	1.1	0.0	MITSUI SUMITOMO INS USA INC
N/A	N/A	--	--	--	--	--	--	--	--	--	--	MLM RRG INC
3.2	2.2	172.9	70.6	-1.5	8.0	68.7	32.8	101.5	103.1	4.4	0.0	MMG INS CO
1.9	1.7	26.7	58.9	-4.5	-8.9	71.6	23.6	95.2	88.8	-8.1	23.4 ●	MMIC INS INC
N/A	N/A	--	--	--	--	--	--	--	--	--	--	MMIC RRG INC
2.1	1.6	94.3	114.3	-5.9	-10.6	70.5	31.8	102.3	107.2	8.5	0.1 ●	MO EMPLOYERS MUTUAL INS CO
1.1	0.8	146.3	44.8	-2.5	1.0	61.9	35.8	97.7	89.1	4.4	0.0	MODERN USA INS CO
2.7	1.8	33.0	14.3	2.9	0.2	130.1	37.5	167.6	69.3	-21.0	0.0	MONARCH NATIONAL INS CO
85.1	39.2	N/A	N/A	N/A	N/A	N/A	N/A	N/A	50.5	0.0	0.0	MONROE GUARANTY INS CO
6.2	5.0	7.3	6.9	N/A	N/A	94.7	89.0	183.7	N/A	0.0	0.0	MONTAUK RRG
0.9	0.6	181.0	170.4	21.3	28.9	100.6	35.7	136.3	85.2	-1.7	0.0	MONTEREY INS CO
100.9	51.5	N/A	N/A	N/A	N/A	N/A	N/A	N/A	N/A	0.0	0.0	MONTGOMERY MUTUAL INS CO
N/A	N/A	--	--	--	--	--	--	--	--	--	--	MONTOUR MUTUAL INS CO
2.1	1.7	53.5	48.0	-13.1	-15.4	5.4	67.8	73.2	153.1	2.6	7.1 ●	MORTGAGE GUARANTY INS CORP
4.2	2.5	2.2	0.3	-0.2	N/A	67.4	58.0	125.4	86.4	-27.2	0.0	MOTOR CLUB INS CO
2.6	1.9	90.6	77.5	4.8	2.0	83.5	42.0	125.5	87.9	1.1	7.3 ●	MOTORISTS COMMERCIAL MUTUAL INS
2.1	1.6	107.4	91.8	5.1	2.0	83.5	40.2	123.7	86.5	1.1	10.0 ●	MOTORISTS MUTUAL INS CO
6.5	4.5	45.4	10.6	1.7	0.2	74.7	20.3	95.0	89.9	1.5	3.8 ●	MOTORS INS CORP
3.6	2.9	64.6	4.0	-1.6	0.3	38.3	40.5	78.8	116.8	-8.4	0.0	MOUND PRAIRIE MUTUAL INS CO
2.3	1.7	12.2	15.0	-3.6	-4.9	26.3	40.7	67.0	120.0	4.1	16.3 ●	MOUNT VERNON FIRE INS CO
1.2	1.2	0.6	0.2	N/A	N/A	68.0	978.1	999 +	10.9	168.4	86.2	MOUNT VERNON SPECIALTY INS CO
2.0	1.6	15.5	39.8	0.1	-1.4	102.8	170.9	273.7	41.5	2.8	0.0	MOUNTAIN LAKE RRG INC
1.4	1.2	292.8	72.6	2.6	-7.3	72.1	21.1	93.2	111.2	14.6	0.0	MOUNTAIN LAUREL ASR CO
1.0	0.7	47.3	82.9	-35.1	-26.7	9.5	35.5	45.0	194.9	2.7	0.0	MOUNTAIN LAUREL RRG INC
N/A	N/A	--	--	--	--	--	--	--	--	--	--	MOUNTAIN STATES COMM INS CO
0.6	0.5	110.9	308.3	4.0	34.6	111.5	28.2	139.7	70.0	7.6	0.0	MOUNTAIN STATES HEALTHCARE RECIP
6.7	6.0	-9.2	N/A	-0.3	11.4	90.4	76.2	166.6	-13.9	-120.9	14.6	MOUNTAIN STATES INDEMNITY CO
2.9	2.0	69.8	31.0	8.1	9.3	66.7	35.8	102.5	161.3	18.1	0.0	MOUNTAIN VALLEY INDEMNITY CO
1.9	1.3	107.7	66.2	-11.6	-8.9	71.4	28.1	99.5	99.2	2.1	7.8	MOUNTAIN WEST FARM BU MUTUAL INS
195.9	176.3	N/A	N/A	N/A	N/A	N/A	N/A	N/A	-51.1	0.0	0.0	MOUNTAINPOINT INS CO
5.8	4.3	63.2	6.1	-12.5	-5.3	46.1	39.7	85.8	100.2	8.2	0.0	MOWER COUNTY FARMERS MUT INS CO
78.0	36.3	N/A	N/A	N/A	N/A	N/A	N/A	N/A	N/A	0.0	0.0	MSA INS CO
2.1	1.7	51.6	84.4	-3.4	-8.6	63.5	39.1	102.6	132.7	4.9	11.8 ●	MT HAWLEY INS CO
2.0	1.3	108.5	26.4	-3.9	N/A	63.0	30.2	93.2	112.6	8.1	0.0	MT MORRIS MUTUAL INS CO
3.3	3.0	N/A	N/A	N/A	N/A	N/A	N/A	N/A	999 +	0.0	0.0	MT WASHINGTON ASR CORP
1.4	0.7	132.3	47.6	3.9	12.9	46.9	42.9	89.8	117.5	25.8	0.0	MULTINATIONAL INS CO
2.1	1.4	103.7	175.4	-3.2	-6.9	84.8	35.0	119.8	119.3	33.7	0.0 ●	MUNICH REINS AMERICA INC
13.5	10.4	0.3	0.1	N/A	N/A	0.5	999 +	999 +	21.2	-37.2	0.0 ●	MUNICIPAL ASR CORP
3.1	2.1	52.1	11.3	-0.4	-3.0	70.8	30.8	101.6	100.5	3.8	0.0	MUNICIPAL MUTUAL INS CO
1.2	0.9	77.8	27.7	-9.4	-1.2	69.6	30.7	100.3	95.3	-3.1	0.0	MUNICIPAL PROPERTY INS CO
3.1	2.3	92.9	60.0	-5.8	-4.8	59.6	33.5	93.1	107.0	2.1	9.6	MUTUAL BENEFIT INS CO
124.6	97.7	2.8	0.1	-0.1	-0.1	1.6	45.6	47.2	182.0	-3.7	0.0	MUTUAL FIRE INS CO OF S BEND
7.8	5.3	14.4	41.7	-4.2	-12.0	62.1	18.4	80.5	119.4	-5.8	0.0 ●	MUTUAL INS CO OF AZ
4.2	3.0	117.0	56.2	4.5	1.5	72.4	29.7	102.1	92.4	2.8	1.4 ●	MUTUAL OF ENUMCLAW INS CO
2.9	1.9	60.0	8.8	-0.6	-1.3	62.7	45.7	108.4	96.4	3.4	0.0	MUTUAL OF WAUSAU INS CORP
4.8	3.8	44.6	91.3	-22.4	-35.0	60.7	9.5	70.2	141.7	-3.1	0.1	MUTUAL RRG INC

999 + Denotes number greater than 999.9%
999 - Denotes number less than -999.99%
● Bullets denote a more detailed analysis is available in Section II.

INSURANCE COMPANY NAME	DOM. STATE	RATING	TOTAL ASSETS ($MIL)	CAPITAL & SURPLUS ($MIL)	ANNUAL NET PREMIUM ($MIL)	NET INCOME ($MIL)	CAPITAL-IZATION INDEX (PTS)	RESERVE ADQ INDEX (PTS)	PROFIT-ABILITY INDEX (PTS)	LIQUIDITY INDEX (PTS)	STAB. INDEX (PTS)	STABILITY FACTORS
MUTUAL SAVINGS FIRE INS CO	AL	D	4.9	4.0	0.0	0.1	10.0	N/A	4.3	10.0	2.2	DR
MUTUALAID EXCHANGE	KS	C+	28.9	15.9	15.4	-1.8	7.6	8.0	3.5	5.4	4.2	DFR
NAMIC INS CO	IN	C+	52.6	29.0	5.3	0.8	9.0	9.1	5.3	7.1	4.6	D
▲NARRAGANSETT BAY INS CO	RI	C	227.3	111.1	47.2	20.3	10.0	5.1	9.1	8.6	3.5	R
▲NASW RRG INC	DC	C	16.6	11.1	4.5	1.0	8.8	5.1	5.1	7.3	3.0	DGT
NATIONAL AMERICAN INS CO	OK	C+	211.7	67.9	83.9	2.6	8.6	6.7	7.2	6.5	4.1	R
NATIONAL AMERICAN INS CO OF CA	CA	U	--	--	--	--	N/A	--	--	--	--	Z
NATIONAL ASSISTED LIVING RRG INC	DC	D+	8.8	4.7	2.4	0.2	7.0	9.8	8.3	7.0	2.2	D
NATIONAL BAIL & SURETY CO	FL	U (1)	--	--	--	--	N/A	--	--	--	--	Z
NATIONAL BUILDERS & CONTRACTORS INS	NV	U	--	--	--	--	N/A	--	--	--	--	Z
NATIONAL BUILDERS INS CO	DE	B	94.4	30.6	23.8	2.3	8.0	9.3	8.9	7.0	6.0	D
▲NATIONAL BUILDING MATERIAL ASR CO	IN	D	6.7	4.7	0.9	0.1	10.0	4.9	5.1	9.0	1.5	DR
NATIONAL CASUALTY CO	OH	B+	418.6	140.8	0.0	5.2	10.0	N/A	7.2	7.0	6.4	
NATIONAL CATHOLIC RRG	VT	D	69.2	15.5	11.5	-1.5	2.0	3.3	3.3	6.2	2.1	CDR
NATIONAL CONTINENTAL INS CO	NY	C	135.0	62.7	12.2	13.0	10.0	9.3	4.6	8.3	3.5	T
NATIONAL DIRECT INS CO	NV	D	6.9	2.3	7.7	0.2	2.1	3.8	3.5	0.6	1.7	CDGL
NATIONAL FARMERS UNION PROP & CAS	WI	C	134.1	42.1	61.0	-2.3	7.3	5.8	3.2	6.2	4.1	FR
NATIONAL FIRE & CASUALTY CO	IL	C	10.3	6.4	2.8	0.1	7.8	9.3	6.6	6.5	2.5	DFRT
NATIONAL FIRE & INDEMNITY EXCHANGE	MO	C-	10.6	5.7	3.7	-0.1	8.8	8.0	3.2	7.0	2.4	DFR
NATIONAL FIRE & MARINE INS CO	NE	C	10,841.0	7,187.2	1,174.6	86.3	8.1	6.3	7.9	8.3	4.1	R
NATIONAL FIRE INS CO OF HARTFORD	IL	C	118.0	118.0	0.0	4.2	10.0	N/A	5.3	9.3	3.8	AR
NATIONAL GENERAL ASR CO	MO	C	41.9	17.4	0.0	0.3	10.0	N/A	6.2	7.0	3.7	DR
NATIONAL GENERAL INS CO	MO	C	69.0	26.4	0.0	1.1	10.0	N/A	5.8	6.9	3.8	R
NATIONAL GENERAL INS ONLINE INC	MO	C	42.6	11.3	0.0	0.1	8.7	N/A	5.9	6.9	3.7	DFR
NATIONAL GENL PREMIER INS CO	CA	B-	35.0	16.8	0.0	0.6	10.0	4.9	7.2	9.8	3.9	DFRT
NATIONAL GUARDIAN RRG INC	HI	C-	10.7	6.4	-0.2	-0.1	9.4	9.9	3.4	6.8	2.5	DRT
NATIONAL HERITAGE INS CO	IL	D+	3.2	1.6	2.8	-0.2	8.1	4.6	1.8	7.3	1.5	DFT
NATIONAL HOME INS CO RRG	CO	U	--	--	--	--	N/A	--	--	--	--	Z
NATIONAL INDEMNITY CO	NE	B	231,374.0	128,563.0	24,030.9	2,079.7	7.8	6.0	8.0	7.0	5.3	
NATIONAL INDEMNITY CO OF MID-AMERICA	IA	C	315.9	252.6	5.9	46.1	8.1	6.2	8.4	10.0	4.3	R
NATIONAL INDEMNITY CO OF THE SOUTH	IA	C+	460.6	266.0	88.7	54.4	8.1	5.8	8.6	9.1	4.4	R
NATIONAL INDEPENDENT TRUCKERS IC	SC	C-	15.3	8.6	4.3	0.3	7.6	5.5	7.8	6.9	2.7	DR
NATIONAL INS ASSN	IN	U	--	--	--	--	N/A	--	--	--	--	Z
NATIONAL INS CO OF WI INC	WI	C	13.6	12.0	0.0	-0.1	10.0	9.6	2.7	10.0	2.7	DFT
NATIONAL INTERSTATE INS CO	OH	C+	1,281.1	301.2	323.4	54.4	7.2	3.9	6.1	6.8	4.7	R
▲NATIONAL INTERSTATE INS CO OF HAWAII	OH	C+	55.9	12.7	9.2	0.7	8.1	4.4	6.1	7.0	4.5	DR
NATIONAL LIABILITY & FIRE INS CO	CT	C+	2,710.1	1,246.3	551.9	522.2	8.3	6.7	7.7	9.0	4.4	R
NATIONAL LLOYDS INS CO	TX	B-	186.9	93.8	110.6	-1.8	9.9	5.3	3.3	6.4	4.8	FR
NATIONAL MEDICAL PROFESSIONAL RRG	SC	U	--	--	--	--	N/A	--	--	--	--	Z
NATIONAL MORTGAGE INS CORP	WI	A-	717.8	344.0	145.1	-36.2	8.3	3.6	2.9	6.9	5.7	FGT
▲NATIONAL MORTGAGE RE INC ONE	WI	B-	34.5	27.1	0.5	0.3	10.0	4.6	3.9	10.0	5.0	DT
NATIONAL MUTUAL INS CO	OH	C	83.4	32.7	40.7	0.1	8.0	8.4	7.7	5.7	4.1	R
▼NATIONAL PUBLIC FINANCE GUAR CORP	NY	D+	3,753.9	2,165.9	13.0	-321.4	10.0	4.2	2.7	9.0	2.4	AF
NATIONAL SECURITY FIRE & CAS CO	AL	B-	73.3	34.2	54.6	-0.9	8.1	6.6	5.6	4.5	4.6	FLR
NATIONAL SERVICE CONTRACT INS CO	DC	C	12.8	10.7	0.7	0.2	10.0	3.6	3.5	10.0	4.3	DR
NATIONAL SPECIALTY INS CO	TX	C+	88.1	50.7	30.0	2.2	10.0	6.0	8.2	7.0	4.8	R
NATIONAL SURETY CORP	IL	C	140.9	73.8	0.0	-0.2	10.0	N/A	2.8	6.9	3.7	FR
NATIONAL TRUST INS CO	IN	C	37.0	37.8	0.0	0.6	10.0	N/A	5.7	8.9	3.4	R
NATIONAL UNION FIRE INS CO	PA	C	25,661.1	6,431.2	5,399.4	-357.4	7.6	2.8	4.3	5.4	4.2	AFR
NATIONAL UNITY INS CO	TX	D	35.9	9.2	27.4	-1.9	2.1	1.3	1.0	0.2	1.9	CDFL
▲NATIONS INS CO	CA	C-	41.6	11.4	18.3	2.2	4.3	4.0	4.7	2.2	3.0	DLT
NATIONWIDE AFFINITY INS CO OF AMER	OH	B	296.7	12.0	0.0	-0.6	7.0	N/A	3.7	7.0	4.8	FT

See Page 27 for explanation of footnotes and
Page 28 for explanation of stability factors.
Arrows denote recent upgrades ▲ or downgrades ▼ (see Section VII for explanations)

92

www.weissratings.com

RISK ADJ. RATIO #1	CAPITAL RATIO #2	PREMIUM TO SURPLUS (%)	RESV. TO SURPLUS (%)	RESV. DEVELOP. 1 YEAR (%)	RESV. DEVELOP. 2 YEAR (%)	LOSS RATIO (%)	EXP. RATIO (%)	COMB RATIO (%)	CASH FROM UNDER-WRITING (%)	NET PREMIUM GROWTH (%)	INVEST. IN AFFIL (%)	INSURANCE COMPANY NAME
9.5	8.6	N/A	N/A	N/A	N/A	N/A	N/A	N/A	183.3	0.0	0.0	MUTUAL SAVINGS FIRE INS CO
1.8	1.4	97.2	14.2	-2.6	-5.1	76.5	35.7	112.2	90.5	18.8	18.5	MUTUALAID EXCHANGE
3.8	2.3	18.2	20.2	-1.4	-8.3	57.7	43.3	101.0	92.3	3.7	0.0	NAMIC INS CO
6.5	5.2	42.5	15.0	-2.1	-7.1	47.6	-2.6	45.0	161.3	-8.6	1.8	NARRAGANSETT BAY INS CO
3.8	2.2	40.8	17.5	1.9	0.3	37.6	32.3	69.9	209.9	12.0	0.0	NASW RRG INC
3.1	2.0	123.6	126.4	-2.9	-4.3	57.6	37.4	95.0	125.2	24.3	0.0	NATIONAL AMERICAN INS CO
N/A	N/A	--	--	--	--	--	--	--	--	--	--	NATIONAL AMERICAN INS CO OF CA
1.8	1.1	51.6	55.2	-20.0	-34.5	49.4	41.2	90.6	120.7	22.8	0.0	NATIONAL ASSISTED LIVING RRG INC
N/A	N/A	--	--	--	--	--	--	--	--	--	--	NATIONAL BAIL & SURETY CO
N/A	N/A	--	--	--	--	--	--	--	--	--	--	NATIONAL BUILDERS & CONTRACTORS
2.6	1.8	77.8	111.0	-4.8	-9.6	62.0	25.2	87.2	160.5	17.2	0.0	NATIONAL BUILDERS INS CO
6.5	5.8	18.2	18.6	0.4	0.9	64.4	30.9	95.3	104.8	11.5	0.0	NATIONAL BUILDING MATERIAL ASR CO
13.2	11.9	N/A	N/A	N/A	N/A	N/A	N/A	N/A	112.4	0.0	0.0 ●	NATIONAL CASUALTY CO
0.5	0.4	74.4	288.1	10.6	2.8	102.6	25.5	128.1	94.2	12.8	0.0	NATIONAL CATHOLIC RRG
8.3	6.1	19.4	40.3	-3.2	-4.8	104.9	-159.9	-55.0	53.6	-8.5	0.0	NATIONAL CONTINENTAL INS CO
0.4	0.3	329.4	147.5	13.5	19.0	81.9	18.2	100.1	96.4	41.1	0.0	NATIONAL DIRECT INS CO
1.8	1.1	144.8	121.0	-4.7	-18.0	75.6	31.2	106.8	85.7	12.2	0.0	NATIONAL FARMERS UNION PROP &
2.5	1.5	44.1	22.9	-5.5	-8.4	72.4	40.3	112.7	85.6	9.6	0.0	NATIONAL FIRE & CASUALTY CO
2.4	2.2	64.3	41.7	1.5	-1.8	62.1	47.6	109.7	84.3	24.3	0.0	NATIONAL FIRE & INDEMNITY
2.7	1.7	16.3	25.9	-1.4	-1.8	85.7	23.3	109.0	176.5	26.4	4.9 ●	NATIONAL FIRE & MARINE INS CO
74.6	30.8	N/A	N/A	N/A	N/A	N/A	N/A	N/A	N/A	0.0	0.0	NATIONAL FIRE INS CO OF HARTFORD
4.3	3.9	N/A	N/A	N/A	N/A	N/A	N/A	N/A	126.9	0.0	0.0	NATIONAL GENERAL ASR CO
4.4	3.9	N/A	N/A	N/A	N/A	N/A	N/A	N/A	86.2	0.0	0.0	NATIONAL GENERAL INS CO
2.3	2.1	N/A	N/A	N/A	N/A	N/A	N/A	N/A	45.1	0.0	0.0	NATIONAL GENERAL INS ONLINE INC
5.2	4.7	N/A	N/A	N/A	N/A	N/A	N/A	N/A	-504.8	0.0	0.0	NATIONAL GENL PREMIER INS CO
5.0	4.3	-3.6	40.3	-7.7	-10.0	198.8	-158.3	40.5	97.7	-120.4	0.0	NATIONAL GUARDIAN RRG INC
2.4	1.7	177.4	12.2	12.3	3.9	69.7	39.4	109.1	88.7	-5.3	0.0	NATIONAL HERITAGE INS CO
N/A	N/A	--	--	--	--	--	--	--	--	--	--	NATIONAL HOME INS CO RRG
1.9	1.6	18.7	21.9	-0.4	-1.7	88.3	50.0	138.3	124.6	20.0	21.7 ●	NATIONAL INDEMNITY CO
3.1	1.9	2.4	5.5	-0.2	0.1	66.0	30.2	96.2	82.7	-11.8	0.0 ●	NATIONAL INDEMNITY CO OF
3.2	1.9	33.3	38.8	1.6	4.1	67.2	22.0	89.2	139.4	30.5	0.0 ●	NATIONAL INDEMNITY CO OF THE
1.7	1.4	50.1	42.2	4.6	7.1	48.0	42.4	90.4	117.5	8.2	0.0	NATIONAL INDEPENDENT TRUCKERS IC
N/A	N/A	--	--	--	--	--	--	--	--	--	--	NATIONAL INS ASSN
13.0	9.4	0.2	12.2	2.2	-8.9	999 +	999 +	999 +	3.0	8.9	0.0	NATIONAL INS CO OF WI INC
1.4	1.1	107.4	147.8	-1.2	3.8	67.0	27.9	94.9	123.3	4.7	16.4 ●	NATIONAL INTERSTATE INS CO
2.0	1.7	72.8	100.3	-0.9	2.5	67.1	30.3	97.4	110.8	4.7	0.0	NATIONAL INTERSTATE INS CO OF
3.0	1.9	44.3	78.8	0.8	0.1	74.3	24.8	99.1	109.4	-1.8	2.5 ●	NATIONAL LIABILITY & FIRE INS CO
3.7	2.9	117.9	16.5	-0.1	-2.1	67.6	39.7	107.3	86.8	-9.9	0.0	NATIONAL LLOYDS INS CO
N/A	N/A	--	--	--	--	--	--	--	--	--	--	NATIONAL MEDICAL PROFESSIONAL
2.1	1.8	42.2	1.9	-0.2	N/A	3.8	113.6	117.4	84.7	11.7	0.0 ●	NATIONAL MORTGAGE INS CORP
13.7	12.4	2.0	0.7	-0.1	-0.1	13.9	107.0	120.9	76.9	121.9	0.0	NATIONAL MORTGAGE RE INC ONE
2.8	1.7	124.8	39.2	-3.5	-7.8	73.8	30.9	104.7	98.6	9.0	0.0	NATIONAL MUTUAL INS CO
7.5	5.9	0.6	10.5	18.6	12.0	273.5	540.2	813.7	4.0	-31.5	7.2 ●	NATIONAL PUBLIC FINANCE GUAR CORP
2.5	1.7	159.7	18.7	-4.0	-5.8	70.1	34.6	104.7	93.4	-0.1	13.9	NATIONAL SECURITY FIRE & CAS CO
14.6	10.1	6.7	N/A	N/A	N/A	N/A	93.1	93.1	113.4	12.6	0.0	NATIONAL SERVICE CONTRACT INS CO
6.1	4.3	59.2	5.5	0.2	-0.2	49.4	41.5	90.9	125.3	7.9	0.0	NATIONAL SPECIALTY INS CO
9.8	8.8	N/A	N/A	N/A	N/A	N/A	N/A	N/A	58.6	0.0	0.0	NATIONAL SURETY CORP
137.7	68.8	N/A	N/A	N/A	N/A	N/A	N/A	N/A	76.0	0.0	0.0	NATIONAL TRUST INS CO
2.1	1.4	84.0	184.3	-11.2	11.9	87.9	38.6	126.5	66.8	11.6	1.2 ●	NATIONAL UNION FIRE INS CO
0.5	0.4	299.1	155.8	48.4	54.1	70.1	44.1	114.2	83.3	-29.1	3.7	NATIONAL UNITY INS CO
0.8	0.6	161.0	104.3	16.2	7.6	79.3	22.5	101.8	101.2	-47.7	0.0	NATIONS INS CO
1.1	1.0	N/A	N/A	N/A	N/A	N/A	N/A	N/A	91.6	0.0	0.0	NATIONWIDE AFFINITY INS CO OF AMER

999 + Denotes number greater than 999.9%
999 - Denotes number less than -999.99%
● Bullets denote a more detailed analysis is available in Section II.

INSURANCE COMPANY NAME	DOM. STATE	RATING	TOTAL ASSETS ($MIL)	CAPITAL & SURPLUS ($MIL)	ANNUAL NET PREMIUM ($MIL)	NET INCOME ($MIL)	CAPITAL-IZATION INDEX (PTS)	RESERVE ADQ INDEX (PTS)	PROFIT-ABILITY INDEX (PTS)	LIQUIDITY INDEX (PTS)	STAB. INDEX (PTS)	STABILITY FACTORS
NATIONWIDE AGRIBUSINESS INS CO	IA	B-	758.6	191.6	0.0	1.5	10.0	N/A	7.5	6.9	5.2	AF
NATIONWIDE ASR CO	OH	B-	131.9	65.0	0.0	3.5	10.0	N/A	7.5	7.0	5.2	AD
NATIONWIDE GENERAL INS CO	OH	B-	406.3	21.3	0.0	-1.8	8.0	N/A	3.7	6.6	4.8	AFT
NATIONWIDE INDEMNITY CO	OH	C+	2,891.2	1,013.2	0.4	89.0	7.2	2.2	3.6	9.7	4.5	FT
NATIONWIDE INS CO OF AM	OH	B-	431.3	155.1	0.0	2.8	10.0	N/A	6.0	7.0	5.2	
▲NATIONWIDE INS CO OF FL	OH	B	33.0	19.6	0.0	1.9	10.0	4.6	1.9	10.0	4.0	DFT
NATIONWIDE LLOYDS	TX	B	41.5	29.2	0.0	0.4	10.0	N/A	6.2	7.0	5.7	DT
▼NATIONWIDE MUTUAL FIRE INS CO	OH	C+	8,598.1	2,380.3	5,206.6	-391.6	7.9	5.9	2.4	5.1	4.8	AFG
NATIONWIDE MUTUAL INS CO	OH	B	35,425.4	12,193.3	12,718.3	-370.8	7.3	5.9	3.5	4.4	6.1	AL
NATIONWIDE P&C INS CO	OH	B-	537.6	39.7	0.0	-4.1	9.8	N/A	3.0	7.0	5.0	AF
NATL TRANSPORTATION INS CO RRG	NC	D	6.8	2.4	4.6	0.2	5.1	3.6	5.7	9.1	1.0	DGT
NAU COUNTRY INS CO	MN	C+	966.9	282.6	469.8	-15.4	7.3	5.9	3.2	6.0	4.3	FRT
NAUTILUS INS CO	AZ	C	268.9	165.8	0.0	4.5	10.0	N/A	6.5	7.0	4.0	R
NAVIGATORS INS CO	NY	B	3,084.5	1,056.6	944.3	76.4	8.1	6.5	8.6	6.9	5.6	T
NAVIGATORS SPECIALTY INS CO	NY	B-	178.6	142.0	0.0	2.9	10.0	N/A	6.8	7.0	5.1	
NAZARETH MUTUAL INS CO	PA	C-	16.0	8.5	7.3	0.8	7.8	4.5	8.3	6.7	2.6	DR
NCMIC INS CO	IA	B	782.8	299.5	168.3	13.2	7.7	9.5	8.8	7.1	5.5	T
NCMIC RRG INC	VT	C	7.5	4.9	0.8	0.6	10.0	5.9	9.2	8.6	3.3	D
NEIGHBORHOOD SPIRIT PROP & CAS CO	CA	C+	271.3	118.9	141.8	1.8	9.8	5.9	5.3	6.5	4.7	FR
NETHERLANDS INS CO	NH	C	99.1	89.7	0.0	1.2	10.0	N/A	6.6	7.0	4.3	R
▼NEVADA CAPITAL INS CO	NV	C	102.3	40.3	43.3	-12.5	7.4	3.7	1.9	5.2	3.6	F
NEVADA DOCS MEDICAL RRG INC	NV	U (5)	--	--	--	--	N/A	--	--	--	--	Z
NEVADA GENERAL INS CO	NV	D	14.5	6.1	6.3	0.1	7.9	4.6	1.2	5.8	2.1	DFT
NEVADA MUTUAL INS CO	NV	D+	18.1	10.1	0.4	0.7	7.5	9.9	5.7	9.6	2.7	DFRT
NEW CENTURY INS CO	TX	C	11.2	6.0	6.3	-0.1	8.1	6.1	4.3	4.0	3.5	DFGL
NEW ENGLAND GUARANTY INS CO INC	VT	U	--	--	--	--	N/A	--	--	--	--	Z
NEW ENGLAND INS CO	CT	U	--	--	--	--	N/A	--	--	--	--	Z
NEW ENGLAND MUTUAL INS CO	MA	B	46.2	42.2	0.0	0.7	10.0	4.7	4.0	7.0	5.5	DT
NEW ENGLAND REINS CORP	CT	U	--	--	--	--	N/A	--	--	--	--	Z
NEW HAMPSHIRE EMPLOYERS INS CO	NH	B-	5.0	4.9	0.0	0.0	10.0	N/A	8.1	7.0	3.5	DFG
▲NEW HAMPSHIRE INS CO	IL	C+	215.9	185.2	0.0	-5.9	10.0	3.4	4.2	7.0	4.5	A
NEW HOME WARRANTY INS CO RRG	DC	C+	23.5	6.7	3.6	0.2	8.2	5.9	4.6	8.0	3.2	DG
NEW HORIZON INS CO	TX	D+	7.3	6.2	1.1	-0.8	8.6	N/A	2.0	5.8	2.5	DFT
▲NEW HORIZONS INS CO OF MO	MO	C+	55.8	27.7	25.4	2.5	7.4	5.2	8.6	6.6	4.5	T
▲NEW JERSEY CASUALTY INS CO	NJ	B	588.0	295.8	57.6	25.2	9.7	7.0	8.9	7.2	5.5	T
NEW JERSEY INDEMNITY INS CO	NJ	C+	77.7	69.7	6.1	1.1	10.0	8.6	7.6	8.5	4.8	DF
NEW JERSEY PHYS UNITED RECIP EXCH	NJ	D+	30.3	11.5	5.1	-1.4	5.0	3.0	1.9	6.9	2.5	DF
NEW JERSEY RE-INS CO	NJ	B	546.4	432.1	11.5	16.2	9.2	6.6	8.2	9.4	5.7	FT
▼NEW JERSEY SKYLANDS INS ASSN	NJ	D-	66.4	8.1	22.0	-2.5	1.0	1.8	1.1	0.1	1.3	CDLT
NEW JERSEY SKYLANDS INS CO	NJ	C-	36.3	9.8	11.9	-0.9	4.0	2.5	2.0	6.0	3.2	DT
NEW LONDON COUNTY MUTUAL INS CO	CT	B-	125.2	68.5	36.2	5.1	8.8	7.9	6.9	6.8	4.7	R
NEW MEXICO ASR CO	NM	C-	6.6	1.6	0.0	-0.2	5.0	N/A	3.4	8.0	2.0	DT
NEW MEXICO BUSINESS INS CO	NM	D	2.1	2.0	0.0	0.0	10.0	N/A	3.8	10.0	0.6	DT
NEW MEXICO COMMERCIAL INS CO	NM	D	2.1	2.0	0.0	0.0	10.0	N/A	4.9	10.0	0.6	DT
NEW MEXICO EMPLOYERS ASR CO	NM	B-	6.2	1.6	0.0	-0.2	5.3	N/A	2.7	10.0	3.5	CDT
NEW MEXICO FOUNDATION INS CO	NM	C	22.9	17.9	0.0	0.0	10.0	N/A	6.7	7.0	3.4	DR
NEW MEXICO MUTUAL CASUALTY CO	NM	C+	407.8	182.8	94.1	19.6	7.6	7.0	8.6	6.9	4.2	T
NEW MEXICO PREMIER INS CO	NM	C	3.9	1.1	0.0	0.0	6.8	N/A	2.9	9.2	2.8	DFT
NEW MEXICO PROPERTY & CASUALTY CO	NM	U	--	--	--	--	N/A	--	--	--	--	Z
▲NEW MEXICO SAFETY CASUALTY CO	NM	C	5.2	2.5	0.0	0.2	8.9	N/A	7.1	9.4	2.3	DT
NEW MEXICO SECURITY INS CO	NM	D+	4.4	1.6	0.0	0.1	7.9	N/A	4.8	9.2	2.0	DT
NEW MEXICO SOUTHWEST CASUALTY CO	NM	C-	17.6	11.0	0.0	-0.2	9.1	N/A	3.9	10.0	3.2	DFR

See Page 27 for explanation of footnotes and Page 28 for explanation of stability factors.

94

www.weissratings.com

Arrows denote recent upgrades ▲ or downgrades ▼ (see Section VII for explanations)

RISK ADJ. RATIO #1	CAPITAL RATIO #2	PREMIUM TO SURPLUS (%)	RESV. TO SURPLUS (%)	RESV. DEVELOP. 1 YEAR (%)	2 YEAR (%)	LOSS RATIO (%)	EXP. RATIO (%)	COMB. RATIO (%)	CASH FROM UNDER-WRITING (%)	NET PREMIUM GROWTH (%)	INVEST. IN AFFIL (%)	INSURANCE COMPANY NAME
14.5	13.0	N/A	N/A	N/A	N/A	N/A	N/A	N/A	-1.0	0.0	0.0	NATIONWIDE AGRIBUSINESS INS CO
8.6	7.7	N/A	N/A	N/A	N/A	N/A	N/A	N/A	391.3	0.0	0.0	NATIONWIDE ASR CO
1.8	1.6	N/A	N/A	N/A	N/A	N/A	N/A	N/A	-25.9	0.0	0.0	NATIONWIDE GENERAL INS CO
2.2	1.7	N/A	180.9	5.3	20.1	999 +	999 +	999 +	0.2	-64.4	0.0 ●	NATIONWIDE INDEMNITY CO
14.6	13.1	N/A	N/A	N/A	N/A	N/A	N/A	N/A	57.9	0.0	0.0	NATIONWIDE INS CO OF AM
7.0	6.3	N/A	N/A	N/A	N/A	N/A	N/A	N/A	999 +	100.0	0.0	NATIONWIDE INS CO OF FL
10.8	9.8	N/A	N/A	N/A	N/A	N/A	N/A	N/A	81.1	0.0	0.0	NATIONWIDE LLOYDS
2.1	1.5	218.7	147.5	0.7	3.3	81.1	28.1	109.2	92.2	122.7	4.2 ●	NATIONWIDE MUTUAL FIRE INS CO
1.3	1.2	104.3	90.1	0.5	2.2	81.1	31.2	112.3	94.4	-21.4	32.5 ●	NATIONWIDE MUTUAL INS CO
3.1	2.8	N/A	N/A	N/A	N/A	N/A	N/A	N/A	281.6	0.0	0.0	NATIONWIDE P&C INS CO
1.0	0.6	188.3	37.8	-0.2	N/A	40.8	27.8	68.6	326.2	N/A	0.0	NATL TRANSPORTATION INS CO RRG
1.8	1.1	166.3	138.9	-4.9	-19.4	75.6	31.2	106.8	85.7	7.7	0.0 ●	NAU COUNTRY INS CO
6.6	7.3	N/A	N/A	N/A	N/A	N/A	N/A	N/A	N/A	0.0	0.0	NAUTILUS INS CO
2.2	1.7	89.4	122.7	-2.7	0.2	67.3	30.5	97.8	125.1	11.8	5.1 ●	NAVIGATORS INS CO
26.7	24.0	N/A	N/A	N/A	N/A	N/A	N/A	N/A	N/A	0.0	0.0	NAVIGATORS SPECIALTY INS CO
2.3	1.5	85.6	20.4	6.0	9.8	41.8	45.0	86.8	117.3	3.5	0.0	NAZARETH MUTUAL INS CO
2.1	1.4	56.2	104.7	1.9	-13.2	67.0	26.2	93.2	131.0	17.3	1.3 ●	NCMIC INS CO
5.1	3.8	16.3	22.8	-15.7	-16.0	-33.0	-66.6	-99.6	-205.8	2.0	0.0	NCMIC RRG INC
4.1	2.9	119.3	70.5	-0.3	1.3	69.4	32.9	102.3	94.2	-3.9	0.0	NEIGHBORHOOD SPIRIT PROP & CAS CO
38.5	34.7	N/A	N/A	N/A	N/A	N/A	N/A	N/A	N/A	0.0	0.0	NETHERLANDS INS CO
2.0	1.2	107.2	101.0	15.0	20.4	100.6	35.7	136.3	85.2	-1.7	0.0	NEVADA CAPITAL INS CO
N/A	N/A	--	--	--	--	--	--	--	--	--	--	NEVADA DOCS MEDICAL RRG INC
2.7	2.1	103.3	67.8	-2.3	-1.4	67.5	25.9	93.4	54.9	-54.4	0.0	NEVADA GENERAL INS CO
2.3	2.1	4.3	47.8	-5.4	-21.9	37.5	-0.9	36.6	21.4	-67.0	33.4	NEVADA MUTUAL INS CO
1.9	1.7	105.5	15.9	-2.7	-1.2	74.6	24.7	99.3	92.6	57.7	0.0	NEW CENTURY INS CO
N/A	N/A	--	--	--	--	--	--	--	--	--	--	NEW ENGLAND GUARANTY INS CO INC
N/A	N/A	--	--	--	--	--	--	--	--	--	--	NEW ENGLAND INS CO
33.1	29.8	N/A	N/A	N/A	N/A	N/A	N/A	N/A	27.5	0.0	0.0	NEW ENGLAND MUTUAL INS CO
N/A	N/A	--	--	--	--	--	--	--	--	--	--	NEW ENGLAND REINS CORP
91.5	68.3	N/A	N/A	N/A	N/A	N/A	N/A	N/A	N/A	0.0	0.0	NEW HAMPSHIRE EMPLOYERS INS CO
32.7	27.0	N/A	N/A	N/A	N/A	N/A	N/A	N/A	N/A	0.0	0.0	NEW HAMPSHIRE INS CO
2.1	1.9	54.1	23.3	6.8	2.3	77.8	14.1	91.9	175.8	0.6	0.0	NEW HOME WARRANTY INS CO RRG
2.6	2.0	17.1	3.0	N/A	N/A	35.6	121.5	157.1	60.6	0.0	0.0	NEW HORIZON INS CO
2.1	1.3	91.6	41.5	-5.8	6.5	51.5	40.5	92.0	119.4	-5.0	0.0	NEW HORIZONS INS CO OF MO
5.2	3.5	19.5	89.7	-4.9	-10.7	40.9	29.3	70.2	141.9	-17.6	0.0 ●	NEW JERSEY CASUALTY INS CO
23.0	19.1	8.8	6.6	-0.8	-2.5	67.9	37.6	105.5	82.2	-14.9	0.0	NEW JERSEY INDEMNITY INS CO
1.0	0.8	44.1	94.6	11.7	21.9	77.0	58.5	135.5	70.8	-12.4	0.0	NEW JERSEY PHYS UNITED RECIP EXCH
4.8	2.8	2.7	24.9	-2.2	-2.1	10.1	33.4	43.5	47.7	-27.8	0.0 ●	NEW JERSEY RE-INS CO
0.3	0.2	270.7	223.5	8.2	22.1	84.9	32.5	117.4	99.6	-2.7	23.4	NEW JERSEY SKYLANDS INS ASSN
0.8	0.6	121.8	100.1	5.8	13.5	84.6	32.4	117.0	91.5	-2.3	0.0	NEW JERSEY SKYLANDS INS CO
2.8	2.2	52.8	19.2	-1.8	-2.9	49.2	40.5	89.7	105.0	1.3	19.8	NEW LONDON COUNTY MUTUAL INS CO
1.0	0.6	N/A	173.3	N/A	N/A	N/A	N/A	N/A	89.0	0.0	0.0	NEW MEXICO ASR CO
58.9	53.0	N/A	1.0	N/A	N/A	N/A	N/A	N/A	63.2	0.0	0.0	NEW MEXICO BUSINESS INS CO
34.1	30.7	N/A	0.6	N/A	N/A	N/A	N/A	N/A	106.7	0.0	0.0	NEW MEXICO COMMERCIAL INS CO
1.1	0.6	N/A	167.4	N/A	N/A	N/A	N/A	N/A	60.1	0.0	0.0	NEW MEXICO EMPLOYERS ASR CO
11.7	5.0	N/A	21.7	N/A	N/A	N/A	N/A	N/A	-14.4	0.0	0.0	NEW MEXICO FOUNDATION INS CO
2.2	1.6	51.5	111.0	-4.1	-10.5	52.5	35.7	88.2	120.3	2.4	10.7	NEW MEXICO MUTUAL CASUALTY CO
1.2	0.9	N/A	110.8	N/A	N/A	N/A	N/A	N/A	257.5	0.0	0.0	NEW MEXICO PREMIER INS CO
N/A	N/A	--	--	--	--	--	--	--	--	--	--	NEW MEXICO PROPERTY & CASUALTY
2.6	2.2	N/A	48.2	N/A	N/A	N/A	N/A	N/A	42.2	0.0	0.0	NEW MEXICO SAFETY CASUALTY CO
1.7	1.5	N/A	62.3	N/A	N/A	N/A	N/A	N/A	67.0	0.0	0.0	NEW MEXICO SECURITY INS CO
6.0	2.4	N/A	45.2	N/A	N/A	N/A	N/A	N/A	-188.4	0.0	0.0	NEW MEXICO SOUTHWEST CASUALTY

999 + Denotes number greater than 999.9%
999 - Denotes number less than -999.99%
● Bullets denote a more detailed analysis is available in Section II.

INSURANCE COMPANY NAME	DOM. STATE	RATING	TOTAL ASSETS ($MIL)	CAPITAL & SURPLUS ($MIL)	ANNUAL NET PREMIUM ($MIL)	NET INCOME ($MIL)	CAPITAL- IZATION INDEX (PTS)	RESERVE ADQ INDEX (PTS)	PROFIT- ABILITY INDEX (PTS)	LIQUIDITY INDEX (PTS)	STAB. INDEX (PTS)	STABILITY FACTORS
NEW SOUTH INS CO	NC	C	62.7	8.4	0.0	0.1	7.1	N/A	6.2	6.6	3.7	DFR
NEW YORK CENTRAL MUTUAL FIRE INS CO	NY	B-	1,177.2	540.0	473.2	22.7	9.6	6.1	8.0	6.6	4.7	R
NEW YORK HEALTHCARE INS CO INC RRG	DC	E+	26.8	3.9	9.2	-1.1	0.0	1.2	1.8	7.9	0.4	CDR
NEW YORK MARINE & GENERAL INS CO	NY	B-	1,746.2	433.9	483.4	20.7	6.7	4.1	3.9	7.0	4.7	GR
▲NEW YORK MUNICIPAL INS RECIPROCAL	NY	B	163.9	65.8	52.3	3.1	8.0	6.3	5.3	6.8	5.5	
▲NEW YORK SCHOOLS INS RECIPROCAL	NY	B+	317.8	182.9	61.8	3.2	10.0	6.5	8.3	7.1	6.4	
NEW YORK TRANSPORTATION INS CORP	NY	U (5)	--	--	--	--	N/A	--	--	--	--	Z
NEWPORT BONDING & SURETY CO	PR	D (4)	4.3	2.5	1.4	0.2	5.0	0.1	3.0	6.1	0.6	DT
NEWPORT INS CO	AZ	U	--	--	--	--	N/A	--	--	--	--	Z
NEXT INSURANCE US CO	DE	U	--	--	--	--	N/A	--	--	--	--	Z
NGM INS CO	FL	B-	2,593.2	1,025.4	1,210.3	-11.3	8.2	3.9	4.4	5.9	4.6	R
NHRMA MUTUAL INS CO	IL	C	40.1	14.6	12.3	1.2	6.6	10.0	8.9	6.7	3.4	DR
NJ MANUFACTURERS INS CO	NJ	B	7,423.2	2,884.4	1,818.5	182.1	8.2	6.6	8.0	6.8	5.7	T
NODAK INS CO	ND	B-	257.6	156.5	160.6	13.9	9.7	8.8	8.5	6.0	4.7	T
NOETIC SPECIALTY INS CO	VT	C	123.9	81.4	11.8	6.9	10.0	9.4	8.8	8.2	3.6	DR
NORCAL MUTUAL INS CO	CA	B-	1,610.5	736.2	395.7	53.6	8.2	6.8	6.8	6.9	4.6	R
NORCAL SPECIALTY INS CO	PA	C-	61.3	48.8	0.0	0.1	10.0	3.9	1.9	9.0	3.1	DT
NORFOLK & DEDHAM MUTUAL FIRE INS CO	MA	C+	453.8	209.3	151.5	10.3	9.3	6.3	6.9	6.8	4.3	R
NORGUARD INS CO	PA	D	1,098.6	238.7	289.4	29.9	1.4	8.8	8.9	2.6	2.0	CGLR
NORMANDY INS CO	FL	D	54.9	13.9	41.2	0.4	1.9	5.1	8.2	4.9	1.9	CDGL
NORTH AMERICAN CAPACITY INS CO	NH	C	173.5	52.4	0.0	-2.5	10.0	3.6	3.9	10.0	3.6	R
NORTH AMERICAN ELITE INS CO	NH	C	139.9	42.0	0.0	2.2	10.0	N/A	8.7	7.0	3.7	FRT
NORTH AMERICAN SPECIALTY INS CO	NH	C	510.4	321.4	0.0	6.8	10.0	6.1	3.6	7.0	3.7	RT
NORTH CAROLINA FARM BU MUTUAL INS	NC	B	2,002.0	1,180.3	833.1	65.5	10.0	8.4	8.2	6.5	5.8	T
▲NORTH CAROLINA GRANGE MUTUAL INS	NC	C	36.2	19.8	18.9	3.7	7.3	7.0	8.7	6.1	3.5	D
▲NORTH COUNTRY INS CO	NY	C+	29.2	20.2	7.7	1.4	10.0	7.9	8.8	7.0	4.2	D
NORTH EAST INS CO	ME	F (5)	35.9	15.7	-6.2	0.0	7.4	1.6	1.3	7.7	0.0	DFRT
NORTH LIGHT SPECIALTY INS CO	IL	B-	89.6	54.6	29.1	2.6	8.8	3.6	7.8	6.7	4.0	T
NORTH PACIFIC INS CO	OR	C	8.5	8.0	0.0	0.1	10.0	N/A	6.4	7.0	4.1	DR
NORTH POINTE INS CO	PA	C-	20.5	11.2	0.0	0.2	10.0	4.1	2.0	7.0	3.1	DRT
NORTH RIVER INS CO	NJ	C-	1,070.3	293.4	410.5	-33.8	5.6	6.2	4.5	7.5	3.3	AR
NORTH STAR GENERAL INS CO	MN	U	--	--	--	--	N/A	--	--	--	--	Z
NORTH STAR MUTUAL INS CO	MN	B-	742.9	456.2	365.9	36.5	10.0	7.7	8.8	6.5	4.7	R
▲NORTHERN MUTUAL INS CO	MI	B-	38.6	26.3	15.1	2.0	8.9	8.7	8.7	6.9	4.7	DR
NORTHERN SECURITY INS CO	VT	C	8.5	8.5	0.0	0.1	10.0	N/A	6.3	7.0	3.7	DR
NORTHFIELD INS CO	IA	C+	391.9	120.2	118.7	8.5	7.9	8.2	4.2	6.9	4.8	
NORTHLAND CASUALTY CO	CT	B	110.6	37.6	32.0	2.4	8.4	8.2	6.9	7.0	5.8	D
NORTHLAND INS CO	CT	B	1,187.8	516.1	278.6	40.8	9.1	7.8	4.5	6.9	6.0	
▲NORTHSTONE INS CO	PA	B-	63.7	12.0	7.5	0.8	6.2	9.7	7.7	7.7	4.6	D
NORTHWEST DENTISTS INS CO	WA	C	24.5	13.9	6.5	2.0	8.1	7.0	5.2	7.2	3.8	D
▲NORTHWEST GF MUTUAL INS CO	SD	D+	20.2	9.6	12.4	1.4	8.2	8.5	7.1	6.5	2.5	D
▲NORTHWESTERN NATL INS CO SEG ACCNT	WI	D-	20.6	1.9	0.4	0.1	0.5	N/A	0.6	6.7	1.0	CDFT
NORTHWESTERN NTL INS CO MILWAUKEE	WI	F	20.6	1.9	0.0	0.0	3.1	N/A	1.8	7.0	0.0	DRT
▲NOVA CASUALTY CO	NY	B-	89.1	88.6	0.0	2.5	8.6	N/A	4.7	10.0	4.9	R
NUCLEAR ELECTRIC INS LTD	DE	A+	5,587.7	4,474.0	228.4	115.1	9.5	4.6	7.8	7.0	8.6	F
NUTMEG INS CO	CT	B-	440.7	257.8	74.9	46.7	10.0	4.9	2.3	7.1	4.8	AT
NW FARMERS MUTUAL INSURANCE CO	NC	D	5.5	4.5	1.4	0.0	8.5	5.0	4.1	7.2	0.9	D
OAK RIVER INS CO	NE	C	809.1	320.3	158.8	97.1	7.4	9.4	8.8	9.1	4.3	R
OAKWOOD INS CO	TN	B	72.1	41.4	0.0	0.5	7.3	5.7	2.4	10.0	4.0	DFT
OASIS RECIPROCAL RRG	VT	B-	15.1	6.2	3.7	1.5	7.1	9.9	9.6	9.2	3.5	DT
OBI AMERICA INS CO	PA	C	15.5	15.4	0.0	0.1	10.0	N/A	4.9	7.0	2.6	DT
OBI NATIONAL INS CO	PA	C+	13.3	13.3	0.0	0.1	10.0	N/A	4.1	7.0	3.3	DT

See Page 27 for explanation of footnotes and Page 28 for explanation of stability factors.

Arrows denote recent upgrades ▲ or downgrades ▼   (see Section VII for explanations)

96

www.weissratings.com

RISK ADJ. CAPITAL RATIO #1	RATIO #2	PREMIUM TO SURPLUS (%)	RESV. TO SURPLUS (%)	RESV. DEVELOP. 1 YEAR (%)	2 YEAR (%)	LOSS RATIO (%)	EXP. RATIO (%)	COMB RATIO (%)	CASH FROM UNDER-WRITING (%)	NET PREMIUM GROWTH (%)	INVEST. IN AFFIL (%)	INSURANCE COMPANY NAME
1.2	1.0	N/A	N/A	N/A	N/A	N/A	N/A	N/A	21.2	0.0	0.0	NEW SOUTH INS CO
3.6	2.7	87.6	58.2	-0.6	0.6	67.3	30.0	97.3	106.2	5.4	4.2 ●	NEW YORK CENTRAL MUTUAL FIRE INS
0.1	0.1	237.8	413.8	78.1	43.4	103.3	15.8	119.1	100.6	48.9	0.0	NEW YORK HEALTHCARE INS CO INC
1.4	1.0	111.4	192.7	6.8	14.4	64.6	31.8	96.4	214.1	22.9	11.0 ●	NEW YORK MARINE & GENERAL INS CO
2.2	1.6	79.5	123.2	0.8	2.6	71.5	27.7	99.2	111.5	0.0	0.0	NEW YORK MUNICIPAL INS RECIPROCAL
4.7	3.3	33.8	54.9	3.9	3.8	84.0	19.7	103.7	115.0	0.5	0.0 ●	NEW YORK SCHOOLS INS RECIPROCAL
N/A	N/A	--	--	--	--	--	--	--	--	--	--	NEW YORK TRANSPORTATION INS
1.0	0.9	55.6	33.1	-3.0	N/A	17.3	86.5	103.8	93.7	0.0	0.0	NEWPORT BONDING & SURETY CO
N/A	N/A	--	--	--	--	--	--	--	--	--	--	NEWPORT INS CO
N/A	N/A	--	--	--	--	--	--	--	--	--	--	NEXT INSURANCE US CO
2.3	1.8	118.0	87.1	4.2	11.2	72.6	31.0	103.6	101.2	13.5	13.3 ●	NGM INS CO
1.6	1.1	83.9	129.0	-19.3	-48.0	76.2	12.0	88.2	128.5	-12.3	10.8	NHRMA MUTUAL INS CO
2.3	1.7	63.0	111.6	0.1	-2.1	77.4	13.4	90.8	115.4	7.6	12.1 ●	NJ MANUFACTURERS INS CO
4.1	3.1	102.6	22.0	-6.7	-6.9	67.4	22.4	89.8	106.1	17.8	9.7	NODAK INS CO
6.1	4.5	14.4	37.4	-9.1	-18.5	12.2	28.2	40.4	93.9	4.8	0.0	NOETIC SPECIALTY INS CO
2.4	1.9	53.7	86.9	4.2	5.0	76.9	22.6	99.5	107.4	17.3	11.5 ●	NORCAL MUTUAL INS CO
20.8	18.6	N/A	10.1	N/A	N/A	N/A	N/A	N/A	999 +	100.0	0.0	NORCAL SPECIALTY INS CO
3.5	2.5	72.4	47.9	-2.1	-7.0	57.3	37.7	95.0	118.3	7.7	3.2	NORFOLK & DEDHAM MUTUAL FIRE INS
0.3	0.3	121.2	130.9	-6.9	-8.9	57.9	24.0	81.9	157.8	26.0	0.0 ●	NORGUARD INS CO
0.4	0.3	296.7	131.4	17.3	4.8	60.7	31.8	92.5	110.4	36.9	0.0	NORMANDY INS CO
5.7	5.1	N/A	1.4	N/A	N/A	999 +	999 +	999 +	-77.4	0.0	0.0	NORTH AMERICAN CAPACITY INS CO
4.7	4.2	N/A	1.2	N/A	N/A	999 +	999 +	999 +	26.4	0.0	0.0	NORTH AMERICAN ELITE INS CO
4.1	3.9	N/A	8.2	0.4	-0.3	999 +	999 +	999 +	4.4	-80.6	19.9 ●	NORTH AMERICAN SPECIALTY INS CO
6.6	4.4	70.6	28.4	-3.0	-3.7	71.9	22.9	94.8	105.0	8.0	0.5 ●	NORTH CAROLINA FARM BU MUTUAL INS
1.9	1.3	95.3	17.3	-6.6	-10.7	45.3	30.3	75.6	125.0	7.7	0.0	NORTH CAROLINA GRANGE MUTUAL INS
6.2	4.7	38.3	17.2	-2.9	-3.8	42.1	39.5	81.6	116.2	3.1	3.5	NORTH COUNTRY INS CO
3.8	3.4	-42.0	N/A	10.6	46.4	108.5	-15.2	93.3	-35.1	-125.3	0.0	NORTH EAST INS CO
4.3	2.2	53.2	16.0	-0.7	0.3	56.1	42.4	98.5	112.8	-38.7	0.0	NORTH LIGHT SPECIALTY INS CO
32.9	29.6	N/A	N/A	N/A	N/A	N/A	N/A	N/A	N/A	0.0	0.0	NORTH PACIFIC INS CO
4.7	4.2	N/A	N/A	N/A	N/A	N/A	N/A	N/A	N/A	100.0	0.0	NORTH POINTE INS CO
1.0	0.8	139.9	193.9	-1.4	-3.3	64.7	35.1	99.8	102.6	3.5	25.1 ●	NORTH RIVER INS CO
N/A	N/A	--	--	--	--	--	--	--	--	--	--	NORTH STAR GENERAL INS CO
6.6	4.4	80.2	22.0	-0.5	-3.8	61.7	26.7	88.4	109.2	4.8	0.6 ●	NORTH STAR MUTUAL INS CO
3.6	2.2	57.4	10.3	-2.0	-2.5	48.2	37.0	85.2	114.9	1.1	0.0	NORTHERN MUTUAL INS CO
68.6	29.4	N/A	N/A	N/A	N/A	N/A	N/A	N/A	N/A	0.0	0.0	NORTHFIELD INS CO
2.3	1.5	98.8	161.9	-2.1	-3.4	69.5	29.1	98.6	108.5	4.9	0.0	NORTHFIELD INS CO
2.9	1.9	85.1	139.4	-1.8	-3.1	69.5	29.1	98.6	108.1	4.9	0.0	NORTHLAND CASUALTY CO
2.8	2.3	54.0	88.4	-1.1	-1.9	69.5	29.2	98.7	106.2	4.9	14.9 ●	NORTHLAND INS CO
1.4	0.9	62.7	192.4	-24.1	-36.7	61.0	37.0	98.0	103.0	4.9	0.0	NORTHSTONE INS CO
2.3	1.7	46.4	50.5	-16.8	1.9	41.8	32.8	74.6	97.6	5.3	0.0	NORTHWEST DENTISTS INS CO
2.5	2.0	129.3	20.7	-4.1	-6.0	48.1	35.5	83.6	121.2	7.8	0.0	NORTHWEST GF MUTUAL INS CO
0.2	0.1	18.9	595.1	N/A	N/A	65.9	222.7	288.6	11.8	-2.8	33.4	NORTHWESTERN NATL INS CO SEG
0.5	0.5	N/A	N/A	N/A	N/A	N/A	N/A	N/A	N/A	0.0	0.0	NORTHWESTERN NTL INS CO
2.1	2.0	N/A	N/A	N/A	N/A	N/A	N/A	N/A	-135.8	0.0	52.7	NOVA CASUALTY CO
4.0	2.8	5.1	6.1	-2.9	-3.9	22.2	17.9	40.1	229.5	-6.9	2.5 ●	NUCLEAR ELECTRIC INS LTD
26.4	23.7	29.1	53.2	-0.1	0.3	68.7	29.9	98.6	110.1	1.6	1.3 ●	NUTMEG INS CO
2.9	1.9	30.3	0.2	-0.1	0.4	55.8	45.6	101.4	95.2	0.0	0.0	NW FARMERS MUTUAL INSURANCE CO
2.6	1.7	49.6	113.8	-14.6	-20.6	53.3	21.3	74.6	182.1	24.9	0.0 ●	OAK RIVER INS CO
3.0	1.2	N/A	73.1	3.4	6.5	999 +	N/A	N/A	-47.4	-100.0	0.0	OAKWOOD INS CO
1.7	1.2	58.8	92.3	-3.4	-30.9	33.4	26.2	59.6	218.1	1.6	0.0	OASIS RECIPROCAL RRG
173.9	86.9	N/A	N/A	N/A	N/A	N/A	N/A	N/A	N/A	0.0	0.0	OBI AMERICA INS CO
148.6	74.2	N/A	N/A	N/A	N/A	N/A	N/A	N/A	N/A	0.0	0.0	OBI NATIONAL INS CO

999 + Denotes number greater than 999.9%
999 - Denotes number less than -999.99%
● Bullets denote a more detailed analysis is available in Section II.

INSURANCE COMPANY NAME	DOM. STATE	RATING	TOTAL ASSETS ($MIL)	CAPITAL & SURPLUS ($MIL)	ANNUAL NET PREMIUM ($MIL)	NET INCOME ($MIL)	CAPITAL-IZATION INDEX (PTS)	RESERVE ADQ INDEX (PTS)	PROFIT-ABILITY INDEX (PTS)	LIQUIDITY INDEX (PTS)	STAB. INDEX (PTS)	STABILITY FACTORS
OBSTETRICIANS & GYNECOLOGISTS RRG	MT	U (5)	--	--	--	--	N/A	--	--	--	--	Z
OCCIDENTAL FIRE & CAS CO OF NC	NC	C-	474.3	224.0	65.2	10.3	6.6	4.0	6.7	7.0	2.7	FRT
OCEAN HARBOR CASUALTY INS CO	FL	B	285.1	66.1	206.3	10.6	6.4	9.8	8.7	2.2	6.3	CL
OCEAN MARINE INDEMNITY INS CO	LA	C-	10.9	7.0	0.5	0.0	8.9	4.5	2.8	6.8	2.6	DFR
OCEANUS INS CO A RRG	SC	F (3)	52.9	6.9	10.8	-0.9	0.9	0.5	0.6	6.0	0.0	CDFR
ODYSSEY REINS CO	CT	C	7,797.1	3,248.8	1,880.8	88.2	7.2	9.4	6.2	7.5	3.7	AR
OGLESBY REINS CO	IL	A+	4,590.7	3,187.0	448.8	-90.2	10.0	3.7	4.5	7.1	8.4	T
OHIC INS CO	OH	U	--	--	--	--	N/A	--	--	--	--	Z
▲OHIO BAR LIABILITY INS CO	OH	B	39.7	30.1	6.7	1.6	10.0	7.8	8.5	8.6	5.1	D
OHIO CASUALTY INS CO	NH	C	6,147.6	1,693.6	2,284.0	-5.2	8.2	5.7	6.3	6.3	3.9	AR
OHIO FARMERS INS CO	OH	B-	3,107.9	2,334.5	352.9	-6.1	7.3	7.4	6.9	6.9	4.6	F
▲OHIO INDEMNITY CO	OH	C+	152.5	45.5	98.6	9.9	7.7	9.3	5.9	6.1	4.5	T
OHIO MUTUAL INS CO	OH	B-	296.3	235.0	59.6	3.0	7.5	7.5	7.3	6.9	4.7	T
OHIO SECURITY INS CO	NH	C-	16.2	15.0	0.0	-0.8	10.0	N/A	3.8	7.0	3.1	ADRT
OKLAHOMA ATTORNEYS MUTUAL INS CO	OK	B	55.9	35.7	5.1	-2.1	9.8	8.0	3.5	7.6	5.3	DF
OKLAHOMA FARM BUREAU MUTUAL INS CO	OK	B-	300.2	112.6	158.9	3.1	8.0	9.3	6.7	5.9	4.7	T
OKLAHOMA P&C INS CO	OK	U	--	--	--	--	N/A	--	--	--	--	Z
▲OKLAHOMA SPECIALTY INS CO	OK	B-	22.1	19.5	0.0	0.5	10.0	N/A	7.9	7.0	4.9	DT
OKLAHOMA SURETY CO	OH	C	17.1	16.5	0.0	0.4	10.0	4.6	6.1	7.0	3.2	DRT
OLD AMERICAN CTY MUTUAL FIRE INS CO	TX	E+	146.7	5.0	39.4	0.0	0.1	4.6	5.1	4.2	0.7	CDFL
OLD AMERICAN INDEMNITY CO	KY	B-	12.2	9.5	0.1	-0.1	10.0	6.0	3.7	7.0	3.5	DRT
OLD DOMINION INS CO	FL	B-	36.1	36.1	0.0	0.7	10.0	N/A	7.1	10.0	4.6	
OLD ELIZABETH MUTUAL FIRE INS CO	PA	U	--	--	--	--	N/A	--	--	--	--	Z
OLD GLORY INS CO	TX	C (1)	23.6	10.2	7.3	0.0	7.2	7.0	4.4	6.6	3.0	DGRT
OLD GUARD INS CO	OH	C+	481.2	218.6	167.2	1.7	9.1	8.3	6.8	6.7	4.6	T
OLD RELIABLE CAS CO	MO	C-	5.6	4.7	0.0	-0.1	10.0	3.6	2.4	9.4	3.3	DFRT
OLD REPUB INS CO	PA	B	2,923.3	1,141.2	459.0	97.3	9.3	6.0	8.8	6.9	6.2	A
OLD REPUB UNION INS CO	IL	B	61.4	53.4	0.1	1.3	8.7	6.2	6.5	7.0	4.3	GRT
OLD REPUBLIC GENERAL INS CORP	IL	B	2,078.8	596.3	224.0	90.7	7.7	8.8	8.9	7.0	6.2	T
OLD REPUBLIC LLOYDS OF TX	TX	B	2.3	0.8	0.7	0.0	7.0	8.9	3.7	7.8	4.9	DT
OLD REPUBLIC SECURITY ASR CO	IL	B	1,023.6	202.6	229.4	1.6	4.8	0.3	3.6	6.2	4.8	CFRT
OLD REPUBLIC SURETY CO	WI	B	127.1	70.5	50.6	11.4	8.2	9.5	8.6	6.9	6.0	T
OLD UNITED CAS CO	KS	C	650.5	240.7	144.1	28.3	10.0	7.3	6.8	9.2	3.7	R
▼OLYMPUS INS CO	FL	D+	78.8	29.3	-4.0	-1.0	2.4	3.8	6.1	9.2	2.7	CR
OMAHA NATIONAL INSURANCE CO	NE	D	3.7	2.9	0.9	-0.1	10.0	N/A	3.0	10.0	0.6	DFT
▼OMEGA INS CO	FL	C-	42.3	13.1	8.4	-4.1	7.5	3.4	1.8	4.7	3.0	DLR
OMEGA ONE INS CO	AL	C	12.1	11.0	0.6	0.0	10.0	8.0	7.5	9.0	2.9	DRT
OMNI INDEMNITY CO	IL	D (1)	68.8	3.6	34.7	-4.9	0.8	1.4	0.3	2.7	2.6	CDFG
OMNI INS CO	IL	C (1)	98.5	10.8	45.8	-7.5	2.6	1.9	0.7	0.0	3.8	CDFL
OMS NATIONAL INS CO RRG	IL	B-	442.8	267.9	64.0	19.6	8.6	8.6	8.6	7.7	4.7	R
ONE ALLIANCE INS CORP	PR	D+(2)	13.8	6.8	2.9	-0.2	5.6	3.6	1.3	6.7	2.2	DFGT
ONECIS INS CO	IL	U	--	--	--	--	N/A	--	--	--	--	Z
ONTARIO INS CO	NY	C	18.2	12.5	4.8	0.6	10.0	8.0	8.2	7.2	3.3	DR
▲ONTARIO REINS CO LTD	GA	C+	31.5	26.2	0.4	0.1	8.1	5.0	6.9	7.6	4.5	D
ONYX INS CO INC A RRG	TN	E+	36.4	7.2	17.1	-3.1	0.9	0.4	2.4	7.3	0.6	CDF
OOIDA RISK RETENTION GROUP INC	VT	C	95.6	24.7	18.4	1.8	7.1	9.6	3.4	6.8	4.3	R
OPHTHALMIC MUTUAL INS CO RRG	VT	B	294.4	213.9	37.2	2.3	10.0	8.6	8.2	7.7	6.1	T
ORANGE COUNTY MEDICAL RECIP INS RRG	AZ	D+	6.0	4.5	0.6	-0.5	8.3	9.3	3.0	9.1	2.3	DF
ORDINARY MUTUAL A RRG CORP	VT	U (5)	--	--	--	--	N/A	--	--	--	--	Z
OREGON AUTOMOBILE INS CO	OR	C	8.3	7.9	0.0	0.1	10.0	N/A	6.1	7.0	3.9	DR
▲OREGON MUTUAL INS CO	OR	C	214.6	72.0	127.8	-4.3	7.9	5.6	2.3	5.4	3.5	FR
ORISKA INS CO	NY	E	37.3	10.8	18.5	-0.5	0.0	2.2	2.9	0.0	0.2	CDFL

See Page 27 for explanation of footnotes and
Page 28 for explanation of stability factors.
Arrows denote recent upgrades ▲ or downgrades ▼   (see Section VII for explanations)

98

www.weissratings.com

RISK ADJ. RATIO #1	CAPITAL RATIO #2	PREMIUM TO SURPLUS (%)	RESV. TO SURPLUS (%)	RESV. DEVELOP. 1 YEAR (%)	RESV. DEVELOP. 2 YEAR (%)	LOSS RATIO (%)	EXP. RATIO (%)	COMB RATIO (%)	CASH FROM UNDER- WRITING (%)	NET PREMIUM GROWTH (%)	INVEST. IN AFFIL (%)	INSURANCE COMPANY NAME
N/A	N/A	--	--	--	--	--	--	--	--	--	--	OBSTETRICIANS & GYNECOLOGISTS
1.2	1.0	29.1	22.2	0.1	4.4	73.4	30.7	104.1	999 +	27.1	41.9 ●	OCCIDENTAL FIRE & CAS CO OF NC
1.2	0.9	312.2	132.7	-11.2	-19.0	63.8	34.6	98.4	113.9	3.9	10.9	OCEAN HARBOR CASUALTY INS CO
3.1	2.2	6.7	51.0	0.2	1.5	155.4	78.6	234.0	29.7	-13.2	0.0	OCEAN MARINE INDEMNITY INS CO
0.2	0.2	141.0	517.3	32.5	81.9	88.8	67.9	156.7	59.6	-53.8	0.0	OCEANUS INS CO A RRG
1.3	1.1	57.9	97.8	-6.9	-12.6	67.4	31.7	99.1	110.4	19.4	32.2 ●	ODYSSEY REINS CO
8.5	4.5	14.1	36.1	-0.4	-2.5	129.1	15.1	144.2	151.5	-50.5	0.0 ●	OGLESBY REINS CO
N/A	N/A	--	--	--	--	--	--	--	--	--	--	OHIC INS CO
5.4	3.7	22.2	19.9	-1.3	-1.2	55.2	29.6	84.8	111.5	5.8	5.4	OHIO BAR LIABILITY INS CO
2.6	1.8	134.9	185.7	4.1	4.6	79.5	29.0	108.5	99.9	7.7	2.1 ●	OHIO CASUALTY INS CO
1.2	1.1	15.1	14.3	N/A	-0.4	73.5	35.1	108.6	96.5	2.6	71.6 ●	OHIO FARMERS INS CO
2.2	1.4	216.8	41.8	-0.7	-10.2	56.8	36.0	92.8	99.3	18.3	0.0	OHIO INDEMNITY CO
1.3	1.3	25.4	11.8	-1.7	-1.7	60.4	33.2	93.6	105.7	5.7	66.8 ●	OHIO MUTUAL INS CO
29.7	26.7	N/A	N/A	N/A	N/A	N/A	N/A	N/A	N/A	0.0	0.0	OHIO SECURITY INS CO
4.0	2.8	14.2	30.5	-1.0	-2.0	113.2	38.7	151.9	61.3	-18.8	0.0	OKLAHOMA ATTORNEYS MUTUAL INS
2.1	1.6	141.1	47.8	-5.5	-9.4	73.7	24.3	98.0	103.3	30.9	13.0	OKLAHOMA FARM BUREAU MUTUAL INS
N/A	N/A	--	--	--	--	--	--	--	--	--	--	OKLAHOMA P&C INS CO
22.0	19.8	N/A	N/A	N/A	N/A	N/A	N/A	N/A	93.3	0.0	0.0	OKLAHOMA SPECIALTY INS CO
70.6	63.6	N/A	N/A	N/A	N/A	N/A	N/A	N/A	N/A	100.0	0.0	OKLAHOMA SURETY CO
0.1	0.1	787.3	N/A	N/A	N/A	N/A	99.0	99.0	97.9	-1.6	0.0	OLD AMERICAN CTY MUTUAL FIRE INS
10.5	9.4	1.2	2.5	0.1	-1.1	142.6	76.0	218.6	-83.0	-77.6	0.0	OLD AMERICAN INDEMNITY CO
57.2	27.1	N/A	N/A	N/A	N/A	N/A	N/A	N/A	37.6	0.0	0.0	OLD DOMINION INS CO
N/A	N/A	--	--	--	--	--	--	--	--	--	--	OLD ELIZABETH MUTUAL FIRE INS CO
1.6	1.1	71.0	95.7	-9.0	-16.3	69.5	53.5	123.0	95.2	-14.5	0.0	OLD GLORY INS CO
3.6	2.4	76.5	72.5	0.2	-2.2	73.5	35.5	109.0	99.6	2.6	0.0	OLD GUARD INS CO
10.7	9.6	N/A	N/A	N/A	0.2	N/A	N/A	N/A	-33.7	0.0	0.0	OLD RELIABLE CAS CO
4.2	2.5	40.2	90.9	2.5	1.4	61.7	28.7	90.4	117.9	-2.5	0.5 ●	OLD REPUB INS CO
3.6	2.1	0.2	6.4	-0.1	-0.1	26.0	240.7	266.7	103.9	-4.2	0.0	OLD REPUB UNION INS CO
3.2	1.8	37.6	182.3	-8.0	-10.4	65.1	6.7	71.8	151.7	21.5	0.0 ●	OLD REPUBLIC GENERAL INS CORP
1.4	1.0	79.0	132.7	-1.3	-4.1	67.5	43.3	110.8	98.2	0.8	0.0	OLD REPUBLIC LLOYDS OF TX
0.9	0.5	113.2	323.7	5.8	25.3	87.0	27.3	114.3	73.2	2.2	0.0	OLD REPUBLIC SECURITY ASR CO
2.4	1.8	71.8	27.3	-8.8	-18.0	7.9	70.1	78.0	118.0	5.7	0.0	OLD REPUBLIC SURETY CO
11.7	6.1	59.9	2.2	-0.4	-0.7	48.0	23.7	71.7	149.1	-4.5	0.0 ●	OLD UNITED CAS CO
0.4	0.4	-13.7	29.7	5.7	1.6	-48.2	710.8	662.6	32.3	76.2	0.0	OLYMPUS INS CO
3.8	2.9	30.2	3.3	N/A	N/A	77.6	21.3	98.9	60.6	0.0	0.0	OMAHA NATIONAL INSURANCE CO
1.9	1.3	63.7	63.5	11.8	10.2	125.3	30.3	155.6	94.4	-22.3	0.0	OMEGA INS CO
9.5	5.8	5.6	3.3	0.1	-0.1	133.6	10.9	144.5	796.9	0.0	0.0	OMEGA ONE INS CO
0.0	0.0	424.0	313.2	33.1	49.3	109.7	28.2	137.9	82.7	54.2	0.0	OMNI INDEMNITY CO
0.1	0.1	207.6	175.8	18.1	26.5	104.4	29.6	134.0	78.8	-30.9	23.1	OMNI INS CO
2.7	2.1	23.9	43.8	-7.0	-8.7	43.8	34.8	78.6	105.2	-4.7	15.8 ●	OMS NATIONAL INS CO RRG
0.9	0.5	40.8	6.2	0.2	N/A	64.2	141.4	205.6	51.1	390.5	0.0	ONE ALLIANCE INS CORP
N/A	N/A	--	--	--	--	--	--	--	--	--	--	ONECIS INS CO
5.6	3.6	38.1	17.9	-3.4	-5.4	54.2	34.4	88.6	115.2	11.6	0.0	ONTARIO INS CO
3.0	1.8	1.7	2.9	-0.2	0.6	58.9	52.7	111.6	82.6	-3.5	0.0	ONTARIO REINS CO LTD
0.3	0.2	238.6	226.8	32.3	108.5	89.2	25.8	115.0	87.6	23.3	0.0	ONYX INS CO INC A RRG
1.6	1.3	74.3	130.3	-22.4	-45.5	59.6	30.3	89.9	101.8	3.7	0.0	OOIDA RISK RETENTION GROUP INC
12.2	7.7	17.4	18.8	N/A	-2.7	63.0	32.8	95.8	107.4	1.9	0.0	OPHTHALMIC MUTUAL INS CO RRG
2.3	1.8	14.0	28.3	8.8	-0.9	188.7	22.9	211.6	82.4	-12.2	0.0	ORANGE COUNTY MEDICAL RECIP INS
N/A	N/A	--	--	--	--	--	--	--	--	--	--	ORDINARY MUTUAL A RRG CORP
39.8	35.8	N/A	N/A	N/A	N/A	N/A	N/A	N/A	N/A	0.0	0.0	OREGON AUTOMOBILE INS CO
2.3	1.6	177.4	93.6	-10.9	-12.4	70.4	39.2	109.6	91.1	3.4	5.2	OREGON MUTUAL INS CO
0.1	0.0	171.1	181.6	-17.9	-9.8	48.5	52.6	101.1	99.3	11.8	0.0	ORISKA INS CO

999 + Denotes number greater than 999.9%
999 - Denotes number less than -999.99%
● Bullets denote a more detailed analysis is available in Section II.

INSURANCE COMPANY NAME	DOM. STATE	RATING	TOTAL ASSETS ($MIL)	CAPITAL & SURPLUS ($MIL)	ANNUAL NET PREMIUM ($MIL)	NET INCOME ($MIL)	CAPITAL-IZATION INDEX (PTS)	RESERVE ADQ INDEX (PTS)	PROFIT-ABILITY INDEX (PTS)	LIQUIDITY INDEX (PTS)	STAB. INDEX (PTS)	STABILITY FACTORS
ORTHOFORUM INS CO	SC	E	25.4	3.5	5.1	0.3	0.0	0.5	2.7	5.6	0.1	CD
▲OSWEGO COUNTY MUTUAL INS CO	NY	C+	29.6	18.0	7.9	1.6	8.7	8.8	8.6	6.9	3.7	D
OTSEGO COUNTY PATRONS CO-OP F R	NY	D	2.2	0.9	0.2	0.2	7.3	7.7	6.5	7.5	1.1	DRT
OTSEGO MUTUAL FIRE INS CO	NY	B	131.8	116.8	4.7	3.7	10.0	7.3	8.2	7.5	6.3	D
▲OWNERS INS CO	OH	A	4,110.4	1,815.5	1,642.5	73.8	10.0	8.1	8.7	6.7	7.5	
P&C CO OF OMAHA	NE	E	12.7	11.0	1.6	0.1	9.1	2.9	4.9	9.5	0.0	DT
P&C INS CO OF HARTFORD	IN	B	237.5	106.2	53.5	11.9	10.0	5.9	5.2	7.0	5.8	A
P&S INS RRG INC	SC	U	--	--	--	--	N/A	--	--	--	--	Z
PACE RRG INC	VT	D+	5.4	3.2	0.1	0.1	8.0	6.0	4.0	6.5	2.1	DGR
PACIFIC COMPENSATION INS CO	CA	C	428.2	116.3	160.1	3.0	4.0	5.1	4.7	6.4	4.1	CRT
PACIFIC EMPLOYERS INS CO	PA	B-	3,687.4	1,063.4	963.4	36.0	8.2	6.0	3.7	6.7	4.9	R
▲PACIFIC INDEMNITY CO	WI	B	6,560.0	2,992.5	863.2	342.3	10.0	8.7	7.0	6.9	5.5	F
PACIFIC INDEMNITY INS CO	GU	C+(1)	35.4	23.3	8.9	1.3	9.5	8.4	8.7	8.2	3.1	DGRT
PACIFIC INS CO LTD	CT	B	676.1	238.0	182.0	21.7	9.2	5.8	8.1	6.8	5.8	A
▲PACIFIC PIONEER INS CO	CA	C	20.0	9.0	4.4	0.2	6.1	5.6	2.9	6.7	2.8	DFRT
PACIFIC PROPERTY & CASUALTY CO	CA	B	90.5	42.9	50.9	0.0	7.9	6.4	5.4	5.5	6.1	
PACIFIC SPECIALTY INS CO	CA	B-	294.4	110.5	165.4	-1.0	7.4	6.4	3.1	3.0	4.6	FLR
▲PACIFIC SPECIALTY PROPERTY & CAS CO	TX	D	6.1	5.4	0.8	0.2	10.0	6.0	4.6	9.2	1.5	DRT
PACIFIC STAR INS CO	WI	C	15.6	10.3	2.5	-0.1	10.0	6.1	3.9	7.6	2.8	DGRT
PACO ASR CO INC	IL	C	64.1	31.4	8.8	1.8	8.1	9.4	3.8	8.1	3.7	DR
PAFCO GENERAL INS CO	IN	F (5)	0.0	0.0	6.3	0.0	1.5	4.9	0.3	2.9	0.0	CDFL
PALADIN REINS CORP	NY	U	--	--	--	--	N/A	--	--	--	--	Z
PALISADES INS CO	NJ	D+	42.5	16.9	0.0	0.2	10.0	N/A	7.7	7.0	2.6	DT
PALISADES P&C INS CO	NJ	D	16.7	12.6	0.0	0.1	10.0	N/A	7.1	7.0	1.5	D
PALISADES SAFETY & INS ASSOC	NJ	C	1,343.7	480.1	616.1	70.9	4.9	9.0	5.4	6.2	3.5	T
PALLADIUM RRG INC	VT	D+	86.1	15.8	27.0	0.1	1.6	4.1	4.1	7.4	2.4	CDT
PALMETTO CASUALTY INS CO	SC	C+	7.1	7.1	0.0	0.1	10.0	N/A	6.9	7.0	3.9	D
▼PALMETTO SURETY CORP	SC	D	15.5	4.1	13.2	-0.4	0.8	9.3	3.8	7.0	1.5	CDFG
▼PALOMAR SPECIALTY INS CO	OR	D-	137.4	61.4	71.5	-4.1	0.8	3.6	3.4	1.7	1.3	CGLT
▲PAN-AMERICAN CASUALTY CO	TX	D+	5.4	5.1	0.0	0.0	10.0	4.6	4.9	10.0	2.5	DRT
PANHANDLE FARMERS MULT INS CO	WV	C-	5.3	2.9	2.8	0.2	8.1	5.0	6.0	6.6	2.0	DR
PARAMOUNT INS CO	MD	D-	13.1	1.8	9.5	0.1	0.5	4.0	2.1	3.6	1.0	CDGL
PARATRANSIT INS CO A MUTUAL RRG	TN	C	31.1	14.8	5.9	0.4	8.2	9.1	7.5	8.5	3.4	DR
▲PARK INS CO	NY	D	36.8	4.0	11.9	2.2	0.0	0.1	2.3	5.7	2.0	CDGT
▲PARTNER REINSURANCE CO OF THE US	NY	B-	4,655.3	1,335.7	929.3	24.1	7.7	9.5	4.4	6.5	4.5	R
PARTNERRE AMERICA INS CO	DE	C+	393.0	110.1	38.4	-4.5	10.0	6.4	3.2	6.7	4.4	R
PARTNERRE INS CO OF NY	NY	C	117.3	109.3	0.0	0.5	9.1	6.5	4.9	8.6	3.8	DFRT
PARTNERS MUTUAL INS CO	WI	C	46.9	13.1	14.1	0.8	7.8	5.6	8.2	6.5	3.3	DR
PASSPORT INS CO	ND	U (5)	--	--	--	--	N/A	--	--	--	--	Z
▲PATONS CO-OP FIRE INS CO	VT	B	144.0	79.4	67.4	5.6	10.0	8.1	8.2	6.5	5.5	T
PATRIOT GENERAL INS CO	WI	B	25.8	25.3	0.0	0.7	10.0	N/A	5.8	10.0	5.7	DT
PATRIOT INS CO	ME	C	130.7	51.4	50.7	4.1	10.0	9.4	8.8	6.6	3.9	T
PATRONS MUTUAL FIRE INS CO OF IN PA	PA	D+	2.8	2.6	0.3	0.0	10.0	8.1	6.2	9.9	2.0	DT
PATRONS MUTUAL INS CO OF CT	CT	C	49.4	21.4	9.8	-0.1	9.9	6.0	5.1	7.0	3.6	DR
PAWTUCKET INS CO	RI	U	--	--	--	--	N/A	--	--	--	--	Z
PCH MUTUAL INS CO INC RRG	VT	D+	7.3	3.0	1.6	-0.2	4.5	7.0	2.9	8.2	2.1	DRT
▲PEACE CHURCH RRG INC	VT	C	21.1	16.3	2.8	0.6	10.0	9.3	7.8	8.4	3.5	DFR
PEACHTREE CASUALTY INS CO	FL	D	16.5	5.1	6.3	-3.0	2.5	2.8	0.7	6.0	1.5	CDFR
PEAK P&C INS CORP	WI	B	48.7	39.1	0.0	0.5	10.0	N/A	5.9	7.0	4.2	R
PEERLESS INDEMNITY INS CO	IL	C+	199.5	192.0	0.0	3.8	10.0	N/A	6.9	7.0	4.3	RT
▲PEERLESS INS CO	NH	B	14,600.0	3,448.5	5,710.0	-54.8	7.6	4.6	5.5	5.9	5.3	
PEKIN INS CO	IL	B+	305.4	132.3	122.8	4.4	10.0	7.9	6.5	6.6	6.0	

See Page 27 for explanation of footnotes and
Page 28 for explanation of stability factors.

100

www.weissratings.com

Arrows denote recent upgrades ▲ or downgrades ▼   (see Section VII for explanations)

RISK ADJ. RATIO #1	CAPITAL RATIO #2	PREMIUM TO SURPLUS (%)	RESV. TO SURPLUS (%)	RESV. DEVELOP. 1 YEAR (%)	RESV. DEVELOP. 2 YEAR (%)	LOSS RATIO (%)	EXP. RATIO (%)	COMB RATIO (%)	CASH FROM UNDER-WRITING (%)	NET PREMIUM GROWTH (%)	INVEST. IN AFFIL (%)	INSURANCE COMPANY NAME
0.1	0.1	146.3	480.6	23.3	64.8	83.0	24.1	107.1	104.9	-24.9	0.0	ORTHOFORUM INS CO
3.4	2.2	44.0	32.4	-6.8	-7.8	47.3	33.5	80.8	113.8	6.9	0.0	OSWEGO COUNTY MUTUAL INS CO
1.6	1.5	17.5	19.5	-2.4	-1.0	79.3	-68.6	10.7	134.2	-74.7	0.0	OTSEGO COUNTY PATRONS CO-OP F R
7.0	4.1	4.0	2.0	-0.3	-0.3	47.6	4.8	52.4	176.6	1.1	0.0	OTSEGO MUTUAL FIRE INS CO
5.9	3.9	90.5	66.1	-2.6	-2.5	69.7	28.8	98.5	102.9	8.1	0.0 ●	OWNERS INS CO
4.0	2.4	14.5	14.5	14.8	15.0	101.0	4.3	105.3	999 +	0.0	0.0	P&C CO OF OMAHA
5.7	3.8	50.4	92.2	-0.4	1.2	68.7	15.0	83.7	110.1	1.6	0.0	P&C INS CO OF HARTFORD
N/A	N/A	--	--	--	--	--	--	--	--	--	--	P&S INS RRG INC
3.3	2.7	3.1	13.7	-6.5	-4.4	-13.0	92.3	79.3	123.8	0.0	0.0	PACE RRG INC
0.8	0.4	137.7	242.8	-0.4	-0.9	74.4	28.5	102.9	141.1	15.8	0.0	PACIFIC COMPENSATION INS CO
2.6	1.8	90.6	163.5	-1.1	2.3	83.9	19.3	103.2	114.3	8.3	4.6 ●	PACIFIC EMPLOYERS INS CO
6.6	4.1	28.8	82.8	-4.5	-9.0	59.0	25.3	84.3	74.1	-19.7	0.0 ●	PACIFIC INDEMNITY CO
4.9	2.9	40.7	14.2	-3.2	-4.3	27.6	40.2	67.8	116.0	0.5	0.5	PACIFIC INDEMNITY INS CO
3.8	2.5	76.5	139.9	-0.7	1.9	68.7	29.8	98.5	110.1	1.6	0.0 ●	PACIFIC INS CO LTD
1.9	1.2	48.3	55.8	11.3	-0.8	90.0	17.2	107.2	63.5	-8.1	0.0	PACIFIC PIONEER INS CO
2.5	1.6	118.8	59.5	-2.1	2.2	79.5	24.7	104.2	99.2	15.8	0.0	PACIFIC PROPERTY & CASUALTY CO
1.7	1.2	149.8	61.5	-2.8	-4.5	67.3	44.7	112.0	88.2	-11.3	2.2	PACIFIC SPECIALTY INS CO
13.9	11.9	14.2	3.3	-0.7	0.8	42.3	32.4	74.7	125.4	24.0	2.2	PACIFIC SPECIALTY PROPERTY & CAS
5.5	4.4	24.0	15.5	-0.5	-2.1	71.2	37.5	108.7	103.3	60.7	0.0	PACIFIC STAR INS CO
2.7	2.3	28.0	76.6	-5.6	-20.8	69.4	22.8	92.2	97.1	-9.8	0.0	PACO ASR CO INC
0.4	0.3	196.2	297.0	7.1	-17.7	95.7	39.4	135.1	51.3	-17.6	0.0	PAFCO GENERAL INS CO
N/A	N/A	--	--	--	--	--	--	--	--	--	--	PALADIN REINS CORP
4.1	3.7	N/A	N/A	N/A	N/A	N/A	N/A	N/A	N/A	0.0	0.0	PALISADES INS CO
9.7	5.6	N/A	N/A	N/A	N/A	N/A	N/A	N/A	N/A	0.0	0.0	PALISADES P&C INS CO
1.0	0.9	128.3	118.5	-5.1	-8.7	74.4	30.7	105.1	96.3	4.9	29.3 ●	PALISADES SAFETY & INS ASSOC
0.5	0.3	171.1	374.4	-67.8	-103.8	68.3	7.7	76.0	307.7	-2.5	0.0	PALLADIUM RRG INC
91.1	45.5	N/A	N/A	N/A	N/A	N/A	N/A	N/A	N/A	0.0	0.0	PALMETTO CASUALTY INS CO
0.2	0.2	324.1	48.9	-5.6	-11.6	17.1	83.7	100.8	92.0	40.4	0.0	PALMETTO SURETY CORP
0.3	0.2	116.5	7.2	-1.9	-0.6	24.6	59.1	83.7	131.6	77.2	0.0	PALOMAR SPECIALTY INS CO
40.2	36.2	N/A	N/A	N/A	N/A	N/A	N/A	N/A	N/A	100.0	0.0	PAN-AMERICAN CASUALTY CO
2.6	1.9	97.6	8.0	3.5	7.6	50.1	40.9	91.0	104.4	2.7	0.0	PANHANDLE FARMERS MULT INS CO
0.2	0.1	523.2	308.9	20.6	6.7	70.6	31.9	102.5	138.9	15.3	0.0	PARAMOUNT INS CO
2.8	1.8	40.1	62.0	-6.7	-11.5	43.9	30.9	74.8	192.8	20.4	0.0	PARATRANSIT INS CO A MUTUAL RRG
0.1	0.0	294.6	385.3	276.0	464.9	128.8	-28.7	100.1	63.8	30.1	0.0	PARK INS CO
2.4	1.5	69.6	170.1	-3.3	-13.8	77.9	31.0	108.9	94.1	-21.8	3.0 ●	PARTNER REINSURANCE CO OF THE US
5.8	3.9	34.9	36.0	4.8	-0.3	126.0	-2.5	123.5	85.2	19.7	0.0	PARTNERRE AMERICA INS CO
6.8	2.7	N/A	46.4	-1.0	-2.2	999 +	999 +	999 +	-33.0	-43.0	0.0	PARTNERRE INS CO OF NY
2.6	1.7	107.2	106.8	0.7	1.0	65.6	32.1	97.7	108.7	2.5	0.0	PARTNERS MUTUAL INS CO
N/A	N/A	--	--	--	--	--	--	--	--	--	--	PASSPORT INS CO
4.7	3.1	84.8	25.5	-4.7	-5.0	61.5	30.0	91.5	103.6	4.1	1.0	PATONS CO-OP FIRE INS CO
102.5	52.4	N/A	N/A	N/A	N/A	N/A	N/A	N/A	-40.5	0.0	0.0	PATRIOT GENERAL INS CO
5.6	3.9	98.7	68.5	-9.1	-12.8	59.0	32.3	91.3	106.3	5.7	0.0	PATRIOT INS CO
12.4	8.8	12.5	3.1	-2.1	-5.0	28.9	70.6	99.5	101.4	5.4	0.0	PATRONS MUTUAL FIRE INS CO OF IN
4.7	2.9	45.6	45.4	-1.7	-0.7	72.2	35.1	107.3	96.5	-1.9	0.0	PATRONS MUTUAL INS CO OF CT
N/A	N/A	--	--	--	--	--	--	--	--	--	--	PAWTUCKET INS CO
1.1	0.9	53.0	86.2	-16.9	-16.0	67.7	70.7	138.4	124.7	-43.9	0.0	PCH MUTUAL INS CO INC RRG
7.6	5.1	17.0	27.4	-2.8	-6.9	51.2	19.8	71.0	87.4	-12.3	0.0	PEACE CHURCH RRG INC
0.6	0.5	124.6	76.8	29.9	41.7	88.3	63.4	151.7	65.1	-24.1	0.0	PEACHTREE CASUALTY INS CO
16.6	14.9	N/A	N/A	N/A	N/A	N/A	N/A	N/A	77.1	0.0	0.0	PEAK P&C INS CORP
96.5	55.4	N/A	N/A	N/A	N/A	N/A	N/A	N/A	N/A	0.0	0.0	PEERLESS INDEMNITY INS CO
1.9	1.4	165.6	228.0	5.0	5.7	79.5	29.0	108.5	100.0	7.7	5.4 ●	PEERLESS INS CO
4.6	3.3	92.8	77.0	-4.2	-1.5	74.2	28.5	102.7	99.1	0.0	3.4 ●	PEKIN INS CO

999 + Denotes number greater than 999.9%
999 - Denotes number less than -999.99%
● Bullets denote a more detailed analysis is available in Section II.

INSURANCE COMPANY NAME	DOM. STATE	RATING	TOTAL ASSETS ($MIL)	CAPITAL & SURPLUS ($MIL)	ANNUAL NET PREMIUM ($MIL)	NET INCOME ($MIL)	CAPITAL-IZATION INDEX (PTS)	RESERVE ADQ INDEX (PTS)	PROFIT-ABILITY INDEX (PTS)	LIQUIDITY INDEX (PTS)	STAB. INDEX (PTS)	STABILITY FACTORS
PELEUS INS CO	VA	D+	92.1	53.6	0.0	0.3	10.0	N/A	7.1	6.7	2.6	FRT
PELICAN INS RRG	VT	C-	17.0	10.8	2.2	-3.1	3.2	5.7	1.7	6.6	3.3	CDFR
PEMCO MUTUAL INS CO	WA	B-	772.8	284.9	453.2	0.6	8.6	5.0	5.6	5.8	4.7	R
PENINSULA INDEMNITY CO	MD	C	12.2	10.2	0.0	0.2	10.0	N/A	7.1	10.0	3.9	DR
▼PENINSULA INS CO	MD	C	95.9	39.4	53.4	-1.1	8.4	4.9	3.1	6.4	4.3	
PENN CHARTER MUTL INS CO	PA	C	16.9	14.6	0.0	0.4	7.4	6.1	6.9	9.8	3.8	D
PENN MILLERS INS CO	PA	C	99.8	42.2	0.0	1.1	10.0	6.4	2.7	7.0	3.7	R
PENN NATIONAL SECURITY INS CO	PA	B-	969.0	336.3	344.6	15.5	9.4	6.2	8.3	6.5	4.7	T
PENN RESERVE INS CO LTD	PA	D	2.1	1.8	0.7	0.1	9.9	N/A	7.8	9.0	1.5	DT
PENN-AMERICA INS CO	PA	C+	127.2	63.1	23.8	-2.6	6.5	6.3	3.0	6.7	4.3	FR
PENN-PATRIOT INS CO	VA	C	50.0	16.6	16.6	-1.6	5.3	5.8	3.2	6.4	3.3	DFGR
PENN-STAR INS CO	PA	C+	121.3	45.4	38.0	-3.6	7.8	6.8	3.7	6.6	4.6	FR
PENNSYLVANIA INS CO	IA	C	72.3	48.6	22.0	4.5	9.2	6.3	8.9	9.1	3.9	DR
PENNSYLVANIA LUMBERMENS MUTUAL INS	PA	B	488.1	132.8	155.2	14.4	7.5	4.5	6.3	6.3	6.1	
PENNSYLVANIA MANUFACTURERS ASN INS	PA	C	1,017.3	343.8	182.1	17.6	8.4	3.1	6.7	6.7	4.2	AR
PENNSYLVANIA MANUFACTURERS IND CO	PA	C	233.7	86.6	60.7	4.5	8.0	3.0	6.0	6.5	4.2	AR
PENNSYLVANIA NTL MUTUAL CAS INS CO	PA	B-	1,307.1	630.2	344.6	23.6	7.8	6.2	7.9	6.8	4.7	R
PENNSYLVANIA PHYSICIANS RECIP INS	PA	U (1)	--	--	--	--	N/A	--	--	--	--	Z
▲PEOPLES TRUST INS CO	FL	D+	254.0	66.4	107.3	9.9	4.1	4.6	2.3	4.3	2.5	L
PERMANENT GEN ASR CORP OF OHIO	WI	C-	226.2	94.8	-63.6	6.8	8.6	5.6	4.4	6.7	3.1	RT
PERMANENT GENERAL ASR CORP	WI	C-	582.2	135.8	-147.5	16.5	10.0	1.8	3.9	2.9	2.9	GLRT
PERSONAL SERVICE INS CO	PA	D (1)	57.3	2.1	13.9	-2.0	1.2	1.3	0.5	0.9	1.6	CDFG
PETROLEUM CAS CO	TX	B-	32.8	23.1	3.7	2.4	5.4	5.8	5.9	9.8	4.9	CD
▲PETROLEUM MARKETERS MGMT INS CO	IA	C+	50.2	28.2	4.5	1.8	7.6	6.3	7.6	7.4	4.5	DG
PFD PHYSICIANS MED RRG A MUTL	MO	C-	24.0	5.0	-73.8	2.1	8.1	9.5	1.9	7.1	3.3	DFRT
PHARMACISTS MUTUAL INS CO	IA	B	319.1	131.4	101.1	15.1	9.3	9.1	8.6	6.6	5.2	F
▼PHENIX MUTUAL FIRE INS CO	NH	C	67.3	18.8	21.7	-3.2	7.3	6.3	2.2	6.0	3.4	DF
PHILADELPHIA CBSP FOR INS OF HOUSES	PA	B-	376.1	300.2	38.6	4.4	7.2	7.3	6.8	6.7	4.7	R
PHILADELPHIA CONTRIBUTIONSHIP INS CO	PA	B-	240.3	144.0	58.1	9.9	8.7	6.3	7.9	6.7	4.7	R
PHILADELPHIA INDEMNITY INS CO	PA	B-	8,653.2	2,316.4	3,024.8	364.1	8.3	8.0	7.9	6.6	4.6	R
PHILADELPHIA REINS CORP	PA	D+	9.4	8.3	1.5	0.3	10.0	5.1	3.7	9.3	2.5	DGRT
▲PHOEBE RECIPROCAL RRG	SC	E+	4.4	3.1	0.4	0.2	9.0	9.3	3.1	8.8	0.5	DFT
PHOENIX FUND INC	NC	F (5)	0.0	0.0	25.2	0.0	0.0	0.3	5.2	5.9	0.0	CDT
PHOENIX INS CO	CT	B	4,210.3	1,625.4	1,142.3	159.2	7.8	8.0	4.4	6.8	6.3	
▲PHYSICIANS CASUALTY RRG INC	AL	E+	12.4	3.6	5.0	0.6	2.2	3.1	8.7	5.3	0.5	DFT
PHYSICIANS IND RRG INC	NV	D	6.5	1.7	2.3	0.5	5.0	10.0	3.4	8.0	1.5	DFT
PHYSICIANS INS A MUTL CO	WA	B-	504.5	250.2	81.1	9.5	10.0	9.4	6.8	7.0	4.7	FR
PHYSICIANS INS CO	FL	D+	14.2	5.6	5.2	-0.7	2.0	4.0	1.5	6.5	2.7	CDR
PHYSICIANS INS MUTUAL	MO	E	4.7	1.1	1.0	0.1	5.2	9.9	2.3	6.7	0.1	DT
▲PHYSICIANS INS PROGRAM	PA	C+	25.8	12.0	3.0	0.2	5.7	7.0	5.9	7.8	4.2	DFR
▲PHYSICIANS PROACTIVE PROTECTION INC	SC	C-	86.1	29.0	9.6	2.5	3.4	4.9	6.0	8.4	3.3	CDR
PHYSICIANS PROFESSIONAL LIABILTY RRG	VT	C+(1)	37.4	19.8	3.8	0.8	9.7	9.5	4.6	7.8	4.2	DFGR
PHYSICIANS RECIPROCAL INSURERS	NY	E-	1,129.2	-311.9	178.7	31.8	0.0	10.0	0.9	7.0	0.0	CFRT
PHYSICIANS REIMBURSEMENT FUND RRG	VT	C	30.0	11.7	2.0	0.5	4.2	10.0	6.0	7.9	3.2	CDR
PHYSICIANS SPECIALTY LTD RRG	SC	U	--	--	--	--	N/A	--	--	--	--	Z
▲PHYSICIANS STANDARD INS CO	KS	C-	3.8	3.1	0.2	-0.4	10.0	7.0	2.0	10.0	2.0	DFT
PIEDMONT MUTUAL INS CO	NC	D+	4.9	3.4	1.9	0.3	7.8	8.0	4.9	7.0	2.1	DR
PIH INS CO A RECIP RRG	HI	B-	21.4	17.1	5.1	3.5	8.3	7.0	8.9	8.2	3.5	D
PILGRIM INS CO	MA	C	101.5	21.4	32.7	1.7	7.0	6.6	6.8	6.7	4.3	DT
▲PINNACLEPOINT INS CO	WV	B-	76.2	12.2	7.5	0.9	6.2	6.1	5.8	8.1	4.2	DT
PIONEER SPECIALTY INS CO	MN	C	71.1	28.4	26.2	1.7	9.1	8.2	8.6	6.4	3.4	FR
▲PIONEER STATE MUTUAL INS CO	MI	B+	608.7	363.2	207.3	22.3	10.0	8.7	8.7	6.8	6.5	

See Page 27 for explanation of footnotes and Page 28 for explanation of stability factors.

Arrows denote recent upgrades ▲ or downgrades ▼   (see Section VII for explanations)

102

www.weissratings.com

RISK ADJ. RATIO #1	CAPITAL RATIO #2	PREMIUM TO SURPLUS (%)	RESV. TO SURPLUS (%)	RESV. DEVELOP. 1 YEAR (%)	RESV. DEVELOP. 2 YEAR (%)	LOSS RATIO (%)	EXP. RATIO (%)	COMB RATIO (%)	CASH FROM UNDER-WRITING (%)	NET PREMIUM GROWTH (%)	INVEST. IN AFFIL (%)	INSURANCE COMPANY NAME
9.7	6.1	N/A	N/A	N/A	N/A	N/A	N/A	N/A	10.2	0.0	0.0	PELEUS INS CO
0.6	0.5	20.5	49.1	23.0	4.7	231.3	62.6	293.9	73.7	-22.3	0.0	PELICAN INS RRG
2.5	2.0	159.1	80.2	2.0	8.4	77.4	24.2	101.6	102.2	7.5	0.5 ●	PEMCO MUTUAL INS CO
14.1	12.7	N/A	N/A	N/A	N/A	N/A	N/A	N/A	-214.1	0.0	0.0	PENINSULA INDEMNITY CO
2.5	1.9	135.6	69.1	12.9	8.4	77.7	27.5	105.2	111.5	5.4	13.2	PENINSULA INS CO
2.2	1.3	0.3	0.3	-0.2	-0.2	72.5	49.4	121.9	71.0	-7.0	0.0	PENN CHARTER MUTL INS CO
6.0	5.4	N/A	49.9	6.6	1.4	N/A	N/A	N/A	-21.8	0.0	0.0	PENN MILLERS INS CO
4.0	2.7	102.5	102.1	0.6	0.8	65.6	33.4	99.0	103.6	2.5	0.0 ●	PENN NATIONAL SECURITY INS CO
4.5	2.9	36.9	9.1	N/A	N/A	79.4	3.3	82.7	122.6	4.8	0.0	PENN RESERVE INS CO LTD
1.0	0.9	37.7	44.7	0.3	-1.4	81.8	39.5	121.3	82.1	-11.7	62.0	PENN-AMERICA INS CO
1.2	0.7	100.0	118.5	0.9	-3.7	81.8	39.5	121.3	79.0	-5.2	0.0	PENN-PATRIOT INS CO
2.4	1.5	83.8	99.2	0.9	-3.8	81.8	39.5	121.3	80.6	-11.7	0.0	PENN-STAR INS CO
3.6	3.0	45.2	46.3	-0.5	2.3	50.2	21.9	72.1	213.0	20.6	0.0	PENNSYLVANIA INS CO
2.4	1.4	116.8	118.9	2.4	6.6	64.4	30.8	95.2	109.1	11.5	0.0	PENNSYLVANIA LUMBERMENS MUTUAL
2.9	1.9	53.0	89.1	3.5	8.4	76.4	23.1	99.5	125.2	14.5	0.0 ●	PENNSYLVANIA MANUFACTURERS ASN
2.3	1.6	70.1	117.9	4.4	10.2	76.4	22.9	99.3	113.1	14.5	0.0	PENNSYLVANIA MANUFACTURERS IND
1.6	1.5	54.7	54.5	0.3	0.4	65.6	33.4	99.0	97.9	2.5	35.0 ●	PENNSYLVANIA NTL MUTUAL CAS INS
N/A	N/A	--	--	--	--	--	--	--	--	--	--	PENNSYLVANIA PHYSICIANS RECIP INS
1.2	0.8	161.5	120.5	-17.1	-0.5	80.7	17.6	98.3	104.7	-4.4	0.0	PEOPLES TRUST INS CO
2.8	2.8	-67.0	N/A	-3.0	6.5	N/A	N/A	N/A	96.3	-144.5	36.3	PERMANENT GEN ASR CORP OF OHIO
10.1	9.1	-108.6	N/A	-2.3	6.0	N/A	N/A	N/A	97.2	-144.5	1.4	PERMANENT GENERAL ASR CORP
0.0	0.0	341.2	257.4	33.2	48.9	108.7	26.7	135.4	78.9	30.9	0.0	PERSONAL SERVICE INS CO
1.2	0.7	16.0	40.1	0.4	0.4	26.0	32.9	58.9	138.2	-24.6	0.0	PETROLEUM CAS CO
2.2	1.3	16.1	15.7	-2.2	-2.3	19.4	46.1	65.5	132.7	3.5	2.1	PETROLEUM MARKETERS MGMT INS CO
1.9	1.7	999 +	49.9	-49.2	-44.0	95.9	2.8	98.7	999 +	-375.3	0.0	PFD PHYSICIANS MED RRG A MUTL
3.8	2.6	76.9	74.4	-8.6	-8.7	66.1	34.6	100.7	95.6	-5.5	1.2	PHARMACISTS MUTUAL INS CO
1.7	1.2	115.5	98.7	4.9	2.1	83.5	41.8	125.3	86.9	1.1	0.0	PHENIX MUTUAL FIRE INS CO
1.3	1.1	12.9	8.1	-0.4	-0.6	65.8	36.6	102.4	99.6	4.9	52.1 ●	PHILADELPHIA CBSP FOR INS OF
3.5	2.1	40.3	23.9	-1.2	-1.7	64.1	28.1	92.2	114.6	4.9	0.0	PHILADELPHIA CONTRIBUTIONSHIP INS
2.4	1.8	130.6	184.1	-3.5	-6.7	63.7	29.2	92.9	125.5	5.3	0.0 ●	PHILADELPHIA INDEMNITY INS CO
4.7	3.9	18.2	1.7	N/A	N/A	11.3	67.4	78.7	259.8	0.0	0.0	PHILADELPHIA REINS CORP
3.7	2.3	12.0	39.7	-4.7	-7.6	86.2	41.8	128.0	70.3	5.6	0.0	PHOEBE RECIPROCAL RRG
0.1	0.1	378.0	273.0	49.1	32.3	71.3	27.2	98.5	133.5	0.0	0.0	PHOENIX FUND INC
1.7	1.5	70.3	115.1	-1.4	-2.4	69.5	29.2	98.7	108.8	4.9	25.3 ●	PHOENIX INS CO
0.5	0.4	137.6	159.3	36.7	98.5	60.3	50.8	111.1	28.5	-34.9	0.0	PHYSICIANS CASUALTY RRG INC
1.2	1.0	132.3	127.9	-15.4	-16.5	32.5	47.2	79.7	100.5	-7.7	0.0	PHYSICIANS IND RRG INC
4.3	3.2	32.4	75.5	-7.7	-15.8	81.0	19.7	100.7	78.1	3.7	2.9 ●	PHYSICIANS INS A MUTL CO
0.4	0.3	92.3	91.4	7.9	2.9	72.3	47.0	119.3	100.3	6.4	0.0	PHYSICIANS INS CO
0.9	0.7	93.2	278.9	-29.6	-15.2	89.4	17.1	106.5	108.0	15.0	0.0	PHYSICIANS INS MUTUAL
1.4	0.8	25.2	96.4	-2.4	-29.7	58.5	56.8	115.3	66.6	-12.6	0.0	PHYSICIANS INS PROGRAM
0.6	0.5	33.0	136.3	1.7	4.0	79.2	23.0	102.2	162.5	18.9	0.0	PHYSICIANS PROACTIVE PROTECTION
3.2	2.8	20.3	47.6	-10.7	-16.9	44.4	68.0	112.4	57.3	-7.5	0.0	PHYSICIANS PROFESSIONAL LIABILTY
-0.4	-0.3	-57.3	-453.7	5.1	-130.6	69.6	37.7	107.3	61.6	-36.1	0.0	PHYSICIANS RECIPROCAL INSURERS
0.8	0.6	17.1	152.8	-31.8	-77.4	37.2	80.8	118.0	91.3	-10.2	0.0	PHYSICIANS REIMBURSEMENT FUND
N/A	N/A	--	--	--	--	--	--	--	--	--	--	PHYSICIANS SPECIALTY LTD RRG
9.8	8.0	4.9	15.7	7.6	7.0	305.3	30.2	335.5	35.4	-0.8	0.0	PHYSICIANS STANDARD INS CO
2.4	1.7	55.5	6.4	-3.6	-3.1	37.3	49.7	87.0	111.9	5.5	0.0	PIEDMONT MUTUAL INS CO
3.6	2.1	29.9	25.4	-11.9	0.8	23.4	14.5	37.9	248.7	13.9	0.0	PIH INS CO A RECIP RRG
1.4	1.0	152.8	82.7	-5.7	-8.2	74.1	23.1	97.2	123.9	3.1	0.0	PILGRIM INS CO
1.5	1.0	61.7	189.4	-23.9	-37.4	61.0	35.7	96.7	97.3	4.9	0.0	PINNACLEPOINT INS CO
3.3	2.4	92.4	73.2	-2.4	-3.5	67.5	30.5	98.0	95.0	-6.1	0.0	PIONEER SPECIALTY INS CO
5.1	3.2	57.1	27.9	-5.6	-7.2	60.3	29.4	89.7	117.2	5.4	0.0 ●	PIONEER STATE MUTUAL INS CO

999 + Denotes number greater than 999.9%
999 - Denotes number less than -999.99%
● Bullets denote a more detailed analysis is available in Section II.

INSURANCE COMPANY NAME	DOM. STATE	RATING	TOTAL ASSETS ($MIL)	CAPITAL & SURPLUS ($MIL)	ANNUAL NET PREMIUM ($MIL)	NET INCOME ($MIL)	CAPITAL-IZATION INDEX (PTS)	RESERVE ADQ INDEX (PTS)	PROFIT-ABILITY INDEX (PTS)	LIQUIDITY INDEX (PTS)	STAB. INDEX (PTS)	STABILITY FACTORS
PLANS LIABILITY INS CO	OH	C	106.7	48.4	1.3	-21.4	1.0	2.0	2.7	8.6	3.3	CDFG
PLATEAU CASUALTY INS CO	TN	C+	45.8	22.4	22.0	2.0	7.5	6.0	8.4	6.5	4.4	DR
▼PLATINUM TRANSPORT INS RRG INC	HI	E-	9.6	-2.1	6.5	-3.6	0.0	3.7	0.2	7.3	0.1	CDGT
PLATTE RIVER INS CO	NE	C	150.8	48.3	40.7	1.9	8.1	4.7	5.1	7.1	3.6	R
▲PLAZA INS CO	IA	B-	65.6	27.7	0.0	0.3	10.0	N/A	6.5	8.1	4.9	FR
▲PLICO INC	OK	C+	110.3	81.9	5.6	1.9	10.0	9.8	6.9	10.0	4.5	R
PLYMOUTH ROCK ASR CORP	MA	B-	684.2	222.5	376.3	15.9	7.5	6.6	6.7	5.7	4.7	R
PMI INS CO	AZ	F	119.4	59.9	18.9	10.9	9.0	4.9	4.1	6.8	0.0	DRT
PMI MORTGAGE INS CO	AZ	F	837.8	-1,367.7	125.8	90.4	0.0	4.9	0.9	7.0	0.0	CFRT
PODIATRY INS CO OF AM	IL	C+	303.2	112.8	56.8	4.3	8.3	9.3	3.8	7.4	4.6	A
▲POINT GUARD INS CO	PR	C	72.1	23.7	53.7	18.5	4.3	4.3	4.2	5.2	3.5	CG
POLICYHOLDERS MUTUAL INS CO	WI	U	--	--	--	--	N/A	--	--	--	--	Z
PONCE DE LEON LTC RRG INC	FL	U	--	--	--	--	N/A	--	--	--	--	Z
POSITIVE PHYSICIANS INS	PA	C	59.0	16.9	13.1	-0.4	5.2	9.9	5.5	7.4	3.7	DGR
POTOMAC INS CO	PA	U	--	--	--	--	N/A	--	--	--	--	Z
PRAETORIAN INS CO	PA	C	453.9	211.8	146.4	-10.1	8.9	5.3	2.4	6.5	4.1	FRT
▲PRE-PAID LEGAL CAS INC	OK	C+	19.7	16.5	47.9	6.1	6.3	7.2	6.9	2.3	3.8	DL
PREFERRED AUTO INS CO	TN	D+	9.7	3.3	3.3	0.1	8.1	9.3	6.1	8.7	2.1	DR
PREFERRED CONTRACTORS INS CO RRG	MT	E	116.3	13.1	7.8	-0.9	0.0	0.3	3.3	6.7	0.1	CDFR
PREFERRED EMPLOYERS INS CO	CA	C	106.2	46.9	0.0	0.9	10.0	N/A	7.0	7.0	4.2	R
PREFERRED MUTUAL INS CO	NY	B	568.1	243.9	249.8	11.7	9.9	8.2	8.5	6.6	6.2	T
▲PREFERRED PROFESSIONAL INS CO	NE	B+	327.4	182.3	33.1	4.6	10.0	9.4	7.6	7.5	6.5	F
PREFERRED PROFESSIONAL RRG	DC	U	--	--	--	--	N/A	--	--	--	--	Z
▲PREMIER GROUP INS CO	TN	B	59.0	38.9	16.9	3.9	9.6	8.7	8.9	7.4	5.3	D
PREMIER INS EXCHANGE RRG	VT	U (5)	--	--	--	--	N/A	--	--	--	--	Z
PREPARED INS CO	FL	D	69.1	20.0	21.3	-15.9	4.3	3.4	2.3	7.5	1.9	DFT
PREVISOR INS CO	CO	C-	10.2	7.9	0.5	-0.7	9.4	3.6	3.3	10.0	2.2	DFGT
PRIME INS CO	IL	B-	127.6	63.4	58.1	7.2	7.1	4.7	8.9	6.9	3.9	GRT
PRIME P&C INS INC	IL	C+	52.3	19.1	28.1	3.4	5.1	4.0	6.5	7.0	3.1	CDGT
▲PRIMEONE INS CO	UT	C-	20.3	8.3	2.5	0.2	7.3	7.0	2.7	7.0	2.2	DT
▲PRIMERO INS CO	NV	C+	16.9	8.9	10.8	0.2	7.6	8.3	3.8	5.8	4.2	DR
PRINCETON EXCESS & SURPLUS LINES INS	DE	C	167.5	65.2	0.0	7.3	10.0	N/A	7.7	6.9	3.6	FR
PRINCETON INS CO	NJ	C	723.1	509.3	28.5	13.3	10.0	8.4	7.7	10.0	3.8	FR
PRIORITY ONE INS CO	TX	C	17.7	10.8	4.1	0.5	8.6	4.3	2.8	6.9	3.7	DFRT
▲PRIVILEGE UNDERWRITERS RECIP EXCH	FL	B	568.0	227.6	208.4	-7.0	7.6	5.5	3.8	6.2	5.5	FGT
PROAIR RRG INC	NV	F (5)	0.5	0.0	0.2	0.0	7.1	6.5	0.1	2.6	0.0	LT
PROASSURANCE CASUALTY CO	MI	C	990.0	294.9	170.4	33.5	8.2	9.5	2.5	7.0	3.7	AR
PROASSURANCE INDEMNTIY CO INC	AL	C-	1,081.0	348.8	187.0	73.2	8.4	9.5	2.3	6.9	3.1	AR
PROASSURANCE SPECIALTY INS CO INC	AL	C	57.0	33.5	0.0	3.3	10.0	N/A	6.2	6.7	3.7	FT
PROBUILDERS SPECIALTY INS CO RRG	DC	U	--	--	--	--	N/A	--	--	--	--	Z
PROCENTURY INS CO	MI	C-	59.9	58.3	0.0	2.4	10.0	1.9	5.4	3.7	3.3	FLRT
PRODUCERS AGRICULTURE INS CO	TX	C	448.8	61.7	0.0	-0.3	10.0	4.5	4.4	0.3	3.9	LRT
PRODUCERS LLOYDS INS CO	TX	C	11.1	6.1	0.0	0.0	10.0	N/A	5.5	10.0	3.6	DFGR
PROFESSIONAL CASUALTY ASSN	PA	C-	36.3	13.6	6.3	0.6	7.1	7.0	6.8	7.2	3.1	DFRT
PROFESSIONAL EXCHANGE ASR CO (A	HI	D	12.7	5.9	3.7	1.5	1.8	6.0	7.9	4.0	1.8	CDL
PROFESSIONAL INS EXCHANGE MUTUAL	UT	C-	8.7	5.5	1.2	0.2	7.4	5.7	6.6	9.1	2.4	D
PROFESSIONAL QUALITY LIABILITY INS	VT	U	--	--	--	--	N/A	--	--	--	--	Z
▲PROFESSIONAL SECURITY INS CO	AZ	B-	82.3	70.3	0.0	1.8	10.0	3.6	5.2	10.0	4.0	FT
PROFESSIONAL SOLUTIONS INS CO	IA	C	24.1	8.4	3.4	0.2	6.2	9.0	3.1	8.6	3.9	DR
PROFESSIONALS ADVOCATE INS CO	MD	B-	142.4	116.1	3.7	4.4	10.0	8.0	8.4	7.7	4.6	DF
PROFESSIONALS RRG INC	MT	D	2.8	1.3	0.4	0.1	8.3	6.9	3.2	9.5	1.1	DT
PROGRESSIVE ADVANCED INS CO	OH	C	530.4	224.5	380.1	14.6	8.4	7.4	8.5	1.8	3.7	LR

See Page 27 for explanation of footnotes and
Page 28 for explanation of stability factors.
Arrows denote recent upgrades ▲ or downgrades ▼   (see Section VII for explanations)

104

www.weissratings.com

RISK ADJ. RATIO #1	CAPITAL RATIO #2	PREMIUM TO SURPLUS (%)	RESV. TO SURPLUS (%)	RESV. DEVELOP. 1 YEAR (%)	RESV. DEVELOP. 2 YEAR (%)	LOSS RATIO (%)	EXP. RATIO (%)	COMB RATIO (%)	CASH FROM UNDER-WRITING (%)	NET PREMIUM GROWTH (%)	INVEST. IN AFFIL (%)	INSURANCE COMPANY NAME
0.3	0.2	2.7	108.7	64.6	62.6	999 +	160.8	999 +	16.5	-56.9	0.0	PLANS LIABILITY INS CO
1.5	1.4	98.2	10.5	3.5	2.3	60.4	29.4	89.8	111.2	1.2	33.3	PLATEAU CASUALTY INS CO
-0.1	-0.0	-308.3	-292.0	63.9	-1.6	132.8	32.0	164.8	156.1	70.3	0.0	PLATINUM TRANSPORT INS RRG INC
2.9	1.7	84.3	82.1	-0.5	-1.6	55.9	43.1	99.0	122.0	8.4	0.0	PLATTE RIVER INS CO
5.0	4.5	N/A	N/A	N/A	N/A	N/A	N/A	N/A	-272.3	0.0	0.0	PLAZA INS CO
7.1	4.4	6.8	18.9	-2.8	-3.4	60.1	29.1	89.2	-297.7	4.0	0.5	PLICO INC
1.9	1.4	169.1	91.5	-6.5	-9.2	74.1	23.2	97.3	106.7	3.1	0.0 ●	PLYMOUTH ROCK ASR CORP
3.1	2.3	31.5	35.7	5.6	11.8	23.9	35.0	58.9	107.7	-17.7	0.0	PMI INS CO
-1.2	-0.8	-9.2	-148.9	3.9	9.3	67.7	-18.1	49.6	51.2	-24.0	7.3	PMI MORTGAGE INS CO
2.6	1.8	50.4	126.7	-1.6	-7.8	89.5	15.5	105.0	115.1	26.5	0.0	PODIATRY INS CO OF AM
0.7	0.7	227.0	35.6	4.7	1.2	77.1	-9.9	67.2	101.1	8.0	0.0	POINT GUARD INS CO
N/A	N/A	--	--	--	--	--	--	--	--	--	--	POLICYHOLDERS MUTUAL INS CO
N/A	N/A	--	--	--	--	--	--	--	--	--	--	PONCE DE LEON LTC RRG INC
0.9	0.8	77.3	191.1	-15.0	-42.1	62.2	50.4	112.6	134.3	37.8	0.0	POSITIVE PHYSICIANS INS
N/A	N/A	--	--	--	--	--	--	--	--	--	--	POTOMAC INS CO
4.1	2.6	69.1	57.8	-2.3	-7.7	75.6	36.0	111.6	89.6	139.6	0.0	PRAETORIAN INS CO
1.3	1.0	289.9	0.5	-0.5	-0.3	38.6	43.6	82.2	121.6	3.2	0.0	PRE-PAID LEGAL CAS INC
1.9	1.7	101.0	78.2	-4.9	-6.1	89.0	5.4	94.4	121.2	15.4	0.0	PREFERRED AUTO INS CO
0.0	0.0	59.8	550.6	174.7	248.6	268.4	-191.7	76.7	14.6	-13.7	0.0	PREFERRED CONTRACTORS INS CO
6.5	5.8	N/A	N/A	N/A	N/A	N/A	N/A	N/A	100.1	0.0	0.0	PREFERRED EMPLOYERS INS CO
4.5	2.9	102.4	60.6	-0.5	-2.1	64.4	32.7	97.1	103.4	17.2	0.0 ●	PREFERRED MUTUAL INS CO
5.9	4.2	18.1	52.5	-1.4	-12.5	80.4	27.5	107.9	77.9	-33.4	0.4 ●	PREFERRED PROFESSIONAL INS CO
N/A	N/A	--	--	--	--	--	--	--	--	--	--	PREFERRED PROFESSIONAL RRG
3.5	2.9	43.5	42.8	-6.1	-8.6	45.8	25.9	71.7	137.3	8.7	0.0	PREMIER GROUP INS CO
N/A	N/A	--	--	--	--	--	--	--	--	--	--	PREMIER INS EXCHANGE RRG
0.9	0.5	106.5	91.3	19.5	17.8	141.0	43.8	184.8	59.3	-18.4	0.0	PREPARED INS CO
3.1	2.6	5.7	6.5	-0.2	-0.3	146.5	130.8	277.3	-18.1	97.5	0.0	PREVISOR INS CO
1.4	1.0	91.6	41.6	3.3	8.8	50.7	21.8	72.5	179.8	92.0	17.7	PRIME INS CO
1.0	0.7	147.0	50.0	N/A	5.3	46.1	13.1	59.2	418.9	231.0	0.0	PRIME P&C INS INC
2.5	1.5	29.6	24.6	-2.5	-16.4	66.1	31.3	97.4	143.5	11.9	0.0	PRIMEONE INS CO
1.5	1.4	121.4	65.0	-1.1	-3.3	82.4	17.4	99.8	89.9	0.5	0.0	PRIMERO INS CO
7.2	6.5	N/A	N/A	N/A	N/A	N/A	N/A	N/A	49.7	0.0	0.0	PRINCETON EXCESS & SURPLUS LINES
7.1	5.0	5.6	27.1	-2.0	-3.7	61.0	17.0	78.0	77.6	-2.0	0.0 ●	PRINCETON INS CO
3.2	2.6	38.5	30.0	-4.2	5.7	50.4	50.7	101.1	79.8	-32.9	12.1	PRIORITY ONE INS CO
2.7	1.7	91.6	24.7	2.3	5.7	69.1	39.6	108.7	94.7	27.4	1.1 ●	PRIVILEGE UNDERWRITERS RECIP
0.0	0.0	44.4	12.2	-1.6	-3.5	64.5	81.9	146.4	101.6	70.3	0.0	PROAIR RRG INC
2.3	1.7	57.8	184.9	-9.5	-19.9	66.8	28.9	95.7	107.3	8.3	0.0 ●	PROASSURANCE CASUALTY CO
2.6	1.9	53.6	166.1	-12.9	-20.7	53.0	19.5	72.5	104.1	-5.5	1.2 ●	PROASSURANCE INDEMNTIY CO INC
8.6	7.7	N/A	20.3	N/A	N/A	N/A	N/A	N/A	999 +	0.0	0.0	PROASSURANCE SPECIALTY INS CO INC
N/A	N/A	--	--	--	--	--	--	--	--	--	--	PROBUILDERS SPECIALTY INS CO RRG
35.9	18.0	N/A	N/A	N/A	N/A	N/A	N/A	N/A	47.0	0.0	0.0	PROCENTURY INS CO
5.2	3.0	N/A	N/A	N/A	N/A	N/A	N/A	N/A	99.8	0.0	0.0	PRODUCERS AGRICULTURE INS CO
3.9	3.5	N/A	N/A	N/A	N/A	N/A	N/A	N/A	-226.5	0.0	0.0	PRODUCERS LLOYDS INS CO
1.5	1.3	46.5	125.9	-3.1	-15.2	54.2	52.9	107.1	46.1	-35.8	0.0	PROFESSIONAL CASUALTY ASSN
0.7	0.4	63.7	120.6	-35.3	-8.9	31.6	28.5	60.1	286.3	-17.7	0.0	PROFESSIONAL EXCHANGE ASR CO (A
2.0	1.2	22.7	46.1	-1.7	-2.3	71.9	45.8	117.7	112.8	2.5	0.0	PROFESSIONAL INS EXCHANGE MUTUAL
N/A	N/A	--	--	--	--	--	--	--	--	--	--	PROFESSIONAL QUALITY LIABILITY INS
12.2	7.0	N/A	N/A	N/A	N/A	N/A	N/A	N/A	486.9	0.0	0.0	PROFESSIONAL SECURITY INS CO
1.2	0.9	40.9	102.9	-8.7	-14.1	81.8	17.5	99.3	105.2	5.8	0.0	PROFESSIONAL SOLUTIONS INS CO
8.3	5.0	3.2	10.0	-0.8	-2.6	70.8	28.7	99.5	41.8	-29.1	0.0	PROFESSIONALS ADVOCATE INS CO
2.3	2.1	28.4	51.5	-12.8	-10.9	30.9	33.0	63.9	299.9	-1.1	0.0	PROFESSIONALS RRG INC
2.1	1.9	169.3	63.5	-0.1	-0.3	73.6	19.1	92.7	104.9	15.8	0.0 ●	PROGRESSIVE ADVANCED INS CO

999 + Denotes number greater than 999.9%
999 - Denotes number less than -999.99%
● Bullets denote a more detailed analysis is available in Section II.

INSURANCE COMPANY NAME	DOM. STATE	RATING	TOTAL ASSETS ($MIL)	CAPITAL & SURPLUS ($MIL)	ANNUAL NET PREMIUM ($MIL)	NET INCOME ($MIL)	CAPITAL-IZATION INDEX (PTS)	RESERVE ADQ INDEX (PTS)	PROFIT-ABILITY INDEX (PTS)	LIQUIDITY INDEX (PTS)	STAB. INDEX (PTS)	STABILITY FACTORS
PROGRESSIVE AMERICAN INS CO	OH	C	585.9	250.3	268.8	11.1	10.0	4.6	8.2	6.4	3.8	FR
PROGRESSIVE BAYSIDE INS CO	OH	C	148.4	42.6	134.4	6.7	7.3	4.7	8.9	5.0	3.5	R
PROGRESSIVE CASUALTY INS CO	OH	B-	8,431.2	2,124.8	6,584.7	370.4	5.8	4.7	9.3	2.4	4.5	LR
PROGRESSIVE CHOICE INS CO	OH	U	--	--	--	--	N/A	--	--	--	--	Z
PROGRESSIVE CLASSIC INS CO	WI	C	452.0	124.9	403.1	16.3	7.2	4.7	8.9	4.1	3.8	LR
PROGRESSIVE COMMERCIAL CASUALTY	OH	U	--	--	--	--	N/A	--	--	--	--	Z
▲PROGRESSIVE COUNTY MUTUAL INS CO	TX	C-	671.6	5.0	0.0	0.0	1.2	N/A	3.9	9.1	3.2	CFR
▲PROGRESSIVE DIRECT INS CO	OH	B-	7,785.7	2,352.7	7,364.1	402.7	7.2	7.5	8.9	1.9	4.5	LR
PROGRESSIVE EXPRESS INS CO	OH	C	251.4	62.5	45.8	1.1	10.0	5.0	7.0	5.6	3.6	FR
PROGRESSIVE FREEDOM INS CO	OH	U	--	--	--	--	N/A	--	--	--	--	Z
PROGRESSIVE GARDEN STATE INS CO	NJ	B	319.8	68.3	63.0	5.5	9.7	6.3	8.8	6.6	6.1	
PROGRESSIVE GULF INS CO	OH	C	313.7	85.4	268.8	14.6	7.3	4.7	7.7	2.8	3.6	LR
PROGRESSIVE HAWAII INS CORP	OH	C	218.5	67.4	204.4	16.7	7.6	9.3	9.6	5.2	3.6	R
PROGRESSIVE MARATHON INS CO	MI	C	594.9	186.0	570.1	29.4	7.1	7.5	9.0	1.7	3.8	LR
PROGRESSIVE MAX INS CO	OH	C	568.7	178.2	570.1	29.9	7.1	7.5	8.9	3.0	3.8	LR
PROGRESSIVE MICHIGAN INS CO	MI	C	618.5	178.2	537.5	28.2	7.3	4.7	8.9	5.1	3.8	R
PROGRESSIVE MOUNTAIN INS CO	OH	C	353.8	88.3	134.4	10.1	9.0	4.6	8.9	6.7	3.7	FR
PROGRESSIVE NORTHERN INS CO	WI	C+	1,866.5	531.4	1,612.6	91.7	7.2	4.7	9.0	3.7	4.4	LR
PROGRESSIVE NORTHWESTERN INS CO	OH	C+	1,812.5	521.2	1,612.6	85.8	7.2	4.7	8.9	5.0	4.4	R
PROGRESSIVE PALOVERDE INS CO	IN	C	161.1	56.1	47.5	2.5	9.7	7.3	8.3	6.5	3.6	R
PROGRESSIVE PREFERRED INS CO	OH	C	931.1	254.0	806.3	43.6	7.2	4.7	8.9	3.1	3.9	LR
PROGRESSIVE PREMIER INS CO OF IL	OH	C	326.6	80.5	190.0	8.5	7.6	7.5	8.9	5.6	4.0	R
▲PROGRESSIVE PROPERTY INS CO	FL	B	91.7	41.6	34.3	5.9	7.9	8.6	6.9	6.6	5.5	DFT
PROGRESSIVE SECURITY INS CO	LA	C	223.3	51.4	45.3	4.8	10.0	6.1	4.6	6.5	3.6	R
PROGRESSIVE SELECT INS CO	OH	C	850.0	222.1	183.3	5.2	10.0	6.0	7.7	4.7	3.9	FLR
PROGRESSIVE SOUTHEASTERN INS CO	IN	C	210.9	74.5	134.4	7.7	8.0	4.6	8.9	2.6	4.0	LR
PROGRESSIVE SPECIALTY INS CO	OH	C	1,166.3	366.4	940.7	63.7	7.5	4.7	7.4	2.9	4.0	LR
PROGRESSIVE UNIVERSAL INS CO	WI	C	440.3	143.4	380.1	22.4	7.4	7.5	8.9	1.3	3.8	LR
PROGRESSIVE WEST INS CO	OH	C	136.1	33.1	29.7	2.8	9.6	5.9	5.5	6.5	3.5	R
▲PROPERTY-OWNERS INS CO	IN	A-	302.7	137.0	125.8	11.9	7.5	5.6	8.6	6.1	7.0	
PROTECTION MUTUAL INS CO	PA	U	--	--	--	--	N/A	--	--	--	--	Z
PROTECTIVE INS CO	IN	A-	885.6	420.4	330.1	20.3	7.2	5.9	7.7	6.3	7.0	
PROTECTIVE P&C INS CO	MO	B-	385.5	169.9	55.8	17.2	10.0	6.4	8.8	6.9	4.9	R
PROTECTIVE SPECIALTY INS CO	IN	B	66.2	60.8	0.1	0.7	10.0	4.3	5.5	10.0	4.8	DT
PROTUCKET INSURANCE CO	RI	U	--	--	--	--	N/A	--	--	--	--	Z
PROVIDENCE MUTUAL FIRE INS CO	RI	B-	207.0	102.0	81.7	4.0	8.7	7.9	4.7	6.5	4.7	R
PROVIDENCE PLANTATIONS INS CO	RI	U (5)	--	--	--	--	N/A	--	--	--	--	Z
PROVIDENCE WASHINGTON INS CO	RI	U	--	--	--	--	N/A	--	--	--	--	Z
PUBLIC SERVICE INS CO	IL	F (4)	295.1	28.3	46.6	-51.3	0.0	1.1	0.2	0.4	0.0	CDFL
▲PUBLIC UTILITY MUTUAL INS CO RRG	VT	E+	7.6	6.7	1.0	0.6	10.0	9.3	8.6	7.6	0.5	DR
PUERTO RICO MED DEFENSE INS CO	PR	D (2)	18.3	4.1	3.2	0.5	2.2	3.5	8.0	7.4	2.2	CDGT
PURE INS CO	FL	B	370.9	189.0	208.4	-10.9	7.6	5.6	3.6	6.3	5.6	T
PYMATUNING MUTUAL FIRE INS CO	PA	D+	3.3	3.2	0.0	-0.1	10.0	N/A	3.1	10.0	2.1	DFT
QBE INS CORP	PA	B	2,054.3	678.0	890.9	-23.7	7.6	5.8	2.9	5.8	5.5	F
QBE REINS CORP	PA	B	1,031.4	773.0	177.0	-3.3	7.5	6.2	3.9	6.4	5.2	F
QBE SEGUROS	PR	D (1)	103.8	15.3	16.8	-0.5	2.3	4.6	3.0	7.0	2.0	CDFR
QBE SPECIALTY INS CO	ND	C-	363.4	117.0	146.4	-5.1	7.8	5.6	2.3	6.2	3.3	FR
QUALITAS INS CO	CA	D	72.6	16.6	35.2	-1.0	1.2	4.3	3.9	6.1	1.5	CDRT
QUALITY CASUALTY INS CO	AL	U	--	--	--	--	N/A	--	--	--	--	Z
QUEEN CITY ASR INC	VT	U (5)	--	--	--	--	N/A	--	--	--	--	Z
QUINCY MUTUAL FIRE INS CO	MA	B	1,774.9	1,190.6	307.0	47.1	9.6	8.0	7.6	6.9	4.7	R
R&Q REINS CO	PA	C	203.5	34.9	0.3	-4.6	0.1	2.2	2.9	9.1	3.5	CDFG

See Page 27 for explanation of footnotes and   106   www.weissratings.com
Page 28 for explanation of stability factors.
Arrows denote recent upgrades ▲ or downgrades ▼   (see Section VII for explanations)

RISK ADJ. RATIO #1	CAPITAL RATIO #2	PREMIUM TO SURPLUS (%)	RESV. TO SURPLUS (%)	RESV. DEVELOP. 1 YEAR (%)	RESV. DEVELOP. 2 YEAR (%)	LOSS RATIO (%)	EXP. RATIO (%)	COMB RATIO (%)	CASH FROM UNDER-WRITING (%)	NET PREMIUM GROWTH (%)	INVEST. IN AFFIL (%)	INSURANCE COMPANY NAME
3.8	3.4	107.4	42.9	0.2	N/A	72.8	19.1	91.9	99.1	17.3	0.0 •	PROGRESSIVE AMERICAN INS CO
1.3	1.1	315.6	126.0	0.5	N/A	72.8	19.7	92.5	118.8	17.3	0.0	PROGRESSIVE BAYSIDE INS CO
1.0	0.8	309.9	123.7	0.5	N/A	72.8	20.2	93.0	119.2	17.3	16.0 •	PROGRESSIVE CASUALTY INS CO
N/A	N/A	--	--	--	--	--	--	--	--	--	--	PROGRESSIVE CHOICE INS CO
1.2	1.1	322.8	128.9	0.5	N/A	72.8	19.4	92.2	115.1	17.3	0.0	PROGRESSIVE CLASSIC INS CO
N/A	N/A	--	--	--	--	--	--	--	--	--	--	PROGRESSIVE COMMERCIAL CASUALTY
0.4	0.2	N/A	N/A	N/A	N/A	N/A	N/A	N/A	-3.4	0.0	0.0	PROGRESSIVE COUNTY MUTUAL INS CO
1.2	1.1	313.0	117.4	-0.2	-0.5	73.6	18.8	92.4	116.8	15.8	0.0 •	PROGRESSIVE DIRECT INS CO
5.6	3.7	73.3	57.7	2.1	2.8	79.1	17.9	97.0	82.4	2.1	0.0	PROGRESSIVE EXPRESS INS CO
N/A	N/A	--	--	--	--	--	--	--	--	--	--	PROGRESSIVE FREEDOM INS CO
3.1	2.8	92.2	55.0	-2.6	-3.3	73.3	15.0	88.3	121.8	9.7	0.0	PROGRESSIVE GARDEN STATE INS CO
1.3	1.1	314.6	125.6	0.5	N/A	72.8	18.6	91.4	108.9	17.3	0.0	PROGRESSIVE GULF INS CO
1.6	1.3	303.5	107.6	6.0	-2.2	69.2	18.5	87.7	118.4	10.4	0.0	PROGRESSIVE HAWAII INS CORP
1.1	1.0	306.6	115.0	-0.2	-0.4	73.6	18.4	92.0	112.8	15.8	0.0	PROGRESSIVE MARATHON INS CO
1.1	1.0	319.9	120.0	-0.2	-0.5	73.6	18.8	92.4	117.1	15.8	0.0	PROGRESSIVE MAX INS CO
1.3	1.2	301.7	120.4	0.5	N/A	72.8	19.5	92.3	113.7	17.3	0.0	PROGRESSIVE MICHIGAN INS CO
2.6	2.3	152.2	60.7	0.2	N/A	72.8	16.6	89.4	86.7	17.3	0.0	PROGRESSIVE MOUNTAIN INS CO
1.3	1.1	303.5	121.2	0.5	N/A	72.8	19.1	91.9	115.6	17.3	0.0 •	PROGRESSIVE NORTHERN INS CO
1.3	1.1	309.4	123.5	0.5	N/A	72.8	19.5	92.3	117.8	17.3	0.0 •	PROGRESSIVE NORTHWESTERN INS CO
3.0	2.7	84.6	31.8	-0.1	-0.1	73.6	19.8	93.4	98.6	15.8	0.0	PROGRESSIVE PALOVERDE INS CO
1.3	1.1	317.4	126.7	0.5	N/A	72.8	19.0	91.8	113.3	17.3	0.0 •	PROGRESSIVE PREFERRED INS CO
1.5	1.4	236.0	88.6	-0.2	-0.4	73.6	19.5	93.1	107.3	15.8	0.0	PROGRESSIVE PREMIER INS CO OF IL
2.6	2.1	82.5	27.5	-3.5	-3.2	50.3	37.6	87.9	71.3	-43.3	0.0	PROGRESSIVE PROPERTY INS CO
4.2	3.7	88.2	30.7	1.0	1.2	73.1	17.2	90.3	120.3	8.2	0.0	PROGRESSIVE SECURITY INS CO
3.9	3.6	82.5	31.3	0.7	1.3	78.6	16.4	95.0	93.2	17.6	0.0	PROGRESSIVE SELECT INS CO
1.8	1.6	180.4	72.0	0.3	N/A	72.8	17.0	89.8	102.0	17.3	0.0	PROGRESSIVE SOUTHEASTERN INS CO
1.5	1.3	256.7	102.5	0.5	N/A	72.8	18.8	91.6	116.6	17.3	0.0 •	PROGRESSIVE SPECIALTY INS CO
1.3	1.2	265.0	99.4	-0.2	-0.4	73.6	16.9	90.5	112.3	15.8	0.0	PROGRESSIVE UNIVERSAL INS CO
3.0	2.7	89.5	33.0	-0.9	1.3	68.0	20.1	88.1	119.6	7.0	0.0	PROGRESSIVE WEST INS CO
2.2	1.3	91.8	44.8	-2.7	-2.6	56.2	33.8	90.0	117.9	5.2	0.0 •	PROPERTY-OWNERS INS CO
N/A	N/A	--	--	--	--	--	--	--	--	--	--	PROTECTION MUTUAL INS CO
1.5	1.1	78.5	81.7	4.4	8.1	74.9	30.1	105.0	108.7	29.1	24.5 •	PROTECTIVE INS CO
8.2	4.9	32.9	6.3	-0.3	-2.5	68.7	20.0	88.7	106.3	-9.6	0.0	PROTECTIVE P&C INS CO
7.4	5.0	0.2	8.8	1.7	3.9	59.7	261.5	321.2	53.4	-90.4	0.0	PROTECTIVE SPECIALTY INS CO
N/A	N/A	--	--	--	--	--	--	--	--	--	--	PROTUCKET INSURANCE CO
3.4	2.1	80.1	48.0	-6.3	-5.1	57.8	39.4	97.2	105.0	3.6	0.6	PROVIDENCE MUTUAL FIRE INS CO
N/A	N/A	--	--	--	--	--	--	--	--	--	--	PROVIDENCE PLANTATIONS INS CO
N/A	N/A	--	--	--	--	--	--	--	--	--	--	PROVIDENCE WASHINGTON INS CO
0.1	0.0	164.9	999 +	32.2	53.8	95.5	133.2	228.7	50.6	-53.4	6.2	PUBLIC SERVICE INS CO
8.4	5.4	14.3	11.0	-8.0	-8.0	4.5	51.3	55.8	168.3	2.4	0.0	PUBLIC UTILITY MUTUAL INS CO RRG
0.9	0.6	85.9	250.0	N/A	-0.1	68.5	39.0	107.5	149.3	-49.6	0.0	PUERTO RICO MED DEFENSE INS CO
2.2	1.4	110.3	29.8	2.4	3.7	68.8	39.4	108.2	103.7	27.4	1.2	PURE INS CO
42.4	40.2	0.1	N/A	N/A	N/A	530.6	999 +	999 +	17.1	-64.4	0.0	PYMATUNING MUTUAL FIRE INS CO
2.1	1.4	131.4	109.8	-4.2	-15.5	75.6	31.2	106.8	85.9	5.2	8.8 •	QBE INS CORP
1.3	1.3	22.9	19.1	-0.7	-2.8	75.6	31.0	106.6	81.3	20.0	71.4 •	QBE REINS CORP
0.6	0.3	119.6	66.3	-39.6	-9.0	37.7	82.2	119.9	70.4	-49.7	0.0	QBE SEGUROS
2.4	1.5	125.2	104.6	-4.1	-10.2	75.6	31.2	106.8	90.8	94.0	0.0	QBE SPECIALTY INS CO
0.4	0.2	212.0	193.4	20.0	8.3	75.3	36.4	111.7	128.6	-14.8	0.0	QUALITAS INS CO
N/A	N/A	--	--	--	--	--	--	--	--	--	--	QUALITY CASUALTY INS CO
N/A	N/A	--	--	--	--	--	--	--	--	--	--	QUEEN CITY ASR INC
4.6	2.9	25.8	21.3	-2.2	-3.6	69.2	35.8	105.0	110.6	-0.2	3.4 •	QUINCY MUTUAL FIRE INS CO
0.3	0.1	0.7	467.6	3.9	-51.6	999 +	485.0	999 +	1.2	N/A	0.0	R&Q REINS CO

999 + Denotes number greater than 999.9%
999 - Denotes number less than -999.99%
• Bullets denote a more detailed analysis is available in Section II.

INSURANCE COMPANY NAME	DOM. STATE	RATING	TOTAL ASSETS ($MIL)	CAPITAL & SURPLUS ($MIL)	ANNUAL NET PREMIUM ($MIL)	NET INCOME ($MIL)	CAPITAL-IZATION INDEX (PTS)	RESERVE ADQ INDEX (PTS)	PROFIT-ABILITY INDEX (PTS)	LIQUIDITY INDEX (PTS)	STAB. INDEX (PTS)	STABILITY FACTORS
R&Q RI INSURANCE CO	RI	U	--	--	--	--	N/A	--	--	--	--	Z
RADIAN GUARANTY INC	PA	D+	4,071.2	1,201.0	706.8	445.1	8.6	4.6	3.5	6.9	2.4	AR
RADIAN GUARANTY REINS INC	PA	U	--	--	--	--	N/A	--	--	--	--	Z
RADIAN INS INC	PA	D+	22.5	19.8	0.5	0.0	10.0	8.9	2.8	10.0	2.4	DFT
RADIAN INVESTOR SURETY INC	PA	U	--	--	--	--	N/A	--	--	--	--	Z
RADIAN MORTGAGE ASR INC	PA	U	--	--	--	--	N/A	--	--	--	--	Z
RADIAN MORTGAGE GUARANTY INC	PA	U	--	--	--	--	N/A	--	--	--	--	Z
RADIAN MORTGAGE INS INC	PA	U (1)	--	--	--	--	N/A	--	--	--	--	Z
RADIAN REINS INC	PA	A-	704.2	328.9	111.1	64.3	10.0	3.9	9.6	8.1	5.7	GT
RADNOR SPECIALTY INS CO	NE	B	54.0	52.8	0.2	-0.2	10.0	N/A	3.9	10.0	4.3	DFGT
RAINIER INS CO	AZ	C+	26.0	21.5	2.8	0.5	10.0	6.5	6.2	9.5	4.7	D
▲RAM MUTUAL INS CO	MN	B	115.1	70.1	49.7	5.2	9.9	8.7	8.8	6.4	5.5	
RAMPART INS CO	NY	U	--	--	--	--	N/A	--	--	--	--	Z
RANCHERS & FARMERS MUTUAL INS CO	TX	D+	36.1	4.8	0.0	0.6	5.5	5.9	8.9	7.0	2.2	DRT
REAL LEGACY ASR CO INC	PR	D+(1)	230.4	29.0	51.1	-5.3	5.6	6.8	1.5	6.6	2.5	RT
REAMSTOWN MUTUAL INS CO	PA	D+	8.8	3.2	5.7	-0.3	6.1	6.5	3.6	4.1	2.1	DFLR
RECOVER INS CO RRG INC	HI	D	2.1	2.0	0.0	-0.1	10.0	N/A	3.4	10.0	0.6	DFT
▲RECREATION RRG INC	VT	D+	3.8	3.0	0.7	0.0	8.6	3.6	6.0	9.3	2.0	DGT
RED CLAY RRG INC	SC	B-	9.2	5.3	1.3	0.5	8.7	9.8	8.7	9.1	3.5	D
▲RED ROCK RISK RETENTION GROUP INC	AZ	C-	6.7	4.6	1.4	-0.1	7.0	2.2	2.9	9.2	2.1	DT
RED SHIELD INS CO	WA	B	40.5	22.6	13.8	0.5	8.4	6.5	7.3	8.3	5.1	D
REDPOINT COUNTY MUTUAL INS CO	TX	C-	46.0	5.0	0.0	0.0	5.2	N/A	7.6	9.1	2.1	DGRT
REDWOOD FIRE & CAS INS CO	NE	C	1,893.7	759.5	424.2	50.7	4.9	8.8	8.7	8.7	4.4	C
REGENT INS CO	WI	C	40.9	32.2	0.0	0.4	10.0	3.9	4.7	10.0	3.5	RT
▲RELIABLE LLOYDS INS CO	TX	B-	19.4	13.3	0.0	1.0	10.0	N/A	8.8	6.9	4.8	DFR
▼RELIAMAX SURETY CO	SD	C	63.0	20.8	23.0	-2.8	8.6	8.1	2.9	6.5	4.1	DF
RENAISSANCE RE US INC	MD	B	1,633.7	523.4	351.8	-3.6	7.3	9.4	5.5	6.8	5.9	T
REPUB MORTGAGE ASSURANCE CO	FL	B	22.8	9.3	1.5	0.8	7.6	6.0	8.5	7.0	4.5	DF
REPUB MORTGAGE INS CO	NC	F	586.4	50.0	88.5	42.2	1.7	5.1	4.7	5.4	0.0	FR
REPUB MRTG GRTY INS CORP	NC	C	139.8	20.3	16.3	8.2	3.3	6.1	7.1	6.0	3.9	CDFR
▲REPUBLIC CREDIT INDEMNITY CO	IL	C-	40.0	7.0	10.7	-0.6	1.5	10.0	1.9	8.8	3.3	CDFT
REPUBLIC FIRE & CASUALTY INS CO	OK	C	8.4	8.4	0.0	0.2	10.0	N/A	6.6	8.2	2.1	DRT
REPUBLIC INDEMNITY CO OF AMERICA	CA	B-	2,267.3	465.1	834.3	126.5	4.8	9.4	7.3	6.2	5.0	AC
REPUBLIC INDEMNITY OF CA	CA	C	26.4	25.4	0.0	0.4	10.0	3.6	3.7	7.0	4.3	RT
REPUBLIC LLOYDS	TX	C	12.4	12.4	0.0	0.1	10.0	N/A	3.9	9.1	2.1	DRT
REPUBLIC RRG	SC	U	--	--	--	--	N/A	--	--	--	--	Z
REPUBLIC UNDERWRITERS INS CO	TX	C	476.7	169.9	39.1	35.4	8.6	6.1	2.8	6.3	3.9	FGRT
REPUBLIC-FRANKLIN INS CO	OH	C+	112.6	54.5	29.1	1.9	10.0	6.4	6.9	6.9	4.4	T
REPUBLIC-VANGUARD INS CO	AZ	B-	25.3	25.2	0.0	0.5	10.0	N/A	6.7	10.0	4.5	DR
▲REPWEST INS CO	AZ	C-	340.6	197.4	47.2	16.3	7.3	5.9	8.5	7.0	3.1	R
RESIDENCE MUTUAL INS CO	CA	C-	131.8	89.2	41.7	6.8	8.0	8.1	8.7	6.9	2.7	R
RESPONSE INDEMNITY CO OF CA	CA	C-	8.3	5.0	3.4	0.2	10.0	5.0	7.6	6.7	2.5	DRT
RESPONSE INS CO	IL	C-	39.3	36.7	0.0	0.1	7.4	N/A	7.0	7.0	2.9	DR
RESPONSE WORLDWIDE DIRECT AUTO INS	IL	U	--	--	--	--	N/A	--	--	--	--	Z
RESPONSE WORLDWIDE INS CO	IL	U	--	--	--	--	N/A	--	--	--	--	Z
RESPONSIVE AUTO INS CO	FL	C	24.8	9.2	20.9	-0.5	4.2	4.6	3.5	5.5	2.9	CDF
▲RESTORATION RRG INC	VT	B	85.0	37.7	14.8	7.4	7.5	9.6	8.8	7.6	5.2	D
▲RETAILERS CASUALTY INS CO	LA	B	82.2	46.9	23.0	5.2	8.6	9.5	8.7	6.7	5.5	D
RETAILERS INS CO	MI	C-	22.5	10.5	9.0	0.4	7.4	9.3	5.1	6.6	3.0	DR
▲RETAILFIRST INS CO	FL	A	325.1	156.3	117.9	9.5	8.5	6.9	8.3	6.5	7.1	
RIDER INS CO	NJ	D+	31.5	9.3	19.0	-1.1	4.0	3.4	1.4	3.6	2.4	DFLR
RIVERPORT INS CO	IA	B	98.6	40.9	0.0	0.8	10.0	N/A	6.4	2.7	5.5	DLT

See Page 27 for explanation of footnotes and Page 28 for explanation of stability factors.

Arrows denote recent upgrades ▲ or downgrades ▼ (see Section VII for explanations)

108

www.weissratings.com

RISK ADJ. RATIO #1	CAPITAL RATIO #2	PREMIUM TO SURPLUS (%)	RESV. TO SURPLUS (%)	RESV. DEVELOP. 1 YEAR (%)	RESV. DEVELOP. 2 YEAR (%)	LOSS RATIO (%)	EXP. RATIO (%)	COMB RATIO (%)	CASH FROM UNDER-WRITING (%)	NET PREMIUM GROWTH (%)	INVEST. IN AFFIL (%)	INSURANCE COMPANY NAME
N/A	N/A	--	--	--	--	--	--	--	--	--	--	R&Q RI INSURANCE CO
4.7	3.3	58.9	36.2	-2.5	0.5	14.7	35.6	50.3	133.9	12.4	0.0 •	RADIAN GUARANTY INC
N/A	N/A	--	--	--	--	--	--	--	--	--	--	RADIAN GUARANTY REINS INC
22.1	19.1	2.6	2.8	-0.2	-7.0	-12.7	121.2	108.5	57.6	-25.9	0.0	RADIAN INS INC
N/A	N/A	--	--	--	--	--	--	--	--	--	--	RADIAN INVESTOR SURETY INC
N/A	N/A	--	--	--	--	--	--	--	--	--	--	RADIAN MORTGAGE ASR INC
N/A	N/A	--	--	--	--	--	--	--	--	--	--	RADIAN MORTGAGE GUARANTY INC
N/A	N/A	--	--	--	--	--	--	--	--	--	--	RADIAN MORTGAGE INS INC
10.8	6.6	33.8	19.5	-8.3	-8.2	18.7	6.4	25.1	159.2	6.5	0.0 •	RADIAN REINS INC
16.2	9.9	0.3	0.2	N/A	N/A	133.7	510.5	644.2	22.7	N/A	0.0	RADNOR SPECIALTY INS CO
5.7	3.4	12.9	15.6	-2.0	-4.8	42.0	45.7	87.7	103.5	11.2	0.0	RAINIER INS CO
5.1	3.3	70.9	26.2	-3.7	-7.2	59.5	29.5	89.0	104.7	2.4	0.0	RAM MUTUAL INS CO
N/A	N/A	--	--	--	--	--	--	--	--	--	--	RAMPART INS CO
1.0	0.9	N/A	0.9	0.3	-2.2	999 +	999 +	999 +	19.3	100.0	0.0	RANCHERS & FARMERS MUTUAL INS CO
1.0	0.6	140.4	70.1	11.2	4.8	69.8	46.6	116.4	113.3	-8.4	-7.6	REAL LEGACY ASR CO INC
1.3	0.8	180.7	34.4	2.6	-3.4	67.4	44.1	111.5	89.3	-2.0	0.0	REAMSTOWN MUTUAL INS CO
17.2	15.6	2.2	0.2	N/A	N/A	28.3	175.4	203.7	44.4	0.0	0.0	RECOVER INS CO RRG INC
3.6	2.0	21.7	13.8	-1.2	N/A	37.2	71.9	109.1	140.7	-20.1	0.0	RECREATION RRG INC
3.3	2.1	24.3	46.2	-12.2	-23.9	14.3	40.4	54.7	200.4	61.7	0.0	RED CLAY RRG INC
1.2	1.0	30.7	43.6	10.7	12.6	94.5	23.3	117.8	132.8	-31.9	0.0	RED ROCK RISK RETENTION GROUP INC
3.0	1.9	61.4	35.5	-4.4	-4.2	45.2	52.2	97.4	104.4	5.8	0.0	RED SHIELD INS CO
0.8	0.7	N/A	N/A	N/A	N/A	N/A	100.0	100.0	91.7	0.0	0.0	REDPOINT COUNTY MUTUAL INS CO
1.2	0.7	55.9	114.2	-8.9	-14.5	67.5	20.6	88.1	176.2	9.9	0.0 •	REDWOOD FIRE & CAS INS CO
14.5	13.0	N/A	N/A	N/A	N/A	N/A	N/A	N/A	N/A	100.0	0.0	REGENT INS CO
7.7	6.9	N/A	N/A	N/A	N/A	N/A	N/A	N/A	94.0	0.0	0.0	RELIABLE LLOYDS INS CO
2.7	2.0	110.8	15.7	-5.9	-2.0	82.8	33.3	116.1	85.6	-19.9	0.0	RELIAMAX SURETY CO
1.8	1.1	67.2	149.8	-6.9	-10.7	76.9	29.3	106.2	90.8	41.5	0.0 •	RENAISSANCE RE US INC
3.2	2.0	16.4	36.2	-6.2	-9.8	59.3	25.2	84.5	53.4	-29.1	0.0	REPUB MORTGAGE ASSURANCE CO
0.8	0.5	177.2	393.3	-62.6	-189.1	59.7	13.9	73.6	52.2	-29.1	0.1	REPUB MORTGAGE INS CO
1.4	0.9	80.3	233.9	-40.6	-88.1	58.1	17.7	75.8	43.8	-26.2	0.0	REPUB MRTG GRTY INS CORP
0.4	0.3	154.2	430.1	-672.2	-813.7	102.2	21.4	123.6	38.8	-28.1	0.0	REPUBLIC CREDIT INDEMNITY CO
98.4	49.2	N/A	N/A	N/A	N/A	N/A	N/A	N/A	N/A	0.0	0.0	REPUBLIC FIRE & CASUALTY INS CO
0.9	0.7	179.4	359.6	-14.3	-22.6	61.6	24.9	86.5	116.7	5.4	1.2 •	REPUBLIC INDEMNITY CO OF AMERICA
56.5	34.4	N/A	N/A	N/A	N/A	N/A	N/A	N/A	N/A	0.0	0.0	REPUBLIC INDEMNITY OF CA
105.2	52.5	N/A	N/A	N/A	N/A	N/A	N/A	N/A	451.1	0.0	0.0	REPUBLIC LLOYDS
N/A	N/A	--	--	--	--	--	--	--	--	--	--	REPUBLIC RRG
2.5	2.3	23.0	N/A	-754.8	-623.6	82.5	23.1	105.6	42.8	434.6	18.1	REPUBLIC UNDERWRITERS INS CO
7.1	4.7	53.5	71.2	-0.6	-1.3	64.4	33.1	97.5	108.4	9.5	0.0	REPUBLIC-FRANKLIN INS CO
65.1	29.0	N/A	N/A	N/A	N/A	N/A	N/A	N/A	N/A	0.0	0.0	REPUBLIC-VANGUARD INS CO
3.6	2.7	23.9	65.0	0.1	0.5	23.1	58.5	81.6	102.2	12.7	0.0	REPWEST INS CO
2.9	1.8	46.7	13.7	-3.8	-3.7	67.7	21.9	89.6	110.9	-1.1	1.6	RESIDENCE MUTUAL INS CO
4.6	3.0	67.4	8.9	0.5	0.4	48.3	40.1	88.4	135.0	17.8	0.0	RESPONSE INDEMNITY CO OF CA
1.2	1.2	N/A	N/A	N/A	N/A	N/A	N/A	N/A	-62.5	0.0	88.8	RESPONSE INS CO
N/A	N/A	--	--	--	--	--	--	--	--	--	--	RESPONSE WORLDWIDE DIRECT AUTO
N/A	N/A	--	--	--	--	--	--	--	--	--	--	RESPONSE WORLDWIDE INS CO
0.8	0.7	228.4	67.7	-3.9	0.9	68.7	33.3	102.0	96.7	11.8	0.0	RESPONSIVE AUTO INS CO
2.2	1.8	39.2	98.5	-28.6	-44.4	37.1	14.9	52.0	205.6	6.0	0.0	RESTORATION RRG INC
3.2	2.5	49.0	53.5	-8.3	-22.4	46.8	33.7	80.5	113.8	-5.3	0.0	RETAILERS CASUALTY INS CO
1.8	1.4	85.9	71.9	-6.4	-13.6	53.5	38.9	92.4	119.2	5.3	0.0	RETAILERS INS CO
2.5	2.0	75.4	91.8	-6.1	-8.4	64.7	28.9	93.6	110.4	6.7	0.0 •	RETAILFIRST INS CO
0.8	0.6	204.4	74.5	5.0	13.4	65.7	38.4	104.1	85.2	50.0	0.0	RIDER INS CO
5.9	5.3	N/A	N/A	N/A	N/A	N/A	N/A	N/A	108.6	0.0	0.0	RIVERPORT INS CO

999 + Denotes number greater than 999.9%
999 - Denotes number less than -999.99%
• Bullets denote a more detailed analysis is available in Section II.

INSURANCE COMPANY NAME	DOM. STATE	RATING	TOTAL ASSETS ($MIL)	CAPITAL & SURPLUS ($MIL)	ANNUAL NET PREMIUM ($MIL)	NET INCOME ($MIL)	CAPITAL-IZATION INDEX (PTS)	RESERVE ADQ INDEX (PTS)	PROFIT-ABILITY INDEX (PTS)	LIQUIDITY INDEX (PTS)	STAB. INDEX (PTS)	STABILITY FACTORS
RLI INS CO	IL	B	1,817.0	864.6	453.1	97.6	7.2	7.8	6.1	6.9	5.7	A
ROCHDALE INS CO	NY	C-	224.7	87.5	31.8	-0.9	8.8	6.0	5.5	0.7	2.9	FLRT
▲ROCKFORD MUTUAL INS CO	IL	B-	80.6	34.5	52.7	-3.9	6.2	7.0	4.3	5.3	5.3	F
ROCKHILL INS CO	AZ	C	157.3	88.7	0.0	-0.2	10.0	N/A	2.9	6.9	4.0	FR
ROCKINGHAM CASUALTY CO	VA	C	30.4	29.4	0.0	0.3	10.0	N/A	6.3	7.0	4.2	R
▲ROCKINGHAM INS CO	VA	B+	144.7	76.8	56.4	4.3	7.1	8.7	7.9	6.2	6.5	
ROCKWOOD CASUALTY INS CO	PA	C-	289.7	120.0	54.6	33.2	8.0	9.4	8.5	7.1	3.3	R
ROMULUS INS RRG INC	SC	D	2.9	2.2	0.8	0.5	8.6	3.5	5.9	9.1	1.4	DT
ROOT INS CO	OH	C	22.1	18.1	1.9	-15.6	7.5	5.3	2.0	8.0	2.7	DFGT
RPX RRG INC	HI	U (3)	--	--	--	--	N/A	--	--	--	--	Z
▲RSUI INDEMNITY CO	NH	B-	3,637.8	1,624.3	670.9	94.4	8.1	8.1	8.6	6.8	4.5	AR
RURAL COMMUNITY INS CO	MN	C+	1,790.7	247.1	0.0	-14.0	9.5	6.2	2.2	6.9	4.4	FRT
RURAL MUTUAL INS CO	WI	B-	484.2	266.5	174.5	28.4	10.0	8.1	8.9	6.7	4.7	R
RURAL TRUST INS CO	TX	C	23.5	13.0	6.0	1.3	7.6	6.2	4.2	6.6	2.5	DFRT
RUSH FIRE INSURANCE CO	LA	D+	4.1	3.3	3.0	0.1	7.1	6.0	7.1	6.3	2.5	DT
RUTGERS CASUALTY INS CO	NJ	C-	23.5	7.5	3.9	-0.3	8.3	5.9	2.1	7.0	2.9	DFR
RUTGERS ENHANCED INS CO	NJ	C-	11.0	4.0	2.6	-0.3	7.8	5.8	2.2	7.5	3.0	DFT
RVI AMERICA INS CO	CT	C	109.4	65.9	5.9	2.8	10.0	5.5	3.8	10.0	3.3	R
▲RVOS FARM MUTUAL INS CO	TX	C	88.5	44.7	53.6	6.3	7.3	5.8	3.7	4.6	3.5	LR
SAFE AUTO INS CO	OH	B	382.4	136.7	359.2	33.8	7.3	6.9	3.8	2.0	5.9	L
▲SAFE HARBOR INS CO	FL	B	83.1	23.6	51.3	-2.5	6.2	5.2	5.4	6.5	5.5	CD
SAFE INS CO	WV	C-	11.7	9.4	2.6	0.4	10.0	8.0	8.6	7.9	2.8	DR
SAFECARD SERVICES INS CO	ND	D	1.9	1.8	0.2	0.1	10.0	3.6	4.7	10.0	1.6	DT
▲SAFECO INS CO OF AMERICA	NH	B	4,863.4	1,503.3	1,713.0	27.2	8.2	5.8	6.4	6.2	5.5	A
SAFECO INS CO OF IL	IL	B	194.6	187.4	0.0	2.2	10.0	N/A	6.5	10.0	5.5	A
SAFECO INS CO OF INDIANA	IN	B	15.8	15.5	0.0	0.2	10.0	N/A	6.3	7.0	5.1	D
SAFECO INS CO OF OREGON	OR	B	14.0	14.0	0.0	0.3	10.0	N/A	7.1	7.0	4.9	DR
SAFECO LLOYDS INS CO	TX	B-	13.3	13.3	0.0	0.2	10.0	N/A	6.5	7.0	4.8	DR
SAFECO NATIONAL INS CO	NH	B-	15.7	14.9	0.0	0.2	10.0	N/A	6.5	7.0	5.0	AD
SAFECO SURPLUS LINES INS CO	NH	U	--	--	--	--	N/A	--	--	--	--	Z
▼SAFEPOINT INS CO	FL	C	175.4	46.1	62.4	-5.3	7.1	2.4	3.6	6.3	3.6	G
SAFETY FIRST INS CO	IL	C	74.7	70.8	1.2	3.1	10.0	7.7	8.1	9.2	4.0	DRT
SAFETY IMPLEMENTATION PROGRAM	NV	U	--	--	--	--	N/A	--	--	--	--	Z
SAFETY INDEMNITY INS CO	MA	C+	127.6	61.0	54.7	3.4	10.0	8.9	5.4	6.7	4.5	T
SAFETY INS CO	MA	B-	1,503.6	617.6	702.9	58.0	8.8	9.1	4.9	6.3	4.7	R
SAFETY NATIONAL CASUALTY CORP	MO	C	7,223.8	2,081.9	882.6	203.6	7.3	3.1	6.5	7.2	3.9	R
▲SAFETY P&C INS CO	MA	C+	47.2	19.6	23.4	1.2	8.1	9.3	5.4	6.5	4.5	D
SAFETY SPECIALTY INS CO	MO	C	89.1	73.5	0.6	3.3	10.0	2.6	3.9	9.6	3.5	DGT
SAFEWAY INS CO	IL	B-	565.8	315.3	221.4	-1.2	7.6	4.4	4.7	5.4	4.5	R
SAFEWAY INS CO OF AL	IL	C	78.5	29.8	43.5	0.0	7.7	3.9	3.1	4.4	4.2	FGLR
SAFEWAY INS CO OF GA	GA	C	76.5	30.3	43.5	-0.4	7.8	4.1	2.8	5.3	4.2	FR
SAFEWAY INS CO OF LA	LA	C+	155.7	60.0	87.0	-0.2	8.8	4.1	3.1	5.9	4.5	GR
SAGAMORE INS CO	IN	B-	169.1	133.0	22.4	2.0	10.0	5.9	6.4	8.4	4.7	T
SAGE RRG INC	NV	D	4.6	1.0	1.9	0.0	5.4	3.9	6.2	8.7	1.1	DT
▲SAINT LUKES HEALTH SYSTEM RRG	SC	C	13.5	8.5	2.3	1.0	7.2	5.9	3.3	7.0	2.9	DFR
SALEM COUNTY MUTUAL FIRE INS CO	NJ	U (5)	--	--	--	--	N/A	--	--	--	--	Z
▲SAMARITAN RRG INC	SC	C+	42.9	24.0	10.0	6.1	7.8	6.3	8.4	7.5	4.2	D
▼SAMSUNG FIRE & MARINE INS CO LTD US	NY	D-	97.6	57.7	13.6	-13.2	5.2	0.6	2.1	7.0	0.9	FRT
SAN ANTONIO INDEMNITY CO	TX	F (5)	0.0	0.0	4.2	0.0	0.3	5.5	1.1	0.0	0.0	CDGL
SAN DIEGO INS CO	CA	U	--	--	--	--	N/A	--	--	--	--	Z
SAN FRANCISCO REINS CO	CA	C	3,390.4	594.8	-437.3	-19.0	8.6	3.0	3.7	7.5	4.0	FRT
SAUCON INSURANCE CO	PA	U	--	--	--	--	N/A	--	--	--	--	Z

See Page 27 for explanation of footnotes and Page 28 for explanation of stability factors.

Arrows denote recent upgrades ▲ or downgrades ▼ (see Section VII for explanations)

110

www.weissratings.com

RISK ADJ. RATIO #1	CAPITAL RATIO #2	PREMIUM TO SURPLUS (%)	RESV. TO SURPLUS (%)	RESV. DEVELOP. 1 YEAR (%)	RESV. DEVELOP. 2 YEAR (%)	LOSS RATIO (%)	EXP. RATIO (%)	COMB RATIO (%)	CASH FROM UNDER-WRITING (%)	NET PREMIUM GROWTH (%)	INVEST. IN AFFIL (%)	INSURANCE COMPANY NAME
1.3	1.1	52.4	62.8	-2.5	-1.4	52.4	42.1	94.5	122.2	-0.7	33.2 •	RLI INS CO
6.9	4.7	36.3	N/A	-444.9	-413.1	107.0	48.1	155.1	38.6	-76.6	0.0	ROCHDALE INS CO
1.5	0.9	152.9	58.9	-5.0	-8.8	71.7	37.7	109.4	94.5	11.0	0.0	ROCKFORD MUTUAL INS CO
3.4	3.3	N/A	N/A	N/A	N/A	N/A	N/A	N/A	-106.1	0.0	25.4	ROCKHILL INS CO
67.5	55.0	N/A	N/A	N/A	N/A	N/A	N/A	N/A	53.1	0.0	0.0	ROCKINGHAM CASUALTY CO
1.2	1.1	73.4	23.8	-5.8	-8.1	55.8	37.3	93.1	110.2	18.1	21.6 •	ROCKINGHAM INS CO
2.7	2.0	45.5	80.5	-11.5	-19.5	36.8	30.0	66.8	152.1	36.1	9.6	ROCKWOOD CASUALTY INS CO
2.5	2.0	34.6	18.4	-0.7	7.5	N/A	17.6	17.6	569.5	35.9	0.0	ROMULUS INS RRG INC
1.5	1.3	10.3	4.3	N/A	-0.4	168.0	814.9	982.9	4.2	N/A	0.0	ROOT INS CO
N/A	N/A	--	--	--	--	--	--	--	--	--	--	RPX RRG INC
2.5	1.7	41.3	90.8	-2.3	-6.0	79.0	28.6	107.6	112.2	-1.5	6.9 •	RSUI INDEMNITY CO
5.2	2.6	N/A	N/A	7.0	0.9	N/A	N/A	N/A	999 +	100.0	0.0 •	RURAL COMMUNITY INS CO
6.9	4.5	65.5	40.1	-2.7	-3.7	59.1	23.3	82.4	119.4	1.8	0.0 •	RURAL MUTUAL INS CO
2.1	1.3	46.2	21.5	-8.0	-1.9	59.4	18.4	77.8	73.3	11.7	0.0	RURAL TRUST INS CO
1.2	1.0	92.2	7.1	-0.6	-0.1	23.5	77.9	101.4	99.3	8.5	0.0	RUSH FIRE INSURANCE CO
2.4	1.8	52.6	92.8	4.4	5.9	80.4	38.2	118.6	70.8	-1.2	0.0	RUTGERS CASUALTY INS CO
2.0	1.5	66.0	116.3	5.3	7.1	80.4	38.4	118.8	76.7	-1.2	0.0	RUTGERS ENHANCED INS CO
10.9	9.8	9.0	7.1	0.3	-0.1	53.3	37.8	91.1	-867.4	-1.1	0.0	RVI AMERICA INS CO
1.9	1.5	119.9	10.8	-6.2	-3.7	62.7	28.3	91.0	97.7	-6.2	24.2	RVOS FARM MUTUAL INS CO
1.3	1.2	262.8	89.3	3.1	2.2	67.7	24.9	92.6	100.5	15.1	0.0	SAFE AUTO INS CO
1.1	0.9	217.5	85.4	-13.2	-13.8	70.3	38.4	108.7	100.2	3.7	0.0	SAFE HARBOR INS CO
5.3	3.2	27.4	8.9	-2.5	-4.3	41.5	46.1	87.6	117.2	-4.9	0.0	SAFE INS CO
18.9	17.1	9.1	0.6	-0.5	-0.6	N/A	11.0	11.0	910.4	0.0	0.0	SAFECARD SERVICES INS CO
2.6	1.8	114.0	156.9	3.5	4.1	79.5	29.0	108.5	99.7	7.7	6.3 •	SAFECO INS CO OF AMERICA
3.5	3.5	N/A	N/A	N/A	N/A	N/A	N/A	N/A	N/A	0.0	29.7	SAFECO INS CO OF IL
102.1	73.2	N/A	N/A	N/A	N/A	N/A	N/A	N/A	N/A	0.0	0.0	SAFECO INS CO OF INDIANA
121.2	60.5	N/A	N/A	N/A	N/A	N/A	N/A	N/A	N/A	0.0	0.0	SAFECO INS CO OF OREGON
233.4	116.7	N/A	N/A	N/A	N/A	N/A	N/A	N/A	N/A	0.0	0.0	SAFECO LLOYDS INS CO
43.9	39.5	N/A	N/A	N/A	N/A	N/A	N/A	N/A	N/A	0.0	0.0	SAFECO NATIONAL INS CO
N/A	N/A	--	--	--	--	--	--	--	--	--	--	SAFECO SURPLUS LINES INS CO
1.5	1.0	135.3	89.6	14.8	24.7	98.2	18.1	116.3	113.1	22.2	0.0	SAFEPOINT INS CO
46.8	22.7	1.7	3.5	-1.2	-1.6	-23.6	35.1	11.5	289.2	5.7	0.0	SAFETY FIRST INS CO
N/A	N/A	--	--	--	--	--	--	--	--	--	--	SAFETY IMPLEMENTATION PROGRAM
5.0	3.4	89.7	56.4	-4.5	-9.3	65.1	29.3	94.4	104.4	1.9	0.0	SAFETY INDEMNITY INS CO
3.1	2.1	113.8	71.5	-5.5	-11.5	65.1	29.4	94.5	104.9	1.9	6.5 •	SAFETY INS CO
1.8	1.3	42.4	204.2	1.9	10.5	88.5	20.5	109.0	192.4	13.4	4.4 •	SAFETY NATIONAL CASUALTY CORP
2.4	1.7	119.4	75.1	-5.9	-12.4	65.1	31.2	96.3	105.3	1.9	0.0	SAFETY P&C INS CO
23.5	18.1	0.8	0.4	N/A	N/A	55.3	-280.0	-224.7	-133.2	176.6	0.0	SAFETY SPECIALTY INS CO
1.5	1.4	70.2	29.0	5.1	7.5	83.5	19.3	102.8	96.6	5.2	44.1 •	SAFEWAY INS CO
1.5	1.4	145.8	60.2	9.7	14.4	83.5	18.4	101.9	88.1	5.2	0.0	SAFEWAY INS CO OF AL
1.6	1.5	143.4	59.2	9.4	13.9	83.5	20.5	104.0	95.0	5.2	0.0	SAFEWAY INS CO OF GA
2.3	2.2	144.9	59.9	9.6	14.2	83.5	20.2	103.7	100.5	5.2	0.0	SAFEWAY INS CO OF LA
17.0	9.3	16.8	12.8	1.0	1.4	75.3	19.8	95.1	145.9	55.5	0.0	SAGAMORE INS CO
0.9	0.8	177.5	207.7	0.1	-9.7	67.9	32.9	100.8	195.9	-2.5	0.0	SAGE RRG INC
2.0	1.5	26.9	50.0	-12.9	-29.6	54.4	16.4	70.8	-1.4	1.3	0.0	SAINT LUKES HEALTH SYSTEM RRG
N/A	N/A	--	--	--	--	--	--	--	--	--	--	SALEM COUNTY MUTUAL FIRE INS CO
2.4	1.5	41.7	45.2	-6.0	-3.8	55.4	12.3	67.7	205.0	6.0	0.0	SAMARITAN RRG INC
1.1	0.6	23.5	209.8	11.2	86.0	99.5	112.3	211.8	25.9	-77.8	0.0	SAMSUNG FIRE & MARINE INS CO LTD
0.2	0.1	394.1	58.1	-14.1	1.3	76.0	26.0	102.0	99.2	75.3	0.0	SAN ANTONIO INDEMNITY CO
N/A	N/A	--	--	--	--	--	--	--	--	--	--	SAN DIEGO INS CO
2.9	2.0	-73.5	204.7	-64.3	-114.3	75.1	-12.1	63.0	-191.2	1.4	0.0 •	SAN FRANCISCO REINS CO
N/A	N/A	--	--	--	--	--	--	--	--	--	--	SAUCON INSURANCE CO

999 + Denotes number greater than 999.9%
999 - Denotes number less than -999.99%
• Bullets denote a more detailed analysis is available in Section II.

INSURANCE COMPANY NAME	DOM. STATE	RATING	TOTAL ASSETS ($MIL)	CAPITAL & SURPLUS ($MIL)	ANNUAL NET PREMIUM ($MIL)	NET INCOME ($MIL)	CAPITAL-IZATION INDEX (PTS)	RESERVE ADQ INDEX (PTS)	PROFIT-ABILITY INDEX (PTS)	LIQUIDITY INDEX (PTS)	STAB. INDEX (PTS)	STABILITY FACTORS
SAUQUOIT VALLEY INS CO	NY	C-	4.9	4.0	0.6	0.1	7.6	7.3	4.1	7.6	2.2	DR
SAVERS P&C INS CO	MO	C-	51.2	50.3	0.0	1.1	10.0	1.8	2.9	7.0	2.9	DRT
SAWGRASS MUTUAL INS CO	FL	F	0.5	0.7	-0.2	-9.2	7.3	3.4	0.5	0.0	0.0	DFLT
▲SC FARM BUREAU MUTUAL INS CO	SC	B-	120.6	65.5	53.2	8.6	9.0	7.9	5.0	6.6	4.7	
SCOR REINS CO	NY	C	3,541.5	820.1	1,158.0	-206.4	5.2	7.0	3.0	6.8	3.4	R
SCOTTSDALE INDEMNITY CO	OH	B	84.5	39.7	0.0	0.5	10.0	N/A	6.8	9.3	5.6	DF
SCOTTSDALE INS CO	OH	B-	2,536.9	737.8	754.7	-40.3	8.1	5.9	3.2	5.9	4.9	A
SCOTTSDALE SURPLUS LINES INS CO	AZ	B	51.6	48.7	0.0	0.6	10.0	N/A	7.2	7.0	6.1	D
SCRUBS MUTUAL ASR CO RRG	NV	D	14.2	3.7	2.4	0.2	2.2	1.6	2.8	9.7	2.1	CDRT
▲SEAVIEW INS CO	CA	C-	23.9	12.8	7.1	2.0	9.1	7.0	7.9	7.4	2.9	D
SEAWAY MUTUAL INS CO	PA	U	--	--	--	--	N/A	--	--	--	--	Z
SECURA INS A MUTUAL CO	WI	B-	1,161.7	431.7	512.9	36.5	8.4	9.2	8.8	6.3	4.7	R
SECURA SUPREME INS CO	WI	C+	141.9	64.8	57.0	4.5	10.0	8.6	8.9	6.7	4.7	T
SECURIAN CASUALTY CO	MN	A-	328.2	118.4	273.5	-0.3	7.6	6.3	7.5	5.1	7.0	L
SECURITY AMERICA RRG INC	VT	E (1)	4.3	1.5	1.6	0.0	0.0	2.6	0.9	2.1	0.1	CDFG
SECURITY FIRST INS CO	FL	B-	252.3	75.9	130.7	2.6	7.3	3.6	2.9	3.9	5.1	FL
▲SECURITY MUTUAL INS CO	NY	B	111.2	61.6	36.6	5.8	10.0	8.3	8.7	6.8	5.5	T
▼SECURITY NATIONAL INS CO	DE	C	1,114.1	109.0	280.4	21.8	0.1	7.1	2.9	2.7	4.2	CLR
SECURITY NATIONAL INS CO	FL	D+	133.1	35.5	0.0	0.3	10.0	4.4	4.0	7.6	2.5	R
SECURITY PLAN FIRE INS CO	LA	D	8.4	7.0	5.0	0.2	8.4	7.9	7.8	7.0	1.8	DR
SELECT INS CO	TX	U	--	--	--	--	N/A	--	--	--	--	Z
SELECT MARKETS INS CO	IL	U	--	--	--	--	N/A	--	--	--	--	Z
SELECT MD RRG INC	MT	D+	1.6	0.8	0.2	0.0	7.8	7.0	2.0	7.0	1.2	DT
SELECT RISK INS CO	PA	C	43.1	18.2	16.6	1.3	8.5	9.0	8.4	6.6	4.3	D
▲SELECTIVE AUTO INS CO OF NJ	NJ	B+	380.7	90.4	142.2	11.3	7.8	9.3	8.8	6.6	6.5	A
▲SELECTIVE CASUALTY INS CO	NJ	B+	452.3	109.0	165.9	13.4	7.9	6.9	8.8	6.4	6.5	
SELECTIVE F&C INS CO	NJ	B	195.7	45.6	71.1	5.6	7.9	6.9	8.8	6.5	6.0	T
SELECTIVE INS CO OF AM	NJ	B	2,434.9	609.7	758.6	84.6	8.2	9.0	8.8	6.7	5.6	A
▲SELECTIVE INS CO OF NEW ENGLAND	NJ	C+	193.6	46.3	71.1	6.3	7.9	9.3	8.8	6.5	4.5	A
SELECTIVE INS CO OF NY	NY	B	442.5	106.5	165.9	13.3	7.9	9.3	8.8	6.4	5.6	A
SELECTIVE INS CO OF SC	IN	B	648.0	144.1	213.4	17.9	8.0	9.3	8.8	6.6	5.6	A
SELECTIVE INS CO OF THE SOUTHEAST	IN	B	507.5	111.8	165.9	14.7	8.0	9.3	8.8	6.6	5.6	A
SELECTIVE WAY INS CO	NJ	B	1,345.7	325.1	497.8	43.6	7.8	9.3	8.8	6.5	5.6	A
SENECA INS CO	NY	D+	181.4	142.5	0.0	-0.3	9.6	3.9	4.9	7.7	2.8	FR
▲SENECA SPECIALTY INS CO	DE	B-	50.8	50.8	0.0	0.6	10.0	N/A	6.4	10.0	4.9	FR
SENIOR AMERICAN INS CO	PA	U (1)	--	--	--	--	N/A	--	--	--	--	Z
SENIORSFIRST RRG INC	NC	U	--	--	--	--	N/A	--	--	--	--	Z
SENTINEL INS CO LTD	CT	B	280.9	196.1	32.1	14.1	10.0	4.9	8.9	7.3	5.8	A
SENTRUITY CASUALTY CO	TX	B	210.7	49.8	10.5	0.7	10.0	6.0	7.9	9.0	5.6	F
▲SENTRY CASUALTY CO	WI	B+	355.9	70.7	52.7	5.7	9.4	7.8	5.3	6.7	6.4	
SENTRY INS A MUTUAL CO	WI	A	8,392.8	5,141.2	1,138.4	267.5	8.7	7.4	6.8	6.9	7.8	
SENTRY LLOYDS OF TX	TX	B	7.2	7.1	0.0	0.1	10.0	N/A	7.2	10.0	4.9	D
▲SENTRY SELECT INS CO	WI	A-	826.6	226.7	210.8	11.4	8.7	8.0	5.2	6.4	7.0	
▼SEQUOIA INDEMNITY CO	NV	C	7.9	7.4	0.3	0.5	10.0	7.0	3.1	9.1	4.2	DFRT
▼SEQUOIA INS CO	CA	C-	152.4	34.0	8.2	9.2	10.0	7.1	1.9	6.4	3.2	FRT
SERVICE AMERICAN INDEMNITY CO	OK	U	--	--	--	--	N/A	--	--	--	--	Z
SERVICE INS CO (FL)	FL	B	61.0	47.3	12.0	4.3	8.5	5.9	8.8	6.9	6.0	
SERVICE INS CO (NJ)	NJ	C-	15.8	8.3	2.3	0.7	10.0	8.4	8.7	8.8	2.7	DR
▲SERVICE LLOYDS INS CO	TX	B	315.8	129.8	87.3	4.4	9.7	9.0	8.4	6.8	4.6	R
▲SEVEN SEAS INS CO	FL	C+	22.8	20.2	20.5	8.7	9.1	6.1	9.5	7.0	4.3	DR
▲SFM MUTUAL INS CO	MN	B+	612.1	147.7	170.2	15.4	6.9	6.6	8.9	6.4	6.5	C
▲SFM SAFE INS CO	MN	D+	5.5	5.1	0.0	0.1	10.0	N/A	4.9	7.0	2.5	DT

See Page 27 for explanation of footnotes and Page 28 for explanation of stability factors.
Arrows denote recent upgrades ▲ or downgrades ▼   (see Section VII for explanations)

112

www.weissratings.com

RISK ADJ. CAPITAL RATIO #1	CAPITAL RATIO #2	PREMIUM TO SURPLUS (%)	RESV. TO SURPLUS (%)	RESV. DEVELOP. 1 YEAR (%)	RESV. DEVELOP. 2 YEAR (%)	LOSS RATIO (%)	EXP. RATIO (%)	COMB RATIO (%)	CASH FROM UNDER-WRITING (%)	NET PREMIUM GROWTH (%)	INVEST. IN AFFIL (%)	INSURANCE COMPANY NAME
2.3	1.4	15.3	6.0	0.5	-0.1	64.6	42.2	106.8	93.7	-1.1	0.0	SAUQUOIT VALLEY INS CO
90.1	40.0	N/A	N/A	N/A	N/A	N/A	N/A	N/A	-284.4	0.0	0.0	SAVERS P&C INS CO
4.2	2.1	-31.8	N/A	-28.5	-10.7	999 +	999 +	999 +	-47.9	-102.7	0.0	SAWGRASS MUTUAL INS CO
3.4	2.9	81.2	14.9	-3.3	-4.0	57.6	29.2	86.8	112.9	-2.9	8.4	SC FARM BUREAU MUTUAL INS CO
1.1	0.6	141.2	230.1	-1.8	-7.3	77.4	43.3	120.7	167.1	3.1	0.0 ●	SCOR REINS CO
6.4	5.7	N/A	N/A	N/A	N/A	N/A	N/A	N/A	-79.5	0.0	0.0	SCOTTSDALE INDEMNITY CO
2.1	1.7	102.3	82.8	0.4	2.0	81.1	30.4	111.5	94.0	-3.2	19.3 ●	SCOTTSDALE INS CO
50.5	45.4	N/A	N/A	N/A	N/A	N/A	N/A	N/A	118.9	0.0	0.0	SCOTTSDALE SURPLUS LINES INS CO
0.5	0.4	65.6	228.9	5.1	11.7	-1.9	92.4	90.5	142.7	-59.1	0.0	SCRUBS MUTUAL ASR CO RRG
3.5	2.8	55.9	3.4	-2.9	-4.1	-1.8	60.3	58.5	164.9	-16.3	0.0	SEAVIEW INS CO
N/A	N/A	--	--	--	--	--	--	--	--	--	--	SEAWAY MUTUAL INS CO
2.7	1.9	118.8	94.1	-6.0	-10.5	61.5	31.2	92.7	115.7	4.4	6.8 ●	SECURA INS A MUTUAL CO
5.3	4.0	87.9	69.7	-4.4	-7.3	61.5	30.4	91.9	113.8	4.4	0.0	SECURA SUPREME INS CO
1.8	1.3	231.0	29.2	0.7	-0.2	60.8	34.4	95.2	117.7	18.1	0.0 ●	SECURIAN CASUALTY CO
0.1	0.1	114.4	167.6	59.3	46.6	140.2	76.7	216.9	48.9	-20.9	0.0	SECURITY AMERICA RRG INC
1.5	1.2	172.2	89.1	-6.3	13.2	86.7	19.5	106.2	81.0	-22.7	0.0	SECURITY FIRST INS CO
5.2	3.8	59.4	37.8	-5.8	-6.4	47.9	39.2	87.1	109.7	1.9	0.0	SECURITY MUTUAL INS CO
0.1	0.1	257.2	299.4	42.4	-119.2	72.4	21.2	93.6	966.7	22.7	0.3	SECURITY NATIONAL INS CO
3.9	3.5	N/A	0.1	-0.1	0.6	N/A	N/A	N/A	-568.4	0.0	0.0	SECURITY NATIONAL INS CO
2.2	1.9	70.9	7.1	-0.4	-2.7	35.0	66.5	101.5	98.9	-1.8	0.0	SECURITY PLAN FIRE INS CO
N/A	N/A	--	--	--	--	--	--	--	--	--	--	SELECT INS CO
N/A	N/A	--	--	--	--	--	--	--	--	--	--	SELECT MARKETS INS CO
1.7	1.5	27.6	60.8	-16.8	-11.9	-5.0	62.3	57.3	69.6	-2.0	0.0	SELECT MD RRG INC
3.1	2.0	91.2	58.9	-5.8	-4.8	59.6	33.5	93.1	107.3	2.1	0.0	SELECT RISK INS CO
2.3	1.6	157.3	210.2	-2.0	-8.3	58.7	33.5	92.2	113.0	6.0	0.0 ●	SELECTIVE AUTO INS CO OF NJ
2.4	1.6	152.3	203.4	-2.0	-8.1	58.7	33.5	92.2	111.5	6.0	0.0 ●	SELECTIVE CASUALTY INS CO
2.4	1.6	155.9	208.3	-2.0	-8.2	58.7	33.5	92.2	106.5	6.0	0.0	SELECTIVE F&C INS CO
2.8	1.8	124.4	166.3	-1.7	-6.6	58.7	33.5	92.2	113.8	6.0	0.0 ●	SELECTIVE INS CO OF AM
2.4	1.6	153.6	205.3	-2.0	-8.2	58.7	33.5	92.2	111.4	6.0	0.0	SELECTIVE INS CO OF NEW ENGLAND
2.4	1.6	155.8	208.2	-2.0	-8.1	58.7	33.5	92.2	112.8	6.0	0.0	SELECTIVE INS CO OF NY
2.5	1.7	148.1	197.8	-1.9	-7.5	58.7	33.3	92.0	114.7	6.0	0.0	SELECTIVE INS CO OF SC
2.5	1.7	148.4	198.3	-1.9	-7.8	58.7	33.3	92.0	115.4	6.0	0.0	SELECTIVE INS CO OF THE SOUTHEAST
2.4	1.6	153.1	204.6	-2.0	-8.2	58.7	33.5	92.2	112.6	6.0	0.0 ●	SELECTIVE WAY INS CO
2.9	2.7	N/A	N/A	N/A	N/A	N/A	N/A	N/A	-51.4	0.0	54.2	SENECA INS CO
53.2	21.4	N/A	N/A	N/A	N/A	N/A	N/A	N/A	N/A	0.0	0.0	SENECA SPECIALTY INS CO
N/A	N/A	--	--	--	--	--	--	--	--	--	--	SENIOR AMERICAN INS CO
N/A	N/A	--	--	--	--	--	--	--	--	--	--	SENIORSFIRST RRG INC
17.6	11.6	16.4	30.0	-0.2	0.5	68.7	-10.0	58.7	110.7	1.6	0.0	SENTINEL INS CO LTD
5.2	4.1	21.0	4.3	1.4	0.6	82.2	42.8	125.0	90.2	-13.0	0.0	SENTRUITY CASUALTY CO
4.0	2.5	74.5	116.0	-1.3	-2.8	74.8	28.6	103.4	111.7	4.7	0.0 ●	SENTRY CASUALTY CO
2.7	2.2	22.1	34.5	-0.4	-1.0	74.8	28.6	103.4	108.7	4.7	20.3 ●	SENTRY INS A MUTUAL CO
147.7	133.0	N/A	N/A	N/A	N/A	N/A	N/A	N/A	999 +	0.0	0.0	SENTRY LLOYDS OF TX
3.3	2.1	93.0	144.8	-1.6	-3.5	74.8	28.6	103.4	96.7	4.7	0.0 ●	SENTRY SELECT INS CO
36.4	32.5	3.9	N/A	-35.6	-32.4	91.5	-97.3	-5.8	12.3	-63.1	0.0	SEQUOIA INDEMNITY CO
4.8	4.2	24.2	N/A	-406.1	-409.1	75.9	10.9	86.8	33.3	260.3	4.9	SEQUOIA INS CO
N/A	N/A	--	--	--	--	--	--	--	--	--	--	SERVICE AMERICAN INDEMNITY CO
3.4	1.9	25.4	4.0	-1.5	0.9	18.9	30.0	48.9	215.4	122.2	0.0	SERVICE INS CO (FL)
4.2	3.5	28.3	10.6	-3.5	-2.2	12.3	53.3	65.6	129.4	-0.5	0.0	SERVICE INS CO (NJ)
3.7	2.8	67.3	56.0	-6.4	-8.0	56.6	44.8	101.4	91.8	6.2	0.0	SERVICE LLOYDS INS CO
2.4	2.4	101.6	6.9	-0.6	-0.7	23.2	12.6	35.8	292.0	13.3	1.3	SEVEN SEAS INS CO
1.3	1.0	115.2	232.1	-1.4	-6.5	71.7	21.0	92.7	124.6	4.3	2.3 ●	SFM MUTUAL INS CO
30.6	27.5	N/A	N/A	N/A	N/A	N/A	N/A	N/A	N/A	0.0	0.0	SFM SAFE INS CO

999 + Denotes number greater than 999.9%
999 - Denotes number less than -999.99%
● Bullets denote a more detailed analysis is available in Section II.

INSURANCE COMPANY NAME	DOM. STATE	RATING	TOTAL ASSETS ($MIL)	CAPITAL & SURPLUS ($MIL)	ANNUAL NET PREMIUM ($MIL)	NET INCOME ($MIL)	CAPITAL-IZATION INDEX (PTS)	RESERVE ADQ INDEX (PTS)	PROFIT-ABILITY INDEX (PTS)	LIQUIDITY INDEX (PTS)	STAB. INDEX (PTS)	STABILITY FACTORS
▲SFM SELECT INS CO	MN	C	4.2	3.5	0.0	0.0	10.0	4.6	5.7	7.0	3.2	DR
▲SHEBOYGAN FALLS INS CO	WI	B-	36.6	13.8	21.7	0.0	7.3	4.9	5.4	6.1	4.8	DR
SHELBY INS CO	TX	F	(5) 0.0	0.0	0.0	0.0	10.0	N/A	2.6	7.0	0.0	
▼SHELTER GENERAL INS CO	MO	C	127.5	58.8	44.8	-5.6	7.7	8.7	2.2	6.2	4.2	FR
SHELTER MUTUAL INS CO	MO	B	3,381.1	1,920.7	1,531.0	43.8	8.2	7.7	6.8	5.8	5.5	
▲SHELTER REINS CO	MO	B	472.9	321.5	114.2	-8.0	9.7	9.3	6.1	6.7	5.5	
SIGMA RRG INC	DC	B-	18.8	7.5	2.4	0.7	7.5	9.3	8.7	9.1	3.5	D
SILVER OAK CASUALTY INC	NE	B-	230.1	87.4	50.1	9.9	8.7	9.3	6.5	7.0	4.6	R
▲SIMED	PR	B	163.1	100.6	17.4	5.6	10.0	8.7	8.0	7.5	5.5	D
SIRIUS AMERICA INS CO	NY	B-	1,337.5	521.8	101.2	-6.4	6.2	6.3	4.1	7.4	4.9	FRT
SLAVONIC INS CO OF TEXAS	TX	U	--	--	--	--	N/A	--	--	--	--	Z
▲SLAVONIC MUTUAL FIRE INS ASN	TX	B-	30.1	29.4	0.9	0.0	10.0	3.6	5.7	7.8	4.8	DFR
SOCIETY INS A MUTUAL CO	WI	B	432.6	153.4	162.6	10.2	8.5	6.7	8.8	6.7	6.0	T
SOMERSET CASUALTY INS CO	PA	D+	44.7	26.4	8.0	2.2	10.0	8.8	8.9	7.4	2.4	DFR
▲SOMPO AMERICA INSURANCE CO	NY	A	1,285.1	571.9	190.6	28.1	9.5	8.6	6.9	7.0	7.5	
SOMPO JAPAN CANOPIUS RE AG	DE	U	(1) --	--	--	--	N/A	--	--	--	--	Z
SOMPO JAPAN NIPPONKOA INS INC	GU	D	11.0	3.3	6.9	0.1	2.2	5.1	7.0	7.7	1.7	CDT
SONNENBERG MUTUAL INS CO	OH	C	27.6	16.4	10.6	0.6	8.6	7.8	8.4	6.8	3.2	DT
SOUTH CAROLINA FARM BUREAU INS	SC	C-	3.7	3.1	0.0	0.0	10.0	N/A	5.8	7.0	2.4	DT
SOUTHERN COUNTY MUTUAL INS CO	TX	C	34.2	30.0	0.0	0.0	10.0	N/A	4.1	8.2	3.8	R
SOUTHERN FARM BUREAU CAS INS CO	MS	B-	2,269.3	1,337.9	961.3	16.3	8.3	7.7	4.0	6.2	4.8	
SOUTHERN FARM BUREAU PROPERTY	MS	U	--	--	--	--	N/A	--	--	--	--	Z
▲SOUTHERN FIDELITY INS CO	FL	B+	196.7	82.1	104.2	-0.1	9.0	6.3	5.4	5.5	6.5	FL
SOUTHERN FIDELITY P&C INC	FL	C+	107.8	27.7	65.8	-4.4	5.3	4.4	3.0	4.7	4.7	FL
SOUTHERN FIRE & CASUALTY CO	WI	C	7.2	7.1	0.0	0.5	10.0	4.1	5.2	7.0	2.7	DRT
▲SOUTHERN GENERAL INS CO	GA	C	51.4	19.9	44.0	1.9	6.6	3.4	2.9	1.4	3.5	DLR
SOUTHERN GUARANTY INS CO	WI	U	--	--	--	--	N/A	--	--	--	--	Z
SOUTHERN INS CO	TX	C	39.4	29.6	1.1	0.6	7.3	4.1	3.7	9.1	3.5	GR
SOUTHERN INS CO OF VA	VA	C+	149.9	54.5	86.7	-3.4	9.0	6.2	2.8	6.3	4.5	R
▲SOUTHERN MUTUAL CHURCH INS CO	SC	B-	70.2	38.6	27.2	5.9	8.4	8.4	8.7	6.8	5.2	T
▲SOUTHERN MUTUAL INS CO	GA	B-	20.3	14.8	0.1	0.6	10.0	4.6	8.0	9.5	5.0	DF
▲SOUTHERN OAK INS CO	FL	B	121.9	56.2	66.9	0.6	8.6	5.6	8.7	6.4	5.5	
SOUTHERN PILOT INS CO	WI	C	7.1	6.9	0.0	0.0	10.0	4.0	2.9	7.0	2.7	DRT
▲SOUTHERN PIONEER PROP & CAS INS CO	AR	B-	49.5	22.0	27.5	0.7	7.2	6.2	5.2	6.6	3.6	DR
SOUTHERN STATES INS EXCHANGE	VA	C+	44.3	18.0	15.8	3.4	7.8	8.8	6.9	6.7	4.0	DR
▼SOUTHERN TRUST INS CO	GA	C	47.1	20.2	35.3	-2.0	7.5	5.8	2.5	5.3	4.1	DFR
SOUTHERN UNDERWRITERS INS CO	OK	C	5.3	5.3	0.0	0.1	10.0	N/A	6.6	7.5	2.1	DRT
SOUTHERN VANGUARD INS CO	TX	C	24.8	10.7	7.7	0.5	7.1	5.4	4.2	6.5	3.1	DR
▲SOUTHERN-OWNERS INS CO	MI	A	821.8	253.9	357.6	16.3	8.3	6.4	8.5	6.6	7.5	
SOUTHLAND LLOYDS INS CO	TX	U	(5) --	--	--	--	N/A	--	--	--	--	Z
SOUTHWEST GENERAL INS CO	NM	D	2.2	1.6	0.4	0.3	9.0	9.3	3.7	8.3	1.2	DFT
SOUTHWEST MARINE & GEN INS CO	AZ	C+	216.4	63.3	30.2	1.9	7.8	3.4	4.1	7.6	4.8	G
SOUTHWEST PHYSICIANS RRG INC	SC	U	--	--	--	--	N/A	--	--	--	--	Z
SPARTA INS CO	CT	D+	228.6	86.3	0.4	12.5	5.1	0.7	1.2	6.6	2.5	DFRT
SPARTAN INS CO	TX	C-	8.0	6.8	3.9	0.8	9.7	7.4	8.6	7.6	2.5	R
▲SPARTAN PROPERTY INS CO	SC	B-	32.4	24.4	10.2	2.7	7.8	5.3	8.0	7.7	5.0	D
SPECIALTY RISK OF AMERICA	IL	C-	16.6	6.4	6.5	0.6	4.1	6.0	5.0	6.7	2.4	D
SPECIALTY SURPLUS INS CO	IL	U	--	--	--	--	N/A	--	--	--	--	Z
SPINNAKER INS CO	IL	B-	48.5	27.9	15.9	-1.1	7.7	4.6	3.3	7.0	3.6	GRT
▼SPIRIT COMMERCIAL AUTO RRG INC	NV	E-	110.9	13.4	64.8	-18.6	0.0	0.1	1.5	0.0	0.2	CDFG
SPIRIT MOUNTAIN INS CO RRG INC	DC	D+	6.1	3.1	1.7	-0.1	8.8	9.9	3.7	9.1	2.2	DR
▲SPRING VALLEY MUTUAL INS CO	MN	E+	4.7	4.7	0.0	0.4	10.0	3.6	6.9	9.8	0.5	DR

See Page 27 for explanation of footnotes and
Page 28 for explanation of stability factors.
Arrows denote recent upgrades ▲ or downgrades ▼   (see Section VII for explanations)

www.weissratings.com

RISK ADJ. RATIO #1	CAPITAL RATIO #2	PREMIUM TO SURPLUS (%)	RESV. TO SURPLUS (%)	RESV. DEVELOP. 1 YEAR (%)	RESV. DEVELOP. 2 YEAR (%)	LOSS RATIO (%)	EXP. RATIO (%)	COMB RATIO (%)	CASH FROM UNDER- WRITING (%)	NET PREMIUM GROWTH (%)	INVEST. IN AFFIL (%)	INSURANCE COMPANY NAME
11.1	10.0	N/A	N/A	N/A	N/A	N/A	N/A	N/A	N/A	0.0	0.0	SFM SELECT INS CO
1.8	1.1	157.3	69.7	-2.1	-2.9	72.8	27.5	100.3	107.1	4.1	0.0	SHEBOYGAN FALLS INS CO
19.5	17.2	N/A	N/A	N/A	N/A	N/A	N/A	N/A	1.9	0.0	0.0	SHELBY INS CO
1.7	1.4	76.3	79.2	-4.4	-11.1	81.2	42.7	123.9	81.4	15.2	7.9	SHELTER GENERAL INS CO
2.3	1.9	79.7	27.2	-1.9	-3.2	73.3	28.2	101.5	100.1	5.7	22.4 ●	SHELTER MUTUAL INS CO
4.2	2.7	35.5	38.4	-4.4	-10.2	98.2	28.4	126.6	96.8	1.0	0.0 ●	SHELTER REINS CO
1.9	1.3	31.7	119.1	-6.7	-9.7	90.3	11.9	102.2	100.5	-1.6	0.0	SIGMA RRG INC
2.8	2.1	57.3	117.1	-5.5	-13.5	60.7	22.8	83.5	134.8	-5.8	0.0	SILVER OAK CASUALTY INC
6.1	4.3	17.3	49.4	-4.2	-7.5	52.8	33.9	86.7	90.1	-6.0	0.0	SIMED
1.6	1.0	19.4	102.4	2.5	1.8	107.6	30.6	138.2	53.6	-53.4	0.0 ●	SIRIUS AMERICA INS CO
N/A	N/A	--	--	--	--	--	--	--	--	--	--	SLAVONIC INS CO OF TEXAS
5.8	5.5	3.1	0.3	-0.1	N/A	134.6	54.5	189.1	55.2	9.8	17.3	SLAVONIC MUTUAL FIRE INS ASN
2.8	2.1	106.0	114.2	-5.5	-7.5	62.4	31.0	93.4	117.5	2.2	0.0	SOCIETY INS A MUTUAL CO
4.1	3.2	30.5	35.8	-4.2	-9.8	39.9	30.6	70.5	93.3	13.6	0.0	SOMERSET CASUALTY INS CO
4.3	2.7	33.3	78.4	-3.9	-6.5	68.7	30.4	99.1	109.1	4.6	1.4 ●	SOMPO AMERICA INSURANCE CO
N/A	N/A	--	--	--	--	--	--	--	--	--	--	SOMPO JAPAN CANOPIUS RE AG
1.0	0.6	206.6	50.1	-6.7	7.8	54.7	38.4	93.1	112.4	14.0	0.0	SOMPO JAPAN NIPPONKOA INS INC
3.4	2.1	64.6	29.5	-1.8	-2.6	69.8	30.6	100.4	103.2	3.8	0.0	SONNENBERG MUTUAL INS CO
10.6	9.5	N/A	N/A	N/A	N/A	N/A	N/A	N/A	N/A	0.0	0.0	SOUTH CAROLINA FARM BUREAU INS
22.6	17.6	N/A	N/A	N/A	N/A	N/A	N/A	N/A	24.6	0.0	0.0	SOUTHERN COUNTY MUTUAL INS CO
1.9	1.8	71.8	31.5	-1.5	-2.0	83.8	19.0	102.8	98.1	10.5	33.4 ●	SOUTHERN FARM BUREAU CAS INS CO
N/A	N/A	--	--	--	--	--	--	--	--	--	--	SOUTHERN FARM BUREAU PROPERTY
3.0	2.3	126.9	37.8	-2.6	-1.9	62.0	39.6	101.6	95.1	4.2	3.3 ●	SOUTHERN FIDELITY INS CO
1.1	0.7	237.2	106.7	14.1	12.8	86.2	25.4	111.6	87.7	-0.2	3.4	SOUTHERN FIDELITY P&C INC
228.7	118.5	N/A	N/A	N/A	N/A	N/A	N/A	N/A	N/A	100.0	0.0	SOUTHERN FIRE & CASUALTY CO
1.2	1.0	221.1	64.1	2.6	24.5	66.7	29.2	95.9	85.9	10.0	0.0	SOUTHERN GENERAL INS CO
N/A	N/A	--	--	--	--	--	--	--	--	--	--	SOUTHERN GUARANTY INS CO
2.1	1.2	3.6	32.2	0.6	9.6	95.8	24.3	120.1	66.4	555.8	0.0	SOUTHERN INS CO
3.2	2.3	159.1	77.8	-1.6	-3.4	75.4	31.8	107.2	104.7	13.1	0.0	SOUTHERN INS CO OF VA
3.2	2.3	70.5	20.0	-8.9	-7.3	45.0	38.9	83.9	120.8	5.1	0.0	SOUTHERN MUTUAL CHURCH INS CO
9.2	8.3	0.4	0.2	0.2	-0.1	63.8	-835.1	-771.3	368.3	-27.4	0.0	SOUTHERN MUTUAL INS CO
2.8	2.2	119.0	34.6	-0.7	-0.2	66.5	30.4	96.9	106.3	11.9	0.0	SOUTHERN OAK INS CO
130.4	84.6	N/A	N/A	N/A	N/A	N/A	N/A	N/A	N/A	100.0	0.0	SOUTHERN PILOT INS CO
1.9	1.2	125.0	54.3	8.6	-0.5	68.5	30.7	99.2	112.4	5.4	0.0	SOUTHERN PIONEER PROP & CAS INS
2.3	1.5	87.6	73.4	-1.5	-1.7	53.1	23.4	76.5	125.0	-1.0	0.0	SOUTHERN STATES INS EXCHANGE
1.9	1.3	175.0	26.1	8.2	6.4	66.8	41.9	108.7	88.5	12.4	0.0	SOUTHERN TRUST INS CO
81.1	38.3	N/A	N/A	N/A	N/A	N/A	N/A	N/A	N/A	0.0	0.0	SOUTHERN UNDERWRITERS INS CO
1.4	1.0	71.4	8.9	-2.0	-2.1	65.7	23.9	89.6	113.5	28.6	0.0	SOUTHERN VANGUARD INS CO
2.5	1.8	140.8	134.4	1.0	5.3	70.5	25.2	95.7	116.7	22.0	0.0 ●	SOUTHERN-OWNERS INS CO
N/A	N/A	--	--	--	--	--	--	--	--	--	--	SOUTHLAND LLOYDS INS CO
3.1	2.6	26.5	12.7	-6.7	-9.5	42.2	120.2	162.4	55.2	-23.8	0.0	SOUTHWEST GENERAL INS CO
2.7	1.5	47.7	80.8	2.4	3.1	64.7	32.3	97.0	311.0	23.1	0.0	SOUTHWEST MARINE & GEN INS CO
N/A	N/A	--	--	--	--	--	--	--	--	--	--	SOUTHWEST PHYSICIANS RRG INC
1.0	0.6	0.5	151.8	-8.0	48.6	-909.7	999 +	514.9	0.6	-93.7	0.0	SPARTA INS CO
3.3	3.0	56.7	1.2	-0.9	-1.2	2.9	67.3	70.2	136.3	14.9	0.0	SPARTAN INS CO
2.5	1.6	41.7	0.9	-0.2	-0.8	5.7	61.6	67.3	154.0	-5.1	0.0	SPARTAN PROPERTY INS CO
1.0	0.6	101.3	97.6	0.1	3.3	58.6	41.1	99.7	95.6	-11.6	0.0	SPECIALTY RISK OF AMERICA
N/A	N/A	--	--	--	--	--	--	--	--	--	--	SPECIALTY SURPLUS INS CO
2.5	1.4	56.8	7.9	-2.1	N/A	38.5	56.7	95.2	133.6	89.6	0.0	SPINNAKER INS CO
0.0	0.0	485.1	543.0	269.4	278.7	116.3	16.3	132.6	68.8	20.2	0.0	SPIRIT COMMERCIAL AUTO RRG INC
2.8	2.3	54.5	46.3	-23.3	-33.1	4.4	62.3	66.7	153.2	-18.1	0.0	SPIRIT MOUNTAIN INS CO RRG INC
76.9	36.5	N/A	N/A	N/A	N/A	N/A	N/A	N/A	-10.1	0.0	0.0	SPRING VALLEY MUTUAL INS CO

999 + Denotes number greater than 999.9%
999 - Denotes number less than -999.99%
● Bullets denote a more detailed analysis is available in Section II.

INSURANCE COMPANY NAME	DOM. STATE	RATING	TOTAL ASSETS ($MIL)	CAPITAL & SURPLUS ($MIL)	ANNUAL NET PREMIUM ($MIL)	NET INCOME ($MIL)	CAPITAL-IZATION INDEX (PTS)	RESERVE ADQ INDEX (PTS)	PROFIT-ABILITY INDEX (PTS)	LIQUIDITY INDEX (PTS)	STAB. INDEX (PTS)	STABILITY FACTORS
▲ST CHARLES INS CO RRG	SC	D	18.0	15.3	2.1	1.4	10.0	9.7	8.8	8.0	1.5	D
ST CLAIR INS CO	NY	U	--	--	--	--	N/A	--	--	--	--	Z
ST JOHNS INS CO	FL	C-	129.5	50.7	39.0	-5.8	2.3	5.5	3.5	1.2	3.0	CFL
▲ST LUKES HEALTH NETWORK INS CO RRG	VT	E+	69.7	21.1	11.5	1.7	2.6	4.0	6.2	6.6	0.5	DF
ST PAUL FIRE & MARINE INS CO	CT	B	18,716.4	5,367.3	5,749.1	712.2	7.7	8.3	3.9	6.6	5.7	
ST PAUL GUARDIAN INS CO	CT	C+	75.8	23.1	22.8	1.6	7.6	8.1	3.8	6.9	4.7	D
ST PAUL MERCURY INS CO	CT	B-	341.2	116.0	91.3	8.6	9.1	8.0	3.8	7.3	4.8	
ST PAUL PROTECTIVE INS CO	CT	B-	518.0	216.2	132.5	12.2	10.0	7.8	4.4	6.9	4.9	
ST PAUL SURPLUS LINES INS CO	DE	C	636.2	183.4	200.9	15.0	4.2	8.3	3.9	6.8	4.0	C
STANDARD & PREFERRED INS CO	NY	U	--	--	--	--	N/A	--	--	--	--	Z
STANDARD CASUALTY CO	TX	C+	37.7	17.3	28.7	0.0	7.5	4.9	3.5	6.0	4.1	DF
STANDARD FIRE INS CO	CT	B	3,766.4	1,189.5	1,105.1	125.4	7.8	8.2	5.5	6.8	6.3	
STANDARD GUARANTY INS CO	DE	B-	314.4	129.8	188.2	28.5	8.2	6.9	3.9	5.7	5.2	
STANDARD P&C INS CO	IL	D+	19.1	11.1	0.0	0.3	10.0	9.5	1.6	9.7	2.8	DFRT
STAR & SHIELD INS EXCHANGE	FL	D	4.4	2.2	1.5	-0.9	3.4	3.6	0.3	5.1	1.4	FT
▼STAR CASUALTY INS CO	FL	D-	23.6	5.2	14.9	1.2	1.4	0.8	1.6	7.4	1.2	CDGT
STAR INS CO	MI	C	1,815.6	563.9	577.3	161.8	7.5	2.5	6.5	6.8	3.6	R
▲STARNET INS CO	DE	C+	242.1	117.1	0.0	2.0	10.0	N/A	4.5	9.5	4.4	R
STARR INDEMNITY & LIABILITY CO	TX	B	4,803.6	1,875.3	1,084.3	4.7	6.3	3.5	5.3	6.8	5.3	C
STARR SPECIALTY INSURANCE CO	TX	U	--	--	--	--	N/A	--	--	--	--	Z
▲STARR SURPLUS LINES INS CO	IL	B	405.0	133.6	37.6	21.2	5.2	4.0	9.1	9.3	5.5	CT
STARSTONE NATIONAL INS CO	DE	C	424.3	111.4	49.8	13.8	7.6	7.0	6.4	7.0	3.7	T
STARSTONE SPECIALTY INS CO	DE	C-	238.0	146.7	16.0	4.3	7.1	3.4	4.1	7.0	3.4	FRT
STATE AUTO INS CO OF OH	OH	C-	29.6	17.4	0.0	0.3	10.0	N/A	6.7	7.0	3.3	ADFR
STATE AUTO INS CO OF WI	WI	B-	15.9	12.2	0.0	0.1	10.0	N/A	5.6	7.0	4.3	ADFR
STATE AUTO P&C INS CO	IA	C+	2,518.9	687.0	995.9	38.0	7.5	5.8	5.4	6.3	4.3	AR
STATE AUTOMOBILE MUTUAL INS CO	OH	C+	2,407.3	778.9	673.7	-18.8	7.0	6.0	2.8	6.0	4.3	A
STATE FARM CTY MUTUAL INS CO OF TX	TX	B-	132.9	23.0	-8.5	4.3	8.8	5.6	1.7	7.0	4.9	DFT
STATE FARM FIRE & CAS CO	IL	B+	39,411.9	17,710.2	16,281.8	1,059.3	8.2	6.2	8.8	5.8	6.7	L
STATE FARM FLORIDA INS CO	FL	B	2,063.4	976.7	589.7	-109.2	10.0	6.3	5.5	6.5	5.4	F
▼STATE FARM GENERAL INS CO	IL	C	7,241.9	3,186.9	1,781.6	-836.9	7.6	6.1	2.2	5.6	4.2	F
▲STATE FARM GUARANTY INS CO	IL	B-	34.5	13.6	0.0	0.1	10.0	N/A	6.2	7.0	4.9	DR
STATE FARM INDEMNITY CO	IL	B	2,301.8	1,275.3	643.6	59.2	10.0	8.5	6.7	6.8	5.4	T
STATE FARM LLOYDS	TX	B	3,358.3	1,194.2	1,692.0	-104.6	8.4	6.2	4.7	5.1	5.5	FL
STATE FARM MUTUAL AUTOMOBILE INS CO	IL	B+	160,732.0	97,005.0	43,171.4	1,701.6	8.1	6.2	4.2	6.5	6.7	
STATE MUTUAL INS CO (ME)	ME	C	13.4	13.2	0.0	0.1	10.0	N/A	7.5	7.0	2.9	DGT
STATE NATIONAL FIRE INS CO	LA	C	4.1	2.4	2.2	-0.2	7.1	7.5	3.1	6.8	2.5	DGT
STATE NATIONAL INS CO	TX	B-	442.9	311.4	45.9	7.6	8.0	5.0	7.5	7.4	4.8	R
▲STATE VOLUNTEER MUTUAL INS CO	TN	B+	1,249.3	606.8	118.9	29.6	10.0	9.3	8.1	8.1	6.5	T
STATES SELF-INSURERS RISK RET GROUP	VT	D-	28.3	9.7	4.4	0.7	0.7	4.1	4.7	7.3	1.2	CDR
STEADFAST INS CO	DE	C+	723.4	508.8	0.0	5.9	9.0	N/A	7.3	6.8	4.7	FR
▲STEADPOINT INS CO	TN	C	26.9	9.7	9.2	2.7	7.1	7.0	9.2	7.1	3.0	DR
STERLING CASUALTY INS CO	CA	D	19.2	6.2	11.5	0.0	5.4	1.5	3.5	7.2	2.1	D
STERLING INS CO	NY	B	198.7	127.5	62.0	13.9	10.0	8.7	8.8	6.9	6.0	T
STERLING INS COOP INC	NY	U	--	--	--	--	N/A	--	--	--	--	Z
▲STICO MUTUAL INS CO RRG	VT	D+	23.1	12.5	2.6	0.1	7.9	9.4	7.4	7.1	2.5	DR
STILLWATER INS CO	CA	B-	399.0	178.0	252.1	-32.3	4.9	6.2	3.6	0.9	4.5	CLR
STILLWATER P&C INS CO	NY	C+	140.4	128.4	2.9	3.6	10.0	3.6	7.9	9.7	4.1	
STONE VALLEY MUTUAL FIRE INS CO	PA	U	--	--	--	--	N/A	--	--	--	--	Z
▼STONEGATE INS CO	IL	D-	26.2	6.8	20.7	0.1	1.7	0.5	5.5	5.3	1.1	DG
▲STONETRUST COMMERCIAL INS CO	NE	B	174.2	72.1	50.0	4.6	7.3	3.9	5.1	6.8	5.5	
STONEWOOD INS CO	NC	C+	105.0	25.2	11.5	0.5	7.2	8.1	3.7	7.0	4.4	RT

See Page 27 for explanation of footnotes and
Page 28 for explanation of stability factors.

Arrows denote recent upgrades ▲ or downgrades ▼   (see Section VII for explanations)

116

www.weissratings.com

RISK ADJ. RATIO #1	CAPITAL RATIO #2	PREMIUM TO SURPLUS (%)	RESV. TO SURPLUS (%)	RESV. DEVELOP. 1 YEAR (%)	RESV. DEVELOP. 2 YEAR (%)	LOSS RATIO (%)	EXP. RATIO (%)	COMB RATIO (%)	CASH FROM UNDER-WRITING (%)	NET PREMIUM GROWTH (%)	INVEST. IN AFFIL (%)	INSURANCE COMPANY NAME
6.0	3.4	14.0	12.0	-11.9	-10.7	12.6	16.0	28.6	482.8	18.0	0.0	ST CHARLES INS CO RRG
N/A	N/A	--	--	--	--	--	--	--	--	--	--	ST CLAIR INS CO
0.4	0.4	77.0	32.7	0.6	2.0	118.2	10.5	128.7	67.0	17.7	0.0	ST JOHNS INS CO
0.8	0.6	54.3	188.0	-19.1	-44.4	83.1	7.9	91.0	73.2	3.9	0.0	ST LUKES HEALTH NETWORK INS CO
2.0	1.5	107.1	178.2	-2.4	-3.7	69.5	29.1	98.6	106.9	4.7	11.6 ●	ST PAUL FIRE & MARINE INS CO
2.1	1.4	98.7	161.7	-2.1	-3.3	69.5	29.2	98.7	107.0	4.9	0.0	ST PAUL GUARDIAN INS CO
3.5	2.3	78.7	129.0	-1.6	-2.7	69.5	29.2	98.7	99.5	4.9	0.0	ST PAUL MERCURY INS CO
4.5	3.0	61.3	100.4	-1.3	-2.1	69.5	29.2	98.7	107.2	4.9	0.0	ST PAUL PROTECTIVE INS CO
0.9	0.6	109.5	179.5	-2.3	-3.7	69.5	29.2	98.7	120.9	4.9	0.0	ST PAUL SURPLUS LINES INS CO
N/A	N/A	--	--	--	--	--	--	--	--	--	--	STANDARD & PREFERRED INS CO
2.0	1.3	166.2	15.5	-1.4	0.7	63.7	40.4	104.1	94.9	0.1	0.0	STANDARD CASUALTY CO
1.9	1.5	92.9	152.3	-2.0	-3.4	69.5	29.3	98.8	107.7	4.9	15.8 ●	STANDARD FIRE INS CO
2.3	1.8	145.1	31.5	-4.4	-14.1	40.2	49.1	89.3	98.2	-5.8	0.0	STANDARD GUARANTY INS CO
6.6	6.0	N/A	N/A	N/A	-28.7	N/A	N/A	N/A	-20.1	-100.0	0.0	STANDARD P&C INS CO
0.8	0.7	66.1	97.2	14.7	2.6	105.1	68.7	173.8	29.5	-77.5	0.0	STAR & SHIELD INS EXCHANGE
0.3	0.3	284.6	90.9	74.9	66.3	96.1	2.5	98.6	131.6	141.0	0.0	STAR CASUALTY INS CO
1.8	1.3	102.4	183.4	1.0	15.2	67.0	35.9	102.9	89.5	-1.7	11.6 ●	STAR INS CO
12.6	11.4	N/A	N/A	N/A	N/A	N/A	N/A	N/A	461.9	0.0	0.0	STARNET INS CO
1.2	0.9	57.8	108.8	12.3	19.5	103.5	19.5	123.0	110.0	8.1	31.5 ●	STARR INDEMNITY & LIABILITY CO
N/A	N/A	--	--	--	--	--	--	--	--	--	--	STARR SPECIALTY INSURANCE CO
1.1	0.7	28.1	89.8	1.1	2.0	77.9	-41.3	36.6	-115.7	-42.7	0.0	STARR SURPLUS LINES INS CO
2.4	1.3	44.7	85.7	-11.2	-4.8	49.2	23.2	72.4	188.6	-46.5	0.0	STARSTONE NATIONAL INS CO
1.3	1.2	10.9	42.5	-0.7	-1.9	74.1	17.1	91.2	85.2	-54.0	54.8	STARSTONE SPECIALTY INS CO
6.5	5.8	N/A	N/A	N/A	N/A	N/A	N/A	N/A	283.4	0.0	0.0	STATE AUTO INS CO OF OH
10.4	9.3	N/A	N/A	N/A	N/A	N/A	N/A	N/A	148.0	0.0	0.0	STATE AUTO INS CO OF WI
2.2	1.3	145.0	144.5	-5.6	-2.4	72.2	35.1	107.3	101.5	-1.9	0.0 ●	STATE AUTO P&C INS CO
1.1	1.0	86.5	86.2	-3.1	-1.3	72.2	35.5	107.7	96.0	-1.9	45.5 ●	STATE AUTOMOBILE MUTUAL INS CO
2.5	2.2	-36.8	24.7	-3.9	6.5	N/A	N/A	N/A	-369.9	-126.0	0.0	STATE FARM CTY MUTUAL INS CO OF TX
3.6	2.3	91.9	41.6	1.7	1.7	73.4	26.3	99.7	100.7	0.7	0.0 ●	STATE FARM FIRE & CAS CO
4.6	3.2	60.4	34.4	-0.6	-0.9	82.7	28.5	111.2	95.1	3.3	0.0 ●	STATE FARM FLORIDA INS CO
2.0	1.3	55.9	67.3	0.2	2.5	156.5	28.8	185.3	68.4	-7.7	0.0 ●	STATE FARM GENERAL INS CO
3.7	3.4	N/A	N/A	N/A	N/A	N/A	N/A	N/A	24.0	0.0	0.0	STATE FARM GUARANTY INS CO
5.7	5.2	50.5	55.7	-3.6	-5.3	77.9	23.3	101.2	98.1	2.0	0.6 ●	STATE FARM INDEMNITY CO
2.3	1.9	141.7	46.4	2.8	0.9	88.5	28.2	116.7	90.1	1.2	0.0 ●	STATE FARM LLOYDS
2.0	1.7	44.5	31.2	-0.3	0.6	84.0	25.1	109.1	100.2	6.7	26.3 ●	STATE FARM MUTUAL AUTOMOBILE INS
18.1	10.5	N/A	N/A	N/A	N/A	N/A	N/A	N/A	N/A	0.0	0.0	STATE MUTUAL INS CO (ME)
1.5	1.0	90.7	9.5	-1.0	-1.4	54.4	50.6	105.0	95.2	39.9	0.0	STATE NATIONAL FIRE INS CO
1.6	1.6	14.8	1.6	0.1	-0.1	49.4	47.5	96.9	135.1	-26.6	52.6 ●	STATE NATIONAL INS CO
4.9	3.5	19.6	77.9	-7.9	-12.6	67.0	18.9	85.9	100.8	6.3	0.0 ●	STATE VOLUNTEER MUTUAL INS CO
0.3	0.2	45.6	151.3	-1.2	5.2	62.0	34.8	96.8	131.7	1.8	0.0	STATES SELF-INSURERS RISK RET
2.3	2.3	N/A	N/A	N/A	N/A	N/A	N/A	N/A	-11.2	0.0	46.3 ●	STEADFAST INS CO
1.5	1.2	95.3	98.7	-14.5	-16.3	28.2	30.3	58.5	132.7	0.4	0.0	STEADPOINT INS CO
1.1	0.9	185.9	80.9	2.8	33.2	72.4	23.9	96.3	277.2	54.2	0.0	STERLING CASUALTY INS CO
7.1	5.1	48.6	19.4	-3.7	-4.8	40.3	33.8	74.1	128.3	3.1	0.2	STERLING INS CO
N/A	N/A	--	--	--	--	--	--	--	--	--	--	STERLING INS COOP INC
2.9	1.9	21.2	39.0	-20.6	-20.1	40.6	64.9	105.5	115.4	-6.3	0.0	STICO MUTUAL INS CO RRG
0.9	0.7	141.7	51.3	5.8	3.3	86.7	32.9	119.6	96.6	13.7	37.7	STILLWATER INS CO
9.9	5.4	2.2	N/A	N/A	N/A	N/A	36.4	36.4	133.5	13.9	0.0	STILLWATER P&C INS CO
N/A	N/A	--	--	--	--	--	--	--	--	--	--	STONE VALLEY MUTUAL FIRE INS CO
0.4	0.3	305.5	137.7	53.8	69.0	64.9	34.5	99.4	129.6	36.1	2.3	STONEGATE INS CO
2.0	1.3	69.3	97.5	-1.7	-1.2	61.3	38.8	100.1	112.0	-5.9	0.0	STONETRUST COMMERCIAL INS CO
1.6	1.1	45.8	99.8	-0.7	-4.1	67.0	36.6	103.6	104.1	-37.5	0.0	STONEWOOD INS CO

999 + Denotes number greater than 999.9%
999 - Denotes number less than -999.99%
● Bullets denote a more detailed analysis is available in Section II.

INSURANCE COMPANY NAME	DOM. STATE	RATING	TOTAL ASSETS ($MIL)	CAPITAL & SURPLUS ($MIL)	ANNUAL NET PREMIUM ($MIL)	NET INCOME ($MIL)	CAPITAL-IZATION INDEX (PTS)	RESERVE ADQ INDEX (PTS)	PROFIT-ABILITY INDEX (PTS)	LIQUIDITY INDEX (PTS)	STAB. INDEX (PTS)	STABILITY FACTORS
STONINGTON INS CO	PA	E+	15.7	14.3	0.0	0.1	10.0	4.0	2.1	7.0	0.6	DT
STRATFORD INS CO	NH	B-	539.9	86.3	22.9	-6.9	7.8	9.3	4.0	6.9	4.1	GRT
STRATHMORE INS CO	NY	C	58.7	26.8	15.9	1.2	8.2	5.9	8.0	6.8	4.1	T
SU INS CO	WI	C	24.1	12.9	16.4	0.1	9.1	6.1	6.7	7.1	3.4	D
▲SUBLIMITY INS CO	OR	B-	40.7	16.0	27.2	-0.3	7.7	5.6	4.5	5.1	5.3	DF
SUBURBAN HEALTH ORG RRG LLC	SC	U	--	--	--	--	N/A	--	--	--	--	Z
SUECIA INS CO	NY	U	--	--	--	--	N/A	--	--	--	--	Z
▲SUMMITPOINT INS CO	WV	B-	59.6	11.5	7.5	0.3	5.9	6.1	5.3	7.8	4.6	D
SUN SURETY INS CO	SD	C-	22.4	10.7	3.8	0.8	8.4	N/A	8.6	7.4	3.0	D
SUNAPEE MUTL FIRE INS CO	NH	B	13.9	13.6	0.0	0.1	10.0	N/A	7.5	7.0	4.0	DGT
SUNDERLAND MARINE INS CO LTD	AK	D+(1)	10.3	5.8	0.3	0.1	8.8	5.8	2.0	10.0	2.4	DFGR
SUNLAND RRG INC	TN	B-	2.4	1.5	0.5	0.0	8.4	8.6	4.5	7.6	3.5	DFT
SUNZ INS CO	FL	E	195.5	37.2	63.3	-0.6	0.4	1.3	5.8	3.2	0.3	CGLR
▲SURETEC INDEMNITY CO	CA	B-	24.1	13.4	4.5	1.1	8.7	5.9	5.8	8.8	4.7	DFT
▲SURETEC INS CO	TX	B+	253.2	102.1	70.0	7.4	8.9	8.5	8.6	8.2	6.5	T
SURETY BONDING CO OF AMERICA	SD	C+	7.7	7.6	0.0	0.1	10.0	N/A	4.1	10.0	4.1	DR
▲SUTTER INS CO	CA	C+	37.2	21.1	16.2	0.6	9.5	6.1	4.0	6.8	4.4	DR
▲SWISS REINS AMERICA CORP	NY	C	14,202.2	3,238.0	1,916.5	121.8	5.2	8.2	3.5	7.7	3.5	R
▲SYNCORA GUARANTEE INC	NY	C+	1,302.1	1,317.6	14.2	70.5	10.0	3.1	6.6	9.6	4.3	FG
▲SYNERGY COMP INS CO	PA	C	41.6	14.7	18.5	0.8	5.9	9.9	8.7	6.7	3.5	DR
▲SYNERGY INS CO	NC	C	74.4	28.6	18.0	6.6	7.4	7.0	9.5	7.1	3.5	R
TANK OWNER MEMBERS INS CO	TX	C	26.7	14.5	5.6	2.9	8.0	9.3	9.4	7.9	3.4	DR
TDC NATIONAL ASR CO	OR	C+	344.8	94.0	19.0	5.4	7.6	6.9	6.5	7.7	4.6	T
TDC SPECIALTY INS CO	DC	C	129.6	95.4	12.8	-7.5	10.0	6.0	3.6	9.1	4.0	FGT
▲TEACHERS AUTO INS CO	NJ	B	28.0	14.3	0.0	0.5	10.0	6.1	7.9	10.0	4.9	D
TEACHERS INS CO	IL	B	356.9	148.7	215.1	6.5	8.2	8.2	5.8	4.9	5.6	AL
▼TECHNOLOGY INS CO	DE	D-	3,773.1	1,098.7	1,322.3	-60.8	0.9	6.0	2.8	1.6	1.2	CGLR
TENNESSEE FARMERS ASR CO	TN	B+	1,505.8	1,044.3	638.6	49.1	10.0	8.0	8.9	6.2	6.1	
TENNESSEE FARMERS MUTUAL INS CO	TN	B+	3,084.6	2,424.4	641.6	68.2	8.3	7.5	8.3	6.7	6.1	
TERRA INS CO (A RRG)	VT	B-	27.2	17.9	7.2	1.8	9.3	5.8	5.4	8.4	4.1	DR
TERRAFIRMA RRG LLC	VT	D+	6.8	4.9	1.4	0.1	8.2	3.9	6.9	6.9	2.3	D
TEXAS BUILDERS INS CO	TX	U	--	--	--	--	N/A	--	--	--	--	Z
TEXAS FAIR PLAN ASSN	TX	E-	73.1	-54.9	74.2	-38.2	0.0	4.0	0.2	7.0	0.0	CDFT
▲TEXAS FARM BUREAU CASUALTY INS CO	TX	A-	1,252.3	678.9	706.6	37.4	10.0	6.1	4.8	5.5	6.9	
▲TEXAS FARM BUREAU MUTUAL INS CO	TX	C+	733.5	328.5	415.6	-6.8	9.1	6.5	4.0	5.4	4.5	F
TEXAS FARM BUREAU UNDERWRITERS	TX	C	81.1	19.8	0.0	0.0	9.2	N/A	5.2	7.0	4.0	D
TEXAS FARMERS INS CO	TX	C+	676.1	87.0	141.8	2.0	8.5	5.6	5.2	0.0	4.8	FGLR
TEXAS HERITAGE INS CO	TX	C	17.4	16.8	-1.5	0.2	10.0	6.1	2.7	7.0	3.8	FRT
TEXAS HOSPITAL INS EXCHANGE	TX	C-	36.3	24.5	7.6	1.6	10.0	10.0	8.5	6.9	2.5	DR
TEXAS INS CO	TX	C	41.6	18.0	22.0	4.2	6.7	6.4	9.4	7.7	3.1	DT
▲TEXAS LAWYERS INS EXCHANGE	TX	B	92.1	64.5	17.4	2.5	10.0	9.4	8.6	7.8	5.5	D
TEXAS MEDICAL INS CO	TX	C-	64.8	33.0	21.6	0.8	7.1	8.9	8.5	7.1	3.3	DRT
THAMES INS CO	CT	C	31.4	18.1	10.8	1.1	8.9	8.0	7.7	6.8	4.2	D
▼THE INS CO	LA	C-	211.6	51.8	47.2	-15.7	5.1	4.1	1.8	6.3	3.2	FR
THIRD COAST INS CO	WI	U	--	--	--	--	N/A	--	--	--	--	Z
TIG INS CO	CA	C	2,465.3	678.6	0.0	-181.1	3.3	2.7	1.8	9.8	3.5	CFRT
TITAN INDEMNITY CO	TX	B-	157.6	145.2	0.0	0.8	7.9	N/A	3.8	7.0	5.0	FT
TITAN INS CO	MI	B-	134.3	100.3	3.0	-1.6	10.0	3.6	4.0	8.5	4.8	T
▲TITAN INS CO INC A RRG	SC	C+	67.5	52.1	-0.7	3.7	8.9	N/A	8.9	10.0	4.5	RT
TITLE INDUSTRY ASR CO RRG	VT	D+	7.9	5.5	1.2	0.6	10.0	7.0	8.9	9.9	2.3	DGR
TM SPECIALTY INS CO	AZ	U	--	--	--	--	N/A	--	--	--	--	Z
TNUS INS CO	NY	B	64.5	57.1	0.0	1.2	10.0	3.6	6.7	9.2	5.5	DT

See Page 27 for explanation of footnotes and
Page 28 for explanation of stability factors.
Arrows denote recent upgrades ▲ or downgrades ▼   (see Section VII for explanations)

118

www.weissratings.com

RISK ADJ. RATIO #1	CAPITAL RATIO #2	PREMIUM TO SURPLUS (%)	RESV. TO SURPLUS (%)	RESV. DEVELOP. 1 YEAR (%)	RESV. DEVELOP. 2 YEAR (%)	LOSS RATIO (%)	EXP. RATIO (%)	COMB RATIO (%)	CASH FROM UNDER-WRITING (%)	NET PREMIUM GROWTH (%)	INVEST. IN AFFIL (%)	INSURANCE COMPANY NAME
24.7	22.2	N/A	N/A	N/A	N/A	N/A	N/A	N/A	N/A	100.0	0.0	STONINGTON INS CO
2.5	1.5	26.5	43.8	-0.3	-1.7	98.1	45.3	143.4	178.7	50.7	0.0	STRATFORD INS CO
2.1	1.8	59.1	80.4	-0.1	3.1	64.0	30.4	94.4	119.4	10.6	0.0	STRATHMORE INS CO
3.4	2.3	126.8	12.3	0.6	-0.7	61.2	38.2	99.4	101.4	6.5	0.0	SU INS CO
1.7	1.4	170.5	58.5	2.9	3.0	77.7	28.9	106.6	91.2	2.3	0.0	SUBLIMITY INS CO
N/A	N/A	--	--	--	--	--	--	--	--	--	--	SUBURBAN HEALTH ORG RRG LLC
N/A	N/A	--	--	--	--	--	--	--	--	--	--	SUECIA INS CO
1.3	0.8	65.3	200.5	-23.8	-37.3	61.0	47.7	108.7	114.0	4.9	0.0	SUMMITPOINT INS CO
2.4	1.9	35.5	N/A	N/A	N/A	-0.6	74.7	74.1	132.9	3.6	19.9	SUN SURETY INS CO
10.7	6.2	N/A	N/A	N/A	N/A	N/A	N/A	N/A	N/A	0.0	0.0	SUNAPEE MUTL FIRE INS CO
4.2	3.7	4.8	N/A	1.9	12.0	-16.9	99.8	82.9	-48.0	-87.4	0.0	SUNDERLAND MARINE INS CO LTD
3.7	3.3	33.8	25.4	-3.2	-4.0	46.7	40.5	87.2	-4.4	-9.8	0.0	SUNLAND RRG INC
0.2	0.1	170.3	98.7	22.2	38.8	54.8	50.0	104.8	117.9	54.1	0.0	SUNZ INS CO
3.3	2.7	33.3	11.3	-8.6	-11.7	12.6	72.8	85.4	85.1	-38.2	0.0	SURETEC INDEMNITY CO
2.7	2.2	68.6	12.2	-1.8	-5.5	18.6	65.1	83.7	125.4	13.5	5.5 ●	SURETEC INS CO
110.2	55.1	N/A	N/A	N/A	N/A	N/A	N/A	N/A	N/A	0.0	0.0	SURETY BONDING CO OF AMERICA
3.7	2.8	77.0	32.4	-7.1	-4.8	59.4	37.8	97.2	97.2	23.8	0.0	SUTTER INS CO
1.2	0.7	59.2	136.8	-0.8	-0.3	72.7	37.2	109.9	175.3	1.8	0.0 ●	SWISS REINS AMERICA CORP
20.3	11.8	1.1	-20.0	-3.1	-16.7	-170.6	316.2	145.6	9.4	73.9	0.0 ●	SYNCORA GUARANTEE INC
1.1	0.9	126.0	110.4	-6.9	-41.0	61.4	29.6	91.0	134.3	24.7	0.0	SYNERGY COMP INS CO
2.5	2.0	62.8	48.1	-21.0	-41.9	22.0	21.4	43.4	173.9	2.7	0.0	SYNERGY INS CO
2.9	1.9	38.6	55.7	-8.5	-13.5	25.2	14.6	39.8	179.9	-2.7	3.7	TANK OWNER MEMBERS INS CO
2.4	1.5	20.3	37.3	-2.0	-10.9	92.9	13.4	106.3	212.1	1.8	0.0	TDC NATIONAL ASR CO
4.7	4.0	13.4	6.5	1.8	3.5	131.5	97.3	228.8	77.7	232.6	3.8	TDC SPECIALTY INS CO
5.0	4.5	N/A	0.4	0.4	0.5	N/A	N/A	N/A	-0.1	0.0	0.0	TEACHERS AUTO INS CO
2.9	1.9	144.7	57.4	0.2	-1.6	76.9	26.2	103.1	98.1	4.5	0.0	TEACHERS INS CO
0.3	0.2	120.4	163.9	129.9	-165.0	80.2	24.3	104.5	130.4	16.0	4.1 ●	TECHNOLOGY INS CO
5.8	4.0	61.2	19.0	-2.2	-3.1	81.6	14.8	96.4	107.8	6.4	1.7 ●	TENNESSEE FARMERS ASR CO
2.2	2.1	26.5	11.3	-0.9	-1.3	81.6	14.3	95.9	111.2	6.4	37.8 ●	TENNESSEE FARMERS MUTUAL INS CO
3.5	2.5	40.0	10.4	1.5	4.1	11.1	56.4	67.5	133.5	-7.0	0.0	TERRA INS CO (A RRG)
2.5	1.7	28.5	33.1	5.4	8.1	65.5	33.7	99.2	106.7	6.1	0.0	TERRAFIRMA RRG LLC
N/A	N/A	--	--	--	--	--	--	--	--	--	--	TEXAS BUILDERS INS CO
-0.6	-0.4	-135.1	-41.1	20.9	-57.4	110.4	40.8	151.2	57.3	-7.7	0.0	TEXAS FAIR PLAN ASSN
4.3	3.4	104.1	35.8	-0.6	-0.5	81.1	17.2	98.3	104.5	2.8	0.0 ●	TEXAS FARM BUREAU CASUALTY INS
2.8	2.4	126.5	19.9	-2.0	-4.9	83.8	21.0	104.8	95.3	-1.8	1.4 ●	TEXAS FARM BUREAU MUTUAL INS CO
2.7	2.4	N/A	N/A	N/A	N/A	N/A	N/A	N/A	N/A	0.0	0.0	TEXAS FARM BUREAU UNDERWRITERS
2.8	2.0	163.1	102.6	0.2	4.2	69.9	31.3	101.2	27.8	-3.9	0.0	TEXAS FARMERS INS CO
49.8	29.8	-9.2	3.2	-0.1	-0.7	111.3	-23.9	87.4	-9.0	-132.8	0.0	TEXAS HERITAGE INS CO
6.1	3.6	30.9	30.2	-5.2	-20.9	38.2	51.0	89.2	99.1	0.6	0.0	TEXAS HOSPITAL INS EXCHANGE
1.1	0.9	122.0	125.0	-1.5	8.5	50.2	21.9	72.1	155.6	20.6	0.0	TEXAS INS CO
10.2	6.4	27.0	27.4	-2.2	-6.1	44.5	14.1	58.6	210.5	2.9	0.1	TEXAS LAWYERS INS EXCHANGE
1.4	1.0	65.3	68.6	3.2	-0.2	65.6	34.8	100.4	152.8	13.7	0.0	TEXAS MEDICAL INS CO
3.7	2.5	59.9	21.8	-2.1	-3.6	49.2	41.8	91.0	114.4	1.3	0.0	THAMES INS CO
1.0	0.7	91.1	254.2	20.6	42.4	114.0	28.7	142.7	78.0	-31.7	0.0	THE INS CO
N/A	N/A	--	--	--	--	--	--	--	--	--	--	THIRD COAST INS CO
0.9	0.6	N/A	242.2	14.6	23.7	999 +	999 +	999 +	0.4	-99.9	14.6 ●	TIG INS CO
1.6	1.5	N/A	N/A	N/A	N/A	N/A	N/A	N/A	149.2	0.0	68.0	TITAN INDEMNITY CO
19.9	16.1	3.0	30.2	-0.3	1.0	234.9	8.8	243.7	42.7	0.0	0.0	TITAN INS CO
2.3	2.2	-1.3	N/A	N/A	N/A	N/A	270.2	270.2	138.4	-108.6	36.1	TITAN INS CO INC A RRG
6.6	4.8	21.8	26.1	-2.8	-1.6	31.0	3.3	34.3	499.9	27.7	0.0	TITLE INDUSTRY ASR CO RRG
N/A	N/A	--	--	--	--	--	--	--	--	--	--	TM SPECIALTY INS CO
29.1	26.1	N/A	1.1	N/A	N/A	N/A	N/A	N/A	-252.7	0.0	0.0	TNUS INS CO

999 + Denotes number greater than 999.9%
999 - Denotes number less than -999.99%
● Bullets denote a more detailed analysis is available in Section II.

INSURANCE COMPANY NAME	DOM. STATE	RATING	TOTAL ASSETS ($MIL)	CAPITAL & SURPLUS ($MIL)	ANNUAL NET PREMIUM ($MIL)	NET INCOME ($MIL)	CAPITAL-IZATION INDEX (PTS)	RESERVE ADQ INDEX (PTS)	PROFIT-ABILITY INDEX (PTS)	LIQUIDITY INDEX (PTS)	STAB. INDEX (PTS)	STABILITY FACTORS
TOA REINS CO OF AMERICA	DE	B+	1,820.3	660.2	423.7	20.5	7.9	6.0	4.8	6.8	6.5	
TOKIO MARINE AMERICA INS CO	NY	A	1,409.5	504.7	287.2	7.8	8.3	6.7	4.6	6.9	7.2	
TOKIO MARINE PACIFIC INS LTD	GU	C	121.0	82.7	149.4	8.0	9.0	8.7	8.0	1.4	3.4	L
TOKIO MARINE SPECIALTY INS CO	DE	C	606.5	190.5	159.2	19.4	9.4	7.6	7.1	6.8	3.9	T
▲TOKIO MILLENNIUM RE AG (US BRANCH)	NY	C	1,226.2	231.2	556.6	-84.4	5.5	4.6	2.2	6.0	3.5	T
TOPA INS CO	CA	B-	199.0	79.0	90.3	-2.2	7.6	6.2	3.8	5.9	4.5	R
TOWER BONDING & SURETY CO	PR	D+	3.7	2.7	1.2	-0.1	7.4	5.0	4.4	6.4	2.0	D
TOWER HEALTH RECIPROCAL RRG	SC	E	6.0	2.1	4.0	0.1	5.1	N/A	5.9	9.1	0.0	DT
TOWER HILL PREFERRED INS CO	FL	D	99.7	45.3	43.0	-2.0	8.8	4.2	3.7	6.4	2.1	R
TOWER HILL PRIME INS CO	FL	D	236.1	98.7	55.1	-26.5	8.9	3.4	3.0	6.2	1.6	FR
▼TOWER HILL SELECT INS CO	FL	C-	75.0	25.3	25.2	-5.0	4.5	2.8	1.9	3.0	3.1	LR
▼TOWER HILL SIGNATURE INS CO	FL	C-	117.7	39.4	60.1	-2.2	2.6	3.5	2.5	1.2	3.3	CL
TOYOTA MOTOR INS CO	IA	C+	557.7	254.1	106.9	10.9	10.0	5.0	8.5	7.4	4.0	R
TRADERS INS CO	MO	C-	83.3	25.8	70.4	3.8	3.1	5.8	8.9	5.9	3.0	CR
TRADEWIND INS CO LTD	HI	C	13.0	8.2	0.0	0.1	10.0	N/A	6.4	10.0	3.8	DFT
TRANS CITY CASUALTY INS CO	AZ	C	18.0	12.7	3.0	0.5	10.0	9.4	8.3	9.4	3.3	DR
▲TRANS PACIFIC INS CO	NY	B+	67.6	54.2	0.0	1.5	10.0	6.0	7.5	7.9	6.0	DT
TRANSAMERICA CASUALTY INS CO	OH	B-	455.5	274.3	370.8	16.1	8.8	5.6	8.5	2.9	5.3	L
▲TRANSATLANTIC REINS CO	NY	B+	14,732.2	4,992.9	3,479.3	21.4	7.7	9.1	6.4	6.7	6.5	A
TRANSGUARD INS CO OF AMERICA INC	IL	B	389.5	154.4	151.5	0.2	7.2	5.6	7.4	7.0	4.6	GRT
TRANSIT GENERAL INS CO	IL	C-	23.0	8.2	10.9	0.9	5.6	7.0	8.9	7.7	2.6	D
TRANSIT GENERAL INS CO OF NY	NY	U	--	--	--	--	N/A	--	--	--	--	Z
▲TRANSIT MUTUAL INS CORP OF WI	WI	D	15.1	11.9	2.7	1.1	10.0	9.4	8.9	8.3	1.4	D
TRANSPORT INS CO	OH	U	--	--	--	--	N/A	--	--	--	--	Z
TRANSPORT RISK SOLUTIONS RRG	SC	U	--	--	--	--	N/A	--	--	--	--	Z
TRANSPORTATION INS CO	IL	C	79.0	78.9	0.0	1.5	10.0	N/A	5.0	9.7	3.8	AR
TRANSPORTATION INS SVCS RRG	SC	D	1.7	0.8	0.5	0.2	7.5	4.0	6.3	6.8	1.1	DT
TRAVCO INS CO	CT	B	217.5	65.9	61.6	4.3	8.5	8.1	3.9	6.8	5.8	
TRAVEL AIR INS CO (KS)	KS	U (5)	--	--	--	--	N/A	--	--	--	--	Z
TRAVELERS CASUALTY & SURETY CO	CT	A-	16,983.8	6,526.1	4,648.6	879.7	7.7	8.0	6.3	6.8	7.2	
▲TRAVELERS CASUALTY & SURETY CO OF	CT	B-	4,232.8	2,016.6	1,491.7	386.9	10.0	9.5	5.3	7.0	4.9	R
TRAVELERS CASUALTY CO	CT	C+	207.4	59.2	66.2	4.8	8.0	8.3	3.9	6.8	4.7	
TRAVELERS CASUALTY CO OF	CT	B	326.1	85.3	107.3	7.4	7.8	8.4	3.8	6.8	5.8	
TRAVELERS CASUALTY INS CO OF	CT	B	1,958.1	532.1	623.3	59.5	7.9	8.4	3.9	6.6	6.1	
TRAVELERS COMMERCIAL CASUALTY CO	CT	B	330.4	89.9	107.3	7.7	7.9	8.4	3.9	6.8	5.9	
TRAVELERS COMMERCIAL INS CO	CT	B	365.0	88.9	107.3	6.1	7.8	8.4	3.9	6.6	5.9	F
TRAVELERS CONSTITUTION STATE INS CO	CT	C+	207.2	59.1	66.2	4.6	8.0	8.3	3.9	7.0	4.7	
TRAVELERS EXCESS & SURPLUS LINES CO	CT	B	219.4	61.7	61.6	4.6	8.3	8.2	4.0	6.7	5.8	F
TRAVELERS HOME & MARINE INS CO	CT	B	370.4	105.6	61.6	5.1	10.0	7.7	3.6	7.0	5.9	
▲TRAVELERS INDEMNITY CO	CT	A-	21,394.5	6,820.2	5,317.6	950.3	7.8	8.0	6.0	6.8	7.2	
TRAVELERS INDEMNITY CO OF AMERICA	CT	B	621.9	178.1	175.8	13.5	8.4	8.2	3.8	6.8	5.9	
TRAVELERS INDEMNITY CO OF CT	CT	B	1,088.9	332.5	312.8	31.4	8.5	8.1	3.8	6.8	6.0	
TRAVELERS LLOYDS INS CO	TX	B	21.2	12.1	0.0	1.1	10.0	N/A	3.5	7.0	4.7	D
TRAVELERS LLOYDS OF TEXAS INS CO	TX	B	19.8	13.5	0.0	1.0	10.0	N/A	4.5	7.0	4.9	D
TRAVELERS PERSONAL INS CO	CT	B	211.6	61.0	61.6	4.1	8.3	8.2	3.9	6.8	4.4	T
TRAVELERS PERSONAL SECURITY INS CO	CT	B	210.7	63.6	61.6	4.3	8.4	8.2	4.1	6.9	5.8	
TRAVELERS PROPERTY CAS OF AMERICA	CT	B	857.4	435.0	82.2	13.5	10.0	7.4	4.0	7.0	5.9	F
TRAVELERS PROPERTY CASUALTY INS CO	CT	B	269.1	74.6	68.5	4.6	8.4	8.2	7.0	6.8	5.4	T
TRENWICK AMERICA REINSURANCE CORP	CT	U	--	--	--	--	N/A	--	--	--	--	Z
▲TREXIS INSURANCE CORP	VA	B+	108.1	50.4	53.2	0.5	9.1	7.8	6.4	6.1	6.5	D
▲TREXIS ONE INSURANCE GROUP	VA	A-	56.6	28.9	26.6	0.4	8.5	7.8	6.5	6.4	6.5	D
TRI-CENTURY INS CO	PA	C+	25.5	9.8	1.0	-0.3	7.4	7.7	3.9	8.2	4.4	DFRT

See Page 27 for explanation of footnotes and Page 28 for explanation of stability factors.

120

www.weissratings.com

Arrows denote recent upgrades ▲ or downgrades ▼ (see Section VII for explanations)

RISK ADJ. RATIO #1	CAPITAL RATIO #2	PREMIUM TO SURPLUS (%)	RESV. TO SURPLUS (%)	RESV. DEVELOP. 1 YEAR (%)	RESV. DEVELOP. 2 YEAR (%)	LOSS RATIO (%)	EXP. RATIO (%)	COMB RATIO (%)	CASH FROM UNDER-WRITING (%)	NET PREMIUM GROWTH (%)	INVEST. IN AFFIL (%)	INSURANCE COMPANY NAME
2.4	1.5	64.2	133.1	1.4	5.1	78.6	28.5	107.1	100.4	6.7	0.0 ●	TOA REINS CO OF AMERICA
2.4	1.8	56.9	156.8	-4.5	-4.7	76.1	37.7	113.8	103.8	-5.1	12.4 ●	TOKIO MARINE AMERICA INS CO
5.4	2.9	180.6	25.0	-15.3	-14.5	82.5	13.3	95.8	103.0	3.8	0.0	TOKIO MARINE PACIFIC INS LTD
3.4	2.6	83.6	117.8	-2.1	-3.6	63.7	29.2	92.9	125.5	5.3	0.0	TOKIO MARINE SPECIALTY INS CO
1.3	0.8	240.8	218.2	14.9	4.3	88.4	30.5	118.9	113.1	3.3	0.0 ●	TOKIO MILLENNIUM RE AG (US BRANCH)
2.0	1.4	114.3	91.0	2.2	-1.4	72.1	34.7	106.8	105.7	24.5	9.7	TOPA INS CO
1.6	1.4	46.6	9.2	-9.0	N/A	N/A	115.5	115.5	92.0	-15.5	0.0	TOWER BONDING & SURETY CO
1.0	0.6	188.0	36.6	N/A	N/A	77.2	3.1	80.3	999 +	0.0	0.0	TOWER HEALTH RECIPROCAL RRG
2.6	2.1	94.8	38.7	6.7	3.2	76.1	34.8	110.9	101.7	12.1	0.0	TOWER HILL PREFERRED INS CO
3.4	2.2	55.9	35.5	8.3	9.1	140.9	28.9	169.8	73.8	47.2	0.0	TOWER HILL PRIME INS CO
0.9	0.6	99.6	66.9	7.6	15.5	96.1	29.1	125.2	94.7	33.4	0.0	TOWER HILL SELECT INS CO
0.6	0.4	152.5	66.9	11.1	13.9	73.8	32.6	106.4	107.3	21.0	0.0	TOWER HILL SIGNATURE INS CO
6.2	5.4	42.1	7.9	0.9	0.6	73.6	17.9	91.5	144.4	19.7	0.0 ●	TOYOTA MOTOR INS CO
0.6	0.5	272.8	128.4	15.3	7.3	76.5	14.7	91.2	115.6	10.3	0.0	TRADERS INS CO
5.4	4.9	N/A	N/A	N/A	N/A	N/A	N/A	N/A	N/A	0.0	3.4	TRADEWIND INS CO LTD
6.2	4.7	23.2	33.8	-8.4	-18.6	40.1	41.3	81.4	122.1	-5.3	1.9	TRANS CITY CASUALTY INS CO
19.3	17.4	N/A	13.4	-0.3	1.4	999 +	999 +	999 +	999 +	N/A	0.0 ●	TRANS PACIFIC INS CO
3.4	2.5	135.2	26.3	-7.0	-4.0	54.3	43.6	97.9	99.7	3.4	0.0 ●	TRANSAMERICA CASUALTY INS CO
2.1	1.4	69.7	155.9	-4.8	-10.3	72.4	35.7	108.1	100.3	-2.7	9.1 ●	TRANSATLANTIC REINS CO
1.8	1.1	98.1	74.9	0.2	11.9	73.4	30.7	104.1	163.6	26.8	0.0	TRANSGUARD INS CO OF AMERICA INC
2.0	1.1	133.1	171.3	-9.1	-27.2	79.9	9.2	89.1	119.3	0.4	5.2	TRANSIT GENERAL INS CO
N/A	N/A	--	--	--	--	--	--	--	--	--	--	TRANSIT GENERAL INS CO OF NY
11.5	7.2	23.0	23.0	-3.6	-13.9	36.3	17.0	53.3	181.2	0.1	0.0	TRANSIT MUTUAL INS CORP OF WI
N/A	N/A	--	--	--	--	--	--	--	--	--	--	TRANSPORT INS CO
N/A	N/A	--	--	--	--	--	--	--	--	--	--	TRANSPORT RISK SOLUTIONS RRG
67.8	28.7	N/A	N/A	N/A	N/A	N/A	N/A	N/A	N/A	0.0	0.0	TRANSPORTATION INS CO
2.2	1.9	61.2	35.9	-16.9	-26.8	10.0	32.0	42.0	315.7	-4.4	0.0	TRANSPORTATION INS SVCS RRG
3.0	2.0	93.5	153.3	-1.9	-3.2	69.5	29.6	99.1	105.0	4.9	0.0	TRAVCO INS CO
N/A	N/A	--	--	--	--	--	--	--	--	--	--	TRAVEL AIR INS CO (KS)
1.6	1.5	71.2	116.7	-1.6	-2.7	69.5	29.1	98.6	107.2	4.9	25.6 ●	TRAVELERS CASUALTY & SURETY CO
4.3	3.2	74.0	49.7	-6.1	-15.8	28.5	40.1	68.6	150.1	5.1	8.6 ●	TRAVELERS CASUALTY & SURETY CO
2.5	1.6	111.9	183.3	-2.3	-3.8	69.5	29.1	98.6	108.3	4.9	0.0	TRAVELERS CASUALTY CO
2.2	1.5	125.8	206.2	-2.6	-4.2	69.5	29.2	98.7	109.0	4.9	0.0	TRAVELERS CASUALTY CO OF
2.4	1.6	117.1	192.0	-2.4	-3.9	69.5	29.3	98.8	104.6	4.9	0.0 ●	TRAVELERS CASUALTY INS CO OF
2.3	1.5	119.3	195.6	-2.5	-4.0	69.5	29.2	98.7	108.5	4.9	0.0	TRAVELERS COMMERCIAL CASUALTY
2.3	1.5	120.7	197.9	-2.5	-4.0	69.5	29.6	99.1	92.3	4.9	0.0	TRAVELERS COMMERCIAL INS CO
2.5	1.6	112.0	183.5	-2.3	-3.8	69.5	29.1	98.6	108.4	4.9	0.0	TRAVELERS CONSTITUTION STATE INS
2.8	1.8	99.9	163.8	-2.1	-3.4	69.5	29.5	99.0	85.2	4.9	0.0	TRAVELERS EXCESS & SURPLUS LINES
4.7	3.1	58.4	95.7	-1.2	-2.0	69.5	31.2	100.7	107.0	4.9	0.0	TRAVELERS HOME & MARINE INS CO
1.8	1.5	78.0	127.9	-1.7	-2.8	69.5	28.3	97.8	110.8	4.9	19.1 ●	TRAVELERS INDEMNITY CO
2.8	1.9	98.7	161.8	-2.1	-3.4	69.5	29.7	99.2	105.4	4.9	0.0	TRAVELERS INDEMNITY CO OF AMERICA
3.0	1.9	94.1	154.2	-2.0	-3.2	69.5	29.5	99.0	99.8	4.9	0.0 ●	TRAVELERS INDEMNITY CO OF CT
5.3	4.7	N/A	N/A	N/A	N/A	N/A	N/A	N/A	-194.0	0.0	0.0	TRAVELERS LLOYDS INS CO
7.6	6.8	N/A	N/A	N/A	N/A	N/A	N/A	N/A	59.2	0.0	0.0	TRAVELERS LLOYDS OF TEXAS INS CO
2.8	1.8	101.0	165.5	-2.1	-3.4	69.5	29.4	98.9	108.6	4.9	0.0	TRAVELERS PERSONAL INS CO
2.9	1.9	96.9	158.7	-2.0	-3.3	69.5	29.1	98.6	114.6	4.9	0.0	TRAVELERS PERSONAL SECURITY INS
14.2	9.3	18.9	31.0	-0.4	-0.7	69.5	33.0	102.5	61.1	4.9	0.0 ●	TRAVELERS PROPERTY CAS OF
3.0	2.0	91.9	150.5	-2.1	-3.4	69.5	29.8	99.3	104.1	4.9	0.0	TRAVELERS PROPERTY CASUALTY INS
N/A	N/A	--	--	--	--	--	--	--	--	--	--	TRENWICK AMERICA REINSURANCE
3.5	2.5	105.5	37.0	-2.2	-3.4	75.2	29.7	104.9	102.7	8.2	0.0 ●	TREXIS INSURANCE CORP
3.1	2.2	91.9	32.2	-2.0	-2.9	75.1	29.1	104.2	101.6	8.2	0.0 ●	TREXIS ONE INSURANCE GROUP
1.6	1.4	10.5	97.6	0.7	-0.5	113.7	50.8	164.5	40.8	-53.3	0.0	TRI-CENTURY INS CO

999 + Denotes number greater than 999.9%
999 - Denotes number less than -999.99%
● Bullets denote a more detailed analysis is available in Section II.

INSURANCE COMPANY NAME	DOM. STATE	RATING		TOTAL ASSETS ($MIL)	CAPITAL & SURPLUS ($MIL)	ANNUAL NET PREMIUM ($MIL)	NET INCOME ($MIL)	CAPITAL-IZATION INDEX (PTS)	RESERVE ADQ INDEX (PTS)	PROFIT-ABILITY INDEX (PTS)	LIQUIDITY INDEX (PTS)	STAB. INDEX (PTS)	STABILITY FACTORS
TRI-STATE CONSUMER INS CO	NY	B		104.1	45.2	25.5	0.7	8.1	9.3	6.5	6.8	6.0	T
TRI-STATE INS CO OF MN	IA	C		60.1	33.4	0.0	0.7	10.0	N/A	6.6	7.0	3.8	T
TRIAD GUARANTY ASR CORP	IL	F	(5)	0.0	0.0	2.5	0.0	6.1	7.1	2.5	6.9	0.0	DFGT
TRIAD GUARANTY INS CORP	IL	F	(5)	0.0	0.0	156.7	0.0	3.0	3.5	0.9	6.5	0.0	FT
▲TRIANGLE INS CO	OK	B-		88.2	30.4	39.7	0.1	7.2	9.4	8.4	4.4	5.1	FL
TRIDENT INSURANCE GROUP INC	MD	U		--	--	--	--	N/A	--	--	--	--	Z
▲TRINITY RISK SOLUTIONS RECIP INS RRG	DC	E+		8.1	4.0	1.5	-0.3	3.4	4.9	2.0	6.8	0.5	DR
▼TRINITY UNIVERSAL INS CO	TX	C+		1,853.3	656.7	1,223.7	7.1	7.5	8.5	3.1	1.7	4.7	ALR
TRIPLE S PROPIEDAD INC	PR	B	(1)	331.6	125.7	87.2	4.0	8.2	6.1	6.5	6.5	4.1	RT
TRISURA SPECIALTY INS CO	OK	U		--	--	--	--	N/A	--	--	--	--	Z
▲TRITON INS CO	TX	B-		453.9	169.9	105.8	31.0	10.0	7.5	5.9	7.4	4.9	R
TRIUMPHE CASUALTY CO	OH	C		60.5	19.1	9.2	1.0	9.5	5.7	6.2	6.9	3.5	DRT
TRUCK INS EXCHANGE	CA	C+		2,107.6	640.8	1,099.3	9.8	5.3	5.5	3.8	2.7	4.8	FLR
TRUMBULL INS CO	CT	B		238.6	109.8	53.5	15.1	10.0	5.9	8.6	7.0	5.8	A
TRUSTGARD INS CO	OH	B-		72.8	72.7	-16.4	4.0	10.0	4.6	8.8	6.9	5.0	FT
TRUSTSTAR INS CO	MD	U	(5)	--	--	--	--	N/A	--	--	--	--	Z
TUDOR INS CO	NH	C		252.1	122.3	22.9	4.7	10.0	8.9	3.1	8.6	4.0	FR
TUSCARORA WAYNE INS CO	PA	B-		114.7	70.5	41.9	3.7	9.8	8.1	8.6	6.8	4.6	R
TWIN CITY FIRE INS CO	IN	B		663.3	273.3	160.6	22.0	10.0	5.9	4.4	7.0	5.8	A
▲TWIN LIGHTS INS CO	NJ	C-		8.7	8.5	0.0	0.1	10.0	N/A	6.8	7.0	3.0	DT
TYPTAP INS CO	FL	C		29.1	24.2	7.2	-0.8	10.0	3.6	3.4	8.1	3.6	DFGT
UC HEALTH RRG A RECPL RRG	DC	U		--	--	--	--	N/A	--	--	--	--	Z
UFB CASUALTY INS CO	IN	B		8.9	8.9	0.0	0.1	10.0	N/A	6.5	10.0	4.8	D
▲UFG SPECIALTY INS CO	IA	C+		43.1	19.6	10.2	0.7	9.9	8.0	5.0	7.0	3.3	DRT
UMIA INS INC	OR	B		224.9	111.4	36.3	9.6	9.0	9.4	6.0	7.0	6.1	F
▲UMIALIK INS CO	AK	B		77.7	26.6	28.4	1.7	9.0	8.2	8.8	6.6	5.5	D
UNDERWRITERS AT LLOYDS (IL)	IL	D		382.6	209.6	69.6	25.8	8.5	4.6	5.6	9.0	2.3	R
▼UNDERWRITERS AT LLOYDS (KY)	KY	D-		165.2	33.4	49.5	18.7	1.0	6.1	5.9	7.5	1.3	C
▼UNDERWRITERS AT LLOYDS (VI)	VI	E+		397.8	75.0	62.1	-347.7	0.5	0.3	1.1	0.8	0.6	CFGL
UNIGARD INDEMNITY CO	WI	U		--	--	--	--	N/A	--	--	--	--	Z
UNIGARD INS CO	WI	C		394.6	96.5	183.1	-5.4	7.0	5.9	2.5	6.0	4.2	FR
UNION INS CO	IA	C		137.6	45.7	0.0	0.9	10.0	N/A	6.9	10.0	4.3	
UNION INS CO OF PROVIDENCE	IA	C		61.2	54.5	0.0	1.5	10.0	4.7	4.6	7.0	4.0	T
UNION MUTUAL FIRE INS CO	VT	B-		242.7	97.2	108.0	5.9	7.7	6.2	8.3	6.5	4.7	T
UNION MUTUAL INS CO	OK	F		5.3	1.2	3.8	0.5	2.9	5.0	0.9	7.5	0.0	DRT
UNION NATIONAL FIRE INS CO	LA	B		9.0	6.2	0.0	0.2	10.0	N/A	5.1	7.0	4.1	DR
UNION STANDARD LLOYDS	TX	C		2.5	0.9	0.0	0.0	7.5	N/A	6.3	10.0	2.8	DT
▼UNIQUE INS CO	IL	E+		101.9	21.2	89.3	-8.4	1.3	0.5	3.2	1.8	0.8	CDFL
UNITED AMERICAS INS CO	NY	U		--	--	--	--	N/A	--	--	--	--	Z
UNITED AUTOMOBILE INS CO	FL	E		263.4	56.0	104.4	0.1	3.9	0.4	2.0	5.1	0.1	FRT
▲UNITED BUS INS CO	GA	D+		12.8	4.4	6.6	0.8	3.3	3.6	2.9	6.6	2.1	DR
UNITED CASUALTY & SURETY CO INC	MA	C-		10.5	8.0	2.1	0.2	9.9	7.7	8.3	9.3	2.5	DR
UNITED CASUALTY INS CO OF AMERICA	IL	B		13.5	10.5	0.0	0.2	10.0	N/A	7.6	10.0	4.4	DR
▲UNITED CENTRAL PA RRG	VT	E+		21.0	10.3	5.6	0.7	4.2	4.8	6.2	8.0	0.5	D
▲UNITED EDUCATORS INS A RECIP RRG	VT	B+		912.3	306.0	149.8	15.6	7.5	8.9	6.9	7.0	6.5	
UNITED EQUITABLE INS CO	IL	D+		25.6	5.8	21.8	0.3	3.6	9.9	5.8	6.2	2.6	T
UNITED FARM FAMILY INS CO	NY	B		44.5	14.0	9.1	0.8	9.7	8.6	8.0	7.6	4.8	D
▲UNITED FARM FAMILY MUTUAL INS CO	IN	B+		1,098.5	462.1	570.9	35.3	9.1	8.2	8.8	5.8	6.4	L
UNITED FINANCIAL CASUALTY CO	OH	B-		3,346.4	721.5	2,249.3	119.1	7.6	6.4	9.2	5.8	4.5	T
UNITED FIRE & CAS CO	IA	B		1,987.8	757.4	652.2	19.3	7.2	8.0	6.9	6.4	5.5	
UNITED FIRE & INDEMNITY CO	TX	C+		55.3	18.4	20.4	0.5	7.7	8.2	6.2	6.7	4.6	D
UNITED FIRE LLOYDS	TX	C+		31.5	9.0	10.2	0.2	7.5	8.7	8.2	6.9	4.2	D

See Page 27 for explanation of footnotes and Page 28 for explanation of stability factors.

122

www.weissratings.com

Arrows denote recent upgrades ▲ or downgrades ▼   (see Section VII for explanations)

RISK ADJ. RATIO #1	CAPITAL RATIO #2	PREMIUM TO SURPLUS (%)	RESV. TO SURPLUS (%)	RESV. DEVELOP. 1 YEAR (%)	RESV. DEVELOP. 2 YEAR (%)	LOSS RATIO (%)	EXP. RATIO (%)	COMB RATIO (%)	CASH FROM UNDER-WRITING (%)	NET PREMIUM GROWTH (%)	INVEST. IN AFFIL (%)	INSURANCE COMPANY NAME
2.4	1.7	56.4	94.8	-4.5	-8.7	71.1	36.3	107.4	95.8	-4.6	0.0	TRI-STATE CONSUMER INS CO
7.9	7.1	N/A	N/A	N/A	N/A	N/A	N/A	N/A	-13.9	0.0	0.0	TRI-STATE INS CO OF MN
1.6	1.3	29.6	92.6	-5.4	-76.8	122.9	39.9	162.8	47.9	-19.1	0.0	TRIAD GUARANTY ASR CORP
0.9	0.7	66.9	208.6	72.1	117.6	223.0	11.0	234.0	51.4	-20.7	1.1	TRIAD GUARANTY INS CORP
2.0	1.3	130.6	101.0	-11.9	-15.7	75.7	28.3	104.0	87.6	-1.6	0.0	TRIANGLE INS CO
N/A	N/A	--	--	--	--	--	--	--	--	--	--	TRIDENT INSURANCE GROUP INC
0.6	0.5	38.5	86.9	-1.0	-2.1	88.2	38.7	126.9	115.7	-0.7	0.0	TRINITY RISK SOLUTIONS RECIP INS
1.7	1.3	186.3	99.4	2.4	-3.4	80.0	29.0	109.0	93.8	2.4	15.5 ●	TRINITY UNIVERSAL INS CO
2.4	1.7	62.4	50.9	-4.7	-3.0	51.2	43.2	94.4	103.9	1.7	0.0	TRIPLE S PROPIEDAD INC
N/A	N/A	--	--	--	--	--	--	--	--	--	--	TRISURA SPECIALTY INS CO
7.6	4.7	62.3	14.2	-1.3	-1.9	35.1	37.0	72.1	126.1	4.2	0.0	TRITON INS CO
3.2	2.6	48.4	66.7	-0.6	1.7	67.1	27.6	94.7	121.0	4.7	0.0	TRIUMPHE CASUALTY CO
0.8	0.7	171.6	110.0	0.5	5.3	70.0	32.9	102.9	93.1	-3.9	48.0 ●	TRUCK INS EXCHANGE
5.9	3.9	48.8	89.2	-0.5	1.3	68.7	5.4	74.1	110.1	1.6	0.0	TRUMBULL INS CO
96.6	44.4	-22.5	N/A	N/A	N/A	N/A	N/A	N/A	-32.3	-139.9	0.0	TRUSTGARD INS CO
N/A	N/A	--	--	--	--	--	--	--	--	--	--	TRUSTSTAR INS CO
4.5	3.0	18.7	31.8	-0.7	-1.4	98.0	21.0	119.0	28.3	50.7	0.0	TUDOR INS CO
3.9	2.8	59.4	23.4	-1.5	-5.4	52.2	40.0	92.2	116.2	4.0	9.0	TUSCARORA WAYNE INS CO
4.9	3.3	58.8	107.5	-0.5	1.3	68.7	24.8	93.5	110.1	1.6	0.0 ●	TWIN CITY FIRE INS CO
9.8	5.7	N/A	N/A	N/A	N/A	N/A	N/A	N/A	N/A	0.0	0.0	TWIN LIGHTS INS CO
16.0	10.2	29.9	N/A	-0.1	N/A	72.5	30.9	103.4	94.3	267.7	0.0	TYPTAP INS CO
N/A	N/A	--	--	--	--	--	--	--	--	--	--	UC HEALTH RRG A RECPL RRG
96.7	48.3	N/A	N/A	N/A	N/A	N/A	N/A	N/A	N/A	0.0	0.0	UFB CASUALTY INS CO
4.6	3.2	52.1	59.4	-1.7	-1.5	72.8	30.4	103.2	109.6	5.6	0.0	UFG SPECIALTY INS CO
3.4	2.3	32.6	84.7	-4.2	-9.0	82.4	16.9	99.3	74.7	-7.5	0.0	UMIA INS INC
3.2	2.3	106.5	78.1	-2.6	-3.9	67.5	28.1	95.6	118.6	21.8	0.0	UMIALIK INS CO
3.3	2.2	33.2	71.6	-1.6	15.8	49.2	18.8	68.0	154.2	-0.4	0.0	UNDERWRITERS AT LLOYDS (IL)
0.3	0.2	148.3	328.0	15.9	-101.4	40.1	25.7	65.8	125.3	32.3	0.0	UNDERWRITERS AT LLOYDS (KY)
0.4	0.2	82.8	415.8	434.1	80.9	639.3	32.2	671.5	47.8	-1.0	0.0	UNDERWRITERS AT LLOYDS (VI)
N/A	N/A	--	--	--	--	--	--	--	--	--	--	UNIGARD INDEMNITY CO
1.6	1.0	189.7	158.5	-6.0	-20.4	75.6	31.2	106.8	85.7	5.1	3.3	UNIGARD INS CO
5.3	4.7	N/A	N/A	N/A	N/A	N/A	N/A	N/A	208.9	0.0	0.0	UNION INS CO
29.9	26.9	N/A	N/A	N/A	N/A	N/A	N/A	N/A	N/A	100.0	0.0	UNION INS CO OF PROVIDENCE
1.7	1.5	111.1	57.3	5.2	7.5	61.1	32.9	94.0	121.8	5.7	21.9	UNION MUTUAL FIRE INS CO
0.9	0.8	324.1	42.3	-36.1	-61.7	59.0	26.1	85.1	98.3	1.6	0.0	UNION MUTUAL INS CO
6.7	6.0	N/A	N/A	N/A	N/A	N/A	N/A	N/A	47.4	0.0	0.0	UNION NATIONAL FIRE INS CO
1.4	1.3	N/A	N/A	N/A	N/A	N/A	N/A	N/A	68.5	0.0	0.0	UNION STANDARD LLOYDS
0.3	0.2	420.6	205.0	86.0	73.7	75.0	36.1	111.1	90.4	46.6	6.4	UNIQUE INS CO
N/A	N/A	--	--	--	--	--	--	--	--	--	--	UNITED AMERICAS INS CO
0.8	0.6	186.5	173.2	46.9	70.8	103.4	2.1	105.5	75.4	-30.7	2.3	UNITED AUTOMOBILE INS CO
1.0	0.7	151.6	78.1	-11.2	0.1	53.6	28.7	82.3	149.7	-0.4	0.0	UNITED BUS INS CO
3.9	3.6	26.8	1.2	-1.4	-2.2	N/A	88.5	88.5	111.3	0.1	0.0	UNITED CASUALTY & SURETY CO INC
10.4	9.3	N/A	N/A	N/A	N/A	N/A	N/A	N/A	63.2	0.0	0.0	UNITED CASUALTY INS CO OF AMERICA
0.8	0.6	54.7	102.8	0.9	-14.1	87.6	7.2	94.8	178.3	33.0	0.0	UNITED CENTRAL PA RRG
1.7	1.3	49.0	146.3	N/A	-9.9	79.1	22.7	101.8	91.0	6.4	0.0 ●	UNITED EDUCATORS INS A RECIP RRG
0.6	0.5	377.7	228.8	-6.9	-70.3	58.9	33.2	92.1	118.7	73.8	0.0	UNITED EQUITABLE INS CO
3.1	2.7	64.6	73.2	-5.6	-8.8	60.0	30.9	90.9	100.6	3.6	0.0	UNITED FARM FAMILY INS CO
3.9	2.6	123.5	53.9	-2.3	-5.1	71.2	27.3	98.5	102.1	4.9	1.5 ●	UNITED FARM FAMILY MUTUAL INS CO
1.9	1.3	311.7	191.3	-0.1	-1.3	73.7	18.8	92.5	121.9	13.5	0.0 ●	UNITED FINANCIAL CASUALTY CO
1.3	1.1	86.1	98.1	-2.4	-2.2	72.8	29.4	102.2	109.3	5.6	33.9 ●	UNITED FIRE & CAS CO
2.2	1.5	111.1	126.6	-2.9	-2.7	72.8	30.4	103.2	116.6	5.6	0.0	UNITED FIRE & INDEMNITY CO
2.1	1.5	113.1	128.9	-3.3	-3.0	72.8	30.4	103.2	114.1	5.6	0.0	UNITED FIRE LLOYDS

999 + Denotes number greater than 999.9%
999 - Denotes number less than -999.99%
● Bullets denote a more detailed analysis is available in Section II.

INSURANCE COMPANY NAME	DOM. STATE	RATING	TOTAL ASSETS ($MIL)	CAPITAL & SURPLUS ($MIL)	ANNUAL NET PREMIUM ($MIL)	NET INCOME ($MIL)	CAPITAL-IZATION INDEX (PTS)	RESERVE ADQ INDEX (PTS)	PROFIT-ABILITY INDEX (PTS)	LIQUIDITY INDEX (PTS)	STAB. INDEX (PTS)	STABILITY FACTORS
UNITED FRONTIER MUTUAL INS CO	NY	C	18.3	11.5	4.7	0.2	8.5	7.9	7.6	7.0	3.1	DR
UNITED GROUP CAPTIVE INS CO	GA	D	1.2	0.7	0.5	0.1	7.8	4.5	3.4	8.2	1.0	DFT
UNITED GUAR RESIDENTIAL INS CO OF NC	NC	C+	53.8	39.6	19.9	525.4	9.3	5.9	1.9	10.0	4.7	DT
UNITED GUARANTY COML INS CO OF NC	NC	U	--	--	--	--	N/A	--	--	--	--	Z
UNITED GUARANTY CREDIT INS CO	NC	U	--	--	--	--	N/A	--	--	--	--	Z
▲UNITED GUARANTY INS CO	NC	B	5.4	5.3	-0.8	8.2	10.0	4.7	1.9	0.0	4.2	FLT
▲UNITED GUARANTY MORTGAGE INDEM CO	NC	C+	48.9	15.1	4.5	13.8	10.0	9.4	1.9	0.0	4.7	DFLR
UNITED GUARANTY MORTGAGE INS CO	NC	B-	23.0	22.9	-0.9	8.9	10.0	4.7	2.1	2.7	3.8	FLT
UNITED GUARANTY MTG INS CO OF NC	NC	B-	22.8	22.7	-0.9	8.9	10.0	4.7	1.9	2.6	3.8	FLT
▼UNITED GUARANTY RESIDENTIAL INS CO	NC	C+	2,607.5	1,004.9	215.1	326.6	10.0	4.9	3.0	6.8	4.4	FRT
UNITED HERITAGE PROP & CAS CO	ID	E+	43.2	15.6	28.1	-0.8	7.3	5.9	3.6	4.8	0.6	DL
▲UNITED HOME INS CO	AR	C	38.3	14.0	33.6	1.1	4.2	6.4	8.2	2.6	2.5	CDLR
UNITED HOME INS CO A RRG	VT	U	--	--	--	--	N/A	--	--	--	--	Z
▼UNITED INSURANCE CO	UT	D+	45.2	11.8	47.2	0.4	2.5	9.4	8.8	0.3	2.6	CDLR
UNITED INTERNATIONAL INS CO	NY	U	--	--	--	--	N/A	--	--	--	--	Z
UNITED NATIONAL INS CO	PA	C	338.5	147.9	71.3	21.0	7.5	6.4	3.3	7.1	4.1	RT
UNITED OHIO INS CO	OH	B-	340.5	172.4	143.6	13.5	10.0	8.4	8.7	6.7	4.7	T
UNITED P&C INS CO	FL	B-	618.2	164.3	406.1	-17.2	5.7	4.1	3.8	2.7	5.1	FL
▲UNITED SECURITY HEALTH & CASUALTY	IL	D+	5.3	4.0	1.0	-0.3	8.2	4.1	2.9	7.1	2.1	DFGT
▲UNITED SERVICES AUTOMOBILE ASN	TX	A-	35,460.0	26,523.2	7,489.8	517.1	7.6	7.3	7.6	6.6	7.1	
▲UNITED SPECIALTY INS CO	DE	B+	330.2	149.0	30.9	5.4	8.8	6.0	8.2	7.6	6.4	GT
UNITED STATES FIDELITY & GUARANTY CO	CT	C-	3,293.0	985.8	1,006.9	82.9	8.4	7.7	2.4	6.7	3.3	
▲UNITED STATES SURETY CO	MD	B	75.4	51.3	18.0	4.9	9.9	9.3	8.6	7.0	5.5	D
UNITED SURETY & INDEMNITY CO	PR	B	107.7	64.3	21.3	8.0	7.7	8.8	6.5	7.0	6.0	T
▲UNITRIN ADVANTAGE INS CO	NY	C	3.3	2.7	0.0	0.1	10.0	N/A	7.4	10.0	3.0	DRT
UNITRIN AUTO & HOME INS CO	NY	D+	73.7	32.6	0.0	1.3	10.0	N/A	4.4	7.0	2.5	R
UNITRIN COUNTY MUTUAL INS CO	TX	B	29.2	4.7	0.0	0.0	7.1	N/A	5.7	10.0	4.1	DFR
UNITRIN DIRECT INS CO	IL	B	11.7	8.2	0.0	0.3	10.0	N/A	5.7	7.0	4.2	DR
UNITRIN DIRECT PROPERTY & CAS CO	IL	B	14.3	10.2	0.0	0.4	10.0	N/A	6.8	7.0	4.4	DR
UNITRIN PREFERRED INS CO	NY	D+	21.1	9.7	0.0	0.3	10.0	N/A	6.0	7.0	2.4	DR
UNITRIN SAFEGUARD INS CO	WI	B	31.8	7.8	0.0	0.3	8.2	N/A	7.9	10.0	4.1	DR
UNIVERSAL FIRE & CASUALTY INS CO	IN	C-	17.2	7.9	3.2	0.5	8.8	N/A	8.3	6.9	2.6	D
UNIVERSAL INS CO	NC	C-	40.9	11.5	23.0	0.5	6.3	4.4	3.9	2.0	2.7	DL
UNIVERSAL INS CO (PR)	PR	B- (2)	896.9	299.3	203.7	6.5	7.5	6.1	6.0	6.6	4.2	RT
UNIVERSAL INS CO OF NORTH AMERICA	FL	C-	116.5	34.4	53.9	-2.1	7.0	6.0	2.0	2.4	3.3	FLO
▼UNIVERSAL NORTH AMERICA INS CO	TX	C-	204.4	70.6	110.1	-2.3	4.0	6.8	3.9	1.3	3.3	CFLR
UNIVERSAL P&C INS CO	FL	D	1,034.0	307.7	733.4	36.2	7.3	6.4	8.5	5.8	2.0	R
▲UNIVERSAL SURETY CO	NE	C+	234.8	191.5	3.0	8.6	8.4	7.4	8.3	9.9	4.5	DR
UNIVERSAL SURETY OF AMERICA	SD	C	14.8	14.8	0.0	0.2	10.0	N/A	4.4	10.0	3.8	DR
UNIVERSAL UNDERWRITERS INS CO	IL	C+	332.2	320.4	0.0	7.3	10.0	N/A	4.4	10.0	4.7	FR
UNIVERSAL UNDERWRITERS OF TX	IL	C+	10.6	9.8	0.0	0.2	10.0	N/A	6.2	7.0	3.2	DRT
UPLAND MUTUAL INS INC	KS	C	31.8	15.7	16.2	1.2	8.4	6.5	8.4	5.7	3.6	DR
▲UPMC HEALTH BENEFITS INC	PA	D+	237.5	110.6	117.7	3.4	3.0	4.6	4.8	5.5	2.5	CG
UPPER HUDSON NATIONAL INS CO	NY	U	--	--	--	--	N/A	--	--	--	--	Z
URGENT CARE ASR CO RRG INC	NV	D	5.2	1.6	1.3	-0.3	3.1	3.2	2.9	2.6	1.5	DFLR
URGENT MD RRG INC	VT	D	10.0	3.1	4.8	0.4	1.1	3.6	8.9	7.3	1.9	CDGT
▲US COASTAL INS CO	NY	C	28.4	9.3	7.5	0.1	5.3	5.0	3.7	7.9	2.8	DT
US COASTAL P&C INS CO	FL	C+	35.3	22.8	12.1	-2.4	7.3	3.6	2.7	7.0	3.2	DGT
US FIRE INS CO	DE	C	4,094.3	1,302.3	1,418.1	-132.0	6.5	6.1	4.4	7.4	3.7	AR
US INS CO OF AMERICA	IL	D+	6.3	3.2	1.0	0.4	5.6	9.9	6.6	6.8	2.0	DR
▲US LEGAL SERVICES INC	TN	D+	3.5	2.9	3.5	0.2	4.6	5.3	8.5	7.2	2.0	DFT
US LIABILITY INS CO	PA	C	1,244.4	827.2	223.2	62.5	7.2	8.5	8.2	7.6	4.3	R

See Page 27 for explanation of footnotes and Page 28 for explanation of stability factors.

124

www.weissratings.com

Arrows denote recent upgrades ▲ or downgrades ▼   (see Section VII for explanations)

RISK ADJ. CAPITAL RATIO #1	RATIO #2	PREMIUM TO SURPLUS (%)	RESV. TO SURPLUS (%)	RESV. DEVELOP. 1 YEAR (%)	RESV. DEVELOP. 2 YEAR (%)	LOSS RATIO (%)	EXP. RATIO (%)	COMB RATIO (%)	CASH FROM UNDER- WRITING (%)	NET PREMIUM GROWTH (%)	INVEST. IN AFFIL (%)	INSURANCE COMPANY NAME
3.1	1.9	40.8	27.3	-0.1	-3.0	57.2	37.2	94.4	120.6	14.0	0.0	UNITED FRONTIER MUTUAL INS CO
2.1	1.6	78.7	70.8	5.6	3.0	66.4	24.5	90.9	88.3	-7.5	0.0	UNITED GROUP CAPTIVE INS CO
7.3	4.7	50.2	26.4	-8.2	-10.0	-90.3	19.5	-70.8	-198.6	-26.6	0.0	UNITED GUAR RESIDENTIAL INS CO OF
N/A	N/A	--	--	--	--	--	--	--	--	--	--	UNITED GUARANTY COML INS CO OF NC
N/A	N/A	--	--	--	--	--	--	--	--	--	--	UNITED GUARANTY CREDIT INS CO
265.1	238.6	-15.0	N/A	-17.6	-8.6	-5.6	-2.7	-8.3	-0.3	-105.6	0.0	UNITED GUARANTY INS CO
4.0	3.6	29.9	N/A	-2.3	-5.6	45.1	-2.2	42.9	29.0	-75.5	0.0	UNITED GUARANTY MORTGAGE INDEM
35.2	24.8	-3.9	5.8	-17.3	-9.0	-5.6	-8.3	-13.9	-3.9	-106.2	0.0	UNITED GUARANTY MORTGAGE INS CO
35.0	24.7	-3.9	5.9	-17.4	-8.6	-5.6	-8.5	-14.1	-3.9	-106.2	0.0	UNITED GUARANTY MTG INS CO OF NC
6.6	4.9	21.4	21.6	-1.4	-2.5	16.6	59.8	76.4	56.1	-60.8	2.1 ●	UNITED GUARANTY RESIDENTIAL INS
1.6	1.2	180.0	49.5	-2.1	-1.5	82.2	28.5	110.7	94.7	18.6	0.0	UNITED HERITAGE PROP & CAS CO
1.0	0.9	240.5	46.6	-11.2	-11.4	66.7	29.6	96.3	101.1	12.2	0.0	UNITED HOME INS CO
N/A	N/A	--	--	--	--	--	--	--	--	--	--	UNITED HOME INS CO A RRG
0.4	0.4	401.3	181.9	-3.2	-12.6	74.3	25.3	99.6	111.5	11.4	0.0	UNITED INSURANCE CO
N/A	N/A	--	--	--	--	--	--	--	--	--	--	UNITED INTERNATIONAL INS CO
1.7	1.3	48.2	57.1	0.4	-2.0	81.8	40.1	121.9	113.3	-11.7	22.8	UNITED NATIONAL INS CO
7.2	5.0	83.3	38.8	-5.5	-5.6	60.4	31.0	91.4	106.8	5.7	0.0	UNITED OHIO INS CO
1.2	0.9	247.2	65.4	2.3	13.1	65.0	43.2	108.2	79.3	1.9	0.0	UNITED P&C INS CO
3.4	2.6	24.7	26.6	-48.0	-44.4	55.9	75.9	131.8	82.0	83.9	0.0	UNITED SECURITY HEALTH & CASUALTY
1.4	1.3	28.2	13.7	-0.1	-0.4	88.4	13.1	101.5	100.5	6.4	59.2 ●	UNITED SERVICES AUTOMOBILE ASN
2.2	2.2	20.8	2.3	0.1	-0.1	49.4	50.4	99.8	132.2	-36.5	33.4 ●	UNITED SPECIALTY INS CO
2.8	1.9	102.1	167.4	-2.1	-2.6	69.5	29.1	98.6	108.3	4.9	3.7 ●	UNITED STATES FIDELITY & GUARANTY
3.9	3.3	35.2	13.6	-12.7	-11.1	6.4	70.6	77.0	97.9	-22.1	0.0	UNITED STATES SURETY CO
3.1	2.0	33.1	9.6	-2.8	-6.7	3.9	58.7	62.6	132.9	-19.1	0.0	UNITED SURETY & INDEMNITY CO
8.9	8.0	N/A	N/A	N/A	N/A	N/A	N/A	N/A	N/A	0.0	0.0	UNITRIN ADVANTAGE INS CO
5.6	5.0	N/A	N/A	N/A	N/A	N/A	N/A	N/A	60.5	0.0	0.0	UNITRIN AUTO & HOME INS CO
1.1	1.0	N/A	N/A	N/A	N/A	N/A	N/A	N/A	-12.9	0.0	0.0	UNITRIN COUNTY MUTUAL INS CO
7.3	6.5	N/A	N/A	N/A	N/A	N/A	N/A	N/A	743.7	0.0	0.0	UNITRIN DIRECT INS CO
7.8	7.0	N/A	N/A	N/A	N/A	N/A	N/A	N/A	99.5	0.0	0.0	UNITRIN DIRECT PROPERTY & CAS CO
3.7	3.3	N/A	N/A	N/A	N/A	N/A	N/A	N/A	66.0	0.0	0.0	UNITRIN PREFERRED INS CO
1.9	1.7	N/A	N/A	N/A	N/A	N/A	N/A	N/A	-3.4	0.0	0.0	UNITRIN SAFEGUARD INS CO
2.7	2.3	40.5	N/A	N/A	N/A	N/A	83.8	83.8	109.4	3.9	0.0	UNIVERSAL FIRE & CASUALTY INS CO
1.3	0.9	198.9	76.6	3.2	-2.0	78.7	20.5	99.2	90.2	-1.6	0.0	UNIVERSAL INS CO
1.8	1.4	78.5	24.4	-1.2	-0.3	66.2	34.5	100.7	102.7	4.8	17.6	UNIVERSAL INS CO (PR)
1.4	1.0	156.7	65.2	-8.5	-18.1	81.4	30.3	111.7	69.5	-16.0	0.0	UNIVERSAL INS CO OF NORTH AMERICA
0.8	0.5	156.0	49.6	-4.5	-7.6	76.6	29.1	105.7	94.0	-2.3	0.0	UNIVERSAL NORTH AMERICA INS CO
1.3	1.2	238.4	21.0	8.8	3.6	55.6	35.2	90.8	117.7	12.4	0.0 ●	UNIVERSAL P&C INS CO
3.5	2.1	1.6	3.4	-0.2	-0.3	12.5	68.6	81.1	154.7	10.5	0.0	UNIVERSAL SURETY CO
78.1	35.5	N/A	N/A	N/A	N/A	N/A	N/A	N/A	N/A	0.0	0.0	UNIVERSAL SURETY OF AMERICA
30.0	25.2	N/A	N/A	N/A	N/A	N/A	N/A	N/A	-274.5	0.0	3.5 ●	UNIVERSAL UNDERWRITERS INS CO
27.5	24.8	N/A	N/A	N/A	N/A	N/A	N/A	N/A	52.4	0.0	0.0	UNIVERSAL UNDERWRITERS OF TX
2.7	2.1	102.8	16.1	-2.1	-1.8	67.6	28.1	95.7	101.1	1.9	0.0	UPLAND MUTUAL INS INC
1.0	0.6	106.4	64.0	22.2	20.5	81.5	19.2	100.7	113.1	16.6	0.0	UPMC HEALTH BENEFITS INC
N/A	N/A	--	--	--	--	--	--	--	--	--	--	UPPER HUDSON NATIONAL INS CO
0.6	0.5	77.6	110.1	19.1	3.0	88.1	39.6	127.7	56.5	-15.2	0.0	URGENT CARE ASR CO RRG INC
0.4	0.2	157.2	159.8	-7.7	N/A	63.7	20.5	84.2	315.8	23.9	0.0	URGENT MD RRG INC
1.2	0.7	81.0	47.1	-2.2	-28.8	65.8	28.5	94.3	160.1	103.1	0.0	US COASTAL INS CO
2.0	1.1	52.8	16.7	-0.4	N/A	77.9	40.8	118.7	127.8	66.8	0.0	US COASTAL P&C INS CO
1.1	0.9	108.9	150.9	-1.2	-3.0	64.7	35.5	100.2	102.9	3.5	28.7 ●	US FIRE INS CO
2.0	1.2	31.8	72.4	-45.7	-64.9	12.4	64.2	76.6	95.4	-3.5	0.0	US INS CO OF AMERICA
0.8	0.7	118.7	8.5	N/A	-1.5	14.5	78.5	93.0	107.1	0.4	0.0	US LEGAL SERVICES INC
1.2	1.1	27.0	26.1	-1.8	-4.3	46.8	42.1	88.9	132.9	9.2	54.9 ●	US LIABILITY INS CO

999 + Denotes number greater than 999.9%
999 - Denotes number less than -999.99%
● Bullets denote a more detailed analysis is available in Section II.

INSURANCE COMPANY NAME	DOM. STATE	RATING	TOTAL ASSETS ($MIL)	CAPITAL & SURPLUS ($MIL)	ANNUAL NET PREMIUM ($MIL)	NET INCOME ($MIL)	CAPITAL-IZATION INDEX (PTS)	RESERVE ADQ INDEX (PTS)	PROFIT-ABILITY INDEX (PTS)	LIQUIDITY INDEX (PTS)	STAB. INDEX (PTS)	STABILITY FACTORS
US LLOYDS INS CO	TX	C	28.7	9.9	24.4	0.3	7.1	4.3	6.6	6.6	2.9	DR
▲US SPECIALTY INS CO	TX	B	1,888.4	587.0	471.5	87.2	7.9	6.5	7.9	6.8	5.4	R
US UNDERWRITERS INS CO	ND	C	163.6	122.1	12.7	4.2	10.0	5.8	5.8	10.0	4.0	R
USA INS CO	MS	C-	16.3	6.7	12.9	0.3	7.5	6.0	3.4	6.4	2.5	DR
USA UNDERWRITERS	MI	C-	10.4	7.1	5.3	0.8	4.0	6.0	5.3	5.9	2.1	DT
USAA CASUALTY INS CO	TX	A-	10,897.7	4,719.6	7,002.9	126.1	8.4	7.6	6.9	3.8	7.1	L
USAA COUNTY MUTUAL INS CO	TX	U	--	--	--	--	N/A	--	--	--	--	Z
USAA GENERAL INDEMNITY CO	TX	B+	4,627.9	1,652.8	3,351.8	37.6	8.2	8.2	5.3	2.4	6.4	L
▲USPLATE GLASS INS CO	IL	B-	33.1	25.7	10.2	0.2	7.4	5.1	8.2	6.7	4.6	DR
UTAH BUSINESS INS CO	UT	D	21.6	5.2	15.3	1.2	2.0	6.9	4.7	5.3	2.1	CDR
UTICA FIRST INS CO	NY	B	291.6	142.5	87.0	10.4	9.7	8.0	8.7	6.7	6.0	T
UTICA LLOYDS OF TX	TX	B	8.3	7.7	0.0	0.4	10.0	N/A	8.2	10.0	4.0	D
UTICA MUTUAL INS CO	NY	B-	2,525.3	929.8	815.9	51.2	8.2	6.6	6.9	6.7	4.9	R
UTICA NATIONAL ASR CO	NY	C	68.9	30.6	19.4	1.2	10.0	6.4	6.9	6.9	4.1	T
▲UTICA NATIONAL INS CO OF OHIO	OH	B-	20.6	15.2	0.0	1.3	10.0	N/A	8.9	7.0	4.9	D
UTICA NATIONAL INS CO OF TX	TX	C	36.3	16.5	9.7	0.6	10.0	6.4	6.9	6.9	3.9	D
UTICA SPECIALTY RISK INS CO	TX	B-	33.6	32.7	0.0	0.8	10.0	N/A	7.3	10.0	3.8	DT
UV INS RRG INC	HI	D+	1.2	0.9	0.3	0.0	7.5	5.9	6.4	9.1	1.3	DT
VA FARM BUREAU TOWN & COUNTRY INS	VA	C+	68.1	24.7	28.3	1.3	8.9	9.3	8.3	6.4	4.5	R
VALLEY FORGE INS CO	PA	C	71.5	71.5	0.0	2.3	10.0	N/A	5.2	8.1	3.8	AR
VALLEY P&C INS CO	OR	B	12.3	8.0	0.0	0.3	10.0	N/A	7.8	7.0	4.1	DR
VANLINER INS CO	MO	B	454.6	134.8	120.1	15.8	8.8	4.1	6.6	6.7	6.2	
VANTAGE CASUALTY INS CO	IN	U	--	--	--	--	N/A	--	--	--	--	Z
VANTAPRO SPECIALTY INS CO	AR	U	--	--	--	--	N/A	--	--	--	--	Z
VASA SPRING GARDEN MUTUAL INS CO	MN	D+	5.3	2.9	3.0	0.1	9.4	6.2	5.3	6.0	2.0	D
VAULT E&S INSURANCE CO	AR	U	--	--	--	--	N/A	--	--	--	--	Z
VAULT RECIPROCAL EXCHANGE	FL	B	49.8	48.3	0.0	-1.6	10.0	N/A	3.3	10.0	4.2	DFT
VEHICULAR SERVICE INS CO RRG	OK	U	--	--	--	--	N/A	--	--	--	--	Z
VELOCITY INS CO A RRG	SC	D	2.7	1.6	0.6	0.1	4.6	3.6	7.2	8.4	1.3	DGT
VERLAN FIRE INS CO	NH	B-	25.4	25.3	0.0	0.5	10.0	N/A	5.5	10.0	5.0	
VERMONT ACCIDENT INS CO	VT	B	15.4	14.7	0.0	0.3	10.0	N/A	7.5	7.0	4.3	DG
VERMONT MUTUAL INS CO	VT	B-	928.3	460.3	416.0	34.9	10.0	8.4	8.7	6.7	4.7	R
VERSANT CASUALTY INS CO	MS	C	50.6	15.8	5.8	1.0	9.4	6.1	8.9	7.0	3.9	D
VERTERRA INS CO	TX	C-	82.3	56.1	14.5	2.4	9.3	6.1	8.2	8.7	3.0	DR
▲VERTI INSURANCE CO	OH	D+	39.5	22.1	15.9	-0.4	8.2	3.5	3.8	7.7	2.5	DGT
VESTA INS CORP	TX	F (5)	0.0	0.0	0.0	0.0	10.0	N/A	3.9	8.1	0.0	DGT
VETERINARY PET INS CO	OH	B	159.4	100.7	0.0	1.8	10.0	4.6	4.1	6.9	4.6	T
▲VFH CAPTIVE INS CO	GA	E+	5.3	0.8	3.3	0.4	1.0	4.7	1.8	0.0	0.5	CDFL
VICTORIA AUTOMOBILE INS CO	OH	B-	10.3	8.1	0.0	0.1	10.0	N/A	3.1	7.0	4.4	DFT
VICTORIA FIRE & CASUALTY CO	OH	C+	58.9	34.0	0.0	7.7	8.5	N/A	2.9	7.0	4.6	T
VICTORIA NATIONAL INS CO	OH	U	--	--	--	--	N/A	--	--	--	--	Z
VICTORIA SELECT INS CO	OH	B-	7.8	5.7	0.0	0.1	10.0	N/A	2.9	7.0	3.8	DFT
VICTORIA SPECIALTY INSURANCE CO	OH	C	7.0	3.6	0.0	0.0	9.8	N/A	3.9	7.0	3.2	DFT
▲VICTORY INS CO	MT	D-	16.4	5.0	6.0	0.1	3.6	1.0	2.8	7.4	1.2	DR
VIGILANT INS CO	NY	B	576.7	327.3	25.4	13.0	10.0	7.6	8.4	7.3	6.0	T
VIKING INS CO OF WI	WI	C	493.9	172.8	105.4	6.7	9.7	7.7	4.7	6.4	3.6	T
VIRGINIA FARM BUREAU FIRE & CAS INS	VA	C	66.4	21.3	33.1	0.7	8.1	9.3	7.4	6.0	4.3	DR
VIRGINIA FARM BUREAU MUTUAL INS CO	VA	B-	402.7	193.6	200.1	20.1	8.1	9.1	8.8	6.3	4.7	R
VIRGINIA PHYSICIANS RRG INC	MT	D	1.8	1.1	0.4	0.1	8.8	9.4	8.1	9.8	1.0	DT
VIRGINIA SURETY CO INC	IL	B	1,439.3	406.3	266.5	9.0	10.0	5.9	8.1	6.9	5.5	
VISION INS CO	TX	D	30.8	14.0	28.9	0.0	3.1	2.6	2.4	2.9	2.0	DLT
VOYAGER INDEMNITY INS CO	GA	C	110.3	50.2	108.6	33.3	8.1	6.9	3.3	6.4	4.2	R

See Page 27 for explanation of footnotes and Page 28 for explanation of stability factors.

126

www.weissratings.com

Arrows denote recent upgrades ▲ or downgrades ▼   (see Section VII for explanations)

RISK ADJ. RATIO #1	CAPITAL RATIO #2	PREMIUM TO SURPLUS (%)	RESV. TO SURPLUS (%)	RESV. DEVELOP. 1 YEAR (%)	RESV. DEVELOP. 2 YEAR (%)	LOSS RATIO (%)	EXP. RATIO (%)	COMB. RATIO (%)	CASH FROM UNDER-WRITING (%)	NET PREMIUM GROWTH (%)	INVEST. IN AFFIL (%)	INSURANCE COMPANY NAME
1.4	1.0	247.6	49.9	-11.7	1.1	51.2	44.3	95.5	100.5	19.5	0.0	US LLOYDS INS CO
2.4	1.6	80.3	152.9	-0.1	1.0	56.7	32.5	89.2	113.7	1.6	0.0 ●	US SPECIALTY INS CO
9.0	7.0	10.4	25.3	-2.8	-3.1	26.9	39.2	66.1	110.0	1.6	0.0	US UNDERWRITERS INS CO
1.4	1.3	191.5	83.4	-1.8	-1.6	74.8	20.7	95.5	98.0	12.4	0.8	USA INS CO
0.7	0.6	74.6	15.1	-3.6	-0.2	31.3	52.0	83.3	119.5	-14.7	0.0	USA UNDERWRITERS
2.4	1.9	148.4	70.3	-1.5	-1.5	88.2	12.3	100.5	103.2	8.2	9.1 ●	USAA CASUALTY INS CO
N/A	N/A	--	--	--	--	--	--	--	--	--	--	USAA COUNTY MUTUAL INS CO
2.3	1.7	202.8	96.1	-2.2	-2.5	87.8	12.4	100.2	112.6	21.8	0.0 ●	USAA GENERAL INDEMNITY CO
1.8	1.2	39.7	3.9	N/A	-0.1	20.9	76.9	97.8	110.2	3.3	0.0	USPLATE GLASS INS CO
0.5	0.4	293.8	254.6	13.6	5.4	57.8	35.5	93.3	105.5	6.0	0.0	UTAH BUSINESS INS CO
3.5	2.8	61.0	61.9	-2.8	-0.9	67.3	26.4	93.7	111.3	4.5	0.0	UTICA FIRST INS CO
26.3	23.7	N/A	N/A	N/A	N/A	N/A	N/A	N/A	N/A	0.0	0.0	UTICA LLOYDS OF TX
2.4	1.8	87.7	116.8	-1.0	-2.2	64.4	33.2	97.6	108.3	9.5	10.4 ●	UTICA MUTUAL INS CO
4.6	3.1	63.5	84.5	-0.7	-1.5	64.4	33.1	97.5	108.5	9.5	0.0	UTICA NATIONAL ASR CO
9.5	8.5	N/A	N/A	N/A	N/A	N/A	N/A	N/A	N/A	0.0	0.0	UTICA NATIONAL INS CO OF OHIO
4.6	3.1	58.9	78.4	-0.6	-1.4	64.4	33.1	97.5	108.4	9.5	0.0	UTICA NATIONAL INS CO OF TX
71.0	32.3	N/A	N/A	N/A	N/A	N/A	N/A	N/A	N/A	0.0	0.0	UTICA SPECIALTY RISK INS CO
1.5	1.3	29.3	24.0	N/A	11.8	9.0	85.9	94.9	116.4	-15.4	0.0	UV INS RRG INC
2.6	2.3	114.8	59.5	-6.2	-8.5	69.1	29.8	98.9	99.8	6.1	0.0	VA FARM BUREAU TOWN & COUNTRY
63.6	27.1	N/A	N/A	N/A	N/A	N/A	N/A	N/A	N/A	0.0	0.0	VALLEY FORGE INS CO
5.9	5.3	N/A	N/A	N/A	N/A	N/A	N/A	N/A	59.4	0.0	0.0	VALLEY P&C INS CO
3.0	2.1	89.1	122.7	-1.0	3.2	67.1	26.3	93.4	103.4	4.7	0.0	VANLINER INS CO
N/A	N/A	--	--	--	--	--	--	--	--	--	--	VANTAGE CASUALTY INS CO
N/A	N/A	--	--	--	--	--	--	--	--	--	--	VANTAPRO SPECIALTY INS CO
3.5	2.8	101.6	9.1	-10.0	-0.9	66.6	31.8	98.4	103.6	21.4	0.0	VASA SPRING GARDEN MUTUAL INS CO
N/A	N/A	--	--	--	--	--	--	--	--	--	--	VAULT E&S INSURANCE CO
81.0	72.9	-0.1	N/A	N/A	N/A	207.2	999 +	999 +	1.3	0.0	0.0	VAULT RECIPROCAL EXCHANGE
N/A	N/A	--	--	--	--	--	--	--	--	--	--	VEHICULAR SERVICE INS CO RRG
0.8	0.7	34.5	46.1	31.4	N/A	69.7	32.5	102.2	159.8	-50.0	0.0	VELOCITY INS CO A RRG
69.7	31.1	N/A	N/A	N/A	N/A	N/A	N/A	N/A	-221.4	0.0	0.0	VERLAN FIRE INS CO
6.1	3.6	N/A	N/A	N/A	N/A	N/A	N/A	N/A	N/A	0.0	0.0	VERMONT ACCIDENT INS CO
4.6	3.0	90.4	34.0	-2.3	-3.0	51.4	37.5	88.9	120.1	8.3	1.1 ●	VERMONT MUTUAL INS CO
3.1	2.6	36.7	8.0	-1.1	-0.4	63.0	38.7	101.7	203.4	-26.8	7.8	VERSANT CASUALTY INS CO
4.5	2.9	25.9	41.2	-1.2	-0.9	65.8	23.2	89.0	149.3	-0.6	0.0	VERTERRA INS CO
3.9	3.2	71.7	36.6	9.7	7.6	79.9	25.5	105.4	98.9	0.4	0.0	VERTI INSURANCE CO
4.8	4.3	N/A	N/A	N/A	N/A	N/A	N/A	N/A	159.8	0.0	0.0	VESTA INS CORP
13.9	12.5	N/A	N/A	N/A	N/A	N/A	N/A	N/A	999 +	100.0	0.2	VETERINARY PET INS CO
0.3	0.2	413.9	438.2	-88.2	-44.1	69.1	21.8	90.9	89.7	-6.4	34.4	VFH CAPTIVE INS CO
10.5	9.5	N/A	N/A	N/A	N/A	N/A	N/A	N/A	236.4	0.0	0.0	VICTORIA AUTOMOBILE INS CO
2.1	2.0	N/A	N/A	N/A	N/A	N/A	N/A	N/A	207.0	0.0	36.1	VICTORIA FIRE & CASUALTY CO
N/A	N/A	--	--	--	--	--	--	--	--	--	--	VICTORIA NATIONAL INS CO
7.6	6.9	N/A	N/A	N/A	N/A	N/A	N/A	N/A	200.1	0.0	0.0	VICTORIA SELECT INS CO
3.2	2.8	N/A	N/A	N/A	N/A	N/A	N/A	N/A	236.4	0.0	0.0	VICTORIA SPECIALTY INSURANCE CO
0.9	0.6	119.5	58.4	-0.4	18.9	64.8	32.6	97.4	113.5	140.0	0.0	VICTORY INS CO
15.6	11.4	7.8	22.0	-0.9	-2.2	62.6	25.4	88.0	184.5	-19.9	5.1 ●	VIGILANT INS CO
3.8	2.7	61.0	95.0	-1.0	-2.2	74.8	28.6	103.4	102.3	4.7	7.7	VIKING INS CO OF WI
1.9	1.7	155.4	69.0	-7.0	-9.6	69.1	25.7	94.8	108.8	7.1	0.0	VIRGINIA FARM BUREAU FIRE & CAS INS
2.1	1.7	103.3	43.0	-5.4	-7.1	54.8	32.9	87.7	112.1	1.8	20.4	VIRGINIA FARM BUREAU MUTUAL INS CO
3.3	2.9	33.7	51.3	-6.3	-8.0	49.0	34.3	83.3	416.0	-2.9	0.0	VIRGINIA PHYSICIANS RRG INC
4.6	3.8	65.6	13.8	1.8	4.1	63.9	30.9	94.8	173.1	480.6	2.2 ●	VIRGINIA SURETY CO INC
0.8	0.6	207.2	114.5	13.6	36.5	71.2	33.0	104.2	95.6	-35.8	0.0	VISION INS CO
3.0	1.7	216.3	29.0	-6.0	-15.6	30.2	23.5	53.7	200.5	1.6	0.0	VOYAGER INDEMNITY INS CO

999 + Denotes number greater than 999.9%
999 - Denotes number less than -999.99%
● Bullets denote a more detailed analysis is available in Section II.

INSURANCE COMPANY NAME	DOM. STATE	RATING	TOTAL ASSETS ($MIL)	CAPITAL & SURPLUS ($MIL)	ANNUAL NET PREMIUM ($MIL)	NET INCOME ($MIL)	CAPITAL-IZATION INDEX (PTS)	RESERVE ADQ INDEX (PTS)	PROFIT-ABILITY INDEX (PTS)	LIQUIDITY INDEX (PTS)	STAB. INDEX (PTS)	STABILITY FACTORS
WADENA INS CO	IA	C	5.5	5.5	0.0	0.1	10.0	N/A	3.4	7.0	3.6	D
WALL ROSE MUTUAL INS CO	PA	D	1.1	0.5	0.3	0.1	7.0	5.9	3.8	7.9	0.8	DT
WARNER INS CO	IL	U	--	--	--	--	N/A	--	--	--	--	Z
WARRANTY UNDERWRITERS INS CO	TX	C-	27.2	14.3	1.8	0.9	8.2	9.8	6.3	7.6	3.0	DFR
WASHINGTON COUNTY CO-OPERATIVE INS	NY	D+	8.6	5.8	1.8	0.1	10.0	7.5	7.9	7.4	2.4	D
WASHINGTON INTL INS CO	NH	C	103.8	82.4	0.0	2.0	10.0	7.6	7.7	9.5	3.5	DFGR
WATFORD INS CO	NJ	C+	23.6	20.1	0.0	-0.2	10.0	N/A	3.1	10.0	4.4	DRT
WATFORD SPECIALTY INS CO	NJ	B	73.2	64.5	1.7	0.3	8.2	N/A	4.5	7.0	4.7	DGT
WAUSAU BUSINESS INS CO	WI	C	34.4	29.3	0.0	0.4	10.0	N/A	7.4	7.0	3.7	ADRT
WAUSAU GENERAL INS CO	WI	C	15.6	12.5	0.0	0.2	10.0	N/A	6.5	10.0	3.0	ADRT
WAUSAU UNDERWRITERS INS CO	WI	C	127.0	69.3	0.0	1.1	10.0	N/A	7.2	7.3	4.1	ART
▲WAWANESA GENERAL INS CO	CA	B	582.0	225.3	404.1	-10.5	7.8	5.0	3.4	2.1	5.4	FLR
▲WAYNE COOPERATIVE INS CO	NY	C+	34.9	17.2	15.2	1.2	8.8	8.5	8.2	6.7	3.8	DR
▲WAYNE MUTUAL INS CO	OH	B-	83.2	41.6	52.2	3.4	9.1	8.2	8.8	6.3	5.3	T
WEA P&C INS CO	WI	C	19.6	5.2	12.4	-0.1	7.3	9.4	3.5	5.9	2.5	D
▲WELLSPAN RRG	VT	D	28.7	11.2	10.5	5.0	7.5	10.0	9.1	7.0	1.5	D
WESCAP INS CO	CO	U (1)	--	--	--	--	N/A	--	--	--	--	Z
▼WESCO INS CO	DE	D	1,621.0	289.7	565.7	-7.4	0.2	7.0	4.1	0.3	2.3	CLR
WEST AMERICAN INS CO	IN	C-	52.3	51.2	0.0	0.7	10.0	N/A	2.9	7.0	3.1	ART
▲WEST BEND MUTUAL INS CO	WI	A-	2,695.9	1,041.1	1,092.0	88.2	8.9	9.0	8.6	6.3	7.0	
WEST BRANCH MUTL INS CO	PA	C+	1.1	0.8	0.3	0.0	7.6	7.3	3.0	8.2	3.0	DT
WEST RIVER INSURANCE CO	SD	C-	18.3	8.1	5.2	1.8	6.7	6.0	7.5	6.8	3.2	DR
WEST VIRGINIA FARMERS MUT INS ASSOC	WV	C-	8.1	6.0	2.0	0.4	9.2	5.2	8.0	6.8	3.1	DR
▲WEST VIRGINIA INS CO	WV	C+	53.7	45.3	11.4	2.5	10.0	7.5	8.1	6.8	4.5	D
▲WEST VIRGINIA MUTUAL INS CO	WV	C	161.7	90.4	15.7	-8.2	8.4	9.3	2.4	7.0	3.5	DFR
WEST VIRGINIA NATIONAL AUTO INS CO	WV	D+	6.0	2.3	5.6	-0.3	4.7	4.9	1.3	2.9	2.0	DFLR
WESTCHESTER FIRE INS CO	PA	C	1,655.7	682.2	339.9	51.3	9.4	4.7	3.6	6.7	4.2	FR
WESTCHESTER SURPLUS LINES INS CO	GA	C	350.2	105.5	44.1	-11.8	8.5	6.4	2.5	6.0	4.0	FR
WESTERN AGRICULTURAL INS CO	IA	B+	213.2	111.9	107.7	9.5	10.0	8.2	8.9	5.9	6.6	L
WESTERN CATHOLIC INS CO RRG	VT	U	--	--	--	--	N/A	--	--	--	--	Z
WESTERN COMMUNITY INS CO	ID	B-	43.3	33.7	0.0	1.6	10.0	N/A	8.2	9.2	4.7	
WESTERN GENERAL INS CO	CA	D+	90.6	23.3	65.4	1.3	2.3	3.0	5.0	2.8	2.7	CDLR
WESTERN HERITAGE INS CO	AZ	B	132.6	115.5	0.0	3.8	10.0	N/A	7.2	8.7	4.5	DFRT
WESTERN HOME INS CO	MN	C	69.3	32.9	26.2	2.5	9.7	8.1	8.8	6.6	3.4	R
WESTERN MUTL INS CO (CA)	CA	C-	90.3	62.5	27.5	2.1	7.3	8.1	8.0	6.7	2.7	R
WESTERN MUTUAL FIRE INS CO	MN	B-	8.1	5.3	2.4	0.3	10.0	5.0	8.9	7.0	3.5	D
WESTERN NATIONAL ASR CO	MN	C	89.3	29.0	26.2	1.7	9.2	8.2	8.8	6.3	4.0	GR
WESTERN NATIONAL MUTUAL INS CO	MN	B-	1,045.2	460.0	417.6	24.3	8.4	8.1	8.5	6.5	4.5	R
▲WESTERN PACIFIC MUT INS CO RISK RET	CO	B	143.1	119.2	4.0	2.9	10.0	8.5	6.8	9.4	5.5	D
WESTERN PROFESSIONAL INS CO	WA	U	--	--	--	--	N/A	--	--	--	--	Z
WESTERN PROTECTORS INS CO	OR	U	--	--	--	--	N/A	--	--	--	--	Z
WESTERN RESERVE MUTUAL CAS CO	OH	B-	203.3	115.7	85.0	4.4	9.9	7.8	8.1	6.1	4.7	T
WESTERN SELECT INS CO	IL	C	17.4	15.4	0.2	0.4	10.0	6.0	5.9	9.5	3.7	D
▲WESTERN SURETY CO	SD	C+	2,043.5	1,527.2	376.3	144.4	10.0	9.2	8.4	7.2	4.4	R
WESTERN WORLD INS CO	NH	C	982.1	376.2	182.9	59.3	6.4	9.4	3.8	7.1	4.1	R
WESTFIELD INS CO	OH	B-	2,937.3	1,278.4	1,002.9	26.2	9.8	8.2	6.8	6.6	4.6	T
WESTFIELD NATIONAL INS CO	OH	B-	696.6	317.2	241.4	5.8	9.6	8.2	6.8	6.6	4.6	T
▲WESTGUARD INS CO	PA	B	1,181.9	613.4	28.9	6.2	7.2	8.0	8.2	10.0	5.5	FT
▲WESTMINSTER AMERICAN INS CO	MD	C+	38.7	19.6	19.6	1.5	7.8	5.9	8.9	8.1	4.1	DR
WESTON INS CO	FL	C	86.1	44.6	5.7	0.1	10.0	5.0	3.7	6.9	4.1	G
WESTPORT INS CORP	MO	B	5,517.6	1,535.5	321.9	93.8	7.1	6.6	4.8	6.8	6.2	F
WHITECAP SURETY CO	MN	D-	1.6	1.4	3.3	0.1	1.8	N/A	8.5	2.8	1.2	CDLT

See Page 27 for explanation of footnotes and
Page 28 for explanation of stability factors.
Arrows denote recent upgrades ▲ or downgrades ▼   (see Section VII for explanations)

128

www.weissratings.com

RISK ADJ. RATIO #1	CAPITAL RATIO #2	PREMIUM TO SURPLUS (%)	RESV. TO SURPLUS (%)	RESV. DEVELOP. 1 YEAR (%)	2 YEAR (%)	LOSS RATIO (%)	EXP. RATIO (%)	COMB RATIO (%)	CASH FROM UNDER-WRITING (%)	NET PREMIUM GROWTH (%)	INVEST. IN AFFIL (%)	INSURANCE COMPANY NAME
104.6	49.4	N/A	N/A	N/A	N/A	N/A	N/A	N/A	104.9	0.0	0.0	WADENA INS CO
1.8	1.2	64.0	10.2	-0.7	-5.2	44.1	40.0	84.1	87.7	12.0	0.0	WALL ROSE MUTUAL INS CO
N/A	N/A	--	--	--	--	--	--	--	--	--	--	WARNER INS CO
3.3	2.3	12.5	41.5	-13.9	-18.7	67.7	78.4	146.1	31.9	-7.5	0.0	WARRANTY UNDERWRITERS INS CO
6.3	5.6	30.3	8.9	-0.1	-1.7	55.6	32.7	88.3	123.6	9.4	0.0	WASHINGTON COUNTY CO-OPERATIVE
22.6	20.3	N/A	3.3	-0.1	-1.9	-747.9	999 +	999 +	35.0	49.0	0.0	WASHINGTON INTL INS CO
14.8	6.0	0.1	N/A	N/A	N/A	61.8	999 +	999 +	-5.5	0.0	0.0	WATFORD INS CO
2.2	1.8	2.7	1.2	N/A	N/A	59.1	133.3	192.4	94.3	102.9	39.7	WATFORD SPECIALTY INS CO
18.9	17.0	N/A	N/A	N/A	N/A	N/A	N/A	N/A	1.0	0.0	0.0	WAUSAU BUSINESS INS CO
12.1	10.9	N/A	N/A	N/A	N/A	N/A	N/A	N/A	-189.9	0.0	0.0	WAUSAU GENERAL INS CO
9.7	8.7	N/A	N/A	N/A	N/A	N/A	N/A	N/A	267.2	0.0	0.0	WAUSAU UNDERWRITERS INS CO
1.9	1.5	179.4	81.6	0.8	-6.9	93.4	13.9	107.3	91.6	12.0	0.0 •	WAWANESA GENERAL INS CO
3.0	2.2	88.5	42.1	-0.3	-1.9	63.0	31.0	94.0	119.8	4.0	0.0	WAYNE COOPERATIVE INS CO
4.0	2.6	125.5	27.0	-5.7	-5.9	55.8	35.5	91.3	113.4	9.0	0.0	WAYNE MUTUAL INS CO
1.5	1.2	237.9	90.9	-4.6	-19.1	71.4	31.3	102.7	100.1	3.2	0.0	WEA P&C INS CO
2.0	1.6	93.4	156.3	-37.5	-69.6	51.3	5.0	56.3	150.9	5.0	0.0	WELLSPAN RRG
N/A	N/A	--	--	--	--	--	--	--	--	--	--	WESCAP INS CO
0.2	0.1	195.3	281.6	63.3	-133.6	83.1	25.3	108.4	359.1	-6.8	8.0 •	WESCO INS CO
108.5	55.5	N/A	N/A	N/A	N/A	N/A	N/A	N/A	N/A	0.0	0.0	WEST AMERICAN INS CO
3.5	2.4	104.9	91.7	-8.0	-8.8	59.8	31.3	91.1	112.4	7.5	0.0 •	WEST BEND MUTUAL INS CO
2.4	1.5	43.6	2.8	-0.4	-0.6	30.1	81.8	111.9	111.9	2.4	0.0	WEST BRANCH MUTL INS CO
2.0	1.6	63.8	87.7	-23.8	-34.6	44.1	17.1	61.2	174.5	-7.8	0.0	WEST RIVER INSURANCE CO
3.5	2.5	33.3	2.5	-1.2	-1.0	27.3	52.2	79.5	124.6	4.7	0.0	WEST VIRGINIA FARMERS MUT INS
12.1	10.0	25.2	3.8	-1.9	-2.5	58.4	20.5	78.9	120.7	0.3	0.0	WEST VIRGINIA INS CO
2.4	1.9	17.4	58.5	4.1	-6.5	142.4	37.9	180.3	51.5	-8.1	0.0	WEST VIRGINIA MUTUAL INS CO
0.7	0.7	242.4	108.6	-2.2	-0.2	78.6	28.8	107.4	90.9	48.7	0.0	WEST VIRGINIA NATIONAL AUTO INS CO
3.9	2.6	49.8	112.9	6.5	11.1	78.2	23.1	101.3	75.2	-6.1	0.0 •	WESTCHESTER FIRE INS CO
2.9	1.9	41.8	85.9	-0.4	-1.9	127.5	24.0	151.5	55.1	2.0	0.0	WESTCHESTER SURPLUS LINES INS CO
5.3	4.0	96.3	35.4	-3.4	-5.8	66.3	26.6	92.9	102.3	2.0	2.0 •	WESTERN AGRICULTURAL INS CO
N/A	N/A	--	--	--	--	--	--	--	--	--	--	WESTERN CATHOLIC INS CO RRG
14.2	12.8	N/A	N/A	N/A	N/A	N/A	N/A	N/A	-53.7	0.0	0.0	WESTERN COMMUNITY INS CO
0.6	0.4	280.6	93.7	16.6	21.1	58.5	39.9	98.4	104.6	10.8	0.0	WESTERN GENERAL INS CO
36.1	32.5	N/A	N/A	N/A	N/A	N/A	N/A	N/A	-76.6	0.0	0.0	WESTERN HERITAGE INS CO
4.0	2.9	79.8	63.3	-2.1	-3.1	67.5	30.6	98.1	104.8	-6.1	0.0	WESTERN HOME INS CO
1.9	1.3	44.1	13.0	-3.8	-3.7	67.7	22.1	89.8	110.9	-1.1	24.3	WESTERN MUTL INS CO (CA)
5.7	4.2	45.6	14.8	0.8	-1.9	69.0	21.1	90.1	107.4	-5.6	0.0	WESTERN MUTUAL FIRE INS CO
3.5	2.5	90.5	71.7	-2.4	-3.5	67.5	30.2	97.7	99.4	-6.1	0.0	WESTERN NATIONAL ASR CO
2.3	1.9	90.8	66.9	-2.3	-3.4	67.5	27.6	95.1	121.8	19.6	18.7 •	WESTERN NATIONAL MUTUAL INS CO
7.8	4.7	3.3	6.2	-3.3	-4.1	26.7	103.9	130.6	70.1	20.5	0.0	WESTERN PACIFIC MUT INS CO RISK
N/A	N/A	--	--	--	--	--	--	--	--	--	--	WESTERN PROFESSIONAL INS CO
N/A	N/A	--	--	--	--	--	--	--	--	--	--	WESTERN PROTECTORS INS CO
4.7	2.9	73.4	33.5	-1.9	-2.8	69.8	30.6	100.4	99.9	3.8	0.2	WESTERN RESERVE MUTUAL CAS CO
21.0	18.9	1.0	1.8	-0.1	0.2	57.6	-70.0	-12.4	212.9	-23.0	0.0	WESTERN SELECT INS CO
8.5	6.5	24.6	17.0	-4.7	-8.7	6.1	54.5	60.6	138.0	1.7	1.1 •	WESTERN SURETY CO
1.1	0.9	48.6	80.8	-0.4	-2.7	98.1	20.3	118.4	66.7	50.7	25.3 •	WESTERN WORLD INS CO
4.3	2.9	78.4	74.3	0.3	-2.2	73.5	33.7	107.2	99.6	2.6	0.0 •	WESTFIELD INS CO
4.0	2.7	76.1	72.1	0.2	-2.1	73.5	35.1	108.6	99.6	2.6	0.0 •	WESTFIELD NATIONAL INS CO
1.3	1.2	4.7	5.0	-0.3	-0.4	57.8	13.0	70.8	999 +	26.0	65.3 •	WESTGUARD INS CO
1.7	1.5	99.9	17.2	8.0	6.1	45.0	35.2	80.2	168.7	22.6	0.0	WESTMINSTER AMERICAN INS CO
7.6	6.8	12.8	1.1	-0.2	-0.5	201.9	-54.0	147.9	121.9	698.1	0.0	WESTON INS CO
1.6	1.0	21.0	69.2	1.5	1.5	77.1	46.0	123.1	65.2	12.1	10.9 •	WESTPORT INS CORP
0.4	0.3	239.5	N/A	N/A	N/A	N/A	96.0	96.0	104.4	-2.4	0.0	WHITECAP SURETY CO

999 + Denotes number greater than 999.9%
999 - Denotes number less than -999.99%
• Bullets denote a more detailed analysis is available in Section II.

INSURANCE COMPANY NAME	DOM. STATE	RATING	TOTAL ASSETS ($MIL)	CAPITAL & SURPLUS ($MIL)	ANNUAL NET PREMIUM ($MIL)	NET INCOME ($MIL)	CAPITAL-IZATION INDEX (PTS)	RESERVE ADQ INDEX (PTS)	PROFIT-ABILITY INDEX (PTS)	LIQUIDITY INDEX (PTS)	STAB. INDEX (PTS)	STABILITY FACTORS
▲WI LAWYERS MUTUAL INS CO	WI	B-	34.8	24.5	3.9	0.9	10.0	8.3	6.8	7.4	4.7	DR
▼WILLIAMSBURG NATIONAL INS CO	MI	D	30.2	29.0	0.0	1.1	10.0	1.8	3.1	0.0	2.2	DFLR
WILMINGTON INS CO	DE	D+	5.1	3.4	0.9	0.0	9.4	6.4	4.7	9.2	2.1	DF
WILSHIRE INS CO	NC	C-	334.5	140.2	112.1	6.2	7.0	3.2	4.5	5.4	2.7	R
▲WILSON MUTUAL INS CO	WI	B	86.1	19.2	21.7	-4.1	7.1	6.3	2.1	5.7	5.4	DF
WINDHAVEN INS CO	FL	D-	218.0	48.6	126.8	-5.8	0.8	1.7	3.8	0.6	1.0	CLR
WINDHAVEN NATIONAL INS CO	TX	C	6.5	5.4	0.4	-0.2	8.1	3.3	3.4	7.1	2.9	DFT
▲WINDSOR MOUNT JOY MUTUAL INS CO	PA	B	87.3	52.8	34.8	3.7	10.0	8.0	8.7	7.5	5.5	T
WISCONSIN COUNTY MUTUAL INS CORP	WI	C	85.6	27.4	25.2	-3.8	6.5	5.6	2.2	6.6	4.0	R
WISCONSIN MUNICIPAL MUTUAL INS CO	WI	C	50.1	30.7	3.2	-0.6	6.0	4.6	2.3	7.5	4.2	DFR
▲WISCONSIN MUTUAL INS CO	WI	B	160.6	92.5	76.1	7.3	10.0	8.4	8.9	6.5	5.5	T
WISCONSIN REINS CORP	WI	C+	96.1	61.1	36.9	3.9	7.8	7.0	8.8	6.4	4.4	FR
▲WOLVERINE MUTUAL INS CO	MI	B-	56.4	23.9	31.9	2.2	8.1	8.5	8.4	6.4	4.6	D
WOODLANDS INS CO	TX	C	29.5	11.2	5.3	0.0	8.0	3.6	4.7	6.6	2.4	DFGT
▲WORK FIRST CASUALTY CO	DE	C	48.0	15.1	18.2	1.6	3.8	5.0	6.9	6.5	3.4	CDR
WORKERS COMPENSATION EXCHANGE	ID	E	8.3	0.5	2.8	0.0	0.1	1.2	3.4	7.2	0.3	CDRT
▲WORKMENS AUTO INS CO	CA	D+	48.2	22.5	29.2	2.4	6.5	2.2	3.9	5.9	2.4	DR
WORTH CASUALTY CO	TX	C	20.4	9.8	0.0	1.4	10.0	3.6	6.0	5.2	3.9	DGR
WRIGHT NATIONAL FLOOD INS CO	TX	B-	37.7	28.7	0.0	4.8	10.0	4.6	8.7	8.0	4.8	
WRM AMERICA INDEMNITY CO	NY	U	--	--	--	--	N/A	--	--	--	--	Z
XL INS AMERICA INC	DE	C	791.3	218.7	211.1	-15.6	7.3	6.4	4.0	6.6	3.8	FR
XL INS CO OF NY INC	NY	C-	240.0	70.6	63.3	-1.8	8.2	6.4	3.0	6.5	3.0	AFR
XL REINS AMERICA INC	NY	C	5,952.3	2,046.6	1,372.0	-10.8	8.3	6.3	4.7	7.4	3.8	AR
▲XL SELECT INS CO	DE	D+	160.3	47.4	42.2	-2.3	8.2	6.4	3.2	6.6	2.5	R
XL SPECIALTY INS CO	DE	C	1,066.4	313.5	126.7	19.4	9.4	6.4	5.7	9.2	3.8	AR
YCI INC	OK	U	--	--	--	--	N/A	--	--	--	--	Z
YEL CO INS	FL	C	15.4	10.7	1.2	1.0	10.0	8.9	5.5	10.0	3.1	D
YELLOWSTONE INS EXCHANGE	VT	C-	19.2	9.5	5.0	0.6	8.1	9.8	5.5	7.5	2.9	DR
YORK INS CO OF MAINE	ME	F (5)	47.0	46.3	0.0	0.0	10.0	N/A	7.5	7.0	0.0	RT
YOSEMITE INS CO	IN	C+	113.7	42.0	13.6	18.5	10.0	6.1	1.9	9.1	4.7	DFT
YOUNG AMERICA INS CO	TX	D	53.2	13.6	44.2	-3.9	1.2	1.2	1.2	0.8	1.6	CDFL
▲ZALE INDEMNITY CO	TX	B-	45.2	18.7	5.2	1.4	7.4	6.3	8.5	5.4	4.6	DR
ZENITH INS CO	CA	C+	1,843.8	571.7	803.9	86.0	6.5	9.5	5.9	7.8	4.4	AR
▲ZEPHYR INS CO	HI	C+	101.3	76.4	27.4	17.0	10.0	3.6	9.3	9.1	4.5	R
ZNAT INS CO	CA	C	68.7	25.8	16.4	2.4	8.3	9.2	5.3	9.3	3.4	AFR
▲ZURICH AMERICAN INS CO	NY	B	31,582.0	7,619.0	4,630.4	828.6	8.0	6.1	5.0	6.8	5.4	R
ZURICH AMERICAN INS CO OF IL	IL	C+	62.3	34.8	0.0	0.6	10.0	N/A	6.1	6.4	4.6	FR

See Page 27 for explanation of footnotes and
Page 28 for explanation of stability factors.   130   www.weissratings.com
Arrows denote recent upgrades ▲ or downgrades ▼   (see Section VII for explanations)

RISK ADJ. RATIO #1	CAPITAL RATIO #2	PREMIUM TO SURPLUS (%)	RESV. TO SURPLUS (%)	RESV. DEVELOP. 1 YEAR (%)	RESV. DEVELOP. 2 YEAR (%)	LOSS RATIO (%)	EXP. RATIO (%)	COMB RATIO (%)	CASH FROM UNDER-WRITING (%)	NET PREMIUM GROWTH (%)	INVEST. IN AFFIL (%)	INSURANCE COMPANY NAME
4.4	3.0	16.1	26.1	-6.0	-8.7	55.6	43.2	98.8	114.5	1.2	0.0	WI LAWYERS MUTUAL INS CO
53.4	37.0	N/A	N/A	N/A	N/A	N/A	N/A	N/A	65.1	0.0	0.0	WILLIAMSBURG NATIONAL INS CO
4.1	2.5	25.7	11.8	1.7	-2.8	53.0	66.1	119.1	80.1	-16.4	0.0	WILMINGTON INS CO
1.6	1.0	80.0	61.1	0.2	11.9	73.3	30.7	104.0	98.9	26.7	0.0	WILSHIRE INS CO
1.6	1.0	113.1	96.7	4.7	2.0	83.5	42.1	125.6	88.8	1.1	0.0	WILSON MUTUAL INS CO
0.3	0.2	260.8	130.2	18.9	15.9	78.4	29.1	107.5	99.7	7.8	0.0	WINDHAVEN INS CO
1.9	1.7	7.7	17.1	4.6	4.7	78.5	62.1	140.6	5.9	0.0	0.0	WINDHAVEN NATIONAL INS CO
3.9	3.1	65.8	17.7	-3.1	-3.6	41.1	43.6	84.7	128.9	6.9	0.0	WINDSOR MOUNT JOY MUTUAL INS CO
1.5	0.9	91.8	154.2	11.7	8.7	93.4	28.9	122.3	109.4	3.6	7.3	WISCONSIN COUNTY MUTUAL INS CORP
1.2	0.8	10.3	34.9	1.2	10.4	116.0	27.7	143.7	69.6	-1.6	5.8	WISCONSIN MUNICIPAL MUTUAL INS CO
6.1	4.4	82.3	32.9	-1.0	-3.9	67.6	22.5	90.1	108.9	4.0	0.0	WISCONSIN MUTUAL INS CO
2.2	1.7	60.4	45.9	-6.7	-13.0	66.6	23.5	90.1	81.9	-7.5	13.3	WISCONSIN REINS CORP
2.6	2.0	133.6	56.0	-7.9	-9.1	60.8	33.7	94.5	97.9	-7.4	0.0	WOLVERINE MUTUAL INS CO
2.5	1.6	47.6	12.7	N/A	-0.1	74.5	33.1	107.6	93.8	209.4	0.0	WOODLANDS INS CO
0.9	0.7	120.0	198.6	-10.0	-14.5	69.7	27.2	96.9	120.9	12.2	0.0	WORK FIRST CASUALTY CO
0.1	0.1	586.4	999 +	-75.6	86.0	94.6	11.6	106.2	109.1	16.5	0.0	WORKERS COMPENSATION EXCHANGE
1.4	1.1	130.0	59.4	-13.9	-19.1	68.7	23.8	92.5	99.2	10.8	0.0	WORKMENS AUTO INS CO
3.9	3.5	N/A	N/A	N/A	N/A	N/A	N/A	N/A	243.9	0.0	0.0	WORTH CASUALTY CO
12.7	11.4	N/A	N/A	N/A	N/A	999 +	999 +	999 +	-7.4	-25.2	0.0	WRIGHT NATIONAL FLOOD INS CO
N/A	N/A	--	--	--	--	--	--	--	--	--	--	WRM AMERICA INDEMNITY CO
1.5	1.2	96.5	158.0	-4.1	-3.6	76.8	27.4	104.2	136.4	26.6	18.2	XL INS AMERICA INC
2.8	1.8	89.7	146.9	-3.2	-3.0	76.8	25.3	102.1	136.5	26.6	0.0	XL INS CO OF NY INC
2.2	1.8	67.0	109.8	-2.5	-2.5	76.8	24.9	101.7	65.9	26.6	17.3 ●	XL REINS AMERICA INC
2.8	1.8	89.2	145.9	-3.3	-3.3	76.8	25.1	101.9	136.5	26.6	0.0	XL SELECT INS CO
4.4	3.2	40.4	66.1	-1.7	-3.5	76.8	0.9	77.7	136.4	26.6	4.9 ●	XL SPECIALTY INS CO
N/A	N/A	--	--	--	--	--	--	--	--	--	--	YCI INC
7.6	6.8	11.2	43.5	-4.0	-8.0	17.5	11.0	28.5	351.6	0.0	0.0	YEL CO INS
2.2	1.7	53.0	78.3	-5.2	-17.9	44.7	53.3	98.0	200.2	-2.0	0.0	YELLOWSTONE INS EXCHANGE
60.4	34.5	N/A	N/A	N/A	N/A	N/A	N/A	N/A	N/A	-100.0	0.0	YORK INS CO OF MAINE
5.5	3.1	32.5	49.7	3.0	2.2	25.7	26.1	51.8	129.2	-56.5	0.0	YOSEMITE INS CO
0.3	0.2	325.7	269.3	26.1	79.5	80.4	36.9	117.3	88.1	-34.2	0.0	YOUNG AMERICA INS CO
1.3	1.2	27.8	5.5	4.8	5.8	15.2	176.6	191.8	107.0	-66.0	40.0	ZALE INDEMNITY CO
1.2	0.9	140.6	195.3	-13.3	-24.4	49.8	32.3	82.1	122.2	1.4	14.2 ●	ZENITH INS CO
9.1	8.0	35.8	N/A	N/A	-0.1	N/A	46.3	46.3	93.8	-8.3	0.0	ZEPHYR INS CO
2.4	1.8	63.7	88.5	-5.8	-11.8	49.8	32.5	82.3	92.5	1.4	0.0	ZNAT INS CO
2.3	1.6	60.8	185.4	-1.7	-3.3	82.5	16.8	99.3	95.2	9.9	7.7 ●	ZURICH AMERICAN INS CO
8.0	7.2	N/A	N/A	N/A	N/A	N/A	N/A	N/A	16.1	0.0	0.0	ZURICH AMERICAN INS CO OF IL

999 + Denotes number greater than 999.9%
999 - Denotes number less than -999.99%
● Bullets denote a more detailed analysis is available in Section II.

Section II

Analysis of Largest Companies

A summary analysis of Weiss Recommended

U.S. Property and Casualty Insurers,

along with the largest companies based on capital and surplus.

Companies are listed in alphabetical order.

Section II Contents

This section contains rating factors, historical data and general information on each of the largest property and casualty insurers in the U.S. that have the most recent quarterly financial information available.

1. Safety Rating	The current rating appears to the right of the company name. Our ratings are designed to distinguish levels of insolvency risk and are measured on a scale from A (Excellent) to F (Failed). Highly-rated companies are, in our opinion, less likely to experience financial difficulties than lower-rated firms. See *About Weiss Safety Ratings* for more information.	

2. Major Rating Factors

A synopsis of the key indexes and sub-factors that have most influenced the rating of a particular insurer. Items are presented in the approximate order of their importance to the rating. There may be additional factors which have influenced the rating but do not appear due to space limitations or confidentiality agreements with insurers.

3. Other Rating Factors

A summary of those Weiss Ratings indexes that were not included as Major Rating Factors, but nevertheless, may have had some impact on the final grade.

4. Principal Business

The major types of policies written by an insurer along with the percentages for each line in relation to the entire book of business. Lines of business written by property and casualty insurers include personal and commercial insurance lines such as homeowners', auto, workers' compensation, commercial multiple peril, medical malpractice and product liability, among others.

5. Principal Investments

The major investments in an insurer's portfolio. These include cash, investment grade bonds, non investment grade bonds, common and preferred stock, and real estate.

6. Investments in Affiliates

The percentage of bonds, common and preferred stocks and other financial instruments an insurer has invested with affiliated companies.

7. Group Affiliation

The name of the group of companies to which a particular insurer belongs.

8. Licensed in

List of the states in which an insurer is licensed to conduct business.

9. Commenced Business

The month and year the company started its operations.

10. Address

The address of an insurer's corporate headquarters. This location may differ from the company's state of domicile.

11. Phone

The telephone number of an insurer's corporate headquarters.

12. Domicile State   The state that has primary regulatory responsibility for this company. You do not have to live in the domicile state to do business with this firm, provided it is registered to do business in your state.

13. NAIC Code   The identification number assigned to an insurer by the National Association of Insurance Commissioners (NAIC).

14. Historical Data   Five years of background data for Weiss Safety Rating, risk-adjusted capital ratios (moderate and severe loss scenarios), total assets, capital, net premium, and net income. See the following page for more details on how to read the historical data table.

15. Customized Graph (or Table)   A graph or table depicting one of the company's major strengths or weaknesses.

How to Read the Historical Data Table

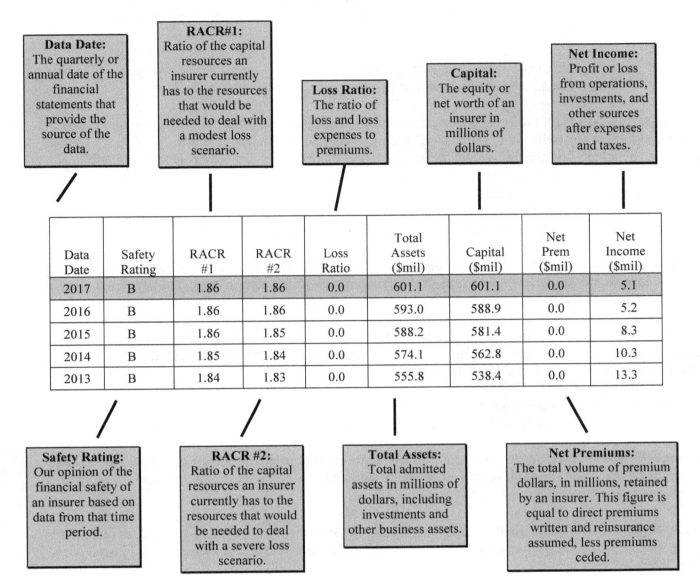

Data Date:
The quarterly or annual date of the financial statements that provide the source of the data.

RACR#1:
Ratio of the capital resources an insurer currently has to the resources that would be needed to deal with a modest loss scenario.

Loss Ratio:
The ratio of loss and loss expenses to premiums.

Capital:
The equity or net worth of an insurer in millions of dollars.

Net Income:
Profit or loss from operations, investments, and other sources after expenses and taxes.

Data Date	Safety Rating	RACR #1	RACR #2	Loss Ratio	Total Assets ($mil)	Capital ($mil)	Net Prem ($mil)	Net Income ($mil)
2017	B	1.86	1.86	0.0	601.1	601.1	0.0	5.1
2016	B	1.86	1.86	0.0	593.0	588.9	0.0	5.2
2015	B	1.86	1.85	0.0	588.2	581.4	0.0	8.3
2014	B	1.85	1.84	0.0	574.1	562.8	0.0	10.3
2013	B	1.84	1.83	0.0	555.8	538.4	0.0	13.3

Safety Rating:
Our opinion of the financial safety of an insurer based on data from that time period.

RACR #2:
Ratio of the capital resources an insurer currently has to the resources that would be needed to deal with a severe loss scenario.

Total Assets:
Total admitted assets in millions of dollars, including investments and other business assets.

Net Premiums:
The total volume of premium dollars, in millions, retained by an insurer. This figure is equal to direct premiums written and reinsurance assumed, less premiums ceded.

Row Descriptions:

Row 1 contains the most recent quarterly data as filed with state regulators and is presented on a year-to-date basis. For example, the figure for year-end premiums includes premiums received through the year-end. **Row 2** consists of data from the same quarter of the prior year so that you can compare current quarterly results to those of a year ago.

Row 3 contains data from the most recent annual statutory filing. **Rows 4-7** include data from year-end statements going back four years from the most recent annual filing so that you can compare current year-end results to those of the previous four years. With the exception of Total Assets and Capital, quarterly data are not comparable with annual data.

Customized Graphs

In the lower right-hand corner of each company section, a customized graph or text block highlights a key factor affecting that company's financial strength. One of nine types of information is found, identified by one of the following headings:

Capital plots the company's reported capital in millions of dollars over the last five years. Volatile changes in capital levels may indicate unstable operations.

Group Affiliation shows the group name, a composite Weiss Safety Rating for the group, and a list of the largest members with their ratings. The composite Safety Rating is made up of the weighted average, by assets, of the individual ratings of each company in the group (including life/health companies, property/casualty companies or HMOs) plus a factor for the financial strength of the holding company, where applicable.

Income Trends shows underwriting and net income results over the last five years.

Liquidity Index evaluates a company's ability to raise the cash necessary to pay claims. Various cash flow scenarios are modeled to determine how the company might fare in the event of an unexpected spike in claims costs.

Rating Indexes illustrate the score and range -- strong, good, fair or weak -- on the five Weiss indexes: Risk-Adjusted Capital Index #2 (Cap2), Stability Index (Stab.), Reserve Adequacy Index (Res.), Profitability Index (Prof.), and Liquidity Index (Liq.).

Reserve Deficiency shows whether the company has set aside sufficient funds to pay claims. A positive number indicates insufficient reserving and a negative number adequate reserving.

Reserves to Capital analyzes the relationship between loss and loss expense reserves to capital. Operating results and capital levels for companies with a high ratio are more susceptible to fluctuations than those with lower ratios.

Risk-Adjusted Capital Ratio #1 answers the question: In each of the past five years, does the insurer have sufficient capital to cover potential losses in its investments and business operations in a *moderate* loss scenario?

Risk-Adjusted Capital Ratio #2 answers the question: In each of the past five years, does the insurer have sufficient capital to cover potential losses in its investments and business operations in a *severe* loss scenario?

21ST CENTURY CENTENNIAL INS CO | B | Good

Major Rating Factors: Good overall profitability index (6.4 on a scale of 0 to 10). Fair expense controls. Return on equity has been low, averaging 1.5% over the past five years. Good overall results on stability tests (5.3) despite weak results on operational trends. Affiliation with Farmers Insurance Group of Companies is a strength.

Other Rating Factors: Strong long-term capitalization index (8.3) based on excellent current risk adjusted capital (severe and moderate loss scenarios), despite some fluctuation in capital levels. Superior liquidity (10.0) with ample operational cash flow and liquid investments.

Principal Business: Auto liability (72%) and auto physical damage (28%).

Principal Investments: Misc. investments (60%) and investment grade bonds (40%).

Investments in Affiliates: 60%

Group Affiliation: Farmers Insurance Group of Companies

Licensed in: All states except PR

Commenced Business: November 1977

Address: 2595 INTERSTATE DRIVE STE 103, Harrisburg, PA 17110

Phone: (302) 252-2000   **Domicile State:** PA   **NAIC Code:** 34789

Data Date	Rating	RACR #1	RACR #2	Loss Ratio %	Total Assets ($mil)	Capital ($mil)	Net Premium ($mil)	Net Income ($mil)
2017	B	1.86	1.86	0.0	601.1	601.1	0.0	5.1
2016	B	1.86	1.86	0.0	593.0	588.9	0.0	5.2
2015	B	1.86	1.85	0.0	588.2	581.4	0.0	8.3
2014	B	1.85	1.84	0.0	574.1	562.8	0.0	10.3
2013	B	1.84	1.83	0.0	555.8	538.4	0.0	13.3

Rating Indexes

21ST CENTURY INS CO | B | Good

Major Rating Factors: Good overall profitability index (6.9 on a scale of 0 to 10). Fair expense controls. Return on equity has been low, averaging 2.5% over the past five years. Good overall results on stability tests (6.0). Stability strengths include good operational trends and excellent risk diversification.

Other Rating Factors: Strong long-term capitalization index (10.0) based on excellent current risk adjusted capital (severe and moderate loss scenarios). Moreover, capital levels have been consistent in recent years. Superior liquidity (10.0) with ample operational cash flow and liquid investments.

Principal Business: Auto liability (63%) and auto physical damage (37%).

Principal Investments: Investment grade bonds (96%), misc. investments (2%), and cash (2%).

Investments in Affiliates: None

Group Affiliation: Farmers Insurance Group of Companies

Licensed in: All states except HI, LA, MA, NH, NM, RI, WY, PR

Commenced Business: December 1968

Address: 2710 GATEWAY OAKS DR STE 150N, Sacramento, CA 95833-3505

Phone: (302) 252-2000   **Domicile State:** CA   **NAIC Code:** 12963

Data Date	Rating	RACR #1	RACR #2	Loss Ratio %	Total Assets ($mil)	Capital ($mil)	Net Premium ($mil)	Net Income ($mil)
2017	B	119.10	54.75	0.0	997.9	996.1	0.0	24.0
2016	B	102.28	46.19	0.0	945.0	934.9	0.0	31.3
2015	B	100.94	45.85	0.0	912.6	902.6	0.0	24.3
2014	B	101.87	48.43	0.0	895.4	880.6	0.0	21.1
2013	B	55.30	36.29	0.0	880.8	861.7	0.0	15.0

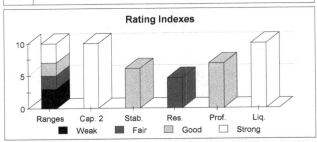

Rating Indexes

21ST CENTURY NORTH AMERICA INS | B | Good

Major Rating Factors: Good overall profitability index (6.0 on a scale of 0 to 10). Fair expense controls. Return on equity has been low, averaging 1.5% over the past five years. Good overall results on stability tests (5.8). Stability strengths include good operational trends and excellent risk diversification.

Other Rating Factors: Fair reserve development (4.9) as reserves have generally been sufficient to cover claims. Strong long-term capitalization index (10.0) based on excellent current risk adjusted capital (severe and moderate loss scenarios), despite some fluctuation in capital levels. Excellent liquidity (7.0) with ample operational cash flow and liquid investments.

Principal Business: Auto liability (68%) and auto physical damage (32%).

Principal Investments: Investment grade bonds (80%), misc. investments (18%), and cash (2%).

Investments in Affiliates: 18%

Group Affiliation: Farmers Insurance Group of Companies

Licensed in: All states except PR

Commenced Business: May 1975

Address: 100 DUFFY AVENUE SUITE 501, Hicksville, NY 11801

Phone: (302) 252-2000   **Domicile State:** NY   **NAIC Code:** 32220

Data Date	Rating	RACR #1	RACR #2	Loss Ratio %	Total Assets ($mil)	Capital ($mil)	Net Premium ($mil)	Net Income ($mil)
2017	B	5.90	5.65	0.0	594.6	572.1	0.0	7.5
2016	B	5.87	5.61	0.0	584.9	563.6	0.0	4.9
2015	B	5.89	5.67	0.0	583.0	556.5	0.0	7.5
2014	B	5.90	5.73	0.0	577.6	545.0	0.0	6.0
2013	B	5.76	5.47	0.0	572.0	532.6	0.0	15.2

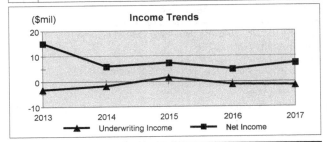

Income Trends

21ST CENTURY PREMIER INS CO   B-   Good

Major Rating Factors: Fair overall results on stability tests (4.9) including weak results on operational trends.

Other Rating Factors: Good overall profitability index (6.3). Weak expense controls. Return on equity has been low, averaging 2.6% over the past five years. Strong long-term capitalization index (10.0) based on excellent current risk adjusted capital (severe and moderate loss scenarios), despite some fluctuation in capital levels. Superior liquidity (10.0) with ample operational cash flow and liquid investments.

Principal Business: Auto liability (56%), auto physical damage (32%), homeowners multiple peril (9%), group accident & health (3%), and other accident & health (1%).

Principal Investments: Investment grade bonds (75%), misc. investments (24%), and cash (1%).

Investments in Affiliates: 24%

Group Affiliation: Farmers Insurance Group of Companies

Licensed in: All states except PR

Commenced Business: April 1866

Address: 2595 INTERSTATE DRIVE STE 103, Harrisburg, PA 17110

Phone: (302) 252-2000   **Domicile State:** PA   **NAIC Code:** 20796

Data Date	Rating	RACR #1	RACR #2	Loss Ratio %	Total Assets ($mil)	Capital ($mil)	Net Premium ($mil)	Net Income ($mil)
2017	B-	4.58	4.52	0.0	289.3	289.3	0.0	4.6
2016	B-	4.59	4.52	0.0	285.2	283.0	0.0	4.5
2015	B-	4.55	4.49	0.0	282.2	279.5	0.0	6.1
2014	B-	4.53	4.43	0.0	275.7	270.6	0.0	8.9
2013	B-	4.58	4.46	0.0	264.5	257.9	0.0	11.3

Rating Indexes

ACCIDENT FUND INS CO OF AMERICA   B-   Good

Major Rating Factors: Fair overall results on stability tests (4.6 on a scale of 0 to 10) including potential drain of affiliation with Blue Cross Blue Shield of Michigan and excessive premium growth. Fair reserve development (4.8) as reserves have generally been sufficient to cover claims.

Other Rating Factors: Good long-term capitalization index (6.5) based on good current risk adjusted capital (moderate loss scenario). Moreover, capital has steadily grown over the last five years. Good liquidity (6.9) with sufficient resources (cash flows and marketable investments) to handle a spike in claims. Excellent profitability (8.9) with operating gains in each of the last five years.

Principal Business: Workers compensation (100%).

Principal Investments: Investment grade bonds (62%), misc. investments (32%), and non investment grade bonds (6%).

Investments in Affiliates: 15%

Group Affiliation: Blue Cross Blue Shield of Michigan

Licensed in: All states except PR

Commenced Business: December 1994

Address: 200 N GRAND AVENUE, Lansing, MI 48933

Phone: (517) 342-4200   **Domicile State:** MI   **NAIC Code:** 10166

Data Date	Rating	RACR #1	RACR #2	Loss Ratio %	Total Assets ($mil)	Capital ($mil)	Net Premium ($mil)	Net Income ($mil)
2017	B-	1.17	0.94	59.8	3,664.5	994.7	1,319.1	126.3
2016	B-	1.27	1.03	63.0	3,114.1	897.4	925.0	93.5
2015	B-	1.26	1.01	64.5	2,780.5	813.8	812.6	107.0
2014	B-	1.31	1.07	72.5	2,387.0	750.9	717.4	62.6
2013	C+	1.46	1.18	65.9	2,257.7	684.1	546.7	30.5

Rating Indexes

ACE AMERICAN INS CO   B-   Good

Major Rating Factors: Fair overall results on stability tests (4.9 on a scale of 0 to 10) including potential drain of affiliation with Chubb Limited. Fair profitability index (3.9). Good expense controls. Return on equity has been fair, averaging 10.9% over the past five years.

Other Rating Factors: History of adequate reserve strength (6.0) as reserves have been consistently at an acceptable level. Good liquidity (6.8) with sufficient resources (cash flows and marketable investments) to handle a spike in claims. Strong long-term capitalization index (7.1) based on excellent current risk adjusted capital (severe and moderate loss scenarios), despite some fluctuation in capital levels.

Principal Business: Other liability (33%), workers compensation (17%), commercial multiple peril (10%), group accident & health (10%), auto liability (8%), fire (5%), and other lines (18%).

Principal Investments: Investment grade bonds (48%), non investment grade bonds (26%), misc. investments (24%), cash (1%), and real estate (1%).

Investments in Affiliates: 15%

Group Affiliation: Chubb Limited

Licensed in: All states, the District of Columbia and Puerto Rico

Commenced Business: January 1946

Address: 436 Walnut Street, Philadelphia, PA 19106

Phone: (215) 640-1000   **Domicile State:** PA   **NAIC Code:** 22667

Data Date	Rating	RACR #1	RACR #2	Loss Ratio %	Total Assets ($mil)	Capital ($mil)	Net Premium ($mil)	Net Income ($mil)
2017	B-	1.46	1.08	83.9	13,606.0	2,531.8	2,002.6	401.0
2016	B-	1.42	1.10	76.5	13,035.8	2,812.4	1,848.6	180.9
2015	B-	1.36	1.09	72.8	12,074.0	2,578.8	1,760.5	214.0
2014	B-	1.57	1.29	77.6	12,150.7	2,992.9	1,656.5	251.2
2013	B-	1.39	1.16	72.2	11,697.3	2,677.0	1,610.8	412.3

Rating Indexes

ACE P&C INS CO   B-   Good

Major Rating Factors: Fair overall results on stability tests (4.9 on a scale of 0 to 10) including potential drain of affiliation with Chubb Limited. History of adequate reserve strength (6.0) as reserves have been consistently at an acceptable level.

Other Rating Factors: Good overall profitability index (5.2). Good expense controls. Return on equity has been fair, averaging 7.5% over the past five years. Good liquidity (6.6) with sufficient resources (cash flows and marketable investments) to handle a spike in claims. Strong long-term capitalization index (8.1) based on excellent current risk adjusted capital (severe and moderate loss scenarios), despite some fluctuation in capital levels.

Principal Business: Allied lines (73%), other liability (21%), auto liability (4%), auto physical damage (1%), and inland marine (1%).

Principal Investments: Investment grade bonds (84%), misc. investments (9%), and non investment grade bonds (7%).

Investments in Affiliates: 3%

Group Affiliation: Chubb Limited

Licensed in: All states, the District of Columbia and Puerto Rico

Commenced Business: August 1819

Address: 436 WALNUT STREET, Philadelphia, PA 19106

Phone: (215) 640-1000   **Domicile State:** PA   **NAIC Code:** 20699

Data Date	Rating	RACR #1	RACR #2	Loss Ratio %	Total Assets ($mil)	Capital ($mil)	Net Premium ($mil)	Net Income ($mil)
2017	B-	2.56	1.70	83.9	8,693.1	1,970.3	1,894.4	157.9
2016	B-	2.90	1.96	76.5	8,192.2	2,157.6	1,748.7	181.2
2015	C+	2.67	1.81	72.8	7,748.8	1,995.9	1,665.3	136.2
2014	C	3.02	2.05	77.6	7,360.7	2,064.4	1,567.0	115.6
2013	C	2.95	2.01	72.2	7,214.1	1,920.5	1,523.8	165.6

Rating Indexes

ACUITY A MUTUAL INS CO *   A-   Excellent

Major Rating Factors: Strong long-term capitalization index (9.4 on a scale of 0 to 10) based on excellent current risk adjusted capital (severe and moderate loss scenarios). Furthermore, this high level of risk adjusted capital has been consistently maintained in previous years. Ample reserve history (8.9) that helps to protect the company against sharp claims increases.

Other Rating Factors: Excellent profitability (8.8) with operating gains in each of the last five years. Excellent overall results on stability tests (7.0). Stability strengths include excellent operational trends and excellent risk diversification. Good liquidity (6.7) with sufficient resources (cash flows and marketable investments) to handle a spike in claims.

Principal Business: Auto liability (24%), workers compensation (20%), auto physical damage (16%), commercial multiple peril (11%), homeowners multiple peril (10%), other liability (10%), and other lines (9%).

Principal Investments: Investment grade bonds (60%), misc. investments (31%), real estate (7%), and non investment grade bonds (3%).

Investments in Affiliates: None

Group Affiliation: None

Licensed in: AL, AZ, AR, CO, DE, GA, ID, IL, IN, IA, KS, KY, ME, MI, MN, MS, MO, MT, NE, NV, NH, NM, ND, OH, OK, OR, PA, SD, TN, TX, UT, VT, VA, WA, WV, WI, WY

Commenced Business: September 1925

Address: 2800 South Taylor Drive, Sheboygan, WI 53081-8470

Phone: (920) 458-9131   **Domicile State:** WI   **NAIC Code:** 14184

Data Date	Rating	RACR #1	RACR #2	Loss Ratio %	Total Assets ($mil)	Capital ($mil)	Net Premium ($mil)	Net Income ($mil)
2017	A-	4.59	2.72	62.0	3,960.1	1,819.8	1,374.3	145.8
2016	B+	4.53	2.69	61.3	3,621.3	1,606.6	1,316.3	145.8
2015	B+	4.33	2.64	61.9	3,349.5	1,429.9	1,269.9	142.0
2014	B	3.83	2.36	65.1	3,101.0	1,323.4	1,189.2	113.2
2013	B	3.77	2.33	62.0	2,826.4	1,202.3	1,074.0	111.1

Risk-Adjusted Capital Ratio #2 (Severe Loss Scenario)

ADMIRAL INS CO   C   Fair

Major Rating Factors: Fair overall results on stability tests (4.1 on a scale of 0 to 10).

Other Rating Factors: Strong long-term capitalization index (8.2) based on excellent current risk adjusted capital (severe and moderate loss scenarios), despite some fluctuation in capital levels. Excellent profitability (7.3) with operating gains in each of the last five years. Return on equity has been excellent over the last five years averaging 28.9%. Excellent liquidity (7.0) with ample operational cash flow and liquid investments.

Principal Business: (Not applicable due to unusual reinsurance transactions.)

Principal Investments: Misc. investments (52%), investment grade bonds (47%), and non investment grade bonds (1%).

Investments in Affiliates: 50%

Group Affiliation: W R Berkley Corp

Licensed in: All states, the District of Columbia and Puerto Rico

Commenced Business: November 1952

Address: 1209 ORANGE STREET, Wilmington, DE 19801-1000

Phone: (480) 951-0905   **Domicile State:** DE   **NAIC Code:** 24856

Data Date	Rating	RACR #1	RACR #2	Loss Ratio %	Total Assets ($mil)	Capital ($mil)	Net Premium ($mil)	Net Income ($mil)
2017	C	1.65	1.78	0.0	749.4	666.0	0.0	10.4
2016	C	1.74	1.88	0.0	737.3	652.1	0.0	10.4
2015	C	1.81	1.92	0.0	710.2	634.0	0.0	8.4
2014	C-	1.82	1.94	0.0	688.5	615.6	0.0	11.2
2013	C-	1.91	2.07	0.0	667.4	597.6	-255.7	826.2

Rating Indexes

AFFILIATED FM INS CO   C+   Fair

Major Rating Factors: Fair overall results on stability tests (4.5 on a scale of 0 to 10). History of adequate reserve strength (6.2) as reserves have been consistently at an acceptable level.

Other Rating Factors: Good liquidity (6.8) with sufficient resources (cash flows and marketable investments) to handle a spike in claims. Strong long-term capitalization index (8.9) based on excellent current risk adjusted capital (severe and moderate loss scenarios). Moreover, capital has steadily grown over the last five years. Excellent profitability (7.7) despite modest operating losses during 2017.

Principal Business: Fire (34%), allied lines (24%), inland marine (23%), commercial multiple peril (9%), boiler & machinery (7%), and ocean marine (2%).

Principal Investments: Misc. investments (53%), investment grade bonds (46%), and cash (1%).

Investments in Affiliates: None

Group Affiliation: Factory Mutual Ins

Licensed in: All states, the District of Columbia and Puerto Rico

Commenced Business: June 1950

Address: 270 Central Avenue, Johnston, RI 02919-4949

Phone: (401) 275-3000   **Domicile State:** RI   **NAIC Code:** 10014

Data Date	Rating	RACR #1	RACR #2	Loss Ratio %	Total Assets ($mil)	Capital ($mil)	Net Premium ($mil)	Net Income ($mil)
2017	C+	3.65	2.27	103.3	3,163.0	1,779.9	457.9	-17.0
2016	C	4.29	2.60	56.9	2,992.9	1,618.7	423.6	83.4
2015	C	4.39	2.71	58.8	2,589.3	1,479.6	420.5	121.6
2014	C	4.35	2.70	52.5	2,528.7	1,397.6	386.6	119.1
2013	C	3.60	2.27	50.6	2,327.1	1,262.1	387.6	124.4

Rating Indexes

AIG PROPERTY CASUALTY CO   C   Fair

Major Rating Factors: Fair overall results on stability tests (4.2 on a scale of 0 to 10) including negative cash flow from operations for 2017 and fair results on operational trends. Strengths include potentially strong support from affiliation with American International Group.

Other Rating Factors: Weak profitability index (1.9). Fair expense controls. Return on equity has been fair, averaging 26.9% over the past five years. Vulnerable liquidity (0.0) as a spike in claims may stretch capacity. Strong long-term capitalization index (10.0) based on excellent current risk adjusted capital (severe and moderate loss scenarios), despite some fluctuation in capital levels.

Principal Business: (Not applicable due to unusual reinsurance transactions.)

Principal Investments: Investment grade bonds (97%), non investment grade bonds (2%), and cash (1%).

Investments in Affiliates: None

Group Affiliation: American International Group

Licensed in: All states except HI, PR

Commenced Business: August 1871

Address: 2595 INTERSTATE DRIVE STE 102, Harrisburg, PA 17110

Phone: (212) 770-7000   **Domicile State:** PA   **NAIC Code:** 19402

Data Date	Rating	RACR #1	RACR #2	Loss Ratio %	Total Assets ($mil)	Capital ($mil)	Net Premium ($mil)	Net Income ($mil)
2017	C	79.62	49.32	0.0	444.0	416.8	-481.9	203.8
2016	C	1.82	1.22	99.8	4,180.0	951.7	806.2	440.2
2015	C	2.16	1.36	88.8	4,730.2	1,312.8	927.5	246.8
2014	C+	2.27	1.45	76.5	5,025.9	1,587.1	1,034.9	158.0
2013	C+	2.30	1.46	76.6	3,656.5	1,166.3	713.5	124.6

American International Group
Composite Group Rating: B

Largest Group Members	Assets ($mil)	Rating
AMERICAN GENERAL LIFE INS CO	178705	B
VARIABLE ANNUITY LIFE INS CO	81665	B
UNITED STATES LIFE INS CO IN NYC	29431	B
NATIONAL UNION FIRE INS CO	25661	C
AMERICAN HOME ASR CO	25640	C

ALAMANCE INS CO   C-   Fair

Major Rating Factors: Weak overall results on stability tests (2.6 on a scale of 0 to 10) including potential drain of affiliation with IFG Companies. Good overall profitability index (5.8). Weak expense controls. Return on equity has been low, averaging 3.0% over the past five years.

Other Rating Factors: Strong long-term capitalization index (7.7) based on excellent current risk adjusted capital (severe and moderate loss scenarios), despite some fluctuation in capital levels. Ample reserve history (7.7) that can protect against increases in claims costs. Excellent liquidity (7.0) with ample operational cash flow and liquid investments.

Principal Business: (This company is a reinsurer.)

Principal Investments: Misc. investments (63%) and investment grade bonds (37%).

Investments in Affiliates: 60%

Group Affiliation: IFG Companies

Licensed in: All states except CA, PR

Commenced Business: December 1998

Address: 400 South Ninth Street, Springfield, IL 62701-1822

Phone: (336) 586-2500   **Domicile State:** IL   **NAIC Code:** 10957

Data Date	Rating	RACR #1	RACR #2	Loss Ratio %	Total Assets ($mil)	Capital ($mil)	Net Premium ($mil)	Net Income ($mil)
2017	C-	1.48	1.45	46.0	466.3	370.5	29.8	9.1
2016	C-	1.47	1.45	47.9	475.0	371.6	27.9	11.7
2015	C-	1.48	1.45	44.4	485.3	373.8	32.8	11.0
2014	C-	1.46	1.43	56.5	488.1	369.5	36.6	8.4
2013	C-	1.45	1.42	50.6	480.6	358.1	40.7	14.7

Rating Indexes

ALASKA NATIONAL INS CO *

B+   **Good**

Major Rating Factors: Good overall results on stability tests (6.5 on a scale of 0 to 10). Strong long-term capitalization index (9.4) based on excellent current risk adjusted capital (severe and moderate loss scenarios). Moreover, capital levels have been consistent in recent years.

Other Rating Factors: Ample reserve history (9.4) that helps to protect the company against sharp claims increases. Excellent profitability (8.9) with operating gains in each of the last five years. Return on equity has been good over the last five years, averaging 12.3%. Excellent liquidity (7.5) with ample operational cash flow and liquid investments.

Principal Business: Workers compensation (77%), commercial multiple peril (6%), auto liability (6%), other liability (5%), inland marine (2%), auto physical damage (1%), and other lines (2%).

Principal Investments: Investment grade bonds (77%), misc. investments (22%), and cash (1%).

Investments in Affiliates: None

Group Affiliation: Alaska National Corp

Licensed in: AL, AK, AZ, CA, CO, FL, HI, ID, IL, IA, KS, LA, MN, MS, MO, MT, NV, NM, ND, OK, OR, SD, TX, UT, WA, WY

Commenced Business: October 1980

Address: 7001 Jewel Lake Road, Anchorage, AK 99502-2800

Phone: (907) 248-2642   **Domicile State:** AK   **NAIC Code:** 38733

Data Date	Rating	RACR #1	RACR #2	Loss Ratio %	Total Assets ($mil)	Capital ($mil)	Net Premium ($mil)	Net Income ($mil)
2017	B+	4.22	2.95	48.2	1,004.7	480.3	226.8	59.4
2016	B	3.83	2.67	56.7	951.4	438.0	221.5	53.4
2015	B	3.48	2.47	56.3	889.0	387.8	228.5	36.4
2014	B	3.10	2.13	55.7	879.8	380.5	212.3	50.5
2013	B	3.18	2.20	51.3	830.4	352.2	200.6	50.3

Rating Indexes

ALFA GENERAL INS CORP *

B+   **Good**

Major Rating Factors: Good liquidity (5.8 on a scale of 0 to 10) with sufficient resources (cash flows and marketable investments) to handle a spike in claims. Good overall results on stability tests (6.4).

Other Rating Factors: Strong long-term capitalization index (9.0) based on excellent current risk adjusted capital (severe and moderate loss scenarios), despite some fluctuation in capital levels. Ample reserve history (7.9) that can protect against increases in claims costs. Fair profitability index (4.9). Fair expense controls. Return on equity has been low, averaging 4.8% over the past five years.

Principal Business: Homeowners multiple peril (49%), auto liability (31%), and auto physical damage (20%).

Principal Investments: Investment grade bonds (50%), misc. investments (47%), cash (2%), and non investment grade bonds (1%).

Investments in Affiliates: None

Group Affiliation: Alfa Ins Group

Licensed in: AL, GA, MS

Commenced Business: January 1983

Address: 2108 East South Boulevard, Montgomery, AL 36116-2015

Phone: (334) 288-3900   **Domicile State:** AL   **NAIC Code:** 41661

Data Date	Rating	RACR #1	RACR #2	Loss Ratio %	Total Assets ($mil)	Capital ($mil)	Net Premium ($mil)	Net Income ($mil)
2017	B+	3.54	2.47	75.6	101.6	51.6	53.2	2.3
2016	B	3.11	2.12	71.2	93.1	48.9	49.2	2.4
2015	B	3.19	2.13	70.7	91.1	49.9	45.5	2.1
2014	B-	3.76	2.52	70.1	95.7	56.9	44.8	2.7
2013	B-	4.59	3.15	66.4	97.4	59.1	43.6	3.4

Liquidity Index

ALFA MUTUAL FIRE INS CO *

B+   **Good**

Major Rating Factors: Good overall profitability index (6.3 on a scale of 0 to 10). Fair expense controls. Good liquidity (5.1) with sufficient resources (cash flows and marketable investments) to handle a spike in claims.

Other Rating Factors: Good overall results on stability tests (6.5). Strong long-term capitalization index (8.4) based on excellent current risk adjusted capital (severe and moderate loss scenarios), despite some fluctuation in capital levels. Ample reserve history (7.7) that can protect against increases in claims costs.

Principal Business: Fire (48%), allied lines (43%), and inland marine (9%).

Principal Investments: Misc. investments (55%), investment grade bonds (41%), non investment grade bonds (2%), cash (1%), and real estate (1%).

Investments in Affiliates: 21%

Group Affiliation: Alfa Ins Group

Licensed in: AL, MD, VA

Commenced Business: August 1946

Address: 2108 East South Boulevard, Montgomery, AL 36116-2015

Phone: (334) 288-3900   **Domicile State:** AL   **NAIC Code:** 19143

Data Date	Rating	RACR #1	RACR #2	Loss Ratio %	Total Assets ($mil)	Capital ($mil)	Net Premium ($mil)	Net Income ($mil)
2017	B+	2.48	2.02	75.1	770.4	437.7	399.0	2.0
2016	B	2.47	2.01	72.1	728.0	420.1	368.8	11.4
2015	B	2.43	1.93	70.6	699.0	409.8	341.5	16.2
2014	B	2.23	1.71	70.2	697.1	419.8	336.0	8.0
2013	B	1.96	1.48	68.6	659.5	399.3	327.1	25.7

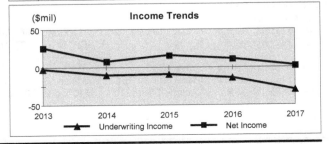

Income Trends

ALFA MUTUAL GENERAL INS CO *

A-   Excellent

Major Rating Factors: Strong long-term capitalization index (9.0 on a scale of 0 to 10) based on excellent current risk adjusted capital (severe and moderate loss scenarios), despite some fluctuation in capital levels. Ample reserve history (7.7) that can protect against increases in claims costs.

Other Rating Factors: Good overall profitability index (6.5). Fair expense controls. Good liquidity (6.3) with sufficient resources (cash flows and marketable investments) to handle a spike in claims. Good overall results on stability tests (6.9).

Principal Business: Homeowners multiple peril (42%), auto liability (33%), auto physical damage (25%), and other liability (1%).

Principal Investments: Misc. investments (51%), investment grade bonds (45%), cash (3%), and non investment grade bonds (1%).

Investments in Affiliates: 1%

Group Affiliation: Alfa Ins Group

Licensed in: AL, GA, MS

Commenced Business: October 1955

Address: 2108 East South Boulevard, Montgomery, AL 36116-2015

Phone: (334) 288-3900   **Domicile State:** AL   **NAIC Code:** 19151

Data Date	Rating	RACR #1	RACR #2	Loss Ratio %	Total Assets ($mil)	Capital ($mil)	Net Premium ($mil)	Net Income ($mil)
2017	A-	4.31	2.93	75.2	115.4	61.9	53.2	2.3
2016	B+	3.57	2.38	72.1	103.3	57.1	49.2	1.8
2015	B+	3.12	2.04	70.7	100.9	56.9	45.5	5.8
2014	B+	2.40	1.57	70.3	99.0	57.9	44.8	3.4
2013	B+	2.35	1.58	68.8	94.8	54.3	43.6	4.1

ALFA MUTUAL INS CO

B   Good

Major Rating Factors: Good overall results on stability tests (6.0 on a scale of 0 to 10). Fair profitability index (3.6) with operating losses during 2017.

Other Rating Factors: Strong long-term capitalization index (7.2) based on excellent current risk adjusted capital (severe and moderate loss scenarios), despite some fluctuation in capital levels. Ample reserve history (7.8) that can protect against increases in claims costs. Vulnerable liquidity (2.8) as a spike in claims may stretch capacity.

Principal Business: Auto physical damage (30%), auto liability (30%), homeowners multiple peril (29%), farmowners multiple peril (7%), commercial multiple peril (3%), and inland marine (1%).

Principal Investments: Misc. investments (69%), investment grade bonds (24%), real estate (4%), non investment grade bonds (2%), and cash (1%).

Investments in Affiliates: 35%

Group Affiliation: Alfa Ins Group

Licensed in: AL, FL, GA, IL, IN, KY, NC, OH, PA, VA

Commenced Business: October 1947

Address: 2108 East South Boulevard, Montgomery, AL 36116-2015

Phone: (334) 288-3900   **Domicile State:** AL   **NAIC Code:** 19135

Data Date	Rating	RACR #1	RACR #2	Loss Ratio %	Total Assets ($mil)	Capital ($mil)	Net Premium ($mil)	Net Income ($mil)
2017	B	1.34	1.16	75.4	1,344.9	499.5	691.5	-9.5
2016	B	1.24	1.07	72.3	1,251.2	451.8	639.3	5.6
2015	B	1.35	1.13	70.5	1,239.6	497.9	592.0	24.9
2014	B	1.38	1.11	70.2	1,275.0	537.8	582.4	12.4
2013	B	1.59	1.25	68.7	1,231.2	580.4	566.7	48.5

ALL AMERICA INS CO *

A-   Excellent

Major Rating Factors: Strong long-term capitalization index (10.0 on a scale of 0 to 10) based on excellent current risk adjusted capital (severe and moderate loss scenarios). Moreover, capital levels have been consistent in recent years. Ample reserve history (9.0) that helps to protect the company against sharp claims increases.

Other Rating Factors: Excellent profitability (8.4) with operating gains in each of the last five years. Good overall results on stability tests (6.9). Affiliation with Central Mutual Ins Group is a strength. Good liquidity (6.8) with sufficient resources (cash flows and marketable investments) to handle a spike in claims.

Principal Business: Commercial multiple peril (56%), auto liability (22%), auto physical damage (11%), workers compensation (7%), and products liability (4%).

Principal Investments: Investment grade bonds (93%) and cash (7%).

Investments in Affiliates: 0%

Group Affiliation: Central Mutual Ins Group

Licensed in: AZ, AR, CA, CO, CT, GA, ID, IL, IN, IA, KY, ME, MD, MA, MI, MN, MS, MT, NV, NH, NJ, NM, NY, NC, OH, OK, OR, SC, TN, TX, UT, VT, VA, WA, WI

Commenced Business: August 1961

Address: 800 SOUTH WASHINGTON STREET, Van Wert, OH 45891-2357

Phone: (419) 238-1010   **Domicile State:** OH   **NAIC Code:** 20222

Data Date	Rating	RACR #1	RACR #2	Loss Ratio %	Total Assets ($mil)	Capital ($mil)	Net Premium ($mil)	Net Income ($mil)
2017	A-	6.42	4.40	65.0	291.6	156.6	106.5	5.8
2016	B+	6.52	4.46	64.0	283.9	152.6	98.8	6.5
2015	B+	6.26	4.32	57.9	275.8	146.0	93.0	11.2
2014	B+	5.95	4.08	59.8	258.8	134.7	85.3	10.3
2013	B+	5.49	3.68	58.4	247.7	124.7	76.6	11.5

ALLIANZ GLOBAL RISKS US INS CO   C   Fair

Major Rating Factors: Fair long-term capitalization index (4.2 on a scale of 0 to 10) based on fair current risk adjusted capital (moderate loss scenario). Fair profitability index (4.5) with operating losses during 2016. Return on equity has been low, averaging 1.4% over the past five years.

Other Rating Factors: Fair overall results on stability tests (4.3) including fair risk adjusted capital in prior years and fair results on operational trends. Good liquidity (5.7) with sufficient resources (cash flows and marketable investments) to handle a spike in claims. Ample reserve history (9.8) that helps to protect the company against sharp claims increases.

Principal Business: Fire (22%), other liability (20%), aircraft (15%), products liability (11%), allied lines (10%), inland marine (8%), and other lines (13%).

Principal Investments: Investment grade bonds (60%), misc. investments (38%), cash (1%), and non investment grade bonds (1%).

Investments in Affiliates: 27%

Group Affiliation: Allianz Ins Group

Licensed in: All states, the District of Columbia and Puerto Rico

Commenced Business: December 1977

Address: 225 W WASHINGTON ST STE 1800, Chicago, IL 60606-3484

Phone: (888) 466-7883   **Domicile State:** IL   **NAIC Code:** 35300

Data Date	Rating	RACR #1	RACR #2	Loss Ratio %	Total Assets ($mil)	Capital ($mil)	Net Premium ($mil)	Net Income ($mil)
2017	C	0.87	0.65	77.2	7,625.6	1,850.6	2,048.5	226.9
2016	C	0.95	0.77	73.3	8,002.5	1,931.8	2,124.9	-268.6
2015	C	1.22	1.06	72.0	4,345.4	1,862.2	1,093.4	32.8
2014	C	0.80	0.51	73.1	3,322.7	759.1	1,236.6	44.4
2013	C-	0.74	0.52	79.5	3,176.9	867.3	868.2	10.0

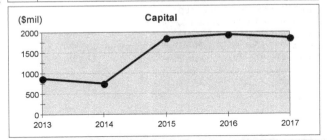

Capital ($mil)

ALLIED WORLD INS CO   C   Fair

Major Rating Factors: Fair overall results on stability tests (3.4 on a scale of 0 to 10) including potential drain of affiliation with Allied World Asr Holding Group. Fair profitability index (3.4) with operating losses during 2017. Return on equity has been low, averaging 1.0% over the past five years.

Other Rating Factors: History of adequate reserve strength (6.0) as reserves have been consistently at an acceptable level. Strong long-term capitalization index (7.7) based on excellent current risk adjusted capital (severe and moderate loss scenarios), despite some fluctuation in capital levels. Excellent liquidity (7.4) with ample operational cash flow and liquid investments.

Principal Business: Other liability (60%), surety (16%), medical malpractice (12%), commercial multiple peril (11%), auto liability (1%), and credit (1%).

Principal Investments: Misc. investments (68%), investment grade bonds (24%), non investment grade bonds (7%), and cash (1%).

Investments in Affiliates: 50%

Group Affiliation: Allied World Asr Holding Group

Licensed in: All states, the District of Columbia and Puerto Rico

Commenced Business: October 1986

Address: 10 FERRY STREET SUITE 313, Concord, NH 3301

Phone: (646) 794-0500   **Domicile State:** NH   **NAIC Code:** 22730

Data Date	Rating	RACR #1	RACR #2	Loss Ratio %	Total Assets ($mil)	Capital ($mil)	Net Premium ($mil)	Net Income ($mil)
2017	C	1.58	1.47	85.6	1,788.1	1,011.6	196.5	-12.9
2016	C	1.79	1.71	74.7	1,713.4	1,030.7	199.4	11.3
2015	C	1.68	1.52	69.1	1,749.6	1,082.3	214.6	15.3
2014	C	1.56	1.40	69.9	1,727.2	1,092.9	198.3	24.7
2013	C	1.57	1.44	67.8	1,687.3	1,044.5	177.2	13.6

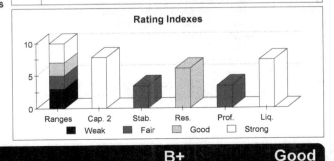

Rating Indexes

ALLIED WORLD SPECIALTY INS CO *   B+   Good

Major Rating Factors: History of adequate reserve strength (5.9 on a scale of 0 to 10) as reserves have been consistently at an acceptable level. Good overall results on stability tests (6.5). Stability strengths include good operational trends and excellent risk diversification.

Other Rating Factors: Strong long-term capitalization index (8.3) based on excellent current risk adjusted capital (severe and moderate loss scenarios), despite some fluctuation in capital levels. Excellent liquidity (8.2) with ample operational cash flow and liquid investments. Fair profitability index (4.3) with operating losses during 2017. Return on equity has been low, averaging 1.8% over the past five years.

Principal Business: Other liability (47%), auto liability (14%), inland marine (11%), commercial multiple peril (10%), fire (7%), auto physical damage (3%), and other lines (8%).

Principal Investments: Investment grade bonds (45%), misc. investments (44%), non investment grade bonds (8%), and cash (3%).

Investments in Affiliates: 28%

Group Affiliation: Allied World Asr Holding Group

Licensed in: All states, the District of Columbia and Puerto Rico

Commenced Business: January 1972

Address: 251 LITTLE FALLS DRIVE, Wilmington, DE 19808

Phone: (646) 794-0500   **Domicile State:** DE   **NAIC Code:** 16624

Data Date	Rating	RACR #1	RACR #2	Loss Ratio %	Total Assets ($mil)	Capital ($mil)	Net Premium ($mil)	Net Income ($mil)
2017	B+	2.24	1.87	85.6	829.1	419.2	109.2	-9.7
2016	B	3.21	2.76	74.7	795.2	413.1	110.8	7.8
2015	B	3.18	2.74	69.1	786.7	405.7	119.2	12.2
2014	B-	2.49	2.00	69.9	752.0	397.4	110.2	13.3
2013	B-	2.98	2.36	67.8	689.3	364.0	98.5	11.0

Reserve Deficiency (as % of capital)

* Adequate & redundant reserves show as negatives

ALLSTATE F&C INS CO

B-   Good

Major Rating Factors: Fair overall results on stability tests (4.9 on a scale of 0 to 10). Strong long-term capitalization index (10.0) based on excellent current risk adjusted capital (severe and moderate loss scenarios), despite some fluctuation in capital levels.

Other Rating Factors: Excellent profitability (7.2) with operating gains in each of the last five years. Excellent expense controls. Superior liquidity (10.0) with ample operational cash flow and liquid investments.

Principal Business: Auto liability (58%), auto physical damage (40%), and homeowners multiple peril (3%).

Principal Investments: Investment grade bonds (98%) and misc. investments (2%).

Investments in Affiliates: None

Group Affiliation: Allstate Group

Licensed in: All states except CA, PR

Commenced Business: May 1973

Address: 2775 SANDERS ROAD, Northbrook, IL 60062-6127

Phone: (847) 402-5000   **Domicile State:** IL   **NAIC Code:** 29688

Data Date	Rating	RACR #1	RACR #2	Loss Ratio %	Total Assets ($mil)	Capital ($mil)	Net Premium ($mil)	Net Income ($mil)
2017	B-	114.10	50.17	0.0	245.1	239.5	0.0	3.6
2016	C+	135.61	60.57	0.0	262.0	258.7	0.0	2.6
2015	C+	129.99	57.65	0.0	215.7	211.2	0.0	2.1
2014	C	136.54	60.77	0.0	175.3	173.9	0.0	1.6
2013	C	130.27	57.28	0.0	148.7	147.5	0.0	2.3

ALLSTATE INS CO *

B+   Good

Major Rating Factors: History of adequate reserve strength (6.1 on a scale of 0 to 10) as reserves have been consistently at an acceptable level. Good liquidity (5.4) with sufficient resources (cash flows and marketable investments) to handle a spike in claims.

Other Rating Factors: Good overall results on stability tests (6.5). Strong long-term capitalization index (7.8) based on excellent current risk adjusted capital (severe and moderate loss scenarios), despite some fluctuation in capital levels. Excellent profitability (8.2) with operating gains in each of the last five years. Return on equity has been good over the last five years, averaging 13.0%.

Principal Business: Homeowners multiple peril (33%), auto liability (31%), auto physical damage (25%), allied lines (4%), commercial multiple peril (4%), other liability (1%), and inland marine (1%).

Principal Investments: Investment grade bonds (55%), misc. investments (34%), non investment grade bonds (12%), and real estate (1%).

Investments in Affiliates: 13%

Group Affiliation: Allstate Group

Licensed in: All states except NJ

Commenced Business: April 1931

Address: 2775 SANDERS ROAD, Northbrook, IL 60062-6127

Phone: (847) 402-5000   **Domicile State:** IL   **NAIC Code:** 19232

Data Date	Rating	RACR #1	RACR #2	Loss Ratio %	Total Assets ($mil)	Capital ($mil)	Net Premium ($mil)	Net Income ($mil)
2017	B+	2.02	1.59	69.4	48,302.5	17,454.4	29,252.0	2,874.4
2016	B	1.89	1.47	71.9	45,624.2	15,559.9	28,491.4	1,379.8
2015	B	1.97	1.52	70.1	43,271.2	15,318.3	27,774.3	1,705.4
2014	B+	2.15	1.68	68.0	43,246.3	16,265.6	26,453.4	2,313.8
2013	A-	2.21	1.72	66.4	43,733.3	17,254.7	25,108.5	2,465.5

* Adequate & redundant reserves show as negatives

ALLSTATE NJ INS CO *

A-   Excellent

Major Rating Factors: Strong long-term capitalization index (8.3 on a scale of 0 to 10) based on excellent current risk adjusted capital (severe and moderate loss scenarios). Furthermore, this high level of risk adjusted capital has been consistently maintained in previous years. Ample reserve history (8.2) that helps to protect the company against sharp claims increases.

Other Rating Factors: Excellent overall results on stability tests (7.1). Stability strengths include good operational trends and excellent risk diversification. Good overall profitability index (6.6). Good expense controls. Return on equity has been excellent over the last five years averaging 16.2%. Good liquidity (6.5) with sufficient resources (cash flows and marketable investments) to handle a spike in claims.

Principal Business: Auto liability (41%), homeowners multiple peril (34%), auto physical damage (20%), allied lines (2%), other liability (2%), commercial multiple peril (1%), and inland marine (1%).

Principal Investments: Investment grade bonds (92%), misc. investments (5%), and non investment grade bonds (4%).

Investments in Affiliates: 5%

Group Affiliation: Allstate Group

Licensed in: IL, NJ, PA

Commenced Business: November 1997

Address: 2775 SANDERS ROAD, Northbrook, IL 60062-6127

Phone: (908) 252-5000   **Domicile State:** IL   **NAIC Code:** 10852

Data Date	Rating	RACR #1	RACR #2	Loss Ratio %	Total Assets ($mil)	Capital ($mil)	Net Premium ($mil)	Net Income ($mil)
2017	A-	2.38	1.97	60.0	2,485.7	831.1	1,128.8	166.8
2016	B+	2.22	1.81	65.6	2,495.4	807.5	1,164.9	123.7
2015	B	2.18	1.78	70.2	2,444.8	774.9	1,157.5	87.6
2014	B	2.22	1.75	63.4	2,478.3	802.8	1,163.9	134.9
2013	B	2.45	1.93	62.4	2,680.7	930.9	1,190.1	162.7

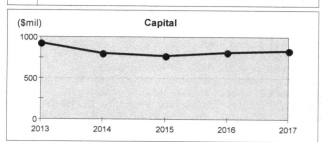

ALTERRA AMERICA INS CO — B — Good

Major Rating Factors: Good overall profitability index (6.0 on a scale of 0 to 10) despite operating losses during 2013, 2014 and 2015. Return on equity has been low, averaging 4.0% over the past five years. Good liquidity (6.9) with sufficient resources (cash flows and marketable investments) to handle a spike in claims.
Other Rating Factors: Good overall results on stability tests (5.2) despite negative cash flow from operations for 2017 and weak results on operational trends. Strong long-term capitalization index (7.7) based on excellent current risk adjusted capital (severe and moderate loss scenarios), despite some fluctuation in capital levels. Ample reserve history (7.0) that can protect against increases in claims costs.
Principal Business: Other liability (72%), inland marine (25%), and commercial multiple peril (3%).
Principal Investments: Investment grade bonds (94%), misc. investments (5%), and cash (1%).
Investments in Affiliates: None
Group Affiliation: Markel Corp
Licensed in: All states except PR
Commenced Business: August 1936
Address: 1209 Orange Street, Wilmington, DE 19801
Phone: (804) 747-0136   **Domicile State:** DE   **NAIC Code:** 21296

Data Date	Rating	RACR #1	RACR #2	Loss Ratio %	Total Assets ($mil)	Capital ($mil)	Net Premium ($mil)	Net Income ($mil)
2017	B	4.47	2.63	N/A	392.6	223.0	29.0	32.6
2016	B-	1.25	0.86	44.7	421.8	193.0	73.8	29.2
2015	B-	0.99	0.60	72.9	454.8	157.2	103.6	-9.5
2014	B	1.15	1.12	81.9	246.5	165.4	22.2	-0.7
2013	B	1.14	1.10	76.1	222.4	150.3	21.3	-4.8

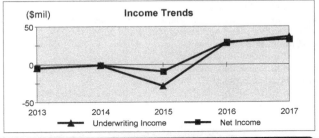

Income Trends ($mil) — Underwriting Income / Net Income

AMBAC ASSURANCE CORP — E — Very Weak

Major Rating Factors: Poor long-term capitalization index (1.8 on a scale of 0 to 10) based on weak current risk adjusted capital (severe and moderate loss scenarios). overall results on stability tests (-0.5) including weak risk adjusted capital in prior years, weak results on operational trends and negative cash flow from operations for 2017.
Other Rating Factors: Fair reserve development (3.0) as reserves have generally been sufficient to cover claims. In 2017, the one year reserve development was 22% deficient. Fair profitability index (3.3) with operating losses during 2013. Return on equity has been fair, averaging 175.0% over the past five years. Superior liquidity (9.0) with ample operational cash flow and liquid investments.
Principal Business: Financial guaranty (99%) and surety (1%).
Principal Investments: Misc. investments (68%), investment grade bonds (31%), and non investment grade bonds (1%).
Investments in Affiliates: 11%
Group Affiliation: AMBAC Financial Group Inc
Licensed in: All states except TN
Commenced Business: March 1970
Address: 2 East Mifflin St, Madison, WI 53703
Phone: (212) 658-7470   **Domicile State:** WI   **NAIC Code:** 18708

Data Date	Rating	RACR #1	RACR #2	Loss Ratio %	Total Assets ($mil)	Capital ($mil)	Net Premium ($mil)	Net Income ($mil)
2017	E	0.73	0.35	360.5	5,445.9	699.6	36.6	123.7
2016	E	0.98	0.45	1.2	5,442.1	976.5	45.2	359.1
2015	E	0.77	0.34	N/A	4,813.4	624.8	53.2	772.3
2014	E	0.36	0.16	N/A	4,451.6	100.0	63.6	724.8
2013	E	0.60	0.30	145.2	5,793.6	840.3	90.3	-235.6

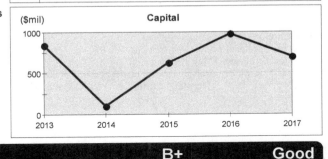

Capital ($mil)

AMERICAN AGRICULTURAL INS CO * — B+ — Good

Major Rating Factors: Good overall profitability index (5.7 on a scale of 0 to 10) despite operating losses during 2017. Return on equity has been fair, averaging 6.5% over the past five years. Good liquidity (6.9) with sufficient resources (cash flows and marketable investments) to handle a spike in claims.
Other Rating Factors: Good overall results on stability tests (6.5). Strong long-term capitalization index (8.0) based on excellent current risk adjusted capital (severe and moderate loss scenarios). Moreover, capital levels have been consistent in recent years. Ample reserve history (7.0) that can protect against increases in claims costs.
Principal Business: Allied lines (100%).
Principal Investments: Investment grade bonds (78%), misc. investments (19%), and cash (3%).
Investments in Affiliates: 0%
Group Affiliation: None
Licensed in: All states except AK, CA, NV
Commenced Business: May 1948
Address: 225 South East Street, Indianapolis, IN 46202
Phone: (847) 969-2900   **Domicile State:** IN   **NAIC Code:** 10103

Data Date	Rating	RACR #1	RACR #2	Loss Ratio %	Total Assets ($mil)	Capital ($mil)	Net Premium ($mil)	Net Income ($mil)
2017	B+	2.43	1.74	87.7	1,338.9	584.8	363.5	-8.6
2016	B	2.43	1.77	73.8	1,249.2	575.9	340.6	29.3
2015	B	2.22	1.61	71.4	1,152.6	541.2	304.9	38.5
2014	C+	2.16	1.59	65.8	1,105.1	525.7	295.4	56.1
2013	C+	1.86	1.38	73.3	1,093.1	489.3	342.2	55.3

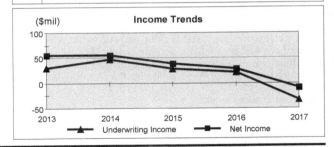

Income Trends ($mil) — Underwriting Income / Net Income

AMERICAN BANKERS INS CO OF FL   B   Good

Major Rating Factors: Good overall results on stability tests (5.8 on a scale of 0 to 10) despite potential drain of affiliation with Assurant Inc. Good liquidity (6.2) with sufficient resources (cash flows and marketable investments) to handle a spike in claims.

Other Rating Factors: Strong long-term capitalization index (8.1) based on excellent current risk adjusted capital (severe and moderate loss scenarios), despite some fluctuation in capital levels. Ample reserve history (8.0) that helps to protect the company against sharp claims increases. Excellent profitability (8.4) with operating gains in each of the last five years. Return on equity has been excellent over the last five years averaging 25.1%.

Principal Business: Other liability (50%), homeowners multiple peril (14%), allied lines (13%), inland marine (11%), credit (4%), credit accident & health (4%), and other lines (4%).

Principal Investments: Investment grade bonds (67%), misc. investments (19%), cash (9%), and non investment grade bonds (5%).

Investments in Affiliates: 1%

Group Affiliation: Assurant Inc

Licensed in: All states, the District of Columbia and Puerto Rico

Commenced Business: October 1947

Address: 11222 QUAIL ROOST DRIVE, Miami, FL 33157-6596

Phone: (305) 253-2244   **Domicile State:** FL   **NAIC Code:** 10111

Data Date	Rating	RACR #1	RACR #2	Loss Ratio %	Total Assets ($mil)	Capital ($mil)	Net Premium ($mil)	Net Income ($mil)
2017	B	3.12	2.21	48.7	2,353.4	561.8	996.8	141.5
2016	B	2.65	1.60	45.2	1,986.3	528.5	915.1	143.6
2015	B	2.06	1.20	39.9	1,877.6	483.2	867.5	142.3
2014	B	2.68	1.55	40.8	1,967.5	563.9	870.1	146.5
2013	B	2.62	1.49	40.1	1,844.9	542.1	884.0	96.5

Rating Indexes

AMERICAN CONTRACTORS INDEMNITY CO *   B+   Good

Major Rating Factors: Good overall results on stability tests (6.5 on a scale of 0 to 10). Stability strengths include good operational trends and excellent risk diversification. Strong long-term capitalization index (10.0) based on excellent current risk adjusted capital (severe and moderate loss scenarios), despite some fluctuation in capital levels.

Other Rating Factors: Ample reserve history (9.6) that helps to protect the company against sharp claims increases. Excellent profitability (8.4) with operating gains in each of the last five years. Return on equity has been excellent over the last five years averaging 18.4%. Excellent liquidity (8.7) with ample operational cash flow and liquid investments.

Principal Business: Surety (100%).

Principal Investments: Investment grade bonds (94%), misc. investments (4%), and cash (2%).

Investments in Affiliates: None

Group Affiliation: HCC Ins Holdings Inc

Licensed in: All states except MA, NH, NC, VT, PR

Commenced Business: May 1994

Address: 601 South Figueroa St 16th Fl, Los Angeles, CA 90017

Phone: (310) 649-0990   **Domicile State:** CA   **NAIC Code:** 10216

Data Date	Rating	RACR #1	RACR #2	Loss Ratio %	Total Assets ($mil)	Capital ($mil)	Net Premium ($mil)	Net Income ($mil)
2017	B+	12.18	8.93	N/A	338.3	128.6	18.1	13.7
2016	B	9.44	6.89	N/A	302.1	117.1	19.3	17.9
2015	B	5.18	4.02	8.3	324.8	113.0	15.5	25.5
2014	B	2.34	1.88	20.6	312.1	86.2	64.3	15.4
2013	B	2.37	1.89	12.6	335.2	89.6	69.1	23.0

($mil)   Capital

AMERICAN FAMILY MUTL INS CO SI *   A-   Excellent

Major Rating Factors: Strong long-term capitalization index (7.7 on a scale of 0 to 10) based on excellent current risk adjusted capital (severe and moderate loss scenarios). Furthermore, this high level of risk adjusted capital has been consistently maintained in previous years. Ample reserve history (8.1) that helps to protect the company against sharp claims increases.

Other Rating Factors: Excellent overall results on stability tests (7.1). Stability strengths include excellent operational trends and excellent risk diversification. Good overall profitability index (6.1). Fair expense controls. Good liquidity (5.7) with sufficient resources (cash flows and marketable investments) to handle a spike in claims.

Principal Business: Homeowners multiple peril (33%), auto liability (28%), auto physical damage (23%), commercial multiple peril (8%), other liability (3%), farmowners multiple peril (2%), and other lines (2%).

Principal Investments: Investment grade bonds (54%), misc. investments (41%), non investment grade bonds (4%), and real estate (2%).

Investments in Affiliates: 16%

Group Affiliation: American Family Ins Group

Licensed in: AZ, CO, FL, GA, ID, IL, IN, IA, KS, MN, MO, MT, NE, NV, NM, NC, ND, OH, OR, SC, SD, TN, TX, UT, VA, WA, WI, WY

Commenced Business: October 1927

Address: 6000 AMERICAN PARKWAY, Madison, WI 53783-0001

Phone: (608) 249-2111   **Domicile State:** WI   **NAIC Code:** 19275

Data Date	Rating	RACR #1	RACR #2	Loss Ratio %	Total Assets ($mil)	Capital ($mil)	Net Premium ($mil)	Net Income ($mil)
2017	A-	1.91	1.49	77.2	17,157.4	6,631.4	8,605.2	103.3
2016	B+	2.17	1.71	68.2	16,193.7	6,867.0	7,291.3	211.7
2015	B+	2.20	1.71	63.5	15,343.9	6,503.1	6,854.8	570.5
2014	B+	2.10	1.66	70.8	14,500.5	6,030.1	6,656.3	659.2
2013	B+	2.17	1.73	72.6	13,229.6	5,791.7	5,595.6	281.2

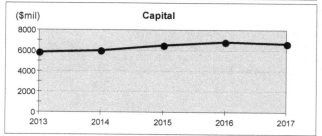

($mil)   Capital

AMERICAN HOME ASR CO   C   Fair

Major Rating Factors: Fair reserve development (3.0 on a scale of 0 to 10) as the level of reserves has at times been insufficient to cover claims. In 2015 and 2016 the two year reserve development was 18% and 22% deficient respectively. Fair profitability index (3.3) with operating losses during 2015, 2016 and 2017. Return on equity has been low, averaging 2.8% over the past five years.

Other Rating Factors: Fair overall results on stability tests (4.2) including negative cash flow from operations for 2017. Good liquidity (6.3) with sufficient resources (cash flows and marketable investments) to handle a spike in claims. Strong long-term capitalization index (7.7) based on excellent current risk adjusted capital (severe and moderate loss scenarios), despite some fluctuation in capital levels.

Principal Business: Fire (47%), workers compensation (15%), allied lines (7%), inland marine (5%), other liability (5%), boiler & machinery (5%), and other lines (15%).

Principal Investments: Investment grade bonds (65%), misc. investments (31%), and non investment grade bonds (4%).

Investments in Affiliates: 1%

Group Affiliation: American International Group

Licensed in: All states except PR

Commenced Business: February 1899

Address: 175 WATER STREET 18TH FLOOR, New York, NY 10038

Phone: (212) 770-7000   **Domicile State:** NY   **NAIC Code:** 19380

Data Date	Rating	RACR #1	RACR #2	Loss Ratio %	Total Assets ($mil)	Capital ($mil)	Net Premium ($mil)	Net Income ($mil)
2017	C	2.35	1.49	96.3	25,639.7	6,237.8	5,030.6	-393.2
2016	C	2.28	1.50	90.5	29,684.9	6,447.6	6,267.6	-243.8
2015	C	2.39	1.63	90.5	26,103.9	6,640.8	5,708.9	-75.2
2014	C+	2.48	1.69	74.2	26,376.9	7,247.9	5,499.4	808.2
2013	C	1.77	1.17	70.0	23,671.1	5,091.7	5,852.4	703.0

Reserve Deficiency (as % of capital)

* Adequate & redundant reserves show as negatives   ■ 1 Yr Dev   □ 2 Yr Dev

AMERICAN INTERSTATE INS CO   B-   Good

Major Rating Factors: Fair overall results on stability tests (4.6 on a scale of 0 to 10) including potential drain of affiliation with Amerisafe Inc. Good overall profitability index (6.7). Good expense controls. Return on equity has been excellent over the last five years averaging 15.2%.

Other Rating Factors: Strong long-term capitalization index (7.8) based on excellent current risk adjusted capital (severe and moderate loss scenarios), despite some fluctuation in capital levels. Ample reserve history (9.4) that helps to protect the company against sharp claims increases. Excellent liquidity (7.0) with ample operational cash flow and liquid investments.

Principal Business: Workers compensation (100%).

Principal Investments: Investment grade bonds (85%), misc. investments (13%), cash (1%), and non investment grade bonds (1%).

Investments in Affiliates: 11%

Group Affiliation: Amerisafe Inc

Licensed in: All states except CT, NJ, OH, PR

Commenced Business: April 1974

Address: 13321 California St Ste 310, Omaha, NE 68154

Phone: (800) 256-9052   **Domicile State:** NE   **NAIC Code:** 31895

Data Date	Rating	RACR #1	RACR #2	Loss Ratio %	Total Assets ($mil)	Capital ($mil)	Net Premium ($mil)	Net Income ($mil)
2017	B-	1.95	1.55	60.5	1,234.5	382.1	274.6	65.5
2016	B-	1.95	1.57	54.1	1,225.5	394.0	291.9	79.0
2015	B-	1.81	1.46	57.1	1,207.7	371.4	301.8	66.9
2014	B-	1.73	1.38	65.2	1,185.6	377.7	305.3	40.3
2013	B-	1.74	1.35	69.4	1,093.7	354.3	284.8	35.3

Rating Indexes

Ranges   Cap. 2   Stab.   Res.   Prof.   Liq.
■ Weak   ■ Fair   □ Good   □ Strong

AMERICAN INTERSTATE INS CO OF TX *   B+   Good

Major Rating Factors: Good overall results on stability tests (6.5 on a scale of 0 to 10). Stability strengths include good operational trends and excellent risk diversification. Strong long-term capitalization index (7.5) based on excellent current risk adjusted capital (severe and moderate loss scenarios), despite some fluctuation in capital levels.

Other Rating Factors: Ample reserve history (9.4) that helps to protect the company against sharp claims increases. Excellent profitability (8.0) with operating gains in each of the last five years. Return on equity has been good over the last five years, averaging 12.3%. Excellent liquidity (7.0) with ample operational cash flow and liquid investments.

Principal Business: Workers compensation (100%).

Principal Investments: Investment grade bonds (96%), misc. investments (3%), and cash (1%).

Investments in Affiliates: None

Group Affiliation: Amerisafe Inc

Licensed in: LA, TX

Commenced Business: January 2005

Address: 211 East 7th Street Suite 620, Austin, TX 78701-3218

Phone: (800) 256-9052   **Domicile State:** TX   **NAIC Code:** 12228

Data Date	Rating	RACR #1	RACR #2	Loss Ratio %	Total Assets ($mil)	Capital ($mil)	Net Premium ($mil)	Net Income ($mil)
2017	B+	1.99	1.51	60.6	68.1	27.3	16.7	3.0
2016	B	2.04	1.57	54.2	67.6	28.7	17.7	4.0
2015	C+	1.68	1.30	58.0	63.4	24.8	18.4	3.4
2014	C	1.32	1.02	65.5	58.3	21.4	18.7	2.3
2013	C	1.21	0.57	69.3	52.7	19.1	17.2	2.3

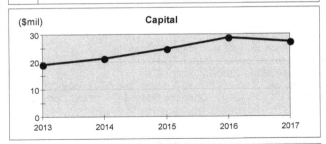

Capital

AMERICAN MODERN HOME INS CO   C+   Fair

Major Rating Factors: Fair overall results on stability tests (4.2 on a scale of 0 to 10) including potential drain of affiliation with Münchener Rückversicherungs-Gesellsc. Fair profitability index (3.4) with operating losses during 2017. Return on equity has been low, averaging 3.6% over the past five years.

Other Rating Factors: Good liquidity (6.4) with sufficient resources (cash flows and marketable investments) to handle a spike in claims. Strong long-term capitalization index (7.9) based on excellent current risk adjusted capital (severe and moderate loss scenarios), despite some fluctuation in capital levels. Ample reserve history (7.7) that can protect against increases in claims costs.

Principal Business: Homeowners multiple peril (44%), inland marine (17%), fire (13%), allied lines (7%), auto physical damage (7%), commercial multiple peril (3%), and other lines (9%).

Principal Investments: Investment grade bonds (46%), misc. investments (44%), real estate (12%), and non investment grade bonds (3%).

Investments in Affiliates: 41%

Group Affiliation: Münchener Rückversicherungs-Gesellsc

Licensed in: All states, the District of Columbia and Puerto Rico

Commenced Business: September 1965

Address: 7000 MIDLAND BLVD, Amelia, OH 45102-2607

Phone: (800) 543-2644   **Domicile State:** OH   **NAIC Code:** 23469

Data Date	Rating	RACR #1	RACR #2	Loss Ratio %	Total Assets ($mil)	Capital ($mil)	Net Premium ($mil)	Net Income ($mil)
2017	C	1.92	1.63	60.5	1,030.7	378.8	305.0	-8.3
2016	C+	1.91	1.50	54.8	1,115.1	406.9	329.0	15.8
2015	C+	2.09	1.62	48.2	1,277.2	436.1	370.2	54.2
2014	C+	1.99	1.51	48.3	1,286.2	380.5	496.5	8.0
2013	C+	2.17	1.66	43.8	1,256.4	373.6	431.7	5.8

Münchener Rückversicherungs-Gesellsc
Composite Group Rating: C+

Largest Group Members	Assets ($mil)	Rating
MUNICH REINS AMERICA INC	18586	C+
MUNICH AMERICAN REASSURANCE CO	7623	C
HARTFORD SM BOIL INSPECTION INS	1214	B-
AMERICAN MODERN HOME INS CO	1031	C+
AMERICAN ALTERNATIVE INS CORP	590	C

AMERICAN MUTUAL SHARE INS CORP   C-   Fair

Major Rating Factors: Weak overall results on stability tests (2.0 on a scale of 0 to 10) including potential drain of affiliation with American Mutual Share Group and negative cash flow from operations for 2017. Good overall profitability index (6.8). Weak expense controls.

Other Rating Factors: Strong long-term capitalization index (10.0) based on excellent current risk adjusted capital (severe and moderate loss scenarios), despite some fluctuation in capital levels. Ample reserve history (9.3) that helps to protect the company against sharp claims increases. Superior liquidity (10.0) with ample operational cash flow and liquid investments.

Principal Business: Aggregate write-ins for other lines of business (100%).

Principal Investments: Investment grade bonds (79%), misc. investments (14%), and cash (7%).

Investments in Affiliates: 9%

Group Affiliation: American Mutual Share Group

Licensed in: AL, AZ, CA, ID, IL, IN, ME, MT, NV, NH, OH, TX

Commenced Business: June 1974

Address: 5656 Frantz Rd, Dublin, OH 43017

Phone: (614) 764-1900   **Domicile State:** OH   **NAIC Code:** 12700

Data Date	Rating	RACR #1	RACR #2	Loss Ratio %	Total Assets ($mil)	Capital ($mil)	Net Premium ($mil)	Net Income ($mil)
2017	C-	10.75	9.70	204.5	257.8	235.0	0.2	1.1
2016	C-	10.01	8.92	N/A	262.8	238.2	0.2	0.1
2015	C-	8.87	7.79	N/A	249.2	219.4	0.2	5.4
2014	C-	8.36	7.32	N/A	230.4	202.3	0.2	11.0
2013	C-	7.89	6.66	N/A	230.2	188.1	0.2	1.6

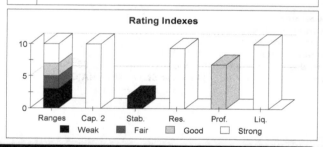

Rating Indexes

AMERICAN NATIONAL PROPERTY & CAS CO *   B+   Good

Major Rating Factors: Good overall profitability index (6.7 on a scale of 0 to 10). Fair expense controls. Return on equity has been low, averaging 4.0% over the past five years. Good liquidity (6.0) with sufficient resources (cash flows and marketable investments) to handle a spike in claims.

Other Rating Factors: Good overall results on stability tests (6.5). Strong long-term capitalization index (8.1) based on excellent current risk adjusted capital (severe and moderate loss scenarios), despite some fluctuation in capital levels. Ample reserve history (8.3) that helps to protect the company against sharp claims increases.

Principal Business: Homeowners multiple peril (25%), auto liability (25%), auto physical damage (16%), credit (13%), other liability (7%), allied lines (5%), and other lines (9%).

Principal Investments: Investment grade bonds (63%), misc. investments (34%), cash (1%), non investment grade bonds (1%), and real estate (1%).

Investments in Affiliates: 19%

Group Affiliation: American National Group Inc

Licensed in: All states except CT, MA, NY

Commenced Business: January 1974

Address: 1949 EAST SUNSHINE, Springfield, MO 65899-0001

Phone: (417) 887-4990   **Domicile State:** MO   **NAIC Code:** 28401

Data Date	Rating	RACR #1	RACR #2	Loss Ratio %	Total Assets ($mil)	Capital ($mil)	Net Premium ($mil)	Net Income ($mil)
2017	B+	2.10	1.70	74.2	1,418.0	656.5	623.1	13.4
2016	B	2.11	1.73	77.2	1,320.1	627.0	542.6	7.1
2015	B	2.15	1.79	70.4	1,275.6	635.9	496.5	33.1
2014	B	2.12	1.75	71.1	1,218.5	596.9	481.3	40.0
2013	B	2.02	1.65	75.2	1,155.6	537.5	468.0	25.4

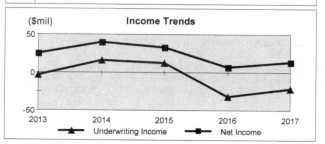

Income Trends

AMERICAN ROAD INS CO | B- | Good

Major Rating Factors: Fair overall results on stability tests (4.5 on a scale of 0 to 10) including potential drain of affiliation with Ford Motor Co. History of adequate reserve strength (6.1) as reserves have been consistently at an acceptable level.

Other Rating Factors: Strong long-term capitalization index (10.0) based on excellent current risk adjusted capital (severe and moderate loss scenarios), despite some fluctuation in capital levels. Excellent profitability (7.5) with operating gains in each of the last five years. Excellent expense controls. Excellent liquidity (7.0) with ample operational cash flow and liquid investments.

Principal Business: (Not applicable due to unusual reinsurance transactions.)

Principal Investments: Investment grade bonds (72%), misc. investments (27%), and cash (1%).

Investments in Affiliates: None

Group Affiliation: Ford Motor Co

Licensed in: All states except PR

Commenced Business: December 1959

Address: One American Road MD 7600, Dearborn, MI 48126-2701

Phone: (313) 337-1102 **Domicile State:** MI **NAIC Code:** 19631

Data Date	Rating	RACR #1	RACR #2	Loss Ratio %	Total Assets ($mil)	Capital ($mil)	Net Premium ($mil)	Net Income ($mil)
2017	B-	22.39	11.95	95.4	711.9	270.4	160.0	9.5
2016	C+	19.38	10.50	99.0	658.8	247.9	157.6	3.7
2015	C+	21.55	11.34	65.0	642.2	251.1	134.6	30.3
2014	C+	22.71	12.29	97.5	556.9	246.6	125.8	3.3
2013	C+	21.22	11.60	64.2	564.2	276.0	118.1	48.6

Rating Indexes

AMERICAN SECURITY INS CO | B- | Good

Major Rating Factors: Fair profitability index (3.4 on a scale of 0 to 10). Weak expense controls. Return on equity has been fair, averaging 32.9% over the past five years. Fair liquidity (3.2) as cash resources may not be adequate to cover a spike in claims.

Other Rating Factors: History of adequate reserve strength (6.4) as reserves have been consistently at an acceptable level. Good overall results on stability tests (5.1) despite negative cash flow from operations for 2017. Stability strengths include good operational trends and excellent risk diversification. Strong long-term capitalization index (7.7) based on excellent current risk adjusted capital (severe and moderate loss scenarios), despite some fluctuation in capital levels.

Principal Business: Allied lines (56%), fire (25%), inland marine (9%), other liability (6%), homeowners multiple peril (3%), and credit (1%).

Principal Investments: Investment grade bonds (60%), misc. investments (41%), non investment grade bonds (5%), and real estate (2%).

Investments in Affiliates: 13%

Group Affiliation: Assurant Inc

Licensed in: All states except NH

Commenced Business: September 1938

Address: 251 LITTLE FALLS DRIVE, Wilmington, DE 19808

Phone: (770) 763-1000 **Domicile State:** DE **NAIC Code:** 42978

Data Date	Rating	RACR #1	RACR #2	Loss Ratio %	Total Assets ($mil)	Capital ($mil)	Net Premium ($mil)	Net Income ($mil)
2017	B-	2.00	1.52	62.5	1,376.3	506.3	849.2	91.8
2016	B-	1.91	1.48	49.0	1,552.5	555.2	945.8	84.2
2015	B-	2.02	1.51	36.6	1,584.9	558.8	1,047.3	298.5
2014	B	1.53	1.20	38.0	1,915.8	661.5	1,369.2	251.2
2013	B	2.55	1.82	33.6	2,078.0	740.8	1,601.9	294.2

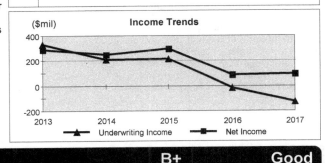

Income Trends

AMERICAN STANDARD INS CO OF WI * | B+ | Good

Major Rating Factors: Good overall profitability index (6.9 on a scale of 0 to 10). Excellent expense controls. Return on equity has been low, averaging 2.3% over the past five years. Good overall results on stability tests (6.4) despite negative cash flow from operations for 2017. Other stability subfactors include potential support from affiliation with American Family Ins Group, good operational trends and excellent risk diversification.

Other Rating Factors: Strong long-term capitalization index (10.0) based on excellent current risk adjusted capital (severe and moderate loss scenarios), despite some fluctuation in capital levels. Excellent liquidity (7.0) with ample operational cash flow and liquid investments.

Principal Business: Auto liability (65%) and auto physical damage (35%).

Principal Investments: Investment grade bonds (92%), misc. investments (6%), and cash (2%).

Investments in Affiliates: None

Group Affiliation: American Family Ins Group

Licensed in: AZ, CO, ID, IL, IN, IA, KS, MN, MO, MT, NE, NV, NM, NC, ND, OH, OR, SC, SD, UT, WA, WI, WY

Commenced Business: September 1961

Address: 6000 AMERICAN PARKWAY, Madison, WI 53783-0001

Phone: (608) 249-2111 **Domicile State:** WI **NAIC Code:** 19283

Data Date	Rating	RACR #1	RACR #2	Loss Ratio %	Total Assets ($mil)	Capital ($mil)	Net Premium ($mil)	Net Income ($mil)
2017	B+	50.40	45.36	0.0	400.9	347.6	0.0	4.5
2016	B+	48.08	43.27	0.0	401.7	343.1	0.0	5.7
2015	B+	37.42	33.68	0.0	443.0	338.3	0.0	9.1
2014	B+	39.45	35.50	0.0	414.8	329.3	0.0	10.3
2013	B+	40.40	36.36	0.0	393.9	318.6	0.0	8.0

Rating Indexes

AMERICAN STRATEGIC INS CO
C   Fair

Major Rating Factors: Fair overall results on stability tests (3.8 on a scale of 0 to 10) including potential drain of affiliation with Progressive Corp. Good overall profitability index (5.1) despite operating losses during 2017. Return on equity has been low, averaging 4.8% over the past five years.

Other Rating Factors: Good liquidity (6.4) with sufficient resources (cash flows and marketable investments) to handle a spike in claims. Strong long-term capitalization index (8.3) based on excellent current risk adjusted capital (severe and moderate loss scenarios). Moreover, capital levels have been consistent in recent years. Ample reserve history (9.3) that helps to protect the company against sharp claims increases.

Principal Business: Homeowners multiple peril (75%), allied lines (18%), fire (4%), and other liability (2%).

Principal Investments: Investment grade bonds (91%), misc. investments (6%), and real estate (4%).

Investments in Affiliates: 1%

Group Affiliation: Progressive Corp

Licensed in: All states except CA, HI, ID, IN, LA, NY, WY, PR

Commenced Business: December 1997

Address: 1 ASI Way, St. Petersburg, FL 33702-2514

Phone: (727) 821-8765   **Domicile State:** FL   **NAIC Code:** 10872

Data Date	Rating	RACR #1	RACR #2	Loss Ratio %	Total Assets ($mil)	Capital ($mil)	Net Premium ($mil)	Net Income ($mil)
2017	C	2.28	1.89	71.0	1,223.1	508.1	779.5	-22.7
2016	C	2.81	2.31	64.5	1,080.0	489.4	618.3	19.8
2015	C	2.68	2.22	57.9	981.8	441.8	576.1	51.5
2014	C	2.34	1.89	63.7	885.3	375.4	500.6	11.3
2013	B-	2.34	1.88	54.1	736.4	307.4	409.5	30.1

Progressive Corp
Composite Group Rating: C+

Largest Group Members	Assets ($mil)	Rating
PROGRESSIVE CASUALTY INS CO	8431	B-
PROGRESSIVE DIRECT INS CO	7786	B-
UNITED FINANCIAL CASUALTY CO	3346	B-
PROGRESSIVE NORTHERN INS CO	1866	C+
PROGRESSIVE NORTHWESTERN INS CO	1813	C+

AMERICAN ZURICH INS CO
C+   Fair

Major Rating Factors: Fair overall results on stability tests (4.7 on a scale of 0 to 10) including fair financial strength of affiliated Zurich Financial Services Group.

Other Rating Factors: Strong long-term capitalization index (10.0) based on excellent current risk adjusted capital (severe and moderate loss scenarios). Moreover, capital levels have been consistent in recent years. Excellent profitability (7.4) with operating gains in each of the last five years. Excellent liquidity (7.5) with ample operational cash flow and liquid investments.

Principal Business: Workers compensation (72%), inland marine (19%), commercial multiple peril (4%), auto liability (2%), other liability (2%), and auto physical damage (1%).

Principal Investments: Investment grade bonds (81%) and misc. investments (19%).

Investments in Affiliates: 15%

Group Affiliation: Zurich Financial Services Group

Licensed in: All states except PR

Commenced Business: September 1981

Address: 1299 ZURICH WAY, Schaumburg, IL 60196-1056

Phone: (847) 605-6000   **Domicile State:** IL   **NAIC Code:** 40142

Data Date	Rating	RACR #1	RACR #2	Loss Ratio %	Total Assets ($mil)	Capital ($mil)	Net Premium ($mil)	Net Income ($mil)
2017	C+	7.17	6.86	0.0	332.8	234.9	0.0	3.6
2016	C+	7.18	6.88	0.0	315.9	230.7	0.0	4.7
2015	C+	7.00	6.72	0.0	314.3	226.3	0.0	4.7
2014	C	4.79	4.61	0.0	264.5	157.5	0.0	2.9
2013	C	4.86	4.71	0.0	234.2	153.3	0.0	3.3

Zurich Financial Services Group
Composite Group Rating: B

Largest Group Members	Assets ($mil)	Rating
ZURICH AMERICAN INS CO	31582	B
ZURICH AMERICAN LIFE INS CO	14227	C
FARMERS NEW WORLD LIFE INS CO	5127	B-
CENTRE LIFE INS CO	1791	B-
RURAL COMMUNITY INS CO	1791	C+

AMERISURE INS CO
B-   Good

Major Rating Factors: Fair overall results on stability tests (4.7 on a scale of 0 to 10) including potential drain of affiliation with Amerisure Companies and negative cash flow from operations for 2017. History of adequate reserve strength (5.2) as reserves have been consistently at an acceptable level.

Other Rating Factors: Good overall profitability index (6.1). Fair expense controls. Return on equity has been low, averaging 3.0% over the past five years. Good liquidity (6.6) with sufficient resources (cash flows and marketable investments) to handle a spike in claims. Strong long-term capitalization index (8.2) based on excellent current risk adjusted capital (severe and moderate loss scenarios), despite some fluctuation in capital levels.

Principal Business: Workers compensation (53%), commercial multiple peril (18%), auto liability (16%), other liability (7%), auto physical damage (4%), and products liability (2%).

Principal Investments: Investment grade bonds (96%), cash (3%), and non investment grade bonds (1%).

Investments in Affiliates: None

Group Affiliation: Amerisure Companies

Licensed in: All states except CA

Commenced Business: September 1968

Address: 26777 Halsted Road, Farmington Hills, MI 48331-3586

Phone: (248) 615-9000   **Domicile State:** MI   **NAIC Code:** 19488

Data Date	Rating	RACR #1	RACR #2	Loss Ratio %	Total Assets ($mil)	Capital ($mil)	Net Premium ($mil)	Net Income ($mil)
2017	B-	2.50	1.77	74.3	875.0	241.8	244.6	2.1
2016	B-	2.57	1.83	69.5	836.4	245.8	244.0	7.5
2015	B-	2.70	1.93	64.5	785.9	238.7	232.8	14.2
2014	B-	2.65	1.87	67.2	752.2	224.5	215.4	8.1
2013	B-	2.57	1.75	73.1	721.6	215.7	199.3	3.4

Rating Indexes

Ranges Cap. 2 Stab. Res. Prof. Liq.

■ Weak ■ Fair □ Good □ Strong

AMERISURE MUTUAL INS CO   B-   Good

Major Rating Factors: Fair overall results on stability tests (4.7 on a scale of 0 to 10) including potential drain of affiliation with Amerisure Companies. History of adequate reserve strength (5.8) as reserves have been consistently at an acceptable level.

Other Rating Factors: Good overall profitability index (6.9). Fair expense controls. Return on equity has been fair, averaging 5.4% over the past five years. Good liquidity (6.8) with sufficient resources (cash flows and marketable investments) to handle a spike in claims. Strong long-term capitalization index (8.3) based on excellent current risk adjusted capital (severe and moderate loss scenarios). Moreover, capital levels have been consistent in recent years.

Principal Business: Workers compensation (53%), commercial multiple peril (17%), other liability (13%), auto liability (10%), auto physical damage (3%), products liability (2%), and inland marine (1%).

Principal Investments: Investment grade bonds (58%), misc. investments (40%), non investment grade bonds (2%), and real estate (1%).

Investments in Affiliates: 13%

Group Affiliation: Amerisure Companies

Licensed in: All states, the District of Columbia and Puerto Rico

Commenced Business: September 1912

Address: 26777 Halsted Road, Farmington Hills, MI 48331-3586

Phone: (248) 615-9000   **Domicile State:** MI   **NAIC Code:** 23396

Data Date	Rating	RACR #1	RACR #2	Loss Ratio %	Total Assets ($mil)	Capital ($mil)	Net Premium ($mil)	Net Income ($mil)
2017	B-	2.48	1.95	74.3	2,369.8	982.5	546.3	35.8
2016	B-	2.34	1.86	69.5	2,231.8	937.9	545.0	40.4
2015	B-	2.26	1.80	64.5	2,124.5	875.2	519.9	71.2
2014	B-	2.25	1.77	67.2	2,069.7	843.0	481.1	48.1
2013	B-	2.16	1.69	73.1	1,981.8	803.8	445.2	41.0

Rating Indexes

AMICA MUTUAL INS CO *   B+   Good

Major Rating Factors: Good overall profitability index (5.5 on a scale of 0 to 10). Good expense controls. Good liquidity (5.3) with sufficient resources (cash flows and marketable investments) to handle a spike in claims.

Other Rating Factors: Good overall results on stability tests (6.8). Strong long-term capitalization index (8.2) based on excellent current risk adjusted capital (severe and moderate loss scenarios), despite some fluctuation in capital levels. Ample reserve history (8.3) that helps to protect the company against sharp claims increases.

Principal Business: Homeowners multiple peril (37%), auto liability (34%), auto physical damage (23%), other liability (3%), earthquake (1%), allied lines (1%), and inland marine (1%).

Principal Investments: Investment grade bonds (56%), misc. investments (43%), non investment grade bonds (1%), and real estate (1%).

Investments in Affiliates: 8%

Group Affiliation: Amica Mutual Group

Licensed in: All states except PR

Commenced Business: April 1907

Address: 100 AMICA WAY, Lincoln, RI 02865-1156

Phone: (800) 652-6422   **Domicile State:** RI   **NAIC Code:** 19976

Data Date	Rating	RACR #1	RACR #2	Loss Ratio %	Total Assets ($mil)	Capital ($mil)	Net Premium ($mil)	Net Income ($mil)
2017	B+	2.66	1.79	79.9	5,384.6	2,669.5	2,273.9	82.7
2016	B+	2.65	1.78	77.9	5,120.6	2,583.7	2,086.5	146.2
2015	B+	2.72	1.84	80.9	4,961.9	2,611.3	1,942.8	56.2
2014	B+	2.97	1.97	66.3	5,061.7	2,759.8	1,841.5	185.5
2013	B+	2.97	1.95	69.9	4,855.2	2,649.7	1,746.7	145.2

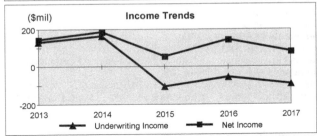

Income Trends

ANSUR AMERICA INS CO *   B+   Good

Major Rating Factors: Good liquidity (6.6 on a scale of 0 to 10) with sufficient resources (cash flows and marketable investments) to handle a spike in claims. Good overall results on stability tests (6.5).

Other Rating Factors: Strong long-term capitalization index (10.0) based on excellent current risk adjusted capital (severe and moderate loss scenarios). Moreover, capital has steadily grown over the last five years. Ample reserve history (9.3) that helps to protect the company against sharp claims increases. Excellent profitability (8.8) with operating gains in each of the last five years.

Principal Business: Commercial multiple peril (36%), workers compensation (27%), auto liability (12%), other liability (11%), auto physical damage (7%), inland marine (5%), and boiler & machinery (2%).

Principal Investments: Investment grade bonds (97%) and misc. investments (4%).

Investments in Affiliates: None

Group Affiliation: Frankenmuth Mutual Group

Licensed in: AL, AR, CO, CT, GA, IL, IN, IA, KS, KY, ME, MI, MS, MO, NE, NV, NM, NC, OH, OK, PA, SC, TN, VT, VA, WA, WV, WI, WY

Commenced Business: October 1999

Address: One Mutual Avenue, Frankenmuth, MI 48787-0001

Phone: (989) 652-6121   **Domicile State:** MI   **NAIC Code:** 10984

Data Date	Rating	RACR #1	RACR #2	Loss Ratio %	Total Assets ($mil)	Capital ($mil)	Net Premium ($mil)	Net Income ($mil)
2017	B+	5.14	3.82	59.0	121.2	46.7	50.7	4.3
2016	B	4.72	3.46	63.3	114.1	43.2	48.0	3.8
2015	B	3.84	2.89	62.1	105.7	39.2	46.2	3.6
2014	B	3.58	2.67	68.9	100.0	35.6	43.9	2.3
2013	B	3.32	2.46	63.2	98.4	33.4	42.1	3.6

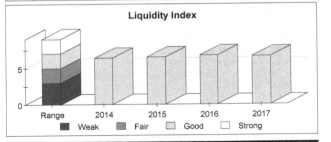

Liquidity Index

ARBELLA MUTUAL INS CO

C+   Fair

Major Rating Factors: Fair overall results on stability tests (4.3 on a scale of 0 to 10) including potential drain of affiliation with Arbella Ins Group. Good overall profitability index (5.7) despite operating losses during 2015.

Other Rating Factors: Good liquidity (6.5) with sufficient resources (cash flows and marketable investments) to handle a spike in claims. Strong long-term capitalization index (8.5) based on excellent current risk adjusted capital (severe and moderate loss scenarios), despite some fluctuation in capital levels. Ample reserve history (8.0) that helps to protect the company against sharp claims increases.

Principal Business: Auto liability (39%), auto physical damage (33%), homeowners multiple peril (24%), fire (1%), other liability (1%), inland marine (1%), and allied lines (1%).

Principal Investments: Investment grade bonds (71%) and misc. investments (29%).

Investments in Affiliates: 14%

Group Affiliation: Arbella Ins Group

Licensed in: MA

Commenced Business: October 1988

Address: 1100 Crown Colony Drive, Quincy, MA 02269-9103

Phone: (617) 328-2800   **Domicile State:** MA   **NAIC Code:** 17000

Data Date	Rating	RACR #1	RACR #2	Loss Ratio %	Total Assets ($mil)	Capital ($mil)	Net Premium ($mil)	Net Income ($mil)
2017	C+	2.64	2.05	60.0	1,462.6	621.1	590.6	49.2
2016	C+	2.51	1.94	64.1	1,404.4	557.6	619.2	41.6
2015	C+	2.38	1.83	82.2	1,334.2	510.5	609.1	-45.0
2014	C+	2.65	2.13	62.9	1,285.7	561.2	577.0	28.6
2013	C+	2.69	2.06	64.5	1,177.8	523.9	496.4	22.8

Rating Indexes

ARCH INS CO

C   Fair

Major Rating Factors: Fair overall results on stability tests (3.4 on a scale of 0 to 10) including potential drain of affiliation with Arch Capital Group Ltd and fair results on operational trends. Good liquidity (6.4) with sufficient resources (cash flows and marketable investments) to handle a spike in claims.

Other Rating Factors: Strong long-term capitalization index (7.9) based on excellent current risk adjusted capital (severe and moderate loss scenarios). Moreover, capital levels have been consistent in recent years. Ample reserve history (9.6) that helps to protect the company against sharp claims increases. Excellent profitability (8.6) with operating gains in each of the last five years.

Principal Business: Other liability (31%), workers compensation (26%), auto liability (11%), inland marine (7%), commercial multiple peril (6%), surety (5%), and other lines (15%).

Principal Investments: Investment grade bonds (76%), misc. investments (22%), and cash (2%).

Investments in Affiliates: 14%

Group Affiliation: Arch Capital Group Ltd

Licensed in: All states, the District of Columbia and Puerto Rico

Commenced Business: June 1980

Address: 2345 GRAND BLVD SUITE 900, Kansas City, MO 64108

Phone: (201) 743-4000   **Domicile State:** MO   **NAIC Code:** 11150

Data Date	Rating	RACR #1	RACR #2	Loss Ratio %	Total Assets ($mil)	Capital ($mil)	Net Premium ($mil)	Net Income ($mil)
2017	C	2.51	2.34	132.5	3,921.9	929.8	-549.1	71.1
2016	C	1.66	1.36	71.5	3,729.3	888.6	793.2	49.7
2015	C	1.56	1.25	68.5	3,545.4	826.5	772.9	52.8
2014	C	1.39	1.07	67.3	3,200.9	778.4	785.5	37.6
2013	C	1.38	1.06	68.2	2,840.9	736.6	659.6	28.7

Rating Indexes

ARCH MORTGAGE INS CO

B   Good

Major Rating Factors: History of adequate reserve strength (5.8 on a scale of 0 to 10) as reserves have been consistently at an acceptable level. Fair profitability index (3.8) with operating losses during 2013, 2014, 2015 and 2016. Average return on equity over the last five years has been poor at -14.0%.

Other Rating Factors: Fair overall results on stability tests (4.5) including excessive premium growth and weak results on operational trends. Strong long-term capitalization index (7.7) based on excellent current risk adjusted capital (severe and moderate loss scenarios), despite some fluctuation in capital levels. Superior liquidity (9.1) with ample operational cash flow and liquid investments.

Principal Business: Mortgage guaranty (100%).

Principal Investments: Investment grade bonds (95%), misc. investments (3%), cash (1%), and non investment grade bonds (1%).

Investments in Affiliates: None

Group Affiliation: Arch Capital Group Ltd

Licensed in: All states, the District of Columbia and Puerto Rico

Commenced Business: December 1981

Address: 33 East Main Street Suite 900, Madison, WI 53703

Phone: (336) 373-0232   **Domicile State:** WI   **NAIC Code:** 40266

Data Date	Rating	RACR #1	RACR #2	Loss Ratio %	Total Assets ($mil)	Capital ($mil)	Net Premium ($mil)	Net Income ($mil)
2017	B	3.07	2.25	17.6	2,134.6	471.9	416.2	12.1
2016	B-	1.16	1.08	3.7	547.5	155.5	88.4	-31.8
2015	C+	1.20	1.09	23.3	436.4	134.5	60.7	-34.8
2014	C+	1.31	1.17	55.3	399.6	152.5	52.6	-34.7
2013	C+	1.45	1.24	67.9	382.1	161.4	87.1	-5.2

Reserve Deficiency (as % of capital)

* Adequate & redundant reserves show as negatives

■ 1 Yr Dev   □ 2 Yr Dev

ARCH REINS CO

C- | **Fair**

Major Rating Factors: Weak overall results on stability tests (2.7 on a scale of 0 to 10) including potential drain of affiliation with Arch Capital Group Ltd. Strong long-term capitalization index (7.8) based on excellent current risk adjusted capital (severe and moderate loss scenarios). Moreover, capital levels have been consistent in recent years.

Other Rating Factors: Ample reserve history (8.1) that helps to protect the company against sharp claims increases. Excellent profitability (7.5) with operating gains in each of the last five years. Excellent liquidity (7.0) with ample operational cash flow and liquid investments.

Principal Business: (This company is a reinsurer.)

Principal Investments: Misc. investments (55%), investment grade bonds (43%), and cash (2%).

Investments in Affiliates: 53%

Group Affiliation: Arch Capital Group Ltd

Licensed in: All states, the District of Columbia and Puerto Rico

Commenced Business: July 1995

Address: 1209 ORANGE STREET, Wilmington, DE 19801

Phone: (973) 898-9575   **Domicile State:** DE   **NAIC Code:** 10348

Data Date	Rating	RACR #1	RACR #2	Loss Ratio %	Total Assets ($mil)	Capital ($mil)	Net Premium ($mil)	Net Income ($mil)
2017	C-	1.53	1.51	60.3	1,987.8	1,287.6	193.9	17.7
2016	C-	1.60	1.57	46.9	2,040.4	1,284.1	215.7	36.9
2015	C-	1.59	1.56	49.2	1,904.9	1,201.4	219.0	32.7
2014	C-	1.61	1.57	52.1	1,736.9	1,104.0	245.5	33.3
2013	C-	1.61	1.58	46.8	1,547.9	1,013.2	204.0	33.0

Rating Indexes

ARCH SPECIALTY INS CO *

B+ | **Good**

Major Rating Factors: History of adequate reserve strength (6.0 on a scale of 0 to 10) as reserves have been consistently at an acceptable level. Good overall profitability index (6.2). Excellent expense controls. Return on equity has been low, averaging 3.0% over the past five years.

Other Rating Factors: Good overall results on stability tests (6.5) despite negative cash flow from operations for 2017. Stability strengths include good operational trends and excellent risk diversification. Strong long-term capitalization index (10.0) based on excellent current risk adjusted capital (severe and moderate loss scenarios), despite some fluctuation in capital levels. Excellent liquidity (7.5) with ample operational cash flow and liquid investments.

Principal Business: Other liability (48%), fire (21%), medical malpractice (13%), products liability (5%), earthquake (5%), allied lines (3%), and other lines (4%).

Principal Investments: Investment grade bonds (93%) and misc. investments (7%).

Investments in Affiliates: None

Group Affiliation: Arch Capital Group Ltd

Licensed in: All states, the District of Columbia and Puerto Rico

Commenced Business: January 1965

Address: 2345 GRAND BLVD SUITE 900, Kansas City, MO 64108

Phone: (201) 743-4000   **Domicile State:** MO   **NAIC Code:** 21199

Data Date	Rating	RACR #1	RACR #2	Loss Ratio %	Total Assets ($mil)	Capital ($mil)	Net Premium ($mil)	Net Income ($mil)
2017	B+	5.76	4.69	N/A	483.4	300.7	0.0	5.7
2016	B	6.01	4.82	N/A	481.0	301.9	0.1	2.1
2015	B	5.76	4.62	N/A	503.0	305.9	0.3	23.3
2014	B	5.61	4.47	N/A	470.6	292.4	0.9	7.7
2013	B	21.66	13.74	N/A	473.5	283.5	0.0	5.6

Reserve Deficiency (as % of capital)

* Adequate & redundant reserves show as negatives

ARGONAUT INS CO

C | **Fair**

Major Rating Factors: Fair overall results on stability tests (3.3 on a scale of 0 to 10) including potential drain of affiliation with Argo Group Intl Holdings Ltd. Fair reserve development (3.5) as the level of reserves has at times been insufficient to cover claims. Deficiencies in the two year reserve development occurred in three of the previous five years and ranged between 16% and 20%.

Other Rating Factors: Good overall profitability index (6.5). Weak expense controls. Return on equity has been fair, averaging 6.3% over the past five years. Good liquidity (6.9) with sufficient resources (cash flows and marketable investments) to handle a spike in claims. Strong long-term capitalization index (7.2) based on excellent current risk adjusted capital (severe and moderate loss scenarios), despite some fluctuation in capital levels.

Principal Business: Other liability (30%), workers compensation (19%), commercial multiple peril (18%), surety (18%), inland marine (4%), auto liability (4%), and other lines (7%).

Principal Investments: Misc. investments (54%), investment grade bonds (39%), and non investment grade bonds (7%).

Investments in Affiliates: 34%

Group Affiliation: Argo Group Intl Holdings Ltd

Licensed in: All states, the District of Columbia and Puerto Rico

Commenced Business: May 1957

Address: 225 W WASHINGTON ST 24TH FL, Chicago, IL 60606

Phone: (800) 470-7958   **Domicile State:** IL   **NAIC Code:** 19801

Data Date	Rating	RACR #1	RACR #2	Loss Ratio %	Total Assets ($mil)	Capital ($mil)	Net Premium ($mil)	Net Income ($mil)
2017	C	1.38	1.17	71.0	1,820.4	872.8	302.0	2.7
2016	C	1.44	1.22	61.8	1,675.0	799.7	223.7	52.0
2015	C	1.72	1.14	70.4	1,268.9	416.1	192.2	38.5
2014	C	1.43	0.94	88.6	1,280.4	390.8	185.2	13.4
2013	C	1.86	1.21	82.8	1,308.9	409.4	196.9	49.8

Rating Indexes

ASPEN AMERICAN INS CO
C+   Fair

Major Rating Factors: Fair reserve development (3.0 on a scale of 0 to 10) as reserves have generally been sufficient to cover claims. In 2017, the two year reserve development was 34% deficient. Fair profitability index (3.6) with operating losses during 2013, 2014, 2015 and 2017. Average return on equity over the last five years has been poor at -4.6%.

Other Rating Factors: Fair overall results on stability tests (4.5). Strong long-term capitalization index (7.6) based on excellent current risk adjusted capital (severe and moderate loss scenarios). Moreover, capital levels have been consistent in recent years. Excellent liquidity (8.3) with ample operational cash flow and liquid investments.

Principal Business: Allied lines (47%), other liability (23%), surety (11%), inland marine (6%), commercial multiple peril (4%), ocean marine (3%), and other lines (5%).

Principal Investments: Misc. investments (50%), investment grade bonds (29%), and cash (21%).

Investments in Affiliates: 29%

Group Affiliation: Aspen Insurance Holdings Ltd

Licensed in: All states, the District of Columbia and Puerto Rico

Commenced Business: December 1990

Address: 1999 BRYAN STREET SUITE 900, Dallas, TX 75201

Phone: (860) 258-3500   **Domicile State:** TX   **NAIC Code:** 43460

Data Date	Rating	RACR #1	RACR #2	Loss Ratio %	Total Assets ($mil)	Capital ($mil)	Net Premium ($mil)	Net Income ($mil)
2017	C+	1.82	1.40	95.6	903.9	506.3	86.5	-5.5
2016	B	2.13	1.59	69.2	881.1	454.5	89.7	14.4
2015	C+	4.99	3.26	83.5	504.9	268.5	69.4	-14.8
2014	C	3.85	2.55	66.9	502.3	262.8	64.0	-24.1
2013	C	6.46	4.35	102.9	443.7	257.5	26.8	-27.4

Reserve Deficiency (as % of capital)

* Adequate & redundant reserves show as negatives

■ 1 Yr Dev   □ 2 Yr Dev

ASSOCIATED INDUSTRIES OF MA MUT INS
B-   Good

Major Rating Factors: Fair overall results on stability tests (4.5 on a scale of 0 to 10) including potential drain of affiliation with AIM Mutual Group. Good liquidity (6.7) with sufficient resources (cash flows and marketable investments) to handle a spike in claims.

Other Rating Factors: Strong long-term capitalization index (8.3) based on excellent current risk adjusted capital (severe and moderate loss scenarios). Moreover, capital levels have been consistent in recent years. Ample reserve history (9.4) that helps to protect the company against sharp claims increases. Excellent profitability (8.8) with operating gains in each of the last five years.

Principal Business: Workers compensation (100%).

Principal Investments: Investment grade bonds (86%) and misc. investments (14%).

Investments in Affiliates: 3%

Group Affiliation: AIM Mutual Group

Licensed in: CT, MA, NH, VT

Commenced Business: January 1989

Address: 54 Third Avenue, Burlington, MA 1803

Phone: (781) 221-1600   **Domicile State:** MA   **NAIC Code:** 33758

Data Date	Rating	RACR #1	RACR #2	Loss Ratio %	Total Assets ($mil)	Capital ($mil)	Net Premium ($mil)	Net Income ($mil)
2017	B-	2.66	1.98	67.1	625.2	237.0	142.2	21.3
2016	B-	2.55	1.90	71.6	593.7	215.0	137.3	19.6
2015	C+	2.39	1.79	71.7	560.3	193.8	132.8	14.7
2014	C	2.31	1.73	74.6	530.9	180.6	129.2	11.6
2013	C	1.99	1.47	76.7	492.9	178.2	126.1	8.0

Rating Indexes

Ranges   Cap. 2   Stab.   Res.   Prof.   Liq.

■ Weak   ■ Fair   ▨ Good   □ Strong

ASSURED GUARANTY CORP
C-   Fair

Major Rating Factors: Weak overall results on stability tests (2.9 on a scale of 0 to 10) including negative cash flow from operations for 2017. Strengths include potentially strong support from affiliation with Assured Guaranty/Financial Sec Asr. A history of deficient reserves (1.5). Underreserving can have an adverse impact on capital and profits. In 2015 and 2016 the two year reserve development was 69% and 134% deficient respectively.

Other Rating Factors: Good overall profitability index (6.9) despite operating losses during 2015. Return on equity has been good over the last five years, averaging 10.4%. Strong long-term capitalization index (10.0) based on excellent current risk adjusted capital (severe and moderate loss scenarios). Moreover, capital levels have been consistent in recent years. Superior liquidity (9.4) with ample operational cash flow and liquid investments.

Principal Business: Financial guaranty (100%).

Principal Investments: Investment grade bonds (85%), non investment grade bonds (8%), misc. investments (4%), cash (2%), and real estate (1%).

Investments in Affiliates: 3%

Group Affiliation: Assured Guaranty/Financial Sec Asr

Licensed in: All states, the District of Columbia and Puerto Rico

Commenced Business: January 1988

Address: 1633 Broadway, New York, NY 10019

Phone: (212) 974-0100   **Domicile State:** MD   **NAIC Code:** 30180

Data Date	Rating	RACR #1	RACR #2	Loss Ratio %	Total Assets ($mil)	Capital ($mil)	Net Premium ($mil)	Net Income ($mil)
2017	C-	12.24	7.84	113.0	3,126.7	2,073.2	21.6	219.1
2016	C-	5.00	4.01	38.1	3,272.0	1,895.6	58.1	107.6
2015	C-	2.81	2.35	74.5	3,791.1	1,454.1	57.2	-52.7
2014	D+	2.98	2.46	N/A	3,888.9	1,421.9	58.6	129.3
2013	D+	2.15	1.82	N/A	2,504.4	692.6	-186.7	211.2

Rating Indexes

Ranges   Cap. 2   Stab.   Res.   Prof.   Liq.

■ Weak   ■ Fair   ▨ Good   □ Strong

ASSURED GUARANTY MUNICIPAL CORP — D+ — Weak

Major Rating Factors: Weak overall results on stability tests (2.4 on a scale of 0 to 10). Strengths include potentially strong support from affiliation with Assured Guaranty/Financial Sec Asr. Strong long-term capitalization index (7.8) based on excellent current risk adjusted capital (severe and moderate loss scenarios), despite some fluctuation in capital levels.

Other Rating Factors: Fair reserve development (4.7) as reserves have generally been sufficient to cover claims. Good overall profitability index (6.1). Excellent expense controls. Return on equity has been good over the last five years, averaging 11.4%. Superior liquidity (9.5) with ample operational cash flow and liquid investments.

Principal Business: Financial guaranty (100%).

Principal Investments: Investment grade bonds (71%), misc. investments (27%), and non investment grade bonds (2%).

Investments in Affiliates: 17%

Group Affiliation: Assured Guaranty/Financial Sec Asr

Licensed in: All states, the District of Columbia and Puerto Rico

Commenced Business: September 1985

Address: 1633 Broadway, New York, NY 10019

Phone: (212) 974-0100   **Domicile State:** NY   **NAIC Code:** 18287

Data Date	Rating	RACR #1	RACR #2	Loss Ratio %	Total Assets ($mil)	Capital ($mil)	Net Premium ($mil)	Net Income ($mil)
2017	D+	2.21	1.51	164.1	5,479.6	2,253.9	261.8	152.4
2016	D+	3.24	1.91	34.8	5,279.1	2,266.6	143.5	190.7
2015	D+	2.85	1.80	59.6	5,788.5	2,440.8	141.8	216.7
2014	D+	2.75	1.69	N/A	5,961.2	2,266.9	173.9	303.9
2013	D+	2.49	1.48	N/A	5,712.1	1,733.1	-191.3	339.6

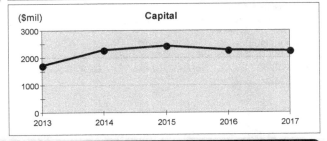

Capital ($mil)

ATLANTIC SPECIALTY INS CO — C+ — Fair

Major Rating Factors: Fair reserve development (3.3 on a scale of 0 to 10) as reserves have generally been sufficient to cover claims. In 2017, the two year reserve development was 19% deficient. Fair overall results on stability tests (4.6) including negative cash flow from operations for 2017.

Other Rating Factors: Good liquidity (6.8) with sufficient resources (cash flows and marketable investments) to handle a spike in claims. Weak profitability index (2.6) with operating losses during 2014 and 2017. Return on equity has been low, averaging 1.8% over the past five years. Strong long-term capitalization index (7.0) based on excellent current risk adjusted capital (severe and moderate loss scenarios), despite some fluctuation in capital levels.

Principal Business: Other liability (24%), commercial multiple peril (12%), ocean marine (12%), group accident & health (11%), inland marine (7%), surety (7%), and other lines (27%).

Principal Investments: Investment grade bonds (49%), misc. investments (44%), non investment grade bonds (5%), and cash (2%).

Investments in Affiliates: 13%

Group Affiliation: White Mountains Group

Licensed in: All states, the District of Columbia and Puerto Rico

Commenced Business: December 1986

Address: 77 Water Street 17th Floor, New York, NY 10005-4488

Phone: (952) 852-2431   **Domicile State:** NY   **NAIC Code:** 27154

Data Date	Rating	RACR #1	RACR #2	Loss Ratio %	Total Assets ($mil)	Capital ($mil)	Net Premium ($mil)	Net Income ($mil)
2017	C+	1.37	1.01	85.3	2,259.6	618.1	555.8	-118.9
2016	B-	1.92	1.48	68.9	2,232.7	624.8	552.8	34.9
2015	C+	1.79	1.37	65.9	2,340.3	622.3	590.1	45.0
2014	C	1.03	0.72	72.2	2,550.9	721.5	1,109.0	-14.1
2013	C	1.33	0.96	54.6	2,258.8	665.8	969.2	116.3

Reserve Deficiency (as % of capital)

* Adequate & redundant reserves show as negatives   ■ 1 Yr Dev   □ 2 Yr Dev

ATLANTIC STATES INS CO — B- — Good

Major Rating Factors: Fair overall results on stability tests (4.7 on a scale of 0 to 10) including potential drain of affiliation with Donegal Mutual Insurance Company. History of adequate reserve strength (5.8) as reserves have been consistently at an acceptable level.

Other Rating Factors: Good overall profitability index (6.8) despite modest operating losses during 2017. Return on equity has been low, averaging 4.6% over the past five years. Good liquidity (6.1) with sufficient resources (cash flows and marketable investments) to handle a spike in claims. Strong long-term capitalization index (8.4) based on excellent current risk adjusted capital (severe and moderate loss scenarios), despite some fluctuation in capital levels.

Principal Business: Auto liability (33%), auto physical damage (21%), commercial multiple peril (18%), workers compensation (13%), and homeowners multiple peril (13%).

Principal Investments: Investment grade bonds (85%), misc. investments (14%), and cash (1%).

Investments in Affiliates: None

Group Affiliation: Donegal Mutual Insurance Company

Licensed in: CT, DC, DE, GA, IL, IN, IA, ME, MD, MI, NE, NH, NY, NC, OH, PA, SC, SD, TN, VT, VA, WV

Commenced Business: October 1986

Address: 1195 River Road, Marietta, PA 17547-0302

Phone: (717) 426-1931   **Domicile State:** PA   **NAIC Code:** 22586

Data Date	Rating	RACR #1	RACR #2	Loss Ratio %	Total Assets ($mil)	Capital ($mil)	Net Premium ($mil)	Net Income ($mil)
2017	B-	2.76	1.96	69.3	793.2	223.2	451.6	-0.3
2016	B-	2.98	2.13	64.1	758.1	227.9	426.3	15.8
2015	B-	2.85	2.08	66.0	705.5	207.6	393.1	13.4
2014	B-	2.82	2.06	68.4	636.4	191.2	371.3	6.1
2013	B-	2.83	2.01	64.7	595.4	186.6	346.9	12.6

Rating Indexes

Ranges   Cap. 2   Stab.   Res.   Prof.   Liq.
■ Weak   ▨ Fair   ▨ Good   □ Strong

ATTORNEYS LIAB ASR SOCIETY INC RRG   D+   Weak

Major Rating Factors: Weak overall results on stability tests (2.4 on a scale of 0 to 10). Fair long-term capitalization index (3.9) based on fair current risk adjusted capital (moderate loss scenario).

Other Rating Factors: Fair reserve development (3.2) as the level of reserves has at times been insufficient to cover claims. In 2014 and 2015 the two year reserve development was 53% and 70% deficient respectively. Good overall profitability index (6.4) despite operating losses during 2013 and 2014. Return on equity has been low, averaging 2.1% over the past five years. Excellent liquidity (7.0) with ample operational cash flow and liquid investments.

Principal Business: Other liability (100%).

Principal Investments: Misc. investments (50%), investment grade bonds (46%), and cash (4%).

Investments in Affiliates: 33%

Group Affiliation: Attorneys Liability Asr Soc Bermuda

Licensed in: All states except PR

Commenced Business: December 1987

Address: 148 College Street Suite 204, Burlington, VT 5401

Phone: (312) 697-6900   **Domicile State:** VT   **NAIC Code:** 10639

Data Date	Rating	RACR #1	RACR #2	Loss Ratio %	Total Assets ($mil)	Capital ($mil)	Net Premium ($mil)	Net Income ($mil)
2017	D+	0.78	0.63	43.3	2,045.4	759.5	199.2	75.3
2016	D	0.46	0.37	79.0	1,933.5	604.5	206.2	37.7
2015	D	0.32	0.26	115.2	1,944.7	557.2	222.9	20.4
2014	D	0.45	0.36	111.6	2,036.0	594.1	243.3	-33.4
2013	C-	4.53	3.11	102.4	239.1	80.3	25.9	-3.2

Capital

AUTO CLUB INDEMNITY CO *   B+   Good

Major Rating Factors: Good overall profitability index (6.4 on a scale of 0 to 10). Excellent expense controls. Return on equity has been low, averaging 1.0% over the past five years. Good overall results on stability tests (5.0). Stability strengths include good operational trends and excellent risk diversification.

Other Rating Factors: Strong long-term capitalization index (7.6) based on excellent current risk adjusted capital (severe and moderate loss scenarios), despite some fluctuation in capital levels. Excellent liquidity (7.9) with ample operational cash flow and liquid investments.

Principal Business: Homeowners multiple peril (99%) and other liability (1%).

Principal Investments: Investment grade bonds (81%) and cash (19%).

Investments in Affiliates: None

Group Affiliation: Auto Club Enterprises Ins Group

Licensed in: TX

Commenced Business: December 1999

Address: 1225 FREEPORT PARKWAY, Coppell, TX 75019-4413

Phone: (714) 850-5111   **Domicile State:** TX   **NAIC Code:** 11008

Data Date	Rating	RACR #1	RACR #2	Loss Ratio %	Total Assets ($mil)	Capital ($mil)	Net Premium ($mil)	Net Income ($mil)
2017	B+	1.54	1.39	0.0	25.7	5.5	0.0	0.1
2016	B+	1.70	1.53	0.0	22.4	5.4	0.0	0.1
2015	B+	1.73	1.55	0.0	21.6	5.4	0.0	0.0
2014	B+	1.80	1.62	0.0	20.0	5.3	0.0	0.0
2013	B+	1.92	1.72	0.0	18.0	5.2	0.0	0.0

Rating Indexes

Ranges   Cap. 2   Stab.   Res.   Prof.   Liq.
■ Weak   ■ Fair   ▨ Good   □ Strong

AUTO CLUB INS ASSN   B   Good

Major Rating Factors: Good overall profitability index (6.9 on a scale of 0 to 10). Fair expense controls. Good liquidity (6.2) with sufficient resources (cash flows and marketable investments) to handle a spike in claims.

Other Rating Factors: Fair overall results on stability tests (4.9) including potential drain of affiliation with Automobile Club of Michigan Group. Fair reserve development (4.9) as reserves have generally been sufficient to cover claims. Strong long-term capitalization index (7.9) based on excellent current risk adjusted capital (severe and moderate loss scenarios), despite some fluctuation in capital levels.

Principal Business: Auto liability (37%), homeowners multiple peril (36%), auto physical damage (26%), and other liability (1%).

Principal Investments: Investment grade bonds (43%), misc. investments (42%), non investment grade bonds (15%), and real estate (1%).

Investments in Affiliates: 16%

Group Affiliation: Automobile Club of Michigan Group

Licensed in: IL, MI, MN, NE, NY, ND, PA, WI

Commenced Business: March 1922

Address: 1 Auto Club Drive, Dearborn, MI 48126

Phone: (313) 336-1234   **Domicile State:** MI   **NAIC Code:** 21202

Data Date	Rating	RACR #1	RACR #2	Loss Ratio %	Total Assets ($mil)	Capital ($mil)	Net Premium ($mil)	Net Income ($mil)
2017	B	2.18	1.68	72.2	4,292.9	1,924.0	1,597.5	158.4
2016	B	2.10	1.66	69.4	4,074.6	1,809.4	1,492.1	97.0
2015	B	1.84	1.49	70.5	3,783.3	1,592.8	1,432.8	127.5
2014	B	1.82	1.46	77.5	3,673.6	1,524.8	1,355.0	51.3
2013	B	1.89	1.53	74.0	3,650.4	1,575.8	1,351.3	48.5

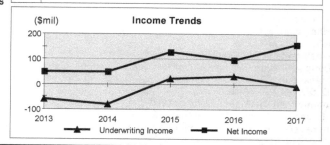

Income Trends

▲ Underwriting Income   ■ Net Income

AUTO CLUB INS CO OF FL *   B+   Good

Major Rating Factors: Good overall profitability index (6.3 on a scale of 0 to 10) despite operating losses during 2017. Return on equity has been fair, averaging 9.1% over the past five years. Good liquidity (6.3) with sufficient resources (cash flows and marketable investments) to handle a spike in claims.

Other Rating Factors: Good overall results on stability tests (6.5) despite negative cash flow from operations for 2017. Strong long-term capitalization index (9.3) based on excellent current risk adjusted capital (severe and moderate loss scenarios), despite some fluctuation in capital levels. Ample reserve history (9.1) that helps to protect the company against sharp claims increases.

Principal Business: Homeowners multiple peril (45%), auto liability (39%), auto physical damage (14%), and other liability (1%).

Principal Investments: Investment grade bonds (91%), non investment grade bonds (6%), and misc. investments (3%).

Investments in Affiliates: None

Group Affiliation: Auto Club Enterprises Ins Group

Licensed in: FL

Commenced Business: December 2007

Address: 14055 Riveredge Drive Ste 500, Tampa, FL 33637

Phone: (888) 929-4222   **Domicile State:** FL   **NAIC Code:** 12813

Data Date	Rating	RACR #1	RACR #2	Loss Ratio %	Total Assets ($mil)	Capital ($mil)	Net Premium ($mil)	Net Income ($mil)
2017	B+	3.38	2.67	86.7	377.9	165.9	197.6	-5.9
2016	B	3.61	2.69	65.7	373.2	173.3	186.1	18.3
2015	C+	3.30	2.45	61.9	347.4	153.1	175.9	19.9
2014	C	3.02	2.24	60.4	318.1	133.6	166.3	19.8
2013	C	2.78	2.08	61.3	281.2	114.3	153.1	12.3

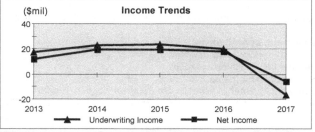
Income Trends

AUTO-OWNERS INS CO *   A   Excellent

Major Rating Factors: Strong long-term capitalization index (8.6 on a scale of 0 to 10) based on excellent current risk adjusted capital (severe and moderate loss scenarios). Furthermore, this high level of risk adjusted capital has been consistently maintained in previous years. Excellent profitability (8.1) with operating gains in each of the last five years.

Other Rating Factors: Excellent overall results on stability tests (7.5). Stability strengths include excellent operational trends and excellent risk diversification. History of adequate reserve strength (6.2) as reserves have been consistently at an acceptable level. Good liquidity (6.8) with sufficient resources (cash flows and marketable investments) to handle a spike in claims.

Principal Business: Homeowners multiple peril (35%), auto liability (19%), auto physical damage (12%), commercial multiple peril (9%), fire (8%), other liability (6%), and other lines (11%).

Principal Investments: Investment grade bonds (50%), misc. investments (49%), non investment grade bonds (1%), and real estate (1%).

Investments in Affiliates: 28%

Group Affiliation: Auto-Owners Group

Licensed in: AL, AZ, AR, CO, FL, GA, ID, IL, IN, IA, KS, KY, MI, MN, MS, MO, NE, NV, NM, NC, ND, OH, OR, PA, SC, SD, TN, UT, VA, WA, WI

Commenced Business: July 1916

Address: 6101 ANACAPRI BOULEVARD, Lansing, MI 48917-3968

Phone: (517) 323-1200   **Domicile State:** MI   **NAIC Code:** 18988

Data Date	Rating	RACR #1	RACR #2	Loss Ratio %	Total Assets ($mil)	Capital ($mil)	Net Premium ($mil)	Net Income ($mil)
2017	A	2.39	2.06	59.0	15,390.4	10,633.7	3,576.5	445.0
2016	A-	2.35	2.05	52.4	14,313.5	9,690.1	3,219.4	454.9
2015	A-	2.44	2.12	51.7	13,117.6	8,777.0	2,873.1	476.6
2014	A-	2.42	2.10	63.1	12,207.7	7,969.1	2,541.0	344.2
2013	A	2.42	2.08	60.9	11,392.8	7,510.8	2,325.4	340.3

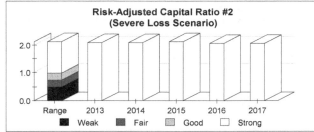
Risk-Adjusted Capital Ratio #2
(Severe Loss Scenario)

AUTOMOBILE INS CO OF HARTFORD CT   B   Good

Major Rating Factors: Good liquidity (6.8 on a scale of 0 to 10) with sufficient resources (cash flows and marketable investments) to handle a spike in claims. Good overall results on stability tests (6.0). Affiliation with Travelers Companies Inc is a strength.

Other Rating Factors: Fair profitability index (4.4). Fair expense controls. Return on equity has been fair, averaging 12.1% over the past five years. Strong long-term capitalization index (8.3) based on excellent current risk adjusted capital (severe and moderate loss scenarios), despite some fluctuation in capital levels. Ample reserve history (8.3) that helps to protect the company against sharp claims increases.

Principal Business: Homeowners multiple peril (40%), auto liability (14%), fire (13%), other liability (12%), auto physical damage (11%), allied lines (10%), and inland marine (1%).

Principal Investments: Investment grade bonds (99%) and misc. investments (1%).

Investments in Affiliates: None

Group Affiliation: Travelers Companies Inc

Licensed in: All states except CA, PR

Commenced Business: August 1968

Address: ONE TOWER SQUARE, Hartford, CT 6183

Phone: (860) 277-0111   **Domicile State:** CT   **NAIC Code:** 19062

Data Date	Rating	RACR #1	RACR #2	Loss Ratio %	Total Assets ($mil)	Capital ($mil)	Net Premium ($mil)	Net Income ($mil)
2017	B	2.77	1.84	69.5	1,028.4	305.9	312.8	22.8
2016	B	2.90	1.89	63.4	1,006.6	316.4	298.3	35.6
2015	B	2.97	1.89	58.7	1,000.8	322.4	284.7	43.1
2014	B	2.97	1.87	60.5	1,013.2	320.8	276.6	43.1
2013	B	2.99	1.90	60.9	1,002.2	317.3	275.9	47.3

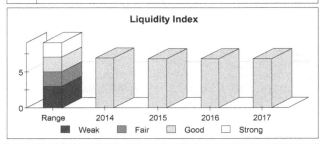
Liquidity Index

AXIS INS CO   B   Good

Major Rating Factors: Good overall results on stability tests (5.2 on a scale of 0 to 10) despite potential drain of affiliation with AXIS Specialty Ltd and negative cash flow from operations for 2017. History of adequate reserve strength (6.9) as reserves have been consistently at an acceptable level.

Other Rating Factors: Good liquidity (6.7) with sufficient resources (cash flows and marketable investments) to handle a spike in claims. Fair profitability index (3.1) with operating losses during 2013, 2014 and 2017. Return on equity has been low, averaging 0.1% over the past five years. Strong long-term capitalization index (7.7) based on excellent current risk adjusted capital (severe and moderate loss scenarios), despite some fluctuation in capital levels.

Principal Business: Other liability (61%), group accident & health (14%), commercial multiple peril (4%), inland marine (4%), allied lines (4%), auto liability (3%), and other lines (11%).

Principal Investments: Investment grade bonds (76%) and misc. investments (24%).

Investments in Affiliates: 21%

Group Affiliation: AXIS Specialty Ltd

Licensed in: All states except PR

Commenced Business: November 1979

Address: 111 South Wacker Dr Ste 3500, Chicago, IL 60606

Phone: (678) 746-9400   **Domicile State:** IL   **NAIC Code:** 37273

Data Date	Rating	RACR #1	RACR #2	Loss Ratio %	Total Assets ($mil)	Capital ($mil)	Net Premium ($mil)	Net Income ($mil)
2017	B	2.05	1.59	77.0	1,465.3	544.7	336.8	-29.8
2016	B	2.05	1.58	68.0	1,505.4	574.5	313.7	13.9
2015	B	1.96	1.29	62.2	1,488.0	565.1	307.5	32.1
2014	C+	1.91	1.28	78.0	1,483.8	578.1	282.3	-2.1
2013	C+	1.79	1.25	80.0	1,366.0	526.2	306.8	-10.1

Rating Indexes

Ranges   Cap. 2   Stab.   Res.   Prof.   Liq.
■ Weak   ■ Fair   □ Good   □ Strong

AXIS REINS CO   C+   Fair

Major Rating Factors: Fair overall results on stability tests (4.2 on a scale of 0 to 10) including potential drain of affiliation with AXIS Specialty Ltd and negative cash flow from operations for 2017. Fair profitability index (4.6) with operating losses during 2017. Return on equity has been low, averaging 3.1% over the past five years.

Other Rating Factors: Good liquidity (6.8) with sufficient resources (cash flows and marketable investments) to handle a spike in claims. Strong long-term capitalization index (7.8) based on excellent current risk adjusted capital (severe and moderate loss scenarios), despite some fluctuation in capital levels. Ample reserve history (9.3) that helps to protect the company against sharp claims increases.

Principal Business: Other liability (89%), allied lines (4%), fidelity (3%), and medical malpractice (2%).

Principal Investments: Investment grade bonds (66%), misc. investments (26%), non investment grade bonds (6%), and cash (2%).

Investments in Affiliates: None

Group Affiliation: AXIS Specialty Ltd

Licensed in: All states, the District of Columbia and Puerto Rico

Commenced Business: January 1992

Address: 1211 Ave of Americas 24th Fl, New York, NY 10036

Phone: (678) 746-9400   **Domicile State:** NY   **NAIC Code:** 20370

Data Date	Rating	RACR #1	RACR #2	Loss Ratio %	Total Assets ($mil)	Capital ($mil)	Net Premium ($mil)	Net Income ($mil)
2017	C+	2.60	1.55	79.1	3,227.4	966.8	612.5	-9.8
2016	C+	2.68	1.63	71.3	3,003.2	896.2	531.8	17.2
2015	C+	2.69	1.64	68.1	2,863.3	860.9	513.4	24.6
2014	C+	2.63	1.62	73.7	2,872.8	864.9	528.4	40.5
2013	C+	2.74	1.71	57.8	2,675.9	822.7	494.2	58.0

Rating Indexes

Ranges   Cap. 2   Stab.   Res.   Prof.   Liq.
■ Weak   ■ Fair   □ Good   □ Strong

BAY STATE INS CO   B-   Good

Major Rating Factors: Fair overall results on stability tests (4.8 on a scale of 0 to 10) including potential drain of affiliation with Andover Group. Strong long-term capitalization index (7.9) based on excellent current risk adjusted capital (severe and moderate loss scenarios), despite some fluctuation in capital levels.

Other Rating Factors: Ample reserve history (7.5) that can protect against increases in claims costs. Excellent profitability (7.9) with operating gains in each of the last five years. Excellent liquidity (7.0) with ample operational cash flow and liquid investments.

Principal Business: Homeowners multiple peril (84%), commercial multiple peril (6%), other liability (5%), and inland marine (4%).

Principal Investments: Misc. investments (87%), investment grade bonds (7%), and cash (6%).

Investments in Affiliates: None

Group Affiliation: Andover Group

Licensed in: CT, IL, ME, MA, NH, NJ, NY, RI

Commenced Business: July 1955

Address: 95 Old River Road, Andover, MA 01810-1078

Phone: (978) 475-3300   **Domicile State:** MA   **NAIC Code:** 19763

Data Date	Rating	RACR #1	RACR #2	Loss Ratio %	Total Assets ($mil)	Capital ($mil)	Net Premium ($mil)	Net Income ($mil)
2017	B-	2.67	1.63	64.3	573.2	367.9	84.4	10.8
2016	B-	3.13	1.89	50.9	476.0	300.0	80.9	15.3
2015	B-	3.23	1.95	68.5	450.4	284.5	77.8	4.8
2014	B-	3.17	1.93	43.4	456.7	287.3	78.5	15.9
2013	B-	3.33	2.06	43.3	412.6	260.3	73.9	16.6

($mil)   Capital

2013   2014   2015   2016   2017

BERKLEY INS CO

B **Good**

Major Rating Factors: Good overall results on stability tests (5.2 on a scale of 0 to 10) despite potential drain of affiliation with W R Berkley Corp. Good liquidity (6.7) with sufficient resources (cash flows and marketable investments) to handle a spike in claims.

Other Rating Factors: Strong long-term capitalization index (7.2) based on excellent current risk adjusted capital (severe and moderate loss scenarios), despite some fluctuation in capital levels. Ample reserve history (7.9) that can protect against increases in claims costs. Excellent profitability (7.0) with operating gains in each of the last five years. Return on equity has been excellent over the last five years averaging 16.7%.

Principal Business: Other liability (74%), surety (17%), other accident & health (5%), auto liability (1%), and medical malpractice (1%).

Principal Investments: Investment grade bonds (55%), misc. investments (42%), non investment grade bonds (2%), and real estate (1%).

Investments in Affiliates: 21%

Group Affiliation: W R Berkley Corp

Licensed in: All states, the District of Columbia and Puerto Rico

Commenced Business: December 1975

Address: 1209 Orange Street, Wilmington, DE 19801

Phone: (203) 542-3800   **Domicile State:** DE   **NAIC Code:** 32603

Data Date	Rating	RACR #1	RACR #2	Loss Ratio %	Total Assets ($mil)	Capital ($mil)	Net Premium ($mil)	Net Income ($mil)
2017	B	1.38	1.16	60.4	18,358.6	5,479.6	5,594.5	698.9
2016	B	1.47	1.24	60.6	17,940.5	5,493.0	5,711.5	702.8
2015	C+	1.44	1.17	56.5	17,109.3	5,295.6	5,338.8	765.4
2014	C	1.40	1.15	59.3	16,934.1	5,437.2	5,070.0	710.5
2013	C	1.38	1.09	61.6	16,122.7	4,907.2	5,744.1	1,493.8

BERKLEY REGIONAL INS CO

C+ **Fair**

Major Rating Factors: Fair overall results on stability tests (4.4 on a scale of 0 to 10) including fair financial strength of affiliated W R Berkley Corp.

Other Rating Factors: Strong long-term capitalization index (8.1) based on excellent current risk adjusted capital (severe and moderate loss scenarios), despite some fluctuation in capital levels. Excellent profitability (7.7) with operating gains in each of the last five years. Superior liquidity (10.0) with ample operational cash flow and liquid investments.

Principal Business: Workers compensation (25%), fidelity (25%), auto liability (17%), commercial multiple peril (15%), auto physical damage (7%), burglary & theft (4%), and other lines (7%).

Principal Investments: Misc. investments (54%) and investment grade bonds (46%).

Investments in Affiliates: 48%

Group Affiliation: W R Berkley Corp

Licensed in: All states except PR

Commenced Business: January 1987

Address: 1209 Orange Street, Wilmington, DE 19801

Phone: (515) 473-3000   **Domicile State:** DE   **NAIC Code:** 29580

Data Date	Rating	RACR #1	RACR #2	Loss Ratio %	Total Assets ($mil)	Capital ($mil)	Net Premium ($mil)	Net Income ($mil)
2017	C+	1.58	1.74	0.0	762.9	728.0	0.0	13.2
2016	C+	1.61	1.77	0.0	748.2	706.9	0.0	13.0
2015	C+	1.73	1.88	0.0	711.6	679.9	0.0	11.6
2014	C+	1.75	1.90	0.0	700.4	666.6	0.0	11.0
2013	C+	1.89	2.08	0.0	681.2	643.2	-547.4	134.5

BERKSHIRE HATHAWAY ASR CORP *

A+ **Excellent**

Major Rating Factors: Strong long-term capitalization index (9.4 on a scale of 0 to 10) based on excellent current risk adjusted capital (severe and moderate loss scenarios). Furthermore, this high level of risk adjusted capital has been consistently maintained in previous years. Excellent profitability (8.7) with operating gains in each of the last five years. Return on equity has been good over the last five years, averaging 12.6%.

Other Rating Factors: Superior liquidity (10.0) with ample operational cash flow and liquid investments. Excellent overall results on stability tests (7.2). Stability strengths include excellent risk diversification. Fair reserve development (4.6) as reserves have generally been sufficient to cover claims.

Principal Business: Financial guaranty (97%) and surety (3%).

Principal Investments: Misc. investments (66%), investment grade bonds (33%), and cash (1%).

Investments in Affiliates: None

Group Affiliation: Berkshire-Hathaway

Licensed in: All states, the District of Columbia and Puerto Rico

Commenced Business: December 2007

Address: Marine Air Terminal LaGuardia, Flushing, NY 11371

Phone: (402) 916-3000   **Domicile State:** NY   **NAIC Code:** 13070

Data Date	Rating	RACR #1	RACR #2	Loss Ratio %	Total Assets ($mil)	Capital ($mil)	Net Premium ($mil)	Net Income ($mil)
2017	A+	4.46	2.66	20.0	2,223.5	1,799.8	9.0	421.3
2016	A+	4.56	2.73	9.7	2,351.4	1,793.8	2.9	254.1
2015	A+	4.18	2.50	N/A	2,176.5	1,449.3	12.9	78.1
2014	A+	4.11	2.46	1.7	2,275.7	1,459.6	2.3	95.2
2013	A+	4.45	2.64	31.1	2,255.6	1,426.8	12.4	195.5

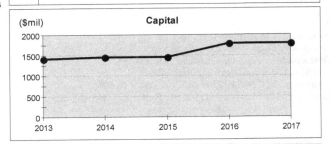

BERKSHIRE HATHAWAY HOMESTATE INS   C+   Fair

Major Rating Factors: Fair overall results on stability tests (4.4 on a scale of 0 to 10) including potential drain of affiliation with Berkshire-Hathaway. Strong long-term capitalization index (7.7) based on excellent current risk adjusted capital (severe and moderate loss scenarios). Moreover, capital levels have been consistent in recent years.

Other Rating Factors: Ample reserve history (8.1) that helps to protect the company against sharp claims increases. Excellent profitability (8.3) with operating gains in each of the last five years. Excellent liquidity (8.3) with ample operational cash flow and liquid investments.

Principal Business: Workers compensation (69%), auto liability (16%), commercial multiple peril (8%), auto physical damage (4%), allied lines (2%), fire (2%), and inland marine (1%).

Principal Investments: Misc. investments (68%), investment grade bonds (21%), and cash (11%).

Investments in Affiliates: None

Group Affiliation: Berkshire-Hathaway

Licensed in: All states except PR

Commenced Business: February 1970

Address: 1314 DOUGLAS ST STE 1300, Omaha, NE 68102-1944

Phone: (402) 393-7255   **Domicile State:** NE   **NAIC Code:** 20044

Data Date	Rating	RACR #1	RACR #2	Loss Ratio %	Total Assets ($mil)	Capital ($mil)	Net Premium ($mil)	Net Income ($mil)
2017	C+	2.92	1.69	61.1	2,938.5	1,660.7	494.0	272.7
2016	C+	2.38	1.41	87.4	2,467.2	1,257.5	441.4	4.0
2015	C+	2.69	1.62	70.4	2,175.0	1,167.7	461.5	55.7
2014	C+	1.63	1.04	64.5	2,008.1	1,159.5	376.5	152.7
2013	C+	1.23	0.80	77.8	1,587.5	963.8	280.1	22.4

Rating Indexes

BERKSHIRE HATHAWAY SPECIALTY INS CO   C+   Fair

Major Rating Factors: Fair reserve development (4.6 on a scale of 0 to 10) as reserves have generally been sufficient to cover claims. Fair profitability index (4.0) with operating losses during 2016. Return on equity has been low, averaging 0.2% over the past five years.

Other Rating Factors: Fair overall results on stability tests (4.6) including fair financial strength of affiliated Berkshire-Hathaway, excessive premium growth and weak results on operational trends. Strong long-term capitalization index (9.4) based on excellent current risk adjusted capital (severe and moderate loss scenarios), despite some fluctuation in capital levels. Superior liquidity (9.6) with ample operational cash flow and liquid investments.

Principal Business: Other liability (52%), other accident & health (9%), surety (5%), auto liability (5%), commercial multiple peril (5%), inland marine (5%), and other lines (19%).

Principal Investments: Misc. investments (63%), investment grade bonds (25%), and cash (12%).

Investments in Affiliates: None

Group Affiliation: Berkshire-Hathaway

Licensed in: All states except PR

Commenced Business: February 1866

Address: 1314 Douglas Street Suite 1400, Omaha, NE 68102-1944

Phone: (402) 916-3000   **Domicile State:** NE   **NAIC Code:** 22276

Data Date	Rating	RACR #1	RACR #2	Loss Ratio %	Total Assets ($mil)	Capital ($mil)	Net Premium ($mil)	Net Income ($mil)
2017	C+	4.65	2.79	84.6	4,950.5	3,749.6	356.0	46.3
2016	C+	4.47	2.69	70.5	4,086.5	3,337.1	267.4	-58.0
2015	C+	4.32	2.60	75.7	3,371.6	3,044.1	95.5	37.7
2014	C+	4.11	2.46	N/A	3,521.6	3,234.1	0.7	7.6
2013	C+	3.20	1.92	156.6	3,357.7	3,106.7	1.6	0.2

Reserve Deficiency (as % of capital)

* Adequate & redundant reserves show as negatives

BITCO GENERAL INS CORP   B   Good

Major Rating Factors: Good overall profitability index (6.7 on a scale of 0 to 10). Good expense controls. Return on equity has been good over the last five years, averaging 10.4%. Good liquidity (6.6) with sufficient resources (cash flows and marketable investments) to handle a spike in claims.

Other Rating Factors: Good overall results on stability tests (6.2) despite excessive premium growth. Strong long-term capitalization index (7.8) based on excellent current risk adjusted capital (severe and moderate loss scenarios), despite some fluctuation in capital levels. Ample reserve history (8.5) that helps to protect the company against sharp claims increases.

Principal Business: Workers compensation (36%), auto liability (21%), commercial multiple peril (18%), other liability (10%), auto physical damage (8%), and inland marine (6%).

Principal Investments: Investment grade bonds (70%), misc. investments (26%), and non investment grade bonds (4%).

Investments in Affiliates: None

Group Affiliation: Old Republic Group

Licensed in: All states except HI, NH, PR

Commenced Business: August 1928

Address: 307 N MICHIGAN AVE, Chicago, IL 60601

Phone: (800) 475-4477   **Domicile State:** IL   **NAIC Code:** 20095

Data Date	Rating	RACR #1	RACR #2	Loss Ratio %	Total Assets ($mil)	Capital ($mil)	Net Premium ($mil)	Net Income ($mil)
2017	B	2.40	1.53	74.1	943.6	293.6	356.3	15.7
2016	B	3.13	1.92	72.5	851.8	295.6	231.5	24.1
2015	B	3.08	1.95	71.9	820.8	275.1	237.6	27.2
2014	B	3.45	2.20	71.2	810.9	288.5	230.2	42.5
2013	A-	3.87	2.49	67.2	788.4	290.2	204.3	39.5

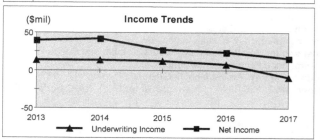

Income Trends

BRICKSTREET MUTUAL INS CO   B   Good

Major Rating Factors: Good liquidity (6.9 on a scale of 0 to 10) with sufficient resources (cash flows and marketable investments) to handle a spike in claims. Good overall results on stability tests (5.5).
Other Rating Factors: Strong long-term capitalization index (8.1) based on excellent current risk adjusted capital (severe and moderate loss scenarios). Moreover, capital has steadily grown over the last five years. Ample reserve history (9.5) that helps to protect the company against sharp claims increases. Excellent profitability (8.4) with operating gains in each of the last five years.
Principal Business: Workers compensation (100%).
Principal Investments: Investment grade bonds (84%), misc. investments (13%), cash (2%), and real estate (1%).
Investments in Affiliates: 3%
Group Affiliation: BrickStreet Mutual Ins
Licensed in: AL, DC, DE, GA, IL, IN, IA, KS, KY, MD, MI, MO, NJ, NC, PA, SC, TN, VA, WV
Commenced Business: January 2006
Address: 400 Quarrier St, Charleston, WV 25301
Phone: (304) 941-1000   **Domicile State:** WV   **NAIC Code:** 12372

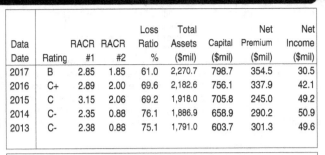

Data Date	Rating	RACR #1	RACR #2	Loss Ratio %	Total Assets ($mil)	Capital ($mil)	Net Premium ($mil)	Net Income ($mil)
2017	B	2.85	1.85	61.0	2,270.7	798.7	354.5	30.5
2016	C+	2.89	2.00	69.6	2,182.6	756.1	337.9	42.1
2015	C	3.15	2.06	69.2	1,918.0	705.8	245.0	49.2
2014	C-	2.35	0.88	76.1	1,886.9	658.9	290.2	50.9
2013	C-	2.38	0.88	75.1	1,791.0	603.7	301.3	49.6

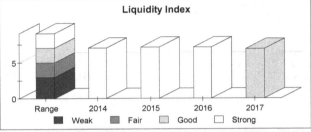

Liquidity Index

BROTHERHOOD MUTUAL INS CO *   B+   Good

Major Rating Factors: Good liquidity (5.1 on a scale of 0 to 10) with sufficient resources (cash flows and marketable investments) to handle a spike in claims. Good overall results on stability tests (6.5).
Other Rating Factors: Strong long-term capitalization index (8.0) based on excellent current risk adjusted capital (severe and moderate loss scenarios). Moreover, capital has steadily grown over the last five years. Excellent profitability (8.3) with operating gains in each of the last five years. Fair reserve development (4.3) as reserves have generally been sufficient to cover claims.
Principal Business: Commercial multiple peril (73%), workers compensation (13%), auto liability (5%), other liability (4%), boiler & machinery (3%), and auto physical damage (2%).
Principal Investments: Misc. investments (47%), investment grade bonds (44%), real estate (5%), and cash (4%).
Investments in Affiliates: None
Group Affiliation: None
Licensed in: All states except PR
Commenced Business: November 1935
Address: 6400 Brotherhood Way, Fort Wayne, IN 46825
Phone: (260) 482-8668   **Domicile State:** IN   **NAIC Code:** 13528

Data Date	Rating	RACR #1	RACR #2	Loss Ratio %	Total Assets ($mil)	Capital ($mil)	Net Premium ($mil)	Net Income ($mil)
2017	B+	2.20	1.65	66.4	644.9	266.2	361.8	8.7
2016	B+	2.17	1.67	62.2	600.7	244.7	341.1	12.2
2015	B	2.35	1.83	61.0	542.0	229.1	304.9	19.1
2014	B	2.02	1.54	66.2	469.7	189.4	277.3	10.0
2013	A-	2.01	1.53	64.5	443.3	178.2	252.5	9.5

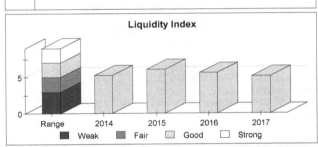

Liquidity Index

BUILD AMERICA MUTUAL ASR CO   C-   Fair

Major Rating Factors: Weak profitability index (2.5) with operating losses during each of the last five years.
Other Rating Factors: Fair overall results on stability tests (3.0) including excessive premium growth, weak results on operational trends and negative cash flow from operations for 2017. Strong long-term capitalization index (10.0) based on excellent current risk adjusted capital (severe and moderate loss scenarios), despite some fluctuation in capital levels. Superior liquidity (10.0) with ample operational cash flow and liquid investments.
Principal Business: Financial guaranty (100%).
Principal Investments: Investment grade bonds (92%), cash (5%), and misc. investments (3%).
Investments in Affiliates: None
Group Affiliation: None
Licensed in: All states except PR
Commenced Business: July 2012
Address: 200 Liberty St 27th Floor, New York, NY 10281
Phone: (212) 235-2500   **Domicile State:** NY   **NAIC Code:** 14380

Data Date	Rating	RACR #1	RACR #2	Loss Ratio %	Total Assets ($mil)	Capital ($mil)	Net Premium ($mil)	Net Income ($mil)
2017	C-	12.42	11.74	0.0	515.0	427.3	8.6	-25.4
2016	D+	10.89	10.36	0.0	496.7	431.5	11.4	-32.7
2015	D+	11.84	11.38	0.0	479.6	437.3	6.3	-32.0
2014	D+	12.00	11.69	0.0	475.7	448.8	3.6	-31.8
2013	D+	14.08	13.68	0.0	486.5	469.0	3.0	-29.3

Rating Indexes

BUILDERS INS (A MUTUAL CAPTIVE CO)   C   Fair

Major Rating Factors: Fair overall results on stability tests (3.5 on a scale of 0 to 10) including potential drain of affiliation with Builders Financial Group Inc. Good liquidity (6.9) with sufficient resources (cash flows and marketable investments) to handle a spike in claims.

Other Rating Factors: Strong long-term capitalization index (8.1) based on excellent current risk adjusted capital (severe and moderate loss scenarios). Moreover, capital has steadily grown over the last five years. Ample reserve history (9.3) that helps to protect the company against sharp claims increases. Excellent profitability (8.6) with operating gains in each of the last five years.

Principal Business: Workers compensation (80%), other liability (12%), and commercial multiple peril (8%).

Principal Investments: Investment grade bonds (66%), misc. investments (31%), real estate (2%), and cash (1%).

Investments in Affiliates: 12%

Group Affiliation: Builders Financial Group Inc

Licensed in: DE, FL, GA, NC, TX

Commenced Business: July 1996

Address: 2410 Paces Ferry Road Ste 300, Atlanta, GA 30339-1802

Phone: (678) 309-4000   **Domicile State:** GA   **NAIC Code:** 10704

Data Date	Rating	RACR #1	RACR #2	Loss Ratio %	Total Assets ($mil)	Capital ($mil)	Net Premium ($mil)	Net Income ($mil)
2017	C	2.44	1.84	62.2	634.4	280.7	168.6	16.8
2016	C	2.40	1.84	59.5	579.3	254.9	154.8	17.6
2015	C	2.30	1.77	54.6	518.1	227.3	144.7	19.9
2014	C	1.96	1.47	62.9	482.6	201.8	141.3	13.9
2013	C	1.78	1.34	69.8	441.6	185.9	125.9	7.2

Rating Indexes

BUILDERS MUTUAL INS CO *   A   Excellent

Major Rating Factors: Strong long-term capitalization index (8.0 on a scale of 0 to 10) based on excellent current risk adjusted capital (severe and moderate loss scenarios). Furthermore, this high level of risk adjusted capital has been consistently maintained in previous years. Excellent profitability (8.8) with operating gains in each of the last five years.

Other Rating Factors: Excellent overall results on stability tests (7.5). Stability strengths include excellent operational trends and excellent risk diversification. History of adequate reserve strength (6.7) as reserves have been consistently at an acceptable level. Good liquidity (6.7) with sufficient resources (cash flows and marketable investments) to handle a spike in claims.

Principal Business: Workers compensation (75%), commercial multiple peril (12%), products liability (4%), other liability (3%), inland marine (3%), auto liability (2%), and auto physical damage (1%).

Principal Investments: Investment grade bonds (69%), misc. investments (27%), cash (2%), and real estate (2%).

Investments in Affiliates: 2%

Group Affiliation: Builders Group

Licensed in: DC, FL, GA, MD, MS, NC, SC, TN, VA, WI

Commenced Business: September 1997

Address: 5580 Centerview Drive, Raleigh, NC 27606

Phone: (919) 845-1976   **Domicile State:** NC   **NAIC Code:** 10844

Data Date	Rating	RACR #1	RACR #2	Loss Ratio %	Total Assets ($mil)	Capital ($mil)	Net Premium ($mil)	Net Income ($mil)
2017	A	2.52	1.78	54.9	859.6	358.2	307.2	41.8
2016	A-	2.25	1.62	63.9	779.8	310.0	284.3	19.6
2015	B+	2.37	1.72	63.1	701.7	281.6	246.8	19.9
2014	B+	2.29	1.63	62.3	638.7	262.6	215.5	18.3
2013	B+	2.24	1.56	61.5	576.4	242.0	181.7	13.4

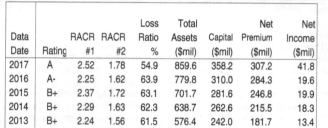

Risk-Adjusted Capital Ratio #2
(Severe Loss Scenario)

CALIFORNIA CASUALTY INDEMNITY EXCH   C+   Fair

Major Rating Factors: Fair overall results on stability tests (4.4 on a scale of 0 to 10) including negative cash flow from operations for 2017. History of adequate reserve strength (6.1) as reserves have been consistently at an acceptable level.

Other Rating Factors: Good liquidity (5.0) with sufficient resources (cash flows and marketable investments) to handle a spike in claims. Weak profitability index (2.2) with operating losses during 2014, 2015, 2016 and 2017. Strong long-term capitalization index (7.7) based on excellent current risk adjusted capital (severe and moderate loss scenarios), despite some fluctuation in capital levels.

Principal Business: Auto physical damage (38%), auto liability (37%), and homeowners multiple peril (25%).

Principal Investments: Investment grade bonds (55%) and misc. investments (47%).

Investments in Affiliates: 30%

Group Affiliation: California Casualty Ins Group

Licensed in: All states except MI, NJ, PR

Commenced Business: January 1914

Address: 1900 Alameda de las Pulgas, San Mateo, CA 94403-1298

Phone: (650) 574-4000   **Domicile State:** CA   **NAIC Code:** 20117

Data Date	Rating	RACR #1	RACR #2	Loss Ratio %	Total Assets ($mil)	Capital ($mil)	Net Premium ($mil)	Net Income ($mil)
2017	C+	1.73	1.45	88.4	575.9	241.6	250.8	-22.8
2016	C+	1.83	1.60	81.6	582.8	273.0	242.1	-7.0
2015	C+	1.87	1.63	84.1	582.3	284.3	238.6	-26.7
2014	C+	2.10	1.89	82.5	557.6	319.1	163.8	-6.2
2013	C+	2.08	1.88	79.4	571.8	336.5	158.7	2.6

Rating Indexes

CALIFORNIA INS CO   B   Good

Major Rating Factors: Good overall results on stability tests (5.4 on a scale of 0 to 10). Stability strengths include good operational trends and excellent risk diversification. History of adequate reserve strength (6.2) as reserves have been consistently at an acceptable level.

Other Rating Factors: Strong long-term capitalization index (9.8) based on excellent current risk adjusted capital (severe and moderate loss scenarios). Moreover, capital has steadily grown over the last five years. Excellent profitability (8.9) with operating gains in each of the last five years. Return on equity has been excellent over the last five years averaging 15.5%. Excellent liquidity (7.9) with ample operational cash flow and liquid investments.

Principal Business: Workers compensation (97%), surety (2%), other liability (1%), and aggregate write-ins for other lines of business (1%).

Principal Investments: Investment grade bonds (81%), misc. investments (15%), and cash (4%).

Investments in Affiliates: None

Group Affiliation: Berkshire-Hathaway

Licensed in: AK, AZ, CA, CT, GA, HI, ID, IL, IN, IA, KS, MD, MO, MT, NV, NJ, NY, NC, ND, OR, PA, TX, UT, VA, WA, WI

Commenced Business: June 1980

Address: 950 Tower Lane 14th Floor, Foster City, CA 94404

Phone: (402) 827-3424   **Domicile State:** CA   **NAIC Code:** 38865

Data Date	Rating	RACR #1	RACR #2	Loss Ratio %	Total Assets ($mil)	Capital ($mil)	Net Premium ($mil)	Net Income ($mil)
2017	B	4.18	3.32	50.0	1,021.4	622.6	307.5	97.2
2016	B	3.63	2.80	43.7	851.1	528.7	255.0	55.0
2015	B-	3.67	2.96	21.1	751.2	468.8	255.3	88.5
2014	B-	2.95	2.30	30.1	631.7	379.8	241.6	65.5
2013	B-	3.98	2.18	32.2	521.1	317.4	186.9	48.9

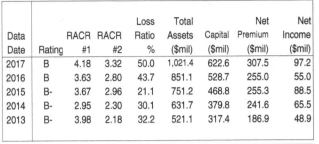

Rating Indexes

CAMBRIDGE MUTUAL FIRE INS CO   B-   Good

Major Rating Factors: Fair overall results on stability tests (4.8 on a scale of 0 to 10) including potential drain of affiliation with Andover Group. Strong long-term capitalization index (8.0) based on excellent current risk adjusted capital (severe and moderate loss scenarios), despite some fluctuation in capital levels.

Other Rating Factors: Ample reserve history (7.6) that can protect against increases in claims costs. Excellent profitability (7.0). Excellent liquidity (7.1) with ample operational cash flow and liquid investments.

Principal Business: Homeowners multiple peril (58%), commercial multiple peril (18%), fire (9%), allied lines (7%), other liability (7%), and inland marine (2%).

Principal Investments: Misc. investments (80%), cash (11%), and investment grade bonds (9%).

Investments in Affiliates: None

Group Affiliation: Andover Group

Licensed in: CT, IL, ME, MA, NH, NJ, NY, RI

Commenced Business: January 1834

Address: 95 Old River Road, Andover, MA 01810-1078

Phone: (978) 475-3300   **Domicile State:** MA   **NAIC Code:** 19771

Data Date	Rating	RACR #1	RACR #2	Loss Ratio %	Total Assets ($mil)	Capital ($mil)	Net Premium ($mil)	Net Income ($mil)
2017	B-	2.66	1.67	64.3	1,012.4	579.5	197.0	56.7
2016	B-	3.32	2.04	50.9	877.5	512.7	188.8	39.4
2015	B-	3.40	2.08	68.5	805.2	474.1	181.5	-9.3
2014	B-	3.23	1.99	43.4	830.2	479.0	183.3	30.1
2013	B-	3.15	2.01	43.3	738.7	421.9	172.5	51.3

Capital

CANAL INS CO   B   Good

Major Rating Factors: Good overall results on stability tests (5.8 on a scale of 0 to 10) despite potential drain of affiliation with Canal Group and negative cash flow from operations for 2017. Good overall profitability index (5.6). Fair expense controls. Return on equity has been low, averaging 3.4% over the past five years.

Other Rating Factors: Fair reserve development (4.9) as reserves have generally been sufficient to cover claims. Strong long-term capitalization index (8.5) based on excellent current risk adjusted capital (severe and moderate loss scenarios), despite some fluctuation in capital levels. Excellent liquidity (7.0) with ample operational cash flow and liquid investments.

Principal Business: Auto liability (72%), auto physical damage (21%), inland marine (6%), and other liability (1%).

Principal Investments: Misc. investments (49%), investment grade bonds (43%), non investment grade bonds (4%), cash (2%), and real estate (2%).

Investments in Affiliates: 6%

Group Affiliation: Canal Group

Licensed in: All states except AK, HI, PR

Commenced Business: March 1939

Address: 400 East Stone Ave, Greenville, SC 29601

Phone: (864) 242-5365   **Domicile State:** SC   **NAIC Code:** 10464

Data Date	Rating	RACR #1	RACR #2	Loss Ratio %	Total Assets ($mil)	Capital ($mil)	Net Premium ($mil)	Net Income ($mil)
2017	B	3.01	2.07	75.6	827.7	453.6	219.4	22.8
2016	B	2.95	2.01	82.9	819.0	439.7	210.0	10.3
2015	B	2.88	2.01	71.6	787.0	428.0	185.5	20.0
2014	B	2.69	1.92	76.9	818.8	447.2	177.4	20.3
2013	B	2.63	1.89	86.6	849.0	444.8	191.9	1.7

Rating Indexes

CAPITOL INDEMNITY CORP

C   Fair

Major Rating Factors: Fair reserve development (4.8 on a scale of 0 to 10) as reserves have generally been sufficient to cover claims. Fair overall results on stability tests (4.1) including fair financial strength of affiliated Alleghany Corp Group.

Other Rating Factors: Good overall profitability index (5.7) despite operating losses during 2013 and 2014. Return on equity has been low, averaging 0.6% over the past five years. Good liquidity (6.7) with sufficient resources (cash flows and marketable investments) to handle a spike in claims. Strong long-term capitalization index (7.3) based on excellent current risk adjusted capital (severe and moderate loss scenarios). Moreover, capital levels have been consistent in recent years.

Principal Business: Commercial multiple peril (47%), other liability (31%), surety (10%), auto liability (7%), auto physical damage (2%), products liability (1%), and other lines (3%).

Principal Investments: Misc. investments (57%), investment grade bonds (42%), and non investment grade bonds (1%).

Investments in Affiliates: 20%

Group Affiliation: Alleghany Corp Group

Licensed in: All states except PR

Commenced Business: June 1960

Address: 1600 Aspen Commons, Middleton, WI 53562-4718

Phone: (608) 829-4200   **Domicile State:** WI   **NAIC Code:** 10472

Data Date	Rating	RACR #1	RACR #2	Loss Ratio %	Total Assets ($mil)	Capital ($mil)	Net Premium ($mil)	Net Income ($mil)
2017	C	1.58	1.18	55.6	592.8	265.3	189.8	11.2
2016	C	1.56	1.18	53.1	520.0	234.2	175.0	8.5
2015	C	1.55	1.18	54.8	478.8	225.5	154.2	5.1
2014	C	1.58	1.21	55.8	462.4	221.9	134.7	-0.9
2013	C	1.69	1.18	65.6	411.2	172.9	120.0	-11.3

Reserve Deficiency (as % of capital)

* Adequate & redundant reserves show as negatives

■ 1 Yr Dev   □ 2 Yr Dev

CASTLE KEY INS CO *

B+   Good

Major Rating Factors: History of adequate reserve strength (6.4 on a scale of 0 to 10) as reserves have been consistently at an acceptable level. Good liquidity (6.7) with sufficient resources (cash flows and marketable investments) to handle a spike in claims.

Other Rating Factors: Good overall results on stability tests (6.4) despite negative cash flow from operations for 2017. Stability strengths include good operational trends and excellent risk diversification. Strong long-term capitalization index (10.0) based on excellent current risk adjusted capital (severe and moderate loss scenarios). Moreover, capital levels have been consistent in recent years. Excellent profitability (8.6) with operating gains in each of the last five years.

Principal Business: Homeowners multiple peril (97%) and inland marine (3%).

Principal Investments: Investment grade bonds (97%) and misc. investments (6%).

Investments in Affiliates: 6%

Group Affiliation: Allstate Group

Licensed in: FL, IL, PA

Commenced Business: November 1988

Address: 2775 SANDERS ROAD, Northbrook, IL 60062-6127

Phone: (727) 573-6800   **Domicile State:** IL   **NAIC Code:** 30511

Data Date	Rating	RACR #1	RACR #2	Loss Ratio %	Total Assets ($mil)	Capital ($mil)	Net Premium ($mil)	Net Income ($mil)
2017	B+	4.54	3.79	71.3	362.5	216.2	122.6	6.7
2016	B	4.41	3.66	71.0	370.5	214.4	122.7	7.5
2015	B-	4.49	3.29	60.5	360.4	206.3	123.0	16.6
2014	B-	2.11	1.53	53.5	360.6	190.0	142.5	26.3
2013	B-	0.77	0.56	50.6	354.0	165.7	153.5	24.4

Reserve Deficiency (as % of capital)

* Adequate & redundant reserves show as negatives

■ 1 Yr Dev   □ 2 Yr Dev

CATASTROPHE REINS CO

C   Fair

Major Rating Factors: Fair overall results on stability tests (3.5 on a scale of 0 to 10).

Other Rating Factors: Strong long-term capitalization index (10.0) based on excellent current risk adjusted capital (severe and moderate loss scenarios), despite some fluctuation in capital levels. Excellent profitability (8.9) with operating gains in each of the last five years. Excellent expense controls. Superior liquidity (9.1) with ample operational cash flow and liquid investments.

Principal Business: (This company is a reinsurer.)

Principal Investments: Investment grade bonds (77%), misc. investments (20%), and non investment grade bonds (3%).

Investments in Affiliates: None

Group Affiliation: USAA Group

Licensed in: TX

Commenced Business: June 2006

Address: 9800 Fredericksburg Road, San Antonio, TX 78288

Phone: (210) 498-1411   **Domicile State:** TX   **NAIC Code:** 12578

Data Date	Rating	RACR #1	RACR #2	Loss Ratio %	Total Assets ($mil)	Capital ($mil)	Net Premium ($mil)	Net Income ($mil)
2017	C	15.28	9.11	39.3	2,013.8	1,886.9	147.0	114.8
2016	D+	15.67	9.00	N/A	1,831.9	1,743.1	148.2	158.1
2015	D	13.80	8.54	N/A	1,775.4	1,659.6	165.5	153.2
2014	D-	9.87	5.93	N/A	1,715.5	1,577.2	178.0	250.6
2013	D-	4.93	3.10	67.6	1,930.5	1,589.2	356.9	136.1

Rating Indexes

■ Weak   ▨ Fair   ▨ Good   □ Strong

CATERPILLAR INS CO *

B+ **Good**

Major Rating Factors: History of adequate reserve strength (6.3 on a scale of 0 to 10) as reserves have been consistently at an acceptable level. Good overall results on stability tests (6.5).

Other Rating Factors: Strong long-term capitalization index (9.4) based on excellent current risk adjusted capital (severe and moderate loss scenarios). Moreover, capital has steadily grown over the last five years. Excellent profitability (8.9) with operating gains in each of the last five years. Return on equity has been good over the last five years, averaging 11.5%. Excellent liquidity (7.0) with ample operational cash flow and liquid investments.

Principal Business: Other liability (92%), aggregate write-ins for other lines of business (5%), and inland marine (3%).

Principal Investments: Investment grade bonds (66%), misc. investments (29%), and cash (5%).

Investments in Affiliates: None

Group Affiliation: Caterpillar Ins Holdings Inc

Licensed in: All states except PR

Commenced Business: February 1963

Address: 237 East High Street, Jefferson City, MO 65101

Phone: (615) 341-8147   **Domicile State:** MO   **NAIC Code:** 11255

Data Date	Rating	RACR #1	RACR #2	Loss Ratio %	Total Assets ($mil)	Capital ($mil)	Net Premium ($mil)	Net Income ($mil)
2017	B+	3.54	2.62	78.2	790.6	347.9	212.3	32.3
2016	B	3.70	2.66	72.4	687.2	316.2	180.7	18.9
2015	B	4.38	3.17	63.5	650.3	286.6	142.5	49.0
2014	B-	3.23	2.60	72.9	660.7	271.9	204.7	31.5
2013	B-	2.62	2.16	55.2	639.6	243.4	214.6	33.2

Reserve Deficiency (as % of capital)

* Adequate & redundant reserves show as negatives

■ 1 Yr Dev   □ 2 Yr Dev

CATLIN SPECIALTY INS CO

C+ **Fair**

Major Rating Factors: Fair overall results on stability tests (4.3 on a scale of 0 to 10) including potential drain of affiliation with XL Group Ltd, negative cash flow from operations for 2017 and weak results on operational trends. Fair reserve development (4.0) as reserves have generally been sufficient to cover claims.

Other Rating Factors: Fair profitability index (3.8) with operating losses during 2015 and 2017. Return on equity has been low, averaging 0.1% over the past five years. Strong long-term capitalization index (8.4) based on excellent current risk adjusted capital (severe and moderate loss scenarios). Moreover, capital levels have been consistent in recent years. Excellent liquidity (7.5) with ample operational cash flow and liquid investments.

Principal Business: Other liability (55%), commercial multiple peril (14%), auto liability (13%), products liability (9%), auto physical damage (6%), fire (1%), and inland marine (1%).

Principal Investments: Investment grade bonds (61%), misc. investments (26%), and cash (13%).

Investments in Affiliates: 15%

Group Affiliation: XL Group Ltd

Licensed in: All states except PR

Commenced Business: January 1942

Address: 1209 Orange St, Wilmington, DE 19801

Phone: (203) 964-5200   **Domicile State:** DE   **NAIC Code:** 15989

Data Date	Rating	RACR #1	RACR #2	Loss Ratio %	Total Assets ($mil)	Capital ($mil)	Net Premium ($mil)	Net Income ($mil)
2017	C+	3.04	2.26	81.9	588.2	244.0	64.8	-7.8
2016	C+	2.46	1.81	86.8	744.0	234.2	50.3	3.5
2015	C+	2.33	1.74	90.9	668.4	213.1	76.8	-6.8
2014	C+	2.01	1.64	76.3	591.4	204.3	86.8	3.0
2013	C+	2.12	1.68	62.0	483.8	201.5	78.0	7.4

XL Group Ltd
Composite Group Rating: C
Largest Group Members

	Assets ($mil)	Rating
XL REINS AMERICA INC	5952	C
GREENWICH INS CO	1250	C
XL SPECIALTY INS CO	1066	C
XL INS AMERICA INC	791	C
CATLIN SPECIALTY INS CO	588	C+

CENTRAL MUTUAL INS CO *

B+ **Good**

Major Rating Factors: Good liquidity (6.6 on a scale of 0 to 10) with sufficient resources (cash flows and marketable investments) to handle a spike in claims. Good overall results on stability tests (6.5).

Other Rating Factors: Strong long-term capitalization index (8.8) based on excellent current risk adjusted capital (severe and moderate loss scenarios). Moreover, capital levels have been consistent in recent years. Ample reserve history (9.1) that helps to protect the company against sharp claims increases. Excellent profitability (8.5) with operating gains in each of the last five years.

Principal Business: Homeowners multiple peril (25%), auto liability (25%), commercial multiple peril (18%), auto physical damage (17%), other liability (6%), inland marine (3%), and other lines (7%).

Principal Investments: Investment grade bonds (55%), misc. investments (38%), cash (4%), and real estate (3%).

Investments in Affiliates: 11%

Group Affiliation: Central Mutual Ins Group

Licensed in: AZ, AR, CA, CO, CT, DE, GA, ID, IL, IN, IA, KY, ME, MD, MA, MI, MN, MS, MT, NV, NH, NJ, NM, NY, NC, OH, OK, OR, PA, SC, TN, TX, UT, VT, VA, WA, WI

Commenced Business: October 1876

Address: 800 SOUTH WASHINGTON STREET, Van Wert, OH 45891-2357

Phone: (419) 238-1010   **Domicile State:** OH   **NAIC Code:** 20230

Data Date	Rating	RACR #1	RACR #2	Loss Ratio %	Total Assets ($mil)	Capital ($mil)	Net Premium ($mil)	Net Income ($mil)
2017	B+	2.97	2.20	65.0	1,618.4	822.0	559.1	34.9
2016	B	2.91	2.18	64.0	1,514.5	743.0	518.8	32.5
2015	B	2.93	2.20	57.9	1,451.2	705.8	488.0	57.0
2014	B	2.79	2.08	59.8	1,359.6	640.1	447.6	50.4
2013	B	2.91	2.14	58.4	1,266.0	619.4	402.3	62.9

Liquidity Index

■ Weak   ▨ Fair   ▢ Good   □ Strong

CENTRAL STATES INDEMNITY CO OF OMAHA

C+ **Fair**

Major Rating Factors: Fair overall results on stability tests (4.5 on a scale of 0 to 10) including potential drain of affiliation with Berkshire-Hathaway. Good overall profitability index (6.8). Weak expense controls. Return on equity has been fair, averaging 5.3% over the past five years.

Other Rating Factors: Strong long-term capitalization index (9.3) based on excellent current risk adjusted capital (severe and moderate loss scenarios), despite some fluctuation in capital levels. Ample reserve history (7.3) that can protect against increases in claims costs. Excellent liquidity (8.4) with ample operational cash flow and liquid investments.

Principal Business: Other accident & health (61%), inland marine (26%), aggregate write-ins for other lines of business (7%), credit accident & health (3%), and aircraft (2%).

Principal Investments: Misc. investments (75%), investment grade bonds (24%), and cash (1%).

Investments in Affiliates: 3%

Group Affiliation: Berkshire-Hathaway

Licensed in: All states, the District of Columbia and Puerto Rico

Commenced Business: June 1977

Address: 1212 North 96th Street, Omaha, NE 68114

Phone: (402) 997-8000   **Domicile State:** NE   **NAIC Code:** 34274

Data Date	Rating	RACR #1	RACR #2	Loss Ratio %	Total Assets ($mil)	Capital ($mil)	Net Premium ($mil)	Net Income ($mil)
2017	C+	3.98	2.53	66.1	542.1	466.0	64.0	63.6
2016	C+	3.82	2.42	60.2	447.9	378.0	59.6	8.0
2015	C+	4.00	2.50	55.4	417.3	354.9	55.0	9.5
2014	C+	4.12	2.63	44.6	435.0	363.7	50.2	11.4
2013	B+	4.34	2.79	36.2	412.3	346.0	43.0	17.7

Berkshire-Hathaway
Composite Group Rating: B

Largest Group Members	Assets ($mil)	Rating
NATIONAL INDEMNITY CO	231374	B
GOVERNMENT EMPLOYEES INS CO	33382	B
COLUMBIA INS CO	24522	U
BERKSHIRE HATHAWAY LIFE INS CO OF NE	19610	C+
GENERAL REINS CORP	16508	C+

CHARTER OAK FIRE INS CO

B **Good**

Major Rating Factors: Good liquidity (6.5 on a scale of 0 to 10) with sufficient resources (cash flows and marketable investments) to handle a spike in claims. Good overall results on stability tests (5.9).

Other Rating Factors: Fair profitability index (3.8). Fair expense controls. Return on equity has been fair, averaging 14.2% over the past five years. Strong long-term capitalization index (7.7) based on excellent current risk adjusted capital (severe and moderate loss scenarios), despite some fluctuation in capital levels. Ample reserve history (8.5) that helps to protect the company against sharp claims increases.

Principal Business: Commercial multiple peril (34%), workers compensation (33%), auto liability (10%), other liability (8%), homeowners multiple peril (6%), auto physical damage (3%), and other lines (7%).

Principal Investments: Investment grade bonds (98%) and misc. investments (2%).

Investments in Affiliates: None

Group Affiliation: Travelers Companies Inc

Licensed in: All states except CA

Commenced Business: October 1935

Address: ONE TOWER SQUARE, Hartford, CT 6183

Phone: (860) 277-0111   **Domicile State:** CT   **NAIC Code:** 25615

Data Date	Rating	RACR #1	RACR #2	Loss Ratio %	Total Assets ($mil)	Capital ($mil)	Net Premium ($mil)	Net Income ($mil)
2017	B	2.23	1.48	69.5	925.9	227.4	290.0	18.3
2016	B	2.41	1.57	63.4	918.0	242.9	276.5	30.9
2015	B	2.54	1.62	58.7	922.9	255.7	263.9	42.1
2014	B	2.53	1.60	60.5	926.1	253.6	256.4	41.7
2013	B	2.50	1.59	60.9	916.9	245.9	255.8	42.6

Liquidity Index

CHESAPEAKE EMPLOYERS INS CO

B **Good**

Major Rating Factors: Good overall results on stability tests (6.3 on a scale of 0 to 10). Stability strengths include good operational trends and excellent risk diversification. Strong long-term capitalization index (7.4) based on excellent current risk adjusted capital (severe and moderate loss scenarios). Moreover, capital has steadily grown over the last five years.

Other Rating Factors: Ample reserve history (9.5) that helps to protect the company against sharp claims increases. Excellent profitability (7.1) with operating gains in each of the last five years. Return on equity has been good over the last five years, averaging 14.4%. Excellent liquidity (7.0) with ample operational cash flow and liquid investments.

Principal Business: Workers compensation (100%).

Principal Investments: Investment grade bonds (75%), misc. investments (21%), and non investment grade bonds (4%).

Investments in Affiliates: None

Group Affiliation: None

Licensed in: MD

Commenced Business: July 1914

Address: 8722 Loch Raven Boulevard, Towson, MD 21286-2235

Phone: (410) 494-2000   **Domicile State:** MD   **NAIC Code:** 11039

Data Date	Rating	RACR #1	RACR #2	Loss Ratio %	Total Assets ($mil)	Capital ($mil)	Net Premium ($mil)	Net Income ($mil)
2017	B	2.76	1.69	51.8	2,317.8	695.3	220.1	140.6
2016	B	1.99	1.22	81.4	2,212.5	543.4	237.4	81.5
2015	B	1.72	1.05	73.1	2,067.8	463.1	231.1	85.4
2014	U	1.41	0.88	83.8	2,005.8	399.7	227.9	50.8
2013	N/A	N/A	N/A	89.3	1,865.6	337.4	225.6	19.3

Rating Indexes

CHUBB CUSTOM INS CO   B-   Good

Major Rating Factors: Fair overall results on stability tests (4.9 on a scale of 0 to 10). Strong long-term capitalization index (10.0) based on excellent current risk adjusted capital (severe and moderate loss scenarios). Moreover, capital levels have been consistent in recent years.

Other Rating Factors: Ample reserve history (7.9) that can protect against increases in claims costs. Excellent profitability (8.5) with operating gains in each of the last five years. Excellent liquidity (7.2) with ample operational cash flow and liquid investments.

Principal Business: Fire (26%), commercial multiple peril (24%), allied lines (16%), other liability (14%), homeowners multiple peril (8%), products liability (5%), and other lines (7%).

Principal Investments: Investment grade bonds (95%), misc. investments (4%), and non investment grade bonds (1%).

Investments in Affiliates: None
Group Affiliation: Chubb Limited
Licensed in: All states, the District of Columbia and Puerto Rico
Commenced Business: December 1980
Address: 202B HALLS MILL RD, Whitehouse Station, NJ 8889
Phone: (215) 640-1000   **Domicile State:** NJ   **NAIC Code:** 38989

Data Date	Rating	RACR #1	RACR #2	Loss Ratio %	Total Assets ($mil)	Capital ($mil)	Net Premium ($mil)	Net Income ($mil)
2017	B-	13.44	8.36	62.6	389.2	223.3	25.4	10.3
2016	B-	11.41	7.18	53.5	372.9	215.0	31.7	12.4
2015	B-	8.99	5.66	55.1	405.5	200.8	48.9	13.5
2014	B-	8.42	5.36	56.7	398.7	187.4	47.0	13.5
2013	B-	7.78	4.98	51.1	346.3	173.9	45.1	14.1

Chubb Limited
Composite Group Rating: C+

Largest Group Members	Assets ($mil)	Rating
FEDERAL INS CO	21770	C+
ACE AMERICAN INS CO	13606	B-
ACE PC INS CO	8693	B-
PACIFIC INDEMNITY CO	6560	B
PACIFIC EMPLOYERS INS CO	3687	B-

CHURCH MUTUAL INS CO *   B+   Good

Major Rating Factors: Good overall profitability index (6.3 on a scale of 0 to 10) despite operating losses during 2013. Good liquidity (6.5) with sufficient resources (cash flows and marketable investments) to handle a spike in claims.

Other Rating Factors: Good overall results on stability tests (6.5). Strong long-term capitalization index (8.3) based on excellent current risk adjusted capital (severe and moderate loss scenarios). Moreover, capital has steadily grown over the last five years. Ample reserve history (8.1) that helps to protect the company against sharp claims increases.

Principal Business: Commercial multiple peril (63%), workers compensation (25%), auto liability (5%), other liability (3%), medical malpractice (2%), auto physical damage (1%), and allied lines (1%).

Principal Investments: Investment grade bonds (66%), misc. investments (32%), cash (1%), and real estate (1%).

Investments in Affiliates: 9%
Group Affiliation: None
Licensed in: All states except PR
Commenced Business: June 1897
Address: 3000 SCHUSTER LANE, Merrill, WI 54452
Phone: (715) 536-5577   **Domicile State:** WI   **NAIC Code:** 18767

Data Date	Rating	RACR #1	RACR #2	Loss Ratio %	Total Assets ($mil)	Capital ($mil)	Net Premium ($mil)	Net Income ($mil)
2017	B+	2.57	1.88	66.6	1,739.8	703.7	730.4	28.5
2016	B	2.77	1.92	55.9	1,625.6	663.8	645.8	49.4
2015	B	2.97	2.12	57.7	1,643.9	585.1	615.7	58.1
2014	B	3.18	2.34	58.2	1,453.6	536.7	589.0	76.0
2013	A	2.71	1.83	63.6	1,357.7	473.2	557.3	-4.9

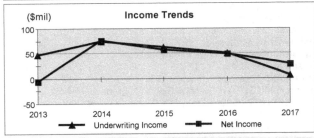

Income Trends — Underwriting Income / Net Income (2013–2017)

CINCINNATI CASUALTY CO   B   Good

Major Rating Factors: Good overall results on stability tests (5.8 on a scale of 0 to 10). Stability strengths include good operational trends and excellent risk diversification. Strong long-term capitalization index (10.0) based on excellent current risk adjusted capital (severe and moderate loss scenarios). Moreover, capital levels have been consistent in recent years.

Other Rating Factors: Excellent profitability (8.0) with operating gains in each of the last five years. Superior liquidity (10.0) with ample operational cash flow and liquid investments.

Principal Business: Workers compensation (38%), commercial multiple peril (33%), other liability (10%), auto liability (9%), auto physical damage (4%), products liability (2%), and other lines (4%).

Principal Investments: Investment grade bonds (69%), misc. investments (30%), and non investment grade bonds (1%).

Investments in Affiliates: None
Group Affiliation: Cincinnati Financial Corp
Licensed in: All states except PR
Commenced Business: March 1973
Address: 6200 SOUTH GILMORE ROAD, Fairfield, OH 45014-5141
Phone: (513) 870-2000   **Domicile State:** OH   **NAIC Code:** 28665

Data Date	Rating	RACR #1	RACR #2	Loss Ratio %	Total Assets ($mil)	Capital ($mil)	Net Premium ($mil)	Net Income ($mil)
2017	B	10.08	5.84	0.0	433.6	392.3	0.0	21.0
2016	B	10.29	5.96	0.0	408.3	359.9	0.0	11.1
2015	B	12.12	6.96	0.0	377.7	336.5	0.0	12.2
2014	B	10.94	6.34	0.0	371.8	330.2	0.0	12.0
2013	B	10.60	6.13	0.0	361.1	316.5	0.0	9.9

Cincinnati Financial Corp
Composite Group Rating: A

Largest Group Members	Assets ($mil)	Rating
CINCINNATI INS CO	12915	A
CINCINNATI LIFE INS CO	4407	B
CINCINNATI SPECIALTY UNDERWRITER	821	A
CINCINNATI CASUALTY CO	434	B
CINCINNATI INDEMNITY CO	133	A-

CINCINNATI INDEMNITY CO *   A-   Excellent

Major Rating Factors: Strong long-term capitalization index (10.0 on a scale of 0 to 10) based on excellent current risk adjusted capital (severe and moderate loss scenarios). Moreover, capital levels have been consistent in recent years. Excellent profitability (7.9) with operating gains in each of the last five years.

Other Rating Factors: Excellent liquidity (7.2) with ample operational cash flow and liquid investments. Good overall results on stability tests (6.9) despite negative cash flow from operations for 2017. Strengths that enhance stability include potential support from affiliation with Cincinnati Financial Corp, good operational trends and excellent risk diversification.

Principal Business: Workers compensation (27%), commercial multiple peril (24%), other liability (15%), auto liability (15%), auto physical damage (7%), allied lines (4%), and other lines (8%).

Principal Investments: Investment grade bonds (70%), misc. investments (25%), cash (3%), and non investment grade bonds (2%).

Investments in Affiliates: None

Group Affiliation: Cincinnati Financial Corp

Licensed in: All states except PR

Commenced Business: January 1989

Address: 6200 SOUTH GILMORE ROAD, Fairfield, OH 45014-5141

Phone: (513) 870-2000   **Domicile State:** OH   **NAIC Code:** 23280

Data Date	Rating	RACR #1	RACR #2	Loss Ratio %	Total Assets ($mil)	Capital ($mil)	Net Premium ($mil)	Net Income ($mil)
2017	A-	11.59	6.66	0.0	133.0	100.0	0.0	4.0
2016	A-	11.23	6.48	0.0	130.3	93.2	0.0	4.1
2015	A-	11.16	6.44	0.0	124.4	87.8	0.0	2.7
2014	A-	10.55	6.12	0.0	123.0	85.6	0.0	3.1
2013	A-	9.53	5.44	0.0	110.7	82.0	0.0	2.4

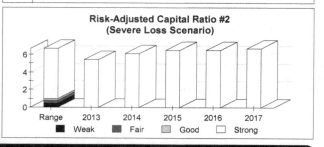

Risk-Adjusted Capital Ratio #2
(Severe Loss Scenario)

■ Weak ■ Fair □ Good □ Strong

CINCINNATI INS CO *   A   Excellent

Major Rating Factors: Excellent overall results on stability tests (7.6 on a scale of 0 to 10). Stability strengths include excellent operational trends and excellent risk diversification. Strong long-term capitalization index (7.9) based on excellent current risk adjusted capital (severe and moderate loss scenarios). Furthermore, this high level of risk adjusted capital has been consistently maintained in previous years.

Other Rating Factors: Ample reserve history (8.2) that helps to protect the company against sharp claims increases. Excellent profitability (8.6) with operating gains in each of the last five years. Good liquidity (6.2) with sufficient resources (cash flows and marketable investments) to handle a spike in claims.

Principal Business: Commercial multiple peril (26%), auto liability (18%), other liability (16%), homeowners multiple peril (14%), auto physical damage (11%), inland marine (3%), and other lines (11%).

Principal Investments: Investment grade bonds (51%), misc. investments (43%), cash (3%), and non investment grade bonds (3%).

Investments in Affiliates: 10%

Group Affiliation: Cincinnati Financial Corp

Licensed in: All states, the District of Columbia and Puerto Rico

Commenced Business: January 1951

Address: 6200 SOUTH GILMORE ROAD, Fairfield, OH 45014-5141

Phone: (513) 870-2000   **Domicile State:** OH   **NAIC Code:** 10677

Data Date	Rating	RACR #1	RACR #2	Loss Ratio %	Total Assets ($mil)	Capital ($mil)	Net Premium ($mil)	Net Income ($mil)
2017	A	2.21	1.61	67.6	12,914.9	5,093.6	4,624.9	401.2
2016	A	2.30	1.70	64.9	12,092.7	4,686.0	4,393.9	434.1
2015	A-	2.36	1.75	60.9	11,194.2	4,412.4	4,189.4	534.1
2014	A-	2.40	1.75	65.5	11,017.2	4,472.2	3,993.2	435.8
2013	A	2.41	1.76	62.1	10,559.8	4,325.7	3,769.2	417.7

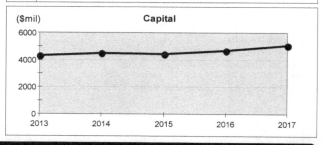

($mil)   Capital

CINCINNATI SPECIALTY UNDERWRITER *   A   Excellent

Major Rating Factors: Strong long-term capitalization index (8.3 on a scale of 0 to 10) based on excellent current risk adjusted capital (severe and moderate loss scenarios). Furthermore, this high level of risk adjusted capital has been consistently maintained in previous years. Ample reserve history (9.4) that helps to protect the company against sharp claims increases.

Other Rating Factors: Excellent profitability (8.8) with operating gains in each of the last five years. Return on equity has been good over the last five years, averaging 13.0%. Excellent liquidity (7.0) with ample operational cash flow and liquid investments. Excellent overall results on stability tests (7.5). Stability strengths include excellent operational trends and excellent risk diversification.

Principal Business: Other liability (74%), products liability (14%), fire (7%), and allied lines (5%).

Principal Investments: Investment grade bonds (76%), misc. investments (15%), cash (8%), and non investment grade bonds (1%).

Investments in Affiliates: None

Group Affiliation: Cincinnati Financial Corp

Licensed in: All states except PR

Commenced Business: November 2007

Address: 1807 NORTH MARKET ST, Wilmington, DE 19802-4810

Phone: (513) 870-2000   **Domicile State:** DE   **NAIC Code:** 13037

Data Date	Rating	RACR #1	RACR #2	Loss Ratio %	Total Assets ($mil)	Capital ($mil)	Net Premium ($mil)	Net Income ($mil)
2017	A	3.35	2.59	41.4	820.6	436.0	219.1	58.5
2016	B+	3.24	1.67	37.6	719.2	372.1	189.8	56.8
2015	B	2.93	1.50	41.9	630.0	306.5	174.7	49.0
2014	B	2.77	1.41	50.5	545.8	265.6	153.3	32.3
2013	B	2.96	1.50	56.7	453.5	228.4	127.7	18.2

Risk-Adjusted Capital Ratio #2
(Severe Loss Scenario)

■ Weak ■ Fair □ Good □ Strong

CITIZENS INS CO OF AM   B   Good

Major Rating Factors: Good overall results on stability tests (5.2 on a scale of 0 to 10) despite potential drain of affiliation with Hanover Ins Group Inc. Good liquidity (6.1) with sufficient resources (cash flows and marketable investments) to handle a spike in claims.

Other Rating Factors: Strong long-term capitalization index (9.9) based on excellent current risk adjusted capital (severe and moderate loss scenarios), despite some fluctuation in capital levels. Ample reserve history (8.0) that helps to protect the company against sharp claims increases. Excellent profitability (7.3) with operating gains in each of the last five years. Return on equity has been good over the last five years, averaging 11.9%.

Principal Business: Commercial multiple peril (32%), homeowners multiple peril (32%), auto liability (14%), auto physical damage (11%), workers compensation (6%), other liability (2%), and other lines (3%).

Principal Investments: Investment grade bonds (75%), misc. investments (19%), and non investment grade bonds (6%).

Investments in Affiliates: None

Group Affiliation: Hanover Ins Group Inc

Licensed in: All states except FL, KY, LA, WY, PR

Commenced Business: August 1974

Address: 808 NORTH HIGHLANDER WAY, Howell, MI 48843-1070

Phone: (508) 853-7200   **Domicile State:** MI   **NAIC Code:** 31534

Data Date	Rating	RACR #1	RACR #2	Loss Ratio %	Total Assets ($mil)	Capital ($mil)	Net Premium ($mil)	Net Income ($mil)
2017	B	4.30	2.97	61.6	1,559.4	699.5	773.2	93.7
2016	B	4.49	3.03	57.7	1,596.2	705.5	714.0	105.5
2015	B	4.36	2.98	58.3	1,526.4	660.4	680.7	100.8
2014	B	4.03	2.69	76.7	1,501.0	633.6	675.3	35.6
2013	B	4.35	3.04	67.1	1,476.6	662.2	679.8	67.9

Rating Indexes

Ranges   Cap. 2   Stab.   Res.   Prof.   Liq.

■ Weak   ■ Fair   ▨ Good   □ Strong

CLEARWATER SELECT INS CO   D   Weak

Major Rating Factors: Weak overall results on stability tests (1.7 on a scale of 0 to 10) including potential drain of affiliation with Fairfax Financial. Fair reserve development (3.5) as the level of reserves has at times been insufficient to cover claims. In 2013 and 2014 the two year reserve development was 401% and 466% deficient respectively.

Other Rating Factors: Good long-term capitalization index (6.2) based on good current risk adjusted capital (moderate loss scenario), despite some fluctuation in capital levels. Excellent profitability (8.7) with operating gains in each of the last five years. Superior liquidity (9.1) with ample operational cash flow and liquid investments.

Principal Business: (This company is a reinsurer.)

Principal Investments: Investment grade bonds (66%), misc. investments (29%), non investment grade bonds (4%), and cash (1%).

Investments in Affiliates: 15%

Group Affiliation: Fairfax Financial

Licensed in: All states except CA, FL

Commenced Business: March 1994

Address: 300 FIRST STAMFORD PLACE, Stamford, CT 6902

Phone: (203) 977-8000   **Domicile State:** CT   **NAIC Code:** 10019

Data Date	Rating	RACR #1	RACR #2	Loss Ratio %	Total Assets ($mil)	Capital ($mil)	Net Premium ($mil)	Net Income ($mil)
2017	D	1.54	1.17	60.3	1,279.8	519.2	215.4	25.8
2016	D	1.49	1.11	57.6	1,193.5	473.4	196.7	54.5
2015	D	0.84	0.68	58.4	1,192.2	476.9	200.4	62.1
2014	D	0.69	0.56	58.4	1,177.7	431.6	222.5	48.3
2013	D	0.11	0.09	93.1	1,111.8	372.6	808.4	2.0

Fairfax Financial
Composite Group Rating: C

Largest Group Members	Assets ($mil)	Rating
ODYSSEY REINS CO	7797	C
US FIRE INS CO	4094	C
TIG INS CO	2465	C
ZENITH INS CO	1844	C+
ALLIED WORLD INS CO	1788	C

COAST NATIONAL INS CO   D+   Weak

Major Rating Factors: Weak overall results on stability tests (2.7 on a scale of 0 to 10) including potential drain of affiliation with Farmers Insurance Group of Companies. Fair reserve development (4.6) as reserves have generally been sufficient to cover claims.

Other Rating Factors: Good overall profitability index (6.6). Excellent expense controls. Return on equity has been low, averaging 1.9% over the past five years. Strong long-term capitalization index (10.0) based on excellent current risk adjusted capital (severe and moderate loss scenarios), despite some fluctuation in capital levels. Superior liquidity (10.0) with ample operational cash flow and liquid investments.

Principal Business: Auto liability (65%) and auto physical damage (35%).

Principal Investments: Investment grade bonds (85%), misc. investments (12%), and cash (3%).

Investments in Affiliates: 12%

Group Affiliation: Farmers Insurance Group of Companies

Licensed in: AZ, CA, FL, GA, MS, NV, OR, PA, TN, WA

Commenced Business: March 1987

Address: 333 S ANITA DR SUITE 150, Orange, CA 92868

Phone: (888) 888-0080   **Domicile State:** CA   **NAIC Code:** 25089

Data Date	Rating	RACR #1	RACR #2	Loss Ratio %	Total Assets ($mil)	Capital ($mil)	Net Premium ($mil)	Net Income ($mil)
2017	D+	8.16	7.55	0.0	589.8	434.8	0.0	8.8
2016	D+	7.97	7.37	0.0	583.3	427.0	0.0	8.9
2015	D+	7.81	7.22	0.0	597.5	418.6	0.0	7.4
2014	D+	7.87	7.35	0.0	609.5	411.3	0.0	6.7
2013	D+	7.94	7.38	N/A	587.0	403.1	0.0	7.1

Farmers Insurance Group of Companies
Composite Group Rating: C

Largest Group Members	Assets ($mil)	Rating
FARMERS INS EXCHANGE	16165	C
MID-CENTURY INS CO	3942	B
FIRE INS EXCHANGE	2864	C+
FOREMOST INS CO	2317	B
TRUCK INS EXCHANGE	2108	C+

COLONY INS CO   C   Fair

Major Rating Factors: Fair overall results on stability tests (3.3 on a scale of 0 to 10) including potential drain of affiliation with Argo Group Intl Holdings Ltd. Good liquidity (6.9) with sufficient resources (cash flows and marketable investments) to handle a spike in claims.

Other Rating Factors: Strong long-term capitalization index (7.4) based on excellent current risk adjusted capital (severe and moderate loss scenarios), despite some fluctuation in capital levels. Ample reserve history (9.2) that helps to protect the company against sharp claims increases. Excellent profitability (8.6) with operating gains in each of the last five years. Return on equity has been good over the last five years, averaging 12.3%.

Principal Business: Other liability (56%), products liability (21%), commercial multiple peril (9%), allied lines (6%), auto liability (3%), auto physical damage (1%), and other lines (4%).

Principal Investments: Investment grade bonds (56%), misc. investments (34%), non investment grade bonds (9%), and cash (1%).

Investments in Affiliates: 5%

Group Affiliation: Argo Group Intl Holdings Ltd

Licensed in: All states except PR

Commenced Business: July 1981

Address: 8720 Stony Point Pkwy Ste 400, Richmond, VA 23235

Phone: (804) 560-2000   **Domicile State:** VA   **NAIC Code:** 39993

Data Date	Rating	RACR #1	RACR #2	Loss Ratio %	Total Assets ($mil)	Capital ($mil)	Net Premium ($mil)	Net Income ($mil)
2017	C	1.84	1.27	56.8	1,698.6	424.5	285.6	18.4
2016	C	1.77	1.22	59.6	1,494.7	368.9	261.8	30.3
2015	C	1.63	1.14	56.1	1,409.4	349.6	278.8	32.4
2014	C	1.88	1.30	43.3	1,318.8	319.8	234.6	81.1
2013	C	1.97	1.40	42.5	1,309.8	324.4	199.8	46.9

Rating Indexes

(Bar chart: Ranges, Cap. 2, Stab., Res., Prof., Liq.; legend: ■ Weak, ■ Fair, ▨ Good, □ Strong)

COLUMBIA CASUALTY CO   C   Fair

Major Rating Factors: Fair overall results on stability tests (3.9 on a scale of 0 to 10) including fair financial strength of affiliated CNA Financial Corp.

Other Rating Factors: Good overall profitability index (6.1). Fair expense controls. Return on equity has been low, averaging 2.7% over the past five years. Strong long-term capitalization index (10.0) based on excellent current risk adjusted capital (severe and moderate loss scenarios), despite some fluctuation in capital levels. Superior liquidity (9.5) with ample operational cash flow and liquid investments.

Principal Business: Other liability (64%), medical malpractice (28%), products liability (3%), commercial multiple peril (3%), and burglary & theft (1%).

Principal Investments: Investment grade bonds (95%) and misc. investments (5%).

Investments in Affiliates: None

Group Affiliation: CNA Financial Corp

Licensed in: All states, the District of Columbia and Puerto Rico

Commenced Business: March 1974

Address: 333 S WABASH AVE, Chicago, IL 60604

Phone: (312) 822-5000   **Domicile State:** IL   **NAIC Code:** 31127

Data Date	Rating	RACR #1	RACR #2	Loss Ratio %	Total Assets ($mil)	Capital ($mil)	Net Premium ($mil)	Net Income ($mil)
2017	C	63.90	28.06	0.0	245.2	245.0	0.0	6.5
2016	C	68.01	28.17	0.0	238.8	238.5	0.0	7.2
2015	C	68.89	28.58	0.0	247.4	247.3	0.0	5.3
2014	C	68.00	28.39	0.0	242.0	241.6	0.0	6.9
2013	C	67.97	28.36	0.0	235.2	234.9	0.0	6.8

CNA Financial Corp
Composite Group Rating: B-
Largest Group Members

	Assets ($mil)	Rating
CONTINENTAL CASUALTY CO	43528	B-
WESTERN SURETY CO	2043	C+
CONTINENTAL INS CO	1776	C
COLUMBIA CASUALTY CO	245	C
AMERICAN CASUALTY CO OF READING	142	C

COMMERCE & INDUSTRY INS CO   C   Fair

Major Rating Factors: Fair overall results on stability tests (4.2 on a scale of 0 to 10) including weak results on operational trends. Strengths include potentially strong support from affiliation with American International Group.

Other Rating Factors: Weak profitability index (1.9). Fair expense controls. Return on equity has been fair, averaging 28.0% over the past five years. Good liquidity (6.8) with sufficient resources (cash flows and marketable investments) to handle a spike in claims. Strong long-term capitalization index (10.0) based on excellent current risk adjusted capital (severe and moderate loss scenarios), despite some fluctuation in capital levels.

Principal Business: Workers compensation (40%), other liability (31%), auto liability (12%), aircraft (11%), homeowners multiple peril (3%), inland marine (1%), and auto physical damage (1%).

Principal Investments: Investment grade bonds (98%) and cash (2%).

Investments in Affiliates: 5%

Group Affiliation: American International Group

Licensed in: All states except PR

Commenced Business: December 1957

Address: 175 WATER STREET 18TH FLOOR, New York, NY 10038

Phone: (212) 770-7000   **Domicile State:** NY   **NAIC Code:** 19410

Data Date	Rating	RACR #1	RACR #2	Loss Ratio %	Total Assets ($mil)	Capital ($mil)	Net Premium ($mil)	Net Income ($mil)
2017	C	22.64	23.28	0.0	419.6	414.8	0.0	2.4
2016	C	11.10	12.02	0.0	387.3	381.9	-521.1	152.8
2015	C	1.92	1.33	91.2	4,142.7	974.0	927.4	650.2
2014	C	2.79	1.87	85.6	4,770.8	1,624.9	590.4	263.8
2013	C	2.05	1.37	73.0	7,339.2	1,905.6	1,569.7	309.1

American International Group
Composite Group Rating: B
Largest Group Members

	Assets ($mil)	Rating
AMERICAN GENERAL LIFE INS CO	178705	B
VARIABLE ANNUITY LIFE INS CO	81665	B
UNITED STATES LIFE INS CO IN NYC	29431	B
NATIONAL UNION FIRE INS CO	25661	C
AMERICAN HOME ASR CO	25640	C

COMMERCE INS CO

B- **Good**

Major Rating Factors: Fair overall results on stability tests (4.8 on a scale of 0 to 10) including potential drain of affiliation with MAPFRE Ins Group. Fair reserve development (4.2) as reserves have generally been sufficient to cover claims.

Other Rating Factors: Fair profitability index (3.8) with small operating losses during 2015. Return on equity has been fair, averaging 6.1% over the past five years. Fair liquidity (3.2) as cash resources may not be adequate to cover a spike in claims. Strong long-term capitalization index (8.0) based on excellent current risk adjusted capital (severe and moderate loss scenarios), despite some fluctuation in capital levels.

Principal Business: Auto liability (50%), auto physical damage (39%), homeowners multiple peril (8%), and fire (1%).

Principal Investments: Investment grade bonds (79%), misc. investments (14%), real estate (6%), and non investment grade bonds (2%).

Investments in Affiliates: 3%

Group Affiliation: MAPFRE Ins Group

Licensed in: CA, CT, FL, ME, MA, NH, NJ, NY, NC, OH, OR, RI, TX, VT

Commenced Business: May 1972

Address: 211 MAIN STREET, Webster, MA 01570-0758

Phone: (508) 943-9000   **Domicile State:** MA   **NAIC Code:** 34754

Data Date	Rating	RACR #1	RACR #2	Loss Ratio %	Total Assets ($mil)	Capital ($mil)	Net Premium ($mil)	Net Income ($mil)
2017	B-	2.06	1.64	79.9	2,246.1	626.3	1,290.8	18.4
2016	C+	2.13	1.75	78.2	2,183.7	621.3	1,285.1	48.0
2015	C	2.37	1.90	84.1	2,235.2	660.6	1,157.6	-1.7
2014	C	2.32	1.91	76.6	2,217.4	682.8	1,370.1	63.7
2013	B-	3.04	2.42	73.5	2,272.1	834.8	1,320.3	88.0

Rating Indexes

(Legend: ■ Weak ■ Fair ▨ Good □ Strong)

(Categories: Ranges, Cap. 2, Stab., Res., Prof., Liq.)

CONCORD GENERAL MUTUAL INS CO

B- **Good**

Major Rating Factors: Fair overall results on stability tests (4.6 on a scale of 0 to 10) including potential drain of affiliation with Concord Group. Good liquidity (6.7) with sufficient resources (cash flows and marketable investments) to handle a spike in claims.

Other Rating Factors: Strong long-term capitalization index (8.2) based on excellent current risk adjusted capital (severe and moderate loss scenarios), despite some fluctuation in capital levels. Ample reserve history (8.4) that helps to protect the company against sharp claims increases. Excellent profitability (7.6) with operating gains in each of the last five years.

Principal Business: Homeowners multiple peril (34%), auto liability (28%), auto physical damage (26%), commercial multiple peril (10%), other liability (2%), and inland marine (1%).

Principal Investments: Misc. investments (62%), investment grade bonds (34%), cash (2%), non investment grade bonds (1%), and real estate (1%).

Investments in Affiliates: 6%

Group Affiliation: Concord Group

Licensed in: ME, NH, SC, VT

Commenced Business: June 1928

Address: 4 BOUTON STREET, Concord, NH 03301-5023

Phone: (603) 224-4086   **Domicile State:** NH   **NAIC Code:** 20672

Data Date	Rating	RACR #1	RACR #2	Loss Ratio %	Total Assets ($mil)	Capital ($mil)	Net Premium ($mil)	Net Income ($mil)
2017	B-	2.84	1.88	62.5	518.0	301.8	170.4	15.0
2016	B-	2.68	1.76	60.5	469.6	245.8	162.5	13.6
2015	B-	2.55	1.71	74.6	438.2	221.6	164.1	0.4
2014	B-	2.60	1.74	72.2	449.5	226.2	167.7	4.4
2013	B-	2.60	1.72	67.4	426.1	211.9	164.6	10.1

Concord Group Composite Group Rating: A Largest Group Members	Assets ($mil)	Rating
AUTO-OWNERS INS CO	15390	A
AUTO-OWNERS LIFE INS CO	4211	B+
OWNERS INS CO	4110	A
HOME-OWNERS INS CO	2324	A
SOUTHERN-OWNERS INS CO	822	A

CONNECTICUT MEDICAL INS CO

B **Good**

Major Rating Factors: Good long-term capitalization index (6.6 on a scale of 0 to 10) based on good current risk adjusted capital (moderate loss scenario). Over the last several years, capital levels have remained relatively consistent. History of adequate reserve strength (6.9) as reserves have been consistently at an acceptable level.

Other Rating Factors: Good overall results on stability tests (5.9) despite negative cash flow from operations for 2017. Stability strengths include good operational trends, good risk adjusted capital for prior years and excellent risk diversification. Fair profitability index (4.3) with operating losses during 2017. Excellent liquidity (7.1) with ample operational cash flow and liquid investments.

Principal Business: Medical malpractice (100%).

Principal Investments: Investment grade bonds (77%) and misc. investments (23%).

Investments in Affiliates: None

Group Affiliation: Connecticut Medical

Licensed in: CT, MA

Commenced Business: October 1984

Address: 80 Glastonbury Boulevard, Glastonbury, CT 6033

Phone: (860) 633-7788   **Domicile State:** CT   **NAIC Code:** 15890

Data Date	Rating	RACR #1	RACR #2	Loss Ratio %	Total Assets ($mil)	Capital ($mil)	Net Premium ($mil)	Net Income ($mil)
2017	B	1.10	0.95	126.9	504.1	307.3	28.3	-6.3
2016	B	1.42	1.22	93.7	492.8	296.7	34.1	3.1
2015	B	1.57	1.35	67.5	476.7	286.8	31.8	8.9
2014	C+	1.65	1.41	63.2	480.2	279.1	31.1	10.7
2013	C+	1.73	1.48	58.6	468.6	264.4	35.9	11.2

Risk-Adjusted Capital Ratio #2
(Severe Loss Scenario)

(Legend: ■ Weak ■ Fair ▨ Good □ Strong)

(Categories: Range, 2013, 2014, 2015, 2016, 2017)

CONTINENTAL CASUALTY CO   B-   Good

Major Rating Factors: Fair overall results on stability tests (4.8 on a scale of 0 to 10) including potential drain of affiliation with CNA Financial Corp. History of adequate reserve strength (6.6) as reserves have been consistently at an acceptable level.

Other Rating Factors: Good overall profitability index (5.4). Fair expense controls. Return on equity has been fair, averaging 8.6% over the past five years. Good liquidity (6.9) with sufficient resources (cash flows and marketable investments) to handle a spike in claims. Strong long-term capitalization index (7.8) based on excellent current risk adjusted capital (severe and moderate loss scenarios), despite some fluctuation in capital levels.

Principal Business: Inland marine (55%), other liability (22%), other accident & health (4%), commercial multiple peril (4%), group accident & health (3%), medical malpractice (2%), and other lines (10%).

Principal Investments: Investment grade bonds (74%), misc. investments (21%), and non investment grade bonds (5%).

Investments in Affiliates: 11%

Group Affiliation: CNA Financial Corp

Licensed in: All states, the District of Columbia and Puerto Rico

Commenced Business: December 1897

Address: 333 S WABASH AVE, Chicago, IL 60604

Phone: (312) 822-5000   **Domicile State:** IL   **NAIC Code:** 20443

Data Date	Rating	RACR #1	RACR #2	Loss Ratio %	Total Assets ($mil)	Capital ($mil)	Net Premium ($mil)	Net Income ($mil)
2017	B-	1.99	1.52	79.7	43,528.3	10,726.2	6,015.6	953.2
2016	C+	2.02	1.53	82.5	43,519.5	10,748.3	5,997.0	1,009.9
2015	C+	2.01	1.54	83.1	43,531.4	10,723.3	6,036.8	1,078.8
2014	C	2.09	1.60	85.1	43,309.7	11,155.2	6,007.1	839.3
2013	C+	2.04	1.59	87.8	42,642.3	11,136.7	6,246.7	788.0

Rating Indexes

Ranges   Cap. 2   Stab.   Res.   Prof.   Liq.
■ Weak   ■ Fair   □ Good   □ Strong

CONTINENTAL INS CO   C   Fair

Major Rating Factors: Fair reserve development (3.7 on a scale of 0 to 10) as reserves have generally been sufficient to cover claims. In 2013, the two year reserve development was 16% deficient. Fair overall results on stability tests (4.3) including fair financial strength of affiliated CNA Financial Corp.

Other Rating Factors: Good overall profitability index (6.5). Weak expense controls. Return on equity has been low, averaging 4.8% over the past five years. Strong long-term capitalization index (10.0) based on excellent current risk adjusted capital (severe and moderate loss scenarios), despite some fluctuation in capital levels. Excellent liquidity (7.0) with ample operational cash flow and liquid investments.

Principal Business: Other liability (37%), commercial multiple peril (15%), workers compensation (14%), ocean marine (9%), auto liability (8%), surety (3%), and other lines (14%).

Principal Investments: Investment grade bonds (88%), misc. investments (10%), cash (1%), and non investment grade bonds (1%).

Investments in Affiliates: 10%

Group Affiliation: CNA Financial Corp

Licensed in: All states, the District of Columbia and Puerto Rico

Commenced Business: December 1977

Address: 100 MATSONFORD RD - STE 200, Radnor, PA 19087

Phone: (312) 822-5000   **Domicile State:** PA   **NAIC Code:** 35289

Data Date	Rating	RACR #1	RACR #2	Loss Ratio %	Total Assets ($mil)	Capital ($mil)	Net Premium ($mil)	Net Income ($mil)
2017	C	6.51	5.19	0.0	1,775.7	1,558.1	0.0	58.5
2016	C	6.35	3.44	0.0	1,667.5	1,500.3	0.0	55.4
2015	C	6.41	3.56	0.0	1,666.9	1,469.3	0.0	53.1
2014	C	5.27	2.92	0.0	1,995.3	1,437.3	0.0	55.8
2013	C	4.78	2.58	0.0	2,345.5	1,366.9	0.0	121.8

Reserve Deficiency (as % of capital)

2013   2014   2015   2016   2017

* Adequate & redundant reserves show as negatives

■ 1 Yr Dev   □ 2 Yr Dev

COPIC INS CO *   B+   Good

Major Rating Factors: Good overall results on stability tests (6.8 on a scale of 0 to 10). Strong long-term capitalization index (9.9) based on excellent current risk adjusted capital (severe and moderate loss scenarios), despite some fluctuation in capital levels.

Other Rating Factors: Ample reserve history (9.3) that helps to protect the company against sharp claims increases. Excellent liquidity (7.5) with ample operational cash flow and liquid investments. Fair profitability index (4.3). Good expense controls. Return on equity has been low, averaging 2.8% over the past five years.

Principal Business: Medical malpractice (95%), other liability (4%), and group accident & health (1%).

Principal Investments: Investment grade bonds (70%), misc. investments (28%), cash (1%), and non investment grade bonds (1%).

Investments in Affiliates: None

Group Affiliation: COPIC Trust

Licensed in: AK, AZ, AR, CO, GA, HI, ID, IL, IA, KS, LA, MN, MO, MT, NE, NV, ND, OK, OR, SD, TX, UT, WI, WY

Commenced Business: September 1984

Address: 7351 E LOWRY BLVD SUITE 400, Denver, CO 80230

Phone: (720) 858-6000   **Domicile State:** CO   **NAIC Code:** 11860

Data Date	Rating	RACR #1	RACR #2	Loss Ratio %	Total Assets ($mil)	Capital ($mil)	Net Premium ($mil)	Net Income ($mil)
2017	B+	4.32	2.90	72.2	603.2	297.7	100.3	7.3
2016	B+	6.06	3.99	63.6	696.8	410.5	100.4	7.0
2015	B	6.43	4.21	56.3	657.3	396.1	82.1	1.9
2014	B	4.75	3.19	49.3	526.5	268.1	81.1	12.8
2013	A-	4.57	3.08	59.4	525.0	260.6	82.0	11.9

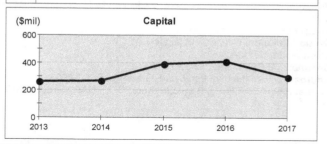

($mil)   Capital

2013   2014   2015   2016   2017

COPPERPOINT MUTUAL INS CO *

A+   **Excellent**

Major Rating Factors: Strong long-term capitalization index (8.3 on a scale of 0 to 10) based on excellent current risk adjusted capital (severe and moderate loss scenarios). Furthermore, this high level of risk adjusted capital has been consistently maintained in previous years. Excellent liquidity (7.1) with ample operational cash flow and liquid investments.

Other Rating Factors: Excellent overall results on stability tests (8.5). Stability strengths include excellent operational trends and excellent risk diversification. History of adequate reserve strength (6.7) as reserves have been consistently at an acceptable level. Good overall profitability index (6.7). Fair expense controls.

Principal Business: Workers compensation (99%).

Principal Investments: Investment grade bonds (69%), misc. investments (28%), cash (1%), non investment grade bonds (1%), and real estate (1%).

Investments in Affiliates: 6%

Group Affiliation: CopperPoint Group

Licensed in: AZ

Commenced Business: January 2013

Address: 3030 N 3RD STREET, Phoenix, AZ 85012

Phone: (602) 631-2240   **Domicile State:** AZ   **NAIC Code:** 14216

Data Date	Rating	RACR #1	RACR #2	Loss Ratio %	Total Assets ($mil)	Capital ($mil)	Net Premium ($mil)	Net Income ($mil)
2017	A+	2.87	1.91	72.7	3,694.0	1,466.9	244.9	74.4
2016	A+	3.31	2.03	76.2	3,606.3	1,351.8	247.6	57.5
2015	A+	3.16	1.96	78.5	3,562.5	1,258.8	242.1	61.9
2014	A+	2.59	1.61	78.2	3,560.4	1,229.7	239.6	51.2
2013	A+	2.22	1.38	89.2	3,536.2	1,186.2	222.5	44.7

Risk-Adjusted Capital Ratio #2
(Severe Loss Scenario)

COUNTRY MUTUAL INS CO *

A-   **Excellent**

Major Rating Factors: Strong long-term capitalization index (10.0 on a scale of 0 to 10) based on excellent current risk adjusted capital (severe and moderate loss scenarios). Furthermore, this high level of risk adjusted capital has been consistently maintained in previous years. Excellent overall results on stability tests (7.3). Stability strengths include excellent operational trends and excellent risk diversification.

Other Rating Factors: History of adequate reserve strength (5.3) as reserves have been consistently at an acceptable level. Good overall profitability index (6.8). Fair expense controls. Good liquidity (6.1) with sufficient resources (cash flows and marketable investments) to handle a spike in claims.

Principal Business: Homeowners multiple peril (39%), auto liability (15%), commercial multiple peril (12%), auto physical damage (11%), farmowners multiple peril (9%), allied lines (6%), and other lines (8%).

Principal Investments: Investment grade bonds (68%), misc. investments (30%), and non investment grade bonds (3%).

Investments in Affiliates: 4%

Group Affiliation: COUNTRY Financial

Licensed in: All states except DC, FL, HI, LA, MS, PR

Commenced Business: November 1925

Address: 1701 N TOWANDA AVENUE, Bloomington, IL 61701-2090

Phone: (309) 821-3000   **Domicile State:** IL   **NAIC Code:** 20990

Data Date	Rating	RACR #1	RACR #2	Loss Ratio %	Total Assets ($mil)	Capital ($mil)	Net Premium ($mil)	Net Income ($mil)
2017	A-	4.61	3.28	73.4	4,850.2	2,567.6	2,314.8	113.3
2016	A-	4.45	3.19	71.6	4,701.9	2,386.1	2,199.8	103.0
2015	A-	4.26	3.05	70.7	4,295.7	2,239.8	2,023.5	120.0
2014	A-	3.74	2.70	70.3	4,255.7	1,964.2	2,055.1	178.0
2013	A-	3.56	2.56	69.3	4,150.3	1,825.5	2,051.7	151.3

Risk-Adjusted Capital Ratio #2
(Severe Loss Scenario)

COURTESY INS CO

B   **Good**

Major Rating Factors: Good overall results on stability tests (5.1 on a scale of 0 to 10) despite potential drain of affiliation with J M Family Enterprise Group. Stability strengths include good operational trends and excellent risk diversification. History of adequate reserve strength (6.0) as reserves have been consistently at an acceptable level.

Other Rating Factors: Good liquidity (6.9) with sufficient resources (cash flows and marketable investments) to handle a spike in claims. Strong long-term capitalization index (10.0) based on excellent current risk adjusted capital (severe and moderate loss scenarios). Moreover, capital levels have been consistent in recent years. Excellent profitability (8.3) with operating gains in each of the last five years.

Principal Business: Aggregate write-ins for other lines of business (29%).

Principal Investments: Investment grade bonds (84%) and misc. investments (16%).

Investments in Affiliates: None

Group Affiliation: J M Family Enterprise Group

Licensed in: All states except MI

Commenced Business: May 1988

Address: 100 Jim Moran Boulevard, Deerfield Beach, FL 33442

Phone: (954) 429-2150   **Domicile State:** FL   **NAIC Code:** 26492

Data Date	Rating	RACR #1	RACR #2	Loss Ratio %	Total Assets ($mil)	Capital ($mil)	Net Premium ($mil)	Net Income ($mil)
2017	B	7.79	4.51	85.0	906.6	401.7	229.6	14.2
2016	B	10.02	5.73	85.7	789.6	377.8	128.8	10.7
2015	B	10.51	5.95	67.6	764.8	360.1	135.6	23.2
2014	B	9.84	5.60	57.9	735.4	341.6	121.7	33.2
2013	B	9.23	5.31	52.7	686.5	308.4	124.9	38.3

Rating Indexes

COVINGTON SPECIALTY INS CO *

B+ **Good**

Major Rating Factors: History of adequate reserve strength (5.9 on a scale of 0 to 10) as reserves have been consistently at an acceptable level. Good overall profitability index (5.3). Fair expense controls. Return on equity has been low, averaging 2.4% over the past five years.

Other Rating Factors: Good liquidity (6.9) with sufficient resources (cash flows and marketable investments) to handle a spike in claims. Good overall results on stability tests (6.5) despite negative cash flow from operations for 2017. Stability strengths include good operational trends and excellent risk diversification. Strong long-term capitalization index (10.0) based on excellent current risk adjusted capital (severe and moderate loss scenarios), despite some fluctuation in capital levels.

Principal Business: Commercial multiple peril (44%), other liability (41%), products liability (6%), allied lines (5%), and fire (4%).

Principal Investments: Investment grade bonds (87%), misc. investments (17%), and non investment grade bonds (1%).

Investments in Affiliates: None

Group Affiliation: Alleghany Corp Group

Licensed in: All states except PR

Commenced Business: February 2008

Address: 900 Elm Street, Manchester, NH 3101

Phone: (404) 231-2366   **Domicile State:** NH   **NAIC Code:** 13027

Data Date	Rating	RACR #1	RACR #2	Loss Ratio %	Total Assets ($mil)	Capital ($mil)	Net Premium ($mil)	Net Income ($mil)
2017	B+	5.26	3.68	73.7	97.9	47.3	14.2	1.3
2016	B	5.31	2.73	69.1	99.9	46.4	14.7	1.5
2015	B	6.05	3.24	67.9	103.4	50.0	16.1	1.3
2014	B	6.59	3.74	63.8	95.6	48.5	15.9	1.6
2013	B	8.60	5.24	66.4	81.7	47.0	13.2	0.1

Reserve Deficiency (as % of capital)

* Adequate & redundant reserves show as negatives

■ 1 Yr Dev
□ 2 Yr Dev

CSAA INS EXCHANGE

B- **Good**

Major Rating Factors: Fair overall results on stability tests (4.8 on a scale of 0 to 10). History of adequate reserve strength (6.3) as reserves have been consistently at an acceptable level.

Other Rating Factors: Good liquidity (5.1) with sufficient resources (cash flows and marketable investments) to handle a spike in claims. Strong long-term capitalization index (8.6) based on excellent current risk adjusted capital (severe and moderate loss scenarios), despite some fluctuation in capital levels. Weak profitability index (2.6) with operating losses during 2015 and 2017.

Principal Business: Auto liability (40%), auto physical damage (37%), homeowners multiple peril (21%), and other liability (1%).

Principal Investments: Investment grade bonds (50%), misc. investments (39%), non investment grade bonds (12%), and real estate (2%).

Investments in Affiliates: 3%

Group Affiliation: CSAA Insurance Group

Licensed in: AZ, CA, IN, MD, NV, NJ, NY, WY

Commenced Business: August 1914

Address: 3055 OAK ROAD, Walnut Creek, CA 94597-2098

Phone: (925) 279-2300   **Domicile State:** CA   **NAIC Code:** 15539

Data Date	Rating	RACR #1	RACR #2	Loss Ratio %	Total Assets ($mil)	Capital ($mil)	Net Premium ($mil)	Net Income ($mil)
2017	B-	3.12	2.04	85.6	7,168.5	3,224.6	3,541.5	-184.2
2016	B-	3.42	2.35	75.0	6,812.9	3,387.8	3,290.5	68.3
2015	B-	3.17	2.19	81.6	6,572.3	3,378.1	3,116.8	-120.8
2014	B	3.51	2.45	73.4	6,983.9	3,749.3	2,899.6	122.6
2013	A-	3.82	2.68	74.1	6,672.1	3,830.2	2,714.9	114.9

Rating Indexes

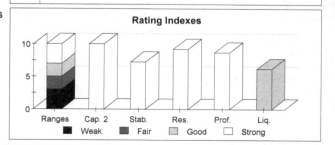

Ranges Cap. 2 Stab. Res. Prof. Liq.

■ Weak ■ Fair ■ Good □ Strong

CUMIS INS SOCIETY INC *

A- **Excellent**

Major Rating Factors: Excellent overall results on stability tests (7.2 on a scale of 0 to 10). Stability strengths include good operational trends and excellent risk diversification. Strong long-term capitalization index (10.0) based on excellent current risk adjusted capital (severe and moderate loss scenarios). Furthermore, this high level of risk adjusted capital has been consistently maintained in previous years.

Other Rating Factors: Ample reserve history (9.2) that helps to protect the company against sharp claims increases. Excellent profitability (8.7) with operating gains in each of the last five years. Good liquidity (6.2) with sufficient resources (cash flows and marketable investments) to handle a spike in claims.

Principal Business: Other liability (70%), fidelity (14%), commercial multiple peril (12%), auto physical damage (2%), credit (1%), and auto liability (1%).

Principal Investments: Investment grade bonds (83%), misc. investments (15%), and non investment grade bonds (2%).

Investments in Affiliates: 5%

Group Affiliation: CUNA Mutual Ins Group

Licensed in: All states, the District of Columbia and Puerto Rico

Commenced Business: June 1960

Address: 2000 HERITAGE WAY, Waverly, IA 50677

Phone: (608) 238-5851   **Domicile State:** IA   **NAIC Code:** 10847

Data Date	Rating	RACR #1	RACR #2	Loss Ratio %	Total Assets ($mil)	Capital ($mil)	Net Premium ($mil)	Net Income ($mil)
2017	A-	4.74	3.53	68.5	2,002.8	911.0	906.7	45.0
2016	B+	5.22	3.81	64.8	1,832.6	869.2	820.9	69.8
2015	B	4.99	3.58	64.4	1,711.8	800.5	826.3	110.9
2014	B	4.48	3.25	63.4	2,062.8	714.9	652.2	80.9
2013	B	4.63	3.27	63.8	1,637.6	621.7	621.0	58.5

Rating Indexes

Ranges Cap. 2 Stab. Res. Prof. Liq.

■ Weak ■ Fair ■ Good □ Strong

CYPRESS INS CO   C+   Fair

Major Rating Factors: Fair overall results on stability tests (4.4 on a scale of 0 to 10) including potential drain of affiliation with Berkshire-Hathaway. Good long-term capitalization index (6.3) based on good current risk adjusted capital (moderate loss scenario), despite some fluctuation in capital levels.

Other Rating Factors: Ample reserve history (9.4) that helps to protect the company against sharp claims increases. Excellent profitability (8.7) with operating gains in each of the last five years. Return on equity has been good over the last five years, averaging 12.3%. Excellent liquidity (8.1) with ample operational cash flow and liquid investments.

Principal Business: Workers compensation (90%), auto liability (7%), auto physical damage (2%), and commercial multiple peril (1%).

Principal Investments: Investment grade bonds (58%), misc. investments (41%), and cash (1%).

Investments in Affiliates: 8%

Group Affiliation: Berkshire-Hathaway

Licensed in: AL, AR, CA, CO, DE, GA, HI, ID, IA, MS, NE, NM, OK, SC, TN, TX, VA

Commenced Business: March 1963

Address: 1 California Street Suite 600, San Francisco, CA 94111

Phone: (888) 495-8949   **Domicile State:** CA   **NAIC Code:** 10855

Data Date	Rating	RACR #1	RACR #2	Loss Ratio %	Total Assets ($mil)	Capital ($mil)	Net Premium ($mil)	Net Income ($mil)
2017	C+	1.50	1.11	64.0	1,764.8	519.2	450.1	105.0
2016	C+	1.00	0.73	68.0	1,499.7	366.0	428.9	76.8
2015	C+	1.21	0.84	77.3	1,284.2	305.7	327.0	6.8
2014	C	1.26	0.85	77.4	1,203.2	311.5	254.3	26.6
2013	C	1.45	1.01	78.9	1,140.2	264.4	271.9	25.3

DAIRYLAND INS CO *   A-   Excellent

Major Rating Factors: Strong long-term capitalization index (9.4 on a scale of 0 to 10) based on excellent current risk adjusted capital (severe and moderate loss scenarios). Furthermore, this high level of risk adjusted capital has been consistently maintained in previous years. Ample reserve history (7.9) that can protect against increases in claims costs.

Other Rating Factors: Excellent overall results on stability tests (7.2). Stability strengths include excellent operational trends and excellent risk diversification. Good overall profitability index (5.6). Fair expense controls. Return on equity has been fair, averaging 6.0% over the past five years. Good liquidity (6.8) with sufficient resources (cash flows and marketable investments) to handle a spike in claims.

Principal Business: Auto liability (70%) and auto physical damage (30%).

Principal Investments: Investment grade bonds (91%), misc. investments (8%), and non investment grade bonds (1%).

Investments in Affiliates: None

Group Affiliation: Sentry Ins Group

Licensed in: All states except CA, DC, HI, LA, NJ, OK, PR

Commenced Business: February 1953

Address: 1800 NORTH POINT DRIVE, Stevens Point, WI 54481

Phone: (715) 346-6000   **Domicile State:** WI   **NAIC Code:** 21164

Data Date	Rating	RACR #1	RACR #2	Loss Ratio %	Total Assets ($mil)	Capital ($mil)	Net Premium ($mil)	Net Income ($mil)
2017	A-	4.02	2.58	74.8	1,400.7	477.0	368.9	29.4
2016	B+	4.26	2.73	73.9	1,272.8	475.4	352.2	24.1
2015	B+	4.57	2.92	72.7	1,239.6	482.0	328.5	29.3
2014	B+	5.05	3.38	74.9	1,194.9	485.3	317.4	34.8
2013	A+	4.86	3.30	76.3	1,163.2	471.7	318.1	25.6

DOCTORS CO AN INTERINS   B-   Good

Major Rating Factors: Fair overall results on stability tests (4.7 on a scale of 0 to 10) including potential drain of affiliation with Doctors Co Group. Fair profitability index (4.8) with operating losses during 2015 and 2016.

Other Rating Factors: Strong long-term capitalization index (7.9) based on excellent current risk adjusted capital (severe and moderate loss scenarios), despite some fluctuation in capital levels. Ample reserve history (8.7) that helps to protect the company against sharp claims increases. Excellent liquidity (7.1) with ample operational cash flow and liquid investments.

Principal Business: Medical malpractice (99%) and other liability (1%).

Principal Investments: Misc. investments (58%), investment grade bonds (37%), non investment grade bonds (4%), and cash (1%).

Investments in Affiliates: 15%

Group Affiliation: Doctors Co Group

Licensed in: All states except PR

Commenced Business: April 1976

Address: 185 GREENWOOD ROAD, Napa, CA 94558

Phone: (707) 226-0100   **Domicile State:** CA   **NAIC Code:** 34495

Data Date	Rating	RACR #1	RACR #2	Loss Ratio %	Total Assets ($mil)	Capital ($mil)	Net Premium ($mil)	Net Income ($mil)
2017	B-	2.18	1.68	77.0	4,409.2	2,138.8	595.9	149.0
2016	B-	2.01	1.63	77.7	4,132.2	1,925.9	602.4	-70.2
2015	B-	1.95	1.54	74.5	3,585.4	1,808.9	622.9	-72.8
2014	B-	1.93	1.53	78.3	3,559.8	1,821.9	644.0	31.3
2013	B-	1.88	1.54	75.1	3,313.2	1,731.7	675.7	27.7

DORINCO REINS CO

C-   **Fair**

Major Rating Factors: Weak overall results on stability tests (2.6 on a scale of 0 to 10) including potential drain of affiliation with Dow Chemical Co and negative cash flow from operations for 2017. Good liquidity (6.8) with sufficient resources (cash flows and marketable investments) to handle a spike in claims.

Other Rating Factors: Strong long-term capitalization index (7.5) based on excellent current risk adjusted capital (severe and moderate loss scenarios), despite some fluctuation in capital levels. Ample reserve history (9.3) that helps to protect the company against sharp claims increases. Excellent profitability (8.6) with operating gains in each of the last five years. Return on equity has been excellent over the last five years averaging 16.0%.

Principal Business: Fire (52%), other liability (47%), and products liability (1%).

Principal Investments: Investment grade bonds (70%), misc. investments (29%), and non investment grade bonds (1%).

Investments in Affiliates: None

Group Affiliation: Dow Chemical Co

Licensed in: AL, AZ, CA, CT, DE, FL, GA, ID, IL, IN, IA, KS, KY, LA, MD, MI, MN, MS, MO, NE, NH, NY, NC, ND, OH, OK, OR, PA, SC, SD, TX, UT, VT, VA, WV, WI, WY

Commenced Business: March 1977

Address: 1320 Waldo Avenue Suite 200, Midland, MI 48674

Phone: (989) 636-0047   **Domicile State:** MI   **NAIC Code:** 33499

Data Date	Rating	RACR #1	RACR #2	Loss Ratio %	Total Assets ($mil)	Capital ($mil)	Net Premium ($mil)	Net Income ($mil)
2017	C-	2.92	1.94	72.8	1,547.9	579.7	157.3	112.1
2016	C-	1.49	1.11	50.9	1,522.9	532.0	172.7	85.5
2015	C-	1.42	1.02	60.2	1,536.2	514.0	153.7	85.8
2014	D+	1.37	1.10	70.8	1,565.9	534.8	171.7	75.0
2013	D+	1.32	1.04	72.9	1,571.4	529.5	196.8	73.2

Rating Indexes

EAGLESTONE REINS CO

C   **Fair**

Major Rating Factors: Fair overall results on stability tests (4.2 on a scale of 0 to 10) including weak risk adjusted capital in prior years and weak results on operational trends. Strengths include potentially strong support from affiliation with American International Group. Fair profitability index (3.7) with operating losses during 2014, 2015 and 2016. Return on equity has been low, averaging 0.2% over the past five years.

Other Rating Factors: Poor long-term capitalization index (1.1) based on weak current risk adjusted capital (severe and moderate loss scenarios). A history of deficient reserves (1.6). Underreserving can have an adverse impact on capital and profits. In the last five years, reserves (two year development) fluctuated between 45% and 28% deficeint. Excellent liquidity (7.0) with ample operational cash flow and liquid investments.

Principal Business: (Not applicable due to unusual reinsurance transactions.)

Principal Investments: Investment grade bonds (98%) and non investment grade bonds (2%).

Investments in Affiliates: None

Group Affiliation: American International Group

Licensed in: DE, IL, NY, PA

Commenced Business: April 1996

Address: 2595 INTERSTATE DRIVE STE 103, Harrisburg, PA 17110

Phone: (212) 770-7000   **Domicile State:** PA   **NAIC Code:** 10651

Data Date	Rating	RACR #1	RACR #2	Loss Ratio %	Total Assets ($mil)	Capital ($mil)	Net Premium ($mil)	Net Income ($mil)
2017	C	0.32	0.26	382.2	6,138.8	1,982.1	-0.1	123.7
2016	C	0.26	0.21	766.6	6,461.9	1,828.4	4.5	-228.8
2015	B	1.63	1.10	N/A	6,792.3	1,858.7	40.4	-3.4
2014	U	2.14	1.37	N/A	5,593.6	1,727.9	0.0	-209.4
2013	B	2.32	1.46	N/A	5,805.7	1,937.4	0.5	377.9

Rating Indexes

ECONOMY FIRE & CAS CO

B-   **Good**

Major Rating Factors: Good overall profitability index (6.8 on a scale of 0 to 10). Fair expense controls. Return on equity has been low, averaging 4.2% over the past five years. Good overall results on stability tests (5.1). Stability strengths include good operational trends and excellent risk diversification.

Other Rating Factors: Strong long-term capitalization index (10.0) based on excellent current risk adjusted capital (severe and moderate loss scenarios), despite some fluctuation in capital levels. Excellent liquidity (7.0) with ample operational cash flow and liquid investments.

Principal Business: Auto liability (50%), auto physical damage (42%), and homeowners multiple peril (7%).

Principal Investments: Investment grade bonds (82%), misc. investments (17%), and real estate (1%).

Investments in Affiliates: 16%

Group Affiliation: MetLife Inc

Licensed in: All states except DC, DE, ME, MA, NJ, RI, SC, PR

Commenced Business: January 1935

Address: 177 South Commons Drive, Freeport, IL 61032

Phone: (401) 827-2400   **Domicile State:** IL   **NAIC Code:** 22926

Data Date	Rating	RACR #1	RACR #2	Loss Ratio %	Total Assets ($mil)	Capital ($mil)	Net Premium ($mil)	Net Income ($mil)
2017	B-	6.58	5.95	0.0	511.9	390.6	0.0	18.0
2016	B-	6.59	6.08	0.0	502.0	381.7	0.0	15.0
2015	B-	6.68	6.13	0.0	477.8	375.5	0.0	12.7
2014	B-	6.75	6.16	0.0	467.9	369.3	0.0	15.1
2013	B-	6.85	6.23	0.0	456.3	362.8	0.0	17.4

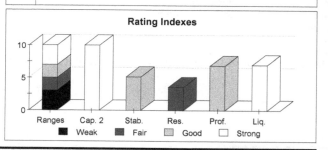

Rating Indexes

ELECTRIC INS CO   C+   Fair

Major Rating Factors: Fair overall results on stability tests (3.4 on a scale of 0 to 10) including potential drain of affiliation with Wilmington Trust. Fair profitability index (3.8). Good expense controls. Return on equity has been fair, averaging 5.6% over the past five years.

Other Rating Factors: Good liquidity (6.8) with sufficient resources (cash flows and marketable investments) to handle a spike in claims. Strong long-term capitalization index (8.8) based on excellent current risk adjusted capital (severe and moderate loss scenarios), despite some fluctuation in capital levels. Ample reserve history (9.3) that helps to protect the company against sharp claims increases.

Principal Business: Auto liability (26%), workers compensation (25%), homeowners multiple peril (24%), auto physical damage (18%), other liability (3%), products liability (2%), and other lines (2%).

Principal Investments: Investment grade bonds (92%), misc. investments (5%), non investment grade bonds (3%), and real estate (1%).

Investments in Affiliates: 2%

Group Affiliation: Wilmington Trust

Licensed in: All states, the District of Columbia and Puerto Rico

Commenced Business: September 1966

Address: 75 Sam Fonzo Drive, Beverly, MA 01915-1000

Phone: (978) 921-2080   **Domicile State:** MA   **NAIC Code:** 21261

Data Date	Rating	RACR #1	RACR #2	Loss Ratio %	Total Assets ($mil)	Capital ($mil)	Net Premium ($mil)	Net Income ($mil)
2017	C	3.81	2.29	82.3	1,424.1	491.5	279.1	32.6
2016	C+	3.57	2.16	76.0	1,488.6	534.1	329.3	30.2
2015	C+	3.62	2.24	81.6	1,507.8	545.5	346.5	23.6
2014	C+	3.68	2.30	82.4	1,467.2	537.6	302.0	25.4
2013	C+	3.16	1.92	79.8	1,448.7	522.6	353.3	33.6

Rating Indexes

EMPLOYERS COMPENSATION INS CO *   A-   Excellent

Major Rating Factors: Strong long-term capitalization index (7.6 on a scale of 0 to 10) based on excellent current risk adjusted capital (severe and moderate loss scenarios). Furthermore, this high level of risk adjusted capital has been consistently maintained in previous years. Ample reserve history (7.8) that can protect against increases in claims costs.

Other Rating Factors: Excellent profitability (7.3) with operating gains in each of the last five years. Excellent liquidity (7.0) with ample operational cash flow and liquid investments. Good overall results on stability tests (6.9). Stability strengths include good operational trends and excellent risk diversification.

Principal Business: Workers compensation (100%).

Principal Investments: Investment grade bonds (94%) and misc. investments (6%).

Investments in Affiliates: None

Group Affiliation: Employers Group Inc

Licensed in: All states except AK, DE, HI, NC, ND, OH, RI, WA, WY, PR

Commenced Business: September 2002

Address: 500 North Brand Boulevard, Glendale, CA 91203-4707

Phone: (775) 327-2700   **Domicile State:** CA   **NAIC Code:** 11512

Data Date	Rating	RACR #1	RACR #2	Loss Ratio %	Total Assets ($mil)	Capital ($mil)	Net Premium ($mil)	Net Income ($mil)
2017	A-	2.03	1.42	59.8	1,091.0	345.3	253.3	48.4
2016	B+	2.15	1.45	62.5	1,083.8	358.3	243.1	38.1
2015	B	1.93	1.27	65.1	1,094.1	335.1	265.0	19.6
2014	B	2.04	1.46	67.4	1,802.2	318.5	185.7	15.7
2013	B	1.69	1.20	73.8	1,712.3	299.0	183.2	8.3

($mil) Capital

EMPLOYERS INS OF WAUSAU   B-   Good

Major Rating Factors: Good overall results on stability tests (5.1 on a scale of 0 to 10) despite potential drain of affiliation with Liberty Mutual Group. History of adequate reserve strength (5.7) as reserves have been consistently at an acceptable level.

Other Rating Factors: Good profitability index (5.0) despite operating losses during 2017. Return on equity has been low, averaging 4.6% over the past five years. Good liquidity (6.2) with sufficient resources (cash flows and marketable investments) to handle a spike in claims. Strong long-term capitalization index (8.0) based on excellent current risk adjusted capital (severe and moderate loss scenarios), despite some fluctuation in capital levels.

Principal Business: Workers compensation (54%), fire (18%), auto liability (11%), allied lines (5%), earthquake (4%), products liability (3%), and other lines (6%).

Principal Investments: Investment grade bonds (78%), misc. investments (19%), and non investment grade bonds (5%).

Investments in Affiliates: 3%

Group Affiliation: Liberty Mutual Group

Licensed in: All states, the District of Columbia and Puerto Rico

Commenced Business: September 1911

Address: 2000 Westwood Drive, Wausau, WI 54401

Phone: (617) 357-9500   **Domicile State:** WI   **NAIC Code:** 21458

Data Date	Rating	RACR #1	RACR #2	Loss Ratio %	Total Assets ($mil)	Capital ($mil)	Net Premium ($mil)	Net Income ($mil)
2017	B-	2.32	1.64	79.5	6,056.4	1,521.5	2,284.0	-48.1
2016	B-	2.54	1.78	69.9	5,614.3	1,585.8	2,119.9	57.9
2015	B-	2.44	1.69	68.4	5,477.2	1,514.4	2,050.6	155.1
2014	B-	2.19	1.51	70.0	5,277.7	1,393.2	2,030.1	119.7
2013	B-	1.83	1.26	73.5	5,599.8	1,283.7	2,427.2	48.9

Rating Indexes

EMPLOYERS MUTUAL CAS CO

B- **Good**

Major Rating Factors: Fair overall results on stability tests (4.8 on a scale of 0 to 10) including potential drain of affiliation with Employers Mutual Group. Good liquidity (6.3) with sufficient resources (cash flows and marketable investments) to handle a spike in claims.

Other Rating Factors: Strong long-term capitalization index (8.0) based on excellent current risk adjusted capital (severe and moderate loss scenarios). Moreover, capital levels have been consistent in recent years. Ample reserve history (7.9) that can protect against increases in claims costs. Excellent profitability (8.1) with operating gains in each of the last five years.

Principal Business: Other liability (21%), auto liability (20%), workers compensation (16%), auto physical damage (10%), allied lines (8%), inland marine (6%), and other lines (19%).

Principal Investments: Misc. investments (49%), investment grade bonds (47%), and real estate (5%).

Investments in Affiliates: 19%

Group Affiliation: Employers Mutual Group

Licensed in: All states except PR

Commenced Business: July 1913

Address: 717 MULBERRY STREET, Des Moines, IA 50309-3872

Phone: (515) 280-2511   **Domicile State:** IA   **NAIC Code:** 21415

Data Date	Rating	RACR #1	RACR #2	Loss Ratio %	Total Assets ($mil)	Capital ($mil)	Net Premium ($mil)	Net Income ($mil)
2017	B-	2.14	1.68	69.7	3,404.4	1,436.6	1,172.9	59.3
2016	B-	2.09	1.66	65.2	3,198.0	1,378.6	1,123.0	65.9
2015	B-	2.08	1.66	65.7	2,890.6	1,276.3	946.0	61.4
2014	B-	2.06	1.65	70.0	2,721.4	1,215.0	902.2	45.4
2013	B-	2.06	1.65	66.7	2,538.0	1,121.9	845.0	56.1

Rating Indexes

ENDURANCE AMERICAN INS CO

B **Good**

Major Rating Factors: History of adequate reserve strength (5.7 on a scale of 0 to 10) as reserves have been consistently at an acceptable level. Good liquidity (6.7) with sufficient resources (cash flows and marketable investments) to handle a spike in claims.

Other Rating Factors: Good overall results on stability tests (5.5). Stability strengths include good operational trends and excellent risk diversification. Fair profitability index (4.2) with operating losses during 2013, 2014 and 2017. Average return on equity over the last five years has been poor at -1.7%. Strong long-term capitalization index (7.4) based on excellent current risk adjusted capital (severe and moderate loss scenarios), despite some fluctuation in capital levels.

Principal Business: Other liability (71%), aircraft (17%), ocean marine (6%), inland marine (4%), commercial multiple peril (2%), and surety (1%).

Principal Investments: Investment grade bonds (72%), misc. investments (20%), and cash (8%).

Investments in Affiliates: 12%

Group Affiliation: Endurance Specialty Holdings

Licensed in: All states except CA, MN, PR

Commenced Business: April 1996

Address: 1209 ORANGE STREET, Wilmington, DE 19801

Phone: (914) 468-8000   **Domicile State:** DE   **NAIC Code:** 10641

Data Date	Rating	RACR #1	RACR #2	Loss Ratio %	Total Assets ($mil)	Capital ($mil)	Net Premium ($mil)	Net Income ($mil)
2017	B	2.75	1.77	94.1	1,794.7	426.9	321.9	-11.9
2016	B-	1.60	1.12	79.3	1,293.3	283.1	253.8	20.3
2015	C+	1.29	0.94	78.4	1,227.4	262.7	233.1	16.5
2014	C	1.31	0.94	87.3	1,243.9	241.2	312.0	-4.9
2013	D+	1.27	0.87	94.4	1,313.8	247.5	362.2	-42.9

Reserve Deficiency (as % of capital)

* Adequate & redundant reserves show as negatives

ENDURANCE ASR CORP *

A- **Excellent**

Major Rating Factors: Strong long-term capitalization index (8.0 on a scale of 0 to 10) based on excellent current risk adjusted capital (severe and moderate loss scenarios). Furthermore, this high level of risk adjusted capital has been consistently maintained in previous years. Ample reserve history (8.6) that helps to protect the company against sharp claims increases.

Other Rating Factors: Excellent liquidity (7.4) with ample operational cash flow and liquid investments. Excellent overall results on stability tests (7.2). Stability strengths include excellent operational trends and excellent risk diversification. Fair profitability index (4.8) with operating losses during 2017. Return on equity has been low, averaging 3.2% over the past five years.

Principal Business: Other liability (53%), aircraft (29%), surety (10%), ocean marine (6%), and inland marine (1%).

Principal Investments: Investment grade bonds (63%), misc. investments (32%), and cash (5%).

Investments in Affiliates: 31%

Group Affiliation: Endurance Specialty Holdings

Licensed in: All states, the District of Columbia and Puerto Rico

Commenced Business: December 2002

Address: 1209 ORANGE STREET, Wilmington, DE 19801

Phone: (914) 468-8000   **Domicile State:** DE   **NAIC Code:** 11551

Data Date	Rating	RACR #1	RACR #2	Loss Ratio %	Total Assets ($mil)	Capital ($mil)	Net Premium ($mil)	Net Income ($mil)
2017	A-	1.84	1.66	73.0	2,059.0	891.5	377.8	-11.3
2016	B+	2.19	1.91	55.9	1,786.4	786.8	299.0	24.2
2015	B	2.24	1.94	47.7	1,642.9	739.3	262.4	35.7
2014	B	2.18	1.89	49.5	1,562.1	674.1	250.9	33.5
2013	B	1.92	1.61	51.2	1,489.7	629.0	263.2	28.4

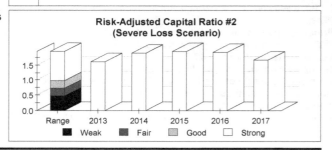

Risk-Adjusted Capital Ratio #2
(Severe Loss Scenario)

ERIE & NIAGARA INS ASSN *   B+   Good

Major Rating Factors: History of adequate reserve strength (6.0 on a scale of 0 to 10) as reserves have been consistently at an acceptable level. Good liquidity (6.9) with sufficient resources (cash flows and marketable investments) to handle a spike in claims.

Other Rating Factors: Good overall results on stability tests (6.5). Strong long-term capitalization index (10.0) based on excellent current risk adjusted capital (severe and moderate loss scenarios). Moreover, capital has steadily grown over the last five years. Excellent profitability (8.8) with operating gains in each of the last five years.

Principal Business: Commercial multiple peril (42%), homeowners multiple peril (26%), farmowners multiple peril (15%), fire (15%), and inland marine (1%).

Principal Investments: Investment grade bonds (75%), misc. investments (21%), cash (3%), and real estate (1%).

Investments in Affiliates: 0%

Group Affiliation: Erie & Niagara Ins Assoc

Licensed in: NY

Commenced Business: January 1875

Address: 8800 SHERIDAN DRIVE, Williamsville, NY 14231-9062

Phone: (716) 632-5433   **Domicile State:** NY   **NAIC Code:** 10374

Data Date	Rating	RACR #1	RACR #2	Loss Ratio %	Total Assets ($mil)	Capital ($mil)	Net Premium ($mil)	Net Income ($mil)
2017	B+	7.32	4.86	43.4	234.3	160.5	70.8	13.0
2016	B	7.38	4.96	40.7	210.6	141.7	66.4	13.5
2015	C+	7.08	4.78	47.0	192.4	125.8	63.4	10.4
2014	C	6.59	4.41	48.1	182.5	115.5	61.1	9.1
2013	C	6.66	4.47	39.2	165.4	106.5	57.3	11.1

Rating Indexes: Ranges, Cap. 2, Stab., Res., Prof., Liq. — Weak, Fair, Good, Strong

ERIE INS CO   B-   Good

Major Rating Factors: Fair overall results on stability tests (4.9 on a scale of 0 to 10) including potential drain of affiliation with Erie Ins Group. Good liquidity (6.5) with sufficient resources (cash flows and marketable investments) to handle a spike in claims.

Other Rating Factors: Strong long-term capitalization index (10.0) based on excellent current risk adjusted capital (severe and moderate loss scenarios). Moreover, capital has steadily grown over the last five years. Ample reserve history (7.8) that can protect against increases in claims costs. Excellent profitability (8.4) with operating gains in each of the last five years.

Principal Business: Homeowners multiple peril (56%), auto liability (19%), auto physical damage (14%), commercial multiple peril (7%), workers compensation (3%), and other liability (1%).

Principal Investments: Investment grade bonds (90%), misc. investments (8%), and non investment grade bonds (2%).

Investments in Affiliates: 5%

Group Affiliation: Erie Ins Group

Licensed in: DC, IL, IN, KY, MD, MN, NY, NC, OH, PA, TN, VA, WV, WI

Commenced Business: January 1973

Address: 100 Erie Insurance Place, Erie, PA 16530

Phone: (814) 870-2000   **Domicile State:** PA   **NAIC Code:** 26263

Data Date	Rating	RACR #1	RACR #2	Loss Ratio %	Total Assets ($mil)	Capital ($mil)	Net Premium ($mil)	Net Income ($mil)
2017	B-	5.32	3.76	68.6	1,039.0	374.3	331.5	22.1
2016	B-	5.29	3.73	68.8	967.7	353.7	312.7	19.5
2015	B-	5.15	3.65	69.4	899.7	334.6	294.6	19.2
2014	B+	5.13	3.66	73.0	839.3	311.9	274.4	12.0
2013	B-	5.04	3.48	69.4	771.8	294.4	252.3	17.1

Erie Ins Group
Composite Group Rating: B

Largest Group Members	Assets ($mil)	Rating
ERIE INS EXCHANGE	16975	B
ERIE FAMILY LIFE INS CO	2433	A-
ERIE INS CO	1039	B-
ERIE INS CO OF NEW YORK	113	B
ERIE INS PC CO	110	B-

ERIE INS EXCHANGE   B   Good

Major Rating Factors: Good overall results on stability tests (5.1 on a scale of 0 to 10) despite potential drain of affiliation with Erie Ins Group. Good liquidity (6.4) with sufficient resources (cash flows and marketable investments) to handle a spike in claims.

Other Rating Factors: Strong long-term capitalization index (9.5) based on excellent current risk adjusted capital (severe and moderate loss scenarios). Moreover, capital levels have been consistent in recent years. Ample reserve history (7.7) that can protect against increases in claims costs. Excellent profitability (8.6) with operating gains in each of the last five years.

Principal Business: Auto liability (34%), auto physical damage (26%), homeowners multiple peril (17%), commercial multiple peril (16%), workers compensation (4%), other liability (3%), and inland marine (1%).

Principal Investments: Investment grade bonds (47%), misc. investments (42%), non investment grade bonds (10%), and real estate (1%).

Investments in Affiliates: 5%

Group Affiliation: Erie Ins Group

Licensed in: AL, CT, DC, DE, GA, IL, IN, IA, KY, ME, MD, MN, MO, MT, NE, NV, NH, NJ, NM, NY, NC, ND, OH, PA, RI, SC, SD, TN, TX, VT, VA, WV, WI, WY

Commenced Business: April 1925

Address: 100 Erie Insurance Place, Erie, PA 16530

Phone: (814) 870-2000   **Domicile State:** PA   **NAIC Code:** 26271

Data Date	Rating	RACR #1	RACR #2	Loss Ratio %	Total Assets ($mil)	Capital ($mil)	Net Premium ($mil)	Net Income ($mil)
2017	B	4.19	2.72	68.6	16,974.6	8,802.8	6,264.4	628.9
2016	B	4.03	2.63	68.8	15,016.9	7,710.6	5,910.0	509.8
2015	B	3.97	2.65	69.4	13,930.7	7,141.5	5,567.1	465.6
2014	B	3.74	2.51	73.0	13,344.7	6,816.6	5,185.5	353.0
2013	B	3.68	2.51	69.4	12,591.7	6,467.0	4,767.7	478.8

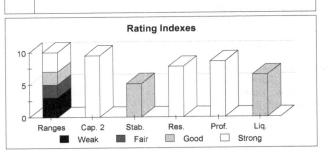

Rating Indexes: Ranges, Cap. 2, Stab., Res., Prof., Liq. — Weak, Fair, Good, Strong

ESSENT GUARANTY INC *

A-   Excellent

Major Rating Factors: Strong long-term capitalization index (10.0 on a scale of 0 to 10) based on excellent current risk adjusted capital (severe and moderate loss scenarios). Furthermore, this high level of risk adjusted capital has been consistently maintained in previous years. Excellent profitability (9.6) with operating gains in each of the last five years. Return on equity has been excellent over the last five years averaging 28.9%.

Other Rating Factors: Excellent liquidity (7.6) with ample operational cash flow and liquid investments. History of adequate reserve strength (5.3) as reserves have been consistently at an acceptable level. Good overall results on stability tests (6.7). Stability strengths include good operational trends and excellent risk diversification.

Principal Business: Mortgage guaranty (100%).

Principal Investments: Investment grade bonds (88%), misc. investments (8%), cash (3%), and non investment grade bonds (1%).

Investments in Affiliates: None

Group Affiliation: Essent Group Ltd

Licensed in: All states except PR

Commenced Business: July 2009

Address: 2 Radnor Corp 100 Matsonford, Radnor, PA 19087

Phone: (877) 673-8190   **Domicile State:** PA   **NAIC Code:** 13634

Data Date	Rating	RACR #1	RACR #2	Loss Ratio %	Total Assets ($mil)	Capital ($mil)	Net Premium ($mil)	Net Income ($mil)
2017	A-	13.19	7.59	5.2	1,756.6	761.0	423.3	261.8
2016	A-	10.85	6.38	3.7	1,323.6	578.9	340.6	216.0
2015	A-	6.05	3.77	3.6	1,072.6	522.2	299.0	172.7
2014	A-	6.33	4.08	2.8	817.3	465.2	239.6	118.2
2013	A-	6.30	4.22	1.9	546.8	346.4	169.8	49.8

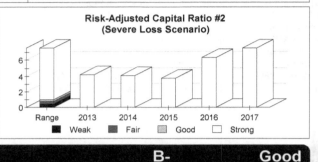

Risk-Adjusted Capital Ratio #2
(Severe Loss Scenario)

EVEREST REINS CO

B-   Good

Major Rating Factors: Fair overall results on stability tests (4.7 on a scale of 0 to 10) including potential drain of affiliation with Everest Reinsurance Group and negative cash flow from operations for 2017. History of adequate reserve strength (6.3) as reserves have been consistently at an acceptable level.

Other Rating Factors: Good overall profitability index (5.3) despite operating losses during 2017. Return on equity has been fair, averaging 10.0% over the past five years. Good liquidity (6.6) with sufficient resources (cash flows and marketable investments) to handle a spike in claims. Strong long-term capitalization index (8.0) based on excellent current risk adjusted capital (severe and moderate loss scenarios), despite some fluctuation in capital levels.

Principal Business: Other liability (63%), group accident & health (16%), surety (13%), other accident & health (6%), credit (1%), and fidelity (1%).

Principal Investments: Investment grade bonds (55%), misc. investments (42%), cash (2%), and non investment grade bonds (1%).

Investments in Affiliates: 5%

Group Affiliation: Everest Reinsurance Group

Licensed in: All states, the District of Columbia and Puerto Rico

Commenced Business: June 1973

Address: 1209 Orange Street, Wilmington, DE 19801

Phone: (908) 604-3000   **Domicile State:** DE   **NAIC Code:** 26921

Data Date	Rating	RACR #1	RACR #2	Loss Ratio %	Total Assets ($mil)	Capital ($mil)	Net Premium ($mil)	Net Income ($mil)
2017	B-	2.40	1.68	105.2	9,486.1	3,391.9	1,741.2	-391.4
2016	B-	3.40	2.18	63.5	10,224.8	3,635.1	2,050.6	523.5
2015	B-	2.61	1.71	58.8	9,979.6	3,210.9	2,079.5	498.5
2014	C+	2.27	1.47	61.7	9,616.2	2,893.0	2,121.8	357.3
2013	C+	1.13	0.93	59.5	9,288.4	2,814.3	2,024.4	540.0

Rating Indexes

EXECUTIVE RISK INDEMNITY INC

B   Good

Major Rating Factors: Good liquidity (6.9 on a scale of 0 to 10) with sufficient resources (cash flows and marketable investments) to handle a spike in claims. Good overall results on stability tests (5.5) despite negative cash flow from operations for 2017. Stability strengths include good operational trends and excellent risk diversification.

Other Rating Factors: Strong long-term capitalization index (9.4) based on excellent current risk adjusted capital (severe and moderate loss scenarios), despite some fluctuation in capital levels. Ample reserve history (8.7) that helps to protect the company against sharp claims increases. Excellent profitability (8.6) with operating gains in each of the last five years. Return on equity has been good over the last five years, averaging 12.9%.

Principal Business: Other liability (67%), homeowners multiple peril (16%), products liability (9%), commercial multiple peril (4%), inland marine (2%), and fidelity (1%).

Principal Investments: Investment grade bonds (83%), misc. investments (16%), and real estate (1%).

Investments in Affiliates: 14%

Group Affiliation: Chubb Limited

Licensed in: All states except PR

Commenced Business: January 1978

Address: 1209 Orange Street, Wilmington, DE 19801-1120

Phone: (215) 640-1000   **Domicile State:** DE   **NAIC Code:** 35181

Data Date	Rating	RACR #1	RACR #2	Loss Ratio %	Total Assets ($mil)	Capital ($mil)	Net Premium ($mil)	Net Income ($mil)
2017	B	3.30	2.70	62.6	3,231.3	1,489.6	406.2	131.3
2016	B-	3.97	2.77	53.6	2,901.4	1,251.0	506.9	189.0
2015	B	3.41	2.32	56.5	3,068.2	1,267.1	782.7	168.4
2014	B	3.42	2.33	56.7	3,024.8	1,258.0	751.6	164.2
2013	B+	3.43	2.34	52.7	2,977.3	1,218.6	721.2	174.1

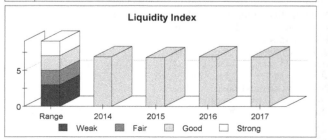

Liquidity Index

FACTORY MUTUAL INS CO　　　　　　　　　B-　　　　Good

Major Rating Factors: Fair overall results on stability tests (4.7 on a scale of 0 to 10) including potential drain of affiliation with Factory Mutual Ins. History of adequate reserve strength (6.2) as reserves have been consistently at an acceptable level.

Other Rating Factors: Good overall profitability index (5.1) despite operating losses during 2017. Good liquidity (6.8) with sufficient resources (cash flows and marketable investments) to handle a spike in claims. Strong long-term capitalization index (8.3) based on excellent current risk adjusted capital (severe and moderate loss scenarios). Moreover, capital levels have been consistent in recent years.

Principal Business: Allied lines (34%), inland marine (31%), boiler & machinery (20%), and fire (15%).

Principal Investments: Misc. investments (73%), investment grade bonds (24%), non investment grade bonds (2%), and cash (1%).

Investments in Affiliates: 20%

Group Affiliation: Factory Mutual Ins

Licensed in: All states, the District of Columbia and Puerto Rico

Commenced Business: December 1835

Address: 270 Central Avenue, Johnston, RI 02919-4949

Phone: (401) 275-3000　　**Domicile State:** RI　　**NAIC Code:** 21482

Data Date	Rating	RACR #1	RACR #2	Loss Ratio %	Total Assets ($mil)	Capital ($mil)	Net Premium ($mil)	Net Income ($mil)
2017	B-	2.34	1.84	109.1	19,155.5	12,501.8	2,894.6	-333.4
2016	B-	2.64	2.04	54.5	16,764.3	11,519.4	2,795.2	601.6
2015	C+	2.57	1.98	58.0	15,682.9	10,546.7	2,782.1	550.1
2014	C	2.50	1.91	50.2	15,070.1	10,141.8	2,838.5	670.8
2013	C	2.48	1.90	50.6	13,795.7	9,153.5	2,824.5	662.5

Rating Indexes

Ranges　Cap. 2　Stab.　Res.　Prof.　Liq.

■ Weak　■ Fair　▨ Good　□ Strong

FARM BU TOWN & COUNTRY INS CO OF MO *　　B+　　Good

Major Rating Factors: Good liquidity (5.4 on a scale of 0 to 10) with sufficient resources (cash flows and marketable investments) to handle a spike in claims. Good overall results on stability tests (6.5).

Other Rating Factors: Strong long-term capitalization index (9.0) based on excellent current risk adjusted capital (severe and moderate loss scenarios). Moreover, capital levels have been consistent in recent years. Ample reserve history (7.6) that can protect against increases in claims costs. Excellent profitability (8.5) with operating gains in each of the last five years. Return on equity has been good over the last five years, averaging 10.5%.

Principal Business: Homeowners multiple peril (28%), farmowners multiple peril (24%), auto physical damage (20%), auto liability (20%), commercial multiple peril (5%), and other liability (1%).

Principal Investments: Investment grade bonds (80%), misc. investments (19%), and cash (1%).

Investments in Affiliates: 5%

Group Affiliation: Missouri Farm Bureau

Licensed in: MO

Commenced Business: April 1946

Address: 701 South Country Club Drive, Jefferson City, MO 65109-4515

Phone: (573) 893-1400　　**Domicile State:** MO　　**NAIC Code:** 26859

Data Date	Rating	RACR #1	RACR #2	Loss Ratio %	Total Assets ($mil)	Capital ($mil)	Net Premium ($mil)	Net Income ($mil)
2017	B+	3.49	2.39	82.2	421.4	191.3	216.1	5.8
2016	B	3.51	2.42	68.8	398.1	186.7	201.5	21.2
2015	B	3.43	2.33	71.8	362.8	163.8	187.9	17.1
2014	B	3.17	2.16	71.0	335.3	148.4	179.5	17.3
2013	B	2.67	1.83	68.8	311.6	131.0	168.4	20.7

Liquidity Index

Range　2014　2015　2016　2017

■ Weak　■ Fair　▨ Good　□ Strong

FARM BUREAU GENERAL INS CO OF MI *　　B+　　Good

Major Rating Factors: History of adequate reserve strength (6.2 on a scale of 0 to 10) as reserves have been consistently at an acceptable level. Good overall profitability index (6.9). Good expense controls. Return on equity has been fair, averaging 5.4% over the past five years.

Other Rating Factors: Good liquidity (5.7) with sufficient resources (cash flows and marketable investments) to handle a spike in claims. Good overall results on stability tests (6.5). Strong long-term capitalization index (9.9) based on excellent current risk adjusted capital (severe and moderate loss scenarios). Moreover, capital levels have been consistent in recent years.

Principal Business: Auto liability (33%), auto physical damage (27%), homeowners multiple peril (25%), commercial multiple peril (6%), workers compensation (3%), inland marine (1%), and other lines (4%).

Principal Investments: Investment grade bonds (84%), misc. investments (17%), and non investment grade bonds (1%).

Investments in Affiliates: None

Group Affiliation: Michigan Farm Bureau

Licensed in: MI

Commenced Business: July 1962

Address: 7373 W SAGINAW, Lansing, MI 48917

Phone: (517) 323-7000　　**Domicile State:** MI　　**NAIC Code:** 21547

Data Date	Rating	RACR #1	RACR #2	Loss Ratio %	Total Assets ($mil)	Capital ($mil)	Net Premium ($mil)	Net Income ($mil)
2017	B+	4.48	3.01	74.3	719.9	321.1	350.9	14.3
2016	B	4.54	3.17	71.2	677.8	300.2	336.4	23.9
2015	B	4.41	3.06	72.1	651.5	273.2	312.7	20.9
2014	B	3.26	2.31	79.7	528.8	178.5	287.3	7.3
2013	B	3.12	2.20	74.8	503.8	170.3	286.4	5.3

Reserve Deficiency (as % of capital)

2013　2014　2015　2016　2017

■ 1 Yr Dev　□ 2 Yr Dev

* Adequate & redundant reserves show as negatives

FARM BUREAU MUTUAL INS CO OF AR | B | Good

Major Rating Factors: Good liquidity (6.1 on a scale of 0 to 10) with sufficient resources (cash flows and marketable investments) to handle a spike in claims. Good overall results on stability tests (6.1). Stability strengths include good operational trends and excellent risk diversification.

Other Rating Factors: Strong long-term capitalization index (10.0) based on excellent current risk adjusted capital (severe and moderate loss scenarios). Moreover, capital levels have been consistent in recent years. Ample reserve history (7.9) that can protect against increases in claims costs. Excellent profitability (8.9) with operating gains in each of the last five years. Return on equity has been good over the last five years, averaging 11.6%.

Principal Business: Homeowners multiple peril (56%), fire (16%), inland marine (16%), allied lines (8%), other liability (2%), and commercial multiple peril (1%).

Principal Investments: Investment grade bonds (93%), misc. investments (8%), and real estate (1%).

Investments in Affiliates: 1%

Group Affiliation: None

Licensed in: AR

Commenced Business: March 1950

Address: 10720 Kanis Road, Little Rock, AR 72211

Phone: (501) 224-4400 **Domicile State:** AR **NAIC Code:** 13757

Data Date	Rating	RACR #1	RACR #2	Loss Ratio %	Total Assets ($mil)	Capital ($mil)	Net Premium ($mil)	Net Income ($mil)
2017	B	6.36	4.67	74.7	408.6	253.3	197.6	13.5
2016	B	6.11	4.29	71.6	402.0	242.4	197.3	17.2
2015	B	5.06	3.47	60.6	387.2	224.9	201.9	32.0
2014	C+	4.58	3.14	71.0	355.5	192.5	195.2	18.9
2013	C+	4.04	2.77	55.3	336.4	172.8	194.5	37.0

Liquidity Index

FARM BUREAU MUTUAL INS CO OF ID | B | Good

Major Rating Factors: History of adequate reserve strength (6.0 on a scale of 0 to 10) as reserves have been consistently at an acceptable level. Good liquidity (6.0) with sufficient resources (cash flows and marketable investments) to handle a spike in claims.

Other Rating Factors: Fair overall results on stability tests (4.7) including potential drain of affiliation with Farm Bureau Group of Idaho and negative cash flow from operations for 2017. Fair profitability index (3.6) with operating losses during 2015 and 2017. Strong long-term capitalization index (8.7) based on excellent current risk adjusted capital (severe and moderate loss scenarios), despite some fluctuation in capital levels.

Principal Business: Auto liability (31%), auto physical damage (26%), homeowners multiple peril (19%), farmowners multiple peril (17%), inland marine (3%), other liability (2%), and allied lines (2%).

Principal Investments: Investment grade bonds (59%), misc. investments (35%), cash (3%), and real estate (3%).

Investments in Affiliates: 21%

Group Affiliation: Farm Bureau Group of Idaho

Licensed in: ID

Commenced Business: May 1947

Address: 275 Tierra Vista Drive, Pocatello, ID 83201

Phone: (208) 232-7914 **Domicile State:** ID **NAIC Code:** 13765

Data Date	Rating	RACR #1	RACR #2	Loss Ratio %	Total Assets ($mil)	Capital ($mil)	Net Premium ($mil)	Net Income ($mil)
2017	B	2.51	2.10	88.9	467.0	241.0	197.7	-13.6
2016	B	2.83	2.37	70.9	470.4	254.1	187.6	13.0
2015	B	2.90	2.40	82.1	447.8	238.5	169.0	-2.9
2014	B	3.08	2.55	77.9	440.3	241.5	162.4	4.8
2013	B+	3.30	2.70	78.2	418.0	233.1	151.7	5.4

Reserve Deficiency (as % of capital)

* Adequate & redundant reserves show as negatives

FARM BUREAU MUTUAL INS CO OF MI * | B+ | Good

Major Rating Factors: Good liquidity (6.0 on a scale of 0 to 10) with sufficient resources (cash flows and marketable investments) to handle a spike in claims. Good overall results on stability tests (6.5).

Other Rating Factors: Strong long-term capitalization index (10.0) based on excellent current risk adjusted capital (severe and moderate loss scenarios). Moreover, capital has steadily grown over the last five years. Ample reserve history (8.4) that helps to protect the company against sharp claims increases. Excellent profitability (8.7) with operating gains in each of the last five years.

Principal Business: Farmowners multiple peril (46%), auto liability (25%), auto physical damage (19%), workers compensation (6%), inland marine (2%), other liability (2%), and boiler & machinery (1%).

Principal Investments: Investment grade bonds (78%), misc. investments (22%), and non investment grade bonds (1%).

Investments in Affiliates: None

Group Affiliation: Michigan Farm Bureau

Licensed in: AL, CA, CT, DE, GA, IL, IN, IA, KS, KY, LA, ME, MD, MA, MI, MN, MO, MT, NE, NH, NJ, NC, ND, OH, OK, OR, PA, RI, SC, SD, TN, TX, UT, VT, VA, WV, WI

Commenced Business: March 1949

Address: 7373 W SAGINAW, Lansing, MI 48917

Phone: (517) 323-7000 **Domicile State:** MI **NAIC Code:** 21555

Data Date	Rating	RACR #1	RACR #2	Loss Ratio %	Total Assets ($mil)	Capital ($mil)	Net Premium ($mil)	Net Income ($mil)
2017	B+	4.96	3.38	65.6	782.4	406.5	352.7	29.1
2016	B	4.41	2.89	66.8	740.3	363.2	357.5	28.7
2015	B	4.22	2.75	65.5	706.3	331.1	345.3	36.7
2014	B-	4.08	2.65	70.8	651.9	290.3	324.9	23.7
2013	B-	3.82	2.49	69.8	630.6	262.8	286.9	21.4

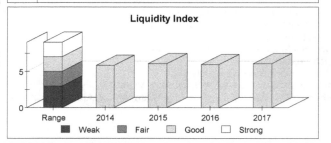

Liquidity Index

FARM BUREAU P&C INS CO *　　　　　　A- 　　Excellent

Major Rating Factors: Excellent overall results on stability tests (7.2 on a scale of 0 to 10). Stability strengths include excellent operational trends and excellent risk diversification. Strong long-term capitalization index (10.0) based on excellent current risk adjusted capital (severe and moderate loss scenarios). Furthermore, this high level of risk adjusted capital has been consistently maintained in previous years.

Other Rating Factors: Ample reserve history (8.2) that helps to protect the company against sharp claims increases. Excellent profitability (8.9) with operating gains in each of the last five years. Return on equity has been good over the last five years, averaging 10.2%. Good liquidity (6.0) with sufficient resources (cash flows and marketable investments) to handle a spike in claims.

Principal Business: Farmowners multiple peril (26%), homeowners multiple peril (23%), auto liability (21%), auto physical damage (20%), commercial multiple peril (4%), other liability (3%), and workers compensation (2%).

Principal Investments: Investment grade bonds (79%), misc. investments (20%), non investment grade bonds (1%), and real estate (1%).

Investments in Affiliates: 6%

Group Affiliation: Iowa Farm Bureau

Licensed in: AZ, ID, IA, KS, MN, MO, NE, NM, SD, UT, WI

Commenced Business: May 1939

Address: 5400 University Avenue, West Des Moines, IA 50266-5997

Phone: (515) 225-5400　　**Domicile State:** IA　　**NAIC Code:** 13773

Data Date	Rating	RACR #1	RACR #2	Loss Ratio %	Total Assets ($mil)	Capital ($mil)	Net Premium ($mil)	Net Income ($mil)
2017	A-	4.62	3.50	66.3	2,532.4	1,303.7	1,238.8	117.1
2016	B+	4.35	3.29	59.9	2,443.5	1,193.5	1,214.8	157.3
2015	B+	3.85	2.91	62.2	2,243.1	1,020.4	1,209.0	129.0
2014	B+	3.57	2.69	70.3	2,036.2	880.6	1,166.7	65.4
2013	A-	3.45	2.57	70.2	1,931.3	802.3	1,127.9	68.6

Rating Indexes

Ranges　Cap. 2　Stab.　Res.　Prof.　Liq.
■ Weak　■ Fair　□ Good　□ Strong

FARM FAMILY CASUALTY INS CO *　　　　　B+ 　　Good

Major Rating Factors: Good overall results on stability tests (6.8 on a scale of 0 to 10). Affiliation with American National Group Inc is a strength. Good liquidity (6.6) with sufficient resources (cash flows and marketable investments) to handle a spike in claims.

Other Rating Factors: Strong long-term capitalization index (9.7) based on excellent current risk adjusted capital (severe and moderate loss scenarios). Moreover, capital levels have been consistent in recent years. Ample reserve history (9.3) that helps to protect the company against sharp claims increases. Excellent profitability (8.4) with operating gains in each of the last five years.

Principal Business: Auto liability (19%), workers compensation (16%), commercial multiple peril (14%), other liability (12%), allied lines (11%), fire (9%), and other lines (20%).

Principal Investments: Investment grade bonds (88%), misc. investments (10%), and non investment grade bonds (2%).

Investments in Affiliates: None

Group Affiliation: American National Group Inc

Licensed in: CT, DE, ME, MD, MA, MO, NH, NJ, NY, PA, RI, VT, VA, WV

Commenced Business: November 1956

Address: 344 ROUTE 9W, Glenmont, NY 12077

Phone: (518) 431-5000　　**Domicile State:** NY　　**NAIC Code:** 13803

Data Date	Rating	RACR #1	RACR #2	Loss Ratio %	Total Assets ($mil)	Capital ($mil)	Net Premium ($mil)	Net Income ($mil)
2017	B+	4.78	3.08	60.0	1,241.7	481.4	444.4	57.6
2016	B+	4.30	2.84	64.4	1,164.4	424.4	428.8	41.4
2015	B+	3.85	2.55	71.0	1,096.5	376.5	407.6	24.9
2014	B+	3.64	2.43	72.8	1,080.0	365.7	392.7	17.5
2013	B+	3.57	2.39	72.1	1,036.7	347.1	371.1	27.6

American National Group Inc
Composite Group Rating: B

Largest Group Members	Assets ($mil)	Rating
AMERICAN NATIONAL INS CO	20147	B
AMERICAN NATIONAL PROPERTY CAS CO	1418	B+
FARM FAMILY LIFE INS CO	1370	B
FARM FAMILY CASUALTY INS CO	1242	B+
STANDARD LIFE ACCIDENT INS CO	522	A-

FARMERS AUTOMOBILE INS ASN *　　　　B+ 　　Good

Major Rating Factors: Good liquidity (6.2 on a scale of 0 to 10) with sufficient resources (cash flows and marketable investments) to handle a spike in claims. Good overall results on stability tests (6.0).

Other Rating Factors: Strong long-term capitalization index (8.0) based on excellent current risk adjusted capital (severe and moderate loss scenarios), despite some fluctuation in capital levels. Ample reserve history (7.8) that can protect against increases in claims costs. Fair profitability index (4.1) with small operating losses during 2016.

Principal Business: Homeowners multiple peril (33%), auto liability (31%), auto physical damage (30%), allied lines (3%), fire (2%), and inland marine (1%).

Principal Investments: Investment grade bonds (67%), misc. investments (29%), cash (2%), and real estate (2%).

Investments in Affiliates: 23%

Group Affiliation: Farmers Automobile Ins Assn

Licensed in: AZ, IL, IN, IA, MI, OH, WI

Commenced Business: April 1921

Address: 2505 COURT STREET, Pekin, IL 61558-0001

Phone: (309) 346-1161　　**Domicile State:** IL　　**NAIC Code:** 24201

Data Date	Rating	RACR #1	RACR #2	Loss Ratio %	Total Assets ($mil)	Capital ($mil)	Net Premium ($mil)	Net Income ($mil)
2017	B+	1.94	1.69	74.2	1,226.6	480.7	491.0	13.9
2016	B+	2.15	1.86	77.7	1,266.9	514.6	491.2	-1.8
2015	B+	2.25	1.95	71.5	1,228.6	519.1	480.8	15.4
2014	B+	2.24	1.95	74.3	1,171.2	491.2	455.1	10.5
2013	B+	2.36	2.06	75.4	1,153.5	497.8	428.5	10.2

Liquidity Index

Range　2014　2015　2016　2017
■ Weak　■ Fair　□ Good　□ Strong

FARMERS INS CO OF OREGON
B   **Good**

Major Rating Factors: Good overall results on stability tests (5.4 on a scale of 0 to 10) despite potential drain of affiliation with Farmers Insurance Group of Companies and negative cash flow from operations for 2017. History of adequate reserve strength (5.6) as reserves have been consistently at an acceptable level.

Other Rating Factors: Good overall profitability index (5.3). Fair expense controls. Return on equity has been low, averaging 3.3% over the past five years. Good liquidity (5.9) with sufficient resources (cash flows and marketable investments) to handle a spike in claims. Strong long-term capitalization index (8.2) based on excellent current risk adjusted capital (severe and moderate loss scenarios), despite some fluctuation in capital levels.

Principal Business: Auto liability (59%), auto physical damage (22%), homeowners multiple peril (12%), commercial multiple peril (4%), earthquake (1%), and allied lines (1%).

Principal Investments: Investment grade bonds (98%) and cash (2%).

Investments in Affiliates: None

Group Affiliation: Farmers Insurance Group of Companies

Licensed in: CA, MI, OR

Commenced Business: October 1970

Address: 23175 NW BENNETT ST, Tigard, OR 97223

Phone: (503) 372-2000   **Domicile State:** OR   **NAIC Code:** 21636

Data Date	Rating	RACR #1	RACR #2	Loss Ratio %	Total Assets ($mil)	Capital ($mil)	Net Premium ($mil)	Net Income ($mil)
2017	B	2.63	1.88	69.7	1,634.6	529.6	992.9	15.5
2016	B	2.53	1.79	71.8	1,691.3	533.1	1,033.3	7.7
2015	B	2.48	1.77	68.7	1,681.5	529.8	1,045.1	18.0
2014	B	2.56	1.85	65.7	1,627.9	514.6	984.4	21.3
2013	B	2.48	1.81	66.8	1,614.9	490.3	954.6	21.9

Farmers Insurance Group of Companies
Composite Group Rating: C

Largest Group Members	Assets ($mil)	Rating
FARMERS INS EXCHANGE	16165	C
MID-CENTURY INS CO	3942	B
FIRE INS EXCHANGE	2864	C+
FOREMOST INS CO	2317	B
TRUCK INS EXCHANGE	2108	C+

FARMERS INS EXCHANGE
C   **Fair**

Major Rating Factors: Fair profitability index (3.7 on a scale of 0 to 10) with operating losses during 2015, 2016 and 2017. Fair overall results on stability tests (4.3) including negative cash flow from operations for 2017.

Other Rating Factors: Vulnerable liquidity (2.6) as a spike in claims may stretch capacity. Good long-term capitalization index (5.3) based on good current risk adjusted capital (severe and moderate loss scenarios). History of adequate reserve strength (5.4) as reserves have been consistently at an acceptable level.

Principal Business: Homeowners multiple peril (33%), auto liability (32%), auto physical damage (19%), commercial multiple peril (10%), other liability (2%), and workers compensation (1%).

Principal Investments: Misc. investments (57%), investment grade bonds (38%), real estate (4%), and non investment grade bonds (1%).

Investments in Affiliates: 48%

Group Affiliation: Farmers Insurance Group of Companies

Licensed in: All states except AK, CT, HI, PR

Commenced Business: April 1928

Address: 6301 OWENSMOUTH AVE, Woodland Hills, CA 91367

Phone: (323) 932-3200   **Domicile State:** CA   **NAIC Code:** 21652

Data Date	Rating	RACR #1	RACR #2	Loss Ratio %	Total Assets ($mil)	Capital ($mil)	Net Premium ($mil)	Net Income ($mil)
2017	C	0.85	0.79	70.0	16,164.8	4,203.1	7,340.6	-65.4
2016	C	0.87	0.80	72.5	16,057.2	4,218.8	7,639.3	-147.9
2015	C	0.89	0.82	69.0	15,566.6	4,206.8	7,726.6	-113.7
2014	C	0.92	0.85	65.8	15,591.3	4,181.5	7,277.2	2.5
2013	C	0.90	0.84	66.8	15,557.1	3,879.7	7,057.1	55.0

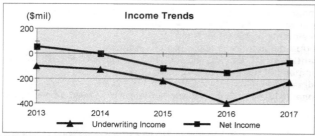

Income Trends — Underwriting Income / Net Income (2013–2017)

FARMERS MUTUAL HAIL INS CO OF IA
B-   **Good**

Major Rating Factors: Fair overall results on stability tests (4.6 on a scale of 0 to 10) including potential drain of affiliation with Farmers Mutual Hail Ins Co and excessive premium growth. Good overall profitability index (5.7) despite operating losses during 2014.

Other Rating Factors: Strong long-term capitalization index (7.6) based on excellent current risk adjusted capital (severe and moderate loss scenarios), despite some fluctuation in capital levels. Ample reserve history (7.9) that can protect against increases in claims costs. Vulnerable liquidity (2.8) as a spike in claims may stretch capacity.

Principal Business: Allied lines (95%), fire (3%), auto liability (1%), auto physical damage (1%), and other liability (1%).

Principal Investments: Misc. investments (57%), investment grade bonds (30%), cash (8%), real estate (3%), and non investment grade bonds (2%).

Investments in Affiliates: 34%

Group Affiliation: Farmers Mutual Hail Ins Co

Licensed in: All states except AK, DC, HI, ME, NV, PR

Commenced Business: March 1893

Address: 6785 WESTOWN PARKWAY, West Des Moines, IA 50266

Phone: (515) 724-5007   **Domicile State:** IA   **NAIC Code:** 13897

Data Date	Rating	RACR #1	RACR #2	Loss Ratio %	Total Assets ($mil)	Capital ($mil)	Net Premium ($mil)	Net Income ($mil)
2017	B-	2.01	1.49	72.8	752.1	450.9	452.8	32.6
2016	B-	2.00	1.54	63.6	703.6	423.8	334.2	45.0
2015	B-	1.67	1.27	77.9	744.5	366.6	360.4	9.4
2014	B-	1.77	1.14	91.0	676.3	309.5	390.2	-31.2
2013	B-	1.98	1.24	85.9	832.8	358.3	431.1	3.9

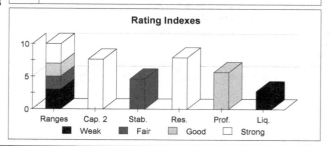

Rating Indexes — Ranges, Cap. 2, Stab., Res., Prof., Liq. (Weak / Fair / Good / Strong)

FARMERS MUTUAL INS CO OF NE *   B+   Good

Major Rating Factors: History of adequate reserve strength (6.3 on a scale of 0 to 10) as reserves have been consistently at an acceptable level. Good overall profitability index (6.1) despite operating losses during 2014.

Other Rating Factors: Good liquidity (6.1) with sufficient resources (cash flows and marketable investments) to handle a spike in claims. Good overall results on stability tests (6.5). Strong long-term capitalization index (10.0) based on excellent current risk adjusted capital (severe and moderate loss scenarios), despite some fluctuation in capital levels.

Principal Business: Farmowners multiple peril (30%), homeowners multiple peril (27%), auto physical damage (21%), auto liability (16%), allied lines (2%), other liability (2%), and fire (2%).

Principal Investments: Investment grade bonds (71%), misc. investments (23%), real estate (5%), and cash (1%).

Investments in Affiliates: None

Group Affiliation: None

Licensed in: IL, IN, IA, KS, NE, ND, SD

Commenced Business: November 1891

Address: 501 S 13th Street, Lincoln, NE 68508

Phone: (402) 434-8300   **Domicile State:** NE   **NAIC Code:** 13889

Data Date	Rating	RACR #1	RACR #2	Loss Ratio %	Total Assets ($mil)	Capital ($mil)	Net Premium ($mil)	Net Income ($mil)
2017	B+	4.31	3.05	69.2	680.3	353.4	343.5	22.0
2016	B	4.25	3.03	65.4	653.5	333.6	327.4	26.4
2015	B	4.08	2.92	65.8	591.0	304.3	315.3	27.3
2014	B	4.31	3.01	83.8	536.2	282.4	267.3	-7.7
2013	B	4.70	3.34	67.1	512.4	293.2	264.9	20.0

Reserve Deficiency (as % of capital)

* Adequate & redundant reserves show as negatives   ■ 1 Yr Dev   □ 2 Yr Dev

FARMINGTON CASUALTY CO   B   Good

Major Rating Factors: Good liquidity (6.7 on a scale of 0 to 10) with sufficient resources (cash flows and marketable investments) to handle a spike in claims. Good overall results on stability tests (6.0). Affiliation with Travelers Companies Inc is a strength.

Other Rating Factors: Fair profitability index (4.2). Fair expense controls. Return on equity has been fair, averaging 13.7% over the past five years. Strong long-term capitalization index (7.8) based on excellent current risk adjusted capital (severe and moderate loss scenarios), despite some fluctuation in capital levels. Ample reserve history (8.5) that helps to protect the company against sharp claims increases.

Principal Business: Workers compensation (65%), homeowners multiple peril (34%), and auto liability (1%).

Principal Investments: Investment grade bonds (97%) and misc. investments (3%).

Investments in Affiliates: 0%

Group Affiliation: Travelers Companies Inc

Licensed in: All states except PR

Commenced Business: October 1982

Address: ONE TOWER SQUARE, Hartford, CT 6183

Phone: (860) 277-0111   **Domicile State:** CT   **NAIC Code:** 41483

Data Date	Rating	RACR #1	RACR #2	Loss Ratio %	Total Assets ($mil)	Capital ($mil)	Net Premium ($mil)	Net Income ($mil)
2017	B	2.31	1.53	69.5	1,031.4	274.5	337.9	25.6
2016	B	2.46	1.61	63.4	1,017.7	289.5	322.2	37.0
2015	B	2.49	1.59	58.7	1,005.4	291.3	307.5	42.0
2014	B	2.48	1.56	60.5	1,009.6	287.7	298.8	46.4
2013	B	2.52	1.60	60.9	1,000.6	287.4	298.1	45.9

Liquidity Index

■ Weak   ■ Fair   □ Good   □ Strong

FCCI INS CO   C+   Fair

Major Rating Factors: Fair overall results on stability tests (4.2 on a scale of 0 to 10) including potential drain of affiliation with FCCI Ins Group. Fair profitability index (4.7) with operating losses during 2016. Return on equity has been low, averaging 3.8% over the past five years.

Other Rating Factors: History of adequate reserve strength (6.3) as reserves have been consistently at an acceptable level. Good liquidity (6.5) with sufficient resources (cash flows and marketable investments) to handle a spike in claims. Strong long-term capitalization index (7.8) based on excellent current risk adjusted capital (severe and moderate loss scenarios), despite some fluctuation in capital levels.

Principal Business: Workers compensation (45%), auto liability (18%), commercial multiple peril (12%), other liability (8%), auto physical damage (5%), surety (4%), and other lines (8%).

Principal Investments: Investment grade bonds (73%), misc. investments (22%), non investment grade bonds (3%), and real estate (2%).

Investments in Affiliates: 7%

Group Affiliation: FCCI Ins Group

Licensed in: AL, AZ, AR, CO, DC, FL, GA, IL, IN, IA, KS, KY, LA, MD, MI, MS, MO, NE, NC, OH, OK, PA, SC, TN, TX, VA

Commenced Business: April 1959

Address: 6300 University Parkway, Sarasota, FL 34240-8424

Phone: (941) 907-3224   **Domicile State:** FL   **NAIC Code:** 10178

Data Date	Rating	RACR #1	RACR #2	Loss Ratio %	Total Assets ($mil)	Capital ($mil)	Net Premium ($mil)	Net Income ($mil)
2017	C+	2.11	1.50	68.6	2,067.1	594.5	799.5	24.5
2016	C+	2.22	1.61	80.6	1,920.9	572.0	750.1	-17.6
2015	C+	2.51	1.83	65.8	1,802.2	581.1	711.1	35.5
2014	C+	2.54	1.85	63.4	1,709.1	578.7	639.2	39.4
2013	C+	2.63	1.90	66.0	1,628.9	552.1	559.1	26.7

Rating Indexes

■ Weak   ■ Fair   □ Good   □ Strong

FEDERAL INS CO

C+   Fair

Major Rating Factors: Fair overall results on stability tests (4.5 on a scale of 0 to 10) including negative cash flow from operations for 2017. Strengths include potentially strong support from affiliation with Chubb Limited. Good liquidity (6.6) with sufficient resources (cash flows and marketable investments) to handle a spike in claims.

Other Rating Factors: Weak profitability index (2.2). Fair expense controls. Return on equity has been fair, averaging 27.7% over the past five years. Strong long-term capitalization index (7.3) based on excellent current risk adjusted capital (severe and moderate loss scenarios), despite some fluctuation in capital levels. Ample reserve history (8.5) that helps to protect the company against sharp claims increases.

Principal Business: Other liability (34%), commercial multiple peril (16%), workers compensation (11%), homeowners multiple peril (10%), group accident & health (4%), surety (4%), and other lines (20%).

Principal Investments: Investment grade bonds (49%), misc. investments (36%), non investment grade bonds (16%), and real estate (1%).

Investments in Affiliates: 27%

Group Affiliation: Chubb Limited

Licensed in: All states, the District of Columbia and Puerto Rico

Commenced Business: March 1901

Address: 202 N Illinois St Suite 2600, Indianapolis, IN 46282

Phone: (215) 640-1000   **Domicile State:** IN   **NAIC Code:** 20281

Data Date	Rating	RACR #1	RACR #2	Loss Ratio %	Total Assets ($mil)	Capital ($mil)	Net Premium ($mil)	Net Income ($mil)
2017	C+	1.40	1.18	59.7	21,770.0	7,296.7	3,532.5	4,948.1
2016	B-	1.28	1.16	52.0	27,371.2	11,423.8	4,708.0	3,239.2
2015	B	1.24	1.15	54.3	32,240.6	13,278.7	7,338.2	2,154.1
2014	B	1.36	1.26	56.8	32,484.3	14,828.4	7,113.5	1,855.3
2013	B+	1.42	1.31	51.7	31,761.3	14,741.3	6,844.9	2,021.9

FEDERATED MUTUAL INS CO

B   Good

Major Rating Factors: Good overall results on stability tests (5.4 on a scale of 0 to 10) despite potential drain of affiliation with Federated Mutual Ins Group. Good liquidity (6.8) with sufficient resources (cash flows and marketable investments) to handle a spike in claims.

Other Rating Factors: Strong long-term capitalization index (9.5) based on excellent current risk adjusted capital (severe and moderate loss scenarios). Moreover, capital has steadily grown over the last five years. Ample reserve history (8.8) that helps to protect the company against sharp claims increases. Excellent profitability (8.4) with operating gains in each of the last five years.

Principal Business: Group accident & health (30%), workers compensation (17%), other liability (15%), auto liability (13%), auto physical damage (5%), commercial multiple peril (5%), and other lines (14%).

Principal Investments: Investment grade bonds (64%), misc. investments (35%), non investment grade bonds (1%), and real estate (1%).

Investments in Affiliates: 17%

Group Affiliation: Federated Mutual Ins Group

Licensed in: All states except HI, PR

Commenced Business: August 1904

Address: 121 EAST PARK SQUARE, Owatonna, MN 55060

Phone: (507) 455-5200   **Domicile State:** MN   **NAIC Code:** 13935

Data Date	Rating	RACR #1	RACR #2	Loss Ratio %	Total Assets ($mil)	Capital ($mil)	Net Premium ($mil)	Net Income ($mil)
2017	B	3.23	2.66	70.9	5,847.9	3,362.5	1,538.1	156.4
2016	B	3.61	2.97	68.8	5,456.8	3,091.1	1,460.6	185.4
2015	B	3.82	3.13	66.9	5,076.2	2,862.4	1,301.0	189.1
2014	B	3.79	3.11	63.2	4,783.7	2,657.1	1,183.9	187.6
2013	A-	3.67	3.00	69.6	4,523.5	2,518.3	1,083.5	127.9

FEDERATED RURAL ELECTRIC INS EXCH *

B+   Good

Major Rating Factors: Good liquidity (6.8 on a scale of 0 to 10) with sufficient resources (cash flows and marketable investments) to handle a spike in claims. Good overall results on stability tests (6.5).

Other Rating Factors: Strong long-term capitalization index (8.9) based on excellent current risk adjusted capital (severe and moderate loss scenarios). Moreover, capital levels have been consistent in recent years. Ample reserve history (9.4) that helps to protect the company against sharp claims increases. Excellent profitability (8.9) with operating gains in each of the last five years. Return on equity has been excellent over the last five years averaging 17.7%.

Principal Business: Other liability (38%), workers compensation (24%), allied lines (14%), auto liability (11%), fire (8%), auto physical damage (3%), and other lines (3%).

Principal Investments: Investment grade bonds (92%), misc. investments (3%), non investment grade bonds (3%), and real estate (3%).

Investments in Affiliates: None

Group Affiliation: None

Licensed in: All states except CT, DC, MA, RI, PR

Commenced Business: July 1959

Address: 7725 RENNER RD, Shawnee, KS 66217-9414

Phone: (913) 541-0150   **Domicile State:** KS   **NAIC Code:** 11118

Data Date	Rating	RACR #1	RACR #2	Loss Ratio %	Total Assets ($mil)	Capital ($mil)	Net Premium ($mil)	Net Income ($mil)
2017	B+	3.45	2.36	74.0	553.2	203.1	122.1	33.0
2016	B	3.02	2.16	78.7	522.7	185.5	123.5	23.5
2015	B	3.29	2.34	71.6	495.0	177.3	120.3	32.6
2014	C+	3.23	2.32	67.6	473.4	167.1	112.3	34.1
2013	C+	2.93	2.10	71.9	458.8	153.3	113.3	31.4

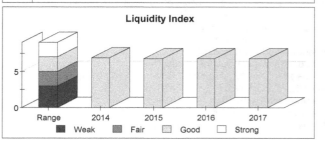

FEDERATED SERVICE INS CO   B-   Good

Major Rating Factors: Good overall results on stability tests (5.2 on a scale of 0 to 10) despite potential drain of affiliation with Federated Mutual Ins Group and negative cash flow from operations for 2017. Good liquidity (6.7) with sufficient resources (cash flows and marketable investments) to handle a spike in claims.
Other Rating Factors: Strong long-term capitalization index (10.0) based on excellent current risk adjusted capital (severe and moderate loss scenarios). Moreover, capital levels have been consistent in recent years. Ample reserve history (9.3) that helps to protect the company against sharp claims increases. Excellent profitability (8.8) with operating gains in each of the last five years.
Principal Business: Auto liability (26%), other liability (23%), workers compensation (19%), auto physical damage (14%), allied lines (7%), fire (5%), and other lines (7%).
Principal Investments: Investment grade bonds (91%), misc. investments (7%), and non investment grade bonds (2%).
Investments in Affiliates: None
Group Affiliation: Federated Mutual Ins Group
Licensed in: All states except HI, NH, NJ, VT, PR
Commenced Business: January 1975
Address: 121 EAST PARK SQUARE, Owatonna, MN 55060
Phone: (507) 455-5200   **Domicile State:** MN   **NAIC Code:** 28304

Data Date	Rating	RACR #1	RACR #2	Loss Ratio %	Total Assets ($mil)	Capital ($mil)	Net Premium ($mil)	Net Income ($mil)
2017	B-	8.23	5.40	70.9	450.4	244.5	128.2	16.2
2016	B-	6.64	4.24	68.8	488.8	228.3	162.3	19.1
2015	B-	6.40	4.08	66.9	455.8	211.2	144.6	20.2
2014	B-	5.82	3.81	63.2	428.3	193.3	131.5	19.6
2013	B	5.31	3.50	69.6	406.0	184.1	120.4	11.6

Federated Mutual Ins Group
Composite Group Rating: B

Largest Group Members	Assets ($mil)	Rating
FEDERATED MUTUAL INS CO	5848	B
FEDERATED LIFE INS CO	1877	A
FEDERATED SERVICE INS CO	450	B-
GRANITE RE INC	61	B

FINANCIAL PACIFIC INS CO *   B+   Good

Major Rating Factors: Good liquidity (6.5 on a scale of 0 to 10) with sufficient resources (cash flows and marketable investments) to handle a spike in claims. Good overall results on stability tests (6.4).
Other Rating Factors: Strong long-term capitalization index (9.7) based on excellent current risk adjusted capital (severe and moderate loss scenarios), despite some fluctuation in capital levels. Ample reserve history (8.0) that helps to protect the company against sharp claims increases. Excellent profitability (7.2) with operating gains in each of the last five years.
Principal Business: Other liability (29%), auto liability (26%), products liability (19%), commercial multiple peril (10%), auto physical damage (6%), inland marine (4%), and other lines (5%).
Principal Investments: Investment grade bonds (95%), cash (2%), real estate (2%), and misc. investments (1%).
Investments in Affiliates: None
Group Affiliation: United Fire & Casualty Group
Licensed in: AK, AZ, AR, CA, CO, FL, ID, IL, IA, KS, MN, MO, MT, NE, NV, NM, ND, OK, OR, SD, TX, UT, WA, WI
Commenced Business: December 1987
Address: 3880 ATHERTON ROAD, Rocklin, CA 95765
Phone: (319) 399-5700   **Domicile State:** CA   **NAIC Code:** 31453

Data Date	Rating	RACR #1	RACR #2	Loss Ratio %	Total Assets ($mil)	Capital ($mil)	Net Premium ($mil)	Net Income ($mil)
2017	B+	4.36	3.08	72.8	261.4	97.6	81.5	3.6
2016	B	4.61	3.01	69.8	232.3	95.1	77.2	5.0
2015	B	4.75	2.98	61.2	227.5	102.1	71.0	17.3
2014	B-	2.93	1.92	66.7	220.0	86.3	64.4	5.0
2013	B-	2.87	1.87	63.3	205.0	81.3	57.8	7.3

Liquidity Index

FINIAL REINS CO   D+   Weak

Major Rating Factors: Weak overall results on stability tests (2.5 on a scale of 0 to 10) including potential drain of affiliation with Berkshire-Hathaway and weak results on operational trends. Fair reserve development (4.6) as reserves have generally been sufficient to cover claims.
Other Rating Factors: Fair profitability index (3.8). Weak expense controls. Return on equity has been fair, averaging 11.2% over the past five years. Strong long-term capitalization index (9.9) based on excellent current risk adjusted capital (severe and moderate loss scenarios), despite some fluctuation in capital levels. Superior liquidity (10.0) with ample operational cash flow and liquid investments.
Principal Business: (This company is a reinsurer.)
Principal Investments: Investment grade bonds (66%), misc. investments (32%), and cash (2%).
Investments in Affiliates: None
Group Affiliation: Berkshire-Hathaway
Licensed in: All states except MS, PR
Commenced Business: February 1993
Address: 100 First Stamford Place, Stamford, CT 06902-6745
Phone: (402) 916-3000   **Domicile State:** CT   **NAIC Code:** 39136

Data Date	Rating	RACR #1	RACR #2	Loss Ratio %	Total Assets ($mil)	Capital ($mil)	Net Premium ($mil)	Net Income ($mil)
2017	D+	5.97	2.90	N/A	1,265.4	780.4	0.2	289.5
2016	D+	5.21	2.80	78.6	1,487.0	975.5	72.4	43.5
2015	D+	5.21	3.30	73.2	1,336.8	881.3	99.4	32.3
2014	D+	6.13	3.75	N/A	1,230.2	848.2	-0.5	29.6
2013	D+	7.17	4.28	N/A	1,257.7	812.1	-2.2	59.1

Rating Indexes

FIRE INS EXCHANGE C+ Fair

Major Rating Factors: Fair profitability index (3.9 on a scale of 0 to 10) with operating losses during 2016 and 2017. Fair overall results on stability tests (4.8).
Other Rating Factors: Good long-term capitalization index (5.2) based on good current risk adjusted capital (severe and moderate loss scenarios). History of adequate reserve strength (5.6) as reserves have been consistently at an acceptable level. Vulnerable liquidity (2.9) as a spike in claims may stretch capacity.
Principal Business: Homeowners multiple peril (66%), commercial multiple peril (16%), allied lines (10%), fire (5%), other liability (1%), and inland marine (1%).
Principal Investments: Misc. investments (75%), investment grade bonds (37%), real estate (8%), and non investment grade bonds (1%).
Investments in Affiliates: 61%
Group Affiliation: Farmers Insurance Group of Companies
Licensed in: AL, AZ, AR, CA, CO, FL, GA, ID, IL, IN, IA, KS, MI, MN, MO, MT, NE, NV, NH, NJ, NM, NY, ND, OH, OK, OR, SD, TN, TX, UT, WA, WI, WY
Commenced Business: November 1942
Address: 6301 OWENSMOUTH AVE, Woodland Hills, CA 91367
Phone: (323) 932-3200   **Domicile State:** CA   **NAIC Code:** 21660

Data Date	Rating	RACR #1	RACR #2	Loss Ratio %	Total Assets ($mil)	Capital ($mil)	Net Premium ($mil)	Net Income ($mil)
2017	C+	0.83	0.77	70.0	2,863.8	787.2	1,063.9	-9.8
2016	C+	0.81	0.76	72.5	2,429.4	777.2	1,107.1	-14.3
2015	C+	0.84	0.79	69.0	2,335.3	786.9	1,119.8	12.5
2014	C+	0.84	0.80	65.8	2,281.7	771.1	1,054.7	6.8
2013	C+	0.83	0.78	66.9	2,254.8	721.3	1,022.8	12.7

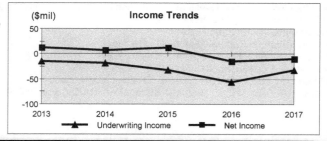

Income Trends

FIREMANS FUND INS CO C+ Fair

Major Rating Factors: Fair profitability index (3.6 on a scale of 0 to 10). Fair expense controls. Return on equity has been fair, averaging 13.1% over the past five years. Fair overall results on stability tests (4.4) including negative cash flow from operations for 2017 and fair results on operational trends.
Other Rating Factors: Strong long-term capitalization index (10.0) based on excellent current risk adjusted capital (severe and moderate loss scenarios), despite some fluctuation in capital levels. Excellent liquidity (7.0) with ample operational cash flow and liquid investments.
Principal Business: Commercial multiple peril (35%), other liability (27%), inland marine (13%), workers compensation (6%), fire (4%), farmowners multiple peril (4%), and other lines (10%).
Principal Investments: Misc. investments (52%), investment grade bonds (42%), cash (5%), and non investment grade bonds (1%).
Investments in Affiliates: 34%
Group Affiliation: Allianz Ins Group
Licensed in: All states, the District of Columbia and Puerto Rico
Commenced Business: September 1864
Address: 1465 N MCDOWELL BLVD STE 100, Petaluma, CA 94954
Phone: (888) 466-7883   **Domicile State:** CA   **NAIC Code:** 21873

Data Date	Rating	RACR #1	RACR #2	Loss Ratio %	Total Assets ($mil)	Capital ($mil)	Net Premium ($mil)	Net Income ($mil)
2017	C+	3.91	3.65	0.0	2,110.0	1,387.4	0.0	99.2
2016	C	3.83	3.53	0.0	2,811.3	1,670.6	-503.1	389.3
2015	C	1.25	0.97	132.5	5,500.4	1,296.3	-1,189.5	292.2
2014	C	1.12	0.75	90.0	9,434.6	2,134.2	2,460.5	62.9
2013	C	1.39	0.92	68.6	9,843.7	2,478.7	2,577.7	237.4

Rating Indexes

Ranges   Cap. 2   Stab.   Res.   Prof.   Liq.
■ Weak   ■ Fair   ▨ Good   □ Strong

FIRST FINANCIAL INS CO C- Fair

Major Rating Factors: Weak overall results on stability tests (2.6 on a scale of 0 to 10) including potential drain of affiliation with IFG Companies. Good overall profitability index (6.2). Weak expense controls. Return on equity has been low, averaging 2.5% over the past five years.
Other Rating Factors: Strong long-term capitalization index (7.3) based on excellent current risk adjusted capital (severe and moderate loss scenarios), despite some fluctuation in capital levels. Ample reserve history (7.7) that can protect against increases in claims costs. Excellent liquidity (7.2) with ample operational cash flow and liquid investments.
Principal Business: Inland marine (73%), auto liability (25%), and auto physical damage (3%).
Principal Investments: Misc. investments (79%) and investment grade bonds (21%).
Investments in Affiliates: 78%
Group Affiliation: IFG Companies
Licensed in: All states except PR
Commenced Business: May 1970
Address: 400 South Ninth Street, Springfield, IL 62701-1822
Phone: (336) 586-2500   **Domicile State:** IL   **NAIC Code:** 11177

Data Date	Rating	RACR #1	RACR #2	Loss Ratio %	Total Assets ($mil)	Capital ($mil)	Net Premium ($mil)	Net Income ($mil)
2017	D+	1.24	1.23	45.8	538.9	429.6	22.3	12.8
2016	C-	1.23	1.20	47.6	551.1	432.6	20.9	12.7
2015	C-	1.21	1.19	35.1	544.2	423.7	24.6	5.6
2014	C-	1.18	1.17	56.3	540.2	406.4	27.4	5.0
2013	C-	1.18	1.17	36.2	533.6	393.5	30.5	16.3

Rating Indexes

Ranges   Cap. 2   Stab.   Res.   Prof.   Liq.
■ Weak   ■ Fair   ▨ Good   □ Strong

FIRST INS CO OF HI LTD

C **Fair**

Major Rating Factors: Fair overall results on stability tests (4.2 on a scale of 0 to 10) including fair financial strength of affiliated Tokio Marine Holdings Inc. History of adequate reserve strength (6.9) as reserves have been consistently at an acceptable level.

Other Rating Factors: Good overall profitability index (6.1). Fair expense controls. Return on equity has been fair, averaging 5.5% over the past five years. Good liquidity (6.7) with sufficient resources (cash flows and marketable investments) to handle a spike in claims. Strong long-term capitalization index (10.0) based on excellent current risk adjusted capital (severe and moderate loss scenarios), despite some fluctuation in capital levels.

Principal Business: Workers compensation (24%), allied lines (21%), other liability (13%), commercial multiple peril (12%), homeowners multiple peril (10%), auto liability (10%), and other lines (9%).

Principal Investments: Investment grade bonds (92%), misc. investments (8%), and non investment grade bonds (1%).

Investments in Affiliates: 4%

Group Affiliation: Tokio Marine Holdings Inc

Licensed in: HI

Commenced Business: September 1982

Address: 1100 Ward Avenue, Honolulu, HI 96814

Phone: (808) 527-7777 **Domicile State:** HI **NAIC Code:** 41742

Data Date	Rating	RACR #1	RACR #2	Loss Ratio %	Total Assets ($mil)	Capital ($mil)	Net Premium ($mil)	Net Income ($mil)
2017	C	5.10	3.42	66.6	661.6	281.5	204.9	15.9
2016	C	4.76	3.33	68.5	664.7	273.1	205.2	6.5
2015	C	5.24	3.75	67.2	640.2	274.9	190.1	15.8
2014	C	5.03	3.55	62.9	631.0	288.8	181.0	20.0
2013	C	5.23	3.66	59.2	640.8	286.4	171.8	19.6

Tokio Marine Holdings Inc
Composite Group Rating: B

Largest Group Members	Assets ($mil)	Rating
RELIANCE STANDARD LIFE INS CO	12173	B
PHILADELPHIA INDEMNITY INS CO	8653	B-
SAFETY NATIONAL CASUALTY CORP	7224	C
HOUSTON CASUALTY CO	3383	B-
US SPECIALTY INS CO	1888	B

FLORIDA FARM BU CASUALTY INS CO

B- **Good**

Major Rating Factors: Fair overall results on stability tests (4.8 on a scale of 0 to 10) including potential drain of affiliation with Southern Farm Bureau Casualty and negative cash flow from operations for 2017. Fair profitability index (4.1) with operating losses during 2016 and 2017. Return on equity has been low, averaging 4.0% over the past five years.

Other Rating Factors: Good liquidity (6.3) with sufficient resources (cash flows and marketable investments) to handle a spike in claims. Strong long-term capitalization index (10.0) based on excellent current risk adjusted capital (severe and moderate loss scenarios), despite some fluctuation in capital levels. Ample reserve history (7.8) that can protect against increases in claims costs.

Principal Business: Homeowners multiple peril (64%), auto liability (26%), and auto physical damage (10%).

Principal Investments: Investment grade bonds (86%), misc. investments (9%), cash (3%), and real estate (2%).

Investments in Affiliates: 3%

Group Affiliation: Southern Farm Bureau Casualty

Licensed in: FL

Commenced Business: July 1974

Address: 5700 SW 34th Street, Gainesville, FL 32608-5330

Phone: (352) 378-8100 **Domicile State:** FL **NAIC Code:** 31216

Data Date	Rating	RACR #1	RACR #2	Loss Ratio %	Total Assets ($mil)	Capital ($mil)	Net Premium ($mil)	Net Income ($mil)
2017	B-	4.51	3.61	88.5	558.0	277.4	263.5	-5.0
2016	B-	4.93	3.71	88.7	557.4	285.8	250.8	-8.2
2015	B-	5.05	3.71	73.4	554.4	292.3	238.6	21.4
2014	B-	4.43	3.19	71.3	532.2	269.0	237.3	24.6
2013	B-	3.02	2.11	73.4	502.8	246.3	235.5	19.9

Southern Farm Bureau Casualty
Composite Group Rating: B-

Largest Group Members	Assets ($mil)	Rating
SOUTHERN FARM BUREAU CAS INS CO	2269	B-
FLORIDA FARM BU CASUALTY INS CO	558	B-
MISSISSIPPI FARM BUREAU CAS INS CO	438	B-
SOUTHERN FARM BUREAU PROPERTY	58	U
LOUISIANA FARM BUREAU CAS INS CO	12	B

FOREMOST INS CO

B **Good**

Major Rating Factors: Good overall results on stability tests (5.5 on a scale of 0 to 10) despite potential drain of affiliation with Farmers Insurance Group of Companies. Stability strengths include good operational trends and excellent risk diversification. Strong long-term capitalization index (10.0) based on excellent current risk adjusted capital (severe and moderate loss scenarios), despite some fluctuation in capital levels.

Other Rating Factors: Ample reserve history (7.2) that can protect against increases in claims costs. Excellent profitability (7.7) with operating gains in each of the last five years. Superior liquidity (9.9) with ample operational cash flow and liquid investments.

Principal Business: Homeowners multiple peril (42%), fire (18%), allied lines (11%), auto physical damage (10%), auto liability (8%), other liability (4%), and other lines (6%).

Principal Investments: Investment grade bonds (83%), misc. investments (9%), real estate (6%), and cash (2%).

Investments in Affiliates: 4%

Group Affiliation: Farmers Insurance Group of Companies

Licensed in: All states except PR

Commenced Business: June 1952

Address: 5600 BEECH TREE LANE, Caledonia, MI 49316-0050

Phone: (616) 942-3000 **Domicile State:** MI **NAIC Code:** 11185

Data Date	Rating	RACR #1	RACR #2	Loss Ratio %	Total Assets ($mil)	Capital ($mil)	Net Premium ($mil)	Net Income ($mil)
2017	B	12.85	8.64	0.0	2,316.6	1,165.6	0.0	44.4
2016	B	9.77	7.10	0.0	2,269.5	1,131.6	0.0	33.8
2015	B	9.74	7.04	0.0	2,172.2	1,093.2	0.0	33.9
2014	B	8.71	6.20	0.0	2,093.3	1,060.1	0.0	27.1
2013	B	10.90	7.99	0.0	1,938.6	1,029.9	0.0	38.5

Rating Indexes

Ranges | Cap. 2 | Stab. | Res. | Prof. | Liq.
■ Weak ■ Fair □ Good □ Strong

FRANKENMUTH MUTUAL INS CO *   B+   Good

Major Rating Factors: Good liquidity (6.7 on a scale of 0 to 10) with sufficient resources (cash flows and marketable investments) to handle a spike in claims. Good overall results on stability tests (6.5).

Other Rating Factors: Strong long-term capitalization index (9.3) based on excellent current risk adjusted capital (severe and moderate loss scenarios). Moreover, capital levels have been consistent in recent years. Ample reserve history (9.2) that helps to protect the company against sharp claims increases. Excellent profitability (8.7) with operating gains in each of the last five years.

Principal Business: Auto liability (23%), commercial multiple peril (22%), auto physical damage (17%), homeowners multiple peril (14%), workers compensation (12%), other liability (5%), and other lines (6%).

Principal Investments: Investment grade bonds (70%), misc. investments (29%), and real estate (2%).

Investments in Affiliates: 14%

Group Affiliation: Frankenmuth Mutual Group

Licensed in: All states except AK, CA, DC, HI, PR

Commenced Business: March 1922

Address: One Mutual Avenue, Frankenmuth, MI 48787-0001

Phone: (989) 652-6121   **Domicile State:** MI   **NAIC Code:** 13986

Data Date	Rating	RACR #1	RACR #2	Loss Ratio %	Total Assets ($mil)	Capital ($mil)	Net Premium ($mil)	Net Income ($mil)
2017	B+	3.10	2.51	59.0	1,351.0	606.7	494.6	44.9
2016	B	3.17	2.61	63.3	1,259.5	556.0	467.8	37.0
2015	B	3.02	2.40	62.1	1,174.2	508.3	450.8	33.2
2014	B	3.06	2.45	68.9	1,107.4	463.8	427.9	22.1
2013	A	3.13	2.51	63.2	1,069.3	445.0	410.9	40.1

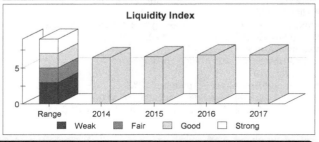

Liquidity Index

FRANKLIN MUTUAL INS CO   B   Good

Major Rating Factors: Good overall results on stability tests (5.6 on a scale of 0 to 10) despite potential drain of affiliation with Franklin Mutual Group. Stability strengths include good operational trends and excellent risk diversification. Strong long-term capitalization index (8.2) based on excellent current risk adjusted capital (severe and moderate loss scenarios), despite some fluctuation in capital levels.

Other Rating Factors: Ample reserve history (7.9) that can protect against increases in claims costs. Excellent profitability (8.1) with operating gains in each of the last five years. Excellent liquidity (7.9) with ample operational cash flow and liquid investments.

Principal Business: Commercial multiple peril (82%), workers compensation (9%), and other liability (7%).

Principal Investments: Misc. investments (82%), investment grade bonds (15%), cash (2%), and real estate (1%).

Investments in Affiliates: 6%

Group Affiliation: Franklin Mutual Group

Licensed in: NJ

Commenced Business: June 1879

Address: 5 Broad St, Branchville, NJ 7826

Phone: (973) 948-8800   **Domicile State:** NJ   **NAIC Code:** 16454

Data Date	Rating	RACR #1	RACR #2	Loss Ratio %	Total Assets ($mil)	Capital ($mil)	Net Premium ($mil)	Net Income ($mil)
2017	B	2.93	1.92	49.8	1,080.4	793.8	119.8	37.9
2016	B	2.70	1.76	52.6	934.5	626.8	119.2	32.9
2015	B	2.73	1.80	60.4	824.4	543.5	112.1	21.7
2014	B	2.59	1.69	64.0	841.4	549.6	112.1	16.4
2013	B	2.63	1.72	39.8	797.0	519.1	104.2	35.3

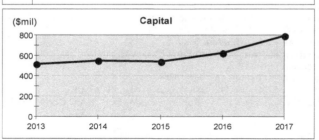

Capital

GARRISON P&C INS CO   B   Good

Major Rating Factors: Good overall results on stability tests (6.3 on a scale of 0 to 10). Fair profitability index (4.8) with operating losses during 2016. Return on equity has been low, averaging 3.9% over the past five years.

Other Rating Factors: Strong long-term capitalization index (8.1) based on excellent current risk adjusted capital (severe and moderate loss scenarios). Moreover, capital has steadily grown over the last five years. Ample reserve history (7.8) that can protect against increases in claims costs. Vulnerable liquidity (2.4) as a spike in claims may stretch capacity.

Principal Business: Auto liability (43%), auto physical damage (32%), homeowners multiple peril (21%), inland marine (1%), allied lines (1%), and fire (1%).

Principal Investments: Investment grade bonds (80%), misc. investments (17%), and non investment grade bonds (3%).

Investments in Affiliates: None

Group Affiliation: USAA Group

Licensed in: All states except PR

Commenced Business: December 1997

Address: 9800 Fredericksburg Road, San Antonio, TX 78288

Phone: (210) 498-1411   **Domicile State:** TX   **NAIC Code:** 21253

Data Date	Rating	RACR #1	RACR #2	Loss Ratio %	Total Assets ($mil)	Capital ($mil)	Net Premium ($mil)	Net Income ($mil)
2017	B	2.33	1.76	88.2	2,277.8	851.4	1,616.1	19.2
2016	B	2.43	1.83	91.8	1,981.5	751.6	1,376.4	-17.9
2015	B	2.49	1.89	86.0	1,707.7	655.3	1,190.8	19.0
2014	B	2.10	1.56	81.3	1,492.6	600.1	1,048.0	43.4
2013	B	2.70	2.06	77.4	1,255.5	506.4	710.0	49.2

Rating Indexes

GEICO ADVANTAGE INS CO   B   Good

Major Rating Factors: History of adequate reserve strength (6.1 on a scale of 0 to 10) as reserves have been consistently at an acceptable level. Fair profitability index (3.1) with operating losses during each of the last five years. Average return on equity over the last five years has been poor at -17.2%.

Other Rating Factors: Fair overall results on stability tests (4.9) including excessive premium growth, weak results on operational trends and negative cash flow from operations for 2017. Strong long-term capitalization index (8.7) based on excellent current risk adjusted capital (severe and moderate loss scenarios), despite some fluctuation in capital levels. Excellent liquidity (7.0) with ample operational cash flow and liquid investments.

Principal Business: Auto liability (59%) and auto physical damage (41%).

Principal Investments: Investment grade bonds (64%) and misc. investments (36%).

Investments in Affiliates: None

Group Affiliation: Berkshire-Hathaway

Licensed in: All states except CA, FL, HI, ME, MA, MI, MN, NY, ND, SD, VT, PR

Commenced Business: November 2011

Address: 1440 KIEWIT PLAZA, Omaha, NE 68131

Phone: (800) 841-3000   **Domicile State:** NE   **NAIC Code:** 14138

Data Date	Rating	RACR #1	RACR #2	Loss Ratio %	Total Assets ($mil)	Capital ($mil)	Net Premium ($mil)	Net Income ($mil)
2017	B	4.03	2.80	106.5	2,911.8	1,633.4	1,228.7	-235.1
2016	B	2.47	1.76	105.9	1,805.2	977.4	788.3	-195.7
2015	B-	1.89	1.39	100.5	1,011.4	532.8	476.5	-115.2
2014	C+	2.49	1.65	103.0	779.7	446.6	192.6	-54.7
2013	C+	4.75	3.61	107.4	629.6	484.6	215.6	-85.3

Reserve Deficiency (as % of capital)

* Adequate & redundant reserves show as negatives   ■ 1 Yr Dev   □ 2 Yr Dev

GEICO CASUALTY CO   C+   Fair

Major Rating Factors: Fair overall results on stability tests (4.5 on a scale of 0 to 10). Weak profitability index (2.9) with operating losses during each of the last five years. Average return on equity over the last five years has been poor at -13.6%.

Other Rating Factors: Vulnerable liquidity (2.5) as a spike in claims may stretch capacity. Strong long-term capitalization index (7.4) based on excellent current risk adjusted capital (severe and moderate loss scenarios), despite some fluctuation in capital levels. Ample reserve history (9.4) that helps to protect the company against sharp claims increases.

Principal Business: Auto liability (60%) and auto physical damage (40%).

Principal Investments: Misc. investments (56%) and investment grade bonds (44%).

Investments in Affiliates: None

Group Affiliation: Berkshire-Hathaway

Licensed in: All states except MI, PR

Commenced Business: May 1983

Address: 5260 WESTERN AVENUE, Chevy Chase, MD 20815-3799

Phone: (800) 841-3000   **Domicile State:** MD   **NAIC Code:** 41491

Data Date	Rating	RACR #1	RACR #2	Loss Ratio %	Total Assets ($mil)	Capital ($mil)	Net Premium ($mil)	Net Income ($mil)
2017	C+	1.71	1.30	90.5	3,526.8	1,108.2	2,171.2	-95.9
2016	C	1.46	1.09	87.3	2,920.5	924.5	1,834.2	-67.0
2015	D+	1.74	1.28	90.8	2,605.9	929.8	1,619.8	-125.3
2014	D	2.45	1.63	83.2	2,347.3	979.9	657.8	-44.1
2013	D-	1.64	1.37	90.9	2,707.2	1,001.0	2,209.4	-342.5

Rating Indexes

Ranges   Cap. 2   Stab.   Res.   Prof.   Liq.

■ Weak   ■ Fair   ▨ Good   □ Strong

GEICO CHOICE INS CO *   B+   Good

Major Rating Factors: History of adequate reserve strength (6.2 on a scale of 0 to 10) as reserves have been consistently at an acceptable level. Good overall results on stability tests (5.0) despite weak results on operational trends and excessive premium growth.

Other Rating Factors: Strong long-term capitalization index (8.0) based on excellent current risk adjusted capital (severe and moderate loss scenarios), despite some fluctuation in capital levels. Fair profitability index (3.2) with operating losses during each of the last five years. Average return on equity over the last five years has been poor at -12.1%. Vulnerable liquidity (2.8) as a spike in claims may stretch capacity.

Principal Business: Auto liability (61%) and auto physical damage (39%).

Principal Investments: Misc. investments (55%) and investment grade bonds (45%).

Investments in Affiliates: None

Group Affiliation: Berkshire-Hathaway

Licensed in: All states except CA, FL, HI, ME, MA, MI, MN, NY, ND, SD, VT, PR

Commenced Business: November 2011

Address: 1440 KIEWIT PLAZA, Omaha, NE 68131

Phone: (800) 841-3000   **Domicile State:** NE   **NAIC Code:** 14139

Data Date	Rating	RACR #1	RACR #2	Loss Ratio %	Total Assets ($mil)	Capital ($mil)	Net Premium ($mil)	Net Income ($mil)
2017	B+	2.28	1.67	94.0	1,134.6	483.1	665.7	-55.2
2016	B+	1.96	1.38	93.2	826.9	361.6	469.2	-48.1
2015	A-	2.37	1.65	93.2	600.9	295.7	315.1	-41.5
2014	A-	2.58	1.65	90.7	411.4	229.4	134.5	-13.9
2013	A-	3.88	2.79	99.4	339.5	236.8	163.6	-37.4

Reserve Deficiency (as % of capital)

* Adequate & redundant reserves show as negatives   ■ 1 Yr Dev   □ 2 Yr Dev

GEICO GENERAL INS CO *   B+   Good

Major Rating Factors: Good overall results on stability tests (5.3 on a scale of 0 to 10). Stability strengths include good operational trends and excellent risk diversification. Strong long-term capitalization index (10.0) based on excellent current risk adjusted capital (severe and moderate loss scenarios). Moreover, capital has steadily grown over the last five years.

Other Rating Factors: Excellent profitability (8.0) with operating gains in each of the last five years. Excellent expense controls. Excellent liquidity (7.0) with ample operational cash flow and liquid investments.

Principal Business: Auto liability (60%) and auto physical damage (40%).

Principal Investments: Investment grade bonds (98%) and misc. investments (2%).

Investments in Affiliates: None

Group Affiliation: Berkshire-Hathaway

Licensed in: All states except PR

Commenced Business: May 1934

Address: 5260 WESTERN AVENUE, Chevy Chase, MD 20815-3799

Phone: (800) 841-3000 **Domicile State:** MD **NAIC Code:** 35882

Data Date	Rating	RACR #1	RACR #2	Loss Ratio %	Total Assets ($mil)	Capital ($mil)	Net Premium ($mil)	Net Income ($mil)
2017	B+	150.20	75.12	0.0	167.6	166.8	0.0	1.0
2016	B+	181.11	90.56	0.0	154.1	153.9	0.0	0.5
2015	B+	18.69	16.82	0.0	209.5	141.4	0.0	0.2
2014	B+	15.86	14.27	0.0	214.8	131.1	0.0	0.3
2013	B+	14.30	12.87	0.0	215.7	123.6	0.0	2.8

Berkshire-Hathaway
Composite Group Rating: B

Largest Group Members	Assets ($mil)	Rating
NATIONAL INDEMNITY CO	231374	B
GOVERNMENT EMPLOYEES INS CO	33382	B
COLUMBIA INS CO	24522	U
BERKSHIRE HATHAWAY LIFE INS CO OF NE	19610	C+
GENERAL REINS CORP	16508	C+

GEICO INDEMNITY CO   B   Good

Major Rating Factors: Good overall results on stability tests (5.3 on a scale of 0 to 10) despite potential drain of affiliation with Berkshire-Hathaway. Good liquidity (6.5) with sufficient resources (cash flows and marketable investments) to handle a spike in claims.

Other Rating Factors: Strong long-term capitalization index (8.0) based on excellent current risk adjusted capital (severe and moderate loss scenarios). Moreover, capital levels have been consistent in recent years. Ample reserve history (9.3) that helps to protect the company against sharp claims increases. Excellent profitability (8.7) with operating gains in each of the last five years. Return on equity has been good over the last five years, averaging 11.8%.

Principal Business: (Not applicable due to unusual reinsurance transactions.)

Principal Investments: Misc. investments (82%) and investment grade bonds (18%).

Investments in Affiliates: 13%

Group Affiliation: Berkshire-Hathaway

Licensed in: All states except PR

Commenced Business: September 1961

Address: 5260 WESTERN AVENUE, Chevy Chase, MD 20815-3799

Phone: (800) 841-3000 **Domicile State:** MD **NAIC Code:** 22055

Data Date	Rating	RACR #1	RACR #2	Loss Ratio %	Total Assets ($mil)	Capital ($mil)	Net Premium ($mil)	Net Income ($mil)
2017	B	2.40	1.73	82.9	10,162.5	6,256.3	2,808.3	1,480.9
2016	B	2.13	1.57	80.7	8,166.9	4,598.2	2,542.6	160.0
2015	B	2.19	1.66	80.3	7,138.7	4,075.9	2,397.8	133.0
2014	B	2.25	1.67	47.4	6,962.8	4,018.3	530.9	409.2
2013	B+	1.75	1.38	73.2	7,811.2	3,636.3	4,411.5	663.6

Rating Indexes

Ranges | Cap. 2 | Stab. | Res. | Prof. | Liq.
■ Weak ▨ Fair ▧ Good □ Strong

GEICO SECURE INS CO *   A-   Excellent

Major Rating Factors: Strong long-term capitalization index (8.2 on a scale of 0 to 10) based on excellent current risk adjusted capital (severe and moderate loss scenarios). Furthermore, this high level of risk adjusted capital has been consistently maintained in previous years. History of adequate reserve strength (5.6) as reserves have been consistently at an acceptable level.

Other Rating Factors: Good liquidity (5.6) with sufficient resources (cash flows and marketable investments) to handle a spike in claims. Good overall results on stability tests (5.7) despite weak results on operational trends and excessive premium growth. Fair profitability index (4.2) with operating losses during each of the last five years. Average return on equity over the last five years has been poor at -3.5%.

Principal Business: Auto liability (67%) and auto physical damage (33%).

Principal Investments: Misc. investments (73%) and investment grade bonds (27%).

Investments in Affiliates: None

Group Affiliation: Berkshire-Hathaway

Licensed in: All states except CA, FL, HI, ME, MA, MI, MN, NY, ND, SD, VT, PR

Commenced Business: November 2011

Address: 1440 KIEWIT PLAZA, Omaha, NE 68131

Phone: (800) 841-3000 **Domicile State:** NE **NAIC Code:** 14137

Data Date	Rating	RACR #1	RACR #2	Loss Ratio %	Total Assets ($mil)	Capital ($mil)	Net Premium ($mil)	Net Income ($mil)
2017	A-	2.69	1.83	83.7	625.3	335.0	294.1	-6.9
2016	A-	2.53	1.70	85.6	489.5	269.1	214.1	-11.6
2015	A-	3.26	2.12	86.7	417.5	269.1	147.3	-13.3
2014	A-	3.65	2.24	80.4	413.6	273.1	66.3	-1.9
2013	A-	7.75	5.16	91.7	322.2	266.6	82.7	-14.3

($mil)   Capital

GENERAL CASUALTY CO OF WI   C+   Fair

Major Rating Factors: Fair liquidity (4.0 on a scale of 0 to 10) as cash resources may not be adequate to cover a spike in claims. Fair overall results on stability tests (4.5) including negative cash flow from operations for 2017.
Other Rating Factors: History of adequate reserve strength (6.8) as reserves have been consistently at an acceptable level. Weak profitability index (2.8) with operating losses during 2013 and 2017. Return on equity has been low, averaging 1.7% over the past five years. Strong long-term capitalization index (7.2) based on excellent current risk adjusted capital (severe and moderate loss scenarios), despite some fluctuation in capital levels.
Principal Business: Commercial multiple peril (34%), auto liability (19%), workers compensation (14%), other liability (9%), auto physical damage (9%), homeowners multiple peril (9%), and other lines (6%).
Principal Investments: Investment grade bonds (71%), misc. investments (35%), and real estate (11%).
Investments in Affiliates: 25%
Group Affiliation: QBE Ins Group Ltd
Licensed in: All states, the District of Columbia and Puerto Rico
Commenced Business: May 1925
Address: One General Drive, Sun Prairie, WI 53596
Phone: (608) 825-5160   **Domicile State:** WI   **NAIC Code:** 24414

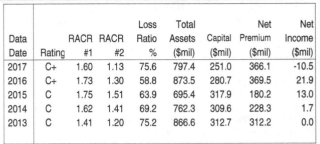

Data Date	Rating	RACR #1	RACR #2	Loss Ratio %	Total Assets ($mil)	Capital ($mil)	Net Premium ($mil)	Net Income ($mil)
2017	C+	1.60	1.13	75.6	797.4	251.0	366.1	-10.5
2016	C+	1.73	1.30	58.8	873.5	280.7	369.5	21.9
2015	C	1.75	1.51	63.9	695.4	317.9	180.2	13.0
2014	C	1.62	1.41	69.2	762.3	309.6	228.3	1.7
2013	C	1.41	1.20	75.2	866.6	312.7	312.2	0.0

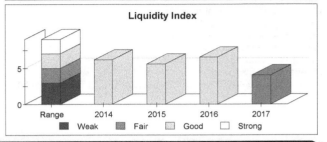

Liquidity Index

Range | 2014 | 2015 | 2016 | 2017
■ Weak ▨ Fair ▢ Good □ Strong

GENERAL REINS CORP   C+   Fair

Major Rating Factors: Fair overall results on stability tests (4.6 on a scale of 0 to 10) including potential drain of affiliation with Berkshire-Hathaway and excessive premium growth. Good overall profitability index (5.8). Weak expense controls. Return on equity has been fair, averaging 5.5% over the past five years.
Other Rating Factors: Strong long-term capitalization index (7.3) based on excellent current risk adjusted capital (severe and moderate loss scenarios), despite some fluctuation in capital levels. Ample reserve history (7.7) that can protect against increases in claims costs. Excellent liquidity (8.7) with ample operational cash flow and liquid investments.
Principal Business: Aircraft (100%).
Principal Investments: Misc. investments (87%), investment grade bonds (12%), and cash (1%).
Investments in Affiliates: 51%
Group Affiliation: Berkshire-Hathaway
Licensed in: All states, the District of Columbia and Puerto Rico
Commenced Business: January 1973
Address: 1209 ORANGE STREET, Wilmington, DE 19801
Phone: (203) 328-5000   **Domicile State:** DE   **NAIC Code:** 22039

Data Date	Rating	RACR #1	RACR #2	Loss Ratio %	Total Assets ($mil)	Capital ($mil)	Net Premium ($mil)	Net Income ($mil)
2017	C+	1.35	1.22	92.8	16,507.9	11,392.5	885.6	300.5
2016	C+	1.46	1.31	54.5	14,780.1	10,660.5	550.2	742.0
2015	C+	1.51	1.34	56.8	15,320.5	11,050.5	548.5	570.7
2014	C+	1.56	1.36	41.8	16,157.5	11,706.6	593.4	538.2
2013	B-	1.51	1.33	30.7	16,219.7	11,561.7	543.0	930.9

Rating Indexes

Ranges | Cap. 2 | Stab. | Res. | Prof. | Liq.
■ Weak ▨ Fair ▢ Good □ Strong

GENERAL STAR INDEMNITY CO   C   Fair

Major Rating Factors: Fair overall results on stability tests (4.0 on a scale of 0 to 10). Strong long-term capitalization index (9.9) based on excellent current risk adjusted capital (severe and moderate loss scenarios), despite some fluctuation in capital levels.
Other Rating Factors: Ample reserve history (8.5) that helps to protect the company against sharp claims increases. Excellent profitability (7.2) with operating gains in each of the last five years. Superior liquidity (9.8) with ample operational cash flow and liquid investments.
Principal Business: Other liability (47%), allied lines (22%), fire (12%), medical malpractice (8%), products liability (6%), homeowners multiple peril (2%), and inland marine (1%).
Principal Investments: Investment grade bonds (56%) and misc. investments (44%).
Investments in Affiliates: None
Group Affiliation: Berkshire-Hathaway
Licensed in: All states, the District of Columbia and Puerto Rico
Commenced Business: May 1979
Address: 1209 ORANGE STREET, Wilmington, DE 19801
Phone: (203) 328-5700   **Domicile State:** DE   **NAIC Code:** 37362

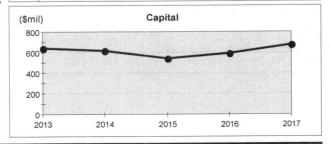

Data Date	Rating	RACR #1	RACR #2	Loss Ratio %	Total Assets ($mil)	Capital ($mil)	Net Premium ($mil)	Net Income ($mil)
2017	C	4.79	2.92	60.4	931.6	677.1	85.2	92.8
2016	C	4.56	2.82	46.6	841.0	595.2	67.7	15.8
2015	C	4.60	2.85	60.3	774.7	543.3	66.8	7.9
2014	C	4.82	3.00	54.6	848.9	616.0	72.3	10.4
2013	B-	6.24	3.84	39.8	859.4	645.8	70.3	47.6

($mil)   **Capital**

2013 | 2014 | 2015 | 2016 | 2017

GENWORTH MORTGAGE INS CORP   C   Fair

Major Rating Factors: Fair overall results on stability tests (4.0 on a scale of 0 to 10). Strengths include potentially strong support from affiliation with Genworth Financial. History of adequate reserve strength (6.1) as reserves have been consistently at an acceptable level.

Other Rating Factors: Strong long-term capitalization index (8.0) based on excellent current risk adjusted capital (severe and moderate loss scenarios), despite some fluctuation in capital levels. Excellent profitability (7.9) with operating gains in each of the last five years. Return on equity has been excellent over the last five years averaging 22.2%. Excellent liquidity (7.0) with ample operational cash flow and liquid investments.

Principal Business: Mortgage guaranty (100%).

Principal Investments: Investment grade bonds (78%), misc. investments (20%), and non investment grade bonds (2%).

Investments in Affiliates: 15%

Group Affiliation: Genworth Financial

Licensed in: All states except PR

Commenced Business: May 1980

Address: 8325 Six Forks Road, Raleigh, NC 27615

Phone: (919) 846-4100   **Domicile State:** NC   **NAIC Code:** 38458

Data Date	Rating	RACR #1	RACR #2	Loss Ratio %	Total Assets ($mil)	Capital ($mil)	Net Premium ($mil)	Net Income ($mil)
2017	C	2.85	2.49	15.5	3,346.0	1,366.5	683.2	449.3
2016	C	1.70	1.46	23.9	2,944.7	1,187.0	675.6	390.4
2015	C	1.42	1.21	35.9	2,627.1	1,073.1	621.1	261.7
2014	C	1.50	1.30	61.0	2,866.0	1,395.8	572.6	179.1
2013	C-	0.88	0.77	77.1	2,390.3	960.3	477.9	77.3

Rating Indexes

GEORGIA FARM BUREAU MUTUAL INS CO   C+   Fair

Major Rating Factors: Fair reserve development (4.3 on a scale of 0 to 10) as reserves have generally been sufficient to cover claims. Fair profitability index (3.6) with operating losses during 2015 and 2016.

Other Rating Factors: Fair overall results on stability tests (4.5) including negative cash flow from operations for 2017. Good liquidity (5.8) with sufficient resources (cash flows and marketable investments) to handle a spike in claims. Strong long-term capitalization index (7.7) based on excellent current risk adjusted capital (severe and moderate loss scenarios), despite some fluctuation in capital levels.

Principal Business: Auto liability (37%), homeowners multiple peril (23%), auto physical damage (21%), farmowners multiple peril (15%), commercial multiple peril (1%), allied lines (1%), and fire (1%).

Principal Investments: Investment grade bonds (82%), misc. investments (14%), and cash (4%).

Investments in Affiliates: 2%

Group Affiliation: Georgia Farm Bureau Ins

Licensed in: GA

Commenced Business: January 1959

Address: 1620 Bass Road, Macon, GA 31210

Phone: (478) 474-8411   **Domicile State:** GA   **NAIC Code:** 14001

Data Date	Rating	RACR #1	RACR #2	Loss Ratio %	Total Assets ($mil)	Capital ($mil)	Net Premium ($mil)	Net Income ($mil)
2017	C+	2.49	1.86	78.5	670.3	238.5	373.9	16.0
2016	C	1.66	1.16	78.3	648.5	211.7	450.0	-17.5
2015	C+	1.85	1.28	73.5	665.6	237.2	437.9	-4.1
2014	C	2.13	1.47	67.7	651.1	260.4	414.2	19.7
2013	C	2.07	1.41	74.3	620.6	258.1	401.4	2.6

Reserve Deficiency (as % of capital)

* Adequate & redundant reserves show as negatives

GNY CUSTOM INS CO *   B+   Good

Major Rating Factors: History of adequate reserve strength (5.0 on a scale of 0 to 10) as reserves have been consistently at an acceptable level. Good overall profitability index (6.9). Fair expense controls. Return on equity has been low, averaging 2.4% over the past five years.

Other Rating Factors: Good overall results on stability tests (6.5). Strong long-term capitalization index (10.0) based on excellent current risk adjusted capital (severe and moderate loss scenarios), despite some fluctuation in capital levels. Superior liquidity (9.2) with ample operational cash flow and liquid investments.

Principal Business: Commercial multiple peril (100%).

Principal Investments: Investment grade bonds (99%) and misc. investments (1%).

Investments in Affiliates: None

Group Affiliation: Greater New York Group

Licensed in: AZ, CT, DC, DE, IL, IN, MD, MA, MI, NJ, NY, NC, OH, PA, VT, VA

Commenced Business: June 2006

Address: 200 Madison Avenue, Phoenix, AZ 85021-4925

Phone: (212) 683-9700   **Domicile State:** AZ   **NAIC Code:** 10814

Data Date	Rating	RACR #1	RACR #2	Loss Ratio %	Total Assets ($mil)	Capital ($mil)	Net Premium ($mil)	Net Income ($mil)
2017	B+	22.50	18.25	64.0	60.5	54.0	3.2	1.2
2016	B+	23.60	18.98	66.5	59.0	52.9	2.9	1.1
2015	B	23.49	18.60	68.7	57.6	51.8	2.7	1.2
2014	B	24.16	18.76	67.6	56.2	50.7	2.5	1.3
2013	B+	24.88	17.89	61.1	54.8	49.5	2.3	1.4

Rating Indexes

GOVERNMENT EMPLOYEES INS CO

B   **Good**

Major Rating Factors: Good overall results on stability tests (5.3 on a scale of 0 to 10) despite potential drain of affiliation with Berkshire-Hathaway. Good liquidity (6.7) with sufficient resources (cash flows and marketable investments) to handle a spike in claims.

Other Rating Factors: Strong long-term capitalization index (8.5) based on excellent current risk adjusted capital (severe and moderate loss scenarios). Moreover, capital levels have been consistent in recent years. Ample reserve history (9.2) that helps to protect the company against sharp claims increases. Excellent profitability (8.7) with operating gains in each of the last five years. Return on equity has been good over the last five years, averaging 12.8%.

Principal Business: Auto liability (59%), auto physical damage (39%), and other liability (3%).

Principal Investments: Misc. investments (81%), investment grade bonds (20%), and non investment grade bonds (1%).

Investments in Affiliates: 1%

Group Affiliation: Berkshire-Hathaway

Licensed in: All states except PR

Commenced Business: December 1937

Address: 5260 WESTERN AVENUE, Chevy Chase, MD 20815-3799

Phone: (800) 841-3000   **Domicile State:** MD   **NAIC Code:** 22063

Data Date	Rating	RACR #1	RACR #2	Loss Ratio %	Total Assets ($mil)	Capital ($mil)	Net Premium ($mil)	Net Income ($mil)
2017	B	3.38	2.09	87.3	33,381.7	20,424.2	7,722.5	4,378.3
2016	B	3.09	1.95	82.9	27,197.9	15,702.6	6,988.3	728.6
2015	B	3.21	2.04	82.3	24,036.2	13,930.5	6,468.3	1,152.6
2014	B	3.43	2.13	36.2	23,472.6	13,443.0	649.5	1,725.3
2013	B+	2.67	1.81	77.3	25,778.8	12,089.8	11,644.8	2,010.1

Rating Indexes

GRANGE MUTUAL CAS CO

B   **Good**

Major Rating Factors: Good overall results on stability tests (5.0 on a scale of 0 to 10) despite potential drain of affiliation with Grange Mutual Casualty Group. Stability strengths include good operational trends and excellent risk diversification. History of adequate reserve strength (6.1) as reserves have been consistently at an acceptable level.

Other Rating Factors: Good liquidity (6.4) with sufficient resources (cash flows and marketable investments) to handle a spike in claims. Strong long-term capitalization index (8.5) based on excellent current risk adjusted capital (severe and moderate loss scenarios). Moreover, capital levels have been consistent in recent years. Excellent profitability (8.7) with operating gains in each of the last five years.

Principal Business: Auto liability (27%), auto physical damage (21%), commercial multiple peril (20%), homeowners multiple peril (19%), farmowners multiple peril (4%), fire (3%), and other lines (6%).

Principal Investments: Investment grade bonds (49%), misc. investments (37%), non investment grade bonds (7%), real estate (4%), and cash (3%).

Investments in Affiliates: 13%

Group Affiliation: Grange Mutual Casualty Group

Licensed in: AL, GA, IL, IN, IA, KS, KY, MN, MO, OH, PA, SC, TN, VA, WI

Commenced Business: April 1935

Address: 671 South High Street, Columbus, OH 43206-1014

Phone: (614) 445-2900   **Domicile State:** OH   **NAIC Code:** 14060

Data Date	Rating	RACR #1	RACR #2	Loss Ratio %	Total Assets ($mil)	Capital ($mil)	Net Premium ($mil)	Net Income ($mil)
2017	B	2.64	1.97	64.7	2,552.6	1,214.5	1,186.5	104.2
2016	B	2.55	1.91	62.3	2,311.7	1,106.8	983.1	82.5
2015	B	2.83	2.06	69.1	2,192.2	1,068.1	1,026.8	57.2
2014	B	3.01	2.22	68.9	2,120.6	1,047.3	1,021.2	33.1
2013	B+	3.02	2.18	67.0	2,011.8	1,010.2	957.4	47.4

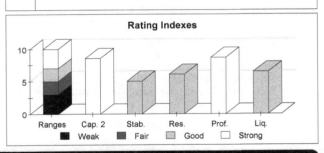

Rating Indexes

GREAT AMERICAN INS CO

B   **Good**

Major Rating Factors: Good overall results on stability tests (5.3 on a scale of 0 to 10) despite potential drain of affiliation with American Financial Group Inc. History of adequate reserve strength (6.5) as reserves have been consistently at an acceptable level.

Other Rating Factors: Good liquidity (6.7) with sufficient resources (cash flows and marketable investments) to handle a spike in claims. Strong long-term capitalization index (7.5) based on excellent current risk adjusted capital (severe and moderate loss scenarios), despite some fluctuation in capital levels. Excellent profitability (7.1) with operating gains in each of the last five years. Return on equity has been excellent over the last five years averaging 19.7%.

Principal Business: Allied lines (48%), other liability (20%), credit (6%), surety (5%), ocean marine (5%), fidelity (4%), and other lines (12%).

Principal Investments: Investment grade bonds (55%), misc. investments (40%), cash (2%), non investment grade bonds (2%), and real estate (1%).

Investments in Affiliates: 8%

Group Affiliation: American Financial Group Inc

Licensed in: All states, the District of Columbia and Puerto Rico

Commenced Business: March 1872

Address: 301 E Fourth Street, Cincinnati, OH 45202

Phone: (513) 369-5000   **Domicile State:** OH   **NAIC Code:** 16691

Data Date	Rating	RACR #1	RACR #2	Loss Ratio %	Total Assets ($mil)	Capital ($mil)	Net Premium ($mil)	Net Income ($mil)
2017	B	1.85	1.31	62.1	7,076.5	1,668.4	2,728.8	446.6
2016	B	1.82	1.40	52.4	6,851.2	1,998.9	2,471.4	349.1
2015	B-	1.76	1.28	55.6	6,110.9	1,550.9	2,354.2	294.2
2014	B-	1.62	1.19	59.0	5,811.7	1,413.6	2,256.9	221.5
2013	B-	1.79	1.31	59.1	5,376.9	1,403.3	2,100.1	273.7

Rating Indexes

GREAT NORTHERN INS CO   B   Good

Major Rating Factors: Good liquidity (6.9 on a scale of 0 to 10) with sufficient resources (cash flows and marketable investments) to handle a spike in claims. Good overall results on stability tests (5.5). Stability strengths include good operational trends and excellent risk diversification.

Other Rating Factors: Strong long-term capitalization index (9.1) based on excellent current risk adjusted capital (severe and moderate loss scenarios), despite some fluctuation in capital levels. Ample reserve history (9.2) that helps to protect the company against sharp claims increases. Excellent profitability (8.7) with operating gains in each of the last five years. Return on equity has been excellent over the last five years averaging 16.1%.

Principal Business: Homeowners multiple peril (41%), commercial multiple peril (23%), inland marine (9%), auto liability (9%), auto physical damage (5%), other liability (5%), and other lines (8%).

Principal Investments: Investment grade bonds (99%) and non investment grade bonds (1%).

Investments in Affiliates: None

Group Affiliation: Chubb Limited

Licensed in: All states except PR

Commenced Business: August 1952

Address: 202 N Illinois St Suite 2600, Indianapolis, IN 46282

Phone: (215) 640-1000   **Domicile State:** IN   **NAIC Code:** 20303

Data Date	Rating	RACR #1	RACR #2	Loss Ratio %	Total Assets ($mil)	Capital ($mil)	Net Premium ($mil)	Net Income ($mil)
2017	B	4.76	2.99	62.6	1,698.4	557.4	203.0	65.2
2016	B-	3.75	2.39	53.6	1,607.6	504.2	253.5	88.0
2015	B	2.87	1.83	56.5	1,647.5	469.2	391.3	81.2
2014	B	2.94	1.88	56.7	1,641.7	477.0	375.8	80.3
2013	B	2.97	1.92	52.7	1,653.1	478.8	360.6	83.4

Liquidity Index

GREAT WEST CASUALTY CO   B   Good

Major Rating Factors: Good liquidity (6.4 on a scale of 0 to 10) with sufficient resources (cash flows and marketable investments) to handle a spike in claims. Good overall results on stability tests (6.2).

Other Rating Factors: Strong long-term capitalization index (8.4) based on excellent current risk adjusted capital (severe and moderate loss scenarios), despite some fluctuation in capital levels. Ample reserve history (9.1) that helps to protect the company against sharp claims increases. Excellent profitability (8.2) with operating gains in each of the last five years. Return on equity has been good over the last five years, averaging 11.9%.

Principal Business: Auto liability (49%), auto physical damage (28%), workers compensation (11%), inland marine (8%), and other liability (4%).

Principal Investments: Investment grade bonds (68%), misc. investments (28%), and non investment grade bonds (4%).

Investments in Affiliates: None

Group Affiliation: Old Republic Group

Licensed in: All states except HI, PR

Commenced Business: April 1956

Address: 1100 WEST 29TH STREET, South Sioux City, NE 68776-3130

Phone: (402) 494-2411   **Domicile State:** NE   **NAIC Code:** 11371

Data Date	Rating	RACR #1	RACR #2	Loss Ratio %	Total Assets ($mil)	Capital ($mil)	Net Premium ($mil)	Net Income ($mil)
2017	B	3.24	1.94	75.3	2,133.2	626.0	900.4	62.7
2016	B	3.51	2.10	74.0	2,015.9	622.3	831.1	63.4
2015	B	3.58	2.20	71.4	1,953.1	586.2	849.2	70.5
2014	B	3.89	2.38	71.4	1,848.4	573.1	787.9	88.9
2013	A-	4.30	2.67	71.3	1,736.6	546.9	712.5	65.1

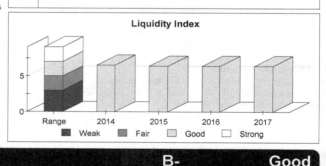

Liquidity Index

GREATER NEW YORK MUTUAL INS CO   B-   Good

Major Rating Factors: Fair overall results on stability tests (4.7 on a scale of 0 to 10) including potential drain of affiliation with Greater New York Group. History of adequate reserve strength (5.9) as reserves have been consistently at an acceptable level.

Other Rating Factors: Good liquidity (6.9) with sufficient resources (cash flows and marketable investments) to handle a spike in claims. Strong long-term capitalization index (8.4) based on excellent current risk adjusted capital (severe and moderate loss scenarios). Moreover, capital levels have been consistent in recent years. Excellent profitability (8.1) with operating gains in each of the last five years.

Principal Business: Commercial multiple peril (96%), workers compensation (2%), and other liability (1%).

Principal Investments: Investment grade bonds (67%), misc. investments (28%), cash (3%), and non investment grade bonds (2%).

Investments in Affiliates: 16%

Group Affiliation: Greater New York Group

Licensed in: All states except AK, CA, FL, HI, TX, PR

Commenced Business: November 1927

Address: 200 Madison Avenue, New York, NY 10016-3904

Phone: (212) 683-9700   **Domicile State:** NY   **NAIC Code:** 22187

Data Date	Rating	RACR #1	RACR #2	Loss Ratio %	Total Assets ($mil)	Capital ($mil)	Net Premium ($mil)	Net Income ($mil)
2017	B-	2.29	1.94	64.0	1,057.8	503.2	266.4	21.7
2016	B-	2.31	1.98	66.5	987.0	472.6	240.8	20.1
2015	B-	2.29	1.97	68.7	942.0	443.9	228.8	13.4
2014	B-	2.37	2.02	67.6	905.4	430.8	213.1	15.6
2013	B-	2.41	2.00	61.1	863.7	414.5	196.7	18.0

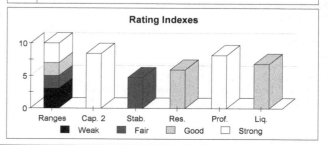

Rating Indexes

GREENWICH INS CO   C   Fair

Major Rating Factors: Fair overall results on stability tests (3.8 on a scale of 0 to 10) including potential drain of affiliation with XL Group Ltd. Fair profitability index (3.9) with operating losses during 2017. Return on equity has been fair, averaging 5.6% over the past five years.

Other Rating Factors: History of adequate reserve strength (6.3) as reserves have been consistently at an acceptable level. Good liquidity (6.7) with sufficient resources (cash flows and marketable investments) to handle a spike in claims. Strong long-term capitalization index (7.5) based on excellent current risk adjusted capital (severe and moderate loss scenarios), despite some fluctuation in capital levels.

Principal Business: Other liability (52%), allied lines (17%), auto liability (14%), group accident & health (6%), aggregate write-ins for other lines of business (3%), commercial multiple peril (3%), and other lines (5%).

Principal Investments: Investment grade bonds (62%), misc. investments (37%), and non investment grade bonds (3%).

Investments in Affiliates: 26%

Group Affiliation: XL Group Ltd

Licensed in: All states, the District of Columbia and Puerto Rico

Commenced Business: May 1946

Address: 1200 Orange Street, Wilmington, DE 19801

Phone: (203) 964-5200   **Domicile State:** DE   **NAIC Code:** 22322

Data Date	Rating	RACR #1	RACR #2	Loss Ratio %	Total Assets ($mil)	Capital ($mil)	Net Premium ($mil)	Net Income ($mil)
2017	C	1.58	1.35	76.8	1,250.4	359.9	253.3	-11.0
2016	C	1.81	1.56	69.3	1,202.5	364.2	200.1	31.1
2015	C	1.63	1.42	71.2	1,088.3	350.4	159.3	21.0
2014	C	1.71	1.51	61.5	1,073.1	397.3	152.0	35.3
2013	C	1.69	1.51	65.3	1,053.3	416.6	159.7	30.8

XL Group Ltd
Composite Group Rating: C
Largest Group Members

	Assets ($mil)	Rating
XL REINS AMERICA INC	5952	C
GREENWICH INS CO	1250	C
XL SPECIALTY INS CO	1066	C
XL INS AMERICA INC	791	C
CATLIN SPECIALTY INS CO	588	C+

GRINNELL MUTUAL REINS CO   B-   Good

Major Rating Factors: Fair overall results on stability tests (4.7 on a scale of 0 to 10) including potential drain of affiliation with Grinnell Mutual Group. Good liquidity (6.1) with sufficient resources (cash flows and marketable investments) to handle a spike in claims.

Other Rating Factors: Strong long-term capitalization index (9.6) based on excellent current risk adjusted capital (severe and moderate loss scenarios). Moreover, capital levels have been consistent in recent years. Ample reserve history (8.0) that helps to protect the company against sharp claims increases. Excellent profitability (8.8) with operating gains in each of the last five years. Return on equity has been good over the last five years, averaging 11.6%.

Principal Business: Commercial multiple peril (19%), other liability (16%), workers compensation (15%), auto liability (15%), allied lines (13%), auto physical damage (13%), and other lines (8%).

Principal Investments: Investment grade bonds (80%), misc. investments (15%), cash (2%), real estate (2%), and non investment grade bonds (1%).

Investments in Affiliates: 2%

Group Affiliation: Grinnell Mutual Group

Licensed in: IL, IN, IA, MN, MO, MT, NE, NY, ND, OH, OK, PA, SD, WI

Commenced Business: April 1909

Address: 4215 HIGHWAY 146 PO BOX 790, Grinnell, IA 50112-0790

Phone: (641) 269-8000   **Domicile State:** IA   **NAIC Code:** 14117

Data Date	Rating	RACR #1	RACR #2	Loss Ratio %	Total Assets ($mil)	Capital ($mil)	Net Premium ($mil)	Net Income ($mil)
2017	B-	4.56	3.28	73.2	1,179.7	613.7	595.8	39.2
2016	B-	3.82	2.65	59.3	1,104.3	589.9	556.5	68.7
2015	B-	3.47	2.38	53.2	1,008.1	517.0	525.1	89.4
2014	B-	3.20	2.25	63.8	913.7	440.1	483.5	58.7
2013	B-	2.90	2.07	65.9	858.6	399.9	451.7	36.8

Rating Indexes

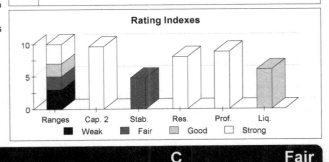

Ranges   Cap. 2   Stab.   Res.   Prof.   Liq.
■ Weak   ■ Fair   ▨ Good   □ Strong

GUIDEONE MUTUAL INS CO   C   Fair

Major Rating Factors: Fair overall results on stability tests (3.8 on a scale of 0 to 10) including negative cash flow from operations for 2017. Strengths include potential support from affiliation with GuideOne Group. Weak profitability index (1.8) with operating losses during 2013, 2016 and 2017.

Other Rating Factors: History of adequate reserve strength (6.6) as reserves have been consistently at an acceptable level. Good liquidity (6.0) with sufficient resources (cash flows and marketable investments) to handle a spike in claims. Strong long-term capitalization index (7.1) based on excellent current risk adjusted capital (severe and moderate loss scenarios), despite some fluctuation in capital levels.

Principal Business: Commercial multiple peril (59%), workers compensation (20%), auto liability (7%), other liability (7%), allied lines (5%), and auto physical damage (2%).

Principal Investments: Investment grade bonds (58%), misc. investments (42%), and real estate (2%).

Investments in Affiliates: 22%

Group Affiliation: GuideOne Group

Licensed in: All states except PR

Commenced Business: April 1947

Address: 1111 Ashworth Road, West Des Moines, IA 50265-3538

Phone: (515) 267-5000   **Domicile State:** IA   **NAIC Code:** 15032

Data Date	Rating	RACR #1	RACR #2	Loss Ratio %	Total Assets ($mil)	Capital ($mil)	Net Premium ($mil)	Net Income ($mil)
2017	C	1.41	1.05	108.9	1,049.1	363.1	260.5	-85.5
2016	B	1.69	1.35	78.6	1,214.7	421.8	353.8	-55.5
2015	B	1.66	1.39	67.1	1,232.0	464.1	360.2	19.6
2014	B-	1.44	1.17	68.0	1,695.2	442.1	355.0	22.3
2013	B-	1.51	1.23	70.5	1,814.5	460.0	334.8	-9.4

Rating Indexes

Ranges   Cap. 2   Stab.   Res.   Prof.   Liq.
■ Weak   ■ Fair   ▨ Good   □ Strong

GUILFORD INS CO

C-   **Fair**

Major Rating Factors: Weak overall results on stability tests (2.6 on a scale of 0 to 10) including potential drain of affiliation with IFG Companies and negative cash flow from operations for 2017. Good overall profitability index (5.6). Weak expense controls. Return on equity has been low, averaging 2.9% over the past five years.

Other Rating Factors: Strong long-term capitalization index (7.9) based on excellent current risk adjusted capital (severe and moderate loss scenarios), despite some fluctuation in capital levels. Ample reserve history (7.9) that can protect against increases in claims costs. Excellent liquidity (7.0) with ample operational cash flow and liquid investments.

Principal Business: Other liability (84%), inland marine (8%), commercial multiple peril (2%), auto liability (2%), allied lines (2%), and fire (2%).

Principal Investments: Misc. investments (52%) and investment grade bonds (48%).

Investments in Affiliates: 50%

Group Affiliation: IFG Companies

Licensed in: All states except CA, PR

Commenced Business: December 1998

Address: 400 South Ninth Street, Springfield, IL 62701-1822

Phone: (336) 586-2500   **Domicile State:** IL   **NAIC Code:** 10956

Data Date	Rating	RACR #1	RACR #2	Loss Ratio %	Total Assets ($mil)	Capital ($mil)	Net Premium ($mil)	Net Income ($mil)
2017	C-	1.65	1.61	46.5	371.3	272.5	29.8	4.3
2016	C-	1.65	1.61	47.9	377.9	274.3	27.9	5.9
2015	C-	1.66	1.62	44.4	386.9	275.2	32.8	9.5
2014	C-	1.63	1.59	56.5	393.3	274.3	36.6	6.9
2013	C-	1.61	1.57	50.6	390.3	267.5	40.7	12.3

Rating Indexes

HANOVER INS CO

B-   **Good**

Major Rating Factors: Fair reserve development (3.1 on a scale of 0 to 10) as the level of reserves has at times been insufficient to cover claims. In 2016 and 2017 the two year reserve development was 17% and 17% deficient respectively. Good overall profitability index (5.6). Fair expense controls. Return on equity has been fair, averaging 9.1% over the past five years.

Other Rating Factors: Good liquidity (5.9) with sufficient resources (cash flows and marketable investments) to handle a spike in claims. Good overall results on stability tests (5.1). Strong long-term capitalization index (7.1) based on excellent current risk adjusted capital (severe and moderate loss scenarios), despite some fluctuation in capital levels.

Principal Business: Other liability (26%), commercial multiple peril (18%), inland marine (16%), homeowners multiple peril (8%), surety (6%), workers compensation (6%), and other lines (19%).

Principal Investments: Investment grade bonds (60%), misc. investments (35%), non investment grade bonds (4%), and real estate (1%).

Investments in Affiliates: 19%

Group Affiliation: Hanover Ins Group Inc

Licensed in: All states except PR

Commenced Business: April 1852

Address: 1 EXEC PARK DR 2ND FL STE 200, Bedford, NH 03110-5905

Phone: (508) 853-7200   **Domicile State:** NH   **NAIC Code:** 22292

Data Date	Rating	RACR #1	RACR #2	Loss Ratio %	Total Assets ($mil)	Capital ($mil)	Net Premium ($mil)	Net Income ($mil)
2017	B-	1.31	1.07	66.4	7,748.1	2,071.7	3,337.1	270.1
2016	B	1.40	1.14	69.5	7,409.3	2,168.2	3,171.5	117.1
2015	B	1.56	1.28	66.4	6,926.3	2,188.0	3,046.3	128.8
2014	B	1.53	1.27	63.3	6,482.1	2,052.4	2,905.8	225.0
2013	B	1.42	1.21	64.8	6,047.1	1,829.7	2,759.4	184.3

Reserve Deficiency (as % of capital)

* Adequate & redundant reserves show as negatives

HARFORD MUTUAL INS CO

B-   **Good**

Major Rating Factors: Fair overall results on stability tests (4.7 on a scale of 0 to 10) including potential drain of affiliation with Harford Group Inc. History of adequate reserve strength (6.1) as reserves have been consistently at an acceptable level.

Other Rating Factors: Strong long-term capitalization index (8.4) based on excellent current risk adjusted capital (severe and moderate loss scenarios), despite some fluctuation in capital levels. Excellent profitability (8.1) with operating gains in each of the last five years. Excellent liquidity (7.0) with ample operational cash flow and liquid investments.

Principal Business: Commercial multiple peril (45%), workers compensation (26%), auto liability (14%), other liability (9%), auto physical damage (5%), and inland marine (1%).

Principal Investments: Investment grade bonds (56%), misc. investments (39%), cash (4%), and real estate (1%).

Investments in Affiliates: 15%

Group Affiliation: Harford Group Inc

Licensed in: DC, DE, GA, MD, NJ, NC, PA, SC, TN, VA, WV

Commenced Business: January 1843

Address: 200 North Main Street, Bel Air, MD 21014-3544

Phone: (410) 838-4000   **Domicile State:** MD   **NAIC Code:** 14141

Data Date	Rating	RACR #1	RACR #2	Loss Ratio %	Total Assets ($mil)	Capital ($mil)	Net Premium ($mil)	Net Income ($mil)
2017	B-	2.45	1.93	61.0	467.1	232.0	134.5	7.8
2016	B-	2.52	1.99	61.2	420.3	208.6	123.6	8.9
2015	B-	2.42	1.89	60.9	384.5	193.4	114.1	10.9
2014	B-	2.52	1.96	62.3	370.6	194.6	104.0	8.8
2013	B-	2.66	2.06	55.6	352.8	187.5	95.3	11.5

Rating Indexes

HARTFORD ACCIDENT & INDEMNITY CO   B   Good

Major Rating Factors: History of adequate reserve strength (5.8 on a scale of 0 to 10) as reserves have been consistently at an acceptable level. Good liquidity (6.6) with sufficient resources (cash flows and marketable investments) to handle a spike in claims.

Other Rating Factors: Good overall results on stability tests (5.5). Fair profitability index (3.6). Fair expense controls. Return on equity has been fair, averaging 15.4% over the past five years. Strong long-term capitalization index (7.4) based on excellent current risk adjusted capital (severe and moderate loss scenarios), despite some fluctuation in capital levels.

Principal Business: Workers compensation (48%), auto liability (25%), auto physical damage (10%), commercial multiple peril (5%), other liability (5%), homeowners multiple peril (4%), and surety (2%).

Principal Investments: Investment grade bonds (68%), misc. investments (30%), and non investment grade bonds (2%).

Investments in Affiliates: 9%

Group Affiliation: Hartford Financial Services Inc

Licensed in: All states, the District of Columbia and Puerto Rico

Commenced Business: August 1913

Address: One Hartford Plaza, Hartford, CT 06155-0001

Phone: (860) 547-5000   **Domicile State:** CT   **NAIC Code:** 22357

Data Date	Rating	RACR #1	RACR #2	Loss Ratio %	Total Assets ($mil)	Capital ($mil)	Net Premium ($mil)	Net Income ($mil)
2017	B	1.76	1.29	68.7	11,906.6	2,833.4	3,499.7	468.1
2016	B	1.99	1.46	70.4	11,604.5	3,154.5	3,444.1	409.9
2015	B	2.09	1.53	66.1	11,521.7	3,276.6	3,444.7	582.3
2014	B	2.18	1.60	67.0	11,348.4	3,324.9	3,349.1	509.1
2013	B	2.18	1.60	68.8	11,122.4	3,271.5	3,252.5	468.7

Reserve Deficiency (as % of capital)

* Adequate & redundant reserves show as negatives   ■ 1 Yr Dev   □ 2 Yr Dev

HARTFORD CASUALTY INS CO   B   Good

Major Rating Factors: History of adequate reserve strength (5.9 on a scale of 0 to 10) as reserves have been consistently at an acceptable level. Good overall profitability index (5.2). Fair expense controls. Return on equity has been fair, averaging 9.5% over the past five years.

Other Rating Factors: Good liquidity (6.8) with sufficient resources (cash flows and marketable investments) to handle a spike in claims. Good overall results on stability tests (5.9). Stability strengths include good operational trends and excellent risk diversification. Strong long-term capitalization index (9.9) based on excellent current risk adjusted capital (severe and moderate loss scenarios), despite some fluctuation in capital levels.

Principal Business: Workers compensation (41%), commercial multiple peril (21%), other liability (13%), auto liability (13%), auto physical damage (6%), surety (2%), and other lines (3%).

Principal Investments: Investment grade bonds (83%), misc. investments (16%), and non investment grade bonds (1%).

Investments in Affiliates: None

Group Affiliation: Hartford Financial Services Inc

Licensed in: All states except PR

Commenced Business: July 1987

Address: 501 Pennsylvania Pkwy Ste 400, Indianapolis, IN 46280-0014

Phone: (860) 547-5000   **Domicile State:** IN   **NAIC Code:** 29424

Data Date	Rating	RACR #1	RACR #2	Loss Ratio %	Total Assets ($mil)	Capital ($mil)	Net Premium ($mil)	Net Income ($mil)
2017	B	4.53	2.93	68.7	2,352.3	886.5	588.8	76.7
2016	B	4.74	3.08	70.4	2,267.2	894.0	579.5	77.9
2015	B	4.80	3.13	66.1	2,249.9	904.4	579.6	95.0
2014	B	4.97	3.23	67.0	2,233.8	913.3	563.5	95.9
2013	B	5.01	3.28	68.8	2,207.0	905.8	547.2	83.6

Reserve Deficiency (as % of capital)

* Adequate & redundant reserves show as negatives   ■ 1 Yr Dev   □ 2 Yr Dev

HARTFORD FIRE INS CO   C+   Fair

Major Rating Factors: Fair overall results on stability tests (4.8 on a scale of 0 to 10). Strengths include potentially strong support from affiliation with Hartford Financial Services Inc. Fair profitability index (3.0). Fair expense controls. Return on equity has been fair, averaging 8.1% over the past five years.

Other Rating Factors: History of adequate reserve strength (5.9) as reserves have been consistently at an acceptable level. Good liquidity (6.9) with sufficient resources (cash flows and marketable investments) to handle a spike in claims. Strong long-term capitalization index (7.8) based on excellent current risk adjusted capital (severe and moderate loss scenarios), despite some fluctuation in capital levels.

Principal Business: Commercial multiple peril (28%), workers compensation (19%), inland marine (13%), other liability (10%), auto liability (10%), surety (9%), and other lines (11%).

Principal Investments: Misc. investments (60%), investment grade bonds (35%), non investment grade bonds (2%), real estate (2%), and cash (1%).

Investments in Affiliates: 28%

Group Affiliation: Hartford Financial Services Inc

Licensed in: All states, the District of Columbia and Puerto Rico

Commenced Business: August 1810

Address: One Hartford Plaza, Hartford, CT 06155-0001

Phone: (860) 547-5000   **Domicile State:** CT   **NAIC Code:** 19682

Data Date	Rating	RACR #1	RACR #2	Loss Ratio %	Total Assets ($mil)	Capital ($mil)	Net Premium ($mil)	Net Income ($mil)
2017	C+	1.88	1.66	75.1	22,855.3	9,916.0	4,442.9	1,257.1
2016	B	1.96	1.41	70.4	25,540.6	12,514.6	4,372.3	526.5
2015	B	2.09	1.48	66.1	25,426.3	13,440.5	4,373.1	1,188.3
2014	B	2.11	1.48	67.0	25,520.2	13,797.4	4,251.7	1,068.2
2013	B	2.16	1.50	68.8	25,684.8	14,081.4	4,129.1	1,006.6

Rating Indexes

Ranges   Cap. 2   Stab.   Res.   Prof.   Liq.

■ Weak   ■ Fair   ▨ Good   □ Strong

HARTFORD INS CO OF IL

B   Good

Major Rating Factors: History of adequate reserve strength (5.8 on a scale of 0 to 10) as reserves have been consistently at an acceptable level. Good liquidity (6.7) with sufficient resources (cash flows and marketable investments) to handle a spike in claims.

Other Rating Factors: Good overall results on stability tests (5.7). Fair profitability index (4.8). Fair expense controls. Return on equity has been fair, averaging 10.9% over the past five years. Strong long-term capitalization index (9.0) based on excellent current risk adjusted capital (severe and moderate loss scenarios), despite some fluctuation in capital levels.

Principal Business: Workers compensation (43%), auto liability (28%), auto physical damage (15%), homeowners multiple peril (12%), and other liability (2%).

Principal Investments: Investment grade bonds (87%), misc. investments (12%), and non investment grade bonds (1%).

Investments in Affiliates: None

Group Affiliation: Hartford Financial Services Inc

Licensed in: CT, HI, IL, MI, NY, PA

Commenced Business: January 1980

Address: 4245 Meridian Parkway, Aurora, IL 60504-7901

Phone: (860) 547-5000   **Domicile State:** IL   **NAIC Code:** 38288

Data Date	Rating	RACR #1	RACR #2	Loss Ratio %	Total Assets ($mil)	Capital ($mil)	Net Premium ($mil)	Net Income ($mil)
2017	B	3.56	2.33	68.7	3,965.3	1,253.5	1,081.3	129.7
2016	B	3.70	2.43	70.4	3,832.8	1,258.0	1,064.1	119.6
2015	B	3.78	2.47	66.1	3,787.8	1,289.3	1,064.3	151.8
2014	B	4.00	2.59	67.0	3,781.9	1,334.8	1,034.8	164.6
2013	B	3.99	2.60	68.8	3,725.2	1,309.1	1,004.9	136.4

Reserve Deficiency (as % of capital)

* Adequate & redundant reserves show as negatives

■ 1 Yr Dev   □ 2 Yr Dev

HARTFORD INS CO OF THE MIDWEST

B   Good

Major Rating Factors: History of adequate reserve strength (5.0 on a scale of 0 to 10) as reserves have been consistently at an acceptable level. Good overall results on stability tests (5.8). Stability strengths include good operational trends and excellent risk diversification.

Other Rating Factors: Strong long-term capitalization index (10.0) based on excellent current risk adjusted capital (severe and moderate loss scenarios). Moreover, capital levels have been consistent in recent years. Excellent profitability (7.9) with operating gains in each of the last five years. Excellent liquidity (7.5) with ample operational cash flow and liquid investments.

Principal Business: Workers compensation (37%), allied lines (23%), auto liability (14%), homeowners multiple peril (13%), auto physical damage (8%), commercial multiple peril (4%), and other liability (1%).

Principal Investments: Investment grade bonds (100%).

Investments in Affiliates: None

Group Affiliation: Hartford Financial Services Inc

Licensed in: All states except PR

Commenced Business: January 1980

Address: 501 Pennsylvania Pkwy Ste 400, Indianapolis, IN 46280-0014

Phone: (860) 547-5000   **Domicile State:** IN   **NAIC Code:** 37478

Data Date	Rating	RACR #1	RACR #2	Loss Ratio %	Total Assets ($mil)	Capital ($mil)	Net Premium ($mil)	Net Income ($mil)
2017	B	27.38	18.02	68.7	636.9	507.8	53.5	17.3
2016	B	27.53	17.58	70.4	617.2	491.4	52.7	18.2
2015	B	26.66	17.49	66.1	595.6	473.3	52.7	20.4
2014	B	25.97	17.00	67.0	581.5	452.9	51.2	21.2
2013	B	25.12	16.51	68.8	550.1	432.1	49.7	19.2

Reserve Deficiency (as % of capital)

* Adequate & redundant reserves show as negatives

■ 1 Yr Dev   □ 2 Yr Dev

HARTFORD SM BOIL INSPECTION & INS

B-   Good

Major Rating Factors: Fair profitability index (3.3 on a scale of 0 to 10). Weak expense controls. Return on equity has been fair, averaging 16.7% over the past five years. Good liquidity (6.7) with sufficient resources (cash flows and marketable investments) to handle a spike in claims.

Other Rating Factors: Good overall results on stability tests (5.1). Stability strengths include good operational trends and excellent risk diversification. Strong long-term capitalization index (8.1) based on excellent current risk adjusted capital (severe and moderate loss scenarios), despite some fluctuation in capital levels. Ample reserve history (8.5) that helps to protect the company against sharp claims increases.

Principal Business: Boiler & machinery (96%), commercial multiple peril (2%), inland marine (1%), and other liability (1%).

Principal Investments: Investment grade bonds (67%), misc. investments (27%), real estate (4%), cash (1%), and non investment grade bonds (1%).

Investments in Affiliates: 17%

Group Affiliation: Münchener Rückversicherungs-Gesellsc

Licensed in: All states, the District of Columbia and Puerto Rico

Commenced Business: October 1866

Address: ONE STATE STREET, Hartford, CT 06102-5024

Phone: (860) 722-1866   **Domicile State:** CT   **NAIC Code:** 11452

Data Date	Rating	RACR #1	RACR #2	Loss Ratio %	Total Assets ($mil)	Capital ($mil)	Net Premium ($mil)	Net Income ($mil)
2017	B-	1.98	1.74	33.1	1,213.5	503.6	676.3	35.9
2016	B	2.97	2.55	29.4	1,256.1	598.9	451.7	97.4
2015	B	3.40	2.89	27.3	1,293.0	635.8	271.5	151.5
2014	B	2.24	1.98	29.4	1,406.6	641.1	771.8	127.8
2013	B	2.30	2.08	26.8	1,372.0	640.9	727.6	105.2

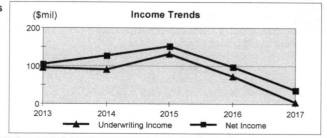

Income Trends

→ Underwriting Income   → Net Income

HARTFORD UNDERWRITERS INS CO   B   Good

Major Rating Factors: History of adequate reserve strength (5.9 on a scale of 0 to 10) as reserves have been consistently at an acceptable level. Good liquidity (6.8) with sufficient resources (cash flows and marketable investments) to handle a spike in claims.

Other Rating Factors: Good overall results on stability tests (5.9). Stability strengths include good operational trends and excellent risk diversification. Fair profitability index (4.4). Fair expense controls. Return on equity has been fair, averaging 9.8% over the past five years. Strong long-term capitalization index (9.4) based on excellent current risk adjusted capital (severe and moderate loss scenarios), despite some fluctuation in capital levels.

Principal Business: Workers compensation (38%), auto liability (32%), auto physical damage (16%), homeowners multiple peril (7%), other liability (2%), commercial multiple peril (2%), and allied lines (1%).

Principal Investments: Investment grade bonds (89%) and misc. investments (11%).

Investments in Affiliates: None

Group Affiliation: Hartford Financial Services Inc

Licensed in: All states except PR

Commenced Business: December 1987

Address: One Hartford Plaza, Hartford, CT 06155-0001

Phone: (860) 547-5000   **Domicile State:** CT   **NAIC Code:** 30104

Data Date	Rating	RACR #1	RACR #2	Loss Ratio %	Total Assets ($mil)	Capital ($mil)	Net Premium ($mil)	Net Income ($mil)
2017	B	3.99	2.63	68.7	1,675.9	581.6	428.2	56.2
2016	B	4.21	2.78	70.4	1,594.1	591.9	421.4	49.7
2015	B	4.36	2.86	66.1	1,590.0	608.8	421.5	66.1
2014	B	4.53	2.97	67.0	1,581.8	620.3	409.8	69.3
2013	B+	4.53	2.99	68.8	1,561.3	611.4	398.0	52.8

Reserve Deficiency (as % of capital)

* Adequate & redundant reserves show as negatives   ■ 1 Yr Dev   □ 2 Yr Dev

HASTINGS MUTUAL INS CO *   B+   Good

Major Rating Factors: History of adequate reserve strength (6.5 on a scale of 0 to 10) as reserves have been consistently at an acceptable level. Good liquidity (6.6) with sufficient resources (cash flows and marketable investments) to handle a spike in claims.

Other Rating Factors: Good overall results on stability tests (6.5). Strong long-term capitalization index (10.0) based on excellent current risk adjusted capital (severe and moderate loss scenarios). Moreover, capital has steadily grown over the last five years. Excellent profitability (8.2) with operating gains in each of the last five years.

Principal Business: Workers compensation (18%), auto liability (18%), commercial multiple peril (17%), farmowners multiple peril (16%), homeowners multiple peril (13%), auto physical damage (12%), and other lines (6%).

Principal Investments: Investment grade bonds (81%), misc. investments (14%), non investment grade bonds (4%), and cash (1%).

Investments in Affiliates: None

Group Affiliation: None

Licensed in: IL, IN, IA, KY, MI, OH, PA, TN, WI

Commenced Business: April 1885

Address: 404 E Woodlawn Ave, Hastings, MI 49058-1091

Phone: (269) 945-3405   **Domicile State:** MI   **NAIC Code:** 14176

Data Date	Rating	RACR #1	RACR #2	Loss Ratio %	Total Assets ($mil)	Capital ($mil)	Net Premium ($mil)	Net Income ($mil)
2017	B+	5.34	3.59	66.0	932.1	446.2	406.6	21.2
2016	B	5.23	3.47	60.8	888.9	422.8	401.8	31.7
2015	B	5.10	3.47	58.2	830.1	386.4	388.6	38.3
2014	B	4.74	3.26	67.9	783.1	354.0	374.2	18.7
2013	A-	4.73	3.30	76.8	759.0	335.5	354.9	3.3

Reserve Deficiency (as % of capital)

* Adequate & redundant reserves show as negatives   ■ 1 Yr Dev   □ 2 Yr Dev

HAWAII EMPLOYERS MUTUAL INS CO   B   Good

Major Rating Factors: History of adequate reserve strength (6.0 on a scale of 0 to 10) as reserves have been consistently at an acceptable level. Good overall profitability index (6.8). Fair expense controls.

Other Rating Factors: Good overall results on stability tests (5.5). Strong long-term capitalization index (10.0) based on excellent current risk adjusted capital (severe and moderate loss scenarios), despite some fluctuation in capital levels. Excellent liquidity (7.0) with ample operational cash flow and liquid investments.

Principal Business: Workers compensation (100%).

Principal Investments: Investment grade bonds (77%), misc. investments (15%), non investment grade bonds (6%), and real estate (2%).

Investments in Affiliates: None

Group Affiliation: None

Licensed in: HI

Commenced Business: October 1996

Address: 1100 Alakea Street Suite 1400, Honolulu, HI 96813-2834

Phone: (808) 524-3642   **Domicile State:** HI   **NAIC Code:** 10781

Data Date	Rating	RACR #1	RACR #2	Loss Ratio %	Total Assets ($mil)	Capital ($mil)	Net Premium ($mil)	Net Income ($mil)
2017	B	5.30	3.66	71.6	396.9	237.7	68.2	4.8
2016	C+	4.73	3.33	71.8	380.9	228.9	71.8	7.2
2015	C	4.28	3.00	72.9	360.6	221.0	67.6	7.5
2014	C-	4.68	3.26	75.8	341.2	217.5	61.3	11.5
2013	C-	5.90	3.93	72.0	313.6	209.4	45.5	9.3

Reserve Deficiency (as % of capital)

* Adequate & redundant reserves show as negatives   ■ 1 Yr Dev   □ 2 Yr Dev

HIGH POINT P&C INS CO   B   Good

Major Rating Factors: Good overall profitability index (6.2 on a scale of 0 to 10). Excellent expense controls. Return on equity has been low, averaging 1.0% over the past five years. Good overall results on stability tests (5.5) despite fair results on operational trends.

Other Rating Factors: Strong long-term capitalization index (7.5) based on excellent current risk adjusted capital (severe and moderate loss scenarios), despite some fluctuation in capital levels. Excellent liquidity (7.0) with ample operational cash flow and liquid investments.

Principal Business: Auto liability (73%) and auto physical damage (27%).

Principal Investments: Misc. investments (89%) and investment grade bonds (11%).

Investments in Affiliates: 78%

Group Affiliation: Palisades Group

Licensed in: NJ

Commenced Business: August 1998

Address: 331 Newman Sprgs Rd Ste 310, Red Bank, NJ 07701-5692

Phone: (732) 978-6000   **Domicile State:** NJ   **NAIC Code:** 10930

Data Date	Rating	RACR #1	RACR #2	Loss Ratio %	Total Assets ($mil)	Capital ($mil)	Net Premium ($mil)	Net Income ($mil)
2017	B	1.36	1.32	0.0	360.6	336.6	0.0	9.1
2016	B	1.69	1.62	0.0	390.9	367.2	0.0	1.3
2015	B	1.81	1.73	0.0	345.1	321.9	0.0	4.1
2014	B	1.68	1.60	0.0	375.6	350.3	0.0	1.8
2013	B	1.98	1.90	0.0	352.0	327.6	0.0	1.0

Rating Indexes

Ranges Cap. 2 Stab. Res. Prof. Liq.
■ Weak ■ Fair ▨ Good □ Strong

HIGH POINT PREFERRED INS CO *   B+   Good

Major Rating Factors: Good overall results on stability tests (6.2 on a scale of 0 to 10). Stability strengths include good operational trends and excellent risk diversification. Strong long-term capitalization index (8.9) based on excellent current risk adjusted capital (severe and moderate loss scenarios), despite some fluctuation in capital levels.

Other Rating Factors: Ample reserve history (8.8) that helps to protect the company against sharp claims increases. Excellent profitability (8.1) with operating gains in each of the last five years. Return on equity has been excellent over the last five years averaging 20.8%. Excellent liquidity (7.0) with ample operational cash flow and liquid investments.

Principal Business: Homeowners multiple peril (91%), allied lines (4%), other liability (3%), inland marine (1%), and fire (1%).

Principal Investments: Investment grade bonds (64%) and misc. investments (36%).

Investments in Affiliates: 5%

Group Affiliation: Palisades Group

Licensed in: NJ, PA

Commenced Business: October 1987

Address: 331 Newman Sprgs Rd Ste 310, Red Bank, NJ 07701-5692

Phone: (732) 978-6000   **Domicile State:** NJ   **NAIC Code:** 28959

Data Date	Rating	RACR #1	RACR #2	Loss Ratio %	Total Assets ($mil)	Capital ($mil)	Net Premium ($mil)	Net Income ($mil)
2017	B+	3.58	2.69	39.0	310.0	186.6	112.6	31.6
2016	B	3.02	2.33	37.9	276.7	152.0	117.0	31.7
2015	B-	2.43	1.90	48.7	251.0	116.0	115.5	28.0
2014	C+	2.75	1.95	37.9	279.8	145.3	98.8	30.5
2013	C+	2.28	1.61	53.4	242.5	107.8	82.5	22.5

($mil)   Capital

2013   2014   2015   2016   2017

HOME-OWNERS INS CO *   A   Excellent

Major Rating Factors: Strong long-term capitalization index (10.0 on a scale of 0 to 10) based on excellent current risk adjusted capital (severe and moderate loss scenarios). Furthermore, this high level of risk adjusted capital has been consistently maintained in previous years. Excellent profitability (8.8) with operating gains in each of the last five years.

Other Rating Factors: Excellent overall results on stability tests (7.5). Stability strengths include good operational trends and excellent risk diversification. History of adequate reserve strength (6.1) as reserves have been consistently at an acceptable level. Good liquidity (6.8) with sufficient resources (cash flows and marketable investments) to handle a spike in claims.

Principal Business: Auto liability (49%), auto physical damage (37%), commercial multiple peril (9%), workers compensation (3%), other liability (2%), and inland marine (1%).

Principal Investments: Investment grade bonds (83%), misc. investments (15%), cash (1%), and non investment grade bonds (1%).

Investments in Affiliates: None

Group Affiliation: Auto-Owners Group

Licensed in: AL, AR, CO, GA, IL, IN, IA, KY, MI, MO, NE, NV, ND, OH, PA, SC, SD, UT, VA, WI

Commenced Business: May 1863

Address: 6101 ANACAPRI BOULEVARD, Lansing, MI 48917-3968

Phone: (517) 323-1200   **Domicile State:** MI   **NAIC Code:** 26638

Data Date	Rating	RACR #1	RACR #2	Loss Ratio %	Total Assets ($mil)	Capital ($mil)	Net Premium ($mil)	Net Income ($mil)
2017	A	5.80	4.41	71.1	2,323.7	1,158.1	905.8	55.1
2016	A-	5.82	4.52	67.6	2,168.8	1,071.3	831.4	80.7
2015	A-	5.27	3.99	66.8	2,063.8	976.4	809.4	102.6
2014	A-	4.42	3.16	72.3	2,104.5	886.7	993.4	89.4
2013	A-	3.77	2.62	69.3	2,069.7	799.4	1,045.3	73.7

Risk-Adjusted Capital Ratio #2
(Severe Loss Scenario)

Range 2013 2014 2015 2016 2017
■ Weak ■ Fair ▨ Good □ Strong

HOSPITALS INS CO   C-   Fair

Major Rating Factors: Fair overall results on stability tests (3.2 on a scale of 0 to 10). Good long-term capitalization index (6.8) based on good current risk adjusted capital (moderate loss scenario), despite some fluctuation in capital levels.

Other Rating Factors: Good liquidity (6.9) with sufficient resources (cash flows and marketable investments) to handle a spike in claims. Ample reserve history (9.8) that helps to protect the company against sharp claims increases. Excellent profitability (8.6) with operating gains in each of the last five years. Excellent expense controls. Return on equity has been excellent over the last five years averaging 15.6%.

Principal Business: Medical malpractice (95%) and other liability (5%).

Principal Investments: Misc. investments (51%), investment grade bonds (45%), non investment grade bonds (3%), and cash (1%).

Investments in Affiliates: None

Group Affiliation: None

Licensed in: NY

Commenced Business: August 1987

Address: 50 Main Street Suite 1220, White Plains, NY 10606

Phone: (914) 220-1800   **Domicile State:** NY   **NAIC Code:** 30317

Data Date	Rating	RACR #1	RACR #2	Loss Ratio %	Total Assets ($mil)	Capital ($mil)	Net Premium ($mil)	Net Income ($mil)
2017	C-	1.33	1.12	63.8	1,671.8	584.0	178.9	62.5
2016	C-	1.20	1.01	54.1	1,568.5	526.6	191.9	61.6
2015	D+	0.99	0.84	88.7	1,472.8	448.2	216.1	11.5
2014	D	1.08	0.92	9.5	1,414.4	460.2	229.2	134.6
2013	D	0.65	0.56	55.3	1,397.5	318.7	234.1	76.5

Capital ($mil)

HOUSING AUTHORITY PROP A MUTUAL CO *   B+   Good

Major Rating Factors: Good overall profitability index (5.3 on a scale of 0 to 10) despite modest operating losses during 2017. Good liquidity (6.9) with sufficient resources (cash flows and marketable investments) to handle a spike in claims.

Other Rating Factors: Good overall results on stability tests (6.5). Strong long-term capitalization index (10.0) based on excellent current risk adjusted capital (severe and moderate loss scenarios), despite some fluctuation in capital levels. Ample reserve history (8.2) that helps to protect the company against sharp claims increases.

Principal Business: Commercial multiple peril (100%).

Principal Investments: Investment grade bonds (70%), misc. investments (25%), cash (4%), and non investment grade bonds (1%).

Investments in Affiliates: 15%

Group Affiliation: Housing Investment Group Inc

Licensed in: All states except AK, HI, PR

Commenced Business: August 1988

Address: 148 College Street, Burlington, VT 5401

Phone: (203) 272-8220   **Domicile State:** VT   **NAIC Code:** 10069

Data Date	Rating	RACR #1	RACR #2	Loss Ratio %	Total Assets ($mil)	Capital ($mil)	Net Premium ($mil)	Net Income ($mil)
2017	B+	3.45	3.09	70.2	181.9	118.5	52.3	-0.4
2016	B	3.76	3.37	68.4	167.4	117.4	43.5	2.2
2015	B	3.87	3.51	51.7	165.0	119.3	41.3	8.7
2014	C+	3.94	3.26	64.2	164.7	116.1	38.4	4.7
2013	C+	4.54	3.70	46.6	165.4	117.1	35.2	10.1

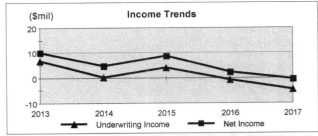

Income Trends ($mil)

HOUSTON CASUALTY CO   B-   Good

Major Rating Factors: Fair overall results on stability tests (4.9 on a scale of 0 to 10). Good profitability index (5.0). Fair expense controls. Return on equity has been good over the last five years, averaging 12.7%.

Other Rating Factors: Good liquidity (6.6) with sufficient resources (cash flows and marketable investments) to handle a spike in claims. Strong long-term capitalization index (7.8) based on excellent current risk adjusted capital (severe and moderate loss scenarios), despite some fluctuation in capital levels. Ample reserve history (7.6) that can protect against increases in claims costs.

Principal Business: Other liability (50%), ocean marine (10%), inland marine (9%), earthquake (6%), products liability (6%), commercial multiple peril (5%), and other lines (14%).

Principal Investments: Investment grade bonds (48%), misc. investments (45%), non investment grade bonds (5%), and cash (2%).

Investments in Affiliates: 37%

Group Affiliation: HCC Ins Holdings Inc

Licensed in: All states, the District of Columbia and Puerto Rico

Commenced Business: June 1981

Address: 13403 Northwest Freeway, Houston, TX 77040

Phone: (713) 462-1000   **Domicile State:** TX   **NAIC Code:** 42374

Data Date	Rating	RACR #1	RACR #2	Loss Ratio %	Total Assets ($mil)	Capital ($mil)	Net Premium ($mil)	Net Income ($mil)
2017	B-	1.82	1.56	64.6	3,382.8	1,865.1	863.0	120.8
2016	B-	1.72	1.54	64.4	3,329.6	1,913.0	860.4	239.2
2015	B-	1.87	1.73	66.4	3,404.1	1,936.9	808.3	313.8
2014	B-	1.72	1.60	51.2	2,960.2	1,891.9	336.7	215.3
2013	B-	1.88	1.71	40.6	2,967.1	1,909.7	301.7	323.6

Rating Indexes

HOUSTON SPECIALTY INS CO
B
Good

Major Rating Factors: Good long-term capitalization index (6.4 on a scale of 0 to 10) based on good current risk adjusted capital (moderate loss scenario), despite some fluctuation in capital levels. History of adequate reserve strength (5.5) as reserves have been consistently at an acceptable level.

Other Rating Factors: Good overall profitability index (5.9) despite operating losses during 2015 and 2016. Return on equity has been low, averaging 3.0% over the past five years. Good liquidity (6.7) with sufficient resources (cash flows and marketable investments) to handle a spike in claims. Good overall results on stability tests (6.1).

Principal Business: Other liability (37%), inland marine (29%), auto liability (19%), allied lines (6%), auto physical damage (5%), commercial multiple peril (2%), and other lines (3%).

Principal Investments: Misc. investments (64%), investment grade bonds (28%), and cash (8%).

Investments in Affiliates: 51%

Group Affiliation: Houston International Ins Group Ltd

Licensed in: All states except PR

Commenced Business: April 2007

Address: 800 Gessner Suite 600, Houston, TX 77024

Phone: (713) 935-4820   **Domicile State:** TX   **NAIC Code:** 12936

Data Date	Rating	RACR #1	RACR #2	Loss Ratio %	Total Assets ($mil)	Capital ($mil)	Net Premium ($mil)	Net Income ($mil)
2017	B	1.09	1.00	50.7	455.8	261.3	91.3	19.6
2016	B	0.99	0.89	69.1	458.0	260.8	111.8	-0.1
2015	B-	1.03	0.91	63.5	497.3	268.9	122.1	-5.8
2014	B	1.01	0.90	61.0	471.1	263.6	74.3	14.0
2013	B	0.78	0.70	51.1	361.7	187.7	109.1	8.2

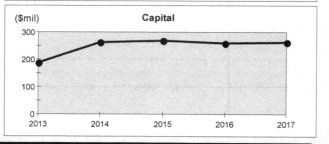

HUDSON INS CO
C-
Fair

Major Rating Factors: Fair profitability index (4.8 on a scale of 0 to 10). Good expense controls. Return on equity has been fair, averaging 5.5% over the past five years. Fair overall results on stability tests (3.3) including weak financial strength of affiliated Fairfax Financial.

Other Rating Factors: Strong long-term capitalization index (8.3) based on excellent current risk adjusted capital (severe and moderate loss scenarios), despite some fluctuation in capital levels. Ample reserve history (7.7) that can protect against increases in claims costs. Excellent liquidity (8.2) with ample operational cash flow and liquid investments.

Principal Business: Allied lines (40%), other liability (35%), auto liability (9%), auto physical damage (7%), surety (7%), medical malpractice (1%), and commercial multiple peril (1%).

Principal Investments: Investment grade bonds (57%), misc. investments (37%), non investment grade bonds (5%), and cash (1%).

Investments in Affiliates: 32%

Group Affiliation: Fairfax Financial

Licensed in: All states, the District of Columbia and Puerto Rico

Commenced Business: December 1918

Address: 1209 ORANGE STREET, Wilmington, DE 19801

Phone: (212) 978-2800   **Domicile State:** DE   **NAIC Code:** 25054

Data Date	Rating	RACR #1	RACR #2	Loss Ratio %	Total Assets ($mil)	Capital ($mil)	Net Premium ($mil)	Net Income ($mil)
2017	C-	2.12	1.87	67.8	1,204.1	428.4	198.4	30.7
2016	C-	2.17	1.91	71.9	1,159.9	453.2	158.6	36.8
2015	C-	2.06	1.87	76.0	1,082.8	457.9	149.4	40.0
2014	C-	2.11	1.91	81.4	1,042.7	440.2	166.6	9.6
2013	C-	2.48	2.22	86.0	819.0	413.9	129.6	6.0

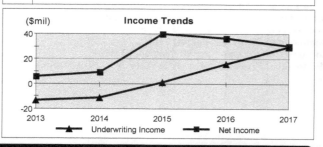

ICI MUTUAL INS CO A RRG *
B+
Good

Major Rating Factors: Good overall results on stability tests (6.5 on a scale of 0 to 10) despite negative cash flow from operations for 2017. Stability strengths include good operational trends and excellent risk diversification. Strong long-term capitalization index (10.0) based on excellent current risk adjusted capital (severe and moderate loss scenarios). Moreover, capital levels have been consistent in recent years.

Other Rating Factors: Ample reserve history (8.7) that helps to protect the company against sharp claims increases. Excellent profitability (8.3) with operating gains in each of the last five years. Excellent liquidity (7.7) with ample operational cash flow and liquid investments.

Principal Business: Other liability (89%) and fidelity (11%).

Principal Investments: Investment grade bonds (78%), misc. investments (17%), cash (4%), and non investment grade bonds (1%).

Investments in Affiliates: 0%

Group Affiliation: None

Licensed in: AZ, CA, CO, CT, DC, FL, GA, IL, IA, KS, MD, MA, MI, MN, MO, NE, NV, NJ, NM, NY, ND, OH, PA, SC, TN, TX, UT, VT, VA, WA, WI

Commenced Business: March 1988

Address: 159 BANK ST 4TH FL, Burlington, VT 5401

Phone: (800) 643-4246   **Domicile State:** VT   **NAIC Code:** 11268

Data Date	Rating	RACR #1	RACR #2	Loss Ratio %	Total Assets ($mil)	Capital ($mil)	Net Premium ($mil)	Net Income ($mil)
2017	B+	10.78	6.55	38.3	367.6	273.1	28.6	8.9
2016	B	10.21	6.41	49.3	355.6	255.0	30.6	6.3
2015	B	11.20	6.98	59.5	340.8	249.1	31.0	3.8
2014	B	12.56	7.50	18.6	333.9	249.6	30.1	12.0
2013	A-	10.76	6.82	17.7	322.1	235.8	29.2	12.5

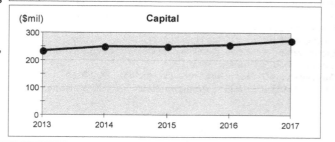

IDS PROPERTY CASUALTY INS CO   B   Good

Major Rating Factors: Good liquidity (5.2 on a scale of 0 to 10) with sufficient resources (cash flows and marketable investments) to handle a spike in claims. Good overall results on stability tests (5.4) despite negative cash flow from operations for 2017.

Other Rating Factors: Fair reserve development (3.8) as reserves have generally been sufficient to cover claims. In 2015, the two year reserve development was 18% deficient. Fair profitability index (3.7) with operating losses during 2014, 2015, 2016 and 2017. Average return on equity over the last five years has been poor at -2.2%. Strong long-term capitalization index (8.7) based on excellent current risk adjusted capital (severe and moderate loss scenarios), despite some fluctuation in capital levels.

Principal Business: Auto liability (39%), homeowners multiple peril (32%), auto physical damage (28%), and other liability (1%).

Principal Investments: Investment grade bonds (99%) and misc. investments (5%).

Investments in Affiliates: 3%

Group Affiliation: Ameriprise Financial Group

Licensed in: All states except PR

Commenced Business: January 1973

Address: 3500 Packerland Drive, De Pere, WI 54115-9070

Phone: (920) 330-5100   **Domicile State:** WI   **NAIC Code:** 29068

Data Date	Rating	RACR #1	RACR #2	Loss Ratio %	Total Assets ($mil)	Capital ($mil)	Net Premium ($mil)	Net Income ($mil)
2017	B	2.96	2.32	92.2	1,789.9	780.6	957.4	-9.7
2016	B-	2.87	2.21	91.2	1,826.3	800.3	1,065.3	-8.4
2015	B-	2.49	1.91	97.7	1,661.8	683.6	1,068.2	-44.4
2014	B	2.25	1.74	95.6	1,414.3	559.9	1,000.9	-25.3
2013	B	2.57	2.13	88.2	1,268.3	530.7	883.7	11.3

Liquidity Index

INDIANA FARMERS MUTUAL INS CO *   B+   Good

Major Rating Factors: Good liquidity (5.7 on a scale of 0 to 10) with sufficient resources (cash flows and marketable investments) to handle a spike in claims. Good overall results on stability tests (6.5).

Other Rating Factors: Strong long-term capitalization index (8.4) based on excellent current risk adjusted capital (severe and moderate loss scenarios). Moreover, capital has steadily grown over the last five years. Ample reserve history (7.0) that can protect against increases in claims costs. Excellent profitability (8.7) with operating gains in each of the last five years. Return on equity has been good over the last five years, averaging 10.6%.

Principal Business: Auto liability (23%), homeowners multiple peril (22%), auto physical damage (18%), farmowners multiple peril (12%), commercial multiple peril (11%), workers compensation (4%), and other lines (8%).

Principal Investments: Investment grade bonds (78%), misc. investments (20%), and cash (2%).

Investments in Affiliates: None

Group Affiliation: None

Licensed in: IL, IN

Commenced Business: August 1877

Address: 10 West 106th Street, Indianapolis, IN 46290-1002

Phone: (317) 846-4211   **Domicile State:** IN   **NAIC Code:** 22624

Data Date	Rating	RACR #1	RACR #2	Loss Ratio %	Total Assets ($mil)	Capital ($mil)	Net Premium ($mil)	Net Income ($mil)
2017	B+	3.67	2.15	63.5	433.3	210.3	211.3	19.6
2016	B	3.26	1.95	69.0	428.4	195.3	198.5	13.5
2015	B	3.01	1.81	59.1	391.0	180.1	189.5	20.8
2014	B	2.91	1.75	62.5	359.6	161.7	180.0	24.4
2013	B+	2.56	1.54	67.3	331.7	139.4	169.5	14.2

Liquidity Index

INFINITY INS CO   B   Good

Major Rating Factors: Good overall results on stability tests (5.3 on a scale of 0 to 10) despite potential drain of affiliation with Infinity Property & Casualty Group. History of adequate reserve strength (6.7) as reserves have been consistently at an acceptable level.

Other Rating Factors: Good overall profitability index (5.4). Good expense controls. Return on equity has been fair, averaging 9.3% over the past five years. Fair liquidity (4.1) as cash resources may not be adequate to cover a spike in claims. Strong long-term capitalization index (7.9) based on excellent current risk adjusted capital (severe and moderate loss scenarios), despite some fluctuation in capital levels.

Principal Business: Auto liability (62%) and auto physical damage (38%).

Principal Investments: Investment grade bonds (76%), misc. investments (13%), non investment grade bonds (9%), and real estate (4%).

Investments in Affiliates: 3%

Group Affiliation: Infinity Property & Casualty Group

Licensed in: All states except KS, LA, NH, NJ, VT, WY, PR

Commenced Business: October 1978

Address: 500 East 96th Street Suite 100, Indianapolis, IN 46240

Phone: (205) 870-4000   **Domicile State:** IN   **NAIC Code:** 22268

Data Date	Rating	RACR #1	RACR #2	Loss Ratio %	Total Assets ($mil)	Capital ($mil)	Net Premium ($mil)	Net Income ($mil)
2017	B	1.86	1.62	77.1	2,043.1	660.1	1,374.4	67.9
2016	B	1.83	1.61	79.0	2,012.7	660.6	1,379.9	62.0
2015	B	1.79	1.59	77.1	1,992.7	652.8	1,360.9	61.4
2014	B	1.84	1.63	75.7	1,991.5	674.6	1,334.7	68.0
2013	B	1.73	1.53	78.2	1,966.4	666.6	1,316.0	47.8

Rating Indexes

INLAND INS CO   C+   Fair

Major Rating Factors: Fair reserve development (3.6 on a scale of 0 to 10) as reserves have generally been sufficient to cover claims. Fair overall results on stability tests (4.5).

Other Rating Factors: Good overall profitability index (6.9). Weak expense controls. Return on equity has been low, averaging 4.6% over the past five years. Strong long-term capitalization index (8.5) based on excellent current risk adjusted capital (severe and moderate loss scenarios), despite some fluctuation in capital levels. Superior liquidity (10.0) with ample operational cash flow and liquid investments.

Principal Business: Surety (100%).

Principal Investments: Misc. investments (87%), investment grade bonds (9%), and cash (4%).

Investments in Affiliates: None

Group Affiliation: Universal Surety

Licensed in: AZ, CO, IA, KS, MN, MO, MT, NE, ND, OK, SD, WY

Commenced Business: November 1958

Address: 601 S 12th Street, Lincoln, NE 68508

Phone: (402) 435-4302   **Domicile State:** NE   **NAIC Code:** 23264

Data Date	Rating	RACR #1	RACR #2	Loss Ratio %	Total Assets ($mil)	Capital ($mil)	Net Premium ($mil)	Net Income ($mil)
2017	C+	3.68	2.19	1.5	300.7	252.9	0.7	8.5
2016	C	3.22	1.92	N/A	273.2	206.9	0.5	11.3
2015	C	3.16	1.89	N/A	240.4	182.8	0.5	8.5
2014	C	3.00	1.79	4.1	262.5	195.7	0.7	8.7
2013	C	2.93	1.75	14.8	254.7	190.0	0.4	9.7

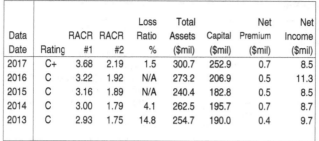

INS CO OF NORTH AMERICA   C   Fair

Major Rating Factors: Fair overall results on stability tests (4.1 on a scale of 0 to 10) including fair financial strength of affiliated Chubb Limited. History of adequate reserve strength (6.0) as reserves have been consistently at an acceptable level.

Other Rating Factors: Good liquidity (6.6) with sufficient resources (cash flows and marketable investments) to handle a spike in claims. Strong long-term capitalization index (7.7) based on excellent current risk adjusted capital (severe and moderate loss scenarios). Moreover, capital levels have been consistent in recent years. Excellent profitability (8.1) with operating gains in each of the last five years.

Principal Business: Other accident & health (29%), other liability (23%), fire (16%), group accident & health (10%), international (8%), ocean marine (5%), and other lines (9%).

Principal Investments: Investment grade bonds (90%), cash (5%), real estate (3%), and misc. investments (2%).

Investments in Affiliates: None

Group Affiliation: Chubb Limited

Licensed in: All states, the District of Columbia and Puerto Rico

Commenced Business: January 1792

Address: 436 WALNUT STREET, Philadelphia, PA 19106

Phone: (215) 640-1000   **Domicile State:** PA   **NAIC Code:** 22713

Data Date	Rating	RACR #1	RACR #2	Loss Ratio %	Total Assets ($mil)	Capital ($mil)	Net Premium ($mil)	Net Income ($mil)
2017	C	2.20	1.45	83.9	999.4	251.2	270.6	6.0
2016	C	2.29	1.53	76.5	944.2	250.2	249.8	16.5
2015	C	2.08	1.40	72.8	883.8	233.6	237.9	8.6
2014	C	2.29	1.53	77.6	869.9	225.2	223.9	12.7
2013	C	1.88	1.26	72.2	787.1	182.8	217.7	15.3

Chubb Limited
Composite Group Rating: C+

Largest Group Members	Assets ($mil)	Rating
FEDERAL INS CO	21770	C+
ACE AMERICAN INS CO	13606	B-
ACE PC INS CO	8693	B-
PACIFIC INDEMNITY CO	6560	B
PACIFIC EMPLOYERS INS CO	3687	B-

INS CO OF THE WEST   C   Fair

Major Rating Factors: Fair overall results on stability tests (3.7 on a scale of 0 to 10) including potential drain of affiliation with American Assets Inc. History of adequate reserve strength (6.4) as reserves have been consistently at an acceptable level.

Other Rating Factors: Good liquidity (6.6) with sufficient resources (cash flows and marketable investments) to handle a spike in claims. Strong long-term capitalization index (7.4) based on excellent current risk adjusted capital (severe and moderate loss scenarios). Moreover, capital has steadily grown over the last five years. Excellent profitability (8.9) with operating gains in each of the last five years. Return on equity has been good over the last five years, averaging 11.1%.

Principal Business: Workers compensation (95%), earthquake (4%), and inland marine (1%).

Principal Investments: Investment grade bonds (62%), misc. investments (30%), cash (4%), and non investment grade bonds (4%).

Investments in Affiliates: 10%

Group Affiliation: American Assets Inc

Licensed in: All states except PR

Commenced Business: May 1972

Address: 15025 INNOVATION DRIVE, San Diego, CA 92128

Phone: (858) 350-2400   **Domicile State:** CA   **NAIC Code:** 27847

Data Date	Rating	RACR #1	RACR #2	Loss Ratio %	Total Assets ($mil)	Capital ($mil)	Net Premium ($mil)	Net Income ($mil)
2017	C	1.88	1.41	65.8	2,570.2	1,034.2	807.7	91.1
2016	C	1.71	1.27	64.9	2,252.8	902.0	812.7	104.0
2015	C	1.47	1.08	63.0	1,917.0	753.3	744.1	90.4
2014	C	1.50	1.07	64.0	1,613.2	658.2	621.4	68.1
2013	C	1.72	1.21	61.1	1,314.5	533.5	514.8	68.8

INTEGON NATIONAL INS CO   B-   Good

Major Rating Factors: Fair overall results on stability tests (4.7 on a scale of 0 to 10) including potential drain of affiliation with AmTrust Financial Services Inc, excessive premium growth and fair results on operational trends. Fair reserve development (4.4) as reserves have generally been sufficient to cover claims.
Other Rating Factors: Fair profitability index (4.0) with operating losses during 2013 and 2015. Return on equity has been low, averaging 0.8% over the past five years. Good liquidity (5.5) with sufficient resources (cash flows and marketable investments) to handle a spike in claims. Strong long-term capitalization index (7.1) based on excellent current risk adjusted capital (severe and moderate loss scenarios). Moreover, capital has steadily grown over the last five years.
Principal Business: Auto liability (39%), auto physical damage (23%), homeowners multiple peril (18%), commercial multiple peril (11%), credit (2%), other liability (2%), and other lines (4%).
Principal Investments: Investment grade bonds (94%), misc. investments (9%), non investment grade bonds (2%), and real estate (1%).
Investments in Affiliates: 5%
Group Affiliation: AmTrust Financial Services Inc
Licensed in: All states except PR
Commenced Business: December 1988
Address: 5630 University Parkway, Winston-salem, NC 27105
Phone: (336) 435-2000   **Domicile State:** NC   **NAIC Code:** 29742

Data Date	Rating	RACR #1	RACR #2	Loss Ratio %	Total Assets ($mil)	Capital ($mil)	Net Premium ($mil)	Net Income ($mil)
2017	B-	1.86	1.32	76.2	3,766.0	970.4	1,384.4	145.4
2016	C+	1.45	1.06	74.3	2,489.2	594.4	1,522.0	50.4
2015	C	1.18	0.85	75.2	2,339.5	448.3	1,155.3	-10.0
2014	C-	1.22	0.97	74.3	1,741.0	332.4	928.7	11.4
2013	D+	1.27	0.96	87.6	1,149.5	159.8	349.1	-33.2

Rating Indexes

INTERINS EXCHANGE *   B+   Good

Major Rating Factors: Good overall results on stability tests (5.8 on a scale of 0 to 10) despite potential drain of affiliation with Auto Club Enterprises Ins Group. History of adequate reserve strength (6.0) as reserves have been consistently at an acceptable level.
Other Rating Factors: Good overall profitability index (6.9). Good expense controls. Good liquidity (6.5) with sufficient resources (cash flows and marketable investments) to handle a spike in claims. Strong long-term capitalization index (9.6) based on excellent current risk adjusted capital (severe and moderate loss scenarios). Moreover, capital levels have been consistent in recent years.
Principal Business: Auto liability (45%), auto physical damage (35%), homeowners multiple peril (18%), and fire (1%).
Principal Investments: Misc. investments (47%), investment grade bonds (42%), non investment grade bonds (10%), and real estate (2%).
Investments in Affiliates: 1%
Group Affiliation: Auto Club Enterprises Ins Group
Licensed in: CA, FL, HI, ME, MI, MO, NH, NM, OH, PA, RI, TX, VT, VA
Commenced Business: October 1912
Address: 3333 FAIRVIEW ROAD, Costa Mesa, CA 92626-1698
Phone: (714) 850-5111   **Domicile State:** CA   **NAIC Code:** 15598

Data Date	Rating	RACR #1	RACR #2	Loss Ratio %	Total Assets ($mil)	Capital ($mil)	Net Premium ($mil)	Net Income ($mil)
2017	B+	4.50	2.76	79.6	10,404.3	6,637.9	3,623.1	71.8
2016	B+	4.72	2.91	79.4	9,326.9	5,911.1	3,261.5	35.6
2015	B+	5.05	3.13	71.9	8,707.0	5,633.7	3,017.0	183.2
2014	B+	5.11	3.16	71.6	8,547.9	5,496.7	2,864.6	200.7
2013	A+	5.26	3.26	71.1	8,106.5	5,214.6	2,752.1	269.8

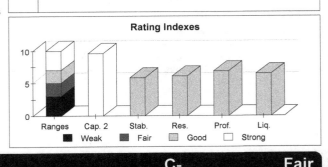

Rating Indexes

IRONSHORE SPECIALTY INS CO   C-   Fair

Major Rating Factors: Weak profitability index (2.6 on a scale of 0 to 10) with operating losses during 2016 and 2017. Return on equity has been low, averaging 2.6% over the past five years. Weak overall results on stability tests (2.8) including weak financial strength of affiliated Ironshore Holdings Inc and negative cash flow from operations for 2017.
Other Rating Factors: Good liquidity (6.9) with sufficient resources (cash flows and marketable investments) to handle a spike in claims. Strong long-term capitalization index (9.2) based on excellent current risk adjusted capital (severe and moderate loss scenarios), despite some fluctuation in capital levels.
Principal Business: Other liability (66%), medical malpractice (10%), homeowners multiple peril (9%), fire (8%), products liability (3%), credit (1%), and other lines (2%).
Principal Investments: Investment grade bonds (58%), misc. investments (30%), and cash (12%).
Investments in Affiliates: None
Group Affiliation: Ironshore Holdings Inc
Licensed in: All states, the District of Columbia and Puerto Rico
Commenced Business: February 1953
Address: 8601 N SCOTTSDALE ROAD STE 300, Scottsdale, AZ 85253
Phone: (617) 357-9500   **Domicile State:** AZ   **NAIC Code:** 25445

Data Date	Rating	RACR #1	RACR #2	Loss Ratio %	Total Assets ($mil)	Capital ($mil)	Net Premium ($mil)	Net Income ($mil)
2017	D+	4.77	4.49	93.8	491.6	297.2	50.8	-29.5
2016	C	2.42	1.56	82.7	1,082.9	349.3	109.7	-0.4
2015	C	2.41	1.46	76.6	987.1	334.0	112.0	20.9
2014	C	2.28	1.40	85.1	974.0	325.8	127.1	31.3
2013	C	2.59	1.58	68.3	832.9	300.3	119.2	21.4

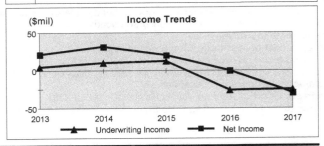

Income Trends

ISMIE MUTUAL INS CO
B-   Good

Major Rating Factors: Fair overall results on stability tests (4.6 on a scale of 0 to 10) including potential drain of affiliation with ISMIE Group and negative cash flow from operations for 2017. Strong long-term capitalization index (10.0) based on excellent current risk adjusted capital (severe and moderate loss scenarios), despite some fluctuation in capital levels.

Other Rating Factors: Ample reserve history (9.4) that helps to protect the company against sharp claims increases. Excellent profitability (7.1) with operating gains in each of the last five years. Excellent liquidity (7.9) with ample operational cash flow and liquid investments.

Principal Business: Medical malpractice (99%) and aggregate write-ins for other lines of business (1%).

Principal Investments: Investment grade bonds (87%), misc. investments (10%), cash (2%), and non investment grade bonds (1%).

Investments in Affiliates: 4%

Group Affiliation: ISMIE Group

Licensed in: AL, AK, AZ, AR, CO, CT, DC, DE, GA, HI, IL, IN, IA, KS, KY, LA, MD, MI, MO, MT, NE, NM, NC, ND, OH, OK, OR, PA, SC, TN, UT, VT, VA, WA, WV, WI

Commenced Business: June 1976

Address: 20 North Michigan Avenue, Chicago, IL 60602-4811

Phone: (312) 782-2749   **Domicile State:** IL   **NAIC Code:** 32921

Data Date	Rating	RACR #1	RACR #2	Loss Ratio %	Total Assets ($mil)	Capital ($mil)	Net Premium ($mil)	Net Income ($mil)
2017	B-	4.49	3.78	71.7	1,403.5	695.5	133.4	12.4
2016	B-	4.51	3.79	61.9	1,468.4	693.3	149.4	24.4
2015	B-	4.15	3.48	57.9	1,525.9	670.1	168.4	37.4
2014	B-	3.73	3.10	53.4	1,625.1	647.4	189.2	34.8
2013	B-	3.66	2.98	37.6	1,616.4	609.9	229.6	80.1

Rating Indexes

■ Weak   ■ Fair   ▨ Good   □ Strong

JEWELERS MUTUAL INS CO
B   Good

Major Rating Factors: Good liquidity (6.8 on a scale of 0 to 10) with sufficient resources (cash flows and marketable investments) to handle a spike in claims. Good overall results on stability tests (6.3).

Other Rating Factors: Strong long-term capitalization index (10.0) based on excellent current risk adjusted capital (severe and moderate loss scenarios). Moreover, capital has steadily grown over the last five years. Ample reserve history (7.6) that can protect against increases in claims costs. Excellent profitability (8.7) with operating gains in each of the last five years.

Principal Business: Inland marine (87%) and commercial multiple peril (13%).

Principal Investments: Investment grade bonds (57%), misc. investments (38%), real estate (3%), and cash (2%).

Investments in Affiliates: 4%

Group Affiliation: None

Licensed in: All states except PR

Commenced Business: June 1914

Address: 24 Jewelers Park Drive, Neenah, WI 54956-3703

Phone: (920) 725-4326   **Domicile State:** WI   **NAIC Code:** 14354

Data Date	Rating	RACR #1	RACR #2	Loss Ratio %	Total Assets ($mil)	Capital ($mil)	Net Premium ($mil)	Net Income ($mil)
2017	B	4.66	3.12	42.8	442.4	282.5	196.3	23.5
2016	B	5.34	3.36	48.4	397.8	247.3	180.6	11.7
2015	B	5.77	3.60	45.0	365.3	226.5	165.9	15.5
2014	B	5.50	3.45	44.2	338.7	207.7	154.0	16.3
2013	A-	5.07	3.14	43.5	304.9	182.6	143.8	17.4

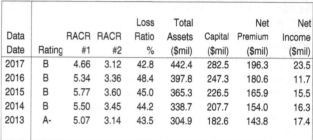

Liquidity Index

■ Weak   ■ Fair   ▨ Good   □ Strong

KENTUCKY FARM BUREAU MUTUAL INS CO
B   Good

Major Rating Factors: Good overall profitability index (6.9 on a scale of 0 to 10). Good expense controls. Good liquidity (6.2) with sufficient resources (cash flows and marketable investments) to handle a spike in claims.

Other Rating Factors: Fair overall results on stability tests (4.8) including potential drain of affiliation with Kentucky Farm Bureau Group. Strong long-term capitalization index (10.0) based on excellent current risk adjusted capital (severe and moderate loss scenarios). Moreover, capital levels have been consistent in recent years. Ample reserve history (7.8) that can protect against increases in claims costs.

Principal Business: Auto liability (35%), homeowners multiple peril (25%), auto physical damage (21%), farmowners multiple peril (11%), commercial multiple peril (6%), and other liability (1%).

Principal Investments: Investment grade bonds (74%), misc. investments (24%), cash (1%), and non investment grade bonds (1%).

Investments in Affiliates: 1%

Group Affiliation: Kentucky Farm Bureau Group

Licensed in: CA, CT, DE, GA, ID, IL, IN, IA, KY, LA, MD, MA, MI, MO, MT, NH, NJ, NC, ND, OH, OK, OR, PA, RI, SD, TX, UT, VT, VA, WA, WV, WI

Commenced Business: December 1943

Address: 9201 Bunsen Parkway, Louisville, KY 40220-3793

Phone: (502) 495-5000   **Domicile State:** KY   **NAIC Code:** 22993

Data Date	Rating	RACR #1	RACR #2	Loss Ratio %	Total Assets ($mil)	Capital ($mil)	Net Premium ($mil)	Net Income ($mil)
2017	B	6.12	4.10	78.5	2,505.4	1,374.7	999.1	71.0
2016	B	5.65	3.76	80.6	2,391.6	1,279.0	937.9	52.6
2015	B	5.58	3.68	79.6	2,286.1	1,226.1	877.8	39.9
2014	B	5.53	3.62	71.1	2,222.2	1,155.1	851.1	120.4
2013	A-	5.04	3.32	67.2	2,119.7	1,066.3	845.5	147.6

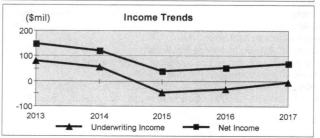

($mil)   Income Trends

▲ Underwriting Income   ■ Net Income

LACKAWANNA AMERICAN INS CO *   B+   Good

Major Rating Factors: History of adequate reserve strength (6.5 on a scale of 0 to 10) as reserves have been consistently at an acceptable level. Good liquidity (6.8) with sufficient resources (cash flows and marketable investments) to handle a spike in claims.

Other Rating Factors: Good overall results on stability tests (6.3). Strong long-term capitalization index (9.1) based on excellent current risk adjusted capital (severe and moderate loss scenarios). Moreover, capital has steadily grown over the last five years. Excellent profitability (8.6) with operating gains in each of the last five years.

Principal Business: Workers compensation (100%).

Principal Investments: Investment grade bonds (97%), misc. investments (2%), and cash (1%).

Investments in Affiliates: None

Group Affiliation: Lackawanna Ins Group

Licensed in: PA

Commenced Business: July 2002

Address: 46 Public Square Suite 501, Wilkes-barre, PA 18701-2609

Phone: (570) 824-1400   **Domicile State:** PA   **NAIC Code:** 11219

Data Date	Rating	RACR #1	RACR #2	Loss Ratio %	Total Assets ($mil)	Capital ($mil)	Net Premium ($mil)	Net Income ($mil)
2017	B+	3.15	2.51	78.0	89.8	43.8	23.0	2.6
2016	B	2.99	2.41	77.2	86.3	41.7	23.1	2.5
2015	C+	2.90	2.35	73.8	84.9	39.1	22.5	2.7
2014	C	2.82	2.27	74.3	79.1	36.4	20.3	2.5
2013	C	2.44	1.94	71.7	74.6	34.1	19.6	2.7

LAMMICO   B   Good

Major Rating Factors: Good overall results on stability tests (6.1 on a scale of 0 to 10). Strong long-term capitalization index (10.0) based on excellent current risk adjusted capital (severe and moderate loss scenarios). Moreover, capital levels have been consistent in recent years.

Other Rating Factors: Ample reserve history (8.7) that helps to protect the company against sharp claims increases. Excellent profitability (8.1) with operating gains in each of the last five years. Excellent liquidity (8.6) with ample operational cash flow and liquid investments.

Principal Business: Medical malpractice (99%) and other liability (1%).

Principal Investments: Investment grade bonds (82%), misc. investments (15%), and cash (3%).

Investments in Affiliates: 0%

Group Affiliation: None

Licensed in: AR, LA, MS, TN

Commenced Business: January 1982

Address: One Galleria Boulevard Ste 700, Metairie, LA 70001

Phone: (504) 831-3756   **Domicile State:** LA   **NAIC Code:** 43656

Data Date	Rating	RACR #1	RACR #2	Loss Ratio %	Total Assets ($mil)	Capital ($mil)	Net Premium ($mil)	Net Income ($mil)
2017	B	5.73	4.31	73.9	432.9	238.8	47.1	7.6
2016	B	5.57	4.28	67.2	431.3	226.6	49.8	9.4
2015	B	5.38	4.17	64.3	427.1	214.9	49.0	11.6
2014	C+	5.12	3.95	63.8	421.5	206.0	49.3	12.3
2013	C+	4.81	3.76	57.6	411.9	194.0	49.4	13.9

LAWYERS MUTUAL INS CO   B   Good

Major Rating Factors: Good overall results on stability tests (6.1 on a scale of 0 to 10). Stability strengths include good operational trends and excellent risk diversification. Strong long-term capitalization index (10.0) based on excellent current risk adjusted capital (severe and moderate loss scenarios). Moreover, capital has steadily grown over the last five years.

Other Rating Factors: Ample reserve history (9.3) that helps to protect the company against sharp claims increases. Excellent profitability (8.7) with operating gains in each of the last five years. Excellent liquidity (7.6) with ample operational cash flow and liquid investments.

Principal Business: Other liability (100%).

Principal Investments: Investment grade bonds (79%), misc. investments (19%), cash (1%), and real estate (1%).

Investments in Affiliates: 0%

Group Affiliation: None

Licensed in: CA

Commenced Business: September 1978

Address: 3110 W Empire Ave, Burbank, CA 91504

Phone: (818) 565-5512   **Domicile State:** CA   **NAIC Code:** 36706

Data Date	Rating	RACR #1	RACR #2	Loss Ratio %	Total Assets ($mil)	Capital ($mil)	Net Premium ($mil)	Net Income ($mil)
2017	B	9.50	5.86	51.6	342.2	239.9	34.7	14.1
2016	B	9.73	6.12	50.4	319.6	224.0	35.2	13.4
2015	C+	9.16	5.82	44.8	308.5	208.7	36.4	15.2
2014	C	8.41	5.40	42.9	303.2	196.0	35.9	16.3
2013	C	6.95	4.43	53.6	296.0	183.2	35.7	14.4

LEXINGTON INS CO

C **Fair**

Major Rating Factors: Fair reserve development (3.0 on a scale of 0 to 10) as reserves have generally been sufficient to cover claims. In 2016, the two year reserve development was 31% deficient. Fair overall results on stability tests (4.2) including negative cash flow from operations for 2017.

Other Rating Factors: Weak profitability index (2.7) with operating losses during 2017. Return on equity has been fair, averaging 7.2% over the past five years. Good liquidity (5.3) with sufficient resources (cash flows and marketable investments) to handle a spike in claims. Strong long-term capitalization index (7.5) based on excellent current risk adjusted capital (severe and moderate loss scenarios), despite some fluctuation in capital levels.

Principal Business: Other liability (27%), fire (23%), allied lines (20%), homeowners multiple peril (10%), inland marine (8%), medical malpractice (4%), and other lines (9%).

Principal Investments: Investment grade bonds (78%), misc. investments (16%), and non investment grade bonds (6%).

Investments in Affiliates: 1%

Group Affiliation: American International Group

Licensed in: All states, the District of Columbia and Puerto Rico

Commenced Business: April 1965

Address: 251 LITTLE FALLS DRIVE, Wilmington, DE 19808

Phone: (617) 330-1100   **Domicile State:** DE   **NAIC Code:** 19437

Data Date	Rating	RACR #1	RACR #2	Loss Ratio %	Total Assets ($mil)	Capital ($mil)	Net Premium ($mil)	Net Income ($mil)
2017	C	2.09	1.36	90.8	21,180.1	5,441.9	4,215.0	-243.1
2016	C	1.92	1.29	99.8	25,180.0	5,857.0	4,837.1	246.4
2015	C+	2.22	1.51	88.8	25,504.7	6,593.0	5,564.4	6.0
2014	C+	2.11	1.45	62.3	25,328.9	6,534.1	6,098.6	862.0
2013	C+	2.85	1.92	69.4	22,120.5	7,224.1	3,755.8	1,660.2

Reserve Deficiency (as % of capital)

* Adequate & redundant reserves show as negatives

■ 1 Yr Dev   □ 2 Yr Dev

LIBERTY INS CORP

C **Fair**

Major Rating Factors: Fair overall results on stability tests (4.3 on a scale of 0 to 10).

Other Rating Factors: Strong long-term capitalization index (10.0) based on excellent current risk adjusted capital (severe and moderate loss scenarios), despite some fluctuation in capital levels. Excellent profitability (7.0) with operating gains in each of the last five years. Superior liquidity (10.0) with ample operational cash flow and liquid investments.

Principal Business: Homeowners multiple peril (68%), workers compensation (19%), other liability (8%), auto liability (1%), and inland marine (1%).

Principal Investments: Investment grade bonds (92%) and misc. investments (8%).

Investments in Affiliates: None

Group Affiliation: Liberty Mutual Group

Licensed in: All states, the District of Columbia and Puerto Rico

Commenced Business: November 1988

Address: 2815 Forbs Avenue Suite 200, Hoffman Estates, IL 60192

Phone: Phone number unavailable   **Domicile State:** IL   **NAIC Code:** 42404

Data Date	Rating	RACR #1	RACR #2	Loss Ratio %	Total Assets ($mil)	Capital ($mil)	Net Premium ($mil)	Net Income ($mil)
2017	C	82.29	71.48	0.0	260.1	245.1	0.0	3.1
2016	C	132.31	64.30	0.0	242.0	240.8	0.0	1.1
2015	C-	135.45	65.78	0.0	244.8	239.7	0.0	16.6
2014	D	96.71	51.72	0.0	232.0	223.2	0.0	8.3
2013	D	135.89	66.60	0.0	218.6	215.4	-215.2	48.2

Liberty Mutual Group Composite Group Rating: B Largest Group Members	Assets ($mil)	Rating
LIBERTY MUTUAL INS CO	46021	B
LIBERTY LIFE ASR CO OF BOSTON	19046	B
PEERLESS INS CO	14600	B
OHIO CASUALTY INS CO	6148	C
EMPLOYERS INS OF WAUSAU	6056	B-

LIBERTY MUTUAL FIRE INS CO

B- **Good**

Major Rating Factors: Good overall results on stability tests (5.0 on a scale of 0 to 10) despite potential drain of affiliation with Liberty Mutual Group. Stability strengths include good operational trends and excellent risk diversification. History of adequate reserve strength (5.7) as reserves have been consistently at an acceptable level.

Other Rating Factors: Good profitability index (5.0) despite operating losses during 2017. Return on equity has been fair, averaging 7.1% over the past five years. Good liquidity (6.0) with sufficient resources (cash flows and marketable investments) to handle a spike in claims. Strong long-term capitalization index (7.7) based on excellent current risk adjusted capital (severe and moderate loss scenarios), despite some fluctuation in capital levels.

Principal Business: Auto liability (28%), homeowners multiple peril (22%), auto physical damage (16%), workers compensation (11%), other liability (9%), fire (5%), and other lines (8%).

Principal Investments: Investment grade bonds (72%), misc. investments (24%), and non investment grade bonds (5%).

Investments in Affiliates: 5%

Group Affiliation: Liberty Mutual Group

Licensed in: All states, the District of Columbia and Puerto Rico

Commenced Business: November 1908

Address: 2000 Westwood Drive, Wausau, WI 54401

Phone: (617) 357-9500   **Domicile State:** WI   **NAIC Code:** 23035

Data Date	Rating	RACR #1	RACR #2	Loss Ratio %	Total Assets ($mil)	Capital ($mil)	Net Premium ($mil)	Net Income ($mil)
2017	B-	2.02	1.44	79.5	6,038.9	1,412.8	2,284.0	-31.0
2016	B-	2.19	1.55	69.9	5,650.7	1,474.6	2,119.9	36.2
2015	B-	2.12	1.48	68.4	5,477.8	1,399.0	2,050.6	252.1
2014	C+	1.93	1.34	70.0	5,297.9	1,302.1	2,030.1	132.2
2013	C+	1.75	1.20	73.5	5,561.6	1,216.3	2,163.5	87.5

Rating Indexes

Ranges   Cap. 2   Stab.   Res.   Prof.   Liq.

■ Weak   ■ Fair   ▨ Good   □ Strong

LIBERTY MUTUAL INS CO   B   Good

Major Rating Factors: Good long-term capitalization index (5.9 on a scale of 0 to 10) based on good current risk adjusted capital (severe and moderate loss scenarios), although results have slipped from the excellent range over the last two years. History of adequate reserve strength (5.9) as reserves have been consistently at an acceptable level.

Other Rating Factors: Good liquidity (5.6) with sufficient resources (cash flows and marketable investments) to handle a spike in claims. Good overall results on stability tests (5.3). Weak profitability index (2.9) with operating losses during 2017. Return on equity has been low, averaging 2.2% over the past five years.

Principal Business: Surety (31%), other liability (25%), auto liability (12%), auto physical damage (11%), inland marine (5%), homeowners multiple peril (4%), and other lines (12%).

Principal Investments: Misc. investments (66%), investment grade bonds (31%), non investment grade bonds (3%), and real estate (1%).

Investments in Affiliates: 44%

Group Affiliation: Liberty Mutual Group

Licensed in: All states, the District of Columbia and Puerto Rico

Commenced Business: July 1912

Address: 175 Berkeley Street, Boston, MA 2116

Phone: (617) 357-9500   **Domicile State:** MA   **NAIC Code:** 23043

Data Date	Rating	RACR #1	RACR #2	Loss Ratio %	Total Assets ($mil)	Capital ($mil)	Net Premium ($mil)	Net Income ($mil)
2017	B	0.92	0.86	79.5	46,020.8	14,531.3	14,275.1	-908.4
2016	B	1.60	1.41	69.9	44,001.9	16,528.2	13,249.4	404.3
2015	B	1.60	1.40	68.4	42,343.2	15,815.3	12,816.1	973.0
2014	B	1.73	1.49	70.0	42,655.2	16,569.3	12,688.4	888.4
2013	B	1.63	1.39	73.5	44,475.8	15,126.4	13,889.2	507.4

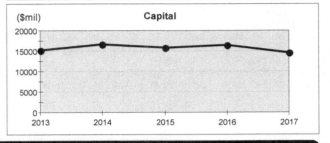

Capital

LION INS CO (FL) *   B+   Good

Major Rating Factors: Good overall results on stability tests (5.1 on a scale of 0 to 10). Stability strengths include excellent operational trends and good risk diversification. Strong long-term capitalization index (8.6) based on excellent current risk adjusted capital (severe and moderate loss scenarios). Moreover, capital has steadily grown over the last five years.

Other Rating Factors: Ample reserve history (8.7) that helps to protect the company against sharp claims increases. Excellent profitability (8.7) with operating gains in each of the last five years. Excellent liquidity (8.3) with ample operational cash flow and liquid investments.

Principal Business: Workers compensation (100%).

Principal Investments: Investment grade bonds (73%), misc. investments (24%), and cash (3%).

Investments in Affiliates: None

Group Affiliation: Jamestown Holdings Corp

Licensed in: AL, AZ, CO, CT, DC, FL, GA, HI, IL, LA, MD, MA, MS, NV, NJ, NM, NC, OK, PA, RI, SC, TN, TX, VA

Commenced Business: June 1986

Address: 2739 US HIGHWAY 19 NORTH, Holiday, FL 34691

Phone: (727) 682-0155   **Domicile State:** FL   **NAIC Code:** 11075

Data Date	Rating	RACR #1	RACR #2	Loss Ratio %	Total Assets ($mil)	Capital ($mil)	Net Premium ($mil)	Net Income ($mil)
2017	B+	3.47	2.08	34.4	264.3	96.9	27.1	6.6
2016	B	2.49	1.55	41.0	253.5	90.0	28.3	6.3
2015	B	3.93	2.34	43.0	244.6	83.4	28.2	6.1
2014	B	5.55	2.35	40.3	208.6	77.6	23.7	4.9
2013	B	5.26	3.38	45.9	192.4	72.4	21.6	4.1

Rating Indexes

■ Weak   ■ Fair   ▨ Good   □ Strong

LUBA CASUALTY INS CO *   B+   Good

Major Rating Factors: Good liquidity (6.9 on a scale of 0 to 10) with sufficient resources (cash flows and marketable investments) to handle a spike in claims. Good overall results on stability tests (6.5). Stability strengths include good operational trends and excellent risk diversification.

Other Rating Factors: Strong long-term capitalization index (8.3) based on excellent current risk adjusted capital (severe and moderate loss scenarios). Moreover, capital levels have been consistent in recent years. Ample reserve history (9.3) that helps to protect the company against sharp claims increases. Excellent profitability (8.8) with operating gains in each of the last five years.

Principal Business: Workers compensation (100%).

Principal Investments: Investment grade bonds (77%), misc. investments (14%), and cash (9%).

Investments in Affiliates: 3%

Group Affiliation: LUBA Group

Licensed in: AR, LA, MS, TX

Commenced Business: January 2006

Address: 2351 Energy Drive Suite 2000, Baton Rouge, LA 70808-2600

Phone: (225) 389-5822   **Domicile State:** LA   **NAIC Code:** 12472

Data Date	Rating	RACR #1	RACR #2	Loss Ratio %	Total Assets ($mil)	Capital ($mil)	Net Premium ($mil)	Net Income ($mil)
2017	B+	2.62	2.08	53.6	228.7	98.6	73.2	7.4
2016	B	2.39	1.90	52.1	224.6	90.9	74.3	9.5
2015	B	2.29	1.82	51.3	219.1	85.5	74.8	10.8
2014	B	2.02	1.60	65.5	212.4	77.3	75.1	5.4
2013	B	1.91	1.53	59.4	214.6	74.0	78.8	8.4

Liquidity Index

■ Weak   ■ Fair   ▨ Good   □ Strong

MAG MUTUAL INS CO

B- **Good**

Major Rating Factors: Fair overall results on stability tests (4.7 on a scale of 0 to 10) including potential drain of affiliation with MAG Mutual Group. Good overall profitability index (6.3). Good expense controls.

Other Rating Factors: Strong long-term capitalization index (9.5) based on excellent current risk adjusted capital (severe and moderate loss scenarios), despite some fluctuation in capital levels. Ample reserve history (9.3) that helps to protect the company against sharp claims increases. Excellent liquidity (7.1) with ample operational cash flow and liquid investments.

Principal Business: Medical malpractice (93%), workers compensation (5%), commercial multiple peril (1%), and other liability (1%).

Principal Investments: Investment grade bonds (64%), misc. investments (34%), cash (1%), and non investment grade bonds (1%).

Investments in Affiliates: 5%

Group Affiliation: MAG Mutual Group

Licensed in: All states except CA, DE, ID, KS, MN, MT, NV, NY, SD, WI, WY, PR

Commenced Business: June 1982

Address: 3535 Piedmont Rd NE Bldg 1, Atlanta, GA 30305-1518

Phone: (404) 842-5600   **Domicile State:** GA   **NAIC Code:** 42617

Data Date	Rating	RACR #1	RACR #2	Loss Ratio %	Total Assets ($mil)	Capital ($mil)	Net Premium ($mil)	Net Income ($mil)
2017	B-	3.70	2.65	73.2	1,718.5	850.0	263.9	29.4
2016	B-	3.20	2.51	71.9	1,773.9	914.9	243.9	15.9
2015	B-	3.25	2.55	71.3	1,719.2	880.7	200.2	40.8
2014	B-	5.19	3.44	74.4	1,635.6	773.3	194.1	45.2
2013	B-	4.96	3.43	64.5	1,609.9	740.3	197.5	52.0

Rating Indexes

Ranges | Cap. 2 | Stab. | Res. | Prof. | Liq.

■ Weak ■ Fair ▨ Good □ Strong

MAIDEN RE NORTH AMERICA INC

C+ **Fair**

Major Rating Factors: Fair reserve development (3.1 on a scale of 0 to 10) as reserves have generally been sufficient to cover claims. In 2017, the two year reserve development was 28% deficient. Fair overall results on stability tests (4.8).

Other Rating Factors: Good overall long-term capitalization (5.4) based on good current risk adjusted capital (severe loss scenario). However, capital levels have fluctuated somewhat during past years. Good profitability index (5.0) despite operating losses during 2013 and 2016. Return on equity has been low, averaging 2.6% over the past five years. Good liquidity (5.5) with sufficient resources (cash flows and marketable investments) to handle a spike in claims.

Principal Business: (This company is a reinsurer.)

Principal Investments: Investment grade bonds (96%), misc. investments (2%), cash (1%), and non investment grade bonds (1%).

Investments in Affiliates: None

Group Affiliation: Maiden Holdings Ltd

Licensed in: All states except PR

Commenced Business: August 2000

Address: PO Box 275 127 A East High St, Jefferson City, MO 65102-0275

Phone: (856) 359-2400   **Domicile State:** MO   **NAIC Code:** 11054

Data Date	Rating	RACR #1	RACR #2	Loss Ratio %	Total Assets ($mil)	Capital ($mil)	Net Premium ($mil)	Net Income ($mil)
2017	C+	1.27	0.82	78.9	1,298.9	301.7	468.3	16.9
2016	B-	1.19	0.69	79.6	1,302.6	291.1	433.2	-11.8
2015	B-	1.31	0.75	69.9	1,240.0	294.3	416.4	17.4
2014	B-	1.46	0.80	68.9	1,216.1	289.2	438.7	16.6
2013	B-	1.55	0.87	75.6	1,159.6	269.6	391.8	-1.3

Reserve Deficiency (as % of capital)

2013 | 2014 | 2015 | 2016 | 2017

* Adequate & redundant reserves show as negatives

■ 1 Yr Dev □ 2 Yr Dev

MARKEL GLOBAL REINS CO *

B+ **Good**

Major Rating Factors: Good liquidity (6.9 on a scale of 0 to 10) with sufficient resources (cash flows and marketable investments) to handle a spike in claims. Good overall results on stability tests (6.5) despite excessive premium growth and fair results on operational trends.

Other Rating Factors: Strong long-term capitalization index (7.0) based on excellent current risk adjusted capital (severe and moderate loss scenarios), despite some fluctuation in capital levels. Ample reserve history (7.5) that can protect against increases in claims costs. Fair profitability index (3.8) with operating losses during 2017. Return on equity has been low, averaging 0.3% over the past five years.

Principal Business: (This company is a reinsurer.)

Principal Investments: Misc. investments (62%), investment grade bonds (37%), and cash (1%).

Investments in Affiliates: 13%

Group Affiliation: Markel Corp

Licensed in: All states except PR

Commenced Business: September 1997

Address: 1209 Orange Street, Wilmington, DE 19801

Phone: (908) 630-2700   **Domicile State:** DE   **NAIC Code:** 10829

Data Date	Rating	RACR #1	RACR #2	Loss Ratio %	Total Assets ($mil)	Capital ($mil)	Net Premium ($mil)	Net Income ($mil)
2017	B+	1.38	1.01	76.6	2,180.9	904.3	613.6	-32.8
2016	B+	2.16	1.45	68.9	1,692.9	804.1	254.7	4.9
2015	B	2.58	1.72	71.7	1,546.4	727.1	211.7	1.7
2014	B+	3.21	2.22	71.4	1,491.6	749.4	220.7	11.6
2013	B+	3.62	2.60	68.0	1,364.7	715.0	186.9	19.6

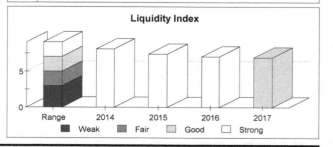

Liquidity Index

Range | 2014 | 2015 | 2016 | 2017

■ Weak ■ Fair ▨ Good □ Strong

MBIA INS CORP   E+   Very Weak

Major Rating Factors: Poor long-term capitalization index (0.5 on a scale of 0 to 10) based on weak current risk adjusted capital (severe and moderate loss scenarios). A history of deficient reserves (1.3) that places pressure on both capital and profits. The one year reserve development was deficient in three of the last five years by between 26% and 149%.

Other Rating Factors: Weak profitability index (1.3) with operating losses during 2013, 2014 and 2016. Average return on equity over the last five years has been poor at -43.0%. Vulnerable liquidity (0.2) as a spike in claims may stretch capacity. Weak overall results on stability tests (0.4) including weak risk adjusted capital in prior years and negative cash flow from operations for 2017.

Principal Business: Financial guaranty (100%).

Principal Investments: Investment grade bonds (74%), cash (20%), and misc. investments (6%).

Investments in Affiliates: 2%

Group Affiliation: MBIA Inc

Licensed in: All states, the District of Columbia and Puerto Rico

Commenced Business: May 1968

Address: 1 Manhattanville Rd Suite 301, Purchase, NY 10577-2100

Phone: (914) 273-4545   **Domicile State:** NY   **NAIC Code:** 12041

Data Date	Rating	RACR #1	RACR #2	Loss Ratio %	Total Assets ($mil)	Capital ($mil)	Net Premium ($mil)	Net Income ($mil)
2017	E+	0.54	0.18	288.6	262.4	236.5	40.7	107.1
2016	E+	0.56	0.19	357.1	514.9	238.2	52.0	-322.6
2015	D	0.77	0.26	81.8	796.8	609.1	87.0	24.6
2014	D	0.75	0.25	131.4	960.2	541.5	104.6	-35.2
2013	D	0.78	0.26	378.6	1,280.1	403.0	133.5	-494.0

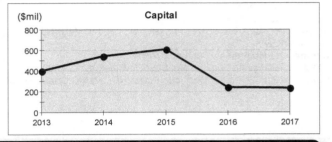

MCIC VERMONT INC RRG   C   Fair

Major Rating Factors: Fair profitability index (4.5 on a scale of 0 to 10). Good expense controls. Fair overall results on stability tests (3.4) including weak risk adjusted capital in prior years.

Other Rating Factors: Poor long-term capitalization index (1.0) based on weak current risk adjusted capital (severe and moderate loss scenarios). A history of deficient reserves (1.7). Underreserving can have an adverse impact on capital and profits. In 2014 and 2015 the two year reserve development was 6273% and 8875% deficient respectively. Good liquidity (6.7) with sufficient resources (cash flows and marketable investments) to handle a spike in claims.

Principal Business: Medical malpractice (96%) and other liability (4%).

Principal Investments: Misc. investments (73%), investment grade bonds (24%), and cash (3%).

Investments in Affiliates: None

Group Affiliation: MCIC Vermont Holdings Inc

Licensed in: CT, DC, FL, MD, MA, NJ, NY, NC, PA, RI, TX, VT, VA

Commenced Business: January 1997

Address: 76 St Paul Street Suite 500, Burlington, VT 05401-4477

Phone: (802) 652-1571   **Domicile State:** VT   **NAIC Code:** 10697

Data Date	Rating	RACR #1	RACR #2	Loss Ratio %	Total Assets ($mil)	Capital ($mil)	Net Premium ($mil)	Net Income ($mil)
2017	C	0.30	0.26	100.7	1,922.5	655.9	337.6	44.6
2016	C	0.23	0.20	97.4	1,650.0	553.5	289.3	19.1
2015	N/A	N/A	N/A	107.2	1,604.3	499.6	230.2	38.3
2014	N/A	N/A	N/A	534.3	1,674.1	576.3	218.5	21.8
2013	E	0.43	0.33	42.7	204.4	10.3	42.2	0.1

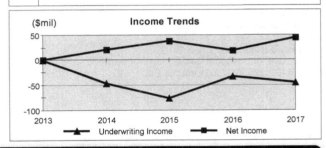

MEDICAL LIABILITY MUTUAL INS CO   D+   Weak

Major Rating Factors: Weak overall results on stability tests (2.4 on a scale of 0 to 10) including negative cash flow from operations for 2017. Strong long-term capitalization index (7.9) based on excellent current risk adjusted capital (severe and moderate loss scenarios). Moreover, capital levels have been consistent in recent years.

Other Rating Factors: Ample reserve history (9.5) that helps to protect the company against sharp claims increases. Excellent profitability (8.7) with operating gains in each of the last five years. Excellent liquidity (7.8) with ample operational cash flow and liquid investments.

Principal Business: (Not applicable due to unusual reinsurance transactions.)

Principal Investments: Investment grade bonds (78%), misc. investments (11%), non investment grade bonds (10%), and cash (1%).

Investments in Affiliates: 0%

Group Affiliation: None

Licensed in: CT, DE, ME, MA, NJ, NY, PA, RI, VT

Commenced Business: May 1977

Address: Two Park Avenue Room 2500, New York, NY 10016

Phone: (212) 576-9801   **Domicile State:** NY   **NAIC Code:** 34231

Data Date	Rating	RACR #1	RACR #2	Loss Ratio %	Total Assets ($mil)	Capital ($mil)	Net Premium ($mil)	Net Income ($mil)
2017	D+	2.19	1.82	85.3	5,430.6	2,204.6	409.9	120.2
2016	D+	2.01	1.69	47.3	5,499.8	2,064.7	393.7	162.7
2015	D+	1.64	1.38	77.6	5,452.2	1,826.9	410.9	114.5
2014	D+	1.52	1.28	78.4	5,881.1	1,783.9	490.3	263.8
2013	D+	1.27	1.08	93.4	5,777.6	1,538.8	533.9	172.2

MEDICAL MUTUAL INS CO OF NC   B-   Good

Major Rating Factors: Fair overall results on stability tests (4.5 on a scale of 0 to 10) including potential drain of affiliation with Medical Ins Group. Strong long-term capitalization index (9.9) based on excellent current risk adjusted capital (severe and moderate loss scenarios), despite some fluctuation in capital levels.

Other Rating Factors: Ample reserve history (9.4) that helps to protect the company against sharp claims increases. Excellent profitability (7.7) with operating gains in each of the last five years. Excellent liquidity (8.7) with ample operational cash flow and liquid investments.

Principal Business: Medical malpractice (100%).

Principal Investments: Investment grade bonds (63%), misc. investments (32%), cash (4%), and non investment grade bonds (1%).

Investments in Affiliates: 3%

Group Affiliation: Medical Ins Group

Licensed in: AL, AR, DC, DE, FL, GA, KY, LA, MD, MS, NJ, NC, OH, PA, SC, TN, TX, VA, WV

Commenced Business: October 1975

Address: 700 Spring Forest Road Ste 400, Raleigh, NC 27609

Phone: (919) 872-7117   **Domicile State:** NC   **NAIC Code:** 32522

Data Date	Rating	RACR #1	RACR #2	Loss Ratio %	Total Assets ($mil)	Capital ($mil)	Net Premium ($mil)	Net Income ($mil)
2017	B-	4.12	2.96	60.4	598.1	288.7	95.0	22.5
2016	B-	3.77	2.71	59.2	555.0	254.8	114.3	24.1
2015	B-	4.50	3.35	57.2	485.7	229.0	64.0	21.8
2014	B-	4.83	3.72	55.0	475.5	221.3	68.7	30.3
2013	B-	6.28	4.56	54.7	598.0	334.2	75.4	26.1

MEDICAL MUTUAL LIAB INS SOC OF MD   B-   Good

Major Rating Factors: Fair overall results on stability tests (4.6 on a scale of 0 to 10) including potential drain of affiliation with Medical Ins Group Of MD. Strong long-term capitalization index (10.0) based on excellent current risk adjusted capital (severe and moderate loss scenarios). Moreover, capital levels have been consistent in recent years.

Other Rating Factors: Ample reserve history (9.4) that helps to protect the company against sharp claims increases. Excellent profitability (7.6) with operating gains in each of the last five years. Excellent liquidity (7.7) with ample operational cash flow and liquid investments.

Principal Business: Medical malpractice (100%).

Principal Investments: Investment grade bonds (80%) and misc. investments (20%).

Investments in Affiliates: 15%

Group Affiliation: Medical Ins Group Of MD

Licensed in: MD, MI, NC, PA

Commenced Business: June 1975

Address: 225 International Circle, Hunt Valley, MD 21030

Phone: (410) 785-0050   **Domicile State:** MD   **NAIC Code:** 32328

Data Date	Rating	RACR #1	RACR #2	Loss Ratio %	Total Assets ($mil)	Capital ($mil)	Net Premium ($mil)	Net Income ($mil)
2017	B-	3.64	3.35	49.6	825.0	414.3	101.0	7.8
2016	B-	3.69	3.36	55.2	806.1	401.5	104.2	10.3
2015	B-	3.68	3.33	53.9	800.7	385.8	108.1	15.1
2014	B-	3.50	3.15	52.2	812.1	369.3	114.5	15.8
2013	B-	3.35	2.99	50.3	804.9	339.9	120.7	3.4

MEDICAL PROFESSIONAL MUTUAL INS CO   B-   Good

Major Rating Factors: Fair overall results on stability tests (4.5 on a scale of 0 to 10) including potential drain of affiliation with Medical Professional Mutual. Good overall profitability index (6.8). Fair expense controls.

Other Rating Factors: Strong long-term capitalization index (8.0) based on excellent current risk adjusted capital (severe and moderate loss scenarios), despite some fluctuation in capital levels. Ample reserve history (9.3) that helps to protect the company against sharp claims increases. Excellent liquidity (7.5) with ample operational cash flow and liquid investments.

Principal Business: Medical malpractice (99%) and other liability (1%).

Principal Investments: Misc. investments (49%), investment grade bonds (42%), non investment grade bonds (8%), and cash (1%).

Investments in Affiliates: 24%

Group Affiliation: Medical Professional Mutual

Licensed in: CO, FL, MA, NY, NC, TN, TX, VA

Commenced Business: July 1975

Address: One Financial Center, Boston, MA 02111-2621

Phone: (617) 330-1755   **Domicile State:** MA   **NAIC Code:** 10206

Data Date	Rating	RACR #1	RACR #2	Loss Ratio %	Total Assets ($mil)	Capital ($mil)	Net Premium ($mil)	Net Income ($mil)
2017	B-	1.93	1.67	82.4	3,134.7	1,638.9	305.1	46.4
2016	B-	1.93	1.66	88.7	3,176.7	1,594.4	250.4	29.4
2015	B-	2.03	1.80	60.0	2,997.3	1,538.2	241.3	72.9
2014	B-	1.93	1.72	65.3	3,012.9	1,474.0	263.6	107.8
2013	B-	2.36	2.01	60.1	3,151.4	1,423.4	277.0	135.3

MEDICAL PROTECTIVE CO   B   Good

Major Rating Factors: Good overall results on stability tests (5.5 on a scale of 0 to 10). Affiliation with Berkshire-Hathaway is a strength. Strong long-term capitalization index (9.3) based on excellent current risk adjusted capital (severe and moderate loss scenarios), despite some fluctuation in capital levels.
Other Rating Factors: Ample reserve history (9.6) that helps to protect the company against sharp claims increases. Excellent profitability (8.7) with operating gains in each of the last five years. Excellent liquidity (8.8) with ample operational cash flow and liquid investments.
Principal Business: Medical malpractice (99%) and other liability (1%).
Principal Investments: Misc. investments (56%), investment grade bonds (41%), and cash (3%).
Investments in Affiliates: None
Group Affiliation: Berkshire-Hathaway
Licensed in: All states, the District of Columbia and Puerto Rico
Commenced Business: January 1910
Address: 5814 Reed Road, Fort Wayne, IN 46835
Phone: (260) 485-9622   **Domicile State:** IN   **NAIC Code:** 11843

Data Date	Rating	RACR #1	RACR #2	Loss Ratio %	Total Assets ($mil)	Capital ($mil)	Net Premium ($mil)	Net Income ($mil)
2017	B	3.98	2.54	58.0	3,318.0	2,021.0	240.0	83.3
2016	B	4.13	2.83	65.0	2,996.1	1,709.5	255.8	109.2
2015	B	4.32	3.00	59.5	2,790.4	1,570.8	226.5	130.1
2014	B	4.98	3.33	114.5	2,699.6	1,589.1	-680.0	140.1
2013	B	2.74	2.15	51.3	3,286.3	1,405.7	366.9	205.3

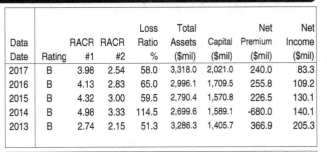

MERCHANTS NATIONAL INS CO *   B+   Good

Major Rating Factors: History of adequate reserve strength (5.6 on a scale of 0 to 10) as reserves have been consistently at an acceptable level. Good overall profitability index (5.9) despite operating losses during 2013. Return on equity has been low, averaging 3.9% over the past five years.
Other Rating Factors: Good liquidity (6.8) with sufficient resources (cash flows and marketable investments) to handle a spike in claims. Good overall results on stability tests (6.5). Strong long-term capitalization index (7.6) based on excellent current risk adjusted capital (severe and moderate loss scenarios). Moreover, capital has steadily grown over the last five years.
Principal Business: Other liability (87%) and products liability (13%).
Principal Investments: Investment grade bonds (73%), misc. investments (26%), and cash (1%).
Investments in Affiliates: 26%
Group Affiliation: Merchants Mutual
Licensed in: All states except AK, AZ, FL, HI, ME, OK, RI, PR
Commenced Business: January 2007
Address: 5 Bedford Farms Suite 101, Bedford, NH 3110
Phone: (716) 849-3333   **Domicile State:** NH   **NAIC Code:** 12775

Data Date	Rating	RACR #1	RACR #2	Loss Ratio %	Total Assets ($mil)	Capital ($mil)	Net Premium ($mil)	Net Income ($mil)
2017	B+	1.80	1.63	58.6	136.0	55.3	44.3	2.6
2016	B	1.75	1.59	59.7	128.4	52.5	41.8	3.3
2015	C+	1.40	1.07	65.3	116.6	40.3	42.0	2.5
2014	C	1.33	1.00	66.0	111.3	37.1	42.5	2.7
2013	C	1.28	0.98	75.5	103.7	34.0	42.3	-1.6

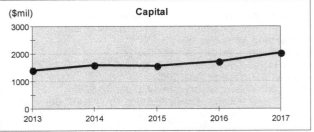

* Adequate & redundant reserves show as negatives   ■ 1 Yr Dev ☐ 2 Yr Dev

MERCHANTS PREFERRED INS CO *   B+   Good

Major Rating Factors: History of adequate reserve strength (5.9 on a scale of 0 to 10) as reserves have been consistently at an acceptable level. Good liquidity (6.8) with sufficient resources (cash flows and marketable investments) to handle a spike in claims.
Other Rating Factors: Good overall results on stability tests (6.3). Strong long-term capitalization index (8.9) based on excellent current risk adjusted capital (severe and moderate loss scenarios). Moreover, capital levels have been consistent in recent years. Excellent profitability (7.9) despite modest operating losses during 2013.
Principal Business: Auto liability (47%), auto physical damage (16%), commercial multiple peril (15%), homeowners multiple peril (11%), and workers compensation (10%).
Principal Investments: Investment grade bonds (98%) and cash (2%).
Investments in Affiliates: None
Group Affiliation: Merchants Mutual
Licensed in: DE, IN, ME, MD, MA, MI, NH, NJ, NY, OH, PA, RI, VT
Commenced Business: February 2007
Address: 250 Main Street, Buffalo, NY 14202-4188
Phone: (716) 849-3333   **Domicile State:** NY   **NAIC Code:** 12901

Data Date	Rating	RACR #1	RACR #2	Loss Ratio %	Total Assets ($mil)	Capital ($mil)	Net Premium ($mil)	Net Income ($mil)
2017	B+	3.63	2.67	58.6	76.4	30.1	22.1	1.6
2016	B	3.61	2.66	59.7	73.3	29.1	20.9	1.4
2015	B-	3.18	1.64	65.3	69.1	27.1	21.0	1.7
2014	C+	3.13	1.59	66.0	68.0	25.8	21.2	1.4
2013	C+	2.99	1.61	75.5	62.8	24.5	21.1	0.0

* Adequate & redundant reserves show as negatives   ■ 1 Yr Dev ☐ 2 Yr Dev

MERCURY CASUALTY CO *
B+   **Good**

Major Rating Factors: History of adequate reserve strength (5.5 on a scale of 0 to 10) as reserves have been consistently at an acceptable level. Good overall profitability index (6.6). Fair expense controls. Return on equity has been good over the last five years, averaging 13.2%.

Other Rating Factors: Good liquidity (6.8) with sufficient resources (cash flows and marketable investments) to handle a spike in claims. Good overall results on stability tests (6.5). Stability strengths include good operational trends and excellent risk diversification. Strong long-term capitalization index (7.7) based on excellent current risk adjusted capital (severe and moderate loss scenarios), despite some fluctuation in capital levels.

Principal Business: Commercial multiple peril (38%), auto liability (23%), homeowners multiple peril (12%), auto physical damage (11%), fire (7%), other liability (5%), and other lines (3%).

Principal Investments: Investment grade bonds (49%), misc. investments (40%), cash (5%), real estate (5%), and non investment grade bonds (1%).

Investments in Affiliates: 36%

Group Affiliation: Mercury General Group

Licensed in: AZ, CA, FL, GA, IL, MI, NV, NJ, NY, OK, PA, TX, VA, WA

Commenced Business: April 1962

Address: 555 West Imperial Highway, Brea, CA 92821

Phone: (714) 671-6600   **Domicile State:** CA   **NAIC Code:** 11908

Data Date	Rating	RACR #1	RACR #2	Loss Ratio %	Total Assets ($mil)	Capital ($mil)	Net Premium ($mil)	Net Income ($mil)
2017	B+	1.72	1.59	79.3	1,877.6	1,071.8	680.7	115.1
2016	B	1.44	1.34	83.2	1,889.0	925.8	753.1	93.9
2015	B	1.50	1.40	77.5	1,849.4	977.7	662.7	119.9
2014	B	1.58	1.46	74.7	1,952.2	1,024.6	735.8	133.9
2013	B+	1.73	1.57	69.4	2,041.5	1,151.3	738.1	226.2

Reserve Deficiency (as % of capital)

* Adequate & redundant reserves show as negatives

■ 1 Yr Dev   □ 2 Yr Dev

MERCURY INS CO *
B+   **Good**

Major Rating Factors: Good overall results on stability tests (6.6 on a scale of 0 to 10). Strong long-term capitalization index (7.5) based on excellent current risk adjusted capital (severe and moderate loss scenarios), despite some fluctuation in capital levels.

Other Rating Factors: Fair reserve development (4.4) as reserves have generally been sufficient to cover claims. Fair profitability index (3.9). Good expense controls. Return on equity has been fair, averaging 10.7% over the past five years. Vulnerable liquidity (2.5) as a spike in claims may stretch capacity.

Principal Business: Auto liability (58%) and auto physical damage (42%).

Principal Investments: Investment grade bonds (86%), misc. investments (13%), and non investment grade bonds (3%).

Investments in Affiliates: None

Group Affiliation: Mercury General Group

Licensed in: CA

Commenced Business: July 1978

Address: 555 West Imperial Highway, Brea, CA 92821

Phone: (714) 671-6600   **Domicile State:** CA   **NAIC Code:** 27553

Data Date	Rating	RACR #1	RACR #2	Loss Ratio %	Total Assets ($mil)	Capital ($mil)	Net Premium ($mil)	Net Income ($mil)
2017	B+	1.47	1.34	74.3	1,708.0	609.8	1,624.5	60.8
2016	B+	1.61	1.49	73.0	1,651.6	631.5	1,560.1	57.7
2015	B+	1.82	1.68	69.6	1,559.3	657.0	1,472.7	90.3
2014	B+	1.84	1.69	70.3	1,561.2	648.7	1,415.9	66.6
2013	A-	1.99	1.81	75.2	1,532.9	652.6	1,350.1	66.5

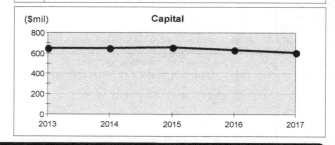

($mil)   Capital

MERRIMACK MUTUAL FIRE INS CO
B-   **Good**

Major Rating Factors: Fair overall results on stability tests (4.8 on a scale of 0 to 10) including potential drain of affiliation with Andover Group. Strong long-term capitalization index (7.7) based on excellent current risk adjusted capital (severe and moderate loss scenarios), despite some fluctuation in capital levels.

Other Rating Factors: Ample reserve history (7.5) that can protect against increases in claims costs. Excellent profitability (7.8) with operating gains in each of the last five years. Excellent liquidity (7.0) with ample operational cash flow and liquid investments.

Principal Business: Homeowners multiple peril (55%), commercial multiple peril (14%), fire (12%), allied lines (9%), other liability (7%), and inland marine (2%).

Principal Investments: Misc. investments (84%), cash (8%), investment grade bonds (6%), and real estate (2%).

Investments in Affiliates: 24%

Group Affiliation: Andover Group

Licensed in: CT, IL, ME, MA, NH, NJ, NY, RI

Commenced Business: April 1828

Address: 95 Old River Road, Andover, MA 01810-1078

Phone: (978) 475-3300   **Domicile State:** MA   **NAIC Code:** 19798

Data Date	Rating	RACR #1	RACR #2	Loss Ratio %	Total Assets ($mil)	Capital ($mil)	Net Premium ($mil)	Net Income ($mil)
2017	B-	1.87	1.44	64.3	1,728.2	1,100.6	281.4	20.7
2016	B-	2.03	1.57	50.9	1,467.0	933.1	269.6	43.7
2015	B-	2.01	1.58	68.5	1,341.1	844.1	259.3	8.7
2014	B	2.02	1.58	43.4	1,363.6	857.8	261.8	49.7
2013	B	2.02	1.58	43.3	1,251.0	785.2	246.4	60.1

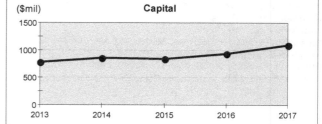

($mil)   Capital

METROPOLITAN GROUP PROP & CAS INS CO   B   Good

Major Rating Factors: Good overall profitability index (5.9 on a scale of 0 to 10). Good expense controls. Return on equity has been low, averaging 4.3% over the past five years. Good overall results on stability tests (5.4). Stability strengths include good operational trends and excellent risk diversification.

Other Rating Factors: Strong long-term capitalization index (10.0) based on excellent current risk adjusted capital (severe and moderate loss scenarios), despite some fluctuation in capital levels. Excellent liquidity (7.0) with ample operational cash flow and liquid investments.

Principal Business: Auto liability (47%), auto physical damage (34%), and homeowners multiple peril (18%).

Principal Investments: Investment grade bonds (98%), misc. investments (1%), and non investment grade bonds (1%).

Investments in Affiliates: None

Group Affiliation: MetLife Inc

Licensed in: All states except HI, KY, ME, MN, NM, NC, OR, VA, WY, PR

Commenced Business: December 1977

Address: 700 Quaker Lane, Warwick, RI 02886-6669

Phone: (401) 827-2400   **Domicile State:** RI   **NAIC Code:** 34339

Data Date	Rating	RACR #1	RACR #2	Loss Ratio %	Total Assets ($mil)	Capital ($mil)	Net Premium ($mil)	Net Income ($mil)
2017	B	35.22	29.17	0.0	687.0	386.2	0.0	12.8
2016	B	38.37	34.53	0.0	695.7	413.7	0.0	28.0
2015	B	27.20	12.43	0.0	651.1	379.2	0.0	3.4
2014	B	22.37	10.27	0.0	611.7	378.3	0.0	25.7
2013	B	16.98	8.60	0.0	582.5	344.9	0.0	13.0

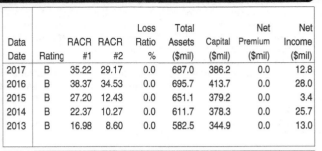

Income Trends

METROPOLITAN P&C INS CO   B-   Good

Major Rating Factors: Fair liquidity (3.2 on a scale of 0 to 10) as cash resources may not be adequate to cover a spike in claims. Good overall profitability index (5.3). Fair expense controls. Return on equity has been fair, averaging 9.5% over the past five years.

Other Rating Factors: Good overall results on stability tests (5.3). Strong long-term capitalization index (7.9) based on excellent current risk adjusted capital (severe and moderate loss scenarios), despite some fluctuation in capital levels. Ample reserve history (7.8) that can protect against increases in claims costs.

Principal Business: Homeowners multiple peril (45%), auto liability (26%), auto physical damage (21%), other liability (3%), other accident & health (2%), inland marine (1%), and other lines (2%).

Principal Investments: Investment grade bonds (70%), misc. investments (28%), and non investment grade bonds (5%).

Investments in Affiliates: 21%

Group Affiliation: MetLife Inc

Licensed in: All states except AK, CA, PR

Commenced Business: December 1972

Address: 700 Quaker Lane, Warwick, RI 02886-6669

Phone: (401) 827-2400   **Domicile State:** RI   **NAIC Code:** 26298

Data Date	Rating	RACR #1	RACR #2	Loss Ratio %	Total Assets ($mil)	Capital ($mil)	Net Premium ($mil)	Net Income ($mil)
2017	B-	1.94	1.58	71.5	6,107.4	2,265.5	3,617.6	246.2
2016	B-	1.97	1.60	74.0	5,630.7	2,271.1	3,558.3	131.3
2015	B-	2.10	1.69	70.2	5,599.1	2,335.5	3,524.3	191.6
2014	B	2.16	1.73	67.3	5,645.6	2,388.0	3,465.7	253.5
2013	B	2.07	1.65	68.8	5,499.7	2,224.9	3,372.1	265.8

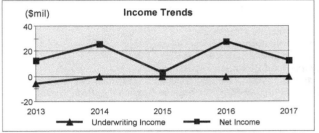

Liquidity Index

MID-CENTURY INS CO   B   Good

Major Rating Factors: Good overall results on stability tests (5.6 on a scale of 0 to 10) despite potential drain of affiliation with Farmers Insurance Group of Companies and negative cash flow from operations for 2017. History of adequate reserve strength (5.9) as reserves have been consistently at an acceptable level.

Other Rating Factors: Good overall profitability index (6.4). Fair expense controls. Return on equity has been low, averaging 4.7% over the past five years. Fair liquidity (4.4) as cash resources may not be adequate to cover a spike in claims. Strong long-term capitalization index (7.6) based on excellent current risk adjusted capital (severe and moderate loss scenarios), despite some fluctuation in capital levels.

Principal Business: Auto liability (41%), auto physical damage (24%), homeowners multiple peril (17%), commercial multiple peril (11%), and workers compensation (7%).

Principal Investments: Investment grade bonds (80%), misc. investments (14%), real estate (4%), and non investment grade bonds (2%).

Investments in Affiliates: 9%

Group Affiliation: Farmers Insurance Group of Companies

Licensed in: All states except AK, ME, PR

Commenced Business: February 1953

Address: 6301 OWENSMOUTH AVE, Woodland Hills, CA 91367

Phone: (323) 932-3200   **Domicile State:** CA   **NAIC Code:** 21687

Data Date	Rating	RACR #1	RACR #2	Loss Ratio %	Total Assets ($mil)	Capital ($mil)	Net Premium ($mil)	Net Income ($mil)
2017	B	2.02	1.48	69.3	3,941.6	1,077.6	2,269.6	48.2
2016	B	1.93	1.42	71.0	3,980.6	1,052.8	2,361.9	28.4
2015	C+	1.88	1.38	68.3	3,904.9	1,023.6	2,388.9	45.1
2014	C	1.86	1.40	65.0	3,765.9	986.4	2,250.0	58.9
2013	C	1.82	1.38	67.2	3,714.7	921.3	2,181.9	56.0

Rating Indexes

MIDDLESEX INS CO *

B+   Good

Major Rating Factors: Good overall profitability index (5.4 on a scale of 0 to 10). Fair expense controls. Return on equity has been fair, averaging 5.5% over the past five years. Good liquidity (6.8) with sufficient resources (cash flows and marketable investments) to handle a spike in claims.

Other Rating Factors: Good overall results on stability tests (6.5). Strong long-term capitalization index (8.8) based on excellent current risk adjusted capital (severe and moderate loss scenarios), despite some fluctuation in capital levels. Ample reserve history (8.0) that helps to protect the company against sharp claims increases.

Principal Business: Workers compensation (43%), auto liability (34%), other liability (7%), auto physical damage (5%), allied lines (4%), fire (3%), and other lines (3%).

Principal Investments: Investment grade bonds (91%) and misc. investments (9%).

Investments in Affiliates: 4%

Group Affiliation: Sentry Ins Group

Licensed in: All states except PR

Commenced Business: March 1826

Address: 1800 NORTH POINT DRIVE, Stevens Point, WI 54481

Phone: (715) 346-6000   **Domicile State:** WI   **NAIC Code:** 23434

Data Date	Rating	RACR #1	RACR #2	Loss Ratio %	Total Assets ($mil)	Capital ($mil)	Net Premium ($mil)	Net Income ($mil)
2017	B+	3.33	2.21	74.8	764.3	244.3	210.8	11.2
2016	B	3.54	2.36	73.9	717.7	246.8	201.2	12.2
2015	B	3.79	2.52	72.7	695.2	249.9	187.7	15.8
2014	B	4.08	2.86	74.9	673.1	251.1	181.4	16.5
2013	B	3.92	2.77	76.3	653.2	242.8	181.8	11.8

Income Trends

MISSISSIPPI FARM BUREAU CAS INS CO

B-   Good

Major Rating Factors: Fair overall results on stability tests (4.8 on a scale of 0 to 10) including potential drain of affiliation with Southern Farm Bureau Casualty. Good liquidity (6.7) with sufficient resources (cash flows and marketable investments) to handle a spike in claims.

Other Rating Factors: Strong long-term capitalization index (10.0) based on excellent current risk adjusted capital (severe and moderate loss scenarios). Moreover, capital has steadily grown over the last five years. Ample reserve history (7.7) that can protect against increases in claims costs. Excellent profitability (8.9) with operating gains in each of the last five years.

Principal Business: Homeowners multiple peril (36%), auto liability (30%), auto physical damage (22%), allied lines (3%), fire (3%), inland marine (2%), and other lines (4%).

Principal Investments: Investment grade bonds (94%), misc. investments (5%), and cash (1%).

Investments in Affiliates: None

Group Affiliation: Southern Farm Bureau Casualty

Licensed in: FL, LA, MS, SC, TX

Commenced Business: September 1986

Address: 6311 Ridgewood Road, Jackson, MS 39211

Phone: (601) 957-3200   **Domicile State:** MS   **NAIC Code:** 27669

Data Date	Rating	RACR #1	RACR #2	Loss Ratio %	Total Assets ($mil)	Capital ($mil)	Net Premium ($mil)	Net Income ($mil)
2017	B-	6.65	5.63	61.0	438.2	289.6	168.0	27.1
2016	B-	6.15	5.18	60.5	426.2	275.8	171.4	30.6
2015	B-	5.45	4.52	59.4	417.6	255.4	175.3	31.6
2014	B-	4.93	4.16	72.9	375.4	228.5	170.2	15.3
2013	B	4.81	3.70	70.4	351.8	212.0	159.2	15.7

Southern Farm Bureau Casualty
Composite Group Rating: B-
Largest Group Members

	Assets ($mil)	Rating
SOUTHERN FARM BUREAU CAS INS CO	2269	B-
FLORIDA FARM BU CASUALTY INS CO	558	B-
MISSISSIPPI FARM BUREAU CAS INS CO	438	B-
SOUTHERN FARM BUREAU PROPERTY	58	U
LOUISIANA FARM BUREAU CAS INS CO	12	B

MITSUI SUMITOMO INS CO OF AMER *

A-   Excellent

Major Rating Factors: Strong long-term capitalization index (9.4 on a scale of 0 to 10) based on excellent current risk adjusted capital (severe and moderate loss scenarios). Furthermore, this high level of risk adjusted capital has been consistently maintained in previous years. Ample reserve history (9.3) that helps to protect the company against sharp claims increases.

Other Rating Factors: Excellent profitability (8.6) with operating gains in each of the last five years. Excellent liquidity (7.0) with ample operational cash flow and liquid investments. Excellent overall results on stability tests (7.0). Stability strengths include excellent operational trends and excellent risk diversification.

Principal Business: Workers compensation (27%), commercial multiple peril (21%), other liability (14%), allied lines (13%), auto liability (6%), ocean marine (6%), and other lines (13%).

Principal Investments: Investment grade bonds (76%), misc. investments (19%), real estate (3%), and cash (2%).

Investments in Affiliates: None

Group Affiliation: MS & AD Ins Group Holdings Inc

Licensed in: All states, the District of Columbia and Puerto Rico

Commenced Business: January 1971

Address: 527 MADISON AVE 18TH FL, New York, NY 10022

Phone: (908) 604-2900   **Domicile State:** NY   **NAIC Code:** 20362

Data Date	Rating	RACR #1	RACR #2	Loss Ratio %	Total Assets ($mil)	Capital ($mil)	Net Premium ($mil)	Net Income ($mil)
2017	A-	4.03	2.59	62.9	975.8	371.9	201.3	30.2
2016	B+	3.94	2.47	66.5	929.6	348.2	199.1	25.5
2015	B+	4.18	2.65	71.2	904.3	335.3	174.4	21.3
2014	B+	3.99	2.58	71.3	900.6	332.3	191.9	20.3
2013	B+	4.02	2.65	73.5	845.2	319.6	182.7	18.5

Risk-Adjusted Capital Ratio #2
(Severe Loss Scenario)

■ Weak   ■ Fair   ▨ Good   ☐ Strong

MMIC INS INC * B+ Good

Major Rating Factors: Good overall results on stability tests (6.5 on a scale of 0 to 10). Stability strengths include good operational trends and excellent risk diversification. Strong long-term capitalization index (7.9) based on excellent current risk adjusted capital (severe and moderate loss scenarios). Moreover, capital levels have been consistent in recent years.

Other Rating Factors: Ample reserve history (9.3) that helps to protect the company against sharp claims increases. Excellent profitability (8.7) with operating gains in each of the last five years. Excellent liquidity (7.0) with ample operational cash flow and liquid investments.

Principal Business: Medical malpractice (95%) and other liability (5%).

Principal Investments: Investment grade bonds (55%), misc. investments (43%), cash (1%), and non investment grade bonds (1%).

Investments in Affiliates: 23%

Group Affiliation: Constellation Inc

Licensed in: AZ, AR, CO, ID, IL, IN, IA, KS, KY, MI, MN, MO, MT, NE, ND, OH, OR, SD, TN, UT, WA, WI, WY

Commenced Business: October 1980

Address: 7701 FRANCE AVE SOUTH STE 500, Minneapolis, MN 55435-5288

Phone: (952) 838-6700 **Domicile State:** MN **NAIC Code:** 16942

Data Date	Rating	RACR #1	RACR #2	Loss Ratio %	Total Assets ($mil)	Capital ($mil)	Net Premium ($mil)	Net Income ($mil)
2017	B+	1.99	1.71	71.6	682.7	362.6	96.8	43.1
2016	B	1.91	1.62	75.2	709.2	339.5	105.4	27.3
2015	B	1.76	1.52	77.4	718.1	327.1	108.7	36.9
2014	B	1.79	1.53	68.8	706.5	310.2	106.5	33.1
2013	A-	1.66	1.40	72.9	708.2	273.6	110.4	14.4

Rating Indexes

MO EMPLOYERS MUTUAL INS CO * B+ Good

Major Rating Factors: Good liquidity (6.5 on a scale of 0 to 10) with sufficient resources (cash flows and marketable investments) to handle a spike in claims. Good overall results on stability tests (6.5).

Other Rating Factors: Strong long-term capitalization index (8.0) based on excellent current risk adjusted capital (severe and moderate loss scenarios), despite some fluctuation in capital levels. Ample reserve history (9.3) that helps to protect the company against sharp claims increases. Excellent profitability (7.6) with operating gains in each of the last five years.

Principal Business: Workers compensation (100%).

Principal Investments: Investment grade bonds (79%), misc. investments (17%), real estate (2%), cash (1%), and non investment grade bonds (1%).

Investments in Affiliates: 0%

Group Affiliation: Missouri Employers Mutual

Licensed in: MO

Commenced Business: March 1995

Address: 101 North Keene St, Columbia, MO 65201

Phone: (573) 499-9714 **Domicile State:** MO **NAIC Code:** 10191

Data Date	Rating	RACR #1	RACR #2	Loss Ratio %	Total Assets ($mil)	Capital ($mil)	Net Premium ($mil)	Net Income ($mil)
2017	B+	2.11	1.64	70.5	695.0	252.8	238.5	10.7
2016	B	2.25	1.74	68.9	667.1	255.2	219.9	15.4
2015	C+	2.12	1.62	62.1	614.5	237.8	202.6	30.6
2014	C	2.10	1.61	72.3	563.2	211.0	189.5	14.9
2013	C	2.01	1.51	72.3	508.8	194.4	166.1	5.9

Liquidity Index

MORTGAGE GUARANTY INS CORP D+ Weak

Major Rating Factors: Weak overall results on stability tests (2.4 on a scale of 0 to 10). Fair reserve development (4.8) as reserves have generally been sufficient to cover claims. In 2013, the two year reserve development was 53% deficient.

Other Rating Factors: Good overall profitability index (5.3) despite operating losses during 2013, 2014 and 2015. Return on equity has been low, averaging 3.1% over the past five years. Good liquidity (6.8) with sufficient resources (cash flows and marketable investments) to handle a spike in claims. Strong long-term capitalization index (7.3) based on excellent current risk adjusted capital (severe and moderate loss scenarios), despite some fluctuation in capital levels.

Principal Business: Mortgage guaranty (100%).

Principal Investments: Investment grade bonds (91%), misc. investments (6%), and non investment grade bonds (3%).

Investments in Affiliates: 7%

Group Affiliation: MGIC Investment Corp

Licensed in: All states, the District of Columbia and Puerto Rico

Commenced Business: March 1979

Address: 250 EAST KILBOURN AVENUE, Milwaukee, WI 53202

Phone: (800) 558-9900 **Domicile State:** WI **NAIC Code:** 29858

Data Date	Rating	RACR #1	RACR #2	Loss Ratio %	Total Assets ($mil)	Capital ($mil)	Net Premium ($mil)	Net Income ($mil)
2017	D+	2.11	1.76	5.4	4,756.2	1,620.4	866.3	271.7
2016	D+	1.14	0.99	26.0	4,475.7	1,504.7	844.0	68.3
2015	D+	1.08	0.92	36.8	4,274.8	1,573.9	905.5	-77.9
2014	D+	1.04	0.87	59.2	4,162.5	1,517.7	758.1	-7.8
2013	D+	0.99	0.79	91.1	4,406.2	1,520.6	793.5	-7.0

Rating Indexes

MOTORISTS COMMERCIAL MUTUAL INS CO *   A-   Excellent

Major Rating Factors: Strong long-term capitalization index (8.4 on a scale of 0 to 10) based on excellent current risk adjusted capital (severe and moderate loss scenarios), despite some fluctuation in capital levels. History of adequate reserve strength (6.3) as reserves have been consistently at an acceptable level.

Other Rating Factors: Good liquidity (6.2) with sufficient resources (cash flows and marketable investments) to handle a spike in claims. Good overall results on stability tests (6.9) despite negative cash flow from operations for 2017. Fair profitability index (3.2) with operating losses during 2017.

Principal Business: Auto liability (30%), commercial multiple peril (23%), auto physical damage (14%), other liability (14%), workers compensation (8%), inland marine (7%), and other lines (5%).

Principal Investments: Investment grade bonds (59%), misc. investments (39%), and real estate (2%).

Investments in Affiliates: 7%

Group Affiliation: Motorists Insurance Group

Licensed in: All states except AL, AK, AR, FL, HI, LA, MS, MT, PR

Commenced Business: January 1900

Address: 471 EAST BROAD STREET, Columbus, OH 43215

Phone: (614) 225-8211   **Domicile State:** OH   **NAIC Code:** 13331

Data Date	Rating	RACR #1	RACR #2	Loss Ratio %	Total Assets ($mil)	Capital ($mil)	Net Premium ($mil)	Net Income ($mil)
2017	A-	2.66	1.91	83.5	368.8	147.5	133.6	-22.4
2016	B+	3.48	2.57	64.1	354.7	156.7	132.2	4.6
2015	B	3.33	2.46	64.5	347.6	150.1	132.7	3.3
2014	B	3.27	2.38	64.0	342.9	146.2	136.9	8.3
2013	B	3.15	2.27	66.8	336.9	140.9	126.0	9.0

MOTORISTS MUTUAL INS CO   C+   Fair

Major Rating Factors: Fair overall results on stability tests (4.5 on a scale of 0 to 10) including negative cash flow from operations for 2017. Strengths include potentially strong support from affiliation with Motorists Insurance Group. History of adequate reserve strength (6.3) as reserves have been consistently at an acceptable level.

Other Rating Factors: Good liquidity (6.0) with sufficient resources (cash flows and marketable investments) to handle a spike in claims. Weak profitability index (2.2) with operating losses during 2017. Strong long-term capitalization index (7.9) based on excellent current risk adjusted capital (severe and moderate loss scenarios), despite some fluctuation in capital levels.

Principal Business: Auto liability (28%), auto physical damage (17%), other liability (16%), homeowners multiple peril (14%), commercial multiple peril (13%), workers compensation (5%), and other lines (7%).

Principal Investments: Investment grade bonds (56%), misc. investments (42%), and real estate (3%).

Investments in Affiliates: 10%

Group Affiliation: Motorists Insurance Group

Licensed in: AL, CA, CT, DE, GA, IL, IN, IA, KY, ME, MD, MA, MI, MO, MT, NE, NH, NJ, NY, NC, ND, OH, OK, OR, PA, RI, SC, SD, TN, TX, UT, VT, VA, WV, WI

Commenced Business: November 1928

Address: 471 EAST BROAD STREET, Columbus, OH 43215

Phone: (614) 225-8211   **Domicile State:** OH   **NAIC Code:** 14621

Data Date	Rating	RACR #1	RACR #2	Loss Ratio %	Total Assets ($mil)	Capital ($mil)	Net Premium ($mil)	Net Income ($mil)
2017	C+	2.19	1.61	83.5	1,370.8	460.7	494.7	-92.4
2016	B+	2.96	2.24	64.1	1,359.7	544.3	489.3	19.7
2015	B+	2.96	2.24	64.5	1,387.4	553.9	491.5	7.8
2014	B+	3.24	2.37	64.0	1,373.9	557.4	500.9	40.4
2013	A-	3.53	2.48	66.8	1,335.8	568.8	480.0	37.9

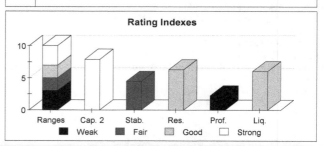

MOTORS INS CORP   D+   Weak

Major Rating Factors: Weak overall results on stability tests (2.5 on a scale of 0 to 10). History of adequate reserve strength (6.4) as reserves have been consistently at an acceptable level.

Other Rating Factors: Good overall profitability index (6.7). Fair expense controls. Return on equity has been fair, averaging 9.9% over the past five years. Strong long-term capitalization index (10.0) based on excellent current risk adjusted capital (severe and moderate loss scenarios), despite some fluctuation in capital levels. Excellent liquidity (7.5) with ample operational cash flow and liquid investments.

Principal Business: Auto physical damage (64%).

Principal Investments: Investment grade bonds (66%), cash (21%), misc. investments (12%), and non investment grade bonds (1%).

Investments in Affiliates: 4%

Group Affiliation: Ally Financial Inc

Licensed in: All states except PR

Commenced Business: November 1939

Address: 500 WOODWARD AVE 14TH FLOOR, Detroit, MI 48226

Phone: (313) 656-5437   **Domicile State:** MI   **NAIC Code:** 22012

Data Date	Rating	RACR #1	RACR #2	Loss Ratio %	Total Assets ($mil)	Capital ($mil)	Net Premium ($mil)	Net Income ($mil)
2017	D+	6.50	4.53	74.7	2,030.5	867.8	394.1	76.2
2016	D	5.04	3.45	71.5	2,038.0	745.5	388.3	50.4
2015	D	4.49	3.07	54.7	2,077.4	746.8	420.5	115.1
2014	C	5.19	3.53	72.1	2,458.7	1,059.9	475.5	84.4
2013	C	4.35	2.71	66.9	2,605.0	1,095.6	462.9	117.7

MOUNT VERNON FIRE INS CO   C   Fair

Major Rating Factors: Fair overall results on stability tests (4.3 on a scale of 0 to 10). Strong long-term capitalization index (8.0) based on excellent current risk adjusted capital (severe and moderate loss scenarios). Moreover, capital levels have been consistent in recent years.
Other Rating Factors: Ample reserve history (8.4) that helps to protect the company against sharp claims increases. Excellent profitability (8.6) with operating gains in each of the last five years. Superior liquidity (9.0) with ample operational cash flow and liquid investments.
Principal Business: Other liability (79%), fire (17%), homeowners multiple peril (1%), products liability (1%), and inland marine (1%).
Principal Investments: Misc. investments (79%) and investment grade bonds (21%).
Investments in Affiliates: 16%
Group Affiliation: Berkshire-Hathaway
Licensed in: All states except PR
Commenced Business: December 1958
Address: 1190 Devon Park Drive, Wayne, PA 19087
Phone: (800) 523-5545   **Domicile State:** PA   **NAIC Code:** 26522

Data Date	Rating	RACR #1	RACR #2	Loss Ratio %	Total Assets ($mil)	Capital ($mil)	Net Premium ($mil)	Net Income ($mil)
2017	C	2.36	1.73	26.3	775.0	579.4	70.9	148.2
2016	C	2.09	1.61	43.2	643.0	445.4	68.1	18.7
2015	C	2.09	1.64	37.8	580.2	399.7	67.7	17.0
2014	C	1.97	1.53	33.8	586.9	395.2	67.3	18.0
2013	B-	1.84	1.48	33.5	526.4	348.2	63.0	24.1

Rating Indexes

MT HAWLEY INS CO   C   Fair

Major Rating Factors: Fair profitability index (4.2 on a scale of 0 to 10). Weak expense controls. Return on equity has been fair, averaging 15.0% over the past five years. Fair overall results on stability tests (4.0).
Other Rating Factors: Good liquidity (6.9) with sufficient resources (cash flows and marketable investments) to handle a spike in claims. Strong long-term capitalization index (8.1) based on excellent current risk adjusted capital (severe and moderate loss scenarios), despite some fluctuation in capital levels. Ample reserve history (9.1) that helps to protect the company against sharp claims increases.
Principal Business: Other liability (56%), allied lines (15%), fire (9%), earthquake (6%), medical malpractice (6%), inland marine (6%), and products liability (1%).
Principal Investments: Investment grade bonds (77%), misc. investments (21%), cash (1%), and non investment grade bonds (1%).
Investments in Affiliates: 12%
Group Affiliation: RLI Corp
Licensed in: All states, the District of Columbia and Puerto Rico
Commenced Business: December 1979
Address: 9025 N Lindbergh Drive, Peoria, IL 61615
Phone: (309) 692-1000   **Domicile State:** IL   **NAIC Code:** 37974

Data Date	Rating	RACR #1	RACR #2	Loss Ratio %	Total Assets ($mil)	Capital ($mil)	Net Premium ($mil)	Net Income ($mil)
2017	C	2.19	1.72	63.5	945.8	441.2	227.7	19.3
2016	C	2.40	1.88	44.8	884.6	452.5	217.0	58.2
2015	C	2.31	1.82	37.4	861.2	447.8	208.2	85.5
2014	C	2.27	1.79	32.3	874.2	461.1	209.5	111.8
2013	C	2.63	2.01	26.0	925.3	523.0	202.9	76.0

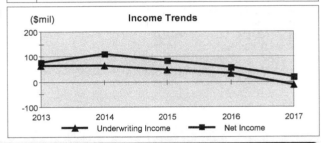

($mil) Income Trends

MUNICH REINS AMERICA INC   C+   Fair

Major Rating Factors: Fair overall results on stability tests (4.4 on a scale of 0 to 10). Good liquidity (6.7) with sufficient resources (cash flows and marketable investments) to handle a spike in claims.
Other Rating Factors: Weak profitability index (2.6) with operating losses during 2017. Return on equity has been fair, averaging 6.0% over the past five years. Strong long-term capitalization index (7.6) based on excellent current risk adjusted capital (severe and moderate loss scenarios), despite some fluctuation in capital levels. Ample reserve history (8.8) that helps to protect the company against sharp claims increases.
Principal Business: Surety (100%).
Principal Investments: Investment grade bonds (89%), misc. investments (6%), non investment grade bonds (4%), and real estate (1%).
Investments in Affiliates: None
Group Affiliation: Münchener Rückversicherungs-Gesellsc
Licensed in: All states, the District of Columbia and Puerto Rico
Commenced Business: April 1917
Address: 251 LITTLE FALLS DR, Wilmington, DE 19808
Phone: (609) 243-4200   **Domicile State:** DE   **NAIC Code:** 10227

Data Date	Rating	RACR #1	RACR #2	Loss Ratio %	Total Assets ($mil)	Capital ($mil)	Net Premium ($mil)	Net Income ($mil)
2017	C+	2.17	1.42	84.8	18,585.6	4,019.2	4,167.9	-617.2
2016	C+	3.21	2.03	65.4	17,710.3	4,819.5	3,117.7	301.0
2015	C+	3.08	1.95	62.4	17,497.9	4,957.4	3,120.4	436.6
2014	C+	2.83	1.72	57.2	16,484.8	5,254.8	3,247.7	781.7
2013	C+	2.31	1.40	57.1	16,840.8	5,288.0	3,195.8	806.1

Rating Indexes

MUNICIPAL ASR CORP

E+   **Very Weak**

Major Rating Factors: Weak profitability index (1.9). Weak expense controls. Return on equity has been fair, averaging 14.4% over the past five years.

Other Rating Factors: Weak overall results on stability tests (0.5). Strong long-term capitalization index (10.0) based on excellent current risk adjusted capital (severe and moderate loss scenarios), despite some fluctuation in capital levels. Superior liquidity (10.0) with ample operational cash flow and liquid investments.

Principal Business: Financial guaranty (100%).

Principal Investments: Investment grade bonds (95%), misc. investments (4%), and non investment grade bonds (1%).

Investments in Affiliates: None

Group Affiliation: Assured Guaranty Ltd

Licensed in: All states except PR

Commenced Business: October 2008

Address: 1633 Broadway, New York, NY 10019

Phone: (212) 974-0100   **Domicile State:** NY   **NAIC Code:** 13559

Data Date	Rating	RACR #1	RACR #2	Loss Ratio %	Total Assets ($mil)	Capital ($mil)	Net Premium ($mil)	Net Income ($mil)
2017	E+	13.51	10.40	0.5	823.6	270.4	0.7	32.3
2016	E	22.54	17.09	0.0	1,104.8	486.9	1.2	141.6
2015	A+	48.25	27.40	0.0	1,509.3	729.5	-4.8	101.9
2014	A+	37.58	22.45	0.0	1,519.8	611.5	-5.0	74.8
2013	A+	3.74	2.27	0.0	1,516.2	514.4	709.9	25.7

Rating Indexes

MUTUAL INS CO OF AZ *

B+   **Good**

Major Rating Factors: Good overall results on stability tests (6.5 on a scale of 0 to 10). Stability strengths include good operational trends and excellent risk diversification. Strong long-term capitalization index (10.0) based on excellent current risk adjusted capital (severe and moderate loss scenarios). Moreover, capital levels have been consistent in recent years.

Other Rating Factors: Ample reserve history (9.3) that helps to protect the company against sharp claims increases. Excellent profitability (8.0) with operating gains in each of the last five years. Excellent liquidity (7.7) with ample operational cash flow and liquid investments.

Principal Business: Medical malpractice (100%).

Principal Investments: Investment grade bonds (82%) and misc. investments (18%).

Investments in Affiliates: None

Group Affiliation: None

Licensed in: AZ, CA, CO, NV, NM, UT

Commenced Business: March 1976

Address: 2602 East Thomas Road, Phoenix, AZ 85016-8202

Phone: (602) 956-5276   **Domicile State:** AZ   **NAIC Code:** 32832

Data Date	Rating	RACR #1	RACR #2	Loss Ratio %	Total Assets ($mil)	Capital ($mil)	Net Premium ($mil)	Net Income ($mil)
2017	B+	7.80	5.32	62.1	1,105.9	665.4	95.8	23.4
2016	B	7.51	5.09	56.9	1,067.7	623.6	101.7	25.3
2015	B	7.31	5.15	53.7	1,038.1	588.8	105.2	28.0
2014	B	7.02	4.95	57.9	1,017.4	565.6	105.4	27.4
2013	A	6.77	4.81	63.3	1,008.0	536.5	109.5	20.9

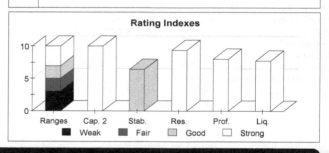

Rating Indexes

MUTUAL OF ENUMCLAW INS CO *

B+   **Good**

Major Rating Factors: History of adequate reserve strength (6.3 on a scale of 0 to 10) as reserves have been consistently at an acceptable level. Good liquidity (6.1) with sufficient resources (cash flows and marketable investments) to handle a spike in claims.

Other Rating Factors: Good overall results on stability tests (6.5) despite negative cash flow from operations for 2017. Strong long-term capitalization index (9.8) based on excellent current risk adjusted capital (severe and moderate loss scenarios), despite some fluctuation in capital levels. Fair profitability index (4.5) with operating losses during 2015. Return on equity has been low, averaging 1.6% over the past five years.

Principal Business: Auto liability (30%), commercial multiple peril (20%), homeowners multiple peril (18%), auto physical damage (13%), farmowners multiple peril (12%), other liability (3%), and other lines (3%).

Principal Investments: Investment grade bonds (82%), misc. investments (16%), cash (1%), and real estate (1%).

Investments in Affiliates: 1%

Group Affiliation: Enumclaw Ins Group

Licensed in: AK, AZ, CO, ID, MT, NV, NM, OR, UT, WA

Commenced Business: March 1898

Address: 4000 KRUSE WAY PLACE BLDG 3, Lake Oswego, OR 97035

Phone: (360) 825-2591   **Domicile State:** OR   **NAIC Code:** 14761

Data Date	Rating	RACR #1	RACR #2	Loss Ratio %	Total Assets ($mil)	Capital ($mil)	Net Premium ($mil)	Net Income ($mil)
2017	B+	4.29	3.02	72.4	748.3	338.3	395.8	7.5
2016	B	4.23	3.00	70.0	745.3	326.3	385.1	9.9
2015	B	3.45	2.48	77.5	697.0	290.0	376.1	-11.6
2014	B	3.86	2.80	68.1	666.7	302.9	350.2	11.3
2013	B	4.05	2.99	68.4	634.8	286.9	331.0	8.0

Reserve Deficiency (as % of capital)

* Adequate & redundant reserves show as negatives

NATIONAL CASUALTY CO *   B+   Good

Major Rating Factors: Good overall results on stability tests (6.4 on a scale of 0 to 10). Strengths include potential support from affiliation with Nationwide Corp, good operational trends and excellent risk diversification. Strong long-term capitalization index (10.0) based on excellent current risk adjusted capital (severe and moderate loss scenarios), despite some fluctuation in capital levels.

Other Rating Factors: Excellent profitability (7.2) with operating gains in each of the last five years. Excellent liquidity (7.0) with ample operational cash flow and liquid investments.

Principal Business: Inland marine (35%), auto liability (21%), other liability (14%), commercial multiple peril (10%), auto physical damage (7%), workers compensation (7%), and other lines (6%).

Principal Investments: Investment grade bonds (97%) and misc. investments (3%).

Investments in Affiliates: None
Group Affiliation: Nationwide Corp
Licensed in: All states except PR
Commenced Business: December 1904
Address: ONE W NATIONWIDE BLVD 1-04-701, Columbus, OH 43215-2220
Phone: (480) 365-4000   **Domicile State:** OH   **NAIC Code:** 11991

Data Date	Rating	RACR #1	RACR #2	Loss Ratio %	Total Assets ($mil)	Capital ($mil)	Net Premium ($mil)	Net Income ($mil)
2017	B+	13.28	11.95	0.0	418.6	140.8	0.0	5.2
2016	B+	12.28	11.06	0.0	487.1	138.1	0.0	3.2
2015	B+	14.13	12.72	0.0	288.5	134.1	0.0	5.5
2014	B+	13.70	12.33	0.0	285.4	130.1	0.0	3.0
2013	B+	13.26	11.93	0.0	280.9	125.9	0.0	2.7

Nationwide Corp Composite Group Rating: B- Largest Group Members	Assets ($mil)	Rating
NATIONWIDE LIFE INS CO	145670	B-
NATIONWIDE MUTUAL INS CO	35425	B
NATIONWIDE LIFE ANNUITY INS CO	20608	C
NATIONWIDE MUTUAL FIRE INS CO	8598	C+
JEFFERSON NATIONAL LIFE INS CO	5817	C

NATIONAL FIRE & MARINE INS CO   C   Fair

Major Rating Factors: Fair overall results on stability tests (4.1 on a scale of 0 to 10). History of adequate reserve strength (6.3) as reserves have been consistently at an acceptable level.

Other Rating Factors: Strong long-term capitalization index (8.1) based on excellent current risk adjusted capital (severe and moderate loss scenarios), despite some fluctuation in capital levels. Excellent profitability (7.9) with operating gains in each of the last five years. Excellent liquidity (8.3) with ample operational cash flow and liquid investments.

Principal Business: Other liability (49%), medical malpractice (17%), allied lines (11%), fire (9%), auto liability (4%), earthquake (3%), and other lines (7%).

Principal Investments: Misc. investments (81%), investment grade bonds (17%), and cash (2%).

Investments in Affiliates: 5%
Group Affiliation: Berkshire-Hathaway
Licensed in: All states, the District of Columbia and Puerto Rico
Commenced Business: January 1950
Address: 1314 Douglas Street Suite 1400, Omaha, NE 68102-1944
Phone: (402) 916-3000   **Domicile State:** NE   **NAIC Code:** 20079

Data Date	Rating	RACR #1	RACR #2	Loss Ratio %	Total Assets ($mil)	Capital ($mil)	Net Premium ($mil)	Net Income ($mil)
2017	C	2.77	1.79	85.7	10,841.0	7,187.2	1,174.6	86.3
2016	C	2.70	1.78	58.3	8,875.2	5,515.7	929.0	919.0
2015	C	2.53	1.67	44.7	8,664.8	5,695.9	822.2	327.2
2014	C	2.40	1.58	49.2	8,437.0	5,604.7	710.9	657.8
2013	C	2.57	1.70	69.8	7,335.1	5,010.4	316.5	233.2

Rating Indexes

NATIONAL INDEMNITY CO   B   Good

Major Rating Factors: Good overall results on stability tests (5.3 on a scale of 0 to 10) despite potential drain of affiliation with Berkshire-Hathaway. Stability strengths include good operational trends and excellent risk diversification. History of adequate reserve strength (6.0) as reserves have been consistently at an acceptable level.

Other Rating Factors: Strong long-term capitalization index (7.8) based on excellent current risk adjusted capital (severe and moderate loss scenarios), despite some fluctuation in capital levels. Excellent profitability (8.0) with operating gains in each of the last five years. Excellent liquidity (7.0) with ample operational cash flow and liquid investments.

Principal Business: Auto liability (67%), auto physical damage (15%), aircraft (11%), inland marine (4%), surety (3%), and other liability (1%).

Principal Investments: Misc. investments (84%), investment grade bonds (15%), and cash (1%).

Investments in Affiliates: 22%
Group Affiliation: Berkshire-Hathaway
Licensed in: All states except PR
Commenced Business: May 1940
Address: 1314 Douglas Street Suite 1400, Omaha, NE 68102-1944
Phone: (402) 916-3000   **Domicile State:** NE   **NAIC Code:** 20087

Data Date	Rating	RACR #1	RACR #2	Loss Ratio %	Total Assets ($mil)	Capital ($mil)	Net Premium ($mil)	Net Income ($mil)
2017	B	1.94	1.63	88.3	231,374.0	128,563.0	24,030.9	2,079.7
2016	B	1.80	1.51	77.3	178,623.0	101,286.0	20,030.1	7,577.1
2015	B	1.81	1.52	75.1	161,777.0	89,828.6	18,456.6	7,270.9
2014	B-	1.66	1.43	79.3	166,985.0	93,997.7	26,655.0	12,007.5
2013	B-	2.24	1.87	49.2	151,912.0	97,226.1	5,650.4	8,390.8

Rating Indexes

NATIONAL INDEMNITY CO OF MID-AMERICA   C   Fair

Major Rating Factors: Fair overall results on stability tests (4.3 on a scale of 0 to 10). History of adequate reserve strength (6.2) as reserves have been consistently at an acceptable level.

Other Rating Factors: Strong long-term capitalization index (8.1) based on excellent current risk adjusted capital (severe and moderate loss scenarios), despite some fluctuation in capital levels. Excellent profitability (8.4) with operating gains in each of the last five years. Superior liquidity (10.0) with ample operational cash flow and liquid investments.

Principal Business: Auto liability (49%), other liability (30%), auto physical damage (14%), allied lines (5%), inland marine (1%), fire (1%), and commercial multiple peril (1%).

Principal Investments: Misc. investments (84%) and cash (16%).

Investments in Affiliates: None

Group Affiliation: Berkshire-Hathaway

Licensed in: IA, MN, NE, ND, PA

Commenced Business: July 1971

Address: 2213 2nd Street, Coralville, IA 52241-1205

Phone: (402) 916-3000   **Domicile State:** IA   **NAIC Code:** 20060

Data Date	Rating	RACR #1	RACR #2	Loss Ratio %	Total Assets ($mil)	Capital ($mil)	Net Premium ($mil)	Net Income ($mil)
2017	C	3.18	1.91	66.0	315.9	252.6	5.9	46.1
2016	C	2.69	1.62	58.6	264.1	188.3	6.7	7.6
2015	C	2.62	1.58	92.6	235.9	168.1	6.6	4.0
2014	C	2.60	1.56	50.9	238.9	170.3	7.1	18.6
2013	B-	2.98	1.79	2.5	231.6	166.1	5.7	19.5

Berkshire-Hathaway
Composite Group Rating: B
Largest Group Members

	Assets ($mil)	Rating
NATIONAL INDEMNITY CO	231374	B
GOVERNMENT EMPLOYEES INS CO	33382	B
COLUMBIA INS CO	24522	U
BERKSHIRE HATHAWAY LIFE INS CO OF NE	19610	C+
GENERAL REINS CORP	16508	C+

NATIONAL INDEMNITY CO OF THE SOUTH   C+   Fair

Major Rating Factors: Fair overall results on stability tests (4.4 on a scale of 0 to 10) including potential drain of affiliation with Berkshire-Hathaway. History of adequate reserve strength (5.8) as reserves have been consistently at an acceptable level.

Other Rating Factors: Strong long-term capitalization index (8.1) based on excellent current risk adjusted capital (severe and moderate loss scenarios). Moreover, capital levels have been consistent in recent years. Excellent profitability (8.6) with operating gains in each of the last five years. Superior liquidity (9.1) with ample operational cash flow and liquid investments.

Principal Business: Auto liability (84%), auto physical damage (9%), aircraft (3%), and inland marine (3%).

Principal Investments: Misc. investments (58%), investment grade bonds (28%), and cash (14%).

Investments in Affiliates: None

Group Affiliation: Berkshire-Hathaway

Licensed in: AL, FL, GA, IA, NE, NJ, TN, PR

Commenced Business: October 1983

Address: 2213 2ND STREET, Coralville, IA 52241-1205

Phone: (402) 916-3000   **Domicile State:** IA   **NAIC Code:** 42137

Data Date	Rating	RACR #1	RACR #2	Loss Ratio %	Total Assets ($mil)	Capital ($mil)	Net Premium ($mil)	Net Income ($mil)
2017	C+	3.22	1.94	67.2	460.6	266.0	88.7	54.4
2016	C+	2.65	1.64	74.3	378.5	198.3	67.9	10.3
2015	C+	2.52	1.58	72.8	355.8	179.1	102.8	6.8
2014	C+	2.69	1.64	71.7	319.2	177.4	84.2	0.7
2013	C+	3.17	1.91	55.2	256.9	167.3	33.0	6.1

Berkshire-Hathaway
Composite Group Rating: B
Largest Group Members

	Assets ($mil)	Rating
NATIONAL INDEMNITY CO	231374	B
GOVERNMENT EMPLOYEES INS CO	33382	B
COLUMBIA INS CO	24522	U
BERKSHIRE HATHAWAY LIFE INS CO OF NE	19610	C+
GENERAL REINS CORP	16508	C+

NATIONAL INTERSTATE INS CO   C+   Fair

Major Rating Factors: Fair overall results on stability tests (4.7 on a scale of 0 to 10) including potential drain of affiliation with American Financial Group Inc. Fair reserve development (3.9) as reserves have generally been sufficient to cover claims.

Other Rating Factors: Good overall profitability index (6.1). Fair expense controls. Return on equity has been fair, averaging 7.3% over the past five years. Good liquidity (6.8) with sufficient resources (cash flows and marketable investments) to handle a spike in claims. Strong long-term capitalization index (7.2) based on excellent current risk adjusted capital (severe and moderate loss scenarios), despite some fluctuation in capital levels.

Principal Business: Auto liability (55%), workers compensation (21%), auto physical damage (13%), other liability (9%), inland marine (1%), and commercial multiple peril (1%).

Principal Investments: Investment grade bonds (66%), misc. investments (29%), real estate (3%), cash (1%), and non investment grade bonds (1%).

Investments in Affiliates: 16%

Group Affiliation: American Financial Group Inc

Licensed in: All states except PR

Commenced Business: March 1989

Address: 3250 Interstate Drive, Richfield, OH 44286

Phone: (330) 659-8900   **Domicile State:** OH   **NAIC Code:** 32620

Data Date	Rating	RACR #1	RACR #2	Loss Ratio %	Total Assets ($mil)	Capital ($mil)	Net Premium ($mil)	Net Income ($mil)
2017	C+	1.41	1.15	67.0	1,281.1	301.2	323.4	54.4
2016	C+	1.51	1.25	70.2	1,286.5	337.0	309.0	16.1
2015	C+	1.43	1.18	75.1	1,200.1	295.6	295.3	12.5
2014	C+	1.45	1.20	78.7	1,117.6	284.7	291.2	5.4
2013	C+	1.52	1.26	70.8	1,054.1	283.4	277.6	21.9

American Financial Group Inc
Composite Group Rating: B-
Largest Group Members

	Assets ($mil)	Rating
GREAT AMERICAN LIFE INS CO	32577	B-
GREAT AMERICAN INS CO	7077	B
ANNUITY INVESTORS LIFE INS CO	3191	A-
REPUBLIC INDEMNITY CO OF AMERICA	2267	B-
NATIONAL INTERSTATE INS CO	1281	C+

NATIONAL LIABILITY & FIRE INS CO   C+   Fair

Major Rating Factors: Fair overall results on stability tests (4.4 on a scale of 0 to 10) including potential drain of affiliation with Berkshire-Hathaway. History of adequate reserve strength (6.7) as reserves have been consistently at an acceptable level.

Other Rating Factors: Strong long-term capitalization index (8.3) based on excellent current risk adjusted capital (severe and moderate loss scenarios), despite some fluctuation in capital levels. Excellent profitability (7.7). Return on equity has been good over the last five years, averaging 11.3%. Superior liquidity (9.0) with ample operational cash flow and liquid investments.

Principal Business: Auto liability (47%), workers compensation (23%), other liability (10%), auto physical damage (9%), aircraft (5%), allied lines (2%), and other lines (3%).

Principal Investments: Misc. investments (48%), investment grade bonds (40%), and cash (12%).

Investments in Affiliates: 3%
Group Affiliation: Berkshire-Hathaway
Licensed in: All states except PR
Commenced Business: December 1958
Address: 100 First Stamford Place, Stamford, CT 06902-6745
Phone: (402) 916-3000   **Domicile State:** CT   **NAIC Code:** 20052

Data Date	Rating	RACR #1	RACR #2	Loss Ratio %	Total Assets ($mil)	Capital ($mil)	Net Premium ($mil)	Net Income ($mil)
2017	C+	3.09	1.95	74.3	2,710.1	1,246.3	551.9	522.2
2016	C+	2.65	1.71	72.7	2,605.4	1,126.6	562.1	89.4
2015	B-	2.86	1.81	68.9	2,377.3	957.1	762.1	-12.5
2014	B-	2.89	1.83	74.2	2,229.9	967.4	631.8	-0.9
2013	B+	4.12	2.55	64.8	1,836.1	899.0	388.3	70.5

Rating Indexes

NATIONAL MORTGAGE INS CORP *   A-   Excellent

Major Rating Factors: Strong long-term capitalization index (8.3 on a scale of 0 to 10) based on excellent current risk adjusted capital (severe and moderate loss scenarios). Furthermore, this high level of risk adjusted capital has been consistently maintained in previous years. Good liquidity (6.9) with sufficient resources (cash flows and marketable investments) to handle a spike in claims.

Other Rating Factors: Good overall results on stability tests (5.7) despite weak results on operational trends, excessive premium growth and negative cash flow from operations for 2017. Fair reserve development (3.6) as reserves have generally been sufficient to cover claims. Weak profitability index (2.9) with operating losses during each of the last five years. Average return on equity over the last five years has been poor at -14.2%.

Principal Business: Mortgage guaranty (100%).
Principal Investments: Investment grade bonds (97%), misc. investments (2%), and cash (1%).
Investments in Affiliates: None
Group Affiliation: NMI Holdings Inc
Licensed in: All states except PR
Commenced Business: N/A
Address: 8040 Excelsior Drive Suite 200, Madison, WI 53717
Phone: (855) 873-2584   **Domicile State:** WI   **NAIC Code:** 13695

Data Date	Rating	RACR #1	RACR #2	Loss Ratio %	Total Assets ($mil)	Capital ($mil)	Net Premium ($mil)	Net Income ($mil)
2017	A-	2.15	1.86	3.8	717.8	344.0	145.1	-36.2
2016	A-	3.01	2.59	2.3	634.8	387.0	129.8	-28.5
2015	A-	4.06	3.43	1.4	487.7	366.9	103.9	-50.3
2014	A-	3.69	3.41	0.6	261.9	223.1	31.3	-47.2
2013	A-	4.93	4.85	0.0	194.2	180.3	3.3	-32.7

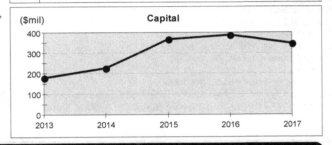

($mil)   Capital

NATIONAL PUBLIC FINANCE GUAR CORP   D+   Weak

Major Rating Factors: Weak profitability index (2.7 on a scale of 0 to 10) with operating losses during 2017. Return on equity has been fair, averaging 5.4% over the past five years. Weak overall results on stability tests (2.4) including negative cash flow from operations for 2017.

Other Rating Factors: Fair reserve development (4.2) as reserves have generally been sufficient to cover claims. Strong long-term capitalization index (10.0) based on excellent current risk adjusted capital (severe and moderate loss scenarios), despite some fluctuation in capital levels. Superior liquidity (9.0) with ample operational cash flow and liquid investments.

Principal Business: Financial guaranty (100%).
Principal Investments: Investment grade bonds (81%), non investment grade bonds (12%), misc. investments (6%), and cash (1%).
Investments in Affiliates: 7%
Group Affiliation: MBIA Inc
Licensed in: All states, the District of Columbia and Puerto Rico
Commenced Business: March 1960
Address: 1 Manhattanville Road Ste 301, Purchase, NY 10577-2100
Phone: (914) 765-3333   **Domicile State:** NY   **NAIC Code:** 23825

Data Date	Rating	RACR #1	RACR #2	Loss Ratio %	Total Assets ($mil)	Capital ($mil)	Net Premium ($mil)	Net Income ($mil)
2017	D+	7.54	5.92	273.5	3,753.9	2,165.9	13.0	-321.4
2016	B	33.03	16.16	41.9	4,355.2	2,730.8	19.0	191.8
2015	B	21.59	13.94	N/A	4,676.6	2,477.5	17.3	283.8
2014	B	25.38	13.47	27.9	5,142.4	2,190.4	13.5	238.1
2013	B	11.85	5.09	18.3	5,339.7	2,086.1	12.1	255.9

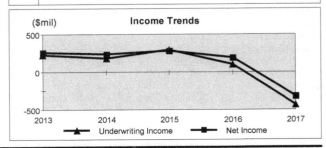

($mil)   Income Trends

NATIONAL UNION FIRE INS CO   C   Fair

Major Rating Factors: Fair profitability index (4.3 on a scale of 0 to 10) with operating losses during 2016 and 2017. Return on equity has been fair, averaging 28.5% over the past five years. Fair overall results on stability tests (4.2) including negative cash flow from operations for 2017.

Other Rating Factors: A history of deficient reserves (2.8). Underreserving can have an adverse impact on capital and profits. In 2015 and 2016 the two year reserve development was 17% and 30% deficient respectively. Good liquidity (5.4) with sufficient resources (cash flows and marketable investments) to handle a spike in claims. Strong long-term capitalization index (7.6) based on excellent current risk adjusted capital (severe and moderate loss scenarios), despite some fluctuation in capital levels.

Principal Business: Other liability (40%), group accident & health (15%), ocean marine (9%), inland marine (6%), workers compensation (6%), auto liability (6%), and other lines (18%).

Principal Investments: Investment grade bonds (64%), misc. investments (32%), and non investment grade bonds (5%).

Investments in Affiliates: 1%

Group Affiliation: American International Group

Licensed in: All states, the District of Columbia and Puerto Rico

Commenced Business: March 1901

Address: 2595 INTERSTATE DRIVE STE 102, Harrisburg, PA 17110

Phone: (212) 770-7000   **Domicile State:** PA   **NAIC Code:** 19445

Data Date	Rating	RACR #1	RACR #2	Loss Ratio %	Total Assets ($mil)	Capital ($mil)	Net Premium ($mil)	Net Income ($mil)
2017	C	2.19	1.42	87.9	25,661.1	6,431.2	5,399.4	-357.4
2016	C	1.99	1.33	99.8	26,517.3	5,967.4	4,837.1	-72.6
2015	C	2.43	1.64	88.8	26,764.2	6,682.8	5,564.4	110.6
2014	C	2.20	1.50	80.2	26,135.8	6,680.8	5,616.6	572.0
2013	C	2.03	1.38	76.7	24,709.6	5,836.5	5,422.5	8,102.0

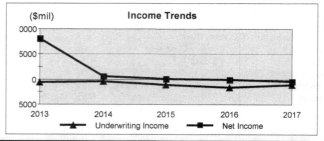

NATIONWIDE INDEMNITY CO   C+   Fair

Major Rating Factors: Fair overall results on stability tests (4.5 on a scale of 0 to 10) including negative cash flow from operations for 2017 and fair results on operational trends. Strengths include potentially strong support from affiliation with Nationwide Corp. Fair profitability index (3.6) with operating losses during 2013 and 2016. Return on equity has been low, averaging 2.4% over the past five years.

Other Rating Factors: A history of deficient reserves (2.2) that places pressure on both capital and profits. In the last five years, reserves (two year development) fluctuated between 26% and 23% deficeint. Strong long-term capitalization index (7.2) based on excellent current risk adjusted capital (severe and moderate loss scenarios), despite some fluctuation in capital levels. Superior liquidity (9.7) with ample operational cash flow and liquid investments.

Principal Business: (This company is a reinsurer.)

Principal Investments: Investment grade bonds (90%), misc. investments (6%), and non investment grade bonds (4%).

Investments in Affiliates: None

Group Affiliation: Nationwide Corp

Licensed in: IL, IA, NY, OH, WI

Commenced Business: April 1994

Address: ONE WEST NATIONWIDE BLVD, Columbus, OH 43215-2220

Phone: (614) 249-7111   **Domicile State:** OH   **NAIC Code:** 10070

Data Date	Rating	RACR #1	RACR #2	Loss Ratio %	Total Assets ($mil)	Capital ($mil)	Net Premium ($mil)	Net Income ($mil)
2017	C+	2.28	1.74	N/A	2,891.2	1,013.2	0.4	89.0
2016	C+	1.63	0.75	N/A	2,981.4	997.6	1.2	-15.6
2015	C+	1.71	0.79	N/A	2,995.0	1,010.1	0.4	54.7
2014	C+	1.84	0.83	N/A	3,165.3	1,044.9	-0.4	4.0
2013	B-	2.21	0.89	N/A	3,251.9	1,069.4	0.2	-8.5

NATIONWIDE MUTUAL FIRE INS CO   C+   Fair

Major Rating Factors: Fair overall results on stability tests (4.8 on a scale of 0 to 10) including excessive premium growth and negative cash flow from operations for 2017. History of adequate reserve strength (5.9) as reserves have been consistently at an acceptable level.

Other Rating Factors: Good liquidity (5.1) with sufficient resources (cash flows and marketable investments) to handle a spike in claims. Weak profitability index (2.4) with operating losses during 2015 and 2017. Strong long-term capitalization index (7.9) based on excellent current risk adjusted capital (severe and moderate loss scenarios), despite some fluctuation in capital levels.

Principal Business: Homeowners multiple peril (50%), auto liability (16%), auto physical damage (10%), commercial multiple peril (7%), other liability (5%), fire (4%), and other lines (7%).

Principal Investments: Investment grade bonds (70%), misc. investments (23%), and non investment grade bonds (7%).

Investments in Affiliates: 4%

Group Affiliation: Nationwide Corp

Licensed in: All states except PR

Commenced Business: April 1934

Address: ONE WEST NATIONWIDE BLVD, Columbus, OH 43215-2220

Phone: (614) 249-7111   **Domicile State:** OH   **NAIC Code:** 23779

Data Date	Rating	RACR #1	RACR #2	Loss Ratio %	Total Assets ($mil)	Capital ($mil)	Net Premium ($mil)	Net Income ($mil)
2017	C+	2.19	1.57	81.1	8,598.1	2,380.3	5,206.6	-391.6
2016	B+	4.83	3.54	74.7	6,121.6	2,671.6	2,338.5	12.4
2015	B+	4.90	3.59	71.1	5,938.4	2,604.3	2,242.5	-10.6
2014	B+	5.00	3.67	71.1	5,733.3	2,559.1	2,163.3	64.1
2013	B+	4.96	3.51	66.2	5,410.1	2,445.1	2,162.4	73.7

NATIONWIDE MUTUAL INS CO   B   Good

Major Rating Factors: History of adequate reserve strength (5.9 on a scale of 0 to 10) as reserves have been consistently at an acceptable level. Good overall results on stability tests (6.1).

Other Rating Factors: Fair profitability index (3.5) with operating losses during 2016 and 2017. Fair liquidity (4.4) as cash resources may not be adequate to cover a spike in claims. Strong long-term capitalization index (7.3) based on excellent current risk adjusted capital (severe and moderate loss scenarios), despite some fluctuation in capital levels.

Principal Business: Auto liability (41%), auto physical damage (26%), commercial multiple peril (12%), other liability (8%), homeowners multiple peril (5%), inland marine (3%), and other lines (6%).

Principal Investments: Misc. investments (58%), investment grade bonds (38%), non investment grade bonds (4%), and real estate (2%).

Investments in Affiliates: 33%
Group Affiliation: Nationwide Corp
Licensed in: All states except PR
Commenced Business: April 1926
Address: ONE WEST NATIONWIDE BLVD, Columbus, OH 43215-2220
Phone: (614) 249-7111   **Domicile State:** OH   **NAIC Code:** 23787

Data Date	Rating	RACR #1	RACR #2	Loss Ratio %	Total Assets ($mil)	Capital ($mil)	Net Premium ($mil)	Net Income ($mil)
2017	B	1.37	1.23	81.1	35,425.4	12,193.3	12,718.3	-370.8
2016	B	1.49	1.31	74.7	37,185.2	12,690.3	16,174.4	-314.6
2015	B	1.45	1.27	71.1	35,923.7	12,315.9	15,510.8	184.1
2014	B	1.46	1.29	71.1	34,711.2	12,138.0	14,962.7	718.4
2013	B	1.49	1.31	66.2	32,675.8	11,792.5	14,630.9	499.8

Reserve Deficiency (as % of capital)

2013   2014   2015   2016   2017

■ 1 Yr Dev   □ 2 Yr Dev

* Adequate & redundant reserves show as negatives

NAU COUNTRY INS CO   C+   Fair

Major Rating Factors: Fair overall results on stability tests (4.3 on a scale of 0 to 10) including potential drain of affiliation with QBE Ins Group Ltd and negative cash flow from operations for 2017. Fair profitability index (3.2) with operating losses during 2013 and 2017. Average return on equity over the last five years has been poor at -0.9%.

Other Rating Factors: History of adequate reserve strength (5.9) as reserves have been consistently at an acceptable level. Good liquidity (6.0) with sufficient resources (cash flows and marketable investments) to handle a spike in claims. Strong long-term capitalization index (7.3) based on excellent current risk adjusted capital (severe and moderate loss scenarios), despite some fluctuation in capital levels.

Principal Business: Allied lines (100%).

Principal Investments: Investment grade bonds (86%), misc. investments (12%), cash (1%), and real estate (1%).

Investments in Affiliates: None
Group Affiliation: QBE Ins Group Ltd
Licensed in: All states except AK, DC, HI, ME, NY, PR
Commenced Business: May 1919
Address: 7333 Sunwood Drive, Ramsey, MN 55303-5119
Phone: (608) 825-5160   **Domicile State:** MN   **NAIC Code:** 25240

Data Date	Rating	RACR #1	RACR #2	Loss Ratio %	Total Assets ($mil)	Capital ($mil)	Net Premium ($mil)	Net Income ($mil)
2017	C+	1.85	1.18	75.6	966.9	282.6	469.8	-15.4
2016	C+	2.50	1.60	58.8	1,342.3	337.2	436.2	14.0
2015	C	2.32	1.54	63.9	1,305.1	309.3	343.9	19.7
2014	C	1.72	1.19	69.2	1,330.5	254.3	415.4	2.0
2013	C	1.53	1.04	75.2	1,300.1	274.8	444.3	-29.0

QBE Ins Group Ltd Composite Group Rating: B Largest Group Members	Assets ($mil)	Rating
QBE INS CORP	2054	B
QBE REINS CORP	1031	B
NAU COUNTRY INS CO	967	C+
GENERAL CASUALTY CO OF WI	797	C+
PRAETORIAN INS CO	454	C

NAVIGATORS INS CO   B   Good

Major Rating Factors: Good overall results on stability tests (5.6 on a scale of 0 to 10) despite potential drain of affiliation with Navigators Group Inc. History of adequate reserve strength (6.5) as reserves have been consistently at an acceptable level.

Other Rating Factors: Good liquidity (6.9) with sufficient resources (cash flows and marketable investments) to handle a spike in claims. Strong long-term capitalization index (8.1) based on excellent current risk adjusted capital (severe and moderate loss scenarios). Moreover, capital levels have been consistent in recent years. Excellent profitability (8.6) with operating gains in each of the last five years.

Principal Business: Other liability (57%), ocean marine (27%), auto liability (8%), inland marine (3%), surety (2%), commercial multiple peril (1%), and auto physical damage (1%).

Principal Investments: Investment grade bonds (81%), misc. investments (14%), non investment grade bonds (3%), and cash (2%).

Investments in Affiliates: 5%
Group Affiliation: Navigators Group Inc
Licensed in: All states, the District of Columbia and Puerto Rico
Commenced Business: March 1983
Address: One Penn Plaza - 32nd Floor, New York, NY 10119-0002
Phone: (203) 905-6090   **Domicile State:** NY   **NAIC Code:** 42307

Data Date	Rating	RACR #1	RACR #2	Loss Ratio %	Total Assets ($mil)	Capital ($mil)	Net Premium ($mil)	Net Income ($mil)
2017	B	2.26	1.74	67.3	3,084.5	1,056.6	944.3	76.4
2016	B	2.34	1.83	60.5	2,808.1	1,026.8	845.0	80.7
2015	B	2.31	1.83	62.4	2,568.5	950.3	757.1	58.7
2014	B	2.33	1.81	61.7	2,454.0	893.9	752.8	72.4
2013	B	2.26	1.70	65.0	2,215.0	804.1	680.0	56.6

Rating Indexes

Ranges   Cap. 2   Stab.   Res.   Prof.   Liq.

■ Weak   ▨ Fair   ▨ Good   □ Strong

NCMIC INS CO   B   Good

Major Rating Factors: Good overall results on stability tests (5.5 on a scale of 0 to 10) despite potential drain of affiliation with NCMIC Group. Strong long-term capitalization index (7.7) based on excellent current risk adjusted capital (severe and moderate loss scenarios). Moreover, capital levels have been consistent in recent years.

Other Rating Factors: Ample reserve history (9.5) that helps to protect the company against sharp claims increases. Excellent profitability (8.8) with operating gains in each of the last five years. Excellent liquidity (7.1) with ample operational cash flow and liquid investments.

Principal Business: Medical malpractice (100%).

Principal Investments: Investment grade bonds (78%) and misc. investments (22%).

Investments in Affiliates: 1%

Group Affiliation: NCMIC Group

Licensed in: All states, the District of Columbia and Puerto Rico

Commenced Business: January 1946

Address: 14001 UNIVERSITY AVENUE, Clive, IA 50325-8258

Phone: (515) 313-4500   **Domicile State:** IA   **NAIC Code:** 15865

Data Date	Rating	RACR #1	RACR #2	Loss Ratio %	Total Assets ($mil)	Capital ($mil)	Net Premium ($mil)	Net Income ($mil)
2017	B	2.15	1.47	67.0	782.8	299.5	168.3	13.2
2016	B	2.68	1.85	52.8	732.7	292.4	143.4	29.2
2015	B	2.20	1.51	58.1	713.0	261.7	145.6	17.7
2014	B	2.23	1.57	50.2	654.9	252.1	147.1	21.1
2013	B	2.68	2.02	50.2	593.9	241.5	102.2	27.2

Rating Indexes

Ranges | Cap. 2 | Stab. | Res. | Prof. | Liq.

■ Weak   ■ Fair   ▢ Good   ☐ Strong

NEW JERSEY CASUALTY INS CO   B   Good

Major Rating Factors: Good overall results on stability tests (5.5 on a scale of 0 to 10). Stability strengths include good operational trends and excellent risk diversification. Strong long-term capitalization index (9.7) based on excellent current risk adjusted capital (severe and moderate loss scenarios). Moreover, capital has steadily grown over the last five years.

Other Rating Factors: Ample reserve history (7.0) that can protect against increases in claims costs. Excellent profitability (8.9) with operating gains in each of the last five years. Excellent liquidity (7.2) with ample operational cash flow and liquid investments.

Principal Business: Workers compensation (100%).

Principal Investments: Investment grade bonds (99%) and misc. investments (1%).

Investments in Affiliates: None

Group Affiliation: NJ Manufacturers

Licensed in: NJ

Commenced Business: April 1999

Address: 301 Sullivan Way, West Trenton, NJ 08628-3496

Phone: (609) 883-1300   **Domicile State:** NJ   **NAIC Code:** 10732

Data Date	Rating	RACR #1	RACR #2	Loss Ratio %	Total Assets ($mil)	Capital ($mil)	Net Premium ($mil)	Net Income ($mil)
2017	B	5.27	3.58	40.9	588.0	295.8	57.6	25.2
2016	B-	4.35	3.01	49.3	577.4	269.7	69.9	24.2
2015	C+	3.58	2.39	60.7	560.1	239.0	79.5	20.3
2014	C	3.09	2.09	56.6	521.4	211.6	88.6	25.8
2013	C	2.33	1.19	74.8	480.9	180.9	84.1	13.9

NJ Manufacturers
Composite Group Rating: B

Largest Group Members	Assets ($mil)	Rating
NJ MANUFACTURERS INS CO	7423	B
NEW JERSEY CASUALTY INS CO	588	B
NEW JERSEY RE-INS CO	546	B
NEW JERSEY INDEMNITY INS CO	78	C+

NEW JERSEY RE-INS CO   B   Good

Major Rating Factors: Good overall results on stability tests (5.7 on a scale of 0 to 10) despite potential drain of affiliation with NJ Manufacturers, negative cash flow from operations for 2017 and fair results on operational trends. History of adequate reserve strength (6.6) as reserves have been consistently at an acceptable level.

Other Rating Factors: Strong long-term capitalization index (9.2) based on excellent current risk adjusted capital (severe and moderate loss scenarios). Moreover, capital levels have been consistent in recent years. Excellent profitability (8.2) with operating gains in each of the last five years. Superior liquidity (9.4) with ample operational cash flow and liquid investments.

Principal Business: Other liability (40%), allied lines (35%), workers compensation (24%), and auto liability (1%).

Principal Investments: Investment grade bonds (99%) and cash (1%).

Investments in Affiliates: None

Group Affiliation: NJ Manufacturers

Licensed in: AL, AK, AZ, CT, DE, FL, GA, IL, IA, KY, ME, MD, MA, MI, MN, MS, MO, MT, NV, NH, NJ, NY, NC, ND, OH, PA, RI, SC, SD, TN, TX, VT, VA, WA, WV, WI

Commenced Business: January 1978

Address: 301 SULLIVAN WAY, West Trenton, NJ 08628-3496

Phone: (609) 883-1300   **Domicile State:** NJ   **NAIC Code:** 35432

Data Date	Rating	RACR #1	RACR #2	Loss Ratio %	Total Assets ($mil)	Capital ($mil)	Net Premium ($mil)	Net Income ($mil)
2017	B	4.82	2.84	10.1	546.4	432.1	11.5	16.2
2016	B	4.11	2.43	67.8	548.6	412.8	16.0	9.0
2015	B	4.06	2.36	95.1	549.8	400.6	21.5	6.2
2014	B	3.86	2.28	33.1	556.8	393.1	33.6	19.8
2013	B	2.99	1.77	47.4	553.6	362.3	37.1	21.1

NJ Manufacturers
Composite Group Rating: B

Largest Group Members	Assets ($mil)	Rating
NJ MANUFACTURERS INS CO	7423	B
NEW JERSEY CASUALTY INS CO	588	B
NEW JERSEY RE-INS CO	546	B
NEW JERSEY INDEMNITY INS CO	78	C+

NEW YORK CENTRAL MUTUAL FIRE INS CO   B-   Good

Major Rating Factors: Fair overall results on stability tests (4.7 on a scale of 0 to 10) including potential drain of affiliation with Central Services Group. History of adequate reserve strength (6.1) as reserves have been consistently at an acceptable level.

Other Rating Factors: Good liquidity (6.6) with sufficient resources (cash flows and marketable investments) to handle a spike in claims. Strong long-term capitalization index (9.6) based on excellent current risk adjusted capital (severe and moderate loss scenarios). Moreover, capital levels have been consistent in recent years. Excellent profitability (8.0) with operating gains in each of the last five years.

Principal Business: Homeowners multiple peril (37%), auto liability (34%), auto physical damage (23%), commercial multiple peril (2%), fire (2%), other liability (2%), and inland marine (1%).

Principal Investments: Investment grade bonds (76%), misc. investments (23%), and real estate (1%).

Investments in Affiliates: 4%

Group Affiliation: Central Services Group

Licensed in: NY

Commenced Business: April 1899

Address: 1899 CENTRAL PLAZA EAST, Edmeston, NY 13335-1899

Phone: (607) 965-8321   **Domicile State:** NY   **NAIC Code:** 14834

Data Date	Rating	RACR #1	RACR #2	Loss Ratio %	Total Assets ($mil)	Capital ($mil)	Net Premium ($mil)	Net Income ($mil)
2017	B-	3.69	2.72	67.3	1,177.2	540.0	473.2	22.7
2016	B-	3.92	2.93	67.1	1,117.7	534.3	448.9	23.3
2015	B-	3.94	2.97	66.9	1,051.1	491.7	422.4	20.0
2014	B-	3.93	2.98	73.7	1,016.7	480.1	420.6	9.7
2013	B-	3.82	2.93	67.9	1,010.8	466.4	421.8	30.7

Rating Indexes

NEW YORK MARINE & GENERAL INS CO   B-   Good

Major Rating Factors: Fair overall results on stability tests (4.7 on a scale of 0 to 10) including potential drain of affiliation with ProSight Specialty Ins Group Inc. Fair reserve development (4.1) as reserves have generally been sufficient to cover claims.

Other Rating Factors: Fair profitability index (3.9) with operating losses during 2015 and 2016. Average return on equity over the last five years has been poor at -0.2%. Good long-term capitalization index (6.7) based on good current risk adjusted capital (moderate loss scenario), despite some fluctuation in capital levels. Excellent liquidity (7.0) with ample operational cash flow and liquid investments.

Principal Business: Other liability (25%), workers compensation (22%), auto liability (16%), commercial multiple peril (9%), ocean marine (5%), inland marine (5%), and other lines (19%).

Principal Investments: Investment grade bonds (76%), misc. investments (15%), non investment grade bonds (5%), and cash (4%).

Investments in Affiliates: 11%

Group Affiliation: ProSight Specialty Ins Group Inc

Licensed in: All states, the District of Columbia and Puerto Rico

Commenced Business: July 1972

Address: 59 Maiden Lane 27th Floor, New York, NY 10038

Phone: (973) 532-1900   **Domicile State:** NY   **NAIC Code:** 16608

Data Date	Rating	RACR #1	RACR #2	Loss Ratio %	Total Assets ($mil)	Capital ($mil)	Net Premium ($mil)	Net Income ($mil)
2017	B-	1.43	1.01	64.6	1,746.2	433.9	483.4	20.7
2016	B-	1.38	0.98	74.5	1,277.9	355.4	393.4	-28.6
2015	B-	1.37	0.98	70.3	1,191.9	379.2	401.2	-8.3
2014	B-	1.10	0.79	57.7	1,062.9	352.6	347.1	12.6
2013	B-	1.21	0.88	60.6	891.7	240.1	270.9	1.8

Rating Indexes

NEW YORK SCHOOLS INS RECIPROCAL *   B+   Good

Major Rating Factors: History of adequate reserve strength (6.5 on a scale of 0 to 10) as reserves have been consistently at an acceptable level. Good overall results on stability tests (6.4).

Other Rating Factors: Strong long-term capitalization index (10.0) based on excellent current risk adjusted capital (severe and moderate loss scenarios). Moreover, capital has steadily grown over the last five years. Excellent profitability (8.3) with operating gains in each of the last five years. Excellent liquidity (7.1) with ample operational cash flow and liquid investments.

Principal Business: Other liability (44%), allied lines (28%), fire (12%), auto liability (8%), auto physical damage (3%), boiler & machinery (3%), and inland marine (2%).

Principal Investments: Investment grade bonds (72%), misc. investments (27%), and cash (1%).

Investments in Affiliates: None

Group Affiliation: None

Licensed in: NY

Commenced Business: July 1989

Address: 333 Earle Ovington Boulevard, Uniondale, NY 11553

Phone: (516) 750-9412   **Domicile State:** NY   **NAIC Code:** 34843

Data Date	Rating	RACR #1	RACR #2	Loss Ratio %	Total Assets ($mil)	Capital ($mil)	Net Premium ($mil)	Net Income ($mil)
2017	B+	4.78	3.35	84.0	317.8	182.9	61.8	3.2
2016	B	4.96	3.54	72.9	297.2	171.3	61.5	11.5
2015	B	4.87	3.50	65.9	279.7	159.0	61.9	13.9
2014	B	4.52	3.29	74.3	266.7	145.7	57.0	7.1
2013	B	4.21	3.16	75.4	259.5	136.9	51.3	9.3

Reserve Deficiency (as % of capital)

* Adequate & redundant reserves show as negatives

NGM INS CO

B- **Good**

Major Rating Factors: Fair overall results on stability tests (4.6 on a scale of 0 to 10) including potential drain of affiliation with Main Street America Group Inc. Fair reserve development (3.9) as reserves have generally been sufficient to cover claims.

Other Rating Factors: Fair profitability index (4.4) with operating losses during 2017. Return on equity has been low, averaging 2.9% over the past five years. Good liquidity (5.9) with sufficient resources (cash flows and marketable investments) to handle a spike in claims. Strong long-term capitalization index (8.2) based on excellent current risk adjusted capital (severe and moderate loss scenarios), despite some fluctuation in capital levels.

Principal Business: Auto liability (31%), homeowners multiple peril (23%), auto physical damage (17%), workers compensation (11%), surety (7%), other liability (5%), and other lines (6%).

Principal Investments: Investment grade bonds (68%), misc. investments (28%), and non investment grade bonds (4%).

Investments in Affiliates: 13%

Group Affiliation: Main Street America Group Inc

Licensed in: All states except AK, CA, HI, MN, PR

Commenced Business: July 1923

Address: 4601 TOUCHTON RD E STE 3400, Jacksonville, FL 32246

Phone: (904) 380-7282   **Domicile State:** FL   **NAIC Code:** 14788

Data Date	Rating	RACR #1	RACR #2	Loss Ratio %	Total Assets ($mil)	Capital ($mil)	Net Premium ($mil)	Net Income ($mil)
2017	B-	2.32	1.80	72.6	2,593.2	1,025.4	1,210.3	-11.3
2016	B-	2.85	2.25	71.9	2,468.0	1,039.4	1,066.2	0.1
2015	B-	2.99	2.31	68.0	2,344.8	1,020.6	967.6	66.2
2014	B-	3.07	2.34	70.6	2,314.4	968.2	968.6	30.3
2013	B-	2.98	2.26	68.2	2,265.3	936.9	1,018.2	53.7

Rating Indexes

NJ MANUFACTURERS INS CO

B **Good**

Major Rating Factors: Good overall results on stability tests (5.7 on a scale of 0 to 10) despite potential drain of affiliation with NJ Manufacturers. History of adequate reserve strength (6.6) as reserves have been consistently at an acceptable level.

Other Rating Factors: Good liquidity (6.8) with sufficient resources (cash flows and marketable investments) to handle a spike in claims. Strong long-term capitalization index (8.2) based on excellent current risk adjusted capital (severe and moderate loss scenarios). Moreover, capital levels have been consistent in recent years. Excellent profitability (8.0) with operating gains in each of the last five years.

Principal Business: Auto liability (39%), workers compensation (25%), auto physical damage (20%), and homeowners multiple peril (14%).

Principal Investments: Investment grade bonds (67%), misc. investments (32%), and real estate (1%).

Investments in Affiliates: 12%

Group Affiliation: NJ Manufacturers

Licensed in: CT, DE, ME, NJ, NY, PA, RI

Commenced Business: July 1913

Address: 301 SULLIVAN WAY, West Trenton, NJ 08628-3496

Phone: (609) 883-1300   **Domicile State:** NJ   **NAIC Code:** 12122

Data Date	Rating	RACR #1	RACR #2	Loss Ratio %	Total Assets ($mil)	Capital ($mil)	Net Premium ($mil)	Net Income ($mil)
2017	B	2.33	1.77	77.4	7,423.2	2,884.4	1,818.5	182.1
2016	B	2.36	1.79	82.0	6,957.2	2,655.6	1,689.5	24.8
2015	B	2.39	1.82	78.6	6,687.0	2,445.0	1,629.6	79.7
2014	B-	2.48	1.87	79.7	6,568.2	2,379.9	1,660.1	162.5
2013	B-	2.38	1.80	83.1	6,282.4	2,273.9	1,597.6	123.6

Rating Indexes

NORCAL MUTUAL INS CO

B- **Good**

Major Rating Factors: Fair overall results on stability tests (4.6 on a scale of 0 to 10) including potential drain of affiliation with NORCAL Mutual. History of adequate reserve strength (6.8) as reserves have been consistently at an acceptable level.

Other Rating Factors: Good overall profitability index (6.8). Good expense controls. Good liquidity (6.9) with sufficient resources (cash flows and marketable investments) to handle a spike in claims. Strong long-term capitalization index (8.2) based on excellent current risk adjusted capital (severe and moderate loss scenarios). Moreover, capital levels have been consistent in recent years.

Principal Business: Medical malpractice (100%).

Principal Investments: Investment grade bonds (63%), misc. investments (33%), and non investment grade bonds (4%).

Investments in Affiliates: 12%

Group Affiliation: NORCAL Mutual

Licensed in: All states except NY, PR

Commenced Business: November 1975

Address: 560 Davis Street Suite 200, San Francisco, CA 94105

Phone: (415) 397-9700   **Domicile State:** CA   **NAIC Code:** 33200

Data Date	Rating	RACR #1	RACR #2	Loss Ratio %	Total Assets ($mil)	Capital ($mil)	Net Premium ($mil)	Net Income ($mil)
2017	B-	2.45	1.92	76.9	1,610.5	736.2	395.7	53.6
2016	B-	2.66	2.07	77.7	1,562.1	705.1	337.5	136.1
2015	B-	1.69	1.46	80.3	1,610.5	670.1	314.1	25.8
2014	B-	1.87	1.58	74.9	1,359.3	642.1	207.8	16.8
2013	B-	1.86	1.56	79.3	1,323.3	634.2	212.3	31.6

Rating Indexes

NORGUARD INS CO   D   Weak

Major Rating Factors: Poor long-term capitalization index (1.4 on a scale of 0 to 10) based on weak current risk adjusted capital (severe and moderate loss scenarios). Vulnerable liquidity (2.6) as a spike in claims may stretch capacity.
Other Rating Factors: Weak overall results on stability tests (2.0) including weak risk adjusted capital in prior years. Ample reserve history (8.8) that helps to protect the company against sharp claims increases. Excellent profitability (8.9) with operating gains in each of the last five years. Return on equity has been good over the last five years, averaging 10.6%.
Principal Business: Workers compensation (94%) and commercial multiple peril (5%).
Principal Investments: Investment grade bonds (68%), misc. investments (19%), and cash (13%).
Investments in Affiliates: None
Group Affiliation: Berkshire-Hathaway
Licensed in: All states except WY, PR
Commenced Business: April 1988
Address: 16 SOUTH RIVER STREET, Wilkes-barre, PA 18702
Phone: Phone number unavailable   **Domicile State:** PA   **NAIC Code:** 31470

Data Date	Rating	RACR #1	RACR #2	Loss Ratio %	Total Assets ($mil)	Capital ($mil)	Net Premium ($mil)	Net Income ($mil)
2017	D	0.39	0.30	57.9	1,098.6	238.7	289.4	29.9
2016	D	0.39	0.29	59.0	760.7	198.4	229.7	18.4
2015	D	0.41	0.31	59.9	615.7	166.2	188.3	19.8
2014	D+	0.52	0.40	62.7	482.7	162.4	121.3	12.1
2013	C	0.94	0.74	66.9	426.9	151.0	62.6	17.8

Risk-Adjusted Capital Ratio #1
(Moderate Loss Scenario)

Range 2013 2014 2015 2016 2017

■ Weak   ▨ Fair   □ Good

NORTH AMERICAN SPECIALTY INS CO   C   Fair

Major Rating Factors: Fair overall results on stability tests (3.7 on a scale of 0 to 10) including potential drain of affiliation with Swiss Reinsurance. Fair profitability index (3.6). Excellent expense controls. Return on equity has been low, averaging 1.9% over the past five years.
Other Rating Factors: History of adequate reserve strength (6.1) as reserves have been consistently at an acceptable level. Strong long-term capitalization index (10.0) based on excellent current risk adjusted capital (severe and moderate loss scenarios), despite some fluctuation in capital levels. Excellent liquidity (7.0) with ample operational cash flow and liquid investments.
Principal Business: Surety (37%), other liability (33%), inland marine (19%), ocean marine (8%), auto liability (1%), fire (1%), and other lines (2%).
Principal Investments: Investment grade bonds (78%) and misc. investments (22%).
Investments in Affiliates: 20%
Group Affiliation: Swiss Reinsurance
Licensed in: All states, the District of Columbia and Puerto Rico
Commenced Business: October 1974
Address: 900 ELM STREET, Manchester, NH 3101
Phone: (913) 676-5200   **Domicile State:** NH   **NAIC Code:** 29874

Data Date	Rating	RACR #1	RACR #2	Loss Ratio %	Total Assets ($mil)	Capital ($mil)	Net Premium ($mil)	Net Income ($mil)
2017	C	4.14	3.91	N/A	510.4	321.4	0.0	6.8
2016	C	4.15	3.91	N/A	488.1	313.6	0.2	7.2
2015	C	5.34	4.93	16.6	576.7	395.3	2.8	9.5
2014	C	5.35	4.92	34.3	547.3	384.2	14.2	6.4
2013	C	5.38	4.98	8.4	514.2	373.0	11.4	4.6

Swiss Reinsurance Composite Group Rating: C Largest Group Members	Assets ($mil)	Rating
SWISS REINS AMERICA CORP	14202	C
SWISS RE LIFE HEALTH AMER INC	14134	C
WESTPORT INS CORP	5518	B
NORTH AMERICAN SPECIALTY INS CO	510	C
NORTH AMERICAN CAPACITY INS CO	174	C

NORTH CAROLINA FARM BU MUTUAL INS CO   B   Good

Major Rating Factors: Good overall results on stability tests (5.8 on a scale of 0 to 10) despite potential drain of affiliation with NC Farm Bureau Ins. Good liquidity (6.5) with sufficient resources (cash flows and marketable investments) to handle a spike in claims.
Other Rating Factors: Strong long-term capitalization index (10.0) based on excellent current risk adjusted capital (severe and moderate loss scenarios). Moreover, capital levels have been consistent in recent years. Ample reserve history (8.4) that helps to protect the company against sharp claims increases. Excellent profitability (8.2) with operating gains in each of the last five years.
Principal Business: Auto liability (30%), homeowners multiple peril (29%), auto physical damage (25%), allied lines (3%), farmowners multiple peril (3%), other liability (2%), and other lines (7%).
Principal Investments: Investment grade bonds (83%) and misc. investments (18%).
Investments in Affiliates: 1%
Group Affiliation: NC Farm Bureau Ins
Licensed in: NC
Commenced Business: October 1953
Address: 5301 GLENWOOD AVENUE, Raleigh, NC 27612
Phone: (919) 782-1705   **Domicile State:** NC   **NAIC Code:** 14842

Data Date	Rating	RACR #1	RACR #2	Loss Ratio %	Total Assets ($mil)	Capital ($mil)	Net Premium ($mil)	Net Income ($mil)
2017	B	6.62	4.40	72.0	2,002.0	1,180.3	833.1	65.5
2016	B	6.69	4.45	80.5	1,895.4	1,107.2	771.2	8.6
2015	B	6.02	4.06	68.5	1,815.1	1,077.2	716.6	78.8
2014	B-	5.77	3.90	68.0	1,740.3	1,008.9	675.7	94.7
2013	B-	3.87	2.60	68.5	1,664.7	933.1	737.3	86.8

Rating Indexes

Ranges   Cap. 2   Stab.   Res.   Prof.   Liq.

■ Weak   ■ Fair   ▨ Good   □ Strong

NORTH RIVER INS CO   C-   Fair

Major Rating Factors: Fair profitability index (4.5 on a scale of 0 to 10) with operating losses during 2016 and 2017. Return on equity has been fair, averaging 7.8% over the past five years. Fair overall results on stability tests (3.3) including weak financial strength of affiliated Fairfax Financial.

Other Rating Factors: Good overall long-term capitalization (5.6) based on good current risk adjusted capital (moderate loss scenario). However, capital levels have fluctuated somewhat during past years. History of adequate reserve strength (6.2) as reserves have been consistently at an acceptable level. Excellent liquidity (7.5) with ample operational cash flow and liquid investments.

Principal Business: Other liability (37%), workers compensation (30%), inland marine (8%), commercial multiple peril (7%), auto liability (7%), products liability (7%), and other lines (5%).

Principal Investments: Investment grade bonds (58%), misc. investments (35%), and non investment grade bonds (7%).

Investments in Affiliates: 25%

Group Affiliation: Fairfax Financial

Licensed in: All states except PR

Commenced Business: October 1972

Address: 305 MADISON AVENUE, Township Of Morris, NJ 7960

Phone: (973) 490-6600   **Domicile State:** NJ   **NAIC Code:** 21105

Data Date	Rating	RACR #1	RACR #2	Loss Ratio %	Total Assets ($mil)	Capital ($mil)	Net Premium ($mil)	Net Income ($mil)
2017	C-	1.09	0.83	64.7	1,070.3	293.4	410.5	-33.8
2016	C-	1.19	0.87	63.7	1,051.4	285.0	396.8	-6.6
2015	C-	1.31	1.02	64.1	1,030.5	306.2	365.6	55.3
2014	C-	1.16	0.92	67.5	945.8	264.8	296.7	4.4
2013	C-	1.13	0.89	71.4	938.2	263.1	281.3	87.7

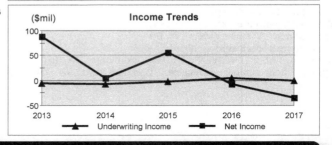

NORTH STAR MUTUAL INS CO   B-   Good

Major Rating Factors: Fair overall results on stability tests (4.7 on a scale of 0 to 10) including potential drain of affiliation with North Star Companies. Good liquidity (6.5) with sufficient resources (cash flows and marketable investments) to handle a spike in claims.

Other Rating Factors: Strong long-term capitalization index (10.0) based on excellent current risk adjusted capital (severe and moderate loss scenarios). Moreover, capital has steadily grown over the last five years. Ample reserve history (7.7) that can protect against increases in claims costs. Excellent profitability (8.8) with operating gains in each of the last five years. Return on equity has been good over the last five years, averaging 10.5%.

Principal Business: Allied lines (23%), homeowners multiple peril (23%), auto physical damage (14%), auto liability (13%), farmowners multiple peril (12%), other liability (6%), and other lines (9%).

Principal Investments: Investment grade bonds (79%), misc. investments (18%), real estate (2%), and cash (1%).

Investments in Affiliates: 1%

Group Affiliation: North Star Companies

Licensed in: IA, KS, MN, NE, ND, OK, SD, WI

Commenced Business: February 1920

Address: 269 Barstad Road South, Cottonwood, MN 56229-0000

Phone: (507) 423-6262   **Domicile State:** MN   **NAIC Code:** 14850

Data Date	Rating	RACR #1	RACR #2	Loss Ratio %	Total Assets ($mil)	Capital ($mil)	Net Premium ($mil)	Net Income ($mil)
2017	B-	6.61	4.41	61.7	742.9	456.2	365.9	36.5
2016	B-	6.40	4.32	56.1	694.3	409.0	349.1	47.0
2015	B-	5.90	4.01	49.2	637.4	361.9	338.6	57.4
2014	B-	4.93	3.40	63.0	566.7	306.5	317.4	29.0
2013	B-	4.61	3.18	64.3	520.2	280.0	288.7	20.9

NORTHLAND INS CO   B   Good

Major Rating Factors: Good liquidity (6.9 on a scale of 0 to 10) with sufficient resources (cash flows and marketable investments) to handle a spike in claims. Good overall results on stability tests (6.0). Affiliation with Travelers Companies Inc is a strength.

Other Rating Factors: Fair profitability index (4.5). Fair expense controls. Return on equity has been fair, averaging 10.2% over the past five years. Strong long-term capitalization index (9.1) based on excellent current risk adjusted capital (severe and moderate loss scenarios), despite some fluctuation in capital levels. Ample reserve history (7.8) that can protect against increases in claims costs.

Principal Business: Auto liability (63%), auto physical damage (26%), inland marine (10%), and other liability (1%).

Principal Investments: Investment grade bonds (85%) and misc. investments (17%).

Investments in Affiliates: 15%

Group Affiliation: Travelers Companies Inc

Licensed in: All states except AK, PR

Commenced Business: March 1948

Address: ONE TOWER SQUARE, Hartford, CT 6183

Phone: (860) 277-0111   **Domicile State:** CT   **NAIC Code:** 24015

Data Date	Rating	RACR #1	RACR #2	Loss Ratio %	Total Assets ($mil)	Capital ($mil)	Net Premium ($mil)	Net Income ($mil)
2017	B	2.88	2.37	69.5	1,187.8	516.1	278.6	40.8
2016	B	2.92	2.41	63.4	1,176.9	535.1	265.6	52.7
2015	B	2.96	2.42	58.7	1,171.6	544.0	253.5	62.1
2014	B	2.97	2.41	60.5	1,166.2	538.9	246.3	60.6
2013	B	2.97	2.43	60.9	1,157.6	533.3	245.7	56.8

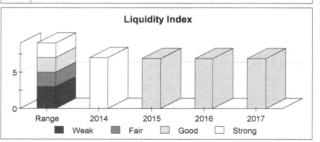

NUCLEAR ELECTRIC INS LTD *   A+   Excellent

Major Rating Factors: Strong long-term capitalization index (9.5 on a scale of 0 to 10) based on excellent current risk adjusted capital (severe and moderate loss scenarios). Furthermore, this high level of risk adjusted capital has been consistently maintained in previous years. Excellent profitability (7.8) with operating gains in each of the last five years.

Other Rating Factors: Excellent liquidity (7.0) with ample operational cash flow and liquid investments. Excellent overall results on stability tests (8.6). Stability strengths include excellent risk diversification. Fair reserve development (4.6) as reserves have generally been sufficient to cover claims.

Principal Business: Commercial multiple peril (100%).

Principal Investments: Misc. investments (65%), investment grade bonds (32%), and cash (3%).

Investments in Affiliates: 3%

Group Affiliation: None

Licensed in: DE

Commenced Business: September 1980

Address: 1201 Market St Ste 1200, Wilmington, DE 19801-1807

Phone: (302) 888-3000   **Domicile State:** DE   **NAIC Code:** 34215

Data Date	Rating	RACR #1	RACR #2	Loss Ratio %	Total Assets ($mil)	Capital ($mil)	Net Premium ($mil)	Net Income ($mil)
2017	A+	4.01	2.80	22.2	5,587.7	4,474.0	228.4	115.1
2016	A+	3.60	2.58	18.8	5,050.9	4,049.0	245.3	271.9
2015	U	3.55	2.54	124.5	4,761.0	3,796.2	204.3	22.6
2014	U	N/A	N/A	140.0	5,208.3	3,882.1	210.8	66.6
2013	U	3.41	2.49	100.2	5,028.1	3,843.9	205.2	178.5

Capital ($mil) chart, 2013–2017

NUTMEG INS CO   B-   Good

Major Rating Factors: Fair overall results on stability tests (4.8 on a scale of 0 to 10). Strengths include potentially strong support from affiliation with Hartford Financial Services Inc. Fair reserve development (4.9) as reserves have generally been sufficient to cover claims.

Other Rating Factors: Strong long-term capitalization index (10.0) based on excellent current risk adjusted capital (severe and moderate loss scenarios), despite some fluctuation in capital levels. Excellent liquidity (7.1) with ample operational cash flow and liquid investments. Weak profitability index (2.3) with operating losses during 2016. Return on equity has been fair, averaging 8.4% over the past five years.

Principal Business: N/A

Principal Investments: Investment grade bonds (96%) and misc. investments (4%).

Investments in Affiliates: 1%

Group Affiliation: Hartford Financial Services Inc

Licensed in: All states except PR

Commenced Business: December 1980

Address: One Hartford Plaza, Hartford, CT 06155-0001

Phone: (860) 547-5000   **Domicile State:** CT   **NAIC Code:** 39608

Data Date	Rating	RACR #1	RACR #2	Loss Ratio %	Total Assets ($mil)	Capital ($mil)	Net Premium ($mil)	Net Income ($mil)
2017	C+	26.40	23.76	68.7	440.7	257.8	74.9	46.7
2016	C	56.41	50.77	70.4	825.4	581.5	73.7	-62.8
2015	D	54.75	49.28	66.1	706.6	530.6	73.8	102.6
2014	D	0.06	0.04	67.0	448.1	280.2	71.7	11.8
2013	C-	26.77	24.09	68.8	421.7	256.6	69.6	28.3

Hartford Financial Services Inc
Composite Group Rating: C+

Largest Group Members	Assets ($mil)	Rating
HARTFORD LIFE INS CO	109357	C+
HARTFORD LIFE ANNUITY INS CO	36379	B-
HARTFORD FIRE INS CO	22855	C+
HARTFORD LIFE ACCIDENT INS CO	12936	C
HARTFORD ACCIDENT INDEMNITY CO	11907	B

OAK RIVER INS CO   C   Fair

Major Rating Factors: Fair overall results on stability tests (4.3 on a scale of 0 to 10). Strong long-term capitalization index (7.4) based on excellent current risk adjusted capital (severe and moderate loss scenarios). Moreover, capital levels have been consistent in recent years.

Other Rating Factors: Ample reserve history (9.4) that helps to protect the company against sharp claims increases. Excellent profitability (8.8) with operating gains in each of the last five years. Return on equity has been good over the last five years, averaging 12.8%. Superior liquidity (9.1) with ample operational cash flow and liquid investments.

Principal Business: Workers compensation (84%), auto liability (11%), auto physical damage (2%), commercial multiple peril (2%), allied lines (1%), and inland marine (1%).

Principal Investments: Investment grade bonds (48%), misc. investments (37%), and cash (15%).

Investments in Affiliates: None

Group Affiliation: Berkshire-Hathaway

Licensed in: All states except OR, PR

Commenced Business: December 1993

Address: 1314 DOUGLAS ST STE 1300, Omaha, NE 68102-1944

Phone: (402) 393-7255   **Domicile State:** NE   **NAIC Code:** 34630

Data Date	Rating	RACR #1	RACR #2	Loss Ratio %	Total Assets ($mil)	Capital ($mil)	Net Premium ($mil)	Net Income ($mil)
2017	C	2.63	1.73	53.3	809.1	320.3	158.8	97.1
2016	C	1.85	1.18	61.3	665.6	230.0	127.2	18.6
2015	C	1.83	1.20	60.5	594.7	200.4	110.9	18.2
2014	C-	0.60	0.37	67.1	571.1	191.9	108.0	16.0
2013	C	1.64	1.07	66.3	527.4	170.9	111.9	14.0

Berkshire-Hathaway
Composite Group Rating: B

Largest Group Members	Assets ($mil)	Rating
NATIONAL INDEMNITY CO	231374	B
GOVERNMENT EMPLOYEES INS CO	33382	B
COLUMBIA INS CO	24522	U
BERKSHIRE HATHAWAY LIFE INS CO OF NE	19610	C+
GENERAL REINS CORP	16508	C+

OCCIDENTAL FIRE & CAS CO OF NC
C-   Fair

Major Rating Factors: Weak overall results on stability tests (2.7 on a scale of 0 to 10) including potential drain of affiliation with IAT Reinsurance Co Ltd and negative cash flow from operations for 2017. Fair reserve development (4.0) as reserves have generally been sufficient to cover claims.
Other Rating Factors: Good long-term capitalization index (6.6) based on good current risk adjusted capital (moderate loss scenario), despite some fluctuation in capital levels. Good overall profitability index (6.7) with small operating losses during 2014. Return on equity has been low, averaging 3.3% over the past five years. Excellent liquidity (7.0) with ample operational cash flow and liquid investments.
Principal Business: Homeowners multiple peril (38%), inland marine (24%), auto liability (21%), auto physical damage (9%), allied lines (5%), fire (2%), and commercial multiple peril (1%).
Principal Investments: Misc. investments (81%), investment grade bonds (15%), non investment grade bonds (3%), and cash (1%).
Investments in Affiliates: 42%
Group Affiliation: IAT Reinsurance Co Ltd
Licensed in: All states except HI, PR
Commenced Business: January 1962
Address: 702 OBERLIN ROAD, Raleigh, NC 27605-0800
Phone: (919) 833-1600   **Domicile State:** NC   **NAIC Code:** 23248

Data Date	Rating	RACR #1	RACR #2	Loss Ratio %	Total Assets ($mil)	Capital ($mil)	Net Premium ($mil)	Net Income ($mil)
2017	C-	1.24	1.04	73.4	474.3	224.0	65.2	10.3
2016	C-	1.08	0.86	76.6	602.8	172.7	51.3	7.7
2015	C-	1.14	0.92	70.4	542.2	145.5	123.4	2.8
2014	C-	1.15	0.95	70.8	518.0	162.9	155.0	-1.4
2013	C-	1.18	0.99	64.9	420.4	155.0	121.8	10.0

Rating Indexes

ODYSSEY REINS CO
C   Fair

Major Rating Factors: Fair overall results on stability tests (3.7 on a scale of 0 to 10) including potential drain of affiliation with Fairfax Financial. Good overall profitability index (6.2). Fair expense controls. Return on equity has been fair, averaging 6.2% over the past five years.
Other Rating Factors: Strong long-term capitalization index (7.2) based on excellent current risk adjusted capital (severe and moderate loss scenarios), despite some fluctuation in capital levels. Ample reserve history (9.4) that helps to protect the company against sharp claims increases. Excellent liquidity (7.5) with ample operational cash flow and liquid investments.
Principal Business: Surety (100%).
Principal Investments: Misc. investments (51%), investment grade bonds (42%), cash (3%), non investment grade bonds (3%), and real estate (1%).
Investments in Affiliates: 32%
Group Affiliation: Fairfax Financial
Licensed in: All states, the District of Columbia and Puerto Rico
Commenced Business: September 1986
Address: 300 FIRST STAMFORD PLACE, Stamford, CT 6902
Phone: (203) 977-8000   **Domicile State:** CT   **NAIC Code:** 23680

Data Date	Rating	RACR #1	RACR #2	Loss Ratio %	Total Assets ($mil)	Capital ($mil)	Net Premium ($mil)	Net Income ($mil)
2017	C	1.32	1.12	67.4	7,797.1	3,248.8	1,880.8	88.2
2016	C	1.50	1.26	55.3	7,162.6	3,193.9	1,575.2	158.4
2015	C	1.48	1.24	52.2	7,308.2	3,288.5	1,575.5	449.6
2014	C	1.41	1.13	51.8	7,577.4	3,248.7	1,799.8	191.7
2013	C	1.63	1.23	29.2	7,448.0	3,102.5	1,267.5	112.5

Rating Indexes

OGLESBY REINS CO *
A+   Excellent

Major Rating Factors: Strong long-term capitalization index (10.0 on a scale of 0 to 10) based on excellent current risk adjusted capital (severe and moderate loss scenarios). Furthermore, this high level of risk adjusted capital has been consistently maintained in previous years. Excellent liquidity (7.1) with ample operational cash flow and liquid investments.
Other Rating Factors: Excellent overall results on stability tests (8.4). Stability strengths include excellent risk diversification. Fair reserve development (3.7) as reserves have generally been sufficient to cover claims. Fair profitability index (4.5) with operating losses during 2017. Return on equity has been low, averaging 2.6% over the past five years.
Principal Business: (This company is a reinsurer.)
Principal Investments: Investment grade bonds (95%) and misc. investments (5%).
Investments in Affiliates: None
Group Affiliation: State Farm Group
Licensed in: IL, TX
Commenced Business: July 2011
Address: One State Farm Plaza, Bloomington, IL 61710
Phone: (309) 766-2311   **Domicile State:** IL   **NAIC Code:** 14103

Data Date	Rating	RACR #1	RACR #2	Loss Ratio %	Total Assets ($mil)	Capital ($mil)	Net Premium ($mil)	Net Income ($mil)
2017	A+	8.52	4.56	129.1	4,590.7	3,187.0	448.8	-90.2
2016	A+	13.96	9.98	67.5	4,410.3	3,267.6	907.1	145.0
2015	A+	12.04	9.41	72.0	3,998.0	3,119.4	1,206.2	34.4
2014	A+	48.48	43.38	0.0	3,171.6	3,071.8	177.2	146.4
2013	A+	52.33	46.32	0.0	3,022.7	2,923.9	155.3	161.7

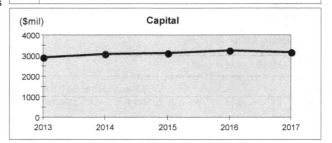

($mil)   Capital

OHIO CASUALTY INS CO   C   Fair

Major Rating Factors: Fair overall results on stability tests (3.9 on a scale of 0 to 10) including potential drain of affiliation with Liberty Mutual Group. History of adequate reserve strength (5.7) as reserves have been consistently at an acceptable level.

Other Rating Factors: Good overall profitability index (6.3) despite operating losses during 2017. Return on equity has been fair, averaging 9.0% over the past five years. Good liquidity (6.3) with sufficient resources (cash flows and marketable investments) to handle a spike in claims. Strong long-term capitalization index (8.2) based on excellent current risk adjusted capital (severe and moderate loss scenarios), despite some fluctuation in capital levels.

Principal Business: Other liability (36%), commercial multiple peril (21%), surety (12%), inland marine (11%), auto liability (8%), workers compensation (7%), and other lines (5%).

Principal Investments: Investment grade bonds (78%), misc. investments (19%), and non investment grade bonds (5%).

Investments in Affiliates: 2%

Group Affiliation: Liberty Mutual Group

Licensed in: All states except PR

Commenced Business: March 1920

Address: 62 Maple Avenue, Keene, NH 3431

Phone: (617) 357-9500   **Domicile State:** NH   **NAIC Code:** 24074

Data Date	Rating	RACR #1	RACR #2	Loss Ratio %	Total Assets ($mil)	Capital ($mil)	Net Premium ($mil)	Net Income ($mil)
2017	C	2.61	1.82	79.5	6,147.6	1,693.6	2,284.0	-5.2
2016	C	2.98	2.01	69.9	5,641.6	1,721.9	2,119.9	73.2
2015	C	2.82	1.87	68.4	5,578.6	1,637.4	2,050.6	157.4
2014	C	2.56	1.68	70.0	5,408.2	1,529.8	2,030.1	133.7
2013	C	2.34	1.52	73.5	5,639.6	1,384.1	1,791.9	313.5

Rating Indexes

OHIO FARMERS INS CO   B-   Good

Major Rating Factors: Fair overall results on stability tests (4.6 on a scale of 0 to 10) including potential drain of affiliation with Westfield Companies and negative cash flow from operations for 2017. Good overall profitability index (6.9) despite operating losses during 2017.

Other Rating Factors: Good liquidity (6.9) with sufficient resources (cash flows and marketable investments) to handle a spike in claims. Strong long-term capitalization index (7.3) based on excellent current risk adjusted capital (severe and moderate loss scenarios). Moreover, capital levels have been consistent in recent years. Ample reserve history (7.4) that can protect against increases in claims costs.

Principal Business: Surety (100%).

Principal Investments: Misc. investments (81%), investment grade bonds (16%), real estate (2%), and cash (1%).

Investments in Affiliates: 72%

Group Affiliation: Westfield Companies

Licensed in: All states except AK, CA, CT, HI, ID, ME, NH, OR, PR

Commenced Business: July 1848

Address: One Park Circle, Westfield Center, OH 44251-5001

Phone: (330) 887-0101   **Domicile State:** OH   **NAIC Code:** 24104

Data Date	Rating	RACR #1	RACR #2	Loss Ratio %	Total Assets ($mil)	Capital ($mil)	Net Premium ($mil)	Net Income ($mil)
2017	B-	1.20	1.17	73.5	3,107.9	2,334.5	352.9	-6.1
2016	B-	1.23	1.20	62.3	2,964.7	2,211.9	343.8	63.0
2015	B-	1.23	1.20	62.7	2,701.1	1,997.1	336.1	22.0
2014	B-	1.22	1.19	63.5	2,595.1	1,902.4	329.3	39.3
2013	B-	1.25	1.21	59.8	2,404.6	1,808.7	318.3	21.1

Rating Indexes

OHIO MUTUAL INS CO   B-   Good

Major Rating Factors: Fair overall results on stability tests (4.7 on a scale of 0 to 10) including potential drain of affiliation with Ohio Mutual Group. Good liquidity (6.9) with sufficient resources (cash flows and marketable investments) to handle a spike in claims.

Other Rating Factors: Strong long-term capitalization index (7.5) based on excellent current risk adjusted capital (severe and moderate loss scenarios). Moreover, capital has steadily grown over the last five years. Ample reserve history (7.5) that can protect against increases in claims costs. Excellent profitability (7.3) with operating gains in each of the last five years.

Principal Business: Auto liability (36%), auto physical damage (32%), homeowners multiple peril (23%), farmowners multiple peril (5%), and fire (4%).

Principal Investments: Misc. investments (73%), investment grade bonds (25%), cash (1%), and real estate (1%).

Investments in Affiliates: 67%

Group Affiliation: Ohio Mutual Group

Licensed in: CT, IN, IA, KS, ME, MN, NE, NH, OH, OR, RI, TN, VT, VA, WI

Commenced Business: March 1901

Address: 1725 HOPLEY AVENUE, Bucyrus, OH 44820-0111

Phone: (419) 562-3011   **Domicile State:** OH   **NAIC Code:** 10202

Data Date	Rating	RACR #1	RACR #2	Loss Ratio %	Total Assets ($mil)	Capital ($mil)	Net Premium ($mil)	Net Income ($mil)
2017	B-	1.36	1.32	60.4	296.3	235.0	59.6	3.0
2016	B-	1.35	1.31	61.7	276.6	217.6	56.4	3.3
2015	B-	1.36	1.32	61.6	256.8	201.3	53.5	2.9
2014	B-	1.37	1.32	64.0	239.7	187.5	51.9	2.4
2013	B-	1.35	1.31	65.8	227.4	177.8	49.4	1.8

Rating Indexes

OLD REPUB INS CO   B   Good

Major Rating Factors: History of adequate reserve strength (6.0 on a scale of 0 to 10) as reserves have been consistently at an acceptable level. Good liquidity (6.9) with sufficient resources (cash flows and marketable investments) to handle a spike in claims.
Other Rating Factors: Good overall results on stability tests (6.2). Strong long-term capitalization index (9.3) based on excellent current risk adjusted capital (severe and moderate loss scenarios). Moreover, capital levels have been consistent in recent years. Excellent profitability (8.8) with operating gains in each of the last five years.
Principal Business: Workers compensation (38%), other liability (17%), inland marine (11%), auto liability (9%), credit (7%), aircraft (6%), and other lines (12%).
Principal Investments: Investment grade bonds (69%), misc. investments (26%), non investment grade bonds (4%), and cash (1%).
Investments in Affiliates: 1%
Group Affiliation: Old Republic Group
Licensed in: All states, the District of Columbia and Puerto Rico
Commenced Business: April 1935
Address: 133 OAKLAND AVENUE, Greensburg, PA 15601-0789
Phone: (724) 834-5000   **Domicile State:** PA   **NAIC Code:** 24147

Data Date	Rating	RACR #1	RACR #2	Loss Ratio %	Total Assets ($mil)	Capital ($mil)	Net Premium ($mil)	Net Income ($mil)
2017	B	4.21	2.55	61.7	2,923.3	1,141.2	459.0	97.3
2016	B	4.13	2.54	54.7	2,813.8	1,106.9	470.7	106.5
2015	B	4.16	2.58	53.5	2,668.8	1,034.0	420.9	98.9
2014	B+	3.85	2.35	61.7	2,609.4	1,035.8	400.4	105.6
2013	A-	4.02	2.48	52.2	2,472.7	937.8	365.4	107.4

Reserve Deficiency (as % of capital)

2013   2014   2015   2016   2017

* Adequate & redundant reserves show as negatives

■ 1 Yr Dev
□ 2 Yr Dev

OLD REPUBLIC GENERAL INS CORP   B   Good

Major Rating Factors: Good overall results on stability tests (6.2 on a scale of 0 to 10). Stability strengths include good operational trends and excellent risk diversification. Strong long-term capitalization index (7.7) based on excellent current risk adjusted capital (severe and moderate loss scenarios). Moreover, capital levels have been consistent in recent years.
Other Rating Factors: Ample reserve history (8.8) that helps to protect the company against sharp claims increases. Excellent profitability (8.9) with operating gains in each of the last five years. Excellent expense controls. Return on equity has been good over the last five years, averaging 12.4%. Excellent liquidity (7.0) with ample operational cash flow and liquid investments.
Principal Business: Workers compensation (62%), other liability (27%), auto liability (9%), and auto physical damage (2%).
Principal Investments: Investment grade bonds (82%), misc. investments (14%), non investment grade bonds (3%), and cash (1%).
Investments in Affiliates: None
Group Affiliation: Old Republic Group
Licensed in: All states, the District of Columbia and Puerto Rico
Commenced Business: January 1961
Address: 307 NORTH MICHIGAN AVENUE, Chicago, IL 60601
Phone: (312) 346-8100   **Domicile State:** IL   **NAIC Code:** 24139

Data Date	Rating	RACR #1	RACR #2	Loss Ratio %	Total Assets ($mil)	Capital ($mil)	Net Premium ($mil)	Net Income ($mil)
2017	B	3.23	1.89	65.2	2,078.8	596.3	224.0	90.7
2016	B	2.86	1.28	85.0	2,021.2	556.8	184.4	53.0
2015	B	2.48	1.14	81.7	2,004.0	500.2	311.4	60.6
2014	B	2.50	1.18	88.8	1,925.7	494.1	303.1	62.8
2013	A-	2.74	1.63	83.2	1,730.6	431.7	286.3	54.2

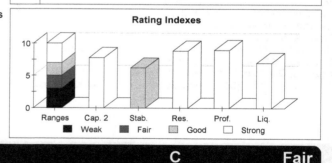

Rating Indexes

Ranges   Cap. 2   Stab.   Res.   Prof.   Liq.

■ Weak   ■ Fair   ▦ Good   □ Strong

OLD UNITED CAS CO   C   Fair

Major Rating Factors: Fair overall results on stability tests (3.7 on a scale of 0 to 10) including fair financial strength of affiliated Berkshire-Hathaway. Good overall profitability index (6.8). Fair expense controls. Return on equity has been good over the last five years, averaging 12.1%.
Other Rating Factors: Strong long-term capitalization index (10.0) based on excellent current risk adjusted capital (severe and moderate loss scenarios), despite some fluctuation in capital levels. Ample reserve history (7.3) that can protect against increases in claims costs. Superior liquidity (9.2) with ample operational cash flow and liquid investments.
Principal Business: (Not applicable due to unusual reinsurance transactions.)
Principal Investments: Investment grade bonds (87%), misc. investments (8%), and non investment grade bonds (5%).
Investments in Affiliates: None
Group Affiliation: Berkshire-Hathaway
Licensed in: All states except PR
Commenced Business: April 1989
Address: 8500 Shawnee Mission Pkwy #200, Merriam, KS 66202
Phone: (913) 895-0200   **Domicile State:** KS   **NAIC Code:** 37060

Data Date	Rating	RACR #1	RACR #2	Loss Ratio %	Total Assets ($mil)	Capital ($mil)	Net Premium ($mil)	Net Income ($mil)
2017	C	11.78	6.10	48.0	650.5	240.7	144.1	28.3
2016	C	6.45	3.58	46.7	605.3	209.7	150.9	20.9
2015	C	6.61	3.57	43.4	540.1	184.1	141.7	33.2
2014	B-	8.20	4.44	43.3	656.6	335.4	126.5	39.0
2013	B-	8.22	4.39	44.7	603.8	302.6	119.9	27.3

Berkshire-Hathaway Composite Group Rating: B Largest Group Members	Assets ($mil)	Rating
NATIONAL INDEMNITY CO	231374	B
GOVERNMENT EMPLOYEES INS CO	33382	B
COLUMBIA INS CO	24522	U
BERKSHIRE HATHAWAY LIFE INS CO OF NE	19610	C+
GENERAL REINS CORP	16508	C+

OMS NATIONAL INS CO RRG   B-   Good

Major Rating Factors: Fair overall results on stability tests (4.7 on a scale of 0 to 10) including potential drain of affiliation with OMS National Ins. Strong long-term capitalization index (8.6) based on excellent current risk adjusted capital (severe and moderate loss scenarios). Moreover, capital levels have been consistent in recent years.

Other Rating Factors: Ample reserve history (8.6) that helps to protect the company against sharp claims increases. Excellent profitability (8.6) with operating gains in each of the last five years. Excellent liquidity (7.7) with ample operational cash flow and liquid investments.

Principal Business: Medical malpractice (100%).

Principal Investments: Investment grade bonds (55%), misc. investments (44%), and cash (1%).

Investments in Affiliates: 16%

Group Affiliation: OMS National Ins

Licensed in: All states except PR

Commenced Business: April 1988

Address: 6133 N RIVER ROAD SUITE 650, Rosemont, IL 60018-5173

Phone: (847) 384-0041   **Domicile State:** IL   **NAIC Code:** 44121

Data Date	Rating	RACR #1	RACR #2	Loss Ratio %	Total Assets ($mil)	Capital ($mil)	Net Premium ($mil)	Net Income ($mil)
2017	B-	2.74	2.18	43.8	442.8	267.9	64.0	19.6
2016	B-	2.59	2.08	61.4	419.0	238.3	67.2	13.8
2015	B-	2.50	2.03	68.0	384.3	216.8	63.8	8.9
2014	B-	2.46	1.98	67.9	374.8	215.1	65.7	12.9
2013	B-	2.43	1.98	51.3	342.9	191.5	69.9	21.4

OWNERS INS CO *   A   Excellent

Major Rating Factors: Strong long-term capitalization index (10.0 on a scale of 0 to 10) based on excellent current risk adjusted capital (severe and moderate loss scenarios). Furthermore, this high level of risk adjusted capital has been consistently maintained in previous years. Ample reserve history (8.1) that helps to protect the company against sharp claims increases.

Other Rating Factors: Excellent profitability (8.7) with operating gains in each of the last five years. Excellent overall results on stability tests (7.5). Stability strengths include good operational trends and excellent risk diversification. Good liquidity (6.7) with sufficient resources (cash flows and marketable investments) to handle a spike in claims.

Principal Business: Auto liability (34%), commercial multiple peril (23%), auto physical damage (23%), workers compensation (7%), other liability (5%), homeowners multiple peril (4%), and other lines (4%).

Principal Investments: Investment grade bonds (83%), misc. investments (15%), cash (1%), and non investment grade bonds (1%).

Investments in Affiliates: None

Group Affiliation: Auto-Owners Group

Licensed in: AL, AZ, AR, CO, FL, GA, ID, IL, IN, IA, KS, KY, MI, MN, MS, MO, NE, NV, NM, NC, ND, OH, OR, PA, SC, SD, TN, UT, VA, WA, WI

Commenced Business: December 1975

Address: 2325 NORTH COLE STREET, Lima, OH 45801-2305

Phone: (517) 323-1200   **Domicile State:** OH   **NAIC Code:** 32700

Data Date	Rating	RACR #1	RACR #2	Loss Ratio %	Total Assets ($mil)	Capital ($mil)	Net Premium ($mil)	Net Income ($mil)
2017	A	5.95	3.99	69.8	4,110.4	1,815.5	1,642.5	73.8
2016	A-	5.57	3.78	68.6	3,924.6	1,696.8	1,519.1	123.2
2015	A-	4.31	2.89	61.6	3,883.0	1,557.7	1,705.9	179.7
2014	A-	3.79	2.48	68.4	3,721.9	1,395.5	1,690.1	96.2
2013	A+	3.73	2.44	67.5	3,510.8	1,292.1	1,617.0	120.6

PACIFIC EMPLOYERS INS CO   B-   Good

Major Rating Factors: Fair overall results on stability tests (4.9 on a scale of 0 to 10) including potential drain of affiliation with Chubb Limited. Fair profitability index (3.7). Good expense controls. Return on equity has been fair, averaging 5.9% over the past five years.

Other Rating Factors: History of adequate reserve strength (6.0) as reserves have been consistently at an acceptable level. Good liquidity (6.7) with sufficient resources (cash flows and marketable investments) to handle a spike in claims. Strong long-term capitalization index (8.2) based on excellent current risk adjusted capital (severe and moderate loss scenarios), despite some fluctuation in capital levels.

Principal Business: Homeowners multiple peril (49%), inland marine (12%), other liability (11%), auto liability (7%), workers compensation (6%), auto physical damage (5%), and other lines (9%).

Principal Investments: Investment grade bonds (91%), misc. investments (6%), and cash (3%).

Investments in Affiliates: 5%

Group Affiliation: Chubb Limited

Licensed in: All states, the District of Columbia and Puerto Rico

Commenced Business: October 1923

Address: 436 WALNUT STREET, Philadelphia, PA 19106

Phone: (215) 640-1000   **Domicile State:** PA   **NAIC Code:** 22748

Data Date	Rating	RACR #1	RACR #2	Loss Ratio %	Total Assets ($mil)	Capital ($mil)	Net Premium ($mil)	Net Income ($mil)
2017	B-	2.64	1.80	83.9	3,687.4	1,063.4	963.4	36.0
2016	B-	3.41	2.36	76.5	3,774.2	1,319.9	889.3	114.6
2015	B-	3.10	2.17	72.8	3,541.6	1,240.4	846.9	69.5
2014	B-	3.12	2.20	77.6	3,390.5	1,170.2	796.9	48.4
2013	B-	3.27	2.31	72.2	3,309.0	1,141.6	774.9	89.1

PACIFIC INDEMNITY CO   B   Good

Major Rating Factors: Good liquidity (6.9 on a scale of 0 to 10) with sufficient resources (cash flows and marketable investments) to handle a spike in claims. Good overall results on stability tests (5.5) despite negative cash flow from operations for 2017. Stability strengths include good operational trends and excellent risk diversification.

Other Rating Factors: Strong long-term capitalization index (10.0) based on excellent current risk adjusted capital (severe and moderate loss scenarios), despite some fluctuation in capital levels. Ample reserve history (8.7) that helps to protect the company against sharp claims increases. Excellent profitability (7.0) with operating gains in each of the last five years. Return on equity has been good over the last five years, averaging 14.2%.

Principal Business: Homeowners multiple peril (43%), workers compensation (26%), inland marine (12%), other liability (4%), commercial multiple peril (4%), auto physical damage (3%), and other lines (7%).

Principal Investments: Investment grade bonds (97%) and misc. investments (3%).

Investments in Affiliates: None

Group Affiliation: Chubb Limited

Licensed in: All states except PR

Commenced Business: February 1926

Address: 330 East Kilbourn Ave Ste 1450, Milwaukee, WI 53202

Phone: (215) 640-1000   **Domicile State:** WI   **NAIC Code:** 20346

Data Date	Rating	RACR #1	RACR #2	Loss Ratio %	Total Assets ($mil)	Capital ($mil)	Net Premium ($mil)	Net Income ($mil)
2017	B	6.60	4.13	59.0	6,560.0	2,992.5	863.2	342.3
2016	B-	5.52	3.53	53.2	6,555.2	2,926.6	1,074.5	417.9
2015	B	4.47	2.85	56.7	6,916.0	2,930.2	1,691.9	449.7
2014	B	4.38	2.80	56.2	6,822.4	2,922.2	1,624.5	421.6
2013	B+	4.16	2.69	52.5	6,640.5	2,771.4	1,568.7	425.6

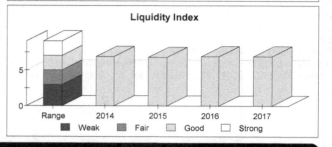

Liquidity Index

PACIFIC INS CO LTD   B   Good

Major Rating Factors: History of adequate reserve strength (5.8 on a scale of 0 to 10) as reserves have been consistently at an acceptable level. Good liquidity (6.8) with sufficient resources (cash flows and marketable investments) to handle a spike in claims.

Other Rating Factors: Good overall results on stability tests (5.8). Strong long-term capitalization index (9.2) based on excellent current risk adjusted capital (severe and moderate loss scenarios), despite some fluctuation in capital levels. Excellent profitability (8.1) with operating gains in each of the last five years. Return on equity has been good over the last five years, averaging 10.3%.

Principal Business: Other liability (65%), workers compensation (29%), auto liability (4%), and auto physical damage (2%).

Principal Investments: Investment grade bonds (95%) and misc. investments (5%).

Investments in Affiliates: None

Group Affiliation: Hartford Financial Services Inc

Licensed in: All states, the District of Columbia and Puerto Rico

Commenced Business: January 1995

Address: One Hartford Plaza, Hartford, CT 06155-0001

Phone: (860) 547-5000   **Domicile State:** CT   **NAIC Code:** 10046

Data Date	Rating	RACR #1	RACR #2	Loss Ratio %	Total Assets ($mil)	Capital ($mil)	Net Premium ($mil)	Net Income ($mil)
2017	B	3.81	2.52	68.7	676.1	238.0	182.0	21.7
2016	B	3.62	2.40	70.4	660.7	219.2	179.1	20.4
2015	B	3.67	2.43	66.1	638.0	222.3	179.1	24.6
2014	B	3.84	2.54	67.0	635.6	227.2	174.2	28.5
2013	B	3.76	2.50	68.8	619.3	218.5	169.1	20.3

Reserve Deficiency (as % of capital)

* Adequate & redundant reserves show as negatives
■ 1 Yr Dev □ 2 Yr Dev

PALISADES SAFETY & INS ASSOC   C   Fair

Major Rating Factors: Fair overall results on stability tests (3.5 on a scale of 0 to 10) including potential drain of affiliation with Palisades Group. Fair long-term capitalization index (4.9) based on good current risk adjusted capital (moderate loss scenario). Over the last several years, capital levels have remained relatively consistent.

Other Rating Factors: Good overall profitability index (5.4) despite operating losses during 2014, 2015 and 2016. Good liquidity (6.2) with sufficient resources (cash flows and marketable investments) to handle a spike in claims. Ample reserve history (9.0) that helps to protect the company against sharp claims increases.

Principal Business: Auto liability (72%) and auto physical damage (28%).

Principal Investments: Misc. investments (64%) and investment grade bonds (38%).

Investments in Affiliates: 29%

Group Affiliation: Palisades Group

Licensed in: NJ

Commenced Business: May 1992

Address: 200 Connell Dr Suite 3000, Red Bank, NJ 7701

Phone: (732) 978-6000   **Domicile State:** NJ   **NAIC Code:** 22050

Data Date	Rating	RACR #1	RACR #2	Loss Ratio %	Total Assets ($mil)	Capital ($mil)	Net Premium ($mil)	Net Income ($mil)
2017	C	1.04	0.90	74.4	1,343.7	480.1	616.1	70.9
2016	C	0.83	0.71	76.9	1,244.1	412.9	587.5	-11.6
2015	C	0.77	0.65	75.9	1,159.7	366.8	575.4	-8.9
2014	C	0.70	0.59	75.4	1,172.0	376.5	553.4	-9.5
2013	C	0.66	0.57	73.3	1,143.6	344.3	545.3	17.0

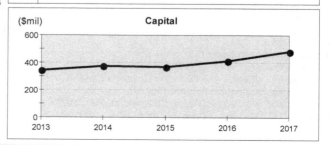

Capital

PARTNER REINSURANCE CO OF THE US   B-   Good

Major Rating Factors: Fair overall results on stability tests (4.5 on a scale of 0 to 10) including potential drain of affiliation with Giovanni Agnelli e C Sapaz. Fair profitability index (4.4). Fair expense controls. Return on equity has been fair, averaging 9.6% over the past five years.
Other Rating Factors: Good liquidity (6.5) with sufficient resources (cash flows and marketable investments) to handle a spike in claims. Strong long-term capitalization index (7.7) based on excellent current risk adjusted capital (severe and moderate loss scenarios), despite some fluctuation in capital levels. Ample reserve history (9.5) that helps to protect the company against sharp claims increases.
Principal Business: (This company is a reinsurer.)
Principal Investments: Investment grade bonds (76%), misc. investments (14%), non investment grade bonds (8%), and cash (2%).
Investments in Affiliates: 3%
Group Affiliation: Giovanni Agnelli e C Sapaz
Licensed in: All states except PR
Commenced Business: May 1980
Address: 245 PARK AVE 39TH FL #39058, New York, NY 10167
Phone: (203) 485-4200   **Domicile State:** NY   **NAIC Code:** 38636

Data Date	Rating	RACR #1	RACR #2	Loss Ratio %	Total Assets ($mil)	Capital ($mil)	Net Premium ($mil)	Net Income ($mil)
2017	B-	2.46	1.53	77.9	4,655.3	1,335.7	929.3	24.1
2016	C+	2.73	1.73	67.2	4,822.9	1,463.8	1,188.2	71.7
2015	C	2.00	1.28	61.8	4,865.9	1,405.1	1,201.8	219.2
2014	C-	1.86	1.20	62.8	4,742.6	1,420.0	1,203.9	236.0
2013	C-	1.68	1.09	66.6	4,886.7	1,332.0	1,139.4	122.7

Rating Indexes

PEERLESS INS CO   B   Good

Major Rating Factors: Good overall profitability index (5.5 on a scale of 0 to 10) despite operating losses during 2017. Return on equity has been fair, averaging 5.1% over the past five years. Good liquidity (5.9) with sufficient resources (cash flows and marketable investments) to handle a spike in claims.
Other Rating Factors: Good overall results on stability tests (5.3). Fair reserve development (4.6) as reserves have generally been sufficient to cover claims. Strong long-term capitalization index (7.6) based on excellent current risk adjusted capital (severe and moderate loss scenarios), despite some fluctuation in capital levels.
Principal Business: Commercial multiple peril (26%), auto liability (15%), inland marine (12%), workers compensation (12%), other liability (10%), homeowners multiple peril (8%), and other lines (16%).
Principal Investments: Investment grade bonds (70%), misc. investments (27%), and non investment grade bonds (5%).
Investments in Affiliates: 5%
Group Affiliation: Liberty Mutual Group
Licensed in: All states except HI, PR
Commenced Business: November 1903
Address: 62 Maple Avenue, Keene, NH 3431
Phone: (617) 357-9500   **Domicile State:** NH   **NAIC Code:** 24198

Data Date	Rating	RACR #1	RACR #2	Loss Ratio %	Total Assets ($mil)	Capital ($mil)	Net Premium ($mil)	Net Income ($mil)
2017	B	1.95	1.40	79.5	14,600.0	3,448.5	5,710.0	-54.8
2016	B-	2.21	1.55	69.9	13,330.8	3,538.9	5,299.8	154.3
2015	B-	2.07	1.44	68.4	13,172.4	3,316.7	5,126.4	304.6
2014	B-	1.88	1.30	70.0	12,800.9	3,058.9	5,075.4	247.2
2013	B-	1.60	1.09	73.5	13,621.2	2,786.4	5,827.5	151.5

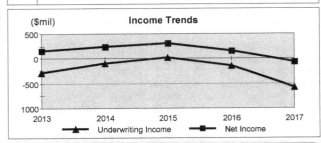

Income Trends

PEKIN INS CO *   B+   Good

Major Rating Factors: Good overall results on stability tests (6.0 on a scale of 0 to 10). Affiliation with Farmers Automobile Ins Assn is a strength. Good overall profitability index (6.5). Fair expense controls. Return on equity has been low, averaging 3.4% over the past five years.
Other Rating Factors: Good liquidity (6.6) with sufficient resources (cash flows and marketable investments) to handle a spike in claims. Strong long-term capitalization index (10.0) based on excellent current risk adjusted capital (severe and moderate loss scenarios), despite some fluctuation in capital levels. Ample reserve history (7.9) that can protect against increases in claims costs.
Principal Business: Commercial multiple peril (25%), auto liability (21%), workers compensation (19%), auto physical damage (15%), homeowners multiple peril (12%), other liability (4%), and other lines (3%).
Principal Investments: Investment grade bonds (89%) and misc. investments (11%).
Investments in Affiliates: 3%
Group Affiliation: Farmers Automobile Ins Assn
Licensed in: AZ, IL, IN, IA, MI, OH, WI
Commenced Business: July 1961
Address: 2505 COURT STREET, Pekin, IL 61558-0001
Phone: (309) 346-1161   **Domicile State:** IL   **NAIC Code:** 24228

Data Date	Rating	RACR #1	RACR #2	Loss Ratio %	Total Assets ($mil)	Capital ($mil)	Net Premium ($mil)	Net Income ($mil)
2017	B+	4.68	3.31	74.2	305.4	132.3	122.8	4.4
2016	B+	4.62	3.27	77.7	312.2	128.3	122.8	1.2
2015	B+	4.60	3.27	71.5	295.9	125.7	120.2	5.5
2014	B+	4.63	3.29	74.3	281.2	118.7	113.8	5.5
2013	B+	4.79	3.39	75.4	281.9	117.1	107.1	4.4

Rating Indexes

PEMCO MUTUAL INS CO

B-   **Good**

Major Rating Factors: Fair overall results on stability tests (4.7 on a scale of 0 to 10) including potential drain of affiliation with PEMCO Corp. History of adequate reserve strength (5.0) as reserves have been consistently at an acceptable level.

Other Rating Factors: Good overall profitability index (5.6) despite operating losses during 2013. Good liquidity (5.8) with sufficient resources (cash flows and marketable investments) to handle a spike in claims. Strong long-term capitalization index (8.6) based on excellent current risk adjusted capital (severe and moderate loss scenarios). Moreover, capital levels have been consistent in recent years.

Principal Business: Auto liability (47%), homeowners multiple peril (24%), auto physical damage (24%), other liability (2%), fire (2%), and inland marine (1%).

Principal Investments: Investment grade bonds (79%), real estate (10%), misc. investments (8%), and cash (3%).

Investments in Affiliates: 1%

Group Affiliation: PEMCO Corp

Licensed in: ID, OR, WA

Commenced Business: February 1949

Address: 1300 Dexter Avenue N, Seattle, WA 98109-3571

Phone: (206) 628-4290   **Domicile State:** WA   **NAIC Code:** 24341

Data Date	Rating	RACR #1	RACR #2	Loss Ratio %	Total Assets ($mil)	Capital ($mil)	Net Premium ($mil)	Net Income ($mil)
2017	B-	2.54	2.04	77.4	772.8	284.9	453.2	0.6
2016	B-	2.70	2.20	80.7	740.7	282.0	421.5	24.1
2015	B-	2.71	2.18	77.0	706.8	259.0	396.6	10.2
2014	B-	2.81	2.33	77.5	687.4	254.5	370.1	24.0
2013	B-	2.82	2.34	72.2	629.4	237.4	346.0	-3.3

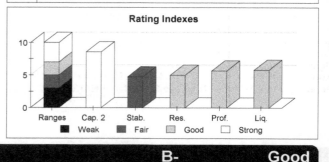

Rating Indexes

PENN NATIONAL SECURITY INS CO

B-   **Good**

Major Rating Factors: Fair overall results on stability tests (4.7 on a scale of 0 to 10) including potential drain of affiliation with Pennsylvania National Ins Group. History of adequate reserve strength (6.2) as reserves have been consistently at an acceptable level.

Other Rating Factors: Good liquidity (6.5) with sufficient resources (cash flows and marketable investments) to handle a spike in claims. Strong long-term capitalization index (9.4) based on excellent current risk adjusted capital (severe and moderate loss scenarios). Moreover, capital levels have been consistent in recent years. Excellent profitability (8.3) with operating gains in each of the last five years.

Principal Business: Workers compensation (24%), auto liability (23%), other liability (13%), fire (12%), commercial multiple peril (10%), auto physical damage (7%), and other lines (11%).

Principal Investments: Investment grade bonds (94%) and misc. investments (6%).

Investments in Affiliates: None

Group Affiliation: Pennsylvania National Ins Group

Licensed in: AL, DC, DE, MD, NJ, NC, PA, SC, TN, VA

Commenced Business: January 1989

Address: Two North Second Street, Harrisburg, PA 17101

Phone: (717) 234-4941   **Domicile State:** PA   **NAIC Code:** 32441

Data Date	Rating	RACR #1	RACR #2	Loss Ratio %	Total Assets ($mil)	Capital ($mil)	Net Premium ($mil)	Net Income ($mil)
2017	B-	4.09	2.79	65.6	969.0	336.3	344.6	15.5
2016	B-	3.81	2.65	64.2	950.4	320.2	336.1	22.9
2015	B-	3.56	2.50	65.0	914.5	299.7	330.9	13.3
2014	B-	3.46	2.43	64.8	894.1	287.2	326.5	18.4
2013	B-	3.04	2.07	65.5	843.2	282.1	315.8	10.3

Rating Indexes

PENNSYLVANIA MANUFACTURERS ASN INS

C   **Fair**

Major Rating Factors: Fair reserve development (3.1 on a scale of 0 to 10) as the level of reserves has at times been insufficient to cover claims. Deficiencies in the two year reserve development occurred in three of the previous five years and ranged between 18% and 22%. Fair overall results on stability tests (4.2).

Other Rating Factors: Good overall profitability index (6.7) with small operating losses during 2014. Return on equity has been low, averaging 3.0% over the past five years. Good liquidity (6.7) with sufficient resources (cash flows and marketable investments) to handle a spike in claims. Strong long-term capitalization index (8.4) based on excellent current risk adjusted capital (severe and moderate loss scenarios), despite some fluctuation in capital levels.

Principal Business: Workers compensation (65%), inland marine (14%), auto liability (11%), commercial multiple peril (4%), other liability (4%), and auto physical damage (2%).

Principal Investments: Investment grade bonds (74%), misc. investments (24%), and non investment grade bonds (4%).

Investments in Affiliates: None

Group Affiliation: Old Republic Group

Licensed in: All states, the District of Columbia and Puerto Rico

Commenced Business: July 1964

Address: 380 SENTRY PARKWAY, Blue Bell, PA 19422-0754

Phone: (610) 397-5000   **Domicile State:** PA   **NAIC Code:** 12262

Data Date	Rating	RACR #1	RACR #2	Loss Ratio %	Total Assets ($mil)	Capital ($mil)	Net Premium ($mil)	Net Income ($mil)
2017	C	2.91	1.99	76.4	1,017.3	343.8	182.1	17.6
2016	C	2.63	1.79	78.6	929.6	283.7	159.1	0.3
2015	C	2.65	1.79	83.1	821.9	251.7	134.7	6.0
2014	C	2.93	2.12	91.2	834.0	266.1	149.5	-2.1
2013	C	2.86	2.11	79.9	761.2	224.5	135.6	18.0

Reserve Deficiency (as % of capital)

* Adequate & redundant reserves show as negatives

PENNSYLVANIA NTL MUTUAL CAS INS CO   B-   Good

Major Rating Factors: Fair overall results on stability tests (4.7 on a scale of 0 to 10) including potential drain of affiliation with Pennsylvania National Ins Group. History of adequate reserve strength (6.2) as reserves have been consistently at an acceptable level.

Other Rating Factors: Good liquidity (6.8) with sufficient resources (cash flows and marketable investments) to handle a spike in claims. Strong long-term capitalization index (7.8) based on excellent current risk adjusted capital (severe and moderate loss scenarios). Moreover, capital levels have been consistent in recent years. Excellent profitability (7.9) with operating gains in each of the last five years.

Principal Business: Auto liability (25%), auto physical damage (17%), homeowners multiple peril (15%), other liability (14%), workers compensation (9%), commercial multiple peril (7%), and other lines (13%).

Principal Investments: Investment grade bonds (48%), misc. investments (47%), and cash (5%).

Investments in Affiliates: 35%

Group Affiliation: Pennsylvania National Ins Group

Licensed in: All states except CA, CT, HI, NV, NH, ND, WY, PR

Commenced Business: April 1920

Address: Two North Second Street, Harrisburg, PA 17101

Phone: (717) 234-4941   **Domicile State:** PA   **NAIC Code:** 14990

Data Date	Rating	RACR #1	RACR #2	Loss Ratio %	Total Assets ($mil)	Capital ($mil)	Net Premium ($mil)	Net Income ($mil)
2017	B-	1.69	1.54	65.6	1,307.1	630.2	344.6	23.6
2016	B-	1.71	1.56	64.2	1,279.7	612.0	336.1	29.4
2015	B-	1.71	1.56	65.0	1,233.6	571.4	330.9	14.6
2014	B-	1.72	1.55	64.8	1,192.6	558.8	326.5	23.8
2013	B-	1.65	1.47	65.5	1,125.8	541.2	315.8	22.4

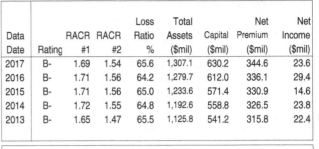

Rating Indexes

PHILADELPHIA CBSP FOR INS OF HOUSES   B-   Good

Major Rating Factors: Fair overall results on stability tests (4.7 on a scale of 0 to 10) including potential drain of affiliation with Philadelphia Contrib Group. Good overall profitability index (6.8) with small operating losses during 2016. Return on equity has been low, averaging 1.5% over the past five years.

Other Rating Factors: Good liquidity (6.7) with sufficient resources (cash flows and marketable investments) to handle a spike in claims. Strong long-term capitalization index (7.2) based on excellent current risk adjusted capital (severe and moderate loss scenarios), despite some fluctuation in capital levels. Ample reserve history (7.3) that can protect against increases in claims costs.

Principal Business: (This company is a reinsurer.)

Principal Investments: Misc. investments (97%), real estate (1%), cash (1%), and investment grade bonds (1%).

Investments in Affiliates: 52%

Group Affiliation: Philadelphia Contrib Group

Licensed in: NJ, PA

Commenced Business: March 1753

Address: 210 SOUTH FOURTH STREET, Philadelphia, PA 19106-9232

Phone: (888) 627-1752   **Domicile State:** PA   **NAIC Code:** 17930

Data Date	Rating	RACR #1	RACR #2	Loss Ratio %	Total Assets ($mil)	Capital ($mil)	Net Premium ($mil)	Net Income ($mil)
2017	B-	1.36	1.19	65.8	376.1	300.2	38.6	4.4
2016	B-	1.32	1.15	71.6	329.2	251.9	36.8	-0.7
2015	B-	1.31	1.14	75.1	309.5	233.1	36.6	1.1
2014	B-	1.32	1.13	85.2	326.3	245.0	37.1	8.3
2013	B-	1.30	1.10	63.0	316.6	234.8	35.8	6.0

Rating Indexes

PHILADELPHIA INDEMNITY INS CO   B-   Good

Major Rating Factors: Fair overall results on stability tests (4.6 on a scale of 0 to 10) including potential drain of affiliation with Tokio Marine Holdings Inc. Good liquidity (6.6) with sufficient resources (cash flows and marketable investments) to handle a spike in claims.

Other Rating Factors: Strong long-term capitalization index (8.3) based on excellent current risk adjusted capital (severe and moderate loss scenarios), despite some fluctuation in capital levels. Ample reserve history (8.0) that helps to protect the company against sharp claims increases. Excellent profitability (7.9) with operating gains in each of the last five years. Return on equity has been good over the last five years, averaging 14.6%.

Principal Business: Commercial multiple peril (53%), other liability (22%), auto liability (14%), auto physical damage (5%), surety (4%), and allied lines (1%).

Principal Investments: Investment grade bonds (82%), misc. investments (11%), non investment grade bonds (6%), and cash (1%).

Investments in Affiliates: None

Group Affiliation: Tokio Marine Holdings Inc

Licensed in: All states except PR

Commenced Business: March 1927

Address: One Bala Plaza Suite 100, Bala Cynwyd, PA 19004-1403

Phone: (610) 206-7836   **Domicile State:** PA   **NAIC Code:** 18058

Data Date	Rating	RACR #1	RACR #2	Loss Ratio %	Total Assets ($mil)	Capital ($mil)	Net Premium ($mil)	Net Income ($mil)
2017	B-	2.46	1.86	63.7	8,653.2	2,316.4	3,024.8	364.1
2016	B-	2.52	1.89	60.9	8,081.0	2,271.5	2,872.8	347.7
2015	B-	2.30	1.73	60.5	7,361.5	2,047.5	2,696.2	311.2
2014	B-	2.55	1.92	61.5	7,182.2	2,337.4	2,553.3	306.1
2013	B	2.66	2.02	61.0	6,526.1	2,156.7	2,351.5	293.5

Rating Indexes

PHOENIX INS CO

B   Good

Major Rating Factors: Good liquidity (6.8 on a scale of 0 to 10) with sufficient resources (cash flows and marketable investments) to handle a spike in claims. Good overall results on stability tests (6.3).
Other Rating Factors: Fair profitability index (4.4). Fair expense controls. Return on equity has been fair, averaging 12.9% over the past five years. Strong long-term capitalization index (7.8) based on excellent current risk adjusted capital (severe and moderate loss scenarios), despite some fluctuation in capital levels. Ample reserve history (8.0) that helps to protect the company against sharp claims increases.
Principal Business: Workers compensation (34%), commercial multiple peril (28%), auto liability (12%), other liability (7%), homeowners multiple peril (7%), inland marine (5%), and other lines (7%).
Principal Investments: Investment grade bonds (70%), misc. investments (29%), and non investment grade bonds (1%).
Investments in Affiliates: 25%
Group Affiliation: Travelers Companies Inc
Licensed in: All states except CA, PR
Commenced Business: July 1850
Address: ONE TOWER SQUARE, Hartford, CT 6183
Phone: (860) 277-0111   **Domicile State:** CT   **NAIC Code:** 25623

Data Date	Rating	RACR #1	RACR #2	Loss Ratio %	Total Assets ($mil)	Capital ($mil)	Net Premium ($mil)	Net Income ($mil)
2017	B	1.70	1.50	69.5	4,210.3	1,625.4	1,142.3	159.2
2016	B	1.77	1.57	63.4	4,184.1	1,718.4	1,088.9	215.9
2015	B	1.77	1.56	58.7	4,175.2	1,746.0	1,039.8	312.8
2014	B	1.62	1.45	60.5	4,196.2	1,739.4	1,009.4	207.8
2013	B	1.53	1.37	60.9	4,009.4	1,579.1	1,006.9	194.5

Liquidity Index

PHYSICIANS INS A MUTL CO

B-   Good

Major Rating Factors: Fair overall results on stability tests (4.7 on a scale of 0 to 10) including potential drain of affiliation with Washington State Health and negative cash flow from operations for 2017. Good overall profitability index (6.8). Good expense controls.
Other Rating Factors: Strong long-term capitalization index (10.0) based on excellent current risk adjusted capital (severe and moderate loss scenarios), despite some fluctuation in capital levels. Ample reserve history (9.4) that helps to protect the company against sharp claims increases. Excellent liquidity (7.0) with ample operational cash flow and liquid investments.
Principal Business: Medical malpractice (85%), aggregate write-ins for other lines of business (14%), and other liability (1%).
Principal Investments: Investment grade bonds (79%), misc. investments (20%), and cash (1%).
Investments in Affiliates: 3%
Group Affiliation: Washington State Health
Licensed in: AK, AZ, CA, CO, GA, HI, ID, IL, MI, MT, NV, NM, OR, UT, WA, WY, PR
Commenced Business: December 1981
Address: 1301 Second Avenue Suite 2700, Seattle, WA 98101
Phone: (206) 343-7300   **Domicile State:** WA   **NAIC Code:** 40738

Data Date	Rating	RACR #1	RACR #2	Loss Ratio %	Total Assets ($mil)	Capital ($mil)	Net Premium ($mil)	Net Income ($mil)
2017	B-	4.38	3.25	81.1	504.5	250.2	81.1	9.5
2016	B-	4.07	3.12	82.2	502.3	232.1	78.2	8.1
2015	B-	4.08	3.15	84.4	471.0	220.0	76.3	6.9
2014	B-	4.08	3.16	82.1	468.3	222.6	76.7	11.6
2013	B-	4.11	3.20	85.2	454.0	211.9	72.9	5.6

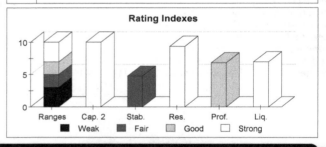

Rating Indexes

PIONEER STATE MUTUAL INS CO *

B+   Good

Major Rating Factors: Good liquidity (6.8 on a scale of 0 to 10) with sufficient resources (cash flows and marketable investments) to handle a spike in claims. Good overall results on stability tests (6.5).
Other Rating Factors: Strong long-term capitalization index (10.0) based on excellent current risk adjusted capital (severe and moderate loss scenarios). Moreover, capital has steadily grown over the last five years. Ample reserve history (8.7) that helps to protect the company against sharp claims increases. Excellent profitability (8.7) with operating gains in each of the last five years.
Principal Business: Auto liability (38%), auto physical damage (25%), homeowners multiple peril (25%), farmowners multiple peril (5%), commercial multiple peril (4%), workers compensation (1%), and other liability (1%).
Principal Investments: Investment grade bonds (60%), misc. investments (37%), cash (2%), and real estate (1%).
Investments in Affiliates: None
Group Affiliation: None
Licensed in: IN, MI
Commenced Business: June 1908
Address: 1510 North Elms Road, Flint, MI 48532-2000
Phone: (810) 733-2300   **Domicile State:** MI   **NAIC Code:** 18309

Data Date	Rating	RACR #1	RACR #2	Loss Ratio %	Total Assets ($mil)	Capital ($mil)	Net Premium ($mil)	Net Income ($mil)
2017	B+	5.16	3.24	60.4	608.7	363.2	207.3	22.3
2016	B	5.12	3.24	60.1	550.7	323.5	196.7	25.7
2015	B	4.96	3.16	60.6	499.5	292.4	183.3	20.0
2014	B	4.69	2.98	66.3	472.2	277.9	174.4	16.0
2013	A	4.51	2.84	64.4	448.4	260.0	171.1	13.6

Liquidity Index

PLYMOUTH ROCK ASR CORP

B-   **Good**

Major Rating Factors: Fair overall results on stability tests (4.7 on a scale of 0 to 10) including potential drain of affiliation with Plymouth Rock Ins Group. History of adequate reserve strength (6.6) as reserves have been consistently at an acceptable level.

Other Rating Factors: Good overall profitability index (6.7) despite operating losses during 2015. Return on equity has been fair, averaging 6.8% over the past five years. Good liquidity (5.7) with sufficient resources (cash flows and marketable investments) to handle a spike in claims. Strong long-term capitalization index (7.5) based on excellent current risk adjusted capital (severe and moderate loss scenarios), despite some fluctuation in capital levels.

Principal Business: Auto liability (56%) and auto physical damage (44%).

Principal Investments: Misc. investments (58%), investment grade bonds (41%), and cash (1%).

Investments in Affiliates: None

Group Affiliation: Plymouth Rock Ins Group

Licensed in: CT, MA, RI

Commenced Business: October 1983

Address: 695 ATLANTIC AVENUE, Boston, MA 02111-2217

Phone: (617) 720-1620   **Domicile State:** MA   **NAIC Code:** 14737

Data Date	Rating	RACR #1	RACR #2	Loss Ratio %	Total Assets ($mil)	Capital ($mil)	Net Premium ($mil)	Net Income ($mil)
2017	B-	1.91	1.41	74.1	684.2	222.5	376.3	15.9
2016	B-	1.72	1.31	76.3	605.8	186.6	365.1	5.9
2015	B-	1.61	1.22	77.8	535.7	161.2	339.1	-2.1
2014	B-	1.71	1.27	78.2	501.0	162.0	315.6	31.3
2013	B-	2.01	1.64	73.1	440.6	152.8	288.7	8.3

Rating Indexes

PREFERRED MUTUAL INS CO

B   **Good**

Major Rating Factors: Good liquidity (6.6 on a scale of 0 to 10) with sufficient resources (cash flows and marketable investments) to handle a spike in claims. Good overall results on stability tests (6.2).

Other Rating Factors: Strong long-term capitalization index (9.9) based on excellent current risk adjusted capital (severe and moderate loss scenarios). Moreover, capital levels have been consistent in recent years. Ample reserve history (8.2) that helps to protect the company against sharp claims increases. Excellent profitability (8.5) with operating gains in each of the last five years.

Principal Business: Homeowners multiple peril (41%), auto liability (19%), commercial multiple peril (18%), auto physical damage (14%), other liability (3%), fire (2%), and other lines (3%).

Principal Investments: Investment grade bonds (80%), misc. investments (15%), non investment grade bonds (6%), and real estate (1%).

Investments in Affiliates: None

Group Affiliation: None

Licensed in: CT, MA, NH, NJ, NY, NC, OH, PA, RI, SC

Commenced Business: January 1897

Address: One Preferred Way, New Berlin, NY 13411

Phone: (607) 847-6161   **Domicile State:** NY   **NAIC Code:** 15024

Data Date	Rating	RACR #1	RACR #2	Loss Ratio %	Total Assets ($mil)	Capital ($mil)	Net Premium ($mil)	Net Income ($mil)
2017	B	4.59	2.93	64.4	568.1	243.9	249.8	11.7
2016	B	4.98	3.14	60.4	539.1	234.6	213.2	16.2
2015	B	4.54	2.99	67.8	522.7	212.7	204.4	18.6
2014	B	4.38	2.89	68.2	502.3	200.1	199.9	14.3
2013	B	3.43	2.25	65.5	484.8	185.3	193.6	13.3

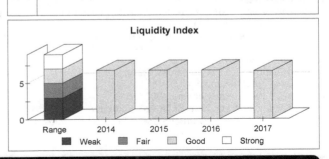

Liquidity Index

PREFERRED PROFESSIONAL INS CO *

B+   **Good**

Major Rating Factors: Good overall results on stability tests (6.5 on a scale of 0 to 10) despite negative cash flow from operations for 2017. Stability strengths include good operational trends and excellent risk diversification. Strong long-term capitalization index (10.0) based on excellent current risk adjusted capital (severe and moderate loss scenarios), despite some fluctuation in capital levels.

Other Rating Factors: Ample reserve history (9.4) that helps to protect the company against sharp claims increases. Excellent profitability (7.6) with operating gains in each of the last five years. Excellent liquidity (7.5) with ample operational cash flow and liquid investments.

Principal Business: Medical malpractice (88%), workers compensation (6%), and other liability (5%).

Principal Investments: Investment grade bonds (76%), misc. investments (21%), and cash (3%).

Investments in Affiliates: 0%

Group Affiliation: Medical Professional Mutual

Licensed in: All states except PR

Commenced Business: July 1976

Address: 11605 MIRACLE HILLS DR STE 200, Omaha, NE 68154-4467

Phone: (402) 392-1566   **Domicile State:** NE   **NAIC Code:** 36234

Data Date	Rating	RACR #1	RACR #2	Loss Ratio %	Total Assets ($mil)	Capital ($mil)	Net Premium ($mil)	Net Income ($mil)
2017	B+	5.94	4.26	80.4	327.4	182.3	33.1	4.6
2016	B	5.27	3.99	59.4	325.6	170.2	49.6	11.8
2015	B	6.07	4.46	77.8	295.1	156.9	36.4	7.3
2014	C+	5.47	3.92	54.2	311.4	150.7	42.3	17.5
2013	C+	5.80	3.95	26.5	408.9	206.1	45.3	34.2

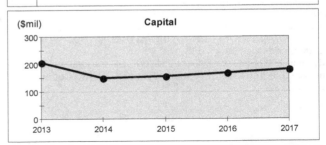

Capital

PRINCETON INS CO — C — Fair

Major Rating Factors: Fair overall results on stability tests (3.8 on a scale of 0 to 10) including fair financial strength of affiliated Berkshire Hathaway and negative cash flow from operations for 2017. Strong long-term capitalization index (10.0) based on excellent current risk adjusted capital (severe and moderate loss scenarios). Moreover, capital levels have been consistent in recent years.

Other Rating Factors: Ample reserve history (8.4) that helps to protect the company against sharp claims increases. Excellent profitability (7.7) with operating gains in each of the last five years. Superior liquidity (10.0) with ample operational cash flow and liquid investments.

Principal Business: (Not applicable due to unusual reinsurance transactions.)

Principal Investments: Investment grade bonds (68%), misc. investments (21%), cash (9%), non investment grade bonds (1%), and real estate (1%).

Investments in Affiliates: None

Group Affiliation: Berkshire Hathaway

Licensed in: AZ, CT, DC, DE, GA, IL, IN, MD, MI, NJ, NY, NC, PA, SC, VA, WA, WV

Commenced Business: February 1982

Address: 746 Alexander Road, Princeton, NJ 8540

Phone: (609) 452-9404   **Domicile State:** NJ   **NAIC Code:** 42226

Data Date	Rating	RACR #1	RACR #2	Loss Ratio %	Total Assets ($mil)	Capital ($mil)	Net Premium ($mil)	Net Income ($mil)
2017	C	7.19	5.02	61.1	723.1	509.3	28.5	13.3
2016	C	6.70	4.97	65.8	689.6	475.9	29.1	18.8
2015	C	6.89	5.14	79.3	666.4	463.9	31.0	12.1
2014	C	6.60	4.76	78.1	665.0	460.7	33.1	13.9
2013	C	8.15	6.06	104.5	628.5	438.8	35.1	12.6

Berkshire Hathaway
Composite Group Rating: B

Largest Group Members	Assets ($mil)	Rating
NATIONAL INDEMNITY CO	231374	B
GOVERNMENT EMPLOYEES INS CO	33382	B
COLUMBIA INS CO	24522	U
BERKSHIRE HATHAWAY LIFE INS CO OF NE	19610	C+
GENERAL REINS CORP	16508	C+

PRIVILEGE UNDERWRITERS RECIP EXCH — B — Good

Major Rating Factors: History of adequate reserve strength (5.5 on a scale of 0 to 10) as reserves have been consistently at an acceptable level. Good liquidity (6.2) with sufficient resources (cash flows and marketable investments) to handle a spike in claims.

Other Rating Factors: Good overall results on stability tests (5.5) despite negative cash flow from operations for 2017 and fair results on operational trends. Fair profitability index (3.8) with operating losses during each of the last five years. Strong long-term capitalization index (7.6) based on excellent current risk adjusted capital (severe and moderate loss scenarios). Moreover, capital has steadily grown over the last five years.

Principal Business: Homeowners multiple peril (58%), auto physical damage (13%), auto liability (10%), other liability (9%), inland marine (8%), earthquake (1%), and ocean marine (1%).

Principal Investments: Investment grade bonds (81%), misc. investments (13%), cash (4%), and non investment grade bonds (2%).

Investments in Affiliates: 1%

Group Affiliation: PURE Companies Group

Licensed in: All states except ID, PR

Commenced Business: January 2007

Address: 800 Corporate Drive-Suite 420, Fort Lauderdale, FL 33334

Phone: (914) 328-7388   **Domicile State:** FL   **NAIC Code:** 12873

Data Date	Rating	RACR #1	RACR #2	Loss Ratio %	Total Assets ($mil)	Capital ($mil)	Net Premium ($mil)	Net Income ($mil)
2017	B	2.73	1.72	69.1	568.0	227.6	208.4	-7.0
2016	B-	2.42	1.56	60.9	410.8	157.1	163.6	-5.8
2015	B-	1.69	0.99	60.6	325.0	98.6	138.0	-20.4
2014	B-	1.57	0.93	55.3	220.0	68.7	96.5	-13.7
2013	B-	1.63	0.96	51.9	171.7	60.1	74.4	-9.4

Reserve Deficiency (as % of capital)

* Adequate & redundant reserves show as negatives
■ 1 Yr Dev   □ 2 Yr Dev

PROASSURANCE CASUALTY CO — C — Fair

Major Rating Factors: Fair overall results on stability tests (3.7 on a scale of 0 to 10). Weak profitability index (2.5). Fair expense controls. Return on equity has been fair, averaging 12.4% over the past five years.

Other Rating Factors: Strong long-term capitalization index (8.2) based on excellent current risk adjusted capital (severe and moderate loss scenarios), despite some fluctuation in capital levels. Ample reserve history (9.5) that helps to protect the company against sharp claims increases. Excellent liquidity (7.0) with ample operational cash flow and liquid investments.

Principal Business: Medical malpractice (99%) and other liability (1%).

Principal Investments: Investment grade bonds (60%), misc. investments (34%), and non investment grade bonds (6%).

Investments in Affiliates: None

Group Affiliation: ProAssurance Corp

Licensed in: AL, CA, CT, DE, FL, GA, IL, IN, IA, KS, KY, MD, MA, MI, MN, MS, MO, NE, NV, NJ, NY, ND, OH, PA, SC, SD, TN, VT, VA, WV, WI

Commenced Business: June 1980

Address: 2600 PROFESSIONALS DRIVE, Okemos, MI 48864

Phone: (205) 877-4400   **Domicile State:** MI   **NAIC Code:** 38954

Data Date	Rating	RACR #1	RACR #2	Loss Ratio %	Total Assets ($mil)	Capital ($mil)	Net Premium ($mil)	Net Income ($mil)
2017	C	2.36	1.77	66.8	990.0	294.9	170.4	33.5
2016	B-	3.28	2.42	63.0	1,092.9	406.8	157.3	39.8
2015	B-	3.48	2.62	59.9	1,139.9	443.6	151.1	51.5
2014	B-	4.06	3.09	44.5	1,274.1	534.1	158.1	81.4
2013	B-	3.66	2.80	52.4	1,342.0	523.6	166.0	72.1

Rating Indexes

Ranges   Cap. 2   Stab.   Res.   Prof.   Liq.
■ Weak   ■ Fair   ▨ Good   □ Strong

PROASSURANCE INDEMNTIY CO INC   C-   Fair

Major Rating Factors: Weak profitability index (2.3 on a scale of 0 to 10). Good expense controls. Return on equity has been fair, averaging 18.3% over the past five years. Fair overall results on stability tests (3.1).

Other Rating Factors: Good liquidity (6.9) with sufficient resources (cash flows and marketable investments) to handle a spike in claims. Strong long-term capitalization index (8.4) based on excellent current risk adjusted capital (severe and moderate loss scenarios), despite some fluctuation in capital levels. Ample reserve history (9.5) that helps to protect the company against sharp claims increases.

Principal Business: Medical malpractice (99%) and other liability (1%).

Principal Investments: Investment grade bonds (60%), misc. investments (35%), and non investment grade bonds (6%).

Investments in Affiliates: 1%

Group Affiliation: ProAssurance Corp

Licensed in: All states except NY, PR

Commenced Business: April 1977

Address: 100 BROOKWOOD PLACE, Birmingham, AL 35209

Phone: (205) 877-4400   **Domicile State:** AL   **NAIC Code:** 33391

Data Date	Rating	RACR #1	RACR #2	Loss Ratio %	Total Assets ($mil)	Capital ($mil)	Net Premium ($mil)	Net Income ($mil)
2017	C-	2.63	1.92	53.0	1,081.0	348.8	187.0	73.2
2016	C	3.05	2.23	52.5	1,247.2	464.8	197.8	83.7
2015	C+	3.75	2.87	52.2	1,382.6	556.3	197.4	84.1
2014	B-	4.38	3.39	43.7	1,539.3	667.3	213.6	120.3
2013	B-	4.72	3.65	26.8	1,718.4	753.7	240.0	147.5

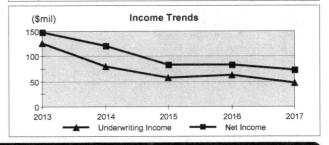

Income Trends

PROGRESSIVE ADVANCED INS CO   C   Fair

Major Rating Factors: Fair overall results on stability tests (3.7 on a scale of 0 to 10) including potential drain of affiliation with Progressive Group. Vulnerable liquidity (1.8) as a spike in claims may stretch capacity.

Other Rating Factors: Strong long-term capitalization index (8.4) based on excellent current risk adjusted capital (severe and moderate loss scenarios). Moreover, capital has steadily grown over the last five years. Ample reserve history (7.4) that can protect against increases in claims costs. Excellent profitability (8.5) with operating gains in each of the last five years.

Principal Business: Auto liability (64%), auto physical damage (35%), and inland marine (1%).

Principal Investments: Investment grade bonds (97%) and non investment grade bonds (3%).

Investments in Affiliates: None

Group Affiliation: Progressive Group

Licensed in: All states except CT, MA, MI, MN, NJ, WY, PR

Commenced Business: August 1930

Address: 6300 WILSON MILLS ROAD W33, Cleveland, OH 44143-2182

Phone: (440) 461-5000   **Domicile State:** OH   **NAIC Code:** 11851

Data Date	Rating	RACR #1	RACR #2	Loss Ratio %	Total Assets ($mil)	Capital ($mil)	Net Premium ($mil)	Net Income ($mil)
2017	C	2.11	1.96	73.6	530.4	224.5	380.1	14.6
2016	C	2.24	2.10	76.5	467.6	199.0	328.2	9.2
2015	C	2.16	2.03	74.5	396.0	167.4	285.0	9.9
2014	C	2.11	1.98	74.3	355.3	147.2	256.3	11.0
2013	C	2.03	1.91	72.4	318.8	129.0	229.7	11.6

Progressive Group
Composite Group Rating: C+

Largest Group Members	Assets ($mil)	Rating
PROGRESSIVE CASUALTY INS CO	8431	B-
PROGRESSIVE DIRECT INS CO	7786	B-
UNITED FINANCIAL CASUALTY CO	3346	B-
PROGRESSIVE NORTHERN INS CO	1866	C+
PROGRESSIVE NORTHWESTERN INS CO	1813	C+

PROGRESSIVE AMERICAN INS CO   C   Fair

Major Rating Factors: Fair overall results on stability tests (3.8 on a scale of 0 to 10) including potential drain of affiliation with Progressive Group and negative cash flow from operations for 2017. Fair reserve development (4.6) as reserves have generally been sufficient to cover claims.

Other Rating Factors: Good liquidity (6.4) with sufficient resources (cash flows and marketable investments) to handle a spike in claims. Strong long-term capitalization index (10.0) based on excellent current risk adjusted capital (severe and moderate loss scenarios). Moreover, capital levels have been consistent in recent years. Excellent profitability (8.2) with operating gains in each of the last five years.

Principal Business: Auto liability (70%), auto physical damage (27%), inland marine (2%), and other liability (1%).

Principal Investments: Investment grade bonds (100%).

Investments in Affiliates: None

Group Affiliation: Progressive Group

Licensed in: AR, CO, FL, GA, HI, IL, IN, KY, ME, MD, MA, MI, MS, MO, MT, NM, NY, NC, ND, OH, OK, UT, VA, WA, WI

Commenced Business: April 1979

Address: 6300 WILSON MILLS ROAD W33, Cleveland, OH 44143-2182

Phone: (440) 461-5000   **Domicile State:** OH   **NAIC Code:** 24252

Data Date	Rating	RACR #1	RACR #2	Loss Ratio %	Total Assets ($mil)	Capital ($mil)	Net Premium ($mil)	Net Income ($mil)
2017	C	3.80	3.40	72.8	585.9	250.3	268.8	11.1
2016	C	3.86	3.49	75.3	493.8	209.3	229.2	7.4
2015	C	3.69	3.35	71.7	427.4	182.8	206.1	12.1
2014	C	3.61	3.29	71.8	416.2	175.4	199.7	12.2
2013	C	3.40	3.10	72.9	390.1	158.5	190.1	8.3

Progressive Group
Composite Group Rating: C+

Largest Group Members	Assets ($mil)	Rating
PROGRESSIVE CASUALTY INS CO	8431	B-
PROGRESSIVE DIRECT INS CO	7786	B-
UNITED FINANCIAL CASUALTY CO	3346	B-
PROGRESSIVE NORTHERN INS CO	1866	C+
PROGRESSIVE NORTHWESTERN INS CO	1813	C+

PROGRESSIVE CASUALTY INS CO

B-   Good

Major Rating Factors: Fair overall results on stability tests (4.5 on a scale of 0 to 10) including potential drain of affiliation with Progressive Group. Fair reserve development (4.7) as reserves have generally been sufficient to cover claims.
Other Rating Factors: Good long-term capitalization index (5.8) based on good current risk adjusted capital (moderate loss scenario). Moreover, capital levels have been consistent over the last several years. Excellent profitability (9.3) with operating gains in each of the last five years. Return on equity has been excellent over the last five years averaging 25.7%. Vulnerable liquidity (2.4) as a spike in claims may stretch capacity.
Principal Business: Auto liability (67%), auto physical damage (29%), inland marine (2%), and other liability (1%).
Principal Investments: Investment grade bonds (55%), misc. investments (36%), real estate (7%), and non investment grade bonds (2%).
Investments in Affiliates: 16%
Group Affiliation: Progressive Group
Licensed in: All states except PR
Commenced Business: December 1956
Address: 6300 WILSON MILLS ROAD W33, Cleveland, OH 44143-2182
Phone: (440) 461-5000   **Domicile State:** OH   **NAIC Code:** 24260

Data Date	Rating	RACR #1	RACR #2	Loss Ratio %	Total Assets ($mil)	Capital ($mil)	Net Premium ($mil)	Net Income ($mil)
2017	B-	1.02	0.86	72.8	8,431.2	2,124.8	6,584.7	370.4
2016	B-	1.04	0.87	75.3	6,967.1	1,818.9	5,614.2	321.5
2015	B-	0.98	0.81	71.7	6,245.6	1,610.1	5,050.3	450.8
2014	C+	0.98	0.83	71.8	6,061.7	1,611.4	4,891.7	528.0
2013	C+	0.94	0.80	72.9	5,781.0	1,543.1	4,657.8	501.3

PROGRESSIVE DIRECT INS CO

B-   Good

Major Rating Factors: Fair overall results on stability tests (4.5 on a scale of 0 to 10) including potential drain of affiliation with Progressive Group. Strong long-term capitalization index (7.2) based on excellent current risk adjusted capital (severe and moderate loss scenarios). Moreover, capital has steadily grown over the last five years.
Other Rating Factors: Ample reserve history (7.5) that can protect against increases in claims costs. Excellent profitability (8.9) with operating gains in each of the last five years. Return on equity has been excellent over the last five years averaging 16.2%. Vulnerable liquidity (1.9) as a spike in claims may stretch capacity.
Principal Business: Auto liability (64%), auto physical damage (35%), and inland marine (1%).
Principal Investments: Investment grade bonds (79%), misc. investments (18%), real estate (2%), and non investment grade bonds (1%).
Investments in Affiliates: None
Group Affiliation: Progressive Group
Licensed in: All states except TX, PR
Commenced Business: January 1987
Address: 6300 WILSON MILLS ROAD W33, Cleveland, OH 44143-2182
Phone: (440) 461-5000   **Domicile State:** OH   **NAIC Code:** 16322

Data Date	Rating	RACR #1	RACR #2	Loss Ratio %	Total Assets ($mil)	Capital ($mil)	Net Premium ($mil)	Net Income ($mil)
2017	B-	1.26	1.14	73.6	7,785.7	2,352.7	7,364.1	402.7
2016	C+	1.32	1.20	76.5	6,727.5	2,065.4	6,358.9	263.9
2015	C	1.30	1.17	74.5	5,835.3	1,783.1	5,521.8	265.6
2014	C-	1.26	1.14	74.3	5,180.2	1,571.5	4,966.6	253.6
2013	C-	1.26	1.13	72.4	4,724.2	1,433.3	4,450.2	286.3

PROGRESSIVE NORTHERN INS CO

C+   Fair

Major Rating Factors: Fair overall results on stability tests (4.4 on a scale of 0 to 10) including potential drain of affiliation with Progressive Group. Fair reserve development (4.7) as reserves have generally been sufficient to cover claims.
Other Rating Factors: Fair liquidity (3.7) as cash resources may not be adequate to cover a spike in claims. Strong long-term capitalization index (7.2) based on excellent current risk adjusted capital (severe and moderate loss scenarios). Moreover, capital levels have been consistent in recent years. Excellent profitability (9.0) with operating gains in each of the last five years. Return on equity has been excellent over the last five years averaging 19.6%.
Principal Business: Auto liability (60%), auto physical damage (36%), inland marine (2%), homeowners multiple peril (1%), and other liability (1%).
Principal Investments: Investment grade bonds (84%) and misc. investments (16%).
Investments in Affiliates: None
Group Affiliation: Progressive Group
Licensed in: All states except AL, AR, CA, FL, MA, MO, NJ, ND, TN, TX, PR
Commenced Business: March 1981
Address: 301 S BEDFORD ST STE 1, Madison, WI 53703
Phone: (440) 461-5000   **Domicile State:** WI   **NAIC Code:** 38628

Data Date	Rating	RACR #1	RACR #2	Loss Ratio %	Total Assets ($mil)	Capital ($mil)	Net Premium ($mil)	Net Income ($mil)
2017	C+	1.33	1.15	72.8	1,866.5	531.4	1,612.6	91.7
2016	C+	1.34	1.18	75.3	1,576.4	442.4	1,374.9	61.0
2015	C+	1.32	1.16	71.7	1,408.4	396.9	1,236.8	88.2
2014	C+	1.30	1.16	71.8	1,349.2	385.8	1,198.0	90.7
2013	C+	1.30	1.15	72.9	1,305.4	370.7	1,140.7	78.6

Progressive Group Composite Group Rating: C+ Largest Group Members	Assets ($mil)	Rating
PROGRESSIVE CASUALTY INS CO	8431	B-
PROGRESSIVE DIRECT INS CO	7786	B-
UNITED FINANCIAL CASUALTY CO	3346	B-
PROGRESSIVE NORTHERN INS CO	1866	C+
PROGRESSIVE NORTHWESTERN INS CO	1813	C+

PROGRESSIVE NORTHWESTERN INS CO   C+   Fair

Major Rating Factors: Fair overall results on stability tests (4.4 on a scale of 0 to 10) including potential drain of affiliation with Progressive Group. Fair reserve development (4.7) as reserves have generally been sufficient to cover claims.
Other Rating Factors: Good liquidity (5.0) with sufficient resources (cash flows and marketable investments) to handle a spike in claims. Strong long-term capitalization index (7.2) based on excellent current risk adjusted capital (severe and moderate loss scenarios). Moreover, capital levels have been consistent in recent years. Excellent profitability (8.9) with operating gains in each of the last five years. Return on equity has been excellent over the last five years averaging 18.5%.
Principal Business: Auto liability (54%), auto physical damage (41%), inland marine (3%), and other liability (2%).
Principal Investments: Investment grade bonds (86%), misc. investments (13%), and non investment grade bonds (1%).
Investments in Affiliates: None
Group Affiliation: Progressive Group
Licensed in: All states except AL, FL, IL, MA, NH, PA, VT, WY, PR
Commenced Business: September 1983
Address: 6300 WILSON MILLS ROAD W33, Cleveland, OH 44143-2182
Phone: (440) 461-5000   **Domicile State:** OH   **NAIC Code:** 42919

Data Date	Rating	RACR #1	RACR #2	Loss Ratio %	Total Assets ($mil)	Capital ($mil)	Net Premium ($mil)	Net Income ($mil)
2017	C+	1.30	1.13	72.8	1,812.5	521.2	1,612.6	85.8
2016	C+	1.34	1.18	75.3	1,537.7	441.6	1,374.9	57.6
2015	C+	1.31	1.16	71.7	1,372.0	396.2	1,236.8	84.5
2014	C+	1.30	1.15	71.8	1,313.5	387.6	1,198.0	92.9
2013	C+	1.30	1.13	72.9	1,267.5	371.6	1,140.7	66.0

Progressive Group
Composite Group Rating: C+

Largest Group Members	Assets ($mil)	Rating
PROGRESSIVE CASUALTY INS CO	8431	B-
PROGRESSIVE DIRECT INS CO	7786	B-
UNITED FINANCIAL CASUALTY CO	3346	B-
PROGRESSIVE NORTHERN INS CO	1866	C+
PROGRESSIVE NORTHWESTERN INS CO	1813	C+

PROGRESSIVE PREFERRED INS CO   C   Fair

Major Rating Factors: Fair overall results on stability tests (3.9 on a scale of 0 to 10) including potential drain of affiliation with Progressive Group. Fair reserve development (4.7) as reserves have generally been sufficient to cover claims.
Other Rating Factors: Fair liquidity (3.1) as cash resources may not be adequate to cover a spike in claims. Strong long-term capitalization index (7.2) based on excellent current risk adjusted capital (severe and moderate loss scenarios). Moreover, capital levels have been consistent in recent years. Excellent profitability (8.9) with operating gains in each of the last five years. Return on equity has been excellent over the last five years averaging 19.2%.
Principal Business: Auto liability (61%), auto physical damage (36%), inland marine (2%), other liability (1%), and homeowners multiple peril (1%).
Principal Investments: Investment grade bonds (98%) and non investment grade bonds (2%).
Investments in Affiliates: None
Group Affiliation: Progressive Group
Licensed in: AK, AZ, CO, DC, DE, GA, HI, ID, IN, IA, KY, ME, MD, MI, MN, MS, MO, MT, NE, NV, NJ, NM, NY, NC, OH, OK, OR, PA, RI, SC, SD, TN, TX, UT, VA, WA, WV
Commenced Business: April 1980
Address: 6300 WILSON MILLS ROAD W33, Cleveland, OH 44143-2182
Phone: (440) 461-5000   **Domicile State:** OH   **NAIC Code:** 37834

Data Date	Rating	RACR #1	RACR #2	Loss Ratio %	Total Assets ($mil)	Capital ($mil)	Net Premium ($mil)	Net Income ($mil)
2017	C	1.30	1.16	72.8	931.1	254.0	806.3	43.6
2016	C	1.37	1.24	75.3	793.2	221.7	687.5	27.6
2015	C	1.35	1.23	71.7	705.5	198.7	618.4	43.0
2014	C	1.35	1.23	71.8	677.1	195.9	599.0	49.6
2013	C	1.32	1.20	72.9	652.5	183.7	570.3	35.4

Progressive Group
Composite Group Rating: C+

Largest Group Members	Assets ($mil)	Rating
PROGRESSIVE CASUALTY INS CO	8431	B-
PROGRESSIVE DIRECT INS CO	7786	B-
UNITED FINANCIAL CASUALTY CO	3346	B-
PROGRESSIVE NORTHERN INS CO	1866	C+
PROGRESSIVE NORTHWESTERN INS CO	1813	C+

PROGRESSIVE SPECIALTY INS CO   C   Fair

Major Rating Factors: Fair overall results on stability tests (4.0 on a scale of 0 to 10) including potential drain of affiliation with Progressive Group. Fair reserve development (4.7) as reserves have generally been sufficient to cover claims.
Other Rating Factors: Vulnerable liquidity (2.9) as a spike in claims may stretch capacity. Strong long-term capitalization index (7.5) based on excellent current risk adjusted capital (severe and moderate loss scenarios), despite some fluctuation in capital levels. Excellent profitability (7.4) with operating gains in each of the last five years. Return on equity has been excellent over the last five years averaging 18.1%.
Principal Business: Auto liability (63%), auto physical damage (34%), inland marine (1%), and homeowners multiple peril (1%).
Principal Investments: Investment grade bonds (73%), misc. investments (26%), and non investment grade bonds (1%).
Investments in Affiliates: None
Group Affiliation: Progressive Group
Licensed in: All states except LA, MA, NH, NC, WY, PR
Commenced Business: May 1976
Address: 6300 WILSON MILLS ROAD W33, Cleveland, OH 44143-2182
Phone: (440) 461-5000   **Domicile State:** OH   **NAIC Code:** 32786

Data Date	Rating	RACR #1	RACR #2	Loss Ratio %	Total Assets ($mil)	Capital ($mil)	Net Premium ($mil)	Net Income ($mil)
2017	C	1.54	1.31	72.8	1,166.3	366.4	940.7	63.7
2016	C	1.35	1.17	75.3	943.0	263.4	802.0	38.1
2015	C	1.49	1.29	71.7	864.7	266.4	721.5	48.3
2014	C	1.78	1.54	71.8	880.2	314.1	698.8	56.9
2013	C	2.27	1.96	72.9	941.3	386.2	665.4	87.0

Progressive Group
Composite Group Rating: C+

Largest Group Members	Assets ($mil)	Rating
PROGRESSIVE CASUALTY INS CO	8431	B-
PROGRESSIVE DIRECT INS CO	7786	B-
UNITED FINANCIAL CASUALTY CO	3346	B-
PROGRESSIVE NORTHERN INS CO	1866	C+
PROGRESSIVE NORTHWESTERN INS CO	1813	C+

PROPERTY-OWNERS INS CO *

A-   Excellent

Major Rating Factors: Strong long-term capitalization index (7.5 on a scale of 0 to 10) based on excellent current risk adjusted capital (severe and moderate loss scenarios). Furthermore, this high level of risk adjusted capital has been consistently maintained in previous years. Excellent profitability (8.6) with operating gains in each of the last five years.

Other Rating Factors: Excellent overall results on stability tests (7.0). Stability strengths include good operational trends and excellent risk diversification. History of adequate reserve strength (5.6) as reserves have been consistently at an acceptable level. Good liquidity (6.1) with sufficient resources (cash flows and marketable investments) to handle a spike in claims.

Principal Business: Homeowners multiple peril (45%), commercial multiple peril (26%), auto liability (8%), workers compensation (6%), auto physical damage (5%), inland marine (3%), and other lines (7%).

Principal Investments: Investment grade bonds (88%), misc. investments (10%), cash (1%), and non investment grade bonds (1%).

Investments in Affiliates: None

Group Affiliation: Auto-Owners Group

Licensed in: AL, AR, GA, IL, IN, IA, KY, MI, MO, NE, NV, ND, SC, SD, UT, VA, WI

Commenced Business: September 1976

Address: 3950 WEST DELPHI PIKE, Marion, IN 46952-9266

Phone: (517) 323-1200   **Domicile State:** IN   **NAIC Code:** 32905

Data Date	Rating	RACR #1	RACR #2	Loss Ratio %	Total Assets ($mil)	Capital ($mil)	Net Premium ($mil)	Net Income ($mil)
2017	A-	2.22	1.32	56.2	302.7	137.0	125.8	11.9
2016	B+	2.14	1.27	56.5	280.6	124.1	119.5	5.6
2015	B+	3.46	1.99	60.7	232.4	115.7	78.9	6.5
2014	B+	3.53	2.09	64.6	216.2	109.6	72.4	5.0
2013	A	3.83	2.21	55.5	209.7	104.5	70.0	9.0

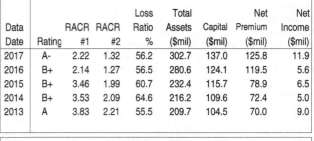

Risk-Adjusted Capital Ratio #2
(Severe Loss Scenario)

■ Weak   ■ Fair   ▨ Good   ☐ Strong

PROTECTIVE INS CO *

A-   Excellent

Major Rating Factors: Strong long-term capitalization index (7.2 on a scale of 0 to 10) based on excellent current risk adjusted capital (severe and moderate loss scenarios). Furthermore, this high level of risk adjusted capital has been consistently maintained in previous years. Excellent profitability (7.7) with operating gains in each of the last five years.

Other Rating Factors: Excellent overall results on stability tests (7.0). Stability strengths include excellent operational trends and excellent risk diversification. History of adequate reserve strength (5.9) as reserves have been consistently at an acceptable level. Good liquidity (6.3) with sufficient resources (cash flows and marketable investments) to handle a spike in claims.

Principal Business: Workers compensation (33%), auto liability (24%), other liability (19%), auto physical damage (16%), group accident & health (5%), and surety (1%).

Principal Investments: Misc. investments (63%), investment grade bonds (28%), non investment grade bonds (8%), and real estate (3%).

Investments in Affiliates: 25%

Group Affiliation: Protective Ins Group

Licensed in: All states, the District of Columbia and Puerto Rico

Commenced Business: December 1954

Address: 111 Congressional Blvd Ste 500, Carmel, IN 46032

Phone: (317) 636-9800   **Domicile State:** IN   **NAIC Code:** 12416

Data Date	Rating	RACR #1	RACR #2	Loss Ratio %	Total Assets ($mil)	Capital ($mil)	Net Premium ($mil)	Net Income ($mil)
2017	A-	1.53	1.17	74.9	885.6	420.4	330.1	20.3
2016	B+	1.59	1.24	65.7	785.4	398.0	255.7	23.2
2015	B	1.54	1.13	57.4	753.5	389.4	233.2	27.1
2014	B	1.51	1.09	56.7	791.8	397.4	235.5	29.7
2013	A-	1.42	1.03	57.6	741.1	375.8	228.0	28.6

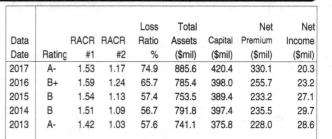

($mil)   Capital

QBE INS CORP

B   Good

Major Rating Factors: History of adequate reserve strength (5.8 on a scale of 0 to 10) as reserves have been consistently at an acceptable level. Good liquidity (5.8) with sufficient resources (cash flows and marketable investments) to handle a spike in claims.

Other Rating Factors: Good overall results on stability tests (5.5) despite negative cash flow from operations for 2017. Stability strengths include good operational trends and excellent risk diversification. Strong long-term capitalization index (7.6) based on excellent current risk adjusted capital (severe and moderate loss scenarios), despite some fluctuation in capital levels. Weak profitability index (2.9) with operating losses during 2013 and 2017. Average return on equity over the last five years has been poor at -0.9%.

Principal Business: Group accident & health (22%), other liability (21%), homeowners multiple peril (16%), commercial multiple peril (11%), workers compensation (8%), allied lines (6%), and other lines (17%).

Principal Investments: Investment grade bonds (68%) and misc. investments (33%).

Investments in Affiliates: 9%

Group Affiliation: QBE Ins Group Ltd

Licensed in: All states except PR

Commenced Business: October 1980

Address: 600 N 2ND STE 401, Harrisburg, PA 17101

Phone: (608) 825-5160   **Domicile State:** PA   **NAIC Code:** 39217

Data Date	Rating	RACR #1	RACR #2	Loss Ratio %	Total Assets ($mil)	Capital ($mil)	Net Premium ($mil)	Net Income ($mil)
2017	B	2.16	1.43	75.6	2,054.3	678.0	890.9	-23.7
2016	B	2.48	1.70	58.8	2,325.0	748.9	846.9	27.7
2015	B-	2.46	1.81	63.9	2,134.5	735.7	597.0	28.8
2014	C+	2.08	1.58	69.2	2,113.3	681.2	742.1	4.2
2013	C	1.95	1.49	75.2	2,138.2	678.7	750.5	-61.1

Reserve Deficiency (as % of capital)

* Adequate & redundant reserves show as negatives

■ 1 Yr Dev   ☐ 2 Yr Dev

QBE REINS CORP   B   Good

Major Rating Factors: Good overall results on stability tests (5.2 on a scale of 0 to 10) despite potential drain of affiliation with QBE Ins Group Ltd and negative cash flow from operations for 2017. Stability strengths include good operational trends and excellent risk diversification. History of adequate reserve strength (6.2) as reserves have been consistently at an acceptable level.

Other Rating Factors: Good liquidity (6.4) with sufficient resources (cash flows and marketable investments) to handle a spike in claims. Fair profitability index (3.9) with operating losses during 2017. Return on equity has been low, averaging 0.4% over the past five years. Strong long-term capitalization index (7.5) based on excellent current risk adjusted capital (severe and moderate loss scenarios), despite some fluctuation in capital levels.

Principal Business: (This company is a reinsurer.)

Principal Investments: Misc. investments (92%), investment grade bonds (7%), and cash (1%).

Investments in Affiliates: 71%

Group Affiliation: QBE Ins Group Ltd

Licensed in: All states, the District of Columbia and Puerto Rico

Commenced Business: October 1964

Address: 600 N 2ND STE 401, Harrisburg, PA 17101

Phone: (608) 825-5160   **Domicile State:** PA   **NAIC Code:** 10219

Data Date	Rating	RACR #1	RACR #2	Loss Ratio %	Total Assets ($mil)	Capital ($mil)	Net Premium ($mil)	Net Income ($mil)
2017	B-	1.37	1.34	75.6	1,031.4	773.0	177.0	-3.3
2016	B	1.39	1.36	58.8	1,171.1	863.6	147.5	1.1
2015	B	1.33	1.31	63.9	1,147.8	813.3	186.6	11.9
2014	B	1.44	1.41	69.2	1,176.1	826.8	168.3	5.0
2013	B	1.40	1.36	75.2	1,232.9	814.7	210.4	0.0

Rating Indexes

QUINCY MUTUAL FIRE INS CO   B   Good

Major Rating Factors: Good liquidity (6.9 on a scale of 0 to 10) with sufficient resources (cash flows and marketable investments) to handle a spike in claims. Fair overall results on stability tests (4.7) including potential drain of affiliation with Quincy Mutual Group.

Other Rating Factors: Strong long-term capitalization index (9.6) based on excellent current risk adjusted capital (severe and moderate loss scenarios), despite some fluctuation in capital levels. Ample reserve history (8.0) that helps to protect the company against sharp claims increases. Excellent profitability (7.6) with operating gains in each of the last five years.

Principal Business: Homeowners multiple peril (30%), auto liability (26%), auto physical damage (20%), commercial multiple peril (18%), allied lines (3%), and fire (2%).

Principal Investments: Misc. investments (59%), investment grade bonds (35%), non investment grade bonds (4%), cash (1%), and real estate (1%).

Investments in Affiliates: 3%

Group Affiliation: Quincy Mutual Group

Licensed in: CT, ME, MA, NH, NJ, NY, PA, RI

Commenced Business: May 1851

Address: 57 Washington Street, Quincy, MA 2169

Phone: (617) 770-5100   **Domicile State:** MA   **NAIC Code:** 15067

Data Date	Rating	RACR #1	RACR #2	Loss Ratio %	Total Assets ($mil)	Capital ($mil)	Net Premium ($mil)	Net Income ($mil)
2017	B	4.66	2.95	69.2	1,774.9	1,190.6	307.0	47.1
2016	B	4.42	2.81	52.4	1,619.5	1,079.9	307.7	62.0
2015	B	3.95	2.50	78.5	1,508.0	977.0	313.3	14.6
2014	B	3.82	2.40	45.2	1,510.5	994.7	269.3	77.0
2013	B	3.71	2.30	55.6	1,471.1	927.1	296.3	49.8

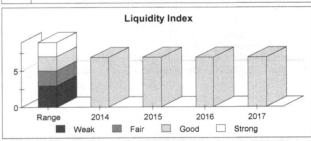

Liquidity Index

RADIAN GUARANTY INC   D+   Weak

Major Rating Factors: Weak overall results on stability tests (2.4 on a scale of 0 to 10). Fair reserve development (4.6) as reserves have generally been sufficient to cover claims. In 2013, the two year reserve development was 27% deficient.

Other Rating Factors: Fair profitability index (3.5) with operating losses during 2013. Return on equity has been fair, averaging 27.3% over the past five years. Good liquidity (6.9) with sufficient resources (cash flows and marketable investments) to handle a spike in claims. Strong long-term capitalization index (8.6) based on excellent current risk adjusted capital (severe and moderate loss scenarios), despite some fluctuation in capital levels.

Principal Business: Mortgage guaranty (100%).

Principal Investments: Investment grade bonds (89%), misc. investments (7%), non investment grade bonds (3%), and cash (1%).

Investments in Affiliates: None

Group Affiliation: Radian Group Inc

Licensed in: All states except PR

Commenced Business: April 1977

Address: 1500 MARKET STREET, Philadelphia, PA 19102

Phone: (800) 523-1988   **Domicile State:** PA   **NAIC Code:** 33790

Data Date	Rating	RACR #1	RACR #2	Loss Ratio %	Total Assets ($mil)	Capital ($mil)	Net Premium ($mil)	Net Income ($mil)
2017	D+	4.73	3.30	14.7	4,071.2	1,201.0	706.8	445.1
2016	D+	2.22	1.86	22.7	3,900.1	1,349.7	628.7	480.8
2015	D+	2.04	1.73	22.2	4,009.0	1,686.5	845.7	754.8
2014	D	0.85	0.76	33.0	3,643.3	1,325.2	797.5	273.7
2013	D	0.66	0.59	81.6	3,657.5	1,317.8	814.4	-23.8

Rating Indexes

RADIAN REINS INC *

A-   Excellent

Major Rating Factors: Strong long-term capitalization index (10.0 on a scale of 0 to 10) based on excellent current risk adjusted capital (severe and moderate loss scenarios). Furthermore, this high level of risk adjusted capital has been consistently maintained in previous years. Excellent profitability (9.6) despite modest operating losses during 2015. Excellent expense controls.

Other Rating Factors: Excellent liquidity (8.1) with ample operational cash flow and liquid investments. Good overall results on stability tests (5.7) despite weak results on operational trends. Fair reserve development (3.9) as reserves have generally been sufficient to cover claims.

Principal Business: Mortgage guaranty (100%).

Principal Investments: Investment grade bonds (93%), misc. investments (4%), non investment grade bonds (2%), and cash (1%).

Investments in Affiliates: None

Group Affiliation: Radian Group Inc

Licensed in: PA

Commenced Business: December 2015

Address: 1500 MARKET STREET, Philadelphia, PA 19102

Phone: (800) 523-1988   **Domicile State:** PA   **NAIC Code:** 15842

Data Date	Rating	RACR #1	RACR #2	Loss Ratio %	Total Assets ($mil)	Capital ($mil)	Net Premium ($mil)	Net Income ($mil)
2017	A-	10.81	6.64	18.8	704.2	328.9	111.1	64.3
2016	A-	3.16	2.09	21.7	491.9	147.6	104.3	60.3
2015	U	1.95	1.33	34.9	466.6	138.7	63.9	-1.0
2014	N/A	N/A	N/A	0.0	0.0	0.0	0.0	0.0
2013	N/A	N/A	N/A	0.0	0.0	0.0	0.0	0.0

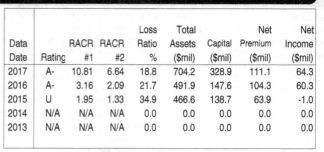

Risk-Adjusted Capital Ratio #2
(Severe Loss Scenario)

REDWOOD FIRE & CAS INS CO

C   Fair

Major Rating Factors: Fair long-term capitalization index (4.9 on a scale of 0 to 10) based on good current risk adjusted capital (severe loss scenario). Moreover, capital levels have been consistent over the last several years. Fair overall results on stability tests (4.4).

Other Rating Factors: Ample reserve history (8.8) that helps to protect the company against sharp claims increases. Excellent profitability (8.7) with operating gains in each of the last five years. Excellent liquidity (8.7) with ample operational cash flow and liquid investments.

Principal Business: Workers compensation (85%), auto liability (11%), and auto physical damage (3%).

Principal Investments: Investment grade bonds (52%), misc. investments (32%), and cash (16%).

Investments in Affiliates: None

Group Affiliation: Berkshire-Hathaway

Licensed in: All states except PR

Commenced Business: January 1970

Address: 1314 DOUGLAS ST STE 1300, Omaha, NE 68102-1944

Phone: (402) 393-7255   **Domicile State:** NE   **NAIC Code:** 11673

Data Date	Rating	RACR #1	RACR #2	Loss Ratio %	Total Assets ($mil)	Capital ($mil)	Net Premium ($mil)	Net Income ($mil)
2017	C+	1.27	0.76	67.5	1,893.7	759.5	424.2	50.7
2016	C	0.94	0.58	63.8	1,655.1	637.3	386.1	53.0
2015	C	0.78	0.49	70.2	1,428.0	552.8	401.2	46.8
2014	C	0.73	0.47	72.6	1,257.7	533.3	377.0	5.1
2013	C	0.93	0.59	66.9	1,031.3	506.0	286.9	49.2

Risk-Adjusted Capital Ratio #1
(Moderate Loss Scenario)

RENAISSANCE RE US INC

B   Good

Major Rating Factors: Good overall profitability index (5.5 on a scale of 0 to 10) despite operating losses during 2017. Return on equity has been fair, averaging 9.5% over the past five years. Good liquidity (6.8) with sufficient resources (cash flows and marketable investments) to handle a spike in claims.

Other Rating Factors: Good overall results on stability tests (5.9) despite fair results on operational trends. Strong long-term capitalization index (7.3) based on excellent current risk adjusted capital (severe and moderate loss scenarios), despite some fluctuation in capital levels. Ample reserve history (9.4) that helps to protect the company against sharp claims increases.

Principal Business: (This company is a reinsurer.)

Principal Investments: Investment grade bonds (87%), misc. investments (10%), and cash (3%).

Investments in Affiliates: None

Group Affiliation: RenaissanceRe Holdings Ltd

Licensed in: All states, the District of Columbia and Puerto Rico

Commenced Business: December 1995

Address: 140 Broadway Suite 4200, New York, NY 10005

Phone: (212) 238-9600   **Domicile State:** MD   **NAIC Code:** 10357

Data Date	Rating	RACR #1	RACR #2	Loss Ratio %	Total Assets ($mil)	Capital ($mil)	Net Premium ($mil)	Net Income ($mil)
2017	B	1.80	1.19	76.9	1,633.7	523.4	351.8	-3.6
2016	B	3.12	1.98	55.8	1,492.8	523.3	248.6	43.3
2015	B-	2.74	1.71	51.6	1,508.0	521.5	323.7	58.8
2014	B-	2.67	1.66	52.3	1,564.7	531.4	339.3	62.1
2013	B-	2.46	1.53	43.4	1,620.3	549.2	395.4	93.2

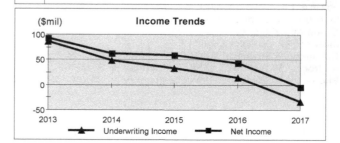

Income Trends

REPUBLIC INDEMNITY CO OF AMERICA   B-   Good

Major Rating Factors: Fair long-term capitalization (4.8 on a scale of 0 to 10) based on fair current risk adjusted capital (moderate loss scenario), although results have slipped from the good range over the last two years. Good liquidity (6.2) with sufficient resources (cash flows and marketable investments) to handle a spike in claims.

Other Rating Factors: Good overall results on stability tests (5.0) despite fair risk adjusted capital in prior years. Ample reserve history (9.4) that helps to protect the company against sharp claims increases. Excellent profitability (7.3) with operating gains in each of the last five years. Return on equity has been excellent over the last five years averaging 15.7%.

Principal Business: Workers compensation (100%).

Principal Investments: Investment grade bonds (79%), misc. investments (19%), cash (1%), and non investment grade bonds (1%).

Investments in Affiliates: 1%

Group Affiliation: American Financial Group Inc

Licensed in: All states except CT, MA, MN, NH, NJ, NY, ND, PA, VT, WY, PR

Commenced Business: March 1973

Address: 15821 Ventura Blvd Ste 370, Encino, CA 91436

Phone: (818) 990-9860   **Domicile State:** CA   **NAIC Code:** 22179

Data Date	Rating	RACR #1	RACR #2	Loss Ratio %	Total Assets ($mil)	Capital ($mil)	Net Premium ($mil)	Net Income ($mil)
2017	B-	0.96	0.72	61.6	2,267.3	465.1	834.3	126.5
2016	B-	1.10	0.83	64.1	2,300.3	532.3	791.2	104.5
2015	C+	1.10	0.82	65.0	2,292.4	537.3	793.3	98.9
2014	C+	1.13	0.83	67.0	2,229.5	503.6	665.9	6.7
2013	C+	1.72	1.24	68.6	847.7	252.3	209.3	30.4

RETAILFIRST INS CO *   A   Excellent

Major Rating Factors: Strong long-term capitalization index (8.5 on a scale of 0 to 10) based on excellent current risk adjusted capital (severe and moderate loss scenarios). Furthermore, this high level of risk adjusted capital has been consistently maintained in previous years. Excellent profitability (8.3) with operating gains in each of the last five years.

Other Rating Factors: Excellent overall results on stability tests (7.1). Stability strengths include excellent operational trends and excellent risk diversification. History of adequate reserve strength (6.9) as reserves have been consistently at an acceptable level. Good liquidity (6.5) with sufficient resources (cash flows and marketable investments) to handle a spike in claims.

Principal Business: Workers compensation (100%).

Principal Investments: Investment grade bonds (84%), misc. investments (15%), and real estate (1%).

Investments in Affiliates: None

Group Affiliation: RetailFirst Mutual Holdings Inc

Licensed in: FL

Commenced Business: January 1979

Address: 2310 Commerce Point Drive, Lakeland, FL 33801

Phone: (863) 665-6060   **Domicile State:** FL   **NAIC Code:** 10700

Data Date	Rating	RACR #1	RACR #2	Loss Ratio %	Total Assets ($mil)	Capital ($mil)	Net Premium ($mil)	Net Income ($mil)
2017	A	2.58	2.01	64.7	325.1	156.3	117.9	9.5
2016	B+	2.53	1.98	69.9	303.0	145.0	110.5	7.2
2015	B	2.64	2.07	68.0	285.5	137.1	100.0	6.9
2014	B	2.45	1.89	69.8	284.9	138.7	100.0	6.8
2013	A-	2.22	1.68	71.1	265.2	130.4	94.8	2.9

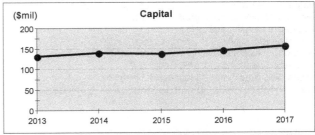

RLI INS CO   B   Good

Major Rating Factors: Good overall results on stability tests (5.7 on a scale of 0 to 10) despite potential drain of affiliation with RLI Corp. Stability strengths include good operational trends and excellent risk diversification. Good overall profitability index (6.1). Weak expense controls. Return on equity has been excellent over the last five years averaging 19.4%.

Other Rating Factors: Good liquidity (6.9) with sufficient resources (cash flows and marketable investments) to handle a spike in claims. Strong long-term capitalization index (7.2) based on excellent current risk adjusted capital (severe and moderate loss scenarios), despite some fluctuation in capital levels. Ample reserve history (7.8) that can protect against increases in claims costs.

Principal Business: Other liability (39%), surety (21%), auto liability (17%), inland marine (6%), ocean marine (5%), commercial multiple peril (3%), and other lines (10%).

Principal Investments: Misc. investments (54%), investment grade bonds (38%), non investment grade bonds (5%), real estate (2%), and cash (1%).

Investments in Affiliates: 33%

Group Affiliation: RLI Corp

Licensed in: All states, the District of Columbia and Puerto Rico

Commenced Business: November 1960

Address: 9025 N Lindbergh Drive, Peoria, IL 61615

Phone: (309) 692-1000   **Domicile State:** IL   **NAIC Code:** 13056

Data Date	Rating	RACR #1	RACR #2	Loss Ratio %	Total Assets ($mil)	Capital ($mil)	Net Premium ($mil)	Net Income ($mil)
2017	B	1.36	1.16	52.4	1,817.0	864.6	453.1	97.6
2016	B	1.34	1.16	52.1	1,753.4	860.0	456.3	107.3
2015	B	1.37	1.18	47.4	1,725.1	865.3	450.9	183.2
2014	B	1.31	1.14	50.6	1,707.0	849.3	437.6	238.4
2013	B	1.25	1.12	50.8	1,679.4	859.2	413.2	205.9

ROCKINGHAM INS CO *

B+   Good

Major Rating Factors: Good liquidity (6.2 on a scale of 0 to 10) with sufficient resources (cash flows and marketable investments) to handle a spike in claims. Good overall results on stability tests (6.5). Stability strengths include excellent operational trends and good risk diversification.

Other Rating Factors: Strong long-term capitalization index (7.1) based on excellent current risk adjusted capital (severe and moderate loss scenarios). Moreover, capital levels have been consistent in recent years. Ample reserve history (8.7) that helps to protect the company against sharp claims increases. Excellent profitability (7.9) despite modest operating losses during 2013.

Principal Business: Homeowners multiple peril (55%), farmowners multiple peril (18%), fire (15%), and other liability (12%).

Principal Investments: Investment grade bonds (52%), misc. investments (43%), cash (4%), and real estate (1%).

Investments in Affiliates: 22%

Group Affiliation: Rockingham Group

Licensed in: MA, NY, PA, VA

Commenced Business: May 1968

Address: 633 East Market Street, Harrisonburg, VA 22801

Phone: (540) 434-5344   **Domicile State:** VA   **NAIC Code:** 10214

Data Date	Rating	RACR #1	RACR #2	Loss Ratio %	Total Assets ($mil)	Capital ($mil)	Net Premium ($mil)	Net Income ($mil)
2017	B+	1.28	1.12	55.8	144.7	76.8	56.4	4.3
2016	B	1.20	1.06	61.2	133.3	68.9	47.7	2.5
2015	B-	1.09	0.96	62.3	121.8	63.6	44.0	2.8
2014	C+	1.08	0.95	61.3	116.7	61.6	40.0	2.6
2013	C+	1.03	0.90	69.0	107.7	58.6	36.4	-0.4

Liquidity Index

RSUI INDEMNITY CO

B-   Good

Major Rating Factors: Fair overall results on stability tests (4.5 on a scale of 0 to 10) including potential drain of affiliation with Alleghany Corp Group. Good liquidity (6.8) with sufficient resources (cash flows and marketable investments) to handle a spike in claims.

Other Rating Factors: Strong long-term capitalization index (8.1) based on excellent current risk adjusted capital (severe and moderate loss scenarios), despite some fluctuation in capital levels. Ample reserve history (8.1) that helps to protect the company against sharp claims increases. Excellent profitability (8.6) with operating gains in each of the last five years. Return on equity has been good over the last five years, averaging 11.0%.

Principal Business: Other liability (73%), allied lines (15%), fire (8%), inland marine (2%), and earthquake (2%).

Principal Investments: Misc. investments (48%), investment grade bonds (46%), and non investment grade bonds (6%).

Investments in Affiliates: 7%

Group Affiliation: Alleghany Corp Group

Licensed in: All states except PR

Commenced Business: December 1977

Address: 900 Elm Street, Manchester, NH 3101

Phone: (404) 231-2366   **Domicile State:** NH   **NAIC Code:** 22314

Data Date	Rating	RACR #1	RACR #2	Loss Ratio %	Total Assets ($mil)	Capital ($mil)	Net Premium ($mil)	Net Income ($mil)
2017	B-	2.50	1.70	79.0	3,637.8	1,624.3	670.9	94.4
2016	C+	2.47	1.75	53.4	3,401.7	1,529.3	681.0	175.2
2015	C+	2.36	1.69	53.8	3,329.0	1,481.6	720.4	201.0
2014	C+	2.45	1.75	51.8	3,286.8	1,466.1	764.3	197.5
2013	C+	2.68	1.92	53.4	3,323.2	1,492.4	765.1	160.2

Rating Indexes

RURAL COMMUNITY INS CO

C+   Fair

Major Rating Factors: Fair overall results on stability tests (4.4 on a scale of 0 to 10) including weak results on operational trends and negative cash flow from operations for 2017. Strengths include potentially strong support from affiliation with Zurich Insurance Group Ltd. History of adequate reserve strength (6.2) as reserves have been consistently at an acceptable level.

Other Rating Factors: Good liquidity (6.9) with sufficient resources (cash flows and marketable investments) to handle a spike in claims. Weak profitability index (2.2) with operating losses during 2017. Return on equity has been low, averaging 3.9% over the past five years. Strong long-term capitalization index (9.5) based on excellent current risk adjusted capital (severe and moderate loss scenarios), despite some fluctuation in capital levels.

Principal Business: Allied lines (100%).

Principal Investments: Investment grade bonds (95%), cash (4%), and misc. investments (1%).

Investments in Affiliates: None

Group Affiliation: Zurich Insurance Group Ltd

Licensed in: All states except PR

Commenced Business: April 1980

Address: 3501 THURSTON AVENUE, Anoka, MN 55303

Phone: (847) 605-6000   **Domicile State:** MN   **NAIC Code:** 39039

Data Date	Rating	RACR #1	RACR #2	Loss Ratio %	Total Assets ($mil)	Capital ($mil)	Net Premium ($mil)	Net Income ($mil)
2017	C+	5.28	2.64	0.0	1,790.7	247.1	0.0	-14.0
2016	C+	5.66	2.83	N/A	1,753.7	267.0	-35.3	19.2
2015	B	13.89	7.16	79.1	3,680.0	693.8	362.9	76.1
2014	B	10.11	5.84	91.2	3,758.2	618.5	380.1	21.1
2013	B	9.16	5.06	92.9	5,245.2	599.8	491.5	20.9

Zurich Insurance Group Ltd Composite Group Rating: B Largest Group Members	Assets ($mil)	Rating
ZURICH AMERICAN INS CO	31582	B
ZURICH AMERICAN LIFE INS CO	14227	C
FARMERS NEW WORLD LIFE INS CO	5127	B-
CENTRE LIFE INS CO	1791	B-
RURAL COMMUNITY INS CO	1791	C+

RURAL MUTUAL INS CO   B-   Good

Major Rating Factors: Fair overall results on stability tests (4.7 on a scale of 0 to 10) including potential drain of affiliation with Wisconsin Farm Bureau Federation. Good liquidity (6.7) with sufficient resources (cash flows and marketable investments) to handle a spike in claims.

Other Rating Factors: Strong long-term capitalization index (10.0) based on excellent current risk adjusted capital (severe and moderate loss scenarios). Moreover, capital has steadily grown over the last five years. Ample reserve history (8.1) that helps to protect the company against sharp claims increases. Excellent profitability (8.9) with operating gains in each of the last five years. Return on equity has been good over the last five years, averaging 10.3%.

Principal Business: Farmowners multiple peril (32%), workers compensation (17%), commercial multiple peril (15%), auto liability (14%), auto physical damage (11%), homeowners multiple peril (9%), and allied lines (1%).

Principal Investments: Investment grade bonds (86%), misc. investments (13%), and non investment grade bonds (1%).

Investments in Affiliates: None

Group Affiliation: Wisconsin Farm Bureau Federation

Licensed in: IL, MN, WI

Commenced Business: June 1935

Address: 1241 JOHN Q HAMMONS DR STE 200, Madison, WI 53717-1929

Phone: (608) 836-5525   **Domicile State:** WI   **NAIC Code:** 15091

Data Date	Rating	RACR #1	RACR #2	Loss Ratio %	Total Assets ($mil)	Capital ($mil)	Net Premium ($mil)	Net Income ($mil)
2017	B-	6.92	4.57	59.1	484.2	266.5	174.5	28.4
2016	B-	6.41	4.32	57.7	460.1	241.7	171.4	24.9
2015	B-	6.18	4.19	59.9	419.9	213.5	162.6	21.3
2014	C+	5.99	4.08	59.8	385.9	194.0	152.9	20.0
2013	C+	5.74	3.93	59.7	356.6	176.5	144.7	18.1

Rating Indexes

SAFECO INS CO OF AMERICA   B   Good

Major Rating Factors: History of adequate reserve strength (5.8 on a scale of 0 to 10) as reserves have been consistently at an acceptable level. Good overall profitability index (6.4). Fair expense controls. Return on equity has been fair, averaging 6.8% over the past five years.

Other Rating Factors: Good liquidity (6.2) with sufficient resources (cash flows and marketable investments) to handle a spike in claims. Good overall results on stability tests (5.5). Strong long-term capitalization index (8.2) based on excellent current risk adjusted capital (severe and moderate loss scenarios). Moreover, capital levels have been consistent in recent years.

Principal Business: Homeowners multiple peril (42%), auto liability (20%), auto physical damage (17%), allied lines (7%), other liability (5%), fire (5%), and other lines (3%).

Principal Investments: Investment grade bonds (72%), misc. investments (23%), and non investment grade bonds (6%).

Investments in Affiliates: 6%

Group Affiliation: Liberty Mutual Group

Licensed in: All states except PR

Commenced Business: October 1953

Address: 62 Maple Avenue, Keene, NH 3431

Phone: (617) 357-9500   **Domicile State:** NH   **NAIC Code:** 24740

Data Date	Rating	RACR #1	RACR #2	Loss Ratio %	Total Assets ($mil)	Capital ($mil)	Net Premium ($mil)	Net Income ($mil)
2017	B	2.61	1.89	79.5	4,863.4	1,503.3	1,713.0	27.2
2016	B-	2.72	1.93	69.9	4,485.1	1,497.9	1,589.9	46.9
2015	B-	2.56	1.80	68.4	4,356.9	1,393.4	1,537.9	103.6
2014	B-	2.33	1.61	70.0	4,233.3	1,278.9	1,522.6	106.8
2013	B-	2.18	1.48	73.5	4,747.1	1,188.7	1,349.1	154.8

Reserve Deficiency (as % of capital)

* Adequate & redundant reserves show as negatives

SAFETY INS CO   B-   Good

Major Rating Factors: Fair overall results on stability tests (4.7 on a scale of 0 to 10) including potential drain of affiliation with Safety Group. Fair profitability index (4.9) with operating losses during 2015. Return on equity has been fair, averaging 6.7% over the past five years.

Other Rating Factors: Good liquidity (6.3) with sufficient resources (cash flows and marketable investments) to handle a spike in claims. Strong long-term capitalization index (8.8) based on excellent current risk adjusted capital (severe and moderate loss scenarios), despite some fluctuation in capital levels. Ample reserve history (9.1) that helps to protect the company against sharp claims increases.

Principal Business: Auto liability (50%), auto physical damage (35%), homeowners multiple peril (8%), commercial multiple peril (3%), other liability (1%), allied lines (1%), and fire (1%).

Principal Investments: Investment grade bonds (71%), misc. investments (20%), and non investment grade bonds (11%).

Investments in Affiliates: 7%

Group Affiliation: Safety Group

Licensed in: ME, MA, NH

Commenced Business: January 1980

Address: 20 Custom House Street, Boston, MA 2110

Phone: (617) 951-0600   **Domicile State:** MA   **NAIC Code:** 39454

Data Date	Rating	RACR #1	RACR #2	Loss Ratio %	Total Assets ($mil)	Capital ($mil)	Net Premium ($mil)	Net Income ($mil)
2017	B-	3.15	2.19	65.1	1,503.6	617.6	702.9	58.0
2016	B-	3.22	2.25	65.3	1,480.5	604.8	689.8	57.2
2015	B-	3.15	2.21	83.0	1,434.6	571.0	671.6	-12.2
2014	B-	3.67	2.72	66.5	1,430.1	630.0	661.4	51.2
2013	B+	3.72	2.71	65.7	1,396.8	628.0	627.8	53.1

Rating Indexes

SAFETY NATIONAL CASUALTY CORP
C   Fair

Major Rating Factors: Fair reserve development (3.1 on a scale of 0 to 10) as the level of reserves has at times been insufficient to cover claims. In 2014 and 2013 the two year reserve development was 16% and 45% deficient respectively. Fair overall results on stability tests (3.9).

Other Rating Factors: Good overall profitability index (6.5). Good expense controls. Return on equity has been fair, averaging 9.9% over the past five years. Strong long-term capitalization index (7.3) based on excellent current risk adjusted capital (severe and moderate loss scenarios). Moreover, capital has steadily grown over the last five years. Excellent liquidity (7.2) with ample operational cash flow and liquid investments.

Principal Business: Workers compensation (24%), auto liability (5%), other liability (4%), and products liability (1%).

Principal Investments: Investment grade bonds (54%), misc. investments (29%), non investment grade bonds (16%), and cash (1%).

Investments in Affiliates: 4%

Group Affiliation: Tokio Marine Holdings Inc

Licensed in: All states, the District of Columbia and Puerto Rico

Commenced Business: December 1942

Address: 1832 Schuetz Road, St. Louis, MO 63146-3540

Phone: (314) 995-5300   **Domicile State:** MO   **NAIC Code:** 15105

Data Date	Rating	RACR #1	RACR #2	Loss Ratio %	Total Assets ($mil)	Capital ($mil)	Net Premium ($mil)	Net Income ($mil)
2017	C	1.85	1.30	88.5	7,223.8	2,081.9	882.6	203.6
2016	C	1.71	1.26	84.6	6,435.2	1,812.6	778.4	190.5
2015	C	1.54	1.16	86.1	5,611.3	1,527.0	728.9	159.3
2014	C	1.46	1.10	87.8	4,985.1	1,367.6	671.2	110.2
2013	C	1.39	1.06	78.4	4,183.6	1,153.8	664.9	122.7

Reserve Deficiency (as % of capital)

* Adequate & redundant reserves show as negatives

■ 1 Yr Dev
□ 2 Yr Dev

SAFEWAY INS CO
B-   Good

Major Rating Factors: Fair overall results on stability tests (4.5 on a scale of 0 to 10) including potential drain of affiliation with Safeway Ins Group. Fair reserve development (4.4) as reserves have generally been sufficient to cover claims.

Other Rating Factors: Fair profitability index (4.7) with operating losses during 2013, 2016 and 2017. Return on equity has been low, averaging 2.2% over the past five years. Good liquidity (5.4) with sufficient resources (cash flows and marketable investments) to handle a spike in claims. Strong long-term capitalization index (7.6) based on excellent current risk adjusted capital (severe and moderate loss scenarios), despite some fluctuation in capital levels.

Principal Business: Auto liability (63%) and auto physical damage (37%).

Principal Investments: Misc. investments (67%), investment grade bonds (25%), cash (7%), and real estate (1%).

Investments in Affiliates: 44%

Group Affiliation: Safeway Ins Group

Licensed in: AL, AK, AZ, CA, CO, DC, DE, FL, GA, ID, IL, IN, IA, KS, LA, ME, MD, MA, MI, MN, MS, MO, MT, NE, NV, NJ, NM, ND, OK, OR, PA, SC, SD, TX, UT, WA, WV, WI, WY

Commenced Business: December 1962

Address: 790 Pasquinelli Drive, Westmont, IL 60559-1254

Phone: (630) 887-8300   **Domicile State:** IL   **NAIC Code:** 12521

Data Date	Rating	RACR #1	RACR #2	Loss Ratio %	Total Assets ($mil)	Capital ($mil)	Net Premium ($mil)	Net Income ($mil)
2017	B-	1.56	1.41	83.5	565.8	315.3	221.4	-1.2
2016	B-	1.56	1.42	86.1	468.3	287.9	210.5	-5.5
2015	B-	1.72	1.57	82.2	463.6	302.1	204.4	33.3
2014	B-	1.53	1.41	76.0	446.1	298.8	167.5	7.3
2013	B-	1.47	1.35	79.1	417.0	279.3	156.1	-0.3

Rating Indexes

Ranges   Cap. 2   Stab.   Res.   Prof.   Liq.

■ Weak   ■ Fair   ▨ Good   □ Strong

SAN FRANCISCO REINS CO
C   Fair

Major Rating Factors: Fair reserve development (3.0 on a scale of 0 to 10) as the level of reserves has at times been insufficient to cover claims. In 2016 and 2015 the two year reserve development was 2508% and 3048% deficient respectively. Fair profitability index (3.7) with operating losses during 2015, 2016 and 2017. Average return on equity over the last five years has been poor at -1.1%.

Other Rating Factors: Fair overall results on stability tests (4.0) including weak results on operational trends and negative cash flow from operations for 2017. Strong long-term capitalization index (8.6) based on excellent current risk adjusted capital (severe and moderate loss scenarios), despite some fluctuation in capital levels. Excellent liquidity (7.5) with ample operational cash flow and liquid investments.

Principal Business: (This company is a reinsurer.)

Principal Investments: Investment grade bonds (99%) and misc. investments (1%).

Investments in Affiliates: None

Group Affiliation: Allianz Ins Group

Licensed in: All states except PR

Commenced Business: August 1964

Address: 1465 N MCDOWELL BLVD STE 100, Petaluma, CA 94954-6516

Phone: (415) 899-2000   **Domicile State:** CA   **NAIC Code:** 21911

Data Date	Rating	RACR #1	RACR #2	Loss Ratio %	Total Assets ($mil)	Capital ($mil)	Net Premium ($mil)	Net Income ($mil)
2017	C	2.92	2.04	75.1	3,390.4	594.8	-437.3	-19.0
2016	C	2.03	1.36	76.5	3,539.8	613.9	-443.3	-22.1
2015	C+	0.75	0.54	100.0	2,931.1	655.9	2,282.7	-14.9
2014	U	18.37	5.88	0.0	98.4	74.5	0.0	1.8
2013	U	18.21	5.90	0.0	96.5	73.0	0.0	0.7

Reserve Deficiency (as % of capital)

* Adequate & redundant reserves show as negatives

■ 1 Yr Dev
□ 2 Yr Dev

SCOR REINS CO   C   Fair

Major Rating Factors: Fair overall results on stability tests (3.4 on a scale of 0 to 10) including potential drain of affiliation with SCOR Reinsurance Group and fair risk adjusted capital in prior years. Good long-term capitalization index (5.2) based on fair current risk adjusted capital (severe loss scenario), although results have slipped from the excellent range over the last two years.

Other Rating Factors: Fair profitability index (3.0) with operating losses during 2017. Return on equity has been low, averaging 2.8% over the past five years. Good liquidity (6.8) with sufficient resources (cash flows and marketable investments) to handle a spike in claims. Ample reserve history (7.0) that can protect against increases in claims costs.

Principal Business: (This company is a reinsurer.)

Principal Investments: Investment grade bonds (95%), misc. investments (4%), and cash (1%).

Investments in Affiliates: None

Group Affiliation: SCOR Reinsurance Group

Licensed in: All states, the District of Columbia and Puerto Rico

Commenced Business: September 1985

Address: 199 WATER STREET SUITE 2100, New York, NY 10038-3526

Phone: (212) 480-1900   **Domicile State:** NY   **NAIC Code:** 30058

Data Date	Rating	RACR #1	RACR #2	Loss Ratio %	Total Assets ($mil)	Capital ($mil)	Net Premium ($mil)	Net Income ($mil)
2017	C	1.11	0.69	77.4	3,541.5	820.1	1,158.0	-206.4
2016	C	1.87	1.11	53.2	3,163.1	1,102.9	1,123.7	60.7
2015	D+	1.94	1.26	48.6	2,749.2	962.2	846.9	126.6
2014	D	1.30	0.85	54.8	2,269.6	704.3	798.2	75.1
2013	D	1.39	0.90	62.3	2,364.7	676.4	755.6	66.6

Capital

SCOTTSDALE INS CO   B-   Good

Major Rating Factors: Fair profitability index (3.2 on a scale of 0 to 10) with operating losses during 2017. Return on equity has been low, averaging 0.3% over the past five years. Fair overall results on stability tests (4.9).

Other Rating Factors: History of adequate reserve strength (5.9) as reserves have been consistently at an acceptable level. Good liquidity (5.9) with sufficient resources (cash flows and marketable investments) to handle a spike in claims. Strong long-term capitalization index (8.1) based on excellent current risk adjusted capital (severe and moderate loss scenarios), despite some fluctuation in capital levels.

Principal Business: Other liability (50%), commercial multiple peril (23%), allied lines (9%), auto liability (6%), homeowners multiple peril (5%), fire (3%), and other lines (4%).

Principal Investments: Investment grade bonds (81%), misc. investments (23%), and non investment grade bonds (1%).

Investments in Affiliates: 19%

Group Affiliation: Nationwide Corp

Licensed in: All states, the District of Columbia and Puerto Rico

Commenced Business: July 1982

Address: ONE WEST NATIONWIDE BLVD, Columbus, OH 43215-2220

Phone: (480) 365-4000   **Domicile State:** OH   **NAIC Code:** 41297

Data Date	Rating	RACR #1	RACR #2	Loss Ratio %	Total Assets ($mil)	Capital ($mil)	Net Premium ($mil)	Net Income ($mil)
2017	B-	2.10	1.76	81.1	2,536.9	737.8	754.7	-40.3
2016	B-	2.23	1.88	74.7	2,683.3	775.3	779.5	17.0
2015	B-	2.27	1.92	71.1	2,313.3	766.1	747.5	8.5
2014	B-	2.30	1.95	71.1	2,222.6	764.9	721.1	9.9
2013	B-	2.42	1.99	66.2	2,133.3	716.4	707.1	16.2

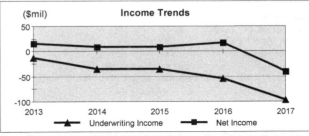

Income Trends

Underwriting Income — Net Income

SECURA INS A MUTUAL CO   B-   Good

Major Rating Factors: Fair overall results on stability tests (4.7 on a scale of 0 to 10) including potential drain of affiliation with SECURA Group. Good liquidity (6.3) with sufficient resources (cash flows and marketable investments) to handle a spike in claims.

Other Rating Factors: Strong long-term capitalization index (8.4) based on excellent current risk adjusted capital (severe and moderate loss scenarios). Moreover, capital levels have been consistent in recent years. Ample reserve history (9.2) that helps to protect the company against sharp claims increases. Excellent profitability (8.8) with operating gains in each of the last five years.

Principal Business: Workers compensation (26%), commercial multiple peril (26%), auto liability (15%), farmowners multiple peril (11%), auto physical damage (8%), other liability (8%), and other lines (6%).

Principal Investments: Investment grade bonds (70%), misc. investments (27%), real estate (3%), and non investment grade bonds (1%).

Investments in Affiliates: 7%

Group Affiliation: SECURA Group

Licensed in: AZ, AR, CO, ID, IL, IN, IA, KS, KY, MI, MN, MO, MT, NE, NV, NM, ND, OH, OK, OR, PA, SD, TN, UT, WA, WI, WY

Commenced Business: May 1900

Address: 2401 S Memorial Drive, Appleton, WI 54915

Phone: (920) 739-3161   **Domicile State:** WI   **NAIC Code:** 22543

Data Date	Rating	RACR #1	RACR #2	Loss Ratio %	Total Assets ($mil)	Capital ($mil)	Net Premium ($mil)	Net Income ($mil)
2017	B-	2.70	1.98	61.6	1,161.7	431.7	512.9	36.5
2016	B-	2.59	1.89	59.9	1,090.1	404.2	491.3	27.7
2015	B-	2.50	1.84	60.1	1,018.7	353.1	462.5	24.7
2014	B-	2.53	1.84	62.6	940.4	332.9	424.4	37.9
2013	B-	2.58	1.87	59.4	872.1	321.7	387.1	45.3

Rating Indexes

Ranges Cap. 2 Stab. Res. Prof. Liq.

■ Weak   ■ Fair   ▨ Good   □ Strong

SECURIAN CASUALTY CO *   A-   Excellent

Major Rating Factors: Strong long-term capitalization index (7.6 on a scale of 0 to 10) based on excellent current risk adjusted capital (severe and moderate loss scenarios). Furthermore, this high level of risk adjusted capital has been consistently maintained in previous years. Excellent profitability (7.5) despite modest operating losses during 2017.

Other Rating Factors: Excellent overall results on stability tests (7.0). Stability strengths include good operational trends and excellent risk diversification. History of adequate reserve strength (6.3) as reserves have been consistently at an acceptable level. Good liquidity (5.1) with sufficient resources (cash flows and marketable investments) to handle a spike in claims.

Principal Business: Inland marine (52%), other liability (38%), and credit (9%).

Principal Investments: Investment grade bonds (92%), misc. investments (5%), and cash (3%).

Investments in Affiliates: None

Group Affiliation: Securian Financial Group

Licensed in: All states except PR

Commenced Business: August 1994

Address: 400 ROBERT STREET NORTH, St. Paul, MN 55101-2098

Phone: (651) 665-3500   **Domicile State:** MN   **NAIC Code:** 10054

Data Date	Rating	RACR #1	RACR #2	Loss Ratio %	Total Assets ($mil)	Capital ($mil)	Net Premium ($mil)	Net Income ($mil)
2017	A-	1.82	1.37	60.8	328.2	118.4	273.5	-0.3
2016	B+	2.12	1.61	55.5	275.8	120.1	231.6	4.6
2015	B	2.48	1.91	49.4	224.1	112.9	180.8	9.2
2014	B	1.83	1.37	48.1	193.3	102.6	150.1	10.8
2013	B	2.31	1.76	46.8	173.9	101.1	122.2	10.1

SELECTIVE AUTO INS CO OF NJ *   B+   Good

Major Rating Factors: Good liquidity (6.6 on a scale of 0 to 10) with sufficient resources (cash flows and marketable investments) to handle a spike in claims. Good overall results on stability tests (6.5).

Other Rating Factors: Strong long-term capitalization index (7.8) based on excellent current risk adjusted capital (severe and moderate loss scenarios). Moreover, capital levels have been consistent in recent years. Ample reserve history (9.3) that helps to protect the company against sharp claims increases. Excellent profitability (8.8) with operating gains in each of the last five years. Return on equity has been good over the last five years, averaging 11.2%.

Principal Business: Auto liability (49%), homeowners multiple peril (29%), auto physical damage (20%), and other liability (2%).

Principal Investments: Investment grade bonds (97%) and misc. investments (3%).

Investments in Affiliates: None

Group Affiliation: Selective Ins

Licensed in: NJ, NC

Commenced Business: July 2006

Address: 40 WANTAGE AVENUE, Branchville, NJ 7890

Phone: (973) 948-3000   **Domicile State:** NJ   **NAIC Code:** 11074

Data Date	Rating	RACR #1	RACR #2	Loss Ratio %	Total Assets ($mil)	Capital ($mil)	Net Premium ($mil)	Net Income ($mil)
2017	B+	2.38	1.63	58.7	380.7	90.4	142.2	11.3
2016	B	2.38	1.61	57.4	365.8	86.7	134.2	11.5
2015	B	2.23	1.51	57.7	345.8	77.5	124.2	10.8
2014	B-	2.09	1.40	62.4	328.4	70.9	113.1	9.1
2013	B-	2.03	1.34	64.5	316.9	68.0	108.7	2.5

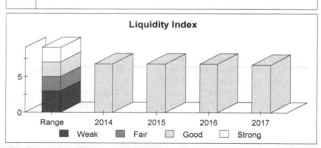

SELECTIVE CASUALTY INS CO *   B+   Good

Major Rating Factors: History of adequate reserve strength (6.9 on a scale of 0 to 10) as reserves have been consistently at an acceptable level. Good liquidity (6.4) with sufficient resources (cash flows and marketable investments) to handle a spike in claims.

Other Rating Factors: Good overall results on stability tests (6.5). Strong long-term capitalization index (7.9) based on excellent current risk adjusted capital (severe and moderate loss scenarios). Moreover, capital levels have been consistent in recent years. Excellent profitability (8.8) with operating gains in each of the last five years. Return on equity has been good over the last five years, averaging 11.5%.

Principal Business: Workers compensation (32%), other liability (24%), auto liability (16%), homeowners multiple peril (7%), products liability (6%), allied lines (4%), and other lines (12%).

Principal Investments: Investment grade bonds (95%) and misc. investments (5%).

Investments in Affiliates: None

Group Affiliation: Selective Ins Group Inc

Licensed in: NJ

Commenced Business: July 2012

Address: 40 Wantage Ave, Branchville, NJ 7890

Phone: (973) 948-3000   **Domicile State:** NJ   **NAIC Code:** 14376

Data Date	Rating	RACR #1	RACR #2	Loss Ratio %	Total Assets ($mil)	Capital ($mil)	Net Premium ($mil)	Net Income ($mil)
2017	B+	2.46	1.68	58.7	452.3	109.0	165.9	13.4
2016	B	2.37	1.61	57.4	431.5	101.0	156.6	12.6
2015	B	2.30	1.56	57.7	413.4	92.3	144.9	12.1
2014	B	2.11	1.41	62.4	391.6	82.7	132.0	9.6
2013	B	2.08	1.37	64.5	376.2	80.5	126.8	6.6

* Adequate & redundant reserves show as negatives

SELECTIVE INS CO OF AM   B   Good

Major Rating Factors: Good overall results on stability tests (5.6 on a scale of 0 to 10) despite potential drain of affiliation with Selective Ins. Good liquidity (6.7) with sufficient resources (cash flows and marketable investments) to handle a spike in claims.

Other Rating Factors: Strong long-term capitalization index (8.2) based on excellent current risk adjusted capital (severe and moderate loss scenarios). Moreover, capital has steadily grown over the last five years. Ample reserve history (9.0) that helps to protect the company against sharp claims increases. Excellent profitability (8.8) with operating gains in each of the last five years. Return on equity has been good over the last five years, averaging 13.7%.

Principal Business: Other liability (25%), auto liability (16%), workers compensation (15%), allied lines (11%), auto physical damage (7%), fire (6%), and other lines (20%).

Principal Investments: Investment grade bonds (75%), misc. investments (17%), non investment grade bonds (7%), and cash (1%).

Investments in Affiliates: None

Group Affiliation: Selective Ins

Licensed in: All states except FL, ID, LA, OK, PR

Commenced Business: April 1926

Address: 40 WANTAGE AVENUE, Branchville, NJ 7890

Phone: (973) 948-3000   **Domicile State:** NJ   **NAIC Code:** 12572

Data Date	Rating	RACR #1	RACR #2	Loss Ratio %	Total Assets ($mil)	Capital ($mil)	Net Premium ($mil)	Net Income ($mil)
2017	B	2.89	1.88	58.7	2,434.9	609.7	758.6	84.6
2016	B	2.83	1.85	57.4	2,314.2	568.6	715.9	72.2
2015	B	2.67	1.77	57.7	2,140.7	520.8	662.4	69.6
2014	B-	2.60	1.70	62.4	2,044.6	493.0	603.3	83.9
2013	B-	2.47	1.59	64.5	1,951.0	463.4	579.7	53.1

Rating Indexes

SELECTIVE WAY INS CO   B   Good

Major Rating Factors: Good overall results on stability tests (5.6 on a scale of 0 to 10) despite potential drain of affiliation with Selective Ins. Good liquidity (6.5) with sufficient resources (cash flows and marketable investments) to handle a spike in claims.

Other Rating Factors: Strong long-term capitalization index (7.8) based on excellent current risk adjusted capital (severe and moderate loss scenarios). Moreover, capital levels have been consistent in recent years. Ample reserve history (9.3) that helps to protect the company against sharp claims increases. Excellent profitability (8.8) with operating gains in each of the last five years. Return on equity has been good over the last five years, averaging 13.6%.

Principal Business: Other liability (26%), auto liability (20%), workers compensation (15%), allied lines (8%), auto physical damage (7%), fire (7%), and other lines (18%).

Principal Investments: Investment grade bonds (91%) and misc. investments (9%).

Investments in Affiliates: None

Group Affiliation: Selective Ins

Licensed in: AZ, CA, CO, DC, DE, GA, MD, MI, NH, NJ, NM, NY, NC, PA, SC, UT, VT, VA

Commenced Business: November 1973

Address: 40 WANTAGE AVENUE, Branchville, NJ 7890

Phone: (973) 948-3000   **Domicile State:** NJ   **NAIC Code:** 26301

Data Date	Rating	RACR #1	RACR #2	Loss Ratio %	Total Assets ($mil)	Capital ($mil)	Net Premium ($mil)	Net Income ($mil)
2017	B	2.42	1.64	58.7	1,345.7	325.1	497.8	43.6
2016	B	2.40	1.62	57.4	1,294.2	309.5	469.8	41.2
2015	B	2.22	1.49	57.7	1,215.0	272.6	434.7	42.3
2014	B	2.07	1.38	62.4	1,167.4	250.3	395.9	37.0
2013	B	2.09	1.36	64.5	1,124.5	250.3	380.4	27.5

Rating Indexes

SENTRY CASUALTY CO *   B+   Good

Major Rating Factors: Good overall profitability index (5.3 on a scale of 0 to 10). Fair expense controls. Return on equity has been fair, averaging 7.3% over the past five years. Good liquidity (6.7) with sufficient resources (cash flows and marketable investments) to handle a spike in claims.

Other Rating Factors: Good overall results on stability tests (6.4). Strong long-term capitalization index (9.4) based on excellent current risk adjusted capital (severe and moderate loss scenarios), despite some fluctuation in capital levels. Ample reserve history (7.8) that can protect against increases in claims costs.

Principal Business: Workers compensation (99%).

Principal Investments: Investment grade bonds (97%), misc. investments (2%), and non investment grade bonds (1%).

Investments in Affiliates: None

Group Affiliation: Sentry Ins Group

Licensed in: All states except PR

Commenced Business: August 1973

Address: 1800 NORTH POINT DRIVE, Stevens Point, WI 54481

Phone: (715) 346-6000   **Domicile State:** WI   **NAIC Code:** 28460

Data Date	Rating	RACR #1	RACR #2	Loss Ratio %	Total Assets ($mil)	Capital ($mil)	Net Premium ($mil)	Net Income ($mil)
2017	B+	4.05	2.57	74.8	355.9	70.7	52.7	5.7
2016	B	4.39	2.80	73.9	296.2	71.8	50.3	4.6
2015	B	4.68	2.97	72.7	272.5	71.9	46.9	5.3
2014	B	5.10	3.39	74.9	261.5	71.4	45.3	5.4
2013	B+	5.18	3.50	76.3	240.3	73.0	45.4	5.0

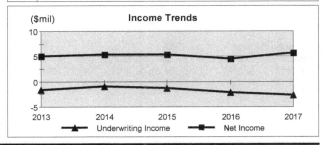

Income Trends

SENTRY INS A MUTUAL CO *   A   Excellent

Major Rating Factors: Strong long-term capitalization index (8.7 on a scale of 0 to 10) based on excellent current risk adjusted capital (severe and moderate loss scenarios). Furthermore, this high level of risk adjusted capital has been consistently maintained in previous years. Ample reserve history (7.4) that can protect against increases in claims costs.

Other Rating Factors: Excellent overall results on stability tests (7.8). Stability strengths include excellent operational trends and excellent risk diversification. Good overall profitability index (6.8). Fair expense controls. Good liquidity (6.9) with sufficient resources (cash flows and marketable investments) to handle a spike in claims.

Principal Business: Auto liability (31%), workers compensation (31%), allied lines (9%), other liability (8%), auto physical damage (7%), products liability (5%), and other lines (9%).

Principal Investments: Misc. investments (55%), investment grade bonds (42%), non investment grade bonds (3%), and real estate (1%).

Investments in Affiliates: 20%
Group Affiliation: Sentry Ins Group
Licensed in: All states, the District of Columbia and Puerto Rico
Commenced Business: August 1914
Address: 1800 NORTH POINT DRIVE, Stevens Point, WI 54481
Phone: (715) 346-6000   **Domicile State:** WI   **NAIC Code:** 24988

Data Date	Rating	RACR #1	RACR #2	Loss Ratio %	Total Assets ($mil)	Capital ($mil)	Net Premium ($mil)	Net Income ($mil)
2017	A	2.77	2.28	74.8	8,392.8	5,141.2	1,138.4	267.5
2016	A	2.62	2.18	73.9	7,587.3	4,723.5	1,086.7	238.1
2015	A	2.49	2.10	72.7	7,214.6	4,404.3	1,014.2	297.6
2014	A	2.34	1.99	74.9	6,981.3	4,164.4	997.7	272.5
2013	A	2.34	2.01	76.3	6,632.0	4,075.3	999.7	308.4

SENTRY SELECT INS CO *   A-   Excellent

Major Rating Factors: Strong long-term capitalization index (8.7 on a scale of 0 to 10) based on excellent current risk adjusted capital (severe and moderate loss scenarios). Furthermore, this high level of risk adjusted capital has been consistently maintained in previous years. Ample reserve history (8.0) that helps to protect the company against sharp claims increases.

Other Rating Factors: Excellent overall results on stability tests (7.0). Stability strengths include excellent operational trends and excellent risk diversification. Good overall profitability index (5.2). Fair expense controls. Return on equity has been fair, averaging 5.7% over the past five years. Good liquidity (6.4) with sufficient resources (cash flows and marketable investments) to handle a spike in claims.

Principal Business: Auto liability (44%), auto physical damage (16%), inland marine (15%), other liability (9%), workers compensation (5%), allied lines (4%), and other lines (6%).

Principal Investments: Investment grade bonds (92%), misc. investments (6%), and non investment grade bonds (2%).

Investments in Affiliates: None
Group Affiliation: Sentry Ins Group
Licensed in: All states except PR
Commenced Business: August 1929
Address: 1800 NORTH POINT DRIVE, Stevens Point, WI 54481
Phone: (715) 346-6000   **Domicile State:** WI   **NAIC Code:** 21180

Data Date	Rating	RACR #1	RACR #2	Loss Ratio %	Total Assets ($mil)	Capital ($mil)	Net Premium ($mil)	Net Income ($mil)
2017	A-	3.34	2.14	74.8	826.6	226.7	210.8	11.4
2016	B+	3.63	2.33	73.9	707.0	231.4	201.2	11.6
2015	B+	3.87	2.48	72.7	679.1	232.0	187.7	11.9
2014	B+	4.30	2.89	74.9	658.6	235.1	181.4	19.0
2013	B+	4.12	2.81	76.3	641.3	227.5	181.8	12.4

SFM MUTUAL INS CO *   B+   Good

Major Rating Factors: Good long-term capitalization index (6.9 on a scale of 0 to 10) based on good current risk adjusted capital (moderate loss scenario). Moreover, capital has steadily grown over the last five years. History of adequate reserve strength (6.6) as reserves have been consistently at an acceptable level.

Other Rating Factors: Good liquidity (6.4) with sufficient resources (cash flows and marketable investments) to handle a spike in claims. Good overall results on stability tests (6.5). Excellent profitability (8.9) with operating gains in each of the last five years.

Principal Business: Workers compensation (100%).

Principal Investments: Investment grade bonds (86%), misc. investments (13%), and non investment grade bonds (1%).

Investments in Affiliates: 2%
Group Affiliation: SFM Group
Licensed in: AL, AZ, CO, FL, IL, IN, IA, KS, MI, MN, MO, MT, NE, NV, OK, SD, TN, WI
Commenced Business: April 1984
Address: 3500 American Blvd W Ste 700, Bloomington, MN 55431-4434
Phone: (952) 838-4200   **Domicile State:** MN   **NAIC Code:** 11347

Data Date	Rating	RACR #1	RACR #2	Loss Ratio %	Total Assets ($mil)	Capital ($mil)	Net Premium ($mil)	Net Income ($mil)
2017	B+	1.38	1.03	71.7	612.1	147.7	170.2	15.4
2016	B	1.33	1.00	73.0	574.3	136.1	163.2	10.3
2015	B	1.29	0.97	74.3	532.3	121.4	148.9	10.4
2014	C+	1.19	0.90	78.1	502.1	110.1	151.0	8.6
2013	C+	1.16	0.88	78.7	477.0	101.2	141.2	9.1

SHELTER MUTUAL INS CO   B   Good

Major Rating Factors: Good overall results on stability tests (5.5 on a scale of 0 to 10) despite potential drain of affiliation with Shelter Ins Companies. Good overall profitability index (6.8). Fair expense controls.

Other Rating Factors: Good liquidity (5.8) with sufficient resources (cash flows and marketable investments) to handle a spike in claims. Strong long-term capitalization index (8.2) based on excellent current risk adjusted capital (severe and moderate loss scenarios). Moreover, capital levels have been consistent in recent years. Ample reserve history (7.7) that can protect against increases in claims costs.

Principal Business: Auto liability (32%), homeowners multiple peril (27%), auto physical damage (24%), allied lines (6%), fire (3%), farmowners multiple peril (2%), and other lines (5%).

Principal Investments: Investment grade bonds (57%), misc. investments (44%), and real estate (1%).

Investments in Affiliates: 22%

Group Affiliation: Shelter Ins Companies

Licensed in: AL, AR, CO, DE, GA, ID, IL, IN, IA, KS, KY, LA, MD, MA, MN, MS, MO, MT, NE, NV, NH, NJ, NY, NC, OH, OK, OR, PA, SC, SD, TN, TX, VT, VA, WV, WI, WY

Commenced Business: January 1946

Address: 1817 WEST BROADWAY, Columbia, MO 65218-0001

Phone: (573) 214-8441   **Domicile State:** MO   **NAIC Code:** 23388

Data Date	Rating	RACR #1	RACR #2	Loss Ratio %	Total Assets ($mil)	Capital ($mil)	Net Premium ($mil)	Net Income ($mil)
2017	B	2.34	1.91	73.3	3,381.1	1,920.7	1,531.0	43.8
2016	B	2.25	1.86	73.9	3,305.5	1,877.1	1,449.1	46.1
2015	B	2.19	1.77	69.4	3,114.8	1,787.8	1,379.7	80.1
2014	B	2.15	1.72	69.7	2,973.8	1,682.7	1,323.6	66.8
2013	B	2.03	1.62	74.2	2,756.5	1,566.9	1,208.2	65.5

Rating Indexes

SHELTER REINS CO   B   Good

Major Rating Factors: Good overall profitability index (6.1 on a scale of 0 to 10) despite operating losses during 2017. Return on equity has been fair, averaging 7.9% over the past five years. Good liquidity (6.7) with sufficient resources (cash flows and marketable investments) to handle a spike in claims.

Other Rating Factors: Good overall results on stability tests (5.5). Strong long-term capitalization index (9.7) based on excellent current risk adjusted capital (severe and moderate loss scenarios), despite some fluctuation in capital levels. Ample reserve history (9.3) that helps to protect the company against sharp claims increases.

Principal Business: Earthquake (100%).

Principal Investments: Investment grade bonds (89%), misc. investments (10%), and cash (1%).

Investments in Affiliates: None

Group Affiliation: Shelter Ins Companies

Licensed in: CA, IA, KS, MD, MI, MN, MO, ND, PA, SD, TN, WI, PR

Commenced Business: November 1986

Address: 1817 WEST BROADWAY, Columbia, MO 65218-0001

Phone: (573) 214-8441   **Domicile State:** MO   **NAIC Code:** 26557

Data Date	Rating	RACR #1	RACR #2	Loss Ratio %	Total Assets ($mil)	Capital ($mil)	Net Premium ($mil)	Net Income ($mil)
2017	B	4.24	2.77	98.2	472.9	321.5	114.2	-8.0
2016	B-	5.29	3.42	44.3	447.3	326.8	113.0	32.2
2015	C+	4.10	2.72	46.7	422.3	296.7	103.5	28.1
2014	C	3.51	2.30	46.1	405.7	271.0	103.4	27.2
2013	C	2.94	2.00	40.6	383.0	245.4	98.0	30.5

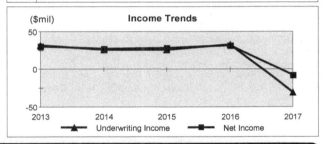

Income Trends

SIRIUS AMERICA INS CO   B-   Good

Major Rating Factors: Fair overall results on stability tests (4.9 on a scale of 0 to 10) including potential drain of affiliation with China Minsheng Investment Co Ltd, negative cash flow from operations for 2017 and fair results on operational trends. Fair profitability index (4.1) with operating losses during 2017. Return on equity has been fair, averaging 9.5% over the past five years.

Other Rating Factors: Good long-term capitalization index (6.2) based on good current risk adjusted capital (moderate loss scenario), despite some fluctuation in capital levels. History of adequate reserve strength (6.3) as reserves have been consistently at an acceptable level. Excellent liquidity (7.4) with ample operational cash flow and liquid investments.

Principal Business: Group accident & health (99%) and commercial multiple peril (1%).

Principal Investments: Investment grade bonds (74%), misc. investments (25%), and cash (1%).

Investments in Affiliates: None

Group Affiliation: China Minsheng Investment Co Ltd

Licensed in: All states, the District of Columbia and Puerto Rico

Commenced Business: January 1980

Address: 140 BROADWAY - 32ND FLOOR, New York, NY 10005-1108

Phone: (212) 312-2500   **Domicile State:** NY   **NAIC Code:** 38776

Data Date	Rating	RACR #1	RACR #2	Loss Ratio %	Total Assets ($mil)	Capital ($mil)	Net Premium ($mil)	Net Income ($mil)
2017	B-	1.60	1.01	107.6	1,337.5	521.8	101.2	-6.4
2016	B-	0.96	0.69	73.8	1,395.1	544.3	217.3	82.7
2015	C+	1.42	0.87	53.7	1,387.6	517.6	283.9	74.7
2014	C+	1.58	0.94	45.1	1,550.5	620.6	267.2	56.1
2013	C+	2.14	1.21	48.9	1,559.4	548.4	252.8	55.9

Rating Indexes

SOMPO AMERICA INSURANCE CO *

A   Excellent

Major Rating Factors: Strong long-term capitalization index (9.5 on a scale of 0 to 10) based on excellent current risk adjusted capital (severe and moderate loss scenarios). Furthermore, this high level of risk adjusted capital has been consistently maintained in previous years. Ample reserve history (8.6) that helps to protect the company against sharp claims increases.

Other Rating Factors: Excellent liquidity (7.0) with ample operational cash flow and liquid investments. Excellent overall results on stability tests (7.5). Stability strengths include excellent operational trends and excellent risk diversification. Good overall profitability index (6.9). Fair expense controls. Return on equity has been low, averaging 4.1% over the past five years.

Principal Business: Workers compensation (29%), allied lines (20%), other liability (10%), ocean marine (7%), commercial multiple peril (7%), auto liability (6%), and other lines (20%).

Principal Investments: Investment grade bonds (73%), misc. investments (25%), and cash (2%).

Investments in Affiliates: 1%

Group Affiliation: Sompo Holdings Inc

Licensed in: All states, the District of Columbia and Puerto Rico

Commenced Business: January 1963

Address: 777 Third Ave 24th Floor, New York, NY 10017

Phone: (704) 759-2200   **Domicile State:** NY   **NAIC Code:** 11126

Data Date	Rating	RACR #1	RACR #2	Loss Ratio %	Total Assets ($mil)	Capital ($mil)	Net Premium ($mil)	Net Income ($mil)
2017	A	4.36	2.75	68.7	1,285.1	571.9	190.6	28.1
2016	B+	4.68	2.96	61.2	1,229.5	558.7	182.3	34.7
2015	B	4.23	2.66	64.8	1,177.6	488.7	183.0	38.1
2014	B	3.55	2.48	62.8	1,238.5	598.3	191.4	8.8
2013	B	2.44	1.86	67.7	1,187.9	555.2	197.2	1.0

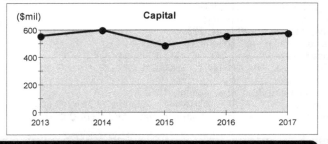

Capital

SOUTHERN FARM BUREAU CAS INS CO

B-   Good

Major Rating Factors: Fair overall results on stability tests (4.8 on a scale of 0 to 10) including potential drain of affiliation with Southern Farm Bureau Casualty. Fair profitability index (4.0) with operating losses during 2016. Return on equity has been low, averaging 1.0% over the past five years.

Other Rating Factors: Good liquidity (6.2) with sufficient resources (cash flows and marketable investments) to handle a spike in claims. Strong long-term capitalization index (8.3) based on excellent current risk adjusted capital (severe and moderate loss scenarios), despite some fluctuation in capital levels. Ample reserve history (7.7) that can protect against increases in claims costs.

Principal Business: Auto physical damage (49%), auto liability (47%), other liability (4%), and allied lines (1%).

Principal Investments: Investment grade bonds (54%), misc. investments (46%), and real estate (1%).

Investments in Affiliates: 33%

Group Affiliation: Southern Farm Bureau Casualty

Licensed in: AR, CO, FL, LA, MS, SC

Commenced Business: September 1947

Address: 1800 East County Line Road, Ridgeland, MS 39157

Phone: (601) 957-7777   **Domicile State:** MS   **NAIC Code:** 18325

Data Date	Rating	RACR #1	RACR #2	Loss Ratio %	Total Assets ($mil)	Capital ($mil)	Net Premium ($mil)	Net Income ($mil)
2017	B-	1.99	1.85	83.8	2,269.3	1,337.9	961.3	16.3
2016	B-	1.98	1.84	92.2	2,161.6	1,287.4	870.0	-50.3
2015	B-	2.13	1.98	83.9	2,150.3	1,317.8	838.3	9.8
2014	B-	2.21	2.03	79.5	2,094.5	1,275.6	841.7	50.7
2013	B-	2.29	2.09	80.3	1,998.3	1,235.9	825.8	36.4

Rating Indexes

SOUTHERN FIDELITY INS CO *

B+   Good

Major Rating Factors: History of adequate reserve strength (6.3 on a scale of 0 to 10) as reserves have been consistently at an acceptable level. Good overall profitability index (5.4) despite modest operating losses during 2017. Return on equity has been fair, averaging 7.0% over the past five years.

Other Rating Factors: Good liquidity (5.5) with sufficient resources (cash flows and marketable investments) to handle a spike in claims. Good overall results on stability tests (6.5) despite negative cash flow from operations for 2017. Stability strengths include good operational trends and good risk diversification. Strong long-term capitalization index (9.0) based on excellent current risk adjusted capital (severe and moderate loss scenarios), despite some fluctuation in capital levels.

Principal Business: (Not applicable due to unusual reinsurance transactions.)

Principal Investments: Investment grade bonds (94%), real estate (8%), and misc. investments (4%).

Investments in Affiliates: 3%

Group Affiliation: Southern Fidelity Holding LLC

Licensed in: FL, LA, MS, SC

Commenced Business: April 2005

Address: 2255 Killearn Center Boulevard, Tallahassee, FL 32312

Phone: (850) 521-3080   **Domicile State:** FL   **NAIC Code:** 10136

Data Date	Rating	RACR #1	RACR #2	Loss Ratio %	Total Assets ($mil)	Capital ($mil)	Net Premium ($mil)	Net Income ($mil)
2017	B+	3.02	2.33	62.0	196.7	82.1	104.2	-0.1
2016	B	3.42	2.60	55.1	192.5	86.3	100.0	1.3
2015	B	3.30	2.54	46.7	191.2	86.9	106.9	6.7
2014	C+	3.07	2.37	37.2	187.4	82.3	113.5	10.7
2013	C+	2.12	1.19	35.6	182.6	72.1	111.1	9.2

Reserve Deficiency (as % of capital)

* Adequate & redundant reserves show as negatives

SOUTHERN-OWNERS INS CO *　　　　　　　　　　　　　A　　Excellent

Major Rating Factors: Strong long-term capitalization index (8.3 on a scale of 0 to 10) based on excellent current risk adjusted capital (severe and moderate loss scenarios). Furthermore, this high level of risk adjusted capital has been consistently maintained in previous years. Excellent profitability (8.5) with operating gains in each of the last five years.

Other Rating Factors: Excellent overall results on stability tests (7.5). Stability strengths include excellent operational trends and excellent risk diversification. History of adequate reserve strength (6.4) as reserves have been consistently at an acceptable level. Good liquidity (6.6) with sufficient resources (cash flows and marketable investments) to handle a spike in claims.

Principal Business: Auto liability (40%), other liability (25%), auto physical damage (15%), commercial multiple peril (12%), workers compensation (4%), homeowners multiple peril (2%), and inland marine (2%).

Principal Investments: Investment grade bonds (87%), misc. investments (11%), cash (1%), and non investment grade bonds (1%).

Investments in Affiliates: None

Group Affiliation: Auto-Owners Group

Licensed in: FL, MI

Commenced Business: June 1995

Address: 6101 ANACAPRI BOULEVARD, Lansing, MI 48917-3968

Phone: (517) 323-1200　　**Domicile State:** MI　　**NAIC Code:** 10190

Data Date	Rating	RACR #1	RACR #2	Loss Ratio %	Total Assets ($mil)	Capital ($mil)	Net Premium ($mil)	Net Income ($mil)
2017	A	2.52	1.88	70.5	821.8	253.9	357.6	16.3
2016	A-	2.66	1.96	75.5	739.3	232.2	293.2	7.2
2015	B+	2.88	2.08	65.1	665.7	219.5	266.1	24.4
2014	B+	2.64	1.93	70.9	628.8	198.2	247.1	13.1
2013	A	2.73	2.04	74.0	573.8	184.6	224.9	13.5

Risk-Adjusted Capital Ratio #2
(Severe Loss Scenario)

ST PAUL FIRE & MARINE INS CO　　　　　　　　　　　B　　Good

Major Rating Factors: Good liquidity (6.6 on a scale of 0 to 10) with sufficient resources (cash flows and marketable investments) to handle a spike in claims. Good overall results on stability tests (5.7).

Other Rating Factors: Fair profitability index (3.9). Fair expense controls. Return on equity has been fair, averaging 17.3% over the past five years. Strong long-term capitalization index (7.7) based on excellent current risk adjusted capital (severe and moderate loss scenarios), despite some fluctuation in capital levels. Ample reserve history (8.3) that helps to protect the company against sharp claims increases.

Principal Business: Other liability (45%), auto liability (21%), products liability (9%), fire (8%), auto physical damage (6%), inland marine (5%), and other lines (5%).

Principal Investments: Investment grade bonds (73%), misc. investments (17%), non investment grade bonds (5%), and real estate (5%).

Investments in Affiliates: 12%

Group Affiliation: Travelers Companies Inc

Licensed in: All states, the District of Columbia and Puerto Rico

Commenced Business: April 1925

Address: ONE TOWER SQUARE, Hartford, CT 6183

Phone: (860) 277-0111　　**Domicile State:** CT　　**NAIC Code:** 24767

Data Date	Rating	RACR #1	RACR #2	Loss Ratio %	Total Assets ($mil)	Capital ($mil)	Net Premium ($mil)	Net Income ($mil)
2017	B	2.04	1.52	69.6	18,716.4	5,367.3	5,749.1	712.2
2016	B	2.06	1.53	63.8	18,558.7	5,558.2	5,490.5	1,199.4
2015	B	1.90	1.45	58.8	18,297.6	5,563.3	5,252.1	1,186.8
2014	B	1.58	1.28	60.3	18,917.2	5,994.1	5,123.4	933.7
2013	B	1.57	1.29	60.5	18,566.3	5,914.7	5,131.4	883.9

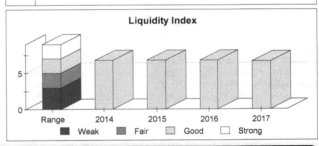

Liquidity Index

STANDARD FIRE INS CO　　　　　　　　　　　　　　B　　Good

Major Rating Factors: Good overall profitability index (5.5 on a scale of 0 to 10). Fair expense controls. Return on equity has been excellent over the last five years averaging 16.2%. Good liquidity (6.8) with sufficient resources (cash flows and marketable investments) to handle a spike in claims.

Other Rating Factors: Good overall results on stability tests (6.3). Affiliation with Travelers Companies Inc is a strength. Strong long-term capitalization index (7.8) based on excellent current risk adjusted capital (severe and moderate loss scenarios), despite some fluctuation in capital levels. Ample reserve history (8.2) that helps to protect the company against sharp claims increases.

Principal Business: Auto liability (45%), auto physical damage (27%), homeowners multiple peril (16%), workers compensation (7%), ocean marine (1%), allied lines (1%), and other lines (2%).

Principal Investments: Investment grade bonds (71%), misc. investments (25%), and non investment grade bonds (4%).

Investments in Affiliates: 16%

Group Affiliation: Travelers Companies Inc

Licensed in: All states, the District of Columbia and Puerto Rico

Commenced Business: March 1910

Address: ONE TOWER SQUARE, Hartford, CT 6183

Phone: (860) 277-0111　　**Domicile State:** CT　　**NAIC Code:** 19070

Data Date	Rating	RACR #1	RACR #2	Loss Ratio %	Total Assets ($mil)	Capital ($mil)	Net Premium ($mil)	Net Income ($mil)
2017	B	1.93	1.52	69.5	3,766.4	1,189.5	1,105.1	125.4
2016	B	1.94	1.54	63.4	3,679.1	1,201.8	1,053.7	202.4
2015	B	1.90	1.49	58.7	3,583.9	1,185.5	1,005.7	204.8
2014	B	1.96	1.53	60.5	3,627.1	1,215.2	977.2	228.2
2013	B	2.02	1.60	60.9	3,605.3	1,234.8	974.8	217.9

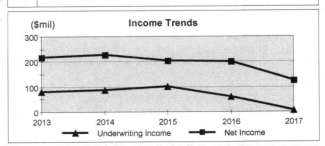

Income Trends

STAR INS CO   C   Fair

Major Rating Factors: Fair overall results on stability tests (3.6 on a scale of 0 to 10). A history of deficient reserves (2.5). Underreserving can have an adverse impact on capital and profits. Deficiencies in the two year reserve development occurred in three of the previous five years and ranged between 15% and 33%.

Other Rating Factors: Good overall profitability index (6.5) despite operating losses during 2015. Return on equity has been fair, averaging 6.9% over the past five years. Good liquidity (6.8) with sufficient resources (cash flows and marketable investments) to handle a spike in claims. Strong long-term capitalization index (7.5) based on excellent current risk adjusted capital (severe and moderate loss scenarios), despite some fluctuation in capital levels.

Principal Business: Workers compensation (72%), commercial multiple peril (9%), auto liability (7%), inland marine (7%), other liability (2%), and auto physical damage (2%).

Principal Investments: Investment grade bonds (69%), misc. investments (23%), non investment grade bonds (7%), and cash (1%).

Investments in Affiliates: 12%

Group Affiliation: Meadowbrook Ins Group

Licensed in: All states except PR

Commenced Business: November 1985

Address: 26255 American Drive, Southfield, MI 48034

Phone: (248) 358-1100   **Domicile State:** MI   **NAIC Code:** 18023

Data Date	Rating	RACR #1	RACR #2	Loss Ratio %	Total Assets ($mil)	Capital ($mil)	Net Premium ($mil)	Net Income ($mil)
2017	C	1.80	1.30	67.0	1,815.6	563.9	577.3	161.8
2016	C	1.33	1.06	64.6	1,915.4	508.3	587.1	16.2
2015	C	2.13	1.74	77.1	946.4	314.1	213.0	-9.8
2014	C	2.15	1.82	66.4	963.8	324.3	211.6	14.7
2013	C	2.10	1.73	79.2	1,000.3	309.6	245.7	3.9

Rating Indexes

STARR INDEMNITY & LIABILITY CO   B   Good

Major Rating Factors: Good long-term capitalization index (6.3 on a scale of 0 to 10) based on good current risk adjusted capital (moderate loss scenario). Good overall profitability index (5.3). Good expense controls. Return on equity has been low, averaging 2.6% over the past five years.

Other Rating Factors: Good liquidity (6.8) with sufficient resources (cash flows and marketable investments) to handle a spike in claims. Good overall results on stability tests (5.3). Stability strengths include excellent operational trends, good risk adjusted capital for prior years and excellent risk diversification. Fair reserve development (3.5) as reserves have generally been sufficient to cover claims. In 2017, the two year reserve development was 20% deficient.

Principal Business: Workers compensation (33%), other liability (30%), aircraft (12%), ocean marine (9%), auto liability (7%), inland marine (3%), and other lines (6%).

Principal Investments: Investment grade bonds (51%), misc. investments (46%), cash (2%), and non investment grade bonds (1%).

Investments in Affiliates: 32%

Group Affiliation: Starr International Co Inc

Licensed in: All states, the District of Columbia and Puerto Rico

Commenced Business: May 1919

Address: 8401 N Central Expressway #890, Dallas, TX 75225

Phone: (646) 227-6400   **Domicile State:** TX   **NAIC Code:** 38318

Data Date	Rating	RACR #1	RACR #2	Loss Ratio %	Total Assets ($mil)	Capital ($mil)	Net Premium ($mil)	Net Income ($mil)
2017	B	1.20	0.91	103.5	4,803.6	1,875.3	1,084.3	4.7
2016	B	1.37	1.14	85.9	4,442.3	1,922.5	1,003.2	98.8
2015	B	1.33	1.12	75.0	4,002.0	1,847.6	1,078.1	73.8
2014	B	1.30	1.12	78.2	3,755.1	1,832.3	1,015.8	54.6
2013	B-	1.35	1.13	81.6	3,467.4	1,865.1	847.3	13.2

Capital

STATE AUTO P&C INS CO   C+   Fair

Major Rating Factors: Fair overall results on stability tests (4.3 on a scale of 0 to 10) including potential drain of affiliation with State Auto Mutual Group. History of adequate reserve strength (5.8) as reserves have been consistently at an acceptable level.

Other Rating Factors: Good overall profitability index (5.4) despite operating losses during 2014. Return on equity has been low, averaging 4.1% over the past five years. Good liquidity (6.3) with sufficient resources (cash flows and marketable investments) to handle a spike in claims. Strong long-term capitalization index (7.5) based on excellent current risk adjusted capital (severe and moderate loss scenarios), despite some fluctuation in capital levels.

Principal Business: Homeowners multiple peril (26%), auto liability (20%), commercial multiple peril (19%), auto physical damage (13%), other liability (7%), allied lines (5%), and other lines (10%).

Principal Investments: Investment grade bonds (76%), misc. investments (22%), and cash (2%).

Investments in Affiliates: None

Group Affiliation: State Auto Mutual Group

Licensed in: All states except CA, NH, NM, WA, PR

Commenced Business: April 1950

Address: 1300 Woodland Avenue, West Des Moines, IA 50265

Phone: (614) 464-5000   **Domicile State:** IA   **NAIC Code:** 25127

Data Date	Rating	RACR #1	RACR #2	Loss Ratio %	Total Assets ($mil)	Capital ($mil)	Net Premium ($mil)	Net Income ($mil)
2017	C+	2.21	1.38	72.2	2,518.9	687.0	995.9	38.0
2016	C+	2.11	1.28	73.1	2,482.6	682.5	1,014.7	19.3
2015	C	2.11	1.34	68.5	2,355.6	655.3	999.2	52.3
2014	C-	2.08	1.28	71.6	2,291.5	628.9	937.0	-13.6
2013	C-	2.19	1.40	68.5	2,066.5	607.7	833.3	39.6

Rating Indexes

STATE AUTOMOBILE MUTUAL INS CO   C+   Fair

Major Rating Factors: Fair overall results on stability tests (4.3 on a scale of 0 to 10) including potential drain of affiliation with State Auto Mutual Group. History of adequate reserve strength (6.0) as reserves have been consistently at an acceptable level.
Other Rating Factors: Good liquidity (6.0) with sufficient resources (cash flows and marketable investments) to handle a spike in claims. Weak profitability index (2.8) with operating losses during 2013, 2014, 2016 and 2017. Strong long-term capitalization index (7.0) based on excellent current risk adjusted capital (severe and moderate loss scenarios), despite some fluctuation in capital levels.
Principal Business: Auto liability (20%), auto physical damage (14%), homeowners multiple peril (13%), farmowners multiple peril (13%), other liability (11%), commercial multiple peril (9%), and other lines (20%).
Principal Investments: Misc. investments (61%), investment grade bonds (37%), cash (1%), and real estate (1%).
Investments in Affiliates: 46%
Group Affiliation: State Auto Mutual Group
Licensed in: All states except PR
Commenced Business: September 1921
Address: 518 East Broad Street, Columbus, OH 43215
Phone: (614) 464-5000   **Domicile State:** OH   **NAIC Code:** 25135

Data Date	Rating	RACR #1	RACR #2	Loss Ratio %	Total Assets ($mil)	Capital ($mil)	Net Premium ($mil)	Net Income ($mil)
2017	C+	1.13	1.00	72.2	2,407.3	778.9	673.7	-18.8
2016	C+	1.15	1.02	73.1	2,461.1	822.6	686.4	-14.6
2015	C+	1.19	1.08	68.5	2,386.4	824.7	675.9	5.2
2014	C+	1.21	1.10	71.5	2,352.1	816.8	633.8	-17.6
2013	C+	1.33	1.22	68.5	2,205.9	866.3	563.7	-2.8

STATE FARM FIRE & CAS CO *   B+   Good

Major Rating Factors: Good overall results on stability tests (6.7 on a scale of 0 to 10). Affiliation with State Farm Group is a strength. History of adequate reserve strength (6.2) as reserves have been consistently at an acceptable level.
Other Rating Factors: Good liquidity (5.8) with sufficient resources (cash flows and marketable investments) to handle a spike in claims. Strong long-term capitalization index (8.2) based on excellent current risk adjusted capital (severe and moderate loss scenarios). Moreover, capital has steadily grown over the last five years. Excellent profitability (8.8) with operating gains in each of the last five years. Return on equity has been good over the last five years, averaging 13.2%.
Principal Business: Homeowners multiple peril (71%), auto liability (8%), commercial multiple peril (6%), auto physical damage (4%), other liability (3%), inland marine (3%), and other lines (4%).
Principal Investments: Investment grade bonds (81%) and misc. investments (19%).
Investments in Affiliates: None
Group Affiliation: State Farm Group
Licensed in: All states except PR
Commenced Business: June 1935
Address: One State Farm Plaza, Bloomington, IL 61710
Phone: (309) 766-2311   **Domicile State:** IL   **NAIC Code:** 25143

Data Date	Rating	RACR #1	RACR #2	Loss Ratio %	Total Assets ($mil)	Capital ($mil)	Net Premium ($mil)	Net Income ($mil)
2017	B+	3.61	2.36	73.4	39,411.9	17,710.2	16,281.8	1,059.3
2016	B+	2.71	1.67	65.2	38,352.5	16,354.7	16,167.1	1,713.6
2015	B	2.41	1.49	60.8	35,495.7	14,196.8	15,914.0	2,543.8
2014	B-	2.15	1.34	65.9	33,481.0	12,193.8	15,917.6	1,853.0
2013	B-	1.99	1.23	63.5	31,460.7	10,951.2	15,276.5	1,803.8

STATE FARM FLORIDA INS CO   B   Good

Major Rating Factors: Good overall results on stability tests (5.4 on a scale of 0 to 10) despite negative cash flow from operations for 2017. Stability strengths include good operational trends and excellent risk diversification. History of adequate reserve strength (6.3) as reserves have been consistently at an acceptable level.
Other Rating Factors: Good overall profitability index (5.5) despite operating losses during 2017. Return on equity has been good over the last five years, averaging 10.8%. Good liquidity (6.5) with sufficient resources (cash flows and marketable investments) to handle a spike in claims. Strong long-term capitalization index (10.0) based on excellent current risk adjusted capital (severe and moderate loss scenarios), despite some fluctuation in capital levels.
Principal Business: Homeowners multiple peril (87%), inland marine (5%), other liability (5%), and commercial multiple peril (3%).
Principal Investments: Investment grade bonds (88%) and misc. investments (12%).
Investments in Affiliates: None
Group Affiliation: State Farm Group
Licensed in: FL, IL
Commenced Business: December 1998
Address: 7401 Cypress Gardens Blvd, Winter Haven, FL 33888
Phone: (863) 318-3000   **Domicile State:** FL   **NAIC Code:** 10739

Data Date	Rating	RACR #1	RACR #2	Loss Ratio %	Total Assets ($mil)	Capital ($mil)	Net Premium ($mil)	Net Income ($mil)
2017	B	4.69	3.23	82.7	2,063.4	976.7	589.7	-109.2
2016	B	5.04	3.54	48.4	2,096.0	1,083.7	570.7	72.6
2015	C+	4.45	3.14	42.1	1,991.9	1,033.8	584.0	179.8
2014	C	3.79	2.63	36.2	1,915.6	894.5	588.7	155.1
2013	C-	1.60	1.13	40.8	1,793.7	734.6	575.4	174.5

STATE FARM GENERAL INS CO
C   Fair

Major Rating Factors: Fair overall results on stability tests (4.2 on a scale of 0 to 10) including negative cash flow from operations for 2017. Weak profitability index (2.2) with operating losses during 2017. Return on equity has been low, averaging 0.3% over the past five years.

Other Rating Factors: History of adequate reserve strength (6.1) as reserves have been consistently at an acceptable level. Good liquidity (5.6) with sufficient resources (cash flows and marketable investments) to handle a spike in claims. Strong long-term capitalization index (7.6) based on excellent current risk adjusted capital (severe and moderate loss scenarios), despite some fluctuation in capital levels.

Principal Business: Homeowners multiple peril (71%), commercial multiple peril (16%), other liability (8%), inland marine (3%), and earthquake (1%).

Principal Investments: Investment grade bonds (96%) and misc. investments (4%).

Investments in Affiliates: None
Group Affiliation: State Farm Group
Licensed in: All states except CT, MA, RI, PR
Commenced Business: May 1962
Address: One State Farm Plaza, Bloomington, IL 61710
Phone: (309) 766-2311   **Domicile State:** IL   **NAIC Code:** 25151

Data Date	Rating	RACR #1	RACR #2	Loss Ratio %	Total Assets ($mil)	Capital ($mil)	Net Premium ($mil)	Net Income ($mil)
2017	C	2.02	1.38	156.5	7,241.9	3,186.9	1,781.6	-836.9
2016	B	6.68	4.40	75.3	7,112.1	4,076.0	1,930.7	128.7
2015	B	6.66	4.33	71.5	6,918.7	3,991.2	1,904.2	174.0
2014	B	6.35	4.11	57.6	6,714.9	3,821.2	1,893.1	352.2
2013	B	5.25	3.31	55.5	6,388.1	3,452.6	1,919.0	379.9

Rating Indexes

Ranges   Cap. 2   Stab.   Res.   Prof.   Liq.
■ Weak   ▩ Fair   ▦ Good   □ Strong

STATE FARM INDEMNITY CO
B   Good

Major Rating Factors: Good overall results on stability tests (5.4 on a scale of 0 to 10). Affiliation with State Farm Group is a strength. Good overall profitability index (6.7). Good expense controls. Return on equity has been fair, averaging 5.1% over the past five years.

Other Rating Factors: Good liquidity (6.8) with sufficient resources (cash flows and marketable investments) to handle a spike in claims. Strong long-term capitalization index (10.0) based on excellent current risk adjusted capital (severe and moderate loss scenarios). Moreover, capital levels have been consistent in recent years. Ample reserve history (8.5) that helps to protect the company against sharp claims increases.

Principal Business: Auto liability (72%) and auto physical damage (28%).

Principal Investments: Investment grade bonds (97%) and misc. investments (3%).

Investments in Affiliates: 1%
Group Affiliation: State Farm Group
Licensed in: IL, NJ
Commenced Business: March 1991
Address: One State Farm Plaza, Bloomington, IL 61710
Phone: (973) 739-5000   **Domicile State:** IL   **NAIC Code:** 43796

Data Date	Rating	RACR #1	RACR #2	Loss Ratio %	Total Assets ($mil)	Capital ($mil)	Net Premium ($mil)	Net Income ($mil)
2017	B	5.75	5.23	78.0	2,301.8	1,275.3	643.6	59.2
2016	B	5.54	5.04	83.3	2,245.4	1,218.6	631.2	29.7
2015	B	5.42	4.95	82.5	2,219.7	1,194.6	621.0	78.1
2014	B-	4.95	4.36	81.1	2,158.4	1,113.6	610.1	56.0
2013	B-	4.72	4.14	75.6	2,098.9	1,061.7	603.6	74.5

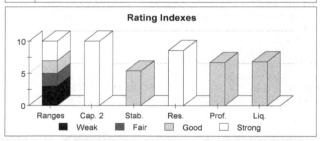

Rating Indexes

Ranges   Cap. 2   Stab.   Res.   Prof.   Liq.
■ Weak   ▩ Fair   ▦ Good   □ Strong

STATE FARM LLOYDS
B   Good

Major Rating Factors: History of adequate reserve strength (6.2 on a scale of 0 to 10) as reserves have been consistently at an acceptable level. Good liquidity (5.1) with sufficient resources (cash flows and marketable investments) to handle a spike in claims.

Other Rating Factors: Good overall results on stability tests (5.5) despite negative cash flow from operations for 2017. Stability strengths include good operational trends and excellent risk diversification. Fair profitability index (4.7) with operating losses during 2014 and 2017. Strong long-term capitalization index (8.4) based on excellent current risk adjusted capital (severe and moderate loss scenarios), despite some fluctuation in capital levels.

Principal Business: Homeowners multiple peril (93%), commercial multiple peril (5%), and farmowners multiple peril (2%).

Principal Investments: Investment grade bonds (96%) and misc. investments (5%).

Investments in Affiliates: None
Group Affiliation: State Farm Group
Licensed in: TX
Commenced Business: June 1983
Address: 1251 State Street Suite 1000, Richardson, TX 75082
Phone: (972) 732-5000   **Domicile State:** TX   **NAIC Code:** 43419

Data Date	Rating	RACR #1	RACR #2	Loss Ratio %	Total Assets ($mil)	Capital ($mil)	Net Premium ($mil)	Net Income ($mil)
2017	B	2.31	1.93	88.5	3,358.3	1,194.2	1,692.0	-104.6
2016	B	2.69	2.26	60.4	3,531.0	1,341.1	1,671.2	205.5
2015	B	2.64	2.22	63.0	3,250.8	1,213.8	1,572.6	412.2
2014	B-	1.67	1.21	51.1	3,490.8	1,039.5	1,799.7	-54.3
2013	B-	2.26	1.93	53.5	3,075.5	1,105.4	1,712.7	215.2

Reserve Deficiency (as % of capital)

2013   2014   2015   2016   2017

* Adequate & redundant reserves show as negatives   ■ 1 Yr Dev   □ 2 Yr Dev

STATE FARM MUTUAL AUTOMOBILE INS CO *   B+   Good

Major Rating Factors: History of adequate reserve strength (6.2 on a scale of 0 to 10) as reserves have been consistently at an acceptable level. Good liquidity (6.5) with sufficient resources (cash flows and marketable investments) to handle a spike in claims.

Other Rating Factors: Good overall results on stability tests (6.7). Strong long-term capitalization index (8.1) based on excellent current risk adjusted capital (severe and moderate loss scenarios). Moreover, capital levels have been consistent in recent years. Fair profitability index (4.2) with operating losses during 2016.

Principal Business: Auto liability (58%), auto physical damage (39%), other accident & health (2%), and group accident & health (1%).

Principal Investments: Misc. investments (69%) and investment grade bonds (31%).

Investments in Affiliates: 26%

Group Affiliation: State Farm Group

Licensed in: All states except PR

Commenced Business: June 1922

Address: One State Farm Plaza, Bloomington, IL 61710

Phone: (309) 766-2311   **Domicile State:** IL   **NAIC Code:** 25178

Data Date	Rating	RACR #1	RACR #2	Loss Ratio %	Total Assets ($mil)	Capital ($mil)	Net Premium ($mil)	Net Income ($mil)
2017	B+	2.06	1.77	84.0	160,732.0	97,005.0	43,171.4	1,701.6
2016	B+	1.96	1.71	91.9	147,697.0	87,573.9	40,455.0	-2,553.8
2015	B+	2.03	1.76	84.5	138,495.0	82,630.7	37,511.4	2,137.2
2014	B+	2.10	1.79	82.2	138,798.0	79,876.9	36,928.5	1,045.8
2013	B+	2.18	1.84	79.9	129,338.0	75,678.9	35,163.3	1,836.5

Reserve Deficiency (as % of capital)

* Adequate & redundant reserves show as negatives

■ 1 Yr Dev   □ 2 Yr Dev

STATE NATIONAL INS CO   B-   Good

Major Rating Factors: Fair overall results on stability tests (4.8 on a scale of 0 to 10) including potential drain of affiliation with TX State National Group. History of adequate reserve strength (5.0) as reserves have been consistently at an acceptable level.

Other Rating Factors: Strong long-term capitalization index (8.0) based on excellent current risk adjusted capital (severe and moderate loss scenarios). Moreover, capital has steadily grown over the last five years. Excellent profitability (7.5) with operating gains in each of the last five years. Excellent liquidity (7.4) with ample operational cash flow and liquid investments.

Principal Business: Workers compensation (27%), auto physical damage (26%), auto liability (16%), commercial multiple peril (12%), homeowners multiple peril (4%), other liability (3%), and other lines (12%).

Principal Investments: Misc. investments (60%), investment grade bonds (25%), cash (12%), and real estate (3%).

Investments in Affiliates: 53%

Group Affiliation: TX State National Group

Licensed in: All states except PR

Commenced Business: September 1984

Address: 1900 L Don Dodson Dr, Bedford, TX 76021

Phone: (817) 265-2000   **Domicile State:** TX   **NAIC Code:** 12831

Data Date	Rating	RACR #1	RACR #2	Loss Ratio %	Total Assets ($mil)	Capital ($mil)	Net Premium ($mil)	Net Income ($mil)
2017	B-	1.69	1.65	49.4	442.9	311.4	45.9	7.6
2016	B-	1.63	1.56	47.6	369.7	269.4	62.6	6.5
2015	B-	1.92	1.81	49.1	319.3	229.8	56.2	5.6
2014	C+	1.94	1.84	42.5	290.7	215.8	52.2	3.2
2013	C+	1.94	1.81	40.3	218.8	155.6	42.0	2.5

TX State National Group
Composite Group Rating: B+
Largest Group Members

	Assets ($mil)	Rating
MARKEL GLOBAL REINS CO	2181	B+
MARKEL AMERICAN INS CO	586	C
STATE NATIONAL INS CO	443	B-
ALTERRA AMERICA INS CO	393	B
UNITED SPECIALTY INS CO	330	B+

STATE VOLUNTEER MUTUAL INS CO *   B+   Good

Major Rating Factors: Good overall results on stability tests (6.5 on a scale of 0 to 10). Stability strengths include good operational trends and excellent risk diversification. Strong long-term capitalization index (10.0) based on excellent current risk adjusted capital (severe and moderate loss scenarios). Moreover, capital levels have been consistent in recent years.

Other Rating Factors: Ample reserve history (9.3) that helps to protect the company against sharp claims increases. Excellent profitability (8.1) with operating gains in each of the last five years. Excellent liquidity (8.1) with ample operational cash flow and liquid investments.

Principal Business: Medical malpractice (100%).

Principal Investments: Investment grade bonds (80%), misc. investments (19%), and non investment grade bonds (1%).

Investments in Affiliates: None

Group Affiliation: None

Licensed in: AL, AR, GA, IN, KY, MS, MO, NC, TN, VA

Commenced Business: May 1976

Address: 101 Westpark Drive Suite 300, Brentwood, TN 37027

Phone: (615) 377-1999   **Domicile State:** TN   **NAIC Code:** 33049

Data Date	Rating	RACR #1	RACR #2	Loss Ratio %	Total Assets ($mil)	Capital ($mil)	Net Premium ($mil)	Net Income ($mil)
2017	B+	4.90	3.56	67.0	1,249.3	606.8	118.9	29.6
2016	B	4.69	3.51	79.3	1,211.1	567.0	111.8	22.4
2015	B	4.43	3.39	79.5	1,193.2	538.0	113.4	25.5
2014	B	4.03	2.96	84.6	1,199.1	516.6	114.6	21.5
2013	A+	3.65	2.76	89.0	1,186.2	496.7	122.2	17.4

Rating Indexes

Ranges   Cap. 2   Stab.   Res.   Prof.   Liq.

■ Weak   ▨ Fair   ▥ Good   □ Strong

STEADFAST INS CO   C+   Fair

Major Rating Factors: Fair overall results on stability tests (4.7 on a scale of 0 to 10) including fair financial strength of affiliated Zurich Financial Services Group and negative cash flow from operations for 2017. Good liquidity (6.8) with sufficient resources (cash flows and marketable investments) to handle a spike in claims.

Other Rating Factors: Strong long-term capitalization index (9.0) based on excellent current risk adjusted capital (severe and moderate loss scenarios), despite some fluctuation in capital levels. Excellent profitability (7.3) with operating gains in each of the last five years.

Principal Business: Other liability (52%), auto liability (19%), commercial multiple peril (8%), medical malpractice (7%), fire (5%), allied lines (4%), and other lines (6%).

Principal Investments: Investment grade bonds (52%) and misc. investments (48%).

Investments in Affiliates: 46%

Group Affiliation: Zurich Financial Services Group

Licensed in: All states, the District of Columbia and Puerto Rico

Commenced Business: May 1988

Address: 251 LITTLE FALLS DRIVE, Wilmington, DE 19808

Phone: (847) 605-6000   **Domicile State:** DE   **NAIC Code:** 26387

Data Date	Rating	RACR #1	RACR #2	Loss Ratio %	Total Assets ($mil)	Capital ($mil)	Net Premium ($mil)	Net Income ($mil)
2017	C+	2.38	2.35	0.0	723.4	508.8	0.0	5.9
2016	C+	2.38	2.35	0.0	605.9	498.7	0.0	6.5
2015	C+	2.42	2.39	0.0	660.2	499.6	0.0	7.9
2014	C	3.03	2.98	0.0	528.8	436.2	0.0	9.1
2013	C	3.06	3.00	0.0	602.2	430.0	0.0	5.1

Zurich Financial Services Group
Composite Group Rating: B

Largest Group Members	Assets ($mil)	Rating
ZURICH AMERICAN INS CO	31582	B
ZURICH AMERICAN LIFE INS CO	14227	C
FARMERS NEW WORLD LIFE INS CO	5127	B-
CENTRE LIFE INS CO	1791	B-
RURAL COMMUNITY INS CO	1791	C+

SURETEC INS CO *   B+   Good

Major Rating Factors: Good overall results on stability tests (6.5 on a scale of 0 to 10). Strong long-term capitalization index (8.9) based on excellent current risk adjusted capital (severe and moderate loss scenarios). Moreover, capital levels have been consistent in recent years.

Other Rating Factors: Ample reserve history (8.5) that helps to protect the company against sharp claims increases. Excellent profitability (8.6) with operating gains in each of the last five years. Return on equity has been good over the last five years, averaging 12.9%. Excellent liquidity (8.2) with ample operational cash flow and liquid investments.

Principal Business: Surety (100%).

Principal Investments: Investment grade bonds (78%), misc. investments (18%), cash (3%), and non investment grade bonds (1%).

Investments in Affiliates: 6%

Group Affiliation: SureTec Financial Corp

Licensed in: All states except PR

Commenced Business: July 1998

Address: 1330 POST OAK BLVD SUITE 1100, Houston, TX 77056

Phone: (713) 812-0800   **Domicile State:** TX   **NAIC Code:** 10916

Data Date	Rating	RACR #1	RACR #2	Loss Ratio %	Total Assets ($mil)	Capital ($mil)	Net Premium ($mil)	Net Income ($mil)
2017	B+	2.72	2.24	18.6	253.2	102.1	70.0	7.4
2016	B	3.16	2.53	12.6	227.9	94.5	61.7	13.1
2015	C+	3.33	2.66	12.5	220.9	86.6	59.3	12.5
2014	C	3.50	2.86	10.1	175.6	81.9	54.4	12.2
2013	C	3.31	2.57	17.4	157.6	78.0	44.2	11.0

SureTec Financial Corp
Composite Group Rating: B+

Largest Group Members	Assets ($mil)	Rating
MARKEL GLOBAL REINS CO	2181	B+
MARKEL AMERICAN INS CO	586	C
STATE NATIONAL INS CO	443	B-
ALTERRA AMERICA INS CO	393	B
UNITED SPECIALTY INS CO	330	B+

SWISS REINS AMERICA CORP   C   Fair

Major Rating Factors: Fair profitability index (3.5 on a scale of 0 to 10). Weak expense controls. Return on equity has been fair, averaging 10.5% over the past five years. Fair overall results on stability tests (3.5).

Other Rating Factors: Good overall long-term capitalization (5.2) based on good current risk adjusted capital (moderate loss scenario). However, capital levels have fluctuated during prior years. Ample reserve history (8.2) that helps to protect the company against sharp claims increases. Excellent liquidity (7.7) with ample operational cash flow and liquid investments.

Principal Business: (This company is a reinsurer.)

Principal Investments: Investment grade bonds (87%) and misc. investments (13%).

Investments in Affiliates: None

Group Affiliation: Swiss Reinsurance

Licensed in: All states, the District of Columbia and Puerto Rico

Commenced Business: September 1940

Address: 175 KING STREET, Armonk, NY 10504-1606

Phone: (914) 828-8000   **Domicile State:** NY   **NAIC Code:** 25364

Data Date	Rating	RACR #1	RACR #2	Loss Ratio %	Total Assets ($mil)	Capital ($mil)	Net Premium ($mil)	Net Income ($mil)
2017	C	1.20	0.78	72.7	14,202.2	3,238.0	1,916.5	121.8
2016	C-	1.00	0.74	57.2	12,927.2	3,352.3	1,882.9	406.4
2015	B-	1.07	0.79	50.4	12,795.5	3,581.1	1,987.4	389.8
2014	B-	1.30	0.93	48.9	13,109.1	4,259.8	1,881.8	498.1
2013	B-	1.50	1.03	39.0	11,409.4	4,619.3	1,965.0	644.9

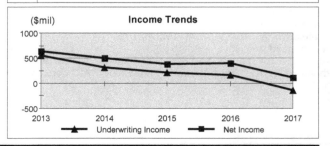

Income Trends

SYNCORA GUARANTEE INC

C+   **Fair**

Major Rating Factors: Fair overall results on stability tests (4.3 on a scale of 0 to 10) including potential drain of affiliation with Syncora Holdings Ltd, excessive premium growth and negative cash flow from operations for 2017. Fair reserve development (3.1) as the level of reserves has at times been insufficient to cover claims. In 2015 and 2014 the two year reserve development was 97% and 185% deficient respectively.

Other Rating Factors: Good overall profitability index (6.6) despite operating losses during 2014. Return on equity has been good over the last five years, averaging 12.5%. Strong long-term capitalization index (10.0) based on excellent current risk adjusted capital (severe and moderate loss scenarios), despite some fluctuation in capital levels. Superior liquidity (9.6) with ample operational cash flow and liquid investments.

Principal Business: Financial guaranty (100%).

Principal Investments: Investment grade bonds (79%), misc. investments (10%), non investment grade bonds (9%), and cash (2%).

Investments in Affiliates: None

Group Affiliation: Syncora Holdings Ltd

Licensed in: All states except AK, FL, OH, TN, PR

Commenced Business: January 1872

Address: 135 West 50th Street, New York, NY 10020

Phone: (212) 478-3400   **Domicile State:** NY   **NAIC Code:** 20311

Data Date	Rating	RACR #1	RACR #2	Loss Ratio %	Total Assets ($mil)	Capital ($mil)	Net Premium ($mil)	Net Income ($mil)
2017	C+	20.32	11.87	N/A	1,302.1	1,317.6	14.2	70.5
2016	E-	16.94	9.53	N/A	1,460.9	1,188.3	18.1	45.3
2015	E-	20.05	12.07	N/A	1,249.4	1,087.0	12.8	209.0
2014	E-	6.94	4.99	240.3	1,219.5	856.0	19.1	-52.7
2013	E-	11.39	8.21	N/A	1,034.5	973.3	23.7	391.5

Rating Indexes

TECHNOLOGY INS CO

D-   **Weak**

Major Rating Factors: Poor long-term capitalization index (0.9 on a scale of 0 to 10) based on weak current risk adjusted capital (severe and moderate loss scenarios), although results have slipped from the good range over the last two years. Weak profitability index (2.8) with operating losses during 2014 and 2017. Average return on equity over the last five years has been poor at -23.8%.

Other Rating Factors: Vulnerable liquidity (1.6) as a spike in claims may stretch capacity. Weak overall results on stability tests (1.2) including weak risk adjusted capital in prior years and weak results on operational trends. History of adequate reserve strength (6.0) as reserves have been consistently at an acceptable level.

Principal Business: Workers compensation (84%), allied lines (6%), auto liability (5%), commercial multiple peril (3%), inland marine (1%), auto physical damage (1%), and other liability (1%).

Principal Investments: Investment grade bonds (80%), misc. investments (13%), cash (6%), and non investment grade bonds (1%).

Investments in Affiliates: 4%

Group Affiliation: AmTrust Financial Services Inc

Licensed in: All states, the District of Columbia and Puerto Rico

Commenced Business: July 1991

Address: 2711 CENTERVILLE RD STE 400, Wilmington, DE 19808

Phone: (212) 220-7120   **Domicile State:** DE   **NAIC Code:** 42376

Data Date	Rating	RACR #1	RACR #2	Loss Ratio %	Total Assets ($mil)	Capital ($mil)	Net Premium ($mil)	Net Income ($mil)
2017	D-	0.36	0.23	80.2	3,773.1	1,098.7	1,322.3	-60.8
2016	C	1.17	0.82	64.8	2,350.0	577.1	1,140.4	53.9
2015	C	1.08	0.78	71.0	1,981.5	478.7	985.0	0.3
2014	C	2.25	1.63	N/A	1,502.4	479.4	-250.2	-622.6
2013	C	1.62	1.11	67.1	1,132.6	236.5	485.6	16.6

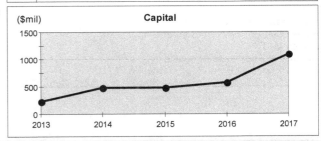

Capital

TENNESSEE FARMERS ASR CO *

B+   **Good**

Major Rating Factors: Good overall results on stability tests (6.1 on a scale of 0 to 10). Affiliation with Tennessee Farmers Mutual is a strength. Good liquidity (6.2) with sufficient resources (cash flows and marketable investments) to handle a spike in claims.

Other Rating Factors: Strong long-term capitalization index (10.0) based on excellent current risk adjusted capital (severe and moderate loss scenarios). Moreover, capital has steadily grown over the last five years. Ample reserve history (8.0) that helps to protect the company against sharp claims increases. Excellent profitability (8.9) with operating gains in each of the last five years. Return on equity has been good over the last five years, averaging 13.1%.

Principal Business: (This company is a reinsurer.)

Principal Investments: Investment grade bonds (87%) and misc. investments (13%).

Investments in Affiliates: 2%

Group Affiliation: Tennessee Farmers Mutual

Licensed in: TN

Commenced Business: August 1991

Address: 147 Bear Creek Pike, Columbia, TN 38401-2266

Phone: (931) 388-7872   **Domicile State:** TN   **NAIC Code:** 41220

Data Date	Rating	RACR #1	RACR #2	Loss Ratio %	Total Assets ($mil)	Capital ($mil)	Net Premium ($mil)	Net Income ($mil)
2017	B+	5.86	4.05	81.6	1,505.8	1,044.3	638.6	49.1
2016	B+	5.64	3.93	72.2	1,431.3	984.3	600.4	91.2
2015	B+	4.64	3.20	66.4	1,302.5	874.5	586.1	122.4
2014	B+	4.08	2.82	67.6	1,156.6	743.4	570.9	108.6
2013	B+	2.77	1.92	65.9	1,014.2	635.5	555.8	144.0

Rating Indexes

TENNESSEE FARMERS MUTUAL INS CO *

B+   **Good**

Major Rating Factors: Good overall results on stability tests (6.1 on a scale of 0 to 10). Affiliation with Tennessee Farmers Mutual is a strength. Good liquidity (6.7) with sufficient resources (cash flows and marketable investments) to handle a spike in claims.

Other Rating Factors: Strong long-term capitalization index (8.3) based on excellent current risk adjusted capital (severe and moderate loss scenarios). Moreover, capital has steadily grown over the last five years. Ample reserve history (7.5) that can protect against increases in claims costs. Excellent profitability (8.3) with operating gains in each of the last five years.

Principal Business: Homeowners multiple peril (31%), auto physical damage (27%), auto liability (26%), farmowners multiple peril (9%), fire (4%), other liability (2%), and commercial multiple peril (1%).

Principal Investments: Investment grade bonds (54%) and misc. investments (47%).

Investments in Affiliates: 38%

Group Affiliation: Tennessee Farmers Mutual

Licensed in: TN

Commenced Business: December 1952

Address: 147 Bear Creek Pike, Columbia, TN 38401-2266

Phone: (931) 388-7872   **Domicile State:** TN   **NAIC Code:** 15245

Data Date	Rating	RACR #1	RACR #2	Loss Ratio %	Total Assets ($mil)	Capital ($mil)	Net Premium ($mil)	Net Income ($mil)
2017	B+	2.29	2.13	81.6	3,084.6	2,424.4	641.6	68.2
2016	B+	1.84	1.75	72.0	2,885.1	2,285.2	603.3	110.4
2015	B+	1.84	1.74	65.8	2,658.9	2,074.6	589.2	141.4
2014	B+	1.80	1.70	67.5	2,410.2	1,807.5	574.3	134.8
2013	B+	1.80	1.67	66.8	2,191.9	1,650.4	559.4	159.8

Rating Indexes

TEXAS FARM BUREAU CASUALTY INS CO *

A-   **Excellent**

Major Rating Factors: Strong long-term capitalization index (10.0 on a scale of 0 to 10) based on excellent current risk adjusted capital (severe and moderate loss scenarios), despite some fluctuation in capital levels. History of adequate reserve strength (6.1) as reserves have been consistently at an acceptable level.

Other Rating Factors: Good liquidity (5.5) with sufficient resources (cash flows and marketable investments) to handle a spike in claims. Good overall results on stability tests (6.9). Fair profitability index (4.8) with operating losses during 2015 and 2016. Return on equity has been low, averaging 2.5% over the past five years.

Principal Business: Auto physical damage (50%), auto liability (48%), and other liability (3%).

Principal Investments: Investment grade bonds (64%) and misc. investments (39%).

Investments in Affiliates: None

Group Affiliation: TX Farm Bureau Mutual

Licensed in: TX

Commenced Business: August 2007

Address: 7420 Fish Pond Road, Waco, TX 76710

Phone: (254) 772-3030   **Domicile State:** TX   **NAIC Code:** 13004

Data Date	Rating	RACR #1	RACR #2	Loss Ratio %	Total Assets ($mil)	Capital ($mil)	Net Premium ($mil)	Net Income ($mil)
2017	A-	4.30	3.44	81.1	1,252.3	678.9	706.6	37.4
2016	B+	4.21	3.42	86.9	1,230.3	653.5	687.1	-3.4
2015	B+	4.39	3.56	88.3	1,180.6	647.8	644.4	-8.6
2014	B+	4.71	3.83	82.3	1,154.8	657.1	620.8	28.4
2013	A	4.80	3.83	81.5	1,099.9	645.0	583.4	28.0

Capital

TEXAS FARM BUREAU MUTUAL INS CO

C+   **Fair**

Major Rating Factors: Fair profitability index (4.0 on a scale of 0 to 10) with operating losses during 2013, 2014 and 2017. Fair overall results on stability tests (4.5) including negative cash flow from operations for 2017.

Other Rating Factors: History of adequate reserve strength (6.5) as reserves have been consistently at an acceptable level. Good liquidity (5.4) with sufficient resources (cash flows and marketable investments) to handle a spike in claims. Strong long-term capitalization index (9.1) based on excellent current risk adjusted capital (severe and moderate loss scenarios), despite some fluctuation in capital levels.

Principal Business: Auto liability (34%), auto physical damage (32%), homeowners multiple peril (32%), and other liability (1%).

Principal Investments: Investment grade bonds (86%), misc. investments (12%), and cash (2%).

Investments in Affiliates: 1%

Group Affiliation: TX Farm Bureau Mutual

Licensed in: TX

Commenced Business: February 1950

Address: 7420 Fish Pond Road, Waco, TX 76710

Phone: (254) 772-3030   **Domicile State:** TX   **NAIC Code:** 25380

Data Date	Rating	RACR #1	RACR #2	Loss Ratio %	Total Assets ($mil)	Capital ($mil)	Net Premium ($mil)	Net Income ($mil)
2017	C+	2.83	2.41	83.9	733.5	328.5	415.6	-6.8
2016	C	2.95	2.51	74.8	755.5	346.5	423.3	22.9
2015	D+	2.82	2.38	76.5	741.3	326.8	407.5	20.1
2014	D	2.81	2.36	79.7	705.1	309.8	389.1	-6.8
2013	D	3.28	2.75	82.6	659.9	313.0	343.1	-19.4

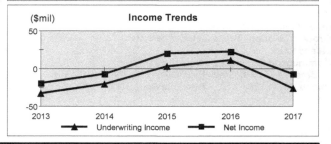

Income Trends

TIG INS CO　　　　　　　　　　　　　　　　　C　　　　Fair

Major Rating Factors: Fair long-term capitalization index (3.3 on a scale of 0 to 10) based on fair current risk adjusted capital (moderate loss scenario). Fair overall results on stability tests (3.5) including weak results on operational trends, negative cash flow from operations for 2017 and fair risk adjusted capital in prior years.

Other Rating Factors: A history of deficient reserves (2.7) that places pressure on both capital and profits. Deficiencies in the two year reserve development occurred in three of the previous five years and ranged between 18% and 24%. Weak profitability index (1.8) with operating losses during 2013, 2016 and 2017. Return on equity has been fair, averaging 6.0% over the past five years. Superior liquidity (9.8) with ample operational cash flow and liquid investments.

Principal Business: (Not applicable due to unusual reinsurance transactions.)

Principal Investments: Misc. investments (48%), investment grade bonds (48%), cash (2%), and non investment grade bonds (2%).

Investments in Affiliates: 15%

Group Affiliation: Fairfax Financial

Licensed in: All states except PR

Commenced Business: April 1915

Address: 7676 HAZARD CENTER DR STE 210, San Diego, CA 92108

Phone: (603) 656-2233　　**Domicile State:** CA　　**NAIC Code:** 25534

Data Date	Rating	RACR #1	RACR #2	Loss Ratio %	Total Assets ($mil)	Capital ($mil)	Net Premium ($mil)	Net Income ($mil)
2017	C	0.90	0.65	N/A	2,465.3	678.6	0.0	-181.1
2016	C	0.87	0.60	235.1	2,818.4	736.0	63.5	-46.1
2015	U	0.78	0.49	N/A	3,191.1	777.1	0.6	32.1
2014	D	0.45	0.32	N/A	3,546.0	996.6	-29.7	673.3
2013	D	0.40	0.31	N/A	2,444.8	850.0	1.0	-74.2

Capital ($mil)

TOA REINS CO OF AMERICA *　　　　　　　　B+　　　Good

Major Rating Factors: History of adequate reserve strength (6.0 on a scale of 0 to 10) as reserves have been consistently at an acceptable level. Good liquidity (6.8) with sufficient resources (cash flows and marketable investments) to handle a spike in claims.

Other Rating Factors: Good overall results on stability tests (6.5). Strong long-term capitalization index (7.9) based on excellent current risk adjusted capital (severe and moderate loss scenarios), despite some fluctuation in capital levels. Fair profitability index (4.8). Fair expense controls. Return on equity has been fair, averaging 7.2% over the past five years.

Principal Business: (This company is a reinsurer.)

Principal Investments: Investment grade bonds (81%), misc. investments (17%), cash (1%), and non investment grade bonds (1%).

Investments in Affiliates: None

Group Affiliation: Toa Reinsurance Co Ltd Japan

Licensed in: All states except PR

Commenced Business: January 1972

Address: 251 LITTLE FALLS DRIVE, Wilmington, DE 19808

Phone: (973) 898-9480　　**Domicile State:** DE　　**NAIC Code:** 42439

Data Date	Rating	RACR #1	RACR #2	Loss Ratio %	Total Assets ($mil)	Capital ($mil)	Net Premium ($mil)	Net Income ($mil)
2017	B+	2.43	1.58	78.7	1,820.3	660.2	423.7	20.5
2016	B+	2.60	1.71	76.3	1,775.2	669.3	397.0	18.5
2015	B+	2.68	1.77	64.1	1,715.4	672.4	363.9	63.3
2014	B+	2.66	1.76	61.7	1,773.3	714.6	351.5	72.8
2013	B+	2.14	1.43	65.1	1,779.4	682.4	403.1	70.7

Reserve Deficiency (as % of capital)

* Adequate & redundant reserves show as negatives

■ 1 Yr Dev　　□ 2 Yr Dev

TOKIO MARINE AMERICA INS CO *　　　　　A　　Excellent

Major Rating Factors: Strong long-term capitalization index (8.3 on a scale of 0 to 10) based on excellent current risk adjusted capital (severe and moderate loss scenarios). Furthermore, this high level of risk adjusted capital has been consistently maintained in previous years. Excellent overall results on stability tests (7.2). Stability strengths include excellent operational trends and excellent risk diversification.

Other Rating Factors: History of adequate reserve strength (6.7) as reserves have been consistently at an acceptable level. Good liquidity (6.9) with sufficient resources (cash flows and marketable investments) to handle a spike in claims. Fair profitability index (4.6). Fair expense controls. Return on equity has been low, averaging 2.7% over the past five years.

Principal Business: Auto liability (17%), ocean marine (14%), fire (12%), workers compensation (9%), other liability (8%), allied lines (8%), and other lines (32%).

Principal Investments: Investment grade bonds (85%), misc. investments (12%), cash (2%), and non investment grade bonds (1%).

Investments in Affiliates: 12%

Group Affiliation: Tokio Marine Holdings Inc

Licensed in: All states, the District of Columbia and Puerto Rico

Commenced Business: September 1999

Address: 1221 AVE OF THE AMERICAS #1500, New York, NY 10020-1001

Phone: (610) 227-1253　　**Domicile State:** NY　　**NAIC Code:** 10945

Data Date	Rating	RACR #1	RACR #2	Loss Ratio %	Total Assets ($mil)	Capital ($mil)	Net Premium ($mil)	Net Income ($mil)
2017	A-	2.45	1.84	76.1	1,409.5	504.7	287.2	7.8
2016	A	2.55	1.91	75.4	1,444.6	539.3	302.7	0.0
2015	A	2.27	1.73	78.0	1,360.5	510.6	308.5	17.8
2014	A	2.98	1.90	76.7	1,349.2	497.3	248.0	25.4
2013	A	2.78	1.85	73.8	1,383.5	514.4	275.0	16.0

Capital ($mil)

TOKIO MILLENNIUM RE AG (US BRANCH)   C   Fair

Major Rating Factors: Fair reserve development (4.6 on a scale of 0 to 10) as reserves have generally been sufficient to cover claims. Fair overall results on stability tests (3.5) including weak results on operational trends and excessive premium growth.

Other Rating Factors: Weak profitability index (2.2) with operating losses during 2014, 2015, 2016 and 2017. Good overall long-term capitalization (5.5) based on good current risk adjusted capital (moderate loss scenario). However, capital levels have fluctuated somewhat during past years. Good liquidity (6.0) with sufficient resources (cash flows and marketable investments) to handle a spike in claims.

Principal Business: (This company is a reinsurer.)

Principal Investments: Investment grade bonds (94%) and misc. investments (6%).

Investments in Affiliates: None

Group Affiliation: Tokio Marine Holdings Inc

Licensed in: All states except PR

Commenced Business: June 2014

Address: 1177 Ave of Americas 41st Fl, New York, NY 10036

Phone: (203) 658-1900   **Domicile State:** NY   **NAIC Code:** 15529

Data Date	Rating	RACR #1	RACR #2	Loss Ratio %	Total Assets ($mil)	Capital ($mil)	Net Premium ($mil)	Net Income ($mil)
2017	C	1.36	0.81	88.4	1,226.2	231.2	556.6	-84.4
2016	C	1.56	0.88	65.2	1,011.7	194.7	538.6	-23.6
2015	C+	1.91	0.97	60.0	817.3	217.9	647.4	-119.7
2014	U	5.10	2.78	60.6	222.6	102.8	121.9	-46.8
2013	N/A	N/A	N/A	0.0	0.0	0.0	0.0	0.0

Reserve Deficiency (as % of capital)

* Adequate & redundant reserves show as negatives   ■ 1 Yr Dev   □ 2 Yr Dev

TOYOTA MOTOR INS CO   C+   Fair

Major Rating Factors: Fair overall results on stability tests (4.0 on a scale of 0 to 10) including potential drain of affiliation with Toyota Motor Corp. History of adequate reserve strength (5.0) as reserves have been consistently at an acceptable level.

Other Rating Factors: Strong long-term capitalization index (10.0) based on excellent current risk adjusted capital (severe and moderate loss scenarios). Moreover, capital levels have been consistent in recent years. Excellent profitability (8.5) with operating gains in each of the last five years. Excellent liquidity (7.4) with ample operational cash flow and liquid investments.

Principal Business: Other liability (82%), credit (5%), and aggregate write-ins for other lines of business (1%).

Principal Investments: Investment grade bonds (89%), cash (9%), misc. investments (1%), and non investment grade bonds (1%).

Investments in Affiliates: None

Group Affiliation: Toyota Motor Corp

Licensed in: All states except PR

Commenced Business: December 1909

Address: 5005 North River Boulevard NE, Cedar Rapids, IA 52411

Phone: (469) 486-5355   **Domicile State:** IA   **NAIC Code:** 37621

Data Date	Rating	RACR #1	RACR #2	Loss Ratio %	Total Assets ($mil)	Capital ($mil)	Net Premium ($mil)	Net Income ($mil)
2017	C+	6.27	5.47	73.6	557.7	254.1	106.9	10.9
2016	C+	7.53	6.55	66.1	518.6	246.9	89.2	16.6
2015	C+	7.24	5.88	48.8	493.8	229.1	91.8	16.3
2014	C	9.12	7.65	43.3	453.0	211.4	79.7	14.9
2013	C	9.87	8.12	38.0	420.0	194.9	65.6	17.1

Rating Indexes

Ranges   Cap. 2   Stab.   Res.   Prof.   Liq.

■ Weak   ■ Fair   ▨ Good   □ Strong

TRANS PACIFIC INS CO *   B+   Good

Major Rating Factors: History of adequate reserve strength (6.0 on a scale of 0 to 10) as reserves have been consistently at an acceptable level. Good overall results on stability tests (6.0). Stability strengths include good operational trends and excellent risk diversification.

Other Rating Factors: Strong long-term capitalization index (10.0) based on excellent current risk adjusted capital (severe and moderate loss scenarios), despite some fluctuation in capital levels. Excellent profitability (7.5) despite modest operating losses during 2013. Excellent expense controls. Excellent liquidity (7.9) with ample operational cash flow and liquid investments.

Principal Business: Workers compensation (76%), commercial multiple peril (15%), other liability (6%), products liability (1%), and auto liability (1%).

Principal Investments: Investment grade bonds (93%), misc. investments (4%), and cash (3%).

Investments in Affiliates: None

Group Affiliation: Tokio Marine Holdings Inc

Licensed in: All states except LA, NH, NM, VT, PR

Commenced Business: January 1982

Address: 1221 AVE OF THE AMERICAS #1500, New York, NY 10020-1001

Phone: (610) 227-1253   **Domicile State:** NY   **NAIC Code:** 41238

Data Date	Rating	RACR #1	RACR #2	Loss Ratio %	Total Assets ($mil)	Capital ($mil)	Net Premium ($mil)	Net Income ($mil)
2017	B+	19.37	17.44	N/A	67.6	54.2	0.0	1.5
2016	B	15.83	11.89	N/A	71.0	52.7	0.0	1.1
2015	B	14.09	9.91	N/A	73.0	51.5	0.0	1.5
2014	B	14.87	7.39	N/A	68.1	49.6	0.0	1.5
2013	B	14.41	6.89	N/A	65.1	47.2	-0.4	-0.2

Reserve Deficiency (as % of capital)

* Adequate & redundant reserves show as negatives   ■ 1 Yr Dev   □ 2 Yr Dev

TRANSAMERICA CASUALTY INS CO   B-   Good

Major Rating Factors: History of adequate reserve strength (5.6 on a scale of 0 to 10) as reserves have been consistently at an acceptable level. Good overall results on stability tests (5.3).

Other Rating Factors: Strong long-term capitalization index (8.8) based on excellent current risk adjusted capital (severe and moderate loss scenarios). Moreover, capital has steadily grown over the last five years. Excellent profitability (8.5) with operating gains in each of the last five years. Vulnerable liquidity (2.9) as a spike in claims may stretch capacity.

Principal Business: (Not applicable due to unusual reinsurance transactions.)

Principal Investments: Investment grade bonds (77%), misc. investments (22%), and non investment grade bonds (3%).

Investments in Affiliates: None

Group Affiliation: AEGON USA Inc

Licensed in: All states except PR

Commenced Business: April 1958

Address: 366 E Broad Street, Columbus, OH 43215

Phone: (319) 355-8511   **Domicile State:** OH   **NAIC Code:** 10952

Data Date	Rating	RACR #1	RACR #2	Loss Ratio %	Total Assets ($mil)	Capital ($mil)	Net Premium ($mil)	Net Income ($mil)
2017	B-	3.44	2.54	54.3	455.5	274.3	370.8	16.1
2016	B-	2.68	1.87	59.3	395.5	179.5	358.5	11.2
2015	B-	3.49	2.27	59.7	355.6	166.5	318.0	12.9
2014	B-	3.04	1.90	61.8	312.4	129.9	275.0	15.0
2013	B-	2.68	1.73	62.5	324.6	118.1	236.0	4.1

Reserve Deficiency (as % of capital)

* Adequate & redundant reserves show as negatives   ■ 1 Yr Dev □ 2 Yr Dev

TRANSATLANTIC REINS CO *   B+   Good

Major Rating Factors: Good overall profitability index (6.4 on a scale of 0 to 10). Weak expense controls. Return on equity has been good over the last five years, averaging 10.0%. Good liquidity (6.7) with sufficient resources (cash flows and marketable investments) to handle a spike in claims.

Other Rating Factors: Good overall results on stability tests (6.5). Strong long-term capitalization index (7.7) based on excellent current risk adjusted capital (severe and moderate loss scenarios), despite some fluctuation in capital levels. Ample reserve history (9.1) that helps to protect the company against sharp claims increases.

Principal Business: (This company is a reinsurer.)

Principal Investments: Investment grade bonds (63%), misc. investments (31%), cash (3%), and non investment grade bonds (3%).

Investments in Affiliates: 9%

Group Affiliation: Alleghany Corp Group

Licensed in: All states, the District of Columbia and Puerto Rico

Commenced Business: January 1953

Address: ONE LIBERTY PLAZA 165 BROADWAY, New York, NY 10006

Phone: (212) 365-2200   **Domicile State:** NY   **NAIC Code:** 19453

Data Date	Rating	RACR #1	RACR #2	Loss Ratio %	Total Assets ($mil)	Capital ($mil)	Net Premium ($mil)	Net Income ($mil)
2017	B+	2.15	1.47	72.4	14,732.2	4,992.9	3,479.3	21.4
2016	B	2.15	1.48	58.2	14,019.4	4,908.7	3,574.2	541.7
2015	B	2.17	1.52	53.3	13,834.9	4,816.9	2,967.9	512.5
2014	B	2.10	1.44	55.0	14,574.6	4,770.5	2,986.8	562.1
2013	B	2.02	1.39	55.2	15,013.0	4,718.9	2,977.0	770.4

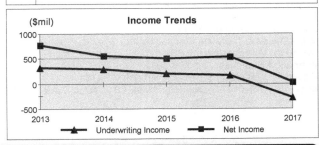

Income Trends ($mil)

—▲— Underwriting Income   —■— Net Income

TRAVELERS CASUALTY & SURETY CO *   A-   Excellent

Major Rating Factors: Excellent overall results on stability tests (7.2 on a scale of 0 to 10). Stability strengths include excellent operational trends and excellent risk diversification. Strong long-term capitalization index (7.7) based on excellent current risk adjusted capital (severe and moderate loss scenarios). Furthermore, this high level of risk adjusted capital has been consistently maintained in previous years.

Other Rating Factors: Ample reserve history (8.0) that helps to protect the company against sharp claims increases. Good overall profitability index (6.3). Fair expense controls. Return on equity has been excellent over the last five years averaging 17.4%. Good liquidity (6.8) with sufficient resources (cash flows and marketable investments) to handle a spike in claims.

Principal Business: Workers compensation (75%), surety (15%), homeowners multiple peril (8%), fire (1%), and other liability (1%).

Principal Investments: Investment grade bonds (67%), misc. investments (32%), and non investment grade bonds (1%).

Investments in Affiliates: 26%

Group Affiliation: Travelers Companies Inc

Licensed in: All states, the District of Columbia and Puerto Rico

Commenced Business: May 1907

Address: ONE TOWER SQUARE, Hartford, CT 6183

Phone: (860) 277-0111   **Domicile State:** CT   **NAIC Code:** 19038

Data Date	Rating	RACR #1	RACR #2	Loss Ratio %	Total Assets ($mil)	Capital ($mil)	Net Premium ($mil)	Net Income ($mil)
2017	A-	1.69	1.50	69.5	16,983.8	6,526.1	4,648.6	879.7
2016	A-	1.68	1.49	63.4	16,564.3	6,485.8	4,432.6	1,183.9
2015	A-	1.65	1.45	58.7	16,273.6	6,376.3	4,230.7	1,259.2
2014	A-	1.63	1.43	60.5	16,436.2	6,469.5	4,111.2	1,141.3
2013	A-	1.75	1.53	60.9	16,464.4	6,558.6	4,101.0	1,165.6

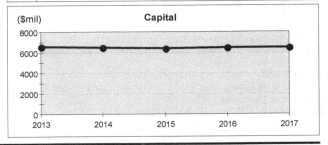

Capital ($mil)

TRAVELERS CASUALTY & SURETY CO OF AM B- Good

Major Rating Factors: Fair overall results on stability tests (4.9 on a scale of 0 to 10). Good overall profitability index (5.3). Weak expense controls. Return on equity has been excellent over the last five years averaging 23.4%.

Other Rating Factors: Strong long-term capitalization index (10.0) based on excellent current risk adjusted capital (severe and moderate loss scenarios), despite some fluctuation in capital levels. Ample reserve history (9.5) that helps to protect the company against sharp claims increases. Excellent liquidity (7.0) with ample operational cash flow and liquid investments.

Principal Business: Other liability (49%), surety (39%), fidelity (10%), and burglary & theft (3%).

Principal Investments: Investment grade bonds (91%), misc. investments (9%), and non investment grade bonds (1%).

Investments in Affiliates: 9%

Group Affiliation: Travelers Companies Inc

Licensed in: All states, the District of Columbia and Puerto Rico

Commenced Business: July 1974

Address: ONE TOWER SQUARE, Hartford, CT 6183

Phone: (860) 277-0111 **Domicile State:** CT **NAIC Code:** 31194

Data Date	Rating	RACR #1	RACR #2	Loss Ratio %	Total Assets ($mil)	Capital ($mil)	Net Premium ($mil)	Net Income ($mil)
2017	B-	4.30	3.24	28.5	4,232.8	2,016.6	1,491.7	386.9
2016	C+	4.61	3.47	20.3	4,195.8	2,088.2	1,419.8	461.9
2015	C+	5.05	3.66	20.9	4,184.9	2,103.6	1,372.9	470.0
2014	C+	4.62	3.46	9.0	4,225.2	2,114.7	1,408.3	565.8
2013	C+	4.75	3.18	13.9	4,147.5	1,881.7	1,293.9	500.5

Rating Indexes

TRAVELERS CASUALTY INS CO OF AMERICA B Good

Major Rating Factors: Good liquidity (6.6 on a scale of 0 to 10) with sufficient resources (cash flows and marketable investments) to handle a spike in claims. Good overall results on stability tests (6.1).

Other Rating Factors: Fair profitability index (3.9). Fair expense controls. Return on equity has been fair, averaging 14.8% over the past five years. Strong long-term capitalization index (7.9) based on excellent current risk adjusted capital (severe and moderate loss scenarios), despite some fluctuation in capital levels. Ample reserve history (8.4) that helps to protect the company against sharp claims increases.

Principal Business: Commercial multiple peril (66%), workers compensation (17%), auto liability (13%), and auto physical damage (4%).

Principal Investments: Investment grade bonds (95%) and misc. investments (5%).

Investments in Affiliates: None

Group Affiliation: Travelers Companies Inc

Licensed in: All states except PR

Commenced Business: October 1971

Address: ONE TOWER SQUARE, Hartford, CT 6183

Phone: (860) 277-0111 **Domicile State:** CT **NAIC Code:** 19046

Data Date	Rating	RACR #1	RACR #2	Loss Ratio %	Total Assets ($mil)	Capital ($mil)	Net Premium ($mil)	Net Income ($mil)
2017	B	2.44	1.62	69.5	1,958.1	532.1	623.3	59.5
2016	B	2.61	1.70	63.4	1,937.0	560.0	594.4	67.8
2015	B	2.73	1.73	58.7	1,942.2	586.0	567.3	104.2
2014	B	2.66	1.67	60.5	1,918.5	566.2	551.1	91.4
2013	B	2.62	1.66	60.9	1,893.1	549.8	549.8	91.5

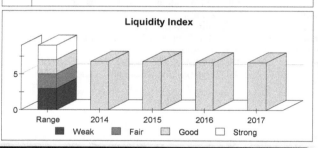

Liquidity Index

TRAVELERS INDEMNITY CO * A- Excellent

Major Rating Factors: Strong long-term capitalization index (7.8 on a scale of 0 to 10) based on excellent current risk adjusted capital (severe and moderate loss scenarios). Furthermore, this high level of risk adjusted capital has been consistently maintained in previous years. Ample reserve history (8.0) that helps to protect the company against sharp claims increases.

Other Rating Factors: Excellent overall results on stability tests (7.2). Stability strengths include excellent operational trends and excellent risk diversification. Good overall profitability index (6.0). Fair expense controls. Return on equity has been excellent over the last five years averaging 15.4%. Good liquidity (6.8) with sufficient resources (cash flows and marketable investments) to handle a spike in claims.

Principal Business: Workers compensation (22%), other liability (20%), commercial multiple peril (14%), auto liability (13%), allied lines (11%), fire (8%), and other lines (12%).

Principal Investments: Investment grade bonds (76%), misc. investments (24%), non investment grade bonds (2%), and real estate (2%).

Investments in Affiliates: 19%

Group Affiliation: Travelers Companies Inc

Licensed in: All states, the District of Columbia and Puerto Rico

Commenced Business: May 1906

Address: ONE TOWER SQUARE, Hartford, CT 6183

Phone: (860) 277-0111 **Domicile State:** CT **NAIC Code:** 25658

Data Date	Rating	RACR #1	RACR #2	Loss Ratio %	Total Assets ($mil)	Capital ($mil)	Net Premium ($mil)	Net Income ($mil)
2017	A-	1.86	1.57	69.5	21,394.5	6,820.2	5,317.6	950.3
2016	B+	1.84	1.55	63.4	21,180.5	7,003.5	5,070.5	1,100.1
2015	B+	1.78	1.49	58.7	20,817.8	6,844.6	4,840.0	1,164.1
2014	B	1.73	1.46	60.5	20,724.5	6,633.4	4,704.2	942.2
2013	B	1.82	1.52	60.9	20,662.6	6,706.1	4,531.6	1,065.7

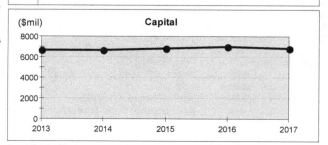

Capital

TRAVELERS INDEMNITY CO OF CT

B   **Good**

Major Rating Factors: Good liquidity (6.8 on a scale of 0 to 10) with sufficient resources (cash flows and marketable investments) to handle a spike in claims. Good overall results on stability tests (6.0).

Other Rating Factors: Fair profitability index (3.8). Fair expense controls. Return on equity has been fair, averaging 12.5% over the past five years. Strong long-term capitalization index (8.5) based on excellent current risk adjusted capital (severe and moderate loss scenarios), despite some fluctuation in capital levels. Ample reserve history (8.1) that helps to protect the company against sharp claims increases.

Principal Business: Workers compensation (29%), commercial multiple peril (27%), auto liability (23%), other liability (11%), auto physical damage (6%), farmowners multiple peril (2%), and other lines (2%).

Principal Investments: Investment grade bonds (97%) and misc. investments (3%).

Investments in Affiliates: None

Group Affiliation: Travelers Companies Inc

Licensed in: All states, the District of Columbia and Puerto Rico

Commenced Business: September 1860

Address: ONE TOWER SQUARE, Hartford, CT 6183

Phone: (860) 277-0111   **Domicile State:** CT   **NAIC Code:** 25682

Data Date	Rating	RACR #1	RACR #2	Loss Ratio %	Total Assets ($mil)	Capital ($mil)	Net Premium ($mil)	Net Income ($mil)
2017	B	3.00	1.99	69.5	1,088.9	332.5	312.8	31.4
2016	B	3.16	2.06	63.4	1,084.1	345.1	298.3	38.0
2015	B	3.25	2.07	58.7	1,075.7	354.4	284.7	46.2
2014	B	3.53	2.22	60.5	1,117.8	383.1	276.6	56.6
2013	B	3.43	2.18	60.9	1,082.4	365.6	275.9	51.8

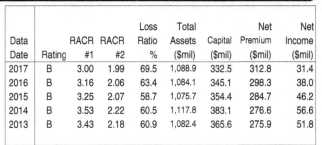

Liquidity Index

Range / 2014 / 2015 / 2016 / 2017
Weak ■ Fair ■ Good ☐ Strong ☐

TRAVELERS PROPERTY CAS OF AMERICA

B   **Good**

Major Rating Factors: Good overall results on stability tests (5.9 on a scale of 0 to 10) despite negative cash flow from operations for 2017. Affiliation with Travelers Companies Inc is a strength. Fair profitability index (4.0). Fair expense controls. Return on equity has been low, averaging 3.8% over the past five years.

Other Rating Factors: Strong long-term capitalization index (10.0) based on excellent current risk adjusted capital (severe and moderate loss scenarios), despite some fluctuation in capital levels. Ample reserve history (7.4) that can protect against increases in claims costs. Excellent liquidity (7.0) with ample operational cash flow and liquid investments.

Principal Business: Workers compensation (31%), other liability (20%), commercial multiple peril (16%), auto liability (8%), inland marine (8%), fire (4%), and other lines (13%).

Principal Investments: Investment grade bonds (98%) and misc. investments (2%).

Investments in Affiliates: None

Group Affiliation: Travelers Companies Inc

Licensed in: All states, the District of Columbia and Puerto Rico

Commenced Business: August 1971

Address: ONE TOWER SQUARE, Hartford, CT 6183

Phone: (860) 277-0111   **Domicile State:** CT   **NAIC Code:** 25674

Data Date	Rating	RACR #1	RACR #2	Loss Ratio %	Total Assets ($mil)	Capital ($mil)	Net Premium ($mil)	Net Income ($mil)
2017	B	14.25	9.35	69.5	857.4	435.0	82.2	13.5
2016	B	14.45	9.35	63.4	837.1	436.9	78.4	16.1
2015	B	14.66	9.30	58.7	848.4	443.9	74.8	19.7
2014	B	16.67	10.46	60.5	933.2	505.0	72.7	18.4
2013	B	16.40	10.35	60.9	907.0	487.0	72.5	20.2

Travelers Companies Inc
Composite Group Rating: A-
Largest Group Members

Largest Group Members	Assets ($mil)	Rating
TRAVELERS INDEMNITY CO	21394	A-
ST PAUL FIRE MARINE INS CO	18716	B
TRAVELERS CASUALTY SURETY CO	16984	A-
TRAVELERS CASUALTY SURETY CO OF AM	4233	B-
PHOENIX INS CO	4210	B

TREXIS INSURANCE CORP *

B+   **Good**

Major Rating Factors: Good overall profitability index (6.4 on a scale of 0 to 10). Fair expense controls. Return on equity has been low, averaging 3.1% over the past five years. Good liquidity (6.1) with sufficient resources (cash flows and marketable investments) to handle a spike in claims.

Other Rating Factors: Good overall results on stability tests (6.5). Stability strengths include good operational trends and excellent risk diversification. Strong long-term capitalization index (9.1) based on excellent current risk adjusted capital (severe and moderate loss scenarios), despite some fluctuation in capital levels. Ample reserve history (7.8) that can protect against increases in claims costs.

Principal Business: Auto liability (75%) and auto physical damage (25%).

Principal Investments: Investment grade bonds (52%), misc. investments (41%), cash (5%), and non investment grade bonds (2%).

Investments in Affiliates: None

Group Affiliation: Alfa Ins Group

Licensed in: AL, AR, IN, KY, MO, OH, TN, TX, VA

Commenced Business: January 2005

Address: 2108 East South Boulevard, Montgomery, AL 36116-2015

Phone: (334) 288-3900   **Domicile State:** VA   **NAIC Code:** 12188

Data Date	Rating	RACR #1	RACR #2	Loss Ratio %	Total Assets ($mil)	Capital ($mil)	Net Premium ($mil)	Net Income ($mil)
2017	B+	3.57	2.54	75.2	108.1	50.4	53.2	0.5
2016	B	3.63	2.56	72.1	104.1	50.7	49.2	1.5
2015	B	3.01	2.06	70.7	95.5	44.4	45.5	1.2
2014	C+	3.33	2.31	70.4	96.7	47.3	44.8	1.2
2013	C+	3.40	2.26	68.5	93.4	45.9	43.6	2.8

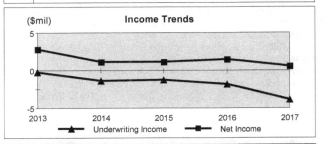

($mil)   Income Trends

2013 / 2014 / 2015 / 2016 / 2017
▲ Underwriting Income ■ Net Income

TREXIS ONE INSURANCE GROUP *

A-   Excellent

Major Rating Factors: Strong long-term capitalization index (8.5 on a scale of 0 to 10) based on excellent current risk adjusted capital (severe and moderate loss scenarios). Furthermore, this high level of risk adjusted capital has been consistently maintained in previous years. Ample reserve history (7.8) that can protect against increases in claims costs.

Other Rating Factors: Good overall profitability index (6.5). Fair expense controls. Return on equity has been low, averaging 3.9% over the past five years. Good liquidity (6.4) with sufficient resources (cash flows and marketable investments) to handle a spike in claims. Good overall results on stability tests (6.5). Stability strengths include good operational trends and excellent risk diversification.

Principal Business: Auto liability (73%) and auto physical damage (27%).

Principal Investments: Investment grade bonds (60%), misc. investments (32%), and cash (8%).

Investments in Affiliates: None

Group Affiliation: Alfa Ins Group

Licensed in: AL, AR, GA, IN, KY, MS, MO, OH, TN, TX, VA

Commenced Business: December 1999

Address: 2108 East South Boulevard, Montgomery, AL 36116-2015

Phone: (334) 288-3900   **Domicile State:** VA   **NAIC Code:** 11004

Data Date	Rating	RACR #1	RACR #2	Loss Ratio %	Total Assets ($mil)	Capital ($mil)	Net Premium ($mil)	Net Income ($mil)
2017	A-	3.16	2.25	75.1	56.6	28.9	26.6	0.4
2016	B+	3.17	2.24	72.2	53.8	27.9	24.6	0.8
2015	B	2.81	1.90	70.7	50.8	26.2	22.8	1.0
2014	C+	2.35	1.61	70.4	52.8	26.8	22.4	0.6
2013	C+	1.45	1.00	68.8	43.4	18.6	21.8	1.8

TRINITY UNIVERSAL INS CO

C+   Fair

Major Rating Factors: Fair overall results on stability tests (4.7 on a scale of 0 to 10). Strengths include potentially strong support from affiliation with Kemper Corporation. Fair profitability index (3.1). Fair expense controls. Return on equity has been fair, averaging 8.8% over the past five years.

Other Rating Factors: Vulnerable liquidity (1.7) as a spike in claims may stretch capacity. Strong long-term capitalization index (7.5) based on excellent current risk adjusted capital (severe and moderate loss scenarios), despite some fluctuation in capital levels. Ample reserve history (8.5) that helps to protect the company against sharp claims increases.

Principal Business: Homeowners multiple peril (39%), auto liability (32%), auto physical damage (25%), other liability (2%), inland marine (1%), and fire (1%).

Principal Investments: Investment grade bonds (48%), misc. investments (46%), and non investment grade bonds (8%).

Investments in Affiliates: 16%

Group Affiliation: Kemper Corporation

Licensed in: AL, AZ, AR, CA, CO, DE, FL, GA, ID, IL, IN, IA, KS, KY, LA, MI, MN, MS, MO, MT, NE, NH, NM, NY, NC, OH, OK, OR, PA, SC, TN, TX, UT, VA, WA, WV, WI, WY

Commenced Business: February 1926

Address: 8360 LBJ FREEWAY SUITE 400, Dallas, TX 75243-1134

Phone: (904) 245-5600   **Domicile State:** TX   **NAIC Code:** 19887

Data Date	Rating	RACR #1	RACR #2	Loss Ratio %	Total Assets ($mil)	Capital ($mil)	Net Premium ($mil)	Net Income ($mil)
2017	C+	1.74	1.30	80.0	1,853.3	656.7	1,223.7	7.1
2016	B	2.15	1.64	71.5	1,900.8	771.4	1,194.5	70.0
2015	B	2.16	1.64	68.4	1,964.7	817.4	1,210.9	89.7
2014	B	2.27	1.69	67.8	2,200.1	943.4	1,279.5	82.5
2013	B	2.19	1.62	66.7	2,380.9	984.1	1,435.7	138.5

TRUCK INS EXCHANGE

C+   Fair

Major Rating Factors: Fair profitability index (3.8 on a scale of 0 to 10) with operating losses during 2014, 2015 and 2016. Fair overall results on stability tests (4.8) including negative cash flow from operations for 2017.

Other Rating Factors: Good overall long-term capitalization (5.3) based on good current risk adjusted capital (severe and moderate loss scenarios). However, capital levels have fluctuated somewhat during past years. History of adequate reserve strength (5.5) as reserves have been consistently at an acceptable level. Vulnerable liquidity (2.7) as a spike in claims may stretch capacity.

Principal Business: Commercial multiple peril (40%), homeowners multiple peril (22%), workers compensation (12%), other liability (11%), auto liability (10%), and auto physical damage (4%).

Principal Investments: Misc. investments (54%), investment grade bonds (52%), non investment grade bonds (1%), and real estate (1%).

Investments in Affiliates: 48%

Group Affiliation: Farmers Insurance Group of Companies

Licensed in: All states except PR

Commenced Business: February 1935

Address: 6301 OWENSMOUTH AVE, Woodland Hills, CA 91367

Phone: (323) 932-3200   **Domicile State:** CA   **NAIC Code:** 21709

Data Date	Rating	RACR #1	RACR #2	Loss Ratio %	Total Assets ($mil)	Capital ($mil)	Net Premium ($mil)	Net Income ($mil)
2017	C+	0.86	0.79	70.0	2,107.6	640.8	1,099.3	9.8
2016	C+	0.84	0.77	72.5	2,143.6	615.7	1,144.0	-19.6
2015	C+	0.88	0.80	69.0	2,164.8	624.1	1,157.1	-6.9
2014	C+	0.90	0.83	65.8	2,077.6	618.7	1,089.8	-7.3
2013	C+	0.86	0.80	66.9	1,933.4	563.5	1,056.9	1.5

TWIN CITY FIRE INS CO

B **Good**

Major Rating Factors: History of adequate reserve strength (5.9 on a scale of 0 to 10) as reserves have been consistently at an acceptable level. Good overall results on stability tests (5.8).

Other Rating Factors: Fair profitability index (4.4). Good expense controls. Return on equity has been fair, averaging 8.9% over the past five years. Strong long-term capitalization index (10.0) based on excellent current risk adjusted capital (severe and moderate loss scenarios), despite some fluctuation in capital levels. Excellent liquidity (7.0) with ample operational cash flow and liquid investments.

Principal Business: Workers compensation (42%), other liability (22%), commercial multiple peril (13%), auto liability (10%), auto physical damage (6%), products liability (4%), and homeowners multiple peril (2%).

Principal Investments: Investment grade bonds (99%) and misc. investments (1%).

Investments in Affiliates: None

Group Affiliation: Hartford Financial Services Inc

Licensed in: All states except PR

Commenced Business: July 1987

Address: 501 Pennsylvania Pkwy Ste 400, Indianapolis, IN 46280-0014

Phone: (860) 547-5000 **Domicile State:** IN **NAIC Code:** 29459

Data Date	Rating	RACR #1	RACR #2	Loss Ratio %	Total Assets ($mil)	Capital ($mil)	Net Premium ($mil)	Net Income ($mil)
2017	B	4.97	3.31	68.7	663.3	273.3	160.6	22.0
2016	B	5.30	3.53	70.4	675.5	281.3	158.0	21.0
2015	B	5.45	3.61	66.1	653.2	286.6	158.1	27.6
2014	B	5.60	3.71	67.0	650.4	288.9	153.7	27.6
2013	B	5.67	3.77	68.8	641.7	288.1	149.2	27.7

Reserve Deficiency (as % of capital)

* Adequate & redundant reserves show as negatives

■ 1 Yr Dev
□ 2 Yr Dev

UNITED EDUCATORS INS A RECIP RRG *

B+ **Good**

Major Rating Factors: Good overall profitability index (6.9 on a scale of 0 to 10). Good expense controls. Good overall results on stability tests (6.5).

Other Rating Factors: Strong long-term capitalization index (7.5) based on excellent current risk adjusted capital (severe and moderate loss scenarios). Moreover, capital levels have been consistent in recent years. Ample reserve history (8.9) that helps to protect the company against sharp claims increases. Excellent liquidity (7.0) with ample operational cash flow and liquid investments.

Principal Business: Other liability (100%).

Principal Investments: Investment grade bonds (75%), misc. investments (24%), and non investment grade bonds (1%).

Investments in Affiliates: None

Group Affiliation: None

Licensed in: All states, the District of Columbia and Puerto Rico

Commenced Business: March 1987

Address: 76 St Paul Street Suite 500, Burlington, VT 05401-4477

Phone: (301) 907-4908 **Domicile State:** VT **NAIC Code:** 10020

Data Date	Rating	RACR #1	RACR #2	Loss Ratio %	Total Assets ($mil)	Capital ($mil)	Net Premium ($mil)	Net Income ($mil)
2017	B+	1.73	1.37	79.1	912.3	306.0	149.8	15.6
2016	B	1.60	1.24	78.3	903.2	291.2	140.9	22.4
2015	C+	1.63	1.32	78.2	874.5	284.3	144.6	23.4
2014	C	1.74	1.41	77.3	820.4	281.8	139.0	26.1
2013	C	1.68	1.35	76.9	759.7	254.5	123.7	37.7

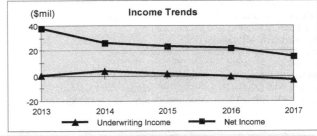

Income Trends

▲ Underwriting Income ■ Net Income

UNITED FARM FAMILY MUTUAL INS CO *

B+ **Good**

Major Rating Factors: Good liquidity (5.8 on a scale of 0 to 10) with sufficient resources (cash flows and marketable investments) to handle a spike in claims. Good overall results on stability tests (6.4).

Other Rating Factors: Strong long-term capitalization index (9.1) based on excellent current risk adjusted capital (severe and moderate loss scenarios). Moreover, capital levels have been consistent in recent years. Ample reserve history (8.2) that helps to protect the company against sharp claims increases. Excellent profitability (8.8) with operating gains in each of the last five years. Return on equity has been good over the last five years, averaging 10.5%.

Principal Business: Auto liability (26%), homeowners multiple peril (23%), auto physical damage (21%), farmowners multiple peril (14%), commercial multiple peril (8%), allied lines (3%), and other lines (4%).

Principal Investments: Investment grade bonds (74%), misc. investments (24%), and cash (2%).

Investments in Affiliates: 2%

Group Affiliation: Indiana Farm Bureau Inc

Licensed in: IN, OH

Commenced Business: February 1935

Address: 225 South East Street, Indianapolis, IN 46202-4056

Phone: (317) 692-7200 **Domicile State:** IN **NAIC Code:** 15288

Data Date	Rating	RACR #1	RACR #2	Loss Ratio %	Total Assets ($mil)	Capital ($mil)	Net Premium ($mil)	Net Income ($mil)
2017	B+	3.91	2.61	71.2	1,098.5	462.1	570.9	35.3
2016	B	3.54	2.38	69.7	1,056.6	447.9	544.4	32.9
2015	B	3.40	2.30	65.9	1,015.2	414.4	536.4	55.9
2014	B-	3.18	2.18	71.5	956.8	357.1	509.6	46.9
2013	B-	2.89	2.00	72.6	915.0	323.7	503.3	35.8

Liquidity Index

■ Weak ▨ Fair ▤ Good □ Strong

UNITED FINANCIAL CASUALTY CO   B-   Good

Major Rating Factors: Fair overall results on stability tests (4.5 on a scale of 0 to 10) including potential drain of affiliation with Progressive Group. History of adequate reserve strength (6.4) as reserves have been consistently at an acceptable level.

Other Rating Factors: Good liquidity (5.8) with sufficient resources (cash flows and marketable investments) to handle a spike in claims. Strong long-term capitalization index (7.6) based on excellent current risk adjusted capital (severe and moderate loss scenarios). Moreover, capital levels have been consistent in recent years. Excellent profitability (9.2) with operating gains in each of the last five years. Return on equity has been excellent over the last five years averaging 20.4%.

Principal Business: Auto liability (66%), auto physical damage (32%), and inland marine (2%).

Principal Investments: Investment grade bonds (87%) and misc. investments (13%).

Investments in Affiliates: None

Group Affiliation: Progressive Group

Licensed in: All states except PR

Commenced Business: August 1984

Address: 6300 WILSON MILLS ROAD W33, Cleveland, OH 44143-2182

Phone: (440) 461-5000   **Domicile State:** OH   **NAIC Code:** 11770

Data Date	Rating	RACR #1	RACR #2	Loss Ratio %	Total Assets ($mil)	Capital ($mil)	Net Premium ($mil)	Net Income ($mil)
2017	B-	1.96	1.37	73.8	3,346.4	721.5	2,249.3	119.1
2016	B-	2.13	1.50	74.1	2,896.7	664.4	1,981.2	114.5
2015	B-	1.98	1.40	70.0	2,507.6	554.7	1,742.6	146.4
2014	C+	2.07	1.49	69.3	2,301.1	546.1	1,619.0	162.0
2013	C+	1.96	1.41	75.3	2,137.9	492.0	1,501.7	60.4

Rating Indexes

UNITED FIRE & CAS CO   B   Good

Major Rating Factors: Good overall results on stability tests (5.5 on a scale of 0 to 10) despite potential drain of affiliation with United Fire & Casualty Group. Good overall profitability index (6.9). Fair expense controls. Return on equity has been fair, averaging 5.4% over the past five years.

Other Rating Factors: Good liquidity (6.4) with sufficient resources (cash flows and marketable investments) to handle a spike in claims. Strong long-term capitalization index (7.2) based on excellent current risk adjusted capital (severe and moderate loss scenarios), despite some fluctuation in capital levels. Ample reserve history (8.0) that helps to protect the company against sharp claims increases.

Principal Business: Other liability (20%), auto liability (20%), workers compensation (11%), auto physical damage (10%), products liability (9%), allied lines (7%), and other lines (23%).

Principal Investments: Misc. investments (55%), investment grade bonds (40%), cash (3%), and real estate (2%).

Investments in Affiliates: 34%

Group Affiliation: United Fire & Casualty Group

Licensed in: All states except DE, NH, PR

Commenced Business: January 1947

Address: 118 SECOND AVENUE SE, Cedar Rapids, IA 52401

Phone: (319) 399-5700   **Domicile State:** IA   **NAIC Code:** 13021

Data Date	Rating	RACR #1	RACR #2	Loss Ratio %	Total Assets ($mil)	Capital ($mil)	Net Premium ($mil)	Net Income ($mil)
2017	B	1.31	1.14	72.8	1,987.8	757.4	652.2	19.3
2016	B	1.38	1.20	69.8	1,893.9	770.9	617.6	44.1
2015	B	1.31	1.13	61.2	1,777.9	722.4	564.5	37.9
2014	B	1.19	1.02	66.7	1,661.9	685.9	523.1	33.0
2013	B	1.18	1.01	63.3	1,558.7	665.8	469.8	58.9

Rating Indexes

UNITED GUARANTY RESIDENTIAL INS CO   C+   Fair

Major Rating Factors: Fair reserve development (4.9 on a scale of 0 to 10) as reserves have generally been sufficient to cover claims. In 2013, the two year reserve development was 19% deficient. Fair profitability index (3.0). Weak expense controls. Return on equity has been fair, averaging 21.7% over the past five years.

Other Rating Factors: Fair overall results on stability tests (4.4) including negative cash flow from operations for 2017. Good liquidity (6.8) with sufficient resources (cash flows and marketable investments) to handle a spike in claims. Strong long-term capitalization index (10.0) based on excellent current risk adjusted capital (severe and moderate loss scenarios), despite some fluctuation in capital levels.

Principal Business: Mortgage guaranty (100%).

Principal Investments: Investment grade bonds (90%), misc. investments (7%), non investment grade bonds (2%), and cash (1%).

Investments in Affiliates: 2%

Group Affiliation: American International Group

Licensed in: All states except PR

Commenced Business: December 1963

Address: 230 NORTH ELM STREET, Greensboro, NC 27401

Phone: (336) 373-0232   **Domicile State:** NC   **NAIC Code:** 15873

Data Date	Rating	RACR #1	RACR #2	Loss Ratio %	Total Assets ($mil)	Capital ($mil)	Net Premium ($mil)	Net Income ($mil)
2017	C+	6.61	4.98	16.6	2,607.5	1,004.9	215.1	326.6
2016	C+	2.53	2.14	17.8	3,307.9	1,186.5	548.8	335.2
2015	C	2.76	2.22	20.7	3,550.4	1,351.3	564.8	314.6
2014	C-	2.58	2.05	27.4	3,247.7	1,383.8	791.3	254.6
2013	D+	2.58	2.01	64.7	3,059.3	1,465.7	799.9	88.4

Reserve Deficiency (as % of capital)

* Adequate & redundant reserves show as negatives

UNITED SERVICES AUTOMOBILE ASN *   A-   Excellent

Major Rating Factors: Strong long-term capitalization index (7.6 on a scale of 0 to 10) based on excellent current risk adjusted capital (severe and moderate loss scenarios). Furthermore, this high level of risk adjusted capital has been consistently maintained in previous years. Ample reserve history (7.3) that can protect against increases in claims costs.

Other Rating Factors: Excellent profitability (7.6) with operating gains in each of the last five years. Excellent overall results on stability tests (7.1). Stability strengths include excellent operational trends and excellent risk diversification. Good liquidity (6.6) with sufficient resources (cash flows and marketable investments) to handle a spike in claims.

Principal Business: Homeowners multiple peril (34%), auto liability (32%), auto physical damage (26%), allied lines (3%), other liability (2%), inland marine (2%), and fire (1%).

Principal Investments: Misc. investments (73%), investment grade bonds (25%), real estate (3%), and non investment grade bonds (1%).

Investments in Affiliates: 59%
Group Affiliation: USAA Group
Licensed in: All states, the District of Columbia and Puerto Rico
Commenced Business: June 1922
Address: 9800 Fredericksburg Road, San Antonio, TX 78288
Phone: (210) 498-2211   **Domicile State:** TX   **NAIC Code:** 25941

Data Date	Rating	RACR #1	RACR #2	Loss Ratio %	Total Assets ($mil)	Capital ($mil)	Net Premium ($mil)	Net Income ($mil)
2017	A-	1.46	1.39	88.5	35,460.0	26,523.2	7,489.8	517.1
2016	B+	1.47	1.40	90.1	33,796.5	25,341.0	7,038.1	373.4
2015	A-	1.49	1.42	79.3	32,549.4	24,363.6	6,812.7	757.2
2014	A-	1.48	1.39	78.7	30,991.0	22,854.4	6,640.0	850.9
2013	A+	1.48	1.40	73.4	28,667.0	20,754.5	6,189.3	922.6

Risk-Adjusted Capital Ratio #2
(Severe Loss Scenario)

Range 2013 2014 2015 2016 2017
■ Weak ▩ Fair ▨ Good □ Strong

UNITED SPECIALTY INS CO *   B+   Good

Major Rating Factors: History of adequate reserve strength (6.0 on a scale of 0 to 10) as reserves have been consistently at an acceptable level. Good overall results on stability tests (6.4). Stability strengths include good operational trends and excellent risk diversification.

Other Rating Factors: Strong long-term capitalization index (8.8) based on excellent current risk adjusted capital (severe and moderate loss scenarios). Moreover, capital has steadily grown over the last five years. Excellent profitability (8.2) with operating gains in each of the last five years. Excellent liquidity (7.6) with ample operational cash flow and liquid investments.

Principal Business: Other liability (46%), commercial multiple peril (25%), auto liability (20%), earthquake (2%), auto physical damage (2%), inland marine (2%), and other lines (3%).

Principal Investments: Investment grade bonds (43%), misc. investments (39%), and cash (18%).

Investments in Affiliates: 33%
Group Affiliation: TX State National Group
Licensed in: All states except PR
Commenced Business: March 2006
Address: 160 Greentree Drive Suite 101, Dover, DE 19904
Phone: (817) 265-2000   **Domicile State:** DE   **NAIC Code:** 12537

Data Date	Rating	RACR #1	RACR #2	Loss Ratio %	Total Assets ($mil)	Capital ($mil)	Net Premium ($mil)	Net Income ($mil)
2017	B+	2.29	2.21	49.4	330.2	149.0	30.9	5.4
2016	B	5.84	4.93	47.6	200.5	128.7	48.7	5.2
2015	B	7.85	5.17	49.1	137.8	79.8	43.7	7.0
2014	B-	6.52	4.85	42.5	121.3	75.0	40.6	2.4
2013	B-	4.56	3.33	40.3	90.5	53.8	32.6	1.9

Reserve Deficiency (as % of capital)

2013 2014 2015 2016 2017
■ 1 Yr Dev □ 2 Yr Dev
* Adequate & redundant reserves show as negatives

UNITED STATES FIDELITY & GUARANTY CO   C-   Fair

Major Rating Factors: Weak profitability index (2.4 on a scale of 0 to 10). Fair expense controls. Return on equity has been fair, averaging 11.7% over the past five years. Fair overall results on stability tests (3.3).

Other Rating Factors: Good liquidity (6.7) with sufficient resources (cash flows and marketable investments) to handle a spike in claims. Strong long-term capitalization index (8.4) based on excellent current risk adjusted capital (severe and moderate loss scenarios), despite some fluctuation in capital levels. Ample reserve history (7.7) that can protect against increases in claims costs.

Principal Business: Surety (-15%).

Principal Investments: Investment grade bonds (95%), misc. investments (4%), and non investment grade bonds (1%).

Investments in Affiliates: 4%
Group Affiliation: Travelers Companies Inc
Licensed in: All states, the District of Columbia and Puerto Rico
Commenced Business: August 1896
Address: ONE TOWER SQUARE, Hartford, CT 6183
Phone: (860) 277-0111   **Domicile State:** CT   **NAIC Code:** 25887

Data Date	Rating	RACR #1	RACR #2	Loss Ratio %	Total Assets ($mil)	Capital ($mil)	Net Premium ($mil)	Net Income ($mil)
2017	C-	2.82	1.92	69.5	3,293.0	985.8	1,006.9	82.9
2016	C-	3.01	2.02	63.4	3,252.1	1,043.3	960.1	129.7
2015	C	4.08	2.67	58.7	3,565.3	1,408.9	916.4	284.3
2014	B	7.00	4.58	60.5	4,677.4	2,466.2	890.3	206.8
2013	B	7.16	4.72	60.9	4,653.9	2,484.4	888.1	224.2

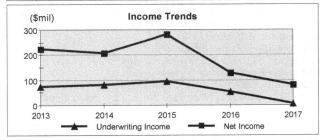

($mil)   Income Trends

2013 2014 2015 2016 2017
▲ Underwriting Income   ■ Net Income

UNIVERSAL P&C INS CO   D   Weak

Major Rating Factors: Weak overall results on stability tests (2.0 on a scale of 0 to 10). History of adequate reserve strength (6.4) as reserves have been consistently at an acceptable level.

Other Rating Factors: Good liquidity (5.8) with sufficient resources (cash flows and marketable investments) to handle a spike in claims. Strong long-term capitalization index (7.3) based on excellent current risk adjusted capital (severe and moderate loss scenarios), despite some fluctuation in capital levels. Excellent profitability (8.5) with operating gains in each of the last five years. Return on equity has been excellent over the last five years averaging 17.4%.

Principal Business: Homeowners multiple peril (93%), allied lines (5%), and fire (1%).

Principal Investments: Investment grade bonds (71%), misc. investments (25%), real estate (3%), and cash (1%).

Investments in Affiliates: None

Group Affiliation: Universal Insurance Holdings Inc

Licensed in: AL, DE, FL, GA, HI, IN, IA, MD, MA, MI, MN, NH, NJ, NY, NC, PA, SC, VA, WV

Commenced Business: December 1997

Address: 1110 West Commercial Boulevard, Fort Lauderdale, FL 33309

Phone: (954) 958-1200   **Domicile State:** FL   **NAIC Code:** 10861

Data Date	Rating	RACR #1	RACR #2	Loss Ratio %	Total Assets ($mil)	Capital ($mil)	Net Premium ($mil)	Net Income ($mil)
2017	D	1.39	1.20	55.6	1,034.0	307.7	733.4	36.2
2016	D	1.63	1.40	49.9	889.3	313.8	652.3	57.7
2015	D	1.30	1.11	40.9	816.3	257.0	623.0	52.9
2014	D-	1.52	1.27	42.1	626.8	200.2	385.3	38.5
2013	E+	0.26	0.19	46.1	553.6	161.8	260.0	27.7

Rating Indexes

UNIVERSAL UNDERWRITERS INS CO   C+   Fair

Major Rating Factors: Fair profitability index (4.4 on a scale of 0 to 10) with small operating losses during 2016. Return on equity has been low, averaging 1.7% over the past five years. Fair overall results on stability tests (4.7) including fair financial strength of affiliated Zurich Financial Services Group and negative cash flow from operations for 2017.

Other Rating Factors: Strong long-term capitalization index (10.0) based on excellent current risk adjusted capital (severe and moderate loss scenarios), despite some fluctuation in capital levels. Superior liquidity (10.0) with ample operational cash flow and liquid investments.

Principal Business: Auto physical damage (19%), other liability (15%), auto liability (3%), and allied lines (1%).

Principal Investments: Investment grade bonds (90%), misc. investments (9%), and cash (1%).

Investments in Affiliates: 4%

Group Affiliation: Zurich Financial Services Group

Licensed in: All states except PR

Commenced Business: January 1982

Address: 1299 ZURICH WAY, Schaumburg, IL 60196-1056

Phone: (847) 605-6000   **Domicile State:** IL   **NAIC Code:** 41181

Data Date	Rating	RACR #1	RACR #2	Loss Ratio %	Total Assets ($mil)	Capital ($mil)	Net Premium ($mil)	Net Income ($mil)
2017	C+	30.00	25.21	0.0	332.2	320.4	0.0	7.3
2016	C+	30.25	25.02	0.0	328.9	322.6	0.0	-2.9
2015	C+	10.35	9.61	0.0	379.9	339.6	0.0	9.5
2014	C	10.14	8.78	0.0	363.8	338.9	0.0	8.6
2013	C	10.82	9.95	0.0	386.2	336.1	0.0	5.2

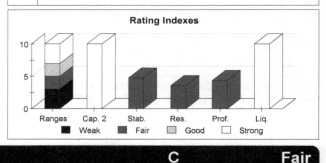

Rating Indexes

US FIRE INS CO   C   Fair

Major Rating Factors: Fair overall results on stability tests (3.7 on a scale of 0 to 10) including potential drain of affiliation with Fairfax Financial. Fair profitability index (4.4) with operating losses during 2013 and 2017. Return on equity has been low, averaging 2.6% over the past five years.

Other Rating Factors: Good long-term capitalization index (6.5) based on good current risk adjusted capital (moderate loss scenario). Moreover, capital levels have been consistent over the last several years. History of adequate reserve strength (6.1) as reserves have been consistently at an acceptable level. Excellent liquidity (7.4) with ample operational cash flow and liquid investments.

Principal Business: Group accident & health (30%), inland marine (22%), other liability (12%), auto liability (10%), workers compensation (9%), commercial multiple peril (6%), and other lines (11%).

Principal Investments: Investment grade bonds (50%), misc. investments (43%), cash (3%), real estate (3%), and non investment grade bonds (1%).

Investments in Affiliates: 29%

Group Affiliation: Fairfax Financial

Licensed in: All states, the District of Columbia and Puerto Rico

Commenced Business: April 1824

Address: 1209 ORANGE STREET, Wilmington, DE 19801

Phone: (973) 490-6600   **Domicile State:** DE   **NAIC Code:** 21113

Data Date	Rating	RACR #1	RACR #2	Loss Ratio %	Total Assets ($mil)	Capital ($mil)	Net Premium ($mil)	Net Income ($mil)
2017	C	1.15	0.94	64.7	4,094.3	1,302.3	1,418.1	-132.0
2016	C	1.35	1.04	63.7	3,949.6	1,218.9	1,370.7	32.3
2015	C	1.45	1.14	64.1	3,736.1	1,178.0	1,262.9	94.5
2014	C	1.62	1.14	67.5	3,248.6	898.6	1,025.1	195.7
2013	C	1.14	0.87	71.4	3,154.5	812.1	971.7	-75.7

Rating Indexes

US LIABILITY INS CO   C   Fair

Major Rating Factors: Fair overall results on stability tests (4.3 on a scale of 0 to 10). Strong long-term capitalization index (7.2) based on excellent current risk adjusted capital (severe and moderate loss scenarios), despite some fluctuation in capital levels.

Other Rating Factors: Ample reserve history (8.5) that helps to protect the company against sharp claims increases. Excellent profitability (8.2) with operating gains in each of the last five years. Excellent liquidity (7.6) with ample operational cash flow and liquid investments.

Principal Business: Other liability (81%), fire (17%), products liability (1%), and inland marine (1%).

Principal Investments: Misc. investments (81%) and investment grade bonds (19%).

Investments in Affiliates: 55%
Group Affiliation: Berkshire-Hathaway
Licensed in: All states except ND, PR
Commenced Business: May 1951
Address: 1190 Devon Park Drive, Wayne, PA 19087
Phone: (800) 523-5545   **Domicile State:** PA   **NAIC Code:** 25895

Data Date	Rating	RACR #1	RACR #2	Loss Ratio %	Total Assets ($mil)	Capital ($mil)	Net Premium ($mil)	Net Income ($mil)
2017	C	1.25	1.15	46.8	1,244.4	827.2	223.2	62.5
2016	C	1.19	1.07	38.8	1,015.3	647.3	204.3	25.2
2015	C	1.31	1.18	37.7	897.2	559.2	187.2	24.4
2014	C	1.35	1.22	51.1	885.9	563.3	169.7	4.6
2013	C	1.50	1.35	47.9	811.3	537.5	144.8	25.0

US SPECIALTY INS CO   B   Good

Major Rating Factors: History of adequate reserve strength (6.5 on a scale of 0 to 10) as reserves have been consistently at an acceptable level. Good liquidity (6.8) with sufficient resources (cash flows and marketable investments) to handle a spike in claims.

Other Rating Factors: Good overall results on stability tests (5.4). Strong long-term capitalization index (7.9) based on excellent current risk adjusted capital (severe and moderate loss scenarios), despite some fluctuation in capital levels. Excellent profitability (7.9) with operating gains in each of the last five years. Return on equity has been excellent over the last five years averaging 18.4%.

Principal Business: Other liability (57%), surety (13%), aircraft (8%), commercial multiple peril (6%), ocean marine (4%), credit (3%), and other lines (8%).

Principal Investments: Investment grade bonds (78%), misc. investments (11%), non investment grade bonds (10%), and cash (1%).

Investments in Affiliates: None
Group Affiliation: HCC Ins Holdings Inc
Licensed in: All states except PR
Commenced Business: April 1987
Address: 13403 Northwest Freeway, Houston, TX 77040
Phone: (713) 462-1000   **Domicile State:** TX   **NAIC Code:** 29599

Data Date	Rating	RACR #1	RACR #2	Loss Ratio %	Total Assets ($mil)	Capital ($mil)	Net Premium ($mil)	Net Income ($mil)
2017	B	2.49	1.60	56.7	1,888.4	587.0	471.5	87.2
2016	B-	2.37	1.53	59.7	1,792.1	518.2	464.1	76.2
2015	B-	2.47	1.63	55.7	1,792.8	525.7	436.2	94.1
2014	B-	2.71	1.76	47.0	1,890.8	577.1	420.1	133.2
2013	B-	2.56	1.66	51.5	1,928.6	580.3	440.5	124.8

USAA CASUALTY INS CO *   A-   Excellent

Major Rating Factors: Strong long-term capitalization index (8.4 on a scale of 0 to 10) based on excellent current risk adjusted capital (severe and moderate loss scenarios). Furthermore, this high level of risk adjusted capital has been consistently maintained in previous years. Ample reserve history (7.6) that can protect against increases in claims costs.

Other Rating Factors: Excellent overall results on stability tests (7.1). Stability strengths include excellent operational trends and excellent risk diversification. Good overall profitability index (6.9) with small operating losses during 2016. Return on equity has been low, averaging 4.3% over the past five years. Fair liquidity (3.8) as cash resources may not be adequate to cover a spike in claims.

Principal Business: Auto liability (38%), homeowners multiple peril (29%), auto physical damage (28%), inland marine (2%), allied lines (1%), other liability (1%), and fire (1%).

Principal Investments: Investment grade bonds (67%), misc. investments (30%), non investment grade bonds (2%), and cash (1%).

Investments in Affiliates: 9%
Group Affiliation: USAA Group
Licensed in: All states except PR
Commenced Business: December 1990
Address: 9800 Fredericksburg Road, San Antonio, TX 78288
Phone: (210) 498-1411   **Domicile State:** TX   **NAIC Code:** 25968

Data Date	Rating	RACR #1	RACR #2	Loss Ratio %	Total Assets ($mil)	Capital ($mil)	Net Premium ($mil)	Net Income ($mil)
2017	A-	2.48	1.92	88.2	10,897.7	4,719.6	7,002.9	126.1
2016	A-	2.63	2.03	91.8	10,315.4	4,489.8	6,412.1	-36.6
2015	A-	2.99	2.31	86.0	9,848.0	4,451.8	5,838.6	183.3
2014	A-	2.86	2.16	81.3	8,699.0	4,392.2	4,836.8	338.4
2013	A+	2.90	2.20	77.4	8,445.8	4,168.8	4,756.9	319.9

USAA GENERAL INDEMNITY CO *

B+   Good

Major Rating Factors: Good overall profitability index (5.3 on a scale of 0 to 10) despite operating losses during 2016. Return on equity has been fair, averaging 5.9% over the past five years. Good overall results on stability tests (6.4).

Other Rating Factors: Strong long-term capitalization index (8.2) based on excellent current risk adjusted capital (severe and moderate loss scenarios). Moreover, capital has steadily grown over the last five years. Ample reserve history (8.2) that helps to protect the company against sharp claims increases. Vulnerable liquidity (2.4) as a spike in claims may stretch capacity.

Principal Business: Auto liability (40%), auto physical damage (33%), homeowners multiple peril (21%), allied lines (5%), inland marine (1%), and fire (1%).

Principal Investments: Investment grade bonds (77%), misc. investments (18%), non investment grade bonds (3%), and cash (2%).

Investments in Affiliates: None

Group Affiliation: USAA Group

Licensed in: All states, the District of Columbia and Puerto Rico

Commenced Business: August 1972

Address: 9800 Fredericksburg Road, San Antonio, TX 78288

Phone: (210) 498-1411   **Domicile State:** TX   **NAIC Code:** 18600

Data Date	Rating	RACR #1	RACR #2	Loss Ratio %	Total Assets ($mil)	Capital ($mil)	Net Premium ($mil)	Net Income ($mil)
2017	B+	2.34	1.77	87.8	4,627.9	1,652.8	3,351.8	37.6
2016	B+	2.58	1.95	91.7	4,001.4	1,482.0	2,752.8	-23.1
2015	B+	2.78	2.10	85.9	3,503.7	1,303.6	2,289.9	66.0
2014	B+	1.92	1.42	81.2	2,933.6	1,096.7	2,176.6	108.4
2013	B+	1.99	1.53	77.3	2,256.6	835.6	1,633.0	117.0

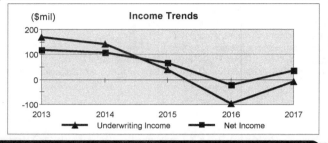

UTICA MUTUAL INS CO

B-   Good

Major Rating Factors: Fair overall results on stability tests (4.9 on a scale of 0 to 10) including potential drain of affiliation with Utica National Ins Group. History of adequate reserve strength (6.6) as reserves have been consistently at an acceptable level.

Other Rating Factors: Good overall profitability index (6.9). Fair expense controls. Good liquidity (6.7) with sufficient resources (cash flows and marketable investments) to handle a spike in claims. Strong long-term capitalization index (8.2) based on excellent current risk adjusted capital (severe and moderate loss scenarios). Moreover, capital levels have been consistent in recent years.

Principal Business: Other liability (24%), workers compensation (22%), commercial multiple peril (20%), auto liability (20%), auto physical damage (8%), homeowners multiple peril (3%), and other lines (3%).

Principal Investments: Investment grade bonds (67%), misc. investments (26%), non investment grade bonds (5%), cash (1%), and real estate (1%).

Investments in Affiliates: 10%

Group Affiliation: Utica National Ins Group

Licensed in: All states, the District of Columbia and Puerto Rico

Commenced Business: July 1914

Address: 180 GENESEE STREET, New Hartford, NY 13413

Phone: (315) 734-2000   **Domicile State:** NY   **NAIC Code:** 25976

Data Date	Rating	RACR #1	RACR #2	Loss Ratio %	Total Assets ($mil)	Capital ($mil)	Net Premium ($mil)	Net Income ($mil)
2017	B-	2.49	1.84	64.5	2,525.3	929.8	815.9	51.2
2016	B-	2.44	1.82	65.5	2,382.3	866.1	745.1	45.7
2015	B-	2.32	1.75	65.5	2,293.5	811.9	689.9	38.0
2014	B-	2.23	1.66	66.2	2,228.8	805.9	627.9	34.0
2013	B-	2.27	1.65	65.5	2,130.1	775.1	579.5	29.9

VERMONT MUTUAL INS CO

B-   Good

Major Rating Factors: Fair overall results on stability tests (4.7 on a scale of 0 to 10) including potential drain of affiliation with Vermont Mutual Group. Good liquidity (6.7) with sufficient resources (cash flows and marketable investments) to handle a spike in claims.

Other Rating Factors: Strong long-term capitalization index (10.0) based on excellent current risk adjusted capital (severe and moderate loss scenarios). Moreover, capital levels have been consistent in recent years. Ample reserve history (8.4) that helps to protect the company against sharp claims increases. Excellent profitability (8.7) with operating gains in each of the last five years.

Principal Business: Homeowners multiple peril (41%), commercial multiple peril (23%), auto physical damage (12%), auto liability (11%), fire (5%), allied lines (4%), and other lines (4%).

Principal Investments: Investment grade bonds (72%), misc. investments (22%), cash (4%), and non investment grade bonds (2%).

Investments in Affiliates: 1%

Group Affiliation: Vermont Mutual Group

Licensed in: CT, ME, MA, NH, NY, RI, VT

Commenced Business: March 1828

Address: 89 State Street, Montpelier, VT 5602

Phone: (802) 223-2341   **Domicile State:** VT   **NAIC Code:** 26018

Data Date	Rating	RACR #1	RACR #2	Loss Ratio %	Total Assets ($mil)	Capital ($mil)	Net Premium ($mil)	Net Income ($mil)
2017	B-	4.69	3.04	51.4	928.3	460.3	416.0	34.9
2016	B-	4.61	3.00	51.1	843.3	416.0	384.0	34.3
2015	B-	4.62	3.03	64.7	753.7	376.5	358.5	13.1
2014	C+	4.49	2.91	51.1	753.1	367.8	343.3	43.2
2013	C+	4.12	2.64	54.0	690.7	328.2	313.7	25.9

VIGILANT INS CO

B   **Good**

Major Rating Factors: Good overall results on stability tests (6.0 on a scale of 0 to 10). Stability strengths include good operational trends and excellent risk diversification. Strong long-term capitalization index (10.0) based on excellent current risk adjusted capital (severe and moderate loss scenarios). Moreover, capital levels have been consistent in recent years.

Other Rating Factors: Ample reserve history (7.6) that can protect against increases in claims costs. Excellent profitability (8.4) with operating gains in each of the last five years. Excellent liquidity (7.3) with ample operational cash flow and liquid investments.

Principal Business: Homeowners multiple peril (46%), workers compensation (15%), commercial multiple peril (14%), inland marine (8%), other liability (7%), auto physical damage (3%), and other lines (7%).

Principal Investments: Investment grade bonds (94%), misc. investments (5%), and non investment grade bonds (1%).

Investments in Affiliates: 5%

Group Affiliation: Chubb Limited

Licensed in: All states except PR

Commenced Business: October 1939

Address: 1133 AVE OF AMERICAS 41ST FL, New York, NY 10036

Phone: (215) 640-1000   **Domicile State:** NY   **NAIC Code:** 20397

Data Date	Rating	RACR #1	RACR #2	Loss Ratio %	Total Assets ($mil)	Capital ($mil)	Net Premium ($mil)	Net Income ($mil)
2017	B	15.62	11.48	62.6	576.7	327.3	25.4	13.0
2016	B	11.60	9.38	53.5	508.0	319.5	31.7	15.2
2015	B	9.88	7.48	56.5	514.8	306.2	48.9	22.0
2014	B	6.05	5.29	56.7	502.5	292.3	47.0	23.3
2013	B	5.10	4.72	52.7	467.9	264.9	45.1	16.7

Chubb Limited
Composite Group Rating: C+

Largest Group Members	Assets ($mil)	Rating
FEDERAL INS CO	21770	C+
ACE AMERICAN INS CO	13606	B-
ACE PC INS CO	8693	B-
PACIFIC INDEMNITY CO	6560	B
PACIFIC EMPLOYERS INS CO	3687	B-

VIRGINIA SURETY CO INC

B   **Good**

Major Rating Factors: History of adequate reserve strength (5.9 on a scale of 0 to 10) as reserves have been consistently at an acceptable level. Good liquidity (6.9) with sufficient resources (cash flows and marketable investments) to handle a spike in claims.

Other Rating Factors: Good overall results on stability tests (5.5). Stability strengths include good operational trends and excellent risk diversification. Strong long-term capitalization index (10.0) based on excellent current risk adjusted capital (severe and moderate loss scenarios), despite some fluctuation in capital levels. Excellent profitability (8.1) with operating gains in each of the last five years. Return on equity has been good over the last five years, averaging 14.2%.

Principal Business: Other liability (91%), inland marine (2%), and credit (1%).

Principal Investments: Investment grade bonds (77%), cash (16%), and misc. investments (7%).

Investments in Affiliates: 2%

Group Affiliation: Onex Corp

Licensed in: All states, the District of Columbia and Puerto Rico

Commenced Business: July 1982

Address: 175 W Jackson, Chicago, IL 60604

Phone: (312) 356-3000   **Domicile State:** IL   **NAIC Code:** 40827

Data Date	Rating	RACR #1	RACR #2	Loss Ratio %	Total Assets ($mil)	Capital ($mil)	Net Premium ($mil)	Net Income ($mil)
2017	B	4.67	3.89	63.9	1,439.3	406.3	266.5	9.0
2016	B	9.25	6.42	62.8	1,169.8	410.0	45.9	64.9
2015	B	4.05	3.59	62.7	1,147.0	363.6	299.6	44.5
2014	C+	3.15	2.78	64.0	1,022.7	300.8	329.7	50.4
2013	C+	2.85	2.48	55.3	1,007.8	309.2	341.8	73.6

Reserve Deficiency (as % of capital)

* Adequate & redundant reserves show as negatives   ■ 1 Yr Dev   □ 2 Yr Dev

---

WAWANESA GENERAL INS CO

B   **Good**

Major Rating Factors: History of adequate reserve strength (5.0 on a scale of 0 to 10) as reserves have been consistently at an acceptable level. Good overall results on stability tests (5.4) despite negative cash flow from operations for 2017.

Other Rating Factors: Fair profitability index (3.4) with operating losses during 2013, 2015, 2016 and 2017. Average return on equity over the last five years has been poor at -4.3%. Strong long-term capitalization index (7.8) based on excellent current risk adjusted capital (severe and moderate loss scenarios), despite some fluctuation in capital levels. Vulnerable liquidity (2.1) as a spike in claims may stretch capacity.

Principal Business: Auto liability (54%), auto physical damage (37%), homeowners multiple peril (8%), and earthquake (1%).

Principal Investments: Investment grade bonds (83%), non investment grade bonds (13%), misc. investments (3%), and cash (1%).

Investments in Affiliates: None

Group Affiliation: Wawanesa Ins Group

Licensed in: CA, OR

Commenced Business: January 1997

Address: 9050 FRIARS ROAD SUITE 420, San Diego, CA 92108-5865

Phone: (858) 874-5421   **Domicile State:** CA   **NAIC Code:** 10683

Data Date	Rating	RACR #1	RACR #2	Loss Ratio %	Total Assets ($mil)	Capital ($mil)	Net Premium ($mil)	Net Income ($mil)
2017	B	1.94	1.50	93.4	582.0	225.3	404.1	-10.5
2016	B-	2.31	1.80	94.7	610.6	237.4	360.8	-6.7
2015	C+	1.89	1.50	102.5	590.3	195.5	365.9	-30.8
2014	C+	2.67	2.13	91.9	583.0	240.2	343.4	5.3
2013	C+	2.73	2.17	94.6	558.2	235.1	331.1	-1.3

Reserve Deficiency (as % of capital)

* Adequate & redundant reserves show as negatives   ■ 1 Yr Dev   □ 2 Yr Dev

WESCO INS CO   D   Weak

Major Rating Factors: Weak overall results on stability tests (2.3 on a scale of 0 to 10) including weak risk adjusted capital in prior years. Strengths include potentially strong support from affiliation with AmTrust Financial Services Inc. Poor long-term capitalization index (0.2) based on weak current risk adjusted capital (severe and moderate loss scenarios), although results have slipped from the good range over the last two years.

Other Rating Factors: Vulnerable liquidity (0.3) as a spike in claims may stretch capacity. Fair profitability index (4.1) with operating losses during 2017. Return on equity has been low, averaging 4.5% over the past five years. Ample reserve history (7.0) that can protect against increases in claims costs.

Principal Business: Workers compensation (33%), commercial multiple peril (14%), auto liability (13%), other liability (8%), auto physical damage (3%), other accident & health (2%), and other lines (28%).

Principal Investments: Investment grade bonds (77%), misc. investments (20%), and cash (3%).

Investments in Affiliates: 8%

Group Affiliation: AmTrust Financial Services Inc

Licensed in: All states, the District of Columbia and Puerto Rico

Commenced Business: May 1963

Address: 2711 CENTERVILLE ROAD STE 400, Wilmington, DE 19808

Phone: (212) 220-7120   **Domicile State:** DE   **NAIC Code:** 25011

Data Date	Rating	RACR #1	RACR #2	Loss Ratio %	Total Assets ($mil)	Capital ($mil)	Net Premium ($mil)	Net Income ($mil)
2017	D	0.21	0.13	83.1	1,621.0	289.7	565.7	-7.4
2016	B-	1.33	0.84	67.5	1,903.7	363.5	607.0	5.9
2015	C+	1.98	1.26	64.1	1,743.4	333.5	416.8	13.1
2014	C+	4.16	2.41	72.7	1,113.6	215.5	182.6	14.2
2013	C+	5.29	3.08	63.2	804.1	166.8	114.8	21.4

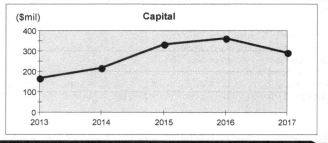

Capital

WEST BEND MUTUAL INS CO *   A-   Excellent

Major Rating Factors: Strong long-term capitalization index (8.9 on a scale of 0 to 10) based on excellent current risk adjusted capital (severe and moderate loss scenarios). Furthermore, this high level of risk adjusted capital has been consistently maintained in previous years. Ample reserve history (9.0) that helps to protect the company against sharp claims increases.

Other Rating Factors: Excellent profitability (8.6) with operating gains in each of the last five years. Excellent overall results on stability tests (7.0). Stability strengths include excellent operational trends and excellent risk diversification. Good liquidity (6.3) with sufficient resources (cash flows and marketable investments) to handle a spike in claims.

Principal Business: Workers compensation (23%), other liability (16%), auto liability (16%), homeowners multiple peril (12%), auto physical damage (11%), allied lines (7%), and other lines (15%).

Principal Investments: Investment grade bonds (71%), misc. investments (19%), non investment grade bonds (6%), real estate (3%), and cash (1%).

Investments in Affiliates: None

Group Affiliation: None

Licensed in: IL, IN, IA, KS, KY, MI, MN, MO, NE, OH, PA, TN, WI

Commenced Business: May 1894

Address: 1900 South 18th Avenue, West Bend, WI 53095

Phone: (262) 334-5571   **Domicile State:** WI   **NAIC Code:** 15350

Data Date	Rating	RACR #1	RACR #2	Loss Ratio %	Total Assets ($mil)	Capital ($mil)	Net Premium ($mil)	Net Income ($mil)
2017	A-	3.53	2.47	59.8	2,695.9	1,041.1	1,092.0	88.2
2016	B+	3.08	2.11	65.5	2,520.9	947.0	1,016.1	40.1
2015	B+	3.18	2.20	59.3	2,329.3	878.2	960.5	44.8
2014	B+	3.48	2.24	63.6	2,171.2	823.1	895.0	57.5
2013	A-	3.27	2.11	61.1	1,975.4	690.7	814.3	62.8

Risk-Adjusted Capital Ratio #2 (Severe Loss Scenario)

WESTCHESTER FIRE INS CO   C   Fair

Major Rating Factors: Fair reserve development (4.7 on a scale of 0 to 10) as reserves have generally been sufficient to cover claims. Fair profitability index (3.6). Fair expense controls. Return on equity has been fair, averaging 7.9% over the past five years.

Other Rating Factors: Fair overall results on stability tests (4.2) including fair financial strength of affiliated Chubb Limited and negative cash flow from operations for 2017. Good liquidity (6.7) with sufficient resources (cash flows and marketable investments) to handle a spike in claims. Strong long-term capitalization index (9.4) based on excellent current risk adjusted capital (severe and moderate loss scenarios), despite some fluctuation in capital levels.

Principal Business: Other liability (58%), surety (25%), inland marine (8%), products liability (3%), fidelity (2%), auto liability (1%), and other lines (4%).

Principal Investments: Investment grade bonds (83%), non investment grade bonds (15%), and misc. investments (4%).

Investments in Affiliates: None

Group Affiliation: Chubb Limited

Licensed in: All states, the District of Columbia and Puerto Rico

Commenced Business: April 1967

Address: 436 WALNUT STREET, Philadelphia, PA 19106

Phone: (215) 640-1000   **Domicile State:** PA   **NAIC Code:** 10030

Data Date	Rating	RACR #1	RACR #2	Loss Ratio %	Total Assets ($mil)	Capital ($mil)	Net Premium ($mil)	Net Income ($mil)
2017	C	3.98	2.61	78.2	1,655.7	682.2	339.9	51.3
2016	C	3.66	2.47	76.5	1,764.4	702.8	361.8	22.9
2015	C+	3.98	2.65	60.1	1,797.9	731.4	374.1	53.0
2014	C	4.92	3.23	56.5	2,011.9	906.1	342.6	81.9
2013	C	4.31	2.96	46.7	2,056.1	906.6	226.4	114.1

Reserve Deficiency (as % of capital)

* Adequate & redundant reserves show as negatives

WESTERN AGRICULTURAL INS CO *   B+   Good

Major Rating Factors: Good liquidity (5.9 on a scale of 0 to 10) with sufficient resources (cash flows and marketable investments) to handle a spike in claims. Good overall results on stability tests (6.6). Affiliation with Iowa Farm Bureau is a strength.

Other Rating Factors: Strong long-term capitalization index (10.0) based on excellent current risk adjusted capital (severe and moderate loss scenarios). Moreover, capital has steadily grown over the last five years. Ample reserve history (8.2) that helps to protect the company against sharp claims increases. Excellent profitability (8.9) with operating gains in each of the last five years. Return on equity has been good over the last five years, averaging 10.1%.

Principal Business: Allied lines (48%), homeowners multiple peril (12%), auto liability (9%), auto physical damage (9%), commercial multiple peril (8%), farmowners multiple peril (7%), and other lines (6%).

Principal Investments: Investment grade bonds (92%), misc. investments (8%), and non investment grade bonds (1%).

Investments in Affiliates: 2%

Group Affiliation: Iowa Farm Bureau

Licensed in: AL, AZ, AR, CO, ID, IL, IN, IA, KS, MI, MN, MO, MT, NE, NV, NM, ND, OH, OK, SC, SD, TN, TX, UT, VA, WI, WY

Commenced Business: January 1972

Address: 5400 University Avenue, West Des Moines, IA 50266-5997

Phone: (515) 225-5400   **Domicile State:** IA   **NAIC Code:** 27871

Data Date	Rating	RACR #1	RACR #2	Loss Ratio %	Total Assets ($mil)	Capital ($mil)	Net Premium ($mil)	Net Income ($mil)
2017	B+	5.36	4.05	66.3	213.2	111.9	107.7	9.5
2016	B+	4.91	3.70	59.9	211.0	103.0	105.6	13.1
2015	B+	4.33	3.25	62.3	190.4	88.9	105.1	11.1
2014	B+	4.00	3.00	70.3	182.7	77.4	101.5	5.8
2013	B+	3.93	2.92	70.2	171.2	70.7	98.1	6.4

Liquidity Index

WESTERN NATIONAL MUTUAL INS CO   B-   Good

Major Rating Factors: Fair overall results on stability tests (4.5 on a scale of 0 to 10) including potential drain of affiliation with Western National Mutual. Good liquidity (6.5) with sufficient resources (cash flows and marketable investments) to handle a spike in claims.

Other Rating Factors: Strong long-term capitalization index (8.4) based on excellent current risk adjusted capital (severe and moderate loss scenarios). Moreover, capital has steadily grown over the last five years. Ample reserve history (8.1) that helps to protect the company against sharp claims increases. Excellent profitability (8.5) with operating gains in each of the last five years.

Principal Business: Workers compensation (20%), auto liability (20%), homeowners multiple peril (16%), auto physical damage (15%), other liability (11%), products liability (5%), and other lines (13%).

Principal Investments: Investment grade bonds (59%), misc. investments (37%), real estate (3%), and non investment grade bonds (1%).

Investments in Affiliates: 19%

Group Affiliation: Western National Mutual

Licensed in: AK, AZ, AR, CA, CO, DE, ID, IL, IN, IA, KS, MD, MI, MN, MO, MT, NE, NV, NJ, NM, ND, OH, OK, OR, PA, RI, SD, TX, UT, WA, WI, WY

Commenced Business: June 1915

Address: 4700 WEST 77TH ST, Edina, MN 55435

Phone: (952) 835-5350   **Domicile State:** MN   **NAIC Code:** 15377

Data Date	Rating	RACR #1	RACR #2	Loss Ratio %	Total Assets ($mil)	Capital ($mil)	Net Premium ($mil)	Net Income ($mil)
2017	B-	2.36	1.94	67.5	1,045.2	460.0	417.6	24.3
2016	B-	2.49	2.11	65.5	956.3	433.5	349.2	28.1
2015	B-	2.47	2.10	65.2	845.5	390.6	340.6	28.2
2014	B-	2.44	2.08	65.7	762.5	350.0	285.0	23.4
2013	B-	2.16	1.78	68.7	696.0	314.2	256.3	15.7

Rating Indexes

WESTERN SURETY CO   C+   Fair

Major Rating Factors: Fair overall results on stability tests (4.4 on a scale of 0 to 10) including fair financial strength of affiliated CNA Financial Corp. Strong long-term capitalization index (10.0) based on excellent current risk adjusted capital (severe and moderate loss scenarios), despite some fluctuation in capital levels.

Other Rating Factors: Ample reserve history (9.2) that helps to protect the company against sharp claims increases. Excellent profitability (8.4) with operating gains in each of the last five years. Return on equity has been good over the last five years, averaging 10.4%. Excellent liquidity (7.2) with ample operational cash flow and liquid investments.

Principal Business: Surety (92%), fidelity (7%), and other liability (1%).

Principal Investments: Investment grade bonds (98%) and misc. investments (2%).

Investments in Affiliates: 1%

Group Affiliation: CNA Financial Corp

Licensed in: All states, the District of Columbia and Puerto Rico

Commenced Business: July 1900

Address: 101 S REID STREET, Sioux Falls, SD 57103

Phone: (312) 822-5000   **Domicile State:** SD   **NAIC Code:** 13188

Data Date	Rating	RACR #1	RACR #2	Loss Ratio %	Total Assets ($mil)	Capital ($mil)	Net Premium ($mil)	Net Income ($mil)
2017	C+	8.58	6.59	6.1	2,043.5	1,527.2	376.3	144.4
2016	C	7.86	5.99	14.7	1,998.8	1,452.4	370.2	129.6
2015	C	7.42	5.79	21.8	1,823.7	1,323.3	295.8	116.5
2014	C	6.57	4.94	10.6	1,998.3	1,368.0	433.7	164.2
2013	C	5.67	4.30	9.2	1,856.4	1,205.6	418.4	152.7

Capital

WESTERN WORLD INS CO

C   Fair

Major Rating Factors: Fair profitability index (3.8 on a scale of 0 to 10). Fair expense controls. Return on equity has been fair, averaging 8.4% over the past five years. Fair overall results on stability tests (4.1).

Other Rating Factors: Good overall long-term capitalization (6.4) based on good current risk adjusted capital (moderate loss scenario). However, capital levels have fluctuated during prior years. Ample reserve history (9.4) that helps to protect the company against sharp claims increases. Excellent liquidity (7.1) with ample operational cash flow and liquid investments.

Principal Business: Other liability (44%), commercial multiple peril (24%), allied lines (18%), products liability (10%), homeowners multiple peril (2%), medical malpractice (1%), and inland marine (1%).

Principal Investments: Investment grade bonds (60%), misc. investments (32%), non investment grade bonds (5%), and cash (3%).

Investments in Affiliates: 25%

Group Affiliation: Western World Group

Licensed in: All states, the District of Columbia and Puerto Rico

Commenced Business: April 1964

Address: 300 KIMBALL DRIVE SUITE 500, Parsippany, NJ 7054

Phone: (201) 847-8600   **Domicile State:** NH   **NAIC Code:** 13196

Data Date	Rating	RACR #1	RACR #2	Loss Ratio %	Total Assets ($mil)	Capital ($mil)	Net Premium ($mil)	Net Income ($mil)
2017	C	1.17	0.93	98.1	982.1	376.2	182.9	59.3
2016	C	1.61	1.46	68.3	868.9	416.7	121.4	3.4
2015	C	1.66	1.49	72.3	916.5	421.0	96.7	22.3
2014	C	1.58	1.33	28.9	1,047.6	452.1	239.9	80.3
2013	C	1.39	1.19	69.0	1,047.0	367.7	201.7	7.8

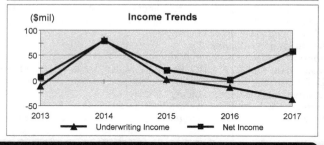

WESTFIELD INS CO

B-   Good

Major Rating Factors: Fair overall results on stability tests (4.6 on a scale of 0 to 10) including potential drain of affiliation with Westfield Companies. Good overall profitability index (6.8). Fair expense controls. Return on equity has been fair, averaging 7.5% over the past five years.

Other Rating Factors: Good liquidity (6.6) with sufficient resources (cash flows and marketable investments) to handle a spike in claims. Strong long-term capitalization index (9.8) based on excellent current risk adjusted capital (severe and moderate loss scenarios). Moreover, capital levels have been consistent in recent years. Ample reserve history (8.2) that helps to protect the company against sharp claims increases.

Principal Business: Commercial multiple peril (29%), auto liability (23%), auto physical damage (11%), other liability (10%), farmowners multiple peril (6%), homeowners multiple peril (6%), and other lines (16%).

Principal Investments: Investment grade bonds (63%) and misc. investments (37%).

Investments in Affiliates: None

Group Affiliation: Westfield Companies

Licensed in: All states except CA, PR

Commenced Business: July 1929

Address: One Park Circle, Westfield Center, OH 44251-5001

Phone: (330) 887-0101   **Domicile State:** OH   **NAIC Code:** 24112

Data Date	Rating	RACR #1	RACR #2	Loss Ratio %	Total Assets ($mil)	Capital ($mil)	Net Premium ($mil)	Net Income ($mil)
2017	B-	4.32	2.90	73.5	2,937.3	1,278.4	1,002.9	26.2
2016	B-	4.46	2.96	62.3	2,739.6	1,177.3	977.1	82.3
2015	B-	4.26	2.89	62.7	2,594.4	1,092.4	955.3	70.9
2014	B-	4.14	2.78	63.5	2,536.1	1,043.0	935.9	93.3
2013	B-	3.76	2.50	59.8	2,450.5	991.2	904.7	127.7

WESTFIELD NATIONAL INS CO

B-   Good

Major Rating Factors: Fair overall results on stability tests (4.6 on a scale of 0 to 10) including potential drain of affiliation with Westfield Companies. Good overall profitability index (6.8). Fair expense controls. Return on equity has been fair, averaging 6.1% over the past five years.

Other Rating Factors: Good liquidity (6.6) with sufficient resources (cash flows and marketable investments) to handle a spike in claims. Strong long-term capitalization index (9.6) based on excellent current risk adjusted capital (severe and moderate loss scenarios). Moreover, capital levels have been consistent in recent years. Ample reserve history (8.2) that helps to protect the company against sharp claims increases.

Principal Business: Homeowners multiple peril (27%), auto liability (23%), auto physical damage (19%), commercial multiple peril (15%), other liability (6%), workers compensation (6%), and other lines (4%).

Principal Investments: Investment grade bonds (72%) and misc. investments (28%).

Investments in Affiliates: None

Group Affiliation: Westfield Companies

Licensed in: AL, AZ, AR, CA, CO, DC, DE, FL, GA, ID, IL, IN, IA, KS, KY, MD, MI, MN, MS, MO, MT, NE, NV, NM, NC, ND, OH, OK, PA, SC, SD, TN, TX, UT, VA, WA, WV, WI, WY

Commenced Business: April 1968

Address: One Park Circle, Westfield Center, OH 44251-5001

Phone: (330) 887-0101   **Domicile State:** OH   **NAIC Code:** 24120

Data Date	Rating	RACR #1	RACR #2	Loss Ratio %	Total Assets ($mil)	Capital ($mil)	Net Premium ($mil)	Net Income ($mil)
2017	B-	4.07	2.76	73.5	696.6	317.2	241.4	5.8
2016	B-	4.25	2.83	62.3	659.5	300.4	235.2	18.3
2015	B-	4.10	2.79	62.7	613.4	272.8	230.0	16.5
2014	B-	3.92	2.62	63.5	598.7	263.1	225.3	16.6
2013	B+	3.75	2.51	59.8	571.9	243.2	217.8	25.2

Westfield Companies Composite Group Rating: B- Largest Group Members	Assets ($mil)	Rating
OHIO FARMERS INS CO	3108	B-
WESTFIELD INS CO	2937	B-
WESTFIELD NATIONAL INS CO	697	B-
OLD GUARD INS CO	481	C+
AMERICAN SELECT INS CO	272	C

WESTGUARD INS CO   B   Good

Major Rating Factors: Good overall results on stability tests (5.5 on a scale of 0 to 10) despite negative cash flow from operations for 2017, fair results on operational trends and excessive premium growth. Strong long-term capitalization index (7.2) based on excellent current risk adjusted capital (severe and moderate loss scenarios). Moreover, capital has steadily grown over the last five years.

Other Rating Factors: Ample reserve history (8.0) that helps to protect the company against sharp claims increases. Excellent profitability (8.2) with operating gains in each of the last five years. Superior liquidity (10.0) with ample operational cash flow and liquid investments.

Principal Business: Workers compensation (100%).

Principal Investments: Misc. investments (85%), investment grade bonds (11%), cash (3%), and real estate (1%).

Investments in Affiliates: 65%

Group Affiliation: Berkshire-Hathaway

Licensed in: NY, PA, WV

Commenced Business: July 2004

Address: 16 SOUTH RIVER STREET, Wilkes-barre, PA 18702

Phone: (570) 825-9900   **Domicile State:** PA   **NAIC Code:** 11981

Data Date	Rating	RACR #1	RACR #2	Loss Ratio %	Total Assets ($mil)	Capital ($mil)	Net Premium ($mil)	Net Income ($mil)
2017	B	1.34	1.26	57.8	1,181.9	613.4	28.9	6.2
2016	B-	1.30	1.19	58.9	955.0	509.2	23.0	1.6
2015	C+	1.30	1.19	60.0	780.5	430.9	19.0	0.3
2014	C+	1.09	1.06	63.2	607.1	309.1	11.9	1.2
2013	C	0.82	0.57	67.8	35.1	14.6	6.2	1.4

Rating Indexes

WESTPORT INS CORP   B   Good

Major Rating Factors: History of adequate reserve strength (6.6 on a scale of 0 to 10) as reserves have been consistently at an acceptable level. Good liquidity (6.8) with sufficient resources (cash flows and marketable investments) to handle a spike in claims.

Other Rating Factors: Good overall results on stability tests (6.2) despite negative cash flow from operations for 2017. Affiliation with Swiss Reinsurance is a strength. Fair profitability index (4.8). Weak expense controls. Return on equity has been fair, averaging 9.9% over the past five years. Strong long-term capitalization index (7.1) based on excellent current risk adjusted capital (severe and moderate loss scenarios), despite some fluctuation in capital levels.

Principal Business: Group accident & health (32%), allied lines (26%), other liability (20%), fire (11%), earthquake (6%), boiler & machinery (2%), and other lines (3%).

Principal Investments: Investment grade bonds (82%) and misc. investments (18%).

Investments in Affiliates: 11%

Group Affiliation: Swiss Reinsurance

Licensed in: All states, the District of Columbia and Puerto Rico

Commenced Business: September 1981

Address: 237 EAST HIGH STREET, Jefferson City, MO 65101-3206

Phone: (913) 676-5200   **Domicile State:** MO   **NAIC Code:** 39845

Data Date	Rating	RACR #1	RACR #2	Loss Ratio %	Total Assets ($mil)	Capital ($mil)	Net Premium ($mil)	Net Income ($mil)
2017	B	1.61	1.04	77.1	5,517.6	1,535.5	321.9	93.8
2016	B	1.78	1.23	80.1	4,730.1	1,558.6	287.1	189.7
2015	B-	1.48	1.03	61.5	4,693.0	1,505.3	281.6	177.3
2014	C+	1.56	1.08	67.9	5,215.7	1,630.5	135.9	160.8
2013	C+	1.25	0.85	62.2	5,454.1	1,769.4	580.1	167.8

Reserve Deficiency (as % of capital)

* Adequate & redundant reserves show as negatives

XL REINS AMERICA INC   C   Fair

Major Rating Factors: Fair overall results on stability tests (3.8 on a scale of 0 to 10) including potential drain of affiliation with XL Group Ltd. Fair profitability index (4.7) with operating losses during 2017.

Other Rating Factors: History of adequate reserve strength (6.3) as reserves have been consistently at an acceptable level. Strong long-term capitalization index (8.3) based on excellent current risk adjusted capital (severe and moderate loss scenarios), despite some fluctuation in capital levels. Excellent liquidity (7.4) with ample operational cash flow and liquid investments.

Principal Business: Other liability (100%).

Principal Investments: Investment grade bonds (72%), misc. investments (26%), and cash (2%).

Investments in Affiliates: 17%

Group Affiliation: XL Group Ltd

Licensed in: All states, the District of Columbia and Puerto Rico

Commenced Business: October 1929

Address: 200 LIBERTY STREET, New York, NY 10281

Phone: (203) 964-5200   **Domicile State:** NY   **NAIC Code:** 20583

Data Date	Rating	RACR #1	RACR #2	Loss Ratio %	Total Assets ($mil)	Capital ($mil)	Net Premium ($mil)	Net Income ($mil)
2017	C	2.29	1.84	76.8	5,952.3	2,046.6	1,372.0	-10.8
2016	C	2.35	1.91	69.3	6,274.1	2,076.3	1,083.7	90.9
2015	C	2.96	2.22	71.2	5,307.7	2,021.6	862.6	83.0
2014	C	3.07	2.34	61.5	5,627.6	2,233.6	823.4	219.8
2013	C	2.94	2.26	65.3	5,527.8	2,244.5	865.2	161.4

Rating Indexes

XL SPECIALTY INS CO

C   **Fair**

Major Rating Factors: Fair overall results on stability tests (3.8 on a scale of 0 to 10) including potential drain of affiliation with XL Group Ltd. History of adequate reserve strength (6.4) as reserves have been consistently at an acceptable level.

Other Rating Factors: Good overall profitability index (5.7) despite operating losses during 2015. Return on equity has been fair, averaging 5.8% over the past five years. Strong long-term capitalization index (9.4) based on excellent current risk adjusted capital (severe and moderate loss scenarios), despite some fluctuation in capital levels. Superior liquidity (9.2) with ample operational cash flow and liquid investments.

Principal Business: Other liability (55%), workers compensation (11%), inland marine (11%), ocean marine (7%), aircraft (6%), aggregate write-ins for other lines of business (5%), and other lines (6%).

Principal Investments: Investment grade bonds (77%), cash (16%), and misc. investments (7%).

Investments in Affiliates: 5%

Group Affiliation: XL Group Ltd

Licensed in: All states, the District of Columbia and Puerto Rico

Commenced Business: December 1979

Address: 1209 Orange Street, Wilmington, DE 19801

Phone: (203) 964-5200   **Domicile State:** DE   **NAIC Code:** 37885

Data Date	Rating	RACR #1	RACR #2	Loss Ratio %	Total Assets ($mil)	Capital ($mil)	Net Premium ($mil)	Net Income ($mil)
2017	C	4.48	3.24	76.8	1,066.4	313.5	126.7	19.4
2016	C	4.32	3.21	69.3	920.4	283.3	100.0	4.6
2015	C	2.14	1.59	71.2	462.2	132.7	79.6	-2.5
2014	C	2.31	1.72	61.5	432.7	143.2	76.0	9.0
2013	C	2.46	1.83	65.3	440.6	158.3	79.9	26.3

XL Group Ltd
Composite Group Rating: C

Largest Group Members	Assets ($mil)	Rating
XL REINS AMERICA INC	5952	C
GREENWICH INS CO	1250	C
XL SPECIALTY INS CO	1066	C
XL INS AMERICA INC	791	C
CATLIN SPECIALTY INS CO	588	C+

ZENITH INS CO

C+   **Fair**

Major Rating Factors: Fair overall results on stability tests (4.4 on a scale of 0 to 10) including potential drain of affiliation with Fairfax Financial. Good long-term capitalization index (6.5) based on good current risk adjusted capital (moderate loss scenario).

Other Rating Factors: Good overall profitability index (5.9) despite operating losses during 2013. Return on equity has been good over the last five years, averaging 14.2%. Ample reserve history (9.5) that helps to protect the company against sharp claims increases. Excellent liquidity (7.8) with ample operational cash flow and liquid investments.

Principal Business: Workers compensation (91%), commercial multiple peril (4%), auto liability (2%), other liability (2%), fire (1%), and auto physical damage (1%).

Principal Investments: Investment grade bonds (62%), misc. investments (34%), real estate (2%), cash (1%), and non investment grade bonds (1%).

Investments in Affiliates: 14%

Group Affiliation: Fairfax Financial

Licensed in: All states except PR

Commenced Business: December 1950

Address: 21255 CALIFA STREET, Woodland Hills, CA 91367

Phone: (818) 713-1000   **Domicile State:** CA   **NAIC Code:** 13269

Data Date	Rating	RACR #1	RACR #2	Loss Ratio %	Total Assets ($mil)	Capital ($mil)	Net Premium ($mil)	Net Income ($mil)
2017	C+	1.20	0.94	49.8	1,843.8	571.7	803.9	86.0
2016	C+	1.31	1.01	44.6	1,824.6	563.6	792.7	115.2
2015	C+	1.43	1.07	46.6	1,908.8	621.7	754.9	121.0
2014	C	1.37	1.02	52.8	1,834.1	564.5	703.4	110.7
2013	C-	1.12	0.82	62.4	1,783.8	515.8	677.5	-18.1

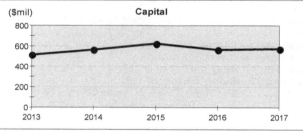

Capital ($mil)

ZURICH AMERICAN INS CO

B   **Good**

Major Rating Factors: History of adequate reserve strength (6.1 on a scale of 0 to 10) as reserves have been consistently at an acceptable level. Good profitability index (5.0). Good expense controls. Return on equity has been good over the last five years, averaging 10.7%.

Other Rating Factors: Good liquidity (6.8) with sufficient resources (cash flows and marketable investments) to handle a spike in claims. Good overall results on stability tests (5.4) despite fair financial strength of affiliated Zurich Financial Services Group. Strong long-term capitalization index (8.0) based on excellent current risk adjusted capital (severe and moderate loss scenarios), despite some fluctuation in capital levels.

Principal Business: Workers compensation (29%), other liability (22%), auto liability (11%), commercial multiple peril (7%), allied lines (6%), inland marine (5%), and other lines (20%).

Principal Investments: Investment grade bonds (67%), misc. investments (23%), non investment grade bonds (5%), and real estate (5%).

Investments in Affiliates: 8%

Group Affiliation: Zurich Financial Services Group

Licensed in: All states, the District of Columbia and Puerto Rico

Commenced Business: January 1913

Address: 4 WTC 150 GREENWICH ST, New York, NY 10007

Phone: (847) 605-6000   **Domicile State:** NY   **NAIC Code:** 16535

Data Date	Rating	RACR #1	RACR #2	Loss Ratio %	Total Assets ($mil)	Capital ($mil)	Net Premium ($mil)	Net Income ($mil)
2017	B	2.38	1.65	82.5	31,582.0	7,619.0	4,630.4	828.6
2016	B-	2.45	1.71	78.5	31,002.9	7,851.7	4,215.2	968.8
2015	B-	2.53	1.71	81.4	30,471.5	7,765.5	4,540.4	597.9
2014	C+	2.71	1.86	78.0	30,309.7	8,015.4	4,739.7	1,000.5
2013	C+	2.76	1.90	74.6	30,184.0	7,798.4	4,733.6	772.8

Reserve Deficiency (as % of capital)

* Adequate & redundant reserves show as negatives

■ 1 Yr Dev   □ 2 Yr Dev

Section III

Weiss
Recommended Companies

A compilation of those

U.S. Property and Casualty Insurers

receiving a Weiss Safety Rating

of A+, A, A- or B+.

Companies are listed in alphabetical order.

Section III Contents

This section provides a list of recommended carriers (based strictly on financial safety) along with additional information you should have when shopping for insurance. It contains all insurers receiving a Safety Rating of A+, A, A- or B+. If an insurer is not on this list, it should not be automatically assumed that the firm is weak. Indeed, there are many firms that have not achieved a B+ or better rating but are in relatively good condition with adequate resources to cover their risk during an average recession. Not being included in this list should not be construed as a recommendation to cancel a policy.

Left Pages

1. Safety Rating	Our rating is measured on a scale from A to F and considers a wide range of factors. Highly-rated companies are, in our opinion, less likely to experience financial difficulties than lower rated firms. See *About Weiss Safety Ratings* for more information.
2. Insurance Company Name	The legally-registered name, which can sometimes differ from the name that the company uses for advertising. An insurer's name can be very similar to the name of other companies which may not be on our Recommended List, so make sure you note the exact name before contacting your agent.
3. Address	The address of the main office where you can contact the firm for additional financial data or for the location of local branches and/or registered agents.
4. Telephone Number	The number to call for additional financial data or for the phone numbers of local branches and/or registered agents.

Right Pages

The right-side pages present the percentage of the company's business that is involved in each type of insurance. Specifically, the numbers shown are the amounts of direct premium (received directly from policyholders) for each line of business as a percent of total premiums.

1. Domicile State	The state which has primary regulatory responsibility for the company. It may differ from the location of the company's corporate headquarters. You do not have to be living in the domicile state to purchase insurance from this firm, provided it is licensed to do business in your state.
2. Auto	Coverage for damage to a policyholder's own automobile and for the financial loss from auto-related bodily injury or property damage.
3. Homeowners Multiple Peril	Package policies for homeowners providing a broad spectrum of property and liability coverages.

4. Farmowners Multiple Peril — Package policies for farm or ranch owners providing a broad spectrum of property and liability coverages.

5. Commercial Multiple Peril — Package policies for businesses and other commercial establishments providing a broad spectrum of property and liability coverages.

6. Commercial Auto Liability — Coverage against financial loss because of a business auto related injuries or damages to third parties.

7. Other Liability — Encompasses all third-party liability coverages not included in other business areas. It can include among others: professional liability, environmental liability, product liability, umbrella liability, general liability.

8. Medical Malpractice — Errors and omissions liability coverages for persons engaged in the practice of medicine, surgery, dentistry, nursing, pharmacy, or other health care services. Also covers health care institutions.

9. Workers' Compensation — Liability coverage issued to employers which provides for the payment of medical care, disability income or possible additional liability amounts to employees who are injured on the job.

10. Accident and Health — This includes three categories: (1) group accident and health, which consists of medical and hospitalization insurance plans under which a number of persons and their dependents are insured under a single policy issued to an employer or a common associated entity; (2) credit accident and health, which makes certain debt payments, usually for car or home loans, in the case of accident or illness; and (3) other accident and health, issued to individuals, to pay health care benefits or loss of income due to accidental injury or death.

11. Other — Fire, allied lines, mortgage guaranty, ocean marine, inland marine, financial guaranty, product liability, aircraft, fidelity, surety, glass, burglary and theft, boiler and machinery, credit, international, reinsurance, aggregate write-ins for other lines of business and other miscellaneous types of insurance.

Weiss Safety Ratings are not deemed to be a recommendation concerning the purchase or sale of the securities of any insurance company that is publicly owned.

RATING	INSURANCE COMPANY NAME	ADDRESS	CITY	STATE	ZIP	PHONE
A-	ACUITY A MUTUAL INS CO	2800 SOUTH TAYLOR DRIVE	SHEBOYGAN	WI	53081	(920) 458-9131
B+	ALASKA NATIONAL INS CO	7001 JEWEL LAKE ROAD	ANCHORAGE	AK	99502	(907) 248-2642
B+	ALFA GENERAL INS CORP	2108 EAST SOUTH BOULEVARD	MONTGOMERY	AL	36116	(334) 288-3900
B+	ALFA MUTUAL FIRE INS CO	2108 EAST SOUTH BOULEVARD	MONTGOMERY	AL	36116	(334) 288-3900
A-	ALFA MUTUAL GENERAL INS CO	2108 EAST SOUTH BOULEVARD	MONTGOMERY	AL	36116	(334) 288-3900
A-	ALL AMERICA INS CO	800 SOUTH WASHINGTON STREET	VAN WERT	OH	45891	(419) 238-1010
B+	ALLIED WORLD SPECIALTY INS CO	251 LITTLE FALLS DRIVE	WILMINGTON	DE	19808	(646) 794-0500
B+	ALLSTATE INS CO	2775 SANDERS ROAD	NORTHBROOK	IL	60062	(847) 402-5000
A-	ALLSTATE NJ INS CO	2775 SANDERS ROAD	NORTHBROOK	IL	60062	(908) 252-5000
B+	AMERICAN AGRICULTURAL INS CO	225 SOUTH EAST STREET	INDIANAPOLIS	IN	46202	(847) 969-2900
B+	AMERICAN CONTRACTORS INDEMNITY CO	601 SOUTH FIGUEROA ST 16TH FL	LOS ANGELES	CA	90017	(310) 649-0990
A-	AMERICAN FAMILY MUTL INS CO SI	6000 AMERICAN PARKWAY	MADISON	WI	53783	(608) 249-2111
B+	AMERICAN INTERSTATE INS CO OF TX	211 EAST 7TH STREET SUITE 620	AUSTIN	TX	78701	(800) 256-9052
B+	AMERICAN NATIONAL PROPERTY & CAS CO	1949 EAST SUNSHINE	SPRINGFIELD	MO	65899	(417) 887-4990
B+	AMERICAN STANDARD INS CO OF WI	6000 AMERICAN PARKWAY	MADISON	WI	53783	(608) 249-2111
B+	AMICA MUTUAL INS CO	100 AMICA WAY	LINCOLN	RI	02865	(800) 652-6422
B+	ANSUR AMERICA INS CO	ONE MUTUAL AVENUE	FRANKENMUTH	MI	48787	(989) 652-6121
B+	ARCH SPECIALTY INS CO	2345 GRAND BLVD SUITE 900	KANSAS CITY	MO	64108	(201) 743-4000
B+	AUTO CLUB INDEMNITY CO	1225 FREEPORT PARKWAY	COPPELL	TX	75019	(714) 850-5111
B+	AUTO CLUB INS CO OF FL	14055 RIVEREDGE DRIVE STE 500	TAMPA	FL	33637	(888) 929-4222
A	AUTO-OWNERS INS CO	6101 ANACAPRI BOULEVARD	LANSING	MI	48917	(517) 323-1200
A+	BERKSHIRE HATHAWAY ASR CORP	MARINE AIR TERMINAL LAGUARDIA	FLUSHING	NY	11371	(402) 916-3000
B+	BROTHERHOOD MUTUAL INS CO	6400 BROTHERHOOD WAY	FORT WAYNE	IN	46825	(260) 482-8668
A	BUILDERS MUTUAL INS CO	5580 CENTERVIEW DRIVE	RALEIGH	NC	27606	(919) 845-1976
B+	CASTLE KEY INS CO	2775 SANDERS ROAD	NORTHBROOK	IL	60062	(727) 573-6800
B+	CATERPILLAR INS CO	237 EAST HIGH STREET	JEFFERSON CITY	MO	65101	(615) 341-8147
B+	CENTRAL MUTUAL INS CO	800 SOUTH WASHINGTON STREET	VAN WERT	OH	45891	(419) 238-1010
B+	CHURCH MUTUAL INS CO	3000 SCHUSTER LANE	MERRILL	WI	54452	(715) 536-5577
A-	CINCINNATI INDEMNITY CO	6200 SOUTH GILMORE ROAD	FAIRFIELD	OH	45014	(513) 870-2000
A	CINCINNATI INS CO	6200 SOUTH GILMORE ROAD	FAIRFIELD	OH	45014	(513) 870-2000
A	CINCINNATI SPECIALTY UNDERWRITER	BRANDYWINE VILLAGE 1807 NORTH	WILMINGTON	DE	19802	(513) 870-2000
A+	CITIZENS PROPERTY INS CORP	2101 MARYLAND CIRCLE	TALLAHASSEE	FL	32303	(850) 513-3700
B+	COPIC INS CO	7351 E LOWRY BLVD SUITE 400	DENVER	CO	80230	(720) 858-6000
A+	COPPERPOINT MUTUAL INS CO	3030 N 3RD STREET	PHOENIX	AZ	85012	(602) 631-2240
A-	COUNTRY MUTUAL INS CO	1701 N TOWANDA AVENUE	BLOOMINGTON	IL	61701	(309) 821-3000
B+	COVINGTON SPECIALTY INS CO	900 ELM STREET	MANCHESTER	NH	3101	(404) 231-2366
A-	CUMIS INS SOCIETY INC	2000 HERITAGE WAY	WAVERLY	IA	50677	(608) 238-5851
A-	DAIRYLAND INS CO	1800 NORTH POINT DRIVE	STEVENS POINT	WI	54481	(715) 346-6000
A-	EMPLOYERS COMPENSATION INS CO	500 NORTH BRAND BOULEVARD	GLENDALE	CA	91203	(775) 327-2700
A-	ENDURANCE ASR CORP	1209 ORANGE STREET	WILMINGTON	DE	19801	(914) 468-8000
B+	ERIE & NIAGARA INS ASSN	8800 SHERIDAN DRIVE	WILLIAMSVILLE	NY	14231	(716) 632-5433
A-	ESSENT GUARANTY INC	2 RADNOR CORP 100 MATSONFORD	RADNOR	PA	19087	(877) 673-8190
B+	FARM BU TOWN & COUNTRY INS CO OF MO	701 SOUTH COUNTRY CLUB DRIVE	JEFFERSON CITY	MO	65109	(573) 893-1400
B+	FARM BUREAU GENERAL INS CO OF MI	7373 W SAGINAW	LANSING	MI	48917	(517) 323-7000
B+	FARM BUREAU MUTUAL INS CO OF MI	7373 W SAGINAW	LANSING	MI	48917	(517) 323-7000
A-	FARM BUREAU P&C INS CO	5400 UNIVERSITY AVENUE	WEST DES MOINES	IA	50266	(515) 225-5400
B+	FARM FAMILY CASUALTY INS CO	344 ROUTE 9W	GLENMONT	NY	12077	(518) 431-5000
B+	FARMERS AUTOMOBILE INS ASN	2505 COURT STREET	PEKIN	IL	61558	(309) 346-1161
B+	FARMERS MUTUAL INS CO OF NE	501 S 13TH STREET	LINCOLN	NE	68508	(402) 434-8300
B+	FEDERATED RURAL ELECTRIC INS EXCH	7725 RENNER RD	SHAWNEE	KS	66217	(913) 541-0150
B+	FINANCIAL PACIFIC INS CO	3880 ATHERTON ROAD	ROCKLIN	CA	95765	(319) 399-5700
B+	FRANKENMUTH MUTUAL INS CO	ONE MUTUAL AVENUE	FRANKENMUTH	MI	48787	(989) 652-6121
B+	GEICO CHOICE INS CO	1440 KIEWIT PLAZA	OMAHA	NE	68131	(800) 841-3000
B+	GEICO GENERAL INS CO	5260 WESTERN AVENUE	CHEVY CHASE	MD	20815	(800) 841-3000
A-	GEICO SECURE INS CO	1440 KIEWIT PLAZA	OMAHA	NE	68131	(800) 841-3000
B+	GNY CUSTOM INS CO	2338 WEST ROYAL PALM RD STE J	PHOENIX	AZ	85021	(212) 683-9700

DOM. STATE	AUTO	HOME MULT. PERIL	FARM MULT. PERIL	COMM. MULT. PERIL	COMM. AUTO LIAB.	OTHER LIABILITY	MED MALPRAC.	WORK. COMP.	ACCID. & HEALTH	OTHER	INSURANCE COMPANY NAME
WI	24	10	0	11	15	10	0	20	0	9	ACUITY A MUTUAL INS CO
AK	1	0	0	6	6	5	0	77	0	4	ALASKA NATIONAL INS CO
AL	51	49	0	0	0	0	0	0	0	0	ALFA GENERAL INS CORP
AL	0	0	0	0	0	0	0	0	0	100	ALFA MUTUAL FIRE INS CO
AL	58	42	0	0	0	1	0	0	0	0	ALFA MUTUAL GENERAL INS CO
OH	11	0	0	56	22	0	0	7	0	4	ALL AMERICA INS CO
DE	3	0	0	10	14	47	3	0	0	23	ALLIED WORLD SPECIALTY INS CO
IL	52	33	0	4	4	1	0	0	0	5	ALLSTATE INS CO
IL	55	34	0	1	5	2	0	0	0	3	ALLSTATE NJ INS CO
IN	0	0	0	0	0	0	0	0	0	100	AMERICAN AGRICULTURAL INS CO
CA	0	0	0	0	0	0	0	0	0	100	AMERICAN CONTRACTORS INDEMNITY CO
WI	50	33	2	8	1	3	0	1	1	1	AMERICAN FAMILY MUTL INS CO SI
TX	0	0	0	0	0	0	0	100	0	0	AMERICAN INTERSTATE INS CO OF TX
MO	40	25	0	5	1	7	0	0	0	22	AMERICAN NATIONAL PROPERTY & CAS CO
WI	100	0	0	0	0	0	0	0	0	0	AMERICAN STANDARD INS CO OF WI
RI	57	37	0	0	0	3	0	0	0	3	AMICA MUTUAL INS CO
MI	7	0	0	36	12	11	0	27	0	8	ANSUR AMERICA INS CO
MO	0	0	0	3	0	48	13	0	0	36	ARCH SPECIALTY INS CO
TX	0	99	0	0	0	1	0	0	0	0	AUTO CLUB INDEMNITY CO
FL	53	45	0	0	0	1	0	0	0	0	AUTO CLUB INS CO OF FL
MI	23	35	1	9	8	6	0	5	0	13	AUTO-OWNERS INS CO
NY	0	0	0	0	0	0	0	0	0	100	BERKSHIRE HATHAWAY ASR CORP
IN	2	0	0	73	5	4	0	13	0	3	BROTHERHOOD MUTUAL INS CO
NC	1	0	0	12	2	3	0	75	0	7	BUILDERS MUTUAL INS CO
IL	0	97	0	0	0	0	0	0	0	3	CASTLE KEY INS CO
MO	0	0	0	0	0	92	0	0	0	8	CATERPILLAR INS CO
OH	35	25	0	18	6	6	0	1	0	8	CENTRAL MUTUAL INS CO
WI	1	0	0	63	5	3	2	25	0	1	CHURCH MUTUAL INS CO
OH	7	0	0	24	15	15	1	27	0	12	CINCINNATI INDEMNITY CO
OH	20	14	0	26	9	16	1	2	0	12	CINCINNATI INS CO
DE	0	0	0	0	0	74	0	0	0	26	CINCINNATI SPECIALTY UNDERWRITER
FL	0	52	0	0	0	0	0	0	0	48	CITIZENS PROPERTY INS CORP
CO	0	0	0	0	0	4	95	0	1	0	COPIC INS CO
AZ	0	0	0	0	0	0	0	99	0	0	COPPERPOINT MUTUAL INS CO
IL	24	39	9	12	2	3	0	4	0	8	COUNTRY MUTUAL INS CO
NH	0	0	0	44	0	41	0	0	0	15	COVINGTON SPECIALTY INS CO
IA	2	0	0	12	1	70	0	0	0	15	CUMIS INS SOCIETY INC
WI	100	0	0	0	0	0	0	0	0	0	DAIRYLAND INS CO
CA	0	0	0	0	0	0	0	100	0	0	EMPLOYERS COMPENSATION INS CO
DE	0	0	0	0	0	53	0	0	0	46	ENDURANCE ASR CORP
NY	0	26	15	42	0	0	0	0	0	16	ERIE & NIAGARA INS ASSN
PA	0	0	0	0	0	0	0	0	0	100	ESSENT GUARANTY INC
MO	39	28	24	5	1	1	0	0	0	1	FARM BU TOWN & COUNTRY INS CO OF MO
MI	58	25	0	6	2	1	0	3	0	4	FARM BUREAU GENERAL INS CO OF MI
MI	39	0	46	0	5	2	0	6	0	3	FARM BUREAU MUTUAL INS CO OF MI
IA	40	23	26	4	1	3	0	2	0	1	FARM BUREAU P&C INS CO
NY	16	5	0	14	12	12	0	16	0	25	FARM FAMILY CASUALTY INS CO
IL	61	33	0	0	0	0	0	0	0	6	FARMERS AUTOMOBILE INS ASN
NE	37	27	30	0	1	2	0	0	0	4	FARMERS MUTUAL INS CO OF NE
KS	3	0	0	0	11	38	0	24	0	23	FEDERATED RURAL ELECTRIC INS EXCH
CA	6	0	0	10	26	29	0	0	0	28	FINANCIAL PACIFIC INS CO
MI	32	14	0	22	8	5	0	12	0	6	FRANKENMUTH MUTUAL INS CO
NE	100	0	0	0	0	0	0	0	0	0	GEICO CHOICE INS CO
MD	100	0	0	0	0	0	0	0	0	0	GEICO GENERAL INS CO
NE	100	0	0	0	0	0	0	0	0	0	GEICO SECURE INS CO
AZ	0	0	0	100	0	0	0	0	0	0	GNY CUSTOM INS CO

RATING	INSURANCE COMPANY NAME	ADDRESS	CITY	STATE	ZIP	PHONE
B+	HASTINGS MUTUAL INS CO	404 E WOODLAWN AVE	HASTINGS	MI	49058	(269) 945-3405
B+	HIGH POINT PREFERRED INS CO	331 NEWMAN SPRGS RD STE 310	RED BANK	NJ	07701	(732) 978-6000
A	HOME-OWNERS INS CO	6101 ANACAPRI BOULEVARD	LANSING	MI	48917	(517) 323-1200
B+	HOUSING AUTHORITY PROP A MUTUAL CO	148 COLLEGE STREET	BURLINGTON	VT	5401	(203) 272-8220
B+	ICI MUTUAL INS CO A RRG	159 BANK ST 4TH FL	BURLINGTON	VT	5401	(800) 643-4246
B+	INDIANA FARMERS MUTUAL INS CO	10 WEST 106TH STREET	INDIANAPOLIS	IN	46290	(317) 846-4211
B+	INTERINS EXCHANGE	3333 FAIRVIEW ROAD	COSTA MESA	CA	92626	(714) 850-5111
B+	LACKAWANNA AMERICAN INS CO	46 PUBLIC SQUARE SUITE 501	WILKES-BARRE	PA	18701	(570) 824-1400
B+	LION INS CO (FL)	2739 US HIGHWAY 19 NORTH	HOLIDAY	FL	34691	(727) 682-0155
B+	LUBA CASUALTY INS CO	2351 ENERGY DRIVE SUITE 2000	BATON ROUGE	LA	70808	(225) 389-5822
B+	MARKEL GLOBAL REINS CO	1209 ORANGE STREET	WILMINGTON	DE	19801	(908) 630-2700
B+	MERCHANTS NATIONAL INS CO	5 BEDFORD FARMS SUITE 101	BEDFORD	NH	3110	(716) 849-3333
B+	MERCHANTS PREFERRED INS CO	250 MAIN STREET	BUFFALO	NY	14202	(716) 849-3333
B+	MERCURY CASUALTY CO	555 WEST IMPERIAL HIGHWAY	BREA	CA	92821	(714) 671-6600
B+	MERCURY INS CO	555 WEST IMPERIAL HIGHWAY	BREA	CA	92821	(714) 671-6600
B+	MIDDLESEX INS CO	1800 NORTH POINT DRIVE	STEVENS POINT	WI	54481	(715) 346-6000
A-	MITSUI SUMITOMO INS CO OF AMER	527 MADISON AVE 18TH FL	NEW YORK	NY	10022	(908) 604-2900
B+	MMIC INS INC	7701 FRANCE AVE SOUTH STE 500	MINNEAPOLIS	MN	55435	(952) 838-6700
B+	MO EMPLOYERS MUTUAL INS CO	101 NORTH KEENE ST	COLUMBIA	MO	65201	(573) 499-9714
A-	MOTORISTS COMMERCIAL MUTUAL INS CO	471 EAST BROAD STREET	COLUMBUS	OH	43215	(614) 225-8211
B+	MUTUAL INS CO OF AZ	2602 EAST THOMAS ROAD	PHOENIX	AZ	85016	(602) 956-5276
B+	MUTUAL OF ENUMCLAW INS CO	4000 KRUSE WAY PLACE BLDG 3	LAKE OSWEGO	OR	97035	(360) 825-2591
B+	NATIONAL CASUALTY CO	ONE W NATIONWIDE BLVD 1-04-701	COLUMBUS	OH	43215	(480) 365-4000
A-	NATIONAL MORTGAGE INS CORP	8040 EXCELSIOR DRIVE SUITE 200	MADISON	WI	53717	(855) 873-2584
B+	NEW YORK SCHOOLS INS RECIPROCAL	333 EARLE OVINGTON BOULEVARD	UNIONDALE	NY	11553	(516) 750-9412
A+	NUCLEAR ELECTRIC INS LTD	1201 MARKET ST STE 1200	WILMINGTON	DE	19801	(302) 888-3000
A+	OGLESBY REINS CO	ONE STATE FARM PLAZA	BLOOMINGTON	IL	61710	(309) 766-2311
A	OWNERS INS CO	2325 NORTH COLE STREET	LIMA	OH	45801	(517) 323-1200
B+	PEKIN INS CO	2505 COURT STREET	PEKIN	IL	61558	(309) 346-1161
B+	PIONEER STATE MUTUAL INS CO	1510 NORTH ELMS ROAD	FLINT	MI	48532	(810) 733-2300
B+	PREFERRED PROFESSIONAL INS CO	11605 MIRACLE HILLS DR STE 200	OMAHA	NE	68154	(402) 392-1566
A-	PROPERTY-OWNERS INS CO	3950 WEST DELPHI PIKE	MARION	IN	46952	(517) 323-1200
A-	PROTECTIVE INS CO	111 CONGRESSIONAL BLVD STE 500	CARMEL	IN	46032	(317) 636-9800
A-	RADIAN REINS INC	1500 MARKET STREET	PHILADELPHIA	PA	19102	(800) 523-1988
A	RETAILFIRST INS CO	2310 COMMERCE POINT DRIVE	LAKELAND	FL	33801	(863) 665-6060
B+	ROCKINGHAM INS CO	633 EAST MARKET STREET	HARRISONBURG	VA	22801	(540) 434-5344
A-	SECURIAN CASUALTY CO	400 ROBERT STREET NORTH	ST. PAUL	MN	55101	(651) 665-3500
B+	SELECTIVE AUTO INS CO OF NJ	40 WANTAGE AVENUE	BRANCHVILLE	NJ	7890	(973) 948-3000
B+	SELECTIVE CASUALTY INS CO	40 WANTAGE AVE	BRANCHVILLE	NJ	7890	(973) 948-3000
B+	SENTRY CASUALTY CO	1800 NORTH POINT DRIVE	STEVENS POINT	WI	54481	(715) 346-6000
A	SENTRY INS A MUTUAL CO	1800 NORTH POINT DRIVE	STEVENS POINT	WI	54481	(715) 346-6000
A-	SENTRY SELECT INS CO	1800 NORTH POINT DRIVE	STEVENS POINT	WI	54481	(715) 346-6000
B+	SFM MUTUAL INS CO	3500 AMERICAN BLVD W STE 700	BLOOMINGTON	MN	55431	(952) 838-4200
A	SOMPO AMERICA INSURANCE CO	777 THIRD AVE 24TH FLOOR	NEW YORK	NY	10017	(704) 759-2200
B+	SOUTHERN FIDELITY INS CO	2750 CHANCELLORSVIILE DR	TALLAHASSEE	FL	32312	(850) 521-3080
A	SOUTHERN-OWNERS INS CO	6101 ANACAPRI BOULEVARD	LANSING	MI	48917	(517) 323-1200
B+	STATE FARM FIRE & CAS CO	ONE STATE FARM PLAZA	BLOOMINGTON	IL	61710	(309) 766-2311
B+	STATE FARM MUTUAL AUTOMOBILE INS CO	ONE STATE FARM PLAZA	BLOOMINGTON	IL	61710	(309) 766-2311
B+	STATE VOLUNTEER MUTUAL INS CO	101 WESTPARK DRIVE SUITE 300	BRENTWOOD	TN	37027	(615) 377-1999
B+	SURETEC INS CO	1330 POST OAK BLVD SUITE 1100	HOUSTON	TX	77056	(713) 812-0800
B+	TENNESSEE FARMERS ASR CO	147 BEAR CREEK PIKE	COLUMBIA	TN	38401	(931) 388-7872
B+	TENNESSEE FARMERS MUTUAL INS CO	147 BEAR CREEK PIKE	COLUMBIA	TN	38401	(931) 388-7872
A-	TEXAS FARM BUREAU CASUALTY INS CO	7420 FISH POND ROAD	WACO	TX	76710	(254) 772-3030
B+	TOA REINS CO OF AMERICA	251 LITTLE FALLS DRIVE	WILMINGTON	DE	19808	(973) 898-9480
A	TOKIO MARINE AMERICA INS CO	1221 AVE OF THE AMERICAS #1500	NEW YORK	NY	10020	(610) 227-1253
B+	TRANS PACIFIC INS CO	1221 AVE OF THE AMERICAS #1500	NEW YORK	NY	10020	(610) 227-1253

DOM. STATE	AUTO	HOME MULT. PERIL	FARM MULT. PERIL	COMM. MULT. PERIL	COMM. AUTO LIAB.	OTHER LIABILITY	MED MALPRAC.	WORK. COMP.	ACCID. & HEALTH	OTHER	INSURANCE COMPANY NAME
MI	24	13	16	17	7	4	0	18	0	2	HASTINGS MUTUAL INS CO
NJ	0	91	0	0	0	3	0	0	0	6	HIGH POINT PREFERRED INS CO
MI	83	0	0	9	3	2	0	3	0	1	HOME-OWNERS INS CO
VT	0	0	0	100	0	0	0	0	0	0	HOUSING AUTHORITY PROP A MUTUAL CO
VT	0	0	0	0	0	89	0	0	0	11	ICI MUTUAL INS CO A RRG
IN	38	22	12	11	3	3	0	4	0	6	INDIANA FARMERS MUTUAL INS CO
CA	81	18	0	0	0	0	0	0	0	1	INTERINS EXCHANGE
PA	0	0	0	0	0	0	0	100	0	0	LACKAWANNA AMERICAN INS CO
FL	0	0	0	0	0	0	0	100	0	0	LION INS CO (FL)
LA	0	0	0	0	0	0	0	100	0	0	LUBA CASUALTY INS CO
DE (*)	0	0	0	0	0	0	0	0	0	0	MARKEL GLOBAL REINS CO
NH	0	0	0	0	0	87	0	0	0	13	MERCHANTS NATIONAL INS CO
NY	29	11	0	15	34	0	0	10	0	0	MERCHANTS PREFERRED INS CO
CA	25	12	0	38	9	5	0	0	0	10	MERCURY CASUALTY CO
CA	100	0	0	0	0	0	0	0	0	0	MERCURY INS CO
WI	32	0	0	1	8	7	0	43	0	10	MIDDLESEX INS CO
NY	2	0	0	21	6	14	0	27	0	30	MITSUI SUMITOMO INS CO OF AMER
MN	0	0	0	0	0	5	95	0	0	0	MMIC INS INC
MO	0	0	0	0	0	0	0	100	0	0	MO EMPLOYERS MUTUAL INS CO
OH	14	0	0	23	30	14	0	8	0	11	MOTORISTS COMMERCIAL MUTUAL INS CO
AZ	0	0	0	0	0	0	100	0	0	0	MUTUAL INS CO OF AZ
OR	33	18	12	20	11	3	0	0	0	3	MUTUAL OF ENUMCLAW INS CO
OH	7	0	0	10	21	14	0	7	0	38	NATIONAL CASUALTY CO
WI	0	0	0	0	0	0	0	0	0	100	NATIONAL MORTGAGE INS CORP
NY	3	0	0	0	8	44	0	0	0	45	NEW YORK SCHOOLS INS RECIPROCAL
DE	0	0	0	100	0	0	0	0	0	0	NUCLEAR ELECTRIC INS LTD
IL (*)	0	0	0	0	0	0	0	0	0	0	OGLESBY REINS CO
OH	44	4	1	23	13	5	0	7	0	3	OWNERS INS CO
IL	26	12	0	25	11	4	0	19	0	3	PEKIN INS CO
MI	62	25	5	4	1	1	0	1	0	1	PIONEER STATE MUTUAL INS CO
NE	0	0	0	0	0	5	88	6	0	0	PREFERRED PROFESSIONAL INS CO
IN	5	45	2	26	8	3	0	6	0	6	PROPERTY-OWNERS INS CO
IN	16	0	0	0	24	19	0	33	5	1	PROTECTIVE INS CO
PA	0	0	0	0	0	0	0	0	0	100	RADIAN REINS INC
FL	0	0	0	0	0	0	0	100	0	0	RETAILFIRST INS CO
VA	0	55	18	0	0	12	0	0	0	15	ROCKINGHAM INS CO
MN	0	0	0	0	0	38	0	0	0	61	SECURIAN CASUALTY CO
NJ	70	29	0	0	0	2	0	0	0	0	SELECTIVE AUTO INS CO OF NJ
NJ	4	7	0	3	16	24	0	32	0	15	SELECTIVE CASUALTY INS CO
WI	0	0	0	0	0	0	0	99	0	0	SENTRY CASUALTY CO
WI	25	0	0	2	14	8	0	31	0	19	SENTRY INS A MUTUAL CO
WI	16	0	0	0	44	9	0	5	2	24	SENTRY SELECT INS CO
MN	0	0	0	0	0	0	0	100	0	0	SFM MUTUAL INS CO
NY	3	0	0	7	6	10	0	29	0	45	SOMPO AMERICA INSURANCE CO
FL	0	68	0	0	0	0	0	0	0	32	SOUTHERN FIDELITY INS CO
MI	53	2	0	12	2	25	0	4	0	2	SOUTHERN-OWNERS INS CO
IL	13	71	1	6	0	3	0	1	0	4	STATE FARM FIRE & CAS CO
IL	97	0	0	0	1	0	0	0	3	0	STATE FARM MUTUAL AUTOMOBILE INS CO
TN	0	0	0	0	0	0	100	0	0	0	STATE VOLUNTEER MUTUAL INS CO
TX	0	0	0	0	0	0	0	0	0	100	SURETEC INS CO
TN (*)	0	0	0	0	0	0	0	0	0	0	TENNESSEE FARMERS ASR CO
TN	52	31	9	1	0	2	0	0	0	5	TENNESSEE FARMERS MUTUAL INS CO
TX	95	0	0	0	2	3	0	0	0	0	TEXAS FARM BUREAU CASUALTY INS CO
DE (*)	0	0	0	0	0	0	0	0	0	0	TOA REINS CO OF AMERICA
NY	9	3	0	6	15	8	0	9	0	51	TOKIO MARINE AMERICA INS CO
NY	0	0	0	15	1	6	0	76	0	1	TRANS PACIFIC INS CO

(*) Denotes reinsurers, companies that do not sell to consumers

RATING	INSURANCE COMPANY NAME	ADDRESS	CITY	STATE	ZIP	PHONE
B+	TRANSATLANTIC REINS CO	ONE LIBERTY PLAZA 165 BROADWAY	NEW YORK	NY	10006	(212) 365-2200
A-	TRAVELERS CASUALTY & SURETY CO	ONE TOWER SQUARE	HARTFORD	CT	6183	(860) 277-0111
A-	TRAVELERS INDEMNITY CO	ONE TOWER SQUARE	HARTFORD	CT	6183	(860) 277-0111
B+	TREXIS INSURANCE CORP	2108 EAST SOUTH BOULEVARD	MONTGOMERY	AL	36116	(334) 288-3900
A-	TREXIS ONE INSURANCE GROUP	2108 EAST SOUTH BOULEVARD	MONTGOMERY	AL	36116	(334) 288-3900
B+	UNITED EDUCATORS INS A RECIP RRG	76 ST PAUL STREET SUITE 500	BURLINGTON	VT	05401	(301) 907-4908
B+	UNITED FARM FAMILY MUTUAL INS CO	225 SOUTH EAST STREET	INDIANAPOLIS	IN	46202	(317) 692-7200
A-	UNITED SERVICES AUTOMOBILE ASN	9800 FREDERICKSBURG ROAD	SAN ANTONIO	TX	78288	(210) 498-2211
B+	UNITED SPECIALTY INS CO	160 GREENTREE DRIVE SUITE 101	DOVER	DE	19904	(817) 265-2000
A-	USAA CASUALTY INS CO	9800 FREDERICKSBURG ROAD	SAN ANTONIO	TX	78288	(210) 498-1411
B+	USAA GENERAL INDEMNITY CO	9800 FREDERICKSBURG ROAD	SAN ANTONIO	TX	78288	(210) 498-1411
A-	WEST BEND MUTUAL INS CO	1900 SOUTH 18TH AVENUE	WEST BEND	WI	53095	(262) 334-5571
B+	WESTERN AGRICULTURAL INS CO	5400 UNIVERSITY AVENUE	WEST DES MOINES	IA	50266	(515) 225-5400

DOM. STATE	AUTO	HOME MULT. PERIL	FARM MULT. PERIL	COMM. MULT. PERIL	COMM. AUTO LIAB.	OTHER LIABILITY	MED MALPRAC.	WORK. COMP.	ACCID. & HEALTH	OTHER	INSURANCE COMPANY NAME
NY (*)	0	0	0	0	0	0	0	0	0	0	TRANSATLANTIC REINS CO
CT	0	8	0	0	0	1	0	75	0	16	TRAVELERS CASUALTY & SURETY CO
CT	4	2	1	14	13	20	0	22	0	23	TRAVELERS INDEMNITY CO
VA	100	0	0	0	0	0	0	0	0	0	TREXIS INSURANCE CORP
VA	100	0	0	0	0	0	0	0	0	0	TREXIS ONE INSURANCE GROUP
VT	0	0	0	0	0	100	0	0	0	0	UNITED EDUCATORS INS A RECIP RRG
IN	46	23	14	8	1	1	0	2	0	3	UNITED FARM FAMILY MUTUAL INS CO
TX	58	34	0	0	0	2	0	0	0	6	UNITED SERVICES AUTOMOBILE ASN
DE	2	0	0	25	20	46	0	0	0	7	UNITED SPECIALTY INS CO
TX	66	29	0	0	0	1	0	0	0	4	USAA CASUALTY INS CO
TX	72	21	0	0	0	0	0	0	0	6	USAA GENERAL INDEMNITY CO
WI	20	12	0	4	7	16	0	23	0	17	WEST BEND MUTUAL INS CO
IA	16	12	7	8	2	1	0	5	0	48	WESTERN AGRICULTURAL INS CO

Section IV

Weiss
Recommended Companies
by Type of Business

A compilation of those

U.S. Property and Casualty Insurers

receiving a Weiss Safety Rating

of A+, A, A- or B+.

Companies are ranked by Safety Rating
in each line of business where they have received
more than $1 million in direct premiums.

Section IV Contents

This section is broken into six subsections, each presenting a list of the recommended carriers receiving at least $1 million in direct premiums from a particular line of business: Auto, Commercial Multiple Peril, Fire and Allied, Homeowners Multiple Peril, Medical Malpractice, and Workers' Compensation. Recommended companies are those insurers receiving a Safety Rating of A+, A, A- or B+. If an insurer is not on this list, it should not be automatically assumed that the firm is weak. Indeed, there are many firms that have not achieved a B+ or better rating but are in relatively good condition with adequate resources to cover their risk during an average recession. Not being included in this list should not be construed as a recommendation to cancel policies.

Companies are ranked within each line of business by their Safety Rating. However, companies with the same rating should be viewed as having the same relative financial strength regardless of their ranking in these tables. While the specific order in which they appear on the page is based upon differences in our underlying indexes, you can assume that companies with the same rating have differences that are only minor and relatively inconsequential.

The six lines of business covered in this section are defined as follows:

Auto: Coverage for auto physical damage and auto liability. Auto physical covers damage to the policyholder's own automobile. Auto liability covers against financial loss from lawsuits (and legal settlements) for auto-related bodily injuries or property damage caused by the insured.

Commercial Multiple Peril: Package policies for business and other commercial establishments providing a broad spectrum of property and liability coverages.

Fire & Allied: Coverage for losses caused by fire, lightning, sprinkler damage, windstorm, and water damage.

Homeowners Multiple Peril: Package policies for homeowners providing a broad spectrum of property and liability coverages.

Medical Malpractice: Errors and omissions liability coverages for persons engaged in the practice of medicine, surgery, dentistry, nursing, pharmacy, or other health care services. Also covers health care institutions.

Workers' Compensation: Liability coverage issued to employers which provides for the payment of medical care, certain disability income benefits and possible additional liability amounts to employees who are injured on the job.

Column definitions are as follows:

1. **Insurance Company Name**   The legally-registered name, which can sometimes differ from the name that the company uses for advertising. An insurer's name can be very similar to the name of other companies which may not be on our Recommended List, so make sure you note the exact name before contacting your agent.

2. **Domicile State**   The state which has primary regulatory responsibility for the company. It may differ from the location of the company's corporate headquarters. You do not have to be living in the domicile state to purchase insurance from this firm, provided it is licensed to do business in your state.

3. **Total Premiums**   Total direct premiums received by the company during the year for all types of policies.

4. **Policy-Type Premium**   Direct premiums received by the company for a specific type of insurance coverage, such as Auto Premiums. Companies that have less than $1,000,000 in this type of premium are not listed.

5. **Maximum Benefit**   Conservative consumers may want to limit the size of their policy with this company to the amount shown. This figure is based on the view that a policy's maximum benefits per risk should not exceed 1% of the company's capital and surplus.

Weiss Safety Ratings are not deemed to be a recommendation concerning the purchase or sale of the securities of any insurance company that is publicly owned.

Auto

INSURANCE COMPANY NAME	DOMICILE STATE	TOTAL PREMIUM ($)	AUTO PREMIUM ($)	MAXIMUM BENEFIT ($)
Rating: A				
AUTO-OWNERS INS CO	MI	3,392,231,672	1,057,487,314	100,000,000
BUILDERS MUTUAL INS CO	NC	281,706,184	6,911,269	3,000,000
CINCINNATI INS CO	OH	3,849,648,295	1,134,856,243	50,000,000
HOME-OWNERS INS CO	MI	1,066,575,609	910,099,124	10,000,000
OWNERS INS CO	OH	1,826,529,041	1,046,901,714	20,000,000
SENTRY INS A MUTUAL CO	WI	493,791,071	192,170,038	50,000,000
SOMPO AMERICA INSURANCE CO	NY	360,298,964	32,660,082	6,000,000
SOUTHERN-OWNERS INS CO	MI	413,981,058	229,605,489	2,000,000
TOKIO MARINE AMERICA INS CO	NY	396,609,646	92,490,290	5,000,000
Rating: A-				
ACUITY A MUTUAL INS CO	WI	1,438,731,591	565,298,542	20,000,000
ALFA MUTUAL GENERAL INS CO	AL	63,206,716	36,490,288	600,000
ALL AMERICA INS CO	OH	46,242,836	15,013,671	1,000,000
ALLSTATE NJ INS CO	IL	435,231,008	262,002,077	8,000,000
AMERICAN FAMILY MUTL INS CO SI	WI	4,950,971,638	2,527,867,735	70,000,000
CINCINNATI INDEMNITY CO	OH	419,169,085	88,180,281	1,000,000
COUNTRY MUTUAL INS CO	IL	1,672,711,150	429,295,719	20,000,000
CUMIS INS SOCIETY INC	IA	471,924,544	13,855,014	9,000,000
DAIRYLAND INS CO	WI	134,591,133	134,591,133	5,000,000
FARM BUREAU P&C INS CO	IA	1,215,284,377	498,415,883	10,000,000
GEICO SECURE INS CO	NE	418,377,184	418,377,183	3,000,000
MITSUI SUMITOMO INS CO OF AMER	NY	266,119,333	20,253,913	4,000,000
MOTORISTS COMMERCIAL MUTUAL INS CO	OH	39,917,755	17,670,882	1,000,000
PROPERTY-OWNERS INS CO	IN	166,623,133	21,584,919	1,000,000
PROTECTIVE INS CO	IN	464,111,054	188,010,381	4,000,000
SENTRY SELECT INS CO	WI	539,955,634	323,507,415	2,000,000
TEXAS FARM BUREAU CASUALTY INS CO	TX	226,838,280	221,010,191	7,000,000
TRAVELERS INDEMNITY CO	CT	1,879,580,132	318,025,052	70,000,000
TREXIS ONE INSURANCE GROUP	VA	87,493,682	87,493,682	300,000
UNITED SERVICES AUTOMOBILE ASN	TX	7,853,691,472	4,564,405,118	300,000,000
USAA CASUALTY INS CO	TX	6,292,183,641	4,178,073,173	50,000,000
WEST BEND MUTUAL INS CO	WI	1,193,687,552	318,777,349	10,000,000
Rating: B+				
ALASKA NATIONAL INS CO	AK	264,038,363	19,750,061	5,000,000
ALFA GENERAL INS CORP	AL	32,386,507	16,433,207	500,000
ALLIED WORLD SPECIALTY INS CO	DE	199,847,231	34,141,874	4,000,000
ALLSTATE INS CO	IL	5,996,500,280	3,371,344,117	200,000,000
AMERICAN NATIONAL PROPERTY & CAS CO	MO	793,465,149	323,983,432	6,000,000
AMERICAN STANDARD INS CO OF WI	WI	125,399,166	125,399,166	3,000,000
AMICA MUTUAL INS CO	RI	2,281,617,395	1,291,957,781	30,000,000
ANSUR AMERICA INS CO	MI	26,041,261	4,791,619	500,000
ARCH SPECIALTY INS CO	MO	475,197,282	1,323,174	3,000,000
AUTO CLUB INS CO OF FL	FL	226,083,963	120,384,372	2,000,000
BROTHERHOOD MUTUAL INS CO	IN	451,977,509	32,071,620	3,000,000
CENTRAL MUTUAL INS CO	OH	673,746,987	276,942,087	8,000,000

Auto (Continued)

INSURANCE COMPANY NAME	DOMICILE STATE	TOTAL PREMIUM ($)	AUTO PREMIUM ($)	MAXIMUM BENEFIT ($)
Rating: B+ (Continued)				
CHURCH MUTUAL INS CO	WI	705,909,975	47,586,234	7,000,000
FARM BU TOWN & COUNTRY INS CO OF MO	MO	229,794,467	91,679,637	2,000,000
FARM BUREAU GENERAL INS CO OF MI	MI	620,854,082	374,608,308	3,000,000
FARM BUREAU MUTUAL INS CO OF MI	MI	166,283,282	72,386,773	4,000,000
FARM FAMILY CASUALTY INS CO	NY	388,973,285	107,910,055	5,000,000
FARMERS AUTOMOBILE INS ASN	IL	239,851,502	146,280,895	5,000,000
FARMERS MUTUAL INS CO OF NE	NE	378,696,914	140,815,275	3,000,000
FEDERATED RURAL ELECTRIC INS EXCH	KS	162,723,134	22,922,780	2,000,000
FINANCIAL PACIFIC INS CO	CA	100,488,107	32,452,996	1,000,000
FRANKENMUTH MUTUAL INS CO	MI	618,338,109	248,573,310	6,000,000
GEICO CHOICE INS CO	NE	823,653,004	823,653,004	5,000,000
GEICO GENERAL INS CO	MD	9,564,314,407	9,564,314,408	2,000,000
HASTINGS MUTUAL INS CO	MI	445,407,392	134,530,632	4,000,000
INDIANA FARMERS MUTUAL INS CO	IN	225,800,638	93,833,871	2,000,000
INTERINS EXCHANGE	CA	3,011,288,317	2,428,296,596	70,000,000
MERCHANTS PREFERRED INS CO	NY	72,113,706	45,107,290	300,000
MERCURY CASUALTY CO	CA	199,388,764	68,781,184	10,000,000
MERCURY INS CO	CA	1,625,426,454	1,625,426,454	6,000,000
MIDDLESEX INS CO	WI	147,883,566	58,293,228	2,000,000
MUTUAL OF ENUMCLAW INS CO	OR	292,603,584	127,378,596	3,000,000
NATIONAL CASUALTY CO	OH	917,033,219	260,791,723	1,000,000
NEW YORK SCHOOLS INS RECIPROCAL	NY	94,082,094	10,707,929	2,000,000
PEKIN INS CO	IL	408,535,379	148,726,985	1,000,000
PIONEER STATE MUTUAL INS CO	MI	235,258,956	149,818,460	4,000,000
SELECTIVE AUTO INS CO OF NJ	NJ	65,282,773	45,464,974	900,000
SELECTIVE CASUALTY INS CO	NJ	177,251,308	34,606,488	1,000,000
STATE FARM FIRE & CAS CO	IL	19,295,387,976	2,472,212,786	200,000,000
STATE FARM MUTUAL AUTOMOBILE INS CO	IL	40,077,551,346	39,058,334,165	***,***,***
TENNESSEE FARMERS MUTUAL INS CO	TN	1,271,582,958	665,314,502	20,000,000
TREXIS INSURANCE CORP	VA	176,063,738	176,063,737	500,000
UNITED FARM FAMILY MUTUAL INS CO	IN	617,838,753	291,607,838	5,000,000
UNITED SPECIALTY INS CO	DE	900,346,690	196,882,879	1,000,000
USAA GENERAL INDEMNITY CO	TX	3,948,737,002	2,856,322,649	20,000,000
WESTERN AGRICULTURAL INS CO	IA	289,423,154	52,390,225	1,000,000

Commercial Multiple Peril

INSURANCE COMPANY NAME	DOMICILE STATE	TOTAL PREMIUM ($)	COMM. MULT. PERIL PREMIUM ($)	MAXIMUM BENEFIT ($)
Rating: A+				
NUCLEAR ELECTRIC INS LTD	DE	204,773,622	204,773,622	40,000,000
Rating: A				
AUTO-OWNERS INS CO	MI	3,392,231,672	481,762,689	100,000,000
BUILDERS MUTUAL INS CO	NC	281,706,184	43,492,911	3,000,000
CINCINNATI INS CO	OH	3,849,648,295	1,603,346,456	50,000,000
CINCINNATI SPECIALTY UNDERWRITER	DE	229,849,825	168,983,901	4,000,000
HOME-OWNERS INS CO	MI	1,066,575,609	111,976,449	10,000,000
OWNERS INS CO	OH	1,826,529,041	513,435,252	20,000,000
SENTRY INS A MUTUAL CO	WI	493,791,071	50,548,542	50,000,000
SOMPO AMERICA INSURANCE CO	NY	360,298,964	61,145,844	6,000,000
SOUTHERN-OWNERS INS CO	MI	413,981,058	153,174,633	2,000,000
TOKIO MARINE AMERICA INS CO	NY	396,609,646	55,897,122	5,000,000
Rating: A-				
ACUITY A MUTUAL INS CO	WI	1,438,731,591	303,838,592	20,000,000
ALL AMERICA INS CO	OH	46,242,836	26,084,534	1,000,000
ALLSTATE NJ INS CO	IL	435,231,008	13,216,665	8,000,000
AMERICAN FAMILY MUTL INS CO SI	WI	4,950,971,638	541,743,964	70,000,000
CINCINNATI INDEMNITY CO	OH	419,169,085	163,953,667	1,000,000
COUNTRY MUTUAL INS CO	IL	1,672,711,150	245,701,317	20,000,000
CUMIS INS SOCIETY INC	IA	471,924,544	386,538,644	9,000,000
ENDURANCE ASR CORP	DE	95,453,870	51,311,107	9,000,000
FARM BUREAU P&C INS CO	IA	1,215,284,377	78,574,984	10,000,000
MITSUI SUMITOMO INS CO OF AMER	NY	266,119,333	92,885,079	4,000,000
MOTORISTS COMMERCIAL MUTUAL INS CO	OH	39,917,755	14,627,677	1,000,000
PROPERTY-OWNERS INS CO	IN	166,623,133	48,481,422	1,000,000
PROTECTIVE INS CO	IN	464,111,054	89,209,820	4,000,000
SECURIAN CASUALTY CO	MN	298,718,137	114,688,882	1,000,000
SENTRY SELECT INS CO	WI	539,955,634	49,566,584	2,000,000
TEXAS FARM BUREAU CASUALTY INS CO	TX	226,838,280	5,828,089	7,000,000
TRAVELERS CASUALTY & SURETY CO	CT	292,108,298	2,150,241	60,000,000
TRAVELERS INDEMNITY CO	CT	1,879,580,132	654,604,516	70,000,000
UNITED SERVICES AUTOMOBILE ASN	TX	7,853,691,472	144,482,159	300,000,000
USAA CASUALTY INS CO	TX	6,292,183,641	65,542,528	50,000,000
WEST BEND MUTUAL INS CO	WI	1,193,687,552	247,641,031	10,000,000
Rating: B+				
ALASKA NATIONAL INS CO	AK	264,038,363	30,853,353	5,000,000
ALLIED WORLD SPECIALTY INS CO	DE	199,847,231	114,801,311	4,000,000
ALLSTATE INS CO	IL	5,996,500,280	306,711,108	200,000,000
AMERICAN NATIONAL PROPERTY & CAS CO	MO	793,465,149	92,064,295	6,000,000
AMICA MUTUAL INS CO	RI	2,281,617,395	66,303,544	30,000,000
ANSUR AMERICA INS CO	MI	26,041,261	12,295,924	500,000
ARCH SPECIALTY INS CO	MO	475,197,282	241,696,314	3,000,000
AUTO CLUB INS CO OF FL	FL	226,083,963	2,803,128	2,000,000

Commercial Multiple Peril (Continued)

INSURANCE COMPANY NAME	DOMICILE STATE	TOTAL PREMIUM ($)	COMM. MULT. PERIL PREMIUM ($)	MAXIMUM BENEFIT ($)
Rating: B+ **(Continued)**				
BROTHERHOOD MUTUAL INS CO	IN	451,977,509	348,351,970	3,000,000
CATERPILLAR INS CO	MO	389,955,389	357,985,508	3,000,000
CENTRAL MUTUAL INS CO	OH	673,746,987	162,536,577	8,000,000
CHURCH MUTUAL INS CO	WI	705,909,975	465,290,143	7,000,000
COPIC INS CO	CO	85,649,611	3,429,569	3,000,000
COVINGTON SPECIALTY INS CO	NH	143,564,134	121,427,236	500,000
ERIE & NIAGARA INS ASSN	NY	75,293,802	31,735,889	2,000,000
FARM BU TOWN & COUNTRY INS CO OF MO	MO	229,794,467	15,118,720	2,000,000
FARM BUREAU GENERAL INS CO OF MI	MI	620,854,082	44,378,209	3,000,000
FARM BUREAU MUTUAL INS CO OF MI	MI	166,283,282	2,769,014	4,000,000
FARM FAMILY CASUALTY INS CO	NY	388,973,285	102,038,629	5,000,000
FARMERS MUTUAL INS CO OF NE	NE	378,696,914	6,324,829	3,000,000
FEDERATED RURAL ELECTRIC INS EXCH	KS	162,723,134	61,074,731	2,000,000
FINANCIAL PACIFIC INS CO	CA	100,488,107	39,694,542	1,000,000
FRANKENMUTH MUTUAL INS CO	MI	618,338,109	168,375,687	6,000,000
HASTINGS MUTUAL INS CO	MI	445,407,392	90,596,896	4,000,000
HIGH POINT PREFERRED INS CO	NJ	103,887,606	3,136,531	2,000,000
HOUSING AUTHORITY PROP A MUTUAL CO	VT	61,721,653	61,721,653	1,000,000
ICI MUTUAL INS CO A RRG	VT	80,248,575	71,061,818	3,000,000
INDIANA FARMERS MUTUAL INS CO	IN	225,800,638	32,130,062	2,000,000
INTERINS EXCHANGE	CA	3,011,288,317	14,582,126	70,000,000
MERCHANTS NATIONAL INS CO	NH	8,408,536	7,336,142	500,000
MERCHANTS PREFERRED INS CO	NY	72,113,706	11,222,513	300,000
MERCURY CASUALTY CO	CA	199,388,764	86,502,269	10,000,000
MIDDLESEX INS CO	WI	147,883,566	11,070,192	2,000,000
MMIC INS INC	MN	108,681,405	5,835,206	4,000,000
MUTUAL OF ENUMCLAW INS CO	OR	292,603,584	68,761,810	3,000,000
NATIONAL CASUALTY CO	OH	917,033,219	215,433,507	1,000,000
NEW YORK SCHOOLS INS RECIPROCAL	NY	94,082,094	41,434,328	2,000,000
PEKIN INS CO	IL	408,535,379	120,860,664	1,000,000
PIONEER STATE MUTUAL INS CO	MI	235,258,956	10,196,197	4,000,000
PREFERRED PROFESSIONAL INS CO	NE	69,155,315	3,419,786	2,000,000
ROCKINGHAM INS CO	VA	29,886,487	3,586,700	800,000
SELECTIVE AUTO INS CO OF NJ	NJ	65,282,773	1,162,165	900,000
SELECTIVE CASUALTY INS CO	NJ	177,251,308	48,746,303	1,000,000
STATE FARM FIRE & CAS CO	IL	19,295,387,976	1,769,703,049	200,000,000
STATE FARM MUTUAL AUTOMOBILE INS CO	IL	40,077,551,346	3,807,627	*** *** ***
TENNESSEE FARMERS MUTUAL INS CO	TN	1,271,582,958	33,300,236	20,000,000
TRANS PACIFIC INS CO	NY	21,308,385	4,414,821	500,000
UNITED EDUCATORS INS A RECIP RRG	VT	187,800,302	187,800,302	3,000,000
UNITED FARM FAMILY MUTUAL INS CO	IN	617,838,753	58,470,164	5,000,000
UNITED SPECIALTY INS CO	DE	900,346,690	640,610,643	1,000,000
USAA GENERAL INDEMNITY CO	TX	3,948,737,002	14,709,737	20,000,000
WESTERN AGRICULTURAL INS CO	IA	289,423,154	27,683,079	1,000,000

Fire & Allied

INSURANCE COMPANY NAME	DOMICILE STATE	TOTAL PREMIUM ($)	FIRE & ALLIED PREMIUM ($)	MAXIMUM BENEFIT ($)
Rating: A+				
CITIZENS PROPERTY INS CORP	FL	893,989,776	433,088,954	70,000,000
Rating: A				
AUTO-OWNERS INS CO	MI	3,392,231,672	336,087,759	100,000,000
CINCINNATI INS CO	OH	3,849,648,295	163,628,792	50,000,000
CINCINNATI SPECIALTY UNDERWRITER	DE	229,849,825	28,073,936	4,000,000
HOME-OWNERS INS CO	MI	1,066,575,609	2,624,679	10,000,000
OWNERS INS CO	OH	1,826,529,041	10,643,257	20,000,000
SENTRY INS A MUTUAL CO	WI	493,791,071	64,830,057	50,000,000
SOMPO AMERICA INSURANCE CO	NY	360,298,964	90,887,703	6,000,000
TOKIO MARINE AMERICA INS CO	NY	396,609,646	79,983,412	5,000,000
Rating: A-				
ACUITY A MUTUAL INS CO	WI	1,438,731,591	78,120,354	20,000,000
ALLSTATE NJ INS CO	IL	435,231,008	9,315,848	8,000,000
AMERICAN FAMILY MUTL INS CO SI	WI	4,950,971,638	16,803,276	70,000,000
CINCINNATI INDEMNITY CO	OH	419,169,085	32,823,135	1,000,000
COUNTRY MUTUAL INS CO	IL	1,672,711,150	109,745,161	20,000,000
MITSUI SUMITOMO INS CO OF AMER	NY	266,119,333	35,862,165	4,000,000
SENTRY SELECT INS CO	WI	539,955,634	33,403,722	2,000,000
TRAVELERS CASUALTY & SURETY CO	CT	292,108,298	3,463,119	60,000,000
TRAVELERS INDEMNITY CO	CT	1,879,580,132	348,518,271	70,000,000
UNITED SERVICES AUTOMOBILE ASN	TX	7,853,691,472	343,484,667	300,000,000
USAA CASUALTY INS CO	TX	6,292,183,641	135,220,736	50,000,000
WEST BEND MUTUAL INS CO	WI	1,193,687,552	123,837,474	10,000,000
Rating: B+				
ALASKA NATIONAL INS CO	AK	264,038,363	3,563,275	5,000,000
ALFA MUTUAL FIRE INS CO	AL	14,470,934	13,134,327	4,000,000
ALLIED WORLD SPECIALTY INS CO	DE	199,847,231	16,398,663	4,000,000
ALLSTATE INS CO	IL	5,996,500,280	254,966,206	200,000,000
AMERICAN AGRICULTURAL INS CO	IN	45,734,542	45,734,542	6,000,000
AMERICAN NATIONAL PROPERTY & CAS CO	MO	793,465,149	48,917,672	6,000,000
AMICA MUTUAL INS CO	RI	2,281,617,395	32,472,855	30,000,000
ARCH SPECIALTY INS CO	MO	475,197,282	117,316,633	3,000,000
CENTRAL MUTUAL INS CO	OH	673,746,987	18,954,507	8,000,000
CHURCH MUTUAL INS CO	WI	705,909,975	5,457,381	7,000,000
COVINGTON SPECIALTY INS CO	NH	143,564,134	12,914,563	500,000
ERIE & NIAGARA INS ASSN	NY	75,293,802	11,412,407	2,000,000
FARM BUREAU GENERAL INS CO OF MI	MI	620,854,082	7,941,049	3,000,000
FARM FAMILY CASUALTY INS CO	NY	388,973,285	77,988,731	5,000,000
FARMERS AUTOMOBILE INS ASN	IL	239,851,502	10,988,019	5,000,000
FARMERS MUTUAL INS CO OF NE	NE	378,696,914	12,571,515	3,000,000
FEDERATED RURAL ELECTRIC INS EXCH	KS	162,723,134	35,388,765	2,000,000
FINANCIAL PACIFIC INS CO	CA	100,488,107	3,603,098	1,000,000
FRANKENMUTH MUTUAL INS CO	MI	618,338,109	4,936,384	6,000,000
HASTINGS MUTUAL INS CO	MI	445,407,392	6,808,365	4,000,000

Fire & Allied (Continued)

INSURANCE COMPANY NAME	DOMICILE STATE	TOTAL PREMIUM ($)	FIRE & ALLIED PREMIUM ($)	MAXIMUM BENEFIT ($)
Rating: B+ (Continued)				
HIGH POINT PREFERRED INS CO	NJ	103,887,606	4,585,107	2,000,000
INDIANA FARMERS MUTUAL INS CO	IN	225,800,638	4,077,413	2,000,000
INTERINS EXCHANGE	CA	3,011,288,317	21,992,083	70,000,000
MERCURY CASUALTY CO	CA	199,388,764	16,900,512	10,000,000
MIDDLESEX INS CO	WI	147,883,566	11,282,297	2,000,000
MUTUAL OF ENUMCLAW INS CO	OR	292,603,584	3,077,987	3,000,000
NATIONAL CASUALTY CO	OH	917,033,219	7,979,714	1,000,000
NEW YORK SCHOOLS INS RECIPROCAL	NY	94,082,094	37,614,052	2,000,000
PEKIN INS CO	IL	408,535,379	5,210,198	1,000,000
PIONEER STATE MUTUAL INS CO	MI	235,258,956	2,288,444	4,000,000
ROCKINGHAM INS CO	VA	29,886,487	4,495,642	800,000
SELECTIVE CASUALTY INS CO	NJ	177,251,308	11,468,263	1,000,000
SOUTHERN FIDELITY INS CO	FL	153,725,618	49,112,519	800,000
STATE FARM FIRE & CAS CO	IL	19,295,387,976	43,369,540	200,000,000
TENNESSEE FARMERS MUTUAL INS CO	TN	1,271,582,958	63,904,022	20,000,000
UNITED FARM FAMILY MUTUAL INS CO	IN	617,838,753	21,468,255	5,000,000
UNITED SPECIALTY INS CO	DE	900,346,690	11,277,777	1,000,000
USAA GENERAL INDEMNITY CO	TX	3,948,737,002	198,583,759	20,000,000
WESTERN AGRICULTURAL INS CO	IA	289,423,154	139,223,611	1,000,000

Homeowners Multiple Peril

INSURANCE COMPANY NAME	DOMICILE STATE	TOTAL PREMIUM ($)	HOME OWNERS PREMIUM ($)	MAXIMUM BENEFIT ($)
Rating:　　A+				
CITIZENS PROPERTY INS CORP	FL	893,989,776	460,900,822	70,000,000
Rating:　　A				
AUTO-OWNERS INS CO	MI	3,392,231,672	1,199,687,815	100,000,000
CINCINNATI INS CO	OH	3,849,648,295	547,289,896	50,000,000
HOME-OWNERS INS CO	MI	1,066,575,609	4,690,008	10,000,000
OWNERS INS CO	OH	1,826,529,041	67,911,257	20,000,000
SOUTHERN-OWNERS INS CO	MI	413,981,058	7,498,016	2,000,000
TOKIO MARINE AMERICA INS CO	NY	396,609,646	10,519,490	5,000,000
Rating:　　A-				
ACUITY A MUTUAL INS CO	WI	1,438,731,591	144,291,849	20,000,000
ALFA MUTUAL GENERAL INS CO	AL	63,206,716	26,245,327	600,000
ALLSTATE NJ INS CO	IL	435,231,008	146,294,257	8,000,000
AMERICAN FAMILY MUTL INS CO SI	WI	4,950,971,638	1,639,677,650	70,000,000
COUNTRY MUTUAL INS CO	IL	1,672,711,150	659,915,424	20,000,000
FARM BUREAU P&C INS CO	IA	1,215,284,377	283,895,618	10,000,000
PROPERTY-OWNERS INS CO	IN	166,623,133	74,650,270	1,000,000
TRAVELERS CASUALTY & SURETY CO	CT	292,108,298	23,590,715	60,000,000
TRAVELERS INDEMNITY CO	CT	1,879,580,132	44,088,390	70,000,000
UNITED SERVICES AUTOMOBILE ASN	TX	7,853,691,472	2,640,956,770	300,000,000
USAA CASUALTY INS CO	TX	6,292,183,641	1,798,829,565	50,000,000
WEST BEND MUTUAL INS CO	WI	1,193,687,552	143,815,728	10,000,000
Rating:　　B+				
ALFA GENERAL INS CORP	AL	32,386,507	15,953,300	500,000
ALLSTATE INS CO	IL	5,996,500,280	2,001,980,535	200,000,000
AMERICAN NATIONAL PROPERTY & CAS CO	MO	793,465,149	200,198,557	6,000,000
AMICA MUTUAL INS CO	RI	2,281,617,395	847,664,627	30,000,000
AUTO CLUB INDEMNITY CO	TX	127,370,935	126,279,999	50,000
AUTO CLUB INS CO OF FL	FL	226,083,963	102,330,015	2,000,000
CASTLE KEY INS CO	IL	99,518,236	96,250,259	2,000,000
CENTRAL MUTUAL INS CO	OH	673,746,987	171,114,469	8,000,000
CHURCH MUTUAL INS CO	WI	705,909,975	1,105,348	7,000,000
ERIE & NIAGARA INS ASSN	NY	75,293,802	19,941,551	2,000,000
FARM BU TOWN & COUNTRY INS CO OF MO	MO	229,794,467	65,453,606	2,000,000
FARM BUREAU GENERAL INS CO OF MI	MI	620,854,082	157,197,785	3,000,000
FARM FAMILY CASUALTY INS CO	NY	388,973,285	21,143,690	5,000,000
FARMERS AUTOMOBILE INS ASN	IL	239,851,502	79,681,041	5,000,000
FARMERS MUTUAL INS CO OF NE	NE	378,696,914	102,078,057	3,000,000
FRANKENMUTH MUTUAL INS CO	MI	618,338,109	85,661,172	6,000,000
HASTINGS MUTUAL INS CO	MI	445,407,392	57,509,194	4,000,000
HIGH POINT PREFERRED INS CO	NJ	103,887,606	94,842,589	2,000,000
INDIANA FARMERS MUTUAL INS CO	IN	225,800,638	49,367,666	2,000,000
INTERINS EXCHANGE	CA	3,011,288,317	540,985,025	70,000,000

Homeowners Multiple Peril (Continued)

INSURANCE COMPANY NAME	DOMICILE STATE	TOTAL PREMIUM ($)	HOME OWNERS PREMIUM ($)	MAXIMUM BENEFIT ($)
Rating: B+ (Continued)				
MERCHANTS PREFERRED INS CO	NY	72,113,706	8,189,138	300,000
MERCURY CASUALTY CO	CA	199,388,764	23,683,400	10,000,000
MUTUAL OF ENUMCLAW INS CO	OR	292,603,584	53,271,044	3,000,000
PEKIN INS CO	IL	408,535,379	49,746,978	1,000,000
PIONEER STATE MUTUAL INS CO	MI	235,258,956	58,712,040	4,000,000
ROCKINGHAM INS CO	VA	29,886,487	16,293,019	800,000
SELECTIVE AUTO INS CO OF NJ	NJ	65,282,773	18,633,460	900,000
SELECTIVE CASUALTY INS CO	NJ	177,251,308	11,793,654	1,000,000
SOUTHERN FIDELITY INS CO	FL	153,725,618	104,575,120	800,000
STATE FARM FIRE & CAS CO	IL	19,295,387,976	13,725,923,822	200,000,000
TENNESSEE FARMERS MUTUAL INS CO	TN	1,271,582,958	390,200,638	20,000,000
UNITED FARM FAMILY MUTUAL INS CO	IN	617,838,753	143,289,924	5,000,000
UNITED SPECIALTY INS CO	DE	900,346,690	1,522,532	1,000,000
USAA GENERAL INDEMNITY CO	TX	3,948,737,002	835,336,305	20,000,000
WESTERN AGRICULTURAL INS CO	IA	289,423,154	34,319,577	1,000,000

Medical Malpractice

INSURANCE COMPANY NAME	DOMICILE STATE	TOTAL PREMIUM ($)	MEDICAL MALPRACTICE PREMIUM ($)	MAXIMUM BENEFIT ($)
Rating: A				
CINCINNATI INS CO	OH	3,849,648,295	29,417,774	50,000,000
Rating: A-				
CINCINNATI INDEMNITY CO	OH	419,169,085	2,598,815	1,000,000
Rating: B+				
ALLIED WORLD SPECIALTY INS CO	DE	199,847,231	5,327,188	4,000,000
ARCH SPECIALTY INS CO	MO	475,197,282	61,010,866	3,000,000
CHURCH MUTUAL INS CO	WI	705,909,975	11,035,838	7,000,000
COPIC INS CO	CO	85,649,611	81,291,362	3,000,000
MMIC INS INC	MN	108,681,405	102,846,199	4,000,000
MUTUAL INS CO OF AZ	AZ	103,835,992	103,835,992	7,000,000
PREFERRED PROFESSIONAL INS CO	NE	69,155,315	61,044,838	2,000,000
STATE FARM FIRE & CAS CO	IL	19,295,387,976	2,602,811	200,000,000
STATE VOLUNTEER MUTUAL INS CO	TN	125,843,731	125,749,659	6,000,000
UNITED SPECIALTY INS CO	DE	900,346,690	1,192,950	1,000,000

Workers' Compensation

INSURANCE COMPANY NAME	DOMICILE STATE	TOTAL PREMIUM ($)	WORKERS' COMPENSATION PREMIUM ($)	MAXIMUM BENEFIT ($)
Rating: A+				
COPPERPOINT MUTUAL INS CO	AZ	46,640,941	46,387,290	10,000,000
Rating: A				
AUTO-OWNERS INS CO	MI	3,392,231,672	170,616,205	100,000,000
BUILDERS MUTUAL INS CO	NC	281,706,184	211,565,976	3,000,000
CINCINNATI INS CO	OH	3,849,648,295	85,743,842	50,000,000
HOME-OWNERS INS CO	MI	1,066,575,609	27,675,919	10,000,000
OWNERS INS CO	OH	1,826,529,041	127,183,030	20,000,000
RETAILFIRST INS CO	FL	93,156,984	93,156,984	1,000,000
SENTRY INS A MUTUAL CO	WI	493,791,071	151,659,794	50,000,000
SOMPO AMERICA INSURANCE CO	NY	360,298,964	104,277,484	6,000,000
SOUTHERN-OWNERS INS CO	MI	413,981,058	15,545,991	2,000,000
TOKIO MARINE AMERICA INS CO	NY	396,609,646	33,897,412	5,000,000
Rating: A-				
ACUITY A MUTUAL INS CO	WI	1,438,731,591	291,790,090	20,000,000
ALL AMERICA INS CO	OH	46,242,836	3,240,918	1,000,000
AMERICAN FAMILY MUTL INS CO SI	WI	4,950,971,638	52,758,611	70,000,000
CINCINNATI INDEMNITY CO	OH	419,169,085	115,017,942	1,000,000
COUNTRY MUTUAL INS CO	IL	1,672,711,150	62,002,309	20,000,000
EMPLOYERS COMPENSATION INS CO	CA	51,726,826	51,726,826	3,000,000
FARM BUREAU P&C INS CO	IA	1,215,284,377	28,060,395	10,000,000
MITSUI SUMITOMO INS CO OF AMER	NY	266,119,333	72,172,734	4,000,000
MOTORISTS COMMERCIAL MUTUAL INS CO	OH	39,917,755	3,011,300	1,000,000
PROPERTY-OWNERS INS CO	IN	166,623,133	9,674,086	1,000,000
PROTECTIVE INS CO	IN	464,111,054	155,205,133	4,000,000
SENTRY SELECT INS CO	WI	539,955,634	26,799,373	2,000,000
TRAVELERS CASUALTY & SURETY CO	CT	292,108,298	218,439,390	60,000,000
TRAVELERS INDEMNITY CO	CT	1,879,580,132	407,343,330	70,000,000
WEST BEND MUTUAL INS CO	WI	1,193,687,552	277,034,029	10,000,000
Rating: B+				
ALASKA NATIONAL INS CO	AK	264,038,363	202,900,969	5,000,000
AMERICAN NATIONAL PROPERTY & CAS CO	MO	793,465,149	2,851,681	6,000,000
ANSUR AMERICA INS CO	MI	26,041,261	6,967,832	500,000
BROTHERHOOD MUTUAL INS CO	IN	451,977,509	57,155,382	3,000,000
CENTRAL MUTUAL INS CO	OH	673,746,987	7,908,742	8,000,000
CHURCH MUTUAL INS CO	WI	705,909,975	175,373,352	7,000,000
FARM BUREAU GENERAL INS CO OF MI	MI	620,854,082	21,589,486	3,000,000
FARM BUREAU MUTUAL INS CO OF MI	MI	166,283,282	9,301,457	4,000,000
FARM FAMILY CASUALTY INS CO	NY	388,973,285	60,637,521	5,000,000
FEDERATED RURAL ELECTRIC INS EXCH	KS	162,723,134	38,345,636	2,000,000
FRANKENMUTH MUTUAL INS CO	MI	618,338,109	77,284,729	6,000,000
HASTINGS MUTUAL INS CO	MI	445,407,392	82,057,345	4,000,000
INDIANA FARMERS MUTUAL INS CO	IN	225,800,638	9,781,551	2,000,000
LACKAWANNA AMERICAN INS CO	PA	65,518,154	65,518,154	400,000
LION INS CO (FL)	FL	19,060,114	19,060,114	1,000,000
LUBA CASUALTY INS CO	LA	72,644,126	72,644,126	1,000,000

Workers' Compensation (Continued)

INSURANCE COMPANY NAME	DOMICILE STATE	TOTAL PREMIUM ($)	WORKERS' COMPENSATION PREMIUM ($)	MAXIMUM BENEFIT ($)
MERCHANTS PREFERRED INS CO	NY	72,113,706	7,373,844	300,000
MIDDLESEX INS CO	WI	147,883,566	64,022,913	2,000,000
MO EMPLOYERS MUTUAL INS CO	MO	233,293,848	233,293,848	2,000,000
NATIONAL CASUALTY CO	OH	917,033,219	60,660,323	1,000,000
PEKIN INS CO	IL	408,535,379	77,961,841	1,000,000
PIONEER STATE MUTUAL INS CO	MI	235,258,956	2,249,951	4,000,000
PREFERRED PROFESSIONAL INS CO	NE	69,155,315	4,316,741	2,000,000
SELECTIVE CASUALTY INS CO	NJ	177,251,308	56,102,541	1,000,000
SENTRY CASUALTY CO	WI	192,846,020	191,643,944	700,000
SFM MUTUAL INS CO	MN	152,206,680	151,778,429	1,000,000
STATE FARM FIRE & CAS CO	IL	19,295,387,976	269,195,999	200,000,000
TRANS PACIFIC INS CO	NY	21,308,385	16,291,074	500,000
UNITED FARM FAMILY MUTUAL INS CO	IN	617,838,753	14,867,264	5,000,000
WESTERN AGRICULTURAL INS CO	IA	289,423,154	14,007,367	1,000,000

Section V

Weiss Recommended Companies by State

A compilation of those

U.S. Property and Casualty Insurers

receiving a Weiss Safety Rating

of A+, A, A- or B+.

Companies are ranked by Safety Rating
in each state where they are licensed to do business.

Section V Contents

This section provides a list of the recommended carriers licensed to do business in each state. It contains all insurers receiving a Safety Rating of A+, A, A- or B+. If an insurer is not on this list, it should not be automatically assumed that the firm is weak. Indeed, there are many firms that have not achieved a B+ or better rating but are in relatively good condition with adequate resources to cover their risk during an average recession. Not being included in this list should not be construed as a recommendation to cancel policies.

Companies are ranked within each state by their Safety Rating. However, companies with the same rating should be viewed as having the same relative safety regardless of their ranking in this table. While the specific order in which they appear on the page is based upon differences in our underlying indexes, you can assume that companies with the same rating have differences that are only minor and relatively inconsequential.

1. **Insurance Company Name**   The legally-registered name, which can sometimes differ from the name that the company uses for advertising. An insurer's name can be very similar to the name of other companies which may not be on our Recommended List, so make sure you note the exact name before contacting your agent.

2. **Domicile State**   The state which has primary regulatory responsibility for the company. It may differ from the location of the company's corporate headquarters. You do not have to be living in the domicile state to purchase insurance from this firm, provided it is licensed to do business in your state.

3. **Total Assets**   All assets admitted by state insurance regulators in millions of dollars. This includes investments and current business assets such as receivables from agents and reinsurers.

Weiss Safety Ratings are not deemed to be a recommendation concerning the purchase or sale of the securities of any insurance company that is publicly owned.

Alabama

INSURANCE COMPANY NAME	DOM. STATE	TOTAL ASSETS ($MIL)
Rating: A+		
BERKSHIRE HATHAWAY ASR CORP	NY	2,223.5
Rating: A		
AUTO-OWNERS INS CO	MI	15,390.4
CINCINNATI INS CO	OH	12,914.9
CINCINNATI SPECIALTY UNDERWRITER	DE	820.6
HOME-OWNERS INS CO	MI	2,323.7
OWNERS INS CO	OH	4,110.4
SENTRY INS A MUTUAL CO	WI	8,392.8
SOMPO AMERICA INSURANCE CO	NY	1,285.1
TOKIO MARINE AMERICA INS CO	NY	1,409.5
Rating: A-		
ACUITY A MUTUAL INS CO	WI	3,960.1
ALFA MUTUAL GENERAL INS CO	AL	115.4
CINCINNATI INDEMNITY CO	OH	133.0
COUNTRY MUTUAL INS CO	IL	4,850.2
CUMIS INS SOCIETY INC	IA	2,002.8
DAIRYLAND INS CO	WI	1,400.7
EMPLOYERS COMPENSATION INS CO	CA	1,091.0
ENDURANCE ASR CORP	DE	2,059.0
ESSENT GUARANTY INC	PA	1,756.6
GEICO SECURE INS CO	NE	625.3
MITSUI SUMITOMO INS CO OF AMER	NY	975.8
NATIONAL MORTGAGE INS CORP	WI	717.8
PROPERTY-OWNERS INS CO	IN	302.7
PROTECTIVE INS CO	IN	885.6
SECURIAN CASUALTY CO	MN	328.2
SENTRY SELECT INS CO	WI	826.6
TRAVELERS CASUALTY & SURETY CO	CT	16,983.8
TRAVELERS INDEMNITY CO	CT	21,394.5
TREXIS ONE INSURANCE GROUP	VA	56.6
UNITED SERVICES AUTOMOBILE ASN	TX	35,460.0
USAA CASUALTY INS CO	TX	10,897.7
Rating: B+		
ALASKA NATIONAL INS CO	AK	1,004.7
ALFA GENERAL INS CORP	AL	101.6
ALFA MUTUAL FIRE INS CO	AL	770.4
ALLIED WORLD SPECIALTY INS CO	DE	829.1
ALLSTATE INS CO	IL	48,302.5
AMERICAN AGRICULTURAL INS CO	IN	1,338.9
AMERICAN CONTRACTORS INDEMNITY CO	CA	338.3
AMERICAN NATIONAL PROPERTY & CAS CO	MO	1,418.0
AMICA MUTUAL INS CO	RI	5,384.6
ANSUR AMERICA INS CO	MI	121.2
ARCH SPECIALTY INS CO	MO	483.4
BROTHERHOOD MUTUAL INS CO	IN	644.9
CATERPILLAR INS CO	MO	790.6
CHURCH MUTUAL INS CO	WI	1,739.8
COVINGTON SPECIALTY INS CO	NH	97.9
FARM BUREAU MUTUAL INS CO OF MI	MI	782.4
FEDERATED RURAL ELECTRIC INS EXCH	KS	553.2
FRANKENMUTH MUTUAL INS CO	MI	1,351.0
GEICO CHOICE INS CO	NE	1,134.6
GEICO GENERAL INS CO	MD	167.6

INSURANCE COMPANY NAME	DOM. STATE	TOTAL ASSETS ($MIL)
HOUSING AUTHORITY PROP A MUTUAL CO	VT	181.9
LION INS CO (FL)	FL	264.3
MARKEL GLOBAL REINS CO	DE	2,180.9
MERCHANTS NATIONAL INS CO	NH	136.0
MIDDLESEX INS CO	WI	764.3
NATIONAL CASUALTY CO	OH	418.6
PREFERRED PROFESSIONAL INS CO	NE	327.4
SENTRY CASUALTY CO	WI	355.9
SFM MUTUAL INS CO	MN	612.1
STATE FARM FIRE & CAS CO	IL	39,411.9
STATE FARM MUTUAL AUTOMOBILE INS CO	IL	160,732.0
STATE VOLUNTEER MUTUAL INS CO	TN	1,249.3
SURETEC INS CO	TX	253.2
TOA REINS CO OF AMERICA	DE	1,820.3
TRANS PACIFIC INS CO	NY	67.6
TRANSATLANTIC REINS CO	NY	14,732.2
TREXIS INSURANCE CORP	VA	108.1
UNITED EDUCATORS INS A RECIP RRG	VT	912.3
UNITED SPECIALTY INS CO	DE	330.2
USAA GENERAL INDEMNITY CO	TX	4,627.9
WESTERN AGRICULTURAL INS CO	IA	213.2

Alaska

INSURANCE COMPANY NAME	DOM. STATE	TOTAL ASSETS ($MIL)
Rating: A+		
BERKSHIRE HATHAWAY ASR CORP	NY	2,223.5
Rating: A		
CINCINNATI INS CO	OH	12,914.9
CINCINNATI SPECIALTY UNDERWRITER	DE	820.6
SENTRY INS A MUTUAL CO	WI	8,392.8
SOMPO AMERICA INSURANCE CO	NY	1,285.1
TOKIO MARINE AMERICA INS CO	NY	1,409.5
Rating: A-		
CINCINNATI INDEMNITY CO	OH	133.0
COUNTRY MUTUAL INS CO	IL	4,850.2
CUMIS INS SOCIETY INC	IA	2,002.8
DAIRYLAND INS CO	WI	1,400.7
ENDURANCE ASR CORP	DE	2,059.0
ESSENT GUARANTY INC	PA	1,756.6
GEICO SECURE INS CO	NE	625.3
MITSUI SUMITOMO INS CO OF AMER	NY	975.8
NATIONAL MORTGAGE INS CORP	WI	717.8
PROTECTIVE INS CO	IN	885.6
SECURIAN CASUALTY CO	MN	328.2
SENTRY SELECT INS CO	WI	826.6
TRAVELERS CASUALTY & SURETY CO	CT	16,983.8
TRAVELERS INDEMNITY CO	CT	21,394.5
UNITED SERVICES AUTOMOBILE ASN	TX	35,460.0
USAA CASUALTY INS CO	TX	10,897.7
Rating: B+		
ALASKA NATIONAL INS CO	AK	1,004.7
ALLIED WORLD SPECIALTY INS CO	DE	829.1
ALLSTATE INS CO	IL	48,302.5
AMERICAN CONTRACTORS INDEMNITY CO	CA	338.3
AMERICAN NATIONAL PROPERTY & CAS CO	MO	1,418.0
AMICA MUTUAL INS CO	RI	5,384.6
ARCH SPECIALTY INS CO	MO	483.4
BROTHERHOOD MUTUAL INS CO	IN	644.9
CATERPILLAR INS CO	MO	790.6
CHURCH MUTUAL INS CO	WI	1,739.8
COPIC INS CO	CO	603.2
COVINGTON SPECIALTY INS CO	NH	97.9
FEDERATED RURAL ELECTRIC INS EXCH	KS	553.2
FINANCIAL PACIFIC INS CO	CA	261.4
GEICO CHOICE INS CO	NE	1,134.6
GEICO GENERAL INS CO	MD	167.6
MARKEL GLOBAL REINS CO	DE	2,180.9
MIDDLESEX INS CO	WI	764.3
MUTUAL OF ENUMCLAW INS CO	OR	748.3
NATIONAL CASUALTY CO	OH	418.6
PREFERRED PROFESSIONAL INS CO	NE	327.4
SENTRY CASUALTY CO	WI	355.9
STATE FARM FIRE & CAS CO	IL	39,411.9
STATE FARM MUTUAL AUTOMOBILE INS CO	IL	160,732.0
SURETEC INS CO	TX	253.2
TOA REINS CO OF AMERICA	DE	1,820.3
TRANS PACIFIC INS CO	NY	67.6
TRANSATLANTIC REINS CO	NY	14,732.2

INSURANCE COMPANY NAME	DOM. STATE	TOTAL ASSETS ($MIL)
UNITED EDUCATORS INS A RECIP RRG	VT	912.3
UNITED SPECIALTY INS CO	DE	330.2
USAA GENERAL INDEMNITY CO	TX	4,627.9

Arizona

INSURANCE COMPANY NAME	DOM. STATE	TOTAL ASSETS ($MIL)
Rating: **A+**		
BERKSHIRE HATHAWAY ASR CORP	NY	2,223.5
COPPERPOINT MUTUAL INS CO	AZ	3,694.0
Rating: **A**		
AUTO-OWNERS INS CO	MI	15,390.4
CINCINNATI INS CO	OH	12,914.9
CINCINNATI SPECIALTY UNDERWRITER	DE	820.6
OWNERS INS CO	OH	4,110.4
SENTRY INS A MUTUAL CO	WI	8,392.8
SOMPO AMERICA INSURANCE CO	NY	1,285.1
TOKIO MARINE AMERICA INS CO	NY	1,409.5
Rating: **A-**		
ACUITY A MUTUAL INS CO	WI	3,960.1
ALL AMERICA INS CO	OH	291.6
AMERICAN FAMILY MUTL INS CO SI	WI	17,157.4
CINCINNATI INDEMNITY CO	OH	133.0
COUNTRY MUTUAL INS CO	IL	4,850.2
CUMIS INS SOCIETY INC	IA	2,002.8
DAIRYLAND INS CO	WI	1,400.7
EMPLOYERS COMPENSATION INS CO	CA	1,091.0
ENDURANCE ASR CORP	DE	2,059.0
ESSENT GUARANTY INC	PA	1,756.6
FARM BUREAU P&C INS CO	IA	2,532.4
GEICO SECURE INS CO	NE	625.3
MITSUI SUMITOMO INS CO OF AMER	NY	975.8
MOTORISTS COMMERCIAL MUTUAL INS CO	OH	368.8
NATIONAL MORTGAGE INS CORP	WI	717.8
PROTECTIVE INS CO	IN	885.6
SECURIAN CASUALTY CO	MN	328.2
SENTRY SELECT INS CO	WI	826.6
TRAVELERS CASUALTY & SURETY CO	CT	16,983.8
TRAVELERS INDEMNITY CO	CT	21,394.5
UNITED SERVICES AUTOMOBILE ASN	TX	35,460.0
USAA CASUALTY INS CO	TX	10,897.7
Rating: **B+**		
ALASKA NATIONAL INS CO	AK	1,004.7
ALLIED WORLD SPECIALTY INS CO	DE	829.1
ALLSTATE INS CO	IL	48,302.5
AMERICAN AGRICULTURAL INS CO	IN	1,338.9
AMERICAN CONTRACTORS INDEMNITY CO	CA	338.3
AMERICAN NATIONAL PROPERTY & CAS CO	MO	1,418.0
AMERICAN STANDARD INS CO OF WI	WI	400.9
AMICA MUTUAL INS CO	RI	5,384.6
ARCH SPECIALTY INS CO	MO	483.4
BROTHERHOOD MUTUAL INS CO	IN	644.9
CATERPILLAR INS CO	MO	790.6
CENTRAL MUTUAL INS CO	OH	1,618.4
CHURCH MUTUAL INS CO	WI	1,739.8
COPIC INS CO	CO	603.2
COVINGTON SPECIALTY INS CO	NH	97.9
FARMERS AUTOMOBILE INS ASN	IL	1,226.6
FEDERATED RURAL ELECTRIC INS EXCH	KS	553.2
FINANCIAL PACIFIC INS CO	CA	261.4
FRANKENMUTH MUTUAL INS CO	MI	1,351.0

INSURANCE COMPANY NAME	DOM. STATE	TOTAL ASSETS ($MIL)
GEICO CHOICE INS CO	NE	1,134.6
GEICO GENERAL INS CO	MD	167.6
GNY CUSTOM INS CO	AZ	60.5
HOUSING AUTHORITY PROP A MUTUAL CO	VT	181.9
ICI MUTUAL INS CO A RRG	VT	367.6
LION INS CO (FL)	FL	264.3
MARKEL GLOBAL REINS CO	DE	2,180.9
MERCURY CASUALTY CO	CA	1,877.6
MIDDLESEX INS CO	WI	764.3
MMIC INS INC	MN	682.7
MUTUAL INS CO OF AZ	AZ	1,105.9
MUTUAL OF ENUMCLAW INS CO	OR	748.3
NATIONAL CASUALTY CO	OH	418.6
PEKIN INS CO	IL	305.4
PREFERRED PROFESSIONAL INS CO	NE	327.4
SENTRY CASUALTY CO	WI	355.9
SFM MUTUAL INS CO	MN	612.1
STATE FARM FIRE & CAS CO	IL	39,411.9
STATE FARM MUTUAL AUTOMOBILE INS CO	IL	160,732.0
SURETEC INS CO	TX	253.2
TOA REINS CO OF AMERICA	DE	1,820.3
TRANS PACIFIC INS CO	NY	67.6
TRANSATLANTIC REINS CO	NY	14,732.2
UNITED EDUCATORS INS A RECIP RRG	VT	912.3
UNITED SPECIALTY INS CO	DE	330.2
USAA GENERAL INDEMNITY CO	TX	4,627.9
WESTERN AGRICULTURAL INS CO	IA	213.2

Arkansas

INSURANCE COMPANY NAME	DOM. STATE	TOTAL ASSETS ($MIL)
Rating: A+		
BERKSHIRE HATHAWAY ASR CORP	NY	2,223.5
Rating: A		
AUTO-OWNERS INS CO	MI	15,390.4
CINCINNATI INS CO	OH	12,914.9
CINCINNATI SPECIALTY UNDERWRITER	DE	820.6
HOME-OWNERS INS CO	MI	2,323.7
OWNERS INS CO	OH	4,110.4
SENTRY INS A MUTUAL CO	WI	8,392.8
SOMPO AMERICA INSURANCE CO	NY	1,285.1
TOKIO MARINE AMERICA INS CO	NY	1,409.5
Rating: A-		
ACUITY A MUTUAL INS CO	WI	3,960.1
ALL AMERICA INS CO	OH	291.6
CINCINNATI INDEMNITY CO	OH	133.0
COUNTRY MUTUAL INS CO	IL	4,850.2
CUMIS INS SOCIETY INC	IA	2,002.8
DAIRYLAND INS CO	WI	1,400.7
EMPLOYERS COMPENSATION INS CO	CA	1,091.0
ENDURANCE ASR CORP	DE	2,059.0
ESSENT GUARANTY INC	PA	1,756.6
GEICO SECURE INS CO	NE	625.3
MITSUI SUMITOMO INS CO OF AMER	NY	975.8
NATIONAL MORTGAGE INS CORP	WI	717.8
PROPERTY-OWNERS INS CO	IN	302.7
PROTECTIVE INS CO	IN	885.6
SECURIAN CASUALTY CO	MN	328.2
SENTRY SELECT INS CO	WI	826.6
TRAVELERS CASUALTY & SURETY CO	CT	16,983.8
TRAVELERS INDEMNITY CO	CT	21,394.5
TREXIS ONE INSURANCE GROUP	VA	56.6
UNITED SERVICES AUTOMOBILE ASN	TX	35,460.0
USAA CASUALTY INS CO	TX	10,897.7
Rating: B+		
ALLIED WORLD SPECIALTY INS CO	DE	829.1
ALLSTATE INS CO	IL	48,302.5
AMERICAN AGRICULTURAL INS CO	IN	1,338.9
AMERICAN CONTRACTORS INDEMNITY CO	CA	338.3
AMERICAN NATIONAL PROPERTY & CAS CO	MO	1,418.0
AMICA MUTUAL INS CO	RI	5,384.6
ANSUR AMERICA INS CO	MI	121.2
ARCH SPECIALTY INS CO	MO	483.4
BROTHERHOOD MUTUAL INS CO	IN	644.9
CATERPILLAR INS CO	MO	790.6
CENTRAL MUTUAL INS CO	OH	1,618.4
CHURCH MUTUAL INS CO	WI	1,739.8
COPIC INS CO	CO	603.2
COVINGTON SPECIALTY INS CO	NH	97.9
FEDERATED RURAL ELECTRIC INS EXCH	KS	553.2
FINANCIAL PACIFIC INS CO	CA	261.4
FRANKENMUTH MUTUAL INS CO	MI	1,351.0
GEICO CHOICE INS CO	NE	1,134.6
GEICO GENERAL INS CO	MD	167.6
HOUSING AUTHORITY PROP A MUTUAL CO	VT	181.9

INSURANCE COMPANY NAME	DOM. STATE	TOTAL ASSETS ($MIL)
LUBA CASUALTY INS CO	LA	228.7
MARKEL GLOBAL REINS CO	DE	2,180.9
MERCHANTS NATIONAL INS CO	NH	136.0
MIDDLESEX INS CO	WI	764.3
MMIC INS INC	MN	682.7
NATIONAL CASUALTY CO	OH	418.6
PREFERRED PROFESSIONAL INS CO	NE	327.4
SENTRY CASUALTY CO	WI	355.9
STATE FARM FIRE & CAS CO	IL	39,411.9
STATE FARM MUTUAL AUTOMOBILE INS CO	IL	160,732.0
STATE VOLUNTEER MUTUAL INS CO	TN	1,249.3
SURETEC INS CO	TX	253.2
TOA REINS CO OF AMERICA	DE	1,820.3
TRANS PACIFIC INS CO	NY	67.6
TRANSATLANTIC REINS CO	NY	14,732.2
TREXIS INSURANCE CORP	VA	108.1
UNITED EDUCATORS INS A RECIP RRG	VT	912.3
UNITED SPECIALTY INS CO	DE	330.2
USAA GENERAL INDEMNITY CO	TX	4,627.9
WESTERN AGRICULTURAL INS CO	IA	213.2

California

INSURANCE COMPANY NAME	DOM. STATE	TOTAL ASSETS ($MIL)
Rating: A+		
BERKSHIRE HATHAWAY ASR CORP	NY	2,223.5
Rating: A		
CINCINNATI INS CO	OH	12,914.9
CINCINNATI SPECIALTY UNDERWRITER	DE	820.6
SENTRY INS A MUTUAL CO	WI	8,392.8
SOMPO AMERICA INSURANCE CO	NY	1,285.1
TOKIO MARINE AMERICA INS CO	NY	1,409.5
Rating: A-		
ALL AMERICA INS CO	OH	291.6
CINCINNATI INDEMNITY CO	OH	133.0
COUNTRY MUTUAL INS CO	IL	4,850.2
CUMIS INS SOCIETY INC	IA	2,002.8
EMPLOYERS COMPENSATION INS CO	CA	1,091.0
ENDURANCE ASR CORP	DE	2,059.0
ESSENT GUARANTY INC	PA	1,756.6
MITSUI SUMITOMO INS CO OF AMER	NY	975.8
MOTORISTS COMMERCIAL MUTUAL INS CO	OH	368.8
NATIONAL MORTGAGE INS CORP	WI	717.8
PROTECTIVE INS CO	IN	885.6
SECURIAN CASUALTY CO	MN	328.2
SENTRY SELECT INS CO	WI	826.6
TRAVELERS CASUALTY & SURETY CO	CT	16,983.8
TRAVELERS INDEMNITY CO	CT	21,394.5
UNITED SERVICES AUTOMOBILE ASN	TX	35,460.0
USAA CASUALTY INS CO	TX	10,897.7
Rating: B+		
ALASKA NATIONAL INS CO	AK	1,004.7
ALLIED WORLD SPECIALTY INS CO	DE	829.1
ALLSTATE INS CO	IL	48,302.5
AMERICAN CONTRACTORS INDEMNITY CO	CA	338.3
AMERICAN NATIONAL PROPERTY & CAS CO	MO	1,418.0
AMICA MUTUAL INS CO	RI	5,384.6
ARCH SPECIALTY INS CO	MO	483.4
BROTHERHOOD MUTUAL INS CO	IN	644.9
CATERPILLAR INS CO	MO	790.6
CENTRAL MUTUAL INS CO	OH	1,618.4
CHURCH MUTUAL INS CO	WI	1,739.8
COVINGTON SPECIALTY INS CO	NH	97.9
FARM BUREAU MUTUAL INS CO OF MI	MI	782.4
FEDERATED RURAL ELECTRIC INS EXCH	KS	553.2
FINANCIAL PACIFIC INS CO	CA	261.4
GEICO GENERAL INS CO	MD	167.6
HOUSING AUTHORITY PROP A MUTUAL CO	VT	181.9
ICI MUTUAL INS CO A RRG	VT	367.6
INTERINS EXCHANGE	CA	10,404.3
MARKEL GLOBAL REINS CO	DE	2,180.9
MERCHANTS NATIONAL INS CO	NH	136.0
MERCURY CASUALTY CO	CA	1,877.6
MERCURY INS CO	CA	1,708.0
MIDDLESEX INS CO	WI	764.3
MUTUAL INS CO OF AZ	AZ	1,105.9
NATIONAL CASUALTY CO	OH	418.6
PREFERRED PROFESSIONAL INS CO	NE	327.4

INSURANCE COMPANY NAME	DOM. STATE	TOTAL ASSETS ($MIL)
SENTRY CASUALTY CO	WI	355.9
STATE FARM FIRE & CAS CO	IL	39,411.9
STATE FARM MUTUAL AUTOMOBILE INS CO	IL	160,732.0
SURETEC INS CO	TX	253.2
TOA REINS CO OF AMERICA	DE	1,820.3
TRANS PACIFIC INS CO	NY	67.6
TRANSATLANTIC REINS CO	NY	14,732.2
UNITED EDUCATORS INS A RECIP RRG	VT	912.3
UNITED SPECIALTY INS CO	DE	330.2
USAA GENERAL INDEMNITY CO	TX	4,627.9

Colorado

INSURANCE COMPANY NAME	DOM. STATE	TOTAL ASSETS ($MIL)
Rating: A+		
BERKSHIRE HATHAWAY ASR CORP	NY	2,223.5
Rating: A		
AUTO-OWNERS INS CO	MI	15,390.4
CINCINNATI INS CO	OH	12,914.9
CINCINNATI SPECIALTY UNDERWRITER	DE	820.6
HOME-OWNERS INS CO	MI	2,323.7
OWNERS INS CO	OH	4,110.4
SENTRY INS A MUTUAL CO	WI	8,392.8
SOMPO AMERICA INSURANCE CO	NY	1,285.1
TOKIO MARINE AMERICA INS CO	NY	1,409.5
Rating: A-		
ACUITY A MUTUAL INS CO	WI	3,960.1
ALL AMERICA INS CO	OH	291.6
AMERICAN FAMILY MUTL INS CO SI	WI	17,157.4
CINCINNATI INDEMNITY CO	OH	133.0
COUNTRY MUTUAL INS CO	IL	4,850.2
CUMIS INS SOCIETY INC	IA	2,002.8
DAIRYLAND INS CO	WI	1,400.7
EMPLOYERS COMPENSATION INS CO	CA	1,091.0
ENDURANCE ASR CORP	DE	2,059.0
ESSENT GUARANTY INC	PA	1,756.6
GEICO SECURE INS CO	NE	625.3
MITSUI SUMITOMO INS CO OF AMER	NY	975.8
MOTORISTS COMMERCIAL MUTUAL INS CO	OH	368.8
NATIONAL MORTGAGE INS CORP	WI	717.8
PROTECTIVE INS CO	IN	885.6
SECURIAN CASUALTY CO	MN	328.2
SENTRY SELECT INS CO	WI	826.6
TRAVELERS CASUALTY & SURETY CO	CT	16,983.8
TRAVELERS INDEMNITY CO	CT	21,394.5
UNITED SERVICES AUTOMOBILE ASN	TX	35,460.0
USAA CASUALTY INS CO	TX	10,897.7
Rating: B+		
ALASKA NATIONAL INS CO	AK	1,004.7
ALLIED WORLD SPECIALTY INS CO	DE	829.1
ALLSTATE INS CO	IL	48,302.5
AMERICAN AGRICULTURAL INS CO	IN	1,338.9
AMERICAN CONTRACTORS INDEMNITY CO	CA	338.3
AMERICAN NATIONAL PROPERTY & CAS CO	MO	1,418.0
AMERICAN STANDARD INS CO OF WI	WI	400.9
AMICA MUTUAL INS CO	RI	5,384.6
ANSUR AMERICA INS CO	MI	121.2
ARCH SPECIALTY INS CO	MO	483.4
BROTHERHOOD MUTUAL INS CO	IN	644.9
CATERPILLAR INS CO	MO	790.6
CENTRAL MUTUAL INS CO	OH	1,618.4
CHURCH MUTUAL INS CO	WI	1,739.8
COPIC INS CO	CO	603.2
COVINGTON SPECIALTY INS CO	NH	97.9
FEDERATED RURAL ELECTRIC INS EXCH	KS	553.2
FINANCIAL PACIFIC INS CO	CA	261.4
FRANKENMUTH MUTUAL INS CO	MI	1,351.0
GEICO CHOICE INS CO	NE	1,134.6

INSURANCE COMPANY NAME	DOM. STATE	TOTAL ASSETS ($MIL)
GEICO GENERAL INS CO	MD	167.6
HOUSING AUTHORITY PROP A MUTUAL CO	VT	181.9
ICI MUTUAL INS CO A RRG	VT	367.6
LION INS CO (FL)	FL	264.3
MARKEL GLOBAL REINS CO	DE	2,180.9
MERCHANTS NATIONAL INS CO	NH	136.0
MIDDLESEX INS CO	WI	764.3
MMIC INS INC	MN	682.7
MUTUAL INS CO OF AZ	AZ	1,105.9
MUTUAL OF ENUMCLAW INS CO	OR	748.3
NATIONAL CASUALTY CO	OH	418.6
PREFERRED PROFESSIONAL INS CO	NE	327.4
SENTRY CASUALTY CO	WI	355.9
SFM MUTUAL INS CO	MN	612.1
STATE FARM FIRE & CAS CO	IL	39,411.9
STATE FARM MUTUAL AUTOMOBILE INS CO	IL	160,732.0
SURETEC INS CO	TX	253.2
TOA REINS CO OF AMERICA	DE	1,820.3
TRANS PACIFIC INS CO	NY	67.6
TRANSATLANTIC REINS CO	NY	14,732.2
UNITED EDUCATORS INS A RECIP RRG	VT	912.3
UNITED SPECIALTY INS CO	DE	330.2
USAA GENERAL INDEMNITY CO	TX	4,627.9
WESTERN AGRICULTURAL INS CO	IA	213.2

Connecticut

INSURANCE COMPANY NAME	DOM. STATE	TOTAL ASSETS ($MIL)
Rating: A+		
BERKSHIRE HATHAWAY ASR CORP	NY	2,223.5
Rating: A		
CINCINNATI INS CO	OH	12,914.9
CINCINNATI SPECIALTY UNDERWRITER	DE	820.6
SENTRY INS A MUTUAL CO	WI	8,392.8
SOMPO AMERICA INSURANCE CO	NY	1,285.1
TOKIO MARINE AMERICA INS CO	NY	1,409.5
Rating: A-		
ALL AMERICA INS CO	OH	291.6
CINCINNATI INDEMNITY CO	OH	133.0
COUNTRY MUTUAL INS CO	IL	4,850.2
CUMIS INS SOCIETY INC	IA	2,002.8
DAIRYLAND INS CO	WI	1,400.7
EMPLOYERS COMPENSATION INS CO	CA	1,091.0
ENDURANCE ASR CORP	DE	2,059.0
ESSENT GUARANTY INC	PA	1,756.6
GEICO SECURE INS CO	NE	625.3
MITSUI SUMITOMO INS CO OF AMER	NY	975.8
MOTORISTS COMMERCIAL MUTUAL INS CO	OH	368.8
NATIONAL MORTGAGE INS CORP	WI	717.8
PROTECTIVE INS CO	IN	885.6
SECURIAN CASUALTY CO	MN	328.2
SENTRY SELECT INS CO	WI	826.6
TRAVELERS CASUALTY & SURETY CO	CT	16,983.8
TRAVELERS INDEMNITY CO	CT	21,394.5
UNITED SERVICES AUTOMOBILE ASN	TX	35,460.0
USAA CASUALTY INS CO	TX	10,897.7
Rating: B+		
ALLIED WORLD SPECIALTY INS CO	DE	829.1
ALLSTATE INS CO	IL	48,302.5
AMERICAN AGRICULTURAL INS CO	IN	1,338.9
AMERICAN CONTRACTORS INDEMNITY CO	CA	338.3
AMICA MUTUAL INS CO	RI	5,384.6
ANSUR AMERICA INS CO	MI	121.2
ARCH SPECIALTY INS CO	MO	483.4
BROTHERHOOD MUTUAL INS CO	IN	644.9
CATERPILLAR INS CO	MO	790.6
CENTRAL MUTUAL INS CO	OH	1,618.4
CHURCH MUTUAL INS CO	WI	1,739.8
COVINGTON SPECIALTY INS CO	NH	97.9
FARM BUREAU MUTUAL INS CO OF MI	MI	782.4
FARM FAMILY CASUALTY INS CO	NY	1,241.7
FRANKENMUTH MUTUAL INS CO	MI	1,351.0
GEICO CHOICE INS CO	NE	1,134.6
GEICO GENERAL INS CO	MD	167.6
GNY CUSTOM INS CO	AZ	60.5
HOUSING AUTHORITY PROP A MUTUAL CO	VT	181.9
ICI MUTUAL INS CO A RRG	VT	367.6
LION INS CO (FL)	FL	264.3
MARKEL GLOBAL REINS CO	DE	2,180.9
MERCHANTS NATIONAL INS CO	NH	136.0
MIDDLESEX INS CO	WI	764.3
NATIONAL CASUALTY CO	OH	418.6

INSURANCE COMPANY NAME	DOM. STATE	TOTAL ASSETS ($MIL)
PREFERRED PROFESSIONAL INS CO	NE	327.4
SENTRY CASUALTY CO	WI	355.9
STATE FARM FIRE & CAS CO	IL	39,411.9
STATE FARM MUTUAL AUTOMOBILE INS CO	IL	160,732.0
SURETEC INS CO	TX	253.2
TOA REINS CO OF AMERICA	DE	1,820.3
TRANS PACIFIC INS CO	NY	67.6
TRANSATLANTIC REINS CO	NY	14,732.2
UNITED EDUCATORS INS A RECIP RRG	VT	912.3
UNITED SPECIALTY INS CO	DE	330.2
USAA GENERAL INDEMNITY CO	TX	4,627.9

Delaware

INSURANCE COMPANY NAME	DOM. STATE	TOTAL ASSETS ($MIL)
Rating: A+		
BERKSHIRE HATHAWAY ASR CORP	NY	2,223.5
NUCLEAR ELECTRIC INS LTD	DE	5,587.7
Rating: A		
CINCINNATI INS CO	OH	12,914.9
CINCINNATI SPECIALTY UNDERWRITER	DE	820.6
SENTRY INS A MUTUAL CO	WI	8,392.8
SOMPO AMERICA INSURANCE CO	NY	1,285.1
TOKIO MARINE AMERICA INS CO	NY	1,409.5
Rating: A-		
ACUITY A MUTUAL INS CO	WI	3,960.1
CINCINNATI INDEMNITY CO	OH	133.0
COUNTRY MUTUAL INS CO	IL	4,850.2
CUMIS INS SOCIETY INC	IA	2,002.8
DAIRYLAND INS CO	WI	1,400.7
ENDURANCE ASR CORP	DE	2,059.0
ESSENT GUARANTY INC	PA	1,756.6
GEICO SECURE INS CO	NE	625.3
MITSUI SUMITOMO INS CO OF AMER	NY	975.8
MOTORISTS COMMERCIAL MUTUAL INS CO	OH	368.8
NATIONAL MORTGAGE INS CORP	WI	717.8
PROTECTIVE INS CO	IN	885.6
SECURIAN CASUALTY CO	MN	328.2
SENTRY SELECT INS CO	WI	826.6
TRAVELERS CASUALTY & SURETY CO	CT	16,983.8
TRAVELERS INDEMNITY CO	CT	21,394.5
UNITED SERVICES AUTOMOBILE ASN	TX	35,460.0
USAA CASUALTY INS CO	TX	10,897.7
Rating: B+		
ALLIED WORLD SPECIALTY INS CO	DE	829.1
ALLSTATE INS CO	IL	48,302.5
AMERICAN AGRICULTURAL INS CO	IN	1,338.9
AMERICAN CONTRACTORS INDEMNITY CO	CA	338.3
AMERICAN NATIONAL PROPERTY & CAS CO	MO	1,418.0
AMICA MUTUAL INS CO	RI	5,384.6
ARCH SPECIALTY INS CO	MO	483.4
BROTHERHOOD MUTUAL INS CO	IN	644.9
CATERPILLAR INS CO	MO	790.6
CENTRAL MUTUAL INS CO	OH	1,618.4
CHURCH MUTUAL INS CO	WI	1,739.8
COVINGTON SPECIALTY INS CO	NH	97.9
FARM BUREAU MUTUAL INS CO OF MI	MI	782.4
FARM FAMILY CASUALTY INS CO	NY	1,241.7
FEDERATED RURAL ELECTRIC INS EXCH	KS	553.2
FRANKENMUTH MUTUAL INS CO	MI	1,351.0
GEICO CHOICE INS CO	NE	1,134.6
GEICO GENERAL INS CO	MD	167.6
GNY CUSTOM INS CO	AZ	60.5
HOUSING AUTHORITY PROP A MUTUAL CO	VT	181.9
MARKEL GLOBAL REINS CO	DE	2,180.9
MERCHANTS NATIONAL INS CO	NH	136.0
MERCHANTS PREFERRED INS CO	NY	76.4
MIDDLESEX INS CO	WI	764.3
NATIONAL CASUALTY CO	OH	418.6

INSURANCE COMPANY NAME	DOM. STATE	TOTAL ASSETS ($MIL)
PREFERRED PROFESSIONAL INS CO	NE	327.4
SENTRY CASUALTY CO	WI	355.9
STATE FARM FIRE & CAS CO	IL	39,411.9
STATE FARM MUTUAL AUTOMOBILE INS CO	IL	160,732.0
SURETEC INS CO	TX	253.2
TOA REINS CO OF AMERICA	DE	1,820.3
TRANS PACIFIC INS CO	NY	67.6
TRANSATLANTIC REINS CO	NY	14,732.2
UNITED EDUCATORS INS A RECIP RRG	VT	912.3
UNITED SPECIALTY INS CO	DE	330.2
USAA GENERAL INDEMNITY CO	TX	4,627.9

District Of Columbia

INSURANCE COMPANY NAME	DOM. STATE	TOTAL ASSETS ($MIL)
Rating: A+		
BERKSHIRE HATHAWAY ASR CORP	NY	2,223.5
Rating: A		
BUILDERS MUTUAL INS CO	NC	859.6
CINCINNATI INS CO	OH	12,914.9
CINCINNATI SPECIALTY UNDERWRITER	DE	820.6
SENTRY INS A MUTUAL CO	WI	8,392.8
SOMPO AMERICA INSURANCE CO	NY	1,285.1
TOKIO MARINE AMERICA INS CO	NY	1,409.5
Rating: A-		
CINCINNATI INDEMNITY CO	OH	133.0
CUMIS INS SOCIETY INC	IA	2,002.8
EMPLOYERS COMPENSATION INS CO	CA	1,091.0
ENDURANCE ASR CORP	DE	2,059.0
ESSENT GUARANTY INC	PA	1,756.6
GEICO SECURE INS CO	NE	625.3
MITSUI SUMITOMO INS CO OF AMER	NY	975.8
MOTORISTS COMMERCIAL MUTUAL INS CO	OH	368.8
NATIONAL MORTGAGE INS CORP	WI	717.8
PROTECTIVE INS CO	IN	885.6
SECURIAN CASUALTY CO	MN	328.2
SENTRY SELECT INS CO	WI	826.6
TRAVELERS CASUALTY & SURETY CO	CT	16,983.8
TRAVELERS INDEMNITY CO	CT	21,394.5
UNITED SERVICES AUTOMOBILE ASN	TX	35,460.0
USAA CASUALTY INS CO	TX	10,897.7
Rating: B+		
ALLIED WORLD SPECIALTY INS CO	DE	829.1
ALLSTATE INS CO	IL	48,302.5
AMERICAN AGRICULTURAL INS CO	IN	1,338.9
AMERICAN CONTRACTORS INDEMNITY CO	CA	338.3
AMERICAN NATIONAL PROPERTY & CAS CO	MO	1,418.0
AMICA MUTUAL INS CO	RI	5,384.6
ARCH SPECIALTY INS CO	MO	483.4
BROTHERHOOD MUTUAL INS CO	IN	644.9
CATERPILLAR INS CO	MO	790.6
CHURCH MUTUAL INS CO	WI	1,739.8
COVINGTON SPECIALTY INS CO	NH	97.9
GEICO CHOICE INS CO	NE	1,134.6
GEICO GENERAL INS CO	MD	167.6
GNY CUSTOM INS CO	AZ	60.5
HOUSING AUTHORITY PROP A MUTUAL CO	VT	181.9
ICI MUTUAL INS CO A RRG	VT	367.6
LION INS CO (FL)	FL	264.3
MARKEL GLOBAL REINS CO	DE	2,180.9
MERCHANTS NATIONAL INS CO	NH	136.0
MIDDLESEX INS CO	WI	764.3
NATIONAL CASUALTY CO	OH	418.6
PREFERRED PROFESSIONAL INS CO	NE	327.4
SENTRY CASUALTY CO	WI	355.9
STATE FARM FIRE & CAS CO	IL	39,411.9
STATE FARM MUTUAL AUTOMOBILE INS CO	IL	160,732.0
SURETEC INS CO	TX	253.2
TOA REINS CO OF AMERICA	DE	1,820.3

INSURANCE COMPANY NAME	DOM. STATE	TOTAL ASSETS ($MIL)
TRANS PACIFIC INS CO	NY	67.6
TRANSATLANTIC REINS CO	NY	14,732.2
UNITED EDUCATORS INS A RECIP RRG	VT	912.3
UNITED SPECIALTY INS CO	DE	330.2
USAA GENERAL INDEMNITY CO	TX	4,627.9

Florida

INSURANCE COMPANY NAME	DOM. STATE	TOTAL ASSETS ($MIL)
Rating:	**A+**	
BERKSHIRE HATHAWAY ASR CORP	NY	2,223.5
CITIZENS PROPERTY INS CORP	FL	11,362.5
Rating:	**A**	
AUTO-OWNERS INS CO	MI	15,390.4
BUILDERS MUTUAL INS CO	NC	859.6
CINCINNATI INS CO	OH	12,914.9
CINCINNATI SPECIALTY UNDERWRITER	DE	820.6
OWNERS INS CO	OH	4,110.4
RETAILFIRST INS CO	FL	325.1
SENTRY INS A MUTUAL CO	WI	8,392.8
SOMPO AMERICA INSURANCE CO	NY	1,285.1
SOUTHERN-OWNERS INS CO	MI	821.8
TOKIO MARINE AMERICA INS CO	NY	1,409.5
Rating:	**A-**	
AMERICAN FAMILY MUTL INS CO SI	WI	17,157.4
CINCINNATI INDEMNITY CO	OH	133.0
CUMIS INS SOCIETY INC	IA	2,002.8
DAIRYLAND INS CO	WI	1,400.7
EMPLOYERS COMPENSATION INS CO	CA	1,091.0
ENDURANCE ASR CORP	DE	2,059.0
ESSENT GUARANTY INC	PA	1,756.6
MITSUI SUMITOMO INS CO OF AMER	NY	975.8
NATIONAL MORTGAGE INS CORP	WI	717.8
PROTECTIVE INS CO	IN	885.6
SECURIAN CASUALTY CO	MN	328.2
SENTRY SELECT INS CO	WI	826.6
TRAVELERS CASUALTY & SURETY CO	CT	16,983.8
TRAVELERS INDEMNITY CO	CT	21,394.5
UNITED SERVICES AUTOMOBILE ASN	TX	35,460.0
USAA CASUALTY INS CO	TX	10,897.7
Rating:	**B+**	
ALASKA NATIONAL INS CO	AK	1,004.7
ALLIED WORLD SPECIALTY INS CO	DE	829.1
ALLSTATE INS CO	IL	48,302.5
AMERICAN AGRICULTURAL INS CO	IN	1,338.9
AMERICAN CONTRACTORS INDEMNITY CO	CA	338.3
AMERICAN NATIONAL PROPERTY & CAS CO	MO	1,418.0
AMICA MUTUAL INS CO	RI	5,384.6
ARCH SPECIALTY INS CO	MO	483.4
AUTO CLUB INS CO OF FL	FL	377.9
BROTHERHOOD MUTUAL INS CO	IN	644.9
CASTLE KEY INS CO	IL	362.5
CATERPILLAR INS CO	MO	790.6
CHURCH MUTUAL INS CO	WI	1,739.8
COVINGTON SPECIALTY INS CO	NH	97.9
FEDERATED RURAL ELECTRIC INS EXCH	KS	553.2
FINANCIAL PACIFIC INS CO	CA	261.4
FRANKENMUTH MUTUAL INS CO	MI	1,351.0
GEICO GENERAL INS CO	MD	167.6
HOUSING AUTHORITY PROP A MUTUAL CO	VT	181.9
ICI MUTUAL INS CO A RRG	VT	367.6
INTERINS EXCHANGE	CA	10,404.3
LION INS CO (FL)	FL	264.3

INSURANCE COMPANY NAME	DOM. STATE	TOTAL ASSETS ($MIL)
MARKEL GLOBAL REINS CO	DE	2,180.9
MERCURY CASUALTY CO	CA	1,877.6
MIDDLESEX INS CO	WI	764.3
NATIONAL CASUALTY CO	OH	418.6
PREFERRED PROFESSIONAL INS CO	NE	327.4
SENTRY CASUALTY CO	WI	355.9
SFM MUTUAL INS CO	MN	612.1
SOUTHERN FIDELITY INS CO	FL	196.7
STATE FARM FIRE & CAS CO	IL	39,411.9
STATE FARM MUTUAL AUTOMOBILE INS CO	IL	160,732.0
SURETEC INS CO	TX	253.2
TOA REINS CO OF AMERICA	DE	1,820.3
TRANS PACIFIC INS CO	NY	67.6
TRANSATLANTIC REINS CO	NY	14,732.2
UNITED EDUCATORS INS A RECIP RRG	VT	912.3
UNITED SPECIALTY INS CO	DE	330.2
USAA GENERAL INDEMNITY CO	TX	4,627.9

Georgia

INSURANCE COMPANY NAME	DOM. STATE	TOTAL ASSETS ($MIL)
Rating: A+		
BERKSHIRE HATHAWAY ASR CORP	NY	2,223.5
Rating: A		
AUTO-OWNERS INS CO	MI	15,390.4
BUILDERS MUTUAL INS CO	NC	859.6
CINCINNATI INS CO	OH	12,914.9
CINCINNATI SPECIALTY UNDERWRITER	DE	820.6
HOME-OWNERS INS CO	MI	2,323.7
OWNERS INS CO	OH	4,110.4
SENTRY INS A MUTUAL CO	WI	8,392.8
SOMPO AMERICA INSURANCE CO	NY	1,285.1
TOKIO MARINE AMERICA INS CO	NY	1,409.5
Rating: A-		
ACUITY A MUTUAL INS CO	WI	3,960.1
ALFA MUTUAL GENERAL INS CO	AL	115.4
ALL AMERICA INS CO	OH	291.6
AMERICAN FAMILY MUTL INS CO SI	WI	17,157.4
CINCINNATI INDEMNITY CO	OH	133.0
COUNTRY MUTUAL INS CO	IL	4,850.2
CUMIS INS SOCIETY INC	IA	2,002.8
DAIRYLAND INS CO	WI	1,400.7
EMPLOYERS COMPENSATION INS CO	CA	1,091.0
ENDURANCE ASR CORP	DE	2,059.0
ESSENT GUARANTY INC	PA	1,756.6
GEICO SECURE INS CO	NE	625.3
MITSUI SUMITOMO INS CO OF AMER	NY	975.8
MOTORISTS COMMERCIAL MUTUAL INS CO	OH	368.8
NATIONAL MORTGAGE INS CORP	WI	717.8
PROPERTY-OWNERS INS CO	IN	302.7
PROTECTIVE INS CO	IN	885.6
SECURIAN CASUALTY CO	MN	328.2
SENTRY SELECT INS CO	WI	826.6
TRAVELERS CASUALTY & SURETY CO	CT	16,983.8
TRAVELERS INDEMNITY CO	CT	21,394.5
TREXIS ONE INSURANCE GROUP	VA	56.6
UNITED SERVICES AUTOMOBILE ASN	TX	35,460.0
USAA CASUALTY INS CO	TX	10,897.7
Rating: B+		
ALFA GENERAL INS CORP	AL	101.6
ALLIED WORLD SPECIALTY INS CO	DE	829.1
ALLSTATE INS CO	IL	48,302.5
AMERICAN AGRICULTURAL INS CO	IN	1,338.9
AMERICAN CONTRACTORS INDEMNITY CO	CA	338.3
AMERICAN NATIONAL PROPERTY & CAS CO	MO	1,418.0
AMICA MUTUAL INS CO	RI	5,384.6
ANSUR AMERICA INS CO	MI	121.2
ARCH SPECIALTY INS CO	MO	483.4
BROTHERHOOD MUTUAL INS CO	IN	644.9
CATERPILLAR INS CO	MO	790.6
CENTRAL MUTUAL INS CO	OH	1,618.4
CHURCH MUTUAL INS CO	WI	1,739.8
COPIC INS CO	CO	603.2
COVINGTON SPECIALTY INS CO	NH	97.9
FARM BUREAU MUTUAL INS CO OF MI	MI	782.4

INSURANCE COMPANY NAME	DOM. STATE	TOTAL ASSETS ($MIL)
FEDERATED RURAL ELECTRIC INS EXCH	KS	553.2
FRANKENMUTH MUTUAL INS CO	MI	1,351.0
GEICO CHOICE INS CO	NE	1,134.6
GEICO GENERAL INS CO	MD	167.6
HOUSING AUTHORITY PROP A MUTUAL CO	VT	181.9
ICI MUTUAL INS CO A RRG	VT	367.6
LION INS CO (FL)	FL	264.3
MARKEL GLOBAL REINS CO	DE	2,180.9
MERCHANTS NATIONAL INS CO	NH	136.0
MERCURY CASUALTY CO	CA	1,877.6
MIDDLESEX INS CO	WI	764.3
NATIONAL CASUALTY CO	OH	418.6
PREFERRED PROFESSIONAL INS CO	NE	327.4
SENTRY CASUALTY CO	WI	355.9
STATE FARM FIRE & CAS CO	IL	39,411.9
STATE FARM MUTUAL AUTOMOBILE INS CO	IL	160,732.0
STATE VOLUNTEER MUTUAL INS CO	TN	1,249.3
SURETEC INS CO	TX	253.2
TOA REINS CO OF AMERICA	DE	1,820.3
TRANS PACIFIC INS CO	NY	67.6
TRANSATLANTIC REINS CO	NY	14,732.2
UNITED EDUCATORS INS A RECIP RRG	VT	912.3
UNITED SPECIALTY INS CO	DE	330.2
USAA GENERAL INDEMNITY CO	TX	4,627.9

Hawaii

INSURANCE COMPANY NAME	DOM. STATE	TOTAL ASSETS ($MIL)	INSURANCE COMPANY NAME	DOM. STATE	TOTAL ASSETS ($MIL)
Rating: **A+**					
BERKSHIRE HATHAWAY ASR CORP	NY	2,223.5			
Rating: **A**					
CINCINNATI INS CO	OH	12,914.9			
CINCINNATI SPECIALTY UNDERWRITER	DE	820.6			
SENTRY INS A MUTUAL CO	WI	8,392.8			
SOMPO AMERICA INSURANCE CO	NY	1,285.1			
TOKIO MARINE AMERICA INS CO	NY	1,409.5			
Rating: **A-**					
CINCINNATI INDEMNITY CO	OH	133.0			
CUMIS INS SOCIETY INC	IA	2,002.8			
ENDURANCE ASR CORP	DE	2,059.0			
ESSENT GUARANTY INC	PA	1,756.6			
MITSUI SUMITOMO INS CO OF AMER	NY	975.8			
NATIONAL MORTGAGE INS CORP	WI	717.8			
PROTECTIVE INS CO	IN	885.6			
SECURIAN CASUALTY CO	MN	328.2			
SENTRY SELECT INS CO	WI	826.6			
TRAVELERS CASUALTY & SURETY CO	CT	16,983.8			
TRAVELERS INDEMNITY CO	CT	21,394.5			
UNITED SERVICES AUTOMOBILE ASN	TX	35,460.0			
USAA CASUALTY INS CO	TX	10,897.7			
Rating: **B+**					
ALASKA NATIONAL INS CO	AK	1,004.7			
ALLIED WORLD SPECIALTY INS CO	DE	829.1			
ALLSTATE INS CO	IL	48,302.5			
AMERICAN AGRICULTURAL INS CO	IN	1,338.9			
AMERICAN CONTRACTORS INDEMNITY CO	CA	338.3			
AMERICAN NATIONAL PROPERTY & CAS CO	MO	1,418.0			
AMICA MUTUAL INS CO	RI	5,384.6			
ARCH SPECIALTY INS CO	MO	483.4			
BROTHERHOOD MUTUAL INS CO	IN	644.9			
CATERPILLAR INS CO	MO	790.6			
CHURCH MUTUAL INS CO	WI	1,739.8			
COPIC INS CO	CO	603.2			
COVINGTON SPECIALTY INS CO	NH	97.9			
FEDERATED RURAL ELECTRIC INS EXCH	KS	553.2			
GEICO GENERAL INS CO	MD	167.6			
INTERINS EXCHANGE	CA	10,404.3			
LION INS CO (FL)	FL	264.3			
MARKEL GLOBAL REINS CO	DE	2,180.9			
MIDDLESEX INS CO	WI	764.3			
NATIONAL CASUALTY CO	OH	418.6			
PREFERRED PROFESSIONAL INS CO	NE	327.4			
SENTRY CASUALTY CO	WI	355.9			
STATE FARM FIRE & CAS CO	IL	39,411.9			
STATE FARM MUTUAL AUTOMOBILE INS CO	IL	160,732.0			
SURETEC INS CO	TX	253.2			
TOA REINS CO OF AMERICA	DE	1,820.3			
TRANS PACIFIC INS CO	NY	67.6			
TRANSATLANTIC REINS CO	NY	14,732.2			
UNITED EDUCATORS INS A RECIP RRG	VT	912.3			
UNITED SPECIALTY INS CO	DE	330.2			
USAA GENERAL INDEMNITY CO	TX	4,627.9			

Idaho

INSURANCE COMPANY NAME	DOM. STATE	TOTAL ASSETS ($MIL)
Rating: A+		
BERKSHIRE HATHAWAY ASR CORP	NY	2,223.5
Rating: A		
AUTO-OWNERS INS CO	MI	15,390.4
CINCINNATI INS CO	OH	12,914.9
CINCINNATI SPECIALTY UNDERWRITER	DE	820.6
OWNERS INS CO	OH	4,110.4
SENTRY INS A MUTUAL CO	WI	8,392.8
SOMPO AMERICA INSURANCE CO	NY	1,285.1
TOKIO MARINE AMERICA INS CO	NY	1,409.5
Rating: A-		
ACUITY A MUTUAL INS CO	WI	3,960.1
ALL AMERICA INS CO	OH	291.6
AMERICAN FAMILY MUTL INS CO SI	WI	17,157.4
CINCINNATI INDEMNITY CO	OH	133.0
COUNTRY MUTUAL INS CO	IL	4,850.2
CUMIS INS SOCIETY INC	IA	2,002.8
DAIRYLAND INS CO	WI	1,400.7
EMPLOYERS COMPENSATION INS CO	CA	1,091.0
ENDURANCE ASR CORP	DE	2,059.0
ESSENT GUARANTY INC	PA	1,756.6
FARM BUREAU P&C INS CO	IA	2,532.4
GEICO SECURE INS CO	NE	625.3
MITSUI SUMITOMO INS CO OF AMER	NY	975.8
MOTORISTS COMMERCIAL MUTUAL INS CO	OH	368.8
NATIONAL MORTGAGE INS CORP	WI	717.8
PROTECTIVE INS CO	IN	885.6
SECURIAN CASUALTY CO	MN	328.2
SENTRY SELECT INS CO	WI	826.6
TRAVELERS CASUALTY & SURETY CO	CT	16,983.8
TRAVELERS INDEMNITY CO	CT	21,394.5
UNITED SERVICES AUTOMOBILE ASN	TX	35,460.0
USAA CASUALTY INS CO	TX	10,897.7
Rating: B+		
ALASKA NATIONAL INS CO	AK	1,004.7
ALLIED WORLD SPECIALTY INS CO	DE	829.1
ALLSTATE INS CO	IL	48,302.5
AMERICAN AGRICULTURAL INS CO	IN	1,338.9
AMERICAN CONTRACTORS INDEMNITY CO	CA	338.3
AMERICAN NATIONAL PROPERTY & CAS CO	MO	1,418.0
AMERICAN STANDARD INS CO OF WI	WI	400.9
AMICA MUTUAL INS CO	RI	5,384.6
ARCH SPECIALTY INS CO	MO	483.4
BROTHERHOOD MUTUAL INS CO	IN	644.9
CATERPILLAR INS CO	MO	790.6
CENTRAL MUTUAL INS CO	OH	1,618.4
CHURCH MUTUAL INS CO	WI	1,739.8
COPIC INS CO	CO	603.2
COVINGTON SPECIALTY INS CO	NH	97.9
FEDERATED RURAL ELECTRIC INS EXCH	KS	553.2
FINANCIAL PACIFIC INS CO	CA	261.4
FRANKENMUTH MUTUAL INS CO	MI	1,351.0
GEICO CHOICE INS CO	NE	1,134.6
GEICO GENERAL INS CO	MD	167.6

INSURANCE COMPANY NAME	DOM. STATE	TOTAL ASSETS ($MIL)
HOUSING AUTHORITY PROP A MUTUAL CO	VT	181.9
MARKEL GLOBAL REINS CO	DE	2,180.9
MERCHANTS NATIONAL INS CO	NH	136.0
MIDDLESEX INS CO	WI	764.3
MMIC INS INC	MN	682.7
MUTUAL OF ENUMCLAW INS CO	OR	748.3
NATIONAL CASUALTY CO	OH	418.6
PREFERRED PROFESSIONAL INS CO	NE	327.4
SENTRY CASUALTY CO	WI	355.9
STATE FARM FIRE & CAS CO	IL	39,411.9
STATE FARM MUTUAL AUTOMOBILE INS CO	IL	160,732.0
SURETEC INS CO	TX	253.2
TOA REINS CO OF AMERICA	DE	1,820.3
TRANS PACIFIC INS CO	NY	67.6
TRANSATLANTIC REINS CO	NY	14,732.2
UNITED EDUCATORS INS A RECIP RRG	VT	912.3
UNITED SPECIALTY INS CO	DE	330.2
USAA GENERAL INDEMNITY CO	TX	4,627.9
WESTERN AGRICULTURAL INS CO	IA	213.2

Illinois

INSURANCE COMPANY NAME	DOM. STATE	TOTAL ASSETS ($MIL)
Rating: A+		
BERKSHIRE HATHAWAY ASR CORP	NY	2,223.5
OGLESBY REINS CO	IL	4,590.7
Rating: A		
AUTO-OWNERS INS CO	MI	15,390.4
CINCINNATI INS CO	OH	12,914.9
CINCINNATI SPECIALTY UNDERWRITER	DE	820.6
HOME-OWNERS INS CO	MI	2,323.7
OWNERS INS CO	OH	4,110.4
SENTRY INS A MUTUAL CO	WI	8,392.8
SOMPO AMERICA INSURANCE CO	NY	1,285.1
TOKIO MARINE AMERICA INS CO	NY	1,409.5
Rating: A-		
ACUITY A MUTUAL INS CO	WI	3,960.1
ALL AMERICA INS CO	OH	291.6
ALLSTATE NJ INS CO	IL	2,485.7
AMERICAN FAMILY MUTL INS CO SI	WI	17,157.4
CINCINNATI INDEMNITY CO	OH	133.0
COUNTRY MUTUAL INS CO	IL	4,850.2
CUMIS INS SOCIETY INC	IA	2,002.8
DAIRYLAND INS CO	WI	1,400.7
EMPLOYERS COMPENSATION INS CO	CA	1,091.0
ENDURANCE ASR CORP	DE	2,059.0
ESSENT GUARANTY INC	PA	1,756.6
GEICO SECURE INS CO	NE	625.3
MITSUI SUMITOMO INS CO OF AMER	NY	975.8
MOTORISTS COMMERCIAL MUTUAL INS CO	OH	368.8
NATIONAL MORTGAGE INS CORP	WI	717.8
PROPERTY-OWNERS INS CO	IN	302.7
PROTECTIVE INS CO	IN	885.6
SECURIAN CASUALTY CO	MN	328.2
SENTRY SELECT INS CO	WI	826.6
TRAVELERS CASUALTY & SURETY CO	CT	16,983.8
TRAVELERS INDEMNITY CO	CT	21,394.5
UNITED SERVICES AUTOMOBILE ASN	TX	35,460.0
USAA CASUALTY INS CO	TX	10,897.7
WEST BEND MUTUAL INS CO	WI	2,695.9
Rating: B+		
ALASKA NATIONAL INS CO	AK	1,004.7
ALLIED WORLD SPECIALTY INS CO	DE	829.1
ALLSTATE INS CO	IL	48,302.5
AMERICAN AGRICULTURAL INS CO	IN	1,338.9
AMERICAN CONTRACTORS INDEMNITY CO	CA	338.3
AMERICAN NATIONAL PROPERTY & CAS CO	MO	1,418.0
AMERICAN STANDARD INS CO OF WI	WI	400.9
AMICA MUTUAL INS CO	RI	5,384.6
ANSUR AMERICA INS CO	MI	121.2
ARCH SPECIALTY INS CO	MO	483.4
BROTHERHOOD MUTUAL INS CO	IN	644.9
CASTLE KEY INS CO	IL	362.5
CATERPILLAR INS CO	MO	790.6
CENTRAL MUTUAL INS CO	OH	1,618.4
CHURCH MUTUAL INS CO	WI	1,739.8
COPIC INS CO	CO	603.2

INSURANCE COMPANY NAME	DOM. STATE	TOTAL ASSETS ($MIL)
COVINGTON SPECIALTY INS CO	NH	97.9
FARM BUREAU MUTUAL INS CO OF MI	MI	782.4
FARMERS AUTOMOBILE INS ASN	IL	1,226.6
FARMERS MUTUAL INS CO OF NE	NE	680.3
FEDERATED RURAL ELECTRIC INS EXCH	KS	553.2
FINANCIAL PACIFIC INS CO	CA	261.4
FRANKENMUTH MUTUAL INS CO	MI	1,351.0
GEICO CHOICE INS CO	NE	1,134.6
GEICO GENERAL INS CO	MD	167.6
GNY CUSTOM INS CO	AZ	60.5
HASTINGS MUTUAL INS CO	MI	932.1
HOUSING AUTHORITY PROP A MUTUAL CO	VT	181.9
ICI MUTUAL INS CO A RRG	VT	367.6
INDIANA FARMERS MUTUAL INS CO	IN	433.3
LION INS CO (FL)	FL	264.3
MARKEL GLOBAL REINS CO	DE	2,180.9
MERCHANTS NATIONAL INS CO	NH	136.0
MERCURY CASUALTY CO	CA	1,877.6
MIDDLESEX INS CO	WI	764.3
MMIC INS INC	MN	682.7
NATIONAL CASUALTY CO	OH	418.6
PEKIN INS CO	IL	305.4
PREFERRED PROFESSIONAL INS CO	NE	327.4
SENTRY CASUALTY CO	WI	355.9
SFM MUTUAL INS CO	MN	612.1
STATE FARM FIRE & CAS CO	IL	39,411.9
STATE FARM MUTUAL AUTOMOBILE INS CO	IL	160,732.0
SURETEC INS CO	TX	253.2
TOA REINS CO OF AMERICA	DE	1,820.3
TRANS PACIFIC INS CO	NY	67.6
TRANSATLANTIC REINS CO	NY	14,732.2
UNITED EDUCATORS INS A RECIP RRG	VT	912.3
UNITED SPECIALTY INS CO	DE	330.2
USAA GENERAL INDEMNITY CO	TX	4,627.9
WESTERN AGRICULTURAL INS CO	IA	213.2

Indiana

INSURANCE COMPANY NAME	DOM. STATE	TOTAL ASSETS ($MIL)
Rating:	**A+**	
BERKSHIRE HATHAWAY ASR CORP	NY	2,223.5
Rating:	**A**	
AUTO-OWNERS INS CO	MI	15,390.4
CINCINNATI INS CO	OH	12,914.9
CINCINNATI SPECIALTY UNDERWRITER	DE	820.6
HOME-OWNERS INS CO	MI	2,323.7
OWNERS INS CO	OH	4,110.4
SENTRY INS A MUTUAL CO	WI	8,392.8
SOMPO AMERICA INSURANCE CO	NY	1,285.1
TOKIO MARINE AMERICA INS CO	NY	1,409.5
Rating:	**A-**	
ACUITY A MUTUAL INS CO	WI	3,960.1
ALL AMERICA INS CO	OH	291.6
AMERICAN FAMILY MUTL INS CO SI	WI	17,157.4
CINCINNATI INDEMNITY CO	OH	133.0
COUNTRY MUTUAL INS CO	IL	4,850.2
CUMIS INS SOCIETY INC	IA	2,002.8
DAIRYLAND INS CO	WI	1,400.7
EMPLOYERS COMPENSATION INS CO	CA	1,091.0
ENDURANCE ASR CORP	DE	2,059.0
ESSENT GUARANTY INC	PA	1,756.6
GEICO SECURE INS CO	NE	625.3
MITSUI SUMITOMO INS CO OF AMER	NY	975.8
MOTORISTS COMMERCIAL MUTUAL INS CO	OH	368.8
NATIONAL MORTGAGE INS CORP	WI	717.8
PROPERTY-OWNERS INS CO	IN	302.7
PROTECTIVE INS CO	IN	885.6
SECURIAN CASUALTY CO	MN	328.2
SENTRY SELECT INS CO	WI	826.6
TRAVELERS CASUALTY & SURETY CO	CT	16,983.8
TRAVELERS INDEMNITY CO	CT	21,394.5
TREXIS ONE INSURANCE GROUP	VA	56.6
UNITED SERVICES AUTOMOBILE ASN	TX	35,460.0
USAA CASUALTY INS CO	TX	10,897.7
WEST BEND MUTUAL INS CO	WI	2,695.9
Rating:	**B+**	
ALLIED WORLD SPECIALTY INS CO	DE	829.1
ALLSTATE INS CO	IL	48,302.5
AMERICAN AGRICULTURAL INS CO	IN	1,338.9
AMERICAN CONTRACTORS INDEMNITY CO	CA	338.3
AMERICAN NATIONAL PROPERTY & CAS CO	MO	1,418.0
AMERICAN STANDARD INS CO OF WI	WI	400.9
AMICA MUTUAL INS CO	RI	5,384.6
ANSUR AMERICA INS CO	MI	121.2
ARCH SPECIALTY INS CO	MO	483.4
BROTHERHOOD MUTUAL INS CO	IN	644.9
CATERPILLAR INS CO	MO	790.6
CENTRAL MUTUAL INS CO	OH	1,618.4
CHURCH MUTUAL INS CO	WI	1,739.8
COVINGTON SPECIALTY INS CO	NH	97.9
FARM BUREAU MUTUAL INS CO OF MI	MI	782.4
FARMERS AUTOMOBILE INS ASN	IL	1,226.6
FARMERS MUTUAL INS CO OF NE	NE	680.3

INSURANCE COMPANY NAME	DOM. STATE	TOTAL ASSETS ($MIL)
FEDERATED RURAL ELECTRIC INS EXCH	KS	553.2
FRANKENMUTH MUTUAL INS CO	MI	1,351.0
GEICO CHOICE INS CO	NE	1,134.6
GEICO GENERAL INS CO	MD	167.6
GNY CUSTOM INS CO	AZ	60.5
HASTINGS MUTUAL INS CO	MI	932.1
HOUSING AUTHORITY PROP A MUTUAL CO	VT	181.9
INDIANA FARMERS MUTUAL INS CO	IN	433.3
MARKEL GLOBAL REINS CO	DE	2,180.9
MERCHANTS NATIONAL INS CO	NH	136.0
MERCHANTS PREFERRED INS CO	NY	76.4
MIDDLESEX INS CO	WI	764.3
MMIC INS INC	MN	682.7
NATIONAL CASUALTY CO	OH	418.6
PEKIN INS CO	IL	305.4
PIONEER STATE MUTUAL INS CO	MI	608.7
PREFERRED PROFESSIONAL INS CO	NE	327.4
SENTRY CASUALTY CO	WI	355.9
SFM MUTUAL INS CO	MN	612.1
STATE FARM FIRE & CAS CO	IL	39,411.9
STATE FARM MUTUAL AUTOMOBILE INS CO	IL	160,732.0
STATE VOLUNTEER MUTUAL INS CO	TN	1,249.3
SURETEC INS CO	TX	253.2
TOA REINS CO OF AMERICA	DE	1,820.3
TRANS PACIFIC INS CO	NY	67.6
TRANSATLANTIC REINS CO	NY	14,732.2
TREXIS INSURANCE CORP	VA	108.1
UNITED EDUCATORS INS A RECIP RRG	VT	912.3
UNITED FARM FAMILY MUTUAL INS CO	IN	1,098.5
UNITED SPECIALTY INS CO	DE	330.2
USAA GENERAL INDEMNITY CO	TX	4,627.9
WESTERN AGRICULTURAL INS CO	IA	213.2

Iowa

INSURANCE COMPANY NAME	DOM. STATE	TOTAL ASSETS ($MIL)
Rating:	**A+**	
BERKSHIRE HATHAWAY ASR CORP	NY	2,223.5
Rating:	**A**	
AUTO-OWNERS INS CO	MI	15,390.4
CINCINNATI INS CO	OH	12,914.9
CINCINNATI SPECIALTY UNDERWRITER	DE	820.6
HOME-OWNERS INS CO	MI	2,323.7
OWNERS INS CO	OH	4,110.4
SENTRY INS A MUTUAL CO	WI	8,392.8
SOMPO AMERICA INSURANCE CO	NY	1,285.1
TOKIO MARINE AMERICA INS CO	NY	1,409.5
Rating:	**A-**	
ACUITY A MUTUAL INS CO	WI	3,960.1
ALL AMERICA INS CO	OH	291.6
AMERICAN FAMILY MUTL INS CO SI	WI	17,157.4
CINCINNATI INDEMNITY CO	OH	133.0
COUNTRY MUTUAL INS CO	IL	4,850.2
CUMIS INS SOCIETY INC	IA	2,002.8
DAIRYLAND INS CO	WI	1,400.7
EMPLOYERS COMPENSATION INS CO	CA	1,091.0
ENDURANCE ASR CORP	DE	2,059.0
ESSENT GUARANTY INC	PA	1,756.6
FARM BUREAU P&C INS CO	IA	2,532.4
GEICO SECURE INS CO	NE	625.3
MITSUI SUMITOMO INS CO OF AMER	NY	975.8
MOTORISTS COMMERCIAL MUTUAL INS CO	OH	368.8
NATIONAL MORTGAGE INS CORP	WI	717.8
PROPERTY-OWNERS INS CO	IN	302.7
PROTECTIVE INS CO	IN	885.6
SECURIAN CASUALTY CO	MN	328.2
SENTRY SELECT INS CO	WI	826.6
TRAVELERS CASUALTY & SURETY CO	CT	16,983.8
TRAVELERS INDEMNITY CO	CT	21,394.5
UNITED SERVICES AUTOMOBILE ASN	TX	35,460.0
USAA CASUALTY INS CO	TX	10,897.7
WEST BEND MUTUAL INS CO	WI	2,695.9
Rating:	**B+**	
ALASKA NATIONAL INS CO	AK	1,004.7
ALLIED WORLD SPECIALTY INS CO	DE	829.1
ALLSTATE INS CO	IL	48,302.5
AMERICAN AGRICULTURAL INS CO	IN	1,338.9
AMERICAN CONTRACTORS INDEMNITY CO	CA	338.3
AMERICAN NATIONAL PROPERTY & CAS CO	MO	1,418.0
AMERICAN STANDARD INS CO OF WI	WI	400.9
AMICA MUTUAL INS CO	RI	5,384.6
ANSUR AMERICA INS CO	MI	121.2
ARCH SPECIALTY INS CO	MO	483.4
BROTHERHOOD MUTUAL INS CO	IN	644.9
CATERPILLAR INS CO	MO	790.6
CENTRAL MUTUAL INS CO	OH	1,618.4
CHURCH MUTUAL INS CO	WI	1,739.8
COPIC INS CO	CO	603.2
COVINGTON SPECIALTY INS CO	NH	97.9
FARM BUREAU MUTUAL INS CO OF MI	MI	782.4

INSURANCE COMPANY NAME	DOM. STATE	TOTAL ASSETS ($MIL)
FARMERS AUTOMOBILE INS ASN	IL	1,226.6
FARMERS MUTUAL INS CO OF NE	NE	680.3
FEDERATED RURAL ELECTRIC INS EXCH	KS	553.2
FINANCIAL PACIFIC INS CO	CA	261.4
FRANKENMUTH MUTUAL INS CO	MI	1,351.0
GEICO CHOICE INS CO	NE	1,134.6
GEICO GENERAL INS CO	MD	167.6
HASTINGS MUTUAL INS CO	MI	932.1
HOUSING AUTHORITY PROP A MUTUAL CO	VT	181.9
ICI MUTUAL INS CO A RRG	VT	367.6
MARKEL GLOBAL REINS CO	DE	2,180.9
MERCHANTS NATIONAL INS CO	NH	136.0
MIDDLESEX INS CO	WI	764.3
MMIC INS INC	MN	682.7
NATIONAL CASUALTY CO	OH	418.6
PEKIN INS CO	IL	305.4
PREFERRED PROFESSIONAL INS CO	NE	327.4
SENTRY CASUALTY CO	WI	355.9
SFM MUTUAL INS CO	MN	612.1
STATE FARM FIRE & CAS CO	IL	39,411.9
STATE FARM MUTUAL AUTOMOBILE INS CO	IL	160,732.0
SURETEC INS CO	TX	253.2
TOA REINS CO OF AMERICA	DE	1,820.3
TRANS PACIFIC INS CO	NY	67.6
TRANSATLANTIC REINS CO	NY	14,732.2
UNITED EDUCATORS INS A RECIP RRG	VT	912.3
UNITED SPECIALTY INS CO	DE	330.2
USAA GENERAL INDEMNITY CO	TX	4,627.9
WESTERN AGRICULTURAL INS CO	IA	213.2

Kansas

INSURANCE COMPANY NAME	DOM. STATE	TOTAL ASSETS ($MIL)
Rating: **A+**		
BERKSHIRE HATHAWAY ASR CORP	NY	2,223.5
Rating: **A**		
AUTO-OWNERS INS CO	MI	15,390.4
CINCINNATI INS CO	OH	12,914.9
CINCINNATI SPECIALTY UNDERWRITER	DE	820.6
OWNERS INS CO	OH	4,110.4
SENTRY INS A MUTUAL CO	WI	8,392.8
SOMPO AMERICA INSURANCE CO	NY	1,285.1
TOKIO MARINE AMERICA INS CO	NY	1,409.5
Rating: **A-**		
ACUITY A MUTUAL INS CO	WI	3,960.1
AMERICAN FAMILY MUTL INS CO SI	WI	17,157.4
CINCINNATI INDEMNITY CO	OH	133.0
COUNTRY MUTUAL INS CO	IL	4,850.2
CUMIS INS SOCIETY INC	IA	2,002.8
DAIRYLAND INS CO	WI	1,400.7
EMPLOYERS COMPENSATION INS CO	CA	1,091.0
ENDURANCE ASR CORP	DE	2,059.0
ESSENT GUARANTY INC	PA	1,756.6
FARM BUREAU P&C INS CO	IA	2,532.4
GEICO SECURE INS CO	NE	625.3
MITSUI SUMITOMO INS CO OF AMER	NY	975.8
MOTORISTS COMMERCIAL MUTUAL INS CO	OH	368.8
NATIONAL MORTGAGE INS CORP	WI	717.8
PROTECTIVE INS CO	IN	885.6
SECURIAN CASUALTY CO	MN	328.2
SENTRY SELECT INS CO	WI	826.6
TRAVELERS CASUALTY & SURETY CO	CT	16,983.8
TRAVELERS INDEMNITY CO	CT	21,394.5
UNITED SERVICES AUTOMOBILE ASN	TX	35,460.0
USAA CASUALTY INS CO	TX	10,897.7
WEST BEND MUTUAL INS CO	WI	2,695.9
Rating: **B+**		
ALASKA NATIONAL INS CO	AK	1,004.7
ALLIED WORLD SPECIALTY INS CO	DE	829.1
ALLSTATE INS CO	IL	48,302.5
AMERICAN AGRICULTURAL INS CO	IN	1,338.9
AMERICAN CONTRACTORS INDEMNITY CO	CA	338.3
AMERICAN NATIONAL PROPERTY & CAS CO	MO	1,418.0
AMERICAN STANDARD INS CO OF WI	WI	400.9
AMICA MUTUAL INS CO	RI	5,384.6
ANSUR AMERICA INS CO	MI	121.2
ARCH SPECIALTY INS CO	MO	483.4
BROTHERHOOD MUTUAL INS CO	IN	644.9
CATERPILLAR INS CO	MO	790.6
CHURCH MUTUAL INS CO	WI	1,739.8
COPIC INS CO	CO	603.2
COVINGTON SPECIALTY INS CO	NH	97.9
FARM BUREAU MUTUAL INS CO OF MI	MI	782.4
FARMERS MUTUAL INS CO OF NE	NE	680.3
FEDERATED RURAL ELECTRIC INS EXCH	KS	553.2
FINANCIAL PACIFIC INS CO	CA	261.4
FRANKENMUTH MUTUAL INS CO	MI	1,351.0

INSURANCE COMPANY NAME	DOM. STATE	TOTAL ASSETS ($MIL)
GEICO CHOICE INS CO	NE	1,134.6
GEICO GENERAL INS CO	MD	167.6
HOUSING AUTHORITY PROP A MUTUAL CO	VT	181.9
ICI MUTUAL INS CO A RRG	VT	367.6
MARKEL GLOBAL REINS CO	DE	2,180.9
MERCHANTS NATIONAL INS CO	NH	136.0
MIDDLESEX INS CO	WI	764.3
MMIC INS INC	MN	682.7
NATIONAL CASUALTY CO	OH	418.6
PREFERRED PROFESSIONAL INS CO	NE	327.4
SENTRY CASUALTY CO	WI	355.9
SFM MUTUAL INS CO	MN	612.1
STATE FARM FIRE & CAS CO	IL	39,411.9
STATE FARM MUTUAL AUTOMOBILE INS CO	IL	160,732.0
SURETEC INS CO	TX	253.2
TOA REINS CO OF AMERICA	DE	1,820.3
TRANS PACIFIC INS CO	NY	67.6
TRANSATLANTIC REINS CO	NY	14,732.2
UNITED EDUCATORS INS A RECIP RRG	VT	912.3
UNITED SPECIALTY INS CO	DE	330.2
USAA GENERAL INDEMNITY CO	TX	4,627.9
WESTERN AGRICULTURAL INS CO	IA	213.2

Kentucky

INSURANCE COMPANY NAME	DOM. STATE	TOTAL ASSETS ($MIL)
Rating: A+		
BERKSHIRE HATHAWAY ASR CORP	NY	2,223.5
Rating: A		
AUTO-OWNERS INS CO	MI	15,390.4
CINCINNATI INS CO	OH	12,914.9
CINCINNATI SPECIALTY UNDERWRITER	DE	820.6
HOME-OWNERS INS CO	MI	2,323.7
OWNERS INS CO	OH	4,110.4
SENTRY INS A MUTUAL CO	WI	8,392.8
SOMPO AMERICA INSURANCE CO	NY	1,285.1
TOKIO MARINE AMERICA INS CO	NY	1,409.5
Rating: A-		
ACUITY A MUTUAL INS CO	WI	3,960.1
ALL AMERICA INS CO	OH	291.6
CINCINNATI INDEMNITY CO	OH	133.0
COUNTRY MUTUAL INS CO	IL	4,850.2
CUMIS INS SOCIETY INC	IA	2,002.8
DAIRYLAND INS CO	WI	1,400.7
EMPLOYERS COMPENSATION INS CO	CA	1,091.0
ENDURANCE ASR CORP	DE	2,059.0
ESSENT GUARANTY INC	PA	1,756.6
GEICO SECURE INS CO	NE	625.3
MITSUI SUMITOMO INS CO OF AMER	NY	975.8
MOTORISTS COMMERCIAL MUTUAL INS CO	OH	368.8
NATIONAL MORTGAGE INS CORP	WI	717.8
PROPERTY-OWNERS INS CO	IN	302.7
PROTECTIVE INS CO	IN	885.6
SECURIAN CASUALTY CO	MN	328.2
SENTRY SELECT INS CO	WI	826.6
TRAVELERS CASUALTY & SURETY CO	CT	16,983.8
TRAVELERS INDEMNITY CO	CT	21,394.5
TREXIS ONE INSURANCE GROUP	VA	56.6
UNITED SERVICES AUTOMOBILE ASN	TX	35,460.0
USAA CASUALTY INS CO	TX	10,897.7
WEST BEND MUTUAL INS CO	WI	2,695.9
Rating: B+		
ALLIED WORLD SPECIALTY INS CO	DE	829.1
ALLSTATE INS CO	IL	48,302.5
AMERICAN AGRICULTURAL INS CO	IN	1,338.9
AMERICAN CONTRACTORS INDEMNITY CO	CA	338.3
AMERICAN NATIONAL PROPERTY & CAS CO	MO	1,418.0
AMICA MUTUAL INS CO	RI	5,384.6
ANSUR AMERICA INS CO	MI	121.2
ARCH SPECIALTY INS CO	MO	483.4
BROTHERHOOD MUTUAL INS CO	IN	644.9
CATERPILLAR INS CO	MO	790.6
CENTRAL MUTUAL INS CO	OH	1,618.4
CHURCH MUTUAL INS CO	WI	1,739.8
COVINGTON SPECIALTY INS CO	NH	97.9
FARM BUREAU MUTUAL INS CO OF MI	MI	782.4
FEDERATED RURAL ELECTRIC INS EXCH	KS	553.2
FRANKENMUTH MUTUAL INS CO	MI	1,351.0
GEICO CHOICE INS CO	NE	1,134.6
GEICO GENERAL INS CO	MD	167.6

INSURANCE COMPANY NAME	DOM. STATE	TOTAL ASSETS ($MIL)
HASTINGS MUTUAL INS CO	MI	932.1
HOUSING AUTHORITY PROP A MUTUAL CO	VT	181.9
MARKEL GLOBAL REINS CO	DE	2,180.9
MERCHANTS NATIONAL INS CO	NH	136.0
MIDDLESEX INS CO	WI	764.3
MMIC INS INC	MN	682.7
NATIONAL CASUALTY CO	OH	418.6
PREFERRED PROFESSIONAL INS CO	NE	327.4
SENTRY CASUALTY CO	WI	355.9
STATE FARM FIRE & CAS CO	IL	39,411.9
STATE FARM MUTUAL AUTOMOBILE INS CO	IL	160,732.0
STATE VOLUNTEER MUTUAL INS CO	TN	1,249.3
SURETEC INS CO	TX	253.2
TOA REINS CO OF AMERICA	DE	1,820.3
TRANS PACIFIC INS CO	NY	67.6
TRANSATLANTIC REINS CO	NY	14,732.2
TREXIS INSURANCE CORP	VA	108.1
UNITED EDUCATORS INS A RECIP RRG	VT	912.3
UNITED SPECIALTY INS CO	DE	330.2
USAA GENERAL INDEMNITY CO	TX	4,627.9

Louisiana

INSURANCE COMPANY NAME	DOM. STATE	TOTAL ASSETS ($MIL)
Rating: **A+**		
BERKSHIRE HATHAWAY ASR CORP	NY	2,223.5
Rating: **A**		
CINCINNATI INS CO	OH	12,914.9
CINCINNATI SPECIALTY UNDERWRITER	DE	820.6
SENTRY INS A MUTUAL CO	WI	8,392.8
SOMPO AMERICA INSURANCE CO	NY	1,285.1
TOKIO MARINE AMERICA INS CO	NY	1,409.5
Rating: **A-**		
CINCINNATI INDEMNITY CO	OH	133.0
CUMIS INS SOCIETY INC	IA	2,002.8
EMPLOYERS COMPENSATION INS CO	CA	1,091.0
ENDURANCE ASR CORP	DE	2,059.0
ESSENT GUARANTY INC	PA	1,756.6
GEICO SECURE INS CO	NE	625.3
MITSUI SUMITOMO INS CO OF AMER	NY	975.8
NATIONAL MORTGAGE INS CORP	WI	717.8
PROTECTIVE INS CO	IN	885.6
SECURIAN CASUALTY CO	MN	328.2
SENTRY SELECT INS CO	WI	826.6
TRAVELERS CASUALTY & SURETY CO	CT	16,983.8
TRAVELERS INDEMNITY CO	CT	21,394.5
UNITED SERVICES AUTOMOBILE ASN	TX	35,460.0
USAA CASUALTY INS CO	TX	10,897.7
Rating: **B+**		
ALASKA NATIONAL INS CO	AK	1,004.7
ALLIED WORLD SPECIALTY INS CO	DE	829.1
ALLSTATE INS CO	IL	48,302.5
AMERICAN AGRICULTURAL INS CO	IN	1,338.9
AMERICAN CONTRACTORS INDEMNITY CO	CA	338.3
AMERICAN INTERSTATE INS CO OF TX	TX	68.1
AMERICAN NATIONAL PROPERTY & CAS CO	MO	1,418.0
AMICA MUTUAL INS CO	RI	5,384.6
ARCH SPECIALTY INS CO	MO	483.4
BROTHERHOOD MUTUAL INS CO	IN	644.9
CATERPILLAR INS CO	MO	790.6
CHURCH MUTUAL INS CO	WI	1,739.8
COPIC INS CO	CO	603.2
COVINGTON SPECIALTY INS CO	NH	97.9
FARM BUREAU MUTUAL INS CO OF MI	MI	782.4
FEDERATED RURAL ELECTRIC INS EXCH	KS	553.2
FRANKENMUTH MUTUAL INS CO	MI	1,351.0
GEICO CHOICE INS CO	NE	1,134.6
GEICO GENERAL INS CO	MD	167.6
HOUSING AUTHORITY PROP A MUTUAL CO	VT	181.9
LION INS CO (FL)	FL	264.3
LUBA CASUALTY INS CO	LA	228.7
MARKEL GLOBAL REINS CO	DE	2,180.9
MERCHANTS NATIONAL INS CO	NH	136.0
MIDDLESEX INS CO	WI	764.3
NATIONAL CASUALTY CO	OH	418.6
PREFERRED PROFESSIONAL INS CO	NE	327.4
SENTRY CASUALTY CO	WI	355.9
SOUTHERN FIDELITY INS CO	FL	196.7

INSURANCE COMPANY NAME	DOM. STATE	TOTAL ASSETS ($MIL)
STATE FARM FIRE & CAS CO	IL	39,411.9
STATE FARM MUTUAL AUTOMOBILE INS CO	IL	160,732.0
SURETEC INS CO	TX	253.2
TOA REINS CO OF AMERICA	DE	1,820.3
TRANSATLANTIC REINS CO	NY	14,732.2
UNITED EDUCATORS INS A RECIP RRG	VT	912.3
UNITED SPECIALTY INS CO	DE	330.2
USAA GENERAL INDEMNITY CO	TX	4,627.9

Maine

INSURANCE COMPANY NAME	DOM. STATE	TOTAL ASSETS ($MIL)
Rating:	**A+**	
BERKSHIRE HATHAWAY ASR CORP	NY	2,223.5
Rating:	**A**	
CINCINNATI INS CO	OH	12,914.9
CINCINNATI SPECIALTY UNDERWRITER	DE	820.6
SENTRY INS A MUTUAL CO	WI	8,392.8
SOMPO AMERICA INSURANCE CO	NY	1,285.1
TOKIO MARINE AMERICA INS CO	NY	1,409.5
Rating:	**A-**	
ACUITY A MUTUAL INS CO	WI	3,960.1
ALL AMERICA INS CO	OH	291.6
CINCINNATI INDEMNITY CO	OH	133.0
COUNTRY MUTUAL INS CO	IL	4,850.2
CUMIS INS SOCIETY INC	IA	2,002.8
DAIRYLAND INS CO	WI	1,400.7
EMPLOYERS COMPENSATION INS CO	CA	1,091.0
ENDURANCE ASR CORP	DE	2,059.0
ESSENT GUARANTY INC	PA	1,756.6
MITSUI SUMITOMO INS CO OF AMER	NY	975.8
MOTORISTS COMMERCIAL MUTUAL INS CO	OH	368.8
NATIONAL MORTGAGE INS CORP	WI	717.8
PROTECTIVE INS CO	IN	885.6
SECURIAN CASUALTY CO	MN	328.2
SENTRY SELECT INS CO	WI	826.6
TRAVELERS CASUALTY & SURETY CO	CT	16,983.8
TRAVELERS INDEMNITY CO	CT	21,394.5
UNITED SERVICES AUTOMOBILE ASN	TX	35,460.0
USAA CASUALTY INS CO	TX	10,897.7
Rating:	**B+**	
ALLIED WORLD SPECIALTY INS CO	DE	829.1
ALLSTATE INS CO	IL	48,302.5
AMERICAN AGRICULTURAL INS CO	IN	1,338.9
AMERICAN CONTRACTORS INDEMNITY CO	CA	338.3
AMERICAN NATIONAL PROPERTY & CAS CO	MO	1,418.0
AMICA MUTUAL INS CO	RI	5,384.6
ANSUR AMERICA INS CO	MI	121.2
ARCH SPECIALTY INS CO	MO	483.4
BROTHERHOOD MUTUAL INS CO	IN	644.9
CATERPILLAR INS CO	MO	790.6
CENTRAL MUTUAL INS CO	OH	1,618.4
CHURCH MUTUAL INS CO	WI	1,739.8
COVINGTON SPECIALTY INS CO	NH	97.9
FARM BUREAU MUTUAL INS CO OF MI	MI	782.4
FARM FAMILY CASUALTY INS CO	NY	1,241.7
FEDERATED RURAL ELECTRIC INS EXCH	KS	553.2
FRANKENMUTH MUTUAL INS CO	MI	1,351.0
GEICO GENERAL INS CO	MD	167.6
HOUSING AUTHORITY PROP A MUTUAL CO	VT	181.9
INTERINS EXCHANGE	CA	10,404.3
MARKEL GLOBAL REINS CO	DE	2,180.9
MERCHANTS PREFERRED INS CO	NY	76.4
MIDDLESEX INS CO	WI	764.3
NATIONAL CASUALTY CO	OH	418.6
PREFERRED PROFESSIONAL INS CO	NE	327.4

INSURANCE COMPANY NAME	DOM. STATE	TOTAL ASSETS ($MIL)
SENTRY CASUALTY CO	WI	355.9
STATE FARM FIRE & CAS CO	IL	39,411.9
STATE FARM MUTUAL AUTOMOBILE INS CO	IL	160,732.0
SURETEC INS CO	TX	253.2
TOA REINS CO OF AMERICA	DE	1,820.3
TRANS PACIFIC INS CO	NY	67.6
TRANSATLANTIC REINS CO	NY	14,732.2
UNITED EDUCATORS INS A RECIP RRG	VT	912.3
UNITED SPECIALTY INS CO	DE	330.2
USAA GENERAL INDEMNITY CO	TX	4,627.9

Maryland

INSURANCE COMPANY NAME	DOM. STATE	TOTAL ASSETS ($MIL)
Rating:	**A+**	
BERKSHIRE HATHAWAY ASR CORP	NY	2,223.5
Rating:	**A**	
BUILDERS MUTUAL INS CO	NC	859.6
CINCINNATI INS CO	OH	12,914.9
CINCINNATI SPECIALTY UNDERWRITER	DE	820.6
SENTRY INS A MUTUAL CO	WI	8,392.8
SOMPO AMERICA INSURANCE CO	NY	1,285.1
TOKIO MARINE AMERICA INS CO	NY	1,409.5
Rating:	**A-**	
ALL AMERICA INS CO	OH	291.6
CINCINNATI INDEMNITY CO	OH	133.0
COUNTRY MUTUAL INS CO	IL	4,850.2
CUMIS INS SOCIETY INC	IA	2,002.8
DAIRYLAND INS CO	WI	1,400.7
EMPLOYERS COMPENSATION INS CO	CA	1,091.0
ENDURANCE ASR CORP	DE	2,059.0
ESSENT GUARANTY INC	PA	1,756.6
GEICO SECURE INS CO	NE	625.3
MITSUI SUMITOMO INS CO OF AMER	NY	975.8
MOTORISTS COMMERCIAL MUTUAL INS CO	OH	368.8
NATIONAL MORTGAGE INS CORP	WI	717.8
PROTECTIVE INS CO	IN	885.6
SECURIAN CASUALTY CO	MN	328.2
SENTRY SELECT INS CO	WI	826.6
TRAVELERS CASUALTY & SURETY CO	CT	16,983.8
TRAVELERS INDEMNITY CO	CT	21,394.5
UNITED SERVICES AUTOMOBILE ASN	TX	35,460.0
USAA CASUALTY INS CO	TX	10,897.7
Rating:	**B+**	
ALFA MUTUAL FIRE INS CO	AL	770.4
ALLIED WORLD SPECIALTY INS CO	DE	829.1
ALLSTATE INS CO	IL	48,302.5
AMERICAN AGRICULTURAL INS CO	IN	1,338.9
AMERICAN CONTRACTORS INDEMNITY CO	CA	338.3
AMERICAN NATIONAL PROPERTY & CAS CO	MO	1,418.0
AMICA MUTUAL INS CO	RI	5,384.6
ARCH SPECIALTY INS CO	MO	483.4
BROTHERHOOD MUTUAL INS CO	IN	644.9
CATERPILLAR INS CO	MO	790.6
CENTRAL MUTUAL INS CO	OH	1,618.4
CHURCH MUTUAL INS CO	WI	1,739.8
COVINGTON SPECIALTY INS CO	NH	97.9
FARM BUREAU MUTUAL INS CO OF MI	MI	782.4
FARM FAMILY CASUALTY INS CO	NY	1,241.7
FEDERATED RURAL ELECTRIC INS EXCH	KS	553.2
FRANKENMUTH MUTUAL INS CO	MI	1,351.0
GEICO CHOICE INS CO	NE	1,134.6
GEICO GENERAL INS CO	MD	167.6
GNY CUSTOM INS CO	AZ	60.5
HOUSING AUTHORITY PROP A MUTUAL CO	VT	181.9
ICI MUTUAL INS CO A RRG	VT	367.6
LION INS CO (FL)	FL	264.3
MARKEL GLOBAL REINS CO	DE	2,180.9

INSURANCE COMPANY NAME	DOM. STATE	TOTAL ASSETS ($MIL)
MERCHANTS NATIONAL INS CO	NH	136.0
MERCHANTS PREFERRED INS CO	NY	76.4
MIDDLESEX INS CO	WI	764.3
NATIONAL CASUALTY CO	OH	418.6
PREFERRED PROFESSIONAL INS CO	NE	327.4
SENTRY CASUALTY CO	WI	355.9
STATE FARM FIRE & CAS CO	IL	39,411.9
STATE FARM MUTUAL AUTOMOBILE INS CO	IL	160,732.0
SURETEC INS CO	TX	253.2
TOA REINS CO OF AMERICA	DE	1,820.3
TRANS PACIFIC INS CO	NY	67.6
TRANSATLANTIC REINS CO	NY	14,732.2
UNITED EDUCATORS INS A RECIP RRG	VT	912.3
UNITED SPECIALTY INS CO	DE	330.2
USAA GENERAL INDEMNITY CO	TX	4,627.9

Massachusetts

INSURANCE COMPANY NAME	DOM. STATE	TOTAL ASSETS ($MIL)
Rating: A+		
BERKSHIRE HATHAWAY ASR CORP	NY	2,223.5
Rating: A		
CINCINNATI INS CO	OH	12,914.9
CINCINNATI SPECIALTY UNDERWRITER	DE	820.6
SENTRY INS A MUTUAL CO	WI	8,392.8
SOMPO AMERICA INSURANCE CO	NY	1,285.1
TOKIO MARINE AMERICA INS CO	NY	1,409.5
Rating: A-		
ALL AMERICA INS CO	OH	291.6
CINCINNATI INDEMNITY CO	OH	133.0
COUNTRY MUTUAL INS CO	IL	4,850.2
CUMIS INS SOCIETY INC	IA	2,002.8
DAIRYLAND INS CO	WI	1,400.7
EMPLOYERS COMPENSATION INS CO	CA	1,091.0
ENDURANCE ASR CORP	DE	2,059.0
ESSENT GUARANTY INC	PA	1,756.6
MITSUI SUMITOMO INS CO OF AMER	NY	975.8
MOTORISTS COMMERCIAL MUTUAL INS CO	OH	368.8
NATIONAL MORTGAGE INS CORP	WI	717.8
PROTECTIVE INS CO	IN	885.6
SECURIAN CASUALTY CO	MN	328.2
SENTRY SELECT INS CO	WI	826.6
TRAVELERS CASUALTY & SURETY CO	CT	16,983.8
TRAVELERS INDEMNITY CO	CT	21,394.5
UNITED SERVICES AUTOMOBILE ASN	TX	35,460.0
USAA CASUALTY INS CO	TX	10,897.7
Rating: B+		
ALLIED WORLD SPECIALTY INS CO	DE	829.1
ALLSTATE INS CO	IL	48,302.5
AMERICAN AGRICULTURAL INS CO	IN	1,338.9
AMICA MUTUAL INS CO	RI	5,384.6
ARCH SPECIALTY INS CO	MO	483.4
BROTHERHOOD MUTUAL INS CO	IN	644.9
CATERPILLAR INS CO	MO	790.6
CENTRAL MUTUAL INS CO	OH	1,618.4
CHURCH MUTUAL INS CO	WI	1,739.8
COVINGTON SPECIALTY INS CO	NH	97.9
FARM BUREAU MUTUAL INS CO OF MI	MI	782.4
FARM FAMILY CASUALTY INS CO	NY	1,241.7
FRANKENMUTH MUTUAL INS CO	MI	1,351.0
GEICO GENERAL INS CO	MD	167.6
GNY CUSTOM INS CO	AZ	60.5
HOUSING AUTHORITY PROP A MUTUAL CO	VT	181.9
ICI MUTUAL INS CO A RRG	VT	367.6
LION INS CO (FL)	FL	264.3
MARKEL GLOBAL REINS CO	DE	2,180.9
MERCHANTS NATIONAL INS CO	NH	136.0
MERCHANTS PREFERRED INS CO	NY	76.4
MIDDLESEX INS CO	WI	764.3
NATIONAL CASUALTY CO	OH	418.6
PREFERRED PROFESSIONAL INS CO	NE	327.4
ROCKINGHAM INS CO	VA	144.7
SENTRY CASUALTY CO	WI	355.9

INSURANCE COMPANY NAME	DOM. STATE	TOTAL ASSETS ($MIL)
STATE FARM FIRE & CAS CO	IL	39,411.9
STATE FARM MUTUAL AUTOMOBILE INS CO	IL	160,732.0
SURETEC INS CO	TX	253.2
TOA REINS CO OF AMERICA	DE	1,820.3
TRANS PACIFIC INS CO	NY	67.6
TRANSATLANTIC REINS CO	NY	14,732.2
UNITED EDUCATORS INS A RECIP RRG	VT	912.3
UNITED SPECIALTY INS CO	DE	330.2
USAA GENERAL INDEMNITY CO	TX	4,627.9

Michigan

INSURANCE COMPANY NAME	DOM. STATE	TOTAL ASSETS ($MIL)
Rating: A+		
BERKSHIRE HATHAWAY ASR CORP	NY	2,223.5
Rating: A		
AUTO-OWNERS INS CO	MI	15,390.4
CINCINNATI INS CO	OH	12,914.9
CINCINNATI SPECIALTY UNDERWRITER	DE	820.6
HOME-OWNERS INS CO	MI	2,323.7
OWNERS INS CO	OH	4,110.4
SENTRY INS A MUTUAL CO	WI	8,392.8
SOMPO AMERICA INSURANCE CO	NY	1,285.1
SOUTHERN-OWNERS INS CO	MI	821.8
TOKIO MARINE AMERICA INS CO	NY	1,409.5
Rating: A-		
ACUITY A MUTUAL INS CO	WI	3,960.1
ALL AMERICA INS CO	OH	291.6
CINCINNATI INDEMNITY CO	OH	133.0
COUNTRY MUTUAL INS CO	IL	4,850.2
CUMIS INS SOCIETY INC	IA	2,002.8
DAIRYLAND INS CO	WI	1,400.7
EMPLOYERS COMPENSATION INS CO	CA	1,091.0
ENDURANCE ASR CORP	DE	2,059.0
ESSENT GUARANTY INC	PA	1,756.6
MITSUI SUMITOMO INS CO OF AMER	NY	975.8
MOTORISTS COMMERCIAL MUTUAL INS CO	OH	368.8
NATIONAL MORTGAGE INS CORP	WI	717.8
PROPERTY-OWNERS INS CO	IN	302.7
PROTECTIVE INS CO	IN	885.6
SECURIAN CASUALTY CO	MN	328.2
SENTRY SELECT INS CO	WI	826.6
TRAVELERS CASUALTY & SURETY CO	CT	16,983.8
TRAVELERS INDEMNITY CO	CT	21,394.5
UNITED SERVICES AUTOMOBILE ASN	TX	35,460.0
USAA CASUALTY INS CO	TX	10,897.7
WEST BEND MUTUAL INS CO	WI	2,695.9
Rating: B+		
ALLIED WORLD SPECIALTY INS CO	DE	829.1
ALLSTATE INS CO	IL	48,302.5
AMERICAN AGRICULTURAL INS CO	IN	1,338.9
AMERICAN CONTRACTORS INDEMNITY CO	CA	338.3
AMERICAN NATIONAL PROPERTY & CAS CO	MO	1,418.0
AMICA MUTUAL INS CO	RI	5,384.6
ANSUR AMERICA INS CO	MI	121.2
ARCH SPECIALTY INS CO	MO	483.4
BROTHERHOOD MUTUAL INS CO	IN	644.9
CATERPILLAR INS CO	MO	790.6
CENTRAL MUTUAL INS CO	OH	1,618.4
CHURCH MUTUAL INS CO	WI	1,739.8
COVINGTON SPECIALTY INS CO	NH	97.9
FARM BUREAU GENERAL INS CO OF MI	MI	719.9
FARM BUREAU MUTUAL INS CO OF MI	MI	782.4
FARMERS AUTOMOBILE INS ASN	IL	1,226.6
FEDERATED RURAL ELECTRIC INS EXCH	KS	553.2
FRANKENMUTH MUTUAL INS CO	MI	1,351.0
GEICO GENERAL INS CO	MD	167.6

INSURANCE COMPANY NAME	DOM. STATE	TOTAL ASSETS ($MIL)
GNY CUSTOM INS CO	AZ	60.5
HASTINGS MUTUAL INS CO	MI	932.1
HOUSING AUTHORITY PROP A MUTUAL CO	VT	181.9
ICI MUTUAL INS CO A RRG	VT	367.6
INTERINS EXCHANGE	CA	10,404.3
MARKEL GLOBAL REINS CO	DE	2,180.9
MERCHANTS NATIONAL INS CO	NH	136.0
MERCHANTS PREFERRED INS CO	NY	76.4
MERCURY CASUALTY CO	CA	1,877.6
MIDDLESEX INS CO	WI	764.3
MMIC INS INC	MN	682.7
NATIONAL CASUALTY CO	OH	418.6
PEKIN INS CO	IL	305.4
PIONEER STATE MUTUAL INS CO	MI	608.7
PREFERRED PROFESSIONAL INS CO	NE	327.4
SENTRY CASUALTY CO	WI	355.9
SFM MUTUAL INS CO	MN	612.1
STATE FARM FIRE & CAS CO	IL	39,411.9
STATE FARM MUTUAL AUTOMOBILE INS CO	IL	160,732.0
SURETEC INS CO	TX	253.2
TOA REINS CO OF AMERICA	DE	1,820.3
TRANS PACIFIC INS CO	NY	67.6
TRANSATLANTIC REINS CO	NY	14,732.2
UNITED EDUCATORS INS A RECIP RRG	VT	912.3
UNITED SPECIALTY INS CO	DE	330.2
USAA GENERAL INDEMNITY CO	TX	4,627.9
WESTERN AGRICULTURAL INS CO	IA	213.2

Minnesota

INSURANCE COMPANY NAME	DOM. STATE	TOTAL ASSETS ($MIL)
Rating: A+		
BERKSHIRE HATHAWAY ASR CORP	NY	2,223.5
Rating: A		
AUTO-OWNERS INS CO	MI	15,390.4
CINCINNATI INS CO	OH	12,914.9
CINCINNATI SPECIALTY UNDERWRITER	DE	820.6
OWNERS INS CO	OH	4,110.4
SENTRY INS A MUTUAL CO	WI	8,392.8
SOMPO AMERICA INSURANCE CO	NY	1,285.1
TOKIO MARINE AMERICA INS CO	NY	1,409.5
Rating: A-		
ACUITY A MUTUAL INS CO	WI	3,960.1
ALL AMERICA INS CO	OH	291.6
AMERICAN FAMILY MUTL INS CO SI	WI	17,157.4
CINCINNATI INDEMNITY CO	OH	133.0
COUNTRY MUTUAL INS CO	IL	4,850.2
CUMIS INS SOCIETY INC	IA	2,002.8
DAIRYLAND INS CO	WI	1,400.7
EMPLOYERS COMPENSATION INS CO	CA	1,091.0
ENDURANCE ASR CORP	DE	2,059.0
ESSENT GUARANTY INC	PA	1,756.6
FARM BUREAU P&C INS CO	IA	2,532.4
MITSUI SUMITOMO INS CO OF AMER	NY	975.8
MOTORISTS COMMERCIAL MUTUAL INS CO	OH	368.8
NATIONAL MORTGAGE INS CORP	WI	717.8
PROTECTIVE INS CO	IN	885.6
SECURIAN CASUALTY CO	MN	328.2
SENTRY SELECT INS CO	WI	826.6
TRAVELERS CASUALTY & SURETY CO	CT	16,983.8
TRAVELERS INDEMNITY CO	CT	21,394.5
UNITED SERVICES AUTOMOBILE ASN	TX	35,460.0
USAA CASUALTY INS CO	TX	10,897.7
WEST BEND MUTUAL INS CO	WI	2,695.9
Rating: B+		
ALASKA NATIONAL INS CO	AK	1,004.7
ALLIED WORLD SPECIALTY INS CO	DE	829.1
ALLSTATE INS CO	IL	48,302.5
AMERICAN AGRICULTURAL INS CO	IN	1,338.9
AMERICAN CONTRACTORS INDEMNITY CO	CA	338.3
AMERICAN NATIONAL PROPERTY & CAS CO	MO	1,418.0
AMERICAN STANDARD INS CO OF WI	WI	400.9
AMICA MUTUAL INS CO	RI	5,384.6
ARCH SPECIALTY INS CO	MO	483.4
BROTHERHOOD MUTUAL INS CO	IN	644.9
CATERPILLAR INS CO	MO	790.6
CENTRAL MUTUAL INS CO	OH	1,618.4
CHURCH MUTUAL INS CO	WI	1,739.8
COPIC INS CO	CO	603.2
COVINGTON SPECIALTY INS CO	NH	97.9
FARM BUREAU MUTUAL INS CO OF MI	MI	782.4
FEDERATED RURAL ELECTRIC INS EXCH	KS	553.2
FINANCIAL PACIFIC INS CO	CA	261.4
FRANKENMUTH MUTUAL INS CO	MI	1,351.0
GEICO GENERAL INS CO	MD	167.6

INSURANCE COMPANY NAME	DOM. STATE	TOTAL ASSETS ($MIL)
HOUSING AUTHORITY PROP A MUTUAL CO	VT	181.9
ICI MUTUAL INS CO A RRG	VT	367.6
MARKEL GLOBAL REINS CO	DE	2,180.9
MERCHANTS NATIONAL INS CO	NH	136.0
MIDDLESEX INS CO	WI	764.3
MMIC INS INC	MN	682.7
NATIONAL CASUALTY CO	OH	418.6
PREFERRED PROFESSIONAL INS CO	NE	327.4
SENTRY CASUALTY CO	WI	355.9
SFM MUTUAL INS CO	MN	612.1
STATE FARM FIRE & CAS CO	IL	39,411.9
STATE FARM MUTUAL AUTOMOBILE INS CO	IL	160,732.0
SURETEC INS CO	TX	253.2
TOA REINS CO OF AMERICA	DE	1,820.3
TRANS PACIFIC INS CO	NY	67.6
TRANSATLANTIC REINS CO	NY	14,732.2
UNITED EDUCATORS INS A RECIP RRG	VT	912.3
UNITED SPECIALTY INS CO	DE	330.2
USAA GENERAL INDEMNITY CO	TX	4,627.9
WESTERN AGRICULTURAL INS CO	IA	213.2

Mississippi

INSURANCE COMPANY NAME	DOM. STATE	TOTAL ASSETS ($MIL)
Rating: A+		
BERKSHIRE HATHAWAY ASR CORP	NY	2,223.5
Rating: A		
AUTO-OWNERS INS CO	MI	15,390.4
BUILDERS MUTUAL INS CO	NC	859.6
CINCINNATI INS CO	OH	12,914.9
CINCINNATI SPECIALTY UNDERWRITER	DE	820.6
OWNERS INS CO	OH	4,110.4
SENTRY INS A MUTUAL CO	WI	8,392.8
SOMPO AMERICA INSURANCE CO	NY	1,285.1
TOKIO MARINE AMERICA INS CO	NY	1,409.5
Rating: A-		
ACUITY A MUTUAL INS CO	WI	3,960.1
ALFA MUTUAL GENERAL INS CO	AL	115.4
ALL AMERICA INS CO	OH	291.6
CINCINNATI INDEMNITY CO	OH	133.0
CUMIS INS SOCIETY INC	IA	2,002.8
DAIRYLAND INS CO	WI	1,400.7
EMPLOYERS COMPENSATION INS CO	CA	1,091.0
ENDURANCE ASR CORP	DE	2,059.0
ESSENT GUARANTY INC	PA	1,756.6
GEICO SECURE INS CO	NE	625.3
MITSUI SUMITOMO INS CO OF AMER	NY	975.8
NATIONAL MORTGAGE INS CORP	WI	717.8
PROTECTIVE INS CO	IN	885.6
SECURIAN CASUALTY CO	MN	328.2
SENTRY SELECT INS CO	WI	826.6
TRAVELERS CASUALTY & SURETY CO	CT	16,983.8
TRAVELERS INDEMNITY CO	CT	21,394.5
TREXIS ONE INSURANCE GROUP	VA	56.6
UNITED SERVICES AUTOMOBILE ASN	TX	35,460.0
USAA CASUALTY INS CO	TX	10,897.7
Rating: B+		
ALASKA NATIONAL INS CO	AK	1,004.7
ALFA GENERAL INS CORP	AL	101.6
ALLIED WORLD SPECIALTY INS CO	DE	829.1
ALLSTATE INS CO	IL	48,302.5
AMERICAN AGRICULTURAL INS CO	IN	1,338.9
AMERICAN CONTRACTORS INDEMNITY CO	CA	338.3
AMERICAN NATIONAL PROPERTY & CAS CO	MO	1,418.0
AMICA MUTUAL INS CO	RI	5,384.6
ANSUR AMERICA INS CO	MI	121.2
ARCH SPECIALTY INS CO	MO	483.4
BROTHERHOOD MUTUAL INS CO	IN	644.9
CATERPILLAR INS CO	MO	790.6
CENTRAL MUTUAL INS CO	OH	1,618.4
CHURCH MUTUAL INS CO	WI	1,739.8
COVINGTON SPECIALTY INS CO	NH	97.9
FEDERATED RURAL ELECTRIC INS EXCH	KS	553.2
FRANKENMUTH MUTUAL INS CO	MI	1,351.0
GEICO CHOICE INS CO	NE	1,134.6
GEICO GENERAL INS CO	MD	167.6
HOUSING AUTHORITY PROP A MUTUAL CO	VT	181.9
LION INS CO (FL)	FL	264.3

INSURANCE COMPANY NAME	DOM. STATE	TOTAL ASSETS ($MIL)
LUBA CASUALTY INS CO	LA	228.7
MARKEL GLOBAL REINS CO	DE	2,180.9
MERCHANTS NATIONAL INS CO	NH	136.0
MIDDLESEX INS CO	WI	764.3
NATIONAL CASUALTY CO	OH	418.6
PREFERRED PROFESSIONAL INS CO	NE	327.4
SENTRY CASUALTY CO	WI	355.9
SOUTHERN FIDELITY INS CO	FL	196.7
STATE FARM FIRE & CAS CO	IL	39,411.9
STATE FARM MUTUAL AUTOMOBILE INS CO	IL	160,732.0
STATE VOLUNTEER MUTUAL INS CO	TN	1,249.3
SURETEC INS CO	TX	253.2
TOA REINS CO OF AMERICA	DE	1,820.3
TRANS PACIFIC INS CO	NY	67.6
TRANSATLANTIC REINS CO	NY	14,732.2
UNITED EDUCATORS INS A RECIP RRG	VT	912.3
UNITED SPECIALTY INS CO	DE	330.2
USAA GENERAL INDEMNITY CO	TX	4,627.9

Missouri

INSURANCE COMPANY NAME	DOM. STATE	TOTAL ASSETS ($MIL)
Rating:	**A+**	
BERKSHIRE HATHAWAY ASR CORP	NY	2,223.5
Rating:	**A**	
AUTO-OWNERS INS CO	MI	15,390.4
CINCINNATI INS CO	OH	12,914.9
CINCINNATI SPECIALTY UNDERWRITER	DE	820.6
HOME-OWNERS INS CO	MI	2,323.7
OWNERS INS CO	OH	4,110.4
SENTRY INS A MUTUAL CO	WI	8,392.8
SOMPO AMERICA INSURANCE CO	NY	1,285.1
TOKIO MARINE AMERICA INS CO	NY	1,409.5
Rating:	**A-**	
ACUITY A MUTUAL INS CO	WI	3,960.1
AMERICAN FAMILY MUTL INS CO SI	WI	17,157.4
CINCINNATI INDEMNITY CO	OH	133.0
COUNTRY MUTUAL INS CO	IL	4,850.2
CUMIS INS SOCIETY INC	IA	2,002.8
DAIRYLAND INS CO	WI	1,400.7
EMPLOYERS COMPENSATION INS CO	CA	1,091.0
ENDURANCE ASR CORP	DE	2,059.0
ESSENT GUARANTY INC	PA	1,756.6
FARM BUREAU P&C INS CO	IA	2,532.4
GEICO SECURE INS CO	NE	625.3
MITSUI SUMITOMO INS CO OF AMER	NY	975.8
MOTORISTS COMMERCIAL MUTUAL INS CO	OH	368.8
NATIONAL MORTGAGE INS CORP	WI	717.8
PROPERTY-OWNERS INS CO	IN	302.7
PROTECTIVE INS CO	IN	885.6
SECURIAN CASUALTY CO	MN	328.2
SENTRY SELECT INS CO	WI	826.6
TRAVELERS CASUALTY & SURETY CO	CT	16,983.8
TRAVELERS INDEMNITY CO	CT	21,394.5
TREXIS ONE INSURANCE GROUP	VA	56.6
UNITED SERVICES AUTOMOBILE ASN	TX	35,460.0
USAA CASUALTY INS CO	TX	10,897.7
WEST BEND MUTUAL INS CO	WI	2,695.9
Rating:	**B+**	
ALASKA NATIONAL INS CO	AK	1,004.7
ALLIED WORLD SPECIALTY INS CO	DE	829.1
ALLSTATE INS CO	IL	48,302.5
AMERICAN AGRICULTURAL INS CO	IN	1,338.9
AMERICAN CONTRACTORS INDEMNITY CO	CA	338.3
AMERICAN NATIONAL PROPERTY & CAS CO	MO	1,418.0
AMERICAN STANDARD INS CO OF WI	WI	400.9
AMICA MUTUAL INS CO	RI	5,384.6
ANSUR AMERICA INS CO	MI	121.2
ARCH SPECIALTY INS CO	MO	483.4
BROTHERHOOD MUTUAL INS CO	IN	644.9
CATERPILLAR INS CO	MO	790.6
CHURCH MUTUAL INS CO	WI	1,739.8
COPIC INS CO	CO	603.2
COVINGTON SPECIALTY INS CO	NH	97.9
FARM BU TOWN & COUNTRY INS CO OF MO	MO	421.4
FARM BUREAU MUTUAL INS CO OF MI	MI	782.4

INSURANCE COMPANY NAME	DOM. STATE	TOTAL ASSETS ($MIL)
FARM FAMILY CASUALTY INS CO	NY	1,241.7
FEDERATED RURAL ELECTRIC INS EXCH	KS	553.2
FINANCIAL PACIFIC INS CO	CA	261.4
FRANKENMUTH MUTUAL INS CO	MI	1,351.0
GEICO CHOICE INS CO	NE	1,134.6
GEICO GENERAL INS CO	MD	167.6
HOUSING AUTHORITY PROP A MUTUAL CO	VT	181.9
ICI MUTUAL INS CO A RRG	VT	367.6
INTERINS EXCHANGE	CA	10,404.3
MARKEL GLOBAL REINS CO	DE	2,180.9
MERCHANTS NATIONAL INS CO	NH	136.0
MIDDLESEX INS CO	WI	764.3
MMIC INS INC	MN	682.7
MO EMPLOYERS MUTUAL INS CO	MO	695.0
NATIONAL CASUALTY CO	OH	418.6
PREFERRED PROFESSIONAL INS CO	NE	327.4
SENTRY CASUALTY CO	WI	355.9
SFM MUTUAL INS CO	MN	612.1
STATE FARM FIRE & CAS CO	IL	39,411.9
STATE FARM MUTUAL AUTOMOBILE INS CO	IL	160,732.0
STATE VOLUNTEER MUTUAL INS CO	TN	1,249.3
SURETEC INS CO	TX	253.2
TOA REINS CO OF AMERICA	DE	1,820.3
TRANS PACIFIC INS CO	NY	67.6
TRANSATLANTIC REINS CO	NY	14,732.2
TREXIS INSURANCE CORP	VA	108.1
UNITED EDUCATORS INS A RECIP RRG	VT	912.3
UNITED SPECIALTY INS CO	DE	330.2
USAA GENERAL INDEMNITY CO	TX	4,627.9
WESTERN AGRICULTURAL INS CO	IA	213.2

Montana

INSURANCE COMPANY NAME	DOM. STATE	TOTAL ASSETS ($MIL)
Rating:	**A+**	
BERKSHIRE HATHAWAY ASR CORP	NY	2,223.5
Rating:	**A**	
CINCINNATI INS CO	OH	12,914.9
CINCINNATI SPECIALTY UNDERWRITER	DE	820.6
SENTRY INS A MUTUAL CO	WI	8,392.8
SOMPO AMERICA INSURANCE CO	NY	1,285.1
TOKIO MARINE AMERICA INS CO	NY	1,409.5
Rating:	**A-**	
ACUITY A MUTUAL INS CO	WI	3,960.1
ALL AMERICA INS CO	OH	291.6
AMERICAN FAMILY MUTL INS CO SI	WI	17,157.4
CINCINNATI INDEMNITY CO	OH	133.0
COUNTRY MUTUAL INS CO	IL	4,850.2
CUMIS INS SOCIETY INC	IA	2,002.8
DAIRYLAND INS CO	WI	1,400.7
EMPLOYERS COMPENSATION INS CO	CA	1,091.0
ENDURANCE ASR CORP	DE	2,059.0
ESSENT GUARANTY INC	PA	1,756.6
GEICO SECURE INS CO	NE	625.3
MITSUI SUMITOMO INS CO OF AMER	NY	975.8
NATIONAL MORTGAGE INS CORP	WI	717.8
PROTECTIVE INS CO	IN	885.6
SECURIAN CASUALTY CO	MN	328.2
SENTRY SELECT INS CO	WI	826.6
TRAVELERS CASUALTY & SURETY CO	CT	16,983.8
TRAVELERS INDEMNITY CO	CT	21,394.5
UNITED SERVICES AUTOMOBILE ASN	TX	35,460.0
USAA CASUALTY INS CO	TX	10,897.7
Rating:	**B+**	
ALASKA NATIONAL INS CO	AK	1,004.7
ALLIED WORLD SPECIALTY INS CO	DE	829.1
ALLSTATE INS CO	IL	48,302.5
AMERICAN AGRICULTURAL INS CO	IN	1,338.9
AMERICAN CONTRACTORS INDEMNITY CO	CA	338.3
AMERICAN NATIONAL PROPERTY & CAS CO	MO	1,418.0
AMERICAN STANDARD INS CO OF WI	WI	400.9
AMICA MUTUAL INS CO	RI	5,384.6
ARCH SPECIALTY INS CO	MO	483.4
BROTHERHOOD MUTUAL INS CO	IN	644.9
CATERPILLAR INS CO	MO	790.6
CENTRAL MUTUAL INS CO	OH	1,618.4
CHURCH MUTUAL INS CO	WI	1,739.8
COPIC INS CO	CO	603.2
COVINGTON SPECIALTY INS CO	NH	97.9
FARM BUREAU MUTUAL INS CO OF MI	MI	782.4
FEDERATED RURAL ELECTRIC INS EXCH	KS	553.2
FINANCIAL PACIFIC INS CO	CA	261.4
FRANKENMUTH MUTUAL INS CO	MI	1,351.0
GEICO CHOICE INS CO	NE	1,134.6
GEICO GENERAL INS CO	MD	167.6
HOUSING AUTHORITY PROP A MUTUAL CO	VT	181.9
MARKEL GLOBAL REINS CO	DE	2,180.9
MERCHANTS NATIONAL INS CO	NH	136.0

INSURANCE COMPANY NAME	DOM. STATE	TOTAL ASSETS ($MIL)
MIDDLESEX INS CO	WI	764.3
MMIC INS INC	MN	682.7
MUTUAL OF ENUMCLAW INS CO	OR	748.3
NATIONAL CASUALTY CO	OH	418.6
PREFERRED PROFESSIONAL INS CO	NE	327.4
SENTRY CASUALTY CO	WI	355.9
SFM MUTUAL INS CO	MN	612.1
STATE FARM FIRE & CAS CO	IL	39,411.9
STATE FARM MUTUAL AUTOMOBILE INS CO	IL	160,732.0
SURETEC INS CO	TX	253.2
TOA REINS CO OF AMERICA	DE	1,820.3
TRANS PACIFIC INS CO	NY	67.6
TRANSATLANTIC REINS CO	NY	14,732.2
UNITED EDUCATORS INS A RECIP RRG	VT	912.3
UNITED SPECIALTY INS CO	DE	330.2
USAA GENERAL INDEMNITY CO	TX	4,627.9
WESTERN AGRICULTURAL INS CO	IA	213.2

Nebraska

INSURANCE COMPANY NAME	DOM. STATE	TOTAL ASSETS ($MIL)
Rating: A+		
BERKSHIRE HATHAWAY ASR CORP	NY	2,223.5
Rating: A		
AUTO-OWNERS INS CO	MI	15,390.4
CINCINNATI INS CO	OH	12,914.9
CINCINNATI SPECIALTY UNDERWRITER	DE	820.6
HOME-OWNERS INS CO	MI	2,323.7
OWNERS INS CO	OH	4,110.4
SENTRY INS A MUTUAL CO	WI	8,392.8
SOMPO AMERICA INSURANCE CO	NY	1,285.1
TOKIO MARINE AMERICA INS CO	NY	1,409.5
Rating: A-		
ACUITY A MUTUAL INS CO	WI	3,960.1
AMERICAN FAMILY MUTL INS CO SI	WI	17,157.4
CINCINNATI INDEMNITY CO	OH	133.0
COUNTRY MUTUAL INS CO	IL	4,850.2
CUMIS INS SOCIETY INC	IA	2,002.8
DAIRYLAND INS CO	WI	1,400.7
EMPLOYERS COMPENSATION INS CO	CA	1,091.0
ENDURANCE ASR CORP	DE	2,059.0
ESSENT GUARANTY INC	PA	1,756.6
FARM BUREAU P&C INS CO	IA	2,532.4
GEICO SECURE INS CO	NE	625.3
MITSUI SUMITOMO INS CO OF AMER	NY	975.8
MOTORISTS COMMERCIAL MUTUAL INS CO	OH	368.8
NATIONAL MORTGAGE INS CORP	WI	717.8
PROPERTY-OWNERS INS CO	IN	302.7
PROTECTIVE INS CO	IN	885.6
SECURIAN CASUALTY CO	MN	328.2
SENTRY SELECT INS CO	WI	826.6
TRAVELERS CASUALTY & SURETY CO	CT	16,983.8
TRAVELERS INDEMNITY CO	CT	21,394.5
UNITED SERVICES AUTOMOBILE ASN	TX	35,460.0
USAA CASUALTY INS CO	TX	10,897.7
WEST BEND MUTUAL INS CO	WI	2,695.9
Rating: B+		
ALLIED WORLD SPECIALTY INS CO	DE	829.1
ALLSTATE INS CO	IL	48,302.5
AMERICAN AGRICULTURAL INS CO	IN	1,338.9
AMERICAN CONTRACTORS INDEMNITY CO	CA	338.3
AMERICAN NATIONAL PROPERTY & CAS CO	MO	1,418.0
AMERICAN STANDARD INS CO OF WI	WI	400.9
AMICA MUTUAL INS CO	RI	5,384.6
ANSUR AMERICA INS CO	MI	121.2
ARCH SPECIALTY INS CO	MO	483.4
BROTHERHOOD MUTUAL INS CO	IN	644.9
CATERPILLAR INS CO	MO	790.6
CHURCH MUTUAL INS CO	WI	1,739.8
COPIC INS CO	CO	603.2
COVINGTON SPECIALTY INS CO	NH	97.9
FARM BUREAU MUTUAL INS CO OF MI	MI	782.4
FARMERS MUTUAL INS CO OF NE	NE	680.3
FEDERATED RURAL ELECTRIC INS EXCH	KS	553.2
FINANCIAL PACIFIC INS CO	CA	261.4

INSURANCE COMPANY NAME	DOM. STATE	TOTAL ASSETS ($MIL)
FRANKENMUTH MUTUAL INS CO	MI	1,351.0
GEICO CHOICE INS CO	NE	1,134.6
GEICO GENERAL INS CO	MD	167.6
HOUSING AUTHORITY PROP A MUTUAL CO	VT	181.9
ICI MUTUAL INS CO A RRG	VT	367.6
MARKEL GLOBAL REINS CO	DE	2,180.9
MERCHANTS NATIONAL INS CO	NH	136.0
MIDDLESEX INS CO	WI	764.3
MMIC INS INC	MN	682.7
NATIONAL CASUALTY CO	OH	418.6
PREFERRED PROFESSIONAL INS CO	NE	327.4
SENTRY CASUALTY CO	WI	355.9
SFM MUTUAL INS CO	MN	612.1
STATE FARM FIRE & CAS CO	IL	39,411.9
STATE FARM MUTUAL AUTOMOBILE INS CO	IL	160,732.0
SURETEC INS CO	TX	253.2
TOA REINS CO OF AMERICA	DE	1,820.3
TRANS PACIFIC INS CO	NY	67.6
TRANSATLANTIC REINS CO	NY	14,732.2
UNITED EDUCATORS INS A RECIP RRG	VT	912.3
UNITED SPECIALTY INS CO	DE	330.2
USAA GENERAL INDEMNITY CO	TX	4,627.9
WESTERN AGRICULTURAL INS CO	IA	213.2

Nevada

INSURANCE COMPANY NAME	DOM. STATE	TOTAL ASSETS ($MIL)
Rating: A+		
BERKSHIRE HATHAWAY ASR CORP	NY	2,223.5
Rating: A		
AUTO-OWNERS INS CO	MI	15,390.4
CINCINNATI INS CO	OH	12,914.9
CINCINNATI SPECIALTY UNDERWRITER	DE	820.6
HOME-OWNERS INS CO	MI	2,323.7
OWNERS INS CO	OH	4,110.4
SENTRY INS A MUTUAL CO	WI	8,392.8
SOMPO AMERICA INSURANCE CO	NY	1,285.1
TOKIO MARINE AMERICA INS CO	NY	1,409.5
Rating: A-		
ACUITY A MUTUAL INS CO	WI	3,960.1
ALL AMERICA INS CO	OH	291.6
AMERICAN FAMILY MUTL INS CO SI	WI	17,157.4
CINCINNATI INDEMNITY CO	OH	133.0
COUNTRY MUTUAL INS CO	IL	4,850.2
CUMIS INS SOCIETY INC	IA	2,002.8
DAIRYLAND INS CO	WI	1,400.7
EMPLOYERS COMPENSATION INS CO	CA	1,091.0
ENDURANCE ASR CORP	DE	2,059.0
ESSENT GUARANTY INC	PA	1,756.6
GEICO SECURE INS CO	NE	625.3
MITSUI SUMITOMO INS CO OF AMER	NY	975.8
MOTORISTS COMMERCIAL MUTUAL INS CO	OH	368.8
NATIONAL MORTGAGE INS CORP	WI	717.8
PROPERTY-OWNERS INS CO	IN	302.7
PROTECTIVE INS CO	IN	885.6
SECURIAN CASUALTY CO	MN	328.2
SENTRY SELECT INS CO	WI	826.6
TRAVELERS CASUALTY & SURETY CO	CT	16,983.8
TRAVELERS INDEMNITY CO	CT	21,394.5
UNITED SERVICES AUTOMOBILE ASN	TX	35,460.0
USAA CASUALTY INS CO	TX	10,897.7
Rating: B+		
ALASKA NATIONAL INS CO	AK	1,004.7
ALLIED WORLD SPECIALTY INS CO	DE	829.1
ALLSTATE INS CO	IL	48,302.5
AMERICAN CONTRACTORS INDEMNITY CO	CA	338.3
AMERICAN NATIONAL PROPERTY & CAS CO	MO	1,418.0
AMERICAN STANDARD INS CO OF WI	WI	400.9
AMICA MUTUAL INS CO	RI	5,384.6
ANSUR AMERICA INS CO	MI	121.2
ARCH SPECIALTY INS CO	MO	483.4
BROTHERHOOD MUTUAL INS CO	IN	644.9
CATERPILLAR INS CO	MO	790.6
CENTRAL MUTUAL INS CO	OH	1,618.4
CHURCH MUTUAL INS CO	WI	1,739.8
COPIC INS CO	CO	603.2
COVINGTON SPECIALTY INS CO	NH	97.9
FEDERATED RURAL ELECTRIC INS EXCH	KS	553.2
FINANCIAL PACIFIC INS CO	CA	261.4
FRANKENMUTH MUTUAL INS CO	MI	1,351.0
GEICO CHOICE INS CO	NE	1,134.6

INSURANCE COMPANY NAME	DOM. STATE	TOTAL ASSETS ($MIL)
GEICO GENERAL INS CO	MD	167.6
HOUSING AUTHORITY PROP A MUTUAL CO	VT	181.9
ICI MUTUAL INS CO A RRG	VT	367.6
LION INS CO (FL)	FL	264.3
MARKEL GLOBAL REINS CO	DE	2,180.9
MERCHANTS NATIONAL INS CO	NH	136.0
MERCURY CASUALTY CO	CA	1,877.6
MIDDLESEX INS CO	WI	764.3
MUTUAL INS CO OF AZ	AZ	1,105.9
MUTUAL OF ENUMCLAW INS CO	OR	748.3
NATIONAL CASUALTY CO	OH	418.6
PREFERRED PROFESSIONAL INS CO	NE	327.4
SENTRY CASUALTY CO	WI	355.9
SFM MUTUAL INS CO	MN	612.1
STATE FARM FIRE & CAS CO	IL	39,411.9
STATE FARM MUTUAL AUTOMOBILE INS CO	IL	160,732.0
SURETEC INS CO	TX	253.2
TOA REINS CO OF AMERICA	DE	1,820.3
TRANS PACIFIC INS CO	NY	67.6
TRANSATLANTIC REINS CO	NY	14,732.2
UNITED EDUCATORS INS A RECIP RRG	VT	912.3
UNITED SPECIALTY INS CO	DE	330.2
USAA GENERAL INDEMNITY CO	TX	4,627.9
WESTERN AGRICULTURAL INS CO	IA	213.2

New Hampshire

INSURANCE COMPANY NAME	DOM. STATE	TOTAL ASSETS ($MIL)
Rating: A+		
BERKSHIRE HATHAWAY ASR CORP	NY	2,223.5
Rating: A		
CINCINNATI INS CO	OH	12,914.9
CINCINNATI SPECIALTY UNDERWRITER	DE	820.6
SENTRY INS A MUTUAL CO	WI	8,392.8
SOMPO AMERICA INSURANCE CO	NY	1,285.1
TOKIO MARINE AMERICA INS CO	NY	1,409.5
Rating: A-		
ACUITY A MUTUAL INS CO	WI	3,960.1
ALL AMERICA INS CO	OH	291.6
CINCINNATI INDEMNITY CO	OH	133.0
COUNTRY MUTUAL INS CO	IL	4,850.2
CUMIS INS SOCIETY INC	IA	2,002.8
DAIRYLAND INS CO	WI	1,400.7
EMPLOYERS COMPENSATION INS CO	CA	1,091.0
ENDURANCE ASR CORP	DE	2,059.0
ESSENT GUARANTY INC	PA	1,756.6
GEICO SECURE INS CO	NE	625.3
MITSUI SUMITOMO INS CO OF AMER	NY	975.8
MOTORISTS COMMERCIAL MUTUAL INS CO	OH	368.8
NATIONAL MORTGAGE INS CORP	WI	717.8
PROTECTIVE INS CO	IN	885.6
SECURIAN CASUALTY CO	MN	328.2
SENTRY SELECT INS CO	WI	826.6
TRAVELERS CASUALTY & SURETY CO	CT	16,983.8
TRAVELERS INDEMNITY CO	CT	21,394.5
UNITED SERVICES AUTOMOBILE ASN	TX	35,460.0
USAA CASUALTY INS CO	TX	10,897.7
Rating: B+		
ALLIED WORLD SPECIALTY INS CO	DE	829.1
ALLSTATE INS CO	IL	48,302.5
AMERICAN AGRICULTURAL INS CO	IN	1,338.9
AMERICAN NATIONAL PROPERTY & CAS CO	MO	1,418.0
AMICA MUTUAL INS CO	RI	5,384.6
ARCH SPECIALTY INS CO	MO	483.4
BROTHERHOOD MUTUAL INS CO	IN	644.9
CATERPILLAR INS CO	MO	790.6
CENTRAL MUTUAL INS CO	OH	1,618.4
CHURCH MUTUAL INS CO	WI	1,739.8
COVINGTON SPECIALTY INS CO	NH	97.9
FARM BUREAU MUTUAL INS CO OF MI	MI	782.4
FARM FAMILY CASUALTY INS CO	NY	1,241.7
FEDERATED RURAL ELECTRIC INS EXCH	KS	553.2
FRANKENMUTH MUTUAL INS CO	MI	1,351.0
GEICO CHOICE INS CO	NE	1,134.6
GEICO GENERAL INS CO	MD	167.6
HOUSING AUTHORITY PROP A MUTUAL CO	VT	181.9
INTERINS EXCHANGE	CA	10,404.3
MARKEL GLOBAL REINS CO	DE	2,180.9
MERCHANTS NATIONAL INS CO	NH	136.0
MERCHANTS PREFERRED INS CO	NY	76.4
MIDDLESEX INS CO	WI	764.3
NATIONAL CASUALTY CO	OH	418.6

INSURANCE COMPANY NAME	DOM. STATE	TOTAL ASSETS ($MIL)
PREFERRED PROFESSIONAL INS CO	NE	327.4
SENTRY CASUALTY CO	WI	355.9
STATE FARM FIRE & CAS CO	IL	39,411.9
STATE FARM MUTUAL AUTOMOBILE INS CO	IL	160,732.0
SURETEC INS CO	TX	253.2
TOA REINS CO OF AMERICA	DE	1,820.3
TRANSATLANTIC REINS CO	NY	14,732.2
UNITED EDUCATORS INS A RECIP RRG	VT	912.3
UNITED SPECIALTY INS CO	DE	330.2
USAA GENERAL INDEMNITY CO	TX	4,627.9

New Jersey

INSURANCE COMPANY NAME	DOM. STATE	TOTAL ASSETS ($MIL)
Rating: A+		
BERKSHIRE HATHAWAY ASR CORP	NY	2,223.5
Rating: A		
CINCINNATI INS CO	OH	12,914.9
CINCINNATI SPECIALTY UNDERWRITER	DE	820.6
SENTRY INS A MUTUAL CO	WI	8,392.8
SOMPO AMERICA INSURANCE CO	NY	1,285.1
TOKIO MARINE AMERICA INS CO	NY	1,409.5
Rating: A-		
ALL AMERICA INS CO	OH	291.6
ALLSTATE NJ INS CO	IL	2,485.7
CINCINNATI INDEMNITY CO	OH	133.0
COUNTRY MUTUAL INS CO	IL	4,850.2
CUMIS INS SOCIETY INC	IA	2,002.8
EMPLOYERS COMPENSATION INS CO	CA	1,091.0
ENDURANCE ASR CORP	DE	2,059.0
ESSENT GUARANTY INC	PA	1,756.6
GEICO SECURE INS CO	NE	625.3
MITSUI SUMITOMO INS CO OF AMER	NY	975.8
MOTORISTS COMMERCIAL MUTUAL INS CO	OH	368.8
NATIONAL MORTGAGE INS CORP	WI	717.8
PROTECTIVE INS CO	IN	885.6
SECURIAN CASUALTY CO	MN	328.2
SENTRY SELECT INS CO	WI	826.6
TRAVELERS CASUALTY & SURETY CO	CT	16,983.8
TRAVELERS INDEMNITY CO	CT	21,394.5
UNITED SERVICES AUTOMOBILE ASN	TX	35,460.0
USAA CASUALTY INS CO	TX	10,897.7
Rating: B+		
ALLIED WORLD SPECIALTY INS CO	DE	829.1
AMERICAN AGRICULTURAL INS CO	IN	1,338.9
AMERICAN CONTRACTORS INDEMNITY CO	CA	338.3
AMERICAN NATIONAL PROPERTY & CAS CO	MO	1,418.0
AMICA MUTUAL INS CO	RI	5,384.6
ARCH SPECIALTY INS CO	MO	483.4
BROTHERHOOD MUTUAL INS CO	IN	644.9
CATERPILLAR INS CO	MO	790.6
CENTRAL MUTUAL INS CO	OH	1,618.4
CHURCH MUTUAL INS CO	WI	1,739.8
COVINGTON SPECIALTY INS CO	NH	97.9
FARM BUREAU MUTUAL INS CO OF MI	MI	782.4
FARM FAMILY CASUALTY INS CO	NY	1,241.7
FEDERATED RURAL ELECTRIC INS EXCH	KS	553.2
FRANKENMUTH MUTUAL INS CO	MI	1,351.0
GEICO CHOICE INS CO	NE	1,134.6
GEICO GENERAL INS CO	MD	167.6
GNY CUSTOM INS CO	AZ	60.5
HIGH POINT PREFERRED INS CO	NJ	310.0
HOUSING AUTHORITY PROP A MUTUAL CO	VT	181.9
ICI MUTUAL INS CO A RRG	VT	367.6
LION INS CO (FL)	FL	264.3
MARKEL GLOBAL REINS CO	DE	2,180.9
MERCHANTS NATIONAL INS CO	NH	136.0
MERCHANTS PREFERRED INS CO	NY	76.4

INSURANCE COMPANY NAME	DOM. STATE	TOTAL ASSETS ($MIL)
MERCURY CASUALTY CO	CA	1,877.6
MIDDLESEX INS CO	WI	764.3
NATIONAL CASUALTY CO	OH	418.6
PREFERRED PROFESSIONAL INS CO	NE	327.4
SELECTIVE AUTO INS CO OF NJ	NJ	380.7
SELECTIVE CASUALTY INS CO	NJ	452.3
SENTRY CASUALTY CO	WI	355.9
STATE FARM FIRE & CAS CO	IL	39,411.9
STATE FARM MUTUAL AUTOMOBILE INS CO	IL	160,732.0
SURETEC INS CO	TX	253.2
TOA REINS CO OF AMERICA	DE	1,820.3
TRANS PACIFIC INS CO	NY	67.6
TRANSATLANTIC REINS CO	NY	14,732.2
UNITED EDUCATORS INS A RECIP RRG	VT	912.3
UNITED SPECIALTY INS CO	DE	330.2
USAA GENERAL INDEMNITY CO	TX	4,627.9

New Mexico

INSURANCE COMPANY NAME	DOM. STATE	TOTAL ASSETS ($MIL)
Rating: A+		
BERKSHIRE HATHAWAY ASR CORP	NY	2,223.5
Rating: A		
AUTO-OWNERS INS CO	MI	15,390.4
CINCINNATI INS CO	OH	12,914.9
CINCINNATI SPECIALTY UNDERWRITER	DE	820.6
OWNERS INS CO	OH	4,110.4
SENTRY INS A MUTUAL CO	WI	8,392.8
SOMPO AMERICA INSURANCE CO	NY	1,285.1
TOKIO MARINE AMERICA INS CO	NY	1,409.5
Rating: A-		
ACUITY A MUTUAL INS CO	WI	3,960.1
ALL AMERICA INS CO	OH	291.6
AMERICAN FAMILY MUTL INS CO SI	WI	17,157.4
CINCINNATI INDEMNITY CO	OH	133.0
COUNTRY MUTUAL INS CO	IL	4,850.2
CUMIS INS SOCIETY INC	IA	2,002.8
DAIRYLAND INS CO	WI	1,400.7
EMPLOYERS COMPENSATION INS CO	CA	1,091.0
ENDURANCE ASR CORP	DE	2,059.0
ESSENT GUARANTY INC	PA	1,756.6
FARM BUREAU P&C INS CO	IA	2,532.4
GEICO SECURE INS CO	NE	625.3
MITSUI SUMITOMO INS CO OF AMER	NY	975.8
MOTORISTS COMMERCIAL MUTUAL INS CO	OH	368.8
NATIONAL MORTGAGE INS CORP	WI	717.8
PROTECTIVE INS CO	IN	885.6
SECURIAN CASUALTY CO	MN	328.2
SENTRY SELECT INS CO	WI	826.6
TRAVELERS CASUALTY & SURETY CO	CT	16,983.8
TRAVELERS INDEMNITY CO	CT	21,394.5
UNITED SERVICES AUTOMOBILE ASN	TX	35,460.0
USAA CASUALTY INS CO	TX	10,897.7
Rating: B+		
ALASKA NATIONAL INS CO	AK	1,004.7
ALLIED WORLD SPECIALTY INS CO	DE	829.1
ALLSTATE INS CO	IL	48,302.5
AMERICAN AGRICULTURAL INS CO	IN	1,338.9
AMERICAN CONTRACTORS INDEMNITY CO	CA	338.3
AMERICAN NATIONAL PROPERTY & CAS CO	MO	1,418.0
AMERICAN STANDARD INS CO OF WI	WI	400.9
AMICA MUTUAL INS CO	RI	5,384.6
ANSUR AMERICA INS CO	MI	121.2
ARCH SPECIALTY INS CO	MO	483.4
BROTHERHOOD MUTUAL INS CO	IN	644.9
CATERPILLAR INS CO	MO	790.6
CENTRAL MUTUAL INS CO	OH	1,618.4
CHURCH MUTUAL INS CO	WI	1,739.8
COVINGTON SPECIALTY INS CO	NH	97.9
FEDERATED RURAL ELECTRIC INS EXCH	KS	553.2
FINANCIAL PACIFIC INS CO	CA	261.4
FRANKENMUTH MUTUAL INS CO	MI	1,351.0
GEICO CHOICE INS CO	NE	1,134.6
GEICO GENERAL INS CO	MD	167.6

INSURANCE COMPANY NAME	DOM. STATE	TOTAL ASSETS ($MIL)
HOUSING AUTHORITY PROP A MUTUAL CO	VT	181.9
ICI MUTUAL INS CO A RRG	VT	367.6
INTERINS EXCHANGE	CA	10,404.3
LION INS CO (FL)	FL	264.3
MARKEL GLOBAL REINS CO	DE	2,180.9
MERCHANTS NATIONAL INS CO	NH	136.0
MIDDLESEX INS CO	WI	764.3
MUTUAL INS CO OF AZ	AZ	1,105.9
MUTUAL OF ENUMCLAW INS CO	OR	748.3
NATIONAL CASUALTY CO	OH	418.6
PREFERRED PROFESSIONAL INS CO	NE	327.4
SENTRY CASUALTY CO	WI	355.9
STATE FARM FIRE & CAS CO	IL	39,411.9
STATE FARM MUTUAL AUTOMOBILE INS CO	IL	160,732.0
SURETEC INS CO	TX	253.2
TOA REINS CO OF AMERICA	DE	1,820.3
TRANSATLANTIC REINS CO	NY	14,732.2
UNITED EDUCATORS INS A RECIP RRG	VT	912.3
UNITED SPECIALTY INS CO	DE	330.2
USAA GENERAL INDEMNITY CO	TX	4,627.9
WESTERN AGRICULTURAL INS CO	IA	213.2

New York

INSURANCE COMPANY NAME	DOM. STATE	TOTAL ASSETS ($MIL)
Rating:	**A+**	
BERKSHIRE HATHAWAY ASR CORP	NY	2,223.5
Rating:	**A**	
CINCINNATI INS CO	OH	12,914.9
CINCINNATI SPECIALTY UNDERWRITER	DE	820.6
SENTRY INS A MUTUAL CO	WI	8,392.8
SOMPO AMERICA INSURANCE CO	NY	1,285.1
TOKIO MARINE AMERICA INS CO	NY	1,409.5
Rating:	**A-**	
ALL AMERICA INS CO	OH	291.6
CINCINNATI INDEMNITY CO	OH	133.0
COUNTRY MUTUAL INS CO	IL	4,850.2
CUMIS INS SOCIETY INC	IA	2,002.8
DAIRYLAND INS CO	WI	1,400.7
EMPLOYERS COMPENSATION INS CO	CA	1,091.0
ENDURANCE ASR CORP	DE	2,059.0
ESSENT GUARANTY INC	PA	1,756.6
MITSUI SUMITOMO INS CO OF AMER	NY	975.8
MOTORISTS COMMERCIAL MUTUAL INS CO	OH	368.8
NATIONAL MORTGAGE INS CORP	WI	717.8
PROTECTIVE INS CO	IN	885.6
SECURIAN CASUALTY CO	MN	328.2
SENTRY SELECT INS CO	WI	826.6
TRAVELERS CASUALTY & SURETY CO	CT	16,983.8
TRAVELERS INDEMNITY CO	CT	21,394.5
UNITED SERVICES AUTOMOBILE ASN	TX	35,460.0
USAA CASUALTY INS CO	TX	10,897.7
Rating:	**B+**	
ALLIED WORLD SPECIALTY INS CO	DE	829.1
ALLSTATE INS CO	IL	48,302.5
AMERICAN AGRICULTURAL INS CO	IN	1,338.9
AMERICAN CONTRACTORS INDEMNITY CO	CA	338.3
AMICA MUTUAL INS CO	RI	5,384.6
ARCH SPECIALTY INS CO	MO	483.4
BROTHERHOOD MUTUAL INS CO	IN	644.9
CATERPILLAR INS CO	MO	790.6
CENTRAL MUTUAL INS CO	OH	1,618.4
CHURCH MUTUAL INS CO	WI	1,739.8
COVINGTON SPECIALTY INS CO	NH	97.9
ERIE & NIAGARA INS ASSN	NY	234.3
FARM FAMILY CASUALTY INS CO	NY	1,241.7
FEDERATED RURAL ELECTRIC INS EXCH	KS	553.2
FRANKENMUTH MUTUAL INS CO	MI	1,351.0
GEICO GENERAL INS CO	MD	167.6
GNY CUSTOM INS CO	AZ	60.5
HOUSING AUTHORITY PROP A MUTUAL CO	VT	181.9
ICI MUTUAL INS CO A RRG	VT	367.6
MARKEL GLOBAL REINS CO	DE	2,180.9
MERCHANTS NATIONAL INS CO	NH	136.0
MERCHANTS PREFERRED INS CO	NY	76.4
MERCURY CASUALTY CO	CA	1,877.6
MIDDLESEX INS CO	WI	764.3
NATIONAL CASUALTY CO	OH	418.6
NEW YORK SCHOOLS INS RECIPROCAL	NY	317.8

INSURANCE COMPANY NAME	DOM. STATE	TOTAL ASSETS ($MIL)
PREFERRED PROFESSIONAL INS CO	NE	327.4
ROCKINGHAM INS CO	VA	144.7
SENTRY CASUALTY CO	WI	355.9
STATE FARM FIRE & CAS CO	IL	39,411.9
STATE FARM MUTUAL AUTOMOBILE INS CO	IL	160,732.0
SURETEC INS CO	TX	253.2
TOA REINS CO OF AMERICA	DE	1,820.3
TRANS PACIFIC INS CO	NY	67.6
TRANSATLANTIC REINS CO	NY	14,732.2
UNITED EDUCATORS INS A RECIP RRG	VT	912.3
UNITED SPECIALTY INS CO	DE	330.2
USAA GENERAL INDEMNITY CO	TX	4,627.9

North Carolina

INSURANCE COMPANY NAME	DOM. STATE	TOTAL ASSETS ($MIL)
Rating: A+		
BERKSHIRE HATHAWAY ASR CORP	NY	2,223.5
Rating: A		
AUTO-OWNERS INS CO	MI	15,390.4
BUILDERS MUTUAL INS CO	NC	859.6
CINCINNATI INS CO	OH	12,914.9
CINCINNATI SPECIALTY UNDERWRITER	DE	820.6
OWNERS INS CO	OH	4,110.4
SENTRY INS A MUTUAL CO	WI	8,392.8
SOMPO AMERICA INSURANCE CO	NY	1,285.1
TOKIO MARINE AMERICA INS CO	NY	1,409.5
Rating: A-		
ALL AMERICA INS CO	OH	291.6
AMERICAN FAMILY MUTL INS CO SI	WI	17,157.4
CINCINNATI INDEMNITY CO	OH	133.0
COUNTRY MUTUAL INS CO	IL	4,850.2
CUMIS INS SOCIETY INC	IA	2,002.8
DAIRYLAND INS CO	WI	1,400.7
ENDURANCE ASR CORP	DE	2,059.0
ESSENT GUARANTY INC	PA	1,756.6
GEICO SECURE INS CO	NE	625.3
MITSUI SUMITOMO INS CO OF AMER	NY	975.8
MOTORISTS COMMERCIAL MUTUAL INS CO	OH	368.8
NATIONAL MORTGAGE INS CORP	WI	717.8
PROTECTIVE INS CO	IN	885.6
SECURIAN CASUALTY CO	MN	328.2
SENTRY SELECT INS CO	WI	826.6
TRAVELERS CASUALTY & SURETY CO	CT	16,983.8
TRAVELERS INDEMNITY CO	CT	21,394.5
UNITED SERVICES AUTOMOBILE ASN	TX	35,460.0
USAA CASUALTY INS CO	TX	10,897.7
Rating: B+		
ALLIED WORLD SPECIALTY INS CO	DE	829.1
ALLSTATE INS CO	IL	48,302.5
AMERICAN AGRICULTURAL INS CO	IN	1,338.9
AMERICAN NATIONAL PROPERTY & CAS CO	MO	1,418.0
AMERICAN STANDARD INS CO OF WI	WI	400.9
AMICA MUTUAL INS CO	RI	5,384.6
ANSUR AMERICA INS CO	MI	121.2
ARCH SPECIALTY INS CO	MO	483.4
BROTHERHOOD MUTUAL INS CO	IN	644.9
CATERPILLAR INS CO	MO	790.6
CENTRAL MUTUAL INS CO	OH	1,618.4
CHURCH MUTUAL INS CO	WI	1,739.8
COVINGTON SPECIALTY INS CO	NH	97.9
FARM BUREAU MUTUAL INS CO OF MI	MI	782.4
FEDERATED RURAL ELECTRIC INS EXCH	KS	553.2
FRANKENMUTH MUTUAL INS CO	MI	1,351.0
GEICO CHOICE INS CO	NE	1,134.6
GEICO GENERAL INS CO	MD	167.6
GNY CUSTOM INS CO	AZ	60.5
HOUSING AUTHORITY PROP A MUTUAL CO	VT	181.9
LION INS CO (FL)	FL	264.3
MARKEL GLOBAL REINS CO	DE	2,180.9

INSURANCE COMPANY NAME	DOM. STATE	TOTAL ASSETS ($MIL)
MERCHANTS NATIONAL INS CO	NH	136.0
MIDDLESEX INS CO	WI	764.3
NATIONAL CASUALTY CO	OH	418.6
PREFERRED PROFESSIONAL INS CO	NE	327.4
SELECTIVE AUTO INS CO OF NJ	NJ	380.7
SENTRY CASUALTY CO	WI	355.9
STATE FARM FIRE & CAS CO	IL	39,411.9
STATE FARM MUTUAL AUTOMOBILE INS CO	IL	160,732.0
STATE VOLUNTEER MUTUAL INS CO	TN	1,249.3
SURETEC INS CO	TX	253.2
TOA REINS CO OF AMERICA	DE	1,820.3
TRANS PACIFIC INS CO	NY	67.6
TRANSATLANTIC REINS CO	NY	14,732.2
UNITED EDUCATORS INS A RECIP RRG	VT	912.3
UNITED SPECIALTY INS CO	DE	330.2
USAA GENERAL INDEMNITY CO	TX	4,627.9

North Dakota

INSURANCE COMPANY NAME	DOM. STATE	TOTAL ASSETS ($MIL)
Rating: A+		
BERKSHIRE HATHAWAY ASR CORP	NY	2,223.5
Rating: A		
AUTO-OWNERS INS CO	MI	15,390.4
CINCINNATI INS CO	OH	12,914.9
CINCINNATI SPECIALTY UNDERWRITER	DE	820.6
HOME-OWNERS INS CO	MI	2,323.7
OWNERS INS CO	OH	4,110.4
SENTRY INS A MUTUAL CO	WI	8,392.8
SOMPO AMERICA INSURANCE CO	NY	1,285.1
TOKIO MARINE AMERICA INS CO	NY	1,409.5
Rating: A-		
ACUITY A MUTUAL INS CO	WI	3,960.1
AMERICAN FAMILY MUTL INS CO SI	WI	17,157.4
CINCINNATI INDEMNITY CO	OH	133.0
COUNTRY MUTUAL INS CO	IL	4,850.2
CUMIS INS SOCIETY INC	IA	2,002.8
DAIRYLAND INS CO	WI	1,400.7
ENDURANCE ASR CORP	DE	2,059.0
ESSENT GUARANTY INC	PA	1,756.6
MITSUI SUMITOMO INS CO OF AMER	NY	975.8
MOTORISTS COMMERCIAL MUTUAL INS CO	OH	368.8
NATIONAL MORTGAGE INS CORP	WI	717.8
PROPERTY-OWNERS INS CO	IN	302.7
PROTECTIVE INS CO	IN	885.6
SECURIAN CASUALTY CO	MN	328.2
SENTRY SELECT INS CO	WI	826.6
TRAVELERS CASUALTY & SURETY CO	CT	16,983.8
TRAVELERS INDEMNITY CO	CT	21,394.5
UNITED SERVICES AUTOMOBILE ASN	TX	35,460.0
USAA CASUALTY INS CO	TX	10,897.7
Rating: B+		
ALASKA NATIONAL INS CO	AK	1,004.7
ALLIED WORLD SPECIALTY INS CO	DE	829.1
ALLSTATE INS CO	IL	48,302.5
AMERICAN AGRICULTURAL INS CO	IN	1,338.9
AMERICAN CONTRACTORS INDEMNITY CO	CA	338.3
AMERICAN NATIONAL PROPERTY & CAS CO	MO	1,418.0
AMERICAN STANDARD INS CO OF WI	WI	400.9
AMICA MUTUAL INS CO	RI	5,384.6
ARCH SPECIALTY INS CO	MO	483.4
BROTHERHOOD MUTUAL INS CO	IN	644.9
CATERPILLAR INS CO	MO	790.6
CHURCH MUTUAL INS CO	WI	1,739.8
COPIC INS CO	CO	603.2
COVINGTON SPECIALTY INS CO	NH	97.9
FARM BUREAU MUTUAL INS CO OF MI	MI	782.4
FARMERS MUTUAL INS CO OF NE	NE	680.3
FEDERATED RURAL ELECTRIC INS EXCH	KS	553.2
FINANCIAL PACIFIC INS CO	CA	261.4
FRANKENMUTH MUTUAL INS CO	MI	1,351.0
GEICO GENERAL INS CO	MD	167.6
HOUSING AUTHORITY PROP A MUTUAL CO	VT	181.9
ICI MUTUAL INS CO A RRG	VT	367.6

INSURANCE COMPANY NAME	DOM. STATE	TOTAL ASSETS ($MIL)
MARKEL GLOBAL REINS CO	DE	2,180.9
MERCHANTS NATIONAL INS CO	NH	136.0
MIDDLESEX INS CO	WI	764.3
MMIC INS INC	MN	682.7
NATIONAL CASUALTY CO	OH	418.6
PREFERRED PROFESSIONAL INS CO	NE	327.4
SENTRY CASUALTY CO	WI	355.9
STATE FARM FIRE & CAS CO	IL	39,411.9
STATE FARM MUTUAL AUTOMOBILE INS CO	IL	160,732.0
SURETEC INS CO	TX	253.2
TOA REINS CO OF AMERICA	DE	1,820.3
TRANS PACIFIC INS CO	NY	67.6
TRANSATLANTIC REINS CO	NY	14,732.2
UNITED EDUCATORS INS A RECIP RRG	VT	912.3
UNITED SPECIALTY INS CO	DE	330.2
USAA GENERAL INDEMNITY CO	TX	4,627.9
WESTERN AGRICULTURAL INS CO	IA	213.2

Ohio

INSURANCE COMPANY NAME	DOM. STATE	TOTAL ASSETS ($MIL)
Rating: A+		
BERKSHIRE HATHAWAY ASR CORP	NY	2,223.5
Rating: A		
AUTO-OWNERS INS CO	MI	15,390.4
CINCINNATI INS CO	OH	12,914.9
CINCINNATI SPECIALTY UNDERWRITER	DE	820.6
HOME-OWNERS INS CO	MI	2,323.7
OWNERS INS CO	OH	4,110.4
SENTRY INS A MUTUAL CO	WI	8,392.8
SOMPO AMERICA INSURANCE CO	NY	1,285.1
TOKIO MARINE AMERICA INS CO	NY	1,409.5
Rating: A-		
ACUITY A MUTUAL INS CO	WI	3,960.1
ALL AMERICA INS CO	OH	291.6
AMERICAN FAMILY MUTL INS CO SI	WI	17,157.4
CINCINNATI INDEMNITY CO	OH	133.0
COUNTRY MUTUAL INS CO	IL	4,850.2
CUMIS INS SOCIETY INC	IA	2,002.8
DAIRYLAND INS CO	WI	1,400.7
ENDURANCE ASR CORP	DE	2,059.0
ESSENT GUARANTY INC	PA	1,756.6
GEICO SECURE INS CO	NE	625.3
MITSUI SUMITOMO INS CO OF AMER	NY	975.8
MOTORISTS COMMERCIAL MUTUAL INS CO	OH	368.8
NATIONAL MORTGAGE INS CORP	WI	717.8
PROTECTIVE INS CO	IN	885.6
SECURIAN CASUALTY CO	MN	328.2
SENTRY SELECT INS CO	WI	826.6
TRAVELERS CASUALTY & SURETY CO	CT	16,983.8
TRAVELERS INDEMNITY CO	CT	21,394.5
TREXIS ONE INSURANCE GROUP	VA	56.6
UNITED SERVICES AUTOMOBILE ASN	TX	35,460.0
USAA CASUALTY INS CO	TX	10,897.7
WEST BEND MUTUAL INS CO	WI	2,695.9
Rating: B+		
ALLIED WORLD SPECIALTY INS CO	DE	829.1
ALLSTATE INS CO	IL	48,302.5
AMERICAN AGRICULTURAL INS CO	IN	1,338.9
AMERICAN CONTRACTORS INDEMNITY CO	CA	338.3
AMERICAN NATIONAL PROPERTY & CAS CO	MO	1,418.0
AMERICAN STANDARD INS CO OF WI	WI	400.9
AMICA MUTUAL INS CO	RI	5,384.6
ANSUR AMERICA INS CO	MI	121.2
ARCH SPECIALTY INS CO	MO	483.4
BROTHERHOOD MUTUAL INS CO	IN	644.9
CATERPILLAR INS CO	MO	790.6
CENTRAL MUTUAL INS CO	OH	1,618.4
CHURCH MUTUAL INS CO	WI	1,739.8
COVINGTON SPECIALTY INS CO	NH	97.9
FARM BUREAU MUTUAL INS CO OF MI	MI	782.4
FARMERS AUTOMOBILE INS ASN	IL	1,226.6
FEDERATED RURAL ELECTRIC INS EXCH	KS	553.2
FRANKENMUTH MUTUAL INS CO	MI	1,351.0
GEICO CHOICE INS CO	NE	1,134.6

INSURANCE COMPANY NAME	DOM. STATE	TOTAL ASSETS ($MIL)
GEICO GENERAL INS CO	MD	167.6
GNY CUSTOM INS CO	AZ	60.5
HASTINGS MUTUAL INS CO	MI	932.1
HOUSING AUTHORITY PROP A MUTUAL CO	VT	181.9
ICI MUTUAL INS CO A RRG	VT	367.6
INTERINS EXCHANGE	CA	10,404.3
MARKEL GLOBAL REINS CO	DE	2,180.9
MERCHANTS NATIONAL INS CO	NH	136.0
MERCHANTS PREFERRED INS CO	NY	76.4
MIDDLESEX INS CO	WI	764.3
MMIC INS INC	MN	682.7
NATIONAL CASUALTY CO	OH	418.6
PEKIN INS CO	IL	305.4
PREFERRED PROFESSIONAL INS CO	NE	327.4
SENTRY CASUALTY CO	WI	355.9
STATE FARM FIRE & CAS CO	IL	39,411.9
STATE FARM MUTUAL AUTOMOBILE INS CO	IL	160,732.0
SURETEC INS CO	TX	253.2
TOA REINS CO OF AMERICA	DE	1,820.3
TRANS PACIFIC INS CO	NY	67.6
TRANSATLANTIC REINS CO	NY	14,732.2
TREXIS INSURANCE CORP	VA	108.1
UNITED EDUCATORS INS A RECIP RRG	VT	912.3
UNITED FARM FAMILY MUTUAL INS CO	IN	1,098.5
UNITED SPECIALTY INS CO	DE	330.2
USAA GENERAL INDEMNITY CO	TX	4,627.9
WESTERN AGRICULTURAL INS CO	IA	213.2

Oklahoma

INSURANCE COMPANY NAME	DOM. STATE	TOTAL ASSETS ($MIL)
Rating: A+		
BERKSHIRE HATHAWAY ASR CORP	NY	2,223.5
Rating: A		
CINCINNATI INS CO	OH	12,914.9
CINCINNATI SPECIALTY UNDERWRITER	DE	820.6
SENTRY INS A MUTUAL CO	WI	8,392.8
SOMPO AMERICA INSURANCE CO	NY	1,285.1
TOKIO MARINE AMERICA INS CO	NY	1,409.5
Rating: A-		
ACUITY A MUTUAL INS CO	WI	3,960.1
ALL AMERICA INS CO	OH	291.6
CINCINNATI INDEMNITY CO	OH	133.0
COUNTRY MUTUAL INS CO	IL	4,850.2
CUMIS INS SOCIETY INC	IA	2,002.8
EMPLOYERS COMPENSATION INS CO	CA	1,091.0
ENDURANCE ASR CORP	DE	2,059.0
ESSENT GUARANTY INC	PA	1,756.6
GEICO SECURE INS CO	NE	625.3
MITSUI SUMITOMO INS CO OF AMER	NY	975.8
MOTORISTS COMMERCIAL MUTUAL INS CO	OH	368.8
NATIONAL MORTGAGE INS CORP	WI	717.8
PROTECTIVE INS CO	IN	885.6
SECURIAN CASUALTY CO	MN	328.2
SENTRY SELECT INS CO	WI	826.6
TRAVELERS CASUALTY & SURETY CO	CT	16,983.8
TRAVELERS INDEMNITY CO	CT	21,394.5
UNITED SERVICES AUTOMOBILE ASN	TX	35,460.0
USAA CASUALTY INS CO	TX	10,897.7
Rating: B+		
ALASKA NATIONAL INS CO	AK	1,004.7
ALLIED WORLD SPECIALTY INS CO	DE	829.1
ALLSTATE INS CO	IL	48,302.5
AMERICAN AGRICULTURAL INS CO	IN	1,338.9
AMERICAN CONTRACTORS INDEMNITY CO	CA	338.3
AMERICAN NATIONAL PROPERTY & CAS CO	MO	1,418.0
AMICA MUTUAL INS CO	RI	5,384.6
ANSUR AMERICA INS CO	MI	121.2
ARCH SPECIALTY INS CO	MO	483.4
BROTHERHOOD MUTUAL INS CO	IN	644.9
CATERPILLAR INS CO	MO	790.6
CENTRAL MUTUAL INS CO	OH	1,618.4
CHURCH MUTUAL INS CO	WI	1,739.8
COPIC INS CO	CO	603.2
COVINGTON SPECIALTY INS CO	NH	97.9
FARM BUREAU MUTUAL INS CO OF MI	MI	782.4
FEDERATED RURAL ELECTRIC INS EXCH	KS	553.2
FINANCIAL PACIFIC INS CO	CA	261.4
FRANKENMUTH MUTUAL INS CO	MI	1,351.0
GEICO CHOICE INS CO	NE	1,134.6
GEICO GENERAL INS CO	MD	167.6
HOUSING AUTHORITY PROP A MUTUAL CO	VT	181.9
LION INS CO (FL)	FL	264.3
MARKEL GLOBAL REINS CO	DE	2,180.9
MERCURY CASUALTY CO	CA	1,877.6

INSURANCE COMPANY NAME	DOM. STATE	TOTAL ASSETS ($MIL)
MIDDLESEX INS CO	WI	764.3
NATIONAL CASUALTY CO	OH	418.6
PREFERRED PROFESSIONAL INS CO	NE	327.4
SENTRY CASUALTY CO	WI	355.9
SFM MUTUAL INS CO	MN	612.1
STATE FARM FIRE & CAS CO	IL	39,411.9
STATE FARM MUTUAL AUTOMOBILE INS CO	IL	160,732.0
SURETEC INS CO	TX	253.2
TOA REINS CO OF AMERICA	DE	1,820.3
TRANS PACIFIC INS CO	NY	67.6
TRANSATLANTIC REINS CO	NY	14,732.2
UNITED EDUCATORS INS A RECIP RRG	VT	912.3
UNITED SPECIALTY INS CO	DE	330.2
USAA GENERAL INDEMNITY CO	TX	4,627.9
WESTERN AGRICULTURAL INS CO	IA	213.2

Oregon

INSURANCE COMPANY NAME	DOM. STATE	TOTAL ASSETS ($MIL)
Rating:	**A+**	
BERKSHIRE HATHAWAY ASR CORP	NY	2,223.5
Rating:	**A**	
AUTO-OWNERS INS CO	MI	15,390.4
CINCINNATI INS CO	OH	12,914.9
CINCINNATI SPECIALTY UNDERWRITER	DE	820.6
OWNERS INS CO	OH	4,110.4
SENTRY INS A MUTUAL CO	WI	8,392.8
SOMPO AMERICA INSURANCE CO	NY	1,285.1
TOKIO MARINE AMERICA INS CO	NY	1,409.5
Rating:	**A-**	
ACUITY A MUTUAL INS CO	WI	3,960.1
ALL AMERICA INS CO	OH	291.6
AMERICAN FAMILY MUTL INS CO SI	WI	17,157.4
CINCINNATI INDEMNITY CO	OH	133.0
COUNTRY MUTUAL INS CO	IL	4,850.2
CUMIS INS SOCIETY INC	IA	2,002.8
DAIRYLAND INS CO	WI	1,400.7
EMPLOYERS COMPENSATION INS CO	CA	1,091.0
ENDURANCE ASR CORP	DE	2,059.0
ESSENT GUARANTY INC	PA	1,756.6
GEICO SECURE INS CO	NE	625.3
MITSUI SUMITOMO INS CO OF AMER	NY	975.8
MOTORISTS COMMERCIAL MUTUAL INS CO	OH	368.8
NATIONAL MORTGAGE INS CORP	WI	717.8
PROTECTIVE INS CO	IN	885.6
SECURIAN CASUALTY CO	MN	328.2
SENTRY SELECT INS CO	WI	826.6
TRAVELERS CASUALTY & SURETY CO	CT	16,983.8
TRAVELERS INDEMNITY CO	CT	21,394.5
UNITED SERVICES AUTOMOBILE ASN	TX	35,460.0
USAA CASUALTY INS CO	TX	10,897.7
Rating:	**B+**	
ALASKA NATIONAL INS CO	AK	1,004.7
ALLIED WORLD SPECIALTY INS CO	DE	829.1
ALLSTATE INS CO	IL	48,302.5
AMERICAN AGRICULTURAL INS CO	IN	1,338.9
AMERICAN CONTRACTORS INDEMNITY CO	CA	338.3
AMERICAN NATIONAL PROPERTY & CAS CO	MO	1,418.0
AMERICAN STANDARD INS CO OF WI	WI	400.9
AMICA MUTUAL INS CO	RI	5,384.6
ARCH SPECIALTY INS CO	MO	483.4
BROTHERHOOD MUTUAL INS CO	IN	644.9
CATERPILLAR INS CO	MO	790.6
CENTRAL MUTUAL INS CO	OH	1,618.4
CHURCH MUTUAL INS CO	WI	1,739.8
COPIC INS CO	CO	603.2
COVINGTON SPECIALTY INS CO	NH	97.9
FARM BUREAU MUTUAL INS CO OF MI	MI	782.4
FEDERATED RURAL ELECTRIC INS EXCH	KS	553.2
FINANCIAL PACIFIC INS CO	CA	261.4
FRANKENMUTH MUTUAL INS CO	MI	1,351.0
GEICO CHOICE INS CO	NE	1,134.6
GEICO GENERAL INS CO	MD	167.6

INSURANCE COMPANY NAME	DOM. STATE	TOTAL ASSETS ($MIL)
HOUSING AUTHORITY PROP A MUTUAL CO	VT	181.9
MARKEL GLOBAL REINS CO	DE	2,180.9
MERCHANTS NATIONAL INS CO	NH	136.0
MIDDLESEX INS CO	WI	764.3
MMIC INS INC	MN	682.7
MUTUAL OF ENUMCLAW INS CO	OR	748.3
NATIONAL CASUALTY CO	OH	418.6
PREFERRED PROFESSIONAL INS CO	NE	327.4
SENTRY CASUALTY CO	WI	355.9
STATE FARM FIRE & CAS CO	IL	39,411.9
STATE FARM MUTUAL AUTOMOBILE INS CO	IL	160,732.0
SURETEC INS CO	TX	253.2
TOA REINS CO OF AMERICA	DE	1,820.3
TRANS PACIFIC INS CO	NY	67.6
TRANSATLANTIC REINS CO	NY	14,732.2
UNITED EDUCATORS INS A RECIP RRG	VT	912.3
UNITED SPECIALTY INS CO	DE	330.2
USAA GENERAL INDEMNITY CO	TX	4,627.9

Pennsylvania

INSURANCE COMPANY NAME	DOM. STATE	TOTAL ASSETS ($MIL)
Rating: **A+**		
BERKSHIRE HATHAWAY ASR CORP	NY	2,223.5
Rating: **A**		
AUTO-OWNERS INS CO	MI	15,390.4
CINCINNATI INS CO	OH	12,914.9
CINCINNATI SPECIALTY UNDERWRITER	DE	820.6
HOME-OWNERS INS CO	MI	2,323.7
OWNERS INS CO	OH	4,110.4
SENTRY INS A MUTUAL CO	WI	8,392.8
SOMPO AMERICA INSURANCE CO	NY	1,285.1
TOKIO MARINE AMERICA INS CO	NY	1,409.5
Rating: **A-**		
ACUITY A MUTUAL INS CO	WI	3,960.1
ALLSTATE NJ INS CO	IL	2,485.7
CINCINNATI INDEMNITY CO	OH	133.0
COUNTRY MUTUAL INS CO	IL	4,850.2
CUMIS INS SOCIETY INC	IA	2,002.8
DAIRYLAND INS CO	WI	1,400.7
EMPLOYERS COMPENSATION INS CO	CA	1,091.0
ENDURANCE ASR CORP	DE	2,059.0
ESSENT GUARANTY INC	PA	1,756.6
GEICO SECURE INS CO	NE	625.3
MITSUI SUMITOMO INS CO OF AMER	NY	975.8
MOTORISTS COMMERCIAL MUTUAL INS CO	OH	368.8
NATIONAL MORTGAGE INS CORP	WI	717.8
PROTECTIVE INS CO	IN	885.6
RADIAN REINS INC	PA	704.2
SECURIAN CASUALTY CO	MN	328.2
SENTRY SELECT INS CO	WI	826.6
TRAVELERS CASUALTY & SURETY CO	CT	16,983.8
TRAVELERS INDEMNITY CO	CT	21,394.5
UNITED SERVICES AUTOMOBILE ASN	TX	35,460.0
USAA CASUALTY INS CO	TX	10,897.7
WEST BEND MUTUAL INS CO	WI	2,695.9
Rating: **B+**		
ALLIED WORLD SPECIALTY INS CO	DE	829.1
ALLSTATE INS CO	IL	48,302.5
AMERICAN AGRICULTURAL INS CO	IN	1,338.9
AMERICAN CONTRACTORS INDEMNITY CO	CA	338.3
AMERICAN NATIONAL PROPERTY & CAS CO	MO	1,418.0
AMICA MUTUAL INS CO	RI	5,384.6
ANSUR AMERICA INS CO	MI	121.2
ARCH SPECIALTY INS CO	MO	483.4
BROTHERHOOD MUTUAL INS CO	IN	644.9
CASTLE KEY INS CO	IL	362.5
CATERPILLAR INS CO	MO	790.6
CENTRAL MUTUAL INS CO	OH	1,618.4
CHURCH MUTUAL INS CO	WI	1,739.8
COVINGTON SPECIALTY INS CO	NH	97.9
FARM BUREAU MUTUAL INS CO OF MI	MI	782.4
FARM FAMILY CASUALTY INS CO	NY	1,241.7
FEDERATED RURAL ELECTRIC INS EXCH	KS	553.2
FRANKENMUTH MUTUAL INS CO	MI	1,351.0
GEICO CHOICE INS CO	NE	1,134.6

INSURANCE COMPANY NAME	DOM. STATE	TOTAL ASSETS ($MIL)
GEICO GENERAL INS CO	MD	167.6
GNY CUSTOM INS CO	AZ	60.5
HASTINGS MUTUAL INS CO	MI	932.1
HIGH POINT PREFERRED INS CO	NJ	310.0
HOUSING AUTHORITY PROP A MUTUAL CO	VT	181.9
ICI MUTUAL INS CO A RRG	VT	367.6
INTERINS EXCHANGE	CA	10,404.3
LACKAWANNA AMERICAN INS CO	PA	89.8
LION INS CO (FL)	FL	264.3
MARKEL GLOBAL REINS CO	DE	2,180.9
MERCHANTS NATIONAL INS CO	NH	136.0
MERCHANTS PREFERRED INS CO	NY	76.4
MERCURY CASUALTY CO	CA	1,877.6
MIDDLESEX INS CO	WI	764.3
NATIONAL CASUALTY CO	OH	418.6
PREFERRED PROFESSIONAL INS CO	NE	327.4
ROCKINGHAM INS CO	VA	144.7
SENTRY CASUALTY CO	WI	355.9
STATE FARM FIRE & CAS CO	IL	39,411.9
STATE FARM MUTUAL AUTOMOBILE INS CO	IL	160,732.0
SURETEC INS CO	TX	253.2
TOA REINS CO OF AMERICA	DE	1,820.3
TRANS PACIFIC INS CO	NY	67.6
TRANSATLANTIC REINS CO	NY	14,732.2
UNITED EDUCATORS INS A RECIP RRG	VT	912.3
UNITED SPECIALTY INS CO	DE	330.2
USAA GENERAL INDEMNITY CO	TX	4,627.9

Rhode Island

INSURANCE COMPANY NAME	DOM. STATE	TOTAL ASSETS ($MIL)
Rating: A+		
BERKSHIRE HATHAWAY ASR CORP	NY	2,223.5
Rating: A		
CINCINNATI INS CO	OH	12,914.9
CINCINNATI SPECIALTY UNDERWRITER	DE	820.6
SENTRY INS A MUTUAL CO	WI	8,392.8
SOMPO AMERICA INSURANCE CO	NY	1,285.1
TOKIO MARINE AMERICA INS CO	NY	1,409.5
Rating: A-		
CINCINNATI INDEMNITY CO	OH	133.0
COUNTRY MUTUAL INS CO	IL	4,850.2
CUMIS INS SOCIETY INC	IA	2,002.8
DAIRYLAND INS CO	WI	1,400.7
ENDURANCE ASR CORP	DE	2,059.0
ESSENT GUARANTY INC	PA	1,756.6
GEICO SECURE INS CO	NE	625.3
MITSUI SUMITOMO INS CO OF AMER	NY	975.8
MOTORISTS COMMERCIAL MUTUAL INS CO	OH	368.8
NATIONAL MORTGAGE INS CORP	WI	717.8
PROTECTIVE INS CO	IN	885.6
SECURIAN CASUALTY CO	MN	328.2
SENTRY SELECT INS CO	WI	826.6
TRAVELERS CASUALTY & SURETY CO	CT	16,983.8
TRAVELERS INDEMNITY CO	CT	21,394.5
UNITED SERVICES AUTOMOBILE ASN	TX	35,460.0
USAA CASUALTY INS CO	TX	10,897.7
Rating: B+		
ALLIED WORLD SPECIALTY INS CO	DE	829.1
ALLSTATE INS CO	IL	48,302.5
AMERICAN AGRICULTURAL INS CO	IN	1,338.9
AMERICAN CONTRACTORS INDEMNITY CO	CA	338.3
AMERICAN NATIONAL PROPERTY & CAS CO	MO	1,418.0
AMICA MUTUAL INS CO	RI	5,384.6
ARCH SPECIALTY INS CO	MO	483.4
BROTHERHOOD MUTUAL INS CO	IN	644.9
CATERPILLAR INS CO	MO	790.6
CHURCH MUTUAL INS CO	WI	1,739.8
COVINGTON SPECIALTY INS CO	NH	97.9
FARM BUREAU MUTUAL INS CO OF MI	MI	782.4
FARM FAMILY CASUALTY INS CO	NY	1,241.7
FRANKENMUTH MUTUAL INS CO	MI	1,351.0
GEICO CHOICE INS CO	NE	1,134.6
GEICO GENERAL INS CO	MD	167.6
HOUSING AUTHORITY PROP A MUTUAL CO	VT	181.9
INTERINS EXCHANGE	CA	10,404.3
LION INS CO (FL)	FL	264.3
MARKEL GLOBAL REINS CO	DE	2,180.9
MERCHANTS PREFERRED INS CO	NY	76.4
MIDDLESEX INS CO	WI	764.3
NATIONAL CASUALTY CO	OH	418.6
PREFERRED PROFESSIONAL INS CO	NE	327.4
SENTRY CASUALTY CO	WI	355.9
STATE FARM FIRE & CAS CO	IL	39,411.9
STATE FARM MUTUAL AUTOMOBILE INS CO	IL	160,732.0

INSURANCE COMPANY NAME	DOM. STATE	TOTAL ASSETS ($MIL)
SURETEC INS CO	TX	253.2
TOA REINS CO OF AMERICA	DE	1,820.3
TRANS PACIFIC INS CO	NY	67.6
TRANSATLANTIC REINS CO	NY	14,732.2
UNITED EDUCATORS INS A RECIP RRG	VT	912.3
UNITED SPECIALTY INS CO	DE	330.2
USAA GENERAL INDEMNITY CO	TX	4,627.9

South Carolina

INSURANCE COMPANY NAME	DOM. STATE	TOTAL ASSETS ($MIL)
Rating: A+		
BERKSHIRE HATHAWAY ASR CORP	NY	2,223.5
Rating: A		
AUTO-OWNERS INS CO	MI	15,390.4
BUILDERS MUTUAL INS CO	NC	859.6
CINCINNATI INS CO	OH	12,914.9
CINCINNATI SPECIALTY UNDERWRITER	DE	820.6
HOME-OWNERS INS CO	MI	2,323.7
OWNERS INS CO	OH	4,110.4
SENTRY INS A MUTUAL CO	WI	8,392.8
SOMPO AMERICA INSURANCE CO	NY	1,285.1
TOKIO MARINE AMERICA INS CO	NY	1,409.5
Rating: A-		
ALL AMERICA INS CO	OH	291.6
AMERICAN FAMILY MUTL INS CO SI	WI	17,157.4
CINCINNATI INDEMNITY CO	OH	133.0
COUNTRY MUTUAL INS CO	IL	4,850.2
CUMIS INS SOCIETY INC	IA	2,002.8
DAIRYLAND INS CO	WI	1,400.7
EMPLOYERS COMPENSATION INS CO	CA	1,091.0
ENDURANCE ASR CORP	DE	2,059.0
ESSENT GUARANTY INC	PA	1,756.6
GEICO SECURE INS CO	NE	625.3
MITSUI SUMITOMO INS CO OF AMER	NY	975.8
MOTORISTS COMMERCIAL MUTUAL INS CO	OH	368.8
NATIONAL MORTGAGE INS CORP	WI	717.8
PROPERTY-OWNERS INS CO	IN	302.7
PROTECTIVE INS CO	IN	885.6
SECURIAN CASUALTY CO	MN	328.2
SENTRY SELECT INS CO	WI	826.6
TRAVELERS CASUALTY & SURETY CO	CT	16,983.8
TRAVELERS INDEMNITY CO	CT	21,394.5
UNITED SERVICES AUTOMOBILE ASN	TX	35,460.0
USAA CASUALTY INS CO	TX	10,897.7
Rating: B+		
ALLIED WORLD SPECIALTY INS CO	DE	829.1
ALLSTATE INS CO	IL	48,302.5
AMERICAN AGRICULTURAL INS CO	IN	1,338.9
AMERICAN CONTRACTORS INDEMNITY CO	CA	338.3
AMERICAN NATIONAL PROPERTY & CAS CO	MO	1,418.0
AMERICAN STANDARD INS CO OF WI	WI	400.9
AMICA MUTUAL INS CO	RI	5,384.6
ANSUR AMERICA INS CO	MI	121.2
ARCH SPECIALTY INS CO	MO	483.4
BROTHERHOOD MUTUAL INS CO	IN	644.9
CATERPILLAR INS CO	MO	790.6
CENTRAL MUTUAL INS CO	OH	1,618.4
CHURCH MUTUAL INS CO	WI	1,739.8
COVINGTON SPECIALTY INS CO	NH	97.9
FARM BUREAU MUTUAL INS CO OF MI	MI	782.4
FEDERATED RURAL ELECTRIC INS EXCH	KS	553.2
FRANKENMUTH MUTUAL INS CO	MI	1,351.0
GEICO CHOICE INS CO	NE	1,134.6
GEICO GENERAL INS CO	MD	167.6

INSURANCE COMPANY NAME	DOM. STATE	TOTAL ASSETS ($MIL)
HOUSING AUTHORITY PROP A MUTUAL CO	VT	181.9
ICI MUTUAL INS CO A RRG	VT	367.6
LION INS CO (FL)	FL	264.3
MARKEL GLOBAL REINS CO	DE	2,180.9
MERCHANTS NATIONAL INS CO	NH	136.0
MIDDLESEX INS CO	WI	764.3
NATIONAL CASUALTY CO	OH	418.6
PREFERRED PROFESSIONAL INS CO	NE	327.4
SENTRY CASUALTY CO	WI	355.9
SOUTHERN FIDELITY INS CO	FL	196.7
STATE FARM FIRE & CAS CO	IL	39,411.9
STATE FARM MUTUAL AUTOMOBILE INS CO	IL	160,732.0
SURETEC INS CO	TX	253.2
TOA REINS CO OF AMERICA	DE	1,820.3
TRANS PACIFIC INS CO	NY	67.6
TRANSATLANTIC REINS CO	NY	14,732.2
UNITED EDUCATORS INS A RECIP RRG	VT	912.3
UNITED SPECIALTY INS CO	DE	330.2
USAA GENERAL INDEMNITY CO	TX	4,627.9
WESTERN AGRICULTURAL INS CO	IA	213.2

South Dakota

INSURANCE COMPANY NAME	DOM. STATE	TOTAL ASSETS ($MIL)
Rating: **A+**		
BERKSHIRE HATHAWAY ASR CORP	NY	2,223.5
Rating: **A**		
AUTO-OWNERS INS CO	MI	15,390.4
CINCINNATI INS CO	OH	12,914.9
CINCINNATI SPECIALTY UNDERWRITER	DE	820.6
HOME-OWNERS INS CO	MI	2,323.7
OWNERS INS CO	OH	4,110.4
SENTRY INS A MUTUAL CO	WI	8,392.8
SOMPO AMERICA INSURANCE CO	NY	1,285.1
TOKIO MARINE AMERICA INS CO	NY	1,409.5
Rating: **A-**		
ACUITY A MUTUAL INS CO	WI	3,960.1
AMERICAN FAMILY MUTL INS CO SI	WI	17,157.4
CINCINNATI INDEMNITY CO	OH	133.0
COUNTRY MUTUAL INS CO	IL	4,850.2
CUMIS INS SOCIETY INC	IA	2,002.8
DAIRYLAND INS CO	WI	1,400.7
EMPLOYERS COMPENSATION INS CO	CA	1,091.0
ENDURANCE ASR CORP	DE	2,059.0
ESSENT GUARANTY INC	PA	1,756.6
FARM BUREAU P&C INS CO	IA	2,532.4
MITSUI SUMITOMO INS CO OF AMER	NY	975.8
MOTORISTS COMMERCIAL MUTUAL INS CO	OH	368.8
NATIONAL MORTGAGE INS CORP	WI	717.8
PROPERTY-OWNERS INS CO	IN	302.7
PROTECTIVE INS CO	IN	885.6
SECURIAN CASUALTY CO	MN	328.2
SENTRY SELECT INS CO	WI	826.6
TRAVELERS CASUALTY & SURETY CO	CT	16,983.8
TRAVELERS INDEMNITY CO	CT	21,394.5
UNITED SERVICES AUTOMOBILE ASN	TX	35,460.0
USAA CASUALTY INS CO	TX	10,897.7
Rating: **B+**		
ALASKA NATIONAL INS CO	AK	1,004.7
ALLIED WORLD SPECIALTY INS CO	DE	829.1
ALLSTATE INS CO	IL	48,302.5
AMERICAN AGRICULTURAL INS CO	IN	1,338.9
AMERICAN CONTRACTORS INDEMNITY CO	CA	338.3
AMERICAN NATIONAL PROPERTY & CAS CO	MO	1,418.0
AMERICAN STANDARD INS CO OF WI	WI	400.9
AMICA MUTUAL INS CO	RI	5,384.6
ARCH SPECIALTY INS CO	MO	483.4
BROTHERHOOD MUTUAL INS CO	IN	644.9
CATERPILLAR INS CO	MO	790.6
CHURCH MUTUAL INS CO	WI	1,739.8
COPIC INS CO	CO	603.2
COVINGTON SPECIALTY INS CO	NH	97.9
FARM BUREAU MUTUAL INS CO OF MI	MI	782.4
FARMERS MUTUAL INS CO OF NE	NE	680.3
FEDERATED RURAL ELECTRIC INS EXCH	KS	553.2
FINANCIAL PACIFIC INS CO	CA	261.4
FRANKENMUTH MUTUAL INS CO	MI	1,351.0
GEICO GENERAL INS CO	MD	167.6

INSURANCE COMPANY NAME	DOM. STATE	TOTAL ASSETS ($MIL)
HOUSING AUTHORITY PROP A MUTUAL CO	VT	181.9
MARKEL GLOBAL REINS CO	DE	2,180.9
MERCHANTS NATIONAL INS CO	NH	136.0
MIDDLESEX INS CO	WI	764.3
MMIC INS INC	MN	682.7
NATIONAL CASUALTY CO	OH	418.6
PREFERRED PROFESSIONAL INS CO	NE	327.4
SENTRY CASUALTY CO	WI	355.9
SFM MUTUAL INS CO	MN	612.1
STATE FARM FIRE & CAS CO	IL	39,411.9
STATE FARM MUTUAL AUTOMOBILE INS CO	IL	160,732.0
SURETEC INS CO	TX	253.2
TOA REINS CO OF AMERICA	DE	1,820.3
TRANS PACIFIC INS CO	NY	67.6
TRANSATLANTIC REINS CO	NY	14,732.2
UNITED EDUCATORS INS A RECIP RRG	VT	912.3
UNITED SPECIALTY INS CO	DE	330.2
USAA GENERAL INDEMNITY CO	TX	4,627.9
WESTERN AGRICULTURAL INS CO	IA	213.2

Tennessee

INSURANCE COMPANY NAME	DOM. STATE	TOTAL ASSETS ($MIL)
Rating: A+		
BERKSHIRE HATHAWAY ASR CORP	NY	2,223.5
Rating: A		
AUTO-OWNERS INS CO	MI	15,390.4
BUILDERS MUTUAL INS CO	NC	859.6
CINCINNATI INS CO	OH	12,914.9
CINCINNATI SPECIALTY UNDERWRITER	DE	820.6
OWNERS INS CO	OH	4,110.4
SENTRY INS A MUTUAL CO	WI	8,392.8
SOMPO AMERICA INSURANCE CO	NY	1,285.1
TOKIO MARINE AMERICA INS CO	NY	1,409.5
Rating: A-		
ACUITY A MUTUAL INS CO	WI	3,960.1
ALL AMERICA INS CO	OH	291.6
AMERICAN FAMILY MUTL INS CO SI	WI	17,157.4
CINCINNATI INDEMNITY CO	OH	133.0
COUNTRY MUTUAL INS CO	IL	4,850.2
CUMIS INS SOCIETY INC	IA	2,002.8
DAIRYLAND INS CO	WI	1,400.7
EMPLOYERS COMPENSATION INS CO	CA	1,091.0
ENDURANCE ASR CORP	DE	2,059.0
ESSENT GUARANTY INC	PA	1,756.6
GEICO SECURE INS CO	NE	625.3
MITSUI SUMITOMO INS CO OF AMER	NY	975.8
MOTORISTS COMMERCIAL MUTUAL INS CO	OH	368.8
NATIONAL MORTGAGE INS CORP	WI	717.8
PROTECTIVE INS CO	IN	885.6
SECURIAN CASUALTY CO	MN	328.2
SENTRY SELECT INS CO	WI	826.6
TRAVELERS CASUALTY & SURETY CO	CT	16,983.8
TRAVELERS INDEMNITY CO	CT	21,394.5
TREXIS ONE INSURANCE GROUP	VA	56.6
UNITED SERVICES AUTOMOBILE ASN	TX	35,460.0
USAA CASUALTY INS CO	TX	10,897.7
WEST BEND MUTUAL INS CO	WI	2,695.9
Rating: B+		
ALLIED WORLD SPECIALTY INS CO	DE	829.1
ALLSTATE INS CO	IL	48,302.5
AMERICAN AGRICULTURAL INS CO	IN	1,338.9
AMERICAN CONTRACTORS INDEMNITY CO	CA	338.3
AMERICAN NATIONAL PROPERTY & CAS CO	MO	1,418.0
AMICA MUTUAL INS CO	RI	5,384.6
ANSUR AMERICA INS CO	MI	121.2
ARCH SPECIALTY INS CO	MO	483.4
BROTHERHOOD MUTUAL INS CO	IN	644.9
CATERPILLAR INS CO	MO	790.6
CENTRAL MUTUAL INS CO	OH	1,618.4
CHURCH MUTUAL INS CO	WI	1,739.8
COVINGTON SPECIALTY INS CO	NH	97.9
FARM BUREAU MUTUAL INS CO OF MI	MI	782.4
FEDERATED RURAL ELECTRIC INS EXCH	KS	553.2
FRANKENMUTH MUTUAL INS CO	MI	1,351.0
GEICO CHOICE INS CO	NE	1,134.6
GEICO GENERAL INS CO	MD	167.6

INSURANCE COMPANY NAME	DOM. STATE	TOTAL ASSETS ($MIL)
HASTINGS MUTUAL INS CO	MI	932.1
HOUSING AUTHORITY PROP A MUTUAL CO	VT	181.9
ICI MUTUAL INS CO A RRG	VT	367.6
LION INS CO (FL)	FL	264.3
MARKEL GLOBAL REINS CO	DE	2,180.9
MERCHANTS NATIONAL INS CO	NH	136.0
MIDDLESEX INS CO	WI	764.3
MMIC INS INC	MN	682.7
NATIONAL CASUALTY CO	OH	418.6
PREFERRED PROFESSIONAL INS CO	NE	327.4
SENTRY CASUALTY CO	WI	355.9
SFM MUTUAL INS CO	MN	612.1
STATE FARM FIRE & CAS CO	IL	39,411.9
STATE FARM MUTUAL AUTOMOBILE INS CO	IL	160,732.0
STATE VOLUNTEER MUTUAL INS CO	TN	1,249.3
SURETEC INS CO	TX	253.2
TENNESSEE FARMERS ASR CO	TN	1,505.8
TENNESSEE FARMERS MUTUAL INS CO	TN	3,084.6
TOA REINS CO OF AMERICA	DE	1,820.3
TRANS PACIFIC INS CO	NY	67.6
TRANSATLANTIC REINS CO	NY	14,732.2
TREXIS INSURANCE CORP	VA	108.1
UNITED EDUCATORS INS A RECIP RRG	VT	912.3
UNITED SPECIALTY INS CO	DE	330.2
USAA GENERAL INDEMNITY CO	TX	4,627.9
WESTERN AGRICULTURAL INS CO	IA	213.2

Texas

INSURANCE COMPANY NAME	DOM. STATE	TOTAL ASSETS ($MIL)
Rating: **A+**		
BERKSHIRE HATHAWAY ASR CORP	NY	2,223.5
OGLESBY REINS CO	IL	4,590.7
Rating: **A**		
CINCINNATI INS CO	OH	12,914.9
CINCINNATI SPECIALTY UNDERWRITER	DE	820.6
SENTRY INS A MUTUAL CO	WI	8,392.8
SOMPO AMERICA INSURANCE CO	NY	1,285.1
TOKIO MARINE AMERICA INS CO	NY	1,409.5
Rating: **A-**		
ACUITY A MUTUAL INS CO	WI	3,960.1
ALL AMERICA INS CO	OH	291.6
AMERICAN FAMILY MUTL INS CO SI	WI	17,157.4
CINCINNATI INDEMNITY CO	OH	133.0
COUNTRY MUTUAL INS CO	IL	4,850.2
CUMIS INS SOCIETY INC	IA	2,002.8
DAIRYLAND INS CO	WI	1,400.7
EMPLOYERS COMPENSATION INS CO	CA	1,091.0
ENDURANCE ASR CORP	DE	2,059.0
ESSENT GUARANTY INC	PA	1,756.6
GEICO SECURE INS CO	NE	625.3
MITSUI SUMITOMO INS CO OF AMER	NY	975.8
MOTORISTS COMMERCIAL MUTUAL INS CO	OH	368.8
NATIONAL MORTGAGE INS CORP	WI	717.8
PROTECTIVE INS CO	IN	885.6
SECURIAN CASUALTY CO	MN	328.2
SENTRY SELECT INS CO	WI	826.6
TEXAS FARM BUREAU CASUALTY INS CO	TX	1,252.3
TRAVELERS CASUALTY & SURETY CO	CT	16,983.8
TRAVELERS INDEMNITY CO	CT	21,394.5
TREXIS ONE INSURANCE GROUP	VA	56.6
UNITED SERVICES AUTOMOBILE ASN	TX	35,460.0
USAA CASUALTY INS CO	TX	10,897.7
Rating: **B+**		
ALASKA NATIONAL INS CO	AK	1,004.7
ALLIED WORLD SPECIALTY INS CO	DE	829.1
ALLSTATE INS CO	IL	48,302.5
AMERICAN AGRICULTURAL INS CO	IN	1,338.9
AMERICAN CONTRACTORS INDEMNITY CO	CA	338.3
AMERICAN INTERSTATE INS CO OF TX	TX	68.1
AMERICAN NATIONAL PROPERTY & CAS CO	MO	1,418.0
AMICA MUTUAL INS CO	RI	5,384.6
ARCH SPECIALTY INS CO	MO	483.4
AUTO CLUB INDEMNITY CO	TX	25.7
BROTHERHOOD MUTUAL INS CO	IN	644.9
CATERPILLAR INS CO	MO	790.6
CENTRAL MUTUAL INS CO	OH	1,618.4
CHURCH MUTUAL INS CO	WI	1,739.8
COPIC INS CO	CO	603.2
COVINGTON SPECIALTY INS CO	NH	97.9
FARM BUREAU MUTUAL INS CO OF MI	MI	782.4
FEDERATED RURAL ELECTRIC INS EXCH	KS	553.2
FINANCIAL PACIFIC INS CO	CA	261.4
FRANKENMUTH MUTUAL INS CO	MI	1,351.0

INSURANCE COMPANY NAME	DOM. STATE	TOTAL ASSETS ($MIL)
GEICO CHOICE INS CO	NE	1,134.6
GEICO GENERAL INS CO	MD	167.6
HOUSING AUTHORITY PROP A MUTUAL CO	VT	181.9
ICI MUTUAL INS CO A RRG	VT	367.6
INTERINS EXCHANGE	CA	10,404.3
LION INS CO (FL)	FL	264.3
LUBA CASUALTY INS CO	LA	228.7
MARKEL GLOBAL REINS CO	DE	2,180.9
MERCHANTS NATIONAL INS CO	NH	136.0
MERCURY CASUALTY CO	CA	1,877.6
MIDDLESEX INS CO	WI	764.3
NATIONAL CASUALTY CO	OH	418.6
PREFERRED PROFESSIONAL INS CO	NE	327.4
SENTRY CASUALTY CO	WI	355.9
STATE FARM FIRE & CAS CO	IL	39,411.9
STATE FARM MUTUAL AUTOMOBILE INS CO	IL	160,732.0
SURETEC INS CO	TX	253.2
TOA REINS CO OF AMERICA	DE	1,820.3
TRANS PACIFIC INS CO	NY	67.6
TRANSATLANTIC REINS CO	NY	14,732.2
TREXIS INSURANCE CORP	VA	108.1
UNITED EDUCATORS INS A RECIP RRG	VT	912.3
UNITED SPECIALTY INS CO	DE	330.2
USAA GENERAL INDEMNITY CO	TX	4,627.9
WESTERN AGRICULTURAL INS CO	IA	213.2

Utah

INSURANCE COMPANY NAME	DOM. STATE	TOTAL ASSETS ($MIL)
Rating:	**A+**	
BERKSHIRE HATHAWAY ASR CORP	NY	2,223.5
Rating:	**A**	
AUTO-OWNERS INS CO	MI	15,390.4
CINCINNATI INS CO	OH	12,914.9
CINCINNATI SPECIALTY UNDERWRITER	DE	820.6
HOME-OWNERS INS CO	MI	2,323.7
OWNERS INS CO	OH	4,110.4
SENTRY INS A MUTUAL CO	WI	8,392.8
SOMPO AMERICA INSURANCE CO	NY	1,285.1
TOKIO MARINE AMERICA INS CO	NY	1,409.5
Rating:	**A-**	
ACUITY A MUTUAL INS CO	WI	3,960.1
ALL AMERICA INS CO	OH	291.6
AMERICAN FAMILY MUTL INS CO SI	WI	17,157.4
CINCINNATI INDEMNITY CO	OH	133.0
COUNTRY MUTUAL INS CO	IL	4,850.2
CUMIS INS SOCIETY INC	IA	2,002.8
DAIRYLAND INS CO	WI	1,400.7
EMPLOYERS COMPENSATION INS CO	CA	1,091.0
ENDURANCE ASR CORP	DE	2,059.0
ESSENT GUARANTY INC	PA	1,756.6
FARM BUREAU P&C INS CO	IA	2,532.4
GEICO SECURE INS CO	NE	625.3
MITSUI SUMITOMO INS CO OF AMER	NY	975.8
MOTORISTS COMMERCIAL MUTUAL INS CO	OH	368.8
NATIONAL MORTGAGE INS CORP	WI	717.8
PROPERTY-OWNERS INS CO	IN	302.7
PROTECTIVE INS CO	IN	885.6
SECURIAN CASUALTY CO	MN	328.2
SENTRY SELECT INS CO	WI	826.6
TRAVELERS CASUALTY & SURETY CO	CT	16,983.8
TRAVELERS INDEMNITY CO	CT	21,394.5
UNITED SERVICES AUTOMOBILE ASN	TX	35,460.0
USAA CASUALTY INS CO	TX	10,897.7
Rating:	**B+**	
ALASKA NATIONAL INS CO	AK	1,004.7
ALLIED WORLD SPECIALTY INS CO	DE	829.1
ALLSTATE INS CO	IL	48,302.5
AMERICAN AGRICULTURAL INS CO	IN	1,338.9
AMERICAN CONTRACTORS INDEMNITY CO	CA	338.3
AMERICAN NATIONAL PROPERTY & CAS CO	MO	1,418.0
AMERICAN STANDARD INS CO OF WI	WI	400.9
AMICA MUTUAL INS CO	RI	5,384.6
ARCH SPECIALTY INS CO	MO	483.4
BROTHERHOOD MUTUAL INS CO	IN	644.9
CATERPILLAR INS CO	MO	790.6
CENTRAL MUTUAL INS CO	OH	1,618.4
CHURCH MUTUAL INS CO	WI	1,739.8
COPIC INS CO	CO	603.2
COVINGTON SPECIALTY INS CO	NH	97.9
FARM BUREAU MUTUAL INS CO OF MI	MI	782.4
FEDERATED RURAL ELECTRIC INS EXCH	KS	553.2
FINANCIAL PACIFIC INS CO	CA	261.4

INSURANCE COMPANY NAME	DOM. STATE	TOTAL ASSETS ($MIL)
FRANKENMUTH MUTUAL INS CO	MI	1,351.0
GEICO CHOICE INS CO	NE	1,134.6
GEICO GENERAL INS CO	MD	167.6
HOUSING AUTHORITY PROP A MUTUAL CO	VT	181.9
ICI MUTUAL INS CO A RRG	VT	367.6
MARKEL GLOBAL REINS CO	DE	2,180.9
MERCHANTS NATIONAL INS CO	NH	136.0
MIDDLESEX INS CO	WI	764.3
MMIC INS INC	MN	682.7
MUTUAL INS CO OF AZ	AZ	1,105.9
MUTUAL OF ENUMCLAW INS CO	OR	748.3
NATIONAL CASUALTY CO	OH	418.6
PREFERRED PROFESSIONAL INS CO	NE	327.4
SENTRY CASUALTY CO	WI	355.9
STATE FARM FIRE & CAS CO	IL	39,411.9
STATE FARM MUTUAL AUTOMOBILE INS CO	IL	160,732.0
SURETEC INS CO	TX	253.2
TOA REINS CO OF AMERICA	DE	1,820.3
TRANS PACIFIC INS CO	NY	67.6
TRANSATLANTIC REINS CO	NY	14,732.2
UNITED EDUCATORS INS A RECIP RRG	VT	912.3
UNITED SPECIALTY INS CO	DE	330.2
USAA GENERAL INDEMNITY CO	TX	4,627.9
WESTERN AGRICULTURAL INS CO	IA	213.2

Vermont

INSURANCE COMPANY NAME	DOM. STATE	TOTAL ASSETS ($MIL)
Rating: **A+**		
BERKSHIRE HATHAWAY ASR CORP	NY	2,223.5
Rating: **A**		
CINCINNATI INS CO	OH	12,914.9
CINCINNATI SPECIALTY UNDERWRITER	DE	820.6
SENTRY INS A MUTUAL CO	WI	8,392.8
SOMPO AMERICA INSURANCE CO	NY	1,285.1
TOKIO MARINE AMERICA INS CO	NY	1,409.5
Rating: **A-**		
ACUITY A MUTUAL INS CO	WI	3,960.1
ALL AMERICA INS CO	OH	291.6
CINCINNATI INDEMNITY CO	OH	133.0
COUNTRY MUTUAL INS CO	IL	4,850.2
CUMIS INS SOCIETY INC	IA	2,002.8
DAIRYLAND INS CO	WI	1,400.7
EMPLOYERS COMPENSATION INS CO	CA	1,091.0
ENDURANCE ASR CORP	DE	2,059.0
ESSENT GUARANTY INC	PA	1,756.6
MITSUI SUMITOMO INS CO OF AMER	NY	975.8
MOTORISTS COMMERCIAL MUTUAL INS CO	OH	368.8
NATIONAL MORTGAGE INS CORP	WI	717.8
PROTECTIVE INS CO	IN	885.6
SECURIAN CASUALTY CO	MN	328.2
SENTRY SELECT INS CO	WI	826.6
TRAVELERS CASUALTY & SURETY CO	CT	16,983.8
TRAVELERS INDEMNITY CO	CT	21,394.5
UNITED SERVICES AUTOMOBILE ASN	TX	35,460.0
USAA CASUALTY INS CO	TX	10,897.7
Rating: **B+**		
ALLIED WORLD SPECIALTY INS CO	DE	829.1
ALLSTATE INS CO	IL	48,302.5
AMERICAN AGRICULTURAL INS CO	IN	1,338.9
AMERICAN NATIONAL PROPERTY & CAS CO	MO	1,418.0
AMICA MUTUAL INS CO	RI	5,384.6
ANSUR AMERICA INS CO	MI	121.2
ARCH SPECIALTY INS CO	MO	483.4
BROTHERHOOD MUTUAL INS CO	IN	644.9
CATERPILLAR INS CO	MO	790.6
CENTRAL MUTUAL INS CO	OH	1,618.4
CHURCH MUTUAL INS CO	WI	1,739.8
COVINGTON SPECIALTY INS CO	NH	97.9
FARM BUREAU MUTUAL INS CO OF MI	MI	782.4
FARM FAMILY CASUALTY INS CO	NY	1,241.7
FEDERATED RURAL ELECTRIC INS EXCH	KS	553.2
FRANKENMUTH MUTUAL INS CO	MI	1,351.0
GEICO GENERAL INS CO	MD	167.6
GNY CUSTOM INS CO	AZ	60.5
HOUSING AUTHORITY PROP A MUTUAL CO	VT	181.9
ICI MUTUAL INS CO A RRG	VT	367.6
INTERINS EXCHANGE	CA	10,404.3
MARKEL GLOBAL REINS CO	DE	2,180.9
MERCHANTS NATIONAL INS CO	NH	136.0
MERCHANTS PREFERRED INS CO	NY	76.4
MIDDLESEX INS CO	WI	764.3

INSURANCE COMPANY NAME	DOM. STATE	TOTAL ASSETS ($MIL)
NATIONAL CASUALTY CO	OH	418.6
PREFERRED PROFESSIONAL INS CO	NE	327.4
SENTRY CASUALTY CO	WI	355.9
STATE FARM FIRE & CAS CO	IL	39,411.9
STATE FARM MUTUAL AUTOMOBILE INS CO	IL	160,732.0
SURETEC INS CO	TX	253.2
TOA REINS CO OF AMERICA	DE	1,820.3
TRANSATLANTIC REINS CO	NY	14,732.2
UNITED EDUCATORS INS A RECIP RRG	VT	912.3
UNITED SPECIALTY INS CO	DE	330.2
USAA GENERAL INDEMNITY CO	TX	4,627.9

Virginia

INSURANCE COMPANY NAME	DOM. STATE	TOTAL ASSETS ($MIL)
Rating: A+		
BERKSHIRE HATHAWAY ASR CORP	NY	2,223.5
Rating: A		
AUTO-OWNERS INS CO	MI	15,390.4
BUILDERS MUTUAL INS CO	NC	859.6
CINCINNATI INS CO	OH	12,914.9
CINCINNATI SPECIALTY UNDERWRITER	DE	820.6
HOME-OWNERS INS CO	MI	2,323.7
OWNERS INS CO	OH	4,110.4
SENTRY INS A MUTUAL CO	WI	8,392.8
SOMPO AMERICA INSURANCE CO	NY	1,285.1
TOKIO MARINE AMERICA INS CO	NY	1,409.5
Rating: A-		
ACUITY A MUTUAL INS CO	WI	3,960.1
ALL AMERICA INS CO	OH	291.6
AMERICAN FAMILY MUTL INS CO SI	WI	17,157.4
CINCINNATI INDEMNITY CO	OH	133.0
COUNTRY MUTUAL INS CO	IL	4,850.2
CUMIS INS SOCIETY INC	IA	2,002.8
DAIRYLAND INS CO	WI	1,400.7
EMPLOYERS COMPENSATION INS CO	CA	1,091.0
ENDURANCE ASR CORP	DE	2,059.0
ESSENT GUARANTY INC	PA	1,756.6
GEICO SECURE INS CO	NE	625.3
MITSUI SUMITOMO INS CO OF AMER	NY	975.8
MOTORISTS COMMERCIAL MUTUAL INS CO	OH	368.8
NATIONAL MORTGAGE INS CORP	WI	717.8
PROPERTY-OWNERS INS CO	IN	302.7
PROTECTIVE INS CO	IN	885.6
SECURIAN CASUALTY CO	MN	328.2
SENTRY SELECT INS CO	WI	826.6
TRAVELERS CASUALTY & SURETY CO	CT	16,983.8
TRAVELERS INDEMNITY CO	CT	21,394.5
TREXIS ONE INSURANCE GROUP	VA	56.6
UNITED SERVICES AUTOMOBILE ASN	TX	35,460.0
USAA CASUALTY INS CO	TX	10,897.7
Rating: B+		
ALFA MUTUAL FIRE INS CO	AL	770.4
ALLIED WORLD SPECIALTY INS CO	DE	829.1
ALLSTATE INS CO	IL	48,302.5
AMERICAN AGRICULTURAL INS CO	IN	1,338.9
AMERICAN CONTRACTORS INDEMNITY CO	CA	338.3
AMERICAN NATIONAL PROPERTY & CAS CO	MO	1,418.0
AMICA MUTUAL INS CO	RI	5,384.6
ANSUR AMERICA INS CO	MI	121.2
ARCH SPECIALTY INS CO	MO	483.4
BROTHERHOOD MUTUAL INS CO	IN	644.9
CATERPILLAR INS CO	MO	790.6
CENTRAL MUTUAL INS CO	OH	1,618.4
CHURCH MUTUAL INS CO	WI	1,739.8
COVINGTON SPECIALTY INS CO	NH	97.9
FARM BUREAU MUTUAL INS CO OF MI	MI	782.4
FARM FAMILY CASUALTY INS CO	NY	1,241.7
FEDERATED RURAL ELECTRIC INS EXCH	KS	553.2

INSURANCE COMPANY NAME	DOM. STATE	TOTAL ASSETS ($MIL)
FRANKENMUTH MUTUAL INS CO	MI	1,351.0
GEICO CHOICE INS CO	NE	1,134.6
GEICO GENERAL INS CO	MD	167.6
GNY CUSTOM INS CO	AZ	60.5
HOUSING AUTHORITY PROP A MUTUAL CO	VT	181.9
ICI MUTUAL INS CO A RRG	VT	367.6
INTERINS EXCHANGE	CA	10,404.3
LION INS CO (FL)	FL	264.3
MARKEL GLOBAL REINS CO	DE	2,180.9
MERCHANTS NATIONAL INS CO	NH	136.0
MERCURY CASUALTY CO	CA	1,877.6
MIDDLESEX INS CO	WI	764.3
NATIONAL CASUALTY CO	OH	418.6
PREFERRED PROFESSIONAL INS CO	NE	327.4
ROCKINGHAM INS CO	VA	144.7
SENTRY CASUALTY CO	WI	355.9
STATE FARM FIRE & CAS CO	IL	39,411.9
STATE FARM MUTUAL AUTOMOBILE INS CO	IL	160,732.0
STATE VOLUNTEER MUTUAL INS CO	TN	1,249.3
SURETEC INS CO	TX	253.2
TOA REINS CO OF AMERICA	DE	1,820.3
TRANS PACIFIC INS CO	NY	67.6
TRANSATLANTIC REINS CO	NY	14,732.2
TREXIS INSURANCE CORP	VA	108.1
UNITED EDUCATORS INS A RECIP RRG	VT	912.3
UNITED SPECIALTY INS CO	DE	330.2
USAA GENERAL INDEMNITY CO	TX	4,627.9
WESTERN AGRICULTURAL INS CO	IA	213.2

Washington

INSURANCE COMPANY NAME	DOM. STATE	TOTAL ASSETS ($MIL)
Rating: A+		
BERKSHIRE HATHAWAY ASR CORP	NY	2,223.5
Rating: A		
AUTO-OWNERS INS CO	MI	15,390.4
CINCINNATI INS CO	OH	12,914.9
CINCINNATI SPECIALTY UNDERWRITER	DE	820.6
OWNERS INS CO	OH	4,110.4
SENTRY INS A MUTUAL CO	WI	8,392.8
SOMPO AMERICA INSURANCE CO	NY	1,285.1
TOKIO MARINE AMERICA INS CO	NY	1,409.5
Rating: A-		
ACUITY A MUTUAL INS CO	WI	3,960.1
ALL AMERICA INS CO	OH	291.6
AMERICAN FAMILY MUTL INS CO SI	WI	17,157.4
CINCINNATI INDEMNITY CO	OH	133.0
COUNTRY MUTUAL INS CO	IL	4,850.2
CUMIS INS SOCIETY INC	IA	2,002.8
DAIRYLAND INS CO	WI	1,400.7
ENDURANCE ASR CORP	DE	2,059.0
ESSENT GUARANTY INC	PA	1,756.6
GEICO SECURE INS CO	NE	625.3
MITSUI SUMITOMO INS CO OF AMER	NY	975.8
MOTORISTS COMMERCIAL MUTUAL INS CO	OH	368.8
NATIONAL MORTGAGE INS CORP	WI	717.8
PROTECTIVE INS CO	IN	885.6
SECURIAN CASUALTY CO	MN	328.2
SENTRY SELECT INS CO	WI	826.6
TRAVELERS CASUALTY & SURETY CO	CT	16,983.8
TRAVELERS INDEMNITY CO	CT	21,394.5
UNITED SERVICES AUTOMOBILE ASN	TX	35,460.0
USAA CASUALTY INS CO	TX	10,897.7
Rating: B+		
ALASKA NATIONAL INS CO	AK	1,004.7
ALLIED WORLD SPECIALTY INS CO	DE	829.1
ALLSTATE INS CO	IL	48,302.5
AMERICAN AGRICULTURAL INS CO	IN	1,338.9
AMERICAN CONTRACTORS INDEMNITY CO	CA	338.3
AMERICAN NATIONAL PROPERTY & CAS CO	MO	1,418.0
AMERICAN STANDARD INS CO OF WI	WI	400.9
AMICA MUTUAL INS CO	RI	5,384.6
ANSUR AMERICA INS CO	MI	121.2
ARCH SPECIALTY INS CO	MO	483.4
BROTHERHOOD MUTUAL INS CO	IN	644.9
CATERPILLAR INS CO	MO	790.6
CENTRAL MUTUAL INS CO	OH	1,618.4
CHURCH MUTUAL INS CO	WI	1,739.8
COVINGTON SPECIALTY INS CO	NH	97.9
FEDERATED RURAL ELECTRIC INS EXCH	KS	553.2
FINANCIAL PACIFIC INS CO	CA	261.4
FRANKENMUTH MUTUAL INS CO	MI	1,351.0
GEICO CHOICE INS CO	NE	1,134.6
GEICO GENERAL INS CO	MD	167.6
HOUSING AUTHORITY PROP A MUTUAL CO	VT	181.9
ICI MUTUAL INS CO A RRG	VT	367.6

INSURANCE COMPANY NAME	DOM. STATE	TOTAL ASSETS ($MIL)
MARKEL GLOBAL REINS CO	DE	2,180.9
MERCHANTS NATIONAL INS CO	NH	136.0
MERCURY CASUALTY CO	CA	1,877.6
MIDDLESEX INS CO	WI	764.3
MMIC INS INC	MN	682.7
MUTUAL OF ENUMCLAW INS CO	OR	748.3
NATIONAL CASUALTY CO	OH	418.6
PREFERRED PROFESSIONAL INS CO	NE	327.4
SENTRY CASUALTY CO	WI	355.9
STATE FARM FIRE & CAS CO	IL	39,411.9
STATE FARM MUTUAL AUTOMOBILE INS CO	IL	160,732.0
SURETEC INS CO	TX	253.2
TOA REINS CO OF AMERICA	DE	1,820.3
TRANS PACIFIC INS CO	NY	67.6
TRANSATLANTIC REINS CO	NY	14,732.2
UNITED EDUCATORS INS A RECIP RRG	VT	912.3
UNITED SPECIALTY INS CO	DE	330.2
USAA GENERAL INDEMNITY CO	TX	4,627.9

West Virginia

INSURANCE COMPANY NAME	DOM. STATE	TOTAL ASSETS ($MIL)
Rating: A+		
BERKSHIRE HATHAWAY ASR CORP	NY	2,223.5
Rating: A		
CINCINNATI INS CO	OH	12,914.9
CINCINNATI SPECIALTY UNDERWRITER	DE	820.6
SENTRY INS A MUTUAL CO	WI	8,392.8
SOMPO AMERICA INSURANCE CO	NY	1,285.1
TOKIO MARINE AMERICA INS CO	NY	1,409.5
Rating: A-		
ACUITY A MUTUAL INS CO	WI	3,960.1
CINCINNATI INDEMNITY CO	OH	133.0
COUNTRY MUTUAL INS CO	IL	4,850.2
CUMIS INS SOCIETY INC	IA	2,002.8
DAIRYLAND INS CO	WI	1,400.7
EMPLOYERS COMPENSATION INS CO	CA	1,091.0
ENDURANCE ASR CORP	DE	2,059.0
ESSENT GUARANTY INC	PA	1,756.6
GEICO SECURE INS CO	NE	625.3
MITSUI SUMITOMO INS CO OF AMER	NY	975.8
MOTORISTS COMMERCIAL MUTUAL INS CO	OH	368.8
NATIONAL MORTGAGE INS CORP	WI	717.8
PROTECTIVE INS CO	IN	885.6
SECURIAN CASUALTY CO	MN	328.2
SENTRY SELECT INS CO	WI	826.6
TRAVELERS CASUALTY & SURETY CO	CT	16,983.8
TRAVELERS INDEMNITY CO	CT	21,394.5
UNITED SERVICES AUTOMOBILE ASN	TX	35,460.0
USAA CASUALTY INS CO	TX	10,897.7
Rating: B+		
ALLIED WORLD SPECIALTY INS CO	DE	829.1
ALLSTATE INS CO	IL	48,302.5
AMERICAN AGRICULTURAL INS CO	IN	1,338.9
AMERICAN CONTRACTORS INDEMNITY CO	CA	338.3
AMERICAN NATIONAL PROPERTY & CAS CO	MO	1,418.0
AMICA MUTUAL INS CO	RI	5,384.6
ANSUR AMERICA INS CO	MI	121.2
ARCH SPECIALTY INS CO	MO	483.4
BROTHERHOOD MUTUAL INS CO	IN	644.9
CATERPILLAR INS CO	MO	790.6
CHURCH MUTUAL INS CO	WI	1,739.8
COVINGTON SPECIALTY INS CO	NH	97.9
FARM BUREAU MUTUAL INS CO OF MI	MI	782.4
FARM FAMILY CASUALTY INS CO	NY	1,241.7
FEDERATED RURAL ELECTRIC INS EXCH	KS	553.2
FRANKENMUTH MUTUAL INS CO	MI	1,351.0
GEICO CHOICE INS CO	NE	1,134.6
GEICO GENERAL INS CO	MD	167.6
HOUSING AUTHORITY PROP A MUTUAL CO	VT	181.9
MARKEL GLOBAL REINS CO	DE	2,180.9
MERCHANTS NATIONAL INS CO	NH	136.0
MIDDLESEX INS CO	WI	764.3
NATIONAL CASUALTY CO	OH	418.6
PREFERRED PROFESSIONAL INS CO	NE	327.4
SENTRY CASUALTY CO	WI	355.9

INSURANCE COMPANY NAME	DOM. STATE	TOTAL ASSETS ($MIL)
STATE FARM FIRE & CAS CO	IL	39,411.9
STATE FARM MUTUAL AUTOMOBILE INS CO	IL	160,732.0
SURETEC INS CO	TX	253.2
TOA REINS CO OF AMERICA	DE	1,820.3
TRANS PACIFIC INS CO	NY	67.6
TRANSATLANTIC REINS CO	NY	14,732.2
UNITED EDUCATORS INS A RECIP RRG	VT	912.3
UNITED SPECIALTY INS CO	DE	330.2
USAA GENERAL INDEMNITY CO	TX	4,627.9

Wisconsin

INSURANCE COMPANY NAME	DOM. STATE	TOTAL ASSETS ($MIL)
Rating: A+		
BERKSHIRE HATHAWAY ASR CORP	NY	2,223.5
Rating: A		
AUTO-OWNERS INS CO	MI	15,390.4
BUILDERS MUTUAL INS CO	NC	859.6
CINCINNATI INS CO	OH	12,914.9
CINCINNATI SPECIALTY UNDERWRITER	DE	820.6
HOME-OWNERS INS CO	MI	2,323.7
OWNERS INS CO	OH	4,110.4
SENTRY INS A MUTUAL CO	WI	8,392.8
SOMPO AMERICA INSURANCE CO	NY	1,285.1
TOKIO MARINE AMERICA INS CO	NY	1,409.5
Rating: A-		
ACUITY A MUTUAL INS CO	WI	3,960.1
ALL AMERICA INS CO	OH	291.6
AMERICAN FAMILY MUTL INS CO SI	WI	17,157.4
CINCINNATI INDEMNITY CO	OH	133.0
COUNTRY MUTUAL INS CO	IL	4,850.2
CUMIS INS SOCIETY INC	IA	2,002.8
DAIRYLAND INS CO	WI	1,400.7
EMPLOYERS COMPENSATION INS CO	CA	1,091.0
ENDURANCE ASR CORP	DE	2,059.0
ESSENT GUARANTY INC	PA	1,756.6
FARM BUREAU P&C INS CO	IA	2,532.4
GEICO SECURE INS CO	NE	625.3
MITSUI SUMITOMO INS CO OF AMER	NY	975.8
MOTORISTS COMMERCIAL MUTUAL INS CO	OH	368.8
NATIONAL MORTGAGE INS CORP	WI	717.8
PROPERTY-OWNERS INS CO	IN	302.7
PROTECTIVE INS CO	IN	885.6
SECURIAN CASUALTY CO	MN	328.2
SENTRY SELECT INS CO	WI	826.6
TRAVELERS CASUALTY & SURETY CO	CT	16,983.8
TRAVELERS INDEMNITY CO	CT	21,394.5
UNITED SERVICES AUTOMOBILE ASN	TX	35,460.0
USAA CASUALTY INS CO	TX	10,897.7
WEST BEND MUTUAL INS CO	WI	2,695.9
Rating: B+		
ALLIED WORLD SPECIALTY INS CO	DE	829.1
ALLSTATE INS CO	IL	48,302.5
AMERICAN AGRICULTURAL INS CO	IN	1,338.9
AMERICAN CONTRACTORS INDEMNITY CO	CA	338.3
AMERICAN NATIONAL PROPERTY & CAS CO	MO	1,418.0
AMERICAN STANDARD INS CO OF WI	WI	400.9
AMICA MUTUAL INS CO	RI	5,384.6
ANSUR AMERICA INS CO	MI	121.2
ARCH SPECIALTY INS CO	MO	483.4
BROTHERHOOD MUTUAL INS CO	IN	644.9
CATERPILLAR INS CO	MO	790.6
CENTRAL MUTUAL INS CO	OH	1,618.4
CHURCH MUTUAL INS CO	WI	1,739.8
COPIC INS CO	CO	603.2
COVINGTON SPECIALTY INS CO	NH	97.9
FARM BUREAU MUTUAL INS CO OF MI	MI	782.4

INSURANCE COMPANY NAME	DOM. STATE	TOTAL ASSETS ($MIL)
FARMERS AUTOMOBILE INS ASN	IL	1,226.6
FEDERATED RURAL ELECTRIC INS EXCH	KS	553.2
FINANCIAL PACIFIC INS CO	CA	261.4
FRANKENMUTH MUTUAL INS CO	MI	1,351.0
GEICO CHOICE INS CO	NE	1,134.6
GEICO GENERAL INS CO	MD	167.6
HASTINGS MUTUAL INS CO	MI	932.1
HOUSING AUTHORITY PROP A MUTUAL CO	VT	181.9
ICI MUTUAL INS CO A RRG	VT	367.6
MARKEL GLOBAL REINS CO	DE	2,180.9
MERCHANTS NATIONAL INS CO	NH	136.0
MIDDLESEX INS CO	WI	764.3
MMIC INS INC	MN	682.7
NATIONAL CASUALTY CO	OH	418.6
PEKIN INS CO	IL	305.4
PREFERRED PROFESSIONAL INS CO	NE	327.4
SENTRY CASUALTY CO	WI	355.9
SFM MUTUAL INS CO	MN	612.1
STATE FARM FIRE & CAS CO	IL	39,411.9
STATE FARM MUTUAL AUTOMOBILE INS CO	IL	160,732.0
SURETEC INS CO	TX	253.2
TOA REINS CO OF AMERICA	DE	1,820.3
TRANS PACIFIC INS CO	NY	67.6
TRANSATLANTIC REINS CO	NY	14,732.2
UNITED EDUCATORS INS A RECIP RRG	VT	912.3
UNITED SPECIALTY INS CO	DE	330.2
USAA GENERAL INDEMNITY CO	TX	4,627.9
WESTERN AGRICULTURAL INS CO	IA	213.2

Wyoming

INSURANCE COMPANY NAME	DOM. STATE	TOTAL ASSETS ($MIL)
Rating:	**A+**	
BERKSHIRE HATHAWAY ASR CORP	NY	2,223.5
Rating:	**A**	
CINCINNATI INS CO	OH	12,914.9
CINCINNATI SPECIALTY UNDERWRITER	DE	820.6
SENTRY INS A MUTUAL CO	WI	8,392.8
SOMPO AMERICA INSURANCE CO	NY	1,285.1
TOKIO MARINE AMERICA INS CO	NY	1,409.5
Rating:	**A-**	
ACUITY A MUTUAL INS CO	WI	3,960.1
AMERICAN FAMILY MUTL INS CO SI	WI	17,157.4
CINCINNATI INDEMNITY CO	OH	133.0
COUNTRY MUTUAL INS CO	IL	4,850.2
CUMIS INS SOCIETY INC	IA	2,002.8
DAIRYLAND INS CO	WI	1,400.7
ENDURANCE ASR CORP	DE	2,059.0
ESSENT GUARANTY INC	PA	1,756.6
GEICO SECURE INS CO	NE	625.3
MITSUI SUMITOMO INS CO OF AMER	NY	975.8
MOTORISTS COMMERCIAL MUTUAL INS CO	OH	368.8
NATIONAL MORTGAGE INS CORP	WI	717.8
PROTECTIVE INS CO	IN	885.6
SECURIAN CASUALTY CO	MN	328.2
SENTRY SELECT INS CO	WI	826.6
TRAVELERS CASUALTY & SURETY CO	CT	16,983.8
TRAVELERS INDEMNITY CO	CT	21,394.5
UNITED SERVICES AUTOMOBILE ASN	TX	35,460.0
USAA CASUALTY INS CO	TX	10,897.7
Rating:	**B+**	
ALASKA NATIONAL INS CO	AK	1,004.7
ALLIED WORLD SPECIALTY INS CO	DE	829.1
ALLSTATE INS CO	IL	48,302.5
AMERICAN AGRICULTURAL INS CO	IN	1,338.9
AMERICAN CONTRACTORS INDEMNITY CO	CA	338.3
AMERICAN NATIONAL PROPERTY & CAS CO	MO	1,418.0
AMERICAN STANDARD INS CO OF WI	WI	400.9
AMICA MUTUAL INS CO	RI	5,384.6
ANSUR AMERICA INS CO	MI	121.2
ARCH SPECIALTY INS CO	MO	483.4
BROTHERHOOD MUTUAL INS CO	IN	644.9
CATERPILLAR INS CO	MO	790.6
CHURCH MUTUAL INS CO	WI	1,739.8
COPIC INS CO	CO	603.2
COVINGTON SPECIALTY INS CO	NH	97.9
FEDERATED RURAL ELECTRIC INS EXCH	KS	553.2
FRANKENMUTH MUTUAL INS CO	MI	1,351.0
GEICO CHOICE INS CO	NE	1,134.6
GEICO GENERAL INS CO	MD	167.6
HOUSING AUTHORITY PROP A MUTUAL CO	VT	181.9
MARKEL GLOBAL REINS CO	DE	2,180.9
MERCHANTS NATIONAL INS CO	NH	136.0
MIDDLESEX INS CO	WI	764.3
MMIC INS INC	MN	682.7
NATIONAL CASUALTY CO	OH	418.6

INSURANCE COMPANY NAME	DOM. STATE	TOTAL ASSETS ($MIL)
PREFERRED PROFESSIONAL INS CO	NE	327.4
SENTRY CASUALTY CO	WI	355.9
STATE FARM FIRE & CAS CO	IL	39,411.9
STATE FARM MUTUAL AUTOMOBILE INS CO	IL	160,732.0
SURETEC INS CO	TX	253.2
TOA REINS CO OF AMERICA	DE	1,820.3
TRANS PACIFIC INS CO	NY	67.6
TRANSATLANTIC REINS CO	NY	14,732.2
UNITED EDUCATORS INS A RECIP RRG	VT	912.3
UNITED SPECIALTY INS CO	DE	330.2
USAA GENERAL INDEMNITY CO	TX	4,627.9
WESTERN AGRICULTURAL INS CO	IA	213.2

Section VI

All Companies
Listed by Rating

A list of all rated and unrated

U.S. Property and Casualty Insurers.

Companies are ranked by Weiss Safety Rating
and then listed alphabetically within each rating category.

Section VI Contents

This section sorts all companies by their Safety Rating and then lists them alphabetically within each rating category. The purpose of this section is to provide in one place all of those companies receiving a given rating. Companies with the same rating should be viewed as having the same relative financial strength regardless of their order in this table.

1. **Insurance Company Name**

   The legally registered name, which can sometimes differ from the name that the company uses for advertising. An insurer's name can be very similar to that of another, so verify the company's exact name and state of domicile to make sure you are looking at the correct company.

2. **Domicile State**

   The state which has primary regulatory responsibility for the company. It may differ from the location of the company's corporate headquarters. You do not have to be living in the domicile state to purchase insurance from this firm, provided it is licensed to do business in your state.

3. **Total Assets**

   All assets admitted by state insurance regulators in millions of dollars. This includes investments and current business assets such as receivables from agents and reinsurers.

INSURANCE COMPANY NAME	DOM. STATE	TOTAL ASSETS ($MIL)
Rating: A+		
BERKSHIRE HATHAWAY ASR CORP	NY	2,223.5
CITIZENS PROPERTY INS CORP	FL	11,362.5
COPPERPOINT MUTUAL INS CO	AZ	3,694.0
NUCLEAR ELECTRIC INS LTD	DE	5,587.7
OGLESBY REINS CO	IL	4,590.7
Rating: A		
AUTO-OWNERS INS CO	MI	15,390.4
BUILDERS MUTUAL INS CO	NC	859.6
CINCINNATI INS CO	OH	12,914.9
CINCINNATI SPECIALTY UNDERWRITER	DE	820.6
HOME-OWNERS INS CO	MI	2,323.7
OWNERS INS CO	OH	4,110.4
RETAILFIRST INS CO	FL	325.1
SENTRY INS A MUTUAL CO	WI	8,392.8
SOMPO AMERICA INSURANCE CO	NY	1,285.1
SOUTHERN-OWNERS INS CO	MI	821.8
TOKIO MARINE AMERICA INS CO	NY	1,409.5
Rating: A-		
ACUITY A MUTUAL INS CO	WI	3,960.1
ALFA MUTUAL GENERAL INS CO	AL	115.4
ALL AMERICA INS CO	OH	291.6
ALLSTATE NJ INS CO	IL	2,485.7
AMERICAN FAMILY MUTL INS CO SI	WI	17,157.4
CINCINNATI INDEMNITY CO	OH	133.0
COUNTRY MUTUAL INS CO	IL	4,850.2
CUMIS INS SOCIETY INC	IA	2,002.8
DAIRYLAND INS CO	WI	1,400.7
EMPLOYERS COMPENSATION INS CO	CA	1,091.0
ENDURANCE ASR CORP	DE	2,059.0
ESSENT GUARANTY INC	PA	1,756.6
FARM BUREAU P&C INS CO	IA	2,532.4
GEICO SECURE INS CO	NE	625.3
MITSUI SUMITOMO INS CO OF AMER	NY	975.8
MOTORISTS COMMERCIAL MUTUAL INS CO	OH	368.8
NATIONAL MORTGAGE INS CORP	WI	717.8
PROPERTY-OWNERS INS CO	IN	302.7
PROTECTIVE INS CO	IN	885.6
RADIAN REINS INC	PA	704.2
SECURIAN CASUALTY CO	MN	328.2
SENTRY SELECT INS CO	WI	826.6
TEXAS FARM BUREAU CASUALTY INS CO	TX	1,252.3
TRAVELERS CASUALTY & SURETY CO	CT	16,983.8
TRAVELERS INDEMNITY CO	CT	21,394.5
TREXIS ONE INSURANCE GROUP	VA	56.6
UNITED SERVICES AUTOMOBILE ASN	TX	35,460.0
USAA CASUALTY INS CO	TX	10,897.7
WEST BEND MUTUAL INS CO	WI	2,695.9
Rating: B+		
ALASKA NATIONAL INS CO	AK	1,004.7
ALFA GENERAL INS CORP	AL	101.6
ALFA MUTUAL FIRE INS CO	AL	770.4
ALLIED WORLD SPECIALTY INS CO	DE	829.1
ALLSTATE INS CO	IL	48,302.5

INSURANCE COMPANY NAME	DOM. STATE	TOTAL ASSETS ($MIL)
AMERICAN AGRICULTURAL INS CO	IN	1,338.9
AMERICAN CONTRACTORS INDEMNITY CO	CA	338.3
AMERICAN INTERSTATE INS CO OF TX	TX	68.1
AMERICAN NATIONAL PROPERTY & CAS CO	MO	1,418.0
AMERICAN STANDARD INS CO OF WI	WI	400.9
AMICA MUTUAL INS CO	RI	5,384.6
ANSUR AMERICA INS CO	MI	121.2
ARCH SPECIALTY INS CO	MO	483.4
AUTO CLUB INDEMNITY CO	TX	25.7
AUTO CLUB INS CO OF FL	FL	377.9
BROTHERHOOD MUTUAL INS CO	IN	644.9
CASTLE KEY INS CO	IL	362.5
CATERPILLAR INS CO	MO	790.6
CENTRAL MUTUAL INS CO	OH	1,618.4
CHURCH MUTUAL INS CO	WI	1,739.8
COPIC INS CO	CO	603.2
COVINGTON SPECIALTY INS CO	NH	97.9
ERIE & NIAGARA INS ASSN	NY	234.3
FARM BU TOWN & COUNTRY INS CO OF MO	MO	421.4
FARM BUREAU GENERAL INS CO OF MI	MI	719.9
FARM BUREAU MUTUAL INS CO OF MI	MI	782.4
FARM FAMILY CASUALTY INS CO	NY	1,241.7
FARMERS AUTOMOBILE INS ASN	IL	1,226.6
FARMERS MUTUAL INS CO OF NE	NE	680.3
FEDERATED RURAL ELECTRIC INS EXCH	KS	553.2
FINANCIAL PACIFIC INS CO	CA	261.4
FRANKENMUTH MUTUAL INS CO	MI	1,351.0
GEICO CHOICE INS CO	NE	1,134.6
GEICO GENERAL INS CO	MD	167.6
GNY CUSTOM INS CO	AZ	60.5
HASTINGS MUTUAL INS CO	MI	932.1
HIGH POINT PREFERRED INS CO	NJ	310.0
HOUSING AUTHORITY PROP A MUTUAL CO	VT	181.9
ICI MUTUAL INS CO A RRG	VT	367.6
INDIANA FARMERS MUTUAL INS CO	IN	433.3
INTERINS EXCHANGE	CA	10,404.3
LACKAWANNA AMERICAN INS CO	PA	89.8
LION INS CO (FL)	FL	264.3
LUBA CASUALTY INS CO	LA	228.7
MARKEL GLOBAL REINS CO	DE	2,180.9
MERCHANTS NATIONAL INS CO	NH	136.0
MERCHANTS PREFERRED INS CO	NY	76.4
MERCURY CASUALTY CO	CA	1,877.6
MERCURY INS CO	CA	1,708.0
MIDDLESEX INS CO	WI	764.3
MMIC INS INC	MN	682.7
MO EMPLOYERS MUTUAL INS CO	MO	695.0
MUTUAL INS CO OF AZ	AZ	1,105.9
MUTUAL OF ENUMCLAW INS CO	OR	748.3
NATIONAL CASUALTY CO	OH	418.6
NEW YORK SCHOOLS INS RECIPROCAL	NY	317.8
PEKIN INS CO	IL	305.4
PIONEER STATE MUTUAL INS CO	MI	608.7
PREFERRED PROFESSIONAL INS CO	NE	327.4
ROCKINGHAM INS CO	VA	144.7
SELECTIVE AUTO INS CO OF NJ	NJ	380.7

INSURANCE COMPANY NAME	DOM. STATE	TOTAL ASSETS ($MIL)	INSURANCE COMPANY NAME	DOM. STATE	TOTAL ASSETS ($MIL)
Rating: B+ (Continued)			AMERICAN MODERN PROPERTY & CASUALTY	OH	34.1
SELECTIVE CASUALTY INS CO	NJ	452.3	AMERICAN MODERN SURPLUS LINES INS CO	OH	62.7
SENTRY CASUALTY CO	WI	355.9	AMERICAN NATIONAL GENERAL INS CO	MO	109.5
SFM MUTUAL INS CO	MN	612.1	AMERICAN NATIONAL LLOYDS INS CO	TX	86.7
SOUTHERN FIDELITY INS CO	FL	196.7	AMERICAN NATL COUNTY MUT INS CO	TX	25.6
STATE FARM FIRE & CAS CO	IL	39,411.9	AMERICAN RELIABLE INS CO	AZ	219.2
STATE FARM MUTUAL AUTOMOBILE INS CO	IL	160,732.0	AMERICAN STANDARD INS CO OF OH	WI	13.0
STATE VOLUNTEER MUTUAL INS CO	TN	1,249.3	AMERICAN STATES INS CO OF TX	TX	14.2
SURETEC INS CO	TX	253.2	AMERICAN STATES LLOYDS INS CO	TX	3.7
TENNESSEE FARMERS ASR CO	TN	1,505.8	AMERIPRISE INS CO	WI	50.1
TENNESSEE FARMERS MUTUAL INS CO	TN	3,084.6	AMEX ASSURANCE CO	IL	218.2
TOA REINS CO OF AMERICA	DE	1,820.3	AMICA P&C INS CO	RI	84.1
TRANS PACIFIC INS CO	NY	67.6	ANPAC LOUISIANA INS CO	LA	134.7
TRANSATLANTIC REINS CO	NY	14,732.2	ARAG INS CO	IA	82.9
TREXIS INSURANCE CORP	VA	108.1	ARCH MORTGAGE GUARANTY CO	WI	50.9
UNITED EDUCATORS INS A RECIP RRG	VT	912.3	ARCH MORTGAGE INS CO	WI	2,134.6
UNITED FARM FAMILY MUTUAL INS CO	IN	1,098.5	ARMED FORCES INS EXCHANGE	KS	139.4
UNITED SPECIALTY INS CO	DE	330.2	ASURE WORLDWIDE INS CO	MI	44.0
USAA GENERAL INDEMNITY CO	TX	4,627.9	ATLANTIC CHARTER INS CO	MA	178.4
WESTERN AGRICULTURAL INS CO	IA	213.2	AUTO CLUB INS ASSN	MI	4,292.9
Rating: B			AUTO CLUB SOUTH INS CO	FL	134.7
21ST CENTURY ADVANTAGE INS CO	MN	29.6	AUTOMOBILE INS CO OF HARTFORD CT	CT	1,028.4
21ST CENTURY ASR CO	DE	70.5	AXIS INS CO	IL	1,465.3
21ST CENTURY CASUALTY CO	CA	12.5	BANKERS SPECIALTY INS CO	LA	55.6
21ST CENTURY CENTENNIAL INS CO	PA	601.1	BARNSTABLE COUNTY MUTUAL INS CO	MA	112.7
21ST CENTURY INDEMNITY INS CO	PA	69.3	BCS INS CO	OH	276.6
21ST CENTURY INS CO	CA	997.9	BEAR RIVER MUTUAL INS CO	UT	279.0
21ST CENTURY NATIONAL INS CO INC	NY	25.4	BEAZLEY INS CO	CT	317.1
21ST CENTURY NORTH AMERICA INS	NY	594.6	BENCHMARK INS CO	KS	347.3
21ST CENTURY PACIFIC INS	CO	44.4	BERKLEY INS CO	DE	18,358.6
21ST CENTURY PINNACLE INS CO	NJ	42.9	BITCO GENERAL INS CORP	IL	943.6
21ST CENTURY PREFERRED INS CO	PA	42.4	BITCO NATIONAL INS CO	IL	427.6
21ST CENTURY SECURITY INS CO	PA	200.8	BRETHREN MUTUAL INS CO	MD	274.8
360 INS CO	WY	33.6	BRICKSTREET MUTUAL INS CO	WV	2,270.7
ADVANTAGE WORKERS COMP INS CO	IN	508.1	BUSINESSFIRST INS CO	FL	45.0
ALFA ALLIANCE INS CORP	VA	37.2	CALIFORNIA AUTOMOBILE INS CO	CA	802.1
ALFA INS CORP	AL	95.8	CALIFORNIA GENERAL UNDERWRITERS INS	CA	21.8
ALFA MUTUAL INS CO	AL	1,344.9	CALIFORNIA HEALTHCARE INS CO INC RRG	HI	127.2
ALLIED P&C INS CO	IA	400.3	CALIFORNIA INS CO	CA	1,021.4
ALLSTATE COUNTY MUTUAL INS CO	TX	14.7	CANAL INDEMNITY CO	SC	49.5
ALLSTATE INDEMNITY CO	IL	115.2	CANAL INS CO	SC	827.7
ALLSTATE P&C INS CO	IL	236.7	CANOPIUS US INS INC	DE	211.4
ALLSTATE TEXAS LLOYDS	TX	17.3	CARING COMMUNITIES RECIP RRG	DC	91.2
ALLSTATE VEHICLE & PROPERTY INS CO	IL	63.1	CAROLINA MUTUAL INS INC	NC	94.7
ALPHA P&C INS CO	WI	30.1	CASTLE KEY INDEMNITY CO	IL	16.8
ALTERRA AMERICA INS CO	DE	392.6	CENTENNIAL CASUALTY CO	AL	125.2
AMERICAN BANKERS INS CO OF FL	FL	2,353.4	CHARTER INDEMNITY CO	TX	11.1
AMERICAN CAPITAL ASSR CORP	FL	122.6	CHARTER OAK FIRE INS CO	CT	925.9
AMERICAN COASTAL INS CO	FL	327.2	CHEROKEE INS CO	MI	541.6
AMERICAN EQUITY SPECIALTY INS CO	CT	78.4	CHESAPEAKE EMPLOYERS INS CO	MD	2,317.8
AMERICAN FAMILY INS CO	WI	64.8	CHUBB INDEMNITY INS CO	NY	397.6
AMERICAN FREEDOM INS CO	IL	51.6	CHUBB INS CO OF NJ	NJ	97.2
AMERICAN HALLMARK INS CO OF TX	TX	423.5	CHUBB INS CO OF PR	PR	146.4
AMERICAN MERCURY INS CO	OK	368.7	CHUBB LLOYDS INS CO OF TX	TX	52.8
AMERICAN MERCURY LLOYDS INS CO	TX	6.3	CHUBB NATIONAL INS CO	IN	406.1
			CINCINNATI CASUALTY CO	OH	433.6

INSURANCE COMPANY NAME	DOM. STATE	TOTAL ASSETS ($MIL)	INSURANCE COMPANY NAME	DOM. STATE	TOTAL ASSETS ($MIL)
			FOREMOST INS CO	MI	2,316.6
Rating: B (Continued)			FORTUITY INS CO	MI	44.7
CITIZENS INS CO OF AM	MI	1,559.4	FRANKLIN MUTUAL INS CO	NJ	1,080.4
CM VANTAGE SPECIALTY INS CO	WI	61.7	FREEDOM SPECIALTY INS CO	OH	57.9
COLONIAL COUNTY MUTUAL INS CO	TX	130.0	GARRISON P&C INS CO	TX	2,277.8
COMMUNITY HOSPITAL ALTERNATIVE RRG	VT	251.1	GEICO ADVANTAGE INS CO	NE	2,911.8
COMPWEST INS CO	CA	251.1	GEICO INDEMNITY CO	MD	10,162.5
CONNECTICUT MEDICAL INS CO	CT	504.1	GENWORTH MORTGAGE REINS CORP	NC	15.3
CONTRACTORS BONDING & INS CO	IL	211.8	GENWORTH MTG INS CORP OF NC	NC	394.9
CONTROLLED RISK INS CO OF VT RRG	VT	60.9	GEORGIA FARM BUREAU CASUALTY INS CO	GA	3.6
CONVENTUS INTER-INS	NJ	93.2	GERMANTOWN MUTUAL INS CO	WI	113.0
COURTESY INS CO	FL	906.6	GOLDEN BEAR INS CO	CA	154.9
COVERYS SPECIALTY INS CO	NJ	64.6	GOODVILLE MUTUAL CAS CO	PA	274.0
CRESTBROOK INS CO	OH	176.1	GOVERNMENT EMPLOYEES INS CO	MD	33,381.7
CUMIS SPECIALTY INS CO INC	IA	57.0	GOVERNMENTAL INTERINS	IL	64.6
DAIRYLAND COUNTY MUTUAL INS CO OF TX	TX	21.0	GRANGE MUTUAL CAS CO	OH	2,552.6
DB INS CO LTD US GUAM BRANCH	GU	78.8	GRANGE P&C INS CO	OH	44.2
DENTISTS INS CO	CA	351.6	GRANITE RE INC	OK	60.9
DRIVE NEW JERSEY INS CO	NJ	186.4	GREAT AMERICAN INS CO	OH	7,076.5
DRYDEN MUTUAL INS CO	NY	217.7	GREAT MIDWEST INS CO	TX	215.3
EASTERN ADVANTAGE ASR CO	PA	61.2	GREAT NORTHERN INS CO	IN	1,698.4
EASTERN DENTISTS INS CO RRG	VT	58.2	GREAT WEST CASUALTY CO	NE	2,133.2
ECONOMY PREFERRED INS CO	IL	61.2	GREEN MOUNTAIN INS CO	VT	13.4
ECONOMY PREMIER ASR CO	IL	80.9	GUARANTEE CO OF NORTH AMERICA USA	MI	230.5
ENCOMPASS INDEMNITY CO	IL	27.9	HALLMARK SPECIALTY INS CO	OK	250.9
ENDURANCE AMERICAN INS CO	DE	1,794.7	HARTFORD ACCIDENT & INDEMNITY CO	CT	11,906.6
ERIE INS CO OF NEW YORK	NY	112.9	HARTFORD CASUALTY INS CO	IN	2,352.3
ERIE INS EXCHANGE	PA	16,974.6	HARTFORD INS CO OF IL	IL	3,965.3
ESSENT GUARANTY OF PA INC	PA	93.1	HARTFORD INS CO OF THE MIDWEST	IN	636.9
EULER HERMES NORTH AMERICA INS CO	MD	445.6	HARTFORD INS CO OF THE SOUTHEAST	CT	192.2
EXECUTIVE RISK INDEMNITY INC	DE	3,231.3	HARTFORD LLOYDS INS CO	TX	76.4
FAIR AMERICAN SELECT INS CO	DE	112.8	HARTFORD SM BOIL INSPECTION IC OF CT	CT	15.3
FALLS LAKE NATIONAL INS CO	OH	321.9	HARTFORD UNDERWRITERS INS CO	CT	1,675.9
FARM BUREAU INS OF NC INC	NC	10.0	HAULERS INS CO	TN	77.8
FARM BUREAU MUTUAL INS CO OF AR	AR	408.6	HAWAII EMPLOYERS MUTUAL INS CO	HI	396.9
FARM BUREAU MUTUAL INS CO OF ID	ID	467.0	HAWAIIAN INS & GUARANTY CO LTD	HI	28.4
FARM CREDIT SYS ASSOC CAPTIVE INS CO	CO	113.3	HDI SPECIALTY INSURANCE CO	IL	48.5
FARMERS & MECH MUTUAL INS CO	PA	6.4	HEALTHCARE UNDERWRITERS GRP MUT OH	OH	86.2
FARMERS & MECHANICS MUTUAL IC OF WV	WV	70.1	HIGH POINT P&C INS CO	NJ	360.6
FARMERS INS CO OF OREGON	OR	1,634.6	HOMELAND INS CO OF DE	DE	52.8
FARMERS INS HAWAII INC	HI	100.6	HORACE MANN INS CO	IL	526.7
FARMERS MUTUAL F I C OF SALEM CTY	NJ	158.7	HORACE MANN P&C INS CO	IL	304.7
FARMERS UNION MUTUAL INS CO	ND	121.3	HOUSING AUTHORITY RISK RET GROUP INC	VT	313.6
FARMINGTON CASUALTY CO	CT	1,031.4	HOUSTON SPECIALTY INS CO	TX	455.8
FARMLAND MUTUAL INS CO	IA	559.9	HSB SPECIALTY INS CO	CT	56.2
FEDERATED MUTUAL INS CO	MN	5,847.9	HUDSON EXCESS INS CO	DE	76.7
FFVA MUTUAL INS CO	FL	336.2	HYUNDAI MARINE & FIRE INS CO LTD	CA	103.5
FIRST COLONIAL INS CO	FL	300.3	IDS PROPERTY CASUALTY INS CO	WI	1,789.9
FIRST FLORIDIAN AUTO & HOME INS CO	FL	259.6	ILLINOIS INS CO	IA	60.4
FIRST GUARD INS CO	AZ	31.9	IMT INS CO	IA	396.0
FIRST NATIONAL INS CO OF AMERICA	NH	57.7	INFINITY INS CO	IN	2,043.1
FIRSTCOMP INS CO	NE	261.3	INS CO OF ILLINOIS	IL	23.3
FLORIDA FAMILY INS CO	FL	106.8	INTEGRITY MUTUAL INS CO	WI	109.3
FLORIDA FARM BUREAU GENERAL INS CO	FL	12.0	INTERNATIONAL FIDELITY INS CO	NJ	219.8
FLORIDA PENINSULA INS CO	FL	304.7	IOWA AMERICAN INS CO	IA	24.3
FMH AG RISK INS CO	IA	123.2	JEWELERS MUTUAL INS CO	WI	442.4

INSURANCE COMPANY NAME	DOM. STATE	TOTAL ASSETS ($MIL)	INSURANCE COMPANY NAME	DOM. STATE	TOTAL ASSETS ($MIL)
Rating: B (Continued)			NJ MANUFACTURERS INS CO	NJ	7,423.2
KANSAS MEDICAL MUTUAL INS CO	KS	155.0	NORTH CAROLINA FARM BU MUTUAL INS CO	NC	2,002.0
KEMPER INDEPENDENCE INS CO	IL	97.5	NORTHLAND CASUALTY CO	CT	110.6
KENTUCKY EMPLOYERS MUTUAL INS	KY	994.0	NORTHLAND INS CO	CT	1,187.8
KENTUCKY FARM BUREAU MUTUAL INS CO	KY	2,505.4	OAKWOOD INS CO	TN	72.1
KINSALE INS CO	AR	578.1	OCEAN HARBOR CASUALTY INS CO	FL	285.1
KNIGHT SPECIALTY INS CO	DE	82.3	OHIO BAR LIABILITY INS CO	OH	39.7
LAMMICO	LA	432.9	OKLAHOMA ATTORNEYS MUTUAL INS CO	OK	55.9
LAWYERS MUTUAL INS CO	CA	342.2	OLD REPUB INS CO	PA	2,923.3
LAWYERS MUTUAL LIAB INS CO OF NC	NC	109.5	OLD REPUB UNION INS CO	IL	61.4
LEAGUE OF WI MUNICIPALITIES MUT INS	WI	70.7	OLD REPUBLIC GENERAL INS CORP	IL	2,078.8
LIBERTY LLOYDS OF TX INS CO	TX	6.6	OLD REPUBLIC LLOYDS OF TX	TX	2.3
LIBERTY MUTUAL INS CO	MA	46,020.8	OLD REPUBLIC SECURITY ASR CO	IL	1,023.6
LIBERTY MUTUAL PERSONAL INS CO	MA	12.8	OLD REPUBLIC SURETY CO	WI	127.1
LOUISIANA FARM BUREAU CAS INS CO	LA	12.2	OPHTHALMIC MUTUAL INS CO RRG	VT	294.4
LOUISIANA FARM BUREAU MUTUAL INS CO	LA	228.3	OTSEGO MUTUAL FIRE INS CO	NY	131.8
LYNDON SOUTHERN INS CO	DE	191.9	P&C INS CO OF HARTFORD	IN	237.5
MANUFACTURING TECHNOLOGY MUT INS CO	MI	63.0	PACIFIC INDEMNITY CO	WI	6,560.0
MEDICAL INS EXCHANGE OF CALIFORNIA	CA	405.4	PACIFIC INS CO LTD	CT	676.1
MEDICAL LIABILITY ALLIANCE	MO	83.3	PACIFIC PROPERTY & CASUALTY CO	CA	90.5
MEDICAL MUTUAL INS CO OF MAINE	ME	312.8	PATONS CO-OP FIRE INS CO	VT	144.0
MEDICAL PROTECTIVE CO	IN	3,318.0	PATRIOT GENERAL INS CO	WI	25.8
MENDAKOTA INS CO	MN	11.1	PEAK P&C INS CORP	WI	48.7
MERCHANTS BONDING CO (MUTUAL)	IA	200.4	PEERLESS INS CO	NH	14,600.0
MERCURY COUNTY MUTUAL INS CO	TX	11.7	PENNSYLVANIA LUMBERMENS MUTUAL INS	PA	488.1
MERCURY INDEMNITY CO OF GEORGIA	GA	16.2	PHARMACISTS MUTUAL INS CO	IA	319.1
MERCURY INS CO OF GA	GA	22.2	PHOENIX INS CO	CT	4,210.3
MERCURY INS CO OF IL	IL	36.3	PREFERRED MUTUAL INS CO	NY	568.1
MET LLOYDS INS CO OF TX	TX	94.4	PREMIER GROUP INS CO	TN	59.0
METROPOLITAN CASUALTY INS CO	RI	234.9	PRIVILEGE UNDERWRITERS RECIP EXCH	FL	568.0
METROPOLITAN DIRECT PROP & CAS INS	RI	173.8	PROGRESSIVE GARDEN STATE INS CO	NJ	319.8
METROPOLITAN GENERAL INS CO	RI	42.4	PROGRESSIVE PROPERTY INS CO	FL	91.7
METROPOLITAN GROUP PROP & CAS INS CO	RI	687.0	PROTECTIVE SPECIALTY INS CO	IN	66.2
MIAMI MUTUAL INS CO	OH	61.2	PURE INS CO	FL	370.9
MID-CENTURY INS CO	CA	3,941.6	QBE INS CORP	PA	2,054.3
MIDWEST BUILDERS CASUALTY MUTUAL CO	KS	103.3	QBE REINS CORP	PA	1,031.4
MIDWEST FAMILY MUTUAL INS CO	IA	242.6	QUINCY MUTUAL FIRE INS CO	MA	1,774.9
MILFORD CASUALTY INS CO	DE	44.8	RADNOR SPECIALTY INS CO	NE	54.0
MILLERS CAPITAL INS CO	PA	145.9	RAM MUTUAL INS CO	MN	115.1
MINNESOTA LAWYERS MUTUAL INS CO	MN	188.7	RED SHIELD INS CO	WA	40.5
MMG INS CO	ME	276.6	RENAISSANCE RE US INC	MD	1,633.7
MOTOR CLUB INS CO	RI	53.5	REPUB MORTGAGE ASSURANCE CO	FL	22.8
MOUNTAIN WEST FARM BU MUTUAL INS CO	WY	382.9	RESTORATION RRG INC	VT	85.0
NATIONAL BUILDERS INS CO	DE	94.4	RETAILERS CASUALTY INS CO	LA	82.2
NATIONAL INDEMNITY CO	NE	231,374.0	RIVERPORT INS CO	IA	98.6
NATIONWIDE AFFINITY INS CO OF AMER	OH	296.7	RLI INS CO	IL	1,817.0
NATIONWIDE INS CO OF FL	OH	33.0	SAFE AUTO INS CO	OH	382.4
NATIONWIDE LLOYDS	TX	41.5	SAFE HARBOR INS CO	FL	83.1
NATIONWIDE MUTUAL INS CO	OH	35,425.4	SAFECO INS CO OF AMERICA	NH	4,863.4
NAVIGATORS INS CO	NY	3,084.5	SAFECO INS CO OF IL	IL	194.6
NCMIC INS CO	IA	782.8	SAFECO INS CO OF INDIANA	IN	15.8
NEW ENGLAND MUTUAL INS CO	MA	46.2	SAFECO INS CO OF OREGON	OR	14.0
NEW JERSEY CASUALTY INS CO	NJ	588.0	SCOTTSDALE INDEMNITY CO	OH	84.5
NEW JERSEY RE-INS CO	NJ	546.4	SCOTTSDALE SURPLUS LINES INS CO	AZ	51.6
NEW YORK MUNICIPAL INS RECIPROCAL	NY	163.9	SECURITY MUTUAL INS CO	NY	111.2
			SELECTIVE F&C INS CO	NJ	195.7

INSURANCE COMPANY NAME	DOM. STATE	TOTAL ASSETS ($MIL)	INSURANCE COMPANY NAME	DOM. STATE	TOTAL ASSETS ($MIL)
Rating: B (Continued)			UNITED FARM FAMILY INS CO	NY	44.5
SELECTIVE INS CO OF AM	NJ	2,434.9	UNITED FIRE & CAS CO	IA	1,987.8
SELECTIVE INS CO OF NY	NY	442.5	UNITED GUARANTY INS CO	NC	5.4
SELECTIVE INS CO OF SC	IN	648.0	UNITED STATES SURETY CO	MD	75.4
SELECTIVE INS CO OF THE SOUTHEAST	IN	507.5	UNITED SURETY & INDEMNITY CO	PR	107.7
SELECTIVE WAY INS CO	NJ	1,345.7	UNITRIN COUNTY MUTUAL INS CO	TX	29.2
SENTINEL INS CO LTD	CT	280.9	UNITRIN DIRECT INS CO	IL	11.7
SENTRUITY CASUALTY CO	TX	210.7	UNITRIN DIRECT PROPERTY & CAS CO	IL	14.3
SENTRY LLOYDS OF TX	TX	7.2	UNITRIN SAFEGUARD INS CO	WI	31.8
SERVICE INS CO (FL)	FL	61.0	US SPECIALTY INS CO	TX	1,888.4
SERVICE LLOYDS INS CO	TX	315.8	UTICA FIRST INS CO	NY	291.6
SHELTER MUTUAL INS CO	MO	3,381.1	UTICA LLOYDS OF TX	TX	8.3
SHELTER REINS CO	MO	472.9	VALLEY P&C INS CO	OR	12.3
SIMED	PR	163.1	VANLINER INS CO	MO	454.6
SOCIETY INS A MUTUAL CO	WI	432.6	VAULT RECIPROCAL EXCHANGE	FL	49.8
SOUTHERN OAK INS CO	FL	121.9	VERMONT ACCIDENT INS CO	VT	15.4
ST PAUL FIRE & MARINE INS CO	CT	18,716.4	VETERINARY PET INS CO	OH	159.4
STANDARD FIRE INS CO	CT	3,766.4	VIGILANT INS CO	NY	576.7
STARR INDEMNITY & LIABILITY CO	TX	4,803.6	VIRGINIA SURETY CO INC	IL	1,439.3
STARR SURPLUS LINES INS CO	IL	405.0	WATFORD SPECIALTY INS CO	NJ	73.2
STATE FARM FLORIDA INS CO	FL	2,063.4	WAWANESA GENERAL INS CO	CA	582.0
STATE FARM INDEMNITY CO	IL	2,301.8	WESTERN HERITAGE INS CO	AZ	132.6
STATE FARM LLOYDS	TX	3,358.3	WESTERN PACIFIC MUT INS CO RISK RET	CO	143.1
STERLING INS CO	NY	198.7	WESTGUARD INS CO	PA	1,181.9
STONETRUST COMMERCIAL INS CO	NE	174.2	WESTPORT INS CORP	MO	5,517.6
SUNAPEE MUTL FIRE INS CO	NH	13.9	WILSON MUTUAL INS CO	WI	86.1
TEACHERS AUTO INS CO	NJ	28.0	WINDSOR MOUNT JOY MUTUAL INS CO	PA	87.3
TEACHERS INS CO	IL	356.9	WISCONSIN MUTUAL INS CO	WI	160.6
TEXAS LAWYERS INS EXCHANGE	TX	92.1	ZURICH AMERICAN INS CO	NY	31,582.0
TNUS INS CO	NY	64.5	**Rating: B-**		
TRANSGUARD INS CO OF AMERICA INC	IL	389.5	21ST CENTURY PREMIER INS CO	PA	289.3
TRAVCO INS CO	CT	217.5	ACCIDENT FUND INS CO OF AMERICA	MI	3,664.5
TRAVELERS CASUALTY CO OF CONNECTICUT	CT	326.1	ACCREDITED SURETY & CAS CO INC	FL	148.7
TRAVELERS CASUALTY INS CO OF AMERICA	CT	1,958.1	ACE AMERICAN INS CO	PA	13,606.0
TRAVELERS COMMERCIAL CASUALTY CO	CT	330.4	ACE P&C INS CO	PA	8,693.1
TRAVELERS COMMERCIAL INS CO	CT	365.0	AFFILIATES INS RECIPROCAL A RRG	VT	7.3
TRAVELERS EXCESS & SURPLUS LINES CO	CT	219.4	AGENCY INS CO OF MD INC	MD	177.4
TRAVELERS HOME & MARINE INS CO	CT	370.4	AGRICULTURAL WORKERS MUT AUTO INS CO	TX	90.5
TRAVELERS INDEMNITY CO OF AMERICA	CT	621.9	AIG INS CO - PR	PR	150.1
TRAVELERS INDEMNITY CO OF CT	CT	1,088.9	AIOI NISSAY DOWA INS CO OF AMERICA	NY	137.7
TRAVELERS LLOYDS INS CO	TX	21.2	AIX SPECIALTY INS CO	DE	56.9
TRAVELERS LLOYDS OF TEXAS INS CO	TX	19.8	ALABAMA MUNICIPAL INS CORP	AL	120.1
TRAVELERS PERSONAL INS CO	CT	211.6	ALAMANCE FARMERS MUTUAL INS CO	NC	8.9
TRAVELERS PERSONAL SECURITY INS CO	CT	210.7	ALLEGANY CO-OP INS CO	NY	55.4
TRAVELERS PROPERTY CAS OF AMERICA	CT	857.4	ALLEGHENYPOINT INSURANCE CO	PA	34.1
TRAVELERS PROPERTY CASUALTY INS CO	CT	269.1	ALLIED EASTERN INDEMNITY CO	PA	95.6
TRI-STATE CONSUMER INS CO	NY	104.1	ALLIED WORLD ASR CO (US) INC	DE	337.7
TRIPLE S PROPIEDAD INC	PR	331.6	ALLSTATE F&C INS CO	IL	245.1
TRUMBULL INS CO	CT	238.6	ALLSTATE NJ P&C INS CO	IL	76.1
TWIN CITY FIRE INS CO	IN	663.3	ALLSTATE NORTHBROOK INDEMNITY CO	IL	59.0
UFB CASUALTY INS CO	IN	8.9	ALPS PROPERTY & CASUALTY INS CO	MT	131.2
UMIA INS INC	OR	224.9	AMALGAMATED CASUALTY INS CO	DC	59.7
UMIALIK INS CO	AK	77.7	AMCO INS CO	IA	959.5
UNION NATIONAL FIRE INS CO	LA	9.0	AMERICAN COMMERCE INS CO	OH	340.7
UNITED CASUALTY INS CO OF AMERICA	IL	13.5	AMERICAN ECONOMY INS CO	IN	72.3

INSURANCE COMPANY NAME	DOM. STATE	TOTAL ASSETS ($MIL)	INSURANCE COMPANY NAME	DOM. STATE	TOTAL ASSETS ($MIL)
Rating: B- (Continued)			DEALERS ASR CO	OH	117.1
AMERICAN EUROPEAN INS CO	NH	138.1	DEPOSITORS INS CO	IA	291.1
AMERICAN INTER FIDELITY EXCHANGE RRG	IN	105.6	DOCTORS CO AN INTERINS	CA	4,409.2
AMERICAN INTERSTATE INS CO	NE	1,234.5	ECONOMY FIRE & CAS CO	IL	511.9
AMERICAN MINING INS CO	IA	40.8	EMC REINS CO	IA	492.3
AMERICAN MODERN INS CO OF FLORIDA	FL	35.4	EMCASCO INS CO	IA	510.9
AMERICAN PLATINUM PROP & CAS INS CO	FL	22.4	EMPIRE BONDING & INS CO	NY	4.0
AMERICAN ROAD INS CO	MI	711.9	EMPLOYERS INS OF WAUSAU	WI	6,056.4
AMERICAN SECURITY INS CO	DE	1,376.3	EMPLOYERS MUTUAL CAS CO	IA	3,404.4
AMERICAN STATES INS CO	IN	143.5	ENCOMPASS HOME & AUTO INS CO	IL	19.1
AMERICAN STATES PREFERRED INS CO	IN	23.5	ENCOMPASS INDEPENDENT INS CO	IL	6.2
AMERISURE INS CO	MI	875.0	ENCOMPASS INS CO OF AM	IL	20.2
AMERISURE MUTUAL INS CO	MI	2,369.8	ENCOMPASS PROPERTY & CASUALTY CO	IL	10.2
AMTRUST INS CO OF KANSAS INC	KS	106.2	ENDURANCE AMERICAN SPECIALTY INS CO	DE	453.7
ARCH INDEMNITY INS CO	MO	102.3	ENDURANCE RISK SOLUTIONS ASR CO	DE	255.9
ARECA INS EXCHANGE	AK	28.4	ERIE INS CO	PA	1,039.0
ARISE BOILER INSPECT & INS CO RRG	KY	4.2	ERIE INS P&C CO	PA	110.4
ARROW MUTUAL LIABILITY INS CO	MA	45.9	EVEREST PREMIER INSURANCE CO	DE	25.7
ASI ASR CORP	FL	128.4	EVEREST REINS CO	DE	9,486.1
ASI HOME INS CORP	FL	17.6	EVERETT CASH MUTUAL INS CO	PA	131.7
ASSOCIATED INDUSTRIES OF MA MUT INS	MA	625.2	EXECUTIVE RISK SPECIALTY INS CO	CT	288.7
ATLANTIC CASUALTY INS CO	NC	286.4	FACTORY MUTUAL INS CO	RI	19,155.5
ATLANTIC STATES INS CO	PA	793.2	FAIR AMERICAN INS & REINS CO	NY	211.3
AVEMCO INS CO	MD	87.6	FARMERS & MERCHANTS MUTUAL FIRE I C	MI	32.2
BAY STATE INS CO	MA	573.2	FARMERS ALLIANCE MUTUAL INS CO	KS	319.2
BELL UNITED INS CO	NV	34.8	FARMERS INS CO OF FLEMINGTON	NJ	70.6
BENEFIT SECURITY INS CO	IL	9.3	FARMERS INS CO OF WA	WA	528.5
BLACKBOARD SPECIALTY INS CO	DE	149.1	FARMERS MUTUAL HAIL INS CO OF IA	IA	752.1
BLOOMINGTON COMP INS CO	MN	16.6	FARMERS SPECIALTY INS CO	MI	51.5
BONDEX INS CO	NJ	8.8	FARMERS UNION MUTUAL INS CO	MT	66.4
BRIDGEFIELD EMPLOYERS INS CO	FL	122.4	FBALLIANCE INS CO	IL	43.9
BUILDERS PREMIER INS CO	NC	12.2	FEDERATED SERVICE INS CO	MN	450.4
CALLICOON CO-OPERATIVE INS CO	NY	32.5	FINANCIAL INDEMNITY CO	IL	102.8
CAMBRIDGE MUTUAL FIRE INS CO	MA	1,012.4	FINGER LAKES FIRE & CASUALTY CO	NY	43.9
CAMPMED CAS & INDEM CO INC OF MD	NH	20.1	FIRE DISTRICTS OF NY MUT INS CO INC	NY	94.5
CAPITOL CASUALTY CO	NE	32.3	FIRST MEDICAL INS CO RRG	VT	114.1
CASCO INDEMNITY CO	ME	32.0	FLORIDA FARM BU CASUALTY INS CO	FL	558.0
CENSTAT CASUALTY CO	NE	25.3	FLORIDA LAWYERS MUTUAL INS CO	FL	90.6
CENTER MUTUAL INS CO	ND	57.7	FMI INS CO	NJ	53.5
CENTURION CASUALTY CO	IA	39.8	FORESTRY MUTUAL INS CO	NC	61.0
CHUBB CUSTOM INS CO	NJ	389.2	FORTRESS INS CO	IL	142.2
CITIES & VILLAGES MUTUAL INS CO	WI	52.1	FRANDISCO P&C INS CO	GA	117.8
CM REGENT INS CO	PA	190.9	GEICO MARINE INS CO	MD	149.5
COLONIAL SURETY CO	PA	62.0	GENERAL AUTOMOBILE INS CO	WI	98.7
COLUMBIA LLOYDS INS CO	TX	50.4	GENERAL INS CO OF AM	NH	118.9
COLUMBIA MUTUAL INS CO	MO	381.2	GENERAL STAR NATIONAL INS CO	DE	237.8
COMMERCE INS CO	MA	2,246.1	GERMAN AMERICAN FARM MUTUAL	TX	4.7
CONCORD GENERAL MUTUAL INS CO	NH	518.0	GRANGE INS ASSN	WA	295.2
CONTINENTAL CASUALTY CO	IL	43,528.3	GRANITE STATE INS CO	IL	35.8
COOPERATIVA D SEGUROS MULTIPLES D PR	PR	518.2	GRAY INS CO	LA	299.8
COPPERPOINT GENERAL INS CO	AZ	15.3	GREATER NEW YORK MUTUAL INS CO	NY	1,057.8
COPPERPOINT WESTERN INS CO	AZ	8.6	GRINNELL MUTUAL REINS CO	IA	1,179.7
CSAA INS EXCHANGE	CA	7,168.5	GUIDEONE NATIONAL INS CO	IA	52.8
CUMBERLAND INS CO	NJ	104.7	HANOVER INS CO	NH	7,748.1
CUMBERLAND MUTUAL FIRE INS CO	NJ	287.2	HARCO NATIONAL INS CO	IL	606.1
			HARFORD MUTUAL INS CO	MD	467.1

INSURANCE COMPANY NAME	DOM. STATE	TOTAL ASSETS ($MIL)
Rating: B- (Continued)		
HARTFORD SM BOIL INSPECTION & INS	CT	1,213.5
HCC SPECIALTY INS CO	OK	22.0
HEALTH PROVIDERS INS RECIPROCAL RRG	HI	79.7
HERITAGE INDEMNITY CO	CA	68.6
HERITAGE P&C INS CO	FL	618.4
HIGH POINT SAFETY & INS CO	NJ	67.5
HORACE MANN LLOYDS	TX	4.5
HOUSING ENTERPRISE INS CO	VT	78.3
HOUSTON CASUALTY CO	TX	3,382.8
IL STATE BAR ASSOC MUTUAL INS CO	IL	80.2
ILLINOIS CASUALTY CO	IL	124.1
ILLINOIS EMCASCO INS CO	IA	378.7
ILLINOIS NATIONAL INS CO	IL	55.4
INDEPENDENCE AMERICAN INS CO	DE	112.9
INDEPENDENT MUTUAL FIRE INS CO	IL	52.2
INFINITY ASSURANCE INS CO	OH	7.0
INFINITY CASUALTY INS CO	OH	7.6
INFINITY SELECT INS CO	IN	6.9
INTEGON NATIONAL INS CO	NC	3,766.0
IOWA MUTUAL INS CO	IA	93.9
IRONSHORE INDEMNITY INC	MN	185.8
ISLAND INS CO LTD	HI	330.4
ISMIE MUTUAL INS CO	IL	1,403.5
JAMES RIVER CASUALTY CO	VA	44.7
KESWICK GUARANTY INC	VI	5.8
KEYSTONE NATIONAL INS CO	PA	19.9
LACKAWANNA CASUALTY CO	PA	240.2
LACKAWANNA NATIONAL INS CO	PA	38.9
LAFAYETTE INS CO	LA	221.2
LAKEVIEW INS CO	FL	33.8
LANCER INDEMNITY CO	NY	30.2
LANCER INS CO	IL	689.1
LANDCAR CASUALTY CO	UT	44.5
LCTA CASUALTY INS CO	LA	71.0
LIBERTY MUTUAL FIRE INS CO	WI	6,038.9
LIGHTHOUSE PROPERTY INS CORP	LA	100.9
LIGHTNING ROD MUTUAL INS CO	OH	300.3
LITITZ MUTUAL INS CO	PA	304.7
LM GENERAL INS CO	IL	11.2
MADISON MUTUAL INS CO	IL	66.3
MAG MUTUAL INS CO	GA	1,718.5
MAISON INS CO	LA	92.0
MARYSVILLE MUTUAL INS CO	KS	51.1
MDOW INS CO	TX	17.9
MEDICAL MUTUAL INS CO OF NC	NC	598.1
MEDICAL MUTUAL LIAB INS SOC OF MD	MD	825.0
MEDICAL PROFESSIONAL MUTUAL INS CO	MA	3,134.7
MEDICUS INS CO	TX	38.2
MEMBERSELECT INS CO	MI	546.9
MEMIC CASUALTY CO	NH	64.8
MERASTAR INS CO	IL	39.6
MERCHANTS MUTUAL INS CO	NY	533.6
MERCHANTS NATIONAL BONDING INC	IA	35.5
MERCURY INS CO OF FL	FL	43.0

INSURANCE COMPANY NAME	DOM. STATE	TOTAL ASSETS ($MIL)
MERRIMACK MUTUAL FIRE INS CO	MA	1,728.2
METROPOLITAN P&C INS CO	RI	6,107.4
MICHIGAN PROFESSIONAL INS EXCHANGE	MI	104.5
MID-CONTINENT EXCESS & SURPLUS INS	DE	18.6
MIDSTATE MUTUAL INS CO	NY	42.5
MISSISSIPPI FARM BUREAU CAS INS CO	MS	438.2
MISSOURI HOSPITAL PLAN	MO	207.4
MITSUI SUMITOMO INS USA INC	NY	139.3
MODERN USA INS CO	FL	64.4
MOUNT VERNON SPECIALTY INS CO	NE	62.3
MSA INS CO	SC	18.8
MUNICIPAL MUTUAL INS CO	WV	38.5
MUTUAL BENEFIT INS CO	PA	228.8
MUTUAL RRG INC	HI	111.4
NATIONAL GENL PREMIER INS CO	CA	35.0
NATIONAL LLOYDS INS CO	TX	186.9
NATIONAL MORTGAGE RE INC ONE	WI	34.5
NATIONAL SECURITY FIRE & CAS CO	AL	73.3
NATIONWIDE AGRIBUSINESS INS CO	IA	758.6
NATIONWIDE ASR CO	OH	131.9
NATIONWIDE GENERAL INS CO	OH	406.3
NATIONWIDE INS CO OF AM	OH	431.3
NATIONWIDE P&C INS CO	OH	537.6
NAVIGATORS SPECIALTY INS CO	NY	178.6
NEW HAMPSHIRE EMPLOYERS INS CO	NH	5.0
NEW LONDON COUNTY MUTUAL INS CO	CT	125.2
NEW MEXICO EMPLOYERS ASR CO	NM	6.2
NEW YORK CENTRAL MUTUAL FIRE INS CO	NY	1,177.2
NEW YORK MARINE & GENERAL INS CO	NY	1,746.2
NGM INS CO	FL	2,593.2
NODAK INS CO	ND	257.6
NORCAL MUTUAL INS CO	CA	1,610.5
NORTH LIGHT SPECIALTY INS CO	IL	89.6
NORTH STAR MUTUAL INS CO	MN	742.9
NORTHERN MUTUAL INS CO	MI	38.6
NORTHSTONE INS CO	PA	63.7
NOVA CASUALTY CO	NY	89.1
NUTMEG INS CO	CT	440.7
OASIS RECIPROCAL RRG	VT	15.1
OHIO FARMERS INS CO	OH	3,107.9
OHIO MUTUAL INS CO	OH	296.3
OKLAHOMA FARM BUREAU MUTUAL INS CO	OK	300.2
OKLAHOMA SPECIALTY INS CO	OK	22.1
OLD AMERICAN INDEMNITY CO	KY	12.2
OLD DOMINION INS CO	FL	36.1
OMS NATIONAL INS CO RRG	IL	442.8
PACIFIC EMPLOYERS INS CO	PA	3,687.4
PACIFIC SPECIALTY INS CO	CA	294.4
PARTNER REINSURANCE CO OF THE US	NY	4,655.3
PEMCO MUTUAL INS CO	WA	772.8
PENN NATIONAL SECURITY INS CO	PA	969.0
PENNSYLVANIA NTL MUTUAL CAS INS CO	PA	1,307.1
PETROLEUM CAS CO	TX	32.8
PHILADELPHIA CBSP FOR INS OF HOUSES	PA	376.1
PHILADELPHIA CONTRIBUTIONSHIP INS CO	PA	240.3
PHILADELPHIA INDEMNITY INS CO	PA	8,653.2

INSURANCE COMPANY NAME	DOM. STATE	TOTAL ASSETS ($MIL)
Rating: B- (Continued)		
PHYSICIANS INS A MUTL CO	WA	504.5
PIH INS CO A RECIP RRG	HI	21.4
PINNACLEPOINT INS CO	WV	76.2
PLAZA INS CO	IA	65.6
PLYMOUTH ROCK ASR CORP	MA	684.2
PRIME INS CO	IL	127.6
PROFESSIONAL SECURITY INS CO	AZ	82.3
PROFESSIONALS ADVOCATE INS CO	MD	142.4
PROGRESSIVE CASUALTY INS CO	OH	8,431.2
PROGRESSIVE DIRECT INS CO	OH	7,785.7
PROTECTIVE P&C INS CO	MO	385.5
PROVIDENCE MUTUAL FIRE INS CO	RI	207.0
RED CLAY RRG INC	SC	9.2
RELIABLE LLOYDS INS CO	TX	19.4
REPUBLIC INDEMNITY CO OF AMERICA	CA	2,267.3
REPUBLIC-VANGUARD INS CO	AZ	25.3
ROCKFORD MUTUAL INS CO	IL	80.6
RSUI INDEMNITY CO	NH	3,637.8
RURAL MUTUAL INS CO	WI	484.2
SAFECO LLOYDS INS CO	TX	13.3
SAFECO NATIONAL INS CO	NH	15.7
SAFETY INS CO	MA	1,503.6
SAFEWAY INS CO	IL	565.8
SAGAMORE INS CO	IN	169.1
SC FARM BUREAU MUTUAL INS CO	SC	120.6
SCOTTSDALE INS CO	OH	2,536.9
SECURA INS A MUTUAL CO	WI	1,161.7
SECURITY FIRST INS CO	FL	252.3
SENECA SPECIALTY INS CO	DE	50.8
SHEBOYGAN FALLS INS CO	WI	36.6
SIGMA RRG INC	DC	18.8
SILVER OAK CASUALTY INC	NE	230.1
SIRIUS AMERICA INS CO	NY	1,337.5
SLAVONIC MUTUAL FIRE INS ASN	TX	30.1
SOUTHERN FARM BUREAU CAS INS CO	MS	2,269.3
SOUTHERN MUTUAL CHURCH INS CO	SC	70.2
SOUTHERN MUTUAL INS CO	GA	20.3
SOUTHERN PIONEER PROP & CAS INS CO	AR	49.5
SPARTAN PROPERTY INS CO	SC	32.4
SPINNAKER INS CO	IL	48.5
ST PAUL MERCURY INS CO	CT	341.2
ST PAUL PROTECTIVE INS CO	CT	518.0
STANDARD GUARANTY INS CO	DE	314.4
STATE AUTO INS CO OF WI	WI	15.9
STATE FARM CTY MUTUAL INS CO OF TX	TX	132.9
STATE FARM GUARANTY INS CO	IL	34.5
STATE NATIONAL INS CO	TX	442.9
STILLWATER INS CO	CA	399.0
STRATFORD INS CO	NH	539.9
SUBLIMITY INS CO	OR	40.7
SUMMITPOINT INS CO	WV	59.6
SUNLAND RRG INC	TN	2.4
SURETEC INDEMNITY CO	CA	24.1
TERRA INS CO (A RRG)	VT	27.2

INSURANCE COMPANY NAME	DOM. STATE	TOTAL ASSETS ($MIL)
TITAN INDEMNITY CO	TX	157.6
TITAN INS CO	MI	134.3
TOPA INS CO	CA	199.0
TRANSAMERICA CASUALTY INS CO	OH	455.5
TRAVELERS CASUALTY & SURETY CO OF AM	CT	4,232.8
TRIANGLE INS CO	OK	88.2
TRITON INS CO	TX	453.9
TRUSTGARD INS CO	OH	72.8
TUSCARORA WAYNE INS CO	PA	114.7
UNION MUTUAL FIRE INS CO	VT	242.7
UNITED FINANCIAL CASUALTY CO	OH	3,346.4
UNITED GUARANTY MORTGAGE INS CO	NC	23.0
UNITED GUARANTY MTG INS CO OF NC	NC	22.8
UNITED OHIO INS CO	OH	340.5
UNITED P&C INS CO	FL	618.2
UNIVERSAL INS CO (PR)	PR	896.9
USPLATE GLASS INS CO	IL	33.1
UTICA MUTUAL INS CO	NY	2,525.3
UTICA NATIONAL INS CO OF OHIO	OH	20.6
UTICA SPECIALTY RISK INS CO	TX	33.6
VERLAN FIRE INS CO	NH	25.4
VERMONT MUTUAL INS CO	VT	928.3
VICTORIA AUTOMOBILE INS CO	OH	10.3
VICTORIA SELECT INS CO	OH	7.8
VIRGINIA FARM BUREAU MUTUAL INS CO	VA	402.7
WAYNE MUTUAL INS CO	OH	83.2
WESTERN COMMUNITY INS CO	ID	43.3
WESTERN MUTUAL FIRE INS CO	MN	8.1
WESTERN NATIONAL MUTUAL INS CO	MN	1,045.2
WESTERN RESERVE MUTUAL CAS CO	OH	203.3
WESTFIELD INS CO	OH	2,937.3
WESTFIELD NATIONAL INS CO	OH	696.6
WI LAWYERS MUTUAL INS CO	WI	34.8
WOLVERINE MUTUAL INS CO	MI	56.4
WRIGHT NATIONAL FLOOD INS CO	TX	37.7
ZALE INDEMNITY CO	TX	45.2
Rating: C+		
ACSTAR INS CO	IL	52.6
ADDISON INS CO	IA	125.3
ADIRONDACK INS EXCHANGE	NY	326.3
AFFILIATED FM INS CO	RI	3,163.0
AGSECURITY INS CO	OK	57.4
AIG SPECIALTY INS CO	IL	115.6
ALLIANCE INDEMNITY CO	KS	10.5
ALLIANCE OF NONPROFITS FOR INS RRG	VT	106.8
ALLIED INS CO OF AMERICA	OH	78.3
ALLMERICA FINANCIAL ALLIANCE INS CO	NH	19.5
ALLMERICA FINANCIAL BENEFIT INS CO	MI	45.3
AMERICA FIRST INS CO	NH	15.0
AMERICA FIRST LLOYD'S INS CO	TX	6.9
AMERICAN AGRI BUSINESS INS CO	TX	715.2
AMERICAN FAMILY HOME INS CO	FL	423.2
AMERICAN FEDERATED INS CO	MS	40.7
AMERICAN GUARANTEE & LIABILITY INS	NY	259.2
AMERICAN INTEGRITY INS CO OF FL	FL	246.3

INSURANCE COMPANY NAME	DOM. STATE	TOTAL ASSETS ($MIL)	INSURANCE COMPANY NAME	DOM. STATE	TOTAL ASSETS ($MIL)
Rating: C+ (Continued)			CRONUS INSURANCE CO	TX	28.8
AMERICAN MODERN HOME INS CO	OH	1,030.7	CRUSADER INS CO	CA	110.8
AMERICAN SOUTHERN INS CO	KS	115.4	CSAA GENERAL INS CO	IN	361.8
AMERICAN SUMMIT INS CO	TX	40.9	CUMIS MORTGAGE REINS CO	WI	37.3
AMERICAN TRADITIONS INS CO	FL	69.0	CYPRESS INS CO	CA	1,764.8
AMERICAN ZURICH INS CO	IL	332.8	DAILY UNDERWRITERS OF AMERICA	PA	47.1
AMERISURE PARTNERS INS CO	MI	88.2	DAKOTA TRUCK UNDERWRITERS	SD	125.4
APPLIED MEDICO LEGAL SOLUTIONS RRG	AZ	152.8	DE SMET FARM MUTUAL INS CO OF SD	SD	27.9
ARBELLA MUTUAL INS CO	MA	1,462.6	DIRECT NATIONAL INS CO	AR	17.1
ARBELLA PROTECTION INS CO	MA	325.7	DISCOVER P&C INS CO	CT	135.4
ARIZONA AUTOMOBILE INS CO	AZ	41.3	DISCOVER SPECIALTY INS CO	CT	108.2
ASI PREFERRED INS CORP	FL	106.7	ELECTRIC INS CO	MA	1,424.1
ASPEN AMERICAN INS CO	TX	903.9	EMPIRE FIRE & MARINE INS CO	NE	50.9
ATLANTIC SPECIALTY INS CO	NY	2,259.6	EMPIRE INDEMNITY INS CO	OK	61.7
ATRADIUS TRADE CREDIT INS CO	MD	117.5	ENCOMPASS INS CO	IL	9.4
AUTO CLUB GROUP INS CO	MI	365.6	ENCOMPASS INS CO OF MA	MA	6.1
AVENTUS INSURANCE CO	TX	33.5	ENCOMPASS INS CO OF NJ	IL	24.6
AXIS REINS CO	NY	3,227.4	ENCOMPASS PROP & CAS INS CO OF NJ	IL	11.1
AXIS SURPLUS INS CO	IL	459.2	ENDEAVOUR INS CO	MA	6.3
BADGER MUTUAL INS CO	WI	180.7	ENUMCLAW P&C INS CO	OR	8.2
BERKLEY REGIONAL INS CO	DE	762.9	EXACT PROPERTY & CASUALTY CO INC	CA	267.7
BERKSHIRE HATHAWAY HOMESTATE INS	NE	2,938.5	FAIRMONT FARMERS MUTUAL INS CO	MN	35.4
BERKSHIRE HATHAWAY SPECIALTY INS CO	NE	4,950.5	FALLS LAKE FIRE & CASUALTY CO	CA	88.0
BREMEN FARMERS MUTUAL INS CO	KS	44.6	FAMILY SECURITY INS CO	HI	83.7
BRISTOL WEST PREFERRED INS CO	MI	22.6	FARMERS INS CO	KS	291.8
BRITISH AMERICAN INS CO	TX	56.3	FARMERS INS CO OF AZ	AZ	44.0
CALIFORNIA CASUALTY INDEMNITY EXCH	CA	575.9	FARMERS INS CO OF IDAHO	ID	188.6
CAMERON MUTUAL INS CO	MO	83.5	FARMERS INS OF COLUMBUS INC	OH	260.2
CAMICO MUTUAL INS CO	CA	91.9	FARMERS MUTUAL FIRE INS CO OF MARBLE	PA	35.4
CAPITOL SPECIALTY INS CORP	WI	150.2	FARMERS NEW CENTURY INS CO	IL	185.5
CATLIN INS CO	TX	181.6	FARMERS REINS CO	CA	202.0
CATLIN SPECIALTY INS CO	DE	588.2	FCCI INS CO	FL	2,067.1
CENTRAL PA PHYSICIANS RRG INC	SC	54.4	FEDERAL INS CO	IN	21,770.0
CENTRAL STATES INDEMNITY CO OF OMAHA	NE	542.1	FIDELITY & DEPOSIT CO OF MARYLAND	MD	214.0
CHUNG KUO INS CO LTD GUAM BRANCH	GU	41.6	FIDELITY & GUARANTY INS	WI	151.3
CITATION INS CO (MA)	MA	256.5	FIDELITY & GUARANTY INS CO	IA	20.1
CITIZENS INS CO OF IL	IL	5.4	FINANCIAL CASUALTY & SURETY INC	TX	24.3
CIVIC PROPERTY & CASUALTY CO INC	CA	268.9	FIRE INS EXCHANGE	CA	2,863.8
CLEAR BLUE INS CO	IL	56.0	FIREMANS FUND INDEMNITY CORP	NJ	15.8
CLEAR BLUE SPECIALTY INS CO	NC	106.5	FIREMANS FUND INS CO	CA	2,110.0
CLOISTER MUTL CAS INS CO	PA	9.9	FIREMANS FUND INS CO OF HI INC	HI	12.4
CMIC RRG	DC	5.4	FIRST LIBERTY INS CORP	IL	22.3
COFACE NORTH AMERICA INS CO	MA	135.9	FIRST MERCURY INS CO	DE	97.6
COLONIAL AMERICAN CAS & SURETY CO	MD	25.1	FIRSTLINE NATIONAL INS CO	MD	102.8
COLORADO CASUALTY INS CO	NH	24.9	FITCHBURG MUTUAL INS CO	MA	140.2
COLORADO FARM BUREAU MUTUAL INS CO	CO	81.3	FLAGSHIP CITY INS CO	PA	50.1
COLUMBIA NATIONAL INS CO	NE	90.7	FOREMOST COUNTY MUTUAL INS CO	TX	81.8
COMMUNITY INS CORP	WI	7.6	FOREMOST LLOYDS OF TEXAS	TX	58.6
CONEMAUGH VALLEY MUTUAL INS CO	PA	14.5	FOREMOST P&C INS CO	MI	56.2
CONSTITUTION INS CO	NY	25.4	FOREMOST SIGNATURE INS CO	MI	61.9
CONSUMERS INS USA INC	TN	65.7	GEICO CASUALTY CO	MD	3,526.8
CONTINENTAL DIVIDE INS CO	CO	18.4	GENERAL CASUALTY CO OF WI	WI	797.4
COPPERPOINT AMERICAN INS CO	AZ	6.5	GENERAL REINS CORP	DE	16,507.9
COPPERPOINT CASUALTY INS CO	AZ	7.1	GEORGIA FARM BUREAU MUTUAL INS CO	GA	670.3
COPPERPOINT INDEMNITY INS CO	AZ	11.0	GERMANIA FARM MUTUAL INS ASN	TX	395.7
			GERMANIA INS CO	TX	82.6

INSURANCE COMPANY NAME	DOM. STATE	TOTAL ASSETS ($MIL)	INSURANCE COMPANY NAME	DOM. STATE	TOTAL ASSETS ($MIL)
Rating: C+ (Continued)			NATIONAL LIABILITY & FIRE INS CO	CT	2,710.1
GERMANTOWN INS CO	PA	98.2	NATIONAL SPECIALTY INS CO	TX	88.1
GRANITE MUTUAL INS CO	VT	4.6	NATIONWIDE INDEMNITY CO	OH	2,891.2
GRAPHIC ARTS MUTUAL INS CO	NY	157.6	NATIONWIDE MUTUAL FIRE INS CO	OH	8,598.1
GRAY CASUALTY & SURETY CO	LA	18.2	NAU COUNTRY INS CO	MN	966.9
GREAT AMERICAN ASR CO	OH	18.5	NEIGHBORHOOD SPIRIT PROP & CAS CO	CA	271.3
GREAT PLAINS CASUALTY INC	IA	23.5	NEW HAMPSHIRE INS CO	IL	215.9
GUIDEONE AMERICA INS CO	IA	12.1	NEW HOME WARRANTY INS CO RRG	DC	23.5
GUIDEONE ELITE INS CO	IA	30.0	NEW HORIZONS INS CO OF MO	MO	55.8
GUIDEONE P&C INS CO	IA	378.4	NEW JERSEY INDEMNITY INS CO	NJ	77.7
GULFSTREAM P&C INS CO	FL	110.1	NEW MEXICO MUTUAL CASUALTY CO	NM	407.8
GUTHRIE RRG	SC	57.9	NORFOLK & DEDHAM MUTUAL FIRE INS CO	MA	453.8
HANOVER LLOYDS INS CO	TX	6.2	NORTH COUNTRY INS CO	NY	29.2
HARTFORD FIRE INS CO	CT	22,855.3	NORTHFIELD INS CO	IA	391.9
HINGHAM MUTUAL FIRE INS CO	MA	68.8	OBI NATIONAL INS CO	PA	13.3
HISCOX INS CO	IL	330.0	OHIO INDEMNITY CO	OH	152.5
HLTHCR PROVIDERS INS CO	SC	81.5	OLD GUARD INS CO	OH	481.2
HOMESITE LLOYDS OF TEXAS	TX	31.2	ONTARIO REINS CO LTD	GA	31.5
HOSPITALITY INS CO	CT	10.5	OSWEGO COUNTY MUTUAL INS CO	NY	29.6
HOUSING & REDEVELOPMENT INS EXCH	PA	44.1	PACIFIC INDEMNITY INS CO	GU	35.4
HOUSING SPECIALTY INS CO	VT	18.1	PALMETTO CASUALTY INS CO	SC	7.1
ILLINOIS FARMERS INS CO	IL	246.7	PARTNERRE AMERICA INS CO	DE	393.0
INFINITY SAFEGUARD INS CO	OH	5.0	PEERLESS INDEMNITY INS CO	IL	199.5
INLAND INS CO	NE	300.7	PENN-AMERICA INS CO	PA	127.2
INS CO OF GREATER NY	NY	128.0	PENN-STAR INS CO	PA	121.3
LEATHERSTOCKING COOP INS CO	NY	43.4	PETROLEUM MARKETERS MGMT INS CO	IA	50.2
LEBANON VALLEY INS CO	PA	26.5	PHYSICIANS INS PROGRAM	PA	25.8
MADISON MUTUAL INS CO	NY	15.1	PHYSICIANS PROFESSIONAL LIABILTY RRG	VT	37.4
MAIDEN RE NORTH AMERICA INC	MO	1,298.9	PLATEAU CASUALTY INS CO	TN	45.8
MAIN STREET AMER PROTECTION INS CO	FL	23.3	PLICO INC	OK	110.3
MAPFRE INS CO OF NY	NY	154.1	PODIATRY INS CO OF AM	IL	303.2
MASSACHUSETTS BAY INS CO	NH	65.2	PRE-PAID LEGAL CAS INC	OK	19.7
MAXUM CASUALTY INS CO	CT	27.6	PRIME P&C INS INC	IL	52.3
MEDICAL SECURITY INS CO	NC	32.0	PRIMERO INS CO	NV	16.9
MEDMAL DIRECT INS CO	FL	43.3	PROGRESSIVE NORTHERN INS CO	WI	1,866.5
MENTAL HEALTH RISK RETENTION GROUP	VT	30.1	PROGRESSIVE NORTHWESTERN INS CO	OH	1,812.5
MERCED PROPERTY & CASUALTY CO	CA	23.4	RAINIER INS CO	AZ	26.0
MERCER INS CO	PA	269.0	REPUBLIC-FRANKLIN INS CO	OH	112.6
MICHIGAN INS CO	MI	154.4	RURAL COMMUNITY INS CO	MN	1,790.7
MICHIGAN MILLERS MUTUAL INS CO	MI	187.6	SAFETY INDEMNITY INS CO	MA	127.6
MID-CONTINENT CAS CO	OH	527.9	SAFETY P&C INS CO	MA	47.2
MIDWEST EMPLOYERS CAS CO	DE	168.8	SAFEWAY INS CO OF LA	LA	155.7
MIDWEST INS CO	IL	96.4	SAMARITAN RRG INC	SC	42.9
MILBANK INS CO	IA	635.9	SECURA SUPREME INS CO	WI	141.9
MILLVILLE MUTUAL INS CO	PA	92.6	SELECTIVE INS CO OF NEW ENGLAND	NJ	193.4
MOTORISTS MUTUAL INS CO	OH	1,370.8	SEVEN SEAS INS CO	FL	22.8
MT MORRIS MUTUAL INS CO	WI	40.7	SOUTHERN FIDELITY P&C INC	FL	107.8
MUNICH REINS AMERICA INC	DE	18,585.6	SOUTHERN INS CO OF VA	VA	149.9
MUTUAL OF WAUSAU INS CORP	WI	25.0	SOUTHERN STATES INS EXCHANGE	VA	44.3
MUTUALAID EXCHANGE	KS	28.9	SOUTHWEST MARINE & GEN INS CO	AZ	216.4
NAMIC INS CO	IN	52.6	ST PAUL GUARDIAN INS CO	CT	75.8
NATIONAL AMERICAN INS CO	OK	211.7	STANDARD CASUALTY CO	TX	37.7
NATIONAL INDEMNITY CO OF THE SOUTH	IA	460.6	STARNET INS CO	DE	242.1
NATIONAL INTERSTATE INS CO	OH	1,281.1	STATE AUTO P&C INS CO	IA	2,518.9
NATIONAL INTERSTATE INS CO OF HAWAII	OH	55.9	STATE AUTOMOBILE MUTUAL INS CO	OH	2,407.3
			STEADFAST INS CO	DE	723.4

INSURANCE COMPANY NAME	DOM. STATE	TOTAL ASSETS ($MIL)	INSURANCE COMPANY NAME	DOM. STATE	TOTAL ASSETS ($MIL)
Rating: C+ (Continued)			ALASKA TIMBER INS EXCHANGE	AK	15.6
STILLWATER P&C INS CO	NY	140.4	ALINSCO INS CO	TX	69.8
STONEWOOD INS CO	NC	105.0	ALLEGHENY CASUALTY CO	NJ	36.1
SURETY BONDING CO OF AMERICA	SD	7.7	ALLIANCE INS CO	KS	25.7
SUTTER INS CO	CA	37.2	ALLIANCE UNITED INS CO	CA	652.9
SYNCORA GUARANTEE INC	NY	1,302.1	ALLIANZ GLOBAL RISKS US INS CO	IL	7,625.6
TDC NATIONAL ASR CO	OR	344.8	ALLIED WORLD INS CO	NH	1,788.1
TEXAS FARM BUREAU MUTUAL INS CO	TX	733.5	ALLIED WORLD NATL ASR CO	NH	320.9
TEXAS FARMERS INS CO	TX	676.1	ALLIED WORLD SURPLUS LINES INS	AR	263.3
TITAN INS CO INC A RRG	SC	67.5	AMERICAN ALTERNATIVE INS CORP	DE	590.3
TOYOTA MOTOR INS CO	IA	557.7	AMERICAN ASSOC OF ORTHODONTIST RRG	AZ	48.2
TRAVELERS CASUALTY CO	CT	207.4	AMERICAN AUTOMOBILE INS CO	MO	126.0
TRAVELERS CONSTITUTION STATE INS CO	CT	207.2	AMERICAN BUILDERS INS CO	DE	146.3
TRI-CENTURY INS CO	PA	25.5	AMERICAN BUS & MERCANTILE INS MUT	DE	68.8
TRINITY UNIVERSAL INS CO	TX	1,853.3	AMERICAN CASUALTY CO OF READING	PA	142.2
TRUCK INS EXCHANGE	CA	2,107.6	AMERICAN EMPIRE INS CO	OH	21.5
UFG SPECIALTY INS CO	IA	43.1	AMERICAN EXCESS INS EXCHANGE RRG	VT	308.3
UNITED FIRE & INDEMNITY CO	TX	55.3	AMERICAN FARMERS & RANCHERS MUTUAL	OK	159.4
UNITED FIRE LLOYDS	TX	31.5	AMERICAN HOME ASR CO	NY	25,639.7
UNITED GUAR RESIDENTIAL INS CO OF NC	NC	53.8	AMERICAN MODERN LLOYDS INS CO	TX	11.6
UNITED GUARANTY MORTGAGE INDEM CO	NC	48.9	AMERICAN MODERN SELECT INS CO	OH	222.3
UNITED GUARANTY RESIDENTIAL INS CO	NC	2,607.5	AMERICAN PET INS CO	NY	75.9
UNIVERSAL SURETY CO	NE	234.8	AMERICAN SAFETY INS CO	GA	16.7
UNIVERSAL UNDERWRITERS INS CO	IL	332.2	AMERICAN SELECT INS CO	OH	271.5
UNIVERSAL UNDERWRITERS OF TX	IL	10.6	AMERICAN SOUTHERN HOME INS CO	FL	135.3
US COASTAL P&C INS CO	FL	35.3	AMERICAN STRATEGIC INS CO	FL	1,223.1
VA FARM BUREAU TOWN & COUNTRY INS CO	VA	68.1	AMERICAN SURETY CO	IN	14.2
VICTORIA FIRE & CASUALTY CO	OH	58.9	AMERICAN WEST INS CO	ND	18.1
WATFORD INS CO	NJ	23.6	AMERICAN WESTERN HOME INS CO	OK	162.7
WAYNE COOPERATIVE INS CO	NY	34.9	AMERICAS INS CO	DC	16.6
WEST BRANCH MUTL INS CO	PA	1.1	AMFED CASUALTY INS CO	MS	5.9
WEST VIRGINIA INS CO	WV	53.7	AMGUARD INS CO	PA	878.8
WESTERN SURETY CO	SD	2,043.5	ANCHOR GENERAL INS CO	CA	98.2
WESTMINSTER AMERICAN INS CO	MD	38.7	ANCHOR SPECIALTY INS CO	TX	18.6
WISCONSIN REINS CORP	WI	96.1	ANTILLES INS CO	PR	69.9
YOSEMITE INS CO	IN	113.7	APPALACHIAN INS CO	RI	326.0
ZENITH INS CO	CA	1,843.8	APPLIED UNDERWRITERS CAPTIVE RISK	IA	847.1
ZEPHYR INS CO	HI	101.3	ARBELLA INDEMNITY INS CO	MA	53.1
ZURICH AMERICAN INS CO OF IL	IL	62.3	ARCH INS CO	MO	3,921.9
Rating: C			ARCHITECTS & ENGINEERS INS CO	DE	22.5
1ST AUTO & CASUALTY INS CO	WI	25.5	ARGONAUT INS CO	IL	1,820.4
1ST CHOICE ADVANTAGE INS CO	PA	21.6	ARTISAN & TRUCKERS CASUALTY CO	WI	346.2
A CENTRAL INS CO	NY	118.3	ASI SELECT AUTO INS CORP	CA	18.3
ACADIA INS CO	NH	164.3	ASI SELECT INS CORP	DE	28.7
ACCESS HOME INS CO	LA	37.8	ASSN CASUALTY INS CO	TX	46.8
ACE FIRE UNDERWRITERS INS CO	PA	119.9	ASSOCIATED EMPLOYERS INS CO	MA	6.8
ACE INS CO OF THE MIDWEST	IN	68.8	ASSOCIATED INDEMNITY CORP	CA	106.4
ADM INS CO	AZ	103.1	ASSOCIATED LOGGERS EXCHANGE	ID	37.6
ADMIRAL INDEMNITY CO	DE	59.5	ASSOCIATED MUTUAL INS CO	NY	28.5
ADMIRAL INS CO	DE	749.4	ATAIN INS CO	TX	88.2
ADRIATIC INS CO	ND	95.4	ATAIN SPECIALTY INS CO	MI	387.9
AGENT ALLIANCE INS CO	AL	67.2	ATLANTA INTERNATIONAL INS CO	NY	96.2
AGRI GENERAL INS CO	IA	99.7	AUTO CLUB FAMILY INS CO	MO	114.7
AGRI INS EXCHANGE RRG	IN	19.3	AUTO CLUB PROPERTY & CASUALTY INS CO	MI	91.2
AIG PROPERTY CASUALTY CO	PA	444.0	AUTOMOBILE CLUB INTERINSURANCE EXCH	MO	422.3
			AXA ART INS CORP	NY	12.7

INSURANCE COMPANY NAME	DOM. STATE	TOTAL ASSETS ($MIL)	INSURANCE COMPANY NAME	DOM. STATE	TOTAL ASSETS ($MIL)
Rating: C (Continued)			COLUMBIA CASUALTY CO	IL	245.2
BALBOA INS CO	CA	77.9	COMMERCE & INDUSTRY INS CO	NY	419.6
BALDWIN MUTUAL INS CO	AL	12.2	COMMERCE WEST INS CO	CA	182.3
BANKERS INDEPENDENT INS CO	PA	20.8	COMMERCIAL ALLIANCE INS CO	TX	104.9
BANKERS INS CO	FL	149.4	COMMUNITIES OF FAITH RRG INC	SC	14.1
BANKERS STANDARD INS CO	PA	762.9	COMMUNITY BLOOD CENTERS EXCHANGE RRG	IN	19.3
BAR PLAN MUTUAL INS CO	MO	41.9	CONSOLIDATED INS CO	IN	14.6
BAR PLAN SURETY & FIDELITY CO	MO	5.5	CONTINENTAL HERITAGE INS CO	FL	29.6
BARNSTABLE COUNTY INS CO	MA	25.0	CONTINENTAL INDEMNITY CO	IA	227.6
BATTLE CREEK MUTUAL INS CO	NE	8.2	CONTINENTAL INS CO	PA	1,775.7
BEARING MIDWEST CASUALTY CO	KS	7.6	CONTINENTAL INS CO OF NJ	NJ	19.1
BERKLEY NATIONAL INS CO	IA	145.9	CONTINENTAL WESTERN INS CO	IA	214.8
BERKLEY REGIONAL SPCLTY INS CO	DE	63.1	COPPERPOINT NATIONAL INS CO	AZ	7.3
BERKSHIRE HATHATWAY DIRECT INS CO	NE	151.8	COUNTRYWAY INS CO	NY	28.2
BLACKBOARD INSURANCE CO	DE	57.0	COVENANT INS CO	CT	89.3
BLOOMFIELD MUTUAL INS CO	MN	12.6	COVERYS RRG INC	DC	28.8
BLUE RIDGE INDEMNITY CO	WI	6.9	CSAA AFFINITY INS CO	AZ	224.3
BOND SAFEGUARD INS CO	SD	90.8	CSAA FIRE & CASUALTY INS CO	IN	116.6
BRIAR CREEK MUTUAL INS CO	PA	14.9	CSE SAFEGUARD INS CO	CA	102.9
BRIDGEFIELD CASUALTY INS CO	FL	56.9	CYPRESS P&C INS CO	FL	89.3
BROADLINE RRG INC	VT	100.1	DAKOTA FIRE INS CO	ND	242.3
BROOME CO OPERATIVE INS CO	NY	22.8	DANBURY INS CO	MA	13.2
BUCKEYE STATE MUTUAL INS CO	OH	55.0	DE SMET INS CO OF SD	SD	16.0
BUILDERS INS (A MUTUAL CAPTIVE CO)	GA	634.4	DENTISTS BENEFITS INS CO	OR	19.0
BUNKER HILL INS CAS CO	MA	12.2	DIAMOND STATE INS CO	IN	97.4
BUNKER HILL INS CO	MA	55.7	DISCOVERY INS CO	NC	30.2
CALIFORNIA CASUALTY & FIRE INS CO	CA	68.0	DISTRICTS MUTL INS & RISK MGMT	WI	25.6
CALIFORNIA CASUALTY INS CO	OR	92.1	DOCTORS CO RRG A RECIPROCAL	DC	27.8
CALIFORNIA MUTUAL INS CO	CA	15.7	DOCTORS DIRECT INS INC	IL	13.5
CAPITOL COUNTY MUTUAL FIRE INS CO	TX	9.6	DORCHESTER INS CO LTD	VI	32.9
CAPITOL INDEMNITY CORP	WI	592.8	DORCHESTER MUTUAL INS CO	MA	99.7
CAPITOL PREFERRED INS CO	FL	56.4	DTRIC INS CO LTD	HI	129.5
CARE WEST INS CO	CA	129.9	DTRIC INS UNDERWRITERS LTD	HI	13.5
CAREGIVERS UNITED LIAB INS CO RRG	SC	43.6	DUBOIS MEDICAL RRG	DC	13.2
CARIBBEAN AMERICAN PROPERTY INS CO	PR	59.4	EAGLESTONE REINS CO	PA	6,138.8
CAROLINA CASUALTY INS CO	IA	176.4	EASTERN MUTUAL INS CO	NY	26.6
CATASTROPHE REINS CO	TX	2,013.8	ELEPHANT INS CO	VA	215.9
CATLIN INDEMNITY CO	DE	108.9	EMC PROPERTY & CASUALTY CO	IA	88.5
CBIA COMP SERVICES INC	CT	24.9	EMERGENCY MEDICINE PROFESSIONAL ASR	NV	18.7
CELINA MUTUAL INS CO	OH	76.8	EMERGENCY PHYSICIANS INS RRG	VT	22.9
CENTAURI SPECIALTY INS CO	FL	143.4	EMPLOYERS ASSURANCE CO	FL	484.8
CENTRAL CO-OPERATIVE INS CO	NY	20.2	EMPLOYERS INS CO OF NV	NV	577.5
CENTURION MEDICAL LIAB PROTECT RRG	AZ	21.0	EMPLOYERS PREFERRED INS CO	FL	966.4
CENTURY SURETY CO	OH	101.1	EQUITY INS CO	TX	86.1
CHAUTAUQUA PATRONS INS CO	NY	22.0	ESSENTIA INS CO	MO	81.8
CHICAGO INS CO	IL	77.2	ESURANCE INS CO	WI	191.5
CIM INS CORP	MI	17.7	ESURANCE INS CO OF NJ	WI	14.0
CITIZENS INS CO OF OHIO	OH	14.7	ESURANCE P&C INS CO	WI	115.2
CITIZENS INS CO OF THE MIDWEST	IN	61.0	EVER-GREENE MUTUAL INS CO	PA	6.4
CITY NATIONAL INS CO	TX	19.1	EVEREST INDEMNITY INS CO	DE	212.5
CIVIL SERVICE EMPLOYEES INS CO	CA	217.2	EVEREST NATIONAL INS CO	DE	808.5
CLERMONT INS CO	IA	27.4	EVEREST SECURITY INS CO	GA	36.3
COLLEGE RRG INC	VT	28.4	EVERGREEN NATIONAL INDEMNITY CO	OH	48.1
COLONIAL LLOYDS	TX	9.7	EXCELSIOR INS CO	NH	36.7
COLONY INS CO	VA	1,698.6	EXCESS SHARE INS CORP	OH	53.3
			EXPLORER INS CO	CA	401.3

INSURANCE COMPANY NAME	DOM. STATE	TOTAL ASSETS ($MIL)	INSURANCE COMPANY NAME	DOM. STATE	TOTAL ASSETS ($MIL)
Rating: C **(Continued)**			GREAT AMERICAN SPIRIT INS CO	OH	17.1
FALLS LAKE GENERAL INS CO	OH	12.2	GREAT DIVIDE INS CO	ND	254.1
FARM BUREAU CNTY MUTUAL INS CO OF TX	TX	18.8	GREENVILLE CASUALTY INS CO INC	SC	9.5
FARMERS & MECHANICS FIRE & CAS INS	WV	12.8	GREENWICH INS CO	DE	1,250.4
FARMERS FIRE INS CO	PA	31.2	GRINNELL SELECT INS CO	IA	37.8
FARMERS INS EXCHANGE	CA	16,164.8	GUIDEONE MUTUAL INS CO	IA	1,049.1
FARMERS MUTUAL F I C OF OKARCHE OK	OK	19.2	GUIDEONE SPECIALTY MUTUAL INS CO	IA	226.6
FARMERS MUTUAL INS CO	WV	17.3	GULF GUARANTY INS CO	MS	4.5
FARMERS MUTUAL OF TENNESSEE	TN	22.6	HALLMARK COUNTY MUTUAL INS CO	TX	5.8
FD INS CO	FL	12.9	HALLMARK NATIONAL INS CO	AZ	87.0
FDM PREFERRED INS CO	NY	10.0	HANOVER AMERICAN INS CO	NH	29.3
FEDERATED NATIONAL INS CO	FL	575.8	HARLEYSVILLE INS CO	OH	167.8
FHM INS CO	FL	72.3	HARLEYSVILLE INS CO OF NEW YORK	OH	59.4
FIRE DISTRICTS INS CO	NY	15.2	HARLEYSVILLE PREFERRED INS CO	OH	118.3
FIREMENS INS CO OF WASHINGTON DC	DE	91.9	HARLEYSVILLE WORCESTER INS CO	OH	181.7
FIRST AMERICAN PROP & CAS INS CO	CA	97.1	HARTLAND MUTUAL INS CO	ND	13.0
FIRST AMERICAN SPECIALTY INS CO	CA	126.7	HAWKEYE-SECURITY INS CO	WI	14.8
FIRST CHOICE CASUALTY INS CO	NV	14.1	HDI GLOBAL INS CO	IL	414.8
FIRST COMMUNITY INS CO	FL	99.4	HEALTH CARE INDEMNITY INC	CO	326.4
FIRST DAKOTA INDEMNITY CO	SD	52.1	HEALTH CARE INDUSTRY LIAB RECIP INS	DC	50.5
FIRST F&C INS OF HI INC	HI	9.3	HIGHMARK CASUALTY INS CO	PA	268.1
FIRST INDEMNITY INS OF HI INC	HI	7.6	HOCHHEIM PRAIRIE CASUALTY INS CO	TX	81.9
FIRST INS CO OF HI LTD	HI	661.6	HOMELAND INS CO OF NY	NY	118.2
FIRST NET INS CO	GU	18.5	HOMEOWNERS CHOICE PROP & CAS INS CO	FL	411.3
FIRST SECURITY INS OF HI INC	HI	5.6	HOMESITE INDEMNITY CO	WI	51.9
FIRST SPECIALTY INS CORP	MO	171.9	HOMESITE INS CO	WI	155.8
FIRST SURETY CORP	WV	37.7	HOMESITE INS CO OF CA	CA	64.3
FLORISTS INS CO	IL	5.7	HOMESITE INS CO OF FL	IL	16.8
FLORISTS MUTUAL INS CO	IL	130.6	HOMESITE INS CO OF GA	GA	27.4
FOUNDERS INS CO (IL)	IL	166.7	HOMESITE INS CO OF IL	IL	11.9
FOUNDERS INS CO (NJ)	NJ	6.6	HOMESITE INS CO OF NY	NY	37.8
FRANKLIN INS CO	PA	31.4	HOMESITE INS CO OF THE MIDWEST	WI	449.7
GEICO COUNTY MUTUAL INS CO	TX	156.4	HOMESTEAD MUTUAL INS CO	WI	10.2
GEM STATE INS CO	ID	12.3	HOOSIER INS CO	IN	7.8
GEMINI INS CO	DE	108.6	HOSPITALITY MUTUAL INS CO	MA	68.9
GENERAL CASUALTY INS CO	WI	9.5	ID COUNTIES RISK MGMT PROGRAM UNDW	ID	73.2
GENERAL STAR INDEMNITY CO	DE	931.6	ILLINOIS UNION INS CO	IL	447.0
GENERALI - US BRANCH	NY	63.3	INDEMNITY CO OF CA	CA	10.8
GENESIS INS CO	DE	184.7	INDEMNITY INS CO OF NORTH AMERICA	PA	485.5
GENWORTH MORTGAGE INS CORP	NC	3,346.0	INDEMNITY NATIONAL INS CO	MS	68.1
GEORGIA CASUALTY & SURETY CO	GA	41.3	INDEPENDENCE CASUALTY INS CO	MA	4.7
GEOVERA SPECIALTY INS CO	DE	90.2	INDEPENDENT SPECIALTY INS CO	DE	69.5
GERMANIA FIRE & CASUALTY CO	TX	32.8	INDIANA INS CO	IN	69.7
GERMANIA SELECT INS CO	TX	211.2	INDIANA LUMBERMENS MUTUAL INS CO	IN	57.0
GOLDEN EAGLE INS CORP	NH	59.2	INFINITY AUTO INS CO	OH	11.6
GOTHAM INS CO	NY	299.3	INFINITY COUNTY MUTUAL INS CO	TX	74.3
GRAIN DEALERS MUTUAL INS CO	IN	12.4	INFINITY INDEMNITY INS CO	IN	6.3
GRANGE INDEMNITY INS CO	OH	58.5	INFINITY PREFERRED INS CO	OH	4.6
GRANGE INS CO OF MI	OH	44.5	INFINITY SECURITY INS CO	IN	5.7
GRANWEST P&C	WA	23.8	INFINITY STANDARD INS CO	IN	7.2
GREAT AMERICAN ALLIANCE INS CO	OH	27.9	INS CO OF NORTH AMERICA	PA	999.4
GREAT AMERICAN E & S INS CO	DE	48.4	INS CO OF THE WEST	CA	2,570.2
GREAT AMERICAN FIDELITY INS CO	DE	48.5	INSURORS INDEMNITY CO	TX	39.7
GREAT AMERICAN INS CO OF NEW YORK	NY	49.7	INSURORS INDEMNITY LLOYDS	TX	5.0
GREAT AMERICAN SECURITY INS CO	OH	15.5	INTEGON CASUALTY INS CO	NC	26.3
			INTEGON GENERAL INS CORP	NC	95.0

INSURANCE COMPANY NAME	DOM. STATE	TOTAL ASSETS ($MIL)	INSURANCE COMPANY NAME	DOM. STATE	TOTAL ASSETS ($MIL)
Rating: C (Continued)			MID-HUDSON CO-OPERTIVE INS CO	NY	28.2
INTEGON INDEMNITY CORP	NC	185.5	MIDSOUTH MUTUAL INS CO	TN	27.4
INTEGON PREFERRED INS CO	NC	99.8	MIDWESTERN INDEMNITY CO	NH	28.1
INTEGRAND ASR CO	PR	126.9	MONARCH NATIONAL INS CO	FL	39.2
INTERBORO INS CO	NY	79.7	MONROE GUARANTY INS CO	IN	52.5
ISLAND PREMIER INS CO LTD	HI	10.5	MONTGOMERY MUTUAL INS CO	MA	54.0
ISMIE INDEMNITY CO	IL	53.8	MOUNT VERNON FIRE INS CO	PA	775.0
JAMES RIVER INS CO	OH	630.4	MOUNTAIN LAUREL ASR CO	OH	183.4
JEFFERSON INS CO	NY	104.6	MOUNTAIN STATES INDEMNITY CO	NM	16.3
KEY RISK INS CO	IA	45.0	MT HAWLEY INS CO	IL	945.8
KINGSTONE INSURANCE CO	NY	197.0	MT WASHINGTON ASR CORP	NH	7.0
LAMMICO RRG INC	DC	6.0	MULTINATIONAL INS CO	PR	71.4
LANDMARK AMERICAN INS CO	NH	355.2	NARRAGANSETT BAY INS CO	RI	227.3
LAWYERS MUTUAL INS CO OF KENTUCKY	KY	23.2	NASW RRG INC	DC	16.6
LE MARS INS CO	IA	66.1	NATIONAL CONTINENTAL INS CO	NY	135.0
LEXINGTON INS CO	DE	21,180.1	NATIONAL FARMERS UNION PROP & CAS CO	WI	134.1
LEXON INS CO	TX	244.5	NATIONAL FIRE & CASUALTY CO	IL	10.3
LIBERTY INS CORP	IL	260.1	NATIONAL FIRE & MARINE INS CO	NE	10,841.0
LIBERTY INS UNDERWRITERS INC	IL	264.1	NATIONAL FIRE INS CO OF HARTFORD	IL	118.0
LIBERTY MUTUAL MID ATLANTIC INS CO	MA	22.8	NATIONAL GENERAL ASR CO	MO	41.9
LIBERTY NORTHWEST INS CORP	OR	59.9	NATIONAL GENERAL INS CO	MO	69.0
LIBERTY PERSONAL INS CO	NH	17.0	NATIONAL GENERAL INS ONLINE INC	MO	42.6
LIBERTY SURPLUS INS CORP	NH	139.7	NATIONAL INDEMNITY CO OF MID-AMERICA	IA	315.9
LIVINGSTON MUTUAL INS CO	PA	3.5	NATIONAL INS CO OF WI INC	WI	13.6
LM INS CORP	IL	124.0	NATIONAL MUTUAL INS CO	OH	83.4
LUTHERAN MUTUAL FIRE INS CO	IL	10.7	NATIONAL SERVICE CONTRACT INS CO RRG	DC	12.8
MA EMPLOYERS INS CO	MA	4.4	NATIONAL SURETY CORP	IL	140.9
MAIN STREET AMERICA ASR CO	FL	44.0	NATIONAL TRUST INS CO	IN	37.0
MANUFACTURERS ALLIANCE INS CO	PA	219.4	NATIONAL UNION FIRE INS CO	PA	25,661.1
MAPFRE INS CO	NJ	80.5	NAUTILUS INS CO	AZ	268.9
MAPFRE INS CO OF FLORIDA	FL	107.5	NCMIC RRG INC	VT	7.5
MAPFRE PAN AMERICAN INS CO	PR	38.3	NETHERLANDS INS CO	NH	99.1
MAPFRE PRAICO INS CO	PR	435.2	NEVADA CAPITAL INS CO	NV	102.3
MAPLE VALLEY MUTUAL INS CO	WI	14.8	NEW CENTURY INS CO	TX	11.2
MARKEL AMERICAN INS CO	VA	585.5	NEW MEXICO FOUNDATION INS CO	NM	22.9
MAXUM INDEMNITY CO	CT	137.3	NEW MEXICO PREMIER INS CO	NM	3.9
MCIC VERMONT INC RRG	VT	1,922.5	NEW MEXICO SAFETY CASUALTY CO	NM	5.2
MCMILLAN WARNER MUTUAL INS CO	WI	18.5	NEW SOUTH INS CO	NC	62.7
MD RRG INC	MT	27.5	NHRMA MUTUAL INS CO	IL	40.1
MDADVANTAGE INS CO OF NJ	NJ	336.8	NOETIC SPECIALTY INS CO	VT	123.9
MEDMARC CASUALTY INS CO	VT	295.6	NORTH AMERICAN CAPACITY INS CO	NH	173.5
MEDPRO RRG	DC	98.6	NORTH AMERICAN ELITE INS CO	NH	139.9
MEEMIC INS CO	MI	286.9	NORTH AMERICAN SPECIALTY INS CO	NH	510.4
MEMBERS INS CO	NC	34.3	NORTH CAROLINA GRANGE MUTUAL INS CO	NC	36.2
MEMIC INDEMNITY CO	NH	528.6	NORTH PACIFIC INS CO	OR	8.5
MENNONITE MUTUAL INS CO	OH	29.0	NORTHERN SECURITY INS CO	VT	8.5
MERCER INS CO OF NJ INC	NJ	92.2	NORTHWEST DENTISTS INS CO	WA	24.5
MERCURY INDEMNITY CO OF AMERICA	FL	52.3	OAK RIVER INS CO	NE	809.1
MERIDIAN SECURITY INS CO	IN	137.7	OBI AMERICA INS CO	PA	15.5
MESA UNDERWRITERS SPECIALTY INS CO	NJ	340.0	ODYSSEY REINS CO	CT	7,797.1
MGA INS CO	TX	299.4	OHIO CASUALTY INS CO	NH	6,147.6
MGIC ASSURANCE CORP	WI	17.8	OKLAHOMA SURETY CO	OH	17.1
MIC GENERAL INS CORP	MI	57.2	OLD GLORY INS CO	TX	23.6
MIC P&C INS CORP	MI	99.7	OLD UNITED CAS CO	KS	650.5
MID-CONTINENT INS CO	OH	21.1	OMEGA ONE INS CO	AL	12.1
			OMNI INS CO	IL	98.5

INSURANCE COMPANY NAME	DOM. STATE	TOTAL ASSETS ($MIL)
Rating: C (Continued)		
ONTARIO INS CO	NY	18.2
OOIDA RISK RETENTION GROUP INC	VT	95.6
OREGON AUTOMOBILE INS CO	OR	8.3
OREGON MUTUAL INS CO	OR	214.6
PACIFIC COMPENSATION INS CO	CA	428.2
PACIFIC PIONEER INS CO	CA	20.0
PACIFIC STAR INS CO	WI	15.6
PACO ASR CO INC	IL	64.1
PALISADES SAFETY & INS ASSOC	NJ	1,343.7
PARATRANSIT INS CO A MUTUAL RRG	TN	31.1
PARTNERRE INS CO OF NY	NY	117.3
PARTNERS MUTUAL INS CO	WI	46.9
PATRIOT INS CO	ME	130.7
PATRONS MUTUAL INS CO OF CT	CT	49.4
PEACE CHURCH RRG INC	VT	21.1
PENINSULA INDEMNITY CO	MD	12.2
PENINSULA INS CO	MD	95.9
PENN CHARTER MUTL INS CO	PA	16.9
PENN MILLERS INS CO	PA	99.8
PENN-PATRIOT INS CO	VA	50.0
PENNSYLVANIA INS CO	IA	72.3
PENNSYLVANIA MANUFACTURERS ASN INS	PA	1,017.3
PENNSYLVANIA MANUFACTURERS IND CO	PA	233.7
PHENIX MUTUAL FIRE INS CO	NH	67.3
PHYSICIANS REIMBURSEMENT FUND RRG	VT	30.0
PILGRIM INS CO	MA	101.5
PIONEER SPECIALTY INS CO	MN	71.1
PLANS LIABILITY INS CO	OH	106.7
PLATTE RIVER INS CO	NE	150.8
POINT GUARD INS CO	PR	72.1
POSITIVE PHYSICIANS INS	PA	59.0
PRAETORIAN INS CO	PA	453.9
PREFERRED EMPLOYERS INS CO	CA	106.2
PRINCETON EXCESS & SURPLUS LINES INS	DE	167.5
PRINCETON INS CO	NJ	723.1
PRIORITY ONE INS CO	TX	17.7
PROASSURANCE CASUALTY CO	MI	990.0
PROASSURANCE SPECIALTY INS CO INC	AL	57.0
PRODUCERS AGRICULTURE INS CO	TX	448.8
PRODUCERS LLOYDS INS CO	TX	11.1
PROFESSIONAL SOLUTIONS INS CO	IA	24.1
PROGRESSIVE ADVANCED INS CO	OH	530.4
PROGRESSIVE AMERICAN INS CO	OH	585.9
PROGRESSIVE BAYSIDE INS CO	OH	148.4
PROGRESSIVE CLASSIC INS CO	WI	452.0
PROGRESSIVE EXPRESS INS CO	OH	251.4
PROGRESSIVE GULF INS CO	OH	313.7
PROGRESSIVE HAWAII INS CORP	OH	218.5
PROGRESSIVE MARATHON INS CO	MI	594.9
PROGRESSIVE MAX INS CO	OH	568.7
PROGRESSIVE MICHIGAN INS CO	MI	618.5
PROGRESSIVE MOUNTAIN INS CO	OH	353.8
PROGRESSIVE PALOVERDE INS CO	IN	161.1
PROGRESSIVE PREFERRED INS CO	OH	931.1

INSURANCE COMPANY NAME	DOM. STATE	TOTAL ASSETS ($MIL)
PROGRESSIVE PREMIER INS CO OF IL	OH	326.6
PROGRESSIVE SECURITY INS CO	LA	223.3
PROGRESSIVE SELECT INS CO	OH	850.0
PROGRESSIVE SOUTHEASTERN INS CO	IN	210.9
PROGRESSIVE SPECIALTY INS CO	OH	1,166.3
PROGRESSIVE UNIVERSAL INS CO	WI	440.3
PROGRESSIVE WEST INS CO	OH	136.1
R&Q REINS CO	PA	203.5
REDWOOD FIRE & CAS INS CO	NE	1,893.7
REGENT INS CO	WI	40.9
RELIAMAX SURETY CO	SD	63.0
REPUB MRTG GRTY INS CORP	NC	139.8
REPUBLIC FIRE & CASUALTY INS CO	OK	8.4
REPUBLIC INDEMNITY OF CA	CA	26.4
REPUBLIC LLOYDS	TX	12.4
REPUBLIC UNDERWRITERS INS CO	TX	476.7
RESPONSIVE AUTO INS CO	FL	24.8
ROCKHILL INS CO	AZ	157.3
ROCKINGHAM CASUALTY CO	VA	30.4
ROOT INS CO	OH	22.1
RURAL TRUST INS CO	TX	23.5
RVI AMERICA INS CO	CT	109.4
RVOS FARM MUTUAL INS CO	TX	88.5
SAFEPOINT INS CO	FL	175.4
SAFETY FIRST INS CO	IL	74.7
SAFETY NATIONAL CASUALTY CORP	MO	7,223.8
SAFETY SPECIALTY INS CO	MO	89.1
SAFEWAY INS CO OF AL	IL	78.5
SAFEWAY INS CO OF GA	GA	76.5
SAINT LUKES HEALTH SYSTEM RRG	SC	13.5
SAN FRANCISCO REINS CO	CA	3,390.4
SCOR REINS CO	NY	3,541.5
SECURITY NATIONAL INS CO	DE	1,114.1
SELECT RISK INS CO	PA	43.1
SEQUOIA INDEMNITY CO	NV	7.9
SFM SELECT INS CO	MN	4.2
SHELTER GENERAL INS CO	MO	127.5
SONNENBERG MUTUAL INS CO	OH	27.6
SOUTHERN COUNTY MUTUAL INS CO	TX	34.2
SOUTHERN FIRE & CASUALTY CO	WI	7.2
SOUTHERN GENERAL INS CO	GA	51.4
SOUTHERN INS CO	TX	39.4
SOUTHERN PILOT INS CO	WI	7.1
SOUTHERN TRUST INS CO	GA	47.1
SOUTHERN UNDERWRITERS INS CO	OK	5.3
SOUTHERN VANGUARD INS CO	TX	24.8
ST PAUL SURPLUS LINES INS CO	DE	636.2
STAR INS CO	MI	1,815.6
STARSTONE NATIONAL INS CO	DE	424.3
STATE FARM GENERAL INS CO	IL	7,241.9
STATE MUTUAL INS CO (ME)	ME	13.4
STATE NATIONAL FIRE INS CO	LA	4.1
STEADPOINT INS CO	TN	26.9
STRATHMORE INS CO	NY	58.7
SU INS CO	WI	24.1
SWISS REINS AMERICA CORP	NY	14,202.2

INSURANCE COMPANY NAME	DOM. STATE	TOTAL ASSETS ($MIL)	INSURANCE COMPANY NAME	DOM. STATE	TOTAL ASSETS ($MIL)
Rating: C **(Continued)**			WESTERN WORLD INS CO	NH	982.1
SYNERGY COMP INS CO	PA	41.6	WESTON INS CO	FL	86.1
SYNERGY INS CO	NC	74.4	WINDHAVEN NATIONAL INS CO	TX	6.5
TANK OWNER MEMBERS INS CO	TX	26.7	WISCONSIN COUNTY MUTUAL INS CORP	WI	85.6
TDC SPECIALTY INS CO	DC	129.6	WISCONSIN MUNICIPAL MUTUAL INS CO	WI	50.1
TEXAS FARM BUREAU UNDERWRITERS	TX	81.1	WOODLANDS INS CO	TX	29.5
TEXAS HERITAGE INS CO	TX	17.4	WORK FIRST CASUALTY CO	DE	48.0
TEXAS INS CO	TX	41.6	WORTH CASUALTY CO	TX	20.4
THAMES INS CO	CT	31.4	XL INS AMERICA INC	DE	791.3
TIG INS CO	CA	2,465.3	XL REINS AMERICA INC	NY	5,952.3
TOKIO MARINE PACIFIC INS LTD	GU	121.0	XL SPECIALTY INS CO	DE	1,066.4
TOKIO MARINE SPECIALTY INS CO	DE	606.5	YEL CO INS	FL	15.4
TOKIO MILLENNIUM RE AG (US BRANCH)	NY	1,226.2	ZNAT INS CO	CA	68.7
TRADEWIND INS CO LTD	HI	13.0	**Rating:** C-		
TRANS CITY CASUALTY INS CO	AZ	18.0	ACCEPTANCE INDEMNITY INS CO	NE	330.6
TRANSPORTATION INS CO	IL	79.0	AFFINITY MUTUAL INS CO	OH	13.9
TRI-STATE INS CO OF MN	IA	60.1	AGCS MARINE INS CO	IL	312.1
TRIUMPHE CASUALTY CO	OH	60.5	AIOI NISSAY DOWA INS CO LTD	GU	35.6
TUDOR INS CO	NH	252.1	ALAMANCE INS CO	IL	466.3
TYPTAP INS CO	FL	29.1	ALLIANZ UNDERWRITERS INS CO	IL	95.2
UNIGARD INS CO	WI	394.6	ALLIED PROFESSIONALS INS CO RRG	AZ	48.2
UNION INS CO	IA	137.6	ALLIED TRUST INS CO	TX	28.0
UNION INS CO OF PROVIDENCE	IA	61.2	AMERICAN EMPIRE SURPLUS LINES INS CO	DE	467.9
UNION STANDARD LLOYDS	TX	2.5	AMERICAN FIRE & CASUALTY CO	NH	46.2
UNITED FRONTIER MUTUAL INS CO	NY	18.3	AMERICAN INS CO	OH	112.7
UNITED HOME INS CO	AR	38.3	AMERICAN MUTUAL SHARE INS CORP	OH	257.8
UNITED NATIONAL INS CO	PA	338.5	AMERICAN RISK INS CO	TX	31.1
UNITRIN ADVANTAGE INS CO	NY	3.3	AMERICAN SENTINEL INS CO	PA	43.3
UNIVERSAL SURETY OF AMERICA	SD	14.8	ANTHRACITE MUTUAL FIRE INS CO	PA	4.3
UPLAND MUTUAL INS INC	KS	31.8	APOLLO MUTUAL FIRE INS CO	PA	4.2
US COASTAL INS CO	NY	28.4	ARCH REINS CO	DE	1,987.8
US FIRE INS CO	DE	4,094.3	ASOC DE SUSCRIPCION CONJUNTA DEL SEG	PR	122.3
US LIABILITY INS CO	PA	1,244.4	ASPIRE GENERAL INS CO	CA	22.7
US LLOYDS INS CO	TX	28.7	ASSOCIATED INDUSTRIES INS CO INC	FL	245.0
US UNDERWRITERS INS CO	ND	163.6	ASSURED GUARANTY CORP	MD	3,126.7
UTICA NATIONAL ASR CO	NY	68.9	ATTORNEYS INS MUTUAL	DC	11.5
UTICA NATIONAL INS CO OF TX	TX	36.3	ATTORNEYS INS MUTUAL RRG	HI	20.3
VALLEY FORGE INS CO	PA	71.5	AXA INS CO	NY	237.5
VERSANT CASUALTY INS CO	MS	50.6	BAR VERMONT RRG INC	VT	31.9
VICTORIA SPECIALTY INSURANCE CO	OH	7.0	BEDFORD PHYSICIANS RRG INC	VT	43.1
VIKING INS CO OF WI	WI	493.9	BERKLEY ASR CO	IA	72.5
VIRGINIA FARM BUREAU FIRE & CAS INS	VA	66.4	BOSTON INDEMNITY CO INC	SD	7.8
VOYAGER INDEMNITY INS CO	GA	110.3	BRIERFIELD INS CO	MS	13.5
WADENA INS CO	IA	5.5	BUILD AMERICA MUTUAL ASR CO	NY	515.0
WASHINGTON INTL INS CO	NH	103.8	BURLINGTON INS CO	IL	345.0
WAUSAU BUSINESS INS CO	WI	34.4	CALIFORNIA CAPITAL INS CO	CA	538.4
WAUSAU GENERAL INS CO	WI	15.6	CALIFORNIA CAS GEN INS CO OF OREGON	OR	111.0
WAUSAU UNDERWRITERS INS CO	WI	127.0	CAMERON NATIONAL INS CO	MO	11.0
WEA P&C INS CO	WI	19.6	CAROLINA FARMERS MUTUAL INS CO	NC	9.8
WEST VIRGINIA MUTUAL INS CO	WV	161.7	CEM INS CO	IL	45.9
WESTCHESTER FIRE INS CO	PA	1,655.7	CENTURY MUTUAL INS CO	NC	10.3
WESTCHESTER SURPLUS LINES INS CO	GA	350.2	CENTURY-NATIONAL INS CO	CA	135.8
WESTERN HOME INS CO	MN	69.3	COASTAL AMERICAN INS CO	MS	9.7
WESTERN NATIONAL ASR CO	MN	89.3	COASTAL SELECT INS CO	CA	105.9
WESTERN SELECT INS CO	IL	17.4	COMPTRUST AGC MUT CAPTIVE INS CO	GA	32.5

INSURANCE COMPANY NAME	DOM. STATE	TOTAL ASSETS ($MIL)	INSURANCE COMPANY NAME	DOM. STATE	TOTAL ASSETS ($MIL)
Rating: C- (Continued)			MFS MUTUAL INS CO	IA	4.2
CONTRACTORS INS CO OF NORTH AMER RRG	HI	37.1	MICHIGAN COMMERCIAL INS MUTUAL	MI	75.2
COREPOINTE INS CO	DE	37.9	MIDDLE STATES INS CO	OK	6.1
CPA MUTL INS CO OF AM (A RRG)	VT	16.2	MILLVILLE INS CO OF NY	NY	2.9
CSAA MID-ATLANTIC INS CO	AZ	38.1	MONTEREY INS CO	CA	78.7
CSAA MID-ATLANTIC INS CO OF NJ	NJ	52.6	MOUNTAINPOINT INS CO	AZ	12.2
DEALERS CHOICE MUTUAL INS INC	NC	23.7	MUNICIPAL PROPERTY INS CO	WI	14.2
DELTA FIRE & CAS INS CO	GA	7.8	NATIONAL FIRE & INDEMNITY EXCHANGE	MO	10.6
DIRECT GENERAL INS CO	IN	188.9	NATIONAL GUARDIAN RRG INC	HI	10.7
DIRECT GENERAL INS CO OF LA	LA	5.5	NATIONAL INDEPENDENT TRUCKERS IC RRG	SC	15.3
DIRECT GENERAL INS CO OF MS	MS	23.0	NATIONS INS CO	CA	41.6
DIRECT INS CO	TN	64.7	NAZARETH MUTUAL INS CO	PA	16.0
DORINCO REINS CO	MI	1,547.9	NEW JERSEY SKYLANDS INS CO	NJ	36.3
EAGLE WEST INS CO	CA	117.9	NEW MEXICO ASR CO	NM	6.6
EASTERN ATLANTIC INS CO	PA	69.4	NEW MEXICO SOUTHWEST CASUALTY CO	NM	17.6
EXCALIBUR NATIONAL INS CO	LA	14.5	NORCAL SPECIALTY INS CO	PA	61.3
FARMERS MUTUAL F I C OF MCCANDLESS	PA	11.9	NORTH POINTE INS CO	PA	20.5
FINANCIAL AMERICAN PROP & CAS INS CO	TX	10.2	NORTH RIVER INS CO	NJ	1,070.3
FIRST ACCEPTANCE INS CO	TX	243.5	OCCIDENTAL FIRE & CAS CO OF NC	NC	474.3
FIRST ACCEPTANCE INS CO OF GEORGIA	GA	89.6	OCEAN MARINE INDEMNITY INS CO	LA	10.9
FIRST FINANCIAL INS CO	IL	538.9	OHIO SECURITY INS CO	NH	16.2
FIRST INDEMNITY OF AMERICA INS CO	NJ	11.9	OLD RELIABLE CAS CO	MO	5.6
FIRST NONPROFIT INS CO	DE	41.1	OMEGA INS CO	FL	42.3
FRANK WINSTON CRUM INS CO	FL	101.0	PANHANDLE FARMERS MULT INS CO	WV	5.3
FREDERICK MUTUAL INS CO	MD	42.5	PELICAN INS RRG	VT	17.0
FRIENDS COVE MUTUAL INS CO	PA	6.0	PERMANENT GEN ASR CORP OF OHIO	WI	226.2
GENERAL SECURITY IND CO OF AZ	AZ	365.7	PERMANENT GENERAL ASR CORP	WI	582.2
GENERAL SECURITY NATIONAL INS CO	NY	416.1	PFD PHYSICIANS MED RRG A MUTL	MO	24.0
GREAT LAKES MUTUAL INS CO	MI	12.6	PHYSICIANS PROACTIVE PROTECTION INC	SC	86.1
GREAT NORTHWEST INS CO	MN	19.4	PHYSICIANS STANDARD INS CO	KS	3.8
GROWERS AUTOMOBILE INS ASN	IN	8.1	PREVISOR INS CO	CO	10.2
GUARDIAN INS CO	VI	37.2	PRIMEONE INS CO	UT	20.3
GUILFORD INS CO	IL	371.3	PROASSURANCE INDEMNTIY CO INC	AL	1,081.0
HARLEYSVILLE INS CO OF NJ	NJ	61.6	PROCENTURY INS CO	MI	59.9
HARLEYSVILLE LAKE STATES INS CO	MI	36.2	PROFESSIONAL CASUALTY ASSN	PA	36.3
HEALTH CARE INS RECPL	MN	27.2	PROFESSIONAL INS EXCHANGE MUTUAL	UT	8.7
HOME STATE COUNTY MUTUAL INS CO	TX	81.2	PROGRESSIVE COUNTY MUTUAL INS CO	TX	671.6
HOSPITALS INS CO	NY	1,671.8	QBE SPECIALTY INS CO	ND	363.4
HUDSON INS CO	DE	1,204.1	RED ROCK RISK RETENTION GROUP INC	AZ	6.7
IMPERIAL F&C INS CO	LA	109.9	REDPOINT COUNTY MUTUAL INS CO	TX	46.0
IMPERIUM INS CO	TX	373.7	REPUBLIC CREDIT INDEMNITY CO	IL	40.0
INDIAN HARBOR INS CO	DE	242.1	REPWEST INS CO	AZ	340.6
INLAND MUTUAL INS CO	WV	7.0	RESIDENCE MUTUAL INS CO	CA	131.8
INSPIRIEN INS CO	AL	34.1	RESPONSE INDEMNITY CO OF CA	CA	8.3
INTEGRITY P&C INS CO	WI	14.0	RESPONSE INS CO	IL	39.3
INTERSTATE FIRE & CAS CO	IL	150.0	RETAILERS INS CO	MI	22.5
IRONSHORE SPECIALTY INS CO	AZ	491.6	ROCHDALE INS CO	NY	224.7
JUNIATA MUTUAL INS CO	PA	9.8	ROCKWOOD CASUALTY INS CO	PA	289.7
KANSAS MUTUAL INS CO	KS	15.3	RUTGERS CASUALTY INS CO	NJ	23.5
KENTUCKY HOSPITAL INS CO RRG	KY	17.7	RUTGERS ENHANCED INS CO	NJ	11.0
KENTUCKY NATIONAL INS CO	KY	34.9	SAFE INS CO	WV	11.7
LAUNDRY OWNERS MUTUAL LIAB INS ASN	PA	16.9	SAUQUOIT VALLEY INS CO	NY	4.9
LIBERTY COUNTY MUTUAL INS CO	TX	7.5	SAVERS P&C INS CO	MO	51.2
MEDICAL ALLIANCE INS CO	IL	9.2	SEAVIEW INS CO	CA	23.9
MENDOTA INS CO	MN	118.6	SEQUOIA INS CO	CA	152.4
			SERVICE INS CO (NJ)	NJ	15.8

INSURANCE COMPANY NAME	DOM. STATE	TOTAL ASSETS ($MIL)	INSURANCE COMPANY NAME	DOM. STATE	TOTAL ASSETS ($MIL)
Rating: C- (Continued)			ATTORNEYS LIAB ASR SOCIETY INC RRG	VT	2,045.4
SOUTH CAROLINA FARM BUREAU INS	SC	3.7	AUSTIN MUTUAL INS CO	MN	59.2
SPARTAN INS CO	TX	8.0	AUTO CLUB COUNTY MUTUAL INS CO	TX	108.7
SPECIALTY RISK OF AMERICA	IL	16.6	BEDIVERE INS CO	PA	240.1
ST JOHNS INS CO	FL	129.5	BONDED BUILDERS INS CO RRG	NV	3.6
STARSTONE SPECIALTY INS CO	DE	238.0	BRISTOL WEST CASUALTY INS CO	OH	18.9
STATE AUTO INS CO OF OH	OH	29.6	BRISTOL WEST INS CO	OH	145.8
SUN SURETY INS CO	SD	22.4	BUNKER HILL PREFERRED INS CO	MA	11.6
TEXAS HOSPITAL INS EXCHANGE	TX	36.3	BUNKER HILL PROPERTY INS CO	MA	11.6
TEXAS MEDICAL INS CO	TX	64.8	BUNKER HILL SECURITY INS CO	MA	11.7
THE INS CO	LA	211.6	CARE RRG INC	DC	21.2
TOWER HILL SELECT INS CO	FL	75.0	CASSATT RISK RETENTION GROUP INC	VT	12.5
TOWER HILL SIGNATURE INS CO	FL	117.7	CASUALTY UNDERWRITERS INS CO	UT	5.1
TRADERS INS CO	MO	83.3	CENTAURI NATIONAL INSURANCE CO	LA	10.7
TRANSIT GENERAL INS CO	IL	23.0	CENTER VALLEY MUTUAL FIRE INS CO	PA	2.6
TWIN LIGHTS INS CO	NJ	8.7	CENTRE COUNTY MUTUAL FIRE INS CO	PA	7.0
UNITED CASUALTY & SURETY CO INC	MA	10.5	CENTURY INS CO GUAM LTD	GU	29.2
UNITED STATES FIDELITY & GUARANTY CO	CT	3,293.0	CGB INS CO	IN	550.2
UNIVERSAL FIRE & CASUALTY INS CO	IN	17.2	CHERRY VALLEY COOPERATIVE INS CO	NY	2.0
UNIVERSAL INS CO	NC	40.9	CLAIM PROFESSIONALS LIAB INS CO RRG	VT	4.7
UNIVERSAL INS CO OF NORTH AMERICA	FL	116.5	CLAVERACK CO-OPERATIVE INS CO	NY	3.1
UNIVERSAL NORTH AMERICA INS CO	TX	204.4	COAST NATIONAL INS CO	CA	589.8
USA INS CO	MS	16.3	COLONY SPECIALTY INS CO	OH	67.9
USA UNDERWRITERS	MI	10.4	COLUMBIA FEDERAL INS CO	DC	3.4
VERTERRA INS CO	TX	82.3	COMCARE PRO INS RECIPROCAL RRG	VT	5.7
WARRANTY UNDERWRITERS INS CO	TX	27.2	COMMUNITY CARE RRG INC	DC	9.3
WEST AMERICAN INS CO	IN	52.3	COMMUNITY MUTUAL INS CO	NY	2.0
WEST RIVER INSURANCE CO	SD	18.3	CONSUMER SPECIALTIES INS CO RRG	VT	4.1
WEST VIRGINIA FARMERS MUT INS ASSOC	WV	8.1	CORNERSTONE NATIONAL INS CO	MO	25.2
WESTERN MUTL INS CO (CA)	CA	90.3	CROWN CAPTIVE INS CO	GA	2.3
WILSHIRE INS CO	NC	334.5	CRUM & FORSTER INDEMNITY CO	DE	53.9
XL INS CO OF NY INC	NY	240.0	CRUM & FORSTER INS CO	NJ	53.2
YELLOWSTONE INS EXCHANGE	VT	19.2	CRUM & FORSTER SPECIALTY INS CO	DE	68.8
			DAN RRG INC	SC	2.5
Rating: D+			EASTGUARD INS CO	PA	180.6
1ST ATLANTIC SURETY CO	NC	4.1	EDISON INS CO	FL	65.9
7710 INS CO	SC	14.8	ELLINGTON MUTUAL INS CO	WI	6.4
ACCEPTANCE CASUALTY INS CO	NE	162.5	ETHIO-AMERICAN INS CO	GA	10.7
ACIG INS CO	IL	503.4	FALCON INS CO	IL	37.1
AEGIS HEALTHCARE RRG INC	DC	5.0	FBALLIANCE INS INC	VA	4.8
AEGIS SECURITY INS CO	PA	148.7	FINIAL REINS CO	CT	1,265.4
AGENTS MUTUAL INS CO	AR	4.5	FIRST FOUNDERS ASR CO	NJ	5.6
ALLEGHENY SURETY CO	PA	4.4	FIRST MUTUAL INS CO	NC	6.7
AMERICAN FOREST CASUALTY CO RRG	VT	9.2	FORT WAYNE MEDICAL ASR CO RRG	AZ	4.1
AMERICAN INDEPENDENT INS CO	PA	108.0	FRANKLIN CASUALTY INS CO RRG	VT	34.3
AMERICAN PROPERTY INS	NJ	24.7	FREEDOM ADVANTAGE INS CO	PA	9.6
AMERICAN SAFETY RRG INC	VT	7.7	GEISINGER INS CORP RRG	VT	23.7
AMERICAN STEAMSHIP O M PROT & IND AS	NY	249.4	GENESEE PATRONS COOP INS	NY	10.7
AMERICAN UNDERWRITERS INS CO	AR	5.9	GENEVA INS CO	IN	4.1
AMERITRUST INS CORP	MI	13.8	GEORGIA MUNICIPAL CAPTIVE INS CO	GA	11.1
AMFIRST SPECIALTY INS CO	MS	2.7	GEOVERA INS CO	CA	92.6
ARGONAUT GREAT CENTRAL INS CO	IL	40.8	GERMAN MUTUAL INS CO	OH	45.0
ASHMERE INS CO	FL	18.0	GLOBAL REINS CORP OF AM	NY	236.9
ASI LLOYDS	TX	222.7	GOAUTO INS CO	LA	52.6
ASSURANCEAMERICA INS CO	NE	79.8	GOOD SHEPHERD RECIPROCAL RRG	SC	10.9
ASSURED GUARANTY MUNICIPAL CORP	NY	5,479.6	GRANGE MUTUAL FIRE INS CO	PA	5.1

INSURANCE COMPANY NAME	DOM. STATE	TOTAL ASSETS ($MIL)
Rating: D+ (Continued)		
GREAT FALLS INS CO	ME	13.4
GULF STATES INS CO (LA)	LA	6.4
HALIFAX MUTUAL INS CO	NC	9.7
HALLMARK INS CO	AZ	308.4
HANOVER FIRE & CASUALTY INS CO	PA	5.8
HARBOR INS CO	OK	11.2
HAY CREEK MUTUAL INS CO	MN	5.9
HEALTH CARE MUT CAPTIVE INS CO	GA	11.9
HEALTHCARE PROFESSIONAL INS CO INC	NY	214.4
HEALTHCARE UNDERWRITING CO RRG	VT	154.9
HEARTLAND MUTUAL INS CO	MN	7.6
HOCHHEIM PRAIRIE FARM MUT INS ASN	TX	122.7
HUDSON SPECIALTY INS CO	NY	367.8
INS CO OF THE SOUTH	GA	51.5
IU HEALTH RRG INC	SC	5.6
LCTA SPECIALTY INSURANCE CO	LA	7.2
LEMONADE INS CO	NY	25.2
LITTLE BLACK MUTUAL INS CO	WI	5.6
LONE STAR ALLIANCE INC A RRG	DC	9.9
LOYA INS CO	TX	289.7
LUBA INDEMNITY INS CO	LA	5.3
MARATHON FINANCIAL INS INC RRG	DE	3.3
MEDICAL LIABILITY MUTUAL INS CO	NY	5,430.6
MEDICAL PROVIDERS MUTUAL INS CO RRG	DC	7.9
MGIC INDEMNITY CORP	WI	147.2
MGIC REINS CORP OF WI	WI	588.2
MIDROX INS CO	NY	8.8
MIDWESTERN EQUITY TITLE INS CO	IN	4.3
MISSOURI VALLEY MUTUAL INS CO	SD	6.3
MORTGAGE GUARANTY INS CORP	WI	4,756.2
MOTORS INS CORP	MI	2,030.5
MOUND PRAIRIE MUTUAL INS CO	MN	7.7
MOUNTAIN STATES HEALTHCARE RECIP RRG	MT	111.9
MOWER COUNTY FARMERS MUT INS CO	MN	5.5
MUTUAL FIRE INS CO OF S BEND TOWNSHP	PA	3.6
NATIONAL ASSISTED LIVING RRG INC	DC	8.8
NATIONAL HERITAGE INS CO	IL	3.2
NATIONAL PUBLIC FINANCE GUAR CORP	NY	3,753.9
NEVADA MUTUAL INS CO	NV	18.1
NEW HORIZON INS CO	TX	7.3
NEW JERSEY PHYS UNITED RECIP EXCH	NJ	30.3
NEW MEXICO SECURITY INS CO	NM	4.4
NORTHWEST GF MUTUAL INS CO	SD	20.2
OLYMPUS INS CO	FL	78.8
ONE ALLIANCE INS CORP	PR	13.8
ORANGE COUNTY MEDICAL RECIP INS RRG	AZ	6.0
PACE RRG INC	VT	5.4
PALISADES INS CO	NJ	42.5
PALLADIUM RRG INC	VT	86.1
PAN-AMERICAN CASUALTY CO	TX	5.4
PATRONS MUTUAL FIRE INS CO OF IN PA	PA	2.8
PCH MUTUAL INS CO INC RRG	VT	7.3
PELEUS INS CO	VA	92.1
PEOPLES TRUST INS CO	FL	254.0

INSURANCE COMPANY NAME	DOM. STATE	TOTAL ASSETS ($MIL)
PHILADELPHIA REINS CORP	PA	9.4
PHYSICIANS INS CO	FL	14.2
PIEDMONT MUTUAL INS CO	NC	4.9
PREFERRED AUTO INS CO	TN	9.7
PYMATUNING MUTUAL FIRE INS CO	PA	3.3
RADIAN GUARANTY INC	PA	4,071.2
RADIAN INS INC	PA	22.5
RANCHERS & FARMERS MUTUAL INS CO	TX	36.1
REAL LEGACY ASR CO INC	PR	230.4
REAMSTOWN MUTUAL INS CO	PA	8.8
RECREATION RRG INC	VT	3.8
RIDER INS CO	NJ	31.5
RUSH FIRE INSURANCE CO	LA	4.1
SECURITY NATIONAL INS CO	FL	133.1
SELECT MD RRG INC	MT	1.6
SENECA INS CO	NY	181.4
SFM SAFE INS CO	MN	5.5
SOMERSET CASUALTY INS CO	PA	44.7
SPARTA INS CO	CT	228.6
SPIRIT MOUNTAIN INS CO RRG INC	DC	6.1
STANDARD P&C INS CO	IL	19.1
STICO MUTUAL INS CO RRG	VT	23.1
SUNDERLAND MARINE INS CO LTD	AK	10.3
TERRAFIRMA RRG LLC	VT	6.8
TITLE INDUSTRY ASR CO RRG	VT	7.9
TOWER BONDING & SURETY CO	PR	3.7
UNITED BUS INS CO	GA	12.8
UNITED EQUITABLE INS CO	IL	25.6
UNITED INSURANCE CO	UT	45.2
UNITED SECURITY HEALTH & CASUALTY	IL	5.3
UNITRIN AUTO & HOME INS CO	NY	73.7
UNITRIN PREFERRED INS CO	NY	21.1
UPMC HEALTH BENEFITS INC	PA	237.5
US INS CO OF AMERICA	IL	6.3
US LEGAL SERVICES INC	TN	3.5
UV INS RRG INC	HI	1.2
VASA SPRING GARDEN MUTUAL INS CO	MN	5.3
VERTI INSURANCE CO	OH	39.5
WASHINGTON COUNTY CO-OPERATIVE INS	NY	8.6
WEST VIRGINIA NATIONAL AUTO INS CO	WV	6.0
WESTERN GENERAL INS CO	CA	90.6
WILMINGTON INS CO	DE	5.1
WORKMENS AUTO INS CO	CA	48.2
XL SELECT INS CO	DE	160.3
Rating: D		
ACADEMIC MEDICAL PROFESSIONALS RRG	VT	4.8
ADVANCED PROVIDERS INS RRG INC	AZ	1.5
ALLIED GUARANTY INS CO RRG	NV	12.7
AMERICAN ACCESS CASUALTY CO	IL	420.6
AMERICAN ALLIANCE CASUALTY CO	IL	38.3
AMERICAN BUILDERS INS CO RRG INC	AL	1.2
AMERICAN COMPENSATION INS CO	MN	73.9
AMERICAN HEARTLAND INS CO	IL	18.3
AMERICAN MILLENNIUM INS CO	NJ	34.4
AMERICAN RESOURCES INS CO INC	OK	23.1

INSURANCE COMPANY NAME	DOM. STATE	TOTAL ASSETS ($MIL)	INSURANCE COMPANY NAME	DOM. STATE	TOTAL ASSETS ($MIL)
Rating: D (Continued)			FULMONT MUTUAL INS CO	NY	2.9
AMERICAN RISK MGMT RRG INC	TN	4.0	GEORGIA TRANSPORTATION CAPTIVE INS	GA	2.9
AMERICAN SERVICE INS CO	IL	207.7	HOMEOWNERS OF AMERICA INS CO	TX	56.4
AMFED NATIONAL INS CO	MS	65.7	HOMESTEAD INS CO	PA	4.9
ANCHOR P&C INS CO	FL	79.8	HORIZON MIDWEST CASUALTY CO	KS	2.7
ARGONAUT-MIDWEST INS CO	IL	22.9	HOSPITALITY RRG INC	VT	6.9
ARI INS CO	PA	72.8	HPIC RRG	SC	1.8
ARIZONA HOME INS CO	AZ	28.8	HUTTERIAN BRETHREN MUTUAL INS CORP	IL	3.3
ARKANSAS MUTUAL INS CO	AR	2.7	INTEGRA INS INC	MN	1.8
ARROWOOD INDEMNITY CO	DE	1,211.0	INTEGRITY SELECT INSURANCE CO	WI	5.1
ASCENDANT COMMERCIAL INS INC	FL	64.0	IQS INS RRG INC	VT	1.6
ASPEN SPECIALTY INS CO	ND	401.7	IRONSHORE RRG (DC) INC	DC	2.0
ASSN OF CERTIFIED MTG ORIG RRG	NV	2.5	ISLAND HOME INS CO	GU	23.9
ATLANTIC BONDING CO	MD	9.5	KAMMCO CASUALTY CO	KS	6.3
ATTPRO RRG RECIPROCAL RRG	DC	3.0	KENSINGTON INS CO	NY	13.9
AVIATION ALLIANCE INS RRG INC	MT	2.9	KENTUCKIANA MEDICAL RRG & INS CO INC	KY	53.9
BROADWAY INS & SURETY CO	NJ	2.7	KNIGHTBROOK INS CO	DE	159.3
CAPACITY INS CO	FL	22.2	LAKE STREET RRG INC	VT	2.4
CAPSON PHYSICIANS INS CO	TX	28.7	LEON HIX INS CO	SC	3.6
CAR RRG INC	TN	1.7	LEXINGTON NATIONAL INS CORP	FL	61.9
CASUALTY CORP OF AMERICA	OK	13.9	LOCUST MUTUAL FIRE INS CO	PA	1.3
CENTURY CASUALTY CO	GA	1.2	LOYA CASUALTY INS CO	CA	120.1
CIRCLE STAR INS CO A RRG	VT	3.1	MACHINERY INS INC	FL	3.0
CITIZENS UNITED RECIP EXCH	NJ	59.6	MAKE TRANSPORTATION INS INC RRG	DE	7.1
CLEARWATER SELECT INS CO	CT	1,279.8	MED MAL RRG INC	TN	4.0
COLLEGE LIAB INS CO LTD RRG	HI	14.2	MEDCHOICE RRG INC	VT	2.6
COMMERCIAL HIRECAR INS CO RRG	TN	6.9	METROMILE INS CO	DE	41.4
COMMUNITY INS CO (PA)	PA	5.8	MIDWEST INS GROUP INC RRG	VT	7.0
COMPASS SPCLTY INS RRG INC	TN	5.4	MISSOURI PROFESSIONALS MUTUAL INS CO	MO	13.0
CONIFER INS CO	MI	121.3	MOUNTAIN LAKE RRG INC	VT	1.6
CONSUMERS COUNTY MUTUAL INS CO	TX	261.6	MOUNTAIN VALLEY INDEMNITY CO	NY	64.1
CONTINENTAL MUTUAL INS CO	PA	1.9	MUTUAL SAVINGS FIRE INS CO	AL	4.9
COUNTY HALL INS CO INC A RRG	NC	18.9	NATIONAL BUILDING MATERIAL ASR CO	IN	6.7
CROWN CAPTIVE INS CO INC	DC	5.0	NATIONAL CATHOLIC RRG	VT	69.2
CRUDEN BAY RRG INC	VT	17.3	NATIONAL DIRECT INS CO	NV	6.9
CYPRESS TEXAS INS CO	TX	63.2	NATIONAL UNITY INS CO	TX	35.9
DELAWARE GRANGE MUTUAL FIRE INS CO	DE	1.6	NATL TRANSPORTATION INS CO RRG	NC	6.8
DELPHI CASUALTY CO	IL	2.3	NEVADA GENERAL INS CO	NV	14.5
DEVELOPERS SURETY & INDEMNITY CO	CA	620.7	NEW MEXICO BUSINESS INS CO	NM	2.1
DIAMOND INS CO	IL	47.3	NEW MEXICO COMMERCIAL INS CO	NM	2.1
DIRECT AUTO INS CO	IL	63.7	NEWPORT BONDING & SURETY CO	PR	4.3
DOCTORS PROF LIAB RRG INC	NC	5.3	NORGUARD INS CO	PA	1,098.6
EAGLE BUILDERS INS CO RRG INC	NC	2.5	NORMANDY INS CO	FL	54.9
EASTERN ALLIANCE INS CO	PA	341.5	NW FARMERS MUTUAL INSURANCE CO	NC	5.5
ECOLE INS CO	AZ	15.1	OMAHA NATIONAL INSURANCE CO	NE	3.7
EMERGENCY CAP MGMT LLC A RRG	VT	9.1	OMNI INDEMNITY CO	IL	68.8
EQUITABLE LIABILITY INS CO	DC	2.5	OTSEGO COUNTY PATRONS CO-OP F R ASN	NY	2.2
FARMERS & MECH MU I ASN OF CECIL CTY	MD	1.1	PACIFIC SPECIALTY PROPERTY & CAS CO	TX	6.1
FARMERS MUTUAL INS CO OF ELLINWOOD	KS	5.2	PALISADES P&C INS CO	NJ	16.7
FARMERS UNION MUTUAL INS CO	AR	4.8	PALMETTO SURETY CORP	SC	15.5
FIRST ACCEPTANCE INS CO OF TN INC	TN	27.5	PARK INS CO	NY	36.8
FIRST BENEFITS INS MUTUAL INC	NC	45.9	PEACHTREE CASUALTY INS CO	FL	16.5
FIRST CHICAGO INS CO	IL	81.5	PENN RESERVE INS CO LTD	PA	2.1
FLORIDA SPECIALTY INS CO	FL	45.5	PERSONAL SERVICE INS CO	PA	57.3
FREMONT INS CO	MI	158.6	PHYSICIANS IND RRG INC	NV	6.5
			PREPARED INS CO	FL	69.1

INSURANCE COMPANY NAME	DOM. STATE	TOTAL ASSETS ($MIL)
Rating: D (Continued)		
PROFESSIONAL EXCHANGE ASR CO (A RRG)	HI	12.7
PROFESSIONALS RRG INC	MT	2.8
PUERTO RICO MED DEFENSE INS CO	PR	18.3
QBE SEGUROS	PR	103.8
QUALITAS INS CO	CA	72.6
RECOVER INS CO RRG INC	HI	2.1
ROMULUS INS RRG INC	SC	2.9
SAFECARD SERVICES INS CO	ND	1.9
SAGE RRG INC	NV	4.6
SCRUBS MUTUAL ASR CO RRG	NV	14.2
SECURITY PLAN FIRE INS CO	LA	8.4
SOMPO JAPAN NIPPONKOA INS INC	GU	11.0
SOUTHWEST GENERAL INS CO	NM	2.2
ST CHARLES INS CO RRG	SC	18.0
STAR & SHIELD INS EXCHANGE	FL	4.4
STERLING CASUALTY INS CO	CA	19.2
TOWER HILL PREFERRED INS CO	FL	99.7
TOWER HILL PRIME INS CO	FL	236.1
TRANSIT MUTUAL INS CORP OF WI	WI	15.1
TRANSPORTATION INS SVCS RRG	SC	1.7
UNDERWRITERS AT LLOYDS (IL)	IL	382.6
UNITED GROUP CAPTIVE INS CO	GA	1.2
UNIVERSAL P&C INS CO	FL	1,034.0
URGENT CARE ASR CO RRG INC	NV	5.2
URGENT MD RRG INC	VT	10.0
UTAH BUSINESS INS CO	UT	21.6
VELOCITY INS CO A RRG	SC	2.7
VIRGINIA PHYSICIANS RRG INC	MT	1.8
VISION INS CO	TX	30.8
WALL ROSE MUTUAL INS CO	PA	1.1
WELLSPAN RRG	VT	28.7
WESCO INS CO	DE	1,621.0
WILLIAMSBURG NATIONAL INS CO	MI	30.2
YOUNG AMERICA INS CO	TX	53.2
Rating: D-		
ALLEGIANT INS CO INC A RRG	HI	30.8
AMERICAN CONTRACTORS INS CO RISK RET	TX	36.4
AMERICAN COUNTRY INS CO	IL	109.7
ARCOA RRG INC	NV	19.4
CLEAR SPRING P&C CO	TX	79.1
COUNTRY-WIDE INS CO	NY	229.5
FARMERS MUTUAL INS CO OF MI	MI	2.0
GATEWAY INS CO	MO	84.4
GLOBAL LIBERTY INS CO OF NY	NY	71.4
HEREFORD INS CO	NY	199.9
KEY INS CO	KS	37.6
MAIDSTONE INS CO	NY	56.7
MIDVALE INDEMNITY CO	WI	14.5
NEW JERSEY SKYLANDS INS ASSN	NJ	66.4
NORTHWESTERN NATL INS CO SEG ACCNT	WI	20.6
PALOMAR SPECIALTY INS CO	OR	137.4
PARAMOUNT INS CO	MD	13.1
SAMSUNG FIRE & MARINE INS CO LTD US	NY	97.6
STAR CASUALTY INS CO	FL	23.6

INSURANCE COMPANY NAME	DOM. STATE	TOTAL ASSETS ($MIL)
STATES SELF-INSURERS RISK RET GROUP	VT	28.3
STONEGATE INS CO	IL	26.2
TECHNOLOGY INS CO	DE	3,773.1
UNDERWRITERS AT LLOYDS (KY)	KY	165.2
VICTORY INS CO	MT	16.4
WHITECAP SURETY CO	MN	1.6
WINDHAVEN INS CO	FL	218.0
Rating: E+		
ACCC INS CO	TX	279.0
ALLIED SERVICES RRG	SC	6.2
AMERICAN TRANSIT INS CO	NY	287.5
CALIFORNIA MEDICAL GROUP INS CO RRG	AZ	16.1
COLUMBIA NATIONAL RRG INC	VT	2.0
CONTINUING CARE RRG INC	VT	4.2
CROSSFIT RRG INC	MT	7.6
DB INS CO LTD (US BRANCH)	HI	283.4
DIST-CO INS CO INC A RRG	HI	3.4
FARMINGTON MUTUAL INS CO	WI	8.2
GABLES RRG INC	VT	9.1
GOLDEN INS CO A RRG	NC	15.2
GOVT TECHNOLOGY INS CO RRG INC	NV	1.2
GRANADA INS CO	FL	42.3
GREEN HILLS INS CO A RRG	VT	12.3
KEYSTONE MUTUAL INS CO	MO	3.3
KOOKMIN BEST INS CO LTD US BR	NY	273.9
LIGHTHOUSE CASUALTY CO	IL	35.6
MAYA ASR CO	NY	16.7
MBIA INS CORP	NY	262.4
MOUNTAIN LAUREL RRG INC	VT	22.4
MUNICIPAL ASR CORP	NY	823.6
NEW YORK HEALTHCARE INS CO INC RRG	DC	26.8
OLD AMERICAN CTY MUTUAL FIRE INS CO	TX	146.7
ONYX INS CO INC A RRG	TN	36.4
PHOEBE RECIPROCAL RRG	SC	4.4
PHYSICIANS CASUALTY RRG INC	AL	12.4
PUBLIC UTILITY MUTUAL INS CO RRG	VT	7.6
SPRING VALLEY MUTUAL INS CO	MN	4.7
ST LUKES HEALTH NETWORK INS CO RRG	VT	69.7
STONINGTON INS CO	PA	15.7
TRINITY RISK SOLUTIONS RECIP INS RRG	DC	8.1
UNDERWRITERS AT LLOYDS (VI)	VI	397.8
UNIQUE INS CO	IL	101.9
UNITED CENTRAL PA RRG	VT	21.0
UNITED HERITAGE PROP & CAS CO	ID	43.2
VFH CAPTIVE INS CO	GA	5.3
Rating: E		
A-ONE COMM INS RRG GROUP INC	TN	22.0
ACCIDENT INS CO	NM	87.3
ALLIED PREMIER INS A RRG	CT	3.0
AMBAC ASSURANCE CORP	WI	5,455.7
AMERICAN LIBERTY INS CO	UT	19.3
APOLLO CASUALTY CO	IL	15.3
ARDELLIS INSURANCE LTD		8.5
BUILDING INDUSTRY INS ASSN INC	VA	23.3
CHEROKEE GUARANTEE CO INC A RRG	AZ	22.9

INSURANCE COMPANY NAME	DOM. STATE	TOTAL ASSETS ($MIL)	INSURANCE COMPANY NAME	DOM. STATE	TOTAL ASSETS ($MIL)
Rating: E (Continued)			IFA INS CO	NJ	3.0
COMMONWEALTH CASUALTY CO	AZ	31.4	LEMIC INS CO	LA	0.0
CUSA RRG INC	VT	3.6	LIBERTY FIRST RRG INS CO	UT	0.0
ECHELON P&C INS CO	IL	14.6	LUMBER MUTUAL INS CO	MA	0.0
EXCELA RECIPROCAL RRG	VT	12.7	LUMBERMENS UNDERWRITING ALLIANCE	MO	354.2
FINANCIAL GUARANTY INS CO	NY	2,340.2	MANHATTAN RE-INS CO	DE	0.0
INNOVATIVE PHYSICIAN SOLUTIONS RRG	VT	5.2	MASSACHUSETTS HOMELAND INS CO	MA	8.9
MONTAUK RRG	VT	3.2	MILLERS CLASSIFIED INS CO	IL	2.7
ORISKA INS CO	NY	37.3	MILLERS FIRST INS CO	IL	7.8
ORTHOFORUM INS CO	SC	25.4	NORTH EAST INS CO	ME	35.9
P&C CO OF OMAHA	NE	12.7	NORTHWESTERN NTL INS CO MILWAUKEE	WI	20.6
PHYSICIANS INS MUTUAL	MO	4.7	OCEANUS INS CO A RRG	SC	52.9
PREFERRED CONTRACTORS INS CO RRG LLC	MT	116.3	PAFCO GENERAL INS CO	IN	0.0
SECURITY AMERICA RRG INC	VT	4.3	PHOENIX FUND INC	NC	0.0
SUNZ INS CO	FL	195.5	PMI INS CO	AZ	119.4
TOWER HEALTH RECIPROCAL RRG	SC	6.0	PMI MORTGAGE INS CO	AZ	837.8
UNITED AUTOMOBILE INS CO	FL	263.4	PROAIR RRG INC	NV	0.5
WORKERS COMPENSATION EXCHANGE	ID	8.3	PUBLIC SERVICE INS CO	IL	295.1
Rating: E-			REPUB MORTGAGE INS CO	NC	586.4
ACADEMIC HLTH PROFESSIONALS INS ASSO	NY	330.7	SAN ANTONIO INDEMNITY CO	TX	0.0
AMERICAN TRUCKING & TRANSP INS RRG	MT	41.1	SAWGRASS MUTUAL INS CO	FL	0.5
CAPITOL INS CO	PA	12.2	SHELBY INS CO	TX	0.0
ELITE TRANSPORTATION RRG INC	VT	9.3	TRIAD GUARANTY ASR CORP	IL	0.0
FAIRWAY PHYSICIANS INS CO RRG	DC	9.5	TRIAD GUARANTY INS CORP	IL	0.0
GLOBAL HAWK INS CO RRG	VT	59.6	UNION MUTUAL INS CO	OK	5.3
INS PLACEMENT FACILITY OF PA	PA	6.9	VESTA INS CORP	TX	0.0
LANCET IND RRG INC	NV	18.2	YORK INS CO OF MAINE	ME	47.0
MISSOURI DOCTORS MUTUAL INS CO	MO	4.4	**Rating: U**		
PHYSICIANS RECIPROCAL INSURERS	NY	1,129.2	21ST CENTURY AUTO INS CO OF NJ	NJ	25.4
PLATINUM TRANSPORT INS RRG INC	HI	9.6	21ST CENTURY INS CO OF THE SW	TX	6.9
SPIRIT COMMERCIAL AUTO RRG INC	NV	110.9	21ST CENTURY SUPERIOR INS CO	CA	31.0
TEXAS FAIR PLAN ASSN	TX	73.1	ACA FINANCIAL GUARANTY CORP	MD	266.9
Rating: F			AETNA INS CO OF CT	CT	16.3
ACCEPTANCE INS CO	NE	11.4	AF&L INS CO	PA	129.3
ACCESS INS CO	TX	214.1	AFFILIATES INS CO	IN	73.8
AFFIRMATIVE CASUALTY INS CO	LA	35.4	AGIC INC	FL	1.3
AFFIRMATIVE DIRECT INS CO	NY	5.1	AIMCO MUTUAL INS CO	NC	7.6
ARGUS FIRE & CASUALTY INS CO	FL	3.6	ALEA NORTH AMERICA INS CO	NY	189.7
CARECONCEPTS INS INC A RRG	MT	3.8	ALLSTATE NORTH AMERICAN INS CO	IL	10.9
CASTLEPOINT FLORIDA INS	FL	10.0	AMBAC ASR CORP SEGREGATED ACCT	WI	9.7
CASTLEPOINT INS CO	NY	178.4	AMERICAN CAR DEALERS RRG INC	HI	1.0
COMMERCIAL MUT INS CO	GA	0.0	AMERICAN EQUITY INS CO	AZ	98.7
CORNERSTONE MUTUAL INS CO	GA	0.0	AMERICAN FEED INDUSTRY INS CO RRG	IA	1.5
DOCTORS & SURGEONS NATL RRG IC	VT	9.1	AMERICAN MEDICAL ASR CO	IL	3.4
FIDUCIARY INS CO OF AMERICA	NY	38.5	AMERICAN PACIFIC INS CO	HI	11.6
FLORIDA SELECT INS CO	FL	0.0	AMERICAN PHYSICIANS ASR CORP	MI	159.7
GALEN INS CO	MO	9.3	AMERICAN SPECIAL RISK INS CO	DE	0.8
GUARANTEE INS CO	FL	400.4	AMSHIELD INS CO	MO	5.7
GULF BUILDERS RRG INC	SC	0.0	ARCH EXCESS & SURPLUS INS CO	MO	69.4
HEALTHCARE PROVIDERS INS EXCH	PA	32.6	ARCH STRUCTURED MRTG INS CO	NC	8.2
HERMITAGE INS CO	NY	167.6	ARGONAUT LTD RISK INS CO	IL	12.0
HIGHLANDS INS CO	TX	0.0	ARGONAUT-SOUTHWEST INS CO	IL	18.5
HOME VALUE INS CO	OH	0.0	ARI CASUALTY CO	NJ	8.4
HOSPITALITY MUT CAPT INS CO	GA	0.0	ARROWOOD SURPLUS LINES INS CO	DE	79.3
			ASCENT INSURANCE CO	IL	2.0

INSURANCE COMPANY NAME	DOM. STATE	TOTAL ASSETS ($MIL)
Rating: U (Continued)		
ASHLAND MUTUAL FIRE INS CO OF PA	PA	0.4
ASPEN SPECIALTY RRG INC	DC	0.3
ASSET PROTECTION PROGRAM RRG INC	SC	1.0
ATRIUM INS CORP	NY	1.6
AUTO CLUB CASUALTY CO	TX	2.9
AUTO-OWNERS SPECIALTY INS CO	DE	28.6
AVIVA INS CO OF CANADA (US BR)	NY	15.7
AWBURY INS CO	DE	1.0
AXIS SPECIALTY INS CO	CT	63.7
BALTIMORE EQUITABLE SOCIETY	MD	173.5
BAY INS RRG INC	SC	1.0
BEACONHARBOR MUTUAL RRG	ME	1.1
BLACK DIAMOND INS CO	NV	0.0
BLUE HILL SPECIALTY INS CO	IL	15.7
BROOKWOOD INS CO	IA	17.6
BTTS INS RRG GROUP INC	SC	0.6
BUCKS COUNTY CONTRIBUTIONSHIP	PA	7.0
CA CASUALTY COMP INS CO	CA	96.6
CAMBRIA COUNTY MUTUAL INS CO	PA	0.4
CATAWBA INS CO	SC	5.9
CATTLEMANS INS CO A RRG	MT	0.6
CENTRE INS CO	DE	50.6
CENTURY INDEMNITY CO	PA	525.6
CHARITABLE SERVICE PROVIDERS RRG	AZ	3.5
CHURCH INS CO	NY	24.2
CIMARRON INSURANCE CO	AZ	13.6
CINCINNATI EQUITABLE INS CO	OH	3.2
CLEARPATH MUTUAL INSURANCE CO	KY	2.3
CLINIC MUTUAL INS CO RRG	HI	4.1
CM SELECT INSURANCE CO	WI	19.8
CODAN INS CO LTD	NY	1.9
COLISEUM REINS CO	DE	277.8
COLONIAL MORTGAGE INS CO	TX	2.7
COLUMBIA INS CO	NE	24,521.5
COMMERCIAL CASUALTY INS CO	IN	65.1
COMMONWEALTH INS CO OF AMERICA	DE	10.5
COMMUNITY HEALTH ALLIANCE RECIP RRG	VT	42.7
COMPASS INS CO	NY	7.4
COMPUTER INS CO	RI	8.3
CONTINENTAL RISK UNDERWRITERS RRG IN	NV	0.4
COPIC A RRG	DC	1.0
COPPERPOINT PREMIER INS CO	AZ	20.2
CRYSTAL RIDGE SPCLTY INS CO	IL	15.3
CRYSTAL RUN RECIPROCAL RRG	VT	17.1
DANIELSON NATIONAL INS CO	CA	6.2
DELTA LLOYDS INS CO OF HOUSTON	TX	7.1
ELIZABETHTOWN INS CO	DE	3.9
EMPIRE INS CO	NY	22.6
EMPLOYERS FIRE INS CO	PA	12.1
EMPLOYERS NATIONAL INS CO (MN)	OK	5.1
ENCOMPASS FLORIDIAN INDEMNITY CO	IL	4.5
ENCOMPASS FLORIDIAN INS CO	IL	4.5
EVEREST DENALI INSURANCE CO	DE	26.2
EVERGREEN USA RRG INC	VT	10.0

INSURANCE COMPANY NAME	DOM. STATE	TOTAL ASSETS ($MIL)
EVERSPAN FINANCIAL GUARANTEE CORP	WI	235.2
EXCALIBUR REINS CORP	PA	9.0
EXECUTIVE INS CO	NY	1.2
FACILITY INS CORP	TX	76.9
FB INS CO	KY	1.3
FCCI ADVANTAGE INS CO	FL	7.4
FCCI COMMERCIAL INS CO	FL	14.9
FFVA SELECT INSURANCE CO	FL	5.1
FIDELITY MOHAWK INS CO	NJ	19.9
FIRST JERSEY CASUALTY INS CO INC	NJ	5.2
FIRST PROFESSIONALS INS CO INC	FL	210.7
FIRST PROTECTIVE INS CO	FL	196.9
FIRST STATE INS CO	CT	238.9
FIRST WASHINGTON INS CO	DC	1.4
FOUNDERS INS CO OF MI	MI	6.1
FRONTLINE INS UNLIMITED CO	IL	35.9
GENWORTH FINANCIAL ASR CORP	NC	8.8
GEORGIA DEALERS INS CO	GA	7.6
GLENCAR INSURANCE CO	WI	21.2
GLOBAL HAWK PPTY CAS INS CO	DE	7.2
GLOBAL INS CO	GA	3.5
GOLDSTREET INS CO	NY	4.7
GOVERNMENT ENTITIES MUTUAL INC	DC	74.0
GRACO RRG INC	SC	0.6
GRAY INDEMNITY CO	TX	6.5
GRAY INS CO OF LOUISIANA	LA	6.0
GREAT AMERICAN CASUALTY INS CO	OH	11.1
GREAT AMERICAN CONTEMPORARY INS CO	OH	10.7
GREAT AMERICAN LLOYDS INS CO	TX	1.4
GREAT AMERICAN PROTECTION INS CO	OH	21.1
GREEN TREE PERPETUAL ASR CO	PA	0.2
GREYHAWK INSURANCE CO	CO	16.5
GREYHAWK SPECIALTY INS CO	RI	1.9
GRINNELL COMPASS INC	IA	5.0
GUILDERLAND REINS CO	NY	4.2
GULF UNDERWRITERS INS CO	CT	53.9
HAMDEN ASR RRG INC	VT	99.6
HANOVER NATIONAL INS CO	NH	12.1
HANOVER NJ INS CO	NH	30.8
HEALTH CARE CASUALTY RRG INC	DC	10.2
HERITAGE CASUALTY INS CO	KS	15.6
HIROAD ASSURANCE CO	IL	9.0
HOME CONSTRUCTION INS CO	NV	5.3
HOMEOWNERS CHOICE ASR CO INC	AL	1.9
HOMESHIELD FIRE & CASUALTY INS CO	OK	1.1
HOUSTON GENERAL INS EXCH	TX	5.2
HOW INS CO A RRG	VA	0.4
ICW NATIONAL INSURANCE CO	CA	15.7
INS CO OF THE AMERICAS	FL	5.9
INSUREMAX INS CO	IN	4.3
INTREPID INS CO	IA	32.2
JM SPECIALTY INSURANCE CO	WI	14.5
JM WOODWORTH RRG INC	NV	5.8
KEMPER FINANCIAL INDEMNITY CO	IL	20.9
LAMORAK INS CO	PA	25.6
LEGAL MUTUAL LIAB INS SOCIETY OF MD	MD	0.5

INSURANCE COMPANY NAME	DOM. STATE	TOTAL ASSETS ($MIL)
Rating: U (Continued)		
LIBERTY AMERICAN INS CO	FL	8.7
LIBERTY AMERICAN SELECT INS CO	FL	6.1
LM P&C INS CO	IN	66.3
LR INS INC	DE	1.6
LVHN RRG	SC	80.4
MADA INS EXCHANGE	MN	0.5
MEDSTAR LIABILITY LTD INS CO INC RRG	DC	3.7
MERCHANTS PROPERTY INS CO OF IN	IN	88.1
MERCURY NATIONAL INS CO	IL	16.1
MERITPLAN INS CO	CA	13.0
MGIC CREDIT ASR CORP	WI	8.7
MICO INS CO	OH	11.6
MID AMERICAN FIRE & CAS CO	NH	8.7
MID-CENTURY INS CO OF TX	TX	39.5
MIDSTATES REINS CORP	IL	75.9
MISSOURI PHYSICIANS ASSOCIATES	MO	1.9
MLM RRG INC	DC	1.0
MMIC RRG INC	DC	0.7
MONTOUR MUTUAL INS CO	PA	0.9
MOUNTAIN STATES COMM INS CO	NM	1.0
NATIONAL AMERICAN INS CO OF CA	CA	24.9
NATIONAL BAIL & SURETY CO	FL	2.0
NATIONAL BUILDERS & CONTRACTORS INS	NV	2.7
NATIONAL HOME INS CO RRG	CO	11.2
NATIONAL INS ASSN	IN	13.8
NATIONAL MEDICAL PROFESSIONAL RRG	SC	2.3
NEVADA DOCS MEDICAL RRG INC	NV	2.6
NEW ENGLAND GUARANTY INS CO INC	VT	46.3
NEW ENGLAND INS CO	CT	19.7
NEW ENGLAND REINS CORP	CT	39.4
NEW MEXICO PROPERTY & CASUALTY CO	NM	1.3
NEW YORK TRANSPORTATION INS CORP	NY	0.0
NEWPORT INS CO	AZ	11.2
NEXT INSURANCE US CO	DE	10.0
NORTH STAR GENERAL INS CO	MN	4.3
OBSTETRICIANS & GYNECOLOGISTS RRG	MT	0.5
OHIC INS CO	OH	98.6
OKLAHOMA P&C INS CO	OK	3.2
OLD ELIZABETH MUTUAL FIRE INS CO	PA	0.6
ONECIS INS CO	IL	22.7
ORDINARY MUTUAL A RRG CORP	VT	1.6
P&S INS RRG INC	SC	0.9
PALADIN REINS CORP	NY	1.3
PASSPORT INS CO	ND	2.0
PAWTUCKET INS CO	RI	7.3
PENNSYLVANIA PHYSICIANS RECIP INS	PA	2.4
PHYSICIANS SPECIALTY LTD RRG	SC	11.0
POLICYHOLDERS MUTUAL INS CO	WI	0.3
PONCE DE LEON LTC RRG INC	FL	5.5
POTOMAC INS CO	PA	10.9
PREFERRED PROFESSIONAL RRG	DC	0.8
PREMIER INS EXCHANGE RRG	VT	7.8
PROBUILDERS SPECIALTY INS CO RRG	DC	12.5
PROFESSIONAL QUALITY LIABILITY INS	VT	2.2

INSURANCE COMPANY NAME	DOM. STATE	TOTAL ASSETS ($MIL)
PROGRESSIVE CHOICE INS CO	OH	6.4
PROGRESSIVE COMMERCIAL CASUALTY CO	OH	8.3
PROGRESSIVE FREEDOM INS CO	OH	5.4
PROTECTION MUTUAL INS CO	PA	0.6
PROTUCKET INSURANCE CO	RI	3.0
PROVIDENCE PLANTATIONS INS CO	RI	1.2
PROVIDENCE WASHINGTON INS CO	RI	159.7
QUALITY CASUALTY INS CO	AL	0.8
QUEEN CITY ASR INC	VT	2,497.4
R&Q RI INSURANCE CO	RI	3.0
RADIAN GUARANTY REINS INC	PA	5.6
RADIAN INVESTOR SURETY INC	PA	4.9
RADIAN MORTGAGE ASR INC	PA	8.7
RADIAN MORTGAGE GUARANTY INC	PA	19.7
RADIAN MORTGAGE INS INC	PA	2.7
RAMPART INS CO	NY	24.8
REPUBLIC RRG	SC	1.7
RESPONSE WORLDWIDE DIRECT AUTO INS	IL	10.5
RESPONSE WORLDWIDE INS CO	IL	11.7
RPX RRG INC	HI	4.8
SAFECO SURPLUS LINES INS CO	NH	44.1
SAFETY IMPLEMENTATION PROGRAM	NV	0.0
SALEM COUNTY MUTUAL FIRE INS CO	NJ	0.0
SAN DIEGO INS CO	CA	71.6
SAUCON INSURANCE CO	PA	21.3
SEAWAY MUTUAL INS CO	PA	2.0
SELECT INS CO	TX	80.4
SELECT MARKETS INS CO	IL	16.2
SENIOR AMERICAN INS CO	PA	11.2
SENIORSFIRST RRG INC	NC	1.0
SERVICE AMERICAN INDEMNITY CO	OK	21.6
SLAVONIC INS CO OF TEXAS	TX	5.2
SOMPO JAPAN CANOPIUS RE AG	DE	25.6
SOUTHERN FARM BUREAU PROPERTY	MS	57.9
SOUTHERN GUARANTY INS CO	WI	30.3
SOUTHLAND LLOYDS INS CO	TX	0.0
SOUTHWEST PHYSICIANS RRG INC	SC	36.9
SPECIALTY SURPLUS INS CO	IL	17.4
ST CLAIR INS CO	NY	0.8
STANDARD & PREFERRED INS CO	NY	10.0
STARR SPECIALTY INSURANCE CO	TX	25.7
STERLING INS COOP INC	NY	0.3
STONE VALLEY MUTUAL FIRE INS CO	PA	0.8
SUBURBAN HEALTH ORG RRG LLC	SC	0.8
SUECIA INS CO	NY	43.5
TEXAS BUILDERS INS CO	TX	12.0
THIRD COAST INS CO	WI	19.3
TM SPECIALTY INS CO	AZ	40.5
TRANSIT GENERAL INS CO OF NY	NY	1.2
TRANSPORT INS CO	OH	37.7
TRANSPORT RISK SOLUTIONS RRG	SC	1.0
TRAVEL AIR INS CO (KS)	KS	5.1
TRENWICK AMERICA REINSURANCE CORP	CT	54.2
TRIDENT INSURANCE GROUP INC	MD	1.9
TRISURA SPECIALTY INS CO	OK	45.3
TRUSTSTAR INS CO	MD	0.6

INSURANCE COMPANY NAME	DOM. STATE	TOTAL ASSETS ($MIL)	INSURANCE COMPANY NAME	DOM. STATE	TOTAL ASSETS ($MIL)
Rating: U (Continued)					
UC HEALTH RRG A RECPL RRG	DC	1.6			
UNIGARD INDEMNITY CO	WI	7.6			
UNITED AMERICAS INS CO	NY	5.2			
UNITED GUARANTY COML INS CO OF NC	NC	61.4			
UNITED GUARANTY CREDIT INS CO	NC	25.5			
UNITED HOME INS CO A RRG	VT	1.3			
UNITED INTERNATIONAL INS CO	NY	4.8			
UPPER HUDSON NATIONAL INS CO	NY	3.0			
USAA COUNTY MUTUAL INS CO	TX	5.5			
VANTAGE CASUALTY INS CO	IN	76.9			
VANTAPRO SPECIALTY INS CO	AR	24.2			
VAULT E&S INSURANCE CO	AR	50.1			
VEHICULAR SERVICE INS CO RRG	OK	2.7			
VICTORIA NATIONAL INS CO	OH	3.6			
WARNER INS CO	IL	15.8			
WESCAP INS CO	CO	3.5			
WESTERN CATHOLIC INS CO RRG	VT	3.1			
WESTERN PROFESSIONAL INS CO	WA	13.7			
WESTERN PROTECTORS INS CO	OR	8.9			
WRM AMERICA INDEMNITY CO	NY	14.7			
YCI INC	OK	8.3			

Section VII

Rating Upgrades and Downgrades

A list of all

U.S. Property and Casualty Insurers

receiving a rating upgrade or downgrade
during the current quarter.

Section VII Contents

This section identifies those companies receiving a rating change since the previous edition of this publication, whether it is a rating upgrade, rating downgrade, newly rated company or the withdrawal of a rating. A rating may be withdrawn due to a merger, dissolution, or liquidation. A rating upgrade or downgrade may entail a change from one letter grade to another, or it may mean the addition or deletion of a plus or minus sign within the same letter grade previously assigned to the company. Ratings are normally updated once each quarter of the year. In some instances, however, a company's rating may be downgraded outside of the normal updates due to overriding circumstances.

Unlike other rating agencies, Weiss ratings are reviewed each and every quarter to ensure that the company's current rating reflects the most recent information available. This allows us to react more promptly and with greater flexibility to changing conditions as they occur. In addition, we are not inhibited to upgrade or downgrade a company as soon as its financial condition warrants the change. You should therefore consider the magnitude of the rating change along with the meaning of the new rating when evaluating the significance of a rating upgrade or downgrade.

1. **Insurance Company Name** — The legally-registered name, which can sometimes differ from the name that the company uses for advertising. An insurer's name can be very similar to that of another, so verify the company's exact name and state of domicile to make sure you are looking at the correct company.

2. **Domicile State** — The state which has primary regulatory responsibility for the company. It may differ from the location of the company's corporate headquarters. You do not have to be living in the domicile state to purchase insurance from this firm, provided it is licensed to do business in your state.

3. **Total Assets** — All assets admitted by state insurance regulators in millions of dollars. This includes investments and current business assets such as receivables from agents and reinsurers.

4. **New Safety Rating** — The rating assigned to the company as of the date of this Guide's publication. Our rating is measured on a scale from A to F and considers a wide range of factors. Highly-rated companies are, in our opinion, less likely to experience financial difficulties than lower-rated firms. See *About Weiss Safety Ratings* for more information.

5. **Previous Safety Rating** — The rating assigned to the company prior to its most recent change.

6. **Date of Change** — The date that the rating upgrade or downgrade officially occurred. Normally, all rating changes are put into effect on a single day each quarter of the year. In some instances, however, a rating may have been changed outside of this normal update.

Withdrawn Ratings

INSURANCE COMPANY NAME	DOM. STATE	TOTAL ASSETS ($MIL)	NEW RATING	PREVIOUS RATING	DATE OF CHANGE
AGRINATIONAL INS CO	VT	971.1	U	D	05/16/18
AHC INSURANCE CO	DE	337.1	U	B-	05/16/18
ALLIANCE NATIONAL INS CO	NY	48.2	U	E	05/16/18
AMERIGUARD RRG INC	VT	15.2	U	C-	05/16/18
ARCH MORTGAGE REINS CO	WI	16.8	U	B-	05/16/18
ARGONAUT-SOUTHWEST INS CO	IL	18.5	U	D	05/16/18
CA CASUALTY COMP INS CO	CA	96.6	U	C+	05/16/18
COLONIAL MORTGAGE INS CO	TX	2.7	U	D+	05/16/18
CONSOLIDATED INS ASSN	TX	2.8	U	U	05/16/18
CONSOLIDATED LLOYDS	TX	0.8	U	U	05/16/18
CRYSTAL RUN RECIPROCAL RRG	VT	17.1	U	E	05/16/18
DELTA LLOYDS INS CO OF HOUSTON	TX	7.1	U	D+	05/16/18
FAITH AFFILIATED RRG INC	VT	5.8	U	E+	05/16/18
GEORGIA DEALERS INS CO	GA	7.6	U	D	05/16/18
GREAT LAKES CASUALTY INS CO	MI	10.3	U	U	05/16/18
GREYHAWK INSURANCE CO	CO	16.5	U	C	05/16/18
HANNAHSTOWN MUTUAL INS CO	PA	4.3	U	D+	05/16/18
HEALTH CARE CASUALTY RRG INC	DC	10.2	U	D	05/16/18
HILLSTAR INS CO	IN	3.6	U	U	05/16/18
INDIANA OLD NATIONAL INS CO	VT	2,179.7	U	C	05/16/18
INSUREMAX INS CO	IN	4.3	U	E	05/16/18
INTREPID INS CO	IA	32.2	U	C	05/16/18
MERCURY NATIONAL INS CO	IL	16.1	U	B	05/16/18
MHA INS CO	MI	562.1	U	C	05/16/18
MONTOUR MUTUAL INS CO	PA	0.9	U	D	05/16/18
MOUNTAIN STATES COMM INS CO	NM	1.0	U	D	05/16/18
PHYSICIANS SPECIALTY LTD RRG	SC	11.0	U	D+	05/16/18
PONCE DE LEON LTC RRG INC	FL	5.5	U	D+	05/16/18
PREMIER INS CO OF MA	CT	252.9	U	B	05/16/18
PREMIER PHYSICIANS INS CO	NV	12.4	U	E	05/16/18
PROGRESSIVE FREEDOM INS CO	OH	5.4	U	C	05/16/18
SENTINEL ASR RRG INC	HI	17.2	U	E	05/16/18
SOUTHERN GUARANTY INS CO	WI	30.3	U	C	05/16/18
SUSSEX INS CO	IL	557.0	U	C+	05/16/18
UNIGARD INDEMNITY CO	WI	7.6	U	C	05/16/18
UNITED GUARANTY CREDIT INS CO	NC	25.5	U	B-	05/16/18
WASHINGTON CASUALTY CO	WA	25.8	U	D-	05/16/18
WESTERN CATHOLIC INS CO RRG	VT	3.1	U	E+	05/16/18
WESTERN PROTECTORS INS CO	OR	8.9	U	C	05/16/18

Rating Upgrades

360 INS CO was upgraded to B from B- in May 2018 based on an increase in the profitability index from a 4.10(fair) to 5.70(good), reserve adequacy index from a 5.30(good) to 6.10(good), and stability index from a 3.80(fair) to 4.10(fair).

A CENTRAL INS CO was upgraded to C from C- in May 2018 based on an increase in the liquidity index from a 6.20(good) to 6.40(good), stability index from a 3.30(fair) to 3.50(fair), and profitability index from a 6.70(good) to 6.80(good).

ACADEMIC MEDICAL PROFESSIONALS RRG was upgraded to D from D- in May 2018 based on an increase in the reserve adequacy index from a 6.90(excellent) to 8.40(excellent), liquidity index from a 9.30(excellent) to 9.60(excellent), and stability index from a 1.30(weak) to 1.50(weak).

ACCEPTANCE CASUALTY INS CO was upgraded to D+ from D in May 2018 based on an increase in the liquidity index from a 6.70(good) to 7.30(excellent) and stability index from a 2.30(weak) to 2.50(weak). Other factors: The company's net asset base increased during the period by 22.2%, from $132.9 million to $162.5 million. Capital and surplus increased during the period by 8.1%, from $62.2 million to $67.2 million.

ACCREDITED SURETY & CAS CO INC was upgraded to B- from C+ in May 2018 based on an increase in the liquidity index from a 7.00(excellent) to 9.40(excellent), capitalization index from a 7.30(excellent) to 9.40(excellent), stability index from a 3.30(fair) to 5.20(good), and profitability index from a 8.00(excellent) to 8.30(excellent). Other factors: The company's net asset base increased during the period by 24.4%, from $119.5 million to $148.7 million. Capital and surplus increased during the period by 98.4%, from $27.5 million to $54.5 million.

ACUITY A MUTUAL INS CO was upgraded to A- from B+ in May 2018 based on an increase in the stability index from a 5.10(good) to 7.00(excellent) and capitalization index from a 9.30(excellent) to 9.40(excellent).

ADIRONDACK INS EXCHANGE was upgraded to C+ from C in May 2018 based on an increase in the profitability index from a 4.70(fair) to 4.90(good), stability index from a 4.30(fair) to 4.50(fair), and reserve adequacy index from a 4.80(fair) to 4.90(good).

ADVANTAGE WORKERS COMP INS CO was upgraded to B from B- in May 2018 based on an increase in the reserve adequacy index from a 4.60(fair) to 5.80(good), profitability index from a 4.40(fair) to 4.60(fair), and stability index from a 4.00(fair) to 4.10(fair).

AEGIS HEALTHCARE RRG INC was upgraded to D+ from D in May 2018 based on an increase in the liquidity index from a 6.40(good) to 6.80(good), profitability index from a 3.00(fair) to 3.30(fair), and capitalization index from a 7.50(excellent) to 7.80(excellent).

AFFILIATED FM INS CO was upgraded to C+ from C in May 2018 based on an increase in the stability index from a 3.60(fair) to 4.50(fair).

AGCS MARINE INS CO was upgraded to C- from D+ in May 2018 based on an increase in the liquidity index from a 0.00(weak) to 7.00(excellent), stability index from a 2.80(weak) to 3.30(fair), profitability index from a 6.40(good) to 6.80(good), and reserve adequacy index from a 3.90(fair) to 4.00(fair).

AGENCY INS CO OF MD INC was upgraded to B- from C+ in May 2018 based on an increase in the profitability index from a 6.40(good) to 8.80(excellent) and stability index from a 3.40(fair) to 5.30(good).

AGENTS MUTUAL INS CO was upgraded to D+ from D in May 2018 based on an increase in the liquidity index from a 3.00(fair) to 6.50(good), capitalization index from a 2.60(weak) to 4.90(good), and profitability index from a 7.40(excellent) to 8.90(excellent).

AGRI GENERAL INS CO was upgraded to C from C- in May 2018 based on an increase in the profitability index from a 2.20(weak) to 2.70(weak) and stability index from a 3.10(fair) to 3.50(fair).

AIOI NISSAY DOWA INS CO LTD was upgraded to C- from D+ in May 2018 based on an increase in the stability index from a 1.30(weak) to 3.20(fair). Other factors: The company's net asset base increased during the period by 6.2%, from $33.5 million to $35.6 million.

AIOI NISSAY DOWA INS CO OF AMERICA was upgraded to B- from C+ in May 2018 based on an increase in the stability index from a 3.40(fair) to 5.30(good) and reserve adequacy index from a 8.80(excellent) to 8.90(excellent).

Rating Upgrades (Continued)

ALABAMA MUNICIPAL INS CORP was upgraded to B- from C+ in May 2018 based on an increase in the stability index from a 3.40(fair) to 4.90(good), liquidity index from a 6.90(excellent) to 7.20(excellent), and capitalization index from a 8.30(excellent) to 8.50(excellent). Other factors: The company's net asset base increased during the period by 6.0%, from $113.3 million to $120.1 million. Capital and surplus increased during the period by 7.8%, from $51.0 million to $55.0 million.

ALASKA NATIONAL INS CO was upgraded to B+ from B in May 2018 based on an increase in the stability index from a 4.70(fair) to 6.50(good), liquidity index from a 7.10(excellent) to 7.50(excellent), capitalization index from a 9.20(excellent) to 9.40(excellent), and profitability index from a 8.80(excellent) to 8.90(excellent).

ALFA GENERAL INS CORP was upgraded to B+ from B in May 2018 based on an increase in the stability index from a 4.60(fair) to 6.40(good), profitability index from a 3.60(fair) to 4.90(good), and capitalization index from a 8.90(excellent) to 9.00(excellent).

ALFA MUTUAL FIRE INS CO was upgraded to B+ from B in May 2018 based on an increase in the profitability index from a 4.70(fair) to 6.30(good) and stability index from a 4.90(good) to 6.50(good).

ALFA MUTUAL GENERAL INS CO was upgraded to A- from B+ in May 2018 based on an increase in the stability index from a 5.00(good) to 6.90(excellent), profitability index from a 6.00(good) to 6.50(good), and reserve adequacy index from a 7.60(excellent) to 7.70(excellent).

ALL AMERICA INS CO was upgraded to A- from B+ in May 2018 based on an increase in the stability index from a 5.00(good) to 6.90(excellent).

ALLEGANY CO-OP INS CO was upgraded to B- from C+ in May 2018 based on an increase in the stability index from a 3.40(fair) to 5.30(good).

ALLEGHENY SURETY CO was upgraded to D+ from D in May 2018 based on an increase in the profitability index from a 2.40(weak) to 3.60(fair), reserve adequacy index from a 3.20(fair) to 3.60(fair), capitalization index from a 7.10(excellent) to 7.20(excellent), and stability index from a 1.90(weak) to 2.00(weak).

ALLEGIANT INS CO INC A RRG was upgraded to D- from E+ in May 2018 based on an increase in the profitability index from a 4.80(fair) to 9.00(excellent), stability index from a 0.50(weak) to 0.90(weak), and reserve adequacy index from a 0.50(weak) to 0.80(weak). Other factors: Capital and surplus increased during the period by 9.2%, from $12.2 million to $13.3 million.

ALLIANCE OF NONPROFITS FOR INS RRG was upgraded to C+ from C in May 2018 based on an increase in the profitability index from a 8.20(excellent) to 8.40(excellent) and stability index from a 4.30(fair) to 4.50(fair).

ALLIED SERVICES RRG was upgraded to E+ from E in May 2018 based on an increase in the reserve adequacy index from a 6.00(good) to 9.50(excellent), stability index from a 0.00(weak) to 0.50(weak), and liquidity index from a 7.00(excellent) to 7.10(excellent).

ALLIED WORLD SPECIALTY INS CO was upgraded to B+ from B in May 2018 based on an increase in the stability index from a 4.70(fair) to 6.50(good) and liquidity index from a 7.00(excellent) to 8.20(excellent).

ALLSTATE F&C INS CO was upgraded to B- from C+ in May 2018 based on an increase in the stability index from a 4.30(fair) to 4.90(good).

ALLSTATE INS CO was upgraded to B+ from B in May 2018 based on an increase in the profitability index from a 4.50(fair) to 8.20(excellent), stability index from a 5.10(good) to 6.50(good), and liquidity index from a 4.20(fair) to 5.40(good).

ALLSTATE NJ INS CO was upgraded to A- from B+ in May 2018 based on an increase in the reserve adequacy index from a 6.80(good) to 8.20(excellent), profitability index from a 5.40(good) to 6.60(good), stability index from a 6.70(good) to 7.10(excellent), liquidity index from a 6.30(good) to 6.50(good), and capitalization index from a 8.20(excellent) to 8.30(excellent).

ALLSTATE NJ P&C INS CO was upgraded to B- from C+ in May 2018 based on an increase in the stability index from a 4.30(fair) to 4.90(good).

ALPS PROPERTY & CASUALTY INS CO was upgraded to B- from C+ in May 2018 based on an increase in the stability index from a 3.40(fair) to 5.30(good) and liquidity index from a 7.40(excellent) to 7.50(excellent).

ALTERRA AMERICA INS CO was upgraded to B from B- in May 2018 based on an increase in the capitalization index from a 4.90(good) to 7.70(excellent), stability index from a 3.60(fair) to 5.20(good), profitability index from a 5.60(good) to 6.00(good), liquidity index from a 6.80(good) to 6.90(excellent), and reserve adequacy index from a 6.90(excellent) to 7.00(excellent).

Rating Upgrades (Continued)

AMCO INS CO was upgraded to B- from C+ in May 2018 based on an increase in the profitability index from a 3.20(fair) to 3.90(fair) and stability index from a 4.50(fair) to 5.00(good).

AMERICAN AGRICULTURAL INS CO was upgraded to B+ from B in May 2018 based on an increase in the stability index from a 6.30(good) to 6.50(good).

AMERICAN COASTAL INS CO was upgraded to B from B- in May 2018 based on an increase in the stability index from a 5.30(good) to 5.50(good).

AMERICAN CONTRACTORS INDEMNITY CO was upgraded to B+ from B in May 2018 based on an increase in the stability index from a 5.70(good) to 6.50(good).

AMERICAN EXCESS INS EXCHANGE RRG was upgraded to C from C- in May 2018 based on an increase in the stability index from a 2.70(weak) to 3.50(fair), capitalization index from a 8.40(excellent) to 9.20(excellent), profitability index from a 3.00(fair) to 3.60(fair), and liquidity index from a 7.10(excellent) to 7.20(excellent).

AMERICAN FAMILY MUTL INS CO SI was upgraded to A- from B+ in May 2018 based on an increase in the stability index from a 5.20(good) to 7.10(excellent) and profitability index from a 5.80(good) to 6.10(good).

AMERICAN FREEDOM INS CO was upgraded to B from B- in May 2018 based on an increase in the capitalization index from a 7.30(excellent) to 8.20(excellent) and liquidity index from a 6.40(good) to 6.60(good).

AMERICAN INTER FIDELITY EXCHANGE RRG was upgraded to B- from C+ in May 2018 based on an increase in the stability index from a 3.20(fair) to 4.80(fair).

AMERICAN INTERSTATE INS CO OF TX was upgraded to B+ from B in May 2018 based on an increase in the stability index from a 6.30(good) to 6.50(good), profitability index from a 7.90(excellent) to 8.00(excellent), and reserve adequacy index from a 9.30(excellent) to 9.40(excellent).

AMERICAN NATIONAL PROPERTY & CAS CO was upgraded to B+ from B in May 2018 based on an increase in the profitability index from a 5.00(good) to 6.70(good), stability index from a 4.90(good) to 6.50(good), and capitalization index from a 8.00(excellent) to 8.10(excellent). Other factors: Capital and surplus increased during the period by 6.8%, from $614.9 million to $656.5 million.

AMERICAN PET INS CO was upgraded to C from C- in May 2018 based on an increase in the stability index from a 3.30(fair) to 3.50(fair). Other factors: The company's net asset base increased during the period by 6.2%, from $71.5 million to $75.9 million.

AMERICAN PLATINUM PROP & CAS INS CO was upgraded to B- from C+ in May 2018 based on an increase in the stability index from a 3.40(fair) to 5.10(good), reserve adequacy index from a 5.10(good) to 6.10(good), and profitability index from a 3.90(fair) to 4.20(fair).

AMERICAN RISK INS CO was upgraded to C- from D+ in May 2018 based on an increase in the liquidity index from a 0.70(weak) to 7.10(excellent), profitability index from a 6.20(good) to 7.50(excellent), reserve adequacy index from a 2.20(weak) to 3.20(fair), stability index from a 2.70(weak) to 3.20(fair), and capitalization index from a 4.70(fair) to 5.10(good).

AMERICAN ROAD INS CO was upgraded to B- from C+ in May 2018 based on an increase in the profitability index from a 4.90(good) to 7.50(excellent) and stability index from a 3.00(fair) to 4.50(fair). Other factors: Capital and surplus increased during the period by 12.8%, from $239.8 million to $270.4 million.

AMFED CASUALTY INS CO was upgraded to C from C- in May 2018 based on an increase in the stability index from a 2.40(weak) to 3.50(fair) and profitability index from a 7.10(excellent) to 7.50(excellent).

AMFED NATIONAL INS CO was upgraded to D from D- in May 2018 based on an increase in the capitalization index from a 0.80(weak) to 3.20(fair), reserve adequacy index from a 0.80(weak) to 1.90(weak), and stability index from a 0.90(weak) to 1.40(weak).

AMFIRST SPECIALTY INS CO was upgraded to D+ from D in May 2018 based on an increase in the stability index from a 0.60(weak) to 2.30(weak), capitalization index from a 9.30(excellent) to 10.00(excellent), and profitability index from a 5.90(good) to 6.50(good).

Rating Upgrades (Continued)

AMICA P&C INS CO was upgraded to B from B- in May 2018 based on an increase in the profitability index from a 3.80(fair) to 6.40(good) and stability index from a 5.30(good) to 5.50(good).

ANSUR AMERICA INS CO was upgraded to B+ from B in May 2018 based on an increase in the stability index from a 4.80(fair) to 6.50(good).

APPLIED MEDICO LEGAL SOLUTIONS RRG was upgraded to C+ from C in May 2018 based on an increase in the stability index from a 4.30(fair) to 4.50(fair) and capitalization index from a 7.10(excellent) to 7.30(excellent).

APPLIED UNDERWRITERS CAPTIVE RISK was upgraded to C from C- in May 2018 based on an increase in the reserve adequacy index from a 4.90(good) to 7.00(excellent), capitalization index from a 5.40(good) to 7.40(excellent), profitability index from a 6.30(good) to 6.70(good), and stability index from a 3.30(fair) to 3.50(fair). Other factors: Capital and surplus increased during the period by 19.1%, from $62.4 million to $74.3 million.

ARAG INS CO was upgraded to B from B- in May 2018 based on an increase in the stability index from a 3.70(fair) to 5.50(good).

ARCH MORTGAGE INS CO was upgraded to B from B- in May 2018 based on an increase in the liquidity index from a 5.90(good) to 9.10(excellent), profitability index from a 2.80(weak) to 3.80(fair), reserve adequacy index from a 5.00(good) to 5.80(good), and capitalization index from a 7.50(excellent) to 7.70(excellent).

ARCH SPECIALTY INS CO was upgraded to B+ from B in May 2018 based on an increase in the stability index from a 4.70(fair) to 6.50(good) and profitability index from a 4.90(good) to 6.20(good).

ARCOA RRG INC was upgraded to D- from E+ in May 2018 based on an increase in the profitability index from a 2.90(fair) to 9.30(excellent), reserve adequacy index from a 3.80(fair) to 5.00(good), liquidity index from a 6.30(good) to 6.90(excellent), stability index from a 0.60(weak) to 1.10(weak), and capitalization index from a 0.80(weak) to 1.20(weak). Other factors: The company's net asset base increased during the period by 5.1%, from $18.5 million to $19.4 million. Capital and surplus increased during the period by 5.5%, from $7.8 million to $8.2 million.

ARECA INS EXCHANGE was upgraded to B- from C+ in May 2018 based on an increase in the stability index from a 3.10(fair) to 4.40(fair), reserve adequacy index from a 5.80(good) to 6.40(good), profitability index from a 3.90(fair) to 4.50(fair), and liquidity index from a 6.90(excellent) to 7.50(excellent).

ARIZONA AUTOMOBILE INS CO was upgraded to C+ from C in May 2018 based on an increase in the profitability index from a 5.10(good) to 5.70(good) and stability index from a 2.90(fair) to 3.10(fair). Other factors: The company's net asset base increased during the period by 38.0%, from $30.0 million to $41.3 million.

ARMED FORCES INS EXCHANGE was upgraded to B from B- in May 2018 based on an increase in the stability index from a 3.80(fair) to 5.50(good), liquidity index from a 6.10(good) to 6.30(good), and capitalization index from a 8.40(excellent) to 8.60(excellent). Other factors: Capital and surplus increased during the period by 7.1%, from $63.1 million to $67.5 million.

ASCENDANT COMMERCIAL INS INC was upgraded to D from D- in May 2018 based on an increase in the profitability index from a 6.90(excellent) to 7.90(excellent), stability index from a 1.00(weak) to 1.50(weak), capitalization index from a 1.40(weak) to 1.90(weak), and reserve adequacy index from a 0.90(weak) to 1.40(weak). Other factors: Capital and surplus increased during the period by 5.1%, from $10.8 million to $11.3 million.

ASI SELECT INS CORP was upgraded to C from C- in May 2018 based on an increase in the stability index from a 3.30(fair) to 3.50(fair).

ASURE WORLDWIDE INS CO was upgraded to B from B- in May 2018 based on an increase in the stability index from a 5.30(good) to 5.40(good) and capitalization index from a 9.30(excellent) to 9.40(excellent).

ATLANTIC BONDING CO was upgraded to D from D- in May 2018 based on an increase in the stability index from a 1.10(weak) to 1.50(weak) and profitability index from a 3.70(fair) to 3.90(fair). Other factors: The company's net asset base increased during the period by 8.9%, from $8.7 million to $9.5 million. Capital and surplus increased during the period by 5.0%, from $8.3 million to $8.7 million.

ATLANTIC CHARTER INS CO was upgraded to B from B- in May 2018 based on an increase in the stability index from a 3.60(fair) to 5.50(good), capitalization index from a 6.20(good) to 6.50(good), and reserve adequacy index from a 9.80(excellent) to 9.90(excellent).

Rating Upgrades (Continued)

ATRADIUS TRADE CREDIT INS CO was upgraded to C+ from C in May 2018 based on an increase in the stability index from a 2.90(fair) to 4.50(fair), profitability index from a 3.20(fair) to 3.50(fair), and reserve adequacy index from a 4.70(fair) to 5.00(good).

ATTORNEYS LIAB ASR SOCIETY INC RRG was upgraded to D+ from D in May 2018 based on an increase in the capitalization index from a 1.80(weak) to 3.90(fair), reserve adequacy index from a 1.70(weak) to 3.20(fair), profitability index from a 5.70(good) to 6.40(good), and stability index from a 1.90(weak) to 2.40(weak). Other factors: Capital and surplus increased during the period by 10.9%, from $684.5 million to $759.5 million.

AUSTIN MUTUAL INS CO was upgraded to D+ from D in May 2018 based on an increase in the reserve adequacy index from a 3.20(fair) to 3.50(fair), profitability index from a 8.40(excellent) to 8.70(excellent), and stability index from a 2.30(weak) to 2.50(weak).

AUTO CLUB INS CO OF FL was upgraded to B+ from B in May 2018 based on an increase in the reserve adequacy index from a 7.00(excellent) to 9.10(excellent), profitability index from a 5.60(good) to 6.30(good), capitalization index from a 8.90(excellent) to 9.30(excellent), and stability index from a 6.30(good) to 6.50(good).

AUTO CLUB SOUTH INS CO was upgraded to B from B- in May 2018 based on an increase in the stability index from a 3.60(fair) to 5.50(good).

AUTO-OWNERS INS CO was upgraded to A from A- in May 2018 based on an increase in the stability index from a 5.70(good) to 7.50(excellent) and reserve adequacy index from a 6.10(good) to 6.20(good).

AVENTUS INSURANCE CO was upgraded to C+ from C in May 2018 based on an increase in the stability index from a 2.90(fair) to 4.20(fair), reserve adequacy index from a 6.50(good) to 6.90(excellent), and liquidity index from a 7.00(excellent) to 7.10(excellent).

AVIATION ALLIANCE INS RRG INC was upgraded to D from E- in May 2018 based on an increase in the profitability index from a 0.60(weak) to 1.90(weak) and stability index from a 0.00(weak) to 1.00(weak). Other factors: The company's net asset base increased during the period by 40.9%, from $2.0 million to $2.9 million. Capital and surplus increased during the period by 119.8%, from $0.5 million to $1.1 million.

BALBOA INS CO was upgraded to C from C- in May 2018 based on an increase in the profitability index from a 1.90(weak) to 3.20(fair) and stability index from a 3.10(fair) to 3.50(fair).

BALDWIN MUTUAL INS CO was upgraded to C from C- in May 2018 based on an increase in the stability index from a 2.30(weak) to 2.90(fair).

BANKERS SPECIALTY INS CO was upgraded to B from B- in May 2018 based on an increase in the capitalization index from a 5.90(good) to 6.20(good), stability index from a 5.30(good) to 5.50(good), and profitability index from a 3.90(fair) to 4.00(fair).

BAR VERMONT RRG INC was upgraded to C- from D+ in May 2018 based on an increase in the stability index from a 2.40(weak) to 2.90(fair) and capitalization index from a 7.70(excellent) to 7.80(excellent). Other factors: Capital and surplus increased during the period by 12.9%, from $19.0 million to $21.5 million.

BEAZLEY INS CO was upgraded to B from B- in May 2018 based on an increase in the stability index from a 3.70(fair) to 5.50(good) and reserve adequacy index from a 8.00(excellent) to 8.10(excellent).

BELL UNITED INS CO was upgraded to B- from C+ in May 2018 based on an increase in the stability index from a 3.10(fair) to 4.70(fair).

BENCHMARK INS CO was upgraded to B from B- in May 2018 based on an increase in the reserve adequacy index from a 6.70(good) to 6.90(excellent) and stability index from a 3.90(fair) to 4.10(fair).

BLOOMFIELD MUTUAL INS CO was upgraded to C from C- in May 2018 based on an increase in the profitability index from a 8.20(excellent) to 8.30(excellent). Other factors: Capital and surplus increased during the period by 5.5%, from $9.2 million to $9.7 million.

BLOOMINGTON COMP INS CO was upgraded to B- from C+ in May 2018 based on an increase in the stability index from a 3.30(fair) to 4.90(good).

Rating Upgrades (Continued)

BOND SAFEGUARD INS CO was upgraded to C from C- in May 2018 based on an increase in the reserve adequacy index from a 2.90(fair) to 4.60(fair), profitability index from a 5.80(good) to 7.00(excellent), stability index from a 2.50(weak) to 3.50(fair), and liquidity index from a 7.30(excellent) to 7.50(excellent). Other factors: The company's net asset base increased during the period by 7.6%, from $84.4 million to $90.8 million.

BOSTON INDEMNITY CO INC was upgraded to C- from D+ in May 2018 based on an increase in the reserve adequacy index from a 6.30(good) to 6.80(good) and capitalization index from a 7.20(excellent) to 7.60(excellent). Other factors: The company's net asset base increased during the period by 11.3%, from $7.0 million to $7.8 million.

BREMEN FARMERS MUTUAL INS CO was upgraded to C+ from C in May 2018 based on an increase in the reserve adequacy index from a 7.00(excellent) to 8.90(excellent), stability index from a 2.90(fair) to 4.50(fair), profitability index from a 8.30(excellent) to 8.80(excellent), and capitalization index from a 7.80(excellent) to 8.00(excellent).

BRICKSTREET MUTUAL INS CO was upgraded to B from B- in May 2018 based on an increase in the profitability index from a 6.90(excellent) to 8.40(excellent) and stability index from a 5.30(good) to 5.50(good).

BRISTOL WEST PREFERRED INS CO was upgraded to C+ from C in May 2018 based on an increase in the reserve adequacy index from a 5.90(good) to 6.20(good) and stability index from a 4.30(fair) to 4.50(fair).

BUILD AMERICA MUTUAL ASR CO was upgraded to C- from D+ in May 2018 based on an increase in the stability index from a 1.10(weak) to 3.00(fair) and profitability index from a 2.20(weak) to 2.50(weak).

BUILDERS MUTUAL INS CO was upgraded to A from A- in May 2018 based on an increase in the stability index from a 7.30(excellent) to 7.50(excellent) and capitalization index from a 7.90(excellent) to 8.00(excellent).

BUILDERS PREMIER INS CO was upgraded to B- from C+ in May 2018 based on an increase in the stability index from a 4.30(fair) to 4.60(fair).

BUSINESSFIRST INS CO was upgraded to B from B- in May 2018 based on an increase in the profitability index from a 8.10(excellent) to 8.40(excellent) and reserve adequacy index from a 6.60(good) to 6.90(excellent).

CALIFORNIA HEALTHCARE INS CO INC RRG was upgraded to B from B- in May 2018 based on an increase in the stability index from a 3.60(fair) to 5.50(good).

CALIFORNIA MEDICAL GROUP INS CO RRG was upgraded to E+ from E in May 2018 based on an increase in the profitability index from a 2.90(fair) to 5.20(good), capitalization index from a 4.30(fair) to 6.30(good), stability index from a 0.00(weak) to 0.50(weak), and liquidity index from a 7.70(excellent) to 7.80(excellent). Other factors: Capital and surplus increased during the period by 19.1%, from $4.1 million to $4.9 million.

CALIFORNIA MUTUAL INS CO was upgraded to C from C- in May 2018 based on an increase in the profitability index from a 5.30(good) to 6.80(good), stability index from a 2.40(weak) to 3.10(fair), liquidity index from a 6.80(good) to 6.90(excellent), and reserve adequacy index from a 6.40(good) to 6.50(good).

CALLICOON CO-OPERATIVE INS CO was upgraded to B- from C+ in May 2018 based on an increase in the stability index from a 3.20(fair) to 5.00(good).

CAMICO MUTUAL INS CO was upgraded to C+ from C in May 2018 based on an increase in the stability index from a 2.90(fair) to 4.50(fair) and profitability index from a 6.30(good) to 6.60(good).

CAMPMED CAS & INDEM CO INC OF MD was upgraded to B- from C+ in May 2018 based on an increase in the liquidity index from a 7.00(excellent) to 10.00(excellent) and stability index from a 4.30(fair) to 4.90(good).

CAPITOL CASUALTY CO was upgraded to B- from C+ in May 2018 based on an increase in the stability index from a 3.20(fair) to 5.00(good) and liquidity index from a 9.20(excellent) to 9.30(excellent). Other factors: Capital and surplus increased during the period by 9.2%, from $27.3 million to $29.8 million.

Rating Upgrades (Continued)

CARE WEST INS CO was upgraded to C from C- in May 2018 based on an increase in the profitability index from a 2.90(fair) to 8.70(excellent), reserve adequacy index from a 3.80(fair) to 5.00(good), capitalization index from a 5.40(good) to 6.50(good), liquidity index from a 6.50(good) to 6.80(good), and stability index from a 3.30(fair) to 3.50(fair).

CAREGIVERS UNITED LIAB INS CO RRG was upgraded to C from C- in May 2018 based on an increase in the profitability index from a 6.40(good) to 7.30(excellent) and stability index from a 3.30(fair) to 3.50(fair).

CARING COMMUNITIES RECIP RRG was upgraded to B from B- in May 2018 based on an increase in the liquidity index from a 8.20(excellent) to 8.90(excellent) and stability index from a 5.30(good) to 5.50(good).

CAROLINA MUTUAL INS INC was upgraded to B from B- in May 2018 based on an increase in the stability index from a 3.50(fair) to 5.40(good).

CASCO INDEMNITY CO was upgraded to B- from C+ in May 2018 based on an increase in the stability index from a 3.20(fair) to 4.90(good) and profitability index from a 8.60(excellent) to 8.70(excellent).

CASTLE KEY INS CO was upgraded to B+ from B in May 2018 based on an increase in the profitability index from a 6.30(good) to 8.60(excellent) and stability index from a 4.50(fair) to 6.40(good).

CASUALTY CORP OF AMERICA was upgraded to D from D- in May 2018 based on an increase in the liquidity index from a 1.00(weak) to 2.60(weak), reserve adequacy index from a 0.50(weak) to 1.60(weak), capitalization index from a 1.40(weak) to 2.20(weak), profitability index from a 3.70(fair) to 4.20(fair), and stability index from a 1.20(weak) to 1.50(weak). Other factors: The company's net asset base increased during the period by 6.1%, from $13.1 million to $13.9 million. Capital and surplus increased during the period by 31.0%, from $3.5 million to $4.6 million.

CATASTROPHE REINS CO was upgraded to C from C- in May 2018 based on an increase in the profitability index from a 8.60(excellent) to 8.90(excellent), stability index from a 3.30(fair) to 3.50(fair), and reserve adequacy index from a 5.30(good) to 5.50(good).

CATERPILLAR INS CO was upgraded to B+ from B in May 2018 based on an increase in the capitalization index from a 9.20(excellent) to 9.40(excellent) and stability index from a 6.30(good) to 6.50(good).

CATLIN INS CO was upgraded to C+ from C in May 2018 based on an increase in the capitalization index from a 4.50(fair) to 6.90(excellent), stability index from a 3.40(fair) to 4.40(fair), and profitability index from a 2.80(weak) to 2.90(fair). Other factors: The company's net asset base increased during the period by 14.0%, from $159.3 million to $181.6 million.

CBIA COMP SERVICES INC was upgraded to C from C- in May 2018 based on an increase in the capitalization index from a 5.40(good) to 6.50(good) and profitability index from a 6.00(good) to 6.60(good). Other factors: Capital and surplus increased during the period by 13.6%, from $9.6 million to $11.0 million.

CEM INS CO was upgraded to C- from D+ in May 2018 based on an increase in the profitability index from a 5.90(good) to 8.30(excellent), reserve adequacy index from a 2.10(weak) to 2.60(weak), and stability index from a 2.70(weak) to 3.10(fair). Other factors: The company's net asset base increased during the period by 8.0%, from $42.5 million to $45.9 million.

CENSTAT CASUALTY CO was upgraded to B- from C+ in May 2018 based on an increase in the stability index from a 3.40(fair) to 5.30(good) and liquidity index from a 8.10(excellent) to 8.40(excellent).

CENTENNIAL CASUALTY CO was upgraded to B from B- in May 2018 based on an increase in the stability index from a 3.80(fair) to 5.50(good) and capitalization index from a 8.30(excellent) to 8.40(excellent). Other factors: Capital and surplus increased during the period by 9.5%, from $75.8 million to $82.9 million.

CENTER MUTUAL INS CO was upgraded to B- from C+ in May 2018 based on an increase in the stability index from a 3.30(fair) to 5.10(good), liquidity index from a 6.00(good) to 6.30(good), and profitability index from a 5.40(good) to 5.70(good). Other factors: The company's net asset base increased during the period by 11.2%, from $51.9 million to $57.7 million.

CENTRAL MUTUAL INS CO was upgraded to B+ from B in May 2018 based on an increase in the stability index from a 4.70(fair) to 6.50(good), capitalization index from a 8.70(excellent) to 8.80(excellent), and profitability index from a 8.40(excellent) to 8.50(excellent).

Rating Upgrades (Continued)

CENTRAL PA PHYSICIANS RRG INC was upgraded to C+ from C in May 2018 based on an increase in the profitability index from a 4.10(fair) to 5.30(good), stability index from a 4.30(fair) to 4.50(fair), and capitalization index from a 7.20(excellent) to 7.40(excellent). Other factors: Capital and surplus increased during the period by 7.7%, from $21.0 million to $22.6 million.

CENTURION MEDICAL LIAB PROTECT RRG was upgraded to C from C- in May 2018 based on an increase in the profitability index from a 8.60(excellent) to 8.70(excellent).

CENTURY CASUALTY CO was upgraded to D from E- in May 2018 based on an increase in the capitalization index from a 7.50(excellent) to 10.00(excellent) and stability index from a 0.10(weak) to 1.50(weak).

CENTURY INS CO GUAM LTD was upgraded to D+ from D in May 2018 based on an increase in the profitability index from a 7.70(excellent) to 8.30(excellent), reserve adequacy index from a 3.70(fair) to 4.20(fair), stability index from a 2.30(weak) to 2.50(weak), and capitalization index from a 7.80(excellent) to 8.00(excellent). Other factors: The company's net asset base increased during the period by 10.7%, from $26.4 million to $29.2 million. Capital and surplus increased during the period by 11.6%, from $16.0 million to $17.8 million.

CGB INS CO was upgraded to D+ from D in May 2018 based on an increase in the stability index from a 2.30(weak) to 2.50(weak).

CHEROKEE INS CO was upgraded to B from B- in May 2018 based on an increase in the liquidity index from a 5.40(good) to 6.00(good), stability index from a 5.30(good) to 5.50(good), capitalization index from a 7.60(excellent) to 7.80(excellent), and reserve adequacy index from a 4.30(fair) to 4.40(fair).

CHERRY VALLEY COOPERATIVE INS CO was upgraded to D+ from D in May 2018 based on an increase in the liquidity index from a 7.90(excellent) to 9.00(excellent).

CHURCH MUTUAL INS CO was upgraded to B+ from B in May 2018 based on an increase in the stability index from a 4.90(good) to 6.50(good) and capitalization index from a 8.20(excellent) to 8.30(excellent).

CINCINNATI SPECIALTY UNDERWRITER was upgraded to A from A- in May 2018 based on an increase in the capitalization index from a 7.90(excellent) to 8.30(excellent), stability index from a 7.30(excellent) to 7.50(excellent), profitability index from a 8.70(excellent) to 8.80(excellent), and liquidity index from a 6.90(excellent) to 7.00(excellent). Other factors: Capital and surplus increased during the period by 5.3%, from $413.9 million to $436.0 million.

CITIES & VILLAGES MUTUAL INS CO was upgraded to B- from C+ in May 2018 based on an increase in the stability index from a 3.30(fair) to 5.00(good).

CLAVERACK CO-OPERATIVE INS CO was upgraded to D+ from D in May 2018 based on an increase in the capitalization index from a 8.00(excellent) to 9.40(excellent), liquidity index from a 6.90(excellent) to 7.90(excellent), stability index from a 1.80(weak) to 1.90(weak), and reserve adequacy index from a 9.30(excellent) to 9.40(excellent).

CLEAR BLUE INS CO was upgraded to C+ from C in May 2018 based on an increase in the profitability index from a 2.90(fair) to 4.00(fair) and liquidity index from a 9.30(excellent) to 10.00(excellent). Other factors: The company's net asset base increased during the period by 13.5%, from $49.3 million to $56.0 million.

CLOISTER MUTL CAS INS CO was upgraded to C+ from C in May 2018 based on an increase in the stability index from a 2.90(fair) to 4.40(fair) and profitability index from a 3.90(fair) to 4.30(fair).

COASTAL SELECT INS CO was upgraded to C- from D+ in May 2018 based on an increase in the capitalization index from a 0.80(weak) to 1.30(weak).

COFACE NORTH AMERICA INS CO was upgraded to C+ from C in May 2018 based on an increase in the stability index from a 2.60(weak) to 4.50(fair), capitalization index from a 7.20(excellent) to 7.80(excellent), and profitability index from a 2.80(weak) to 3.20(fair).

COLONIAL LLOYDS was upgraded to C from C- in May 2018 based on an increase in the profitability index from a 3.90(fair) to 5.90(good), stability index from a 2.60(weak) to 3.50(fair), reserve adequacy index from a 4.30(fair) to 4.80(fair), and liquidity index from a 9.00(excellent) to 9.10(excellent).

Rating Upgrades (Continued)

COLORADO FARM BUREAU MUTUAL INS CO was upgraded to C+ from C in May 2018 based on an increase in the stability index from a 3.30(fair) to 4.50(fair), liquidity index from a 6.20(good) to 6.70(good), and profitability index from a 3.70(fair) to 3.90(fair).

COLUMBIA LLOYDS INS CO was upgraded to B- from C+ in May 2018 based on an increase in the profitability index from a 5.40(good) to 8.90(excellent), stability index from a 3.30(fair) to 5.20(good), and reserve adequacy index from a 5.90(good) to 6.90(excellent). Other factors: The company's net asset base increased during the period by 6.3%, from $47.4 million to $50.4 million. Capital and surplus increased during the period by 8.8%, from $25.5 million to $27.8 million.

COLUMBIA NATIONAL RRG INC was upgraded to E+ from E in May 2018 based on an increase in the stability index from a 0.00(weak) to 0.50(weak).

COMMERCE INS CO was upgraded to B- from C+ in May 2018 based on an increase in the profitability index from a 3.40(fair) to 3.80(fair), liquidity index from a 3.00(fair) to 3.20(fair), and stability index from a 4.60(fair) to 4.80(fair).

COMMUNITY CARE RRG INC was upgraded to D+ from D in May 2018 based on an increase in the stability index from a 0.60(weak) to 1.90(weak), liquidity index from a 7.20(excellent) to 7.90(excellent), profitability index from a 6.70(good) to 7.30(excellent), capitalization index from a 7.10(excellent) to 7.30(excellent), and reserve adequacy index from a 3.60(fair) to 3.80(fair).

COMMUNITY HOSPITAL ALTERNATIVE RRG was upgraded to B from B- in May 2018 based on an increase in the capitalization index from a 8.90(excellent) to 9.50(excellent), liquidity index from a 7.00(excellent) to 7.20(excellent), and stability index from a 5.30(good) to 5.50(good). Other factors: Capital and surplus increased during the period by 11.0%, from $126.4 million to $140.3 million.

COMPWEST INS CO was upgraded to B from B- in May 2018 based on an increase in the stability index from a 5.30(good) to 5.50(good).

CONEMAUGH VALLEY MUTUAL INS CO was upgraded to C+ from C in May 2018 based on an increase in the profitability index from a 6.80(good) to 8.00(excellent), stability index from a 2.80(weak) to 3.80(fair), and capitalization index from a 8.60(excellent) to 9.00(excellent). Other factors: Capital and surplus increased during the period by 5.2%, from $6.7 million to $7.0 million.

CONIFER INS CO was upgraded to D from D- in May 2018 based on an increase in the stability index from a 1.00(weak) to 1.40(weak), capitalization index from a 1.20(weak) to 1.50(weak), and profitability index from a 2.80(weak) to 2.90(fair). Other factors: The company's net asset base increased during the period by 5.8%, from $114.6 million to $121.3 million.

CONSTITUTION INS CO was upgraded to C+ from C in May 2018 based on an increase in the reserve adequacy index from a 3.80(fair) to 4.90(good), stability index from a 3.00(fair) to 3.50(fair), and profitability index from a 8.30(excellent) to 8.60(excellent).

CONTINENTAL CASUALTY CO was upgraded to B- from C+ in May 2018 based on an increase in the stability index from a 3.30(fair) to 4.80(fair), reserve adequacy index from a 6.30(good) to 6.60(good), and profitability index from a 5.30(good) to 5.40(good).

CONTINUING CARE RRG INC was upgraded to E+ from E in May 2018 based on an increase in the liquidity index from a 0.00(weak) to 2.30(weak), profitability index from a 0.70(weak) to 1.30(weak), stability index from a 0.00(weak) to 0.50(weak), and capitalization index from a 1.10(weak) to 1.40(weak). Other factors: Capital and surplus increased during the period by 30.9%, from $1.0 million to $1.4 million.

CONTROLLED RISK INS CO OF VT RRG was upgraded to B from B- in May 2018 based on an increase in the stability index from a 5.30(good) to 5.40(good) and profitability index from a 7.90(excellent) to 8.00(excellent).

CONVENTUS INTER-INS was upgraded to B from B- in May 2018 based on an increase in the stability index from a 5.00(good) to 5.40(good).

COPPERPOINT INDEMNITY INS CO was upgraded to C+ from C in May 2018 based on an increase in the stability index from a 2.80(weak) to 4.10(fair) and profitability index from a 3.40(fair) to 3.60(fair).

COVERYS RRG INC was upgraded to C from C- in May 2018 based on an increase in the liquidity index from a 6.60(good) to 9.20(excellent), capitalization index from a 5.30(good) to 7.40(excellent), profitability index from a 2.50(weak) to 2.90(fair), and reserve adequacy index from a 4.60(fair) to 4.90(good).

COVINGTON SPECIALTY INS CO was upgraded to B+ from B in May 2018 based on an increase in the profitability index from a 4.80(fair) to 5.30(good), capitalization index from a 9.50(excellent) to 10.00(excellent), and stability index from a 6.30(good) to 6.50(good).

Rating Upgrades (Continued)

CROWN CAPTIVE INS CO was upgraded to D+ from D in May 2018 based on an increase in the stability index from a 1.40(weak) to 1.50(weak). Other factors: Capital and surplus increased during the period by 13.3%, from $1.1 million to $1.2 million.

CSAA GENERAL INS CO was upgraded to C+ from C in May 2018 based on an increase in the stability index from a 4.20(fair) to 4.40(fair) and reserve adequacy index from a 6.10(good) to 6.20(good).

DAIRYLAND INS CO was upgraded to A- from B+ in May 2018 based on an increase in the stability index from a 5.30(good) to 7.20(excellent).

DAN RRG INC was upgraded to D+ from D in May 2018 based on an increase in the stability index from a 0.80(weak) to 1.40(weak).

DB INS CO LTD US GUAM BRANCH was upgraded to B from B- in May 2018 based on an increase in the stability index from a 3.80(fair) to 5.50(good). Other factors: The company's net asset base increased during the period by 22.4%, from $64.4 million to $78.8 million.

DISCOVERY INS CO was upgraded to C from C- in May 2018 based on an increase in the reserve adequacy index from a 7.00(excellent) to 9.40(excellent), stability index from a 2.40(weak) to 3.20(fair), liquidity index from a 1.90(weak) to 2.40(weak), and profitability index from a 5.90(good) to 6.00(good).

DIST-CO INS CO INC A RRG was upgraded to E+ from E in May 2018 based on an increase in the stability index from a 0.00(weak) to 0.50(weak) and profitability index from a 6.30(good) to 6.40(good).

DISTRICTS MUTL INS & RISK MGMT was upgraded to C from C- in May 2018 based on an increase in the profitability index from a 5.20(good) to 6.30(good), capitalization index from a 8.60(excellent) to 8.80(excellent), stability index from a 3.30(fair) to 3.40(fair), and liquidity index from a 7.50(excellent) to 7.60(excellent).

DOCTORS CO RRG A RECIPROCAL was upgraded to C from C- in May 2018 based on an increase in the capitalization index from a 5.00(good) to 8.40(excellent), liquidity index from a 7.90(excellent) to 9.50(excellent), and profitability index from a 3.00(fair) to 3.50(fair). Other factors: The company's net asset base increased during the period by 62.3%, from $17.2 million to $27.8 million. Capital and surplus increased during the period by 217.9%, from $4.7 million to $15.0 million.

DRIVE NEW JERSEY INS CO was upgraded to B from B- in May 2018 based on an increase in the reserve adequacy index from a 6.30(good) to 6.60(good) and profitability index from a 8.30(excellent) to 8.50(excellent).

EASTERN ADVANTAGE ASR CO was upgraded to B from B- in May 2018 based on an increase in the capitalization index from a 4.00(fair) to 5.30(good), reserve adequacy index from a 4.60(fair) to 4.70(fair), and liquidity index from a 6.20(good) to 6.30(good). Other factors: The company's net asset base increased during the period by 16.4%, from $52.6 million to $61.2 million.

EASTERN DENTISTS INS CO RRG was upgraded to B from B- in May 2018 based on an increase in the liquidity index from a 6.90(excellent) to 7.10(excellent) and capitalization index from a 7.80(excellent) to 7.90(excellent).

EMPLOYERS INS CO OF NV was upgraded to C from C- in May 2018 based on an increase in the profitability index from a 1.90(weak) to 2.80(weak), stability index from a 3.10(fair) to 3.50(fair), liquidity index from a 6.70(good) to 7.00(excellent), and capitalization index from a 6.90(excellent) to 7.10(excellent). Other factors: Capital and surplus increased during the period by 12.0%, from $177.4 million to $198.7 million.

ENCOMPASS INS CO OF AM was upgraded to B- from C+ in May 2018 based on an increase in the stability index from a 4.30(fair) to 4.90(good).

ENDURANCE AMERICAN INS CO was upgraded to B from B- in May 2018 based on an increase in the capitalization index from a 6.20(good) to 7.40(excellent), profitability index from a 3.60(fair) to 4.20(fair), liquidity index from a 6.20(good) to 6.70(good), and stability index from a 5.30(good) to 5.50(good). Other factors: Capital and surplus increased during the period by 71.1%, from $249.5 million to $426.9 million.

ENDURANCE AMERICAN SPECIALTY INS CO was upgraded to B- from C+ in May 2018 based on an increase in the stability index from a 3.70(fair) to 5.20(good), profitability index from a 3.20(fair) to 4.00(fair), capitalization index from a 4.80(fair) to 5.50(good), and liquidity index from a 6.50(good) to 6.70(good). Other factors: Capital and surplus increased during the period by 6.3%, from $94.1 million to $100.0 million.

Rating Upgrades (Continued)

ENDURANCE RISK SOLUTIONS ASR CO was upgraded to B- from C+ in May 2018 based on an increase in the stability index from a 3.60(fair) to 5.10(good), capitalization index from a 4.30(fair) to 5.10(good), and profitability index from a 3.30(fair) to 4.00(fair). Other factors: Capital and surplus increased during the period by 6.9%, from $63.9 million to $68.3 million.

ERIE & NIAGARA INS ASSN was upgraded to B+ from B in May 2018 based on an increase in the stability index from a 6.30(good) to 6.50(good).

EXECUTIVE RISK INDEMNITY INC was upgraded to B from B- in May 2018 based on an increase in the profitability index from a 6.80(good) to 8.60(excellent), stability index from a 3.70(fair) to 5.50(good), capitalization index from a 8.80(excellent) to 9.40(excellent), and reserve adequacy index from a 8.60(excellent) to 8.70(excellent).

FALLS LAKE FIRE & CASUALTY CO was upgraded to C+ from C in May 2018 based on an increase in the liquidity index from a 6.90(excellent) to 8.50(excellent), profitability index from a 3.90(fair) to 4.30(fair), and reserve adequacy index from a 3.60(fair) to 3.70(fair).

FALLS LAKE NATIONAL INS CO was upgraded to B from B- in May 2018 based on an increase in the liquidity index from a 2.30(weak) to 7.00(excellent), reserve adequacy index from a 6.90(excellent) to 8.50(excellent), stability index from a 3.90(fair) to 5.30(good), and capitalization index from a 6.90(excellent) to 7.30(excellent).

FARM BU TOWN & COUNTRY INS CO OF MO was upgraded to B+ from B in May 2018 based on an increase in the stability index from a 4.60(fair) to 6.50(good), profitability index from a 8.30(excellent) to 8.50(excellent), and capitalization index from a 8.90(excellent) to 9.00(excellent).

FARM BUREAU GENERAL INS CO OF MI was upgraded to B+ from B in May 2018 based on an increase in the stability index from a 4.90(good) to 6.50(good) and capitalization index from a 9.70(excellent) to 9.90(excellent).

FARM BUREAU MUTUAL INS CO OF MI was upgraded to B+ from B in May 2018 based on an increase in the stability index from a 4.60(fair) to 6.50(good), capitalization index from a 9.50(excellent) to 10.00(excellent), profitability index from a 8.40(excellent) to 8.70(excellent), and liquidity index from a 5.90(good) to 6.00(good).

FARM BUREAU P&C INS CO was upgraded to A- from B+ in May 2018 based on an increase in the stability index from a 5.30(good) to 7.20(excellent), capitalization index from a 9.80(excellent) to 10.00(excellent), profitability index from a 8.80(excellent) to 8.90(excellent), and reserve adequacy index from a 8.10(excellent) to 8.20(excellent). Other factors: Capital and surplus increased during the period by 5.6%, from $1234.5 million to $1303.7 million.

FARM CREDIT SYS ASSOC CAPTIVE INS CO was upgraded to B from B- in May 2018 based on an increase in the stability index from a 3.90(fair) to 5.50(good).

FARMERS & MECHANICS MUTUAL IC OF WV was upgraded to B from B- in May 2018 based on an increase in the stability index from a 3.50(fair) to 5.40(good) and reserve adequacy index from a 5.20(good) to 6.10(good).

FARMERS & MERCHANTS MUTUAL FIRE I C was upgraded to B- from C+ in May 2018 based on an increase in the stability index from a 3.20(fair) to 4.90(good) and profitability index from a 6.90(excellent) to 8.00(excellent). Other factors: Capital and surplus increased during the period by 7.9%, from $25.2 million to $27.1 million.

FARMERS INS CO OF FLEMINGTON was upgraded to B- from C+ in May 2018 based on an increase in the stability index from a 3.40(fair) to 5.10(good) and profitability index from a 8.10(excellent) to 8.70(excellent). Other factors: The company's net asset base increased during the period by 6.0%, from $66.6 million to $70.6 million. Capital and surplus increased during the period by 9.2%, from $27.7 million to $30.3 million.

FARMERS MUTUAL F I C OF SALEM CTY was upgraded to B from B- in May 2018 based on an increase in the stability index from a 3.80(fair) to 5.50(good), liquidity index from a 6.90(excellent) to 7.00(excellent), and capitalization index from a 9.50(excellent) to 9.60(excellent). Other factors: Capital and surplus increased during the period by 6.5%, from $76.1 million to $81.0 million.

FARMERS MUTUAL FIRE INS CO OF MARBLE was upgraded to C+ from C in May 2018 based on an increase in the stability index from a 2.90(fair) to 4.40(fair), liquidity index from a 7.00(excellent) to 7.10(excellent), and capitalization index from a 8.50(excellent) to 8.60(excellent). Other factors: Capital and surplus increased during the period by 6.0%, from $23.6 million to $25.1 million.

FARMERS MUTUAL INS CO OF ELLINWOOD was upgraded to D from D- in May 2018 based on an increase in the profitability index from a 4.90(good) to 5.40(good), capitalization index from a 7.60(excellent) to 8.00(excellent), reserve adequacy index from a 4.10(fair) to 4.40(fair), and stability index from a 1.30(weak) to 1.50(weak). Other factors: Capital and surplus increased during the period by 9.8%, from $2.9 million to $3.2 million.

FARMERS MUTUAL INS CO OF NE was upgraded to B+ from B in May 2018 based on an increase in the stability index from a 4.80(fair) to 6.50(good) and profitability index from a 6.00(good) to 6.10(good).

FARMERS UNION MUTUAL INS CO was upgraded to B from B- in May 2018 based on an increase in the stability index from a 3.60(fair) to 5.50(good) and liquidity index from a 6.70(good) to 6.80(good).

FARMERS UNION MUTUAL INS CO was upgraded to B- from C+ in May 2018 based on an increase in the profitability index from a 6.30(good) to 8.30(excellent), stability index from a 3.40(fair) to 5.30(good), and liquidity index from a 6.90(excellent) to 7.00(excellent).

FARMINGTON MUTUAL INS CO was upgraded to E+ from E in May 2018 based on an increase in the stability index from a 0.00(weak) to 0.50(weak) and capitalization index from a 8.60(excellent) to 9.10(excellent). Other factors: The company's net asset base increased during the period by 11.3%, from $7.3 million to $8.2 million.

FBALLIANCE INS INC was upgraded to D+ from D in May 2018 based on an increase in the liquidity index from a 7.00(excellent) to 10.00(excellent) and stability index from a 2.30(weak) to 2.50(weak).

FDM PREFERRED INS CO was upgraded to C from C- in May 2018 based on an increase in the liquidity index from a 8.00(excellent) to 9.00(excellent), capitalization index from a 2.10(weak) to 3.10(fair), stability index from a 2.40(weak) to 3.20(fair), and profitability index from a 8.60(excellent) to 8.80(excellent). Other factors: Capital and surplus increased during the period by 29.3%, from $3.1 million to $3.9 million.

FEDERATED RURAL ELECTRIC INS EXCH was upgraded to B+ from B in May 2018 based on an increase in the capitalization index from a 8.60(excellent) to 8.90(excellent) and stability index from a 6.30(good) to 6.50(good).

FFVA MUTUAL INS CO was upgraded to B from B- in May 2018 based on an increase in the reserve adequacy index from a 5.80(good) to 8.80(excellent), profitability index from a 6.80(good) to 8.90(excellent), stability index from a 5.30(good) to 5.50(good), and capitalization index from a 8.40(excellent) to 8.50(excellent).

FINANCIAL CASUALTY & SURETY INC was upgraded to C+ from C in May 2018 based on an increase in the reserve adequacy index from a 7.00(excellent) to 9.30(excellent), stability index from a 2.80(weak) to 3.90(fair), liquidity index from a 7.20(excellent) to 7.50(excellent), and capitalization index from a 7.30(excellent) to 7.40(excellent).

FINANCIAL PACIFIC INS CO was upgraded to B+ from B in May 2018 based on an increase in the stability index from a 4.50(fair) to 6.40(good) and profitability index from a 7.00(excellent) to 7.20(excellent). Other factors: The company's net asset base increased during the period by 6.5%, from $245.3 million to $261.4 million.

FINGER LAKES FIRE & CASUALTY CO was upgraded to B- from C+ in May 2018 based on an increase in the stability index from a 3.20(fair) to 5.00(good) and capitalization index from a 9.00(excellent) to 9.20(excellent). Other factors: Capital and surplus increased during the period by 6.4%, from $28.4 million to $30.2 million.

FIRE DISTRICTS OF NY MUT INS CO INC was upgraded to B- from C+ in May 2018 based on an increase in the stability index from a 3.30(fair) to 5.20(good), profitability index from a 7.90(excellent) to 8.60(excellent), reserve adequacy index from a 6.20(good) to 6.50(good), capitalization index from a 7.20(excellent) to 7.40(excellent), and liquidity index from a 7.50(excellent) to 7.60(excellent). Other factors: Capital and surplus increased during the period by 26.8%, from $31.4 million to $39.8 million.

FIREMANS FUND INS CO was upgraded to C+ from C in May 2018 based on an increase in the liquidity index from a 5.90(good) to 7.00(excellent), profitability index from a 3.00(fair) to 3.60(fair), capitalization index from a 9.50(excellent) to 10.00(excellent), stability index from a 4.20(fair) to 4.40(fair), and reserve adequacy index from a 5.00(good) to 5.10(good).

FIRST ACCEPTANCE INS CO was upgraded to C- from D+ in May 2018 based on an increase in the capitalization index from a 4.70(fair) to 5.80(good), liquidity index from a 0.60(weak) to 1.10(weak), stability index from a 2.50(weak) to 3.00(fair), and profitability index from a 1.30(weak) to 1.60(weak). Other factors: Capital and surplus increased during the period by 6.0%, from $62.3 million to $66.1 million.

FIRST ACCEPTANCE INS CO OF GEORGIA was upgraded to C- from D+ in May 2018 based on an increase in the profitability index from a 1.40(weak) to 2.40(weak), capitalization index from a 2.50(weak) to 3.30(fair), and stability index from a 2.40(weak) to 2.90(fair).

FIRST CHOICE CASUALTY INS CO was upgraded to C from C- in May 2018 based on an increase in the liquidity index from a 3.30(fair) to 7.10(excellent), reserve adequacy index from a 3.90(fair) to 5.00(good), capitalization index from a 2.30(weak) to 3.40(fair), stability index from a 2.30(weak) to 2.90(fair), and profitability index from a 3.20(fair) to 3.50(fair).

FIRST GUARD INS CO was upgraded to B from B- in May 2018 based on an increase in the reserve adequacy index from a 7.30(excellent) to 7.40(excellent) and liquidity index from a 7.40(excellent) to 7.50(excellent).

FIRST INDEMNITY OF AMERICA INS CO was upgraded to C- from D+ in May 2018 based on an increase in the reserve adequacy index from a 2.80(weak) to 4.30(fair), profitability index from a 6.60(good) to 7.70(excellent), and stability index from a 2.10(weak) to 2.40(weak).

FIRST MEDICAL INS CO RRG was upgraded to B- from C+ in May 2018 based on an increase in the liquidity index from a 6.90(excellent) to 9.00(excellent), profitability index from a 3.30(fair) to 4.30(fair), stability index from a 4.60(fair) to 5.10(good), and capitalization index from a 8.30(excellent) to 8.60(excellent).

FIRST MERCURY INS CO was upgraded to C+ from C in May 2018 based on an increase in the profitability index from a 3.60(fair) to 4.20(fair) and stability index from a 4.30(fair) to 4.50(fair).

FIRST NET INS CO was upgraded to C from C- in May 2018 based on an increase in the profitability index from a 5.10(good) to 5.70(good), capitalization index from a 8.00(excellent) to 8.50(excellent), reserve adequacy index from a 4.10(fair) to 4.30(fair), and stability index from a 3.30(fair) to 3.40(fair).

FIRST SURETY CORP was upgraded to C from C- in May 2018 based on an increase in the capitalization index from a 7.80(excellent) to 8.70(excellent), profitability index from a 4.00(fair) to 4.50(fair), and reserve adequacy index from a 4.90(good) to 5.30(good).

FLORIDA LAWYERS MUTUAL INS CO was upgraded to B- from C+ in May 2018 based on an increase in the stability index from a 3.40(fair) to 4.90(good), liquidity index from a 7.70(excellent) to 8.90(excellent), capitalization index from a 9.10(excellent) to 9.40(excellent), and profitability index from a 8.40(excellent) to 8.70(excellent). Other factors: Capital and surplus increased during the period by 10.6%, from $46.9 million to $51.9 million.

FLORIDA PENINSULA INS CO was upgraded to B from B- in May 2018 based on an increase in the reserve adequacy index from a 5.20(good) to 5.50(good), stability index from a 5.30(good) to 5.50(good), and liquidity index from a 6.80(good) to 6.90(excellent).

FLORISTS MUTUAL INS CO was upgraded to C from C- in May 2018 based on an increase in the profitability index from a 1.70(weak) to 3.00(fair), stability index from a 2.20(weak) to 3.50(fair), reserve adequacy index from a 4.20(fair) to 4.80(fair), and capitalization index from a 7.40(excellent) to 7.70(excellent).

FRANKENMUTH MUTUAL INS CO was upgraded to B+ from B in May 2018 based on an increase in the stability index from a 4.90(good) to 6.50(good) and capitalization index from a 9.20(excellent) to 9.30(excellent).

FULMONT MUTUAL INS CO was upgraded to D from D- in May 2018 based on an increase in the capitalization index from a 3.40(fair) to 4.50(fair).

GABLES RRG INC was upgraded to E+ from E in May 2018 based on an increase in the stability index from a 0.00(weak) to 0.50(weak), profitability index from a 3.00(fair) to 3.30(fair), and liquidity index from a 6.80(good) to 7.00(excellent). Other factors: Capital and surplus increased during the period by 13.2%, from $4.1 million to $4.7 million.

GEICO CASUALTY CO was upgraded to C+ from C in May 2018 based on an increase in the capitalization index from a 7.00(excellent) to 7.40(excellent), stability index from a 4.20(fair) to 4.50(fair), liquidity index from a 2.30(weak) to 2.50(weak), and profitability index from a 2.80(weak) to 2.90(fair). Other factors: Capital and surplus increased during the period by 6.5%, from $1040.9 million to $1108.2 million.

GEICO MARINE INS CO was upgraded to B- from C+ in May 2018 based on an increase in the profitability index from a 2.50(weak) to 4.90(good), stability index from a 3.10(fair) to 3.90(fair), and capitalization index from a 7.40(excellent) to 7.70(excellent). Other factors: Capital and surplus increased during the period by 12.2%, from $48.4 million to $54.3 million.

GEISINGER INS CORP RRG was upgraded to D+ from D in May 2018 based on an increase in the liquidity index from a 8.60(excellent) to 9.00(excellent), stability index from a 2.30(weak) to 2.50(weak), and profitability index from a 5.70(good) to 5.80(good).

GEM STATE INS CO was upgraded to C from C- in May 2018 based on an increase in the profitability index from a 5.90(good) to 6.90(excellent) and stability index from a 2.30(weak) to 2.90(fair).

GENERAL AUTOMOBILE INS CO was upgraded to B- from C+ in May 2018 based on an increase in the liquidity index from a 2.80(weak) to 5.10(good), capitalization index from a 7.30(excellent) to 8.70(excellent), stability index from a 3.80(fair) to 4.90(good), and profitability index from a 3.70(fair) to 3.90(fair).

GENWORTH MTG INS CORP OF NC was upgraded to B from B- in May 2018 based on an increase in the reserve adequacy index from a 5.80(good) to 6.90(excellent) and stability index from a 4.50(fair) to 5.40(good).

GEORGIA FARM BUREAU MUTUAL INS CO was upgraded to C+ from C in May 2018 based on an increase in the liquidity index from a 4.50(fair) to 5.80(good), profitability index from a 2.40(weak) to 3.60(fair), stability index from a 4.00(fair) to 4.50(fair), and capitalization index from a 7.50(excellent) to 7.70(excellent). Other factors: Capital and surplus increased during the period by 5.7%, from $225.7 million to $238.5 million.

GERMAN MUTUAL INS CO was upgraded to D+ from D in May 2018 based on an increase in the profitability index from a 3.40(fair) to 5.20(good), stability index from a 2.30(weak) to 2.50(weak), reserve adequacy index from a 5.90(good) to 6.10(good), and capitalization index from a 7.50(excellent) to 7.60(excellent).

GERMANIA FARM MUTUAL INS ASN was upgraded to C+ from C in May 2018 based on an increase in the profitability index from a 4.20(fair) to 5.30(good) and stability index from a 4.10(fair) to 4.50(fair). Other factors: The company's net asset base increased during the period by 6.0%, from $373.3 million to $395.7 million.

GERMANTOWN MUTUAL INS CO was upgraded to B from B- in May 2018 based on an increase in the stability index from a 3.60(fair) to 5.50(good), reserve adequacy index from a 8.60(excellent) to 8.90(excellent), profitability index from a 8.40(excellent) to 8.60(excellent), and liquidity index from a 6.10(good) to 6.20(good).

GOAUTO INS CO was upgraded to D+ from D in May 2018 based on an increase in the liquidity index from a 2.10(weak) to 6.10(good), reserve adequacy index from a 5.80(good) to 6.30(good), stability index from a 2.30(weak) to 2.50(weak), and profitability index from a 2.70(weak) to 2.90(fair). Other factors: Capital and surplus increased during the period by 16.3%, from $13.8 million to $16.0 million.

GOLDEN BEAR INS CO was upgraded to B from B- in May 2018 based on an increase in the stability index from a 3.60(fair) to 5.50(good) and reserve adequacy index from a 9.60(excellent) to 9.80(excellent).

GOOD SHEPHERD RECIPROCAL RRG was upgraded to D+ from D in May 2018 based on an increase in the profitability index from a 5.30(good) to 9.10(excellent), capitalization index from a 3.40(fair) to 4.90(good), liquidity index from a 7.90(excellent) to 9.20(excellent), reserve adequacy index from a 3.60(fair) to 4.80(fair), and stability index from a 2.30(weak) to 2.50(weak). Other factors: Capital and surplus increased during the period by 11.7%, from $7.4 million to $8.3 million.

GOVT TECHNOLOGY INS CO RRG INC was upgraded to E+ from E in May 2018 based on an increase in the capitalization index from a 3.90(fair) to 7.00(excellent), liquidity index from a 2.90(fair) to 5.80(good), profitability index from a 3.50(fair) to 6.30(good), and stability index from a 0.00(weak) to 0.50(weak). Other factors: Capital and surplus increased during the period by 26.7%, from $0.6 million to $0.8 million.

GRAIN DEALERS MUTUAL INS CO was upgraded to C from C- in May 2018 based on an increase in the stability index from a 2.10(weak) to 3.40(fair). Other factors: Capital and surplus increased during the period by 9.2%, from $9.9 million to $10.8 million.

GRANGE P&C INS CO was upgraded to B from B- in May 2018 based on an increase in the stability index from a 5.30(good) to 5.50(good).

Rating Upgrades (Continued)

GRANITE RE INC was upgraded to B from B- in May 2018 based on an increase in the capitalization index from a 5.30(good) to 7.40(excellent), stability index from a 3.50(fair) to 5.40(good), and profitability index from a 8.60(excellent) to 8.70(excellent). Other factors: The company's net asset base increased during the period by 18.5%, from $51.4 million to $60.9 million. Capital and surplus increased during the period by 51.9%, from $27.4 million to $41.6 million.

GRAY CASUALTY & SURETY CO was upgraded to C+ from C in May 2018 based on an increase in the stability index from a 3.10(fair) to 4.50(fair) and profitability index from a 4.00(fair) to 4.20(fair).

GRAY INS CO was upgraded to B- from C+ in May 2018 based on an increase in the stability index from a 3.50(fair) to 4.70(fair) and capitalization index from a 7.20(excellent) to 7.40(excellent).

GREAT NORTHERN INS CO was upgraded to B from B- in May 2018 based on an increase in the stability index from a 3.60(fair) to 5.50(good), capitalization index from a 8.30(excellent) to 9.10(excellent), profitability index from a 8.40(excellent) to 8.70(excellent), reserve adequacy index from a 9.00(excellent) to 9.20(excellent), and liquidity index from a 6.80(good) to 6.90(excellent).

GREEN HILLS INS CO A RRG was upgraded to E+ from E in May 2018 based on an increase in the stability index from a 0.00(weak) to 0.50(weak).

GREENVILLE CASUALTY INS CO INC was upgraded to C from C- in May 2018 based on an increase in the profitability index from a 2.40(weak) to 2.90(fair).

GROWERS AUTOMOBILE INS ASN was upgraded to C- from D+ in May 2018 based on an increase in the liquidity index from a 9.20(excellent) to 10.00(excellent) and reserve adequacy index from a 4.90(good) to 5.00(good). Other factors: The company's net asset base increased during the period by 6.3%, from $7.6 million to $8.1 million. Capital and surplus increased during the period by 18.1%, from $5.8 million to $6.9 million.

GUIDEONE NATIONAL INS CO was upgraded to B- from C+ in May 2018 based on an increase in the stability index from a 3.90(fair) to 4.90(good) and liquidity index from a 9.10(excellent) to 10.00(excellent).

GUTHRIE RRG was upgraded to C+ from C in May 2018 based on an increase in the profitability index from a 3.70(fair) to 6.50(good), capitalization index from a 4.80(fair) to 7.40(excellent), and liquidity index from a 6.90(excellent) to 7.80(excellent). Other factors: Capital and surplus increased during the period by 10.5%, from $18.0 million to $19.9 million.

HALIFAX MUTUAL INS CO was upgraded to D+ from D in May 2018 based on an increase in the profitability index from a 5.20(good) to 6.40(good), liquidity index from a 6.90(excellent) to 7.20(excellent), stability index from a 2.00(weak) to 2.20(weak), and capitalization index from a 7.50(excellent) to 7.60(excellent). Other factors: Capital and surplus increased during the period by 5.3%, from $4.7 million to $4.9 million.

HALLMARK SPECIALTY INS CO was upgraded to B from B- in May 2018 based on an increase in the stability index from a 3.70(fair) to 5.50(good).

HARTFORD SM BOIL INSPECTION IC OF CT was upgraded to B from B- in May 2018 based on an increase in the stability index from a 3.90(fair) to 4.00(fair).

HASTINGS MUTUAL INS CO was upgraded to B+ from B in May 2018 based on an increase in the stability index from a 4.70(fair) to 6.50(good) and reserve adequacy index from a 5.80(good) to 6.50(good).

HAULERS INS CO was upgraded to B from B- in May 2018 based on an increase in the stability index from a 3.90(fair) to 5.50(good), profitability index from a 6.00(good) to 6.50(good), capitalization index from a 9.60(excellent) to 9.80(excellent), and reserve adequacy index from a 6.90(excellent) to 7.00(excellent).

HAWAII EMPLOYERS MUTUAL INS CO was upgraded to B from B- in May 2018 based on an increase in the stability index from a 5.30(good) to 5.50(good).

Rating Upgrades (Continued)

HAWAIIAN INS & GUARANTY CO LTD was upgraded to B from B- in May 2018 based on an increase in the profitability index from a 6.30(good) to 8.00(excellent) and reserve adequacy index from a 6.00(good) to 6.60(good). Other factors: The company's net asset base increased during the period by 5.5%, from $27.0 million to $28.4 million.

HEALTH CARE INDEMNITY INC was upgraded to C from C- in May 2018 based on an increase in the capitalization index from a 5.80(good) to 7.20(excellent), stability index from a 2.70(weak) to 3.50(fair), and profitability index from a 2.90(fair) to 3.40(fair).

HEALTH CARE INDUSTRY LIAB RECIP INS was upgraded to C from C- in May 2018 based on an increase in the reserve adequacy index from a 5.20(good) to 6.40(good), liquidity index from a 6.90(excellent) to 7.30(excellent), and stability index from a 3.30(fair) to 3.50(fair).

HEALTH CARE MUT CAPTIVE INS CO was upgraded to D+ from D in May 2018 based on an increase in the profitability index from a 2.90(fair) to 8.50(excellent), reserve adequacy index from a 9.40(excellent) to 9.60(excellent), and stability index from a 2.30(weak) to 2.40(weak). Other factors: Capital and surplus increased during the period by 12.6%, from $5.6 million to $6.3 million.

HEALTHCARE UNDERWRITERS GRP MUT OH was upgraded to B from B- in May 2018 based on an increase in the stability index from a 5.30(good) to 5.50(good).

HEALTHCARE UNDERWRITING CO RRG was upgraded to D+ from D in May 2018 based on an increase in the profitability index from a 3.00(fair) to 3.80(fair), stability index from a 2.30(weak) to 2.50(weak), and capitalization index from a 2.90(fair) to 3.10(fair). Other factors: Capital and surplus increased during the period by 44.7%, from $23.5 million to $34.0 million.

HEARTLAND MUTUAL INS CO was upgraded to D+ from D in May 2018 based on an increase in the profitability index from a 6.60(good) to 8.60(excellent), reserve adequacy index from a 6.60(good) to 7.80(excellent), and capitalization index from a 9.80(excellent) to 10.00(excellent). Other factors: Capital and surplus increased during the period by 12.5%, from $4.3 million to $4.8 million.

HERITAGE INDEMNITY CO was upgraded to B- from C+ in May 2018 based on an increase in the reserve adequacy index from a 4.90(good) to 7.10(excellent) and stability index from a 3.00(fair) to 4.90(good).

HERITAGE P&C INS CO was upgraded to B- from C+ in May 2018 based on an increase in the stability index from a 4.10(fair) to 5.10(good), capitalization index from a 3.70(fair) to 4.60(fair), and profitability index from a 4.10(fair) to 4.30(fair).

HIGH POINT PREFERRED INS CO was upgraded to B+ from B in May 2018 based on an increase in the reserve adequacy index from a 7.00(excellent) to 8.80(excellent), stability index from a 4.50(fair) to 6.20(good), profitability index from a 7.20(excellent) to 8.10(excellent), and liquidity index from a 6.60(good) to 7.00(excellent). Other factors: Capital and surplus increased during the period by 5.3%, from $177.2 million to $186.6 million.

HLTHCR PROVIDERS INS CO was upgraded to C+ from C in May 2018 based on an increase in the profitability index from a 7.40(excellent) to 8.70(excellent), stability index from a 4.30(fair) to 4.50(fair), and capitalization index from a 9.20(excellent) to 9.30(excellent). Other factors: Capital and surplus increased during the period by 10.4%, from $46.0 million to $50.8 million.

HOCHHEIM PRAIRIE FARM MUT INS ASN was upgraded to D+ from D in May 2018 based on an increase in the capitalization index from a 5.40(good) to 7.00(excellent), reserve adequacy index from a 4.40(fair) to 5.00(good), stability index from a 2.30(weak) to 2.50(weak), and profitability index from a 1.90(weak) to 2.00(weak). Other factors: Capital and surplus increased during the period by 23.4%, from $43.5 million to $53.7 million.

HOME-OWNERS INS CO was upgraded to A from A- in May 2018 based on an increase in the stability index from a 5.90(good) to 7.50(excellent) and reserve adequacy index from a 6.00(good) to 6.10(good).

HOMESITE LLOYDS OF TEXAS was upgraded to C+ from C in May 2018 based on an increase in the liquidity index from a 6.90(excellent) to 7.00(excellent).

HOSPITALITY RRG INC was upgraded to D from D- in May 2018 based on an increase in the profitability index from a 3.50(fair) to 3.70(fair) and stability index from a 1.30(weak) to 1.50(weak). Other factors: The company's net asset base increased during the period by 27.6%, from $5.4 million to $6.9 million. Capital and surplus increased during the period by 6.2%, from $2.7 million to $2.9 million.

Rating Upgrades (Continued)

HOUSING & REDEVELOPMENT INS EXCH was upgraded to C+ from C in May 2018 based on an increase in the profitability index from a 4.50(fair) to 5.70(good) and stability index from a 2.70(weak) to 3.70(fair). Other factors: Capital and surplus increased during the period by 12.0%, from $14.7 million to $16.5 million.

HOUSING AUTHORITY PROP A MUTUAL CO was upgraded to B+ from B in May 2018 based on an increase in the stability index from a 6.30(good) to 6.50(good).

HOUSING AUTHORITY RISK RET GROUP INC was upgraded to B from B- in May 2018 based on an increase in the stability index from a 4.10(fair) to 5.50(good), profitability index from a 2.90(fair) to 3.60(fair), capitalization index from a 9.10(excellent) to 9.30(excellent), and liquidity index from a 7.10(excellent) to 7.20(excellent).

HOUSING ENTERPRISE INS CO was upgraded to B- from C+ in May 2018 based on an increase in the profitability index from a 3.80(fair) to 5.00(good), capitalization index from a 3.90(fair) to 4.80(fair), stability index from a 4.60(fair) to 5.10(good), and reserve adequacy index from a 6.60(good) to 7.00(excellent). Other factors: Capital and surplus increased during the period by 15.9%, from $29.0 million to $33.6 million.

ICI MUTUAL INS CO A RRG was upgraded to B+ from B in May 2018 based on an increase in the profitability index from a 7.10(excellent) to 8.30(excellent) and stability index from a 6.30(good) to 6.50(good).

IDS PROPERTY CASUALTY INS CO was upgraded to B from B- in May 2018 based on an increase in the stability index from a 4.90(good) to 5.40(good), reserve adequacy index from a 3.30(fair) to 3.80(fair), capitalization index from a 8.40(excellent) to 8.70(excellent), and liquidity index from a 5.10(good) to 5.20(good).

IL STATE BAR ASSOC MUTUAL INS CO was upgraded to B- from C+ in May 2018 based on an increase in the stability index from a 3.40(fair) to 5.30(good), profitability index from a 7.30(excellent) to 8.50(excellent), and liquidity index from a 7.80(excellent) to 8.30(excellent).

ILLINOIS CASUALTY CO was upgraded to B- from C+ in May 2018 based on an increase in the stability index from a 3.30(fair) to 5.10(good), capitalization index from a 7.40(excellent) to 7.90(excellent), liquidity index from a 6.50(good) to 6.60(good), and reserve adequacy index from a 9.30(excellent) to 9.40(excellent).

ILLINOIS INS CO was upgraded to B from B- in May 2018 based on an increase in the stability index from a 3.90(fair) to 5.50(good) and capitalization index from a 7.80(excellent) to 8.10(excellent).

INDEPENDENCE CASUALTY INS CO was upgraded to C from C- in May 2018 based on an increase in the stability index from a 3.30(fair) to 3.50(fair).

INDEPENDENT MUTUAL FIRE INS CO was upgraded to B- from C+ in May 2018 based on an increase in the stability index from a 3.40(fair) to 5.30(good), reserve adequacy index from a 3.60(fair) to 4.60(fair), liquidity index from a 7.00(excellent) to 7.30(excellent), and capitalization index from a 7.60(excellent) to 7.70(excellent). Other factors: The company's net asset base increased during the period by 6.2%, from $49.2 million to $52.2 million. Capital and surplus increased during the period by 10.9%, from $41.8 million to $46.3 million.

INDIANA FARMERS MUTUAL INS CO was upgraded to B+ from B in May 2018 based on an increase in the profitability index from a 5.30(good) to 8.70(excellent), stability index from a 4.60(fair) to 6.50(good), and capitalization index from a 8.30(excellent) to 8.40(excellent).

INLAND INS CO was upgraded to C+ from C in May 2018 based on an increase in the stability index from a 2.70(weak) to 4.50(fair) and capitalization index from a 8.40(excellent) to 8.50(excellent). Other factors: Capital and surplus increased during the period by 16.0%, from $218.1 million to $252.9 million.

INSURORS INDEMNITY CO was upgraded to C from C- in May 2018 based on an increase in the stability index from a 2.80(weak) to 3.50(fair), capitalization index from a 7.60(excellent) to 7.90(excellent), liquidity index from a 7.00(excellent) to 7.30(excellent), and profitability index from a 8.40(excellent) to 8.50(excellent). Other factors: Capital and surplus increased during the period by 8.2%, from $19.5 million to $21.1 million.

INTEGON NATIONAL INS CO was upgraded to B- from C+ in May 2018 based on an increase in the liquidity index from a 1.50(weak) to 5.50(good), profitability index from a 3.10(fair) to 4.00(fair), and reserve adequacy index from a 4.20(fair) to 4.40(fair).

Rating Upgrades (Continued)

INTEGRITY MUTUAL INS CO was upgraded to B from B- in May 2018 based on an increase in the stability index from a 3.80(fair) to 5.50(good) and reserve adequacy index from a 6.00(good) to 6.10(good).

INTEGRITY P&C INS CO was upgraded to C- from D+ in May 2018 based on an increase in the stability index from a 2.10(weak) to 3.10(fair) and profitability index from a 8.70(excellent) to 8.80(excellent).

INTERBORO INS CO was upgraded to C from C- in May 2018 based on an increase in the profitability index from a 6.60(good) to 8.30(excellent), capitalization index from a 7.80(excellent) to 8.70(excellent), liquidity index from a 6.50(good) to 6.80(good), and stability index from a 3.30(fair) to 3.50(fair). Other factors: Capital and surplus increased during the period by 5.1%, from $40.8 million to $42.8 million.

INTERNATIONAL FIDELITY INS CO was upgraded to B from B- in May 2018 based on an increase in the profitability index from a 4.40(fair) to 5.40(good), stability index from a 4.50(fair) to 5.50(good), and reserve adequacy index from a 9.20(excellent) to 9.30(excellent).

JAMES RIVER CASUALTY CO was upgraded to B- from C+ in May 2018 based on an increase in the stability index from a 3.40(fair) to 5.30(good), reserve adequacy index from a 6.80(good) to 8.60(excellent), profitability index from a 6.40(good) to 7.30(excellent), and liquidity index from a 6.50(good) to 6.90(excellent).

JUNIATA MUTUAL INS CO was upgraded to C- from D+ in May 2018 based on an increase in the stability index from a 2.10(weak) to 2.40(weak), capitalization index from a 8.10(excellent) to 8.30(excellent), and profitability index from a 4.70(fair) to 4.90(good). Other factors: The company's net asset base increased during the period by 5.5%, from $9.3 million to $9.8 million. Capital and surplus increased during the period by 7.5%, from $5.5 million to $5.9 million.

KENTUCKIANA MEDICAL RRG & INS CO INC was upgraded to D from D- in May 2018 based on an increase in the profitability index from a 6.60(good) to 7.50(excellent), capitalization index from a 7.70(excellent) to 8.20(excellent), liquidity index from a 8.30(excellent) to 8.70(excellent), and stability index from a 1.30(weak) to 1.50(weak). Other factors: Capital and surplus increased during the period by 7.0%, from $36.5 million to $39.1 million.

KEYSTONE MUTUAL INS CO was upgraded to E+ from E in May 2018 based on an increase in the stability index from a 0.00(weak) to 0.50(weak), profitability index from a 2.40(weak) to 2.80(weak), and capitalization index from a 0.20(weak) to 0.40(weak).

LACKAWANNA AMERICAN INS CO was upgraded to B+ from B in May 2018 based on an increase in the capitalization index from a 9.00(excellent) to 9.10(excellent).

LAKEVIEW INS CO was upgraded to B- from C+ in May 2018 based on an increase in the stability index from a 3.30(fair) to 5.20(good), reserve adequacy index from a 6.10(good) to 6.30(good), profitability index from a 5.40(good) to 5.60(good), and capitalization index from a 8.30(excellent) to 8.40(excellent).

LAMMICO RRG INC was upgraded to C from C- in May 2018 based on an increase in the stability index from a 1.80(weak) to 3.50(fair).

LANCER INDEMNITY CO was upgraded to B- from C+ in May 2018 based on an increase in the stability index from a 3.10(fair) to 4.60(fair), reserve adequacy index from a 3.50(fair) to 4.10(fair), and capitalization index from a 5.90(good) to 6.00(good).

LANDCAR CASUALTY CO was upgraded to B- from C+ in May 2018 based on an increase in the stability index from a 3.10(fair) to 4.60(fair) and profitability index from a 4.80(fair) to 4.90(good).

LAWYERS MUTUAL LIAB INS CO OF NC was upgraded to B from B- in May 2018 based on an increase in the stability index from a 3.80(fair) to 5.50(good).

LEAGUE OF WI MUNICIPALITIES MUT INS was upgraded to B from B- in May 2018 based on an increase in the profitability index from a 6.10(good) to 8.90(excellent) and capitalization index from a 8.20(excellent) to 8.50(excellent). Other factors: Capital and surplus increased during the period by 20.3%, from $32.3 million to $38.8 million.

LEBANON VALLEY INS CO was upgraded to C+ from C in May 2018 based on an increase in the stability index from a 3.00(fair) to 4.50(fair), profitability index from a 5.30(good) to 6.10(good), and reserve adequacy index from a 9.30(excellent) to 9.40(excellent).

Rating Upgrades (Continued)

LEXINGTON NATIONAL INS CORP was upgraded to D from D- in May 2018 based on an increase in the profitability index from a 6.30(good) to 7.40(excellent) and stability index from a 1.30(weak) to 1.50(weak). Other factors: Capital and surplus increased during the period by 11.8%, from $17.3 million to $19.3 million.

LEXON INS CO was upgraded to C from C- in May 2018 based on an increase in the profitability index from a 6.20(good) to 7.90(excellent), reserve adequacy index from a 2.50(weak) to 3.90(fair), liquidity index from a 7.90(excellent) to 8.20(excellent), and stability index from a 3.30(fair) to 3.50(fair). Other factors: The company's net asset base increased during the period by 9.0%, from $224.3 million to $244.5 million.

LION INS CO (FL) was upgraded to B+ from B in May 2018 based on an increase in the capitalization index from a 7.80(excellent) to 8.60(excellent), stability index from a 4.90(good) to 5.10(good), and reserve adequacy index from a 8.60(excellent) to 8.70(excellent).

LONE STAR ALLIANCE INC A RRG was upgraded to D+ from D in May 2018 based on an increase in the liquidity index from a 8.90(excellent) to 10.00(excellent) and reserve adequacy index from a 3.70(fair) to 4.40(fair). Other factors: The company's net asset base increased during the period by 9.1%, from $9.0 million to $9.9 million.

LOYA INS CO was upgraded to D+ from D in May 2018 based on an increase in the liquidity index from a 0.00(weak) to 2.70(weak), stability index from a 2.00(weak) to 2.50(weak), and profitability index from a 1.90(weak) to 2.00(weak).

LUBA CASUALTY INS CO was upgraded to B+ from B in May 2018 based on an increase in the capitalization index from a 8.10(excellent) to 8.30(excellent) and stability index from a 6.30(good) to 6.50(good). Other factors: Capital and surplus increased during the period by 6.9%, from $92.2 million to $98.6 million.

LUBA INDEMNITY INS CO was upgraded to D+ from D in May 2018 based on an increase in the stability index from a 2.30(weak) to 2.50(weak).

MACHINERY INS INC was upgraded to D from D- in May 2018 based on an increase in the stability index from a 0.00(weak) to 1.40(weak) and profitability index from a 5.30(good) to 6.10(good). Other factors: Capital and surplus increased during the period by 6.0%, from $2.7 million to $2.8 million.

MAIDSTONE INS CO was upgraded to D- from E+ in May 2018 based on an increase in the capitalization index from a 0.50(weak) to 2.90(fair), liquidity index from a 4.80(fair) to 5.60(good), stability index from a 0.50(weak) to 1.00(weak), and profitability index from a 0.60(weak) to 0.70(weak). Other factors: The company's net asset base increased during the period by 12.8%, from $50.3 million to $56.7 million. Capital and surplus increased during the period by 229.3%, from $4.4 million to $14.6 million.

MAIN STREET AMER PROTECTION INS CO was upgraded to C+ from C in May 2018 based on an increase in the stability index from a 2.90(fair) to 3.20(fair). Other factors: The company's net asset base increased during the period by 43.0%, from $16.3 million to $23.3 million. Capital and surplus increased during the period by 44.1%, from $16.1 million to $23.1 million.

MAISON INS CO was upgraded to B- from C+ in May 2018 based on an increase in the stability index from a 3.30(fair) to 4.90(good), capitalization index from a 5.60(good) to 6.50(good), profitability index from a 2.90(fair) to 3.40(fair), reserve adequacy index from a 4.90(good) to 5.20(good), and liquidity index from a 6.70(good) to 6.90(excellent). Other factors: The company's net asset base increased during the period by 12.4%, from $81.9 million to $92.0 million. Capital and surplus increased during the period by 7.6%, from $36.0 million to $38.7 million.

MANUFACTURERS ALLIANCE INS CO was upgraded to C from C- in May 2018 based on an increase in the profitability index from a 4.50(fair) to 5.90(good), stability index from a 3.30(fair) to 3.50(fair), capitalization index from a 7.30(excellent) to 7.50(excellent), and reserve adequacy index from a 2.50(weak) to 2.70(weak). Other factors: The company's net asset base increased during the period by 5.1%, from $208.6 million to $219.4 million. Capital and surplus increased during the period by 15.2%, from $65.8 million to $75.8 million.

MANUFACTURING TECHNOLOGY MUT INS CO was upgraded to B from B- in May 2018 based on an increase in the profitability index from a 5.90(good) to 8.90(excellent). Other factors: Capital and surplus increased during the period by 9.3%, from $26.6 million to $29.0 million.

MARYSVILLE MUTUAL INS CO was upgraded to B- from C+ in May 2018 based on an increase in the stability index from a 3.30(fair) to 5.10(good) and capitalization index from a 8.60(excellent) to 8.80(excellent). Other factors: Capital and surplus increased during the period by 5.5%, from $30.0 million to $31.7 million.

Rating Upgrades (Continued)

MD RRG INC was upgraded to C from C- in May 2018 based on an increase in the stability index from a 3.00(fair) to 3.50(fair), capitalization index from a 9.40(excellent) to 9.60(excellent), and profitability index from a 8.50(excellent) to 8.60(excellent). Other factors: The company's net asset base increased during the period by 7.3%, from $25.6 million to $27.5 million. Capital and surplus increased during the period by 8.7%, from $16.5 million to $17.9 million.

MEDPRO RRG was upgraded to C from C- in May 2018 based on an increase in the stability index from a 2.00(weak) to 2.70(weak) and capitalization index from a 4.50(fair) to 4.80(fair).

MEMBERS INS CO was upgraded to C from C- in May 2018 based on an increase in the stability index from a 3.30(fair) to 3.50(fair).

MENDOTA INS CO was upgraded to C- from D+ in May 2018 based on an increase in the stability index from a 2.70(weak) to 3.20(fair) and capitalization index from a 0.30(weak) to 0.70(weak).

MENTAL HEALTH RISK RETENTION GROUP was upgraded to C+ from C in May 2018 based on an increase in the stability index from a 2.80(weak) to 3.90(fair), liquidity index from a 9.10(excellent) to 9.20(excellent), and capitalization index from a 9.00(excellent) to 9.10(excellent).

MERCHANTS NATIONAL BONDING INC was upgraded to B- from C+ in May 2018 based on an increase in the stability index from a 3.20(fair) to 4.20(fair) and reserve adequacy index from a 6.60(good) to 6.90(excellent). Other factors: The company's net asset base increased during the period by 10.8%, from $32.1 million to $35.5 million.

MERCHANTS NATIONAL INS CO was upgraded to B+ from B in May 2018 based on an increase in the reserve adequacy index from a 5.30(good) to 5.60(good), stability index from a 6.20(good) to 6.50(good), profitability index from a 5.80(good) to 5.90(good), capitalization index from a 7.50(excellent) to 7.60(excellent), and liquidity index from a 6.70(good) to 6.80(good).

MERCHANTS PREFERRED INS CO was upgraded to B+ from B in May 2018 based on an increase in the profitability index from a 7.00(excellent) to 7.90(excellent) and reserve adequacy index from a 5.80(good) to 5.90(good).

MERCURY CASUALTY CO was upgraded to B+ from B in May 2018 based on an increase in the profitability index from a 3.70(fair) to 6.60(good) and stability index from a 6.20(good) to 6.50(good).

MERCURY INDEMNITY CO OF AMERICA was upgraded to C from C- in May 2018 based on an increase in the stability index from a 3.30(fair) to 3.50(fair).

MERCURY INS CO OF FL was upgraded to B- from C+ in May 2018 based on an increase in the liquidity index from a 7.00(excellent) to 10.00(excellent) and profitability index from a 6.50(good) to 6.70(good).

MGIC ASSURANCE CORP was upgraded to C from C- in May 2018 based on an increase in the profitability index from a 4.80(fair) to 5.90(good).

MGIC REINS CORP OF WI was upgraded to D+ from D in May 2018 based on an increase in the profitability index from a 2.70(weak) to 4.90(good), capitalization index from a 3.40(fair) to 5.10(good), and stability index from a 2.20(weak) to 2.40(weak). Other factors: Capital and surplus increased during the period by 10.4%, from $175.0 million to $193.2 million.

MICHIGAN MILLERS MUTUAL INS CO was upgraded to C+ from C in May 2018 based on an increase in the stability index from a 3.90(fair) to 4.50(fair), capitalization index from a 7.90(excellent) to 8.10(excellent), and reserve adequacy index from a 3.10(fair) to 3.20(fair). Other factors: Capital and surplus increased during the period by 5.9%, from $56.6 million to $60.0 million.

MICHIGAN PROFESSIONAL INS EXCHANGE was upgraded to B- from C+ in May 2018 based on an increase in the stability index from a 3.40(fair) to 4.90(good).

MID-CONTINENT EXCESS & SURPLUS INS was upgraded to B- from C+ in May 2018 based on an increase in the stability index from a 3.40(fair) to 5.10(good).

MIDDLESEX INS CO was upgraded to B+ from B in May 2018 based on an increase in the stability index from a 4.80(fair) to 6.50(good).

MIDSTATE MUTUAL INS CO was upgraded to B- from C+ in May 2018 based on an increase in the stability index from a 3.30(fair) to 5.00(good), liquidity index from a 6.80(good) to 6.90(excellent), and capitalization index from a 9.90(excellent) to 10.00(excellent).

MIDWEST FAMILY MUTUAL INS CO was upgraded to B from B- in May 2018 based on an increase in the profitability index from a 6.60(good) to 8.90(excellent), stability index from a 3.60(fair) to 5.50(good), and reserve adequacy index from a 6.10(good) to 6.90(excellent).

MIDWEST INS CO was upgraded to C+ from C in May 2018 based on an increase in the reserve adequacy index from a 3.50(fair) to 4.90(good), profitability index from a 8.20(excellent) to 8.40(excellent), stability index from a 4.30(fair) to 4.50(fair), and capitalization index from a 7.20(excellent) to 7.30(excellent).

MILFORD CASUALTY INS CO was upgraded to B from B- in May 2018 based on an increase in the capitalization index from a 2.80(weak) to 9.30(excellent), profitability index from a 4.70(fair) to 8.50(excellent), stability index from a 3.50(fair) to 5.40(good), and reserve adequacy index from a 5.90(good) to 7.10(excellent). Other factors: Capital and surplus increased during the period by 45.8%, from $17.4 million to $25.3 million.

MILLERS CAPITAL INS CO was upgraded to B from B- in May 2018 based on an increase in the stability index from a 3.80(fair) to 5.50(good) and profitability index from a 5.40(good) to 6.00(good).

MISSOURI HOSPITAL PLAN was upgraded to B- from C+ in May 2018 based on an increase in the stability index from a 3.40(fair) to 5.30(good) and profitability index from a 3.80(fair) to 4.20(fair).

MISSOURI PROFESSIONALS MUTUAL INS CO was upgraded to D from E- in May 2018 based on an increase in the liquidity index from a 0.00(weak) to 7.00(excellent), profitability index from a 0.10(weak) to 1.00(weak), and stability index from a 0.00(weak) to 0.60(weak).

MITSUI SUMITOMO INS CO OF AMER was upgraded to A- from B+ in May 2018 based on an increase in the stability index from a 5.10(good) to 7.00(excellent), profitability index from a 7.80(excellent) to 8.60(excellent), capitalization index from a 9.10(excellent) to 9.40(excellent), and liquidity index from a 6.90(excellent) to 7.00(excellent).

MITSUI SUMITOMO INS USA INC was upgraded to B- from C+ in May 2018 based on an increase in the stability index from a 3.20(fair) to 5.10(good), liquidity index from a 8.40(excellent) to 8.60(excellent), and reserve adequacy index from a 8.80(excellent) to 8.90(excellent).

MMIC INS INC was upgraded to B+ from B in May 2018 based on an increase in the stability index from a 4.70(fair) to 6.50(good) and capitalization index from a 7.70(excellent) to 7.90(excellent). Other factors: Capital and surplus increased during the period by 6.3%, from $341.0 million to $362.6 million.

MO EMPLOYERS MUTUAL INS CO was upgraded to B+ from B in May 2018 based on an increase in the profitability index from a 5.60(good) to 7.60(excellent), stability index from a 6.30(good) to 6.50(good), capitalization index from a 7.80(excellent) to 8.00(excellent), and reserve adequacy index from a 9.20(excellent) to 9.30(excellent). Other factors: Capital and surplus increased during the period by 6.3%, from $237.8 million to $252.8 million.

MOTORS INS CORP was upgraded to D+ from D in May 2018 based on an increase in the profitability index from a 3.00(fair) to 6.70(good), stability index from a 0.90(weak) to 2.50(weak), and liquidity index from a 7.10(excellent) to 7.50(excellent). Other factors: Capital and surplus increased during the period by 11.2%, from $780.4 million to $867.8 million.

MOUNTAIN LAUREL RRG INC was upgraded to E+ from E in May 2018 based on an increase in the profitability index from a 2.80(weak) to 4.40(fair), capitalization index from a 3.10(fair) to 4.10(fair), liquidity index from a 7.20(excellent) to 7.70(excellent), and stability index from a 0.30(weak) to 0.50(weak). Other factors: Capital and surplus increased during the period by 32.4%, from $7.6 million to $10.1 million.

MT MORRIS MUTUAL INS CO was upgraded to C+ from C in May 2018 based on an increase in the profitability index from a 8.20(excellent) to 8.40(excellent) and capitalization index from a 7.30(excellent) to 7.40(excellent). Other factors: Capital and surplus increased during the period by 6.2%, from $18.9 million to $20.0 million.

MULTINATIONAL INS CO was upgraded to C from C- in May 2018 based on an increase in the liquidity index from a 5.80(good) to 8.60(excellent), profitability index from a 2.60(weak) to 3.90(fair), stability index from a 2.80(weak) to 3.50(fair), and capitalization index from a 2.80(weak) to 3.40(fair). Other factors: The company's net asset base increased during the period by 89.0%, from $37.8 million to $71.4 million. Capital and surplus increased during the period by 46.1%, from $10.1 million to $14.7 million.

Rating Upgrades (Continued)

MUNICIPAL ASR CORP was upgraded to E+ from E in May 2018 based on an increase in the liquidity index from a 7.00(excellent) to 10.00(excellent) and stability index from a 0.00(weak) to 0.50(weak). Other factors: Capital and surplus increased during the period by 13.5%, from $238.2 million to $270.4 million.

MUNICIPAL MUTUAL INS CO was upgraded to B- from C+ in May 2018 based on an increase in the stability index from a 3.20(fair) to 4.90(good) and liquidity index from a 6.70(good) to 6.80(good).

MUTUAL INS CO OF AZ was upgraded to B+ from B in May 2018 based on an increase in the stability index from a 4.90(good) to 6.50(good).

MUTUAL OF ENUMCLAW INS CO was upgraded to B+ from B in May 2018 based on an increase in the stability index from a 4.70(fair) to 6.50(good).

MUTUAL RRG INC was upgraded to B- from C+ in May 2018 based on an increase in the stability index from a 3.40(fair) to 4.90(good) and liquidity index from a 7.70(excellent) to 7.80(excellent).

NARRAGANSETT BAY INS CO was upgraded to C from C- in May 2018 based on an increase in the profitability index from a 3.90(fair) to 9.10(excellent), liquidity index from a 7.00(excellent) to 8.60(excellent), capitalization index from a 9.10(excellent) to 10.00(excellent), reserve adequacy index from a 4.50(fair) to 5.10(good), and stability index from a 3.30(fair) to 3.50(fair). Other factors: Capital and surplus increased during the period by 5.3%, from $105.5 million to $111.1 million.

NASW RRG INC was upgraded to C from C- in May 2018 based on an increase in the profitability index from a 4.30(fair) to 5.10(good), capitalization index from a 8.10(excellent) to 8.80(excellent), and stability index from a 2.30(weak) to 3.00(fair).

NATIONAL BUILDING MATERIAL ASR CO was upgraded to D from D- in May 2018 based on an increase in the liquidity index from a 6.90(excellent) to 9.00(excellent), stability index from a 1.30(weak) to 1.50(weak), and reserve adequacy index from a 4.80(fair) to 4.90(good). Other factors: Capital and surplus increased during the period by 5.8%, from $4.5 million to $4.7 million.

NATIONAL INTERSTATE INS CO OF HAWAII was upgraded to C+ from C in May 2018 based on an increase in the stability index from a 4.30(fair) to 4.50(fair).

NATIONAL MORTGAGE RE INC ONE was upgraded to B- from C+ in May 2018 based on an increase in the stability index from a 3.70(fair) to 5.00(good), reserve adequacy index from a 3.60(fair) to 4.60(fair), and profitability index from a 3.80(fair) to 3.90(fair).

NATIONS INS CO was upgraded to C- from D+ in May 2018 based on an increase in the profitability index from a 2.60(weak) to 4.70(fair), capitalization index from a 3.60(fair) to 4.30(fair), and stability index from a 2.80(weak) to 3.00(fair).

NATIONWIDE INS CO OF FL was upgraded to B from B- in May 2018 based on an increase in the liquidity index from a 7.10(excellent) to 10.00(excellent).

NEW HAMPSHIRE INS CO was upgraded to C+ from C in May 2018 based on an increase in the profitability index from a 1.90(weak) to 4.20(fair) and stability index from a 4.20(fair) to 4.50(fair).

NEW HORIZONS INS CO OF MO was upgraded to C+ from C in May 2018 based on an increase in the profitability index from a 3.90(fair) to 8.60(excellent) and stability index from a 4.30(fair) to 4.50(fair). Other factors: Capital and surplus increased during the period by 6.0%, from $26.2 million to $27.7 million.

NEW JERSEY CASUALTY INS CO was upgraded to B from B- in May 2018 based on an increase in the reserve adequacy index from a 5.80(good) to 7.00(excellent), capitalization index from a 9.00(excellent) to 9.70(excellent), stability index from a 5.00(good) to 5.50(good), and profitability index from a 8.80(excellent) to 8.90(excellent). Other factors: Capital and surplus increased during the period by 9.7%, from $269.7 million to $295.8 million.

NEW MEXICO SAFETY CASUALTY CO was upgraded to C from C- in May 2018 based on an increase in the liquidity index from a 7.20(excellent) to 9.40(excellent).

Rating Upgrades (Continued)

NEW YORK MUNICIPAL INS RECIPROCAL was upgraded to B from B- in May 2018 based on an increase in the stability index from a 3.60(fair) to 5.50(good) and capitalization index from a 7.90(excellent) to 8.00(excellent). Other factors: Capital and surplus increased during the period by 5.8%, from $62.2 million to $65.8 million.

NEW YORK SCHOOLS INS RECIPROCAL was upgraded to B+ from B in May 2018 based on an increase in the stability index from a 4.50(fair) to 6.40(good).

NORTH CAROLINA GRANGE MUTUAL INS CO was upgraded to C from C- in May 2018 based on an increase in the stability index from a 2.60(weak) to 3.50(fair), liquidity index from a 5.70(good) to 6.10(good), and capitalization index from a 7.00(excellent) to 7.30(excellent). Other factors: The company's net asset base increased during the period by 5.4%, from $34.3 million to $36.2 million. Capital and surplus increased during the period by 7.0%, from $18.5 million to $19.8 million.

NORTH COUNTRY INS CO was upgraded to C+ from C in May 2018 based on an increase in the stability index from a 2.90(fair) to 4.20(fair).

NORTHERN MUTUAL INS CO was upgraded to B- from C+ in May 2018 based on an increase in the reserve adequacy index from a 7.00(excellent) to 8.70(excellent), stability index from a 3.10(fair) to 4.70(fair), capitalization index from a 8.60(excellent) to 8.90(excellent), and liquidity index from a 6.80(good) to 6.90(excellent). Other factors: Capital and surplus increased during the period by 5.1%, from $25.0 million to $26.3 million.

NORTHSTONE INS CO was upgraded to B- from C+ in May 2018 based on an increase in the profitability index from a 4.60(fair) to 7.70(excellent) and stability index from a 3.10(fair) to 4.60(fair).

NORTHWEST GF MUTUAL INS CO was upgraded to D+ from D in May 2018 based on an increase in the capitalization index from a 7.90(excellent) to 8.20(excellent) and stability index from a 2.30(weak) to 2.50(weak).

NORTHWESTERN NATL INS CO SEG ACCNT was upgraded to D- from E- in May 2018 based on an increase in the stability index from a 0.10(weak) to 1.00(weak), profitability index from a 0.10(weak) to 0.60(weak), and capitalization index from a 0.00(weak) to 0.50(weak). Other factors: Capital and surplus increased during the period by 61.6%, from $1.2 million to $1.9 million.

NOVA CASUALTY CO was upgraded to B- from C+ in May 2018 based on an increase in the stability index from a 4.30(fair) to 4.90(good).

OHIO BAR LIABILITY INS CO was upgraded to B from B- in May 2018 based on an increase in the stability index from a 3.90(fair) to 5.10(good) and profitability index from a 8.30(excellent) to 8.50(excellent).

OHIO INDEMNITY CO was upgraded to C+ from C in May 2018 based on an increase in the stability index from a 2.90(fair) to 4.50(fair).

OKLAHOMA SPECIALTY INS CO was upgraded to B- from C+ in May 2018 based on an increase in the stability index from a 3.40(fair) to 4.90(good).

ONTARIO REINS CO LTD was upgraded to C+ from C in May 2018 based on an increase in the profitability index from a 6.70(good) to 6.90(excellent), stability index from a 4.30(fair) to 4.50(fair), and capitalization index from a 7.90(excellent) to 8.10(excellent). Other factors: Capital and surplus increased during the period by 14.4%, from $22.9 million to $26.2 million.

OREGON MUTUAL INS CO was upgraded to C from C- in May 2018 based on an increase in the reserve adequacy index from a 4.80(fair) to 5.60(good), profitability index from a 1.70(weak) to 2.30(weak), stability index from a 3.30(fair) to 3.50(fair), and liquidity index from a 5.30(good) to 5.40(good).

OSWEGO COUNTY MUTUAL INS CO was upgraded to C+ from C in May 2018 based on an increase in the stability index from a 2.70(weak) to 3.70(fair) and capitalization index from a 8.50(excellent) to 8.70(excellent).

OWNERS INS CO was upgraded to A from A- in May 2018 based on an increase in the stability index from a 5.60(good) to 7.50(excellent).

PACIFIC INDEMNITY CO was upgraded to B from B- in May 2018 based on an increase in the stability index from a 3.70(fair) to 5.50(good), capitalization index from a 9.60(excellent) to 10.00(excellent), and reserve adequacy index from a 8.60(excellent) to 8.70(excellent).

Rating Upgrades (Continued)

PACIFIC PIONEER INS CO was upgraded to C from C- in May 2018 based on an increase in the liquidity index from a 4.90(good) to 6.70(good), capitalization index from a 5.40(good) to 6.10(good), stability index from a 2.30(weak) to 2.80(weak), profitability index from a 2.40(weak) to 2.90(fair), and reserve adequacy index from a 5.40(good) to 5.60(good).

PACIFIC SPECIALTY PROPERTY & CAS CO was upgraded to D from D- in May 2018 based on an increase in the stability index from a 1.30(weak) to 1.50(weak). Other factors: Capital and surplus increased during the period by 10.6%, from $4.9 million to $5.4 million.

PAN-AMERICAN CASUALTY CO was upgraded to D+ from D in May 2018 based on an increase in the liquidity index from a 6.80(good) to 10.00(excellent), stability index from a 2.30(weak) to 2.50(weak), and profitability index from a 4.80(fair) to 4.90(good). Other factors: The company's net asset base increased during the period by 5.4%, from $5.1 million to $5.4 million.

PARK INS CO was upgraded to D from E- in May 2018 based on an increase in the liquidity index from a 0.00(weak) to 5.70(good), stability index from a 0.10(weak) to 2.00(weak), and profitability index from a 1.50(weak) to 2.30(weak). Other factors: Capital and surplus increased during the period by 34.4%, from $3.0 million to $4.0 million.

PARTNER REINSURANCE CO OF THE US was upgraded to B- from C+ in May 2018 based on an increase in the stability index from a 4.40(fair) to 4.50(fair).

PATONS CO-OP FIRE INS CO was upgraded to B from B- in May 2018 based on an increase in the stability index from a 3.80(fair) to 5.50(good) and profitability index from a 7.90(excellent) to 8.20(excellent).

PEACE CHURCH RRG INC was upgraded to C from C- in May 2018 based on an increase in the stability index from a 3.30(fair) to 3.50(fair).

PEERLESS INS CO was upgraded to B from B- in May 2018 based on an increase in the stability index from a 3.90(fair) to 5.30(good).

PEOPLES TRUST INS CO was upgraded to D+ from D in May 2018 based on an increase in the liquidity index from a 0.10(weak) to 4.30(fair), capitalization index from a 2.90(fair) to 4.00(fair), profitability index from a 1.60(weak) to 2.30(weak), stability index from a 2.10(weak) to 2.50(weak), and reserve adequacy index from a 4.40(fair) to 4.60(fair). Other factors: The company's net asset base increased during the period by 23.2%, from $206.3 million to $254.0 million. Capital and surplus increased during the period by 33.4%, from $49.8 million to $66.4 million.

PETROLEUM MARKETERS MGMT INS CO was upgraded to C+ from C in May 2018 based on an increase in the profitability index from a 4.30(fair) to 7.60(excellent), stability index from a 4.30(fair) to 4.50(fair), and capitalization index from a 7.50(excellent) to 7.60(excellent). Other factors: The company's net asset base increased during the period by 38.2%, from $36.4 million to $50.2 million. Capital and surplus increased during the period by 8.7%, from $25.9 million to $28.2 million.

PHOEBE RECIPROCAL RRG was upgraded to E+ from E in May 2018 based on an increase in the stability index from a 0.00(weak) to 0.50(weak) and capitalization index from a 8.80(excellent) to 9.00(excellent).

PHYSICIANS CASUALTY RRG INC was upgraded to E+ from E in May 2018 based on an increase in the profitability index from a 6.90(excellent) to 8.70(excellent) and stability index from a 0.00(weak) to 0.50(weak). Other factors: Capital and surplus increased during the period by 11.1%, from $3.3 million to $3.6 million.

PHYSICIANS INS PROGRAM was upgraded to C+ from C in May 2018 based on an increase in the capitalization index from a 4.90(good) to 5.70(good) and reserve adequacy index from a 6.80(good) to 7.00(excellent).

PHYSICIANS PROACTIVE PROTECTION INC was upgraded to C- from D+ in May 2018 based on an increase in the liquidity index from a 7.10(excellent) to 8.40(excellent), stability index from a 2.20(weak) to 3.30(fair), and capitalization index from a 2.50(weak) to 3.40(fair).

PHYSICIANS STANDARD INS CO was upgraded to C- from D+ in May 2018 based on an increase in the reserve adequacy index from a 4.90(good) to 7.00(excellent) and profitability index from a 1.70(weak) to 2.00(weak).

PINNACLEPOINT INS CO was upgraded to B- from C+ in May 2018 based on an increase in the stability index from a 3.10(fair) to 4.20(fair), reserve adequacy index from a 5.00(good) to 6.10(good), and liquidity index from a 7.90(excellent) to 8.10(excellent).

Rating Upgrades (Continued)

PIONEER STATE MUTUAL INS CO was upgraded to B+ from B in May 2018 based on an increase in the stability index from a 4.70(fair) to 6.50(good). Other factors: Capital and surplus increased during the period by 5.4%, from $344.5 million to $363.2 million.

PLAZA INS CO was upgraded to B- from C+ in May 2018 based on an increase in the stability index from a 3.70(fair) to 4.90(good) and liquidity index from a 6.90(excellent) to 8.10(excellent). Other factors: The company's net asset base increased during the period by 28.9%, from $50.9 million to $65.6 million.

PLICO INC was upgraded to C+ from C in May 2018 based on an increase in the liquidity index from a 9.00(excellent) to 10.00(excellent) and stability index from a 3.90(fair) to 4.50(fair).

POINT GUARD INS CO was upgraded to C from C- in May 2018 based on an increase in the liquidity index from a 2.90(fair) to 5.20(good), stability index from a 3.00(fair) to 3.50(fair), and reserve adequacy index from a 3.90(fair) to 4.30(fair). Other factors: The company's net asset base increased during the period by 25.9%, from $57.3 million to $72.1 million.

PREFERRED PROFESSIONAL INS CO was upgraded to B+ from B in May 2018 based on an increase in the stability index from a 4.70(fair) to 6.50(good) and profitability index from a 7.10(excellent) to 7.60(excellent).

PREMIER GROUP INS CO was upgraded to B from B- in May 2018 based on an increase in the liquidity index from a 7.00(excellent) to 7.40(excellent), reserve adequacy index from a 8.60(excellent) to 8.70(excellent), and capitalization index from a 9.50(excellent) to 9.60(excellent).

PRE-PAID LEGAL CAS INC was upgraded to C+ from C in May 2018 based on an increase in the stability index from a 2.80(weak) to 3.80(fair), profitability index from a 6.10(good) to 6.90(excellent), liquidity index from a 1.90(weak) to 2.30(weak), and capitalization index from a 6.10(good) to 6.30(good).

PRIMEONE INS CO was upgraded to C- from D+ in May 2018 based on an increase in the profitability index from a 1.60(weak) to 2.70(weak) and liquidity index from a 6.20(good) to 7.00(excellent). Other factors: The company's net asset base increased during the period by 34.2%, from $15.1 million to $20.3 million. Capital and surplus increased during the period by 7.8%, from $7.7 million to $8.3 million.

PRIMERO INS CO was upgraded to C+ from C in May 2018 based on an increase in the liquidity index from a 5.70(good) to 5.80(good) and capitalization index from a 7.50(excellent) to 7.60(excellent).

PRIVILEGE UNDERWRITERS RECIP EXCH was upgraded to B from B- in May 2018 based on an increase in the stability index from a 4.30(fair) to 5.50(good) and profitability index from a 2.80(weak) to 3.80(fair). Other factors: The company's net asset base increased during the period by 8.9%, from $521.6 million to $568.0 million. Capital and surplus increased during the period by 34.5%, from $169.2 million to $227.6 million.

PROFESSIONAL SECURITY INS CO was upgraded to B- from C+ in May 2018 based on an increase in the liquidity index from a 7.20(excellent) to 10.00(excellent).

PROGRESSIVE COUNTY MUTUAL INS CO was upgraded to C- from D+ in May 2018 based on an increase in the liquidity index from a 2.40(weak) to 9.10(excellent), stability index from a 2.50(weak) to 3.20(fair), and capitalization index from a 1.00(weak) to 1.20(weak).

PROGRESSIVE DIRECT INS CO was upgraded to B- from C+ in May 2018 based on an increase in the stability index from a 4.20(fair) to 4.50(fair) and liquidity index from a 1.70(weak) to 1.90(weak).

PROGRESSIVE PROPERTY INS CO was upgraded to B from B- in May 2018 based on an increase in the capitalization index from a 7.50(excellent) to 7.90(excellent), stability index from a 5.30(good) to 5.50(good), and liquidity index from a 6.50(good) to 6.60(good).

PROPERTY-OWNERS INS CO was upgraded to A- from B+ in May 2018 based on an increase in the stability index from a 5.10(good) to 7.00(excellent) and capitalization index from a 7.30(excellent) to 7.50(excellent).

PUBLIC UTILITY MUTUAL INS CO RRG was upgraded to E+ from E in May 2018 based on an increase in the stability index from a 0.00(weak) to 0.50(weak). Other factors: Capital and surplus increased during the period by 7.2%, from $6.2 million to $6.7 million.

Rating Upgrades (Continued)

RAM MUTUAL INS CO was upgraded to B from B- in May 2018 based on an increase in the stability index from a 3.70(fair) to 5.50(good), capitalization index from a 9.70(excellent) to 9.90(excellent), and profitability index from a 8.70(excellent) to 8.80(excellent).

RECREATION RRG INC was upgraded to D+ from D in May 2018 based on an increase in the profitability index from a 5.90(good) to 6.00(good).

RED ROCK RISK RETENTION GROUP INC was upgraded to C- from D+ in May 2018 based on an increase in the profitability index from a 2.30(weak) to 2.90(fair), liquidity index from a 8.70(excellent) to 9.20(excellent), and reserve adequacy index from a 1.90(weak) to 2.20(weak).

RELIABLE LLOYDS INS CO was upgraded to B- from C+ in May 2018 based on an increase in the stability index from a 3.20(fair) to 4.80(fair). Other factors: The company's net asset base increased during the period by 9.1%, from $17.8 million to $19.4 million.

REPUBLIC CREDIT INDEMNITY CO was upgraded to C- from D+ in May 2018 based on an increase in the reserve adequacy index from a 5.10(good) to 10.00(excellent), capitalization index from a 0.80(weak) to 1.50(weak), stability index from a 2.70(weak) to 3.30(fair), and profitability index from a 1.70(weak) to 1.90(weak).

REPWEST INS CO was upgraded to C- from D+ in May 2018 based on an increase in the capitalization index from a 2.60(weak) to 7.30(excellent), reserve adequacy index from a 4.40(fair) to 5.90(good), and stability index from a 2.60(weak) to 3.10(fair).

RESTORATION RRG INC was upgraded to B from B- in May 2018 based on an increase in the capitalization index from a 7.30(excellent) to 7.50(excellent), liquidity index from a 7.40(excellent) to 7.60(excellent), profitability index from a 8.70(excellent) to 8.80(excellent), and reserve adequacy index from a 9.50(excellent) to 9.60(excellent). Other factors: Capital and surplus increased during the period by 7.2%, from $35.2 million to $37.7 million.

RETAILERS CASUALTY INS CO was upgraded to B from B- in May 2018 based on an increase in the reserve adequacy index from a 7.00(excellent) to 9.50(excellent), stability index from a 5.30(good) to 5.50(good), and capitalization index from a 8.50(excellent) to 8.60(excellent). Other factors: Capital and surplus increased during the period by 6.2%, from $44.1 million to $46.9 million.

RETAILFIRST INS CO was upgraded to A from A- in May 2018 based on an increase in the profitability index from a 8.00(excellent) to 8.30(excellent), reserve adequacy index from a 6.60(good) to 6.90(excellent), and capitalization index from a 8.40(excellent) to 8.50(excellent).

ROCKFORD MUTUAL INS CO was upgraded to B- from C+ in May 2018 based on an increase in the stability index from a 3.40(fair) to 5.30(good) and reserve adequacy index from a 6.80(good) to 7.00(excellent).

ROCKINGHAM INS CO was upgraded to B+ from B in May 2018 based on an increase in the profitability index from a 5.40(good) to 7.90(excellent) and stability index from a 6.30(good) to 6.50(good).

RSUI INDEMNITY CO was upgraded to B- from C+ in May 2018 based on an increase in the stability index from a 2.90(fair) to 4.50(fair), profitability index from a 7.40(excellent) to 8.60(excellent), capitalization index from a 7.90(excellent) to 8.10(excellent), and reserve adequacy index from a 8.00(excellent) to 8.10(excellent). Other factors: Capital and surplus increased during the period by 6.7%, from $1521.9 million to $1624.3 million.

RVOS FARM MUTUAL INS CO was upgraded to C from C- in May 2018 based on an increase in the liquidity index from a 3.20(fair) to 4.60(fair), reserve adequacy index from a 5.40(good) to 5.80(good), capitalization index from a 7.10(excellent) to 7.30(excellent), and stability index from a 3.30(fair) to 3.50(fair). Other factors: Capital and surplus increased during the period by 12.2%, from $39.8 million to $44.7 million.

SAFE HARBOR INS CO was upgraded to B from B- in May 2018 based on an increase in the reserve adequacy index from a 4.00(fair) to 5.20(good) and stability index from a 5.30(good) to 5.50(good).

SAFECO INS CO OF AMERICA was upgraded to B from B- in May 2018 based on an increase in the stability index from a 3.90(fair) to 5.50(good) and profitability index from a 6.10(good) to 6.40(good).

SAFETY P&C INS CO was upgraded to C+ from C in May 2018 based on an increase in the stability index from a 4.30(fair) to 4.50(fair) and reserve adequacy index from a 9.20(excellent) to 9.30(excellent).

Rating Upgrades (Continued)

SAINT LUKES HEALTH SYSTEM RRG was upgraded to C from C- in May 2018 based on an increase in the reserve adequacy index from a 4.90(good) to 5.90(good), liquidity index from a 6.60(good) to 7.00(excellent), profitability index from a 3.00(fair) to 3.30(fair), and capitalization index from a 7.10(excellent) to 7.20(excellent).

SAMARITAN RRG INC was upgraded to C+ from C in May 2018 based on an increase in the profitability index from a 8.00(excellent) to 8.40(excellent). Other factors: Capital and surplus increased during the period by 9.3%, from $21.9 million to $24.0 million.

SC FARM BUREAU MUTUAL INS CO was upgraded to B- from C+ in May 2018 based on an increase in the profitability index from a 3.20(fair) to 5.00(good), stability index from a 3.50(fair) to 4.70(fair), liquidity index from a 5.90(good) to 6.60(good), capitalization index from a 8.70(excellent) to 9.00(excellent), and reserve adequacy index from a 7.80(excellent) to 7.90(excellent). Other factors: The company's net asset base increased during the period by 9.7%, from $110.0 million to $120.6 million. Capital and surplus increased during the period by 21.0%, from $54.1 million to $65.5 million.

SEAVIEW INS CO was upgraded to C- from D+ in May 2018 based on an increase in the stability index from a 1.80(weak) to 2.90(fair), liquidity index from a 7.20(excellent) to 7.40(excellent), and profitability index from a 7.80(excellent) to 7.90(excellent).

SECURITY MUTUAL INS CO was upgraded to B from B- in May 2018 based on an increase in the stability index from a 3.60(fair) to 5.50(good), reserve adequacy index from a 6.80(good) to 8.30(excellent), and liquidity index from a 6.70(good) to 6.80(good).

SELECTIVE AUTO INS CO OF NJ was upgraded to B+ from B in May 2018 based on an increase in the profitability index from a 8.40(excellent) to 8.80(excellent) and stability index from a 6.30(good) to 6.50(good).

SELECTIVE CASUALTY INS CO was upgraded to B+ from B in May 2018 based on an increase in the stability index from a 4.90(good) to 6.50(good), reserve adequacy index from a 6.00(good) to 6.90(excellent), profitability index from a 8.60(excellent) to 8.80(excellent), and capitalization index from a 7.80(excellent) to 7.90(excellent). Other factors: Capital and surplus increased during the period by 7.9%, from $101.0 million to $109.0 million.

SELECTIVE INS CO OF NEW ENGLAND was upgraded to C+ from C in May 2018 based on an increase in the profitability index from a 8.60(excellent) to 8.80(excellent) and stability index from a 4.30(fair) to 4.50(fair).

SENECA SPECIALTY INS CO was upgraded to B- from C+ in May 2018 based on an increase in the stability index from a 4.30(fair) to 4.90(good).

SENTRY CASUALTY CO was upgraded to B+ from B in May 2018 based on an increase in the stability index from a 4.50(fair) to 6.40(good).

SENTRY SELECT INS CO was upgraded to A- from B+ in May 2018 based on an increase in the stability index from a 5.10(good) to 7.00(excellent).

SERVICE LLOYDS INS CO was upgraded to B from B- in May 2018 based on an increase in the profitability index from a 7.80(excellent) to 8.40(excellent), stability index from a 4.00(fair) to 4.60(fair), capitalization index from a 9.50(excellent) to 9.70(excellent), and reserve adequacy index from a 8.90(excellent) to 9.00(excellent).

SEVEN SEAS INS CO was upgraded to C+ from C in May 2018 based on an increase in the stability index from a 2.90(fair) to 4.30(fair) and profitability index from a 8.30(excellent) to 9.50(excellent).

SFM MUTUAL INS CO was upgraded to B+ from B in May 2018 based on an increase in the capitalization index from a 6.50(good) to 6.90(excellent), reserve adequacy index from a 6.20(good) to 6.60(good), and stability index from a 6.30(good) to 6.50(good).

SFM SAFE INS CO was upgraded to D+ from D in May 2018 based on an increase in the stability index from a 2.30(weak) to 2.50(weak).

SFM SELECT INS CO was upgraded to C from C- in May 2018 based on an increase in the stability index from a 2.40(weak) to 3.20(fair) and profitability index from a 5.60(good) to 5.70(good).

SHEBOYGAN FALLS INS CO was upgraded to B- from C+ in May 2018 based on an increase in the stability index from a 3.20(fair) to 4.80(fair), reserve adequacy index from a 4.50(fair) to 4.90(good), and profitability index from a 5.20(good) to 5.40(good).

Rating Upgrades (Continued)

SHELTER REINS CO was upgraded to B from B- in May 2018 based on an increase in the reserve adequacy index from a 7.00(excellent) to 9.30(excellent) and stability index from a 3.80(fair) to 5.50(good).

SIMED was upgraded to B from B- in May 2018 based on an increase in the stability index from a 5.30(good) to 5.50(good).

SLAVONIC MUTUAL FIRE INS ASN was upgraded to B- from C+ in May 2018 based on an increase in the stability index from a 3.30(fair) to 4.80(fair).

SOMPO AMERICA INSURANCE CO was upgraded to A from A- in May 2018 based on an increase in the profitability index from a 5.80(good) to 6.90(excellent) and stability index from a 7.30(excellent) to 7.50(excellent).

SOUTHERN FIDELITY INS CO was upgraded to B+ from B in May 2018 based on an increase in the stability index from a 6.30(good) to 6.50(good).

SOUTHERN GENERAL INS CO was upgraded to C from C- in May 2018 based on an increase in the stability index from a 2.80(weak) to 3.50(fair) and liquidity index from a 0.80(weak) to 1.40(weak). Other factors: Capital and surplus increased during the period by 10.0%, from $18.1 million to $19.9 million.

SOUTHERN MUTUAL CHURCH INS CO was upgraded to B- from C+ in May 2018 based on an increase in the stability index from a 3.40(fair) to 5.20(good), capitalization index from a 8.10(excellent) to 8.40(excellent), and reserve adequacy index from a 8.20(excellent) to 8.40(excellent). Other factors: Capital and surplus increased during the period by 6.4%, from $36.3 million to $38.6 million.

SOUTHERN MUTUAL INS CO was upgraded to B- from C+ in May 2018 based on an increase in the liquidity index from a 7.60(excellent) to 9.50(excellent) and stability index from a 3.20(fair) to 5.00(good). Other factors: The company's net asset base increased during the period by 9.9%, from $18.5 million to $20.3 million.

SOUTHERN OAK INS CO was upgraded to B from B- in May 2018 based on an increase in the capitalization index from a 8.30(excellent) to 8.60(excellent), stability index from a 5.30(good) to 5.50(good), and profitability index from a 8.60(excellent) to 8.70(excellent).

SOUTHERN PIONEER PROP & CAS INS CO was upgraded to B- from C+ in May 2018 based on an increase in the stability index from a 3.10(fair) to 3.60(fair), profitability index from a 4.90(good) to 5.20(good), and capitalization index from a 7.10(excellent) to 7.20(excellent). Other factors: Capital and surplus increased during the period by 6.3%, from $20.7 million to $22.0 million.

SOUTHERN-OWNERS INS CO was upgraded to A from A- in May 2018 based on an increase in the profitability index from a 7.50(excellent) to 8.50(excellent) and stability index from a 7.30(excellent) to 7.50(excellent).

SPARTAN PROPERTY INS CO was upgraded to B- from C+ in May 2018 based on an increase in the stability index from a 3.20(fair) to 5.00(good), profitability index from a 6.30(good) to 8.00(excellent), capitalization index from a 7.50(excellent) to 7.80(excellent), liquidity index from a 7.60(excellent) to 7.70(excellent), and reserve adequacy index from a 5.20(good) to 5.30(good). Other factors: The company's net asset base increased during the period by 10.7%, from $29.3 million to $32.4 million. Capital and surplus increased during the period by 7.8%, from $22.7 million to $24.4 million.

SPRING VALLEY MUTUAL INS CO was upgraded to E+ from E in May 2018 based on an increase in the stability index from a 0.10(weak) to 0.50(weak) and profitability index from a 6.60(good) to 6.90(excellent).

ST CHARLES INS CO RRG was upgraded to D from D- in May 2018 based on an increase in the stability index from a 1.30(weak) to 1.50(weak). Other factors: Capital and surplus increased during the period by 5.1%, from $14.5 million to $15.3 million.

ST LUKES HEALTH NETWORK INS CO RRG was upgraded to E+ from E in May 2018 based on an increase in the capitalization index from a 1.90(weak) to 2.60(weak), reserve adequacy index from a 3.60(fair) to 4.00(fair), stability index from a 0.30(weak) to 0.50(weak), and profitability index from a 6.10(good) to 6.20(good). Other factors: The company's net asset base increased during the period by 12.7%, from $61.8 million to $69.7 million. Capital and surplus increased during the period by 7.3%, from $19.7 million to $21.1 million.

STARNET INS CO was upgraded to C+ from C in May 2018 based on an increase in the liquidity index from a 7.90(excellent) to 9.50(excellent) and stability index from a 4.20(fair) to 4.40(fair).

Rating Upgrades (Continued)

STARR SURPLUS LINES INS CO was upgraded to B from B- in May 2018 based on an increase in the liquidity index from a 6.50(good) to 9.30(excellent), stability index from a 3.70(fair) to 5.50(good), reserve adequacy index from a 3.60(fair) to 4.00(fair), and profitability index from a 8.90(excellent) to 9.10(excellent). Other factors: The company's net asset base increased during the period by 7.6%, from $376.5 million to $405.0 million.

STATE FARM GUARANTY INS CO was upgraded to B- from C+ in May 2018 based on an increase in the stability index from a 4.30(fair) to 4.90(good).

STATE VOLUNTEER MUTUAL INS CO was upgraded to B+ from B in May 2018 based on an increase in the stability index from a 4.90(good) to 6.50(good) and profitability index from a 6.80(good) to 8.10(excellent).

STEADPOINT INS CO was upgraded to C from C- in May 2018 based on an increase in the profitability index from a 7.20(excellent) to 9.20(excellent), liquidity index from a 6.90(excellent) to 7.10(excellent), and capitalization index from a 6.90(excellent) to 7.10(excellent). Other factors: Capital and surplus increased during the period by 15.9%, from $8.4 million to $9.7 million.

STICO MUTUAL INS CO RRG was upgraded to D+ from D in May 2018 based on an increase in the profitability index from a 6.50(good) to 7.40(excellent), stability index from a 1.90(weak) to 2.50(weak), liquidity index from a 7.00(excellent) to 7.10(excellent), and reserve adequacy index from a 9.30(excellent) to 9.40(excellent).

STONETRUST COMMERCIAL INS CO was upgraded to B from B- in May 2018 based on an increase in the stability index from a 5.10(good) to 5.50(good), capitalization index from a 6.90(excellent) to 7.30(excellent), profitability index from a 4.80(fair) to 5.10(good), reserve adequacy index from a 3.70(fair) to 3.90(fair), and liquidity index from a 6.70(good) to 6.80(good). Other factors: Capital and surplus increased during the period by 5.2%, from $68.5 million to $72.1 million.

SUBLIMITY INS CO was upgraded to B- from C+ in May 2018 based on an increase in the stability index from a 3.40(fair) to 5.30(good).

SUMMITPOINT INS CO was upgraded to B- from C+ in May 2018 based on an increase in the stability index from a 3.10(fair) to 4.60(fair) and reserve adequacy index from a 5.00(good) to 6.10(good).

SURETEC INDEMNITY CO was upgraded to B- from C+ in May 2018 based on an increase in the stability index from a 3.10(fair) to 4.70(fair), liquidity index from a 7.60(excellent) to 8.80(excellent), reserve adequacy index from a 4.80(fair) to 5.90(good), and capitalization index from a 8.00(excellent) to 8.70(excellent). Other factors: The company's net asset base increased during the period by 7.5%, from $22.4 million to $24.1 million.

SURETEC INS CO was upgraded to B+ from B in May 2018 based on an increase in the liquidity index from a 7.90(excellent) to 8.20(excellent) and stability index from a 6.30(good) to 6.50(good).

SUTTER INS CO was upgraded to C+ from C in May 2018 based on an increase in the stability index from a 2.90(fair) to 4.40(fair), capitalization index from a 8.80(excellent) to 9.50(excellent), profitability index from a 3.50(fair) to 4.00(fair), liquidity index from a 6.60(good) to 6.80(good), and reserve adequacy index from a 5.90(good) to 6.10(good).

SWISS REINS AMERICA CORP was upgraded to C from C- in May 2018 based on an increase in the stability index from a 2.00(weak) to 3.50(fair), liquidity index from a 7.00(excellent) to 7.70(excellent), capitalization index from a 4.70(fair) to 5.20(good), and profitability index from a 3.20(fair) to 3.50(fair).

SYNCORA GUARANTEE INC was upgraded to C+ from E- in May 2018 based on an increase in the stability index from a 0.00(weak) to 4.30(fair), reserve adequacy index from a 1.90(weak) to 3.10(fair), and profitability index from a 5.40(good) to 6.60(good). Other factors: The company's net asset base increased during the period by 12.0%, from $1162.9 million to $1302.1 million. Capital and surplus increased during the period by 21.7%, from $1082.9 million to $1317.6 million.

SYNERGY COMP INS CO was upgraded to C from C- in May 2018 based on an increase in the stability index from a 3.30(fair) to 3.50(fair).

SYNERGY INS CO was upgraded to C from C- in May 2018 based on an increase in the profitability index from a 5.90(good) to 9.50(excellent) and stability index from a 3.30(fair) to 3.50(fair). Other factors: The company's net asset base increased during the period by 7.5%, from $69.2 million to $74.4 million. Capital and surplus increased during the period by 8.0%, from $26.5 million to $28.6 million.

Rating Upgrades (Continued)

TEACHERS AUTO INS CO was upgraded to B from B- in May 2018 based on an increase in the stability index from a 4.60(fair) to 4.90(good). Other factors: The company's net asset base increased during the period by 9.5%, from $25.5 million to $28.0 million. Capital and surplus increased during the period by 5.2%, from $13.6 million to $14.3 million.

TEXAS FARM BUREAU CASUALTY INS CO was upgraded to A- from B+ in May 2018 based on an increase in the profitability index from a 4.30(fair) to 4.80(fair) and stability index from a 6.60(good) to 6.90(excellent).

TEXAS FARM BUREAU MUTUAL INS CO was upgraded to C+ from C in May 2018 based on an increase in the profitability index from a 3.60(fair) to 4.00(fair), reserve adequacy index from a 6.20(good) to 6.50(good), stability index from a 4.30(fair) to 4.50(fair), and capitalization index from a 9.00(excellent) to 9.10(excellent). Other factors: Capital and surplus increased during the period by 9.5%, from $299.9 million to $328.5 million.

TEXAS LAWYERS INS EXCHANGE was upgraded to B from B- in May 2018 based on an increase in the stability index from a 3.60(fair) to 5.50(good) and liquidity index from a 7.60(excellent) to 7.80(excellent).

TITAN INS CO INC A RRG was upgraded to C+ from C in May 2018 based on an increase in the liquidity index from a 8.40(excellent) to 10.00(excellent), stability index from a 4.30(fair) to 4.50(fair), and capitalization index from a 8.80(excellent) to 8.90(excellent).

TOKIO MILLENNIUM RE AG (US BRANCH) was upgraded to C from C- in May 2018 based on an increase in the capitalization index from a 3.80(fair) to 5.50(good), reserve adequacy index from a 3.60(fair) to 4.60(fair), stability index from a 2.90(fair) to 3.50(fair), and profitability index from a 2.00(weak) to 2.20(weak). Other factors: The company's net asset base increased during the period by 10.5%, from $1109.2 million to $1226.2 million. Capital and surplus increased during the period by 47.7%, from $156.5 million to $231.2 million.

TRANS PACIFIC INS CO was upgraded to B+ from B in May 2018 based on an increase in the profitability index from a 4.90(good) to 7.50(excellent) and stability index from a 4.50(fair) to 6.00(good).

TRANSATLANTIC REINS CO was upgraded to B+ from B in May 2018 based on an increase in the stability index from a 4.80(fair) to 6.50(good), profitability index from a 6.00(good) to 6.40(good), reserve adequacy index from a 8.90(excellent) to 9.10(excellent), and capitalization index from a 7.60(excellent) to 7.70(excellent). Other factors: Capital and surplus increased during the period by 5.3%, from $4743.5 million to $4992.9 million.

TRANSIT MUTUAL INS CORP OF WI was upgraded to D from D- in May 2018 based on an increase in the liquidity index from a 7.60(excellent) to 8.30(excellent) and stability index from a 0.90(weak) to 1.40(weak).

TRAVELERS CASUALTY & SURETY CO OF AM was upgraded to B- from C+ in May 2018 based on an increase in the stability index from a 3.00(fair) to 4.90(good).

TRAVELERS INDEMNITY CO was upgraded to A- from B+ in May 2018 based on an increase in the stability index from a 5.40(good) to 7.20(excellent) and capitalization index from a 7.70(excellent) to 7.80(excellent).

TREXIS INSURANCE CORP was upgraded to B+ from B in May 2018 based on an increase in the profitability index from a 5.00(good) to 6.40(good), stability index from a 6.30(good) to 6.50(good), and reserve adequacy index from a 7.70(excellent) to 7.80(excellent).

TREXIS ONE INSURANCE GROUP was upgraded to A- from B+ in May 2018 based on an increase in the profitability index from a 4.90(good) to 6.50(good).

TRIANGLE INS CO was upgraded to B- from C+ in May 2018 based on an increase in the profitability index from a 6.20(good) to 8.40(excellent), stability index from a 3.30(fair) to 5.10(good), and capitalization index from a 6.10(good) to 7.20(excellent). Other factors: Capital and surplus increased during the period by 5.5%, from $28.8 million to $30.4 million.

TRINITY RISK SOLUTIONS RECIP INS RRG was upgraded to E+ from E in May 2018 based on an increase in the stability index from a 0.00(weak) to 0.50(weak) and reserve adequacy index from a 4.70(fair) to 4.90(good).

TRITON INS CO was upgraded to B- from C+ in May 2018 based on an increase in the profitability index from a 2.90(fair) to 5.90(good), stability index from a 4.20(fair) to 4.90(good), and liquidity index from a 7.20(excellent) to 7.40(excellent).

Rating Upgrades (Continued)

TWIN LIGHTS INS CO was upgraded to C- from D+ in May 2018 based on an increase in the stability index from a 2.50(weak) to 3.00(fair) and profitability index from a 6.40(good) to 6.80(good).

UFG SPECIALTY INS CO was upgraded to C+ from C in May 2018 based on an increase in the capitalization index from a 9.40(excellent) to 9.90(excellent), liquidity index from a 6.60(good) to 7.00(excellent), and profitability index from a 4.90(good) to 5.00(good).

UMIALIK INS CO was upgraded to B from B- in May 2018 based on an increase in the stability index from a 3.80(fair) to 5.50(good). Other factors: The company's net asset base increased during the period by 16.8%, from $66.5 million to $77.7 million.

UNITED BUS INS CO was upgraded to D+ from D in May 2018 based on an increase in the capitalization index from a 2.50(weak) to 3.30(fair) and reserve adequacy index from a 3.50(fair) to 3.60(fair). Other factors: Capital and surplus increased during the period by 27.5%, from $3.4 million to $4.4 million.

UNITED CENTRAL PA RRG was upgraded to E+ from E in May 2018 based on an increase in the profitability index from a 5.10(good) to 6.20(good), liquidity index from a 6.90(excellent) to 8.00(excellent), capitalization index from a 3.80(fair) to 4.20(fair), stability index from a 0.10(weak) to 0.50(weak), and reserve adequacy index from a 4.60(fair) to 4.80(fair).

UNITED EDUCATORS INS A RECIP RRG was upgraded to B+ from B in May 2018 based on an increase in the stability index from a 6.30(good) to 6.50(good) and capitalization index from a 7.30(excellent) to 7.50(excellent).

UNITED FARM FAMILY MUTUAL INS CO was upgraded to B+ from B in May 2018 based on an increase in the profitability index from a 4.90(good) to 8.80(excellent), stability index from a 4.50(fair) to 6.40(good), capitalization index from a 8.70(excellent) to 9.10(excellent), and liquidity index from a 5.50(good) to 5.80(good).

UNITED GUARANTY INS CO was upgraded to B from B- in May 2018 based on an increase in the capitalization index from a 6.70(good) to 10.00(excellent) and reserve adequacy index from a 4.60(fair) to 4.70(fair).

UNITED GUARANTY MORTGAGE INDEM CO was upgraded to C+ from C in May 2018 based on an increase in the reserve adequacy index from a 5.00(good) to 9.40(excellent), stability index from a 4.20(fair) to 4.70(fair), and capitalization index from a 9.50(excellent) to 10.00(excellent). Other factors: The company's net asset base increased during the period by 61.8%, from $30.2 million to $48.9 million.

UNITED HOME INS CO was upgraded to C from C- in May 2018 based on an increase in the profitability index from a 7.30(excellent) to 8.20(excellent), reserve adequacy index from a 5.70(good) to 6.40(good), and capitalization index from a 4.10(fair) to 4.20(fair). Other factors: Capital and surplus increased during the period by 6.7%, from $13.1 million to $14.0 million.

UNITED SECURITY HEALTH & CASUALTY was upgraded to D+ from D in May 2018 based on an increase in the profitability index from a 1.20(weak) to 2.90(fair), capitalization index from a 7.30(excellent) to 8.20(excellent), reserve adequacy index from a 3.60(fair) to 4.10(fair), and stability index from a 2.00(weak) to 2.10(weak).

UNITED SERVICES AUTOMOBILE ASN was upgraded to A- from B+ in May 2018 based on an increase in the stability index from a 5.20(good) to 7.10(excellent) and capitalization index from a 7.50(excellent) to 7.60(excellent).

UNITED SPECIALTY INS CO was upgraded to B+ from B in May 2018 based on an increase in the stability index from a 4.50(fair) to 6.40(good). Other factors: The company's net asset base increased during the period by 6.3%, from $310.5 million to $330.2 million. Capital and surplus increased during the period by 11.3%, from $133.9 million to $149.0 million.

UNITED STATES SURETY CO was upgraded to B from B- in May 2018 based on an increase in the capitalization index from a 9.50(excellent) to 9.90(excellent) and stability index from a 5.30(good) to 5.50(good).

UNITRIN ADVANTAGE INS CO was upgraded to C from C- in May 2018 based on an increase in the liquidity index from a 7.00(excellent) to 10.00(excellent).

UNIVERSAL SURETY CO was upgraded to C+ from C in May 2018 based on an increase in the stability index from a 2.70(weak) to 4.50(fair) and capitalization index from a 8.30(excellent) to 8.40(excellent). Other factors: The company's net asset base increased during the period by 5.0%, from $223.6 million to $234.8 million. Capital and surplus increased during the period by 16.6%, from $164.3 million to $191.5 million.

Rating Upgrades (Continued)

UPMC HEALTH BENEFITS INC was upgraded to D+ from D in May 2018 based on an increase in the capitalization index from a 1.70(weak) to 2.70(weak), profitability index from a 3.80(fair) to 4.80(fair), and stability index from a 2.30(weak) to 2.50(weak). Other factors: Capital and surplus increased during the period by 11.1%, from $99.6 million to $110.6 million.

US COASTAL INS CO was upgraded to C from C- in May 2018 based on an increase in the reserve adequacy index from a 3.60(fair) to 5.00(good), liquidity index from a 6.80(good) to 7.90(excellent), and profitability index from a 3.60(fair) to 3.70(fair).

US LEGAL SERVICES INC was upgraded to D+ from D in May 2018 based on an increase in the stability index from a 1.90(weak) to 2.00(weak) and reserve adequacy index from a 5.20(good) to 5.30(good).

US SPECIALTY INS CO was upgraded to B from B- in May 2018 based on an increase in the profitability index from a 3.80(fair) to 7.90(excellent), stability index from a 3.50(fair) to 5.40(good), and liquidity index from a 6.70(good) to 6.80(good).

USPLATE GLASS INS CO was upgraded to B- from C+ in May 2018 based on an increase in the stability index from a 3.10(fair) to 4.60(fair) and profitability index from a 8.10(excellent) to 8.20(excellent). Other factors: Capital and surplus increased during the period by 6.0%, from $24.3 million to $25.7 million.

UTICA NATIONAL INS CO OF OHIO was upgraded to B- from C+ in May 2018 based on an increase in the profitability index from a 6.70(good) to 8.90(excellent) and stability index from a 3.20(fair) to 4.90(good). Other factors: The company's net asset base increased during the period by 11.3%, from $18.5 million to $20.6 million.

VERTI INSURANCE CO was upgraded to D+ from D in May 2018 based on an increase in the liquidity index from a 5.20(good) to 7.70(excellent), capitalization index from a 6.40(good) to 8.20(excellent), profitability index from a 2.10(weak) to 3.80(fair), and stability index from a 2.30(weak) to 2.50(weak).

VFH CAPTIVE INS CO was upgraded to E+ from E in May 2018 based on an increase in the profitability index from a 0.50(weak) to 1.80(weak), reserve adequacy index from a 3.60(fair) to 4.70(fair), capitalization index from a 0.30(weak) to 1.00(weak), and stability index from a 0.00(weak) to 0.50(weak).

VICTORY INS CO was upgraded to D- from E+ in May 2018 based on an increase in the profitability index from a 2.10(weak) to 2.80(weak), reserve adequacy index from a 0.50(weak) to 1.00(weak), stability index from a 0.80(weak) to 1.20(weak), and liquidity index from a 7.20(excellent) to 7.40(excellent).

WAWANESA GENERAL INS CO was upgraded to B from B- in May 2018 based on an increase in the reserve adequacy index from a 4.40(fair) to 5.00(good) and stability index from a 5.30(good) to 5.40(good).

WAYNE COOPERATIVE INS CO was upgraded to C+ from C in May 2018 based on an increase in the stability index from a 2.80(weak) to 3.80(fair).

WAYNE MUTUAL INS CO was upgraded to B- from C+ in May 2018 based on an increase in the stability index from a 3.40(fair) to 5.30(good) and capitalization index from a 9.00(excellent) to 9.10(excellent).

WELLSPAN RRG was upgraded to D from D- in May 2018 based on an increase in the profitability index from a 7.30(excellent) to 9.10(excellent), stability index from a 1.00(weak) to 1.50(weak), capitalization index from a 7.10(excellent) to 7.50(excellent), and liquidity index from a 6.90(excellent) to 7.00(excellent). Other factors: Capital and surplus increased during the period by 34.0%, from $8.4 million to $11.2 million.

WEST BEND MUTUAL INS CO was upgraded to A- from B+ in May 2018 based on an increase in the stability index from a 5.10(good) to 7.00(excellent), capitalization index from a 8.60(excellent) to 8.90(excellent), and reserve adequacy index from a 8.90(excellent) to 9.00(excellent).

WEST VIRGINIA INS CO was upgraded to C+ from C in May 2018 based on an increase in the stability index from a 4.30(fair) to 4.50(fair).

WEST VIRGINIA MUTUAL INS CO was upgraded to C from C- in May 2018 based on an increase in the stability index from a 3.30(fair) to 3.50(fair).

WESTERN PACIFIC MUT INS CO RISK RET was upgraded to B from B- in May 2018 based on an increase in the stability index from a 3.70(fair) to 5.50(good) and profitability index from a 6.70(good) to 6.80(good).

WESTERN SURETY CO was upgraded to C+ from C in May 2018 based on an increase in the profitability index from a 8.20(excellent) to 8.40(excellent) and stability index from a 4.20(fair) to 4.40(fair).

WESTGUARD INS CO was upgraded to B from B- in May 2018 based on an increase in the stability index from a 4.40(fair) to 5.50(good), profitability index from a 7.50(excellent) to 8.20(excellent), and capitalization index from a 7.00(excellent) to 7.20(excellent). Other factors: Capital and surplus increased during the period by 7.0%, from $573.1 million to $613.4 million.

WESTMINSTER AMERICAN INS CO was upgraded to C+ from C in May 2018 based on an increase in the stability index from a 2.90(fair) to 4.10(fair) and liquidity index from a 7.60(excellent) to 8.10(excellent). Other factors: The company's net asset base increased during the period by 13.5%, from $34.1 million to $38.7 million.

WI LAWYERS MUTUAL INS CO was upgraded to B- from C+ in May 2018 based on an increase in the stability index from a 3.10(fair) to 4.70(fair) and reserve adequacy index from a 8.00(excellent) to 8.30(excellent).

WILSON MUTUAL INS CO was upgraded to B from B- in May 2018 based on an increase in the stability index from a 3.80(fair) to 5.40(good).

WINDSOR MOUNT JOY MUTUAL INS CO was upgraded to B from B- in May 2018 based on an increase in the stability index from a 3.60(fair) to 5.50(good) and liquidity index from a 7.00(excellent) to 7.50(excellent).

WISCONSIN MUTUAL INS CO was upgraded to B from B- in May 2018 based on an increase in the stability index from a 3.90(fair) to 5.50(good) and reserve adequacy index from a 6.90(excellent) to 8.40(excellent).

WOLVERINE MUTUAL INS CO was upgraded to B- from C+ in May 2018 based on an increase in the stability index from a 3.10(fair) to 4.60(fair), profitability index from a 8.00(excellent) to 8.40(excellent), reserve adequacy index from a 8.20(excellent) to 8.50(excellent), capitalization index from a 7.80(excellent) to 8.10(excellent), and liquidity index from a 6.30(good) to 6.40(good).

WORK FIRST CASUALTY CO was upgraded to C from C- in May 2018 based on an increase in the profitability index from a 3.10(fair) to 6.90(excellent), stability index from a 2.50(weak) to 3.40(fair), and liquidity index from a 6.20(good) to 6.50(good). Other factors: Capital and surplus increased during the period by 5.5%, from $14.3 million to $15.1 million.

WORKMENS AUTO INS CO was upgraded to D+ from D in May 2018 based on an increase in the reserve adequacy index from a 0.60(weak) to 2.20(weak), capitalization index from a 5.80(good) to 6.50(good), stability index from a 1.90(weak) to 2.40(weak), profitability index from a 3.60(fair) to 3.90(fair), and liquidity index from a 5.70(good) to 5.90(good). Other factors: Capital and surplus increased during the period by 13.7%, from $19.8 million to $22.5 million.

XL SELECT INS CO was upgraded to D+ from D in May 2018 based on an increase in the stability index from a 2.30(weak) to 2.50(weak) and reserve adequacy index from a 6.30(good) to 6.40(good). Other factors: The company's net asset base increased during the period by 8.3%, from $147.9 million to $160.3 million.

ZALE INDEMNITY CO was upgraded to B- from C+ in May 2018 based on an increase in the stability index from a 3.10(fair) to 4.60(fair), profitability index from a 7.50(excellent) to 8.50(excellent), and capitalization index from a 6.80(good) to 7.40(excellent).

ZEPHYR INS CO was upgraded to C+ from C in May 2018 based on an increase in the stability index from a 4.00(fair) to 4.50(fair) and liquidity index from a 8.70(excellent) to 9.10(excellent).

ZURICH AMERICAN INS CO was upgraded to B from B- in May 2018 based on an increase in the stability index from a 3.50(fair) to 5.40(good), reserve adequacy index from a 6.00(good) to 6.10(good), and capitalization index from a 7.90(excellent) to 8.00(excellent).

Rating Downgrades

ACCC INS CO was downgraded to E+ from D in May 2018 based on a decrease in the reserve adequacy index from a 1.80(weak) to 0.50(weak), stability index from a 2.00(weak) to 0.80(weak), and capitalization index from a 2.20(weak) to 1.90(weak).

ACCESS INS CO, was downgraded to F having been placed into liquidation by the state insurance regulator in March 2018.

AEGIS SECURITY INS CO was downgraded to D+ from C+ in May 2018 based on a decrease in the liquidity index from a 2.80(weak) to 0.70(weak), profitability index from a 5.10(good) to 3.30(fair), capitalization index from a 3.60(fair) to 2.00(weak), stability index from a 3.60(fair) to 2.70(weak), and reserve adequacy index from a 8.40(excellent) to 7.90(excellent).

AMERICAN ACCESS CASUALTY CO was downgraded to D from D+ in May 2018 based on a decrease in the liquidity index from a 2.10(weak) to 0.70(weak), capitalization index from a 2.20(weak) to 1.60(weak), stability index from a 2.80(weak) to 2.20(weak), profitability index from a 4.10(fair) to 3.80(fair), and reserve adequacy index from a 2.00(weak) to 1.90(weak).

AMERICAN COUNTRY INS CO was downgraded to D- from C in May 2018 based on a decrease in the capitalization index from a 6.00(good) to 0.70(weak), liquidity index from a 5.10(good) to 0.50(weak), profitability index from a 5.80(good) to 1.90(weak), stability index from a 3.50(fair) to 1.00(weak), and reserve adequacy index from a 2.30(weak) to 0.70(weak). Other factors: Capital and surplus decreased during the period by 48.3%, from $27.1 million to $18.3 million.

AMERICAN EMPIRE SURPLUS LINES INS CO was downgraded to C- from C in May 2018 based on a decrease in the reserve adequacy index from a 3.10(fair) to 1.90(weak), stability index from a 4.00(fair) to 2.90(fair), liquidity index from a 7.20(excellent) to 6.50(good), and profitability index from a 5.60(good) to 5.00(good).

AMERICAN TRUCKING & TRANSP INS RRG was downgraded to E- from E+ in May 2018 based on a decrease in the liquidity index from a 7.00(excellent) to 2.80(weak), profitability index from a 1.80(weak) to 0.30(weak), reserve adequacy index from a 5.70(good) to 4.90(good), stability index from a 0.70(weak) to 0.10(weak), and capitalization index from a 0.50(weak) to 0.00(weak). Other factors: The company's net asset base decreased during the period by 7.0%, from $43.9 million to $41.1 million. Capital and surplus decreased during the period by 197.4%, from $7.1 million to $2.4 million.

A-ONE COMM INS RRG GROUP INC was downgraded to E from E+ in May 2018 based on a decrease in the reserve adequacy index from a 3.60(fair) to 2.10(weak), stability index from a 0.80(weak) to 0.20(weak), and capitalization index from a 0.50(weak) to 0.10(weak).

ASI ASR CORP was downgraded to B- from B in May 2018 based on a decrease in the liquidity index from a 7.10(excellent) to 6.30(good), stability index from a 5.60(good) to 5.10(good), profitability index from a 3.80(fair) to 3.30(fair), and reserve adequacy index from a 9.50(excellent) to 9.40(excellent). Other factors: The company's net asset base decreased during the period by 9.4%, from $140.5 million to $128.4 million.

ASI PREFERRED INS CORP was downgraded to C+ from B in May 2018 based on a decrease in the stability index from a 5.40(good) to 4.50(fair) and profitability index from a 3.50(fair) to 3.00(fair). Other factors: The company's net asset base decreased during the period by 5.6%, from $112.6 million to $106.7 million. Capital and surplus decreased during the period by 5.7%, from $35.5 million to $33.6 million.

ASPEN AMERICAN INS CO was downgraded to C+ from B in May 2018 based on a decrease in the reserve adequacy index from a 4.80(fair) to 3.00(fair) and profitability index from a 4.20(fair) to 3.60(fair).

ASPEN SPECIALTY INS CO was downgraded to D from D+ in May 2018 based on a decrease in the reserve adequacy index from a 6.20(good) to 3.80(fair), stability index from a 2.70(weak) to 2.20(weak), capitalization index from a 2.00(weak) to 1.50(weak), and liquidity index from a 7.20(excellent) to 6.90(excellent). Other factors: The company's net asset base decreased during the period by 16.6%, from $468.5 million to $401.7 million.

ASSOCIATED INDUSTRIES INS CO INC was downgraded to C- from C in May 2018 based on a decrease in the liquidity index from a 7.40(excellent) to 1.80(weak), profitability index from a 7.20(excellent) to 2.00(weak), and stability index from a 4.30(fair) to 3.20(fair). Other factors: The company's net asset base decreased during the period by 59.4%, from $390.3 million to $245.0 million. Capital and surplus decreased during the period by 133.8%, from $113.1 million to $48.4 million.

BUCKEYE STATE MUTUAL INS CO was downgraded to C from C+ in May 2018 based on a decrease in the profitability index from a 3.30(fair) to 2.30(weak), liquidity index from a 3.20(fair) to 2.40(weak), reserve adequacy index from a 9.30(excellent) to 8.60(excellent), and capitalization index from a 7.20(excellent) to 7.10(excellent). Other factors: The company's net asset base decreased during the period by 5.6%, from $58.0 million to $55.0 million.

CALIFORNIA CAPITAL INS CO was downgraded to C- from B- in May 2018 based on a decrease in the reserve adequacy index from a 5.60(good) to 3.80(fair), stability index from a 4.70(fair) to 3.10(fair), profitability index from a 3.10(fair) to 1.80(weak), liquidity index from a 6.50(good) to 5.80(good), and capitalization index from a 7.50(excellent) to 7.30(excellent). Other factors: Capital and surplus decreased during the period by 13.9%, from $250.4 million to $219.8 million.

CALIFORNIA CAS GEN INS CO OF OREGON was downgraded to C- from C in May 2018 based on a decrease in the liquidity index from a 6.00(good) to 3.10(fair), capitalization index from a 7.20(excellent) to 5.70(good), profitability index from a 1.90(weak) to 1.50(weak), reserve adequacy index from a 6.30(good) to 6.10(good), and stability index from a 3.30(fair) to 3.20(fair). Other factors: Capital and surplus decreased during the period by 15.4%, from $22.1 million to $19.1 million.

CALIFORNIA CASUALTY INS CO was downgraded to C from C+ in May 2018 based on a decrease in the profitability index from a 2.60(weak) to 2.40(weak), liquidity index from a 6.80(good) to 6.60(good), stability index from a 3.90(fair) to 3.70(fair), and reserve adequacy index from a 6.10(good) to 6.00(good). Other factors: The company's net asset base decreased during the period by 5.6%, from $97.3 million to $92.1 million. Capital and surplus decreased during the period by 13.3%, from $62.4 million to $55.1 million.

CIVIL SERVICE EMPLOYEES INS CO was downgraded to C from B- in May 2018 based on a decrease in the profitability index from a 3.10(fair) to 2.20(weak), stability index from a 4.60(fair) to 4.10(fair), liquidity index from a 6.20(good) to 6.00(good), capitalization index from a 8.30(excellent) to 8.20(excellent), and reserve adequacy index from a 6.10(good) to 6.00(good).

COMPTRUST AGC MUT CAPTIVE INS CO was downgraded to C- from C in May 2018 based on a decrease in the capitalization index from a 5.60(good) to 2.80(weak), profitability index from a 4.50(fair) to 3.10(fair), liquidity index from a 6.90(excellent) to 6.30(good), and stability index from a 3.60(fair) to 3.10(fair). Other factors: The company's net asset base decreased during the period by 14.3%, from $37.2 million to $32.5 million. Capital and surplus decreased during the period by 53.0%, from $16.0 million to $10.5 million.

CONSUMERS INS USA INC was downgraded to C+ from B in May 2018 based on a decrease in the stability index from a 5.60(good) to 4.40(fair), profitability index from a 3.80(fair) to 2.80(weak), capitalization index from a 8.60(excellent) to 8.00(excellent), and liquidity index from a 6.90(excellent) to 6.50(good). Other factors: The company's net asset base decreased during the period by 10.2%, from $72.4 million to $65.7 million.

COPIC INS CO was downgraded to B+ from A- in May 2018 based on a decrease in the profitability index from a 7.70(excellent) to 4.30(fair), liquidity index from a 8.10(excellent) to 7.50(excellent), stability index from a 7.30(excellent) to 6.80(good), reserve adequacy index from a 9.40(excellent) to 9.30(excellent), and capitalization index from a 10.00(excellent) to 9.90(excellent). Other factors: The company's net asset base decreased during the period by 26.9%, from $765.4 million to $603.2 million. Capital and surplus decreased during the period by 43.9%, from $428.4 million to $297.7 million.

CORNERSTONE NATIONAL INS CO was downgraded to D+ from C- in May 2018 based on a decrease in the liquidity index from a 3.00(fair) to 0.90(weak), profitability index from a 2.00(weak) to 1.50(weak), and stability index from a 3.00(fair) to 2.70(weak). Other factors: The company's net asset base decreased during the period by 8.9%, from $27.4 million to $25.2 million.

CROSSFIT RRG INC was downgraded to E+ from D in May 2018 based on a decrease in the liquidity index from a 7.00(excellent) to 1.30(weak), profitability index from a 4.80(fair) to 1.80(weak), stability index from a 1.70(weak) to 0.80(weak), and capitalization index from a 1.40(weak) to 0.50(weak). Other factors: Capital and surplus decreased during the period by 25.3%, from $2.0 million to $1.6 million.

CRUSADER INS CO was downgraded to C+ from B- in May 2018 based on a decrease in the reserve adequacy index from a 9.20(excellent) to 6.30(good), liquidity index from a 8.00(excellent) to 6.90(excellent), profitability index from a 3.20(fair) to 2.50(weak), and capitalization index from a 9.70(excellent) to 9.30(excellent). Other factors: Capital and surplus decreased during the period by 8.3%, from $54.6 million to $50.4 million.

CSE SAFEGUARD INS CO was downgraded to C from C+ in May 2018 based on a decrease in the profitability index from a 3.40(fair) to 2.10(weak), capitalization index from a 9.10(excellent) to 8.30(excellent), reserve adequacy index from a 6.20(good) to 5.90(good), and stability index from a 3.70(fair) to 3.60(fair).

DB INS CO LTD (US BRANCH) was downgraded to E+ from D in May 2018 based on a decrease in the stability index from a 1.40(weak) to 0.80(weak) and reserve adequacy index from a 0.90(weak) to 0.50(weak).

Rating Downgrades (Continued)

DIAMOND STATE INS CO was downgraded to C from B- in May 2018 based on a decrease in the capitalization index from a 8.70(excellent) to 7.60(excellent), profitability index from a 3.30(fair) to 2.90(fair), and liquidity index from a 7.00(excellent) to 6.70(good). Other factors: The company's net asset base decreased during the period by 6.3%, from $103.6 million to $97.4 million.

EAGLE WEST INS CO was downgraded to C- from C+ in May 2018 based on a decrease in the profitability index from a 3.50(fair) to 1.50(weak), liquidity index from a 5.80(good) to 3.90(fair), stability index from a 4.70(fair) to 2.90(fair), capitalization index from a 7.50(excellent) to 6.10(good), and reserve adequacy index from a 4.40(fair) to 3.20(fair). Other factors: Capital and surplus decreased during the period by 23.3%, from $43.5 million to $35.2 million.

ECHELON P&C INS CO was downgraded to E from D in May 2018 based on a decrease in the liquidity index from a 5.60(good) to 2.60(weak), stability index from a 2.00(weak) to 0.20(weak), capitalization index from a 1.60(weak) to 0.10(weak), reserve adequacy index from a 2.20(weak) to 1.40(weak), and profitability index from a 1.60(weak) to 0.80(weak). Other factors: Capital and surplus decreased during the period by 69.3%, from $4.1 million to $2.4 million.

EVEREST NATIONAL INS CO was downgraded to C from C+ in May 2018 based on a decrease in the stability index from a 4.50(fair) to 4.00(fair) and reserve adequacy index from a 2.90(fair) to 2.60(weak). Other factors: The company's net asset base decreased during the period by 24.6%, from $1007.7 million to $808.5 million.

FBALLIANCE INS CO was downgraded to B- from B in May 2018 based on a decrease in the stability index from a 4.00(fair) to 3.50(fair) and profitability index from a 2.60(weak) to 2.20(weak).

FD INS CO was downgraded to C from C+ in May 2018 based on a decrease in the stability index from a 4.40(fair) to 2.90(fair) and profitability index from a 3.90(fair) to 2.40(weak). Other factors: The company's net asset base decreased during the period by 118.4%, from $28.2 million to $12.9 million. Capital and surplus decreased during the period by 91.6%, from $21.3 million to $11.1 million.

FEDERAL INS CO was downgraded to C+ from B- in May 2018 based on a decrease in the profitability index from a 3.30(fair) to 2.20(weak) and liquidity index from a 6.80(good) to 6.60(good). Other factors: The company's net asset base decreased during the period by 25.4%, from $27298.2 million to $21770.0 million. Capital and surplus decreased during the period by 62.3%, from $11843.0 million to $7296.7 million.

FIRST ACCEPTANCE INS CO OF TN INC was downgraded to D from D+ in May 2018 based on a decrease in the reserve adequacy index from a 5.80(good) to 3.70(fair), liquidity index from a 1.40(weak) to 0.00(weak), and stability index from a 2.80(weak) to 2.00(weak). Other factors: The company's net asset base decreased during the period by 15.2%, from $31.7 million to $27.5 million.

FIRST NONPROFIT INS CO was downgraded to C- from C in May 2018 based on a decrease in the liquidity index from a 7.10(excellent) to 1.70(weak), profitability index from a 2.30(weak) to 1.90(weak), and stability index from a 3.40(fair) to 3.10(fair). Other factors: The company's net asset base decreased during the period by 45.0%, from $59.5 million to $41.1 million. Capital and surplus decreased during the period by 51.5%, from $23.8 million to $15.7 million.

FLORIDA SPECIALTY INS CO was downgraded to D from C- in May 2018 based on a decrease in the liquidity index from a 6.80(good) to 2.60(weak), reserve adequacy index from a 7.30(excellent) to 6.00(good), stability index from a 2.90(fair) to 2.30(weak), capitalization index from a 4.50(fair) to 4.00(fair), and profitability index from a 1.30(weak) to 1.10(weak). Other factors: Capital and surplus decreased during the period by 13.5%, from $17.0 million to $15.0 million.

GATEWAY INS CO was downgraded to D- from D in May 2018 based on a decrease in the capitalization index from a 3.00(fair) to 0.90(weak), reserve adequacy index from a 2.30(weak) to 0.80(weak), stability index from a 2.30(weak) to 1.20(weak), and profitability index from a 2.90(fair) to 1.80(weak). Other factors: Capital and surplus decreased during the period by 62.5%, from $19.8 million to $12.2 million.

GERMANIA SELECT INS CO was downgraded to C from B- in May 2018 based on a decrease in the liquidity index from a 2.60(weak) to 1.50(weak), stability index from a 5.10(good) to 4.10(fair), reserve adequacy index from a 6.40(good) to 5.80(good), capitalization index from a 8.00(excellent) to 7.70(excellent), and profitability index from a 2.40(weak) to 2.10(weak). Other factors: The company's net asset base decreased during the period by 5.1%, from $222.1 million to $211.2 million. Capital and surplus decreased during the period by 6.7%, from $65.3 million to $61.1 million.

GLOBAL LIBERTY INS CO OF NY was downgraded to D- from D in May 2018 based on a decrease in the capitalization index from a 7.30(excellent) to 2.10(weak), profitability index from a 5.70(good) to 2.00(weak), stability index from a 2.30(weak) to 1.20(weak), liquidity index from a 6.30(good) to 5.20(good), and reserve adequacy index from a 1.80(weak) to 0.80(weak). Other factors: Capital and surplus decreased during the period by 56.4%, from $23.7 million to $15.1 million.

GOLDEN INS CO A RRG was downgraded to E+ from D- in May 2018 based on a decrease in the capitalization index from a 1.60(weak) to 0.30(weak), profitability index from a 2.70(weak) to 1.50(weak), stability index from a 1.30(weak) to 0.50(weak), and liquidity index from a 7.60(excellent) to 7.50(excellent). Other factors: Capital and surplus decreased during the period by 41.8%, from $3.1 million to $2.2 million.

GUARDIAN INS CO was downgraded to C- from C in May 2018 based on a decrease in the profitability index from a 2.70(weak) to 2.00(weak), capitalization index from a 7.50(excellent) to 7.30(excellent), and reserve adequacy index from a 5.90(good) to 5.80(good). Other factors: The company's net asset base decreased during the period by 33.4%, from $49.6 million to $37.2 million. Capital and surplus decreased during the period by 20.4%, from $13.8 million to $11.5 million.

GUIDEONE MUTUAL INS CO was downgraded to C from B- in May 2018 based on a decrease in the reserve adequacy index from a 8.60(excellent) to 6.60(good), stability index from a 4.40(fair) to 3.80(fair), liquidity index from a 6.60(good) to 6.00(good), and profitability index from a 2.20(weak) to 1.80(weak). Other factors: The company's net asset base decreased during the period by 6.3%, from $1114.7 million to $1049.1 million.

GUIDEONE P&C INS CO was downgraded to C+ from B in May 2018 based on a decrease in the reserve adequacy index from a 8.00(excellent) to 6.30(good), capitalization index from a 8.50(excellent) to 8.00(excellent), liquidity index from a 6.80(good) to 6.50(good), and profitability index from a 2.60(weak) to 2.40(weak). Other factors: The company's net asset base decreased during the period by 12.1%, from $424.3 million to $378.4 million.

GUIDEONE SPECIALTY MUTUAL INS CO was downgraded to C from B in May 2018 based on a decrease in the reserve adequacy index from a 8.90(excellent) to 6.70(good), profitability index from a 3.00(fair) to 2.00(weak), capitalization index from a 8.10(excellent) to 7.20(excellent), liquidity index from a 6.60(good) to 6.00(good), and stability index from a 4.40(fair) to 3.90(fair). Other factors: The company's net asset base decreased during the period by 16.4%, from $263.9 million to $226.6 million.

GULFSTREAM P&C INS CO was downgraded to C+ from B- in May 2018 based on a decrease in the reserve adequacy index from a 9.30(excellent) to 8.70(excellent), profitability index from a 3.50(fair) to 2.90(fair), and stability index from a 5.20(good) to 4.70(fair). Other factors: The company's net asset base decreased during the period by 7.9%, from $118.8 million to $110.1 million.

HANOVER INS CO was downgraded to B- from B in May 2018 based on a decrease in the reserve adequacy index from a 3.40(fair) to 3.10(fair) and liquidity index from a 6.00(good) to 5.90(good).

HARLEYSVILLE INS CO OF NJ was downgraded to C- from C in May 2018 based on a decrease in the liquidity index from a 10.00(excellent) to 7.00(excellent), profitability index from a 3.50(fair) to 1.90(weak), stability index from a 3.60(fair) to 3.20(fair), and reserve adequacy index from a 3.90(fair) to 3.60(fair). Other factors: The company's net asset base decreased during the period by 45.2%, from $89.5 million to $61.6 million. Capital and surplus decreased during the period by 120.1%, from $48.4 million to $22.0 million.

HARLEYSVILLE LAKE STATES INS CO was downgraded to C- from C in May 2018 based on a decrease in the profitability index from a 3.60(fair) to 2.00(weak), stability index from a 3.80(fair) to 3.30(fair), and reserve adequacy index from a 3.90(fair) to 3.60(fair). Other factors: The company's net asset base decreased during the period by 68.0%, from $60.7 million to $36.2 million. Capital and surplus decreased during the period by 105.5%, from $39.7 million to $19.3 million.

HARTFORD FIRE INS CO was downgraded to C+ from B in May 2018 based on a decrease in the profitability index from a 3.80(fair) to 3.00(fair), stability index from a 5.10(good) to 4.80(fair), and reserve adequacy index from a 6.00(good) to 5.90(good). Other factors: The company's net asset base decreased during the period by 11.8%, from $25552.7 million to $22855.3 million. Capital and surplus decreased during the period by 25.7%, from $12463.4 million to $9916.0 million.

HARTFORD SM BOIL INSPECTION & INS was downgraded to B- from B in May 2018 based on a decrease in the stability index from a 6.10(good) to 5.10(good), capitalization index from a 8.90(excellent) to 8.10(excellent), profitability index from a 3.90(fair) to 3.30(fair), liquidity index from a 6.90(excellent) to 6.70(good), and reserve adequacy index from a 8.70(excellent) to 8.50(excellent). Other factors: Capital and surplus decreased during the period by 9.3%, from $550.5 million to $503.6 million.

Rating Downgrades (Continued)

HEALTHCARE PROVIDERS INS EXCH, was downgraded to F having been placed into liquidation by the state insurance regulator in January 2018.

HEREFORD INS CO was downgraded to D- from C in May 2018 based on a decrease in the reserve adequacy index from a 3.10(fair) to 0.70(weak), stability index from a 3.20(fair) to 1.10(weak), capitalization index from a 6.40(good) to 4.80(fair), and profitability index from a 5.90(good) to 5.80(good). Other factors: The company's net asset base decreased during the period by 5.2%, from $210.3 million to $199.9 million. Capital and surplus decreased during the period by 5.5%, from $37.8 million to $35.8 million.

HOMEOWNERS OF AMERICA INS CO was downgraded to D from C- in May 2018 based on a decrease in the liquidity index from a 6.90(excellent) to 0.00(weak), stability index from a 3.30(fair) to 2.00(weak), profitability index from a 7.10(excellent) to 6.30(good), and capitalization index from a 7.50(excellent) to 7.40(excellent). Other factors: The company's net asset base decreased during the period by 15.5%, from $65.2 million to $56.4 million.

IOWA MUTUAL INS CO was downgraded to B- from B in May 2018 based on a decrease in the profitability index from a 3.80(fair) to 2.40(weak), reserve adequacy index from a 7.60(excellent) to 6.20(good), liquidity index from a 6.60(good) to 6.20(good), and capitalization index from a 7.50(excellent) to 7.30(excellent). Other factors: The company's net asset base decreased during the period by 11.9%, from $105.1 million to $93.9 million. Capital and surplus decreased during the period by 9.1%, from $30.7 million to $28.1 million.

KEY INS CO was downgraded to D- from D in May 2018 based on a decrease in the reserve adequacy index from a 2.60(weak) to 1.30(weak), stability index from a 1.50(weak) to 1.10(weak), and capitalization index from a 0.60(weak) to 0.30(weak).

LANCER INS CO was downgraded to B- from B in May 2018 based on a decrease in the reserve adequacy index from a 3.50(fair) to 3.30(fair), profitability index from a 6.20(good) to 6.10(good), and liquidity index from a 6.80(good) to 6.70(good).

LE MARS INS CO was downgraded to C from C+ in May 2018 based on a decrease in the liquidity index from a 6.60(good) to 6.10(good), profitability index from a 2.70(weak) to 2.50(weak), and capitalization index from a 7.60(excellent) to 7.50(excellent).

LIGHTHOUSE CASUALTY CO was downgraded to E+ from D- in May 2018 based on a decrease in the reserve adequacy index from a 1.00(weak) to 0.40(weak), stability index from a 1.20(weak) to 0.70(weak), and profitability index from a 2.90(fair) to 2.80(weak).

MAIDEN RE NORTH AMERICA INC was downgraded to C+ from B- in May 2018 based on a decrease in the reserve adequacy index from a 4.30(fair) to 3.10(fair), stability index from a 5.30(good) to 4.80(fair), and liquidity index from a 5.60(good) to 5.50(good).

MEDMAL DIRECT INS CO was downgraded to C+ from B- in May 2018 based on a decrease in the capitalization index from a 7.00(excellent) to 4.60(fair), reserve adequacy index from a 6.40(good) to 4.20(fair), profitability index from a 4.60(fair) to 3.30(fair), and liquidity index from a 7.40(excellent) to 6.90(excellent). Other factors: Capital and surplus decreased during the period by 20.9%, from $20.4 million to $16.8 million.

METROMILE INS CO was downgraded to D from C in May 2018 based on a decrease in the liquidity index from a 9.60(excellent) to 2.90(fair), capitalization index from a 7.30(excellent) to 1.30(weak), and stability index from a 2.50(weak) to 2.00(weak). Other factors: Capital and surplus decreased during the period by 5.5%, from $13.6 million to $12.9 million.

MONTEREY INS CO was downgraded to C- from C+ in May 2018 based on a decrease in the capitalization index from a 6.70(good) to 3.80(fair), liquidity index from a 5.80(good) to 3.50(fair), profitability index from a 3.30(fair) to 1.40(weak), reserve adequacy index from a 4.40(fair) to 3.20(fair), and stability index from a 3.70(fair) to 3.10(fair). Other factors: Capital and surplus decreased during the period by 26.6%, from $27.7 million to $21.9 million.

MOTORISTS MUTUAL INS CO was downgraded to C+ from B+ in May 2018 based on a decrease in the reserve adequacy index from a 7.80(excellent) to 6.30(good), profitability index from a 3.60(fair) to 2.20(weak), stability index from a 5.10(good) to 4.50(fair), capitalization index from a 8.40(excellent) to 7.90(excellent), and liquidity index from a 6.40(good) to 6.00(good). Other factors: The company's net asset base decreased during the period by 5.4%, from $1444.7 million to $1370.8 million. Capital and surplus decreased during the period by 5.3%, from $485.2 million to $460.7 million.

NATIONAL PUBLIC FINANCE GUAR CORP was downgraded to D+ from B in May 2018 based on a decrease in the profitability index from a 5.80(good) to 2.70(weak), stability index from a 5.10(good) to 2.40(weak), reserve adequacy index from a 5.80(good) to 4.20(fair), and liquidity index from a 9.80(excellent) to 9.00(excellent). Other factors: The company's net asset base decreased during the period by 10.6%, from $4151.3 million to $3753.9 million. Capital and surplus decreased during the period by 18.9%, from $2575.1 million to $2165.9 million.

NATIONWIDE MUTUAL FIRE INS CO was downgraded to C+ from B+ in May 2018 based on a decrease in the liquidity index from a 6.40(good) to 5.10(good), capitalization index from a 9.20(excellent) to 7.90(excellent), profitability index from a 3.60(fair) to 2.40(weak), stability index from a 5.10(good) to 4.80(fair), and reserve adequacy index from a 6.00(good) to 5.90(good). Other factors: Capital and surplus decreased during the period by 6.4%, from $2533.3 million to $2380.3 million.

NEVADA CAPITAL INS CO was downgraded to C from B in May 2018 based on a decrease in the stability index from a 5.70(good) to 3.60(fair), profitability index from a 3.60(fair) to 1.90(weak), reserve adequacy index from a 4.90(good) to 3.70(fair), liquidity index from a 6.00(good) to 5.20(good), and capitalization index from a 8.00(excellent) to 7.40(excellent). Other factors: Capital and surplus decreased during the period by 13.9%, from $46.0 million to $40.3 million.

NEW JERSEY SKYLANDS INS ASSN was downgraded to D- from D+ in May 2018 based on a decrease in the liquidity index from a 6.80(good) to 0.10(weak), capitalization index from a 3.00(fair) to 1.00(weak), stability index from a 2.50(weak) to 1.30(weak), profitability index from a 1.70(weak) to 1.10(weak), and reserve adequacy index from a 2.00(weak) to 1.80(weak). Other factors: Capital and surplus decreased during the period by 80.8%, from $14.7 million to $8.1 million.

OLYMPUS INS CO was downgraded to D+ from C in May 2018 based on a decrease in the capitalization index from a 7.90(excellent) to 2.40(weak) and stability index from a 3.80(fair) to 2.70(weak). Other factors: The company's net asset base decreased during the period by 15.3%, from $90.8 million to $78.8 million.

OMEGA INS CO was downgraded to C- from C in May 2018 based on a decrease in the liquidity index from a 7.00(excellent) to 4.70(fair), profitability index from a 3.30(fair) to 1.80(weak), reserve adequacy index from a 3.70(fair) to 3.40(fair), and stability index from a 3.20(fair) to 3.00(fair). Other factors: The company's net asset base decreased during the period by 18.7%, from $50.2 million to $42.3 million. Capital and surplus decreased during the period by 12.1%, from $14.7 million to $13.1 million.

PALMETTO SURETY CORP was downgraded to D from D+ in May 2018 based on a decrease in the liquidity index from a 6.70(good) to 2.00(weak), profitability index from a 4.90(good) to 3.80(fair), capitalization index from a 1.70(weak) to 0.80(weak), and stability index from a 2.10(weak) to 1.50(weak). Other factors: Capital and surplus decreased during the period by 14.2%, from $4.7 million to $4.1 million.

PALOMAR SPECIALTY INS CO was downgraded to D- from C- in May 2018 based on a decrease in the liquidity index from a 6.10(good) to 1.70(weak), capitalization index from a 2.50(weak) to 0.80(weak), stability index from a 2.20(weak) to 1.30(weak), and profitability index from a 4.00(fair) to 3.40(fair). Other factors: Capital and surplus decreased during the period by 5.2%, from $64.5 million to $61.4 million.

PENINSULA INS CO was downgraded to C from C+ in May 2018 based on a decrease in the profitability index from a 4.10(fair) to 3.10(fair), reserve adequacy index from a 5.80(good) to 4.90(good), and capitalization index from a 8.90(excellent) to 8.40(excellent). Other factors: Capital and surplus decreased during the period by 5.9%, from $41.7 million to $39.4 million.

PHENIX MUTUAL FIRE INS CO was downgraded to C from B- in May 2018 based on a decrease in the reserve adequacy index from a 7.90(excellent) to 6.30(good), profitability index from a 3.80(fair) to 2.20(weak), stability index from a 3.90(fair) to 3.40(fair), liquidity index from a 6.40(good) to 6.00(good), and capitalization index from a 7.70(excellent) to 7.30(excellent). Other factors: The company's net asset base decreased during the period by 9.2%, from $73.5 million to $67.3 million. Capital and surplus decreased during the period by 5.2%, from $19.7 million to $18.8 million.

PLATINUM TRANSPORT INS RRG INC was downgraded to E- from D- in May 2018 based on a decrease in the capitalization index from a 1.90(weak) to 0.00(weak), profitability index from a 1.80(weak) to 0.20(weak), liquidity index from a 8.50(excellent) to 7.30(excellent), and stability index from a 0.80(weak) to 0.10(weak).

RELIAMAX SURETY CO was downgraded to C from C+ in May 2018 based on a decrease in the profitability index from a 3.80(fair) to 2.90(fair), liquidity index from a 7.30(excellent) to 6.50(good), stability index from a 4.30(fair) to 4.10(fair), reserve adequacy index from a 8.20(excellent) to 8.10(excellent), and capitalization index from a 8.70(excellent) to 8.60(excellent).

Rating Downgrades (Continued)

SAFEPOINT INS CO was downgraded to C from C+ in May 2018 based on a decrease in the reserve adequacy index from a 3.00(fair) to 2.40(weak), liquidity index from a 6.80(good) to 6.30(good), and capitalization index from a 7.30(excellent) to 7.10(excellent).

SAMSUNG FIRE & MARINE INS CO LTD US was downgraded to D- from D in May 2018 based on a decrease in the stability index from a 2.30(weak) to 0.90(weak), reserve adequacy index from a 1.90(weak) to 0.60(weak), liquidity index from a 8.10(excellent) to 7.00(excellent), and profitability index from a 2.20(weak) to 2.10(weak). Other factors: The company's net asset base decreased during the period by 136.8%, from $231.1 million to $97.6 million. Capital and surplus decreased during the period by 8.1%, from $62.4 million to $57.7 million.

SECURITY NATIONAL INS CO was downgraded to C from B in May 2018 based on a decrease in the capitalization index from a 7.00(excellent) to 0.10(weak), profitability index from a 7.60(excellent) to 2.90(fair), liquidity index from a 6.80(good) to 2.70(weak), and stability index from a 4.70(fair) to 4.20(fair). Other factors: The company's net asset base decreased during the period by 11.8%, from $1245.5 million to $1114.1 million. Capital and surplus decreased during the period by 74.7%, from $190.4 million to $109.0 million.

SEQUOIA INDEMNITY CO was downgraded to C from B- in May 2018 based on a decrease in the profitability index from a 6.30(good) to 3.10(fair). Other factors: The company's net asset base decreased during the period by 52.3%, from $12.0 million to $7.9 million. Capital and surplus decreased during the period by 39.3%, from $10.3 million to $7.4 million.

SEQUOIA INS CO was downgraded to C- from C in May 2018 based on a decrease in the liquidity index from a 9.30(excellent) to 6.40(good) and profitability index from a 3.10(fair) to 1.90(weak). Other factors: The company's net asset base decreased during the period by 51.0%, from $230.1 million to $152.4 million. Capital and surplus decreased during the period by 183.2%, from $96.3 million to $34.0 million.

SHELTER GENERAL INS CO was downgraded to C from C+ in May 2018 based on a decrease in the capitalization index from a 8.40(excellent) to 7.70(excellent), profitability index from a 2.80(weak) to 2.20(weak), and liquidity index from a 6.30(good) to 6.20(good). Other factors: Capital and surplus decreased during the period by 19.3%, from $70.1 million to $58.8 million.

SOUTHERN TRUST INS CO was downgraded to C from B in May 2018 based on a decrease in the profitability index from a 3.80(fair) to 2.50(weak), liquidity index from a 6.20(good) to 5.30(good), stability index from a 4.70(fair) to 4.10(fair), and reserve adequacy index from a 6.10(good) to 5.80(good).

SPIRIT COMMERCIAL AUTO RRG INC was downgraded to E- from E in May 2018 based on a decrease in the liquidity index from a 7.00(excellent) to 0.00(weak) and profitability index from a 2.10(weak) to 1.50(weak). Other factors: Capital and surplus decreased during the period by 34.5%, from $18.0 million to $13.4 million.

STAR CASUALTY INS CO was downgraded to D- from D in May 2018 based on a decrease in the capitalization index from a 2.40(weak) to 1.40(weak), stability index from a 1.80(weak) to 1.20(weak), and reserve adequacy index from a 1.40(weak) to 0.80(weak).

STATE FARM GENERAL INS CO was downgraded to C from B in May 2018 based on a decrease in the profitability index from a 8.40(excellent) to 2.20(weak), capitalization index from a 10.00(excellent) to 7.60(excellent), liquidity index from a 6.70(good) to 5.60(good), stability index from a 5.00(good) to 4.20(fair), and reserve adequacy index from a 6.40(good) to 6.10(good). Other factors: Capital and surplus decreased during the period by 30.3%, from $4152.6 million to $3186.9 million.

STONEGATE INS CO was downgraded to D- from D in May 2018 based on a decrease in the liquidity index from a 6.20(good) to 5.30(good), stability index from a 1.50(weak) to 1.10(weak), and reserve adequacy index from a 0.80(weak) to 0.50(weak). Other factors: The company's net asset base decreased during the period by 14.8%, from $30.1 million to $26.2 million.

TECHNOLOGY INS CO was downgraded to D- from C in May 2018 based on a decrease in the capitalization index from a 5.00(good) to 0.90(weak), liquidity index from a 5.60(good) to 1.60(weak), stability index from a 3.60(fair) to 1.20(weak), and profitability index from a 3.70(fair) to 2.80(weak).

THE INS CO was downgraded to C- from C in May 2018 based on a decrease in the reserve adequacy index from a 7.00(excellent) to 4.10(fair), stability index from a 4.20(fair) to 3.20(fair), capitalization index from a 5.80(good) to 5.10(good), liquidity index from a 6.80(good) to 6.30(good), and profitability index from a 2.10(weak) to 1.80(weak).

TOWER HILL SELECT INS CO was downgraded to C- from C in May 2018 based on a decrease in the liquidity index from a 6.60(good) to 3.00(fair), capitalization index from a 5.90(good) to 4.40(fair), profitability index from a 2.90(fair) to 1.90(weak), stability index from a 4.10(fair) to 3.10(fair), and reserve adequacy index from a 3.10(fair) to 2.80(weak). Other factors: The company's net asset base decreased during the period by 12.4%, from $84.2 million to $75.0 million. Capital and surplus decreased during the period by 13.7%, from $28.7 million to $25.3 million.

TOWER HILL SIGNATURE INS CO was downgraded to C- from C in May 2018 based on a decrease in the liquidity index from a 5.50(good) to 1.20(weak), profitability index from a 3.30(fair) to 2.50(weak), stability index from a 3.90(fair) to 3.30(fair), capitalization index from a 3.10(fair) to 2.60(weak), and reserve adequacy index from a 3.80(fair) to 3.50(fair). Other factors: The company's net asset base decreased during the period by 15.9%, from $136.4 million to $117.7 million.

TRINITY UNIVERSAL INS CO was downgraded to C+ from B in May 2018 based on a decrease in the reserve adequacy index from a 8.90(excellent) to 8.50(excellent), profitability index from a 3.40(fair) to 3.10(fair), and capitalization index from a 7.70(excellent) to 7.50(excellent). Other factors: Capital and surplus decreased during the period by 5.0%, from $689.8 million to $656.7 million.

UNDERWRITERS AT LLOYDS (KY) was downgraded to D- from D in May 2018 based on a decrease in the liquidity index from a 8.80(excellent) to 7.50(excellent), stability index from a 2.30(weak) to 1.30(weak), and capitalization index from a 1.80(weak) to 1.00(weak). Other factors: The company's net asset base decreased during the period by 17.0%, from $193.2 million to $165.2 million.

UNDERWRITERS AT LLOYDS (VI) was downgraded to E+ from C- in May 2018 based on a decrease in the profitability index from a 5.90(good) to 1.10(weak) and stability index from a 3.10(fair) to 0.60(weak).

UNIQUE INS CO was downgraded to E+ from D in May 2018 based on a decrease in the liquidity index from a 3.20(fair) to 1.80(weak), profitability index from a 4.50(fair) to 3.20(fair), reserve adequacy index from a 1.30(weak) to 0.50(weak), and stability index from a 1.50(weak) to 0.80(weak).

UNITED GUARANTY RESIDENTIAL INS CO was downgraded to C+ from B- in May 2018 based on a decrease in the stability index from a 5.00(good) to 4.40(fair) and profitability index from a 3.50(fair) to 3.00(fair).

UNITED INSURANCE CO was downgraded to D+ from C- in May 2018 based on a decrease in the liquidity index from a 0.70(weak) to 0.30(weak), stability index from a 3.00(fair) to 2.60(weak), and capitalization index from a 2.80(weak) to 2.50(weak). Other factors: The company's net asset base decreased during the period by 7.6%, from $48.6 million to $45.2 million. Capital and surplus decreased during the period by 10.8%, from $13.0 million to $11.8 million.

UNIVERSAL NORTH AMERICA INS CO was downgraded to C- from C in May 2018 based on a decrease in the profitability index from a 6.90(excellent) to 3.90(fair), liquidity index from a 2.50(weak) to 1.30(weak), stability index from a 4.20(fair) to 3.30(fair), and capitalization index from a 3.60(fair) to 3.20(fair). Other factors: Capital and surplus decreased during the period by 6.9%, from $75.5 million to $70.6 million.

WESCO INS CO was downgraded to D from B- in May 2018 based on a decrease in the liquidity index from a 6.10(good) to 0.30(weak), capitalization index from a 5.10(good) to 0.20(weak), stability index from a 4.70(fair) to 2.30(weak), and profitability index from a 5.30(good) to 4.10(fair). Other factors: The company's net asset base decreased during the period by 20.3%, from $1949.3 million to $1621.0 million. Capital and surplus decreased during the period by 52.2%, from $440.8 million to $289.7 million.

WILLIAMSBURG NATIONAL INS CO was downgraded to D from C- in May 2018 based on a decrease in the liquidity index from a 7.70(excellent) to 0.00(weak), profitability index from a 4.20(fair) to 3.10(fair), and stability index from a 2.90(fair) to 2.20(weak).

Appendix

State Guaranty Associations

The states have established insurance guaranty associations to help pay claims to policyholders of failed insurance companies. However, there are several cautions which you must be aware of with respect to this coverage:

1. Most of the guaranty associations do not set aside funds in advance. Rather, states assess contributions from other insurance companies after an insolvency occurs.

2. There can be an unacceptably long delay before claims are paid.

3. Each state has different levels and types of coverage, often governed by legislation unique to that state that can sometimes conflict with coverage of other states. Generally speaking, most property and casualty lines of business written by licensed insurers are covered by guaranty associations subject to the conditions and limitations set forth in the various acts. The Guaranty Funds do not cover non-admitted carriers (except in the state of New Jersey). Most state guaranty funds will not cover title, surety, credit, mortgage guarantee or ocean marine insurance.

The table on the following page is designed to help you sort out these issues. However, it is not intended to handle all of them. If your carrier has failed and you need a complete answer, we recommend you contact your State Insurance Official.

Following is a brief explanation of each of the columns in the table.

1.	**Maximum Per Claim**	The maximum amount payable by the State Guaranty Fund on a single covered claim, with the exception of workers' compensation claims, which are paid in full in most states.
2.	**Workers' Comp. Paid in Full**	"Yes" indicates that there is no cap on the amount paid for workers' compensation claims.
3.	**Net Worth Provision**	A net worth provision gives the association the right to seek reimbursement from an insured if the insured's net worth exceeds $50 million, essentially excluding certain large organizations from coverage by the guaranty association. Roughly half of the states have a net worth provision. If a state has a provision, marked "yes", there are other conditions applicable; contact your local department of insurance for further information.
4.	**Guaranty Fund Trigger**	The action that triggers the guaranty fund process.

COVERAGE OF STATE GUARANTY FUNDS

STATE	MAXIMUM PER CLAIM	WORKERS' COMP. PAID IN FULL	NET WORTH PROVISION	GUARANTY FUND TRIGGER		
				FINAL ORDER OF LIQUIDATION WITH FINDING OF INSOLVENCY	FINDING OF INSOLVENCY ONLY	OTHER
Alabama	$150,000	Yes	Yes	X		(16)
Alaska	$500,000	Yes	None	X		
Arizona	$300,000	(8)	None	X		(16)
Arkansas	$300,000	(9)	Yes		X	
California	$500,000	Yes	None	X		
Colorado	$300,000	Yes	Yes	X		(16)
Connecticut	$400,000	Yes	Yes		X	
Delaware	$300,000	Yes	Yes	X		(16)
Dist. of Colombia	$300,000	Yes	Yes	X		(16)
Florida	$300,000 (1)	(10)	None	X		(17)
Georgia	$300,000	Yes	Yes	X		(16)
Hawaii	$300,000	Yes	Yes	X		
Idaho	$300,000	Yes	None	X		
Illinois	$500,000	Yes	Yes	X		(17)
Indiana	$300,000	Yes	Yes	X		(17)
Iowa	$500,000	Yes	yes (15)	X		
Kansas	$300,000	Yes	None	X		
Kentucky	$300,000	Yes	Yes	X		
Louisiana	$500,000	Yes	Yes	X		(18)
Maine	$300,000	Yes	Yes	X		
Maryland	$300,000 (2)	Yes	Yes	X		
Massachusetts	$300,000	Yes	Yes		X	
Michigan	(3)	Yes	Yes	X		(19)
Minnesota	$300,000	Yes	Yes	X		
Mississippi	$300,000	Yes	None	X		(16)
Missouri	$300,000	Yes	Yes	X		(16)
Montana	$300,000	Yes	Yes	X		
Nebraska	$300,000	Yes	None	X		
Nevada	$300,000	Yes	Yes	X		(20)
New Hampshire	$300,000	Yes	Yes	X		(21)
New Jersey	$300,000 (2)	(10)	Yes			(22)
New Mexico	$100,000	Yes	None	X		(16)
New York	$1,000,000 (4)	(10)	None			(23)
North Carolina	$300,000	Yes	Yes	X		(16)
North Dakota	$300,000	(11)	Yes	X		
Ohio	$300,000	(11)	Yes			(24)
Oklahoma	$150,000 (6)	Yes	Yes	X		
Oregon	$300,000	Yes	Yes	X		
Pennsylvania	$300,000	(10)	Yes	X		
Puerto Rico	$300,000	(12)	None	X		(16)
Rhode Island	$500,000	Yes	Yes	X		
South Carolina	$300,000	Yes	Yes		X	(25)
South Dakota	$300,000	Yes	Yes	X		
Tennessee	$100,000	Yes	Yes	X		
Texas	$300,000	Yes	Yes		X	(26)
Utah	$300,000	Yes	Yes			(22)
Vermont	$500,000	Yes	None	X		
Virgin Island	$50,000	(9)	None		X	
Virginia	$300,000	Yes	Yes			(22)
Washington	$300,000	(13)	None			(24)
West Virginia	$300,000	Yes	None			(24)

| Wisconsin | $300,000 (5) | (12) | yes | | | (24) |
| Wyoming | $300,000 (2) | Yes | None | X | | |

NOTES

1. Limit of $100,000 per residential unit for policies covering condominium associations or homeowners' associations. Policies providing coverage for homeowner's insurance shall provide for an additional 200,000 for the portion of covered claim which relates only to the damage to the structure and contents.

2. Maximum claim per occurrence is $300,000.

3. $5,000,000 – Subject to Consumer Price Index.

4. $100,000 – Per claim or claimant

5. $1,000,000/Claim; $5,000,000/Policy (non residents)

6. $150,000 limit per claimant for each covered claim.

7. $300,000 is the limit on a sinlge risk, loss or life.

8. Workers' compensation claims of insolvent insurers paid by Arizona's state fund.

9. Workers' compensation payments subject only to maximu claim amount.

10. Workers' compensation not covered, workers' compensation claims covered by a separate workers' compensation security fund.

11. Workers' compensation insurance written exclusively through monopolistic state fund.

12. Workers' compensation payments subject to both deductible and maximum claim amount.

13. Workers compensation not covered except Longshore Harbor workers'. Workers' compensation insurance written exclusively through monopolistic state fund.

14. Covered clain does not include any claim that would otherwise be a covered clain under this part that has been rejected by any other state guaranty fund on the grounds that an insured's net worth is greater than that allowed under that state's guaranty fund law.

15. Iowa does not cover claim of person whose net worth is greater than that allowed by guaranty fund law of his or her state of residence.

16. Order not stayed or subject to supersedeas.

17. Liquidation order not final until there is no further right of appeal.

18. Associated also obligatd to pay claims of an insurer in rehabilitation upon joint motion of association and receiver; order not stayed or subject to supersedeas.

19. All appeals exhausted

20. Also triggered if the insolvent insurer is involved in a court proceeding to determine its status of solvency, rehabilitation or liquidation, and the court has prohibited the insurer from paying claims for more than thirty days.

21. A new act (NH Act of 2004) was enacted for insolvencies occurring after 8-6-2004 and defines an insolvent insurer as a licensed insurer against whom a final order of liquidation has been entered with a finding of insolvency by a court of competent jurisdiction in the insurer's state of domicile. The prior act requires a finding of insolvency only.

22. Order of liquidation with finding of insolvency.

23. Insolvency of Insurer.

24. Triggered by finding of insolvency and liquidation order.

25. Fails to meet obligation to policyholders and state.

26. Requires separate impairment order.

Although the NCIGF has made every effort to produce the most complete, up-to-date and accurate law summaries possible, this work is meant to be used for reference purposes only. It is not meant as a substitute for an official version of a state statue or for legal advice.

Information provided in the Coverage of State Guaranty Funds chart was obtained from the National Conference of Insurance Guaranty Funds (NCIGF).

State Insurance Commissioners'
Website and Departmental Phone Numbers

State	Official's Title	Website Address	Phone Number
Alabama	Commissioner	www.aldoi.org	(334) 269-3550
Alaska	Director	https://www.commerce.alaska.gov/web/ins/	(800) 467-8725
Arizona	Director	https://insurance.az.gov/	(602) 364-2499
Arkansas	Commissioner	www.insurance.arkansas.gov	(800) 282-9134
California	Commissioner	www.insurance.ca.gov	(800) 927-4357
Colorado	Commissioner	https://www.colorado.gov/dora/division-insurance	(800) 886-7675
Connecticut	Commissioner	http://www.ct.gov/cid/site/default.asp	(800) 203-3447
Delaware	Commissioner	http://delawareinsurance.gov/	(800) 282-8611
Dist. of Columbia	Commissioner	http://disb.dc.gov/	(202) 727-8000
Florida	Commissioner	www.floir.com/	(850) 413-3140
Georgia	Commissioner	www.oci.ga.gov/	(800) 656-2298
Hawaii	Commissioner	http://cca.hawaii.gov/ins/	(808) 586-2790
Idaho	Director	www.doi.idaho.gov	(800) 721-3272
Illinois	Director	www.insurance.illinois.gov/	(866) 445-5364
Indiana	Commissioner	www.in.gov/idoi/	(317) 232-2385
Iowa	Commissioner	www.iid.state.ia.us	(877) 955-1212
Kansas	Commissioner	www.ksinsurance.org	(800) 432-2484
Kentucky	Commissioner	http://insurance.ky.gov/	(800) 595-6053
Louisiana	Commissioner	www.ldi.la.gov/	(800) 259-5300
Maine	Superintendent	www.maine.gov/pfr/insurance/	(800) 300-5000
Maryland	Commissioner	http://insurance.maryland.gov/Pages/default.aspx	(800) 492-6116
Massachusetts	Commissioner	www.mass.gov/ocabr/government/oca-agencies/doi-lp/	(877) 563-4467
Michigan	Director	http://www.michigan.gov/difs	(877) 999-6442
Minnesota	Commissioner	http://mn.gov/commerce/	(651) 539-1500
Mississippi	Commissioner	http://www.mid.ms.gov/	(601) 359-3569
Missouri	Director	www.insurance.mo.gov	(800) 726-7390
Montana	Commissioner	http://csimt.gov/	(800) 332-6148
Nebraska	Director	www.doi.nebraska.gov/	(402) 471-2201
Nevada	Commissioner	www.doi.nv.gov/	(888) 872-3234
New Hampshire	Commissioner	www.nh.gov/insurance/	(800) 852-3416
New Jersey	Commissioner	www.state.nj.us/dobi/	(800) 446-7467
New Mexico	Superintendent	www.osi.state.nm.us/	(855) 427-5674
New York	Superintendent	www.dfs.ny.gov/	(800) 342-3736
North Carolina	Commissioner	www.ncdoi.com	(800) 546-5664
North Dakota	Commissioner	www.nd.gov/ndins/	(800) 247-0560
Ohio	Lieutenant Governor	www.insurance.ohio.gov/	(800) 686-1526
Oklahoma	Commissioner	www.ok.gov/oid/	(800) 522-0071
Oregon	Insurance Commissioner	www.oregon.gov/dcbs/insurance/Pages/index.aspx	(888) 877-4894
Pennsylvania	Commissioner	www.insurance.pa.gov/	(877) 881-6388
Puerto Rico	Commissioner	www.ocs.gobierno.pr	(787) 304-8686
Rhode Island	Superintendent	www.dbr.state.ri.us/divisions/insurance/	(401) 462-9500
South Carolina	Director	www.doi.sc.gov	(803) 737-6160
South Dakota	Director	http://dlr.sd.gov/insurance/default.aspx	(605) 773-3563
Tennessee	Commissioner	www.tn.gov/insurance/	(615) 741-2241
Texas	Commissioner	www.tdi.texas.gov/	(800) 252-3439
Utah	Commissioner	www.insurance.utah.gov	(800) 439-3805
Vermont	Commissioner	www.dfr.vermont.gov/	(802) 828-3301
Virgin Islands	Lieutenant Governor	http://ltg.gov.vi/division-of-banking-and-insurance.html	(340) 774-7166
Virginia	Commissioner	www.scc.virginia.gov/boi/	(804) 371-9741
Washington	Commissioner	www.insurance.wa.gov	(800) 562-6900
West Virginia	Commissioner	www.wvinsurance.gov	(888) 879-9842
Wisconsin	Commissioner	oci.wi.gov	(800) 236-8517
Wyoming	Commissioner	http://doi.wyo.gov/	(800) 438-5768

Risk-Adjusted Capital for Property and Casualty Insurers in Weiss Rating Model

Among the most important indicators used in the analysis of an individual company are our two risk-adjusted capital ratios, which are useful tools in determining exposure to investment, liquidity and insurance risk in relation to the capital the company has to cover those risks.

The first risk-adjusted capital ratio evaluates the company's ability to withstand a moderate loss scenario. The second ratio evaluates the company's ability to withstand a severe loss scenario.

In order to calculate these Risk-Adjusted Capital Ratios, we follow these steps:

1. Capital Resources	First, we find out how much capital a company actually has by adding the company's resources which could be used to cover unexpected losses. These resources are primarily composed of stock issued by the company (capital) and accumulated funds from prior year profits (retained earnings or surplus). Additional credit can also be given for conservative reserving practices and other "hidden capital" where applicable.
	Conservative policy reserves can be an important source of capital and can contribute significantly to the financial strength of a company. Companies that set aside more than is necessary in their reserves year after year are less likely to be over run with claims and forced to dip into capital to pay them. Conversely, a company that understates its reserves year after year will be forced to routinely withdraw from capital to pay claims. Accordingly, we give companies credit for consistent over- reserving and penalize companies for consistent under-reserving.
2. Target Capital	Next, we determine how much capital the company should have to cover moderate losses based upon the company's level of risk in both its insurance business and its investment portfolio. We examine each of the company's risk areas and determine how much capital is needed for each area, based on how risky it is and how much exposure it has in that area. Then we combine these amounts to arrive at a total risk figure.
	Credit is given for the company's diversification, since it is unlikely that "the worst" will happen in all areas at once.
3. Risk-Adjusted Capital Ratio #1	We compare the results of Step 1 with those of Step 2. Specifically, we divide the "capital resources" by the "target capital" and express it in terms of a ratio. This ratio is called RACR #1.
	If a company has a Risk-Adjusted Capital Ratio of 1.0 or more, it means the company has all of the capital we believe it requires to withstand potential losses which could be inflicted by a moderate economic decline. If the company has a ratio of less than 1.0, it does not currently have all of the capital resources we think it needs. During times of financial distress, companies often have access to additional capital through contributions from a parent or holding company, current profits or reductions in dividends. Therefore, we make an allowance for firms with Risk-Adjusted Capital Ratios of somewhat less than 1.0.

4. Risk-Adjusted Capital Ratio #2   We repeat Steps 2 and 3 but now assume a severe loss scenario. This ratio is called RACR #2.

5. Risk-Adjusted Capital Index   We convert RACR #1 and #2 into an index. It is measured on a scale of zero to ten, with ten being the best and seven or better considered strong. A company whose capital resources exactly equal its target capital will have a Risk-Adjusted Capital Ratio of 1.0 and a Risk-Adjusted Capital Index of 7.0.

How We Determine Target Capital

The basic procedure for determining target capital is to identify the risk areas where the company is exposed to loss such as: (1) the risk of receiving more claims than expected; (2) the risk of not being able to collect from reinsurers or others who owe the company money; (3) the risk of losses on investments and (4) the risk of having inadequate reserves. Then we ask questions, such as:

- What is the breakdown of the company's investment portfolio? What types of policies does the company offer? Who owes the company money and how likely are they to pay? What losses has the company experienced on its underwriting (when claims and expenses exceeded premiums)? How accurate have reserve estimates been? What exposure does the company have to catastrophic property losses, such as Hurricane Andrew or the Los Angeles earthquake? What exposure does the company have to catastrophic liability losses such as asbestos pollution?

- For each category, what are the potential losses which could be incurred in both a moderate loss and a severe loss scenario?

- In order to cover those potential losses, how much in capital resources does the company need? It stands to reason that more capital is needed as a cushion for losses on high-risk investments, such as junk bonds, than on low-risk investments, such as AAA-rated utility bonds.

Amounts from each separate risk area are added together and adjustments are made to take into account the low likelihood that all risk areas would suffer severe losses at the same time. Finally, target capital is adjusted for the company's spread of risk in the diversification of its investment portfolio, the size and number of the policies it writes and the diversification of its business.

Table 1 on the next page shows target capital percentages used in Weiss Ratings Risk-Adjusted Capital Ratios #1 and #2 (RACR #1 and RACR #2).

The percentages shown in the table answer the question: How much should the firm hold in capital resources for every $100 it has committed to each category? Several of the items in Table 1 are expressed as ranges. The actual percentages used in the calculation of target capital for an individual company are determined by the levels of risk in the operations, investments or policy obligations of that specific company.

Table 1. Target Capital Percentages

Invested Asset Risk	Weiss Ratings	
	RACR#	RACR#2
Bonds	(%)	(%)
Government guarantee bonds	0	0
Class 1	.5-.75	1-1.5
Class 2	2	5
Class 3	5	15
Class 4	10	30
Class 5	20	60
Class 6	20	60
Preferred Stock	7	9.1
Common Stock		
Unaffiliated	25	33
Affiliated	25-100	33-100
Mortgages	5	15
Real Estate	10	33
Short-term investment	0.5	1
Collateral loans	2	5
Other invested assets	5	10
Credit Risk		
Agents' Balances	0.5	1
Premium Notes	2	5
Receivable Investment Income	2	3
Misc. Non-invested Assets	5	10
Reinsurance Recov. Current	1	1.5
30 to 90 Days Overdue	2	3
90 to 180 Days Overdue	5	7.5
More Than 180 Days Overdue	10	15
Rein Recov on Unpaid Losses	5	7.5
Rein Recov on IBNR	10	15
Rein Recov on UEP	5	7.5
Off Balance Sheet RBC		
Noncontrolled assets	1	2
Guarantee for affiliates	2	5
Contingent Liabilities	2	5
Reserve Risk*		
Homeowner Reserves	19-152	22-176
Private Auto Reserves	10-80	14-108
Commercial Auto Reserves	11-88	14-108
Worker's Comp Reserves	8-60	21-168
Commercial Multiple Peril Res.	19-152	22-176
Medical Malpractice Res.	26-208	39-312
Special Liability Res.	13-100	15-120
Other Liability Res.	24-192	26-208
International Reserves	16-128	19-152
Product Liability Reserves	24-192	39-312
Health Lines Reserves	15-116	23-180
Other Lines Reserves	20-156	25-196
Premium Risk*		
Homeowners NPW	29-260	43-260
Auto Liability NPW	34-304	35-319
Worker's Comp NPW	34-303	40-363
Commercial Multiperil NPW	30-272	39-347
Medical Malpractice NPW	53-478	79-478
Special Liabilities NPW	29-266	32-281
Other Liabilities NPW	38-342	49-441
International NPW	41-373	43-388
Product Liabilities NPW	41-365	52-464
Other Lines NPW	24-220	26-234

* All numbers are shown for illustrative purposes. Figures actually used in the formula vary annually based on industry experience.

Investment Class		Description
Government guaranteed bonds		Guaranteed bonds issued by U.S. and other governments which receive the top rating of state insurance commissioners
Bonds	Class 1	Investment grade bonds rated AAA, AA or A by Moody's or Standard & Poor's or deemed AAA - A equivalent by state insurance regulators
	Class 2	Investment grade bonds with some speculative elements rated BBB or equivalent
	Class 3	Noninvestment grade bonds, rated BB or equivalent
	Class 4	Noninvestment grade bonds, rated B or equivalent
	Class 5	Noninvestment grade bonds, rated CCC, C, C- or equivalent
	Class 6	Noninvestment grade bonds, in or near default
Preferred Stock		
Common Stock		
		Unaffiliated common stock
		Affiliated common stock
Mortgages		
Real Estate		Company occupied and other investment properties
Short-term Investments		All investments whose maturities at the time of acquisition were one year or less
Collateral Loans		Loans made to a company or individual where the underlying security is in the form of bonds, stocks or other marketable securities
Other Invested Assets		Any invested assets that do not fit under the main categories above

Credit Risk

Agents' Balances	Amounts which have been booked as written and billed to agents
Premium Notes	Loans to policyholders for payments of premiums
Receivable Interest Income	Interest income due but not yet received
Misc. Non-invested Income	Misc. income that is not related to invested assets
Reinsurance Recov. Current	Current receivables from reinsurers for their portion of the recorded losses
30 to 90 Days Overdue	Receivables from reinsurers 30 - 90 days overdue
90 to 180 Days Overdue	Receivables from reinsurers 90 - 180 days overdue
More Than 180 Days Overdue	Receivables from reinsurers more than 180 days overdue
Rein. Recov. on Unpaid Losses	Receivables from reinsurers for unpaid losses
Rein. Recov. on IBNR	Receivables from reinsurers for incurred but not reported losses
Rein. Recov. on UEP	Receivables from reinsurers for unearned premium

Off Balance Sheet Risk

Noncontrolled Assets	Assets not subject to complete insurer control
Guarantee for Affiliates	Guarantees on behalf of affiliates
Contingent Liabilities	Liabilities that are likely to happen but are not certain

Table 2. Bond Default Rates - potential losses as a percent of bond portfolio

Bond Rating	(1) Moody's 15 Yr Rate (%)	(2) Moody's 12 Yr Rate (%)	(3) Worst Year (%)	(4) 3 Cum. Recession Years (%)	(5) Weiss 15 Year Rate (%)	(6) Assumed Loss Rate (%)	(7) Losses as % of Holdings (%)	(8) RACR #2 Rate (%)
Aaa	0.73	0.55	0.08	0.24	0.79	50	0.95	1.00
Aa	1.39	1.04	0.13	0.39	1.43	50	1.09	1.00
A	4.05	2.96	0.35	1.05	4.02	55	2.02	1.00
Baa	7.27	5.29	0.67	2.02	7.31	60	5.15	5.00
Ba	23.93	19.57	2.04	6.11	25.68	65	23.71	15.00
B	43.37	39.30	4.99	14.96	54.26	70	43.57	30.00

Comments on Target Capital Percentages

The factors in the RACR calculations can be grouped into five categories: (1) Investment Risks; (2) Credit Risks; (3) Off Balance Sheet Risks; (4) Reserve Risks and (5) Premium Risks. Each of these has numerous subcomponents. The five categories are discussed below along with specific comments on some of the most important subcomponents.

Investment Risks:

Bonds

Target capital percentages for bonds are derived from a model that factors in historical cumulative bond default rates from the last 45 years and the additional loss potential during a prolonged economic decline.

Table 2 shows how this was done for each bond rating classification. A 15-year cumulative default rate is used (column 1). These are historical default rates for 1970-2015 for each bond class, taken from Moody's Annual Default Study. To factor in the additional loss potential of a severe three-year-long economic decline, we reduced the base to Moody's 12-year rate (column 2), determined the worst single year experience (column 3), extended that experience over three years (column 4) and added the historical 12-year rate to the 3-year projection to derive Weiss Ratings 15-year default rate (column 5). The next step was to determine the losses that could be expected from these defaults. This would be equivalent to the capital a company should have to cover those losses. Loss rates were assigned for each bond class (column 6), based on the fact that higher rated issues generally carry less debt and the fact that the debt is also better secured, leading to higher recovery rates upon default.

Column 7 shows losses as a percent of holdings for each bond class. Column 8 shows the target capital percentages that are used in RACR #2 (Table 1, RACR #2 column, Bonds -classes 1 to 6).

Regulations limiting junk bond holdings of insurers to a set percent of assets are a tacit acknowledgement that the reserve requirements used by State Insurance Commissioners are inadequate. If the figure adequately represented full loss potential, there would be no need to limit holdings through legislation since an adequate loss reserve would provide sufficient capital to absorb potential losses.

Affiliate Common Stock
These stocks are often only "paper" assets, difficult to sell, and not truly available to pay insurance claims. The appropriate value of the stock may also be difficult to determine unless the stock is publicly traded.

The target capital rate on affiliate common stock for RACR #2 can vary between 33% and 100% (Table 1, RACR #2 column, Common stock — Affiliated), depending on the financial strength of the affiliate and the prospects for obtaining capital from the affiliate should the need arise.

Credit Risk
This category refers to the financial risk faced if the company cannot collect funds it is owed. These include funds owed to the company by its agents and reinsurers.

Off Balance Sheet Risk
A miscellaneous category of risk that is developed from data not found on the company's balance sheet. It includes risks associated with rapid premium growth, unsettled lawsuits against the company, guarantees to affiliates and investment risks such as interest rate swaps.

Reserve Risk
The risk that reserve estimates are too low to pay all outstanding claims. Target capital percentages used for each line of business are based on the historical experience of both the company and industry, for that line.

Rather than basing our figures solely on the company's average experience over the last nine years, we factor in the company's worst results over the same period. We believe that this gives a more realistic appraisal of the company's loss potential. Of two companies with identical averages, one may have greater ups and downs than the other.

Target capital requirements have been reduced for each line of business in order to reflect the time value of money. As claims are generally paid months or years after premiums are received, insurers invest those premium funds, accumulating investment income until the claims must be paid. The discount given varies from 9% for private auto liability, a "short-tail" line where claims are paid shortly after receipt of premiums, to 21% for medical malpractice, a "long-tail" line where claims are generally paid many years after receipt of premiums.

Premium Risk
The risk that premium levels are not sufficient to pay claims and related expenses. Individual target capital percentages are used for each line of business based on the riskiness of the line and the company's own experience with reserve risk. Target capital requirements are reduced to account for the time value of money, using a technique similar to that used for reserve risk.

Risky Lines of Business and Catastrophic Losses
These include fire, earthquake, multiple peril (including storm damage) and similar personal and commercial property coverages. Even excluding Hurricane Andrew, and other major storms since then, the insured losses from natural disasters since 1989 have been far greater than in previous decades. Yet, too many insurance

companies are basing their risk calculations on the assumption that losses will return to more normal levels. They are not ready for the possibility that the pattern of increasing disasters might be a real, continuing trend.

Also considered high risk lines are medical malpractice, general liability, product liability and other similar liability coverages. Court awards for damages often run into the millions. These settlement amounts can be very difficult to predict. This uncertainty hinders an insurer's ability to accurately assess how much to charge policyholders and how much to set aside to pay claims. Of special concern are large, unexpected liabilities related to environmental damages such as asbestos. Similar risk may lie hidden in coverage for medical equipment and procedures, industrial wastes, carcinogens and other substances found in products previously viewed as benign.

RECENT INDUSTRY FAILURES

2018

Institution	Headquarters	Industry	Date of Failure	Total Assets ($Mil)	Safety Rating
				At Date of Failure	
Healthcare Providers Ins Exch	Pennsylvania	P&C	01/12/18	32.6	E- (Very Weak)
Touchstone Health HMO Inc	New York	Health	04/19/18	12.5	E+ (Very Weak)
Access Ins Co	Texas	P&C	03/18/18	214.1	C (Fair)

2017

Institution	Headquarters	Industry	Date of Failure	At Date of Failure	
				Total Assets ($Mil)	Safety Rating
IFA Ins Co	New Jersey	P&C	03/07/17	8.4	E (Very Weak)
Public Service Ins Co	New York	P&C	03/16/17	278.5	E (Very Weak)
Zoom Health Plan Inc	Oregon	Health	04/26/17	6.0	U (Unrated)
Galen Insurance Co	Missouri	P&C	05/31/17	10.0	E- (Very Weak)
Fiduciary Ins. Co of America	New York	P&C	07/25/17	13.9	E- (Very Weak)
Evergreen Health Inc	Maryland	Health	07/27/17	37.2	E- (Very Weak)
Minuteman Health Inc	Massachusetts	Health	08/02/17	111.7	E- (Very Weak)
Sawgrass Mutual Ins. Co	Florida	P&C	08/22/17	32.3	D+ (Weak)
Guarantee Ins. Co	Florida	P&C	08/28/17	400.4	E+ (Very Weak)
Oceanus Ins. Co A RRG	South Carolina	P&C	09/04/17	52.9	D- (Weak)

2016

| Institution | Headquarters | Industry | Date of Failure | At Date of Failure | |
				Total Assets ($Mil)	Safety Rating
Consumers Choice Health Ins Co	South Carolina	Health	01/06/16	92.4	D (Weak)
Moda Health Plan Inc	Oregon	Health	01/28/16	445.5	D+ (Weak)
Family Health Hawaii MBS	Hawaii	Health	04/07/16	5.5	D (Weak)
Health Republic Ins of NY Corp	New York	Health	04/22/16	525.3	D (Weak)
Coordinated Health Mutual Inc	Ohio	Health	05/26/16	94.9	E (Very Weak)
HealthyCT Inc	Connecticut	Health	07/01/16	112.3	D+ (Weak)
Oregons Health Co-Op	Oregon	Health	07/11/16	46.6	D (Weak)
Land of Lincoln Mut Health Ins Co	Illinois	Health	07/14/16	107.8	D+ (Weak)
Excalibur Reins Corp	Pennsylvania	P&C	07/18/16	9.0	U (Unrated)
Castlepoint Florida Ins	Florida	P&C	07/28/16	100.0	D (Weak)
Castlepoint Insurance Co	New York	P&C	07/28/16	178.4	E (Very Weak)
Castlepoint National Ins Co	California	P&C	07/28/16	355.1	C- (Fair)
Hermitage Insurance Co	New York	P&C	07/28/16	167.6	E+ (Very Weak)
Massachusetts Homeland Ins Co	Massachusetts	P&C	07/28/16	8.9	C (Fair)
North East Insurance Co	Maine	P&C	07/28/16	35.9	D (Weak)
York Ins Co of Maine	Maine	P&C	07/28/16	47.0	C (Fair)
Careconcepts Ins Inc A RRG	Montana	P&C	08/08/16	3.8	E (Very Weak)
Freelancers Consumer Operated	New Jersey	Health	09/12/16	135.3	D+ (Weak)
Doctors & Surgeons Natl RRG IC	Kentucky	P&C	10/07/16	9.1	E+ (Very Weak)
American Medical & Life Ins Co	New York	L&H	12/28/16	4.4	U (Unrated)

2015

Institution	Headquarters	Industry	Date of Failure	At Date of Failure Total Assets ($Mil)	Safety Rating
Millers Classified Ins Co	Illinois	P&C	01/20/15	2.7	E (Very Weak)
Eveready Ins Co	New York	P&C	01/29/15	10.6	E- (Very Weak)
Jordan Funeral and Ins Co, Inc	Alabama	L&H	02/17/15	1.1	U (Unrated)
Drivers Insurance Co	New York	P&C	03/12/15	3.0	E- (Very Weak)
Lumbermens Underwriting Alliance	Missouri	P&C	05/19/15	354.3	E- (Very Weak)
Pinelands Ins Co RRG, Inc	District of Columbia	P&C	08/25/15	4.9	E (Very Weak)
Louisiana Health Cooperative, Inc	Louisiana	Health	09/01/15	59.5	E (Very Weak)
Affirmative Ins Co	Illinois	P&C	09/16/15	181.2	E (Very Weak)
Affirmative Casualty Ins Co	Louisiana	P&C	10/05/15	32.6	D+ (Weak)
Affirmative Direct Ins Co	New York	P&C	10/05/15	5.3	U (Unrated)
Nevada Health Co-op	Nevada	Health	10/14/15	47.9	E- (Very Weak)
WINHealth Partners	Wyoming	Health	10/21/15	34.0	D (Weak)
Kentucky Health Cooperative Inc	Kentucky	Health	10/29/15	189.5	D+ (Weak)
Meritus Mutual Health Partners	Arizona	Health	10/30/15	45.8	D (Weak)
Meritus Health Partners	Arizona	Health	10/30/15	43.0	D+ (Weak)
Regis Ins Co	Pennsylvania	P&C	10/30/15	.6	E- (Very Weak)
Arches Mutual Ins Co	Utah	Health	11/02/15	77.2	D (Weak)
Lincoln General Ins Co	Pennsylvania	P&C	11/05/15	65.6	E- (Very Weak)
Advantage Health Solutions Inc	Indiana	Health	11/06/15	64.2	E (Very Weak)
Colorado Health Ins Coop Inc	Colorado	Health	11/10/15	108.7	D+ (Weak)
Consumers Mutual Ins of Michigan	Michigan	Health	11/13/15	60.4	E- (Very Weak)

2014

Institution	Headquarters	Industry	Date of Failure	At Date of Failure	
				Total Assets ($Mil)	Safety Rating
Union Mutual Ins Co	Oklahoma	P&C	01/24/14	5.1	E+ (Very Weak)
Commonwealth Ins Co	Pennsylvania	P&C	03/20/14	1.1	E (Very Weak)
LEMIC Ins Co	Louisiana	P&C	03/31/14	51.6	D (Weak)
Interstate Bankers Casualty Co	Illinois	P&C	04/16/14	16.2	D+ (Weak)
Freestone Ins Co	Delaware	P&C	04/28/14	421.2	D- (Weak)
Alameda Alliance For Health	California	Health	05/05/14	176.3	D (Weak)
Sunshine State Ins Co	Florida	P&C	06/03/14	22.9	E+ (Very Weak)
Physicians United Plan Inc	Florida	Health	06/09/14	110.7	E (Very Weak)
Red Rock Ins Co	Oklahoma	P&C	08/01/14	28.5	E+ (Very Weak)
DLE Life Ins co	Louisiana	L&H	10/02/14	39.3	D+ (Weak)
Mothe Life Ins Co	Louisiana	L&H	10/02/14	15.2	E- (Very Weak)
First Keystone RRG Inc	South Carolina	P&C	10/21/14	13.6	E+ (Very Weak)
SeeChange Health Ins Co	California	Health	11/19/14	23.4	D (Weak)
PROAIR Risk Retention Grp Inc	Nevada	P&C	11/12/14	0.5	U (Unrated)
Florida Healthcare Plus, Inc	Florida	Health	12/10/14	11.1	U (Unrated)
CoOportunity Health, Inc	Iowa	Health	12/23/14	195.7	U (Unrated)

2013

Institution	Headquarters	Industry	Date of Failure	Total Assets ($Mil)	Safety Rating
				At Date of Failure	
Partnership Health Plan Inc	Wisconsin	Health	01/18/13	27.1	D (Weak)
Driver's Insurance Co	Oklahoma	P&C	02/21/13	33.1	D+ (Weak)
Lewis & Clark LTC RRG	Nevada	P&C	02/28/13	16.4	E (Very Weak)
Pride National Ins Co	Oklahoma	P&C	03/08/13	17.1	E+ (Very Weak)
Santa Fe Auto	Texas	P&C	03/08/13	22.9	E (Very Weak)
Ullico Casualty Co	Delaware	P&C	03/11/13	327.7	D (Weak)
Builders Ins Co Inc	Nevada	P&C	03/15/13	15.0	U (Unrated)
Nevada Contractors Ins Co Inc	Nevada	P&C	03/15/13	49.0	U (Unrated)
Universal Health Care Ins Co Inc	Florida	Health	03/22/13	106.1	C (Fair)
Universal Health Care Inc	Florida	Health	03/25/13	109.0	D (Weak)
Universal HMO of Texas	Texas	Health	04/18/13	15.3	C- (Fair)
Universal Health Care of NV Inc	Nevada	Health	06/03/13	1.9	D+ (Weak)
Liberty First RRG Ins Co	Utah	P&C	08/06/13	2.5	E (Very Weak)
United Contrs Ins Co Inc, RRG	Delaware	P&C	08/22/13	17.0	E (Very Weak)
Advance Physicians Ins RRG, Inc	Arizona	P&C	08/29/13	1.9	D (Weak)
Georgia Mutual Ins Co	Georgia	P&C	09/10/13	3.3	D (Weak)
Ocean Risk Retention Group	D.C.	P&C	09/06/13	7.9	E (Very Weak)
Gertrude Geddes Willis Life Ins Co	Louisiana	L&H	10/24/13	4.9	U (Unrated)
San Antonio Indemnity Co	Texas	P&C	10/31/13	2.8	E+ (Very Weak)
Higginbotham Burial Ins Co	Arkansas	L&H	11/04/13	1.3	U (Unrated)
Indemnity Ins Corp RRG	Delaware	P&C	11/07/13	83.2	D- (Weak)
Concert Health Plan Ins Co	Illinois	L&H	12/10/13	1.8	D- (Weak)
ICM Insurance Co	New York	P&C	12/23/13	5.0	E+ (Very Weak)

Glossary

This glossary contains the most important terms used in this publication.

Admitted Assets	The total of all investments and business interests which are acceptable under statutory accounting rules.
Asset/Liability Matching	Management of cash flows so that investments pay interest or mature at just the right time to meet the need for cash to pay claims and expenses.
Average Recession	A recession involving a decline in real GDP which is approximately equivalent to the average of the postwar recessions of 1957-58, 1960, 1970, 1974-75, 1980, 1981-82, 1990-1991, 2001, and 2007-2009. It is assumed, however, that in today's market, the financial losses suffered from a recession of that magnitude would be greater than those experienced in previous decades. (See also "Severe Recession.")
Capital	Strictly speaking, capital refers to funds raised through the sale of common and preferred stock. Mutual companies have capital in the form of retained earnings. In a more general sense, the term capital is commonly used to refer to a company's equity or net worth, that is, the difference between assets and liabilities (i.e., capital and surplus as shown on the balance sheet).
Capital Resources	The sum of various resources which serve as a capital cushion to losses, including capital and surplus.
Cash and Demand Deposits	Includes cash on hand and on deposit. A negative figure indicates that the company has more checks outstanding than current funds to cover those checks. This is not an unusual situation for an insurance company.
Common and Preferred Stocks	See "Stocks".
Direct Premiums Written	Premiums derived from policies issued directly by the company. This figure excludes the impact of reinsurance.
Safety Rating	Weiss Safety Ratings grade insurers on a scale from A (Excellent) to F (Failed). Ratings for property and casualty insurers are based on five major factors: liquidity, reserve adequacy, capitalization, profitability, and stability of operations.
Five-Year Profitability Index	See "Profitability Index".

Government Securities	Securities issued and/or guaranteed by U.S. and foreign governments which are rated as highest quality (class 1) by state insurance commissioners. Included in this category are bonds issued by governmental agencies and guaranteed with the full faith and credit of the government. Regardless of the issuing entity, they are viewed as being relatively safer than the other investment categories.
Interest Rate Risk	The risk that, due to changes in interest rates, investment income will not meet the needs of policy commitments. This risk can be reduced by effective asset/liability matching.
Invested Assets	The total size of the firm's investment portfolio.
Investments in Affiliates	Includes bonds, preferred stocks and common stocks, as well as other vehicles which many insurance companies use to invest in— and establish a corporate link with—affiliated companies.
Line of Business	Types of insurance coverage such as fire, inland marine, group accident and health, auto physical damage and auto liability. Statutory accounting uses over 30 different lines of business. A particular insurer may write coverage in any or all of these lines.
Liquidity Index	An index, expressed on a scale of zero to ten, with seven or higher considered excellent, that measures a company's ability to raise the necessary cash to settle claims. It is possible for a company to have the resources to pay claims on paper, but be unable to raise the cash. This can occur when a company is owed a great deal of money by its agents or reinsurers, or when it cannot sell its investments at the anticipated price. Our liquidity tests examine how the company might fare under various cash flow scenarios.
Long/Short-Tail Lines	Time periods over which claims are paid out. For example, auto physical damage is considered a short-tail line, since claims are generally paid within one year of an accident. On the other hand, medical malpractice is considered a long-tail line as claims are typically paid five years or more after the occurrence of the incident giving rise to the claim. For the insurer, the risks associated with long-tail lines are greater than with short-tail lines because the period of uncertainty in which unexpected claims can arise is longer.
Moderate Loss Scenario	Possible future events that would result in loss levels comparable to those experienced in recent history. (Compare with "Severe Loss Scenario.")
Net Premiums Written	The dollar volume of premiums retained by the company. This figure is equal to direct premiums written, plus reinsurance assumed, less reinsurance ceded to other companies.

Noninvestment Grade Bonds

Low-rated issues, commonly known as "junk bonds," which carry a high risk as defined by the state insurance commissioners. These include bond classes 3 - 6.

Other Investments

Items not included in any of the other categories, such as premium notes, collateral loans, short-term investments and other miscellaneous items.

Premium Risk

The risk that, for a particular group of policies, premiums will not be sufficient to meet the level of claims and related expenses.

Profitability Index

An index, expressed on a scale of zero to ten, with seven or higher considered excellent, that measures the soundness of the company's operations and the contribution of profits to the company's fiscal strength. The Profitability Index is a composite of five factors: (1) gain or loss on underwriting (core insurance business); (2) gain or loss on overall operations; (3) consistency of operating results; (4) impact of operating results on surplus and (5) expenses in relation to industry averages for the types of policies that the company offers.

Real Estate

Direct real estate investments, including property (a) occupied by the company; (b) acquired through foreclosure of a mortgage and (c) purchased as an investment.

Reinsurance Assumed

Insurance risk acquired by taking on partial or full responsibility for claims on policies written by other companies. (See "Reinsurance Ceded.")

Reinsurance Ceded

Insurance risk sold to another company. When there is a claim on a reinsured policy, the original company generally pays the claim and then is reimbursed by its reinsurer.

Reserve Adequacy Index

An index, expressed on a scale of zero to ten with seven or higher considered excellent, that measures the adequacy of the company's reserves over the last five years. Companies that have a history of inadequate reserves will receive a low score. Reserves are company estimates of unsettled claims in each year, including both claims that have been received but not yet settled, as well as claims that the company expects to receive. A company that underestimates its claims inflates profits and capital. Additionally, chronically deficient reserves call into question the company's ability to manage its policy risk effectively.

Risk-Adjusted Capital

The capital resources that would be needed to deal with unexpected claims or other adverse developments (same as "Target Capital").

Risk-Adjusted Capital Ratio #1

The capital resources which a company currently has, expressed as a ratio, to the resources that would be needed to deal with a moderate loss scenario. (See "Moderate Loss Scenario.")

Risk-Adjusted Capital Ratio #2	The capital resources which a company currently has, expressed as a ratio, to the resources that would be needed to deal with a severe loss scenario. (See "Severe Loss Scenario.")
Severe Loss Scenario	Possible future events that could result in loss levels that are somewhat higher than recent experience. These levels are developed from examination of current trends. (Compare with "Moderate Loss Scenario.")
Severe Recession	A prolonged economic slowdown in which the single worst year of the postwar period is extended for a period of three years. (See also "Average Recession.")
Short-Tail Lines	See "Long/Short-Tail Lines".
Stability Index	An index, measured on a scale of zero to ten, integrating a wide variety of factors that reflect the company's stability and diversification of risk.
State of Domicile	Although most insurance companies are licensed to do business in many states, they have only one state of domicile. This is the state which has primary regulatory responsibility for the company. Use the state of domicile to make absolutely sure that you have the correct company. Bear in mind, however, that this need not be the state where the company's main offices are located.
State Guaranty Funds	Funds that are designed to raise cash from existing insurance carriers to cover policy claims of bankrupt insurance companies.
Stocks	Common and preferred equities, including stocks in affiliates.
Surplus	Accumulated funds from prior years' profits (retained earnings) plus additional amounts paid-in by a parent or other corporation. The term "surplus" is also sometimes used broadly to include capital such as common stock.
Target Capital	See "Risk-Adjusted Capital."
Total Assets	Total admitted assets, including investments and other business assets. (See "Admitted Assets.")